RACIAL AND CULTURAL MINORITIES

An Analysis of Prejudice and Discrimination

Fifth Edition

ENVIRONMENT, DEVELOPMENT, AND PUBLIC POLICY

A series of volumes under the general editorship of
Lawrence Susskind, *Massachusetts Institute of Technology, Cambridge, Massachusetts*

PUBLIC POLICY AND SOCIAL SERVICES

Series Editor:
Gary Marx, *Massachusetts Institute of Technology, Cambridge, Massachusetts*

Other subseries:

ENVIRONMENTAL POLICY AND PLANNING

Series Editor:
Lawrence Susskind, *Massachusetts Institute of Technology, Cambridge, Massachusetts*

CITIES AND DEVELOPMENT

Series Editor:
Lloyd Rodwin, *Massachusetts Institute of Technology, Cambridge, Massachusetts*

RACIAL AND CULTURAL MINORITIES

An Analysis of Prejudice and Discrimination

Fifth Edition

George Eaton Simpson
and
J. Milton Yinger
Oberlin College
Oberlin, Ohio

PLENUM PRESS • NEW YORK AND LONDON

Library of Congress Cataloging in Publication Data

Simpson, George Eaton, 1904–
    Racial and cultural minorities.

    (Environment, development, and public policy. Public policy and social
services)
    Bibliography: p.
    Includes index.
    1. Minorities. 2. Racism. 3. Race discrimination—United States. I.
Yinger, J. Milton (John Milton), 1916–   . II. Title. III. Series.
HT1521.S53 1985   305.8′00973   84-26637
ISBN 0-306-41777-4

First Printing—June 1985
Second Printing—March 1986
Third Printing—June 1987

©1985 Plenum Press, New York
A Division of Plenum Publishing Corporation
233 Spring Street, New York, N.Y. 10013

Printed in the United States of America

To E. B. S. and W. M. Y.

Preface to the Fifth Edition

We need scarcely note that the topic of this book is the stuff of headlines. Around the world, political, economic, educational, military, religious, and social relations of every variety have a racial or ethnic component. One cannot begin to understand the history or contemporary situation of the United States, the Soviet Union, China, Zimbabwe, South Africa, Great Britain, Lebanon, Mexico, Canada—indeed, almost any land—without careful attention to the influence of cultural and racial divisions.

Preparation of this new edition has brought a strong sense of *déjà vu*, with regard both to the persistence of old patterns of discrimination, even if in new guises, and also to the persistence of limited and constraining explanations. We have also found, however, rich new empirical studies, new theoretical perspectives, and greatly expanded activity and analyses from members of minority groups.

Although this edition is an extensive revision, with reference both to the data used and the theoretical approaches examined, we have not shifted from our basically analytical perspective. We strongly support efforts to reduce discrimination and prejudice; but these can be successful only if we try to understand where we are and what forces are creating the existing situation. We hope to reduce the tendency to use declarations and condemnations of other persons' actions as substitutes for an investigation of their causes and consequences.

Books, monographs, and articles dealing with the place of racial and cultural minorities in a social structure are now very numerous. Many of them are of excellent quality, and the scope of their coverage is so wide that no single volume can even hope to indicate the range of materials. Our aim is not simply to sample these materials in order to assess the present status of the scientific study of majority–minority relations. We hope also to contribute to two essential tasks. First, the very quantity of present studies increases the problem of synthesis—of relating the various analyses to each other and to a systematic group of principles that underlie them all. We have not given full attention to the many excellent studies of racial and cultural relations outside of the United States because pressures of space make an adequate worldwide comparative statement impossible within the framework of this volume. It is our hope, however, that the principles developed here can be used in the study of intergroup relations in other parts of the world. If this hope is realized, readers interested in intensive study of a majority–minority situation not dealt with in this volume will have been furnished with some guiding concepts for their own work. They may be less likely to adopt an oversimplified, one-factor view and less likely to study one situation in isolation from the total society of which it is a part.

The second task is to connect the study of majority–minority relations with the whole range of the sciences of human behavior. To study racial and cultural minorities is to be drawn into the critical theoretical and methodological issues of contemporary social science. If we have succeeded in any measure in performing this task, the careful student should gain from this volume not only some understanding of discrimination and prejudice and of the place of minorities in the social structure, but also some knowledge of stratification theory, of the nature of personality, the types of social interaction, the influence of institutions, and the meaning of culture. It is also our hope that she or he will be alerted to some of the problems of methodology faced by social scientists today.

References in footnotes and bibliography can only inadequately express our indebtedness to the hundreds of scholars on whose work we have drawn. In particular we want to thank Gary Marx, Reynolds Farley, and the reference librarians of Oberlin College for their substantial help. Eliot Werner, Senior Editor of Plenum Press, and Christopher Kates, Production Editor, have furnished essential support and encouragement. As for the preparation of the final copy, the work of Phyllis O'Brien and Patt Clarkson is especially appreciated.

GEORGE EATON SIMPSON
J. MILTON YINGER

Contents

PART II: MINORITIES IN THE SOCIAL STRUCTURE:
THE INSTITUTIONAL PATTERNS OF INTERGROUP RELATIONS

PART III: PREJUDICE, DISCRIMINATION, AND DEMOCRATIC VALUES

PART I

Causes and Consequences of Prejudice and Discrimination

In the eight chapters of Part I, our aim is to examine the highly interdependent sources of discrimination and prejudice and to describe their major effects, not only on members of minority groups but on dominant groups as well. To do this effectively we need first to discuss the key concepts in the analysis of majority–minority relations. We shall develop definitions that we believe are powerful and reasonable, but they are not necessarily *true* in some final sense. Definitions are "contructs of convenience" designed to sharpen one's thinking and observation. Readers will know other definitions of *discrimination, minority,* or *race*, for example, and will want to ask which definitions are most helpful in clarifying thought.

Some scholars emphasize one or another of the several sources of discrimination and prejudice as fundamental—sometimes seeing that one as almost exclusively important. We shall emphasize their interaction. That is not to say that in the study of particular problems attention cannot most fruitfully be paid to a given source. We think it is essential, however, that such study be preceded by knowledge of a general theory that takes all the sources into account. We shall argue, indeed, that the consequences are part of the system of discrimination. From this perspective, perhaps the central question that emerges from Part I is this: When do the disadvantages suffered by the members of a minority group feed back into the system that caused them, reenforcing that system; and when do those disadvantages promote opposition, civil rights movements, and social changes that weaken the patterns of discrimination?

1

CHAPTER 1

Types of Majority–Minority Situations

All over the world in the late twentieth century, perhaps more than ever before, the puzzling phenomena of intergroup relations command attention. Civil rights, "internal colonialism," desegregation, integration, discrimination, pluralism, genocide, apartheid—these are terms the student of contemporary life must learn to use. Western European nations discovered that "guest workers," whom they have employed by the millions, are something more than cogs in an economic machine. England, with a steady migration of people from India, Pakistan, Bangladesh, Africa, and the West Indies, found herself faced with problems of a color bar and passed an unprecedented law limiting immigration. Pressures against persons of Indian descent in the new nations of East Africa not only reshaped intergroup relations in those lands but influenced Britain's restrictive immigration policy. The South African government boldly defends a policy of apartheid but keeps stumbling over the problem of economic interdependence among the races. The United States, rapidly becoming a thoroughly urbanized society, discovers that problems of racial inequalities have become nationwide. The Soviet Union not only struggles with questions of equity and control of her own racial and cultural minorities but finds that her ancient fear of the "Mongol hordes," now the Chinese, intrudes into international relations. And, as Lucien Pye observes (1975, p. 502):

What is often overlooked is that the Chinese on their side have an equally powerful historic fear of tribal peoples moving down into their agricultural domains. The Great Wall of China is a monument to this fear, and now that the Chinese are reacting again to a threat from the north it is understandable that the historic imagery of the dangerous "barbarians" of the border regions, that is, some of their national minorities, has again come alive in the Chinese imagination.

How shall we seek to understand developments such as these? To what system of concepts shall we turn? Humankind has always struggled to understand the world, to predict the sequence of events, and to achieve some control over them. This book is an attempt to study one aspect of human behavior from the perspectives of sociology, anthropology, and social psychology, to place the study of intergroup relations within the framework of the social sciences. Good will and a high interest are not sufficient to understand the complicated problems of racial and cultural relations. There is a tendency in most books on this subject—including, perhaps, this one—to speak of heroes and villains rather than of the human condition. We shall try to avoid this tendency. Even when our value positions are clearly evident—for this is not a question of having or not having a point of view—our aim will be to specify the conditions under which various events occur. The vocabulary of praise and blame is inappropriate to our task. Long-established patterns of discrimination are natural events, however much we may

3

regret them, that we shall try to understand. Insofar as our aim is to break up such patterns, we will be successful to the degree that the reader understands their causes rather than in proportion to the vigor of our condemnation of their carriers.

One needs to make no lengthy defense of the importance of the study of minority–majority relations. Pick up the daily newspaper or read the record of an international debate or watch the actions of a crowd: intergroup hostility, discrimination, and prejudice are there, sometimes unrecognized, but more often today defended or attacked—for we are becoming self-conscious about our divisions. The following items from several times and places come almost at random from our files:

> On Christmas Eve [1980], about 50 men in the working-class suburb of Vitry-sur-Seine stormed to a housing unit for black African laborers and used bulldozers to shift mounds of earth against the building's entrances.
> Then in a matter of minutes, the men cut off all electricity, gas and telephone lines to the building while the town's communist mayor stood by and watched.
> The incident illustrated the growing resentment in France against the nation's 4 million foreign laborers.
> The Associated Press, *St. Petersburg Times*, January 2, 1981

> In terms of sheer brutality, few events in post-World War II history can equal the massacre that took place last year in the beautiful central African republic of Burundi. At that time, members of the Bahutu tribe, which makes up 85 percent of the country's population, rose up against the towering Watutsi overlords who have dominated them for centuries. The insurrection failed, and the "Tutsi" government of Col. Michel Micombero exacted a frightful vengeance—slaughtering up to 250,000 "Hutu" men, women, and children.
> *Newsweek*, July 2, 1973

> *Bad Blood: The Tuskegee Syphilis Experiment,* by James H. Jones, examines one of the most shameful medical experiments ever conducted in this country: a 40-year study by the U.S. Public Health Service of the effects of untreated syphilis on 399 black men in Alabama . . . . The men who agreed to participate did so because (1) they were mostly illiterate and didn't understand the terms, (2) they were poor and received free medical care for minor ailments, (3) when they died (usually of neurologic or cardiac complications of the disease), their families received a fifty-dollar burial payment, through a grant from the respected Milbank Memorial Fund . . . . Because the men weren't treated, their wives were also infected and their children were born with congenital syphilis.
> *New York Review of Books*, November 5, 1981

> In Nürnberg's warm, well-lighted courtroom, the lawyers tried to get the point across—these Nazis had killed 6,000,000 Jews . . . . This was no report from a refugee agency. Here it was, right out of the Nazi files. The Gestapo chief Jew catcher, Adolf Eichmann, said that 4,000,000 died in concentration camps

and 2,000,000 were killed by extermination squads. Fat, brutal Hans Frank counted 3,500,000 Jews in Western Poland in 1941, "perhaps 100,000" in 1944. If the untellable crime could ever be told, Nürnberg's evidence, as clear and specific as last week's robbery, had told it. But its immense inhumanity made it almost immune to translation into human terms.
> *Time,* December 24, 1945

Our task is to try to understand such phenomena. Do they have anything in common? What are the factors in group conflict, in cultural difference, in individual personality that account for these expressions of discrimination and prejudice? What various forms does intergroup hostility take?

It would be a mistake to believe that the items cited are fully representative, that antipathy between racial and cultural groups is universal. Opposition to discrimination and the reduction of antagonism are also newsworthy items in the comtemporary scene. We are often tempted to be categorically pessimistic because that shows how sympathetic we are, how unlikely it is that we will be conned by a few small gains or lulled to sleep by partial success. Pessimism can goad us into examining our deepest assumptions (Sieber 1981, pp. 24–25); it can compel us to exercise one of the most important parts of the sociological imagination dealing with the unintended effects of well-intentioned actions (Killian 1971).

Unqualified pessimism, however, can also have unintended consequences. It can reduce ability to win allies, to be effective politically, to maintain morale, to see the full range of changes taking place. Our aim is to be tough-minded but not cynical, to be equally alert to evidence of persistent discrimination and to evidence of its reduction. Thus we need to be aware of such items as the following:

> In 1970 George Wallace "gave Alabama the most blatantly racist gubernatorial campaign of its recent history. But he finished the 70's on the podium with Mr. Arrington [Richard Arrington, the first black Mayor of Birmingham], applauding the kind of political change that represents this decade's signal accomplishment for blacks." At the same time, the 70's were seen as a period in which the economic gains of the 60's were barely maintained among racial minorities.
> *The New York Times,* December 30, 1979

> Twice as many blacks are attending college today as did a decade ago, the Census Bureau reports.
> The new study of school enrollment disclosed that more than a million black students were enrolled at U.S. colleges and universities as of last October.
> Only 522,000 black college students were reported in 1970.

Since 1976, the proportion of college students who are black has been at least equal to the proportions of blacks in the college-age population.

Cleveland, *The Plain Dealer*, May 20, 1981

In South Africa, the 1959 Extension of University Education Act, intended to bar black students from universities attended by whites, is still on the books . . . ; racially separate universities duly came into existence. But non-whites were never driven entirely from the rolls of the major institutions, which still preferred to regard themselves as "open" even though the laws said they had to be restricted to whites, unless a non-white received Government permission to pursue studies in a discipline not represented in the curriculum of the institution dedicated to his particular racial group. But in the last few years the loophole has widened to the point of becoming a gap, practically a tunnel, and a process that elsewhere might be called integration is occurring at an accelerating pace. The number of non-white students at theoretically white universities now exceeds 4,000, twice what it was five years ago.

The New York Times, Spring Survey of Education,
April 26, 1981

The Rapidly Changing Contemporary Scene

The student of race relations is confronted with a rapidly changing situation, both as to the facts of prejudice and discrimination and as to our knowledge of their meaning. In the enormous international struggles of our time, with their power and ideological aspects, the role of minority groups inevitably has become tremendously important. How maintain national unity? How win or preserve the friendship of former colonial peoples? How adjust to the rising literacy, power, and demands of minority groups everywhere? How preserve and extend a democratic ideology in the face of its obvious violations in almost every land? Such questions might, perhaps, have been treated casually a generation ago; they have surged now to the forefront of international attention and cannot be disregarded. The result is a ferment in minority–majority relations of greater importance than the modern world has witnessed before.

In the United States, the national compromise over the "Negro question" that lasted for two generations has been broken by changes in the nature of American society and is being intensely reexamined. Crucial Supreme Court decisions, changes in the practices of labor unions, the migration and industrialization of an important part of the black labor force, the rapid expansion and urbanization

of Hispanic and other minority groups, the demands made by our position on the international scene—these and many other factors are forcing us to work out a new and more effective adjustment among the races and cultural groups (see Barron 1975).

During World War I many people were made aware of the problem of minorities by the discovery here, in times of crisis, of partially assimilated national groups. They were shocked at the failure of the "melting-pot" idea. One reaction was anti-foreignism, a demand for tightened immigration restrictions. Some few, however, began to wonder whether the melting-pot idea might not itself be inadequate, demanding, as it did, Americanization on quite narrow terms. Many of our immigrants, as Rudolph Bourne pointed out, are not simply those who missed the Mayflower and came over on a later boat; when they did come they took a *Maiblume*, a *Fleur de Mai*, a *Fior di Maggio*, or a *Majblomst*. There were national, cultural, religious, and lingual differences to be accommodated. In a world of international tension and publicity, insistent "Americanization" of our national minorities, with the strong implication that their ways of doing things are queer, foolish, and unacceptable, is unlikely to be a successful procedure. Myrdal (1944, p. 1021) observed that "the Negro problem is not only America's greatest failure but also America's incomparably great opportunity for the future." And in the same vein, Bourne declared: "To seek no other goal than the weary old nationalism, belligerent, exclusive, inbreeding . . . is to make patriotism a hollow sham . . . . In a world which has dreamed of internationalism, we find that we have all unawares been building up the first international nation" (in Locke and Stern 1946, pp. 730–31).

Other facets of majority–minority relations are appearing rapidly in the contemporary world. Direct imperialistic domination of "native" peoples ran into self-contradictions and costs that greatly weakened it. Although "internal colonialism"—a concept we shall examine later—requires careful study, the 400-year period of colonial domination, at least by the West, is past. (Russian domination of eastern Europe and parts of Asia, involving the more open use of force, more frequent manipulation of local political movements, and exploitation of an international ideology, shares some aspects of the old pattern.) After World War II, Western nations found that the practical advantages of colonialism had sharply declined just at the time when the costs of maintaining the old pattern had increased vastly. Indigenous labor was no longer so cheap and tractable; local political movements could be stopped only by costly suppression; the defense of colonies against rivals was difficult and expensive. During the period of domination there had been a diffusion of Western ideas of nationalism, democracy, and freedom that armed the colonies against their overlords. Meanwhile, the growth of democratic movements in the mother countries themselves weakened the colonial system. Many people came to the conviction that lack of democracy anywhere endangers world peace (Raymond Kennedy in Linton 1945, pp. 338–46).

These forces, and others, brought important changes to the colonial world. Japan's effort to extend her imperial domination was broken. China freed herself from the extraterritorial privileges that many western nations demanded and held. Scores of new nations have been formed since 1945 from former colonies in Africa, Asia, Oceania, and the Caribbean.

All of this does not mean that domination across national boundaries has decreased but only that the pattern is changing. Major powers continue to attempt to seat and unseat those governments that they consider essential to their interests. Nor does it indicate the growth of democracy, for the decline of imperialism is not necessarily a gain for the majority of human beings; it may represent only a shift in power from an external to an internal ruling class. J. H. Boeke (in Lind 1955, p. 73) describes this situation well:

There is abundant evidence that often new national governments, behind the screen of nationalism, fight colonialism by taking over its policy. But it is no longer colonialism since foreign capitalists have been eliminated. The small villager and the poor consumer who are the victims of this game of puss in the corner have every reason to remember the Dutch proverb that it is all the same whether one is bitten by a she-cat or a he-cat.

Policies concerning industrialization, land-holding, imports, granting of credit, and the like may be primarily in the interests of the new internal elite, as Boeke points out, the masses being paid in slogans of nationalism and anticolonialism.

There are at least modest success stories in Mexico, Brazil, Nigeria (since 1970), Holland, Yugoslavia, the United States, Zimbabwe, and elsewhere; but mainly what we see is that humanity has yet to find ways to achieve full equality for diverse racial and ethnic groups within a pluralistic society. Nevertheless, such a time of change can yield valued insights into the nature of the subject with which we are concerned in this book. Fixed notions of causes and cures are obviously inadequate today. Equipped with tentativeness and modesty we can, with the knowledge available, begin to grasp the basic nature of intergroup relations, of discrimination, of hierarchies of power within and between societies.

The Changing Scientific View of Intergroup Relations

The speed with which majority–minority relations are changing in the contemporary world is matched by the development of scientific theories in the field. The concepts and beliefs of competent scholars only a few decades ago are now looked upon as entirely inadequate, and many of the writings that were most widely read are seen today as scarcely more than elaborate rationalizations for existing stereotypes and prejudices. (This rapid change in our conceptions should encourage us to hold present hypotheses and theories—including those advanced in this book—tentatively. They may prove to be inadequate to account for tomorrow's evidence.)

At various points in the chapters that follow we shall refer to the work of such well-known propagandists as Count de Gobineau, Houston Stewart Chamberlain, Lothrop Stoddard, and Madison Grant. For two or three generations their type of analysis of "race relations" was widely circulated among the literate group and helped to reinforce the traditional views of millions who had never heard of these propagandists (Field 1981; Gutman 1977, pp. 531–44; Fredrickson 1971). The work of such writers was intellectually respectable only a few decades ago. Their contemporary successors, however, have no such standing. The "popular" intellectual supports of prejudice are weakening.

Before World War I, sociological writing about race relations often reflected "not only outmoded conceptions concerning primitive people but all the current popular prejudices concerning the Negro" (Frazier 1947, p. 267). These views were strongly opposed by black scholars and leaders, of whom W. E. B. DuBois was most notable. It was not until the 1930s and 1940s, however, that DuBois and other black social scientists were joined by any significant number of white scholars in efforts to apply the theories and tools of current research to minority–majority relations (Blackwell and Janowitz 1974; Myrdal 1944).

In his excellent account of the history of racialist thinking, Gould (1981, p. 143, see also Chase 1980; Reynolds 1980) observes that, although there has been change in the objects of attention, the strand of biological determinism persists. Society is seen as an accurate reflection, in such thinking, of biology.

We live in a more subtle century, but the basic arguments never seem to change. The crudities of the cranial index have given way to the complexity of intelligence testing. The signs of innate criminality are no longer sought in stigmata of gross anatomy, but in twentieth-century criteria: genes and fine structures of the brain.

These brief references may serve to indicate that theories of majority–minority relations, like those dealing with other aspects of human behavior, are strongly influenced by the surrounding intellectual and moral environment. There are several ways in which this influence on particular theorists—the present authors included—is expressed. The following are particularly notable: (1) the availability or lack of various kinds of empirical research; (2) the focusing of attention by dramatic events; (3) the majority or minority identity of the individual scholars; (4) disciplinary perspectives; (5) various styles or what today are often called paradigm aspects of all theoretical work; (6) the moral-political concerns with which the study of majority–minority relations is connected; (7) research methodologies available, and those deemed sufficiently powerful to be worthy of use (see Banton 1977; Gabriel and Ben-Tovim 1979; Gould 1981; Metzger 1971a).

Insiders and Outsiders

In this list of influences on students of majority–minority relations, one (number three) deserves additional comment here. What has long been observed, but not always dealt with, is the potential effects of a person's own social identity on her or his assumptions, perceptions, and conclusions. We cannot examine the important questions dealt with by the sociology of knowledge (see Mannheim 1936; Merton 1968). We will, however, discuss one of

one of its implications for our topic: What are the effects, or the possible effects, of minority and majority identities on analyses and interpretations of intergroup relations?

In one sense, to be sure, no one is outside minority–majority *relations*. All are involved. In another sense, each of us is an insider and an outsider, depending on time, place, and perspective. If, however, one thinks of insiders as those who bear the brunt of a discriminatory system, then it is minority-group members who are the insiders. It is outsiders, using this definition, who make up the majority of interpreters, possess greater access to research funds and publishing outlets, and do most of the teaching. Some will argue that this outside situation allows greater objectivity and perspective. Insiders may "know" about a problem as a patient knows about a toothache; but that is not sufficient qualification for diagnosis and treatment.

Others argue that those without the ache cannot truly understand; their knowledge is superficial, lacking in realism. Merton, in his seminal article, "Insiders and Outsiders" (1972), observes that the pain, humiliation, and frustration experienced by minority-group members may be so built into social structures that they may be almost invisible to outsiders. The grave difficulties may be described in such bland and neutral terms (*sociological euphemism*, Merton calls it) that the intense human suffering involved is glossed over. Yet insider status by itself scarcely furnishes adequate credentials. Shared experience can furnish insight, but group loyalties can also blind us, as Francis Bacon emphasized long ago.

Many languages draw a distinction, Merton notes, between "acquaintance with" and "knowledge about," between *noscere* and *scire*, *kennen* and *wissen*, *connaître* and *savoir*. A mature social science will help us to blend these two sources of understanding. It will require that outsiders experience as deeply as they can the life conditions of insiders, building upon methods developed in anthropology. Special rules are needed for surveys among minority populations, for identifying the effects of white interviewers among nonwhite groups, for making visible the unstated cultural assumptions (Montero and Levine 1977; Shosteck 1977; Yinger et al. 1977).

Cedrix X (1973, p. 7; see also Ladner 1973; Valentine 1972) introduces an issue of the *Journal of Social Issues* devoted to the problem of objectivity with the statement:

The theme throughout several of the articles is that under the guise of scientific objectivity, a small but powerful group of modern psychologists has fully participated in an attempt to impose their reality onto a group of people having a totally different frame of reference. While the intent may have been scientific, the effect has been political.

Washington (1971, pp. 580–581; see also Goldstein 1971; Lyman 1972; Metzger 1971a, 1971b; Rose 1978; Watson 1976) writes in a similar vein:

> Black Americans themselves have begun to produce competing images of their social reality, images that clash sharply with those by liberal white sociologists . . . . Sociologists have become progressively more bourgeois and remote from the poor, black and white, who are more and more isolated from the rest of society.

Not all minority scholars agree with the implications of these statements. Insiders are far from identical in their views.[1] What we need, in our view, is the strongest possible effort to combine "acquaintance with" and "knowledge about," *noscere* and *scire,* in the thinking of both insiders and outsiders.

Our aim here is to enlarge section one in Figure 1, to push back the boundary marked by the dotted line. In Merton's words:

> When a transition from social conflict to intellectual controversy is achieved, when the perspectives of each group are taken seriously enough to be carefully examined rather than rejected out of hand, there can develop trade offs between the distinctive strengths and weaknesses of Insider and Outsider perspectives that enlarge the chances for a sound and relevant understanding of social life. (1972, p. 40)

Readers need to ask how the identities of the authors of this book—both of whom are rather WASPish—influence their work. More broadly: "What constraints are there within the profession that facilitate or hinder the creative incorporation of hitherto excluded knowledge systems?" (Moore 1973b, p. 65). Readers might also ask themselves how their own insider or outsider identities affect their judgments and interpretations and how, by

giving thought to this issue, their understanding can be enlarged.

It has become increasingly difficult to avoid politicizing the study of minority–majority relations, to steer between special pleading and indifference. Throughout this book we shall attempt to avoid special pleading precisely because we are *not* indifferent.

Emphasis on conflict and power, on economic and political struggle, which will be a major topic in this book as it has been since the first edition 30 years ago, is sometimes given such exclusive attention that important reenforcing and interacting factors are neglected. As Shils (1975, xii; see also Williams 1977) puts it:

> there are not and can never be any human societies which are wholly consensual; nor have there ever been societies so wholly disintegrated that there were no links at all binding many of their individual members together. For a long time there has been a tendency among intellectuals in Western countries to deny this obvious fact. For some reasons, good and bad, they have accepted uncritically a tradition which has depicted modern society as if it were on the verge of the state of nature according to Hobbes. This situation was not improved by the introduction of a vulgar Marxism which unthinkingly made membership in society identical with subjugation by coercion.

Nevertheless, attention to how deeply discrimination is embedded in the very structure of society is essential. Our understanding is greatly enhanced by seeing majority–minority relations as part of systems of social stratification (see, e.g., Blalock 1967; Blauner 1972; Gabriel and Ben-Tovim 1979; Ransford 1977; Rex 1983; Schermerhorn 1970; Shibutani and Kwan 1965). If we cannot speak yet of a mature science of intergroup relations, thoroughly integrated with a systematic science of humanity, we do have fundamental parts of such a discipline and valuable approaches to it that we hope to build upon.

Definitions and Types of Minorities

One of our first tasks is to delimit our area of inquiry, separating it from closely related but distinctive neighboring fields. We need also to define several basic concepts carefully.

---

[1] See Blackwell and Janowitz, *Black Sociologists: Historical and Contemporary Perspectives* (1974), and the perceptive review by Meier (1977). Or see Wilson's *The Declining Significance of Race* (1978), and compare it with the numerous reviews that followed or with the "Statement of the Association of Black Sociologists" (mimeographed, 1978), which declared: "The Association of Black Sociologists is outraged over the misrepresentation of the black experience."

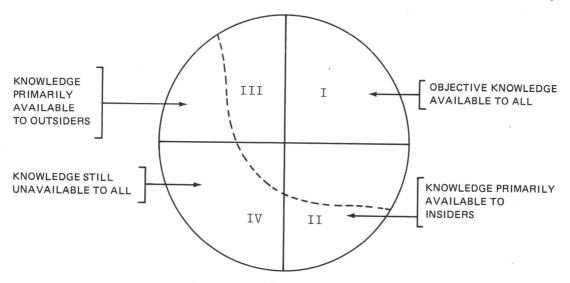

Figure 1-1. Insider and outsider knowledge.

There are many definitions of the primary terms in the study of intergroup relations. Sharp disagreements have frequently resulted from differences in definition, partly because of a misunderstanding of the nature of definitions. Definitions do not reveal what the data in question *really are*. The phenomena of the world are not divided into neat, mutually exclusive types which, if we study hard enough, we can discover. They flow endlessly one into another, by minute gradations; and any definition which tries to draw a sharp line is bound to be arbitrary to some degree. The phenomena included within the definition are not exactly alike, but only more or less alike. Some phenomena excluded are also alike—but presumably less rather than more. In defining relations as complicated as those with which we are dealing in this study, with so many variables involved, one is bound to run into disagreement over what is more and what is less.

Yet definitions are necessary for communication. We must remember simply that they are, to some degree, empirically arbitrary.

The most important concept throughout the book is *minority*. From its definition one can derive its reciprocal, *majority*. Some counties of Mississippi have three times as many black citizens as white. Nonwhites make up an even higher proportion of the population of South Africa. For two centuries a handful of British dominated hundreds of millions

of Indians. Yet we frequently refer to these situations as majority–minority situations—clearly meaning a pattern of relationship, the distribution of power, and not numbers. According to Louis Wirth (in Linton 1945, p. 347):

We may define a minority as a group of people who, because of their physical or cultural characteristics, are singled out from the others in the society in which they live for differential and unequal treatment, and who therefore regard themselves as objects of collective discrimination. The existence of a minority in a society implies the existence of a corresponding dominant group with higher social status and greater privileges. Minority status carries with it the exclusion from full participation in the life of the society.

From the perspective of the individual minority-group member, his status is characterized primarily by its categorical nature; typically he cannot resign or escape by merit. Whatever his unique characteristics, he is treated, in the defining case, simply as one unit of a group by those of dominant status.

Minorities, however, are not all alike. They differ in the symbols that set them apart, in the nature of their relationship to the dominant group, and in their reactions to the situation. It was once thought that the difference in symbols was most important—that the study of racial minorities was different from the study of groups set apart by religion, nationality, or culture. While recognizing that symbolic differences do affect the nature of the interaction, we must see that it is the pattern of relationship that is crucial. Several variables affect the pattern, as Wirth pointed out. A situation in which there is only one minority will be different from one in which there are several. A single minority has to absorb all the anxieties and frustration of the dominant group and become the object of all its power manipulations. Where there are several minorities, as in the United States, some may escape relatively easily; a hierarchy develops among them. The majority will play one minority off against another—and this maneuver will affect the way in which minorities respond to one another.

The degree of difference in culture, language, and race is another variable. The sharper the differences, the more the status pattern tends to persist.

Analysis of majority–minority interaction must also pay attention to the different effects of various types of social structure. John Blue (1959) notes that race relations, for example, develop differently in colonial, imperial, reservation, segregated, and equalitarian or quasi-segregated social systems. Van den Berghe (1970) contrasts the kinds of race relations that develop in a competitive system (typically an urban, industrial setting where the dominant group is numerically larger, is itself stratified into many classes, and is motivated by the ideology of an open, liberal, democratic society) with those that appear in a paternalistic system (where the dominant group is often numerically small, the economy largely agricultural, and the division of labor strictly along racial lines). Lieberson (1961) points out that race relations develop differently in societies where a migrant population has imposed its order from the way they develop in situations where the indigenous population is dominant.

In Europe, the term *minority* is typically applied "to a group of people living on soil which they have occupied from time immemorial, but who, through change of boundaries, have become politically subordinate" (Schermerhorn 1959, p. 179). Such minorities are "cultural nationalities" deprived of political independence. This conception is found in the definition used by the United Nations Subcommission on Prevention and Protection of Minorities (1952, p. 490): Minorities are "those nondominant groups in a population which possess and wish to preserve stable ethnic, religious or linguistic traditions or characteristics markedly different from those of the rest of the population."

Recognizing the complexity of the empirical world—the extent to which the phenomena of our interest shade off into related but distinctive phenomena—how shall we specify the primary defining properties of *minority?* Wagley and Harris (1958, p. 10) suggest five characteristics: (1) minorities are subordinate segments of complex state societies; (2) minorities have special physical or cultural traits that are held in low esteem by the dominant segments of the society; (3) minorities are self-conscious units bound together by the special traits that their members share and by the special disabilities which these bring; (4) membership in a minority is transmitted by a rule of descent which is capable of affiliating succeeding generations even in the absence of readily apparent special cultural or physical traits; (5) minority peoples, by choice or necessity, tend to marry within their group.

Many groups share some of these characteristics. One can argue that they too should be called minorities and studied in a book of this kind. The first three of the five defining characteristics certainly apply, in many contexts, to the aged, women, homosexuals, deviant sociopolitical groups, the physically handicapped, and others. Much can be learned by comparing their situations with those of groups to whom characteristics four and five also apply (see Kasschau 1977; Sagarin 1971). We do not do so here for two reasons: Each of the "near-minorities" faces special circumstances that require focused commentary—a task that would make an encyclopedia out of an already long book. A more substantial reason is that the "rule of descent" ties full minorities to the continuing structures of the stratification system. The continuity of generations, the passing along of status, adds a toughness to the patterns of discrimination applied to minorities. This difference ought not to be exaggerated, however, and studies that climb the abstraction ladder a step or two higher can help us to develop a more general theory of discrimination. The enormous literature dealing with the status of women, for example, can be of great value to the student of racial and cultural minorities.

We must also examine the concept of ethnicity in relation to the definition of the term *minority*. Ethnic groups are not necessarily minority groups, but many of them are; and studies of discrimination have long included, even emphasized, how one's ethnic status and what might be called the ethnic order have influenced the distribution of rewards.

Recently, more attention in the literature on ethnicity has been paid to cultural differences and the value of pluralism, less to the ways in which ethnic differences are implicated in the distribution of power and privilege. We think of an ethnic group as "a segment of a larger society whose members are thought, by themselves and/or others, to have a common origin and to share important segments of a common culture and who, in addition, participate in shared activities in which the common origin and culture are significant ingredients" (Yinger 1976, p. 200). An ethnic group is different from others in the society in some combination of the following characteristics: language, religion, ancestral homeland with its related culture, and race. No one of these traits by itself is sufficient to indicate an ethnic group, but commonly in the contemporary world two or more occur together. Groups that are different by race, as well as by some of the other criteria, are sometimes excluded from the category of ethnic group. That is not our preference. Americans of Korean background, for example, or native Americans, or black Americans (Ronald Taylor 1979) who are racially different from the majority are ethnic groups to the degree that they also differ in religion, language, or attachment to some elements of an ancestral culture. It should be noted, however, that the racial factor adds a symbolically important line of distinction.

The distinction between race and ethnicity, even as analytic concepts, has been blurred in recent years, as in the *Harvard Encyclopedia of American Ethnic Groups* (Thernstrom 1980). This doubtless expresses a desire to oppose racial discrimination, as M. G. Smith (1982, p. 9) suggests. "Abandoning a useful analytic distinction, however, does not exorcise the evil of racism. To relabel race 'ethnicity' does not make it so" (van den Berghe 1978, xv). Some groups, of course, can be distinguished both by their racial and their cultural characteristics.

The terms *ethnic group* and *minority,* we must also emphasize, are not synonyms. The two categories overlap, but they are analytically distinct. Persons of Swedish background in north central America may preserve something of an ancestral identity, but they are scarcely a minority. Minorities may mobilize the rudiments of ethnicity, reviving and partly inventing a shared ancestral culture, in an attempt to improve their situation. The driving force under these conditions, however, is their minority status and the disadvantages it brings. If one's major interest is in discrimination and inequality, it is unfortunate when attention is deflected to ethnicity as the primary term. For that reason we prefer and will normally use, in this context, the terms *cultural minority* and, when racial differences are also involved, *racial minority.*

Of course, the study of ethnicity is important in its own right, even when no discrimination or group hostility is present. However, much of the enormous literature on ethnicity deals, as one theme, with the implication of the ethnic order for the stratification system and thus becomes important for us.[2]

Three Types of Stratification Systems

The value of the criteria for defining *minority* is increased when one uses them in making additional distinctions. Harris (1959) compares *minority* with *caste* and *class* and in doing so notes the need for at least one additional variable. The three terms share many connotations; *caste* and *minority,* particularly, are often used interchangeably. Do we need all three terms? Harris believes that we do if we are to make refined distinctions, and he argues his point by suggesting three continua by which groups can be classified. We might put these into quasi-scales, as in Figure 1-2.

These are subtle distinctions. But we are dealing with complicated phenomena and we need as powerful a vocabulary as we can create. It is well to note that on two of the scales caste and minority are placed close together whereas on the other two minority and class are close.

We must be careful not to place a given system of social relationships in one of these categories and then overlook changing patterns that require reclassification. In India, for example, there is good evidence that acceptance of status has been reduced for lower castes. This means that they have become more "minority-like" (Berreman 1972; Béteille 1965; Schermerhorn 1978; Srinivas 1962, 1969). Although categorical prejudice remains strong, there is some tendency in the United States to respond to Blacks more in terms of their individual characteristics, somewhat less in terms of descent, moving them to that degree from the category of minority toward that of class.

Perhaps these variations around the meaning of caste, minority, and class can be made clearer by

[2]See, for example, Archdeacon 1983; A. Cohen 1974; Banton 1983; DeVos and Romanucci-Ross 1975; Enloe 1973; Glazer and Moynihan 1975; Hechter 1976; King 1983; Léons 1978; Mughan and McAllister 1982; G. Patterson 1979; O. Patterson 1977; Steinberg 1981; R. Taylor 1979; Thernstrom 1980; Yancey et al. 1976; Young 1976.

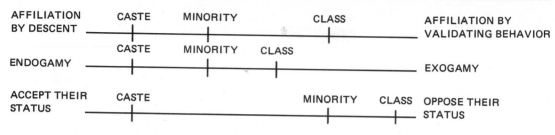

WE MIGHT ADD A FOURTH, A STRUCTURAL COUNTERPART
TO THE THIRD CONTINUUM ABOVE:

FIXED STATUS HIERARCHY VALIDATED BY INSTITUTIONAL STRUCTURE — CASTE —————— MINORITY — CLASS — **FIXED STATUS HIERARCHY OPPOSED BY INSTITUTIONAL STRUCTURE**

Figure 1-2. Relationship among caste, minority, and class.

scaling the four variables in a somewhat different way. In Figure 1-3 we have designated possible profiles from among many that might be drawn.

Such a chart may help us to avoid using only a few nouns that cannot do justice to the full range of facts and it may facilitate the recognition of change. Rather than state what a society really is in its stratification system in terms of a few types, we must locate it along the scale.

Our concern in this book is with minority–majority systems, not with all varieties of stratification. Clearly, however, we will have to make comparative references at many points to caste systems on the one hand and to class systems on the other.

Varieties of Minority Aims

Having distinguished minorities from related types of groups, we must still note that minorities vary widely among themselves. Perhaps they can be most usefully classified on the basis of their ultimate objectives, using Wirth's (1945) classic distinction of four types. (Of course minority aims

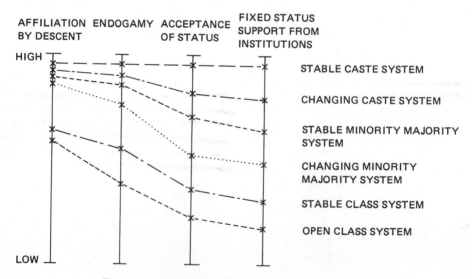

Figure 1-3. Types of stratification systems using four criteria.

cannot be thoroughly discussed without reference to majority aims and larger questions of social structure, as we shall note below.)

1. *Pluralistic:* a minority desiring peaceful existence side by side with the majority and other minorities. Pluralism is often a precondition of a dynamic civilization, for it allows mutual exchange and stimulation. It usually takes the form of a desire for basic political and economic unity along with toleration of cultural, lingual, and religious diversity. Many black Americans, as we shall see, have become more pluralistic in recent years. The awakening of the ethnic minorities of eastern Europe in the late eighteenth century was first of all a cultural renaissance, a change from feelings of inferiority to pride in their distinctness. Where economic and political equality have been achieved or granted, this awakening has continued to be pluralistic. When cultural diversity has been suppressed, the minorities have tended to become secessionistic.

The concept of pluralism varies from setting to setting. In the British scholarly tradition it carries connotations of intergroup conflict and of patterns of subordination and superordination among the separate groups (Furnival 1948; Kuper and Smith 1969). In some societies it implies toleration but little active cooperation among cultural groups, political and economic unity but little exchange and common participation in other matters. This pattern has often been dominant in eastern Europe. Cultural pluralism may imply, however, a more active kind of unity among diverse groups, a reaching out toward common goals, a sharing of their different heritages. This has frequently been the response of ethnic groups in the United States. After they have become thoroughly established in this country, pride in their cultural heritage becomes less defensive and protective. The last shreds of secessionism are gone, but a desire to contribute to the full range of American life out of their earlier experience remains.

2. *Assimilationist:* a minority desiring absorption into the larger society and treatment simply as individuals. Assimilation is likely to occur only when the majority accepts the idea; but it may prevail as a goal even in the face of majority opposition. Assimilationism has been a common tendency among minorities in some settings. Many groups have been divided, however, on the question of the relative desirability of pluralism and assimilation as well as on their perceptions of the options open to them. Thus one finds some evidences of assimilation among Asian and West Indian

immigrants in Birmingham, England, but also evidence of substantial barriers and of nonassimilationist aims among them (Rex and Tomlinson 1979).

Although we shall use the term neutrally—neither applauding it nor lamenting it in general—assimilation has become something of a swearword for some people; for others it distorts our pictures of what is taking place. The latter argue that emphasis on assimilation—with an accompanying view that a tendency toward consensus best describes social process—is not only factually wrong but that it also, intentionally or not, reenforces oppressive systems (e.g., Blauner 1972; Lyman 1972).

Others argue that emphasis on the various separatist policies—with their implicit assumption that conflict is the basic social process—not only obscures assimilationist trends but also, again intentionally or not, reenforces lines of division that perpetuate inequality and hostility (e.g., Kuper 1977; Pettigrew 1969).

We will be commenting on this issue at various points throughout the book. Here we will only remark that there are ideological elements in both points of view, that the evidence is difficult to assess, that both arguments are doubtless true *under different sets of conditions that are not yet well identified,* and that the issues raised by this debate are of great importance intellectually and morally and with reference to public policy.

It is now widely believed that pluralism is the dominant view among minorities in many and probably in most parts of the world. This is not easily documented, however, and we must be aware of the ideological factors that influence our perceptions on this question. Under some conditions assimilationism, purged of its one-way emphasis, tends to reemerge. We must follow the evidence on this closely to try to discover who most strongly supports pluralism and who supports assimilationism. Behind that difference are disagreements over the effects. Some believe that the hidden agenda—or at least the unintended effect—of pluralism is continued discrimination. Others believe that pluralistic groups are better able to fight discrimination. We will be discussing that issue at several points in later chapters.

3. *Secessionist:* a minority that seeks both cultural and political independence. When a friendly plural existence or assimilation is frustrated, a minority may develop a movement dedicated to complete independence. They become discontented with cultural pluralism and antagonistic to

assimilation. Such a movement most often occurs among a minority that has once had political independence—for example, Zionism. There may be some tendencies in this direction among other minorities, however, as illustrated by the Garveyite movement for a separate nation among Afro-Americans and the separatist tendencies of the Black Muslims in their first years.

4. *Militant:* a minority that goes beyond the desire for equality to a desire for domination—the total reversal of statuses. It becomes convinced of its own superiority. (Wirth was using the term to refer to a goal, not to the use of active protest against discrimination, which can be used in efforts to obtain a variety of goals.) When Hitler overran Czechoslovakia, the Sudeten Germans sought domination over the Czechs and Slovaks. When Britain withdrew from Palestine, both Arabs and Jews attempted to establish a dominant status. With the forming of new nations in Asia and Africa there have been many reversals of status.

What we have described are abstract types, not empirical groups or explicitly formulated policies.[3] Although groups might be compared as more or less supportive of a particular aim, we would be better served by information that permitted us to describe profiles. We need to think in terms of the proportionate share of support for these different aims, both within individuals (for many are ambivalent) and among them. If we are to avoid stereotypy, we must also recognize change. Each minority can best be studied in terms of a sequence of profiles, indicating varying aims in response to changing circumstances. Lacking precise information, we can only make an estimate, but the "aim profile" of black Americans might have been characterized by line A, in Figure 1-4, in 1940 and by line B in 1980.

The Origin of Minorities

There are unique elements in the history of every minority, but a few general principles are involved. Since a minority is a group of people that can be distinguished by physical or cultural characteristics, it follows that anything which makes a population more heterogeneous may create a minority

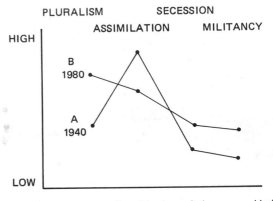

Figure 1-4. Estimate of combinations of aims among black Americans.

situation. The kind of heterogeneity that will be noticed, of course, depends upon national, cultural, religious, and racial ideologies—in other words, on the characteristics of the majority, those with the greatest power and highest status. Migration, cultural contact, conquering armies bring diverse peoples together. This process has doubtless been accelerated by modern technology and transportation. "The genesis of minorities must therefore be sought in the fact that territory, political authority, people, and culture rarely coincide" (Wirth 1945, p. 365).

The development of the nation-state system has been the central fact in the origin of minorities. Both the spread of dominance over formerly separate groups and the common desire to create a homogeneous nation (leading to attempts to repress cultural variation) have created the minority–majority situation. Wagley and Harris (1958, pp. 241–42) view this development against the background of tribal societies:

An individual's world in primitive societies is . . . populated largely by "relatives," all of whom speak the same language, practice the same customs, and belong to the same physical stock. . . . Primitive social organization thus contains no provisions for incorporating into a single unit groups of individuals who are not related by descent or by marriage, who follow different customs, who stress distinctive values, and who, in sum, are an alien people.

Only with the development of the state did human societies become equipped with a form of social organization which could bind masses of culturally and physically heterogeneous "strangers" into a single social entity. . . .

Yet the growth of the state form of organization did not entirely replace the principles by which unity is achieved among primitive peoples. On the contrary, if a thoroughgoing replacement had indeed taken place, minorities, as we know them today, would not exist.

---

[3] In Chapters 6 and 7 minority actions will be discussed in greater detail. For a few sources on these types of minority aims and policies see Alba 1976; Blackwell 1975; Caditz 1976; M. M. Gordon 1964; Murguía 1975; Young 1976.

Many people, even in modern urban and heterogeneous societies, continue to view the world from a "tribal" perspective. The dominant groups particularly "have tended to act as if the state society to which they belong ideally ought to consist of their own physical and cultural type" (Wagley and Harris 1958, p. 242). We need now to examine the various ways in which they have acted on this conviction.

Types of Majority Policy

Majority–minority situations are doubtless ancient. It was with the coming of the era of nationalism, however, with the Renaissance, the rise of trade, and increasing secularization, that the problem of minorities became very important. Merchants and kings were demanding national unity at the same time that minorities were becoming more self-conscious. The theories of national sovereignty and the divine right of kings were manufactured to oppose the universalist claims of the papacy on the one hand and the decentralization of the power of feudalism on the other. In the process of national centralization, institutions were modeled after those of the majority, and the minorities were required, with varying degrees of rigidity, to bring their customs into line. When nationalism began to come to the more diverse peoples of central and eastern Europe, with their histories of imperial domination, the cultural minorities had a strong feeling of unity that resisted the larger nationalism. As McCartney pointed out (1934), the Serb had never been a true part of the Ottoman Empire, but he knew that he was a Serb. Centuries of domination had produced a secessionist feeling that would not easily be worn away (see Kann 1950).

Along with the growth of nationalism, new minority problems were developing as a result of imperialism and a fresh wave of conquests. Even greater diversity—of culture, of religion, of race—was brought into one political framework by the expansion of European power. The dominant groups were faced with new questions of policy with regard to minority groups. Extermination, subjugation, toleration, assimilation—each of these was tried at various times and places, as "external" minorities (the "colonies") were added to "internal" minorities (those within the mother country). England had scarcely worked out a peaceful *modus vivendi* with Scotland and Wales and was still fighting bitterly with Ireland when she was faced with the problems of policy in dealing with American Indians, Asiatic Indians, Arabs, Africans, Malayans, and a host of other peoples. Czarist Russia crossed mountains and plains, rather than oceans, but she absorbed an equally diverse group of minorities, as did many other nations.

With this brief sketch of the rise of internal and external minorities in mind, we may ask: What major types of policies have the dominant groups developed? Six varieties may be seen, sometimes paralleling, sometimes opposing the aims of minorities:

1. Assimilation
   a. Forced
   b. Permitted
2. Pluralism
3. Legal protection of minorities
4. Population transfer
   a. Peaceful transfer
   b. Forced migration
5. Continued subjugation
6. Extermination

A brief discussion of these types of policies will indicate the wide range of responses that dominant groups may make to majority–minority situations.

1. *Assimilation.* One way to "solve" the problem is to eliminate the minority—as a minority. We have noted that this is the aim of some minorities, but their approach to assimilation is often very different. Dominant groups have frequently adopted an extreme ethnocentrism that refused minorities the right to practice their own religion, speak their own language, follow their own customs. The czarist regime went through periods of vigorous Russification during which the only alternatives available to minorities who wished to preserve their identity were rigid segregation, expulsion, or extermination. Perhaps the most extreme manifestation of forced assimilation was the Nazi regime, with its ideology of a monocultural, monolingual, monoracial people ruled by an authoritarian state. The Nazi policy went beyond forced assimilation, of course, for its doctrine of race superiority asserted that some groups were unassimilable. For them, forced population transfers and extermination were the policies adopted.

Thus forced assimilation is an extreme manifestation of ethnocentrism developed into an active policy for the supposed benefit of a national state.

Peaceful assimilation is in marked contrast. It is a long-run policy of cultural and sometimes racial unity; but it permits minorities to absorb the dominant patterns in their own way and at their own speed, and it envisages reciprocal assimilation, a blending of the diverse group, not a one-way adjustment. Brazil has an ideology that looks with favor on the eventual blending of diverse racial types into a Brazilian stock. Gunnar Myrdal declares that the assimilation of many of her minorities is part of the value creed of the United States, although the creed does not have a strong reciprocal emphasis (minorities are to give up their differences) and it tends to exclude racial minorities. The supposed lesser assimilability of racial groups adds a dimension that must be taken into account in any analysis of the American situation.

Gordon uses the term "Anglo-conformity" to refer to what he considers the most prevalent form of American assimilationism. Although the term covers a variety of interpretations, they all assume "the desirability of maintaining English institutions (as modified by the American Revolution), the English language, and English-oriented cultural patterns as dominant and standard in American life" (Gordon 1964, p. 88). This conception has sometimes been related to notions of "Nordic" or "Aryan" superiority, to strong opposition to non-British immigration, and to vigorous Americanization campaigns. There has also been a moderate variant, however, which eschews ideas of racial superiority and accepts immigration from diverse sources, demanding only a fairly rapid adoption of "Anglo-Saxon" culture patterns.

This moderate "Anglo-conformity" view shades off into the "melting-pot" view of assimilation. Conditions in America were different in many ways from those in England; the population was drawn from many nations.

Was it not possible, then, to think of the evolving American society not simply as a slightly modified England but rather as a totally new blend, culturally and biologically, in which the stocks and folkways of Europe were, figuratively speaking, indiscriminantly mixed in the political pot of the emerging nation and melted together by the fires of American influence and interaction into a distinctly new type? (Gordon 1964, p. 115)

This thesis has perhaps been more prominent in America as ideology than as policy; yet for 150 years our immigration laws were based, in part, on it, and the melting-pot idea probably affects, to some degree, the way in which most Americans view their society.

Because conceptualization and measurement of assimilation are not far advanced, one cannot easily compare two groups on the extent of their assimilation (but see, e.g., Alba 1976; Simpson 1968). It is one thing to see it as a majority policy, however widely shared, and something else to see it as an unintended effect of numerous social changes, involving the interaction of majority and minority. Seen in the latter way, assimilation undoubtedly has several dimensions that must be identified. Think of assimilation as a process of boundary reduction that can occur when members of two or more societies or of smaller social groups meet. As a completed process, it means the blending into one of formerly distinguishable groups (Francis 1976, Chapter 20; Simpson 1968). If one thinks of it as a variable, however, assimilation can range from the smallest beginnings of interaction and cultural exchange to the thorough fusion of the groups.

The extent of assimilation depends on the strength of the four subprocesses of which it is constituted: amalgamation (biological), identification (psychological), acculturation (cultural), and integration (structural). These occur in various combinations and sequences, not in a fixed order; and the strength of each is affected by the strength of the others (Yinger 1981).

Gordon (1964) included a similar set of four subprocesses or conditions among what he called the assimilation variables. He also included, however, the absence of prejudice, of discrimination, and of value and power conflict. These are better seen as conditions that influence the extent of assimilation, not as aspects of it. In fact, opposite conditions—the presence of discrimination, for example—can also increase the extent of assimilation under some circumstances.

2. *Pluralism.* Some minorities do not want to be assimilated, to lose their separate identity, whether it be unilaterally or bilaterally. And parallel to the pluralistic aims of such groups is the willingness on the part of some dominant groups to permit cultural variability within the range still consonant with national unity and security. This is frequently the immediate policy of an ultimate assimilationist approach. The Soviet Union sought, and apparently won, the support of scores of cultural and national minorities who had bitterly resented the czarist policy of suppression. In 1917

the Communists appealed to the various minorities by defending the right of cultural atonomy: "Mohammedans of Russia . . . Tartars of the Volga and Crimea; Kirghiz and Sartes of Siberia and Turkestan; Turks and Tartars of Transcaucasia, your beliefs and customs, your national institutions and culture, are hereafter free and inviolable" (quoted by Sidney Webb and Beatrice Webb, in Locke and Stern 1946, p. 673). Stalin, himself a member of a small nationality, was made People's Commissar for Nationalities and was important in the policy that separated statehood from cultural nationality and race. Native languages and arts were not only permitted but encouraged, and the political organization of the Soviet Union reflects, to some degree, cultural units of the population. The Soviet policy was not, however, thoroughly pluralistic, and it has become less so. It opposed the extraterritorial pluralism of the Zionists; religious autonomy was systematically undermined by antireligious propaganda; vigorous insistence upon political and economic orthodoxy reduced the significance of cultural autonomy; and, since the beginning of World War II, a resurgent Russian nationalism has brought some return of the Russification policy of the czars. During that war, some Soviet minorities were forcefully broken up and dispersed; Jews and others have been attacked for being "cosmopolites"; and the theory of the Great Russian as the "elder brother" of the other groups in the Soviet Union implies at best an Orwellian equality, the Russian being "more equal than others" (Azrael 1978; Connor 1984; W. J. Kolarz in Lind 1955, Chapter 9; Rakowska-Harmstone 1977; Wheeler 1962).

Switzerland is probably the outstanding example of a thoroughgoing use of the policy of pluralism. Her experience demonstrates the fact, however, that where pluralism is thoroughly accepted by all the groups involved one no longer has a minority–majority society, but simply a culturally differentiated society. Only a careful measurement of levels of discrimination can indicate where these varieties of pluralism prevail. For several centuries the French and Italian Swiss have not been minorities, in our sense of the term, nor have they given up lingual and cultural differences from the German Swiss, who make up three-fourths of the population. A strong political and economic unity overrides the cultural differences. Geographical location, the presence nearby of large supporting nations for each of the three major groups in the Swiss confederation, a democratic ideology,

and other factors have contributed to this development. The delicacy of the balance, however, may be suggested by the decisive action taken in Switzerland to expel or to curtail the rights of guest workers—who made up such a large share of its less-skilled labor force for two decades or more after World War II—when it appeared that they might become a permanent part of the Swiss population.

There are several dimensions to pluralism, as there are to assimilation. Seen from the perspective of the dominant group, one can envisage situations in which cultural pluralism, but not structural pluralism, is permitted. This is to some degree true in South Africa, which permits black Africans some cultural identity but strongly inhibits the development of separate structures—an indication that pluralism is not necessarily a liberal policy. The government of South Africa supports education in the native tongue, for example, but many black South Africans want education in English, realizing that the "language policy of only educating in tribal languages outside of the major towns is a policy clearly designed to make sure that cultural pluralism and social stratification coincide; that is, that the people do not learn the skills (English) necessary to get more resources. In other words, the language policy perpetuates white supremacy" (Harrington 1978, pp. 2–3).

Some societies insist on structural separation but discourage cultural variation. Or a society may permit rather wide variation in individual beliefs and values, perhaps in the name of civil liberty, provided these do not accumulate into groups that are sharply distinct in culture and structure (see Van den Berghe 1978, Chapter 7; Young 1976; Patterson 1977; Smock and Smock 1975).

Whatever the pattern of pluralism in a society, there comes a point at which the variation is constrained. The critical line may be language; it may be religion. In the modern nation-state it tends to be politicoeconomic. Loyalty is defined in terms of allegiance to the dominant political and economic structures and values. Setting the limits of legitimate opposition is one of the critical tasks of a complex society. The prevailing theory (Yinger 1970, pp. 239–44, 425–30) tries to reconcile two somewhat opposing views of the consequences of pluralism:

On the one hand, well-organized groups with which individuals feel closely identified are regarded as the best means of maximizing freedom, creating channels for the expression of interests, preventing alienation, and achieving some flexibility in the system. On the other hand, cross-cutting memberships that prevent the piling up of differences are considered necessary to safeguard society from splitting into such distinctive units that mobility, political compromise, and national action would be prevented. (p. 244)

The United States has followed a complex and somewhat contradictory course with regard to pluralism. She is sometimes described as basically assimilationist, not only permitting, but demanding conformity to a rather narrow range of options. There is substantial evidence for this description. On the other hand, religious pluralism is now nearly fully the fact as well as the ideal; the country has followed a "hands-off" policy toward the private associations and foreign-language newspapers of many immigrant groups; there is some support for language diversity (later we shall inquire about possible effects); Blacks, Chicanos, Indians, Asians, and others assert their separate identities with some approval and even support from the majority; and pluralism is widely accepted as a value. If America has never been so even-handed in her treatment of different groups as her ideology would imply, neither has she been so utterly indifferent to the range of cultures and peoples as her most severe critics have declared.

3. *Legal protection of minorities.* Closely related to pluralism, or a subdivision of it, is the policy of protecting minorities by legal, constitutional, and diplomatic means. This is often official pluralism, but the emphasis on legal protection implies that there are important groups involved that do not accept the pattern. After World War I, for example, the constitutions of Bulgaria and Turkey guaranteed rights of autonomy for minorities. The Thirteenth, Fourteenth, and Fifteenth Amendments to the United States Constitution, although not pluralistic in aim, sought to protect the equal rights of minorities, primarily Blacks, in a situation that had been unfavorable to that aim. Recent civil rights legislation has similar objectives.

Another variety of legal protection involves international action (Thornberry 1980). This again implies that there are important groups who do not accept the principle of equal rights for minorities and that therefore some coercive legal force is necessary. The Genocide Convention of the United Nations is perhaps more moral than legal in its implications, but it seeks to establish a clear-cut international law against the kind of mass extermination of peoples that was part of Nazi policy. The Versailles Treaty was also concerned with minorities—particularly in the countries of the old Austro-Hungarian Empire, where so many conflicts had originated. One "solution," involved in Woodrow Wilson's famous Fourteen Points, was the "self-determination of peoples." Had this been carried out it would have eliminated "national" minorities by making it possible for each minority to form itself into a nation. It was based on the assumption that a monocultural, monolingual state was most likely to be successful; but it minimized the important economic forces that demanded multigroup unity. It tended to encourage small cultural group self-consciousness rather than large multigroup cooperation. Moreover, it was virtually impossible to carry out, without enormous migrations, for many of the minorities were scattered in small enclaves throughout the area. Nevertheless, the fact that the rights of minorities were given careful consideration represented a significant change in peacemaking. And when the "self-determination" principle was disregarded, as it often was, an additional treaty provision for pluralism within nations was invoked.

Civil and religious liberties, the right of citizenship, language rights, and special attention to the rights of Jews—who had been the most disadvantaged minority in most of these nations—were among the provisions in the treaties.

The United Nations has not followed the lead of the League of Nations in regard to the minorities question, for a number of reasons. The League had applied legal protection clauses mainly to the defeated nations and new nations of eastern Europe. The United Nations, with more attention to worldwide problems, inevitably becomes entangled with questions of diplomacy and international conflict. The United States, eager to hold Latin-American support, has—not altogether consistently—emphasized nonintervention in internal affairs by the United Nations and thus can scarcely support strenuous international efforts to protect minorities within a state. The Soviet Union will not accept international surveillance over states that she wants under her control. Nations which found that some members of their national minorities had been disloyal during World War II—Czechoslovakia, for example—were unwilling to think in terms of their international protection. Nor do the Soviet Union and the United States respond favorably to debate in the United Nations concerning their minority policies. The result of such forces as these has been a deinternationalization of the minorities problem since the days of the League of Nations.

This does not mean that the United Nations is unconcerned with minorities. There has been a shift in emphasis toward human rights—the rights of all individuals as individuals, not as members of groups. And as we shall see below, the United Nations has given attention to the process of population transfer. Active efforts to protect minorities by international legal means, following the pattern of the League of Nations, have, however, been weak. Although the United Nations, through many of its agencies, is interested in the question of minorities and may develop more effective techniques (indirect approaches that reduce the causes of discrimination), its present state of political disarray does not promote optimism.

4. *Population transfer.* Majorities have sometimes adopted a policy of population transfer to attempt to reduce minorities' problems. This matches the secessionist aim of some minorities—both groups hoping for a reduction of tension through physical separation. In a few instances population transfer has been a peaceful process, with some concern for the rights and desires of individual minority–group members and a general interest in improving their situation. More often it has been a thoroughly discriminatory policy aimed at "solving" the problem by driving minority-group members out of an area.

In the early 1920s a fairly successful exchange was made among Greece, Turkey, and Bulgaria. There are many obstacles, however, to the widespread use of this policy. When the transfer is on an exchange basis, many will not want to move. Are they to be compelled to? The minorities may be of unequal size and trained for different occupations. Can they, under such conditions, be absorbed into the new lands? The basic difficulty is that this policy assumes that a homogeneous population will be a more peaceful one, although transfer of minorities does little to reduce the primary causes of conflict. These causes will be discussed in later chapters.

Some Americans have felt that the way to solve the "Negro problem" was to recolonize Negroes in Africa or segregate them in a separate state. Many thousands of Blacks did, in fact, return to Africa during the nineteenth century. The separate state idea is often the manifestation of a vigorous prejudice. Paradoxically, it has sometimes been part of a Communist policy, presumably designed to benefit a minority. And it is sometimes given well-meaning support by persons of relatively mild prejudice mixed with good intentions. When Paul Robeson was graduated from college, wealthy alumni of his school proposed that he cooperate with them, as a leader, in helping to establish a separate geographical area for Negroes in the United States. The response of Robeson was one of strong disagreement. Most Negroes repudiate such a plan. Why, they ask, should we, any more than any other group of individuals, be separated from the total community? Negroes are very old Americans; they are thoroughly identified with America's society. Even the separatist views formerly held by the Black Muslims were oriented more to the transfer of the White than of the Black population.

If population transfer sometimes has good intentions, it far more often expresses only hostility and discrimination as a policy of the majority. The transfer can be of two types, direct and indirect. In the former, the minority involved is specifically required and forced to leave. Many nations and cities drove out Jews in the late medieval period; the United States drove the Indians out of area after area; the British kept the Irish beyond the Pale; the Soviet Union deported millions of her citizens, members of religious and national minorities, during World War II; and Nazi Germany followed a relentless policy, aimed at a homogeneous nation, by forcibly transferring large numbers of persons of many minorities. The indirect policy is so make life so unbearable for members of the minority that they "choose" to migrate. Thus czarist Russia drove out millions of Jews. This was also part of Germany's policy, as it has been of several newly independent African states in dealing with their citizens of Asian background.

After World War II, efforts to reduce minority–majority problems in Europe by population transfer received a great deal of support. During the war some German groups had been brought back to the *Vaterland* and after the war others were expelled. The desire in eastern Europe to drive out a "disloyal minority" showed a great deal of categorical prejudice because there was little effort to distinguish between loyal and disloyal members of the national minorities. (This was paralleled in some measure in the United States, where those of Japanese ancestry, the vast majority of whom were loyal to the United States and most of whom were citizens, were "driven out" of the West into relocation camps.)

It is not always easy to distinguish between immigration (to be discussed later), which often has a push factor, and forced migration. Certainly the latter has been a major factor in recent migration from Cuba, Vietnam, Cambodia, and Ethiopia, for example. It is a tragic fact that "there are probably more refugees in the world today than at any other time in modern history. . . 10 to 13 million" (*Cultural Survival Newsletter,* Spring 1981; see also Glaser and Possony 1979, pp. 415–53).

Population transfer may be effective in a few marginal cases, but in the modern world it can scarcely solve, or in most cases even reduce, the minorities problems. It is based on the monocultural ideal, which in a day of mobility and international communication is progressively less meaningful. To be effective, it would have to block later population movement, despite labor demands or other economic changes, an action that contradicts the growing internationalization of the economy. Even when carried out in a humane way, it violates many of the most basic rights of individuals (Claude 1955, Chapters 8, 10).

5. *Continued subjugation.* The policies just discussed have sought either to incorporate the minorities into a society or to drive them out. Often, however, the dominant group wants neither of these results; it wants the minority groups around, but it wants them kept "in their place," subservient and exploitable. There may be some ultimate promise of equality, but often not even that. Average white South Africans cannot conceive of the time when Blacks will be their equal. Yet they would be dismayed at the thought of a nation without Blacks. Who would do all the hard work?

Many persons in the United States have supported large-scale immigration in the expectation that it would bring cheap labor. Today it is difficult to enforce laws regarding the migration of Mexicans into the United States because many powerful people in the Southwest and elsewhere want an exploitable minority. Were the "wetbacks" not a subjugated minority, were they able to command wages equal to those of American citizens, it would be far less difficult to enforce immigration laws. Much of this volume will be concerned with the subjugation policy employed by majorities.

6. *Extermination.* Conflict between groups sometimes becomes so severe that physical destruction of one by the other becomes an accepted goal. This may have been true of some ancient tribal contacts; it certainly has been true of the contact between hunting and gathering societies and industrial societies. The United States destroyed perhaps two-thirds of the Indian population before her policy changed. The small Tasmanian population was completely wiped out by the British (and by the civilized diseases that they brought to the island). The Boers of South Africa looked upon the Hottentots as scarcely more than animals of the jungle and hunted them ruthlessly. In the late nineteenth and early twentieth centuries, tens of thousands of Armenians who would not convert to Islam were killed by the Turks. And the Hitler regime, between 1933 and 1945, murdered six million Jews.

Other terms, more general in their reference, include extermination within the scope of their meaning but add other violent and hostile acts. Thus victimology, the study of group oppression, emphasizes violence but in its broadest meaning becomes a synonym for discrimination. Genocide, defined literally, is identical with extermination, but its meaning has been extended, particularly in the language of the Convention on Genocide, adopted by the General Assembly of the United Nations. The Convention, which came into force in 1951, after having been ratified by twenty nations, states (Dadrian 1975a, p. 117):

Genocide means any of the following acts committed with intent to destroy, in whole, or in part, a national, ethical, racial or religious group as such:
  (a) killing members of the group;
  (b) causing serious bodily or mental harm to members of the group;
  (c) deliberately inflicting on the group conditions of life calculated to bring about its physical destruction in whole or in part;
  (d) imposing measures intended to prevent births within the group;
  (e) forcibly transferring children of the group.

Over eighty nations have ratified the Convention on Genocide, but the United States is not among them.

Genocide can be aimed at an outside society, whose land or resources the aggressor society wants to seize, or at an internal minority, whom the majority wants to eliminate or is willing to see disappear without any policy decisions specifying that aim. Only the attacks on internal minorities are technically within our subject, but the line is often difficult to draw, as in the case of attacks on North and South American Indians. It is also difficult to distinguish, on this topic as on others, between majority–minority conflict and class conflict (Pettigrew 1981b) or political conflict. The latter is illustrated by Gouldner (1977) in his description of the killing of millions of kulaks and other peasants in the 1930s by the urban-centered Bolshevik power elite and, of course, by Solzhenitsyn in his powerful and influential three-volume work, *The Gulag Archipelago.*

Dadrian (1975b) includes "cultural genocide" within his general definition. Since pressures on minorities to give up aspects of their own culture, religion for example, may succeed to some degree, "non-violent genocide may ensue." This is what we have called *forced assimilation,* which seems more appropriate than extending the meaning of genocide. His definition, nevertheless, is valuable (p. 201):

> Genocide is the successful attempt by a dominant group, vested with formal authority and/or with preponderant access to the overall resources of power, to reduce by coercion or lethal violence the number of a minority group whose ultimate extermination is held desirable and useful and whose respective vulnerability is a major factor contributing to the decision of genocide.

(See also Cohn 1967; Dadrian 1976; Dawidowicz 1975; Fein 1978; Horowitz 1976; Howton 1971; Kuper 1981, 1982.)

These six policies of dominant groups are not, of course, mutually exclusive; many may be practiced simultaneously. Some are conscious long-run plans; some are *ad hoc* adjustments to specific situations; some are by-products (perhaps unintended) of other policies. In some instances they are the official actions of majority-group leaders; in others they are the day-by-day responses of individual members of the dominant group. In this book we shall see many of the policies in operation, from complete acceptance, to toleration, to subjugation, to extermination.

What Is Prejudice?

Our reference, up to this point, has been primarily to the group dimensions of intergroup relations. There are individual dimensions that, although closely connected, require separate definition.

For our purposes, we shall define prejudice as an emotional, rigid attitude (a *pre*disposition to respond to a certain stimulus in a certain way) toward a group of people. They may be a group only in the mind of the prejudiced person; that is,

he categorizes them together, although they may have little similarity or interaction. Prejudices are thus attitudes, but not all attitudes are prejudices. They both contain the element of prejudgment, but prejudiced attitudes have an affective or emotional quality that not all attitudes possess.

Prejudice leads one to select facts for emphasis, blinding one to other facts. It causes one to look upon all members of a "group" as if they were alike. New experiences are fitted into the old categories by selecting only those cues that harmonize with the prejudgment or stereotype. Prejudiced attitudes, because of their emotional quality, are relatively stable and persistent; but this should not be exaggerated. They are, after all, anchored in life experiences that are subject to drastic reorganization.

Prejudice involves not only prejudgment but, as Vickery and Opler (1948) point out, misjudgment as well. It is categorical thinking that systematically misinterprets the facts. Again, not all misjudgment is prejudice. Prejudice is misjudgment of the members of a supposed human group; it is socially oriented action. One may misjudge the speed of an approaching car, but one is anxious to correct the error. Prejudice is a misjudgment that one defends. When a preexisting attitude is so strong and inflexible that it seriously distorts perception and judgment, one has a prejudice.

In discussing the emotional and rigid quality of prejudice, we do not want to give the impression that no cognitive or even rational elements are involved. From one perspective, prejudice can be seen as an effort to give some coherence and order to a puzzling and complex situation, or as an effort to defend some value. Facts and experience may play some part, adding strength to the inflexibility of a prejudgment. We would only emphasize that these cognitive and rational elements are used in the service of attitudes that usually have a strong emotional component (see Chapter 4; see also Hamilton 1981; Tajfel 1969).

The limitation of the meaning of the term *prejudice* to human interaction has some etymological justification. As Kimball Young pointed out (1956, p. 502), the word comes from the Latin *prejudicum*—a preceding judgment: "The word took on special meaning when it came to refer to judicial examination in Rome held prior to a trial as a way of determining the social status of the would-be litigants. . . . This status-defining function of prejudice has never been lost. Prejudice puts an individual 'in his place.'"

Many writers have worked on refinements of the term in order to isolate what seems to be a more homogeneous group of phenomena for inclusion. Communication is made more accurate by limiting a term to homogeneous elements. If I say, "Will you bring me that piece of furniture from the next room," I may get anything from a footstool to a grand piano. If I ask for a small chair, I am quite likely to get what I want. Prejudice is a "furniture" kind of word. As it is normally used, it includes a wide variety of phenomena.

In isolating homogeneous phenomena, one can either talk about types of prejudice (prejudice$_1$, prejudice$_2$, prejudice$_3$) or find different terms to assign to the related, yet different phenomena (prejudice for one type, intolerance for another, stereotypy for a third, for example).

In their valuable analysis of racial attitudes, Apostle, Glock, Piazza, and Suelzle (1983) distinguish among three components: persons' perceptions of racial differences, their explanations of the sources of those differences, "and their prescriptions for what, if anything, should be done to bring about racial equality." Since these attitudes do not necessarily covary, they must be studied separately and the relationships among them examined. (In our judgment, the term *racial attitudes* includes but is not a substitute for the term *prejudice*. Presumably there can be nonprejudiced perceptions, explanations, and prescriptions.)

Robin Williams, Jr. (1947), distinguishes between prejudices based on functional differences in the social order or real differences in value, on the one hand, and those that emphasize stereotypes centered on some symbol, such as skin color, that has no functional significance, on the other. Thus for a democrat to be prejudiced against communists or fascists is different from his being prejudiced against Japanese—not entirely different, to be sure, but sufficiently so to require separation in our vocabularies (prejudice$_1$ and prejudice$_2$). It is the latter type that is the subject of this book.

Some writers prefer, from their theoretical perspectives, to distinguish among the varieties of related phenomena by using different terms, rather than by describing types and degrees of prejudice. The tendency for definitions to reflect theoretical positions is shown clearly by the interpretation of the relationship between prejudice and anti-Semitism that Oliver Cox made. He believed that *economic* forces are the fundamental ones in determining the patterns of intergroup relations. He was concerned primarily with race relations. He used the term *prejudice* to refer to attitudes that facilitate economic exploitation of racial minorities. Thus Cox (1948, p. 393) declared that anti-Semitism is *not* prejudice, but intolerance:

Anti-Semitism, to begin with, is clearly a form of social intolerance, which attitude may be defined as an unwillingness on the part of a dominant group to tolerate the beliefs or practices of a subordinate group because it considers these beliefs and practices to be either inimical to group solidarity or a threat to the continuity of the status quo. Race prejudice, on the other hand, is a social attitude propagated among the public by an exploiting class for the purpose of stigmatizing some group as inferior so that the exploitation of either the group itself or its resources or both may be justified. Persecution and exploitation are the behavior aspects of intolerance and race prejudice respectively.

That economic exploitation is importantly involved in majority–minority relations no one can doubt. That the term *prejudice* may be used to refer only to the attitudes that facilitate economic exploitation is also legitimate. But Cox obscures the similarities between the various types of majority–minority relations and oversimplifies the causal complex. "Religious persecution and racial domination," Cox declared, "are categorically different social facts" (1948, p. 481).

It is wise to emphasize the variety of types of majority–minority relations, to isolate separate causes, and to develop a terminology based on these distinctions. But if this procedure leads to the claim that related phenomena are "categorically different social facts," it will block our ability to see interconnections. Science must search not only for differences that lie behind superficial similarities, but also for similarities that may be disguised by superficial differences.

What Is Discrimination?

Prejudice is an attitude, a *tendency* to respond or a symbolic response. It may never involve overt action toward members of a minority group, either because no situation presents itself or, in situations wherein one might show antipathy, because other attitudes inhibit open expressions of hostility. You may have a strong prejudice against the residents of southwest Euthanasia, but since you have never met one of them, you have had no opportunity to express your attitude. A black man may have a vigorous prejudice against white men but may disguise his feelings or give them indirect expression.

Thus prejudice must not be equated with discrimination although they are closely related.

In a neutral sense, discrimination means simply "to draw a distinction," but this can be done, as the dictionary meanings show, by showing a "faculty for nicely distinguishing," according to generally accepted standards, or by drawing "an unfair or injurious distinction." It is the latter with which we are concerned, that is, the drawing of distinctions in such a way that widely accepted values and procedures are violated. It is apparent from such a definition that a given act can be labeled discriminatory only when particular values or a particular labeling group is specified.

The essence of social discrimination is that there are some who say: we are "nicely distinguishing," while others reply: no, you are drawing "an unfair and injurious distinction." That is, discrimination tends to be supported by secondary, if not by primary, norms and by significant subgroups in a society, thus making it the subject of intergroup and not simply interindividual conflict (Yinger 1968). In Robin Williams's well-known definition (1947, p. 39): "Discrimination may be said to exist to the degree that individuals of a given group who are otherwise formally qualified are not treated in conformity with these nominally universal institutionalized codes."

Antonovsky (1960, p. 81) uses a similar definition: "Discrimination may be defined as the effective injurious treatment of persons on grounds rationally irrelevant to the situation." He notes that discrimination is a "system of social relations," not an isolated individual act. Because discrimination "vitiates the power and knowledge of its victims," their behavior feeds back into and reinforces the system, a point we shall discuss in Chapter 6 (see also Glaser and Possony 1979).

The Relation of Discrimination to Prejudice

To say that prejudice and discrimination are distinct phenomena is not to say that they are empirically separate. One might discriminate against a member of a minority group without feeling any prejudice, but almost certainly it would be because one believes other persons hold a prejudice. A businessman, for example, might refuse to accept clients from a minority group despite his own lack of prejudice because he thinks that their presence would injure his business. In other cases, however, discrimination is the overt expression of prejudice.

Analysis of the relationship between prejudice and discrimination can also prevent an easy assumption of a particular causal connection between them (Warner and Rutledge 1970).

Behind many of the studies of "the prejudiced personality" is the hypothesis that personal needs and insecurities, expressing themselves in prejudices, are the primary cause of discrimination. (It would follow that any important reduction in discrimination requires large-scale reduction of personal insecurity.) There is good evidence, however, that prejudice is in part the *result of discrimination*—a way of rationalizing and getting rid of guilt feelings that arise when one has treated an individual unfairly, according to one's own definition. By emphasizing that the pursuit of power and gain and traditional factors, as well as personal insecurities, are involved in prejudice, we can more readily understand the interaction between prejudice and discrimination.

No one expression of the relationship between prejudice and discrimination is adequate:

1. There can be prejudice without discrimination.
2. There can be discrimination without prejudice.
3. Discrimination can be among the causes of prejudice.
4. Prejudice can be among the causes of discrimination.
5. Probably most frequently they are mutually reinforcing.

The need is for careful specification of the personal and structural conditions under which these various relationships prevail.

Group Conflict and Tension

In a majority–minority social system, prejudice and discrimination are almost always accompanied by tension and often by conflict (Grimshaw 1961). Yet each of these can exist independently of the others. In his comment on group conflict, Williams (1947, p. 36) writes, "Although often closely connected in life situations, these elements have a considerable range of independent variation." There can be a great deal of prejudice and discrimination—for example, in a caste system—with relatively little open conflict. Attempts to reduce discrimination may lead, at least in the short run, to *increased* conflict and efforts to avoid conflict may take the form of accepting patterns of discrimination. On the whole, however, group conflict is an outgrowth of widespread prejudice and discrimination. It is particularly likely to occur in an open-class society, where the suppressed groups have some hope of improving their status and the dominant group has some fear that the minorities may advance (and perhaps ambivalent feelings about whether they ought to advance).

Conclusion

This chapter has been primarily concerned with some basic terms. We have seen that they can be defined in many ways, but we have tried to develop a meaning that will be useful in the study of the relationships with which we are concerned. One term, *race,* will be dealt with separately in the next chapter. This book is not limited to the study of *race relations;* but because that phrase is so frequently used to refer to the larger field of majority–minority relations, and because race is used so broadly and vaguely by many people, we must develop clear-cut definitions.

It is the thesis of this book that relations among races have a great deal in common with relations among groups that think of themselves as different on other grounds—culture, nationality, religion. Race differences are primarily important for what people believe them to be.

A Note on the Use of Group Names

Questions of personal identity, courtesy, accuracy, and fashion are found in the use of group names. Pejorative terms, of course, are symbols and indeed weapons of group conflict. But even in scholarly discourse, one faces difficult problems of communication because of the wide range of connotations that become associated with different group terms. If one adopts a shortcut and refers to "Mexicans" when he has "Americans of Mexican descent" in mind, he runs the risk of seeming to grant them less than full citizenship. Should one

Table 1-1

	Like most	Like least
Negro	38%	11%
Colored people	20%	31%
Blacks	19%	25%
Afro-American	10%	11%

Source: *Newsweek*, June 30, 1969, p. 12.

speak of Indians (who, as someone has said, did not even know they were Indians until Columbus told them), or native Americans, or pre-Columbian Americans?

For a time the sharpest controversy over name in America surrounded the question of the appropriate term for Americans of African or part African descent. When *Newsweek* asked a random sample of Americans of African descent which name they liked most and which name they liked least, four names received 87% of the positive choices (Table 1-1). But those same four names received 78% of the "like least" choices.

Another poll that was taken a little more recently comes from the Detroit Area Study in 1971. A random sample from the area was asked: "Do you have a preference for one of these words: 'Black,' 'Negro,' 'Colored,' or 'Afro-American'?" (Schuman and Hatchett 1974, p. 84). The responses were compared with the respondents' alienation scores—the higher the score, the greater the alienation, indicating the level of distrust of Whites and white institutions (Table 1-2).

Our impression is that *Black* has now become more widely preferred, particularly in middle-class and college groups and in the media. It seems unlikely, however, to become a permanent label, since name changes continually respond to social changes. Controversy over names rages, as Lerone

Table 1-2

	Preference (N)	Percentage	Mean alienation score
Afro-American	21	5.5	6.1
Black	144	38.0	5.1
Negro	89	23.5	4.0
No preference (volunteered)	80	21.1	3.8
Colored	45	11.9	3.6

Bennett notes (in Rose 1970, p. 379), with religious intensity. In his careful review of the historical shifts, he records the swings of usage and the variations in attitudes with which they were associated. He notes W. E. B. Du Bois's reply to a student who criticized the use of the term *Negro* in *Crisis:*

Do not at the outset of your career make the all too common error of mistaking names for things. Names are only conventional signs for identifying things. Things are the reality that counts. If a thing is despised, either because of ignorance or because it is despicable, you will not alter matters by changing the names. If men despise Negroes, they will not despise them less if Negroes are called "colored" or "Afro-Americans."

Du Bois's comment will displease as many as it pleases. His opponents would say that words prefigure and control experience to some degree; they are not simply innocent labels. If someone says that *Negro* is a slave-oriented epithet and should be replaced by *Black,* he will find it irrelevant that *Negro* is derived from the Portuguese and Spanish words for 'black' (see Bennett in Rose 1970, and also Lampe 1982).

In recent years, as persons of Spanish-speaking background have increased rapidly in number in the United States, spread more widely through the occupational system, and become major forces in several regions of the country, many group names have gained currency. *Hispanic, Latino,* and *Spanish-surnamed* are among those used and responded to—with different degrees of enthusiasm or opposition—with reference to the highly diverse population of persons of Mexican, Puerto Rican, Cuban, and other Spanish-speaking backgrounds. Thus Representative Edward Roybal is chairman of the Congressional Hispanic Caucus and also president of the National Association of Latino Elected and Appointed Officials.

Some speak of *La Raza*—"all Spanish-speaking people of the New World collectively, with overtones of a common spirit and destiny" (Samora and Simon 1977, p. 10)—and, we might add, occasionally a touch of chauvinism.

For a number of years, many Americans of Mexican background, particularly the more militant, have thought of themselves as and have preferred to be called *Chicano*—perhaps an altered version of the Aztecs' term for themselves as it sounded in Spanish (Tomas Guillen, Cleveland *Plain Dealer,* July 6, 1980, p. C21). Others, however—the more acculturated and less militant, on one hand, and those who still identify with Mexico, on the other—object to the term *Chicano.* Joan Moore observes (1976) that *Mexican-American* is now the term most widely preferred.

We cannot resolve the problems associated with racial and ethnic labels. Since there are persons within any group who prefer different group titles, any single choice will cause some discomfort. We shall use *Black, Negro,* and *Afro-American* interchangeably when referring to persons of African background.[4] Both *Hispanic* and *Latino* will be used for general reference to persons of Spanish-speaking background, *Chicano* and *Mexican-American* for those of Mexican background. When quoting or drawing directly on another source, we will employ the term of the original author. We trust that the tone of this work will convey our sense of the shared dignity of all humankind. We only hope that this book gets into print before some new "most preferred choice" that we have entirely neglected appears.

---

[4]This raises a question about spelling, which also has its political-moral aspects. We shall capitalize White, Black, Chicano, and the like when they are used as nouns, as group names. When they are used adjectivally, we shall use lower case.

MORE IMPORTANTLY, THE LABELS SIGNIFIGANCE LIES IN WHAT IT MEANS TO THE PERSON. HOW THEY WANT TO BE IDENTIFIED.

CHAPTER 2

The Meaning of Race

The term *race* has many levels of meaning, scientific, administrative, and popular. The meanings are so diverse, even contradictory, that some authors believe the word ought not to be used. While sharing their discomfort over the confusions and distortions, we believe the word is unlikely to disappear from general usage and that therefore it is better to examine it carefully than to disregard it.

Popular Conceptions of Race

Reflecting the views of educated Europeans of the eighteenth and nineteenth centuries, a number of writers tackled the problem of the equality or inequality of the human races and subraces and offered evaluative racial classifications of one kind or another. Among these were Count Henry de Boulainvilliers (1658–1722), Count Joseph Arthur de Gobineau (1816–1882), and Houston Stewart Chamberlain (1855–1927). Boulainvilliers, an aristocratic political writer, declared that there were two races: the nobles, who were descended from the Germanic conquerors (Nordics), and the masses, who were the descendants of the subject Celts and Romans. Opposition to democratic ideas did not disappear in France after the French Revolution, and in 1853–55 Gobineau brought out his famous *Essay on the Inequality of the Human Races*. Gobineau asserted that the different human races are innately unequal in the talent necessary to initiate civilization. In *The Foundations of the Twentieth Century* (1899, 1911) Chamberlain, a native of England married to Richard Wagner's daughter, presented an oversimplified account of the development of European culture. He held that the *Germanen* were incomparably the most important people in world history. According to him, they were the founders of an entirely new civilization, and he deplored the indiscriminate mixing of different human stocks. At the same time, Chamberlain claimed that "whoever reveals himself German by his acts, whatever his genealogical tree, is a German."

Two American authors, Madison Grant (1867–1937) and Lothrop Stoddard (1883–1950), dealt superficially and crudely with so-called racial questions in the first quarter of the twentieth century, but the works of both men were widely read. In *The Passing of a Great Race* (1917), Grant developed the theme that the United States was founded by Anglo-Saxon Protestants, a superior race, and that this country should be reserved for their kind. He was obsessed with the threat that he saw in the increasing proportion of non-Nordic peoples in the population of the United States. In *The Rising Tide of Color Against White World-Supremacy* (1920), Stoddard maintained that there are higher races and lower races, that intermixture produces a race that reverts to the lower type, and that the downfall of the great civilizations has been due to the crossing of higher and lower races. He was alarmed about the danger that might result if people of the white race were to be outnumbered by the rapid multiplication of the "non-white" races.

27

In *Mein Kampf* (1925–27, 1940), Adolf Hitler stated that the human race could be divided into three categories—founders, maintainers, and destroyers of culture, and that the Aryan stock alone could be considered as representing the first category.

Finally, as an example of popular conceptions of race, we cite a black theologian: "Being black in America has very little to do with skin color. To be black means that your heart, your soul, your mind, and your body are where the dispossessed are" (Cone 1969, pp. 39–40).

Administrative Definitions of Race

At times, popular conceptions of race are given official standing, often with far-reaching consequences. Either by legislative act or by bureaucratic practice, certain racial categories are established and governmental actions are based on them. Perhaps the outstanding example of such negative definitions of race was the Nazi dichotomy of Aryan and non-Aryan. In Hitler's Germany to be classified as non-Aryan meant dismissal from civil service and university positions, severe restrictions in the practice of law, medicine, dentistry, and journalism, special identity cards, the adoption of Jewish first names, business and property restrictions and confiscations, deprivation of the rights of citizenship, the prohibition of marriage to an Aryan, concentration camps, and, for millions, death in gas chambers. Less extreme examples of official definitions of race include the distinction in South Africa between "Native" and "Coloured," between "recognized Indians" and others of Indian descent in a number of Latin American countries, and the varying definitions of Native Americans (American Indians) by different agencies of the federal government in the United States.

In recent years, Government agencies administering "affirmative action" programs have based their decisions on whether the people in question are "socially or economically disadvantaged," rather than on some conception of race. Consequently, programs which were intended originally to help Blacks, American Indians, and Hispanic Americans often benefit others. Among these categories are poor Whites, women, and veterans—groups whose plights lie beyond the scope of the present study. As a result of these redefinitions of minority groups, tensions have arisen, especially between Blacks and Mexican-Americans on one hand and women, veterans, and southern and eastern European nationality groups on the other. Representatives of the latter groups claim that their people are underrepresented in positions of responsibility. Black and Hispanic American leaders maintain that the indignities suffered by such groups do not compare with those received by members of their groups.

One problem with administrative racial definitions is that they sometimes benefit those who are not at all disadvantaged. The provisions of most affirmative action programs required of colleges and of companies doing business with the federal government refer specifically to "blacks, Spanish-surnamed Americans, American Indians, and Orientals." Minority enterprises are defined in the Public Works Act of 1976 as those more than half-owned by "citizens of the United States who are Negroes, Spanish-speaking, Orientals, Indians, Eskimos, and Aleuts." A panel studying the attempts of the Office of Minority Enterprise to eliminate abuses in the agency's minority "set-aside" program recommended in 1978 that persons eligible for the program should have suffered "social or economic disadvantage," that is, "chronic, historic and of long standing." It recommended further that a "rebuttable presumption" of such disadvantage be accorded to Blacks, Hispanics, Indians, Orientals, Eskimos, and Aleuts. Others would have to prove that they have been disadvantaged in order to qualify.

While making preparations for taking the 1980 Census, officials of the Bureau of the Census were accused by some demographers of responding to minority pressure by asking detailed ethnic questions intended to increase the number of persons calling themselves members of Hispanic, American Indian, or other deprived groups (Reinhold 1978, pp. 1, 33). Another problem confronting government agencies is how to define an individual of mixed ancestry. In a directive to all federal agencies in 1978, the Office of Federal Statistical Policy instructed them to use "the category which most closely reflects the individual's recognition in his community," at least for the purpose of reporting data.

The general practice of those administering government programs and of college admissions officers is to accept a person's own declaration of his racial or ethnic identity unless it obviously conflicts with reality. Self-definitions are, then, the usual rule.

Self-definitions are not, however, acceptable in some situations. In 1977, the regulations of the Office of Native American Programs in the Department of Health, Education, and Welfare stated:

"American Indian or Indian" means any individual who is a member or a descendant of a member of a North American tribe, band, or organized group of native people who are indigenous to the United States or who otherwise have a special relationship with the United States or a State through treaty agreement, or some other form of recognition. This includes any individual who claims to be an Indian *and who is regarded as such by the Indian community of which he or she claims to be a part.* This definition also includes Alaskan Natives. (*Federal Register*, 42, January 19, 1977, p. 3785; italics added)

There is a large discrepancy between the number of "administrative" or "official" Indians listed by the Bureau of Indian Affairs and those enumerated by the Census Bureau. For the BIA, Indians were those who were members of tribes with federal trust land, who had one-quarter or more Indian blood, and who lived on a federal reservation or nearby. Beginning in 1960, the Census Bureau employed a cultural rather than a legal or "heirship" definition of Indian. Thus, members of a household were permitted to classify themselves racially.

With various rights to education, health care, and other benefits dependent upon tribal or racial identity, the question of who is an Indian will continue to be important and controversial.

In 1980, the concept of race used by the Bureau of the Census

reflects self-identification by respondents; it does not denote any clear-cut scientific definition of biological stock. . . . For persons who could not provide a single response to the race question, the race of the person's mother was used; however, if a single response could not be provided for the person's mother, the first race reported by the person was used. This is a modification of the 1970 census procedure in which the race of the person's father was used.

The category "White" includes persons who indicated their race as White, as well as persons who did not classify themselves in one of the specific race categories listed on the questionnaire but entered a response such as Canadian, German, Italian, Lebanese, or Polish. In the 1980 census, persons who did not classify themselves in one of the specific race categories but marked "Other" and reported entries such as Cuban, Puerto Rican, Mexican, or Dominican were included in the "Other" category; in the 1970 census, most of these persons were included in the "White" category.

The category "Black" includes persons who indicated their race as Black or Negro, as well as persons who did not classify themselves in one of the specific race categories listed on the questionnaire but reported entries such as Jamaican, Black Puerto Rican, West Indian, Haitian, or Nigerian.

The categories "American Indian," "Eskimo," and "Aleut" include persons who classified themselves as such in one of the specific race categories. In addition, persons who did not report themselves in one of the specific categories but entered the name of an Indian tribe were classified as American Indian.

The combined category "Asian and Pacific Islander" includes persons who indicated their race as Japanese, Chinese, Filipino, Korean, Vietnamese, Asian Indian, Hawaiian, Guamanian, or Samoan. Persons who did not report themselves in one of the specific categories but reported a write-in entry indicating one of the nine categories listed above were classified accordingly. For example, entries of Nipponese and Japanese American were classified as Japanese; entries of Taiwanese and Cantonese as Chinese, etc.

The category "Other" includes Asian and Pacific Islander groups not listed separately (e.g., Cambodian, Laotian, Pakistani, Fiji Islander) and other races not included in the specific categories listed on the questionnaire. (*1980 Census of Population: Supplementary Reports,* July 1981, p. 3)

Important differences between the 1980 and 1970 census counts affect the comparability for some groups. People of Spanish origin reported their race differently in the 1980 census than in the 1970 census, and this difference has a marked effect on the counts and comparability for the "White" and "Other" populations.

A much larger proportion of the Spanish origin population in 1980 than in 1970 reported their race as "Other." Second, in 1970, most persons who marked the "Other" race category and wrote in a Spanish designation such as Mexican, Venezuelan, Latino, etc., were reclassified as "White." In 1980, such persons were not reclassified but remained in the "Other" race category. As a result of this procedural change and the differences in reporting by this population, the proportion of the Spanish origin population classified as "Other" in the 1980 census was substantially higher than that in the 1970 census. Nationally, in 1970, only 1 percent of the Spanish origin persons were classified as "Other" race and 93 percent as "White." In 1980, a much larger proportion—40 percent—of Spanish origin persons reported their race as "Other" and only 56 percent reported "White." As a consequence of these differences, 1980 population totals for "White" and "Other" are not comparable with corresponding 1970 figures. (*1980 Census of Population: Supplementary Reports,* July 1981, p. 3)

The 1980 count for Asians and Pacific Islander categories reflects a high level of immigration during the 1970s as well as a number of changes in census procedures.

The Census Bureau identifies a Puerto Rican as someone "born in Puerto Rico or born in the United

States. . . with one or both parents born in Puerto Rico" (Wagenheim 1975, p. 9). According to this definition, the children of Puerto Ricans born in the United States are not Puerto Ricans. When these persons become a larger proportion of the Puerto Rican-derived population, the controversy over definition will increase. If the present census definition prevails for two generations, some Puerto Ricans will be classified with United States Blacks, others will have disappeared into the white population, and it is unclear what will happen to the mixed and largest group in the middle.

The Biological Approach to Race

Biologists and many anthropologists use the term *race* not as a social but as a genetic concept. Although humankind consists of only one species, with all members sharing a great many genetic traits, there are some differences. These differences have little direct behavioral significance. Because of a common perception of their importance, however, it is essential that we examine the biological approach to race with some care.

The Morphology of Race

Among the most widely used characteristics in the traditional physical anthropological approach to race are skin color, hair and eye color, hair texture, nasal index, lip form, head form, and facial index. Skin color has been called the most obvious racial feature; certainly it is, sociologically, the most important one. However, it is one of the most unreliable traits if taken singly, because of the great variation within the major divisions of *Homo sapiens,* because of the overlapping from one group to another, and because of environmental influences. The sources of skin color are five pigments, the main ones being melanin and carotene, and an effect known as scattering. The technique of spectrophotometry permits accurate and objective measurement of skin coloring. Varieties of skin color range from the extremely pale shade of the Lapplanders to the dark brown pigmentation of the inhabitants of the tropical rain forest of Central Africa. A considerable range of difference exists in the filtering ability of human skins, that is, in the ability to prevent the sun's rays from penetrating to the dermal layer where blood vessels,

nerves, and gland cells are located (Molnar 1975, p. 66; Montagu 1974, pp. 328–329).

The commonest pigment in the hair is brown or black, identical with that in the skin, but a diffuse red-gold pigment is sometimes present. An overwhelming majority of the world's population has black hair; blonds are numerically insignificant. Eye color is determined mainly by the pigment in the iris. In general, light and dark coloration in hair and eyes are associated, although there are differences in these associations between the sexes, and combinations of dark hair and blue eyes occur frequently where there has been a crossing of racial stocks.

Hair texture falls into three main categories: ulotrichy (oval, tightly curled strands), leiotrichy (straight, round in cross section), and cymotrichy (wavy, intermediate in cross-section). Typically, these three types of hair form are found in Negroes, Mongoloids, and Whites (Montagu 1974, pp. 329–331).

Nasal index is the relationship between the width of the nose, measured between the wings, and the length from the juncture of the nasal bones and the frontal bone to the juncture of the septum with the upper lip. If the percentage of the width relative to the length is less than 70, the index is called leptorrhine (narrow-nosed); if it is 84 or over, the index is known as platyrrhine (broad-nosed); intermediate indexes are mesorrhine (medium-nosed). On the average, these nasal forms are characteristic of Caucasoids, Negroids, and Mongoloids, respectively. A narrow or a broad nose form is not, however, confined to any one racial group; for example, long narrow noses are found among Negroids living in the East African highlands, while the tropical dwellers in the Congo Basin have wide noses (Molnar 1975, p. 63; Montagu 1974, pp. 321–323).

Lip form refers to lip thickness, which ranges from thin, inverted anthropoidal lips of Caucasoids through the intermediate structures of Mongoloids, to the wide, everted, highly evolved Negroid lips. Here again these differences refer to averages; considerable variation is found within racial categories.

One of the most widely known racial indexes is head form, or the relationship between the width of the head and the length. A percentage of less than 75 indicates dolichocephaly (long-headedness), one of 75–80 mesocephaly (medium-headedness), and over 80 brachycephaly (broadheadedness). The cephalic index has to be discounted as a criterion of race, but it is true that certain populations tend to be more long-headed or more broadheaded than others. On the average, except for the Australian Aborigines, Africans tend to be the most long-headed, and American Indians and Central Europeans are the most broadheaded (Molnar 1975, p. 55).

In the facial index, the length is expressed as a percentage of the width. If this percentage is 88 or above, the person is narrow-faced (leptoprosopic), from 85 to 88 medium-faced (mesoprosopic), and less than 84, broad-faced (euryprosopic). The human face is, however, highly variable in its shape and size, and any scheme used to describe the facial characteristics of certain populations will include only a relatively small percentage of the individuals in the group (Molnar 1975, p. 49).[1]

Genetics and Race

Such characteristics as skin color, face form, head shape, and stature are polygenic traits the exact mode of inheritance of which is not known. Some human phenotypes, however, are known to be the result of the inheritance of identifiable gene combinations. These characteristics can be detected by chemical tests and include twenty or more blood groups, several serum proteins, enzymes, hemoglobin, and the ability to taste or smell certain substances, especially phenylthiocarbamide or PTC (Molnar 1975, pp. 67–88).

Serious difficulties are encountered, however, when attempts are made to define racial groups by specifying differences in the frequency distributions of certain genes. One may ask, which genes, and how many genes should be used to define a so-called racial group? Man has 23 pairs of chromosomes, and if it is assumed that there are 1,250 genes on each chromosome, man has at least 28,750 genes in the chromosomes of his sex cells. In a single mating the theoretical possible combinations between the 23 chromosomes of the male and those of the female are 8,388,608 . . . and the chance of any one such combination being repeated more than once is one in 70,000,000,000,000 (Montagu 1974, pp. 61–62).

Numerous studies have reported the frequencies of a number of genes *within* particular human populations, but the results obtained thus far concerning the relationships *between* populations based on differences in frequency distributions of certain genes is quite inconclusive.

Racial Classifications

The members of *Homo sapiens* are extremely variable creatures constantly undergoing change. These changes can be studied in minute detail in every living, breeding population. The problem of classifying major groups and subgroups of mankind is, however, exceedingly difficult. Usually a classification is based on a combination of characteristics. The number of races designated and the labels used vary from one classifier to another; nevertheless, rough correspondences exist among the classifications. Frequently, classifiers have recognized four major races, divisions, stocks, major groups, or subspecies: Negroid or Black, Archaic white or Australoid, Caucasoid or White, and Mongoloid.

No generally accepted classification of human races based on morphological or morphological and genetical data exists, and it seems unlikely that such a classification will ever be devised. As an aid in visualizing the broad, overall biological differences in the world's populations, we include here two of the most recent attempts at racial classification schema. Baker's (1974; see Table 2-1) includes most of the modern and recently extinct races and subraces, but he omits the Pygmies of Central Africa and the Negritos of the Malay Archipelago because he considers that their affinities with other categories are still obscure and for unexplained reasons North American Indians and Eskimos do not appear in Baker's classification.

Garn's Geographical and Local Races. Garn (1971, pp. 16, 18, 153–166) uses the term *geographical race* to describe broad, geographically delimited population collections, the largest taxonomic unit immediately below the species. Such races are not breeding populations; they are collections of breeding populations. Because gene-exchange has been more intensive within geographical races, and because such races share many selective factors in common, overall resemblances usually are greater within than between them. Garn gives a number of morphological and serological characteristics for each of the nine geographical races he lists. In general, these geographical races correspond with the major continents.

[1] For discussions of other physical characteristics that have been used in racial classifications, including body hair, body odor, cranial capacity, length of arms and legs, see Montagu (1974, pp. 313–320, 323–326, 331–336).

Table 2-1. Baker's Classification of Human Races and Subraces

Races	Subraces		
Names used in Baker's book	Names used by Baker	Alternative names roughly or exactly corresponding	Examples of places where typical specimens can be or have been found
Australasid	Australid	Australian aborigine	Australia
	Melanesid	Melanesian	New Hebrides
	Tasmanid	Tasmanian	Tasmania
Europid	Ainuid	Ainu	Kurile Islands
	Nordid	Nordic	Norway
	Mediterranid	Mediterranean	Southern Italy
	Nordindid	Indo-Afghan	Pakistan
	Orientalid	'Arab'	Arabia
	Armenid	Assyroid	Armenian S.S.R.
	Dinarid	Illyrian	Yugoslavia
	Alpinid	Alpine	Switzerland
	Osteuropid	Est-baltique	Northern Russia
	Turanid	Turki	Kazakh S.S.R.
	Aethiopid	Eastern Hamite	Ethiopia
Negrid	Palaenegrid	Congolese	Zaïre
	Sudanid	Western Sudanese	Senegal
	Nilotid	Eastern Sudanese	Southern Sudan
	Kafrid	Zambesian	Rhodesia
Khoisanid	Khoid	Hottentot	South West Africa
	Sanid	Bushman	Kalahari Desert
Mongolid	Tungid	Mongol	Mongolia
	Sinid	Chinese	Central China
	Palaemongolid	Southern Mongol	Vietnam
Indianid	Zentralid	(No equivalent name)	Mexico
	Andid	Ando-Péruvienne	Peru
	Brasilid	Brasilio-Guarienne	Brasil

Source: John R. Baker, *Race*, Oxford University Press, 1974, p. 625.

Garn's nine geographical races

1. The Amerindian geographical race—a large number of local populations ranging from Alaska to the southern tip of South America
2. The Polynesian geographical race—occupying a large territory in the Pacific, ranging from New Zealand to Hawaii and Easter (Pascua) Island
3. The Micronesian geographical race—occupying a series of small islands in the Pacific
4. The Melanesian-Papuan geographical race—comprising Melanesians, Papuans, and New Guineans
5. The Australian geographical race—comprising a series of local races clearly allied with the extinct Tasmanians

6. The Asiatic geographical race of continental Asia—extending to Japan, Taiwan, the Philippines, Indonesia, Sumatra, Borneo, and Java

7. The Indian geographical race—consisting of a large number of local races, "tribes," and microraces occupying the territory from the Himalayas to the Indian Ocean

8. The European geographical race—including the peoples of Europe, North Africa, and the Middle East

9. The African geographical race—including the local races and microraces of sub-Saharan Africa; includes persons taken as slaves to Southern Arabia.

According to Garn, local races number into the thousands (1971, p. 169), and if one considers the total number of contemporary, local breeding populations (demes) in *Homo sapiens* the number might approximate one million. The latter figure assumes an average population of 3,500 per deme, probably a reasonable assumption (Loehlin, Lindzey, and Spuhler 1975, p. 33). Local races are largely or totally endogamous, and the small amount of geneflow usually comes from contiguous and related local races (Garn 1971, p. 19). Garn (1971, pp. 169–178) illustrates the variety of local races by listing thirty-two groups under five headings: representative large local races; Amerindian groups of local races; puzzling, isolated, numerically small local races; long isolated marginal local races; and "hybrid" local races of recent origin.

According to historical records, some geographical and local races (Garn's definition) have existed for 6,000 years, and prehistoric archeology indicates that some of them have been in existence for 30,000 years. Coon (1962, p. 657) is almost alone in asserting that five major geographic races may have existed for 500,000 years (Loehlin, Lindzey, and Spuhler 1975, p. 37).[2] It should be noted that

Garn's "'hybrid' local races of recent origin" (North American Colored; South African Colored; Ladinos; and Neo-Hawaiian) are relatively new populations (Garn 1971, pp. 177–178).

These outlines of two racial classifications can serve to indicate the great complexity of the subdivisions of *Homo sapiens,* the continuing process of change—both further subdivision and blending—and the need for recognizing how tentative we should be in our views of racial differentiation.

Our conclusion is that the possibility of devising a scientific typology of races based either on morphological or genetic characteristics, or a combination of both, is slight. Obviously, racial differences exist. Mongoloid Asians are visibly different from Negroid Africans and from Caucasoid Europeans. Also, the great regional populations of *Homo sapiens* which resemble each other probably have some common lines of descent. We agree with Leach (1975, pp. 29–30) that all that can be usefully discussed scientifically "are the processes by which racial differentiation comes about, and the environmental and social circumstances which lead to an increase or decrease in such differentiation over time."[3]

A Sociological View of Race

Many important questions pertaining to the human species lie outside our main concerns in this book. Among these are such biological matters as the following: a full account of the evolution of man from lower forms of life; detailed delineations of morphological, genetic, and behavioral similarities between *Homo sapiens* and other animals; how the races of mankind have come into being; and the meaning of genetically determined disease.

Garn (1971, pp. 188–189) gives fourteen reasons for studying race in living man, but they are all biological reasons. Sociologically, racial questions involve the interaction of persons, individually and collectively, who are believed by themselves and others to constitute groups that possess some combination of distinctive biological and/

---

[2]Coon's thesis is that man was a single species over half a million years ago and that this species, *Homo erectus,* "then evolved into *Homo sapiens* not once but five times, as each subspecies, living in its own territory, passed a critical threshold from a more brutal to a more sapient state" (Coon 1962, p. 657). This claim has not been generally accepted (Lehrman 1966, pp. 69, 121–22; Loehlin, Lindzey, and Spuhler 1975, pp. 36–37; and Montagu 1974, pp. 74–81), nor has Coon's view that Congoids (Negroes and pygmies) crossed the sapient line some 500,000 years later than Caucasians (Coon 1962, p. 658).

[3]Mutation, genetic drift, and natural selection are the basic evolutionary processes, but social factors such as celibacy, social class, marriage rules, and assortative mating tend to skew the gene pool in directions which are out of balance with biological process (Alland 1971, p. 20).

or cultural characteristics, regardless of the accuracy of these beliefs. In Chapter 1 we discussed our conception of racial minority, cultural minority, and ethnic group.

The Admixture of Racial Groups

The process of biological amalgamation begins with the first contact of populations of diverse cultural or national backgrounds. Whether it proceeds slowly or rapidly depends upon a number of sociological, psychological, and political factors, some of which are discussed in Chapter 13. Strangers are both fascinating and frightening by virtue of differences in appearance, customs, and, sometimes, in the amount of power they possess. Distaste for the outlandish and fear that outsiders will disrupt the unity of the in-group have often led to strong opposition to fraternization and intermixture. Our concern here is with the alleged harmful biological effects of interbreeding.

The older viewpoints concerning physical disharmonies, defectiveness, and constitutional unbalance are not supported by recent investigations. The identification of identical genes in different races, the genetic heterogeneity of all racial groups, and the unquestioned fact that particular genes and not genotypes or phenotypes are inherited have refuted such beliefs (Loehlin, Lindzey, and Spuhler 1975, p. 21). Geneticists hold that "human populations do not represent coadapted genetic combinations which are disrupted by outcrossing" (Morton, Chung, and Mi 1967, p. 148).

Instead of a loss of biological fitness under hybridization, there appears to be a gain. All of the subpopulations of mankind appear to possess qualities which, when biologically mixed, result in the emergence of novel and fit types (Montagu 1974, p. 233).

It is now thought that the chances for matching defective genes (often carried recessively) are greater within a group than in matings between members of different groups (Montagu 1974, pp. 219–220):

No population has a monopoly of good genes; no population has a monopoly of bad genes; normal and defective genes are found in all populations of human beings. Furthermore, it is most unlikely that the kind of defective genes distributed in one population will be found to occur in anything like as great a frequency, if at all, in another population or ethnic group.

Evidence concerning the salutary effects of race crossing comes from all parts of the world. The admixture of Polynesians, Japanese, Chinese, Koreans, and whites of many nationalities in Hawaii has resulted in very satisfactory physical and mental types. Maori-White mixture in New Zealand has produced healthy and capable hybrids. Hottentot-Boer crossing in Southwest Africa has yielded vigorous hybrids. The same comment may be made about Mongoloid-White crosses, and the hybrids resulting from the mating of Whites and Australian aborigines. Negro-White crossing in the United States has produced a group of hybrids that has survived, increased, and prospered in spite of tremendous social and economic obstacles. The American Negro represents the successful blending of African, European, and American Indian elements into "a perfectly adapted biological type (Montagu 1974, p. 339)."[4]

The biological consequences of race mixture may be summed up in these statements:

1. Race mixture does not produce biologically or mentally inferior offspring.
2. Race mixture tends to produce offspring that equal or exceed their parental groups in vitality, stature, and fertility.
3. Radical crosses between races in the United States, and in certain places outside this country, may occasion serious personal problems for parents and children in the 1980s. Persons of mixed descent may be discriminated against economically and in other ways. The social disadvantages experienced by some hybrids will be discussed in a later chapter, but the evidence does not indicate that such mixing is biologically inadvisable.

Race and Vitality

In discussing this subject, as in discussing race and intelligence, it should be remembered that the black people of the United States constitute a very mixed group racially. Although the white population is by no means a pure race (nearly one-fourth of the persons classified as white may have an element of African ancestry), four-fifths of the black population may have some degree of non-African ancestry (Stuckert 1976, 137–138). In recent censuses, racial classification has been mainly by self-definition. For the most part, those listed as Blacks

[4]For the best available statement on the creative power of race and ethnic mixture, see Montagu 1974, Chapter 10.

regard themselves as persons of African descent, and those listed as Whites consider themselves the descendants of European peoples. Basically, then, these are social rather than genetic definitions. Keeping this caveat in mind, we cite certain national data concerning differential mortality rates among racial groups. Blacks have the highest mortality among racial groups for which national data are available—Whites, Blacks, American Indians, Japanese, Chinese, and others. The black mortality indexes for population 5 years old and over are 28 percent higher than Whites for males and 47 percent higher than Whites for females. For American Indians, the levels are 24 percent and 37 percent above those for white males and females, respectively. For the age range 35 to 64 years, the following age-adjusted differentials (percentage by which each index exceeds that for Whites of the corresponding sex) are found (Sutton 1974, pp. 26–27):

	Male	Female
Negro	66	145
American Indian	28	69

Diseases of the heart are the leading cause of death in the United States among both Whites and Blacks. Studies of one heart condition, hypertension, show that the rates are higher and that the disease is different in black men and women than it is in Whites. According to Finnerty (1974, pp. 99–100), "it develops earlier in life, is frequently more severe, and results in a higher mortality at a younger age, more commonly from strokes than from coronary artery disease." It has been hypothesized that the observed rates of occurrence of coronary disease in Blacks compared with Whites can be accounted for only by taking into account four sex–race groups (white males, black males, white females, black females) in such risk factors as hypertension, hypercholesterolemia, obesity, diabetes, and heavy smoking, singly or in various combinations (Stamler et al. 1974, p. 95). For example, in spite of their situation with respect to the hypertensive risk factor, middle-aged black men have coronary heart disease occurrence rates not significantly higher than those of white men; black women apparently have higher rates than white women.

Prior to the late 1950s, mortality rates for all races and sex groups declined. Later, mortality rates for some age and sex groups increased, with the highest increase appearing among nonwhite males in the age groups between fifteen and forty-four. Rates for these groups greatly exceeded the rates for their white cohorts. The three leading causes of death for young black males, accidents, homicide, and suicide, are closely related to social causes. The next two, heart disease and cancer, are related directly or indirectly to social causes. The stress and strain which young black males experience appear to be associated with physical surroundings, position in society, and emotional adaptation to the values and goals of the culture in which they find themselves (Dennis 1977, pp. 315, 320–321).

Infant mortality is an accurate indicator of the availability and effectiveness of certain types of medical and social services. By 1967 the infant mortality rate in the United States had fallen to 22.4 per 1,000 live births, approximately one-fifth of the rate sixty years earlier. During that period, the mortality rates for nonwhite infants consistently exceeded those for white infants by a ratio of about two to one. In 1967, the white rate was 19.7, the nonwhite rate 35.9. By 1973, the infant mortality rate for Whites had dropped to 15.8 and Blacks and other races (Blacks constitute approximately 90 percent of this group) to 26.2 percent (Bureau of the Census, 1974, p. 126). The high rates for Nonwhites were primarily a function of high rates for Blacks and for American Indians. Infant mortality rates for Native Americans have fallen approximately midway between those for Whites and for Blacks (MacMahon 1974, pp. 190–193). The infant mortality rate for Blacks remained twice as high (23.1) as for Whites (12.0) in 1978 (*Statistical Abstract,* 1981, p. 73).

Although the maternal mortality rate for Blacks and other races in the United States in 1970 was lower than the white rate in 1950, it was still nearly four times as high as the white rate (55.9 per 100,000 births, compared with 14.4). (The rates in 1950 were 221.6 and 61.1 respectively—Bureau of the Census, *Statistical Abstract 1974,* p. 60). In 1978, the maternal death rate for Whites was 6.4 and for blacks, 25.0 (*Statistical Abstract,* 1981, p. 73). Additional data and comments on death rates among Blacks, Mexican Americans, Puerto Ricans, and American Indians are given in the section on health care in Chapter 10.

The great differences between the death rates of Whites and Nonwhites, especially Blacks and American Indians, reflect the disadvantaged status of the latter in the nation. Large mortality differentials within subpopulations suggest that much of the excess mortality of the nonwhite groups could be reduced with increases in levels of living and life-style. At the present time, improved social-economic conditions might contribute more to mortality reduction than additions to and application of biomedical knowledge (Kitagawa and Hauser 1973, pp. 179–180).

The Question of Race and Ability

The controversy concerning alleged racial differences in intelligence quotients died down during the 1940s and 1950s but has been revived in recent years. Part of this revival of interest in group differences in IQ has been an aspect of the opposition of some Whites to school desegregation. The reports of Arthur R. Jensen on racial testing have done much to reactivate old fears and superstitions.

Jensen on Racial Testing

Jensen attributes approximately 80 percent of human intelligence to heredity (1973, p. 50). He asserts also that Blacks in the United States obtain scores on the average about one standard deviation (fifteen IQ points on most intelligence tests) below the average for the white population (1971, p. 20). He claims further that between one-half and three-fourths of the average IQ difference between Blacks and Whites is due to genetic factors and the remainder to environmental factors and their interactions with the genetic differences (1975, p. 363).

According to Jensen, the addition or subtraction of fifteen IQ points from an individual's "potential mental development" has quite different consequences depending on where the resultant IQ falls. Thus, he asserts that fifteen points added to an IQ of 70 might mean the difference between institutionalization or social dependency and self-sufficiency in a job, and fifteen points added to an IQ of 100 might mean the difference between succeeding and failing in college. Predicted also for such an increase in IQ are an average increase in the scale of income and an average increase in IQ points for the individual's children (1973, p. 34).

Jensen acknowledges that neither the black nor the white subpopulation of the United States is homogeneous and states that 20 to 30 percent of

the genes of American Negroes come from white ancestors (1975, pp. 352–353). Actually the African ancestry of American Blacks varies quantitatively from 10 to 90 percent Negroid (Molnar 1975, 149). Jensen does not seem to realize that African ancestry is no more homogeneous than that of the population of Europe or any other geographically defined human population (Alland 1971, pp. 193–195).

After stating that the degree of Caucasian admixture in the black subpopulation of the United States varies from region to region, Jensen asserts that "the average educability" of American Blacks is further below the general average for the United States than is the educability of any other major ethnic or cultural group: Orientals, Mexican-Americans, American Indians, or Puerto Ricans (Jensen 1975, pp. 352–353).

Earlier Reports on Racial Testing

Perspective on the value (or lack of it) of Jensen's conclusions on racial and ethnic intelligence may be gained from a review of earlier comparisons in the United States. In 1912, Henry Goddard, a Princeton University psychologist, reported on an intelligence test that he had given to a representative sample of European immigrants. He found that 83 percent of the Jews trying to enter the United States were feebleminded, that 79 percent of the Italians were feebleminded, and that 87 percent of the Russians were feebleminded. In 1917, he wrote that the number of aliens deported because of feeblemindedness increased approximately 350 percent in 1913 and 57 percent in 1914 over what it had been (Kamin 1973, p. 6; Kamin 1974, p. 16).

In 1921, the National Academy of Science published a large volume, edited by Robert M. Yerkes, summarizing the intelligence testing data gathered on draftees in World War I. Blacks scored much lower than Whites, but the most immediate application of these data was to the question of immigration. A special section dealt with draftees who had been born in European countries. According to the army test scores, the average intelligence of immigrants from England, Holland, Denmark, Scotland, Germany, and Switzerland was quite high. The Russians, the Italians, and the Poles were "all just plain stupid" (Kamin 1973, p. 10). The Poles did not stand higher than the Blacks. "The Slavic and Latin countries," Yerkes reported, "stand low."

In 1923, Carl Brigham, a Princeton University professor of psychology, published *A Study of American Intelligence,* a book which utilized the army immigrant data. Brigham demonstrated that the longer an immigrant had been in the United States, the higher was his IQ. He did not conclude, however, that these results had anything to do with the length of time immigrant groups had been in this country, or with knowing the English language or American culture. Brigham did conclude that there was a close parallel between the proportion of Nordic "blood" and the intelligence of immigrants. He was concerned with the decline of American intelligence in the future because, as Kamin says, he thought that "we have stupid immigrants, and we have stupid blacks as well (Kamin 1973, p. 10; Kamin 1974, pp. 20–22)." Brigham advocated compulsory sterilization of the "defective." (Later, Brigham became secretary to the College Entrance Examination Board and devised the Scholastic Aptitude Test.)

The immigration law of 1924 provided that the number of immigrants coming from a European country should be equal to two percent of the persons from that country residing in the United States in 1920. That law was rationalized on the basis of the tests of innate ability developed by psychologists which showed that Italians, Poles, Russians, and Jews scored 25 or 30 IQ points lower than those whose forebears had come earlier from northwestern Europe. It is noteworthy that this difference is approximately twice as large as that reported by Jensen between Whites and Blacks in the United States.

Hirsch conducted a study (1926) which dealt with the intelligence of children of southeastern European immigrants. As had been the case earlier with Polish, Italian, and Russian immigrants, Hirsch (cited in Kamin 1973, p. 10; see also Kamin 1974, p. 28) found that their children were also inferior. And he added that the law recently passed by Congress should be modified to cover non-quota immigrants, that is, immigrants from Canada or from Mexico:

All mental testing upon children of Spanish Mexican descent has shown that the average intelligence of this group is even lower than the average intelligence of Portuguese and Negro children in this study. Yet Mexicans are flowing into the country. In our immigration from Canada, we are getting the less intelligent, working-class people. The increase in the number of French Canadians is alarming. Whole New England villages and towns are filled with them. The average intelligence of the French Canadian group in our data approaches the level of the average Negro intelligence. Lips thick, mouth coarse, chin poorly formed, sugar loaf heads, goose-bill noses . . . a set of skew-molds discarded by the Creator . . . . Immigration officials . . . report vast troubles in extracting the truth from certain brunette nationalities.

The major domestic issue facing the country in the 1920s was immigration; today the main domestic issue is "the great welfare mess." Both issues have involved economic conflicts and prejudice against racial and cultural minorities. Kamin (1973, p. 10; 1974, p. 29) remarks that there was no shortage of biologists and psychologists in 1920 to guide the House Committee on Immigration and Naturalization and that such professionals are available today to act as teachers. In his view, the data which such teachers now present are no more valid than those presented by their predecessors in the 1920s on the innate intelligence of European nationality groups.

To Jensen (1975, p. 93), the most reasonable hypothesis concerning IQ differences is that Blacks and Whites "differ in the rate and the asymtote of development of the brain processes underlying the general factor common to intelligence items." This conclusion is reminiscent of the contention of some scholars in the nineteenth century that Negroes could never equal Whites in intelligence because, they thought, the sutures of the cranium of Blacks closed earlier, thus preventing the full expansion of the brain. (It was never explained how much white ancestry was necessary to prevent this alleged early closing of these sutures). According to Montagu (1960, p. 614), there are no significant ethnic group or race differences in suture closure.

Race Mixture; Studies of Twins; Within-Group Variation in Intelligence

Jensen's discussion of race mixture is of special interest. He reports first that nationwide testing of youths for induction into the armed services has revealed regional differences in "intellectual ability" and second that Negro IQs have been found to be the lowest in the South and the Southeast and to increase as one moves further north and west. A similar gradient has been found for the white population. This regional variation in IQ is attributed by Jensen to past selective migration of southern Blacks (a finding contrary to that of Klineberg

[1935b, Part II, Chapters 1–3; and 1935a, Chapters 8–9]) and to "the amount of Caucasian admixture" in the black subpopulation. (Jensen states that Caucasian admixture in Negroes in the Deep South is about 10 percent, while in the North and West the range is from 20 to 30 percent, and in the Northwest it is as high as 40 percent [1975, pp. 85–86].) Jensen's speculation stands in sharp contrast to the conclusion reached by Loehlin et al. (1975, pp. 132–133) that recent studies in the United States of interracial matings and ability–blood group correlations "on the whole fail to offer positive support to the hereditarian positions concerning between-group differences."

An important criticism of Jensen's estimate that IQ is 80 percent heritable concerns the twin studies that he cites. Numerous inaccuracies and inconsistensies have been found in the extensive studies made by the late Cyril Burt on identical twins reared apart. By 1976 it was clear that Burt had indeed fabricated some of his data (Gould 1981; Hearnshaw 1979); yet Jensen (1980) continues to cite Burt's studies. Studies by other investigators have not been standardized for age and sex. Gould (1981) concludes that the data are so flawed that no conclusions concerning the heritability of IQ can be drawn from them.

Even if it is assumed, for the sake of argument, that the heritability of IQ is 0.8, another serious criticism can be made concerning Jensen's claim that differences in intelligence among human groups is genetically based. Jensen confuses within- and between-group variation. He asserts that the within-group heritability of IQ is 0.8 for American Whites and that the mean difference in IQ between American Blacks and Whites is fifteen points. He maintains that the black "deficit" is largely genetic in origin because IQ is highly heritable. There is, however, "no necessary relationship between heritability within a group and differences in mean values of two separate groups" (Gould 1975, p. 149).

Environmental Change and Intelligence

The findings of psychologists provide reasonably clear evidence of large-scale changes in intelligence attributable to naturally occurring environmental changes (Brody and Brody 1974, p. 165). For example, intelligence scores have been improving in the United States at a fairly fast rate. According to Brody and Brody:

Comparisons of the Army Alpha tests of World War I and the testing of World War II draftees, as well as large scale testing since World War II, suggest that the change in intelligence over the last 50 years in the U.S. can be conservatively estimated at one standard deviation. . . . This increase is probably related to changes in educational level. What remains to be determined by subsequent research is the future trend of changes in intelligence test score performance. It is not clear if the relatively rapid increase that has occurred over the last 50 years will continue. Nevertheless the generational changes in intelligence that have occurred provide the clearest nonexperimental evidence for changes in intelligence test scores attributable to environmental influences.

A major explanatory concept with respect to differences in temperament and intelligence test responses is the "two cultures" (black and white) hypothesis. Recent studies show that behaviors, beliefs, and attitudes mean different things to those who belong to the two cultures. In the black child's experience at school, little is offered that fits into the background of his or her ghetto culture. Respect for learning has no place in that culture, nor is a high value put upon the ability to think abstractly, nor even upon ordinary school work (Montagu 1974, p. 380). Individuals from the black group who score ten to fifteen points lower on intelligence tests operate in actual situations indistinguishably from their white peers. Clearly, something is happening here that the usual "heredity" or "heredity × environment" explanations do not explain (Dreger 1973, pp. 220–221).

One of the findings of Coleman et al. (1966) was that intelligence and achievement test scores for large numbers of pupils do not appear to be related to the quality of schooling. However, these findings do not include assessment of teacher–pupil and pupil–pupil interaction. Such interactions may result in differences when status variables such as the number of books, age of building, and expenditures per pupil do not. Coleman did report, however, that for the most disadvantaged children and for black children quality of schooling does make a difference in terms of achievement.

As Gordon and Green (1975, pp. 90–91) put it: "Differences in the quality and quantity of schooling in the United States seem to make little difference in your achievement score unless you are poor or black. If you are both, it seems that schooling might make a powerful difference in your scores and your life chances."

The findings of a recent and important study of race, competence, socialization, and social structure in Chicago confirms the view that observed differences in the measured intelligence of black and white children of each sex are not due to innate race differences but rather stem from social factors and complex interactions among these factors (Blau 1981, p. 183). This study found further that the initial observed difference of ten IQ points between the two racial groups was reduced to approximately six points by considering several aspects of socioeconomic status and that it was further reduced to approximately four points when differences in the religious composition of the two races were considered (p. 54).

Questionable Value of IQ Tests for Comparing Racial Intelligence

Extended consideration of the shortcomings of IQ tests themselves is beyond the scope of this work, but a sampling of the numerous criticisms of intelligence testing is essential. In the first place, the widest application has been in the field of education, and success in the United States and Europe tends to be based on a rather narrow portion of the total spectrum of intellectual abilities. It is mainly by the use of this narrow set of abilities that traditional IQ tests predict so well (Jensen 1969, pp. 19–20). Secondly, it has been shown that the mood or attitude of the respondent may make a difference of as much as twenty points. For example, when black testers administer IQ tests, black students perform better, and black students score higher on such tests when they are deceived into believing that their intelligence is not being tested (Montagu 1972a, pp. 1056–1057).

Thirdly, and most important, what IQ tests measure is not simply genetic potentials for intelligence but the expression of the interaction between genetic potentials and the nutritional, socioeconomic, emotional, motivational, and educational experience of the individual (Montagu 1972a, p. 1053; 1974, pp. 381–403).

A very important aspect of racial-cultural testing is that the differences in the averages are much smaller than the variations within any race. High IQs of persons of every race are much higher than the averages of their own or any other race. Similarly, the low variants in every race are much below the average for any race (Dobzhansky 1971, p. 21; Loehlin et al. 1975, p. 257).

Jensen's hypothesis is that "something between one-half and three-fourths of the average IQ difference between American Negroes and Whites is attributable to genetic factors, and the remainder to environmental factors and their interaction" (1975, p. 363). If true, this would mean that the average IQ difference between Blacks and Whites due to genetic factors would be nine points (62.5 percent of 15). Because the white group is far from being a homogeneous group genetically and the black group is even more heterogeneous genetically, the comparison is quite meaningless.

CHAPTER 3

Discrimination and Prejudice as Weapons in Group Conflict

Explanations for discrimination and prejudice are best sought in the general body of sociological, anthropological, and psychological theory about human behavior. In the development of our knowledge, the relationship has been reciprocal: the study of minority–majority relations has been a valuable approach to many social scientific problems; at the same time, the advances in the sciences of human behavior have made possible, and imperative, the reformulation of our explanations of intergroup hostility. One-factor explanations or the perspectives of one discipline are clearly inadequate.

The Roots of Intergroup Hostility

A comprehensive theory can be developed, in our judgment, around three analytically distinct but highly interactive factors, each the subject of several lines of investigation.

Intergroup hostility is, to an important degree, an expression of the struggle for power, income, and prestige. It is built into some of the basic structures of society. Studies of the power arrangements seek to find out who makes the key economic, political, educational, and religious decisions and the ways in which these are facilitated by social structures in such a way that some groups are persistently disadvantaged and harmed (Lenski 1966). In examining some of the evidence that supports the importance of this factor, we shall, in this chapter, pay no attention to the individual characteristics of either majority-group or minority-group members.

In recent years one aspect of the structural approach is the study of the effects of comparative sizes of groups in interaction, without reference to individual tendencies or the nature of the interaction (Blau 1977). This is an attempt, in other words, to isolate the purely structural influence. What are the effects, for example, of one group having only token representation, perhaps with only a single member involved in an interaction? (We should note that *token* in the sense used here refers not to tokenism as a policy or to the perception of underrepresentation, but to a numerical fact.) Kanter (1977) observes that the fact of small numbers in a given category (her studies refer mainly to women) makes them highly visible, tends toward polarization, with the majority exaggerating differences between themselves and the minority, and leads to distorted perceptions among the majority that make minority-group members seem to fit more closely to stereotyped expectations. These majority actions produce efforts on the part of minority persons to reduce their visibility. The majority draws group boundaries more sharply and heightens performance pressure on the minority. The result, Kanter observes, is often "role entrapment" for the minority (see also Spangler, Gordon, and Pipkin 1978; Taylor 1981).

41

Members of a minority experience a number of restrictive effects when they make up a very large proportion of a group as well as when they have only token representation. The effect studied most often is the lower income, compared with majority-group members of equivalent education and experience, when minorities constitute a high ratio (Brown and Fuguitt 1972; Frisbie and Neidert 1977). It is difficult to distinguish the effects of ratios from those of other factors with which ratios may be correlated (except in small-group laboratories, where some experiments with the effects of solo status have been carried out), but the literature on minority–majority proportions calls our attention clearly to the fact that disadvantage is, at least to a small degree, the result of impersonal, structural factors. Many readers can refer to their own experience, both as tokens and as members of majorities, to enhance their understanding of the influence of ratios.

The comparative size of age groups (or cohorts) also affects intergroup relations in largely impersonal, unintended ways. In a later chapter we will discuss the very large difference in unemployment rates between the majority and minorities, particularly Blacks, in the United States. The causes are numerous and complicated but among them is a set of demographic facts interacting with patterns of discrimination. The high rate of unemployment among Blacks is partly the result of the large number of new entrants into the job market in the fifteen-year period between 1967 and 1982, reflecting the large birth cohorts twenty years earlier. There were fewer jobs being created or vacated than there were candidates. The situation was made worse by the fact that black workers were, on the average, younger—that is, had a higher proportion of new workers. With lower average levels of training they were hit more severely by the decrease in the proportion of less skilled jobs. At the same time, women were entering the labor force in large numbers and immigration was at a higher level than it had been in several decades. The impact of these largely impersonal forces was accentuated by persistent discrimination.

There is—or there may be—an optimistic side to this picture (Easterlin 1980). By 1982 the size of the cohorts ready to enter the job market was beginning to fall. A shortage of applicants is already beginning to show up in a few highly skilled fields and is likely to spread into other parts of the economy. The 1994 cohort of twenty-years-olds will be 25 percent smaller than the 1980 cohort. The increase in the number of women entering the labor force is likely to be at a slower rate (since women already make up 40 percent of the labor force, the pool available for further expansion is becoming small). One cannot speak with any confidence about the effects of immigration but the number admitted annually seems unlikely to be any larger, and may well be smaller, than is the case today.

If these estimates are correct, purely impersonal demographic forces will tend to reduce the minority unemployment rate. These effects could, of course, be cancelled out by a depression or by an increase in discrimination but they would still be operating, preventing a bad situation from becoming even worse. If they are not cancelled out, and the unemployment rate drops, we will be wise to remember that we cannot assume that discrimination has been reduced (although it may have been), just as today we must recognize that part of the unemployment situation is the result of impersonal demographic changes.

The structural and macrosociological view has been strongly emphasized in recent years, as it has been in all editions of this book. We think this is essential, because it is easy to personalize explanations. This emphasis can be made too strongly, however. If one is a tenant or worker or student from a minority, it makes a difference whether one's landlord, employer, or teacher is a relatively tolerant or a hostile person, whether his or her behavior is governed by stereotypes, guilt, or self-hatred. This microsociological approach cannot explain why hostility is directed against certain groups or individuals but it helps to account for its intensity and persistence. Thus prejudice and discrimination can partly be understood as manifestations of the tendencies of individuals—tendencies that are being acted out or repressed, of course, in particular situations (Seeman 1981; Yinger 1965b, Chapter 11). When one is focusing analytically on this level one needs to give little attention to the characteristics of the groups against whom prejudice and discrimination are directed; nor need one emphasize the dominant social structures. The attention, rather, should be given to individual members of dominant groups, to study the processes by which they were socialized, the nature of their self-regard, the wants and values instilled by society, the degree to which they are able to fulfill those wants and attain those values. We need to be especially alert to any factors that help to differentiate between the more hostile and the less hostile.

In trying to answer some kinds of questions it makes little difference, for example, that some slave owners were especially cruel and others relatively humane. It is the slave system that must be examined. For other kinds of questions, however, we need a microscope rather than a telescope; we need to see in clear detail the tendencies of the particular individuals involved in an encounter across the majority–minority line.

We ought perhaps to emphasize that the macro-micro distinction is analytic. To throw light on a particular question one may give primary attention to one or the other; one view may lead to more powerful explanations than the other under certain conditions. Both structural and individual factors are involved in all situations, however, and must be taken into account if one seeks a full explanation.

A third analytic factor, indeed, must be added: culture. In almost every society, if not in all, each new generation is taught what are considered to be appropriate beliefs regarding other groups. Such beliefs are part of the folkways; we learn them in the same way that we acquire other beliefs, attitudes, and values. Belief in the superiority of one's own group is as natural to the dominant members of many societies as belief in the rightness of their marriage customs or their political structures. The speech and action of others, one's observation of status differentials among the races, the jokes, the histories, the rewards and punishments for various actions toward members of minority groups all teach one the correct behavior as it is defined by society. One does not have to have any individual experience with members of minority groups. Individuals will often be equipped with ready-made responses in advance of any such experience, or even in the complete absence of contact. In many instances the correct referent in this type of analysis will be to subsocieties, for norms may vary by region, occupation, or ethnic group. Under those conditions we can speak of the subcultural factor in prejudice.

On this level of explanation we need not refer to personality needs or to group conflicts. A person can show intergroup hostility even when she or he has a minimum of the frustrations of which prejudice is an expression and even when economic or political interests, far from being served by the attitude, are actually injured by it, as we shall see later. To be sure, the prejudice may not be so deeply rooted when it is acquired simply as a culture norm and is unsustained by personality and group needs. But for purposes of understanding the causes of intergroup hostility and for any kind of effective action in its reduction, the analytic separation of the cultural factor from the others is important. This "culture norm" theory does not explain the origin of a prejudice as part of a group's culture. One can understand how an attitude toward minority groups can be passed along as tradition, but to explain the origin of that tradition, and perhaps its continuing vitality, one must refer to the individual and group sources. Similarly, one can understand the sources of individual tendencies toward hostility without seeing why specific groups should be used for the expressions of those tendencies. The selection of certain groups as targets can be understood only by analysis of the traditions of the society and the vulnerability of certain groups.

Thus the three factors interact. The importance of the various causes, however, will vary from person to person and from situation to situation. Hostility will be most intense and least subject to change when all three factors are involved. A person brought up in a culture that is rich with traditions of prejudice, who identifies himself or herself with groups that stand to gain, or think they do, from discriminatory actions, and who is insecure and frustrated will have a high probability for hostile intergroup behavior.

We can say that the *probability* is high that such a person will express such hostility, but not that he positively will. Several closely related factors require this qualification. Other influences are doubtless involved that are unmentioned and unmeasured; since they are unmeasured, we cannot know to what degree they affect this result. Moreover, every person is influenced by many unique experiences that make him or her something different from a typical representative of the groups to which he belongs. One may be a member of a group that believes it profits from an exclusionist policy; but he or she may have had experiences that cause him or her to doubt or deny this. Finally, a culture that is rich in traditions of prejudice may also be rich—or at least not lacking—in traditions of nonprejudice. If one has experienced this aspect of culture in more than normal amount, the traditions of prejudice may be offset or counteracted.

Many readers may wonder why no mention has been made of the targets of prejudice in this outline of causes. Are their characteristics not involved? If one asks a prejudiced person why he believes as he does or acts as he does toward the members of a minority group, he will cite *their* characteristics, not his own, as the cause. Is this a wholly irrational response? We think not. Any complete analysis of the system of discrimination will have to take fully into account the influence of minority-group behavior, as we shall do in Chapters 6 and 7. A case could be made for identifying the response of minority-group members to their disprivileged positions as a fourth major cause of hostility. The key word in this sentence, however, is *response*. Although the targets of hostility may develop tendencies that feed back into the system of causes which created the hostility, thus reenforcing those causes, in the first instance the tendencies are the effects of that hostility. A person deprived of opportunity may be lazy, deprived of schools may be ignorant, deprived of hope may be careless—and the depriving majority may then accuse that person of the very characteristics they have brought about. And the ostensible facts will support their claim in some instances. We shall have to give full attention to this process whereby effects become reenforcing causes. But to list them as a primary cause would be to obscure the sequence of events and to mistake the roots of discrimination for its fruit. At this point we need say only that the fruit may furnish seed for further growth. In the life of human beings and their societies—and elsewhere in nature—the *cycle* of causes is of profound importance.

In the next chapter we shall review the evidence that prejudice and discrimination stem, in part, from the tendencies of individuals. Although this is an essential part of an adequate theory of intergroup hostility, it can, and in some cases has, obscured the economic and political conflicts and scarcity-based competitions that can support discrimination and prejudice. It is difficult to resist lodging the explanations of events in individuals—in our heroes or villains—because they are visible. Social structures and processes are abstract. To see them requires a greater effort of the imagination.

In this chapter and throughout the book the structural sources of discrimination will be a major topic of interest. On this level of analysis, knowledge of the extent to which people are ego-alien, threat-oriented, or authoritarian—terms we will examine in the next chapter—is of little value. In recent years it has become fashionable to refer to this group-based source by the phrase "institutional racism" (Knowles and Prewitt 1969). Insofar as this calls attention to the structured sources of discrimination it can contribute to our understanding. It clouds the meaning of *race,* however; and there is some danger that *institutional racism,* or simply *racism,* will be used as an explanatory term when

in fact it designates only a mode of behavior that itself requires explanation.

When human beings come together, they tend both to unite for common purposes and to oppose each other. There is cooperation and accommodation, but there is also competition and conflict; and the cooperating members of one group are often united for purposes of opposition toward another group. Thus the two processes of association and dissociation are opposite sides of the same interaction. Many of the things that human beings desire—prestige, power, income—come in scarce quantity; and much of the social process, both of association and of dissociation, can be understood as an attempt to hold on to or to increase one's share of these scarce values. We cooperate with some in order to compete more effectively with others.[1]

One of the widespread and probably universal results of this process is the stratification of human societies into many ranks, sharing differently in the distribution of prized and scarce values. These ranks may be defined in the folkways and buttressed by tradition and are often maintained by force. But the distribution of values is not permanent; human beings are constantly widening or narrowing their claims. Technological change, culture contact, and new systems of belief continually bring new forces into the "moving equilibrium" that makes up a social order. The entrance of these factors is obviously more rapid in some situations than in others, but they can scarcely be entirely lacking in any main society. To protect their established positions or to improve upon them, human groups are quick to invent or to accept systems of belief and attitudes that justify and explain what they are trying to do. The explanation may be "religious"—the infidel, the barbarian, the pagan deserves no better—or cultural, or national, or based on class distinctions. In our time it is frequently racial, or pseudoracial. In the following pages we shall examine some attempts to use these distinctions as bases for maintaining or improving a group's position in the struggle for prestige, power, and income.

One must avoid exaggerating, as many writers have done, the role of conflict and competition in human life. There are those who think of conflict as the "the father of all things" and those who,

---

[1] There is a rich literature on the place of conflict in societies. See, e.g., Collins 1975; Coser 1954, 1967; Dahrendorf 1959; Giddens 1973; Marx 1963; Simmel 1955.

especially since Darwin's day (despite Darwin, one might add), think of it in moral terms—conflict is good, and without it life would lack both zest and progress. Our position here is simply that conflict and competition are important social processes, natural to human society (as is cooperation) and probably inevitable. That is *not* to say, however, that any specific mode of conflict is inevitable or that any particular group alignment is natural. History is filled with evidence of the shifting pattern of groups among whom conflict occurs and of the wide range of modes of conflict, from violence to rational argument, that characterize human interaction.

Few persons doubt the relationship between economic placement and minority status. In recent years this commonplace observation has been taken apart and examined as one of the elements in a complex, multifactored status-placement process. The question of who gets ahead has been examined in a significant body of literature (Arrow 1971; Blau and Duncan 1967; Duncan, Featherman, and Duncan 1972; Featherman and Hauser 1978; Jencks et al. 1979; Sewell, Hauser, and Featherman 1976).

Our task in this chapter will be to examine some of the ways in which majority and minority status affect the allocation of rewards in a society. Or, to put it somewhat differently, we will illustrate the ways in which economic considerations enter into the system of discrimination.

Discrimination and Prejudice in the Struggle for Power, Prestige, and Income

A fundamental attitude underlying the use of discrimination and prejudice as a group weapon is ethnocentrism—belief in the unique value and rightness of one's own group (Lanternari 1980; Sumner 1906, pp. 13–15). This nearly universal tendency was explained at first by the theory that there was a natural aversion to difference. Having been socialized to the behavior and beliefs of one's own society, seeing them as natural, each individual inevitably judged other behavior and beliefs as unnatural. The very standards by which one judges the value or desirability of any action are part of the culture that the growing individual absorbs; therefore one cannot avoid ethnocentrism. Although this explanation is still regarded as valid, another element which relates it to the topic of this chapter

has been added. Ethnocentrism serves the group in its struggles for power and wealth. (It also serves the individual in his attempt to find personal security.) It flourishes best in conflict situations. In the eighteenth century an East Indian, traveling in England, was received as an honored guest; there was also a general admiration for the Chinese. With the growth of conflicts of power between Britain and the East, however, this attitude faded; there was a loss of appreciation for the civilizations of the eastern lands; ethnocentrism and prejudice grew (Toynbee 1934, vol. 1). To the degree that boundaries (social or physical), group loyalties, and labels coincide—that is, do not cut across each other— ethnocentrism tends to be strong. That situation in pure form is not common in the modern world (Brewer and Campbell 1976; Levine and Campbell 1972), but situations approaching it occur quite frequently, particularly in contacts between races or groups that differ significantly in culture, religion, and language.

To say that ethnocentrism serves groups and individuals is not to say that it is good. We mean only that it contributes to the stability of a social system in a given situation. One may abhor the system thus stabilized. Or the situation may change in such a way that gains from ingroup cohesion are outweighed by the losses from intergroup conflict. Catton (1960–61) points out that "ethnocentrism may have contributed to the futility of many well-meant attempts by statesmen to use the conference table as a functional alternative to war." An attitude of superiority within a society may contribute to a group's dominance at one time but add inflexibility and blindness that weakens their position in a changed situation.

If ethnocentrism is functional in group conflict, as well as being a result of the limitations in perspective that come from the process of socialization, it is an expression of the needs of the powerful people as a ruling group, not simply a reflection of the frustrations of powerless individuals. This is also true of group prejudices within a society; the designation of inferior groups comes from those on top—an expression of their right to rule—as well as from frustrated persons often near the bottom, as an expression of their need for security. Sherif (1948, p. 343) notes:

The scale of hierarchy of prejudice in settled and stable times flows from the politically, economically, and socially strong and eminent down to lower hierarchies of the established order....The most elaborate "race" superiority doctrines are products of already existing organizations of superiority–inferiority relationships and exploitations.

In examining the usefulness of this theory, we must be careful not to limit the study to ethnocentric views that are currently most visible. A few centuries ago it was easier to designate so-called inferior groups by religious than by racial lines of division. In Europe there was relatively little contact with the members of non-Caucasian races, for instance. Differences in religious belief, however, frequently reflected different status positions; social changes and conflicts were accompanied by religious differentiation. At a time when the religious view of life was extremely powerful, it was easy to believe that a religiously different group was inferior. A moment's thought will bring to mind religious and political-ideological prejudices of great strength in the contemporary world as well.

Subsidiary beliefs (subsidiary from the point of view of a theory of prejudice) helped account for the use of *religious* prejudice in *secular* group conflicts. The medieval world believed that life on earth was a brief second, that eternal salvation was the most important thing. Was it not common humanity to kill any Antichrist who might lead thousands to eternal damnation? (Benedict 1940, pp. 220-23). An examination of the setting in which this religious prejudice flourished, however, shows that a strictly religious explanation of the conflict is insufficient. Involved in the Inquisition of the thirteenth century, for example, were many secular gains for the inquisitor—confiscation of property, political gains, weakening of the hold of emerging new ruling groups, avoiding attention to the role of the church in the secular power structure: "Heresy hunting was profitable, and all those who sought riches and power eagerly took advantage of the opportunity, masking their satisfactions behind the dogma that the heretics were guilty of treason against the Almighty" (Benedict 1940, p. 225).

From Religious to Racial Prejudice

In our time, religious lines of demarcation are less useful in group conflict. Religious cleavages coincide less well with political and economic divisions. To be sure, there are cleavages in modern society where religious differentiation and political-economic differentiation do coincide, with something of the same results as were found in the religious wars of medieval Europe. Strictly religious differentiation, however, is less often used for group conflict in modern society because many other lines of distinction cut across religious lines. In a large measure, racial differentiation, or supposed racial differentiation, has come to take its place. We now fight our economic and political opponents not by claiming that they believe the wrong things in religion but by claiming that they are natively inferior.

It was not difficult to make the transition from the religious to the racial line of demarcation. Europe's first extensive contacts with Negroes and Orientals occurred when religious differences were still regarded as vitally important. Relative tolerance in religious matters had not yet developed. The members of other races were, in most cases, not only racially different but also religiously different. If, at first, the white European did not condemn the Negro because he was a Negro, he could condemn him because he was a pagan. But what if the black pagan were converted to Christianity? When there were only a few such persons, the adjustment was not difficult; they could be given a higher status or even admitted to the dominant group. MacCrone (1937, p. 135) states that the earliest practice in South Africa was to free slaves who had been baptized. But in time this threatened to become a costly economic burden and a challenge to the whole status structure. In 1792 the Church Council of Capetown explicitly stated that "neither the law of the land nor the law of the church" required the freeing of converted slaves. Even earlier the same decision had been made in Britain's American colonies. "A series of laws enacted between 1667 and 1671 had systematically removed any lingering doubts whether conversion to Christianity should make a difference in status: henceforth it made none" (Elkins 1959, p. 50). Thus a line of cleavage originally symbolized in part by religion came to be symbolized wholly by race.

The racial line of cleavage had the additional advantage, as a weapon, of relative permanence. Poverty, or occupation, or language, or religion can set a group apart as sharply as skin color or head shape, but the line of distinction may be more difficult for the dominant group to maintain (Benedict 1940, pp. 233–36). George Bernard Shaw has caricatured this difficulty in *Pygmalion* by having a speech expert transform a servant girl into a "duchess" by giving her an Oxford accent. The transformation was not complete, to be sure, for it proved harder to control what she said than to change how she said it. After six months of training she seldom slipped back into cockney accent when she said "the rain in Spain falls mainly in the plain"; but it was a bit disconcerting to her teacher to see how often the weather conditions of southwestern Europe came into her conversation. Nevertheless she could "pass" relatively successfully. Had her skin been black, the most perfect Oxford accent and all the appropriate ideas to go with it would not have sufficed. It might be well to add that even the racial line is far from permanent, for wherever races have come into contact, miscegenation has produced a mixed group. The "line" between the dominant and subordinate races may then be drawn at one of several places, depending on the power needs of the dominant group.

Moreover, among all the ways in which human beings differ, visibility of some differences more than others is a function of attention. It is not the intrinsic quality of the differences, but the way these differences are connected with advantages and disadvantages that make some stand out.

Race prejudice was not only a weapon of imperialism, as in Africa and India, but a weapon of class conflict in many nations. In the eighteenth century the Count de Boulainvilliers, an admirer of feudalism, tried to oppose not only the peasantry but Louis XIV as well by claiming that the nobles, who were losing their autonomous power to the absolute monarch, were of superior "Teuton" blood. To attack their power was to destroy the racial leadership of France. It was not until the nineteenth century, however, that this idea was widely used. In *The Inequality of Human Races,* de Gobineau declared that the hope of the world was the fair-haired Teutons—"Aryans." All the countries of Europe had been swamped by "Gallo-Romans" while the racial aristocrats were being destroyed. The revolutionary movements of 1848 were, to Gobineau, an uprising of racial trash. Since the masses were innately inferior, the democracy and liberalism for which they fought were impossible. Thus he fought a class battle with racism (Gobineau 1915; see also Benedict 1940, pp. 173–79).

The Political and Economic Use of Anti-Semitism.

Out of the political and economic struggles of Europe in the latter half of the nineteenth century there emerged an anti-Semitic program that demonstrates clearly the role of prejudice in group conflict. Overt expressions of anti-Semitism had gradually subsided in western Europe during the eighteenth and first half of the nineteenth centuries. The merchant and industrial middle class had fought its way to power under the banner of democracy and liberalism; it had sought, and won, the support of many Jews. Legal and political discriminations against Jews were generally abolished. By the middle of the nineteenth century, however, the central political-economic battle was no longer between the new middle class and the old feudal aristocracy but had become a struggle between the now powerful middle class and a rising proletarian movement (of many types). Whereas democracy and liberalism had been appropriate ideologies for the earlier struggle, they were embarrassing and difficult concepts for the middle class to use in its conflicts with the proletariat. In this setting anti-Semitism began to revive. In Germany, where the conflicts were sharpest, there was no time between 1870 and 1945 when there was not a frankly anti-Semitic political party. Bismarck, although probably personally disdainful of the intellectual supports to anti-Semitism, nevertheless began to use it to fight the liberal movement. Since several Jews or persons of Jewish parentage had been prominent in his government, it was not religious or cultural difference that led to the new attacks, but the usefulness of Jews as symbols. Finding it difficult to get a positive political program behind which they could unite a sufficiently large following, the conservatives discovered that they could achieve a kind of negative unity by the use of anti-Semitism.

Since the 1870s many other struggles between the political left and right, including some in the United States, have involved anti-Semitism. Gradually the attacks on Jews shifted from a religious and cultural base to a "racial" one. As late as 1899 Chamberlain, in his *Foundations of the Nineteenth Century,* declared that Jews were enemies, not because of biological differences but because of their special ways of thinking and acting. "One can very soon become a Jew." By the time of Hitler, however, anti-Semitism had become thoroughly biologized. Jews were held to be innately inferior and vicious, the destroyers of civilization. Throughout this period anti-Semitism, whether rationalized on cultural or "racial" grounds, was a clear example of the use of prejudice for political and economic purposes.

Discrimination and Prejudice as Weapons in the United States

Most of the preceding material has referred to prejudice as a weapon in the struggles of Europe. No less convincing a demonstration of its role in group conflict can be found in the history of the United States, which was being settled at the very time that racial lines of cleavage were beginning to be drawn. Several factors in American history encouraged the use and elaboration of race prejudice. As the colonists became numerous and began to press deeper into the Indian's lands, sharp conflicts inevitably arose. Few of the settlers seriously considered that the Indians might have some rights to the land. It was easier to develop a picture of the lying, thieving, murdering savage, pagan in religion, racially stupid except for a kind of animal cunning. Such a person had no rights; the only good Indian was a dead Indian. This picture was frequently not held by the trappers and traders who moved individually among the Indians. They gained by friendly contact and therefore tended to judge the Indian differently. But the prejudice of the farmer-settler prevailed, leading to the continuing seizure of Indian lands with a minimum of compensation and the reduction of the Indian population to scarcely more than one-third its original size.

At various points we shall discuss the numerous changes in government policy toward Native Americans, shifting public attitudes, and some of the political and religious movements among Indians. The population has begun to grow rapidly in the last twenty years, to one and a third million by 1980. This is probably about the number who lived in what is now the United States in 1492; but they live on a tiny fraction of the land base they had then. Although discrimination has been reduced, the consequences of past exploitation remain severe.[2]

The Slave System in the United States

Slavery, like other systems of domination, is defended and explained by beliefs congenial to those in power and those who identify with them (Patterson 1982, Chapter 2). These beliefs, often deeply

[2]On Indian-White contacts, see Bahr, Chadwick, and Day 1972; Deloria 1974; Levine and Lurie 1970; Schusky 1980; Sorkin 1978; Spicer 1962; Wax 1971; Wilson 1976; Yinger and Simpson 1978.

embedded in the culture, are scarcely the cause of slavery, although they may help to reinforce it. Human bondage is the clearest illustration of the economic and political factor in discrimination. Most of the ten or eleven million people taken from Africa, mostly to be sent to the New World, were prisoners of war, sold by Africans to European agents. (Estimates of the number vary. Curtin [1969] gives 9,566,000; Rawley [1981] gives 11,345,000 as his estimate.) The economic demand for slaves was an important factor in promoting the wars that produced them.

The structure of domination and its attendant beliefs took some time to evolve, their nature being affected by the economic and political setting. The situation before the American Revolution held the possibilities for several different patterns. Many of the Negroes who came to American first were indentured servants, not slaves; there were also white indentured servants. From this situation it was possible that both black and white bondsmen would move toward freedom as the settlements became more stable or that both would sink into a permanent status of inferiority (whether of slavery or some other legal form), or that one group would break out of servitude while the other was kept in. In the seventeenth century a Virginia court had upheld the right of one Negro to claim the perpetual service of another Negro—showing that no categorical race line had yet been drawn. With the failure of tobacco, rice, and indigo to support the plantation economy, the settlers became lukewarm toward slavery. As Charles Johnson reported (in Thompson 1939, pp. 280–281):

In Granville County, North Carolina, a full-blooded Negro, John Chavis, educated at Princeton, conducted a private school for white children, and was a licentiate under the local Presbytery, preaching to white congregations in the state. One of his pupils became Governor of North Carolina, another was the state's Whig Senator. Two were sons of the Chief Justice of North Carolina. He was not stopped until the Denmark Vesey uprising in South Carolina (the first state to show promise of economic prosperity through the cotton industry) threatened the whole structure of slavery.

Myrdal (1944, p. 86) states that in the first two decades of the nineteenth century the abolitionist movement was as strong in the South as in the North, if not stronger.

Despite these signs of contradictory tendencies in the South, the legal and institutional structure of slavery had developed, since the late seventeenth century, into a system of great clarity and consistency focused primarily on one goal: the maximization of profit. No matter how harsh or beneficent might be the personal relationship of master to slave, and despite the skillful adaptations of slave families and larger kin structures (Gutman 1977), in the last analysis the slave was property, without personal rights, without family rights, without religious rights.

How did a system of such unlimited power develop? Interpretations vary with regard to the harshness of the system, the basic supports for it in the American social, economic, and political structure, and the way in which slaves dealt with it. We will examine the last part of this problem of interpretation in Chapter 6. Here we want only to note the economic and political structure of control that developed around slavery, referring to a few of the interpretations.

U. B. Phillips (1918, 1929), who powerfully influenced the study of slavery for decades, saw it as a relatively natural product of an environment within which a plantation system, with its sharp status contrasts, prospered. His interpretations seem today to be insensitive to the cruelties of slavery and his examination of the feelings and attitudes of black men and women superficial, although his detailed descriptions of slavery as a control system are still useful.

Rejecting Phillips's racialist assumptions, Stanley Elkins examines the way in which slavery was established in a society without prior traditional institutions. The slave was not protected by the feudal immunities that aided even the lowliest of the medieval peasants; the crown was primarily concerned with revenue; competing churches could not command moral leadership. In this open society, however, the road to success was to create a plantation; and for the slave there was little "to prevent unmitigated capitalism from becoming unmitigated slavery....The drive of the law—unembarrassed by the perplexities of competing interests—was to clarify beyond all question, to rationalize, to simplify, and to make more logical and symmetrical the slave's status in society" (Elkins 1959, p. 52). The relationship to England was crucial (pp. 43–44):

Virginia was settled during the very key period in which the English middle class forcibly reduced, by revolution, the power of those standing institutions—the church and the crown—that most directly symbolized society's traditional limitations upon personal success and mobility.

Eugene Genovese has effectively stated a Marxian view that slavery is fundamentally a class system and that the Civil War was the final expression of a reactionary elite attempting to protect its status against major changes in the nation (1965, 1969, 1974).

In *Time on the Cross,* Fogel and Engerman (1974), using the systematic quantitative methods of the cliometrician, examine slavery primarily as a system of production, an economic enterprise. Although they do not use this phrase, they seem to be saying, in opposition to Elkins, that "unmitigated capitalism led to mitigated slavery." In their desire to maximize profits—and plantations were often profitable—the landowners fed the slaves well enough to keep them healthy, had regard for their morale (which meant some support for a stable family system), and trained many of them to be skilled workers and managers. Curtin (1969) estimates that not more than 4.5 percent of the slaves imported into the New World were brought to the United States. Some concern for their health was prompted, if for no other reason, by the fact that good health promoted natural increase, the main source of growth in numbers.

Time on the Cross was widely and on the whole caustically reviewed, because it seemed to go back to John C. Calhoun, or at least to U. B. Phillips, in the picture it drew of a kind of benign slavery that was at the same time a very efficient mode of production (Davis 1974). That was certainly not the authors' intent, although we are inclined to agree with the critics who believe that their cold calculations of efficiency almost completely overlooked the harsh reality of imprisonment. After all, one might also take good care of draft animals or machinery in the name of efficiency. Fogel and Engerman did, however, sweep away a lot of myths surrounding slavery, particularly those related to the presumed childishness and inferiority of slaves (see also Hermann 1981). And Woodward (1974, p. 6) points to another gain that could flow from their discussion:

Had they thought of it, the authors might have pointed out also that the traditional picture of the pitiful, emasculated slave is the standard rationalization of policy makers for modern problems of the black minority. It runs like a litany through "background" papers on welfare, employment, the "matriarchal" family, the public schools. It turns up in Supreme Court opinions and presidential addresses. It has become the conventional way of shifting responsibility for the failings of the free enterprise system to the shoulders of a forgotten and long discredited class of a remote period.

Whatever the unintended effects of the arguments of Fogel and Engerman may be, they have clearly documented the economic base of slavery and shown how the pursuit of gain and power are tied to racial discrimination (see also Higginbotham 1978; Noel 1972; Patterson 1982, Rawick 1972).

If the legal clarity of an unmitigated slave system in the United States was not fully matched by practice in the seventeenth and eighteenth centuries, in the first half of the nineteenth century almost all the ambiguities were eliminated. Economic forces were of great importance in this development. The invention of the cotton gin and other mechanical devices for the processing of cotton cloth began to make cotton agriculture profitable. In 1793, 500,000 pounds of cotton were exported to Europe. The cotton gin was patented in 1794, and the next year six million pounds were exported. By a decade later, 1805, the amount had grown to 40 million pounds, and by 1850 to over one billion pounds (Weatherford and Johnson 1934, p. 136). The effects of this increase were soon felt. The price of cotton rose, the value of slaves doubled, and land values increased sharply; "and with every increase in value the difficulty of breaking the status of Negro slavery increased" (Charles S. Johnson in Thompson 1939, p. 282). The belief in slavery, which had been on the decline for a century or more, began to revive in the South. After 1830 an extensive literature to justify slavery appeared. It attempted to show that slavery was contrary neither to nature nor to religion and that since the Negro was inferior and subhuman, it was even harmonious with democracy. Occasionally a writer would recognize the economic foundation of these beliefs. In *Sociology for the South,* 1854, George Fitzhugh wrote (quoted in Myrdal 1944, p. 1188):

Our Southern patriots at the time of the Revolution, finding Negroes expensive and useless, became warm antislavery men. We, their wiser sons, having learned to make cotton and sugar, find slavery very useful and profitable, and think it a most excellent institution. We of the South advocate slavery, no doubt, from just as selfish motives as induce the Yankees and English to deprecate it.

But Fitzhugh hastened to add, "We have, however, almost all human and divine authority on our side of the argument. The Bible nowhere condemns, and throughout recognizes slavery."

Perhaps we ought to add that something close to slavery persists in the United States, perpetuated by the same drive for profit even if lacking normative support. Ostensibly it is illegal. Three men have recently been sentenced to long prison terms for conspiring to enslave migrant workers, one of whom died while being held in a labor camp (*St. Petersburg Times,* February 3, 1982, p. 3). Most such enslavement, however, goes on under shadowy legal protection or neglect, able to survive because of powerful economic demand for unskilled workers. A story in the *New York Times,* October 19, 1980, noted:

Uncounted thousands of Spanish-speaking aliens who flee to this country each year to escape the crushing poverty of their homelands are being virtually enslaved, bought and sold on sophisticated underground labor exchanges. They are trucked around the country in consignments by self-described labor contractors who deliver them to farmers and growers for hundreds of dollars a head.

Immigration and Minority Status

Throughout history, wherever there has been unoccupied and desirable land, or the possibility of finding a place in a land already occupied, or the chance of avoiding starvation or war, human beings have migrated. Driven by want and oppression or attracted by the chance for a new beginning, migrants have moved in waves or in small bands into new territories. It is a truism to state that America is a land of immigrants, starting with the arrival of persons from eastern Asia, perhaps 20,000 years ago. By the sixteenth century, Europeans began to come in significant numbers and Africans, in forced migration, in the seventeenth. This is scarcely an exclusive American experience, however. Every continent has been affected by extensive migration. And since the sixteenth century it has been one of the major demographic facts around the world. Today, most societies are composed of persons of diverse culture, language, religion, or race.

Although there has been extensive change in the nature of the forces permitting or compelling migration, the process continues. In fact, more migration, in absolute numbers, has occurred during the nineteenth and twentieth centuries than at any other time. Tens of millions of persons have crossed deserts, continents, and oceans, as well as political boundaries. Some have been primarily pulled by hope and ambition; more have been pushed by oppression and poverty. Some have been welcomed and often absorbed into the resident population; others have been less cordially received, even though admitted under the law, and have continued as minorities in a stratified ethnic and racial system (Richmond 1973). Some have entered the new lands legally, others illegally. For many, the migration has been permanent, for others temporary. Each of these four distinctions has many gradations. Thought about together, however, they indicate the variety and complexity of migratory patterns.

If most migrants were rather quickly assimilated, in either a one-way process or a two-way exchange, whatever one thinks of the desirability of such an outcome, they would not be of great interest to us here. That is not the case, however. Humankind has not yet learned how to organize multicultural and multiracial societies very well. Or perhaps it would be more accurate to say that dominant peoples have learned quite well how, under most conditions, to keep migrants in subservient positions (Burawoy 1976). They build their control on top of the inevitable disadvantages that newcomers face, whatever the intent and the actions of the majority, as a result of their newness and their cultural, lingual, and racial differences.

Most of our attention will be focused on American experience with immigration. Minority–majority issues connected with refugees and immigrants are of great importance, however, in many parts of the world today. They require at least illustrative examination if we are to see the American experience in perspective. We will look briefly at two related topics: refugees and recent migration into the countries of Western Europe.

Refugees in the Late Twentieth Century

A testimony to the great importance attached to the problem of refugees is the award, both in 1954 and in 1981, of the Nobel Peace Prize to the United Nations High Commission for Refugees. The Commission, along with other United Nations agencies, the United States Committee for Refugees, other national committees, and numerous religious and philanthropic organizations, can only begin to deal with the enormous problems involved in the present state of intranational and international conflict. The number of refugees varies quite widely year to year, but at no time in recent years has it fallen below 10 million persons. In 1966 the United States Committee for Refugees, in its *World Refugee Report,* counted 11.2 million; in 1981, 12.6 million. Over a million and a half Somalis have fled from Ogaden,

the area disputed between Ethiopia and Somalia; nearly that many Afghans have fled to Pakistan after the Soviet invasion of their homeland. These increases have been offset by an improving situation in Southeast Asia. Cambodia, with its first good harvest in 1980 after many lean years, saw many of its citizens return (see Stein and Tomasi 1981).

In the fall of 1981, the United Nations High Commissioner for Refugees, in *Refugees,* estimated (one should not forget how imprecise these figures may be) the four largest groups of refugees to be the following: Somalis, 1.6 million; Afghans, 1.4 million; Palestinians, 1.0 million; and Vietnamese, .9 million. Only in the case of the Vietnamese has any significant proportion been resettled under secure conditions.

It is necessary also to note the receiving countries, for it is in them that minority status will develop or be avoided. One can learn a great deal about minority-majority relations by observing the differing ways in which societies respond to refugees within their boundaries. The UNHCR has estimated the major receiving countries during the last several years to be those shown in Table 3-1.

Although the distinction is not sharp, one can divide countries receiving refugees into those into which refugees have fled—usually neighboring countries themselves faced by harsh economic or unstable political conditions—and industrialized countries that, out of a mixture of humanitarianism and self-interest, have accepted responsibility for the resettlement of refugees.

It is difficult to exaggerate the anguish of refugees. They are not always, however, to be considered minorities, in our sense of the term. If they are resident in refugee camps under multinational

Table 3-1. Refugee Receiving Countries, Totals as of 1981

Somalia	1,600,000	Lebanon	229,000
Pakistan	1,400,000	Tanzania	156,000
United States	849,000	France	150,000
Jordan	716,000	United Kingdom	148,000
Sudan	500,000	Israel	120,000
Zaire	400,000	Uganda	113,000
Canada	338,000	Cameroon	110,000
Australia	304,000	Malaysia	107,000
China	265,000	Nigeria	105,000
Thailand	241,000	West Germany	94,000

From *Refugees,* Fall 1981.

care and expect soon to return home or if they have little or no contact with the people of the new land and do not think of themselves even temporarily as part of the new society, then their plight is better understood as something other than that of a minority. (This in no way implies, of course, that their plight is therefore less harsh or a less significant fact.) In many cases, however, they are destined to be permanent or long-term residents of the new land. A few of them may quickly be absorbed without being placed in an ethnic stratification system, with its attendant discriminations; but more commonly refugees, like other migrants, find themselves in a minority status.

One cannot distinguish precisely between immigrants and refugees. Using the four criteria mentioned above, one can draw a typological contrast. It is possible to say that refugees are not simply pushed from their homeland but flee impending disaster, whereas the pull of new opportunities is likely to be stronger among immigrants. Refugees are more likely to see themselves, and be seen, as in a temporary situation; they are less likely to be welcomed; and they are more likely to be illegal migrants. None of these clearly distinguishes immigrants from refugees, however. In some cases it is wise to think of certain individuals and groups as both. Persons of Asian background fleeing East African nations for Britain; Haitians and Cubans fleeing to the United States; East Germans or Poles asking for asylum in Western Europe; ethnic Chinese escaping to Malyasia or Thailand from Vietnam—these are refugees who often become immigrants, when their status is regularized in the new lands, even if it is not in all instances transformed into a fully legal status.

The New Era of Migrants to Western Europe and Britain

Europe and Britain have been receiving migrants for millenia, but for many generations prior to the end of World War II, except for France and to a lesser degree Germany, newcomers had been relatively few. After the war, and following struggles for independence in Indonesia, Indochina, Algeria, and sub-Saharan Africa, Western Europe—Holland, France, and Britain particularly—received a flood of migrants, some of them refugees from former colonies. A little later, beginning slowly in the early 1950s and becoming increasingly important as European economies recovered from the war and with the development of the European Common Market, workers from Southern Europe, Turkey, North Africa, and, in Britain's case, from the newly independent states of the Commonwealth, were admitted (Amersfoort 1982; Martin 1980; Mayer 1975). In many cases it would be more accurate to say they were encouraged and recruited: "At the height of the active search for new workers from 1968–1972, Germany had between 500 and 600 labor-recruiting offices scattered throughout the countries of Southern Europe" (Rist 1979b, p. 412). France also had official recruiters. Long-established patterns of individual, and often illegal, migration from Italy and Spain, however, continued to be the primary source of foreign workers to France after World War II (Dignan 1981).

In the mid-1970s a new wave of refugees, this time mainly from Indochina, was added to the population of Western Europe, with the largest number going to France. The common American image of Western European countries as being much more homogeneous, racially and culturally, than the United States, never entirely true, is now wide of the mark. A few additional comments on three societies may serve to illustrate the trends.

The Federal Republic of Germany—West Germany—admitted a large number of East Europeans of German background after World War II. This process continues for the ethnic Germans in the Soviet Union, some 85,000 of whom (out of almost two million) have been permitted to leave, a few thousand per year (*The New York Times*, November 8, 1981, p. 6). Of greater interest for students of minorities, however, is the large number of foreign workers admitted, beginning in 1960. They are, significantly, called "guest workers"—*gastarbeiter*—a term that indicates the predominant legal situation and public expectation that Germany is a temporary residence for them. That has not proved to be the reality. "These new immigrants have found a home in Germany and show no intention of returning to their villages in rural Anatolia or Croatia. Germany is rapidly evolving into a multicultural and ethnically diverse society" (Rist 1979b, p. 401).

At the peak of the guest worker program, 1973, 2,595,000 were resident in Germany. This number does not include the workers' dependents, nor the quarter of a million or more illegal migrants, nor the half-million workers from other Common Market countries. The expectation was that foreign workers would stay in Germany for no more than four years. In 1978, over 26 percent of the foreign workers had been in Germany for ten years or more (Martin 1980, p. 17).

In November, 1973, a ban on further recruitment of foreign workers was adopted by West Germany, partly due to the fact that larger cohorts of Germans were entering the labor force. That did not eliminate the demand for unskilled and semiskilled labor, however. Some work permits continued to be granted under rather stringent controls; the number of illegal migrants increased; a few foreign workers were naturalized; and a second generation—born in Germany and knowing life only in Germany—is beginning to grow to substantial numbers (Rist 1978a). Despite her ambivalence and in the face of numerous legal and cultural restraints, Germany has a diverse immigrant population. Without rather drastic changes of policy, she will also have an immigrant problem. As Rist observes (1979b, p. 413): "To ignore the millions of persons who at present live in the society, but who are not of it, is to insure the perpetuation of marginality and lack of commitment."

The situation in France is different in important ways. France has had a large immigrant population for more than a century. By 1886 a million foreigners were resident in France and for the next several decades immigrants and their children accounted for half of the population growth (Dignan 1981, p. 138). By 1931 there were three million naturalized foreigners and immigrants in France—Italians, Spaniards, Poles, refugees from the Russian revolution, a few from Africa, and persons from many other lands (Dignan 1981).

Events after World War II added significantly to the diversity and size of the French immigrant population (McDonald 1969). Refugees from Algeria and Vietnam were joined by migrants attracted to, and recruited for, the expanding work opportunities. As in Germany, they were welcomed, because "the *immigrés* do what the French won't" (Sheean 1973)—the dirtier, less-well paid jobs of a booming industrial economy. That is not the only story, of course, for among the immigrants to France and to other western nations have been large numbers of professional and technical workers—a brain drain from the poorer lands that has contributed resources of great value to the wealthiest nations.

In the early 1980s, ten per cent of the population of France were immigrants (four million) or naturalized foreigners (one and a half million), with a major proportion coming from Southern Europe (Portugal, Italy, and Spain) or from Northern Africa (Algeria, Morocco, and Tunisia).

Interesting parallels exist between the French and the American immigration experience. Both nations have admitted large numbers and have been havens for many political refugees. Both are relatively tolerant of illegal migration. A "melting-pot" ideology has been predominant in France and in the United States; yet both are beginning to shift toward a more pluralistic view. Strong economic and political opposition to immigration began to develop in both countries in the 1880s and partially succeeded in the United States, between 1924 and 1965, as we shall see. Those who for economic and ideological reasons supported immigration were more willing to compromise, in the United States, in part because restrictions were not applied to the Western Hemisphere. Numerous workers were available from Mexico, Puerto Rico, and the rural South. France, on the other hand, had a much smaller internal reservoir, and her population was twice nearly decimated—in the precise meaning of the word—by World Wars I and II. Finally, immigrant labor in both countries has been economically exploited, often badly housed, and caught up in periods of violent conflict and prejudice. One would need to change only a few words to shift the following description from France to the United States:

French popular objections to Italian immigrations before World War I were the same as present-day objections to Africans. Ironically, the grandchildren of the first wave of persecuted Italian immigrants in France now join in the general chorus that attributes most of the crime and serious social problems in France to the Algerians. (Dignan 1981, p. 141)

American readers are somewhat more familiar with the British immigration picture. The population has been created from many waves of migrants and invaders over a period of several millenia; but except for lines among the English, Irish, Scots, and Welsh, distinctions have been fading for many generations. (Indeed, there is also a British population that is not only English but has Irish, Scotch, and Welsh components. In this period of ethnic consciousness, political struggle, and devolution, however, one hears less commonly of this long-term development.)

Events since 1945 have added great complexity to this already complex situation. Migrants and refugees from the Commonwealth and from former colonies and workers attracted by the expanding postwar economy of the 1950s and 1960s moved into the industrial centers in large numbers. The population is now about four percent nonwhite, with nearly two million immigrants (about two-thirds of the total) and their descendants from Jamaica and Barbados, from Pakistan, India, and the former British colonies of Africa, and more recently from Indochina. It should also be noted that during this same period emigration from Britain was also heavy. Over two million left in the 1965–1975 decade, although 25 or 30 percent of these returned (London *Times,* December 6, 1976, p. 2).

Like Germany and to a lesser degree France, Britain began to limit immigration in the early 1970s and most of the gain in nonwhite population is now by natural increase. That has not eliminated the conflicts over housing, jobs, and education that so often accompany changes in the racial and cultural mixes of a community. Commenting on the rioting, looting, and arson that affected at least 30 cities and towns in Britain in the summer of 1981, R. W. Appel noted (*The New York Times,* July 19, 1981, E2) that the British people, appalled by what they saw, began to arrive at a consensus similar to that expressed by the American Kerner Commission in 1968: "None of us can escape the consequences of the continuing economic and social decay of the central city....The essential fact is that neither existing conditions nor the garrison state offer acceptable alternatives."

The consensus is more on the depth of the problem, however, than on policy. An extensive literature describes the conflicts and discrimination as well as the efforts at amelioration (see e.g., Freeman 1979; Miles and Phizacklea 1979; Patterson 1968; Rex and Tomlinson 1979; Richmond 1973). Because a large proportion of the British postwar immigration has been nonwhite, most of them arriving with full citizenship rights, the importance of race *per se* in the stratification system is being tested, albeit somewhat ambiguously. Will these new Britons, most of whom are working class, rather quickly join the white working class in outlook and activity? Or will worker opposition to them and hostility in the society generally strengthen their presently somewhat nebulous "third world" identities, as Rex argues (Rex and Tomlinson 1979), as the most promising source of the structural changes needed to bring them equality?

Doubtless both trends will occur. It is difficult at this point to judge which is likely to be the stronger.

Immigration into the United States

Although several countries—Australia, New Zealand, Canada, and Argentina, for example—can be thought of as immigrant countries, in terms of the absolute size of the migration the United States heads the list. We are thinking of an immigrant country as one with a relatively small indigenous population that has been settled by a larger migrating population.

Typically the earliest migrants have conquered or harshly driven back the aboriginal people, although not without some exceptions to this rule, making of them the first minority in their own land. Later migrants who differed significantly in culture, language, or race from the first settlers have also found themselves in most instances to be on the lower rungs of the status ladder, even though they are better off economically and often politically than in their lands of origin.

It is sometimes believed that there was no "immigrant problem" in America until the late nineteenth century. Study of early American history will show this to be false. It is easy today to assume that the early immigrants were readily accepted because of their passion for liberty, their thrift, their industry. Their comtemporaries, however, were as likely to complain of the immigrants' foreign ways, criminality, and filth. The agitation of the Know-Nothing Order was directed against the Irish and Germans. The supposed contrast between the "new" immigration (from southern and eastern Europe) and the "old" immigration (from northern Europe) that was drawn so sharply by many writers in the early twentieth century is interestingly paralleled by a writer comparing the "new" and the "old" of 1835 (quoted by Hourwich 1912; see also Archdeacon 1983; Handlin 1951; Jones 1960):

Then our accessions of immigration were real accessions of strength from the ranks of the learned and the good, from the enlightened mechanic and artisan and intelligent husbandman. Now, immigration is the accession of weakness, from the ignorant and vicious, or the priest ridden slaves of Ireland and Germany, or the outcast tenants of the poorhouses and prisons of Europe.

Compare that with the writers of 1910–1920, who were exalting the quality of the early immigrants in order to condemn the newcomers. Lothrop Stoddard, for example, wrote (1920, pp. 162–65):

The white race divides into three main sub-species—the Nordics, the Alpines, and the Mediterraneans. All three are good stocks, ranking in genetic worth well above the various colored races. However, there seems to be no question that the Nordic is far and away the most valuable type....Our country, originally settled almost exclusively by Nordics, was toward the close of the nineteenth century invaded by hordes of immigrant Alpines and Mediterraneans, not to mention Asiatic elements like Levantines and Jews. As a result, the Nordic native American has been crowded out with amazing rapidity by the swarming, prolific aliens.

It is easy to see from such statements that things are not so good as they used to be—and perhaps they never were.

Racial differences or supposed differences, national, religious, or cultural differences, or simply a general "inferiority" are the reasons ordinarily given to explain opposition to immigrants. Nevertheless, the evidence seems to indicate clearly that opposition to immigrants is based to an important degree on economic and political conflicts. There seems to be a direct correlation between the peaks of "nativist" activity and the valleys of economic depression. The Native American party of the 1830s, the Know-Nothing Order of the 1850s, the American Protective Association in the last two decades of the nineteenth century, and the scores of anti-alien, one-hundred-percent-American groups in the 1930s—these all show the tendency to try to bolster a shaky economic situation by opposition to recent immigrant groups. It should be noted, however, that economic forces can encourage attacks on immigration in "good times" (and among the economically powerful), hope of gain rather than fear of loss being the underlying motive.

Restrictive Legislation

The story of legislation that gradually controlled and restricted immigration into the United States after 1882 is a useful case study of the ways in which anti-immigrant action expresses, in part, economic forces. The arguments used were partly racial or biological—continued immigration meant "blood pollution" or "mongrelization"; they were partly religious and cultural—"our capacity to maintain our cherished institutions stands diluted by a stream of alien blood." But the economic factor was occasionally stated in undisguised fashion. "The Chinaman is here because his presence pays, and he will remain and continue to increase so long as there is money in him. When the time comes that he is no longer profitable *that* generation will take care of him and will send him back" (quoted from the *Sacramento Record Union*, January 10, 1879, by Cox 1948, p. 413).

Changing American Policy toward Chinese Immigration Vigorous exclusionist sentiments developed first on the West Coast, where a visible racial minority with a unifying cultural tradition came into economic competition with some of the "native" Whites, who in exploiting the resources of a new area were accustomed to a conflict pattern and a vigilante tradition. When unskilled workers were needed to build railroads and to begin the development of the resources of the West, many Chinese were imported and welcomed. Agitation against the Chinese began, perhaps, in the 1860s. During this decade the Central Pacific Railroad was completed, so that competition for jobs among the unskilled was intensified. The gold boom began to fade and unemployment to rise. Serious economic crises in the 1870s, accompanied by extensive migration of unemployed persons from the East, brought sharper and sharper demands from the white workers that the continuing Chinese immigration be stopped. In 1876 both major parties in California had anti-Chinese planks in their platforms, and a statewide vote in 1879 was overwhelmingly for exclusion (Schreike 1936, pp. 3–22).

The changing economic situation was accompanied by a shifting stereotype of the Chinese. From worthy, industrious, sober, law-abiding citizens they rather suddenly developed into unassimilable, deceitful, servile people smuggling opium.

In 1882 Congress passed a law that suspended all immigration of Chinese labor for ten years. The legislation was renewed from time to time and in 1904 the time limit was removed. The immigration act of 1924 assigned Asiatic countries no quota from the total amount of immigration to be permitted. Even the alien wives of citizens of Oriental ancestry were barred by the clause which stated that "no alien ineligible for citizenship shall be admitted to the United States." Some Chinese were able to enter under various nonquota provisions of the law. Ninety-three thousand, in fact, emigrated to the United States during the first half of the twentieth century (compared with 309,000 during the last half of the nineteenth century), most of them before the 1924 law went into effect (*Report of the Commissioner of Immigration and Naturalization,* 1969). But the failure to grant any quota under the regular immigration procedures was a decisive proclamation of racism: had China been assigned a quota according to the formula contained in the Immigration Act of 1924, she would have been granted approximately 100 immigrants per year. During World War II, in fact, the United States made this gesture to her Chinese ally by giving her a quota of 105 per year.

To bring this story up to date we should note that various provisions of the 1952 and 1965 immigration laws have made it possible for additional Chinese to emigrate to the United States, thus significantly changing the picture (King and Locke 1980). Spouses and dependent children of American citizens are admitted. Persons born in China may now be naturalized. And by provisions of the 1965 act, up to 20,000 per year could enter the United States from "China" (until recently, basically Taiwan). In 1982, each of the "two Chinas" was given a quota of 20,000 per year. Persons of Chinese ancestry have increased rapidly in number from 435,000 in 1970 to 806,000 in 1980. And America's "Chinatowns," once again with numerous young residents, are expressing greater militancy (Lyman 1974).

Changing American Policy toward Japanese Immigration. Responses to Japanese immigrants have followed much the same pattern as those to Chinese immigration. At first they were welcomed; but by 1900 there were demands that the Japanese be excluded which grew more and more insistent. On March 1, 1905, the California legislature, by a vote of 28–0 and 70–0 in the two houses, passed a resolution urging Congress to exclude Japanese from the country (McWilliams 1944, p. 19). In 1906 the San Francisco school board passed a resolution that barred Japanese children from white schools. This was repealed under pressure from the federal government, but continued agitation finally led to the "gentlemen's agreement" of 1907 in which the Japanese government agreed to issue no more passports to skilled or unskilled workers, except those who had previously resided in the United States or their wives or their children under 21 years of age. The immigration of women to become the wives of Japanese

already in the United States was permitted until 1920, when Japan agreed to refuse emigration to the "picture brides." The Immigration Act of 1924 stopped all immigration from Japan.

Anti-Japanese activity had not stopped with the virtual cutting off of immigration by the "gentlemen's agreement." Newspaper headlines and editorials, nativist organizations such as the Native Sons of the Golden West, mob action, political oratory, and legal enactments all continued to show the extent of the prejudice, particularly in California. Gradually the federal government became involved after having tried for several decades to restrain California's anti-Japanese expressions because of the difficulties they created in international diplomacy. By the Immigration Act of 1924, and by the resettlement policy of 1942, the federal government expressed agreement with the racial sentiments involved.

It is our concern to ask at this point: Who profited, or thought they profited, from such moves? Perhaps the most tangible and continuous gains accrued to men running for office or in office who, by striking out at the Japanese, could create in-group feeling, could sponsor a cause, could exploit the tensions of the average voter, and could avoid reference to any of the critical issues which might have two opposing sides that were difficult to occupy simultaneously. Many California politicians during the first half of the twentieth century made use of prejudice against the Japanese to win an election. If the existing fund of prejudice was not enough to make the tactic effective, their supporting newspapers could manufacture enough to help. Before World War II there was a strong correlation between the waves of anti-Japanese agitation and election years. Since the Japanese group was small and politically and economically weak, candidates could attack it almost without fear of reprisals; it was as politically safe to be against the Japanese as to be against sin. Even Woodrow Wilson, speaking in California during the presidential election of 1912, declared: "The whole question is one of assimilation of diverse races. We cannot make a homogeneous population of a people who do not blend with the Caucasian race." McWilliams (1944) reported that the Democratic party distributed over 100,000 copies of this declaration around the state.

There were economic as well as political motives involved in the anti-Japanese activities on the West

Coast after 1900. At various times trade unions and small landowners took part in these agitations, but organized opposition stemmed most directly from the owners of the huge estates that characterize parts of California. These men certainly did not fear the competition of the few Japanese farmers with their relatively small holdings. What they did fear was the opposition of the small white landowners who found it difficult to compete with the estates, the struggles for improvement of their badly paid field hands, the traditions in favor of family-sized farms and homesteads, and federal legislation that prevented them from monopolizing the water supplied through governmentally sponsored irrigation projects. If they could divert attention from their own control of the land by attacking the Japanese farmer as the cause of everybody's difficulties, they might funnel off some of the hostility to which they were vulnerable and get political support for laws favorable to them.

If the farm laborers, working at low wages and often under very poor working conditions, could be persuaded that the Japanese farmers were the cause of their difficulties, they might show less hostility toward the owners of the large estates. Out of this situation came the Alien Land Acts of 1913 and 1920 in California and similar bills in other states. (These statutes, 16 in all, were voided by the Walter–McCarran Act of 1952 which removed barriers to citizenship.) The 1920 act was passed as an initiative measure and approved by a majority of three to one. These two bills did not change the actual landholding situation much, for they could not dispossess alien Japanese of land they already held nor could they apply to the increasing number of second-generation Japanese who were American citizens. It seems likely that few people were interested in enforcing the law anyway, for Japanese "managers" rather than "tenants" appeared, and title to land was transferred to American- or Hawaiian-born Japanese—with little objection from officials (McWilliams 1944, pp. 64-65). The chief gains to economic and political groups came not from the provisions of the bill but from the controversy, the pseudoconflict situation, that was built up in the process of passing the bill. Actually, most of those who voted for the 1920 act, insofar as it was effective at all, suffered from the legislation—the landowner by lower rentals (he had been able to charge the Japanese tenant high rents) and the consumer by higher prices. But the powerful few found the anti-Japanese agitation very useful in their diversionary tactics.

Relocation of Americans of Japanese Ancestry. Economic factors in the prejudice against the Japanese continued to operate in the period of their "relocation" from the West Coast during World War II. After Pearl Harbor the groups that had long agitated against the Japanese lost no time in telling Washington that the presence of 110,000 Japanese on the West Coast, including about 40,000 "enemy aliens" (those born in Japan were ineligible for citizenship), was a grave threat to the safety of the country. There were, of course, many factors involved in President Roosevelt's Executive Order 9066 to evacuate all persons of Japanese ancestry to relocation camps away from the West Coast; but the climate of opinion that had been created by those who saw economic and political gain in anti-Japanese agitation was important in the complex of causes. Persons of Japanese descent who might have been a military danger were already known to the FBI and were taken into custody within a few days. That all the rest, including 70,000 American citizens, should be treated as military threats was an act of unprecedented official racism in the United States.

Judgments differ concerning the importance of various influences that led to the relocation order. The direct pressure of interested economic groups was probably relatively unimportant, although they had helped to create the atmosphere in which such an order was accepted with little protest. tenBroek, Barnhart, and Matson (1954) argue cogently that the direct responsibility must be shared by many groups—the general public, particularly in the West; the military leaders; President Roosevelt and his staff, who concurred with the military decision; the Congress, which reinforced the process with legislation; and finally the courts, especially the Supreme Court, which gave the relocation order what now seems to many students a dubious constitutional sanction. All of these acted out of fear and, in our opinion, bad judgment. But behind the fear and the error stood prejudice, distorting the ability to deal rationally with the situation. Definitive support for the relocation came from the Supreme Court:

The Japanese American cases—*Hirabayashi, Korematsu,* and *Endo*— . . . represent a constitutional yielding to the awe inspired in all men by total war and the new weapons of warfare. They disclose a judicial unwillingness to interfere with—or even to look upon—the actions of the military taken in time of global war, even to the extent of determining whether those actions are substantially or somehow connected with the prosecution of the war. (tenBroek, Barnhart, and Matson 1954, p. 259)

Whatever the role of economic factors in causing the evacuation of Americans of Japanese descent, the economic results were clearcut and severe for the people involved (Commission on Wartime Relocation, 1982, Chapter 4). They suffered a loss variously estimated from 350 to 500 million dollars, with losses averaging nearly $10,000 per family (Bloom and Riemer 1949, Chapter 5). Some of this loss resulted in no gain for anyone: property deterioration, inefficient and incomplete use of skills, costs of property transfer and storage and the like profited no one. Some of the losses to the Japanese-Americans, however, were direct gains to others: property sold in desperation at a fraction of its worth or abandoned completely, vandalism of goods that had to be stored for several years, further monopolization of job and business opportunities by whites—these gave economic incentive to prejudice, to the few who thus profited. The costs to the whole nation were scarcely noticed.[3]

This brief reference to the wartime relocation of Americans of Japanese descent would be incomplete without some mention of the current situation. Gradually, from 1943 on, residents of the relocation centers were allowed to leave, to attend college, to accept jobs, and to enter the armed services, where they achieved outstanding records. After the war, 80 percent of the Japanese-Americans returned to the West Coast, with three-fourths of these going to California. Slowly their claims for property losses received legislative and judicial attention. Congress passed legislation permitting claims up to $100,000 to be settled administratively, without court litigation (*The New York Times*, August 12, 1956, p. 38). It is not yet clear what proportion of the actual losses may ultimately be recovered or general compensation paid. Although several million dollars have been paid—a small fraction of the loss—the issue was still (in 1982!) moot and the subject of study by a presidential panel.

[3]For additional studies of the relocation, see, e.g., Commission on Wartime Relocation and Interment of Civilians 1982; Grodzins 1949; Irons 1984; Leighton 1945; McWilliams 1944; Miyamoto 1973; Thomas 1952; Weglyn 1976.

The Americans of Japanese descent who did not return to the West Coast have been absorbed into many cities with relatively little discrimination and at fairly high job levels (see Bonacich and Modell 1980; Caudill and DeVos 1956; Kitano 1976; Petersen 1971; Sue and Kitano 1973). The Walter–McCarran Act of 1952 brought Japan into the American immigration quota system (185 Japanese were permitted to migrate each year, in addition to spouses and unmarried children) and made foreign-born Japanese eligible for citizenship. With the addition of Hawaii as a state, the status and influence of Americans of Japanese descent improved further. They constitute nearly one-third of the population of Hawaii and are important in its political and economic life. These developments all represent a substantial change from the prewar and wartime situation.

In the country as a whole citizens of Japanese descent increased significantly in number by the addition of an estimated 50,000 brides of American servicemen, brought in by special legal provision outside the quota. This explains the entrance of most of the 66,000 who came to the United States between 1951 and 1965. The quota for this whole period was less than 3,000.

Under the 1965 Immigration Act, to be discussed later, it became possible for Japan to send 20,000 immigrants per year. In fact, however, the total during the 1965–1980 period was less than 60,000. By 1980 the population of Japanese descent had increased to 701,000, from 591,000 in 1970.

The period since World War II has been one of rapid economic advance for Japanese-Americans. Their per capita income is now higher than that of white Americans. Among third-generation citizens, structural, identificational, and marital assimilation has become extensive (Levine and Rhodes 1981; Montero 1980). Along with this, however, are indications of pluralism—family traditionalism and participation in Japanese community affairs—as well as some continuing discrimination (United States Commission on Civil Rights 1980c; Woodrum 1981).

The 1924 Immigration Law. Legal restrictions on Chinese and Japanese immigration were the first steps in a series of policy changes that were brought together in the Quota Act of 1924. There is general agreement that this act, the culmination of decades of agitation to restrict immigration, was partly the product of economic and political forces related to the closing of our frontier, the ideological and power aspects of "manifest destiny" imperialism at the turn of the century, and the postwar tensions and economic difficulties of the early 1920s. In a rather strange combination of forces, industrialists, unionists, farmers, exuberant nationalists, racists, and many intellectuals combined to produce the pressure of legislation (Solomon 1956). The 1924 law not only restricted the number to approximately 150,000 a year but sought to determine the national origin of future immigrants. Immigration from Asia was barred; no quantitative restrictions were placed on migration from the Western Hemisphere; and the 150,000 was divided among other nations in proportion to their supposed representation in our population in 1920. The result was to assign 68.9 percent of the quota to Great Britain, Ireland, and Germany. Immigration from southern and eastern Europe was drastically curtailed.

There is no doubt that immigration from the countries affected was sharply reduced. Migration from the countries under the quota averaged well over 500,000 a year during the first quarter of the twentieth century; in the second quarter of the century the average was scarcely 100,000 per year. Great Britain, with over 40 percent of the quota, seldom used more than a fraction of her assignment, whereas many countries with small quotas had waiting lists for years ahead.

In 1952, our immigration legislation was slightly revised by the Walter–McCarran Immigration and Naturalization Act. The quota system and the quantitative limit were essentially retained, except that Asiatic countries were now assigned their "appropriate" quota, in most instances the minimum number of 100 per year. The total number was raised to approximately 155,000; and resident aliens from the Orient, formerly ineligible for citizenship, were granted naturalization rights. Racial distinctions continued to be drawn, however, not only by the differences in quotas, but by the mode of defining country of origin. A person of German descent, born and living in Brazil, for example, was Brazilian; but a person of Chinese descent, born and living in Brazil, was Chinese. He or she could immigrate to the United States only by obtaining one of the 105 places annually allotted to the Chinese.

The changes in the law slightly reduced the national and racist prejudices it contained—but only slightly. The whole quota system makes sense only if one assumes that there are racial and national differences in desirability, that is, that desirability can be determined by one's race and national origin, not by individual characteristics.

Some Effects of the 1924 Immigration Law. The abrupt reduction of immigration and its redirection by the 1924 law had a number of unanticipated effects. Some of them still affect the United States in important ways. It produced serious diplomatic strains, particularly with the nations of the East. Many economists hold that it sped the approach of the depression of the 1930s and made it worse. It increased the northward migration of black and white workers from the South (with many consequences). And it greatly increased the number of migrants from the Western Hemisphere, particularly from Mexico and Puerto Rico (Davis, Haub and Willette 1983).

Of the 15 million or more persons of Spanish-speaking background in the United States in 1983, over half were of Mexican descent. Several factors encourage the heavy rate of temporary migration and immigration from Mexico, including the country's high rate of population increase (to about 75 million in 1983), contact of many Mexican workers with the *bracero* program for the importation of temporary workers with relatives and friends in the United States, high rates of unemployment and low rates of pay at home, and continued opportunities for work in the United States—an indication of the contributions they make to the American economy, although not without injury to some workers (Burawoy 1976).

With the reduction of immigration that began with the 1924 law, the number of Puerto Ricans entering the country also increased. This is not, strictly speaking, immigration, since Puerto Ricans are American citizens. In 1980 there were approximately two million persons of Puerto Rican birth or Puerto Rican descent living in the United States, nearly half of these in New York City. The rate of migration was particularly heavy in the 1945–1960 period. Since then, as a result of changing economic conditions on the island and of unemployment and discrimination on the mainland, there has been, in some years, a net emigration back to Puerto Rico. On balance, however, the mainland population of Puerto Rican descent has grown significantly.

The Puerto Rican migrant may experience a somewhat briefer period of exploitation than have some earlier groups. The fact that he is a citizen, the greater appreciation today of the nature of culture contact and conflict, the serious efforts being made in New York City and elsewhere to strengthen education for Puerto Ricans, the increase in their political activities (Rogler 1974), and other factors are hopeful aspects of the situation. There is good evidence that movement up the educational ladder and into middle-class occupations is proceeding at a rapid pace among Puerto Ricans. We shall examine some of these trends in later chapters.[4]

Current Immigration Policy and Trends in the United States

After several decades in the background, immigration has once again become a major fact of American experience. In the course of a few months one reads a steady flow of such headlines as these:

- Vietnamese refugees adapt to U.S.
- Give me your rich. New wave of Asian immigrants pumps millions into U.S. economy.
- Immigration flood engulfs well-being of our citizens.
- Deciding how to stop Haitians—and why.
- Illegal aliens pose ever-deepening crisis for the U.S.
- Iranian immigrants, totaling perhaps a million, bring wealth and diversity to the U.S.

These headlines reflect the world scene, but they also flow from the fact that in 1965 American immigration law was revised again. In an era of greater sensitivity to international perspectives and in the context of a vigorous civil rights movement at home, existing legislation seemed more and more anachronistic. The exceptions that had developed around the 1924 and 1952 laws had, in any event, eroded their effects (Reimers 1981). In the 1965 act, national quotas were eliminated and replaced by two international quotas: 170,000 per year for the Eastern Hemisphere, with a maximum of 20,000 from any one country; and 120,000 for the Western Hemisphere, without specific national limitations. (Such limitations were put into effect, however, in 1976, a change the main effect of which has been to reduce legal immigration from Mexico by about half.)

Under the 1965 law, preference is given to relatives of United States citizens or of resident aliens

[4]For accounts of the mixture of discrimination and progress, see Bonilla and Campos 1981; Flores, Attinasi, and Pedraza 1981; Lewis 1966b; Lopez and Petras 1974; Rogler 1972.

and to persons with occupational skills. A few persons in addition to the 290,000 in the two quotas were to be admitted by provisions of the law dealing with dependent children, husbands, wives, and parents of American citizens.

In 1978 the two quotas were combined into one, applying to the whole world, and in 1980 the ceiling was raised to 320,000 per year. In addition a "normal flow" of 50,000 refugees was to be allowed entry each year, with the administration also permitted to admit additional refugees in an emergency (Reimers 1981, p. 6). In the early 1980s emergencies were almost continuous. Indo-Chinese, Cubans, Haitians, and others entered the country in numbers that totaled several times more than the 50,000 normal flow.

The 1965 law sharply reduced the national and racial preferences that were so prominent in the 1924 and 1952 laws. The result has been not only to increase the number of immigrants (Table 3-2) but also to revise drastically the pattern of national origins. These effects are shown in a comparison of the number of immigrants from selected countries at different time periods, as shown in Table 3-3.

Of course, not all of the change illustrated by the shifts among the countries noted in Table 3 can be accounted for by the immigration law. It was, however, a substantial factor, particularly among those countries that increased the number sent from the earlier period to the later ones. The Caribbean has been added to Mexico as a major Western Hemisphere source. And Asians, who for so long were nearly barred from entry, are coming in numbers that significantly transform some of the ethnic communities (Haas 1978; Li 1978; Liu, Lamanna, and Murata 1981). By the 1976–80 period, although Mexico remained the largest source, the four other

Table 3-2. Total Immigration into the United States, by Ten-Year Periods

1901–1910	8,795,000
1911–1920	5,736,000
1921–1930	4,107,000
1931–1940	528,000
1941–1950	1,025,000
1951–1960	2,515,000
1961–1970	3,322,000
1971–1980	4,741,000

United States Committees on the Judiciary, 1981, p. 93; Reimers, 1981, p. 7.

Table 3-3. Immigration into the United States for Selected Countries before and after the 1965 Immigration Act (in thousands)

	1961–1965	1966–1970	1976–1980
Mexico	223	220	303
Canada	175	119	62
Germany	136	69	32
Great Britain	92	104	68
Italy	83	124	35
Cuba	77	180	159
Dominican Republic	35	59	78
Japan	19	19	21
China and Taiwan	17	65	96
Philippines	16	86	197
Portugal	15	65	46
Korea	10	26	153
Jamaica	8	63	78
India	3	28	99
Vietnam	1	4	162

Source: Statistical Analysis Branch, Immigration and Naturalization Service, U.S. Department of Justice.

countries with largest numbers (Canada, Germany, Great Britain, and Italy) had dropped out of the top five and were replaced by the Phillippines, Vietnam, Cuba, and Korea.

Despite the importance of refugees in recent years, with the image they bring of dependence and sharp cultural contrasts, it should be noted that America's most recent immigrants also include persons of higher than average education and occupational skill. For example, before an act of 1976 that led to the phasing out of preferences for physicians, 70,000 had emigrated to the United States, as had thousands of nurses, scientists, and other professionals and skilled workers (Reimers 1981). Most evidence shows that not only they, but the unskilled as well, contribute to the economy.

With enormous differences of levels of living among nations, harsh political and religious conflict in some, and millions of refugees seeking new homes, the laws of immigrant-receiving nations will continue to be modified. Although the 1965 American law, with its several modifications, seems to us to be a significant improvement over the laws it replaced, it carries the costs of the political compromises needed to get it passed. It serves the interests of the richer—both in the country and among the migrants—much more than those of the poorer. One cannot argue on sociological grounds that unlimited and undirected immigration strengthens a society. Starting from the premise that a nation's immigration policy will be an attempt to serve its economic, political, and social interests, we believe that both the number and the direction of flow must necessarily be taken into account; and the diversity of interests must be recognized. Present American laws, however, do not explicitly define the number of immigrants to be permitted nor attempt to specify in rational terms the number who might be absorbed in a given period of time. In particular, policies relating to illegal migrants are ambiguous and poorly enforced. Since this is an issue that seems certain to be on the public agenda for many years, we will outline some of the facts and the policy debate.

Undocumented Workers. Perhaps the major unintended effect of the 1965 immigration law was the rapid increase in the number of illegal aliens in the United States. No one is certain of the exact number (Jorge Bustamante in Bryce-Laporte 1980, pp. 139–44). By 1971 estimates ranged from one to two million. In that year 420,000 were deported, the large majority then, as now, having come in from Mexico (*The New York Times,* October 17, 1971, pp. 1, 58). But many also came from the Caribbean area, entering mainly into Florida and into northern states, crossing over from Canada (*The New York Times,* May 1, 1983, pp. 1, 21). By 1981 estimates ranged from 2 to 12 million, with the range of 3.5 to 6 million given by the Census Bureau being widely accepted as reasonable. During the last several years a million or more "deportable aliens" have been found annually.

Intense interest in such a situation stems from the sense, on one hand, that "we've lost control of our borders," as Attorney General Smith put it (*The New York Times,* August 12, 1981, E22), and the realization, on the other, that undocumented workers are both economically important and highly vulnerable to exploitation. It is difficult for them to complain about wages that are far below scale, about difficult working conditions, inferior housing, and inadequate education for their children, because employers and landlords need only remind them of their illegal status (Bustamante 1972; Crewdson 1983; Samora 1971). In New York City, according to a Department of Labor task force, approximately 400 garment factories employ 10,000 Chinese, some two-thirds of whom are illegal aliens, at wages of $100 to $120 for a 60-hour week. "They are working under the fear that they are going to be turned in" (Blum 1979, p. 40). Not all are working at low wages; some "have been found working as doctors, teaching at a city high school and even—at $9 an hour—painting the Statue of Liberty for the Department of the Interior" (Blum 1979, p. 40). Needless to say, in areas where illegal aliens work almost entirely as crop pickers or in the lowest paid service jobs, no such incomes are earned, except by recruiters and agents, some of whom are themselves undocumented.

All the arguments, pro and con, over legal immigration are magnified when applied to illegal aliens. We can only call attention to some of them here while emphasizing the minority status of undocumented workers. Legal and illegal migration combined furnished approximately one-third of American population growth during the 1970s. Since it included a high proportion of young people, these new residents will probably contribute a larger share to the next generation. Those for whom zero population growth or slow growth is a major policy objective oppose the high levels of immigration, legal and illegal.

A more vigorously debated subject is the effects of undocumented workers on jobs and unemployment. A high proportion of undocumented aliens are young men, drawn to the United States by the hope of finding work and willing to do unskilled labor. (This is less true of those from the Eastern Hemisphere, who are more likely to be professional or skilled workers.) Their employers claim that Americans will not do stoop labor or unskilled service jobs. Others note that America receives a great human resource, "a supply of vigorous, ambitious workers in the prime of their working years without having to assume the full cost of educating them or their children, or caring for them in sickness or old age, or supporting them when they are out of work" (Midgley 1978, p. 15).

Several issues are contained in that quotation. It suggests the degree to which undocumented workers are exploitable. It also raises the questions of jobs and welfare. The country as a whole profits from their work, but the least skilled part of the labor force, those most subject to low wages and unemployment, suffer. The legal resident workers in unskilled jobs, often themselves minority-group members, find their wages depressed by the availability of a substitute work force. Thus minority is pitted against minority while the better off profit (Christina Brinkley-Carter in Bryce-Laporte 1980, pp. 211–21; Stoddard 1976).

Is that profit not reduced by high demands on the welfare system? Most evidence points in the opposite direction. "The millions of illegal aliens who have false Social Security numbers are fattening up the trust fund for the rest of us: while taxes are deducted from their paychecks, they have not established valid accounts which might someday provide them with benefits" (Midgley 1978, p. 15; see also Cornelius 1978; Bustamante 1977). Particular areas, Midgley notes, may suffer from census undercounts of illegal aliens, thus receiving less in revenue-sharing funds while having greater demands on various public services.

America's minority-majority relations cannot be separated from the world situation. Specifically in the case of illegal aliens, it cannot be separated from our relationships with Mexico. Undocumented workers in the United States represent a kind of foreign aid to Mexico amounting to perhaps two or three billion dollars in wages sent to their families. Because it is such a complex domestic political issue, American immigration decisions are typically made without discussions with major sending countries, whose interests are also clearly affected. Thus the 1976 decision to apply to the Western Hemisphere the 20,000 ceiling on immigration from any one country (Mexico had been sending about 40,000 per year) was made with minimum consultation with Mexico. Is such internal decision making in America's interests? If present trends continue, Mexico's population of nearly 75 million will double in the next 25 years. We share with her a long and, for nearly a century and a half, a largely peaceful border—perhaps the only place in the world where a large developed nation touches a large and poor nation (Ehrlich, Bilderback, and Ehrlich 1979). Mexico is becoming a major force in the international relations of the Western Hemisphere. Her oil reserves are probably second only to those of Saudi Arabia. Mexico's situation has been powerfully affected for several generations by the fact that the United States seized almost half of her territory.

Lessons from such facts as these are not easily drawn. Yet surely as a minimum they suggest how closely intertwined the fates of the United States and Mexico are (Hansen 1981; Hirschman 1978;

Riding 1978). Shutting off the hope that many Mexicans feel as a result of the availability, legal or illegal, of migration to the United States would certainly not be without powerful consequences, within each country and between them. Ironically, strongest support for measures to restrict illegal migration comes from some liberal groups—environmentalists, population control groups, and labor unions. They are opposed by Hispanic-American leaders, who find the idea of limitations offensive and perhaps a threat to their growing political influence. Opposition comes also from agribusiness and industries that employ large numbers of unskilled workers, joined, to heighten the irony, by civil libertarians who see no proposals to curtail illegal entry into the country that do not threaten to be oppressive (Midgley 1978).

Others are primarily concerned, not with the fact of a certain level of immigration, but with the lack of control over it, the present inability of the country to make and execute a rational immigration policy.

A million people are waiting in line to enter the United States legally; millions more are eager to jump the line; and the nation must choose which to let through the door....Undocumented farm workers from Mexico, for instance, may be brave and industrious. But each takes a place that, if society were choosing fairly, might be assigned instead to a refugee from Somalia, a sister from Korea or a more deserving Mexican applicant. The country is not now making the choice. (*The New York Times,* March 1, 1981, p. 20)

It is in this tangled situation that America is now seeking to rethink and revise its immigration procedures (see, e.g., Martin 1980; D. S. Massey 1981; United States Commission on Civil Rights 1980d; United States Committees on the Judiciary 1981). Presidents Carter and Reagan have proposed plans that involve several issues: some sort of worker identification, penalties on employers who hire undocumented workers, amnesty for all but the most recent migrants, and tighter control over national borders. How these things are to be done, however, cannot easily be agreed upon. To some, worker identification means police state pass cards or, if Social Security cards are used, a threat to the integrity of the Social Security system. Employers strongly resist the idea of large penalties for hiring undocumented workers and would treat small ones as a cost of doing business (as seems likely with the Reagan administration's proposal of a maximum fine of $1,000 for each illegal entrant hired).

It is unlikely that even a large force could patrol American borders successfully. It may be that it will be easiest to come to agreement on the fact that the several million illegal aliens presently in the country, some of them having been here for many years, need to be given some legitimate status. Such a decision is likely to be made, however, only in conjunction with agreement on a policy dealing with the other issues—something that seems unlikely in the near future. As of autumn, 1984, both the Senate and the House of Representatives have passed bills dealing—somewhat differently—with several of these issues. It remains problematic, however, whether they can soon prepare a statute that is mutually acceptable that will also be acceptable to the President. Meanwhile, illegal aliens will remain a large and important minority group.

Competing Explanations of the Connections between Economic Interests and Discrimination

In their attempts to maintain or increase their share of income, prestige, and power, groups find it easy to invent or accept the idea that other groups are inferior and thus less deserving of life's values. Most students of majority–minority relations recognize, and many emphasize—sometimes to the exclusion of other factors—the economic sources of discrimination. Within the broad area of agreement, however, there is room for a great deal of disagreement about the nature of the connection between economic interests and intergroup hostility and discrimination. Marxist interpretations see minority status as the result of a kind of double-barreled form of exploitation by the dominant groups, with both race, or other minority symbol, and class being involved. Drawing on Marxism, or the radical perspective more generally, but also modifying it in significant ways, theories of "split labor markets" and of "internal colonialism" also emphasize the economic factor in discrimination. Neoclassical economic theorists interpret discrimination primarily as a response to the forces of supply and demand, a market phenomenon, although this interpretation may be modified by attention to individual tendencies to discriminate, the influence of monopoly power, and other variables. Still other interpretations give primary attention to the frustrations of the lower classes of the majority and to their competition for jobs and status with minority-group members.

Each of these theories deserves comment. To the Marxist, the fundamental cause of racial oppression is the drive on the part of ruling groups to maximize their power to exploit, to increase the "surplus value" that they can extract from workers. Prejudice, this explanation states, helps them to justify their course of action and to deflect the attention of the lower classes in the majority from their own powerless state.

"Race prejudice in the United States," Oliver Cox wrote (1948, p. 475), "is the socio-attitudinal matrix supporting a calculated and determined effort of a white ruling class to keep some people or peoples of color and their resources exploitable." Doxey Wilkerson (in Aptheker 1946, pp. 8–10) expresses the same idea: "The Negro people are oppressed because the rulers of our society find it highly profitable to oppress them."

Capitalist societies, Nikolinakos (1973) argues, create racism to assist exploitation. Defenseless workers yield more surplus value; that is, they cannot obtain in wages the total value of their labor. He adds a qualifying statement that takes him toward split labor market theory. The ruling class, he suggests, may create a labor force divided between a privileged segment and an exploited segment, a division that may go so far that the exploited workers create the surplus value and the privileged workers share in its appropriation.

Seen against the facts of exploitation, Marxist arguments seem quite plausible (Greer 1979; History Task Force 1979; Reich 1981). The ease with which they are adapted to different sets of facts, however, should give us pause. As Max Gluckman noted (in Kuper and Smith 1971, p. 395):

In Marxist argument, if the bourgeoisie "exploit" the proletariat, it is in their interests; if they grant concessions in wages and welfare, it is because they see their long-term interests....I feel it is dangerous if we argue that persons serve their own interests...both when they follow one course of action and when they follow an opposite course of action. Analysis then tends to become a system of political beliefs, defended by secondary elaboration of belief.

We must also add that radical interpretations should be directed toward communist as well as capitalist societies. It can well be argued that minorities, and the relatively poor and powerless generally, although they may gain in the degree of economic equality, in some communist societies experience high levels of political inequality and alienation (Connor 1979; Lenski 1978). It is well to ask: From which societies are they fleeing or attempting to flee? To which societies do they go or aspire to go?

Segmented, dual, or split-labor market theories build on the majority-minority conflict and class conflict kind of analysis, but with stronger empirical work and a more complex picture of the forces at work (Cain 1976; Cheng and Bonacich 1984; Marshall 1974; Mukabe 1981). In its simplest form, a split-labor market, as described by Bonacich (1972, 1975), is one with three classes: capitalist, cheap labor, and higher-priced labor. The outcome of this situation is not fixed. If employers are powerful, they can drive out or drastically weaken the position of higher-priced labor, as is the case under slavery. If higher-priced labor is powerful enough, they can drive the cheaper labor out of the labor market or block its entrance. Under other conditions, higher-priced labor can get a kind of compromise with employers under which they win a monopoly over the best jobs. Finally, under such conditions as high demand for labor, political democracy, low ratio of minority workers, and the like, higher- and lower-priced labor may combine in an attempt to reduce the power of employers. In large and complex labor markets all four of these processes may be going on at once, as we believe to be the case in the United States.

A critical problem for students of split-labor markets is the identification of the conditions under which these various processes occur and in what mixtures and comparative strengths. Segmentation in relatively open economic markets is unlikely to be clear-cut (Greenberg 1980). Even less skilled workers can mobilize resources to improve their positions (Hodson and Kaufman 1982). Employers are sometimes ambivalent, for a mixture of profit, legal, and moral reasons. Some of the "dominant" workers are more vulnerable than others to minority-worker competition; and it is not surprising to discover that they are more likely to show high levels of prejudice (Cummings 1980).

It is well to remember that segmented labor markets are often dynamic and rapidly changing. In the United States before 1930 black workers were used by employers to weaken the position of white workers and to undermine their unions. That does not mean, however, that Black–White union efforts were entirely lacking (Marks 1981). Now that black unemployment rates are twice as high as white rates it is important to remember that before 1930 they were often lower. As Bonacich notes, this was a period of several serious race riots, at least partly the result of labor conflict. New Deal labor legislation, however, protected unions and outlawed the use of strike breakers (Bonacich 1976, p. 34; see also Edwards, Reich, and Gordon 1975):

This permitted a coalition to emerge between black and white workers. But in the long run the rising cost of labor drove capital to seek cheaper labor overseas, to make use of internal pockets of unprotected labor or to automate. All three processes hurt black industrial workers disproportionately, leaving a group of hardcore unemployed in the ghettoes.

To some degree the United States has returned, so far as a substantial proportion of black workers is concerned, to a segmented labor market.

That a large proportion of workers in racial and cultural minorities are caught in the lower parts of a split-labor market is readily shown by occupational and income data (see Chapter 9). A related way of looking at the same set of facts is to use the analogy of an "internal colony." The term is part political slogan and part analytic tool. It can be of great value in studying the economic aspects of discrimination if we remember that it is an analogy, with greater power to focus our attention on strategic facts and major issues in some situations than in others.

Although the term goes back at least to the early part of the twentieth century, it began to be used widely to interpret the persistent disadvantages of minorities only in the 1960s. In particular it has been used to examine the question: Why do economic and political disadvantages remain attached, not simply to individuals, but to racial and cultural groups? The concept directs our attention to the disadvantages placed on minority workers, to their exploitation as consumers, and to the subcultural lines of division that mark off the "colony" and are often reenforced by the conflicts associated with colonization.

In an influential paper, Blauner (1969) characterized the colonization complex as one in which (1) the minority has been brought in by force; (2) its culture and social organization are seriously weakened by a policy "which constrains, transforms, or destroys indigenous values, orientations, and ways of life"; (3) the colony is "managed and manipulated" by ethnic outsiders; and (4) the relationship is justified by racist doctrines (see also Carmichael and Hamilton 1967; Clark 1965; Cruse 1968).

It is scarcely surprising that during a period when more and more "external" colonies were winning independence not only analysts, but also internal minorities and their supporters should declare: we are colonies too. "The dark ghettos," Kenneth Clark wrote (1965, p. 11), "are social, political, educational and—above all—economic colonies." As the concept of internal colonies became more widely used, the situations to which it was applied became more diverse (Barrera 1979; Karlovic 1982; Stone 1979). In the most ambitious application, Hechter (1977) argued that in Britain even extensive industrialization and urbanization, social and physical mobility, and the growth of literacy and political participation did not succeed in bringing the Celtic fringe or periphery into the core of British national development. The colony need not have a distinct geographical setting. Hechter (1977, p. 15) quotes Marx: "Every industrial and commercial center in England now possesses a working-class *divided* into two *hostile* camps, English proletarians and Irish proletarians." "The core," Hechter goes on to say, "is seen to dominate the periphery politically and to exploit it materially" (1977, p. 9). Such an observation could have been made with regard to northern domination of the South in the United States, 1865–1930, indicating that the use of the term *internal colony* does not always imply a strictly racial or ethnic division.

Once a cultural or racial group has established dominance, in various historical sequences, it is often able, according to the internal colony theory, to maintain "a cultural division of labor: a system of stratification where objective cultural distinctions are superimposed upon class lines" (Hechter 1977, p. 30).

One gains new insights by seeing minority–majority relations within the framework of an internal-colony model. It is not without weaknesses, however, which we must keep in mind (see Glazer 1971; Moore 1976a). For example, the model can make a colony appear to be more homogeneous in class and culture than it is. It can deflect our attention from the domination over lower classes within the core. It sometimes tends to overlook the processes of integration of core and periphery that can go on alongside the colonization process and in some conditions reverse it.

Classical and neoclassical theories of the placement of majorities and minorities in an economic system start out with a market model, with "the laws of supply and demand"; but modifications are soon added (Pascal 1972; Tobin 1965). One can scarcely quarrel wih the assertion that workers with few skills in a market demanding more and more skills will receive lower wages and have higher rates of unemployment. Improved income of Blacks relative to Whites reflects, from the supply side of the market model, "increased congruency in black–white income-producing characteristics, such as education and region of residence. . . . Newer cohorts of blacks relative to their white counterparts start their careers with higher initial stocks of marketable human capital than their black predecessors already in the labor market" (Smith and Welch 1979, p. 69).

When we ask, why should there be different levels of skill, or why should the skill gap between Blacks and Whites be closing, we have to go beyond the market for an answer, to study political, attitudinal, technical, and other influences on the market. Gary Becker (1971), who was one of the first economists to study discrimination, introduced the idea of a "taste for discrimination" among many Whites as a factor in the market. Presumably they were willing—and through the mechanisms of the market were required—to pay for that taste. This argument has not stood up very well; but the introduction of noneconomic motives has proved to be of value (Arrow 1971) and attention to legislative influences (Stiglitz 1973) and monopolistic conditions (Thurow 1969) have been added.

The model of "the market" that one thinks most accurate, we should note, has strong implications, on economic grounds, for policy choices:

If one thinks of labor markets as fairly competitive, then minimum wage legislation not only results in unemployment of low-skilled workers, but eliminates the strong competitive forces that would naturally have led to the alleviation of economic discrimination among these workers. If one thinks of all capitalists conspiring together to exploit workers of low skills (many of whom may belong to particular groups in the population), then minimum wage legislation is an important element in the reduction of that exploitation. (Stiglitz 1973, pp. 294–95)

The usual situation, we would add, is mixed, so that the effects of minimum wage legislation or other economic policies is problematic.

Economic considerations are important in studying the situation of minorities as consumers as well as workers. Monopoly power, seller prejudice, and buyer prejudice, John Yinger notes (1979, p. 459), all contribute to the greater cost of housing for Blacks:

Only a theory that involves discrimination can explain why blacks are concentrated in a central ghetto, why blacks pay more for comparable housing than whites in the same submarkets, why prices of equivalent housing are higher in the ghetto than in the white interior, and why blacks consume less housing and are much less likely to be home owners than whites with the same characteristics.

The final approach to minority–majority relations in the economy that we shall discuss gives the market little attention and challenges the Marxist view that the upper classes, having the most to gain, are most antagonistic to minorities. Examining the various interpretations of race relations following the American Civil War, Gunnar Myrdal, in his influential *An American Dilemma,* pays far more attention to the fears and attitudes of lower-class Whites than to the economic interests of the powerful. When the feedbox is empty, says a Swedish proverb, the horses bite each other. Myrdal observed that lower classes are not naturally radical, or even liberal; they do not readily take a favorable attitude toward disadvantaged groups.

There have been numerous efforts to test this proposition, so sharply at odds with radical interpretations of majority–minority relations. For the most part they have measured verbal prejudices, not discrimination or control over institutions that preserve discriminatory patterns—a fact that we must keep in mind. Using the methods of attitude research, a number of writers have established that persons in lower socioeconomic strata are more authoritarian, are less supportive of civil liberties, and express prejudice toward more groups. Lipset (1959) reviewed the evidence from many countries and found a consistent pattern of intolerance and prejudice among those of low status. The causes, he suggests (p. 489), are numerous.

A number of elements in the typical social situation of lower-class individuals may be singled out as contributing to authoritarian predispositions: low education, low participation in political organizations or in voluntary organizations of any type, little reading, isolated occupations, economic insecurity, and authoritarian family patterns.

The intolerance should not be identified with a general conservative outlook. Lower-status groups often take liberal positions on economic issues—welfare state measures, graduated income taxes, and the like. The reference here is to their intolerance toward unpopular political groups and racial and ethnic minorities.

In interviews with 2,600 male heads of households in three northern California counties, Cohen and Hodges (1963) discovered that intolerance was highest among the lowest strata. With reference to the most disprivileged person, the lower lower-class member, they report that "it was above all toward the ethnic minority group that he directed his animosity" (p. 321). They agree with Lipset that this expresses in part the need among unsophisticated and poorly trained persons to simplify their world. In political matters they choose the least complex alternative; in intergroup relations they divide the world sharply into "we" and "they." In addition to that tendency, however, Cohen and Hodges suggest that the prejudiced responses of the lower lower-class are not only a denial of the American creed of equality but also a result of it. When they apply the creed to themselves they measure up so poorly that they are strongly motivated to look for other bases of evaluation; ascriptive group membership is readily seized upon.

In a study of a sample of 5,000 Americans, Stouffer (1955) reported that intolerance went up as position on the status ladder (measured by occupation) went down. When this study was repeated two decades later, all but the least well educated (using education as an index of class) had become more tolerant. This doubtless reflects a general shift in the political climate; but we should note that the gains had been most pronounced among the best educated (Nunn, Crockett, and Williams 1978, p. 60; see also Campbell 1971).

The eight General Social Surveys conducted by the National Opinion Research Center, 1972–1980, confirm these results. On a scale which combines measures of attitudes of Whites on intermarriage, school desegregation, interracial socializing, neighborhood integration, and black activism, those higher in socioeconomic status, as measured, for example, by family income or education, were more tolerant. Note the percentages giving nonprejudiced responses (A. Wade Smith 1981a, p. 29):

Family income		Education	
Bottom third	39.3%	Less than high school	
Middle third	48.3%		28.2%
Upper third	61.2%	High school graduate	
			50.1%
		Some college +	70.0%

Specifying the Class–Prejudice Relationship

There are strong evidences for class differentials in prejudice. A number of qualifications must be noted, however, if we are to interpret these evidences correctly (Jackman 1981; Jackman and Senter 1980; Ransford 1972). There are measurement problems involved, particularly when prejudice is determined by verbal tests: measures of authoritarianism may tap the respondents' realistic experiences of deprivation and hostility, rather than or in addition to their attitudes. When education is controlled, class differences in levels of prejudice may be sharply reduced or eliminated (Grabb 1979; Lipsitz 1965). Miller and Riessman (1961; see also Wright 1972) argue, in fact, that many qualities of lower-class life and subculture promote democratic tendencies—support for the underdog, more egalitarian values, perhaps a stronger sense of group solidarity.

Westie and Westie (1957) differentiate the general observation of a relationship between class and prejudice by noting that the class of the persons being responded to is also involved. Lower-class Whites express the greatest feelings of social distance from Blacks, but they make some distinctions among lower-, middle-, and upper-class Blacks. Middle- and upper-class Whites indicate less prejudice and draw larger distinctions among various classes of Blacks (see also Blalock 1967, pp. 61–70, 199–203; Giles, Gatlin, and Cataldo 1976).

In some measure it is not objective class status but the fact of having *fallen into* a lower class status that is the decisive fact (Wilensky and Edwards 1959). Hodge and Treiman, however, found a somewhat more complicated situation (1966). For both upwardly mobile and downwardly mobile persons, prointegration sentiments were in between what one would expect from a knowledge of their class origins and a knowledge of their present class.

Light is thrown on these somewhat ambiguous findings by the introduction of another variable. Silberstein and Seeman (1959) found that it was not downward mobility by itself that was associated with prejudice but downward mobility of those who were highly sensitive to status considerations. Such persons were significantly more anti-Semitic and anti-Negro than stationary worker- or middle-class persons or downwardly mobile persons who were not status-seeking. Middle-class persons showed somewhat less prejudice than did those from the working-class; and those who had climbed into the middle class showed the least of all. Even those climbers who were mobility-oriented exhibited lower levels of prejudice than did the stable middle class. In a further observation on mobility, Pettigrew (1958) found that the downwardly mobile in four small northern towns were more prejudiced than the stationary or upwardly mobile, but in four small southern towns downward social mobility was associated with less prejudice. This suggests that loss of status cuts a person off from the norms of the surrounding community, whatever they are. In the case of the southern sample the result was some alienation from norms of prejudice. Thus the effects of mobility on prejudice are complex and probably not very strong (Seeman 1977), depending on the setting, other attitudes of the individual, and doubtless other variables.

We must qualify further by noting that not all the evidence supports the observed relationship between lower-class status and prejudice. Moreover, most measures of prejudice have been developed and standardized against middle- and upper-class groups; their reliability in measuring the attitudes of lower-class persons with different vocabularies, different styles of response to written documents or to strangers, and different skills in interpersonal relations has not been established. When a cross section of Detroiters were asked to give their opinions of two mutually contradictory propositions, widely separated in the interview, nearly eight percent agreed with both. Whether this is the result of a norm of deference toward the interviewer, as Lenski and Leggett (1960) suggest, or "response set" is not crucial here. What is interesting is that the mutually contradictory responses were most characteristic of those with lower-class standing or with low education. They may get high scores on some measures of prejudice just because they say yes to a stranger interviewing them (and on most scales a yes answer means prejudice). Such data should encourage us to be cautious in our interpretation of statements of comparative levels of prejudice among classes that are based on the measurement of verbal attitudes.

Assessment of the influence of class location on prejudice is further complicated by status inconsistency: many persons are higher by some measures of status than by others; their placement, therefore, is problematic—a fact that influences their attitudes and opinions and the responses of others to them. A person of high education may have a

modest income; or a person belonging to the dominant ethnic group may work at a low-status job.

There is now substantial literature dealing with status inconsistency, much of it concerned with its effects on political attitudes and behavior.[5] Only a few studies have dealt with the implications of status inconsistency for prejudice, and the results have not been entirely compatible (Geschwender 1970; Rush 1967; Treiman 1966). On balance, however, it appears that prejudice is supported by a combination of dominant ethnic status with low income, education, and occupational attainment.

A final qualification is perhaps of greatest importance: We must keep fully in mind the distinction between discrimination and prejudice. It is one thing to note that lower-class Whites get a higher prejudice score on verbal tests. It is another to discover what class of Whites is most discriminatory. Middle- and upper-class people may have more skillful rationalizations and verbal disguises. They may recite the American creed more spontaneously. They may have a great need to seem reasonable and tolerant. Hence their prejudice score may be low. These tendencies, however, could be accompanied by vigorous discrimination against minority-group members—low wages paid to them, high rents charged for slum dwellings, exclusion from business and professional organizations, refusal to rent or sell property to them, ambitious programs to prevent them from voting. If it is true that the powerful, upper-class Whites are the chief defenders—not without exceptions, of course—of the whole institutional structure by which the minority group is exploited, then their more polite verbal behavior may be of relatively little importance. On the other hand, the verbal world is an important world. Inhibitions against the expression of deep prejudice may help to create a situation in which change toward more tolerant action is easier for middle- and upper-class Whites. The way in which prejudices are expressed also strongly affects the responses of minority-group members and thus the whole cycle of interaction.

[5]We cannot examine that literature here, but much of it, even when not concerned with race relations, has indirect relevance for the student of prejudice. In particular, the analysis of the varieties of status inconsistency that promote right-wing extremism on one hand and liberal views on the other are of value. See, e.g., Eitzen 1970; Hope 1975; House and Harkins 1975; Jackson and Curtis 1972; Laumann and Segal 1971; Lenski 1954; Wilson 1979; Zurcher and Wilson 1979.

In discussing class differences in discrimination it is well to note that in one situation the economic or political interests of the upper classes may be served by discrimination, but in another situation they may be served by equality of treatment. As employers, for example, they could profit from free choice among all members of the labor force on the basis of skill. Similarly, the interests of lower-class members may in one instance be served by discrimination whereas in another they demand equalitarianism and solidarity.

On the basis of these several qualifications, let us return to Myrdal's observations concerning the relationship of class and prejudice. He writes (1944, p. 68):

Our hypothesis is that in a society where there are broad social classes, and in addition, more minute distinctions and splits in the lower strata, *the lower class groups will, to a great extent, take care of keeping each other subdued,* thus relieving, to that extent, the higher classes of this otherwise painful task necessary to the monopolization of the power and the advantages.

It will be observed that this hypothesis is contrary to the Marxian theory of class society....A solidarity between poor whites and Negroes has been said to be "natural" and the conflicts to be due to "illusions."...Everything we know about human frustration and aggression, and the displacement of aggression, speaks against it.

In our judgment Myrdal, while making a valuable point, overstates it. When he says that "everything we know about human frustration and aggression" points to vigorous conflict between various divisions within the lower class, he overlooks the fact that some, and in some instances much, of the aggression of lower-class people is directed against the upper classes. As we shall see in Chapter 7, the *apparent* nonaggressiveness of many Blacks toward the dominant Whites hides a great deal of subtle attack. Myrdal is right in noting that a great deal (not all) of the frustrations of the lower-class Whites and Blacks tend to keep them apart. Not all the hostility is displaced, however. Lower-class Whites often feel a bitter resentment against upper-class Whites, and in some instances this is accompanied by a feeling of common fate with lower-class Blacks—even though there is a simultaneous attitude of prejudice.

Marxist theory, and radical theories generally, are correct in pointing out that discrimination brings more gains to the upper classes of the dominant group than to the lower, that sometimes the ruling class consciously manipulates prejudice, that in some situations lower-class Whites will turn away from race prejudice in order to work together with a minority group against the upper class. The theory is one-sided, however, in failing to note that some of the forces encourage nonprejudice among the upper class (greater personal security, a feeling of *noblesse oblige,* and probably their long-run economic interests). Oppositely, the theory is weak in failing to indicate the forces that encourage hostility among lower-class Whites (greater personal insecurity, a richer tradition with regard to violence and aggression, and direct immediate economic competition with minority-group members).

Some Blacks contend, we need also to note, that middle-class Whites are their chief opponents. The complexity of the class-discrimination picture is nicely drawn by Campbell (1961, p. 137):

Who were the people with the brickbats forming the crowd in front of Central High School in Little Rock, screaming and crying, 'They're in. They're in. The niggers are in,' on September 23, 1957? They were the rural and lower class urban riffraff. But who were the people who built a new high school on the western edge of the city and planned to keep its attendance area lily-white, by this act securing a private public school for their kind and releasing Central High School to the residents of the city's inner zones? This was the urban middle class, the Southern moderate. Understanding community processes, and controlling the mechanisms of decision, they had no need to resort to violence; they had alternative methods of securing their ends.

To complete this story, however, we must add that the suburban Hall High School and all other junior and senior high schools in Little Rock were desegregated during the next three or four years. By 1981, 66 percent of the pupils in the public schools were Black. Yet an organization, Parents for Public Schools, with a membership of 1,000 Whites, was campaigning for a return of white students, with some success. In 1980, 43 Whites returned to Central High School from private schools; and in 1981, 39 returned (*The New York Times,* September 13, 1982, p. 15).

One does not have to go far to find support for Murray Kempton's remark (*New York Review of Books,* February 2, 1982, p. 8) that "the genius of our politics is the art of distracting the resentments of a cheated middle class and letting them fall upon a worse-cheated lower class" (or, in terms of our interest, upon minorities). That is a partial truth, however. Situations vary widely; cross-pressures lead us to emphasize now one identity, then another. One can be a member of an integrated union while living in a segregated community, and each identity will affect behavior.

Discrimination is not simply an individual eccentricity; it is tied into social structures and privilege systems. It cannot be removed by paying attention to individual attitudes alone. Change will require significant revision of occupational structures, of access to training, of presently protected economic opportunity channels. Discrimination is a "tough" system in which individual anxiety and group advantage support each other. Out of their interaction, moreover, there comes a shared attitude of prejudice that, once launched, becomes in some measure a force on its own, able to continue, at least for a time, without the support of group conflict or personal insecurity.

CHAPTER 4

The Individual Sources of Discrimination and Prejudice

In Chapter 3 we examined discrimination and prejudice from a macrosocial perspective. Attention was focused primarily on economic and political interests and the institutions through which those interests were expressed. Although some reference to individual tendencies was necessary, they were mainly treated as background for the play of structural forces. We bring them now into the foreground. In this chapter we will be examining the degree to which hostility and discrimination can be accounted for by the study of individual needs, values, and attitudes. Some authors see individual tendencies and microsocial encounters as the major source of discrimination. Others downplay them or even regard the study of them as hindrances to understanding majority–minority relations. We see the structural and individual forces as parts of a single system.

A Field Theory of Personality

To maintain a system approach, we need a theory of personality that sees the individual neither as the independent cause of behavior nor as a simple reflection of other causes. Although single-level approaches are still the most common and those who use a multilevel approach are far from agreement, the outlines of a multidisciplinary theory are found in the work of many cultural anthropologists, psychiatrists, psychologists, and sociologists (Lewin 1935; Coutu 1949; Kluckholn, Murray, and Schneider 1953; Yinger 1965b, Gordon 1978, pp. 3–64; Glassner 1980; Rosenberg and Turner 1981). From this perspective, the heredity versus environment controversy is dismissed as meaningless. Rather than trying to establish which is the major influence, the aim is to find out what the range of biological *potentialities* is, and then to study which of those potentialities are activated by a particular series of experiences in the physical, social, and cultural environments. One of the most important ideas is that personality is best conceived as *process,* not as a collection of fixed traits. As process, it can be understood only by analysis of the flow of behavior that comes from the interaction of the individual with the situation. Which tendencies—from among the numerous and often contradictory tendencies we all possess—will be set in motion cannot be predicted from knowledge of the individual alone. With what reference groups is one most closely identified at the moment? Which of various potentialities are being encouraged by the existing situation, which are being blocked? How do the structured aspects of a role channel behavior? *Role* is a cultural concept designating the expected behavior of a person in a given social relationship. To be sure, there is role-making as well as role-playing. Yet the roles themselves have some structure that influences which of the various tendencies the individual will express. Thus personality thought of as process is *field determined.*

In this chapter we shall describe some of the processes involved in the generation of hostile tendencies but will also note the way in which their expression is affected by situations (see Allport 1954; Bagley and Verma 1979; Harding, Proshansky, Kutner, and Chein 1969).

Although our attention will be focused on discrimination and prejudice, we will draw on theories applicable to a much wider range of phenomena. The principles being developed in studies of *attraction in interpersonal relationships,* for example, are clearly important in the areas of our interest. This is well shown in Backman's comment (1981, p. 241) that "persons will tend, where possible, to notice and distort the characteristics of others in the direction of their current motivational states."

Studies of *status-organizing processes* are also of great importance to majority–minority relations. Those processes have been defined (Berger, Rosenholtz, and Zelditch 1980, p. 479) as processes "in which evaluations of and beliefs about the characteristics of actors become the basis of observable inequalities in face-to-face social interaction." A little thought about that general definition reveals its significance for racial and cultural relations (see Dovidio and Gaertner 1981), as well as for relations in which age, sex, educational level, occupations, and other status characteristics vary.

Knowledge of the effects of a *status characteristic*—"a characteristic of an actor that has two or more states that are differentially evaluated in terms of honor, esteem, or desirability, each of which is associated with distinct moral and performance expectations," as Berger et al. (1980, p. 482) put it—can be used to suggest ways to reduce the effects of the use of an irrelevant characteristic. For example, Cohen and Roper (1972) sought to create an equal-status interaction within four-person interracial groups of junior high school boys. Previous research had shown that in "untreated" groups the racial characteristic became activated—Whites being more likely than Blacks to be active and influential. Cohen and Roper taught the black pupils how to build a radio and then how to teach another pupil to build one. Shifting to another activity, a game called "kill the bull," they informed some of the respondents that the skills involved in learning how to build a radio and to teach others were relevant to playing the game. To reach the goal, repeated decisions had to be made on direction of travel on the game board. In the groups where the white pupils had been told that the radio skills were relevant, there were significant increases in equality, because the expectations of both white and black participants had been altered.

One additional illustration of the relevance of more general theories for the study of majority–minority relations will help us to keep studies that focus directly on prejudiced individuals in perspective. Schelling (1978) has skillfully shown that behavior cannot be explained simply by reference to individual motives and actions seen separately. The whole system of interaction has to be taken into account. The final outcome of the interaction may be, in fact, something that few of the individuals wanted, even though their behavior seemed to be an expression of their own motives and desires.

Imagine a situation, Schelling suggests, in which students are deciding which of two dining halls to select. There are 120 women and 100 men; each prefers a 50–50 ratio, a fact known to all. The women go in first, 60 to each hall. Of the first three-quarters of the men, 40 go to one hall, 35 to the other. Later arrivals, noting the greater equality of number in one hall (60–40), go there, making it more equal (60–50), while the other remains at 60–35. The next 10 men are therefore attracted even more to the first hall, giving it a 60–60 balance, which would be appealing to the last 5. Thus the rooms would end up with 60–65 and 60–35 distributions.

Now suppose, Schelling suggests, that the men are free to change their minds. Since the 60–65 ratio is preferable to 60–35, men will begin to move to the first hall. If 10 move, 60–75 is still preferable to the new 60–25, so others will move. The final outcome, given the assumptions, will be 100–60 in one hall and 0–60 in the other, something nobody wanted (Schelling 1978, pp. 37–38). This "critical mass" phenomenon can readily be seen in operation in race relations (pp. 93–94):

In some schools, the white pupils are being withdrawn because there are too few white pupils; as they leave, white pupils become fewer so that even those who didn't mind yesterday's ratio will leave at today's ratio, leaving behind still fewer, who may leave tomorrow. At other schools, black students, with what is reported to be the same motivation, are leaving because they find themselves too few for safety and comfort, and as they leave they aggravate the fewness for those they leave behind.

It is essential that we keep these interactional and situational factors in mind as we turn to an examination of the individual factors in prejudice and discrimination. We shall return to those factors at the end of the chapter.

Prejudice as a Product of Frustration

One of the most frequent applications of modern social psychological theory to prejudice is found in the frustration–aggression hypothesis and a group of concepts related to it. Every person is a cluster of forces—original organic forces that have been shaped and heavily supplemented by sociocultural forces—pointed toward goals. Seldom, however, do human beings move smoothly toward all the goals that have become part of their life plans. Major and minor frustrations are a continuing part of life. Achievement of these goals may be blocked by other people, by natural forces (illness, for example), by one's own lack of skill or some other personal tendency. We may have mutually contradictory goals, one of which inevitably must be denied.

There is much evidence to indicate that the blocking of goal-directed behavior frequently creates hostile impulses in the individual. In many instances this hostility cannot be directed toward the source of the frustration; there may be no human agent, or the agent may be unknown, or too powerful to strike. The frustration may result from self-contradictory tendencies in the individual. A pattern of beliefs may define the agent as an in-group member, a friend, a protector, so that it is impossible to recognize him or her, consciously, as a source of frustration. Agents may be task leaders, necessary for the attainment of desired goals, yet demanding sacrifices or undertaking actions beyond the level of legitimacy granted them, as Burke (1969) notes in his study of scapegoating. Burke's evidence comes from the small group laboratory. If the principle applies to larger, natural groups, the current lower levels of legitimacy granted political, educational, and occupational task leaders in many parts of the world may be a source, not only of opposition to those leaders but in some contexts of increased scapegoating as well.

One person may be tied to another in an ambivalent relationship of both love and hostility, as is the child to the parent. The hostility in such circumstances may be stored up, or it may be directed toward oneself or toward some substitute target that is more accessible or less able to strike back. In other words, a "free-floating," undirected hostility may result from frustration when the actual frustrating agent cannot be attacked; and the social context often favors displacement of this hostility onto minority-group members.

The newly directed attack does not take place, however, without some emotional and intellectual strains; the irrationality and injustice of such hostility, even from the point of view of prejudiced persons, cannot be completely ignored, although it may not be consciously recognized. The substitute target is, after all, a substitute. In order to make themselves seem reasonable and moral, according to their own standards, those who have shown prejudice or discrimination toward a scapegoat look for justifications. They create or accept convincing reasons for hating or discriminating against members of the minority group. They discover and believe many kinds of evidence that "prove" that the members of that group thoroughly deserve the treatment given them. In a strange but common perversion of the facts they even project onto the scapegoat some of the evil traits (again according to their own definition) which characterize their own behavior, in an attempt to get rid of the feeling of guilt that is too heavy to bear. Finally, to get rid of any sense of doubt and to give an absolute quality to their beliefs, prejudiced persons categorize all the individual members of the minority group by stereotypes, usually furnished by society, which help them to rationalize prejudice toward the whole group, despite the variations that characterize any human group (cf. Zawadski 1948).

In this process, the theory goes on to state, a prejudiced person is not wholly successful in reducing his feelings of hostility. Attacks on a scapegoat, after all, are of little use in reducing the actual source of frustrations. They may, in fact, protect the frustrating agent because attention is diverted, permitting the person or the social situation that is causing the frustration to continue its activities or even to intensify them. Thus, for example, if the true cause of the frustrations of unemployment of an industrial worker is automation or a group of attitudes held by management and/or his fellow workers, but he thinks that he is unemployed because of competition from black workmen, he may displace his hostility onto Blacks while the true cause of his frustrations continues unaffected. There is another reason for the ineffectiveness of this frustration–hostility–displacement (or projection) cycle in reducing hostility. The displacement of hostility on a substitute may well be accompanied by some doubts concerning its effectiveness and justice; and projection of one's own failings onto others almost certainly leaves, at least unconsciously, a sense of guilt and a fear of retaliation. These doubts and feelings of guilt create further anxiety and hostility—the more so because they cannot be consciously recognized—and lead to even further displacement and projection. Such a vicious circle helps to explain the tenacity with which prejudice, once started, survives attempts to reduce it by appeal to reason.

It is clear that this theory of prejudice owes much to Freudian doctrines. Some of the writers who support it continue to interpret the process in classic Freudian terms. Almost any social norm is looked upon as a frustrating restriction of the natural organic man. Frustration and hostility are thus not only widespread and inevitable but basic to the very process of socialization. Non-Freudians contend that the needs of the socialized human being are scarcely to be understood solely by reference to original tendencies. The *channeling* of behavior by culture is not necessarily the *inhibiting* of behavior, for learned patterns are just as natural as biological needs and may be much more urgent. Whatever the balance between innate and acquired needs—the present authors incline toward an emphasis of the latter—it is clear that we all face frustrations of those needs. And out of that frustration may grow prejudice and discrimination.

Prejudice and Displacement

Having stated the "personality approach" in general terms, let us examine some of the evidence for it, looking first at the process of displacement. We must keep in mind that this is only a partial explanation; some of its weaknesses will be discussed in later sections of this chapter.

Displacement is the tendency to direct hostility toward a target that cannot realistically be shown to be the cause of one's difficulties. Thus the authors of *Frustration and Aggression* (Dollard, Miller, and Doob 1939, pp. 55–56) connect the many frustrations of the Germans from 1914 to 1933 with the ease with which they adopted overt anti-Semitism. Defeated in war, their prestige destroyed, forced to accept the Treaty of Versailles and to relinquish their colonies and other territory, they came to the peace only to face depression, a ruinous inflation (which virtually destroyed a middle class that had sought security through frugality), and finally a worldwide economic collapse that deepened their own depression. Direct aggression against the Allies was impossible, but various kinds of displaced aggression appeared. Many joined the Social Democratic and Communist parties to fight the old order, some joined youth movements, and an increasingly large number gave support to Hitler's anti-Semitism and other aggressive moves.

Scapegoating is not sheer displacement, with the target selected at random. One must explore not only the hostility leading to displacement but also the "stimulus qualities of the scapegoat" (Berkowitz and Green 1962). Some are attacked but not others. White and Lippitt (1960) note that in the boys' groups that they studied scapegoating was never against the weakest persons. They interpret this to mean that the attacks were an attempt to recover self-esteem. This required that one attack someone strong and dangerous, yet not too threatening. In other circumstances, with scapegoating performing different functions, weaker or stronger persons may be the targets.

Displacement cannot be explained by reference to the individual's tendencies in isolation from the setting in which they are expressed. It is especially important to know what alternative ways of reducing threat or struggling for status are available.

Prejudice and Projection

Closely associated with the hypothesis that free-floating hostility may be important in prejudice through the process of displacement is the conception that prejudice may be an attempt to help individuals accept the inhibitions that culture imposes on them or to rationalize violations of those inhibitions when they do occur. This idea has been suggested at various points above but now needs explicit formulation. The reasoning of the prejudiced person might be stated briefly in this way: "I must not do that" (show uninhibited aggressive or sexual acts, for example), "but there is no great loss—only inferior people do that anyway." Or "I should not have done that" (joined in mob violence against a member of a minority group or violated the sex code), "but these people are inferior, so I have not really done anything bad." Society is based on interdependence, on the suppression of in-group aggressions, and on defensive-aggressive actions against outgroups. However, hostility toward the in-group is generated in the process of transmitting its patterns of behavior to each member. Such hostility is suppressed by many sanctions and rewards. For the most part, individuals find that such hostile moves are either useless or dangerous and abandon them as overt responses. No one is perfectly socialized, however; each is the record of a battle in which frustration, hostility, and fear have played roles. Control over hostility is one of the chief problems of social life. No society requires the complete renunciation of in-group aggression, of course. There are standardized, culturally defined channels for aggression. In modern American society, economic competition and sports, for example, may serve this function. Moreover, aggression can be suppressed to some degree—one of man's most useful capacities from the point of view of adjustment to society. Seldom, however, does a society rechannel aggressions effectively enough to drain off all hostility. In-group members live in a constant state of readiness for aggressive responses.

Anthropological evidence indicates that human beings can be socialized to widely different cultural standards, including some highly restrictive practices, without endangering social cohesion. More hostility arises when cultural norms, whatever they are, are brought to conscious attention and scrutiny by culture contact, by social and technological change. Then the weight of the inhibitions imposed by society begins to be felt.

Here the familiar process of projection may come into use. Many studies have shown, for example, that a ruling group which has exhibited violent aggression against a minority and has exploited it sexually is likely to be firmly convinced that members of the minority are uniformly violent and sexually unrestrained. MacCrone (1937) states that the sexual life of the "natives" has a perennial fascination for the South African Whites. There is a widespread belief that native men are more potent sexually and native women more voluptuous. This is combined with morbid fear of miscegenation and great emotional fear of rape—a strange combination of beliefs since virtually all sexual contact has been initiated by white men, despite intense social disapproval. The picture of the Blacks as vicious and violent can be intrepreted in the same way, since the Whites have often been ruthless in their use of violent suppression. Having ignored their own standards regarding the use of violence and the control of the sex impulse, the ruling Whites find the strains on their consciences too heavy to bear. They attempt to reduce the tension by projecting the traits of violence and sexuality onto the native group. As already noted, this attempt to reduce strain may not work, for it may be accompanied by a sense of guilt that leads to further anxiety, more hostility, the need for even more projection—and thus a vicious circle which can be broken only by a change of action or of conscience on the part of the projecting person (Dollard 1937, 363-388; Lillian Smith 1949).

We should note that the sexual element in prejudice and discrimination is not seen, by some scholars, as primarily the result of projection. Stember (1976) emphasizes what he sees as direct sexual competition between men of the majority and minority groups. Myrdal (1944, pp. 586–92) modifies the projection argument by seeing sexual fears of the majority as rationalizations, used to justify opposition to social equality. Without social equality Blacks can more readily be kept at a lower status.

One need not assume that the claims of prejudiced persons that those who are supposed to be inferior are violent and sexually uninhibited are entirely false. Such characteristics are not uncommon in the human species. What we must see is that the partial truth of the stereotype of the minority group upon whom a dominant group has projected its own faults helps to reinforce the prejudice, to make it seem reasonable. The functions served by the prejudice are thereby carried on more effectively, unmindful of several complications: actual errors in the picture of the minority group, with gross exaggeration of most other traits; assumption that the traits are innate; categorization of the whole group, without attention to wide individual variations; and an emotional defense of the total picture which shows how important it is to the prejudiced person that the issue not be examined.

Nor should we assume that projection characterizes only majority-group members. Norman Podhoretz (1963) has vividly reminded us that if, as James Baldwin makes tragically clear, Negroes are often faceless to Whites, his experience as a white child in New York was that he was faceless to Negroes. He suggests that if Whites hate Negroes because they project onto them their own wild impulses, Negroes may hate Whites because they project onto them their own tendencies toward submission to authority, discipline, and the desire for achievement—impulses that must be repressed because they can lead only to frustration. He speaks of his own fearful admiration for the toughness and the utter freedom of the Negro boys which led him to believe that it was surely he, not they, who was underprivileged.

From this discussion it should be apparent that the concept of projection, "the attribution of internal characteristics to some external person or objects" (Chase 1960, p. 289), is a complicated one. Empirical work does not give it strong support (Ashmore and DelBoca 1976). A full inquiry must ask: Who projects what self-alienating tendencies onto whom in what circumstances? Knowledge of the guilt and anxiety of the projecting individual by itself is insufficient to answer this question. The groups to which one belongs may furnish some targets and prohibit the use of others. Because it aids the process of repression of our guilt, those whom we have harmed are likely to be the focus of our hostility. By accusing them of the very tendencies we have shown in our dealings with them, we seek to allay our anxieties.

We must be careful to note that this scapegoat theory of prejudice is by no means adequate by itself. There appears to be good evidence that frustration does not always lead to aggression and hostile acts. The theory does not explain how the hostile *impulses* become transformed into hostile *attitudes*—persistent, patterned hostility toward an individual or a group—rather than selecting some new and unique target each time (Newcomb 1947). And it does not explain why this patterning takes the form of prejudice against specific groups. One may say correctly that frustration may well make a person more susceptible to prejudice, that it is one of the forces found where prejudice is most common; but the many other factors involved must be taken into account. Persons in whom the frustrations and guilt feelings we have discussed are at a minimum may nevertheless be prejudiced because of the other factors that we have discussed and shall discuss later.

Personality, Uncertainty, and Status Needs

In many instances writers examining the personality of the prejudiced individual have limited themselves to the discussion of frustration, repression, and closely related topics. There are,

however, a number of other needs which in only a very general sense can be brought into this kind of explanation. Prejudice may be an attempt to bring meaning into a confusing and ambiguous crisis situation. Few of us like the feeling that we do not understand an important situation close to us; yet there are many situations that we cannot understand. If the content of our culture includes prejudices, or if, in a new situation, the media of communication offer prejudices, we may adopt them to try to explain the crisis. Lacking true explanations, we rely on comforting pseudo explanations.

This cognitive element in prejudice has often been forgotten in favor of exclusive attention to the unconscious motives (see, however, Hamilton 1981; Schuman and Harding 1964; Tajfel 1969). To say that there is a cognitive element in prejudice is not to say that it is reasonable or rational but only that it is, in part, an effort to comprehend a complex and often threatening world, sometimes by persons lacking cognitive sophistication (Glock et al. 1975). People categorize in an effort to simplify the complicated world to which they must respond; they assimilate views of those around them, including prejudices, as part of the process of becoming a group member; they search for coherence in a changing intergroup setting by imposing a structure on it, often in a way that justifies various advantages for themselves.

Rubin and Peplau (1973) observed groups of six 19-year-old men as they listened to a live broadcast of the 1971 national draft lottery. On the whole, the listeners were more sympathetic to losers— those who received high priority numbers. This was not true, however, among the respondents who were high on a scale measuring their belief that the world is a just place. Their tendency to justify the lot of others overcame the sympathetic attitude toward the losers. This tendency to see the world as a just and reasonable place may be one of the factors behind the process of "blaming the victim" that one sees, for example, among some middle-class Americans who seek to justify poverty (Ryan 1971). Rubin and Peplau suggest that the same spurious reasoning helps to account for the fact that some Germans were able to be persuaded that those sent to concentration camps were of an impure race and deserved their fate (1973, p. 74).

The sense that the world may be arbitrary poses more than a cognitive problem. It can also be experienced as threatening because it implies that one lacks control. The concept of threat as a source of prejudice has recently been examined in a number of studies. In situations where minorities are becoming more competitive for jobs, housing, and schools, a perceived threat, more than deep-seated personality tendencies on one hand or a "symbolic racism" based on cultural values on the other, may be the major cause of antiminority beliefs and actions. Many recent studies have sought to measure the impact of an attitude based on realistic group conflict or perceived threat. It is a negative attitude, as is prejudice, but it contains "a larger fear and a smaller contempt component," as Ashmore and DelBoca put it. The fear is based on the belief that a minority is trying to usurp the position of the majority, rather than on beliefs about minority inferiority (Ashmore and DelBoca 1976, p. 102). Using attitudes toward school desegregation as his criterion, A. W. Smith (1981a) found that those who felt that their positions were most threatened were the most opposed. General egalitarian attitudes have increased throughout the white population, as shown by numerous polls throughout the last quarter of a century. These attitudes tend to be set aside, however, when respondents are asked if they would have any objection to sending their children to majority-black schools. Smith interprets this, following Blumer (1958) as a response to a threat to group position in a racially stratified system (see also Groves and Rossi 1970; LeVine and Campbell 1972; Wellman 1977).

Not all studies have found that the sense of threat is a dominant factor in intergroup hostility. In their study of two mayoral elections in Los Angeles involving a white and a black candidate, Kinder and Sears found that "the white public's political response to racial issues is based on moral and symbolic challenges to the racial status quo in society generally rather than on any direct, tangible challenge to their own personal lives" (1981, p. 429). Although the explicitly segregationist and white supremacist view "has all but disappeared," Kinder and Sears see it replaced by what they call symbolic racism—"a form of resistance to change in the racial status quo based on moral feelings that blacks violate such traditional American values as individualism and self-reliance, the work ethic, obedience, and discipline" (1981, p. 416). This interpretation brings them close to the cultural explanation that we shall examine in Chapter 5.

Although the psychodynamic, the perceived threat, and the symbolic racism explanations of prejudice are sometimes treated as competitors, we see no reason why all, or some combination of them, might not be involved, in varying strengths in different settings. In the extensive literature on these questions, variation in sample, time, measures used, and issues examined inevitably produce different results. In future research we shall undoubtedly see efforts to discover the conditions under which one or another of these influences, and various combinations, are most likely to occur.

A brief reference to other individual tendencies may indicate the complexity of the personality sources of prejudice. It may be an attempt to enhance one's self-esteem or to remove a threat to self-esteem (Ehrlich 1973, pp. 30–36; Bagley et al. 1979, Chapter 6). In a culture that stresses the opportunities each person has for success but prevents success, by its own definition, for a great many people, a shadowy image of success is created by the dominant group's placing itself categorically, above all members of groups perceived as inferior.

A genteel kind of prejudice may be sustained simply by the need for social acceptance in one's group. "Nice" people have no social contact with Negroes. They wish them no harm; there is little projection or displacement involved; the individuals are well adjusted. Nevertheless, prejudice directs their activities, and the polite "gentlemen's agreements" of various kinds furnish the context in which more vigorous prejudices thrive.

Is There a Prejudiced "Personality Type"?

Some of the research in the field of the social psychology of prejudice has sought to discover the degree to which an attitude of prejudice should be interpreted as a more or less independent *trait* and the degree to which it should be seen as simply one manifestation of a total personality. Social psychology has gone through a long controversy over this question of the generality and the specificity of personality attributes—a controversy that has not yet been closed by the evidence. There have been rather drastic swings from the position that supposed traits, such as intelligence or honesty, were general—expressed themselves in any situation where they applied—to the opposite position that personality was simply a loosely joined bundle of specific responses to specific stimuli. We need not examine that controversy here, except to note the contemporary point of view: Neither extreme should be asserted in a doctrinaire way; specific studies should attempt to measure the degree of generality or specificity; and tendencies should be studied in the context of the situations with which they interact.

For us the question becomes: Is there a "prejudiced personality" that is different from the unprejudiced in major ways, or is prejudice a specific response to a specific stimulus? In recent years the impact of psychiatry and cultural anthropology has encouraged greatly increased attention to the matter of personality integration. In the process of acquiring the responses characteristic of his culture, particularly in the intimate contacts within the family during his earliest years, the individual has built a basic *ego structure*. This is a fundamental attitude toward himself and toward others which, once established, reacts upon objective experiences and strongly influences their meaning for the individual. A person, for example, who in his earliest experiences acquires an attitude of superiority and a tendency toward domination may continue to hold that attitude when the objective situation contradicts it. He may fail in a certain endeavor according to the judgments of others, but he can find for himself reasons that prove that he did not really fail; luck was against him, or the other party was dishonest or had some undue advantage, or the referee was blind—at least he won a moral victory.

The Authoritarian Personality

A great deal of research has sought to test the hypothesis that prejudice is part of a complicated personality syndrome. According to this thesis, prejudice is one manifestation of a basically insecure person, one who is "ego alien"—that is, has repressed many of his own impulses—one who looks upon life as capricious and threatening, and one who looks upon all human relationships in competitive power terms. Prejudice, moreover, is tied in a functional way to many other personality trends, to particular styles of politics, religion, and sex behavior. The authors of *The Authoritarian Personality* (Adorno et al. 1950, p. 971; see also Stanford 1973) write:

The most crucial result of the present study, as it seems to the authors, is the demonstration of close correspondence in the type of approach and outlook a subject is likely to have in a

great variety of areas, ranging from the most intimate features of family and sex adjustment through relationships to other people in general, to religion and to social and political philosophy. Thus a basically hierarchical, authoritarian, exploitive parent–child relationship is apt to carry over into a power-oriented, exploitively dependent attitude toward one's sex partner and one's God and may well culminate in a political philosophy and social outlook which has no room for anything but a desperate clinging to what appears to be strong and a disdainful rejection of whatever is relegated to the bottom.

There is not just one type of prejudiced personality, to be sure (Adorno identifies six types from the evidence in these studies), but many tendencies seem to occur frequently among all the varieties (Adorno et al. 1950, pp. 753 ff.). On the basis of interview materials, Frenkel-Brunswik states that those with high scores on prejudice tests exhibit, among other tendencies, rigidity of outlook (inaccessibility to new experience), intolerance of ambiguity (they want to know the answers), pseudoscientific or antiscientific attitudes (more superstition, reliance on accidents as explanations, attribution of behavior to heredity), suggestibility and gullibility, and autistic thinking in goal behavior (unrealistic views of what will achieve the desired goals). Those low in prejudice, on the other hand, show more flexibility of judgment, greater tolerance of ambiguity, a tendency toward more scientific and naturalistic explanation of events, greater autonomy and self-reliance, and realistic thinking about goal behavior (Adorno et al. 1950, p. 461; see also Martin 1964).

Scores of studies have sought to test and refine, and more recently to qualify, the thesis that prejudice is to an important degree the expression of an insecure personality. They converge on such concepts as self-rejection, repression, a strong concern for power in human relationships, a general "threat orientation," as Newcomb calls it.[1] Many of these studies have introduced new variables and some, as we shall see in the next section, have required extensive modifications of the thesis of *The Authoritarian Personality*.

A Critique of "The Authoritarian Personality"

The scales developed in the Berkeley studies of the authoritarian personality were immediately put

---

[1] For valuable bibliographies, summaries, and evaluations, see Ashmore and DelBoca 1976; Christie and Cook 1958; Kirscht and Dillehay 1967; Stone 1974.

to use in replications and modifications of the original research. The methodology and theoretical perspective of the book have been carefully analyzed. A brief examination of this process of testing and criticism can be of value as a lesson in the way in which science grows, as well as a source of knowledge concerning the personality factors in prejudice.

Broadly speaking, there have been three types of commentary and interpretation: comments on the methodology of the original study, further research that has sought to refine the measurement of the variables that affect the extent of prejudice, and discussion of the adequacy of the theoretical assumptions. These approaches cannot be sharply distinguished, but they can be dicussed separately.

Some Questions of Method. Confidence in the findings of *The Authoritarian Personality* is increased by the wide variety of research instruments used by the authors. The effort to measure several different levels of personality also strengthens the study. There were, however, serious methodological weaknesses. The authors paid little attention to questions of sampling; hence the extent to which their findings could be generalized to a wider group was unknown. Memories of childhood, which they obtained from many interviewees, are not necessarily accurate records of past events. Failure to control such variables as education and group membership sometimes led to unwarranted interpretations of the findings. If a person high on a scale of prejudice (ethnocentrism) admires generals and political figures and one low in prejudice admires scientists and writers, this is not necessarily evidence of a different outlook on life. If a prejudice scale is negatively correlated with education, as many studies (but not all: see Weil 1982) have shown, the difference in selection of admired persons may be a function of the educational differences, not of the attitudes toward minorities. The study also faced serious problems in coding qualitative material. One respondent said: "Very, very fine man—intelligent, and understanding, excellent father, in every way." Is this to be classed as "conventional idealization" or "positive effect" (Christie and Jahoda 1954, p. 159)?

Studies of human behavior based on verbal responses often face serious problems of reliability; today's answer may not be tomorrow's answer, and one is not certain whether the difference represents a change in attitude or the crudity of the measuring device.

A number of studies have indicated that the F scale is not unidimensional; it measures several things at the same time, which is to say that it does not measure any of them very well. If the compound of conventionality, rigidity of mind, cynicism, tendencies toward aggression and projection, and the like is not stable—if the separate parts can vary independently of one another—one cannot measure them by a single scale nor think of them as a single personality characteristic. Factor analyses of the F scale have tended to show that six or seven distinct tendencies are represented (Camilleri 1959; Krug 1961; Krug and Moyer 1961). A general factor may underlie them all or there may be subtypes of authoritarianism. But more careful work on the measuring device is needed before we can speak with confidence.

Despite the seriousness of such methodological problems, they do not refute, in the judgment of most observers, the significance of personality research for the student of prejudice. They do alert us, however, to the need for tentativeness and for further research with more careful methods.

Variables Related to Authoritarianism and Prejudice. There are rather consistent findings with respect to the influence of age, intelligence, and education. Using an abbreviated scale based on *The Authoritarian Personality,* MacKinnon and Centers (1956) found, in general, in a sample of 460 drawn from Los Angeles County census tracts, that agreement with authoritarian items went up as age went up. One should not assume, however, that age *per se* is the central fact, or that age can be interpreted without reference to the social setting in which it is experienced. Persons of similar ages may share a view of the world based on common cultural norms; they may have had a decisive experience—war or depression—at a critical time in their lives. Their views, moreover, are not static. Reviewing seven national surveys taken between 1963 and 1982, Cutler (1983) found that all age cohorts had become more liberal in race relations attitudes (up from an average score of 2.12 to 3.11 on a six-point scale), with the oldest having shifted more than all cohorts except the youngest (see also Nunn, Crockett, and Williams 1978, pp. 84–85).

Numerous studies have indicated that authoritarian tendencies fall as intelligence goes up. Simple correlations are usually of the order of −.50 to −.60, falling to perhaps −.20 when education is held constant (Christie and Cook 1958, p. 176). In early studies this relationship between the measures of intelligence and of authoritarianism was often disregarded. Since authoritarianism was believed to involve many cognitive aspects (rigidity, stereotypy, superstition), the disregard was unfortunate. One could not be certain whether the scores obtained were a result of the level of intelligence or of presumed authoritarian tendencies. Any measure of authoritarianism by such devices as the F scale must control for intelligence, comparing only those persons with similar intelligence scores (Jacobson and Rettig 1959). Even when this is done, one cannot know without developmental knowledge of the persons involved what the time sequence of the variables is. Childhood experiences that promote an authoritarian view of the world may repress intelligence (as measured by IQ tests), or low intelligence may predispose one to an authoritarian view of the world, or both.

The same need for control is strong in the study of the relationship of education to authoritarian tendencies. The evidence for a simple correlation is clear: as education goes up, authoritarianism goes down. One cannot draw from this fact, however, the easy conclusion that education reduces prejudice and promotes tolerance. This relationship may reflect the intelligence variable, or class, or selectivity. There is some evidence that those with authoritarian inclinations are less likely to attend college or to stay in college (Stern, Stein, and Bloom 1956). Even when controls are applied, however, the relationship between education and tolerance hold up (Hyman and Wright 1979; Nunn, Crockett, and Williams 1978, pp. 57–75; Stember 1961). Nevertheless, we must add a caution. There is some evidence, as Jackman and Muha put it (1983, pp. 31–32), that "the leadership of the well educated is restricted to the shaping of more refined and sophisticated intergroup attitudes in the face of subordinate group challenge" (see also Jackman 1981).

The Study of New Variables Related to Authoritarianism. Although the original thesis of *The Authoritarian Personality* has received substantial support, it has been continuously qualified by the study of additional variables. Our interest is particularly in the search for variables that may explain the relationship between authoritarianism and prejudice better than (or along with) the presumed functional connection between them. Taking 29 items from the Berkeley prejudice scales, Sullivan and Adelson rewrote them to refer to "people" or "most people" instead of to Jews, Negroes, or other specific groups. Thus "Jews seem to prefer

the most luxurious, extravagant, and sensual way of living," becomes "People seem to prefer the most luxurious, extravagant, and sensual way of living." Two hundred and twenty-one students at a midwestern university were given this revised M (for misanthropy) scale, along with a 20-item E (ethnocentrism) scale. There was a correlation of .53 between the two. Thus prejudice is correlated, in these data, with a general misanthropy. It appears that for the antidemocratic person "there may be no in-group other than the self" (Sullivan and Adelson 1954).

Response Set as a Factor in Authoritarianism. Several writers have suggested that *response set* or a tendency toward acquiescence can account for part of what appears to be a strong relationship between an authoritarian outlook on life and prejudice. In the original F scale, all items were "agree" items. To get a low authoritarian score on an item, one needed to disagree with the statement. Bass (1955) reversed 28 statements on the original F scale to make what he labeled a G scale. Thus, "People can be divided into two distinct classes, the weak and the strong" became "People cannot be divided into two distinct classes, the weak and the strong." Half of the F items and half of the G were then put into one test and the remainder into another. Sixty-three students were given form 1, then form 2 two weeks later. Twenty-one students were given form 2 first and then form 1. By factor analysis, Bass found that one-fourth of the variance of the F scale could be accounted for by acquiescence. That is, the tendency to accept a positively stated item (however that tendency may be explained) accounted for a large part of the relationship between authoritarianism and prejudice.[2] A number of studies have replicated this finding at levels of strength ranging from one-quarter to three quarters (see Carr 1971; Chapman and Campbell 1959; Peabody 1966; Sanford 1973, pp. 153–55). In her study of a national sample, Jackman (1973) found that acquiescent responses occurred significantly more frequently among the less well educated. The result is to inflate the apparent authoritarianism of the poorly educated when all the items are worded positively because of their greater tendency to say "I agree" to all questions, even opposites.

---

[2]Bass 1955. In this publication, the amount of variance to be accounted for by acquiescence is noted to be .59 rather than .25. Messick and Jackson, however, have indicated an error in Bass's calculations (1957). There is a reply by Bass.

The interpretation of these findings, however, is difficult. Ray (1980) found authoritarianism significantly correlated with racial prejudice even when he used a balanced scale of positively and negatively worded items. Some writers argue that acquiescence is part of authoritarianism in any event, because both are associated with low ego-strength and conformity (Gage, Leavitt, and Stone 1957). In a valuable review of this problem, Christie, Havel, and Seidenberg (1958) note the great difficulty in producing a true reversal of the original questions in both a logical and a psychological sense. Are "familiarity does not breed contempt" or "we are bound to admire and respect a person if we get to know him well" true reversals of the common saying? On the basis of the study of eight samples they conclude that, although acquiescence plays some part in determining the scores on tests when questions are all stated in one way, acquiescence is not identical with authoritarianism (see also Rorer 1965).

Mental Rigidity as a Factor in Authoritarianism. One of the presumed characteristics of the prejudiced person is a general mental rigidity, an inflexibility of mind. In a well-known study closely associated with the authoritarian personality research, Rokeach (1948) tried to discover whether the tendency toward ethnocentrism (categorical judgments in favor of one's own group) was associated with a general rigidity of mind. Having separated a group of University of California students into high and low ethnocentric groups on the basis of a standardized test, he asked them to do a serie of "puzzles," in order to determine the degree to which they would rigidly pursue a complicated method that had been used in illustration, rather than adopt a simple solution. The puzzles were of the familiar variety: If you have 3 jars that hold, respectively, 31, 61, and 4 quarts, how can you measure out 22 quarts? Some of the puzzles could be solved only by a fairly complicated method; others could be solved by a simple procedure. When puzzles requiring complicated solutions were followed by several that could be done simply, Rokeach found that ethnocentric persons tended rigidly to continue to use the complicated method. The difference between those high and those low in ethnocentrism was statistically significant, seeming to demonstrate that ethnocentric individuals are more rigid in their approach to nonsocial as well as to social problems.

Several studies, however, have shown that the relationship between rigidity and ethnocentrism is not a simple one. Jackson, Messick, and Solley (1957) found that rigidity in the jar test was correlated with score on a reverse F as well as on the original F scale (and also that there was a correlation of .35 between scores on the F and reverse-F scales). This study is not strictly comparable with Rokeach's, for the latter employed the E scale of the California research, but it indicates the need for studying response set and acquiescence as well as authoritarian tendencies as variables related to rigidity. A person who gets a high reverse-F score is presumably low in authoritarianism. If he rigidly pursues complicated methods of solving the jar tests, this cannot be part of a syndrome which includes authoritarianism (in which he scores low), but shows a tendency to persist in an established way of doing things.

Not finding the same relationship between rigidity and authoritarianism described by Rokeach, Brown (1953) looked for refinements in the meaning of *rigid*. With hundreds of subjects he had always failed to get a significant correlation between rigidity and authoritarianism (as measured by the California F scale). Were the differences in results due to differences in the atmosphere of the testing situation? Rokeach had made his test in a large lecture class; problems were given as a "test" in bluebooks. Brown had made his measurements in small laboratory groups. He suspected that the former situation created a strong ego-involving atmosphere and that the rigidity was "a defensive situationally dependent rigidity," not a generalized trait. To test this possibility, Brown gave the jar test to two matched groups. For the first group he created an ego-involving atmosphere, stressing the test as a measure of intelligence and motivation, cautioning the subjects repeatedly against looking at the test ahead of time. The experimenter was aloof; he dressed quite formally. The subjects wrote their names before they took the test. For the second group the experimenter created a relaxed atmosphere. He was dressed in sports clothes, treated the test casually, showed little interest in the results, and asked for the names of the subjects only at the end. The results confirmed the hypothesis. The correlation between the F scale (authoritarian) score and the jar test score was significantly higher for the ego-involved group than for the casual group. This does not indicate a lack of difference in rigidity between those high and those low in authoritarianism. But it does indicate the need for careful definition of rigidity and the recognition that results are affected by the situation, not simply by the personalities involved. When the authoritarian is in a relaxed setting, he solves the problems as easily as the equalitarian; when he senses a threat he clings to security (Brown 1953).

Supporting this situational view, Maher (1957) found that he could promote rigidity of response in persons with equalitarian as well as authoritarian tendencies by creating a situation more laden with anxiety than Brown had designed. Where Brown created a formal or austere atmosphere, Maher set up a punishment–reward situation by relating performance to marks in a course. Thus, he suggests, some anxiety may make those with authoritarian tendencies more rigid and much anxiety may make most or all persons more rigid.

By putting some of the studies into a crude tendency-situation field model, we can emphasize the interactions involved (see Table 4-1). Knowledge of tendency or of condition alone could not have predicted the observed results. Their interaction was crucial.

Authoritarianism and Politics. Are certain kinds of political views and actions the logical and necessary expression of authoritarian tendencies? We think that the answer clearly is no. Psychodynamic and motivational influences are doubtless involved in the complex of causes leading to particular political beliefs and activities; but the same individual tendencies can lead to widely different political expressions, depending upon the setting; and persons whose tendencies are quite different can support the same political process.

The importance of combining measures of character with measures of situational influence has been emphasized in recent years by research in

Table 4-1. Likelihood of Mental Rigidity as Measured by the Jar Test

Experimental conditions	Tendencies		Studies
	Authoritarian	Nonauthoritarian	
Relaxed	no	no	Brown
Ego-involving	yes	no	Rokeach, Brown
Anxiety-producing	yes	yes	Maher

political science. As political science has become more behavioral in its approach, it has tended to recapitulate some of the theoretical stages exhibited by psychology and sociology in dealing with related issues. Much of the early work was strongly Freudian: political behavior expressed unconscious hostilities and hidden ambivalences of individuals (Lasswell 1930; Marvick 1977); "private motives are displaced onto a public object and rationalized in terms of public interest" (M. B. Smith 1958, p. 3; see also McClosky and Schaar 1965). This is basically the approach of the authors of *The Authoritarian Personality* when they deal with politics. Few would deny the importance of traditional training, of interests, of location in the social structure. These factors are sometimes treated quite lightly, however, while childhood sexual conflicts, inner drives, and unclear self-images are given major attention. These are the emphases, for example, in the *Journal of Psychohistory*.

We have no doubt that individual tendencies, including unconscious motivations, are involved in the creation of both authoritarian and nonauthoritarian politics. There is now a substantial literature dealing with "political socialization" and with political psychology more generally that examines many of the sources of these tendencies. It rests on a much broader theoretical base than much of the earlier work.[3]

The necessary next stage is to explore the way in which these tendencies combine with various environments to produce the observed political outcomes. The need for such a combination is now widely recognized and is reflected in research.[4] We can no longer be content with formulations that affirm a direct and unqualified relationship between authoritarianism and certain kinds of political behavior. Assuming valid measures of authoritarian tendencies and reliable measures of correlation with particular political outcomes, we must elaborate the relationship, in the sense in which Lazarsfeld uses the term, by introducing numerous other test variables. Various simple forms of elaboration might be sketched in the following ways:

[3]For representative works, see Hyman 1959; Knutson 1972, 1973; Renshon 1974; Schwartz 1973; Wright 1976; and the journal *Political Psychology*.

[4]For a number of works relevant for the study of minority-majority relations even if they do not deal directly with them, see Easton 1965; Greenstein 1968; Lane 1959; Lipset and Raab 1970; Sniderman 1975; Stone 1974.

Authoritarianism → Politics X (.70)

(Read this to mean: A high level of authoritarianism is strongly correlated [.70] with a given political belief or activity [X].)

If this pattern were "specified" it might read

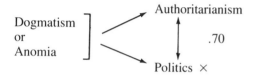

Or the relationship could be "explained" by introducing a preceding variable:

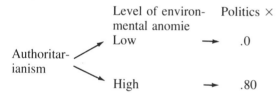

"Interpretation" might produce still a different pattern:

	Level of environmental anomie	Politics ×
Authoritarianism	Low	.0
	High	.80

Dogmatism versus Authoritarianism. One of the most persistent criticisms of *The Authoritarian Personality* has dealt with its tendency to equate authoritarian tendencies with right-wing political philosophy and to assume that a person with a general threat-orientation to the world expressed this characteristic by racial and ethnic prejudices. Are there not left-wing authoritarians? Might not the person who believes the world is hostile and threatening demonstrate this in ways other than prejudice? There are two ways in which one can attempt to answer these questions: One can look for a different personality tendency, probably a more general one, than authoritarianism to explain the range of observations that the original thesis could not explain. Or one can introduce group and situational factors to seek to discover how they affect behavior, as we shall do below. In a major series of studies Rokeach has undertaken the former approach. He holds that authoritarianism as

described by the Berkeley studies is a subspecies of a more general personality syndrome, which he labels *dogmatism*. Although he introduces more situational and field influences than did the authors of *The Authoritarian Personality* (see Rokeach 1960, Chapters 10 and 12; 1968, Chapter 3), his theory is still primarily concerned with the personality level.

Dogmatism, in Rokeach's formulation (1956, p. 3) is

(a) relatively closed cognitive organization of beliefs and disbeliefs about reality, (b) organized around a central set of beliefs about absolute authority which, in turn, (c) provide a framework for patterns of intolerance and qualified tolerance toward others.

Thus Rokeach starts with a person's belief system as a central fact. His "dogmatism scale" is an attempt to devise a measuring instrument on which bigots of the left, center, and right will get the same score. This is an expression of his contention that the *structure* of a belief system (a rigid, closed structure, for example) is distinct from its *content*. One could presumably be dogmatically prejudiced against other races or dogmatically tolerant. The rigid structure does not imply a specific content. Rokeach seeks further to study the *function* of dogmatic belief systems (and all belief systems), proposing that they are defenses against threat and attempts to satsify the need to know the world one lives in. Dogmatism is correlated with authoritarianism, as measured by the F scale, but is factorially discriminable (Kerlinger and Rokeach 1966; see also Ehrlich 1973, pp. 143–46).

A major result of this approach to dogmatism is the proposition that the dogmatic person is much more likely to reject the person who disagrees with him than he is to reject persons because of their group identities—their race or ethnic group, for example. In an ingenious series of studies, Rokeach and others have sought to put this proposition to the test. They have presented evidence to show that when people are confronted with a choice between a person of different race or ethnic group who agrees with them on a major belief and a person of their own race or ethnic group who disagrees with them on a major belief, a large majority will feel more friendly toward the former (Rokeach 1960, Chapter 7; see also Stein 1966). Prejudice against Negroes, according to this view, is importantly based for most people not on categorical racial views but on the perception of the Negro as one who disagrees with or threatens one's belief system.

Additional studies of belief congruence have helped to specify the conditions under which it is strong or weak in its influence on prejudice. Whether or not the perception that a person of another race holds the same beliefs will govern one's attitudes toward that person depends upon the issue involved (interactions of a more personal or intimate source may be more affected by race than belief), other individual perceptions and attitudes (some persons are more sensitive to race than others), the responses of others to the situation (regional differences indicating greater or lesser support for attitudes based on belief congruence), status-organizing processes, and doubtless other variables.

One would expect, from theories of Heider, Newcomb, and others, that most persons would be attracted to those who hold similar values and attitudes and, in the absence of knowledge of strangers' values and attitudes, would attribute one's own to strangers who belong to preferred groups and conflicting values and attitudes to those belonging to disliked groups. That is, the degree of perceived belief congruity may be the dependent, not the independent variable. We must be aware, as Sanford notes (1973, p. 161), that hostility to outsiders is more than a style of thinking, of dogmatism; it expresses deepseated needs and conflicts (see Byrne and Wong 1962).

This is an important avenue of research but it requires careful examination. There is no reason to doubt that belief orientation plays an important part in the behavior of most persons, that race is the definitive criterion in all situations for few, that many "prejudiced" persons will nevertheless prefer a black Christian or American to a white atheist or Communist. But the salience of the choices is strongly affected by the wording of questions and perhaps by response-set (on his Dogmatism scale, Rokeach wrote all questions in such a way that an affirmative answer yielded a high dogmatism score (see Rokeach 1960, pp. 405–17).

What we need are careful observations of behavior outside the laboratory and beyond the pencil-and-paper test that will indicate for whom, and under what conditions, belief systems will override the influence of categorical judgment of groups. Under what conditions, for example, does a white businessman see a black businessman as a businessman? To answer such a question requires the introduction of the kind of situational and group variables on which we shall comment below.

Anomie, Anomia, and Prejudice. Another line of research explores a factor that was implied but not explicitly developed in earlier studies of the highly prejudiced person. Drawing on a long interest in sociology in the concept of *anomie* or normlessness, Srole (1956) hypothesized that this well might be related to the tendency toward prejudice and the rejection of out-groups. There is a vast literature relating anomie, which is a sign of lack of consensus in society, to a personal sense of isolation, to political movements of both right and left, to many of the developments in modern religions—in fact to almost every aspect of life today.[5] Many different responses may be seen as functionally alternative ways of attempting to deal with "the breakdown of the individual's sense of attachment to society" (to use MacIver's phrase). May not our knowledge of prejudice be increased by studying it in this same context?

Srole interviewed a sample of 401 white, native-born adults in an eastern city and asked questions from three different scales. Five questions and their spontaneous comments measured the degree of racial and religious prejudice; five questions, in revised form, were drawn from the Berkeley *F* scale to measure authoritarian tendencies; and five questions were devised to measure feelings of anomia or isolation from others (thought of as the individual counterpart of anomie as a group fact). The degree of anomia was measured by asking respondents the extent to which they agreed with such statements as "There's little use writing to public officials because often they aren't really interested in the problems of the average man" and "These days a person doesn't really know whom he can count on." There was a significant correlation between both authoritarianism and anomia and the scores on the prejudice scale. By means of partial correlation, Srole was able to discover

[5]Unfortunately, key terms are used in widely different ways in this literature. Unless we are quoting, we shall always use *anomie* as a term to refer to a group property, either a gap between the cultural norms and the structured opportunities for fulfilling those norms, as in Merton's definition, or as a quality of a social situation in which there is a low level of agreement on means and ends. *Anomia*, on the other hand, or more satisfactorily, *alienation*, is a quality of individuals. It has several facets that are beginning to be identified. For an attempt to clarify these individual and group dimensions, see Yinger 1973; see also Merton 1968; Seeman 1959.

the degree to which each of the former was *independently* correlated with the prejudice score, that is, the degree to which authoritarianism was correlated with prejudice when the effect of anomia was held constant, and the degree to which anomia was correlated with prejudice when the effect of authoritarianism was held constant. The partial correlation of anomia and prejudice was .35, that of authoritarianism and prejudice, .12. For the sample studied with the scales used, it appears that the sense of isolation was more closely associated with antiminority views than was authoritarianism.

Using the same five-item anomia and authoritarianism scales and a ten-item ethnocentrism scale from the Berkeley studies, Roberts and Rokeach (1956) obtained somewhat different results. With a sample of 86 adults, they found a correlation of .53 between authoritarianism and ethnocentrism when anomia was held constant. Since this study is not an exact replication of Srole's, we cannot know the degree to which differences in samples, in the scales used, in the scoring methods, or other factors affected the results. Nevertheless together they establish the tentative thesis that the prejudiced person is likely to be one who feels isolated and alone (see also Angell 1962; Killian and Grigg 1962; Lutterman and Middleton 1970).

What do such diverse facts mean? Are variations in results due to different samples, different measuring instruments, different variables controlled? Any attempt to answer this question requires a major restatement of the thesis of *The Authoritarian Personality* and the follow-up studies that qualified and refined its interpretation. To that restatement we now turn.

Situational and Group Influences on Prejudice

By way of summary of our examination of the personality theory approach to prejudice and our criticism of *The Authoritarian Personality*, we shall discuss three related ideas: (1) The approach would benefit from the use of the concept of *functional alternatives*. (2) It is insufficiently aware of subcultural and group factors in prejudice. (3) It fails to give adequate attention to situational influences which affect the likelihood that prejudice will be translated into discrimination. These weaknesses

stem from what in our view is an inadequate theory of personality—a theory that emphasizes traits, not process and interaction, a theory that isolates the individual as the unit of analysis when what is needed is a series of concepts that functionally interrelate the individual and the situation of which she or he is a part.

1. *Functional Alternatives.* Persons who are *ego alien*, insecure, suffering from feelings of anomia and powerlessness may, as the authors of *The Authoritarian Personality* indicate, express hostility and prejudice toward minority groups and support fascistic types of totalitarian political movements. They may, however, express their insecurities and seek to resolve their doubts in other ways. What the functional alternatives are for a given individual depends upon his total situation. Shils has argued that in certain circumstances the authoritarian may support the radical left not the reactionary right—indeed, the whole picture of a simple right–left continuum is inadequate, for the two extremes have a great deal in common. The fascist who says that Jews control everything and the communist who contends that big business has absolute power express views that are concretely very different: "Yet looked at from another point of view, they are strikingly similar. Both aver that a small group has with doubtful legitimacy concentrated the power of the country in their hands" (Shils in Christie and Jahoda 1954, p. 32). They may also share an extreme hostility toward outgroups, submissiveness in in-groups, the tendency toward all-or-none judgments, and the vision of the world as a realm of conflict. Some religious movements may be interpreted in part in these same terms. Even some aspects of antiauthoritarian sentiments and organizations can be interpreted as manifestations of hostility and ego alienation. Which expressions of the inner insecurity will be made depends upon the whole range of values and motives of the individual and on the surrounding social situation.

The *left,* it should be emphasized, is highly diverse, as is the *right.* Some segments of it may attract those inclined toward authoritarianism, others the democratically inclined (Stone 1980). We are suggesting only that the close, almost exclusive connection between authoritarianism and right-wing and intolerant politics is not supported by the evidence. This is not to say, of course, that persons attracted to the right are not, in some nonpolitical as well as political ways, different from those attracted to the left (Stone 1980).

2. *Group Differences.* Before one can explain antiminority feelings in terms of a harsh, capricious, and unloving childhood, one must be aware of group structure and of variation in values among the subcultures of a society as well as of differences between groups on a number of demographic measures. If residents of Mississippi have a higher antiblack score than those of Minnesota, this does not prove that they are more authoritarian—more intolerant of ambiguity, more cynical, more rigid, less self-accepting. It may be that they simply express different cultural influences. Middleton (1976) reported that antiblack prejudice was much higher in the South than in the rest of the country, but not anti-Semitism, anti-Catholicism, or anti-immigrant attitudes—a fact, he observes, that "constitutes something of an embarrassment to most personality theories of prejudice" (see also Pettigrew 1958).

Variation in extent of agreement with the idea that there are two different kinds of people in the world, the weak and the strong, may simply indicate differences in actual experience, not deep psychodynamic differences. As Christie says (Christie and Jahoda 1954, p. 175):

Anyone familiar with lower socio-economic groupings can scarcely be unaware of the fact that there is realistic justification for their view that the world is indeed jungle-like and capricious....The acceptance of an item referring to peoople prying into personal affairs may reflect paranoid tendencies among middle-class respondents; it may be reality based among lower-class individuals who are the first to be questioned by police, social workers, and other functionaries of the social structure.

Authoritarianism and prejudice vary also with education, age, sex, religion, nationality, social status, and income (Campbell 1971, Chapter 3; Miles Simpson 1972). Differences in the realities of the situation, in cultural values, in role, in the ways different groups use language and respond to the testing process, and other variables are also involved. Before the extent of personality factors can be measured, other variables must be controlled (see, e.g., Stewart and Hoult 1959). To disregard group membership is to permit all sorts of spurious factors to obscure the actual relationships on the personality level. One might sketch the research needs in an overly simplified way, using only a few variables and dichotomizing those for purposes of brevity; such a scheme is shown in Figure 4-1.

With this scheme the research task would be to compare the eight subgroups under A with their matching subgroups under B. Since they would be "alike" in subculture, socioeconomic status, and educational level, any differences that continued between A and B could more confidently (but not, of course, in this limited design, with great confidence) be attributed to the personality-forming conditions that were the focus of the study. Lacking this, we must hold tentatively to any generalizations concerning personality factors in prejudice.

3. *Interactions of Situation and Tendency.* At various points, we have already introduced the third element in our evaluation of the personality approach to prejudice; but here we shall focus more explicitly on it. Group norms and individual tendencies are not behavior. We can indicate their importance to a larger theory of prejudice and discrimination by examining situational influences on behavior. Thinking of personality as process, not as fixed essence, we are concerned with the way in which it unfolds. Here again the self–other relationships are vital to a theory of personality and an understanding of prejudice.

In part, we are concerned with reemphasizing here the distinction between prejudice and discrimination. How a person will behave cannot be understood solely with reference to his internal attitudes, his verbal expressions of prejudice or nonprejudice. In part, however, we are insisting that even on the personality level, when one is concerned with the prejudices of the individual, situational factors must be taken into account. Personality itself may be thought of in interactional terms. A person *is* what he *does*. To hypothesize some essence previous to the doing is to complicate analysis and make prediction of behavior more difficult.

In a valuable paper on "violence without moral restraint," Kelman (1973, p. 25) shows the importance of taking context into account in explaining the topic of his interest—a class of violent acts that he calls sanctioned massacres. They occur, as he notes, in a genocidal context. Individual characteristics can scarcely account for these attacks on "groups that have not themselves threatened or engaged in hostile actions against the perpetrators of the violence." Kelman notes that three interrelated processes are involved:

(a) processes of authorization, which define the situation as one in which standard moral principles do not apply and the individual is absolved of responsibility to make personal moral

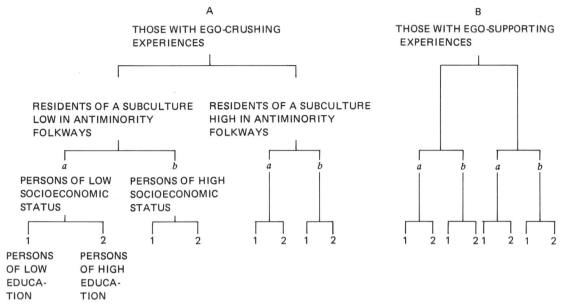

Figure 4-1. Design for a four-variable study.

choices; (b) processes of routinization, which so organize the action that there is no opportunity for raising moral questions and making moral decisions; and (c) processes of dehumanization, which deprive both victim and victimizer of identity and community.

To introduce situations into the explanation of behavior is not to make the individual wholly malleable. It is equally inappropriate to hypothesize some fixed structure for the situation (patterns of roles, norms, group interests) as the determining factor. Situations must also be defined "in process."

In our use of the concept, personality is what personality does; and the doing varies with how a situation is defined, the reference group with which one identifies at the moment, the sanctions and rewards in a given setting, the roles into which one is cast, and the range of tendencies brought by the individual. Many of the problems connected with the development of an adequate theory to deal with tendency, situation, and behavior are revealed in discussions of the concept *attitude*. We shall not review the extensive literature dealing with the concept,[6] but will develop here, in a series of

statements for our own use, a way of summarizing this chapter:

1. Attitudes are individual predispositions to respond to a given event, person, or situation in a given way.

2. Attitudes vary in intensity, as measured by the ease with which they become involved in behavior. Some people will pay a higher price or will require a lower inducement from a situation to act on an attitude than will others.

3. A person generally has several attitudes that relate to a given attitude-object. Within his attitude repertoire there are multiple possibilities for action (Yinger 1965b, pp. 42–45; 250–54). These possibilities may indeed contain mutually contradictory attitudes, whether of equal or unequal intensity.

4. Situations furnish cues and opportunities that call up or activate attitudes (Fendrich 1967b). In any given situation, most attitudes of the participants are latent.

5. An attitude-relevant situation is one that has reward and punishment potential for an individual, either directly because he perceives that potential or indirectly because others who influence him perceive it.

6. A situation generally carries several possible patterns of rewards and punishments, whether of equal or unequal strength. Thus there are multiple possibilities for behavior. (E.g., a white child in a

[6]For important statements relevant to a theory of minority–majority relations see e.g., Deutscher 1973; Fishbein and Ajzen 1975; Hill 1981; Schuman and Johnson 1976; Warner and DeFleur 1969; and Howard Schuman, Martin Fishbein, E. S. Maynes, and Herbert Kelman in Yinger and Cutler 1978, pp. 373–420.

recently integrated school may have a wide range of rewards and sanctions from teachers, parents, white children, black children, and others in the school situation.)

7. Behavior is a *product* of the interaction of attitudes (and other individual influences) and situations. If there are no attitudes or tendencies (expressed symbolically by a zero) or no relevant stimuli from the environment, behavior related to the issue being studied will not occur, for the product of the interaction will be zero. An attitude, no matter what its strength, remains latent if no relevant situation is encountered. A situation also remains latent for any individuals who have no attitudes relevant to it.

Perhaps this sequence of observations can be put into numerical form to illustrate that behavior is a product of the interaction of individuals with certain tendencies and situations with certain potentials for action. A given person may have a weak tendency in one direction, for example, toward friendliness to persons of other races (we shall give that tendency a "score" of 2 on an imaginary 10-point scale) and a strong tendency to discriminate (with a score of 6). Other persons and situational forces, however, set the costs and opportunities for acting out these attitudes. Suppose the supports for friendliness are strong (8) and those for discrimination weak (2). Then behavior will be nondiscriminatory (2 $\times$ 8) even though the stronger attitude supports discrimination (6 $\times$ 2). In another context, however, supports for friendliness may be medium (5) and supports for discrimination, although weaker (3), are not absent. Here we may expect discrimination from the person involved even though the situation seems supportive of friendliness (2 $\times$ 5 vs. 6 $\times$ 3).

All of this is to say that efforts to discover whether individuals are consistent in their attitudes or whether situations govern behavior seem, to us, to formulate the problem in an inadequate way. Behavior is always the result of a transaction between individuals and situations, each having multiple latent possibilities. Which possibilities will become manifest cannot be determined for either individuals or situations without knowledge of the range and intensity of the possibilities in the other. For example, a number of studies have introduced situational variables into their attempts to discover whether or not those with authoritarian tendencies were conformists. These studies show that it is better to ask: Under what conditions do those with

authoritarian and nonauthoritarian tendencies conform (e.g., Malof and Lott 1962; Steiner and Vannoy 1966; Vaughan and White 1966). Although there are doubtless individual differences in tendency to conform, "it seems inappropriate to regard the authoritarian as a person with a 'conformist personality,' for, like the nonauthoritarian, he conforms in some situations but not in others. Moreover, given certain situations he may conform to some people but not to others" (Steiner and Johnson 1963). The person with strong authoritarian tendencies may conform over a wider range of situations, but knowledge of the specific situation is necessary for prediction.

Other lines of investigation reenforce the observation that efforts to predict discriminatory behavior cannot rest on measures of individual prejudices alone. Behavior is "field"-determined (see Warner and DeFleur 1969). It may express sensitivity to different reference groups. Fendrich (1967a) found that readiness to participate in interracial activity was more closely associated with his respondents' perceptions of the attitudes of friends, parents, roommates, and respected older persons than it was with the respondents' own attitudes, although the latter were also of some effect. In another study involving college students, Linn (1965) found no significant relationship between attitudes and interracial behavior. He concluded that involvement with the surrounding liberal environment was a powerful influence—indicating again the need for taking reference groups and other situational forces into account.

Conclusion

Gradually emerging out of the type of material discussed above is a theory of the personality elements in prejudice. Much of our knowledge, however, is still on the descriptive level (but see Tuch 1981). We can expect systematic effort in the years ahead to explain the meaning of several relationships that have been observed but not yet fully explained. The evidence to date indicates that certain types of personality are prejudice-prone; that a wide variety of needs may, in particular social settings, be served by prejudice; that persons' relationships with those around them may strongly influence their attitudes and behavior toward the members of minority groups. These explanations must come into any total theory of prejudice. We must be alert, however, to the weaknesses of this approach.

Prejudice against a group is scarcely a unitary attitude. In most people it varies in strength with the situation being envisaged. In a study of samples from fifteen major cities, for example, the Survey Research Center found that 86 percent said they would not mind at all having a qualified Negro as a supervisor on their job. Yet 51 percent opposed laws to prevent racial discrimination in housing (Campbell 1971, p. 4). By most measures, however, prejudice in the United States has declined quite sharply in the last generation. There is no equivalent evidence that the proportion of persons who are insecure, ego-alien, or alienated from society has also declined. When asked whether they thought white and black students should go to the same schools or to separate schools, the percentage of national samples answering "the same schools" rose from 30 in 1942 to 49 in 1956 to 74 in 1974, and to 86 in 1977. The percentage of nonblacks who would vote for a black for president, if he were nominated by their party and was qualified, rose, between 1958 and 1978, from 38 to 80. In 1963, 50 percent said "not at all" when asked how strongly they would object if a member of their family wanted to bring a black friend home to dinner. By 1980 the percentage was 75.

Not all of the changes have been as large as those cited, and some have been in the opposite direction. When asked to express their agreement or disagreement with the statement that "White people have the right to keep Blacks out of their neighborhoods if they want to, and Blacks should respect that right," 45 percent disagreed or disagreed strongly in 1963; by 1980 67 percent took those positions. Those favoring the busing of children went up, 1970–1978, to only 20 percent from 14 percent. And those who thought the country was spending too little to improve the conditions of Blacks went down, 1973–1978, from 33 to 24 percent. (For these and other data, see Condram 1979; NORC 1980; A. W. Smith 1981b; T. W. Smith 1980.)

These opinion polls do not show, of course, that prejudice has disappeared or that discrimination is declining. It is quite possible, in fact, for the nation to experience rising discrimination at the same time it sees declining prejudice. In Pettigrew's judgment (1981b, p. 252): "White Americans increasingly reject racial injustice in principle, but are reluctant to accept the measures necessary to eliminate the injustice." In Part II we will be examining the evidence with respect to that issue with some care; but here we must at least emphasize that the verbal-attitudinal world is not identical with the behavioral world. The limits to a purely individual approach operate in both directions: There may be relatively equalitarian behavior despite prejudice, or there may be discrimination despite reduced prejudice.

In this chapter we have sought to interpret the personality dimension as part of a larger system of causes. The key to this interpretation is the word *tendency:* To isolate an authoritarian predisposition or a prejudice is not to describe behavior but only to indicate one of the forces at work. Among other things we must also ask: What other tendencies furnish different possibilities? Most persons have complex, even contradictory attitudes. What is the relative salience of the diverse values and attitudes held by an individual? What role is he playing? The concept of role implies that he is bound into a network of interacting persons who are governed, to an important degree, by shared expectations. What is the system of rewards and sanctions in the situation? Without knowledge of potential gains and costs for an individual we cannot predict which of his various tendencies will be brought into play. How are the groups of which he is a member helping to define the situation for him? What kinds of cues are being furnished by leaders?

Such questions are of special importance in understanding prejudice and discrimination in a mobile, heterogeneous society. As Reitzes has excellently shown (1959), in such a society we interact more in the framework of specialized organizations wherein we are engaged not as total persons but as role players. Many contacts in the modern world have limited and specific objectives. Relationships tend to be "contractual," thus allowing fewer individual tendencies to come into play. Large groups with explicit organizational objectives and policies govern our actions in more and more ways. Since these groups often bring together individuals with widely differing personal tendencies, any policy will contradict some of the personal inclinations. Thus labor unions may discriminate in an effort to protect a limited job market despite a low level of prejudice among many of their members. Or unions may develop a nondiscriminatory policy in order to present a united front despite a high level of prejudice among many of their members.

Even in situations that are poorly structured by groups or norms, individuals do not simply "express themselves." They look for clues, for a "definition of the situation" that can guide them in their interaction with others (Kohn and Williams 1956). If there are leaders taking a definite stand, their clues may well be followed; but in the absence of leaders the tentative actions of others may furnish the direction. And this response, in turn, may support the first person's tentative move, this promoting a *group* cycle of causation.

CHAPTER 5

The Cultural Factor in Prejudice and Discrimination

The previous two chapters have shown how discrimination reflects, in part, economic and political conflict and competition as well as the *psychic economy* of individuals—their efforts to deal with a baffling world, hostility, and anxiety. Prejudice represents these forces in symbolic form; it is a readiness to act—whether or not set in motion—in service of those individual and group needs.

Even the most complete analysis of the socioeconomic and personality sources of discrimination and prejudice, however, does not explain why any particular group should be selected as their target. Nor does it explain why prejudice should be found even among individuals and groups who are in virtually no way served by it. There is nothing intrinsic about group conflict or personal insecurity that requires that certain specific groups be the objects of hostility. A group must be socially visible, recognizably distinct from the majority, to be subject to discrimination; but visibility is a function of attention. Blond hair could be as useful as brown skin in setting a person apart. Why have many western societies selected the latter? And why will a stable and secure white person discriminate against a black person, for example, when she or he has a low amount of hostility, has never known a Negro, and has no conceivable economic or political interest to be served? In this chapter we shall attempt to answer these two related questions. We shall see that, in addition to the sources of prejudice and discrimination already discussed, other sociological and historical factors must be taken into account.

An attitude toward a minority group can be seen, from one point of view, as simply one of the folkways, one of the learned ways of responding that are part of the standard cultural equipment. We are taught to be prejudiced against certain groups just as we are taught to dislike certain foods that people in other societies consider great delicacies. Individuals may be equipped with a number of culturally learned responses to minority groups that they are never called upon to use. These responses scarcely can be called functional, except in the general sense of representing the cohesiveness of a culture group. They survive, however, as group-patterned ways of thinking, ready to influence one's responses if an occasion arises. A brief statement concerning the origin and nature of cultural definitions may be of help in the study of this cultural root of prejudice.

Many, perhaps most, of the ways of behaving that are agreed upon by members of a society had their origin in an attempt to meet a specific need. The attempt was not necessarily rational or objectively valid, though it may have been, but somehow it came to be accepted as the appropriate way. Individuals could not possibly bear the strain that would come from trying to decide, for each of the hundreds of actions they perform each day, what the best response might be. Some of these folkways designated by culture perform their functions as well as any alternative form would, for the action is symbolic. So long as everybody accepts the symbol it *works,* even though its meaning may have changed. Shaking hands may originally have been a way of saying, "See, my hand is not on my sword; it is outstretched; I am a friend." Having lost most of its original meaning, it can still serve as the symbol of greeting. Other folkways, however, are not symbolic; they are adjustments to actual circumstances. If used outside the situation in which they developed, therefore, they may serve the functions for which they are intended very badly. Wearing a coat of mail may help one survive the thrusts of the spear of an enemy, but its modern survival, the stiff shirt of formal clothing for men, is hardly adequate to protect one against the barbed remarks or the arrows of love that he may encounter in gatherings to which the dress suit is appropriate.

The things that are important about cultural norms, from our point of view, are their tendency to continue beyond the situation in which they appeared and their coercive power over individuals. These traits were probably overemphasized by the early students of culture, who drew much of their material from primitive, isolated societies and tried to apply their conclusions unmodified to a complex, mobile, urban society. This exaggeration should not cause us, however, to go to the opposite extreme that overemphasizes the speed with which new patterns of thought and behavior are created in the modern world. It is reported that George III of England suffered from a goiter which he felt was disfiguring. His tailor came up with the brilliant thought one day that the goiter could be hidden by a piece of brightly colored silk wrapped around the king's neck. The men of the court, anxious to show the king that they admired his taste, were soon copying the pattern. So today uncomfortable males in many lands wear ties because George III had a goiter.

Folkways change, of course, and today they doubtless change more rapidly than they did formerly; but in varying degrees they continue to control individual behavior and to furnish guides to thought and action. They may have outlived their original meaning, they may even bring pain and discomfort to those who follow them, they may seem absurd to the outsider; but they seldom die out abruptly. To contradict the folkways of one's group is to set oneself apart, to subject oneself to the charges of heresy and eccentricity with which the group tries to maintain its unity. It may be that each member of a group, as an individual, would gladly dispense with a given pattern of behavior, but none can take the first step.

Prejudice as Culture

If this view of one aspect of culture is correct, it may help us to understand prejudice. Attitudes toward minority groups have been started by various circumstances doubtless related to personality and to group conflict, have become fixed as part of the culture—embodied in its lore, developed in its literature, built into its institutions—and have continued even when the original circumstances were drastically changed. The institutional formulation of the folkways of prejudice is especially effective in preserving them for a number of reasons. The basic institutions are so important in the socialization of the individual that they can build into him the very standards by which they themselves are judged. Institutions are the chief symbol of group cohesion; they are surrounded with ritual and an elaborate system of protective beliefs. And the functionaries of institutions, and others who profit most from their pattern of control, are diligent in defense of the institutional framework.

Although in the last two decades, cultural factors in the system of discrimination have been relatively neglected, they have not been completely forgotten. Kuper (1974, p. 11) has emphasized that "ideologies of cultural differences are an almost invariable phenomenon in race relations. They convey racial characterizations and derive from them principles of race relations." There are, he notes, reciprocal ideologies, often describing the "morally repugnant qualities" of the oppressors, that are used by minorities to oppose their situation. Turner and Singleton (1978) note the tendency "to ignore the impact of culture" in recent studies of ethnic oppression. They emphasize the interaction of structural and cultural factors in a review of the various stages of oppression of black Americans and develop a set of systematic theoretical propositions expressing that interaction. (There are, of course, structural and cultural forces opposing discrimination, as we shall discuss later.) Referring to America, Turner and Singleton write (1978, p. 1011): "In a society valuing equality, freedom, achievement, activity, and individualism, structured discrimination is likely to be ligitimated by beliefs emphasizing the inferior nature of those subject to discrimination."

The interdependence of structural and cultural factors in discrimination is well shown by the comparisons drawn by Bagley and his associates (1979, pp. 143–74) among Britain, France, and the Netherlands. The greater tolerance in France, and the Netherlands is partly to be explained by the emphasis on structural assimilation of racial and cultural minorities within the colonies or the metropolitan societies. In contrast with Britain, norms of tolerance emerged from and then influenced the structural arrangements. The Dutch, for example, "conceived of marriage with the native populations as a means for achieving good relations with the conquered populations, and as an instrument for creating a harmonious climate in which colonial exploitation could take place." Mixed marriages were much more common in Indonesia under the Dutch than in India under the British. Anglo-Indians were "treated as natives by the British, and accorded no right or privilege. In contrast, Eurasians in Indonesia were given full status and rights of Dutch citizenship" (Bagley et al. 1979, p. 170).

We applaud such recent emphasis on the cultural factors, having given them a significant place in our interpretation of the perpetuation—or modification—of discrimination. Cultural values and ideologies not only justify existing patterns of dominance. They also persist past the situation within which they developed and help to shape and support new patterns of dominance in new contexts. We ought to note, however, that belief in the persistence of cultural norms supporting particular forms of discrimination and prejudice may be in error: "Most white American adults grossly exaggerate the support among other whites for racial segregation" (O'Gorman 1975, p. 313). Such "pluralistic ignorance"—a shared belief in a nonfact—is itself "a prominent feature of the total culture," as O'Gorman observes. It has its own consequences, mainly, we would guess, by reenforcing the system it misperceives or retarding its rate of change.

In each situation the question is: Why are particular differences seized upon as legitimate ones for marking a group off as inferior? There are two basic factors that help to answer this question. First, those differences that help to distinguish a group whose exploitation will be profitable (in terms of all the gains discussed in Chapters 3 and 4) for the dominant group will be used. Second, each group

has a hierarchy of values, a system of beliefs that it carries into conflict situations. It will most readily set apart another group that differs from it in a high-order value. This is close to what, in recent years, has been called *symbolic racism,* a term we shall comment on below. As the system of values and standardized beliefs changes, so will the pattern of prejudice tend to change.

The Importance of Traditional Prejudices

The existence of wide contrasts between verbal behavior and nonsymbolic behavior should make us cautious in our study of the role of tradition in a theory of prejudice. Equally inadequate, however, would be dismissal of the traditional element in prejudice as a mere survival. It is very much a part of the contemporary process. A traditional prejudice can produce complacence, acquiescence, and a fertile area for the cultivation by interested groups of more vigorous prejudices. Even the relatively innocuous statement or acceptance of a verbal tradition of prejudice can set in motion a chain of events that is highly significant in the relationship between majority- and minority-group members.

1. Acceptance of the tradition by those who are only mildly served by it helps to reinforce the prejudice of those who use it to satisfy more fundamental needs. It is easy to say, "I can scarcely be accused of being prejudiced because of self-interest when those people who obviously have no self-interest express the same prejudice." In other words, anyone who accepts a tradition of prejudice helps to sharpen the sword for those who want to use it.

2. The mild verbal prejudice may govern a person's actions in one of those either-or decisions that have a watershed effect on many subsequent events. Shall the community accept or oppose a segregated school that is gradually appearing because of housing shifts? One with the traditional prejudice may easily assume that segregation is pretty normal and natural. He has nothing in particular to gain or lose by it, but it seems right. Once fixed as a pattern, however, the segregated school has a long sequence of effects on the personalities of the black and white students, on comparative educational and economic opportunities, on the extent and nature of interracial contacts, on the whole life of the community. An action that came about as the result of a mild, verbal, traditional prejudice may have effects as significant in race

relations as actions that result from more deeply rooted prejudice.

3. Finally, traditional attitudes keep alive a mind-set that, when crisis situations arrive, will be strengthened and attached to contemporary needs. Having survived as tradition, the prejudice takes on renewed life as a weapon. Had the traditional prejudice not been available, some other adjustment to the situation might have occurred—an adjustment conceivably more in harmony with the realities of the situation and thus more in the interest of the prejudiced person as well as the target of his hostility. For long periods, anti-Semitism has lingered as tradition, active in the lives of only a small proportion of those who believed it. But when conflict situations and frustrations have arisen, it has been asserted with a renewed force, blocking adjustments that were more in line with the actual problems.

For these reasons the social scientist must study the traditional factor in prejudice. The fact that it is "only verbal" or "skin-deep" should not be allowed to obscure the basic role it often plays. In any complete analysis of prejudice one cannot ignore the casual, verbal, "proper" prejudices of the average person, for they are involved in this important interactional way with the other factors in prejudice. In Chapter 3 we noted the connection of ethnocentrism with systems of domination, internal as well as external. As Lanternari puts it (1980, p. 53):

In a complex society based on class-determined relations of production and characterized by politically organized and expansionistic power *elites* [which is to say, in many, if not most modern societies], ethnocentrism is not limited to naive myths, more or less harmless labels applied to "others."

Dominant cultural standards of the true, the good, and the beautiful are, in our judgment, powerfully involved in the structures of stratification.

Ways of Conceptualizing and Measuring the Culture of Prejudice

Several different research strategies have been used in efforts to measure the culture of prejudice and to identify its social locations. Most of these have been applied primarily to the United States.

Before indicating the major findings of these studies, we should note a number of qualifications: Much of the evidence has been in the form of verbal responses to paper-and-pencil tests. Insofar as these tests are valid, they show that many Americans share a verbal tradition that reflects, or expresses, the majority–minority system of stratification. The pattern varies, to be sure, with income, region, occupation, and education. Yet even minority groups accept it to a degree—rejecting only that part of it that applies to them, and in some instances accepting even that.

The studies do not indicate, for the most part, the degree to which this verbal behavior might be correlated with other behavior; nor do they indicate whether there are important differences among individuals in the ease with which the verbal behavior might be changed. If the analysis in the preceding two chapters is correct, individuals expressing similar culturally anchored verbal opinions about a minority group may vary widely in the extent to which those opinions reach into the core of their personalities. One person may express the "proper" opinions, may sincerely "believe" them, but may act in a way that shows the prejudices have little significance for him or her. Another person may have not only the same traditional prejudices, but a strong contemporary need for their defense. Finally, it should be emphasized that stereotypes, one of the forms of the culture of prejudice, are to some degree anchored to particular societal conditions. They are fairly persistent, as are other elements of culture, but they are not permanent. When major social changes remake the conditions of intergroup relations—as is happening in many parts of the world—old stereotypes are broken up. This is a significant part of the cultural dimension of social change. We must be alert to the conditions under which stereotypes persist and the conditions under which they are revised or discarded.

Social Distance in the Culture of Prejudice

We shall discuss three ways in which the culture of prejudice has been conceptualized: social distance, stereotypes, and symbolic racism. Despite their differences, they share in common the idea that prejudice expresses, in part, standards and values that are widely shared and normative within a group.

Social distance—"the degree of intimacy which group norms allow between any two individuals" (Poole 1927, p. 115)—should be distinguished from personal distance, which is governed, as Poole noted, not by social norms but by considerations of individual welfare and satisfaction. It is the former that concerns us here. It can be measured or inferred, Ehrlich observes (1973, p. 62), in several ways: by the study of rates of behavior—of intermarriage, for example, or residential segregation; by idealized norms—"expressed preference for specified forms of intergroup behavior"; by indications of perceived legitimacy and conventionality of certain degrees of intimacy. Indications of personal distance—degree of readiness to engage in specified forms of intergroup behavior—are also a component of prejudice and a clue to social distance, although conceptually distinct. Most measures of social distance are attained by aggregating individual measures.

Systematic study began with the social distance scale devised by Bogardus. He secured the responses of nearly 2,000 Americans to forty racial, national, and religious groups. The respondents were asked to which step on the following scale they would admit the members of each group:

1. to close kinship by marriage
2. to my club as personal chums
3. to my street as neighbors
4. to employment in my occupation
5. to citizenship in my country
6. as visitors only to my country
7. would exclude from my country

These steps were assumed to be on a quantitative scale that ranged from most favorable to least favorable. It is unlikely that all the respondents would regard the questions in this way or would agree entirely on the amount of social distance expressed by each question, but the instrument is certainly of sufficient precision to give an approximate preference ranking of the forty groups. Near the top were British, native white Americans, and Canadians; then came French, Germans, Norwegians, Swedes, and other north Europeans; then Spaniards, Italians, south and east Europeans, and Jews; and near the bottom Negroes, Japanese, Chinese, Hindus, and Turks (Bogardus 1928, pp. 13–29 ff.).

This pattern appeared, with only minor fluctuations, in several of the early studies. It is interesting to compare the rankings obtained when Bogardus asked 110 businessmen and schoolteachers on the West Coast the degree of social intimacy to which they were willing to admit various ethnic groups with the rankings that Thurstone found in studying the likes and dislikes of 239 midwestern college students (in Newcomb and Hartley 1947, p. 204). Referring only to those groups that appear in both studies, five have identical ranking; nine differ by only one rank; four by two ranks; the largest disagreement is three ranks, which occurs only once. Guilford (1931) found that the students in seven widely separated colleges had the same pattern of prejudice. Hartley (1946) discovered that the women students in Bennington College, Vermont, had the same attitudes toward minority groups as did the black students of Howard University in Washington, D.C. In general he found the same pattern in 1946 that Bogardus had found in 1928 and concluded that "this pattern of prejudice is practically an American institution."

Minority groups themselves tended to share this tradition, although with some variations. Zeligs and Hendrickson (1933) found a correlation of .87 between the rankings of Jewish and non-Jewish children. Compare the rankings that Bogardus obtained from 202 American Negroes and 178 native-born Jews with those found in the study of the businessmen and schoolteachers noted above. In Table 5-1 we have eliminated groups that were

Table 5-1. "Social Distance Scale"

Native white businessmen and schoolteachers	American Negroes	Native-born Jews
1. English	1. Negro	1. Jewish
2. French	2. French	2. English
3. German	3. Spanish	3. French
4. Spanish	4. English	4. German
5. Italian	5. Mexican	5. Spanish
6. Jewish	6. Hindu	6. Italian
7. Greek	7. Japanese	7. Mexican
8. Mexican	8. German	8. Japanese
9. Chinese	9. Italian	9. Turkish
10. Japanese	10. Chinese	10. Greek
11. Negro	11. Jewish	11. Chinese
12. Hindu	12. Greek	12. Hindu
13. Turkish	13. Turkish	13. Negro

Adapted from Bogardus, 1928.

not found in all three studies, so the comparisons should be taken as a rough indication of the degree of similarity in attitudes.)

Evidence of some degree of national culture and continuity comes from the rankings given to many of these same groups by a sample of 491 underclassmen at the University of Hawaii (Yinger 1961). Although over 75 percent of the students were of Asian ancestry (primarily Japanese) and had had little contact with mainland United States, their rankings of the groups on a social distance scale were identical with those of businessmen and school teachers 33 years earlier, except that Japanese and Chinese were raised to the top of the list.

Although the social-distance method of studying the culture of prejudice has been little used in the last several years (but see Starr 1978), several refinements have been added that should be noted. Following his studies of 1926 and 1946, Bogardus continued to examine changes through time by gathering judgments from widely scattered groups of college students and adults in 1956. Although this is not a sample of national opinion (the 2,053 persons studied were mostly under 35 and almost entirely drawn from higher educational levels), it compares with the groups studied by Bogardus earlier. Groups in the upper third of social nearness (largely North European) remained the same, although with somewhat higher scores, due probably to greater social distance expressed toward them by Blacks. Although Jews remained in the middle of the range of groups being ranked and Japanese and Negroes near the bottom, less social distance was expressed toward each of them. On a seven-step scale, the greatest social distance score fell from 3.91 (1926) to 3.61 (1946) to 2.83 (1956), and the average score fell from 2.14 to 2.12 to 2.09 (Bogardus 1958).

A shift in the opposite direction, it should be noted, may have occurred among some minority-group members. This shift had already begun in the early 1950s (Prothro and Jensen 1952). Although the feelings of social distance felt by some Blacks toward Whites have not, to our knowledge, been recently measured by the Bogardus scale, we can infer from various public opinion polls that for a few Blacks, personal distance, at least, has increased. Schuman and Hatchett (1974, p. 7) report, for example, that the percentage of Blacks preferring an "all-Negro" or "mostly Negro" neighborhood increased between 1968 and 1971 by about ten percent. We should note, however, that data

for the earlier year came from two national samples and that for the later year from the Detroit area sample. Even in 1971, only 18.9 percent preferred "all-Negro" or "mostly-Negro" neighborhoods. And in the same time span, the percentage preferring a mixed neighborhood also increased, from 56.5 to 62.0.

Most studies of social distance ask respondents to think of an average or standard member of a group in making their judgment. It is doubtless significant that many persons find little difficulty in doing this. Yet we need to know how they might respond to a differentiated picture of a minority group. Westie (1952) attacked this problem by measuring the differences in responses of white persons to Blacks in various occupations. Sixty lower-class, 56 middle-class, and 58 upper-class Whites, chosen by random-sample blocks in Indianapolis, were interviewed in their homes. The degree of social distance that they felt toward Blacks was measured by a series of four scales which referred to various kinds of interpersonal contact. Lower-class Whites made very little distinction among Blacks in various occupations, whether doctors, bankers, machine operators, or ditch diggers. With a score of 24 representing the maximum social distance, lower-class Whites averaged from 14.03 to 15.10 for the eight occupations listed in the study, a range of only 1.07 scale points. The scores of the middle-class Whites were from 10.91 to 13.09, indicating both less social distance and the willingness to distinguish more sharply among Blacks in various occupational groups. The range for upper-class Whites was from 9.38 to 12.52, again indicating a lower amount of social distance and a greater willingness to differentiate among Negroes of different occupations. Since the white respondents were not classified by education, region of birth, or other variables, we cannot know how much their class standing *per se* influenced the results. But the study indicates the need for measuring the variations in social distance as well as the nationally shared traditions.

Ehrlich (1973, Chapter 3) has well summarized the kinds of criteria that enter into judgments of social distance: socioeconomic status; ethnicity; race; degree of social, political, or moral deviance; other social categories; physical qualities; positive and negative interpersonal qualities. Some of these are purely individual criteria, varying widely in importance from person to person as factors affecting their feelings of personal social distance. Others are tied to the stratification system, to ethnocentrism. They are normative, part of the culture, and as such enter into the majority–minority relations of a society.

Stereotypes in the Culture of Prejudice

Built into the cultures of many societies are guidelines that tell their members not only whom to like and to dislike, whom to feel close to and distant from, but also why these attitudes are appropriate. In the process of growing up individuals learn, by various direct and indirect means, what the qualities of the members of racial, ethnic, religious, and other groups presumably are. Sex stereotypes have been studied intensively recently (Ashmore 1981; Ashmore and DelBoca 1979; Friedman 1977). These "pictures in our heads," to use Walter Lippmann's phrase, vary from those that are widely shared within a group, which we can call *cultural stereotypes,* to those used by particular individuals. Although both reflect and affect intergroup contact, we are mainly concerned here with cultural stereotypes because of their significance for stratification systems and not for individual behavior alone. Nevertheless, we want a definition that covers both shared and individual referents, such as that of Ashmore and DelBoca (in Hamilton 1981, p. 16). They define a stereotype as "a set of beliefs about the personal attributes of a group of people." They leave out, as we believe appropriate, questions of the accuracy, the badness, the extent to which shared, and the rigidity of stereotypes. These are questions for analysis and evaluation, not issues to be settled in the definition itself.

Katz and Braly (1933) initiated an important although somewhat limiting line of research on stereotypes. They asked 25 students to list all the traits they thought typical of Germans, Italians, Irish, English, Negroes, Jews, Americans, Chinese, Japanese, Turks. This list was supplemented by other traits commonly found in the literature. One hundred Princeton students were then asked to select from the 84 characteristics listed the five traits that were typical of each of the ten groups. If there had been no patterning in the pictures that the students had of these groups, 42 (half) of the traits would have received 50 percent of the votes. Oppositely, if the students had agreed perfectly on the five traits that were typical of a group, 2.5 traits would have received 50 percent of the votes. The degree of

uniformity in attitude is shown by the fact that only 4.6 traits were needed to include half of all selections referring to Negroes; only 5.0 to include half the selection of traits referring to Germans; and for the Turks, about whom there was least agreement, only 15.9 traits were required, compared with the 42 that would have occurred on a chance basis. With 84 characteristics to select among, over half the designations were to only five that supposedly typify the Negro: He was seen as superstitious, lazy, happy-go-lucky, ignorant, and musical. Just half of all the traits listed for Germans were selected from five: they were scientifically minded, industrious, stolid, intelligent, and methodical. Over half of all listings for Jews were chosen from six traits: They were shrewd, mercenary, industrious, grasping, intelligent, and ambitious. When it is seen that even these few traits are often virtual synonyms (superstitious and ignorant, scientifically minded and intelligent, mercenary and grasping), the limited picture that these students, half a century ago, had of these groups is emphasized. The pictures can scarcely be a description of reality, for the students had had relatively little contact with some of these groups and probably no contact with a few. That did not prevent them from "knowing" what they were like, for they were the heirs of a tradition that informed them.

Bayton discovered (1941) that 100 Negro students at the Virginia State College had nearly the same picture *of the Negro* that the Princeton students had, although they added a few more favorable traits (e.g., progressive) to the list.

Change and Variation in Stereotypes. Despite evidence of persistence, we must remember that these are the rankings of particular times and places. By the 1960s, forces that sustained a "black is beautiful" theme were furnishing an in-group frame of reference for America's black population more strongly than in the past. With increasing political and economic power and awareness among Blacks, dependence on Whites for standards of self-appraisal sharply declined. In 1969 (June 30, p. 14) *Newsweek* asked a national sample of Negroes: "Do you think that most Negroes agree that 'black is beautiful'?" Seventy-four percent answered yes. In another national sample, only 17 percent of the black respondents agreed with the statement that "generally speaking, Negroes are lazy and don't like to work hard" (Marx 1967a, p. 89), a statement to which 40 percent of Whites in a national sample agreed (Selznick and Steinberg

1969, p. 171). Derbyshire and Brody (1964) found that black stereotypes were largely rejected by a group of Negro college students.

There have been similar shifts in the stereotypes held by Whites. In a follow-up study, Gilbert (1951) found that Princeton students were more resistent to stereotyping in 1950 than in 1932; although the traits put at the top of the list for various national and racial groups tended to be the same, they were checked by fewer students. By 1967, Karlins, Coffman, and Walters (1969) found, in a replication of the earlier studies, that these trends were accentuated. There was still a measurable tendency for judgments to cluster around a few adjectives. Students often protested the measurement, however, and there were major changes in content, particularly with the addition of favorable characteristics to the stereotype. Four of the five traits most frequently assigned to Negroes by the 1933 students were much less likely to be selected in 1967 (see Table 5-2; see also Kurokawa 1971; Maykovich 1972).

These are average evaluations of the 1967 students, and therefore the interpretation is somewhat problematic. Adjectival meanings may have shifted since 1933; and the individuals using an adjective may not give it the degree of favorableness or unfavorableness represented by the mean (for general reviews, see Brigham 1971; Cauthen, Robinson, and Krauss 1971).

It seems probable that there has been some reduction in stereotyping in the United States and a shift toward a more favorable image for many groups (see, e.g., Sue and Kitano 1973; U.S. Commission on Civil Rights 1980a). Why the change? Referring to his 1950 college sample, Gilbert (1951) suggested that the trends reflected in part a changed student body (more persons from the lower classes), the growing influence of social science, a reduction of stereotypes in the entertainment media (Greenberg and Mazingo 1976), but perhaps also simply

Table 5-2. Characteristics Assigned to Negroes by Princeton Students (in percentages)

	1933	1951	1967
Superstitious	84	41	13
Lazy	75	31	26
Happy-go-lucky	38	17	27
Ignorant	38	24	11
Musical	26	33	47

a change in verbal conventions. Each of these factors seems operative. In a content analysis of forty-two works of fiction for children, for example, Gast (1967) discovered little negative stereotyping. Negroes were portrayed as the group most likely to be seeking higher education, and they were not cast in occupational stereotypes, although some other groups were.

Something of this same picture is found in printed advertising in the United States. Blacks are appearing more often in a more favorable light, although the full effect of the shift is not easily determined. Comparing the ads in *Life, Look, The Saturday Evening Post, Time, The New Yorker,* and *Ladies' Home Journal* for 1949–50 and 1967–68, Cox (1969–70), found that, of those ads having identifiable adults, only .57 percent had Blacks in the earlier period, while 2.17 percent of the 1967–68 ads contained Blacks. More importantly, there was a shift in the occupations portrayed. Most Whites in the ads could not be identified by occupation; most Blacks could be. In the earlier period, 6.1 percent were above the skilled labor category; in the later period, 71.3 percent were thus portrayed.

In a more intensive analysis of the themes of ads in *Reader's Digest, Look, Life,* and *Ladies' Home Journal,* Colfax and Sternberg (1972) see a more complicated picture. Despite the greater frequency with which Blacks appeared in the ads, dangers of stereotyping remained. Many of the people classified as professional were entertainers, advertising phonograph records (stereos of a different type, if you will forgive us). The ads seemed to be "the result of a complex interplay of a sense of responsibility and prejudice on the part of various advertisers and their agencies, and their imputation of similar values and motives to their markets" (Colfax and Sternberg 1972, p. 12). Blacks often appeared as tokens, part of a large, mainly white group. About ten percent of the ads dealt with the beneficiaries of private and public welfare. Although more Whites are thus helped, Blacks were disproportionately found in such ads.

Colfax and Sternberg seem to us to underestimate somewhat the change that has taken place. There is substantial truth, however, in their summary (1972, p. 18) that "mass circulation magazine advertising reflects, if not precisely and not always accurately, the values of white America, as it conveys racial stereotypes, subtle and probably unintentional, to tens of millions of predominantly white readers and consumers."

Studies of stereotypes are probably of less value in times of rapid change and among groups—whether on those doing the judging or on those being judged—that are heterogeneous. One person may offer a stereotype as his estimate of how those around him view a group; another may be stating his own view. One person may be thinking of an average or a *modal* member of the stereotyped group, leaving rather wide room for variation; another may think that the description fits most of those in a group. This latter view becomes less likely when a minority group becomes highly diversified by occupation, class, educational level, region, religion, and the like. Such diversity tends to break up the cultural element in prejudice, although it may support or even enhance prejudice based on economic conflict or status anxiety (see Hyman in Katz and Gurin 1969, pp. 11–12).

We should also note that within every society there are some individuals who for a number of reasons turn out to be atypical. They may have acquired a system of beliefs and values from some other frame of reference (a different culture, a thoroughgoing belief in science, or the teachings of religion taken seriously), or they may be simply maladjusted as individuals, with no integrated system of beliefs. From the point of view of the majority, they are heretics, radicals, and eccentrics. They do not share the dominant values of the society, and they frequently do not share its prejudices. No statement of the traditional factors in prejudice should disregard these exceptions.

There are, of course, traditions of nonprejudice as well, traditions of democracy and equality. One cannot say, therefore, that the reduction of the hold of tradition on an individual will, other things being equal, make him less prejudiced. We need to know, further, whether or not the atypical person has experienced an emotional reaction against all cultural norms, why he is atypical, and what aspects of the culture he does accept.

From the evidence in hand it seems clear that although members of a society are still likely to share some beliefs about what various groups are supposed to be like, the process of stereotyping is more complicated than it was formerly thought to be; and, though stereotypes are subject to rather continuous change, strong forces support them in their old and new forms.

Problems of Reliability and Validity in the Measurement of Stereotypes. We must be alert to problems of reliability and validity in the measurement of stereotypes. The many risks that inhere in efforts to record attitudes on fairly objective and simple verbal scales require that we hold the evidence recorded above lightly. A number of studies have shown how responses may be affected by the measuring process. Diab (1963) asked 50 Arab-Moslem students at the American University in Beirut to select adjectives that characterized 13 groups from a list of 99 adjectives. Fifty other students were asked to make their selection with reference to only seven groups (five of them being found also on the first list). Although some of the pictures were similar, there were also important changes. Americans, for example, were characterized by the first 50 students as superficial, rich, materialistic, industrial, and selfish. When several of the low-ranking groups were removed from this list for the second test, Americans tended to be contrasted more specifically with the Russians and on the whole were seen in a more favorable light. The five adjectives most selected by the second group were rich, democratic, materialistic, industrial, and sociable.

The Persistence of Stereotypes. Stereotypes are such a compound of error, exaggeration, omission, and half-truth that they tell us more about the people who believe them and the needs of the group in which they circulate than about the group to which they are supposed to refer. Stereotyped beliefs about the majority also abound in the thinking of minorities, so that interaction is, in part, not among individuals as they are but among individuals as they are thought to be.

Whether held by the majority- or the minority-group member, stereotypes are easy ways of explaining things. They take less effort and give an appearance of order without the difficult work that understanding the full order of things demands. They provide "a common language of discourse," as Ehrlich puts it, a "vocabulary of motives" for those who share them. "As a special language, stereotypes function to reinforce the beliefs and disbeliefs of its users, and to furnish the basis for the development and maintenance of solidarity for the prejudiced" (Ehrlich 1973, p. 21).

Stereotypes, Pettigrew emphasizes (1981a, pp. 316–20), are over determined, with mutually reenforcing supports from sociocultural, psychodynamic, and cognitive influences. Stereotypes affect interaction in ways that restrict disconfirming information and may actually produce confirming experience. Hamilton notes (1979, p. 59) that "the person categories I employ at any given time influence what information I retain and what kinds of inferences I make about the persons I group into those categories" (see also Rothbart in Hamilton 1981, Chapter 5; Grant and Holmes 1981; Howard and Rothbart 1980). Early encounters between members of mutually stereotyping groups often result in selective memories and also in behavioral confirmation, because interaction is guided by what members of each group believe the others are like, helping to initiate a self-fulfilling prophecy (Snyder, Chapter 6, and Rose, Chapter 8, in Hamilton 1981). This is not an uncommon occurrence in the contacts between minorities and the police. Hamiilton (1981, p. 137) observes that we sometimes have to reverse the old adage about seeing and believing to have it read: "I wouldn't have seen it if I hadn't believed it."

The larger social structure enhances the psychodynamic and cognitive sources of stereotype persistence by producing differential contacts, in jobs, schools, churches, and neighborhoods. The mass media accentuate the dramatic, the extreme. "News" by definition is sensational and surprising. Negative events capture attention and are more likely to be remembered; the nonoccurrence of an event—which is after all an event—is scarecely noticed (Pettigrew 1981a, p. 317).

These media influences illustrate, and perhaps enhance, what Pettigrew (1979) has called "the ultimate attribution error": Negative acts of members of outgroups are seen as caused by their permanent, even genetic, dispositions. Their positive acts, however, are explained by situational and transitory forces. They are exceptions, the result of luck, of special advantage, of unusual effort, or of a situation which allowed no other response. Such an attributional bias "would essentially prevent the perceiver from having to confront and cope with disconfirming evidence" (Hamilton 1979, p. 65).

Stereotypes persist in part because they are rough-hewn expressions of the process of classifying or categorizing—a necessary process for any kind of thinking. The word *chair* is an abstraction that leaves out a large number of specific traits of specific chairs in favor of general characteristics. A scientific abstraction, however, differs from a stereotype in including *all* important traits and in selecting those traits on purely rational grounds. The traits assigned to a stereotype are selected, not

usually consciously, for their ability to produce some desired effect or on the basis of an emotional predisposition.

There is doubtless some truth in many stereotypes, but the commonplace application of them as descriptive of the behavior of all the members of a group is in error in several ways:

1. The stereotype gives a highly exaggerated picture of the importance of some few characteristics—whether they be favorable or unfavorable.
2. It invents some supposed traits out of whole cloth, making them seem reasonable by association with other tendencies that may have a kernal of truth.
3. In a negative stereotype, personality tendencies that are favorable, that would have to be mentioned to give a complete picture, are either omitted entirely or insufficiently stressed.
4. The stereotype fails to show how the majority, or other groups, share the same tendencies or have other undesirable characteristics.
5. It fails to give any attention to the cause of the tendencies of the minority group—particularly to the place of the majority itself and its stereotypes in creating the very characteristics being condemned. They are thought of rather as intrinsic or even self-willed traits of the minority.
6. It leaves little room for change; there is a lag in keeping up with the tendencies that actually typify many members of a group.
7. It leaves little room for individual variation, which is always wide in human groups. One does not deal with a group average, but with specific individuals. One of the functions of stereotypes is shown by this failure to adjust to individual differences—to do so would be to destroy the discriminatory value of the stereotype. It is easy for the human mind to overlook completely or to treat as unimportant exceptions the evidence that contradicts a well-established belief (see Lieberson 1982, pp. 63–65).

The stereotyped pictures of the minority groups held by members of dominant groups are not all alike. They differ both because of the various historical circumstances out of which they grew and also because they are related to different kinds of conflict situations. But even stereotypes can be classified. One often can discern a great similarity between the stereotyped pictures of two minority groups who are related in about the same way to a dominant group. One group of stereotypes seems aimed especially at *keeping* a group down, another at *pushing* a group down that has achieved some degree of competitive power. Thus an earlier picture of the American Negro as lazy, shiftless, irresponsible, unable to acquire a skill, and unable to appreciate a higher standard of living is matched by the stereotype of the Polish worker that developed in Germany in the latter part of the last century. The same picture was drawn of the migrants to California from Oklahoma and Arkansas during the 1930s, despite the fact that they were overwhelmingly white Protestant Anglo-Saxons (McWilliams 1948, p. 163).

There is another pattern to the stereotypes of groups that have been more successful in competing with the dominant group. It would be too great a distortion of the fact to label them lazy or unintelligent, so they are pictured as too ambitious and with a crafty kind of self-interested intelligence. In various settings this picture has arisen in connection with Jews, Greeks, Syrians, Armenians, the American Japanese, overseas Chinese, and other groups. Such stereotypes indicate the skill that human beings have in interpreting almost any phenomenon so that it reinforces their established beliefs. Earlier stereotypes of the Jew, now much less harsh (see Wuthnow 1982), showed particularly clearly that it is not what the out-group does or fails to do that causes prejudice. "Superficial appearances notwithstanding, prejudice and discrimination aimed at the out-group are not a result of what the out-group does, but are rooted deep in the structure of our society and the social psychology of its members" (Merton 1968, p. 482). It is a simple matter for most of us to make what we consider virtues in ourselves into vices when they are found in the behavior of a minority-group member. Merton (1968, p. 482) puts the matter sharply:

> The very same behavior undergoes a complete change of evaluation in its transition from the in-group Abe Lincoln to the out-group Abe Cohen or Abe Kurokawa....Did Lincoln work far into the night? This testifies that he was industrious, resolute, perseverant, and eager to realize his capacities to the full. Do the out-group Jews or Japanese keep these same hours? This only bears witness to their sweatshop mentality, their ruthless undercutting of American standards, their unfair competitive practices. Is the in-group hero frugal, thrifty, and sparing? Then the out-group villain is stingy, miserly, and penny-pinching. All honor is due the in-group Abe for his having been smart, shrewd, and intelligent, and, by the same token, all contempt is owing the out-group Abes for their being sharp, cunning, crafty, and too clever by far.

Whether we are dealing with a stereotype that attacks a minority group for failing to be like the majority or with one that accuses the minority group of having virtues—but in excess—the important thing to keep in mind is that these categorical judgments are not dormant traditional items but active ingredients in human interaction, helping to shape experience, to color observations, and finally, as we shall see, to help create the very tendencies with which they were in the first instance justified.

Recent Theoretical and Methodological Work on Stereotypes. Research dealing with stereotypes is developing in various new directions. More comparative work is being undertaken; new instruments, for example multidimensional scaling and the semantic differential, are being employed; comparisons of attitudes toward peoples and toward governments are being developed; questions of validity are being explored; and the relationships between tendencies to stereotype and other qualities—ease in interracial contacts, for example, or acquaintanceship with and liking for a group—are being studied (see, e.g., Ehrlich 1973, Chapter 2; Funk et al. 1976; Hamilton 1981; Miller 1982; Stewart, Powell, and Chetwynd 1979).

The most significant change in the study of stereotypes is the growing tendency to bring it more fully within the framework of general social scientific theory, particularly that of cognitive social psychology. Commenting on the work of Tajfel (1969), Hamilton (1981, p. 336) observes that there is strong evidence that the judgmental and behavioral phenomena of stereotyping can be based on the common processess of categorization alone, not requiring prejudices or self-interest:

> That is, the discriminatory behavior evidenced by Tajfel's subjects occurred in the absence of conditions typically thought to underlie intergroup discrimination—prior hostile attitudes toward the outgroup, intergroup competition, opportunity for personal gain as a result of discriminatory behavior, and so forth.

According to the cognitive perspective "the human capacity for processing information is limited," (i.e., we can be pretty dumb) so that apparent breakdowns in perception and cognition need not be attributed to motivational factors or inadequate available information" (Ashmore and DelBoca in Hamilton 1981, p. 29).

It is possible to overemphasize as well as underemphasize the cognitive aspects of stereotyping—neglecting the affective and the cultural aspects and their interaction with cognition. As our interpretation shows, however, we share the view here, as we did in the discussion of prejudice generally in Chapter 4, that cognitive elements are of great importance in the stereotyping process. In classifying, storing, and retrieving information, to use computer language, stereotypes play a part in ways that make them influential in the formation of our judgments. There is experimental evidence of a tendency to favor members of an in-group, even when persons have been assigned to in- or outgroups on a purely arbitrary basis. And "subjects expected members of the same group to have more similar beliefs...even though they were aware that the group had been arbitrarily formed" (Wilder 1978, p. 13; see also Allen and Wilder 1975; Wilder in Hamilton 1981, Chapter 7).

A number of recent studies have examined the boundaries of the groups to which stereotypes refer. Those boundaries become uncertain in times of change. The very large groups—races, classes, sexes, or ages—which have commonly been the focus of attention are too broad "to capture adequately the actual nature of perceivers' conceptions" (Hamilton 1981, p. 377). When ninety percent of America's black population lived in the South, mainly in rural area, it was relatively easier to use a single stereotype—however inadequate—than it is today. As Taylor suggests (in Hamilton 1981, p. 106), the decline in the Katz–Braly type of stereotyping that we discussed earlier may simply indicate a shift to less encompassing groups.

The behavioral consequences of stereotyping have been a topic of increasing interest. We are concerned here more with the effects on those who use stereotypes, reserving until Chapter 6 most of our comments on the effects on their targets. Although we will not refer directly to the extensive literature on labeling, it raises a large number of theoretical and methodological issues that overlap

our interest here in stereotyping (see, e.g., Gove 1975; Hagan 1973; Mercer 1973; Rosenthal and Jacobson 1968; Scheff 1974). A stereotype is a kind of label. Those who use it act, in many situations, in a way consonant with it. Rubovits and Maehr (1973) studied the actions of women undergraduates enrolled in a teacher-training course as they taught four junior high school students of comparable ability—two of them Black, two White. The teachers were provided with a teaching chart which gave the first names of the students, their IQ scores, and an indication of whether they were from the school's gifted program or from the regular "track." The students were randomly assigned high IQ scores and the "gifted" label. Teacher–student interaction was coded for each 40-minute session by an observer. Black students "were given less attention, ignored more, praised less and criticized more" (Rubovits and Maehr 1973, p. 217). This was somewhat more likely to be the experience of the gifted black students than of those in the regular track.

Word, Zanna, and Cooper (1974) trained white and black "job applicants" to respond in similar ways to job interviews. Nevertheless, the black applicants received less satisfactory interview treatment. There was less eye contact with the interviewer, less expressed interest, more speech errors by the interviewer, and less time given. They found also that this poorer treatment led to poorer interview performance, thus contributing to a vicious circle.

Summarizing their case studies of sixty-one young black men in Boston, Rosenthal and his associates (1976, p. 304) remark that "the most striking and probably the most significant conclusions...are the pervasiveness of stereotyped thinking about them and the destructive results of such thinking." Their observations remind us that the effects of stereotypes on those who hold them cannot be separated from their effects on those who are thus categorized.

Symbolic Racism

The evidence is quite conclusive that feelings of social distance, both normative and personal, of the majority toward minorities in the United States have been reduced in recent years. So also has stereotypy. Does this mean that the cultural supports for prejudice and discrimination have declined? Probably so, but not by the amount that the measures of social distance and stereotypy would lead one to believe (Brigham, Woodmansee, and Cook 1976; Rosenthal 1980). The persistent opposition to residential and school integration, despite increases in both, opposition to affirmative action programs designed to reduce the occupational disadvantages of minorities, and the slow rate of increase in interpersonal contact across racial lines, as illustrative issues, have led some observers to the belief that cultural support for prejudice and discrimination has shifted in the nature of its expression more than it has declined.

This point of view has recently been expressed by the use of the concept of *symbolic racism*. The term has been used primarily to account for the fact that even among suburban Whites who experience little occupational or residential threat from minorities and who shun stereotypes, opposition to minorities continues at quite a high level. Reference has been mainly to antiblack actions, for example, opposition to racial busing or voting against a black mayoral candidate in Los Angeles even by those who "did not score high on the traditional indices of anti-black prejudice" (Ashmore and DelBoca 1976, p. 106; Kinder and Sears 1981). As we noted in Chapter 4, symbolic racism refers to resistance to change in the racial order based on feelings that members of a minority race violate traditional values—self-reliance, the work ethic, obedience, and discipline.

Whites may feel that people should be rewarded on their merits, which in turn should be based on hard work and diligent service. Hence symbolic racism should find its most vociferous expression on political issues that involve "unfair" government assistance to blacks; welfare ("welfare cheats could find work if they tried"); "reverse discrimination" and racial quotas ("blacks should not be given a status they have not earned"); "forced" busing ("whites have worked hard for their neighborhood schools"); or "free" abortions for the poor ("if blacks behaved morally, they would not need abortions"). (Kinder and Sears 1981, p. 416)

Minorities who challenge the status quo are identified by some persons as major forces threatening what are seen as central values. McConahay and Hough (1976) contrast symbolic racism with "red-neck" racism, the latter based on "old-fashioned" stereotypes and prejudice. (We do not like the term because it runs the risk, ironically in a study of stereotyping, of supporting a stereotyped view of the people thus identified. We shall use the term, however, in the purely descriptive sense undoubtedly intended by McConahay and Hough.) Among their respondents, there was little correlation between scores on scales designed to measure red-neck and symbolic racism. They conclude, on the basis of their studies of black–white relationships, that symbolic racism can best be defined as "the expression in terms of abstract ideological symbols and symbolic behaviors of the feeling that blacks are violating cherished values and making illegitimate demands for changes in the racial status quo" (McConahay and Hough 1976 p. 38).

The distinction between symbolic racism on one hand and feelings of social distance and stereotypy on the other is not as sharp as these comments may seem to indicate. Kinder and Sears see the roots of symbolic racism not only in "deep-seated feelings of social morality and propriety," but also "in early-learned racial fears and stereotypes." In a similar way, McConahay and Hough (1976, p. 39) identify three roots of symbolic racism in early socialization: traditional religious and value socialization; socialization to laissez faire political conservatism, and unacknowledged, negative feelings toward Blacks.

This gives symbolic racism a potent one-two-three punch as the independent effects of these residues of socialization are cumulative. Two of the three roots also provide ready-made nonracial rationalizations for symbolic racism behavior.

Although feelings of social distance, stereotyping, and symbolic racism can be distinguished conceptually, they are closely related, and collectively they represent current ways of thinking about the cultural element in prejudice.

"Facts" as the Embodiment and Support of a Tradition of Prejudice

Having noted the important place of essentially false stereotypes in our judgments of minority groups, must we conclude that there are no important differences among human groups? Are our observations so completely distorted by the "pictures in our heads" that reality disappears? Apparently when majority-group members look around for confirmation of the "inferiority" of minority groups, they do not look entirely in vain (Mackie 1973). This point needs careful study, for it has been the subject of much misunderstanding. Most people like to think of themselves as rational. They would probably not accept a tradition of prejudice as readily as they do if they could not, in daily experiences, find support—or what seems to be support—for the validity (granted certain premises) of the tradition. Stereotypes, as we have seen, lend a kind of support; the beliefs and verbalizations of other people, the definitions of roles found in the culture—these are taken by most people as evidence of the inferiority of some groups. And for many people this is all the evidence they ever have, for they lack contact with the minority groups themselves.

Some majority-group members, however, see for themselves. And what do they see? Disregard now the selectivity of perception. Blacks and Chicanos, on the average, for example, live in poorer houses than majority Whites; they perform more menial tasks; they are more often poorly educated. The characteristics of minorities can be made to seem a confirmation of the tradition of prejudice; minority-group members are given an inferior status because that is the only one they deserve or can fill. In other words, these "facts" are the basis of a theory of prejudice. The traits of a minority group are the cause of its low status, not the result of that status.

That this is an inadequate theory our whole discussion to this point should demonstrate. The word *cause,* however, is a slippery concept. Many scientists and philosophers have stopped using it entirely because of the misunderstandings that result from its naive application. Only the use of the concept of many *levels of causation* can prevent the attempt to explain a phenomenon by one surface relationship. Behind each cause is another cause, and behind that another, and the third may, in turn, affect the first. Science is not interested in finding the ultimate cause but in describing the total group of interacting forces that occur in connection with the phenomenon being studied. Some forces, to be sure, may be more important than others. This is determined by a simple criterion: How consistently does the force occur in connection with the phenomenon when other forces are controlled? How well can one predict the occurrence of the phenomenon by analysis of the presumed cause?

The Principle of Cumulation

From this point of view, the attempt to explain prejudice as a result of the inferiority of minority-group members is very inadequate. There can be inferiority without prejudice; and there can be prejudice without inferiority. Even when the two occur together the likelihood is that the majority group assumes a *post hoc, ergo propter hoc* relationship that is not justified. It is reported that during the London blitz in World War II rescue workers were tunneling into a demolished house when they discovered a frightened but unhurt old man sitting in a bathtub. He was shaking his head, looking very puzzled, and mumbling: "I can't understand it! I can't understand it! I pulled out the plug and the house blew up." Majority-group members are less modest. They declare: "We do understand it. We grew up observing the factual inferiority of minority-group members, and our attitudes toward them are simply a result of that fact." Our anology here is not perfect, for presumably the bathtub plug was not a booby trap; it was completely uninvolved in the cycle of forces that led to the demolition of the house. The alleged inferiority of minorities, however, is a booby trap; it helps to detonate discriminatory activities. To be sure, that inferiority is in part the product of prejudice and discrimination in the first place; but *once established,* it becomes a part of the cycle of interaction. This is the interaction that Myrdal has described as "the vicious circle." If a group of forces have created an inferior status for a minority, there will appear, both as rationalization of the discrimination shown and as a result of the fact of observation of that inferior status, an attitude of prejudice toward the minority group. Such prejudice will block members of the group perceived as inferior from the life chances necessary to advancement. By limiting the opportunities of a minority group, by segregating it, by putting it at every competitive disadvantage, the prejudice helps to create the very inferiority by which it seems justified in the minds of the dominant group. Start out by saying that the black man is inferior; use this as the reason for giving him poor schools, poor jobs, poor opportunities for advancement; and one soon proves himself correct by creating and enforcing that very inferiority. This in turn, will deepen the prejudice, which, again, will further restrict the opportunities of the minority person (Myrdal 1944, pp. 75-78).

MacIver (1948, pp. 52–81) and Merton (1968,

pp. 475–90) have shown how the idea of the vicious circle in race relations can be seen as one manifestation of a general principle, the self-fulfilling prophecy. People respond not only to the objective features of a situation, but to their own definition of that situation—to the meaning it has for them. Even though the original definition of the situation is false, it may, by becoming part of the interacting forces, help to make itself true. A rumor (a false definition) spreads that the local bank is insolvent; a run on the bank starts; and, since no bank can immediately honor all claims upon it, the bank has to close. "The rumor is self-confirming." This self-fulfilling postulate is not completely circular, since the original state does not recur, but it illustrates how a belief—and actions based upon it—can produce the very situation with which it is supposed to have started. In other situations the interaction is circular. "The process of international armament may run as follows: armament in country A → fear in country B → armament in country B → fear in country A → armament in country A, and so on ad infinitum → or ad bellum" (MacIver 1948; p. 63). This kind of sequence in race relations would move from discrimination to conditions confirmed or imposed by discrimination back to discrimination.

The various forces with which we have been concerned can be brought within a general field theoretical statement. What we see is a *feedback system* of human events, with primary processes being influenced and often reenforced by their own consequences.

Several observations are required to interpret this system. The forces listed in A and the results listed in B (Figure 5-1) can have consequences other than those noted here. We disregard those other consequences to focus on the discrimination cycle. As we shall see in Part III, the rigidity or continuity implied in the system we have described becomes problematic when that system is seen as part of a larger pattern. The discrimination cycle in the United States is part of a larger system containing various tensions—religious and political norms and values opposed to discrimination, for example. When these are strengthened, a formerly fairly stable smaller system of discrimination tends to break up. Yet it is a "tough" system; it has homeostatic properties that bring it back to "normal" unless the disrupting outer pressures are continuous and strong. Some of those who regret what they see as a conservative bias in this kind of analysis (mistaking the judgment that systems have self-

sustaining qualities for approval of such systems) are also quick to lament the "conservative toughness" of the system of discrimination. In our judgment, field theoretical interpretations of functional systems need not have any conservative bias. Carefully stated, they identify the conditions under which various cycles of causation are broken up (see Yinger 1970, Chapters 5 and 6).

The theory of the vicious circle is, to be sure, only one part of a complex explanation of prejudice. The vicious circle sustains prejudice but does not create it. That the support of "facts" is not essential to prejudice is shown by the elaborate cultural equipment for prejudice that most Americans share even when they know no facts, when they have had no contact with the people to whom the prejudice refers. Nor could appeal to the "facts" justify the categorical nature of prejudice—for the facts are very uncategorical. The "facts" help to sustain prejudice only because of man's capacity for partial observations, rigid ideas, and poor logic.

It should be stated again that in saying the facts of group differences may support prejudice we have taken the point of view of the prejudiced person: *to him* they are a proof of the reasonableness of his attitudes. That he is in error, from the point of view of the scientist, does not prevent his attitude from being a factor in prejudice. We have already noted some of the errors involved in the reasoning that uses the facts of group differences to support prejudice, but it may be well to summarize them.

1. The minority groups are not inferior in any absolute sense, but only relative to the standards of the dominant group. The "proof" that the prejudice is justified, therefore, is convincing only to a person who accepts the values of the dominant group as absolutely valid.

2. Reality is taken *as is* by the prejudiced person. He is scarcely interested in *why* minority groups are "inferior"; or his explanation is likely to be very simple—it is their nature.

This kind of "logic" or use of evidence is doubtless encouraged by the fact that it comes out with the "right" answer—the answer that profits the individual or group using it or corresponds to their established notions. It may be due in part, however, to a cultural pattern of thought. We are gradually discovering that the forms of logic and the kinds of evidences that one will accept are to some degree cultural. The kind of thinking that "explains" prejudice by the "nature" of minority groups is the *substantive mode of mentality,* "the tendency to

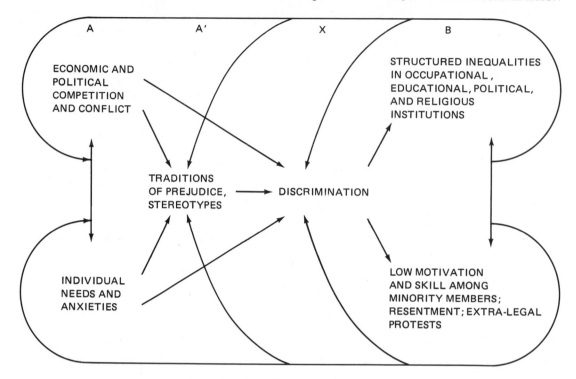

Figure 5-1. The field context of discrimination.

account for or describe events (social and otherwise) in terms of the 'essence' of things instead of in terms of related processes" (Sherif 1948, p. 361). This is an easy kind of thinking; it gives the answer by an examination of surface relationships without concern for the complicated chains of events that preceded those relationships.

More and more people are accepting the *process mode of mentality* (Sherif 1948, pp. 359–61) in dealing with the physical world. If something goes wrong with one's car, he is not likely to say that it is the "nature" of cars to behave that way; he looks for or has an expert look for a disturbance in the usual process. Gradually that way of looking at things is being applied to human behavior. It is less commonly said today then formerly that children behave in a particular way "because it is the nature of children." We are beginning to be interested in the sequence of events that leads to certain behavior. At least a few people are beginning to study criminal behavior and abnormal behavior in the same way. To say that a person commits a crime because he is criminal by nature is as useless a statement as to say that a person or group is in an inferior status because he or it is inferior by

nature. To some degree, this kind of explanation is simply part of our cultural equipment; but there seems to be a trend—however slow in its reference to human behavior—toward the process mode of mentality. Meanwhile "facts" support prejudice.

3. Another error in the assumption that prejudice is simply a description of reality is the use of incomplete and distorted pictures of reality. The truth, the whole truth, and nothing but the truth would support prejudice far less effectively than the part-truth, the half-truth, and error with the truth. Human events are almost always ambiguous, and our preconceived notions assign them the proper interpretation. What is thrifty, businesslike behavior in our gentile neighbor may be stingy, unfair competition from our Jewish competitor. In such circumstances it is difficult to know what "facts" are justifying prejudice. The "sampling errors of experience" give us only a one-sided view of the "facts." We know the Black janitor, but not the Black author; the Mexican field hand, but not the Mexican doctor (Krech and Crutchfield 1948, pp. 466–67).

Thus the facts of group differences are a reinforcement to prejudice only for the superficial and biased observer. Since a high proportion of us are superficial and biased observers, however, an adequate theory of prejudice must take account of this factor.

How Does the Individual Acquire the Traditions of Prejudice?

We have discussed the traditional element in prejudice—its place as part of culture, embodied in stereotypes and supported by selective observation of facts. Now comes the question: How is this tradition transferred to the maturing individuals of a new generation?

It is now universally agreed among scientists that there are no innate antipathies toward the members of different racial, national, religious, or other groups. We have to learn whom to dislike just as we learn other group norms. Babies are iconoclast, with no respect for even the most cherished beliefs of their elders. They are dependent, however, on adults for the satisfaction of most of their needs; adults are likely to reward and punish according to their orthodoxy. Sometimes a child will take quite a bit of punishment before acquiring the proper prejudices. Black and white boys, for example, may have a common interest in a game or sport that for some time brings enough pleasure to outweigh the requests, threats, or punishments that some parents bring upon their children. Prejudice is usually acquired less painfully than that. The very acquisition of language may start a child off with a mind-set favorable to the absorption of the traditions of prejudice. Some things are "white and clean," others are "dirty and black." The more serious conversations of adults that children overhear may refer to the inferiority or undesirable traits of several minority groups. Those traits will be associated with observations of the social segregation of those groups, seeming to confirm their inferiority. Parents may change the subject when a child raises questions about group differences and relationships that the parents do not know how to answer. Thus they convey the impression that the topic is anxiety laden (Ashmore and DelBoca 1976, p. 96).

These influences will be joined, even in the young child, with several of the needs discussed in Chapter 4. The need for belonging, for feeling secure in relation to the groups with which one is most closely identified, will be served by accepting the values of those groups. These feelings, and with them the tendencies toward prejudice, can begin very early in life (Ehrlich 1973, Chapter 5). The prejudices of small children, however, are likely to be inconsistent, because the hierarchy of attitudes has not become well established. One cannot predict which value will come to the fore in a specific instance. A small child may have been taught to dislike Negroes but to like curly hair. He may then show an "inconsistency" in his prejudice by expressing liking for a curly-haired Negro (Horowitz 1939). Gradually the child learns which kinds of attitudes take precedence in his social group. At first he will explain his negative responses on the basis of differences between himself and the disliked person. The older child, however, will increasingly recognize the role of social pressure. If asked why he dislikes the members of a minority group, he will recite the reasons taught him by his culture, by the adults around him—always assuming, of course, that they are strictly his own reasons and that they are the true reasons. He has forgotten the punishment, the threats, the stories and jokes that have given him the prejudice. The cultural norm is now his norm; he is socialized.

The largely unintended instruction from parents is reenforced by signals from schools and the media. Although explicit stereotyping has been reduced, minority underrepresentation—sometimes approaching invisibility—keeps majority-group members unaware of what minority-group members are like, makes it easy for inferences of belief incongruity to develop, and supports feelings of social distance (Ashmore and DelBoca 1976, p. 98). Although visibility in the purely numerical sense has increased, especially on television (Greenberg and Mazingo 1976), story lines—with such notable exceptions as "Roots" and "The Autobiography of Miss Jane Pittman"—continue to portray Blacks, as the United States Civil Rights Commission has reported, in a "disproportionately high number of immature, demeaning, and comical roles" (*The New York Times*, February 18, 1979, p. D35). In England, Bagley observes (1979, p. 157), "Irishmen are portrayed" by British comedians "as stupid and untrustworthy. Asians are cringing and servile."

With the approach of adolescence and the beginning of "dating" the line between proper and improper associates is likely to be drawn more sharply by adults, as contrasted with the more tolerant attitude often shown toward interracial or other intergroup activities among small children. At the same time, the peer influences among adolescents grow in importance.

We do not mean to imply by this discussion that prejudice is the inevitable product of socialization. Tolerance and attitudes of intergroup harmony are also taught. Stereotyped views do change, as we have noted. It is interesting and unfortunate, however, that less is known about the development of attitudes of nonprejudice than about the origins and persistence of stereotypes and social distance.

Conclusion

In this chapter we have examined the role of tradition in sustaining and passing along a prejudice. The analysis of personality needs and group conflicts can go a long way toward answering the question, "Why prejudice and discrimination?" but it cannot explain "Why toward this group?" The choice of a target for group hostility frequently rests upon historical conflicts that have been fixed in tradition. There can also be traditions of nonprejudice, of course, that emerge out of one group of circumstances but survive to affect others. Part of what Myrdal calls "the American creed" is a product of the French and American revolutions—times when concepts of equality were effective weapons for rallying the support of the masses to the middle class. Equality was a useful idea then. Once lodged in the democratic societies, it became fixed in tradition, supported by some institutional structures, and passed on to later generations. Many have found it an embarrassing idea that runs counter to their group or individual interests. Yet they cannot escape all of its influence over them. The idea of equality has some power to react back upon the society that carries it.

In examining the three clusters of factors involved in intergroup hostility, we have noted that the distinctions drawn were analytic. In virtually every case the several elements are interactive and mutually reinforcing. The use of prejudice as an economic weapon strengthens the tradition, and the presence of the tradition makes it easier to employ prejudice in economic conflict. A stereotype facilitates projection; and having projected one's faults onto a minority group, one's belief in the stereotype is stengthened. Moreover, discriminatory acts tend to affect the members of the minority group involved

in such a way as to create superficial justification for the original activity. The often baffling tenacity of prejudice, in the face of emotional and rational appeals, moral arguments, and proof that it is against obvious self-interest, can be understood only by an appreciation of the interaction of the many forces involved and their consequent strength. Myrdal exaggerated the ease with which prejudice can be changed when he said that a change in any one segment of the interacting circle will have effects on all other segments. The impulse toward change may be temporary and local; it may be submerged by the cumulative force of the continuing factors in prejudice. A labor shortage, for example, may temporarily obscure the economic element in discrimination against minority groups, but it will not necessarily produce a long-run reduction in prejudice. The mutually interlocking and sustaining forces of prejudice give it power of recovery. We do not mean that prejudice as a cultural element cannot be reduced but only that it has a strength that one-factor analyses are likely to minimize. As MacIver put it (1948, p. 71):

Hence we must revise the proposition that an upward change anywhere in the lower caste complex will tend to raise all the other conditions within it. Instead we should say that *a favorable change in any one of the distinctive conditions will, if it can be held constant long enough, tend to raise the other conditions and to bring about a readjustment of the whole system in conformity with the favorable change.* By "long enough" we denote the period within which the requisite habituations and reconditionings, the responses of the group to the altered condition, are formed and established. (MacIver's emphasis)

A person may experience a vigorous attack on his or her prejudice—a scientific course of study or close acquaintance with atypical (from his or her point of view) members of a minority group. A slight reshuffling of some of the surface manifestations of the prejudice may be required, some new rationalizations, the granting of a few more "exceptions"; *but these very changes may be a way of protecting the core of the prejudice unaltered unless the challenge is sustained.*

Prejudice is a deep-rooted part of American culture, a vital part of the adjustment system of most individuals, a weapon in economic and political conflict, an example of standard but quite inadequate intellectual functioning, a significant part of the stream of tradition that brings the influences of the past into the present and puts them to use in contemporary conflicts. As we turn to the study of its effects, we must keep steadily in mind the complex and interlocked forces that sustain it.

The next three chapters will examine some of the consequences of discrimination and prejudice, first for those against whom they are directed and then for whose who use them. It is too simple to designate these consequences as effects only, with the factors we have discussed being regarded as the causes. Once established, these consequences become part of the total interaction by which prejudice and discrimination are sustained, part of the total causal complex.

CHAPTER 6

The Consequences of Prejudice and Discrimination

THE RESPONSES OF MINORITY-GROUP MEMBERS

Having discussed the roots of discrimination and prejudice, we turn now to the fruit—to their consequences. Fruits can produce seeds that help to start new roots. That is, we are dealing to some degree with self-reenforcing systems.

There are two closely related but distinguishable consequences of intergroup hostility for minority-group members: the effects on the tendencies of individuals and the effects on the structures and processes of the groups to which they belong and the social processes they participate in. We are not concerned here with specific institutions; these will receive a great deal of attention in Part II. In this chapter and the next we shall refer mainly to the general principles of personality formation and to some degree to the group processes and structures that underlie the specific economic, political, familial, educational, and religious factors that affect the lives of minority-group members.

Does Minority Status Affect Personality?

It is a matter of common observation that on the average members of the minority groups may exhibit ways of behaving that are somewhat different from those of majority-group members. The differences are often exaggerated by the dominant group; it is assumed that they mark the minority group as inferior; the heterogeneity of each group is overlooked, and differences are usually explained, if at all, by inadequate concepts. These errors should not, however, obscure the differences in personality that may result from the important differences in experience. It would be surprising indeed if the whole range of influences at work on the individual who is a member of a minority group did not produce different tendencies from those that result from majority-group membership. It must be added, of course, that minority and majority are likely to have many more values and aspirations and behavioral tendencies in common than differences that separate them. But in a study of prejudice it is primarily the differences that count.

Members of the dominant group are likely to take these differences thoroughly for granted, assuming them to be signs of superiority–inferiority rankings. The task of an adequate sociology and social psychology dealing with this problem is to try to answer four questions.

1. What, specifically, are the differences in personality tendencies? This question cannot be answered by studying the partial and biased stereotypes that are so frequently used as "evidence."

2. What personality tendencies of minority-group members are the result of factors that happen

111

simply to be correlated with minority-group status but are not the direct product of that status? The recency of migration from rural settings may be involved. Many aspects of behavior are the consequences of class status, not simply of prejudice. They are shared with fellow class members of other races and groups. Prejudice doubtless increases the likelihood that a minority-group member will be a member of the lower class and thus lies behind this tendency; but the class factor *per se* must also be considered (Pettigrew 1981b).

3. What value stands are stated or implied in the study of personality? This is an important question, because not only do the members of the dominant group assume that the behavior of the minority group is inferior but most studies, while maintaining objectivity in the explanation of causes of behavior, *assume* the value stand of the dominant group in evaluating the results.

4. The fourth question is the basic one. What are the causes of observed differences in tendencies between members of majority and minority groups? We cannot be content with observing them or taking them for granted. In Chapter 2 we saw that a racial-biological explanation of behavioral differences was virtually useless. Not that biological factors are unimportant, but they do not vary in any important way with race. For any differences in behavior that vary from group to group we must look to differences in experience.

We have avoided the term *trait* in our discussion of personality. Unless carefully defined, it is likely to carry the connotation of a fixed and rigid aspect of personality, perhaps of an innate origin and not varying with the situation in which the person is behaving. The attempt to explain an individual's behavior by an analysis of his traits fails to give sufficient attention to the fact that what a person *is* cannot be defined independently of the whole situation with which he is interacting. Each person has a great many potentialities for behavior. Which ones will appear depends upon the situation, but none can appear for which there is no potentiality. If we look to the traits of members of dominant and minority groups as the "causes" of their behavior, even if we have accounted for them by reference to their differing experiences, we shall add a rigidity to our observations that will block understanding.

Keeping these four questions in mind, we can turn to the study of the personality consequences of prejudice and discrimination, to an examination of the way children acquire basic attitudes toward themselves, toward the norms of the groups of which they are members and the norms of the larger society, and toward those in authority. These aspects of personality are the results of experiences with others, the ways they define roles, the ways in which they encourage children (by their behavior toward them) to look at themselves—all conditioned, of course, by particular inherited tendencies and previous experiences. In Cooley's classic phrase, we have a "looking-glass self," compounded of others' reactions to us, our interpretations of those reactions, and a response to the interpretation. Or, as Mead put it, we know ourselves only by "taking the role of the other," by reacting to ourselves as we imagine others react toward us. We shall need to ask who those "others" are who are especially significant. In time we learn to take the role of the "generalized other"—the norms of society and the groups with which we are associated. We come to see ourselves, to an important degree, in the light of these norms.

Variables That Affect the Responses of Minority-Group Members

Before turning to specific personality consequences of discrimination and prejudice we must take careful note of the many variables that affect the nature of the experience for a minority-group member. We shall draw chiefly upon studies of black Americans, with regard to whom the evidence is more extensive than for other minorities. The same need for subclassifying on the basis of several factors, however, applies to any minority group. Not only the amount and the type but also the meaning of discrimination and prejudice for members of minority groups will vary according to such factors as these: nature of parental advice and training with regard to the dominant group; extent to which minority cultural elements facilitate adaptation or make it difficult (Mirowsky and Ross 1980); level of education; income; occupation; temperament of the individual; amount of minority-group solidarity; nature of minority–majority contact (contrast the experience of the north European immigrant, for example, with that of the American Indian in terms of the kinds of contact they had with the dominant group); region of the country; nature of surrounding group response to discrimination; type of neighborhood (compare the higher frequency of the perception of society as normless in "streetcorner" neighborhoods than in stable communities (Kapsis 1979); age; extent of experience with other intergroup patterns (for example, the Jamaica-born Black in Harlem, the native New Yorker, and the migrant from Georgia will see "the same" situation differently); color variations within the minority group (there is ample evidence that light-skinned and dark-skinned persons have, in many ways, significantly different experiences although this differentiating factor has become less important [Goering 1972; Rosenberg and Simmons 1972; Udry, Bauman, and Chase 1971]).

It is also essential to be aware of the clustering of variables, because what may seem to be a crucial variable may appear so because it is correlated with another. Age is negatively correlated with education, for example. When education is controlled, the effects of age on attitudes of Blacks toward Whites or toward integration are sharply reduced (Brunswick 1970). We cannot discuss every possible combination, for even with subdivision on the basis of only five or six variables there would be hundreds of subgroups; but frequent reference to the different effects of discrimination and prejudice on persons who vary in many ways will help us to avoid stereotypy. It will also alert us to the need to study, not some general Chicano or Native American or Black experience, but the wide range of experiences of persons possessing different tendencies and facing diverse situations.

The world of the minority-group member is shaped not only by individual experiences but also by group responses that are passed along in a stream of culture. The experience of parents and grandparents are built into their personalities, shaping the ways in which they deal with their children and affecting the kinds of advice and the unconsciously chosen influences they furnish to the growing generation. Fear and insecurity and hostility are thus to some degree cumulative, as, of course, are pride and courage.

These references to the variables affecting the responses of minority-group members to their deprivations can well be illustrated by reference to the experience of slavery.

Personality Influences of Slavery

In Chapter 3 we discussed slavery as a system of exploitation and control. Our interest there was in seeing this most severe form of discrimination as an illustration of the economic roots of systems of racial domination. That is only part of the picture, of course. Slavery has personal consequences for all of those involved; and we must note here the range of responses of those who suffered under its yoke—responses that range from angry protest, to creative adjustment to the power of the master, to docile accommodation.

The literature on slavery is enormous, but we will limit ourselves to several important works that have appeared in the last few decades, based on intensive research into the historical records. In addition to the fact that the evidence is complex and ambiguous, perspectives and ideologies influence interpretations of the effects of slavery. Two values—both humane and sympathetic—affect interpretations in opposite ways. Writers who focus on the cruelties of slavery, the crushing impact of discrimination, describe the personality damage. Those who focus on the human capacity to deal with adversity, to deflect negative appraisals, to develop supportive communities, describe the direct and indirect forms of creative resistance by the presumably powerless.

The most influential of the works describing the destructive power of slavery is Stanley Elkins's *Slavery* (1959). Even after due allowance is made for exaggeration and caricature, he observes, there is good evidence that the "Sambo" of fable and story is not wholly a figment of the imagination. In North American there were strong elements of docility, irresponsibility, laziness, and childish dependence among the slaves. How is one to account for such tendencies? Certainly not by reference to the African background, for contemporary research has well documented the energy and vitality of West African tribal life (Herskovits 1962). Nor is slavery *per se* the source of the Sambo tendencies, for they are not to be found, Elkins believed, among the slaves in Latin American societies. In North America, however, the utter dependence of the slave on the master created for him a permanent childlike status. The shock of capture and transport (two-thirds of the fifteen million taken died before reaching the Americas), the annihilation of the social ground for past standards (partly by random purchase and partly by owner design), and most importantly the entrance into a closed system wherein the master had virtually complete power, all combined to force onto the slave a highly constricted mode of adjustment. The master was the overwhelmingly "significant other," on whom all lines of authority converged. He had to be seen by the slave as somehow good, or else the world would be unbearably destructive.

Elkins draws a parallel between the utterly closed condition of North American slavery and the life of the concentration camp. He notes their similar personality consequences. After a time, most of those who survived in the concentration camps of Hitler's Germany took on many of the values of the guards, who wielded the decision of life or death. The prisoners felt utter depersonalization, the loss of past values and identities; they acquired a childlike dependence; their interests and values became those of children (Bettelheim 1943; Milosz 1953).

Once established, such tendencies may be perpetuated, through the socialization of children by parents and by the operation of self-fulfilling cycles. Thus the Sambo of slave days has something in common, Elkins observed, with the plantation field hand a century later. Much of this, of course, can be explained by the perpetuation of the conditions of a fixed low status and of overwhelming dependence.

Stampp (1965) also emphasized "childish" behavior and irresponsibility as outcomes of slavery. He saw them, however, not as deeply ingrained tendencies, but as adjustments that in part disguised resentment and resistance, an observation that Powdermaker (1943) had made earlier. This is a step in the direction of the second interpretation noted above, an interpretation that emphasizes the ability of an oppressed group to fight back, on the psychological level and in its groups. Genovese (1970, p. 35; see also 1974) suggests that we miss many subtle forms of resistance and effective adaptation when we think in terms of "defenseless slaves":

Although any individual at any given moment may be defenseless, a whole people rarely if ever is. A people may be on the defensive and dangerously exposed, but it often finds its own ways to survive and fight back....From this point of view, the most ignorant of the field slaves who followed the conjurer on the plantation was saying no to the boss and seeking a form of cultural autonomy. That the conjurer may in any one case have been a fraud and even a kind of extortionist, and in another case a genuine popular religious leader is, from this point of view, of little importance.

Although primarily interested in slavery as an economic system, Fogel and Engerman (1974) sharply criticize the tendency to view slaves as incompetent. They regard this as a stereotype created, ironically, more by the abolitionists—in their desire to show the cruelty of slavery—than by those who approved of slavery. (It is doubly ironic that in emphasizing the efficiency of slaves as workers, on many levels of skill, Fogel and Engerman tend to neglect the cruelty of any system of human bondage.)

Gutman, in *The Black Family in Slavery and Freedom* (1976), has most persuasively emphasized the adaptibility of slaves, the development of kin networks, the strength and continuity of slave communities. They had the ingenuity and power to prevent themselves from being trapped in the kind of concentration camp situation described by Elkins.

In his excellent comparative study, Patterson (1982, Chapter 3) comes close to combining these two perspectives. Drawing on anthropological studies of pollution, however, he stresses the debasement in slavery—the result of owners' efforts to enhance their own prestige—more than slaves' skills in resisting personal degradation.

It is difficult to separate fact from ideology in dealing with a complex issue when the full range of evidences is lacking. Elkins expressed his sympathy for black Americans by saying that interpretations of the personalities of slaves based on notions of racial inferiority are false. The enormous coercive power of the slave system is the cause. Stampp, Genovese, Gutman, and others, in various ways, express their sympathy by saying that despite the crushing impact of the slave system, America's black population found ways to show resistance, to adjust to enormous burdens, and to make creative responses. We are inclined to think that both of these interpretations are of value, to varying degrees in different times and places. Additional research will doubtless help us to understand slavery more fully; but more importantly it will show the diversity of responses to discrimination and the forms of adaptation and resistance to it under a range of conditions.

Responding to the Culture of the Dominant Group

One of the most important questions in the study of intergroup relations is the likelihood that members of a minority group will, in various circumstances, become assimilated to the dominant culture. When will they take on the pattern of motivation and morality that the majority group considers right? Is that, in fact, a desirable goal to strive for? And desirable or not, will the acquisition of the dominant values and tendencies promote improvement in the status of minority group members? We have seen that prejudiced persons often justify their attitudes and actions by reference to the supposed inferior behavior and ideals of the members of the minority group. Is that inferiority—in terms of the standards of the dominant group—in a significant way the very product of prejudice and discrimination?

There are many problems of policy and morality, as well as of science, in this set of questions. The operation and management of more and more complex societies requires a sharp increase in the proportion of the population able and willing to undertake strenuous educational programs. Yet the motivation for such undertakings is not automatic, even when opportunities are opened up. And the desire to open up such opportunities is not automatic among members of the dominant group, even when the need for enlarging the number of trained persons is clear.

In his assessment of "the positive functions of poverty," Gans (1972) powerfully reminds us that the affluent members of a society are far from eager to eliminate poverty, despite many of their ideals and despite the gains that might accrue to society. There are too many economic, political, social, and cultural advantages that flow to the higher classes (as individuals, although far less certainly as a group) as a result of the presence of the poor. Poverty can be eliminated, he suggests, only when it no longer serves the interests of the affluent, "or when the poor can obtain enough power to change the system of social stratification" (Gans 1972; p. 288; see also Lewis 1978).

Graves lends support to this interpretation in his study of Navajo migrants to Denver. Some of them have become "middle class" in their "future time" orientation, in their sense of an internal locus of control, and in their levels of desire to achieve higher status. Yet they are no more likely, and by some measures are less likely, to improve their status than those who have not acquired such tendencies: "For a middle-class personality is adaptive only within a structural setting which permits the attainment of middle-class goals" (Graves 1974, p. 83).

Is There a "Culture of Poverty"?

The kinds of questions suggested by these references to poverty have been especially important in recent years in the highly diverse literature dealing with "the culture of poverty." Widespread agreement exists on the statement that barriers to social interaction between members of different classes help to maintain fairly well defined and distinctive life-styles. We shall be examining the sources and the degree of persistence of those distinctive life styles by studying the controversy surrounding the concept of the culture of poverty. In doing so we must remember, because of our interest in minority groups, that many of the tendencies of minority-group members are a product of their class status and not specifically of their racial or cultural identities. Discrimination is often involved, of course, in determining a person's class status; the two phenomena therefore are closely related.

There have been two rather distinct phases in the study of class subcultures. Both emphasize the importance of the class structure in creating significantly different learning environments for children in different class locations. The earlier literature, however, tended to view the result as a consequence of isolation and lack of opportunity. More recently there has been an emphasis on the distinctive subculture of the slum or of an impoverished ethnic minority. One might say that the former stressed what was lacking in the experience of a child, the latter emphasized what was present. In an overly simple contrast, the approaches were structural and cultural. Both groups of authors express opposition to discrimination and seek to increase our understanding of the sources of different patterns of behavior. But the "subculture" school adds some elements of the current widespread dismay over the dominant culture and society. If one is unhappy with the "establishment," contrasting styles and policies take on a positive appearance. This perspective helps to control middle-class biases; it is a good antidote to ethnocentrism; it can help enrich our sympathetic understanding of differences in a pluralistic society. We should not forget, however, that the literature on the culture of poverty comes mainly from the pens of middle- and upper-class writers. They are not free from the danger of romanticizing a life-style they do not share, in part as a form of deflected criticism and an expression of disenchantment with the foibles and absurdities of the one they do share (we share much of this disenchantment, but do not want to let it govern our assessment of the sources of those foibles and absurdities).

The isolation stressed by the first school could be either geographical or social. Some of the literature emphasizes class location, without much reference to minority-group status; other studies are concerned with both (see, e.g., Davis and Havighurst 1947; Kohn 1959; Sutherland 1942). If a person from the rural peasantry or the city slums is, from the point of view of the dominant society, careless, without ambition, immoral, or criminal, the causes are to be sought in the personality-forming conditions that he has experienced.

To "explain" or judge the behavior of the adult without a thorough understanding of the experiences of the child is clearly to miss the basic causes. If the dominant elements in a society isolate a segment of the people from contact with the prevailing norms and prevent them from sharing in the rewards that may follow from abiding by those norms, they should not be surprised at the appearance of different standards of conduct and motivations.

The isolation we are referring to is far from complete. A minority group, by definition, cannot be fully isolated from the majority. For persons in a deprived group, in fact, learning how to handle the prejudices and anxieties of members of a dominant group is an essential lesson.

When we turn to studies dealing directly with the culture of poverty, we find a wide range of interpretations. There are some who see the life-style of those in poverty as the cumulative cultural result of the experience of poverty, mingled perhaps with various ethnic elements. The concept was first developed by Oscar Lewis in a number of works (Lewis 1959, 1961, 1966a,b; see also Cohen and Hodges 1963, and Miller 1958; and, for modifications, Irelan, Moles, and O'Shea 1969, and Johnson and Sanday 1971). For Lewis (1966a, p. 19) the phrase "culture of poverty" describes

in positive terms a subculture of Western society with its own structure and rationale, a way of life handed on from generation to generation along family lines. The culture of poverty is not just a matter of deprivation or disorganization, a term signifying the absence of something. It is a culture in the traditional anthropological sense in that it provides human beings with a design for living, with a ready made set of solutions for human problems, and so serves a significant adaptive function.

Where Lewis was suggesting that we ought to see the culture of poverty as a dignified life-style, or at least ought to treat it with anthropological objectivity, others use the concept more critically. In *The Moral Basis of a Backward Society* (1958), Banfield describes the life-style of villagers in southern Italy as a product of "amoral familism" (see also Banfield 1968). Although there are some references to opportunity in Banfield's work, as there are in Lewis's, the emphasis is on a traditional subculture and the individual tendencies that express it—suspicion, inability to cooperate, and failure to plan ahead.

Banfield's work has been sharply criticized, both for its empirical base and for its interpretations (Miller 1974; Muraskin 1974; Silverman 1968). As Valentine (1968), Ryan (1971), and others have noted, the cultural explanation of poverty slips rather easily into a characterological explanation: Poverty is the direct outcome of the low levels of skill, poor work motivation, inadequate willingness to secure necessary training, ignorance, laziness, and other personal characteristics. Poverty is blamed on the poor. Perhaps many of us need this view of the poor as "failures of their own volition"—a fairly easy assumption in a society of highly visible, if not widely available, opportunities—to reassure us of our own personal worth (Michael Lewis 1978). Those who take this view moralistically are likely to say: If the poor would learn how to work and get some skills there would be no problem. Those more sympathetically inclined may say: We need to create programs that will teach them skills, necessary work disciplines, and higher aspirations. But in either case, the emphasis is on individual characteristics of the poor. This is a typical case of the blind man and the elephant, for it touches only part of a complex system. The elephant is clearly very much like a snake? Scarcely. And yet as part of a larger system of explanation, as we shall try to show, it may add to our understanding.

The idea of a culture of poverty can be taken in another, and more creative, direction. Several writers emphasize the interaction of subcultural elements with the experience of discrimination and the high chance of failure. A complex value system has developed as a way of dealing both with training in and aspirations to the dominant patterns and with the realistic chances for failure and frustration. Rodman describes this nicely as a "value stretch." The lower-class person develops an alternative set of values to deal with his difficult situation "without abandoning the general values of the society" (Rodman 1963; Della Fave 1974a, b). This point of view has been expanded in a valuable way in a number of studies. Liebow remarks, for example, that family instability among lower-class Negroes does not so much represent a subcultural style as "the cultural model of the larger society as seen through the prism of repeated failure" (Liebow 1967, p. 221; see also Ball 1968; Patterson 1981, pp. 115-25). The "shadow culture" is subsidiary, less thoroughly internalized, and therefore, according to this argument, the behavior associated with it is more flexible, more sensitive to changes in opportunity than would be behavior based on a thoroughly internalized culture.

Rainwater (1970, pp. 142–143; see also Parker and Kleiner 1970; Waxman 1977) adds a necessary time dimension to the question by tracing the interaction of subcultural norms with the dominant culture in a particular situation:

Norms with their existential concomitants can be regarded as rules for playing a particular game. That game represents one kind of adaptation to the environmental situation in which a group finds itself....
But what if a good many people cannot play the normative game, are in constant communication with each other, and there is generational continuity among them? In that case, the stage is set for the invention and diffusion of substitute games of a wide variety....The substitute adaptations of each generation condition the possibilities subsequent generations have of adapting in terms of the requirements of the normative games.
Nevertheless, in the American context at least it is clear that each generation of Negroes has a strong desire to be able to perform successfully in terms of the norms of the larger society and makes efforts in this direction. The inadequacies of the opportunity structure doom most to failure to achieve in terms of their own desires, and therefore facilitate the adoption of the readily available alternatives.

By the use of two carefully selected national samples, Abell and Lyon (1979) have made a valuable addition to our understanding of the strengths and weaknesses of the concept of a culture of poverty. Is poverty primarily the result of discrimination and other forces that restrict opportunity, or is it simply passed along as the result of socialization to a poverty-adapted community? Primarily the former. "Attitudinally, the poor and the nonpoor do not significantly differ concerning a work ethic and the locus of control" (Abell and Lyon 1979, p. 607; see also Valentine 1978).

Still other studies see the culture of poverty as an excessively rigid concept that overemphasizes value contrasts among the status groups of a society and underemphasizes the situational contrasts, particularly the differences in opportunity, that produce differences in behavior (Coward, Feagin, and Williams 1974; Davidson and Gaitz 1974; Graves 1974; Stack 1974; Suttles 1968; Valentine 1968). What started as support for cultural pluralism and an affirmation of the dignity of the life styles of lower classes and minority groups, these authors suggest, may end up as support for conditions that perpetuate poverty and discrimination (Coser 1969).

Poverty Seen Field Theoretically. In our judgment, these diverse approaches to and criticisms of the concept of a culture of poverty can be made consistent—their contradictions removed and their various omissions filled—only by studying them together in a field theoretical system. *Structure of poverty* refers to the lack of power and the low level of opportunity that characterize some groups. Persistent experience of such conditions, especially when accompanied by a perception of unfairness, can result, in some people, in resignation, resentment, an unwillingness to seek training that is seen as useless under the circumstances (from the outside, these individual tendencies may be seen as laziness and ignorance). We think the phrase *subculture of poverty* should be used to refer only to shared beliefs about how life ought to be organized and directed—that is, to shared norms and values.

If one seeks to answer the question "Who will be poor?" with reference to these three elements seen separately, or analytically, one would say:

1. those living under low-opportunity conditions, whatever their culture or individual tendencies
2. those with certain individual tendencies, whatever the opportunity system around them or the values emphasized in their communities
3. those trained to poverty-oriented norms and participants in communities substantially influenced by those norms

These separate statements, we want to emphasize, are of little value. It is particularly in the interaction of these various elements, in their system quality, that the explanation of both the sources and the consequences of poverty resides.

One possible sequence that illustrates the feedback processes among these elements might run as follows: Low opportunity leads to low motivation and skill which, when widely shared, leads to values adapted to poverty that prevent recognition or pursuit of whatever opportunities do exist or new ones that appear (see Figure 6-1).

We want to emphasize that this is an analytically closed system. Contrary forces are left out. It is a strong system that is not easily breached but it is not in fact closed. Arrows to and from the small "islands" outside the main circle in Figure 6-1 suggest ways in which the cycle of poverty is part of a larger field of forces.

Some of those forces may in fact harden the system, but others tend to weaken it, just as they may be strengthened or weakened by the impact of the system of poverty. These complex possibilities are suggested by the plus and minus symbols. (In Part III we will discuss in more general terms the need to examine the extent to which and the conditions under which systems of inequality are best seen as "open"—as part of larger fields, often containing contrary forces.)

What we are trying to say in Figure 6-1 is that the analysis of the cycle of causes of continuing poverty can best begin with the opportunity structure within which a great deal of discrimination is buried and from which flow various cultural and characterological consequences. Once created, these consequences flow back into the system from which they came and reenforce it. These cybernetic processes are among the most important qualities of human systems. They require that we not draw too sharp a distinction between causes and effects. Once developed, the culture of poverty and the individual tendencies that express it reenforce the conditions from which they came. This is true both in the sense that they influence perception of opportunities and the readiness to take them and in the sense that they affect the level of opportunities. The latter occurs because those outside the culture of poverty (whether of the adaptive and temporary or the more traditional variety) may respond negatively to its values and related behavior, thus being led to restrict opportunities even further.

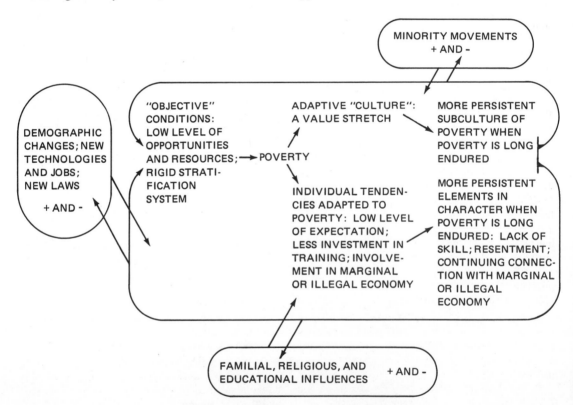

Figure 6–1. The field context of poverty.

A correct statement of this problem is peculiarly important because policies based on a partial statement are bound to be ineffective and often counterproductive. The conservative sees only level 2, the character level. He has no objection to admitting the poor into full participation in society, as soon as they acquire the attitudes, skills, and motivations necessary to perform important functions at a sufficiently high level. The conservative does not make clear how those who are not allowed in the water are going to learn to swim.

The radical correctly sees the isolated characterological argument as "bootstrap thinking." He sees little chance for a change in motivation and skill level until those now trapped in poverty are convinced that their efforts will be rewarded, that opportunities will be opened. After long experience with restricted opportunity, however, many persons will find it difficult to acquire such a conviction. The radical who counts wholly on the need for structural change may give insufficient attention to "character lag."

The liberal is caught between his desire to avoid ethnocentrism and middle-class bias and the fact that some of the values and norms that emerge out of poverty are, as a result of the very fact of their adaptive power, part of a cycle that keeps individuals in poverty. The need is to support an open-minded pluralism without falling into sentimental approval of a life-style that is in some measure a desperate expedient to deal with an extremely difficult situation.

It is in the context of these often powerfully stated partial truths that the United States, indeed the world, struggles in various wars on poverty. Public action in the United States is strongly inhibited by the belief that a "welfare ethic" has obliterated the "work ethic" in the lives of many people, that individual attitudes and motives toward work, partly shaped by the values of their communities, incline many to accept public help over job opportunities. Those who believe this are naturally not inclined to begin with the opportunity system or to look for patterns of discrimination in trying to break up the poverty cycle. They oppose guaranteed minimum incomes and negative income taxes on the ground that they would be disincentives to work—just another drag on the taxpayers.

Fortunately we are getting some tough-minded research that examines such questions and exposes our folklore on poverty (see Covello 1980). It is clear that structural changes in the occupational system have sharply reduced the number of lesser-skill jobs; quite rapidly growing minority populations require expanding job opportunities; and discrimination continues to be a barrier to many. What about attitudes toward work? We will not discuss the numerous findings of the "guaranteed income experiments" (see Haveman 1977; Kershaw and Fair 1976; Watts and Rees 1977a); but the conclusion most relevant for our topic here is quite clear: Most of the poor want to work; they share the work ethic. In the experiments in New Jersey, Pennsylvania, Iowa, and North Carolina the guaranteed income contained a tax that grew as income from work grew until at a fairly low level the tax became as high as the supplement—that is, there was no subsidy. Each family faced a break-even point where it had no more income working than it had not working; but the guaranteed income did not, in most cases, stop them from working. As Linda Greenhouse remarked (*The New York Times,* July 2, 1973, p. E8): "The low-income wage earners in the study kept working even when they were taxed on their earned income at rates that would send members of the middle class scurrying to the nearest tax shelter." In a related line of research, Hill and Ponza (1983) demonstrate that children raised in families strongly dependent on welfare are themselves dependent on welfare in only a very small percentage of cases.

Striving to Achieve the American Dream

It would be unfortunate if our discussion of the concept of the culture of poverty caused us to overlook the extent of striving for educational and occupational advance among minority-group members. Even in fairly remote rural areas decades ago there was hope and aspiration (Johnson 1941, pp. 114–15). It is important also to remember the growing numbers of middle- and upper-class persons in American minority groups. The critical questions for them are not so much those of educational and economic opportunity as of marginality and status discrepancies. In contrast with the middle class so disparagingly described by Frazier in *Black Bourgeoisie* (1957), the more recent studies find minority-group members in the middle class to be more self-confident, more highly educated, and more widely distributed through the range of occupations (Brashler 1978; Kronus 1971; Lieberson 1980; Wilson 1978). This seems to us to represent not simply a shift in the ideology of authors but to a major degree a change in the facts.

Most Chicanos, Blacks, Puerto Ricans, Native Americans, and other minorities, however, although fully in touch with the sights and sounds and promises of an affluent society, are denied full access to achievement in that society by discrimination and by their own responses. The result, inevitably, is a high level of disillusionment and frustration.

Contemporary research on the effects of minority status on personality helps us to spell out some of the conditions under which various results occur. On this issue, as on so many of the issues with which we are concerned in this volume, we must be alert to methodological problems. Many personality tests have been standardized on white, and usually middle-class, populations. Their reliability and validity when applied to minority-group members are often subject to doubt. When comparisons are being made it is often difficult to establish adequate scientific controls across major racial or cultural lines. Are a white student and a black student who have both finished the tenth grade in segregated schools, for example, "equated" for education? In most cases this is doubtless an unwarranted assumption. How should one interpret the different results, in the measurement of attitudes for example, recorded by a black interviewer and a white interviewer for a black population? Most research is carried on by white scholars, who may get traditional or restrained answers from Blacks; yet it would not be wise to assume that answers to black interviewers are more valid. Only as several lines of independent evidence accumulate can we speak with great confidence (Jerome Sattler in Miller and Dreger 1973, pp. 7–32).

Keeping methodological cautions in mind, we shall examine some of the evidence concerning the relationship of minority-group members to the dominant society. Do they have similar definitions of a good job (Shapiro 1977), similar levels of "achievement motive"—the readiness to work hard and postpone satisfactions in order to get ahead? Three generalizations appear to be appropriate on the basis of current evidence: (1) class is as important as or more important than race or ethnic group in determining the strength of achievement motive;

(2) an important line of demarcation can be drawn between the lower-lower and upper-lower class (Glasgow 1980; Valentine 1978); and (3) the desire for achievement is not always accompanied by the values, norms, motivation, and goals related to achievement, nor by the expectation of achievement—and their separation is a strategic fact (Han 1969; Howell and Freese 1981).

A number of concepts are proving of value in the study of motivation: perception of opportunity (Garza 1969), expectancy of success, sense of powerlessness (Seeman 1975), and internal versus external control. The last, as described by Rotter (1966) is the contrast between the belief that rewards follow from one's own behavior and the belief that rewards are the result of external forces beyond one's control.

These are valuable concepts that prompt us to pay careful attention to variation in aspiration and motivation but they have not been thoroughly absorbed into a theory of prejudice and discrimination. The sources and the correlates of high aspiration require further study. And the interactions between individual tendencies and facilitating or inhibiting situations must be examined. Measures of level of achievement motive become more valuable when they are specified by measures of expectancy of success. These two individual tendencies do not necessarily vary together, and the significance of high achievement motive for behavior is quite different for a person with low expectancy of success from what it is for a person with high expectancy of success. These relationships, in turn, are made more meaningful by examining "the social context of ambition"—the context within which achievement motives and feelings of internal or external control are formed (Turner 1964).

Seeman (1963) has shown that the level of alienation, defined in his study as powerlessness, influences the process of learning of information about parole on the part of inmates in a reformatory. As one would predict from Rotter's theory, those who felt most controlled by chance learned less and those who had higher expectations of control over their lives learned more. In a comment on Seeman's research, Coleman (1964, p. 77) notes its significance for the student of race relations: "Seeman's results suggest a general phenomenon that a man is sensitive to the cues of his environment only when he believes he can have some effect upon it." Blacks who have migrated from or live in an environment which gives them little sense of control may have a mind set that makes them insensitive to learning cues—a set that will, in part, be transmitted to their children.

It would be a mistake to conclude from the data in hand that the aspirations of black youth are equivalent to those of white youth in the United States today. When we control for class we should not forget that a vastly larger proportion of Blacks are found in the lower class. And the studies cited refer largely to *upper*-lower-class persons in northern cities. Difficult as their situation is, they have come in touch with the American Dream and have begun to share in at least a few of its promises; their hopes are aroused. There is still a large group, however, for whom even dreams are remote. They stand on the edge of the economy barely sustained by this affluent society; their children go to inferior and segregated, or nearly segregated, schools, whether they live in the North or the South; they are "piled up," sometimes over 50,000 to the square mile, in substandard dwellings in northern cities; or they are cut off by segregation from the agencies of hope and improvement in many parts of the South.

Conditions have undoubtedly improved for many minority-group members in the last generation. Many others are nearly untouched, however, by the economic, political, and educational changes. The strategies to adapt to a life without a future—or only the frustrating future they see prefigured in the lives around them—described by Rohrer and Edmonson (1960), Liebow (1967), Hannerz (1969), and many others are still widely used. Rohrer and Edmonson (1960, p. 160) describe the gang as a defensive and protective male culture. It is not necessarily a criminal organization nor is it a formal group. It is a convergence upon a pattern of life by persons equally in search of self-respect and a meaningful social role:

The psychic economy of the gang demands aggressive independence, a touchy and exaggerated virility, and a deep, protective secrecy. Acceptance by the gang provides almost the only source of security for its members, but such acceptance is conditional upon continual proof that it is merited, and this proof can only be furnished through physical aggressiveness, a restless demonstration of sexual prowess, and a symbolic execution of those illegal deeds that a "sissy" would not perform. These activities victimize women, but it would seem that they are not specifically directed toward women. Rather the enemy of the gang is the world of people (especially men) too unmanly for survival in what has often been described as a social jungle.

In all this there is more than a little reaction-formation, more than a little effort to rid one's self of doubt about one's manhood and worth. The result, however, is to create a style of life, perhaps a counterculture, that aids temporary adjustment but cuts the participants off from alternative ways of struggling with their problems.

The impact of minority status is affected by its entanglement with class status (Moore 1981; Pettigrew 1981b) and by the different sets of experience of men and women (Ladner 1971; Mirandé and Enríquez 1980; Wilkinson and Taylor 1977; Jacquelyne Jackson in Willie, Kramer, and Brown 1973, pp. 185–268). Thus coping strategies vary widely. The point that we want to emphasize here, however, is that the levels of opportunity—the barriers or gateways to jobs, adequate housing, and education—are the decisive facts in shaping those coping strategies. Liebow (1967, p. 66) well describes the situation of those for whom the barriers are high and the gateways few. Among them, low aspirations and lack of plans are not so much the result of "present-orientation" as of bleak prospects:

As for the future, the young streetcorner man has a fairly good picture of it. In Richard or Sea Cat or Arthur he can see himself in his middle twenties; he can look at Tally to see himself at thirty, at Wee Tom to see himself in his middle thirties, and at Budder and Stanton to see himself in his forties. It is a future in which everything is uncertain except the ultimate destruction of his hopes and the eventual realization of his fears. The most he can reasonably look forward to is that these things do not come too soon. Thus, when Richard squanders a week's pay in two days it is not because, like an animal or a child, he is "present-time oriented," unaware of or unconcerned with his future. He does so precisely because he is aware of the future and the hopelessness of it all.

Situational Pressures toward Deviation

One of the consequences of knowing and sharing the hopes and values of a society but being blocked from full participation in that society is an ambivalence toward the nation and its laws. It is difficult for oppressed persons to give full allegiance to a society which itself has not fully accepted them.

It is easy to make the argument that persons of lower status seem to commit more crimes only because they are more likely to be caught or prosecuted, while the "white-collar" crimes of the powerful go undetected or unpunished. "Steal a farthing and go to prison; steal a railroad and go to Parliament." One can even argue that violent crimes "at a distance"—unsafe automobile designs, junk food, and the like—are committed by the powerful in the name of profit. We believe that such an argument contains a great deal of truth. In a different context we would want to examine it carefully. It should not allow us here, however, to be deflected from noting the ways in which minority status creates pressures toward deviation, including crime. Direct violent crime in particular is such a visible and salient fact that it shapes public attitudes and policies in ways that the student of minority–majority relations cannot disregard. It is also important to note that minorities are more likely to be victims of crime (Daniels 1982).

It is difficult to doubt that nonwhites, particularly black men, are overrepresented among those who commit violent crimes (Blau and Blau 1982; Farley 1980; Leonard Savitz in Miller and Dreger 1973, pp. 457–615). Does this stem from the deprivations of minority status? If so, what elements of that status are the crucial sources? Blau and Blau (1982) in their careful study of data from the 125 largest American metropolitan areas are able to show that neither a Southern "tradition of violence" nor poverty—other factors being controlled— increases rates of criminal violence, although they are often cited as causes. The proportion of Blacks in the population scarcely affects the rates. What does increase the rates? It is socioeconomic inequality between races and economic inequality generally. "Pronounced ethnic inequality in resources implies that there are great riches within view but not within reach of many people destined to live in poverty" (Blau and Blau 1982, p. 119). Those differences, moreover, "tend to deprive the lower strata of the strength and resources to organize successful collective action" which might help them to reduce the inequality. We suspect, although without firm evidence, that when a few members of a minority group attain riches, they make the gap experienced by most persons in the lower strata all the more visible and those at the bottom all the more frustrated.

This is not to say that they cannot in any way effectively protest their situation (a topic we will examine in Part III), but some of their protests or adaptations may be ineffectual. For example, one can interpret the numbers racket as a kind of "bank," as Light (1977) does, although it is scarcely an efficient way to raise capital. Those with low and uncertain income, however, and with little help from standard financial institutions design ways to try to help themselves. "You might almost say the numbers is the salvation of Harlem, its Medicare, and its Black Draught, its 666 [two laxatives popular in the South], its little liver pills, its vitamins, its aspirins and its analgesic balm combined" (Langston Hughes, quoted in the *New York Times*, March 1, 1971, p. 1).

With many states having legalized off-track betting or running their own lotteries, it becomes problematic how deviant the numbers racket is.[1] Chance-taking and gambling are quite congruent with some aspects of the dominant world. Among minorities, however, an additional stimulus to gambling is the loss of hope of achieving even a modest success by the more stable methods of work and thrift. The prejudice and discrimination they experience cause them to doubt the rewards of virtue. They turn, rather, to a kind of magic (just as people seem to do everywhere when the odds are heavily against them) in their search for success (McCall 1963).

Light (1977, p. 892) skillfully describes the social context out of which the numbers game emerges and some of its consequences:

Mainstream financial institutions have never been able to provide generally prevailing service levels in poor communities. In the resulting partial-service vacuum, blacks invented numbers gambling. Numbers-gambling banks became sources of capital and a major savings device of urban black communities. In conjunction with the usury industry, numbers banks framed an alternative institutional system for the savings-investment cycle in the slum.

The total result, Light notes, is a mixture of a little philanthropy and some direct business investment by numbers racketeers—helping to fill the gap left by the mainline institutions—but in larger measure usurious loans and, we would add, a heavy tax on the vast majority who are losers for the benefit of those who control the system and the few winners. Rotating credit systems are much more efficient adaptations to the cruel mixture of poverty and majority-bank discrimination faced by many minorities (Light 1972).

[1]This illustrates the problem of defining *deviation* in a period of change, alienation, and loss of legitimacy. It is, in any event, an analytic term not a swearword (Yinger 1982). The presumed moral and legal criteria become suspect in some persons' eyes, who say, in effect: deviation is determined by those who have the power to make their definitions stick. We will examine some of the implications of this question in Part III.

Minorities that experience discrimination are also likely to have higher than average rates of the more traditional delinquencies and crimes (Bahr, Chadwick, and Day 1972, pp. 313–38). There are subtle interactions between the absence of legitimate opportunities and the presence of illegitimate ones Hewitt 1970; Short, Rivera, and Tennyson 1965). When both factors are operative in a society that promises "liberty and justice for all" but rations them severely for members of minorities, deviant responses are not uncommon.

In his well-known essay, "Social Structure and Anomie," Robert Merton (1968, pp. 185–214) discusses the consequences for behavior of a society that places strong emphasis on the desirability of specific goals without placing a corresponding emphasis upon institutionalized procedures. One type of adjustment that people make to such a situation is to strive for goals they have been taught to desire with little regard for the legitimacy of the means used. Analyses of white-collar crime (Geis and Stotland 1980) show this adjustment to be not uncommon among members of the dominant group; but the pressures toward deviation are probably greater on those who have the least opportunity for success by legitimate means.

"Least opportunity" should probably be read as "least relative opportunity," because perceptions and reference groups play an important part. Lefton found, for example (1968, p. 347), that "Negro autoworkers who were economically advantaged registered significantly higher anomia scores than those who were considerably less well off in terms of seniority and employment history." Anomia, which we shall regard here as one possible individual manifestation of the experience of anomie, thus expresses, Lefton notes, frustration as well as despair. It is an indication that modest gains may *increase* the gap between expectations and reality. It would be a mistake, of course, to assume from this discussion that a deviant pattern of motivation and regard for law are the inevitable results of minority-group status in a society or, conversely, that membership in the dominant group is a promise of high motivation and complete honesty.

It is a matter for careful study that most minority-group members, despite the obstacles, continued to strive for improved status and, notwithstanding the unequal protection of the law and resentment against discrimination, are reliable and honest in their relationships with others. The differences in motivation and morality should not be exaggerated, but insofar as they do exist they can be accounted for by the differential sharing in the rewards and encouragement of society.

The Marginal Man and Cultural Participation

An extensive body of literature dealing with the concept of the marginal man offers a number of valuable insights and hypotheses for the study of the effects of minority-group membership (see Gist and Dworkin 1972; Stonequist 1937; Wright and Wright 1972). The consequences of marginality are not limited to minority-group members, of course, for in a rapidly changing society the lack of a stable, continuous, unchallenged set of life definitions makes virtually everyone, to a greater or lesser degree, marginal and likely to exhibit the tendencies characteristic of that condition. But inability to participate fully in the life of society according to one's individual interests and talents complicates this experience for those in minority status. Most discussions of marginality are somewhat impressionistic, so generalizations must be tentative. The consequences vary, moreover, with the height of the barriers to full participation, with the presence or absence of a minority culture to which the marginal person feels attached, and with the degree to which an individual is self-conscious of her or his status between two groups—part of both, yet belonging to neither.

Discussions of marginality do not always distinguish between measures that are used to define the condition and measures of presumed consequences of it. Our interest is primarily in the latter but causal connections are not readily ascertained.

The experience of marginality can be avoided by opting for one or another identity. This may be achieved, however, only at a cost if it involves repression of an important part of self or choices that tend to be irreversible. Wiley illustrates this latter situation by use of the concept of "mobility trap." He uses the metaphor of climbing a tree rather than a social ladder. One can go up, as well as out on a limb, but one reaches a dead-end. To go higher a person must climb down the limb to the trunk. "The essence of the mobility trap is this: the means for moving up within a stratum are contrary to those for moving to the next higher stratum" (Wiley 1967, p. 149). Thus a boy in the slums may advance in a gang by "accumulating tattoos, knife skills and a police record;" but by the very process he will block advancement in the larger society. When mobile ethnics climb the ethnic ladder, they may deprive their group of leadership for a more concerted attack on the marginality and discrimination experienced by their followers.

Keeping these qualifications in mind, we can note some of the personality tendencies that appear to be associated with marginal status. Ambivalence heightens self-consciousness and attention to oneself. This may take the form of selfhatred and an inferiority complex, or it may express itself in egocentrism, withdrawal, and/or "aggressiveness" (Stonequist 1937).

Some writers have emphasized the influence of a marginal role in encouraging a rational instead of a traditional view of life. Robert Park wrote in the introduction to Stonequist's study (1937):

The fate which condemns him to live, at the same time, in two worlds is the same which compels him to assume, in relation to the worlds in which he lives, the role of a cosmopolitan and a stranger. Inevitably he becomes, relatively to his cultural milieu, the individual with the wider horizon, the keener intelligence, the more detached and rational viewpoint.

If thinking comes from perplexity and doubt, from problems posed but not solved by established traditional answers, then indeed the marginal man may take a more rational view of life.

Other authors emphasize the personal instability that they believe is likely to characterize persons who lack a strong feeling of identification with one group. Minority-group members who feel torn between association with the group in which they are categorically placed by prejudice and their feelings of identification with the dominant society may lack some of the security that comes from stable and acceptable group relationships. This generalization must be used with care, however. In modern societies, many persons belong to diverse groups and combine a variety of identities. The very concept of marginality is not well applied to them. Indeed, a "mutable self," as Zurcher (1977) calls it, a self adaptable and flexible in a changing world, may be becoming more common and more appropriate to the comptemporary situation than a person closely tied to an ancestral identity (see Granovetter 1973, 1983; Weimann 1982).

This argument is much more difficult to make, however, if one is thinking not of the secure who have some choice but of the deprived who are threatened by a lack of any strong identity. Several sets of such marginal people have appeared in the late twentieth century. One can be identified by the title of an essay: "The Cruel Legacy: The Children Our GIs Left Behind in Asia" (Lifton 1975; see also Gist and Dworkin 1972; George DeVos in Bryce-Laporte 1980, pp. 321–28). One hundred thousand or more such children—many now grown to adulthood—live in Japan, Korea, Vietnam, and elsewhere in Asia. They are not Americans nor are they accepted fully in societies that stress—to some degree against the facts—their homogeneity of race and culture.

Status Inconsistency as Marginality. Marginality is not limited to the experience of racial or cultural minorities. In recent years the kind of marginality associated with inconsistent status placement has been carefully studied. Since racial and cultural identities are often among the criteria used in examining status inconsistency, the topic is relevant to our interests here (Bagley 1970). A person may have high educational and occupational achievements but relatively low income, or high income and low education, or low racial- or cultural-group status according to a society's dominant standards and high occupational position, or high ethnic status and low income and occupation. Such status inconsistencies have been found to influence many attitudes and values. Liberal political views, for example are associated to some degree, as Lenski noted (1954), with status inconsistency, particularly of the variety that combines high incomes, education, or occupation with low racial and ethnic status, although we would emphasize the complexity of that relationship (Crosbie 1979; Jackson and Curtis 1972; Knoke 1972; Laumann and Segal 1971). Having won some measure of success on the basis of socially designated criteria, a person occupying inconsistent statuses may feel frustrated and cheated at being denied full acceptance. Their liberal attitudes indicate a desire to modify a system that puts them in an unpleasant ambivalent situation. On the other hand, there is some evidence that persons whose ascribed status is higher than their achieved status are inclined toward conservative or in some instances right-wing extremist views.

Thus status inconsistency can be associated with the protest movements of minority-group members and also with the prejudices and reactionary views of dominant-group members whose incomes or occupational attainments are modest.

These statements concerning possible outcomes of status inconsistency must be treated with caution because the evidences are somewhat mixed. Due to the use of different measuring instruments, different status variables, and different populations, the various studies have led to conclusions that are only partly congruent. Marx (1967a, pp. 57–60) found, for example, that among Blacks with at least some college education more of those in high-status occupations were militant (57%) than those in low-status occupations (26%), although he defines the latter as having more discrepant statuses. His data could be interpreted to mean, however, that there is a perceptual element in status inconsistency. When ethnicity is taken into account, well-educated black workers, whether in high- or low-status occupations, experience discrepancy. Were extent of awareness of the discrepancy also measured, as Marx notes, or the effect of available reference groups studied, those in higher-status jobs might be found to be experiencing more inconsistency.

Seen this way, the recent experience of America's mobile and urban black population has led to greater status inconsistency. Although most of them were uniformly low in income, power, education, and other status variables at the beginning of the century, a significant number have climbed one or more of these ladders, thus increasing their inconsistency of status. The civil rights movement and militancy can be read as indicatory of *improvement* in *some* status measures. Whenever this happens to many people in close communication, we have the ingredients for a sharp protest movement or a revolutionary situation.

When one adds more subjective variables, the status inconsistency of many Black, Hispanic, Indian, and other minority Americans is even more readily apparent. Small improvements on the objective scales may lead to soaring hopes and to dreams of dramatic change. A uniformly low-status situation smothers many dreams, as well as repressing motivation, but visible, if modest, improvement releases the imagination. The result may be a split between objective and subjective measures of status—a split as significant as inconsistency among the various objective measures (Yinger 1965a, pp. 10–14).

Such difficulties of interpretation must give us pause in adding the concept of status inconsistency to our examination of the effects of marginality. In our judgment, nevertheless, the concept deserves the careful study of those investigating majority–minority relations.

Illustrations of Marginality. The consequences of marginality vary greatly from group to group, and the interested student will need to explore carefully the different effects, for example, on middle-class Blacks, American Indians (who vary widely, depending on the type of contact with the dominant society and the nature of the aboriginal culture), first-generation immigrants, second-generation immigrants and so forth. Feeling that one's status as a minority-group member is permanent and unchangeable, regardless of one's individual beliefs or behavior, produces influences different than does knowledge or belief that one will, in time, no longer suffer discrimination.

It is, of course, a mistake to attribute all the consequences of marginal position to prejudice. Individuals who stand between two cultural worlds, influenced by two sets of values, often exhibit strong personality effects even when no prejudice is involved. Frequently, however, marginal persons are not only bicultural but recipients of prejudice as well. These two factors interlock and increase the impact of his position.

Studies of American Indians furnish a great deal of information on the consequences of culture contact. As white men came into contact with the Indians, many treated them with harshness and prejudice, looking upon the indigenous cultures as inferior and demanding either rapid assimilation or segregation. Indian leaders, often subjected to the authority of the white stranger, lost the respect and confidence of their people. They felt themselves to be in a cultural vacuum, without incentives or objectives. The indigenous religions were generally condemned and efforts were made to force their replacement by Christianity; but faith in the original beliefs was lost before Christianity was adopted, with resulting personal and social disorganization. This was by no means a universal experience. There were also creative religious responses (see Wallace 1970). The loss of an integrated value system helps to account for the brutality that many settlers claimed was embedded in the very nature of the Indians. The tribes of the Iroquois League, for example, were much less warlike before the white settlers began to seize their lands and undermine their culture. Then the decline of cultural cohesion expressed itself in increased personal aggressiveness and organized violence.

MacGregor (1946, p. 36) has described the disorganizing effects on the American Indians of the reservation policies to which they were subjected in the latter part of the nineteenth century:

Excerpts from the statement of the educational policy for all Indian children at this time are enlightening. The policy was "to civilize," "to humanize," and "to put the children in boarding school where they will learn English" and "not relapse into their former moral and mental stupor." In connection with this statement, the federal superintendent of Indian Schools in 1885 makes one remark which is highly significant in light of this study. "The Indian is the strangest compound of individualism and socialism run to seed. It is this being that we endeavor to make a member of a new social order....To do this we must recreate him, *make a new personality."*

Children were virtually kidnaped to force them into government schools, their hair was cut, and their Indian clothes thrown away. They were forbidden to speak in their own language. Life in the school was under military discipline, and rules were enforced by corporal punishment. Those who persisted in clinging to their old ways and those who ran away and were recaptured were thrown into jail. Parents who objected were also jailed. Where possible, children were kept in school year after year to avoid the influence of their families.

There are, of course many different responses possible to the intrusions of a dominant society, and these vary with the nature of the aboriginal culture, the types of contact, and the particular individuals' experience with both worlds. Among American Indians, patterns have varied from complete assimilation to vigorous resistance to white culture, with many positions in between (see Bahr, Chadwick, and Day 1972; Linton 1940; Spindler and Spindler 1971; Tax 1978; Wax 1971). A resurgent interest in Indian identity, "red power" movements, and continued pride in their heritage on the one hand are balanced on the other by economic pressure on an inadequate land base, by extensive contact with the larger society in schools, the armed forces, and jobs, and by the pull of the dominant culture. Indian students perhaps experience the marginal situation most strongly:

Going down the rough dirt road, from the earthy and easygoing tribal life on the rural reservations to the middle-class upmanship of university life in the cities, these young Indians were like refugees in an unknown country. The university was more than strange. It was foreign and alien.

"Very few of us crossed the gap between the two cultures," Blatchford said [Herbert Blatchford, a Navaho who founded the National Indian Youth Council]. "Those who found it difficult to indulge in the new culture developed into a hybrid group, belonging fully to neither culture." (Steiner 1968, p. 30)

Indian experience of marginality, to be sure, is somewhat different from that of other minorities, particularly those who find return to the homeland costly and unlikely. The picture of marginality as a kind of way station between tribal isolation and complete assimilation now seems especially inadequate to describe American Indians. Their population is growing and is now at least three times as large as it was in 1900. It is being dispersed, but at the same time Indian communities are appearing, both in rural areas and in cities.

About seven percent of America's population is of Spanish-speaking descent. For many persons in this group, cultural marginality is enhanced by the problems of bilinguality, by job discrimination, and by prejudice (see, e.g., Murguía 1975; Poggie 1973; West and Macklin 1979). Difficulties associated with marginality, however, are not simply the result of majority-group rigidity. Some serious dilemmas are involved. How to pay special attention to differential language background, for example, without producing substantial segregation or how to support pluralism and subcultural variation without reinforcing traditions that separate? Efforts to deal with these dilemmas have often leaned toward enforcement of cultural uniformity, but not without some attention to the minority's culture (see Grebler, Moore, and Guzman 1970, especially Part 4).

In recent years, the dilemmas associated with the marginality of many Americans of Mexican descent, as of other minorities, have at least become more visible. Earlier programs, whether characterized by pressure toward assimilation or segregation, are being replaced by attention to the facts of biculturality, its problems, and its possibilities. Although awareness of dilemmas does not automatically produce resolutions, it is a necessary first step. Thus we have seen some gains in recognition of the fact that Spanish is the first language of many Americans and study of the consequences of different school policies in teaching children of Spanish-speaking descent. These range from attempts to get more Spanish-speaking teachers, to treatment of English as the second language, to more fully reciprocal situations in which both pupils and teachers, Spanish- and English-speaking, assist one another in learning the language and culture of the other group. An important tangible expression of these interests is the Bilingual Education Act passed by Congress in 1968. A related action is the 1982 ruling of the Supreme Court (by a 5–4 margin) that illegal aliens are entitled to public education and that laws requiring them to pay tuition are unconstitutional. This can have a significant effect, particularly on the schooling of Spanish-speaking children in Texas, California, and Florida. We shall be discussing bilingualism in our examination of educational institutions and in Part III. Here we want only to call attention to its importance as a factor in marginality, especially for the large, growing, and geographically concentrated population of Spanish-speaking descent (see Burke 1981; Fishman 1976; Lopez 1976; Nunis 1981).

Marginality, we scarely need to observe, is not an American invention. Groups of outsiders, strangers, or "pariahs," as Weber called them, have appeared frequently in history, often to perform commercial functions in a rigidly stratified society. In such a situation, the illiterate peasantry is unable—and the traditional aristocracy is unwilling—to take on tasks that are essential when social change and economic opportunity call for bankers, moneylenders, merchants, and traders. Becker (1956, Chapter 15) documented the frequency of this pattern and the remarkable similarity of the status assigned to the "middleman trading peoples." Greek, Armenian, Turk, Jew, Chinese, Scotsman, Yankee, and others have stepped into the "status gap" at various times and places. Summarizing dozens of studies, Bonacich and Modell (1980, pp. 269–71) show that "middleman minorities" are found throughout the world (see also Bonacich 1973; Walter Zenner in Bryce-Laporte 1980, pp. 413–25; Gary Hamilton 1978; Light 1972). Despite the wide cultural differences and the contrasting setting, these marginal trading peoples have tended to resist assimilation, even after many generations of contact and reciprocally to be the targets of prejudice and discrimination. Those on top in the societies where they work exploit their services but deny them full accreditation; those on the bottom see them as exploiting outsiders. Despite this scapegoat position, however, these groups are often characterized by high achievement. Rinder (1958–59, p. 259) remarks that "location in the status gap is more likely to result in the desirable and creative types of marginality than are marginalities having different etiologies."

We must avoid over-emphasizing the thesis that middleman outsiders are always subject to prejudice and persist indefinitely in their culturally marginal positions. Stryker points out that prejudice is not an inevitable result of the occupation of a marginal trading position. It is in a context of emerging nationalism that identifiable outsiders are easily made the target of random hostilities and the agent of in-group solidarity. Opposition to the Chinese subcommunities in many nations of the Orient in this day of powerful national movements lends support to this thesis. It will be important to watch developments in South America, where the Yankee is already subject to much categorical rejection, and in Africa, as Russians, French, English, Americans, Chinese, and others seek commercial and other opportunities in the status gap. Under more developed and economically secure conditions, however, minorities who enter a society as middleman traders may in a few generations become occupationally diverse. Opposition to them is likely to decline; and in some instances their distinctive cultural identities may tend to fade. Bonacich and Modell (1980) argue persuasively for this sequence of events in their analysis of the experience of Americans of Japanese descent.

The Effects of Prejudice and Discrimination on Self-Attitudes and Racial Identification

Prejudice and discrimination affect not only the attitudes and behavior of minority-group members toward the standards set by the dominant society but also their response to themselves and their groups. Self-regarding attitudes are as much a product of one's social experience as are attitudes toward other persons and toward social norms. At an early age in an interracial society children develop an awareness of themselves as different, particularly with regard to skin color. The timing and the strength of this awareness vary with the social definitions of color differences given by the minority and majority groups; important class, regional, and other variables are involved.

Our analysis will be built largely around the experience of learning that one is of a color different from the dominant group, but this should be seen as illustrative of the whole experience of learning that one belongs to a minority group. It is in the context of slights, rebuffs, forbidden opportunities, restraints, and often violence that the minority-group member shapes that fundamental aspect of personality—a sense of oneself and of one's place in the whole scheme of things.

There has been a steady stream—almost a flood—of research on self-attitudes during the last few decades (Gecas 1982; Porter and Washington 1979; Wylie 1979). Because methods of study, samples used, time, and focus of attention have varied widely, conclusions differ. To some degree they are contradictory, at least on the surface, largely we believe because of delay in recognizing clearly the distinction between group identification and self-esteem. For a young black child to fail to identify himself or herself as black is not necessarily a sign of low self-esteem. We shall examine the evidence for that statement without, however, assuming that the two attitudes are entirely separate.

Research on racial identification was powerfully influenced by the work of Clark and Clark (1947). In a study of 253 Negro children aged three to seven, some from a segregated southern school and some from a mixed school in the North, they found that a high proportion of the children (over 90 percent) were aware of racial differences. Even at these ages, however, there were important differences. When asked to choose, between a white and a Negro doll, "the doll that looks like you," only 20 percent of the lighter-colored children selected the Negro doll, whereas 73 percent of the medium and 81 percent of the dark children identified with the Negro doll. When asked to give their preferences, a majority of the Negro children preferred the white doll.

Older children were more likely than younger children to select the Negro doll as the one with the "nice color," although half of the six- and seven-year-olds still selected the white doll. Even three-year-olds, these data suggest, had acquired some of the valuations of the dominant society. The older children were more ambivalent, as suggested by the comment of a six-year-old who rejected the brown doll by stating that he "'looks bad 'cause he hasn't got a eyelash.'"

Many writers have followed the Clarks' lead to explore race awareness and preferences among a variety of groups, using dolls in some instances but also puppets, photographs, or play-group choices. Problems of methodology and interpretation are severe, with society, class, region, age, sex, time period, measuring instrument, race of experimenter, group pressure, and other variables influencing the results (see, e.g., Adam 1978; Beuf 1977; Crain and Weisman 1972; Goodman 1964; Porter 1971; Porter and Washington 1979; Rosenthal 1974; Williams and Morland 1976).

There is little reason to doubt that racial awareness begins for most children at an early age and that some nonwhites prefer white, not because they "view white as intrinsically better than brown, black, or red" but because "they understand that certain societal avenues are better open to those who *are* white" (Beuf 1977, p. 102). White is good, according to this interpretation, because in a child's mind it is associated, with good reason, with privileges and opportunities.

Some studies tend to slip over, without marking the passage, from the issue of group identification to the issue of self-worth, on the assumption that feelings regarding oneself reflect, to a significant degree, the fact of membership in a deprived group. Lewin argued (1948) that self-hatred is a common outcome of low social evaluation of one's group. It is a mistake to dismiss this connection. The need, however, is to draw a sharp analytic distinction between group identification and feelings of self-worth and then to examine the conditions under which the connection is close and when it is broken. The earlier studies neglected this issue. They seemed to confirm a fairly self-evident fact: the burdens of minority status and its personal consequences lowered self-esteem. Methodological weaknesses, however, raised doubts. The samples used were small and not random; there was seldom a white comparison group; self-esteem was not clearly distinguished from group-esteem (the regard in which one's group was held, compared with other groups).

The climate of opinion also began to change, influencing the kinds of questions that were asked about minority–majority relations. We have noted that in studies of slavery attention shifted from descriptions of its cruelties to descriptions of the creative power of slaves to deflect its cruelties. In a similar fashion, studies of ghetto dialects shifted from emphasis on the ways in which isolation and deprivation led to restrictive and inadequate language patterns to examination of the complexity and richness of these nonstandard language forms. In a parallel way, studies of self-esteem came to the fore. The findings of the group-esteem research were set aside, not only because of their methodological weaknesses and their tendency to assume, rather than to demonstrate, the connection between group- and self-esteem, but also, possibly, because they were less in tune with the feelings of confidence generated by a powerful civil rights movement.

Beginning in the late 1960s a new wave of research, based on larger and more adequate samples (but seldom, we should note, fully adequate samples from national populations) focused on the study of self-esteem, especially of black Americans. Many of the studies concluded that earlier work was seriously in error. Black self-esteem is not lower and is sometimes higher than white self-esteem, as judged by responses to public-opinion type questions. When segregation was introduced as a variable, it was often found to increase, not decrease, the self-esteem of Blacks.

The most extensive work on this question has been done by Rosenberg (1979). He suggests that looking out at the world from the child's perspective we must ask: How much does a child care about a given appraisal? How much confidence does she or he place in it? The reflective appraisals and social comparison of most importance to a child, Rosenberg believes, come from those closest and most supportive, not from a distant and abstract societal judgment.

Rosenberg and Simmons (1972, pp. 11–12) measured self-esteem by asking six questions, ranged in order, by the Guttman technique, from one that was least indicative of low self-esteem to one that was most indicative of low self-esteem. The Guttman technique, it should be noted, selects questions in pretests that fall into a regular scale. That is, persons who answer yes to question six will in most instances also answer yes to all of the preceding questions; those who answer yes to question five will not necessarily answer yes to question six, but will do so to the other questions; and so on down the scale.

In a large sample of Baltimore school children, the percentage of Blacks in low, medium, and high self-esteem categories were 19, 35, and 46; the percentage of Whites were 37, 30, and 33 (Rosenberg and Simmons 1972, p. 5). Similar findings are reported in many other studies, although numerous complexities are suggested (see Heiss and Owens 1972; Katz 1976, Chapter 4; Katz and Zalk 1974; Lorenz 1972; McCarthy and Yancey 1971a). This wave of research successfully refuted the assumption that low levels of identification with one's own group (often to be read to mean high regard for the opportunities afforded dominant-group members) meant low self-esteem. Moreover, strong group identification also occurs under many conditions (Beuf 1977, p. 101):

Plains Indian women, far from being impressed by or envious of white pioneer women, were repulsed by their ways, especially their child-rearing practices, amazed at the severe discipline of a people who "make their own children cry." There are many ways in which blacks, also, can regard whites with something short of mad jealousy.

Poussaint wryly remarks (1974, p. 139): "Blacks have not really believed that white equals goodness and purity." (For valuable commentaries on self-esteem studies, see (Della Fave 1980; Gordon 1973; Hunt 1977; Loudon 1981; June Christmas in Miller and Dreger 1973, pp. 249–72; Taylor and Walsh 1979; Wylie 1979, Chapter 4).

"Mark of Oppression" or Color Blind? Can we begin to select among these competing views or combine their partial truths into a larger truth? It is a serious mistake, in our judgment, to fail to emphasize the "mark of oppression"—the destructive personal consequences of prejudice and discrimination. It is equally a mistake to overlook the support minority children receive from primary groups and the importance of that support for their sense of selfhood (Beuf 1977, p. 124). (We must also study the way in which these two forces interact to affect the kinds of strategies adopted by minority-group members to deal with their disadvantaged situation. That will be a major topic in Chapter 7.)

A number of studies help us to specify the conditions under which self-esteem remains strong despite deprivation. Rosenberg has been interested primarily in global self-esteem, the general sense of self-worth. There are various aspects of this global quality, however. Heiss and Owens (1972) show that feelings of self-esteem vary from one trait to another, depending on the significant others who serve as standards (perhaps parents in one case, friends in another, and a teacher in a third), on the presence or absence of a subcultural standard for a particular trait, and on the availability of a "system-blame" explanation. It has been too easily assumed that system-blame helps to protect a minority-group person from low self-esteem: It's not my fault; I didn't have a chance. Taylor and Walsh (1979) found that those who tended to blame the system had lower, not higher, levels of self-esteem. In some instances, however, system-blame is available and persuasive. If I have no chance to enter an occupation or to get any training for it, I can readily blame the system.

Levels of self-esteem among the members of a minority vary from time to time and place to place.

In the context of a vigorous civil rights movement that is breaking down barriers, one can say with conviction that "Black is beautiful" or can join the Reverend Jesse Jackson in affirming that "I am *somebody*." Using Rosenberg's scale, Yancey, Rigsby, and McCarthy (1972) found that Blacks in Nashville had significantly higher self-esteem scores than Whites; but in Philadelphia, the scores of Whites were higher, although not significantly so. In making these comparisons, the authors controlled for age, sex, education, marital status, and work force participation. That is, Blacks and Whites who were alike with respect to these variables were compared. Clearly it is of little value—although not for that reason always avoided—to compare, on levels of self-esteem, an unemployed, poorly educated, divorced black man with a well-employed, highly educated, happily married white man. Yet, if we can make a rather difficult methodological point, something is lost if we compare only well-matched Blacks and Whites. We have learned one lesson but might lose another if we can say only that a well-educated black man with a good job—that is, one who has escaped the constraints of discrimination—has higher self-esteem than an equally well educated and employed white man, or that a poorly educated, unemployed white man has lower self-esteem than a similar black man. The *average* level of self-esteem could still be lower in a minority group because of the greater frequency of the latter set of conditions in that group. We need both the individual and the group comparisons.

In our judgment, recent work on self-esteem has not so much disproved the "mark of oppression" research as it has clarified the need to distinguish between group identification and self-esteem and then to examine the primary sources of self-esteem for children. It has called attention to the inner resources that people often show in the face of adversity as well as emphasizing the partially protected environment within which the sense of self develops. A warm and rewarding family experience leads to a good start in developing a healthy self-regard. Later, stressful situations can be handled with less crushing impact. A sound ego can develop a kind of external response system to the outer world of conflict. Many black families, Rainwater (1966) observes, are highly adaptive to the difficult environment they face. They promote a self-sufficiency and toughness that protect their members from some of the ego-threatening impact of discrimination.

Robert Coles gives us a vivid illustration of the sense of confidence and control that can be shown by a minority-group member. He describes an occasion at which he sat with a black student at a high school basketball game. The student attended a recently desegregated school, but the opposing school was still segregated. As the only Black in the audience, he attracted a great deal of attention, which turned to serious heckling, cursing, and threatening behavior after the game. Without a quick call to the police there might have been a riot. Coles felt alarmed, sad, and angry, while the black student maintained his composure. Having known the student for several months, Coles felt free to talk with him about the incident:

"I don't know how you can take that sort of treatment; I really don't." He smiled, and looked at me as if he understood my problems and would try to help me as best he could. In a moment he did. He started with gentle criticism of me: "You don't know how I can take it because you haven't ever *had* to take it." He paused. "You see, when I grew up I had to learn to expect that kind of treatment; and I got it, so many times I hate to remember to count them. Well, now I'm getting it again, but it's sweet pain this time, because whatever they may say to me or however they try to hurt me, I know that just by sticking it out I'm going to help end the whole system of segregation; and that can make you go through anything." (Coles 1967, p. 117).

"Sweet pain"—a keenly diagnostic phrase. In a context of "Black is beautiful," of confident assertion of rights with some support from the dominant society, of a declining sense of powerlessness and a growing sense of internal control, discrimination has a less crushing impact. There have always been such creative responses, but they are more likely to prosper in an environment where hope has expanded.

The study of self-esteem must be carried on with full recognition of the influence of the larger society. Adam (1978) is concerned lest the newer studies of self-esteem deflect attention from the study of the negative impact of discrimination. He argues (pp. 49, 51):

Self-esteem has become a psychological abstraction which allows the effects of a racist social structure simply to fade away....The fundamental problem raised by the early writers, of the production and reproduction of the social order, has been side-stepped and ultimately obscured by the redefinition of the self-esteem concept over time.

He says this in response to those who simply dismiss the earlier studies of the personality injury resulting from discrimination, who believe that "discrediting this tradition is, we believe, necessary" (McCarthy and Yancey 1971b, p. 591).

In our view, the tradition of Clark and Clark and the others who documented the personal injuries caused by segregation and discrimination ought not to be discredited but corrected where needed and then built upon. Certainly Rosenberg and the others who have found evidence of positive self-esteem even in the face of discrimination do not believe that their studies allow "the effects of a racist social structure simply to fade away," to repeat Adam's phrase. To find that individuals have ways of coping with prejudice and discrimination is scarcely to deny their negative impact.

We need a framework within which the diverse but not necessarily contradictory findings can be drawn together. Pettigrew (1978, p. 60) has wisely suggested such a framework:

(1) Oppression and subjugation do in fact have "negative" personal consequences for minority individuals that are mediated by behavioral responses shaped through coping with oppression.

(2) There are also some "positive" personal consequences for minority individuals as well as negative personal consequences for majority individuals....

(3) Many of the "negative" consequences for minority group members are reflected in personality traits that in a range of situations can act to maintain, rather than challenge, the repressive social system.

(4) Not all minority group members will be so affected nor are most traits of most minority members so shaped, since a sharp disjunction between the "real" personal self and the racial self is generally possible.

(5) Thus, proud, strong minorities are possible despite "marks of oppression." And this strength becomes increasingly evident as the minority itself effectively challenges the repressive societal system.

The Prejudices of Minority-Group Members

Minority-group members do not escape the tendency toward prejudice. Partly because of the same set of economic, political, cultural, and personal reasons we have discussed in Chapters 3–5 with reference to majority-group members and partly as a consequence of the deprivations they have experienced, those who are targets of intergroup hostility also engage in it.

The hostility of minority-group members is expressed in part toward other minorities and in part toward the dominant group. And when minorities become dominant groups, they sometimes turn quickly to discriminations on their own. Thus many African nations have experienced sharp intertribal conflicts, as attested by the several million refugees, the forced migrations, and the extreme interethnic violence in some areas (Elliott Skinner in Despres, 1975, 131–57; Tandon 1973; Waldron 1981). Some of this is closer to international conflict than minority–majority conflict, since many African nations are new and artificial by historical and cultural standards (it is not for that reason less tragic). Some of it, however, is the continuation of long-standing hostilities. Jews have fled from harsh discrimination in many lands to Israel, where those who are not from the West or the Soviet Union and are called the Oriental Jews find that discrimination has not entirely been left behind (Peres 1971; Rosenstein 1981; Smooha 1978; Yuchtman-Yaar and Semyonov 1979).

In the United States, some Chicanos and Puerto Ricans are at pains to set themselves apart from Blacks. This is an effect not simply of their own minority status but also of their acceptance of the dominant "Anglo" prejudice (Grebler, Moore, and Guzman 1970, pp. 390–94). Guy Johnson has described the intensity with which the Croatian Indians in North Carolina try to distinguish themselves from the Blacks of the area. Whites tend to class Indians and Blacks together, but the Indians strive for a separate status. The large amount of mixture of Black and Indian inheritance has produced sharp internal cleavages, with darker Indians more likely to be prejudiced (Berry 1963; Guy Johnson 1939).

Anti-Semitism among Black Americans. The minority prejudice most discussed in recent years in the United States is probably anti-Semitism among Blacks. The question is a difficult one, with the evidence far from clear. In the 1960s and again in the late 1970s there were some who believed that black opposition to Jews had reached a crisis level. Schlomo Katz introduced a book on *Negro and Jew* (1967, vii) with the statement:

It is now widely accepted as as an incontrovertible fact that, (1) there exists a pronounced anti-Jewish sentiment among the Negro masses in this country, despite the active participation of many idealistic young Jews in the Negro struggle for equal rights, and the moral support given to the Civil Rights movement by organized Jewish groups, and (2) that Jews are reacting to this sentiment with an emotional backlash. Though no exact studies of substantial reliable data about this situation are available, the prevalence of anti-Jewish myths among Negroes is undeniable.

As Katz noted, exact studies are scarce. A national urban sample taken in 1964 found about one-third of both white and black respondents to be high on an anti-Semitism scale (Marx 1967, Chapter 6). Marx noted that most Blacks do not distinguish Jews from other Whites; when they do, Jews are seen more favorably. Brink and Harris (1964, p. 133) noted that Blacks were more favorable to Jews and Catholics than to Protestants when the question was put in terms of religious identities. Later polls found a continuing trend of declining anti-Semitism in the country as a whole. Although Blacks tended to be a little more favorable to Jews in general, their attitudes on issues related to economics were somewhat more negative (Gelb 1980; Quinley and Glock 1979).

These data do not adequately inform us about Black-Jewish relationships, however, because specific issues have led to sharp public controversy, especially among leaders of the two groups. Differences with regard to educational and job opportunities and policies toward Israel and the Palestine Liberation Organization have been expressed in acrimonious terms.

Competition for jobs and educational opportunities became harsher in the 1960s (Weisbord and Stein 1970). This is best understood as competition between Blacks and Whites but because of particular circumstances was frequently interpreted as antagonism between Blacks and Jews specifically:

What the Negro wants is what the White has, and he wants it now. The Whites who have what Negroes are going to want to take next are very often Jews. The stores in Harlem, the teaching and civil service appointments, are rungs on the ladder Negroes have to climb over the toes of Jews, just as they have to make Irish and Italians move over in the construction trades. (Ben Halpern in Shlomo Katz 1967, p. 68)

In this situation a few Blacks sought to exploit anti-Semitism and some Jewish leaders responded with expressions of deep concern. It is understandable that there should be distress at any sign of new or renewed anti-Semitism but it is possible to overread the signs. At the height of controversy over control of New York City schools and access to the City University of New York, the Anti-Defamation League of B'nai B'rith declared that "Raw, undisguised anti-Semitism is at a crisis level in New York City schools" (*The New York Times,* January 23, 1969, p. 1). We think the same evidences could be read to mean, however, that there was a sharp and difficult conflict between Jews and Blacks over control of teaching and administrative positions, over curriculum, and over control of school policy generally. This led some black leaders and would-be leaders to speak in harsh and uncompromising terms, some including severe anti-Semitic statements. Opposition to those statements is on soundest ground when it is carried through in a context in which the realistic basis of conflict and the severe disadvantages of Blacks are recognized. Arthur Hertzberg puts the matter sharply (in Shlomo Katz 1967, p. 74):

The issues between Jews and Negroes are not misunderstandings between the two groups but hard questions about power and position. It is ridiculous to pretend that at this moment in American history, the textures of Jewish and Negro experiences are similar. The Jews are the most vulnerable of the haves, and the Negroes are the most unfortunate of the have-nots. They may have some rhetoric in common; they are together the heirs of moral imperatives; but the real question is what love and justice mean, concretely: how many Jewish school principals are commanded by the joint Negro-Jewish commitment to morality, and Jewish memories of persecution, to go sell shoes, so less well-trained Negroes can hold their jobs.

In the last sentence, Hertzberg leaves his analytic position. Whether Blacks are "less well-trained" depends upon what one wants accomplished. Are they less well trained to motivate black students to stay in school, to be sensitive to the aspirations and perspectives of the black population, to introduce perspectives on American culture and history that express more fully the roles of black men and women? Or, even granted that they are less well trained now, is there any other way to achieve parity than to offer special opportunities for experience to overcome past disprivilege?

The conflicts in New York City were part of a larger shift in intergroup relations. As Oliphant notes (1979, p. 20):

Something began to go wrong toward the end of the 1960s. By then, the civil rights movement had moved beyond attacks on the segregation of public accommodations and the denial of voting rights in the South. The movement went North; blacks were after real power now, and jobs, and control over the institutions and organizations in their own communities.

In addition, some Blacks began to identify more closely with the "third world," not excluding the Palestinians, while most Jews have strong attachments with Israel.

This potential conflict was highlighted in 1979 when Andrew Young, then American Ambassador to the United Nations, made an unauthorized approach to the Palestine Liberation Organization. Other Blacks, including Jesse Jackson and Joseph Lowery, President of the Southern Christian Leadership Conference, followed with similar visits. Some Blacks believed that Young's dismissal as ambassador was instigated by Jewish protests over the visits. On the other side, many Jews saw the visit as harshly anti-Israel and perhaps also as deflected protest against the opposition of some Jews (see Glazer 1978) to affirmative action. Such moderate black leaders as Bayard Rustin and Vernon Jordan, Jr., also condemned the contacts with the PLO (*The New York Times,* October 14, 1979, p. 1, and October 18, 1979, p. A9); and Julius Lester wrote: "The irony is that this new expression of anti-Semitism was spearheaded by the organization founded by Martin Luther King, Jr.—the Southern Christian Leadership Conference....It is hard to believe that Dr. King ever lived" (*The Village Voice,* September 10, 1979, p. 1).

In assessing this issue we will be wise to remember that it is not simply a matter of Black versus Jew. Israel is a state, with interests that collide with the interests of some of the third world states. At home, other interests collide. Dreyfuss, who has both black and Jewish ancestors, observed that "Blacks, envious of the power that Jews wield in America [he refers to the 'image-shaping industries'—film, television, journalism, and book publishing], find it difficult to understand the profound insecurity of Jews about their own role in this country" (Dreyfuss 1979, p. 11).

Through all of this, the majority of Blacks showed relatively little interest in Israel, did not think that Young's dismissal was brought about by Jewish pressure, and saw Jews as friendly to their interests (Gelb 1980). Gelb emphasizes the common interests, the contacts, and the similar voting patterns. This is a valuable corrective to the harsh and, in our judgment, exaggerated picture of conflict found in the press. On the whole, Blacks are less anti-Semitic than Whites. We should not overlook the fact, however, that some perspectives and interests do clash. In the spring of 1984, during his campaign for the Democratic presidential nomination, Jesse Jackson made a careless off-the-cuff and presumably off-the-record ethnic slur against Jews. The attention it received, the sharp criticism it provoked and his belated and somewhat awkward apology revealed again that the interests and perceptions of Jews and Blacks are to some degree at odds. At this particular time in history, both national and international issues, in the minds of some Jews and Blacks, push their shared concerns into the background (Rose 1981).

Other Personality Differences That Are Affected by Minority Status

There is scarcely an aspect of personality that has not been held to vary with race or to be differentially associated with various groups. Dozens of paper-and-pencil and performance tests of various kinds have compared the tendencies or behavior of Blacks, or other racial groups, with those of Whites. Few of them, however, have even approximately solved the complicated methodological problems involved in such studies, and we must be very careful, therefore, in evaluating the results. Many of the studies assume that they are trying to measure a racial difference *per se.* To do this, the influence of all other factors would have to be eliminated by matching the groups compared—an almost impossible task in a society in which the members of minority races are the objects of prejudice and discrimination.

The weaknesses of such studies, however, should not lead one to assume that there are no differences. Other studies of differences among racial groups start from the premise that racial difference, unaffected by experience, is unimportant (or at least unmeasurable at the present time) and seek rather to measure the differences that are the result of differing experience. This is safer scientific ground. The question of perfect matching of the groups is less important in these studies, for the task is to measure the personality consequences precisely when important factors *do* vary. The chief methodological problem in such studies is to know how widely the results may be generalized.

Minority Status and Mental Illness

Illustrative of research of this type is the attempt to discover whether there are differences in types and amounts of mental illness and whether prejudice and discrimination are among the factors that affect the development of personality disorder. It is difficult to give an adequate appraisal of this question because the data on the incidence of mental illness are seldom comparable. How mental illness is defined and the amount of hospitalization vary greatly from time to time and in different places.

There are problems of a technical sort that we shall mention here in order to indicate the complexity of the situation but which we shall not discuss: One must distinguish the prevalence rate (the ratio of any given group that is ill at a particular time) from the incidence rate (the ratio who fall ill in a given time period). Any group that suffers longer neglect, poorer care, or lower community support will have a higher prevalence rate, even if its incidence rate is equal. Diagnostic practices can influence the rates. Physicians may be more likely, for example, to diagnose minority-group or lower-class members as schizophrenic because of the mixture of their symptoms with behavior normal to their situation—greater distrust, suspicion, anger. Groups may vary in the number of alternative ways available to express their anxieties. The wealthy person may be a tolerated eccentric—a luxury that minority-group members cannot afford. Communities may differ, as a result of their subcultures or their resources, in the ways they deal with the illness "role." Mental illness is in part a group fact, with some individuals selected, so to speak, to carry and express the anxieties for a group of interacting persons.

Keeping these difficulties in mind, we may note that contemporary explanations of the causes of mental illness would lead us to expect a higher incidence, at least for many varieties of illness, among oppressed groups. That appears to be the case, at least for the kinds of mental illness which are treated (perhaps too generous a term) in public hospitals and agencies and therefore get into public records.[2]

The higher rates of serious mental illness among many minorities are to be accounted for by their life conditions, their attitudes toward treatment (in a health profession dominated by majority culture and personnel), the facilities available to them, and the kinds of treatment they receive. As Graves remarks (1970, pp. 461–62), "The vast majority of Navajo drunkenness, at least in Denver, can be accounted for *without recourse to the fact that our subjects are Indians*." Oppression leads to pathogenic conditions in minority communities and, in the words of Charles Pinderhughes referring to Blacks, to "more opportunity than Whites to have early experiences of loss, pain, and deprivation which can imprint tragedy-seeking scripts in their personalities." He goes on to say that because of these conditions "usually large numbers of people need psychiatric treatment, serious resistances to treatment are frequently encountered, and patients must return to the same pathogenic circumstances which spawned their pathology" (Pinderhughes in Willie, Kramer, and Brown 1973, pp. 66–67).

From the evidence available we cannot speak with confidence about the relationship of minority status to mental illness. We cannot even state beyond doubt what the comparative incidence rates are, whether of neuroses, which are often thought to be found more often in the middle and upper classes and therefore by correlation among the white population, or of psychoses which generally bear more heavily on the lower classes. Any measure of majority–minority difference in rate must control for class before one can isolate the possible psychic burdens imposed by prejudice and discrimination. One must, indeed, study psychosis rates in the context of possible functionally alternative modes of response to extreme stress—rates of suicide, of outward aggression (thinking of mental illness as inner aggression), of low motivation and aspiration (shutting out and devaluing the harsh world). Such alternative responses may be more available, as a result of socialization and subcultural values, to one group than to another, thus affecting their rates of mental illness.

That contemporary intergroup relations carry a heavy psychic cost we think there is little doubt. That they are measured in higher rates of psychosis for minorities we think is probable. We need more study of this question, however, before these general statements can be formulated into the kind of differentiated statements that science requires. Some of the earlier work that emphasized the "mark of oppression"—the self-destroying impact of discrimination (e.g., Grier and Cobbs 1968; Kardiner and Ovesey 1951; Parker and Kleiner 1966)—tends to overlook the personal resources of the oppressed and the sources of self-esteem we have discussed

---

[2]For a variety of studies of native Americans, Mexican Americans and black Americans see, for example, Bahr, Chadwick, and Day 1972, pp. 345–400; Graves 1970; Hernandez, Haug, and Wagner 1976, pp. 205–96; Indian Health Service Task Force on Alcoholism 1972; Benjamin Malzberg in Klineberg 1944; Levy 1974; Joel See and Kent Miller in Miller and Dreger 1973, pp. 447–66; Pasamanick 1963; Willie, Kramer, and Brown 1973.

earlier. It is essential, however, that we not let this newer view obscure the enormous personality costs a society pays for categorical deprivation.

Minority Status and Intelligence

In Chapter 2 we discussed the evidence regarding differences in group averages in intelligence test scores. There is no need to repeat that account; but it may be useful to summarize several points in order to connect that discussion with our interest here in the consequences of minority status:

1. In every large group there is wide variation in intelligence scores, ranging, in terms of IQ, from under 50 to over 200.

2. Group means, therefore, are of little significance, since it is individuals who are given or denied opportunities. To oppose opportunities for individuals with IQs of 140 because "their group" has an average score of 90 compared with an average among another group of 100 or 105 makes no sense.

3. Scores among races overlap extensively despite wide differences in experience. The interpretation of that overlap is sometimes obscure. A 25 percent overlap between Blacks and Whites, for example, means that 25 percent of the black scores are above the *median* white score.

4. White groups vary widely in average scores, and in a way incapable of interpretation on national grounds, unless one cares to argue that the predominantly "Anglo-Saxon" South represents an inferior national stock.

5. Differences by group averages among young children are small, but they become larger with age, particularly on those tests that rely heavily on language.

6. Intelligence is powerfully affected by health and nutrition in the earliest years of life, indeed even in the prenatal environment. An inadequate supply of protein and other nutriments means, almost literally, a lack of "food for thought." Brain weight growth is most rapid in embryo and in the earliest months. At birth, a human infant's brain has ¼ of adult weight, while the body as a whole has about 1/25 of adult weight. Loehlin, Lindzey, and Spuhler (1975, p. 216) report a study of nutritional adequacy for Blacks and Whites in the rural South. Nutrition is "obviously inadequate" for 60 percent of the Blacks and for 25 percent of the Whites; it is "probably inadequate" for 15 percent of the Blacks and 45 percent of the Whites. This

inadequacy has persisted for decades (Myrdal 1944, p. 375). Class and dietary customs as well as minority status affect levels of nutritional adequacy. We must emphasize the importance of malnutrition for the *world,* not only for minorities. And the enormous number in poverty, even if not the percentage, is likely to grow in the years ahead— a "sociogenically induced tragedy" of malnutrition in Montagu's words (1972a).

The work on nutrition (see Kallen 1973; Loehlin, Lindsey, and Spuhler 1975, pp. 196–229, 310–19; Montagu 1972) gives special point to Gould's emphasis (1981, p. 156): heritability does not mean inevitability. It refers to the passage of traits or tendencies by genetic transmission. But there is a range, from which environmental influences select. Moderate nutritional deficiency, especially after the first few years, does not by itself seriously hamper intellectual development. It does seem, however, to affect emotional development, which can lead to behavior that blocks social interaction and, at least indirectly, the quality of school work.

7. Intellectual and stimulus deprivation, correlated with but not identical to low socioeconomic status, leads to poor concept development and poor verbal skills; these in turn lead to inadequate school performance, alienation from school, and barriers to environmental stimuli; and these lead to poor test performance. IQ can be significantly raised by improving the stimulus richness of the child's environment. In a *Report on Longitudinal Evaluations of Preschool Programs* to the United States Department of Health, Education, and Welfare (1974), Ryan and Bronfenbrenner note the special importance of mothers and their care of children. In some cases, when greater maternal participation was impossible, a trained teacher was assigned to each child, some as young as three months. The teacher was responsible, until the mother could take over, for total care, for cuddling and soothing as well as for learning. "At five and a half years the cared-for children had a mean IQ of 124 points while the uncared for controls had a mean IQ of 94" (Montagu 1975, p. 13). All of this emphasizes that intelligence is a result of a complex organism–environment transaction—a transaction that affects not simply content and style of thought, but its deepest processes.

8. Test conditions, including the identities and expectations of testers and of respondents, affect the result. Intelligence test scores lead to labeling (Beeghley and Butler 1974) with strong effects on

educational opportunities and, reciprocally, on test scores (Mercer 1973; Rosenthal and Jacobson 1968). In schools, labeling becomes joined to official processes of tracking and to unofficial sorting and steering processes, to the effect that educational and test performance is influenced (Erickson 1975; Rist 1970; Rosenbaum 1976).

9. Differences in group averages become progressively smaller as life conditions (income, residence, education, occupation) become more nearly similar. The measures of "similarity," however, are often quite imprecise, the effect of which is usually to make a minority seem more similar to the majority than it is in fact. If, for example, the full range of socioeconomic differences is condensed into three catagories, minority-group members may, on the average, be near the bottom of each category while majority-group members are near the top of "the same" category. Or, in the matching process, important variables may be neglected—variables which, in terms of our interest here, have significance for intelligence. Zena Blau (1981) demonstrates, for example, that aversive discipline of children—the extent of which varies from group to group—strongly affects scholastic achievement.

10. Full equation of conditions is difficult because equivalent income and education do not protect many minority-group members from rebuffs and other ego-crushing conditions that lead to "intellectually defeating personality traits that play a significant role in their ability to score on measures of intelligence" (Roen 1960, p. 150).

11. Intelligence defined solely with reference to the usual tests scarcely gives an adequate picture. If intelligence is skillful adaptation to the stresses and possibilities of one's environment—a functional interpretation—responses of Blacks may measure up well.

12. Tests free of cultural and subcultural influences have yet to be designed—indeed are probably not possible to design (Rosalie Cohen 1969; Eells, Davis, Havighurst, Herrick, and Tyler 1951).

With such a list of qualifications it is obvious that one must speak with caution, but the evidence to date appears to show that, although members of some minority groups do exhibit lower average scores in the abilities that intelligence tests measure, these are best understood as personality consequences of inferior status, not as biological causes of inferior status.

Such, then, are the consequences of minority status. The pressures at work on those who are the targets for prejudice and discrimination require that they develop some mechanisms of adjustment and response. These may be looked upon as further personality consequences of the experiences that come from an inferior position. They are the subject matter of the next chapter.

CHAPTER 7

Types of Response to Prejudice and Discrimination

Probably no two persons respond in exactly the same way to the problems they face as members of a minority group. It is possible, however, to classify the patterns of adjustment into broad types for purposes of analysis and to point out the kinds of persons and groups most likely to adopt each type as the primary mode of response to prejudice and discrimination. Response to the dominant world is not simply a matter of individual trial and error, for the culture of a minority group contains traditional adjustment techniques that are passed on, intentionally and unintentionally, to the oncoming generation. These techniques will vary from group to group; there will be many variations, moreover, within each group. To speak simply of "Americans of Mexican descent," for example, is to miss sharp contrasts among them. Both the nature of their problems and the modes of response are quite different for immigrant farm laborers, second-generation urban dwellers, and those families of Mexican ancestry who have roots in the Southwest going back in some instances 400 years. As Charles S. Johnson pointed out (1943, p. 231) with respect to Blacks, the response to prejudice varies with the regional and cultural setting, social status, the specific situational factors, and the basic personality type of the individuals, among other factors.

Murguia (1975, Chapter 3) identifies additional variables that significantly influence whether a minority group will be primarily assimilative or will, in his terms, seek "decolonization"—that is, will seek some recognition as an equal and in some measure distinctive cultural group. These variables are shown in Table 7-1.

It seems to us wise to add a social psychological perspective to the structural and cultural variables influencing the responses of minority-group members. How one learns the nature of his or her status and adjusts to it ranges all the way from systematic training by parents to entirely informal and accidental acquisition of points of view from small incidents or major crises. Some parents believe it necessary to give their children explicit attitudes concerning their relationship to the dominant world, whether they be attitudes of acceptance or rejection of that relationship. Some may try to teach specific ways of avoiding trouble or of facing trouble if it comes. Others, however, make no conscious effort to equip their children with attitudes or techniques. These are then acquired informally by observation, by the learning of traditional modes of behavior, by the use of peer-group folkways, and by on-the-spot adjustments to members of the dominant group.

What, then, are the basic types of response to prejudice and discrimination? There are four fundamental varieties:

- Avoidance
- Aggression

• Acceptance
• Reform

Several qualifications and clarifications are necessary in the use of such typologies: (1) as analytic types, they do not describe particular individuals, who usually express mixed responses; (2) few specific actions are purely of one type or another; (3) these modes of reponse are subject to change, often quite rapidly, as situations change; (4) they feed back into the system from which they come and thus are causes as well as effects; (5) they are in many ways similar to the modes of response in areas of human behavior other than those of minority–majority relations—for example, ascetic (avoidance), prophetic (aggressive), and mystical (acceptance) religious sects, or value-oriented, power-oriented, and participation-oriented social movements (Turner and Killian 1957, Part 4; Yinger 1970, Chapter 13); (6) they match, to an important degree, the types of minorities discussed in Chapter 1. Types of minorities can be thought of as organized, structured manifestations of *shared* strategies or responses. The kinds of qualifications applicable to a typology of individual responses, of course, must be applied also to types of minorities.

Figure 7-1 may suggest some of the relationships among these responses (or these strategies, if one thinks of them as consciously selected adaptations and policies). Aggression, for example, can shade off toward reformism, as in nonviolent

TYPES OF RESPONSE TO
PREJUDICE AND DISCRIMINATION

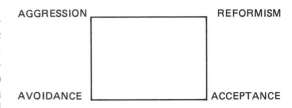

Figures 7–1. Types of response to prejudice and discrimination.

protests, or toward avoidance, as in political or religious movements seeking separation.

One way of looking at these types of response is to see them as different combinations of ways to answer two strategic questions: Can change be accomplished within the established social system? Do minority-group members have access to forces of change? The possible combinations are shown in Table 7-2. Column 3 in the table suggests the kinds of groups that can emerge among those who agree on answers to the two questions, groups that match the minority-group policies discussed in Chapter 1 (see also Crawford and Naditch 1970).

Avoidance

If members of a minority group cannot abolish the status restrictions under which they live, they

Table 7-1. Variables Influencing Minority-Group Response

Toward assimilation		Toward decolonization
	1. Mode of entry	
Voluntary immigration		Conquest
	2. Size, with reference to the majority	
Small		Large
	3. Distribution	
Scattered throughout the host nation		Concentrated in particular areas
	4. Race, with reference to the majority	
Same		Different
	5. Culture, with reference to the majority	
Some language and religion		Different language and religion

Adapted from Murguia, 1975. p. 31.

Table 7-2. Type of Individual and Group Responses to Minority Status

Types of individual response	I Can change be accomplished within the system? Is reform possible?	II Do minority-group members have access to change forces?	III If many agree on the answers, one has a group or social movement of these types:
1. Avoidance	no	no	Secessionist
2. Aggression	no	yes	Militant
3. Acceptance	yes	no	Assimilationist
4. Reformism	yes	yes	Pluralistic

can, at least in some circumstances, avoid situations wherein they must experience the full weight of those restrictions.

Avoidance is a complex response. It can involve movement in either of two opposite directions: People can withdraw or attempt to withdraw from their minority group or, oppositely, they can draw closer to their group while withdrawing so far as possible from contact with the dominant group. With respect to the latter, Jacobson (1977) distinguishes between separatism and avoidance. Separatism is more active and protest-oriented; it is close to aggression and counterposed to integration. Avoidance is movement away from the dominant group rather than movement against it; it is contrasted with approach activities. This distinction is not self-evident, but it emerges from a factor analysis of the responses of high school and junior high school students to thirteen items dealing with intergroup relations. The avoidance response, for example, was most clearly indicated by agreement with the statement: "People should have nothing to do with people of another race if they can help it." Among the black respondents, the clearest case of separation was agreement with the statement: "White people can never fully understand the black condition." Among Latino students, separation was most clearly marked by disagreement with: "Close friendship between Latins and whites is possible" (Jacobson 1977, pp. 1014–15).

Types of Avoidance

1. The most complete form of avoidance, clearly, is to withdraw entirely from the minority group. When the color line is drawn sharply, this adjustment is open to only a small proportion of persons of mixed race. Estimates of the extent of Negro "passing" in the United States, which of necessity are very rough, range from a few thousands to tens of thousands per year. Even with national or religious minorities, passing into the dominant group is often restricted by the presence of identifying characteristics: language accents, names, cultural differences, or knowledge by the dominant community of the family background can inhibit passing. This last factor is strong in societies such as Japan where ancestry is of great importance. Obviously these are much less categorical and permanent differences. Extensive assimilation mixed with pluralism, after three or four generations, has been the rule in the United States and in many other societies, particularly for national minorities. This is less likely to be the case in the short run. Immigrants who discover that their hopes are not being fulfilled and that they are facing major obstacles to status improvement may become more oriented to conflict after three or four years (Portes, Parker, and Cobas 1980).

In situations in which minorities have not wanted to be assimilated but have worked and fought for cultural and/or national independence, this process has, of course, not taken place. In such circumstances relatively few members of a minority group have sought to avoid the penalties of that status by joining the majority. They have, far more often, united to try to win independence or at least a protected position within the larger society for the continuation of their group as a distinct cultural and national population. Having felt a long series of outside imperialisms—Turkish, Austro-Hungarian, German, Russian—most Eastern European minorities have had their group self-consciousness and cohesiveness sharply accentuated. It seems not unreasonable to suppose that the present Russian domination of this area, as well as the highly centralized national domination within the eastern European countries, will face the same kind of group resistance already witnessed, in both external and internal affairs, in Yugoslavia, Great Britain, Iraq, and many other societies.

Racial passing, particularly, and individual assimilation (e.g., a Jew who gives up his religion and leaves the Jewish community) are not guaranteed to permit the individual to avoid all the consequences of minority-group status. There is the danger of discovery, which might destroy the whole pattern of adjustment. There is the problem of relationship to one's old friends and community. To break contact completely is sometimes a painful experience. Some persons who pass develop a sense of guilt that they have deserted their group. They cannot completely break off identification with it. Some members of their former community may look with approval at their decision (happy that they are avoiding some of the hardships of their former status or glad that they are putting something over on the majority group). Others, however, may strongly disapprove and so give those who pass a sense of fear or guilt. A random sample of Blacks in the Detroit area were asked: "Suppose someone you knew told you he could 'pass' into white society, and was going to because of the advantages it would give him. How would you feel toward this person?" The results are tabulated in Table 7-3 according to the race of the interviewer which, however, in this instance had little effect.

Passing is largely limited to urban communities, where one's former status can more readily be hidden.

Despite these difficulties, passing is for a few members of minority groups a decisive way to avoid some of the penalties of their status. Doubtless many more use it temporarily for specific purposes than attempt to cross permanently into the dominant group.

2. Upper-class members of a minority are able to avoid some prejudice and discrimination by sealing themselves off from contact with lower-class members of their group and by insulating themselves from their struggles and problems. They are able to afford well-ordered lives free from contact with the dominant group in large measure and free from dependence upon it. In these circumstances, some upper-class persons develop a complacency about "race problems." Having achieved a satisfactory adjustment, they see no reason to endanger it by being identified with the minority group as a whole. (Many upper-class persons, of course, refuse to make this adjustment and instead become aggressive leaders of the minority.) This kind of avoidance is not wholly successful. Even those who have most successfully reduced the necessity for contact with the dominant group may run into rigid barriers, especially with regard to finding a good place to live and in economic matters. Some have feelings of guilt which make their apparent complacency in the matter somewhat less than wholehearted.

An interesting aspect of the desire to avoid economic involvement with the dominant community is the effort to persuade the members of a minority group to patronize only business and professional people from their own group. Some leaders have developed this into an ideology of a separate economy or a "nation within a nation." This ideology, as found for example among Blacks in the United States, is closely related to the growth of black nationalism. Its appeal has not been large, but for a minority who see in it a mode of adjustment it has often led to support of segregation. It is an attempt to derive "advantages from the disadvantages." Some businessmen have appealed to "race pride" to reduce or eliminate competition.

More extreme nationalist movements among minorities are primarily visible to majorities because of their hostile rhetoric and sometimes their violent actions. We shall refer to them as among the aggressive types of responses. Yet they can be seen partly as an avoidance strategy, with emphasis on separatism (Blair 1977; Hall 1978; Turner and Wilson 1976). Aggression in those cases is used in an effort to break the bonds of dependence and interdependence more than to win greater equality and justice within the dominant society. Such movements among black Americans tend to be small and

Table 7-3. Black Attitudes toward Passing

	To White interviewers ($N = 165$)	To Black interviewers ($N = 330$)
Approve	17%	19%
Don't care	40%	28%
Disapprove	40%	46%
Other	3%	7%

Source: Schuman and Converse, 1971, p. 53.

to fade away after a few years or they modify their goals and methods to become less harsh and separatist. Among Native Americans, separation is more clearly preservationist, in the sense of an effort to reaffirm and rescue viable Indian communities and values, than it is an attempt to create new ways to avoid contact with a discriminatory society (Deloria 1973; Dorris 1981; Ponting and Gibbins 1980, Part 3; George and Louise Spindler in Yinger and Simpson 1978, pp. 73–85). This is to some degree true also of Puerto Rican nationalist movements (Steiner 1974, pp. 397–437). Americans of Mexican descent have not yet shown strong tendencies toward such avoidance policies, although some of the emphasis on the Spanish language carry this possibility (G. Cohen 1982; Nunis 1981).

Empirical study of the strength of the appeal of separatist beliefs and movements is scarce. Turner and Wilson found that "Blacks who favor separation tend to be more alienated, fearful of race genocide, race conscious, and supportive of racial violence than those who endorse interracial cooperation" (1976, p. 139; see also Elder 1971). In a study of a black neighborhood in Cleveland, Dubey (1970) found that from 10 to 16 percent preferred a black to a white person as doctor, nurse, social worker, store owner, and other occupations. From 77 to 84 percent said that race made no difference and from 5 to 11 percent preferred Whites. Only for ministers was there a fairly large vote for a black person, and even then, the majority said that it made no difference (42 percent preferred a Negro; 56 percent thought it made no difference).

3. The avoidance response is made by a few in the development of communities composed only of minority-group people—for example, the all-Negro town of Mound Bayou, Mississippi (Hermann 1981). A more extreme expression of this tendency is the call for a separate nation. The appeal of Zionism among Jews, particularly those in Europe, has been not only positive (the desire to preserve the religiocultural tradition) but also an avoidance response (the desire to lay down the burden of prejudice and discrimination). Negro "Zionism" in the Americas has relied on remote or even fallacious connections with Africa, as in the Ras Tafari movement in the West Indies (Simpson 1955), the Garveyite movement in the United States (Cronon 1955), and more recently the Black Muslims. Since we shall discuss the Muslims in Chapter 15, we need mention here only that their call for a separate nation, their attack on integration, their appeal to the unifying force of a supposed separate black culture not only are expressions of avoidance but contain also powerful themes of aggression against the system. These themes are much less important in the American Muslim Mission, which has evolved from the Black Muslims.

Far more common than separate communities or nations—or dreams of them—are the segregated subcommunities in our cities. They are largely forced upon the minority but to some degree are encouraged by the desire to find an island partly free from the prejudice and discrimination of the dominant group. The people of Harlem, a major city in its own right, can avoid some of the daily and even hourly symbols and experiences of imposed inferiority. The great majority of the residents cannot, however, avoid the fact that the very existence of Harlem as a separate community is largely a result of discrimination. They are still largely dependent upon white employers and white landlords. And even the daily interaction *within* the community is strongly influenced by the fact that it is a segregated area. This fact is always in the background, conditioning the internal status structure, influencing the nature of its leadership, affecting the cohesiveness of the community. Segregated communities have a decided tendency to split into factions, partly because of the intensified internal struggle for status, partly because of disagreements over the best way to deal with the dominant group.

Immigrant communities, faced with the additional problems of language and cultural assimilation, are not to be understood simply as devices for avoiding the pressures of the dominant group. On the one hand, they serve as stepping stones to the new society; on the other, they serve to slow down the transition by acting as a center for the old culture, with native-language papers, schools, and churches and a general emphasis on the common background. The balance of these two tendencies varies from community to community, depending upon the size and type of the immigrant group, the recency of immigration, and the attitudes of the larger society.

Groups not steadily replenished with newcomers often disperse into the larger community. In recent years, large increases in immigration into the United States, as compared with the 1924–1965 period, have reenforced some ethnic communities—for example, those of Chinese or of Spanish-speaking descent. In the latter case, the size and recency of much of the immigration (whether from

Mexico, Puerto Rico, Cuba, or elsewhere), the importance of the Spanish language and related cultural elements, widespread poverty, discrimination, and doubtless other factors contribute to the maintenance of fairly distinctive residential areas. The degree of separation, however, varies widely from city to city. and is sharply reduced as income and educational differentials are reduced (Grebler, Moore,and Guzman 1970, Chapter 12).

4. The desire to escape a highly discriminatory situation has often been a powerful motive ·in the migration of persons of low status. Religious prejudice was one of the factors in the migration of some of the early settlers of America; discrimination against socialist workers encouraged a great many to leave Bismarck's Germany; discrimination and violence in Poland and Russia, particularly after 1880, and in Germany after 1933 caused millions of Jews to seek avoidance by emigration; and one of the propelling forces behind the migration of Blacks from South to North has been the hope of escaping from discrimination and low status. The success of such moves has varied greatly, depending on existing prejudices in the new situation, the ease with which the newcomers could be absorbed economically, the size of the migrating group, the degree to which the migrants desired assimilation or a separate protected status, and other factors. One aspect of this kind of avoidance is the belief—based partly on known facts, partly on fervent hope—that the new land is the promised land, where the great problems of discrimination are solved.

5. For most people the rather intensive avoidance techniques that we have discussed are either impossible or held to be undesirable. Most members of minority groups have to face frequent contact with members of the dominant group. They may try to reduce these contacts by ordering goods from a catalogue or making reservations by telephone or patronizing the businesss and professional people of their own group.

6. Frazier described a somewhat different type of avoidance response. This is an effort not to avoid punishing or humiliating contact with the dominant group, but to escape the feelings of inferiority and futility that the discriminations of the dominant group may have forced upon one's own self-image. Some aspects of this process can have happy results, as judged by the dominant values, whereas other results are unfortunate. There may be strong efforts

at self-improvement and an emphasis on education. There may develop, however, a "world of make-believe," as Frazier (1957b) called it, in which the members of a minority group struggle with their feelings of inferiority in wholly unrealistic terms.

Before we conclude that such responses are especially characteristic of Blacks, however, or of minorities more generally, or are the result of prejudice and discrimination, we must measure the extent to which similar patterns are found among the white bourgeoisie. Blacks certainly have no monopoly on the world of make-believe. In a complex society, most people carry some feelings of inadequacy and inferiority, and many develop awkward ways of responding to those feelings—chauvinism, perhaps, or prejudice; alcoholism or mental illness.

Many avoidance responses carry a strong undertone of aggression, but in a context of accommodation and a sense of powerlessness the aggressive aspect is deflected. Many black youths in the slums are keenly aware of the values and criteria for success in the dominant society. They are also highly sensitive to the barriers that separate them from those values. Some strive for achievement in the system; some react by delinquency or random aggression; but others develop a world of make-believe akin, as Finestone (1957) points out, to that described by Frazier for the black bourgeoisie. They deny the values of the larger society or perhaps raise to a primary level what are generally regarded as secondary and marginal values (Matza and Sykes 1961). Thus they avoid the sense of failure, at least consciously, by creating a world in which *they* are the successful ones. The squares who work hard, stay in school, and keep within the bounds approved by society are the failures. The Cat reverses these tendencies of squares; he rejects work; he seeks for a "hustle"—a way of getting income by the easiest means possible. Life is a search for kicks—any act tabooed by squares—that will heighten the experience of the moment. Thus, the ego-crushing feelings from encounters with the dominant society are turned aside; a private world is built according to one's own plan (Finestone 1957). Like other forms of escape, this one is only minimally successful. If it involves the use of drugs, there is usually a downward spiral of health. It leads easily into illegal activities that, far from helping one avoid the outside world, bring one into painful confrontation with it. And the dismissal of the values of society is often not wholehearted; there is ambivalence, exposed by the intensity of the attack on the world of the squares.

In sum, we see that avoidance as a means of adjustment varies all the way from complete withdrawal to playing a role in a specific incident. The behavior patterns it represents are largely *responses*—the results of the attitudes and behavior of the dominant group; but they also become part of the interaction that affects the dominant group. Seldom is a given action a pure case of avoidance; more often it also contains elements of aggression and protest, and perhaps also of acceptance.

Variables Affecting Types and Extent of Avoidance

At several points we have referred to the fact that avoidance is not equally available to all members of a minority group. Those least dependent on the majority for jobs, housing, protection in the courts, and so forth are most able to avoid painful contact. Segregation therefore does little to aid avoidance, because it is most often found precisely in those places where minorities are most dependent on the dominant group. Other things being equal, the higher the income and occupational status of a minority-group member, the more successfully can she or he avoid direct contact with prejudice. Avoidance, in fact, may become part of the culture of upper-class members of a minority. Even wealthy members of a low-status group, however, cannot avoid all contacts and cannot insulate their children completely from the dominant group. For lower-class members, daily contacts with members of the dominant group in their roles of employer, landlord, merchant, police, or whatever are almost inevitable. They are much less likely to use avoidance as a mode of adjustment, therefore; and when they do use it, the application is of the temporary and partial variety.

Aggression: Striking Back

It seems unlikely that members of minority groups could experience prejudice and discrimination without feeling hostility, a desire to strike back, to attack the source of their frustration or a substitute target. The nature of this aggression varies greatly from person to person and from group to group. Much of it will be unconscious—unrecognized as hostility either by the person using it or by the majority. A great deal will be directed away from the primary source of frustration because of the dangers or difficulties in attacking members of the dominant group. As we shall see, some writers go so far as to interpret almost all responses of minority-group members, no matter how unaggressive they may seem on the surface, in terms of hostility. It does not seem possible, at our present level of knowledge, to accept this hypothesis with complete assurance. But the evidence does point to the need for seeing the relationship between outward, more or less obvious acts of aggression and internal or covert modes of adjustment that seem very different but which, from the point of view of the person using them, serve the same social psychological functions. Majority-group members frequently fail to see the similarity in these different ways of behaving and consequently seriously misunderstand the behavior of minority-group members with whom they come in contact. In fact, the more completely the modes of aggression have to be disguised—in areas wherein overt hostility would be most vigorously suppressed and most violently punished by the dominant group—the more likely are people of high status to misinterpret the behavior of people of low status. It is precisely in such areas that the claim "to know" the minority group is most frequently asserted, because outward behavior is usually more uniform and predictable there. A deeper knowledge of personality, of the feelings, the desires, the motives of the persons of low status, however, will probably be lacking under these conditions.

In a valuable essay Hortense Powdermaker (1943) noted how modes of aggression change with varying conditions. Even the faithful slave and the "meek, unaggressive" Negro that followed him after the Civil War were not, she asserted, lacking in hostility but were simply forced by circumstances and taught by their culture to express their hostility mainly in indirect and hidden ways. The nature of their religion, their internal relationships, even the strong tendency to identify with the master can be interpreted in part as modes of aggression. The slave was dependent upon the white man. His security and the avoidance of pain demanded the white man's good will, so that much of the hatred the Negro felt had to be repressed. There were, of course, direct expressions of hostility. Thousands ran away; others committed crimes against Whites despite brutal punishment; and there were slave revolts. The great majority, however, were ostensibly loyal and expressed their hostility indirectly.

Powdermaker interpreted even the meekness of deference to Whites not as a lack of aggression but as a form of adaptation containing a great deal of aggression, an aggression the expression of which was appropriate to the personalities involved and the nature of the cultural surroundings.

The strength of the black protest movement that developed after World War II has involved more people in more settings, seeking more goals than was thought at all likely when it began. This is testimony, we believe, to the fact that resentment against segregation and discrimination had always been strong, that many earlier forms of response, as Powdermaker noted, were deflected and disguised aggression, that direct protests had been inhibited by powerlessness and fear of reprisals. Now "the lid is off"—attacks on the system are direct, and it seems highly unlikely that they will abate short of substantial change in America's race relations patterns.

Turning now to a wider context, we can discuss briefly some of the many ways in which minority-group members express their resentment against their status and attempt to strike back against their oppressors. These vary with the personalities of the people involved and with the environment. The response that is permitted or likely to be effective in one place might be dangerous or ineffective in another.

Types of Aggression

1. Some individuals become active and aggressive group leaders, professionally championing the claims of the whole group by editing papers, leading protest groups, organizing boycotts, trying to persuade friends among the dominant group to support them economically and politically. (To a few, this furnishes middle- and upper-class status and thus simultaneously aids them in avoiding some of the hardships of the group they defend.)

During this period of protest against America's race relations patterns, we are rediscovering the works of black leaders who opposed those patterns earlier. The tone of protest and the medium of expression vary widely. But through the generations there have been aggressive black leaders who have fought against discrimination. It is not clear, for example, that Andrew Young and Jesse Jackson, or a few years earlier, Eldridge Cleaver and Stokely Carmichael have been in sharper opposition to discrimination than Frederick Douglass in the generation before the Civil War, W. E. B. DuBois in a career spanning the first half of the twentieth century and longer, or Martin Luther King, Jr. (see Bracey, Meier, and Rudwick 1970; Carmichael and Hamilton 1967; Chisholm 1970; Cleaver 1968; Douglass 1882; DuBois 1962; King 1963b; Logan and Winston 1983; Pinkney 1976; Rudwick 1969).

Forms of protest among American Indians have also changed, but the leaders of the current "red power" movement are scarcely more vigorous in their opposition to white domination than Wodziwob, Wovoka, and other leaders of the Ghost Dance (Mooney 1965). There is less historical depth in the work of protest leaders among Americans of Spanish-speaking descent, who have been less prominent until recently. They have been, perhaps, "the invisible minority," as some have called them. But in recent years, with increasing political organization, with demands for education designed to meet their needs, and with the growth of labor organizations, we have seen the appearance of such protest leaders as Rodolfo ("Corky") Gonzales, José Angel Gutierrez, and Cesar Chavez.

The balance of forces leading toward avoidance, acceptance, aggression, or conciliation is clearly shown in the kinds of leaders who come to the fore at different times. Beginning, perhaps, during World War II and becoming steadily more powerful, the movement that we have witnessed in the United States has pushed aside the moderate, accommodating, class-oriented leader in favor of the assertive, impatient, mass-oriented leader. Among ethnic-group leaders and publicists and on college campuses, the issue is often stated in somewhat stereotypical form as a shift from leaders who supported an outmoded "melting pot" ideal to those who emphasize pluralism or the more extreme views of separatism and nationalism. This puts the issue too sharply, for as we have noted protest leaders have not been uncommon in American history; nor are moderates absent from the scene today. But the balance has changed.

New leaders have come to the fore because the context of race relations has changed. The development of an urban, literate constituency, the

Supreme Court and Congressional challenges to segregation, the appearance of independent African nations, and other forces have dramatically changed minority perceptions of what is possible. In a context of hope and aspiration new voices are demanded. A broad attack on the whole range of discriminatory patterns is demanded *now*. A few years ago, not to have been in jail or at the head of a picket line was to risk loss of influence. Thus the heads of the major protest organizations, including those who had worked in the past through negotiation and legal action, joined the demonstration lest those whom they led should get too far ahead of them (a situation that political leaders not uncommonly find themselves in).

This reference is primarily to leaders who were prominent nationally. On the community level, accommodating leadership is less uncommon, because of variation in local conditions and the greater vulnerability of local leaders to reprisals from the dominant group. Yet even on the community level protest, not accommodation, has become the mode. Those who believe that the demand for full equality now is unwise are either fairly quiet or are limited to assertions that demanding rights too aggressively and rapidly will lead to retaliation and failure.

2. Direct physical aggression against one's oppressors occurs in many discriminatory situations. From the days of slavery some Blacks have expressed their resentment by furtive, individual acts of violence. Organized hostility has been uncommon, largely, perhaps, because of a feeling of inevitable failure, partly because of the lack of internal solidarity among the oppressed group, particularly with regard to agreement on the appropriate means of dealing with Whites. The police and the courts have traditionally been likely to side with a member of the dominant group in a case of physical aggression (see Chapter 12). The unlawful use of violence by the dominant group has also been common in American history, inviting retaliation, but even more strongly blocking it (Grimshaw 1969, National Commission on the Causes and Prevention of Violence 1970). The current scene, however, indicates that significant changes may be taking place: Growing power and intensive communication have removed some of the inhibitions against violence in the oppressed groups; the gap between their aspirations and their actual conditions has widened; the lower classes—with stronger subcultural support for violence—have been drawn more fully into the struggle for equality. These forces may combine to increase the frequency with which minority-group members in the United States use physical aggression.

These shifts match laboratory findings that persons assigned a low-status position feel free to express hostility toward those in high-status positions until the situation is manipulated in such a way that they see themselves destined to remain in low status. In a striking, even if not experimentally demonstrated way, the protests of the 1960s turned this relationship around: seeing themselves no longer destined to remain in low status, some black Americans and other minority-group members felt freer to express their hostility. The more difficult times of the 1970s brought doubt. Hostile protests became less frequent in part because of feelings that the civil rights movement had run out of steam and that improvement of status was less likely. (At the same time, we should note that the growing number of skilled and educated persons in the minority groups has helped to open new forms of protest and kept older legal and political forms alive. Technical knowledge of the law and the workings of the political system, for example, is being used in several states to protest as unrepresentative the reapportionment after the 1980 census of state legislative and congressional districts; see Ehrenhalt 1983.)

Hostile aggression has taken several forms: random or spontaneous acts of violence directed mainly against property (most of the people killed during the race riots of the 1960s in the United States were Blacks); more focused and planned, but, as yet, small-scale attacks on the establishment, particularly the police; and a justifying ideology that acclaims violence as a purification ceremony or an effective strategy.

The various forms of violence express in common the reduction in legitimacy accorded the political, legal, economic, and social system by a population that is deeply frustrated and angered (Kelman 1970). This delegitimation is likely to occur in a context of poor performance by elites (e.g., a lagging economy), greater visibility of inequality, and rising self-confidence among the disadvantaged (Della Fave 1980).

There is now a large literature on the violent aggression of recent years, some of it descriptive, but much of it seeking also to identify the variables that most frequently underlie participation in riots or other violent acts of protest. It is a mixture of several conditions that produces violence: (1) severe discrimination and deprivation, made more visible by the mass media, by rising hopes and even by rising achievements (for *relative* deprivation is the key), by population concentration, and by the general affluence of the society; (2) demographic changes that have brought a higher ratio of young, better educated, more self-confident Blacks into close interaction; (3) a general environment that challenges legitimacy, not only with reference to minorities and race relations but also with reference to national war policies, educational procedures, and many other aspects of national life; (4) a reciprocal readiness to talk and act violently by many Whites, in part a continuation of earlier patterns, in part a change produced by the tensions of the civil rights struggles of the last generation; (5) racial isolation that promotes misperceptions and the spread of rumors. These various factors are systematically interrelated. It would be too much to say that severe outbreaks require that all the factors be present in each instance, but the absence of even one of these factors would significantly reduce the likelihood of violence.[1]

There is less adequate evidence on violent aggression that is more focused and planned than spontaneous rebellion against deprivation. An excessively sharp distinction is often drawn between rioting, which is thought to be spontaneous, and insurrection, which is seen as premeditated attack on the social order. On the one hand, riotous destruction is sometimes quite focused, with merchants, employers, or others who are believed to be particularly discriminatory receiving the major attack (Berk and Aldrich 1972; Abudu et al. 1972). On the other hand, insurrection is sometimes a creation of the news media or the police, who in an ambiguous situation find it easy to read the signals in such a way as to confirm their definition of the situation when in fact an outburst has developed out of a particular interaction or has been precipitated by a specific event against a background of distrust and frustration.

[1]For general discussions of intergroup conflict, consult Coser 1972; Gurr 1970; Himes 1980; Kuper 1977; Oppenheimer 1969; Pinkney 1972; Williams 1977. More specifically on the violent conflicts in the United States during the 1960s, see Allen 1970; Button 1978; Campbell 1971; Connery 1968; Feagin and Hahn 1973; Marx 1967a, 1971; National Advisory Commission on Civil Disorders 1968; Schuman and Hatchett 1974; Spilerman 1970, 1976; Stark et al. 1974; Tomlinson 1970.

Nevertheless, an analytic distinction must be maintained between spontaneous and planned violence. There have been armed attacks without immediate provocation being visible. We need systematic study of the conditions that lead to one or the other and to various mixtures. Probably many underlying conditions are the same. Planned insurrections and sniping develop, however, only when additional factors are present: prolonged frustration, unusually harsh harassment from the police, certain personality configurations, and a supporting ideology that violence is not only effective but a positive good.

This last has been furnished by Frantz Fanon and others who see violence as psychologically liberating, as essential to an oppressed population striving to free itself, not only from domination by others but from self-hatred as well. Violence "is a cleansing force. It frees the native from his inferiority complex and from his despair and inaction" (Fanon 1963, p. 73; see also Gendzier 1972; and for a critical view Kuper 1974, Chapter 3). This sentiment is caught up by Jean-Paul Sartre in the preface to Fanon's book (1963, p. 21): "This irrepressible violence is neither sound nor fury, nor the resurrection of savage instincts, nor even the effect of resentment; it is man recreating himself."

People who become involved in planned violence by participation in guerrilla activity are decisively cut off from the dominant society, and thus their loyalty to the violent group is more nearly assured. They are also cut off from part of themselves—from that part that recognizes a shared humanity or shared values and goals with those being attacked. Violence may function to repress feelings of ambivalence.

The critical question concerns the total, long-run consequences of violence (a question we shall raise in the final chapter); but here we see it as one of the responses to serious disprivilege. We are inclined to agree with Bertrand Russell in his attack on the approach of D. H. Lawrence, similar to that of Sartre in the quotation cited, that such "thinking with the blood...led straight to Auschwitz" (in Oppenheimer 1970, p. 60). Nazism also appealed, as Oppenheimer observed, to the unity of the folk and the recovery of self-confidence through violence. The critical question remains: At what cost?

3. Some counterassertion or aggression is more appropriately seen as acting against the whole status system rather than against specific individuals

or situations. Efforts on the part of a member of a minority group to climb the economic ladder, and to demonstrate that climb by purchases appropriate to his new status, are usually interpreted as aggression by the dominant group.

Ostentation is not to be interpreted solely as a means of aggression against a confining definition of economic place. In part it is a mode of self-expression that may become exaggerated under conditions which prevent other modes of self-expression from being used. Thus it is likely to be exaggerated among minority-group members who have made some advancement, particularly in income, but whose activities are blocked from many channels, in the purchase or rental of adequate housing, for example. It should also be noted that the dominant group's interpretation of efforts to climb the economic and occupational ladder as aggression may be reason to hide and disguise, not display, any success in this regard, in order to avoid retaliation from the majority.

4. Members of a minority group can express their hostility by withdrawing trade from the businesses of the dominant group or from those individuals in the group who show the most prejudice and discrimination. This is partly an avoidance device, as we have seen, but it is also a sign of aggression. Where there is legal protection, this way of expressing resentment may take the form of organized boycotts, of "don't buy where you can't work" movements. The opposite side of the coin says: "Support the businesses of fellow Blacks" (see Bracey, Meier, and Rudwick 1970, pp. 235–45, 371–86, 486–503) or help develop a "Black Common Market" by "selective patronage," as several speakers urged to a business conference of black leaders (Cleveland *Plain Dealer,* August 1, 1982, p. E1). Such a strategy is effective only when the minority group has substantial purchasing power and is important to the success of specific individuals in the dominant group.

In some minority–majority situations, the modes of wage payment, of purchasing, and of finding housing are so much under the control of the dominant group that any expression of resentment by members of the minority at the kind of treatment they receive can be made only at the risk of loss of wages or of poorer shopping and housing conditions. This was true, for example, in plantation settings. With the development of an urban economy, however, with its regular wage payments and increased purchasing power, the situation changes.

The boycott becomes a powerful weapon. The legality of its use was upheld in 1982 by the Supreme Court.

5. A form of aggression often used by even the most powerless member of an oppressed group is to work slowly or to leave a job entirely if the treatment is too offensive. Inefficient, lazy, and therefore costly work is a source of a great deal of complaint from members of the dominant group. They usually assume it to be a proof of inferiority, failing to see that, whether by conscious intent or by lack of motivation, it is an expression of hostility and primarily a result of a low ceiling on opportunities. A black field hand or unskilled factory worker or janitor may not dare to stop work entirely, but he can be careless with the white man's time and goods. The situation is somewhat similar to the low efficiency and low motivation sometimes characteristic of buck privates in the Army. They too are caught in a status that many of them resent; they feel hostility that cannot be expressed openly against those who give them orders; their response is to "soldier" on the job, to do only what they are told to do, and that only to the barest minimum. The authors of *The American Soldier* (Stouffer et al. 1949, pp. 502–03) found that the army situation produced among white soldiers many of the same protests that Negroes had long used in reference to their treatment.

High labor turnover can be a similar expression of resentment. It may not be an effective method of hostility, but it brings some satisfaction as a sign of independence. In many situations the unreliability of servants is a source of much complaint but is little understood as an expression of aggression against inferior status.

6. Aggression may be expressed in some circumstances by the withdrawal of the forms of deference and etiquette, by the loss of earlier feelings of affection, and the development of feelings of distrust and suspicion. In societies in which status lines are sharply drawn, violation of prescribed patterns of etiquette are quickly interpreted as aggressive acts. In the South, until recently, variation from established forms of deference—recognized as attacks on the system—were often severely punished. Most Blacks disguised their feelings of distrust and resentment and overtly accepted the required forms (Doyle 1937). Overt acceptance, however, may cover—or indeed fail to cover—resistance to the system. Many Blacks learned the skillful use of etiquette, allaying any

fears on the part of Whites that they did not accept the status patterns, to wring some small advantage from a difficult situation.

When stable patterns of dominance and submission break down, familiar deference forms quickly change because they so obviously represent the old order. George Fox observed in his *Journal* that Quakers refused "hat honor" to emphasize their unwillingness to accept an inferior social status. "The Lord forbade me," he wrote, "to put off my hat to any, high or low." In recent years, some black Americans and others have followed similar practices (e.g., wearing their hats in class) to express their opposition to the status order.

7. Aggressive feelings may be embodied in art. Whether art can and should be used for political purposes and remain art is, of course, a long-standing issue. We think it can be, provided something of the situation of common humanity, and not of one group alone, is involved, and provided the politics are indirect, latent, and secondary to the artistic statement. These rather stern criteria may leave open whether various forms of minority-group expression are art, but that makes them none the less important.

Among the arts, literature is undoubtedly the most clearly involved in expressing the protest theme. Much more reading in of the presumed message is needed, for example, in music (Kofsky 1970). In many settings, literature has been an articulate voice for the deep-seated but unexpressed hostilities of large numbers of people. This may take the form of folk tales and myths or of written literature. Among the American Indians, for example, many of the original myths have gradually taken on a content that helps them express their resentment against the white conquerors, giving support to Malinowski's remark (1926, p. 12): "Myth...is not an idle rhapsody, not an aimless outpouring of vain imaginings, but a hard-working, extremely important cultural force."

Written literature may contain a much more explicit aggressive theme in protest against prejudice and discrimination (see, e.g., Baraka [LeRoi Jones] 1979a, 1979b; Dickstein 1977, pp. 154–182; Jackson 1962; Ludwig and Santibañez 1971; McKay 1953; Sanchez 1973).

Autobiographies and books of personal essays are a rich source of guidance to the person seeking to understand minority experience from "the other side." They do not stand as representative, in any sampling sense, any more than autobiographies of majority-group members are representative. On the current scene, the authors are articulate, angry, and self-confident, doubtless beyond the usual range. Yet several autobiographies have become significant documents of the time, throwing experiences that have been widely shared onto a large screen, bringing a deep sense of personal recognition to minority-group readers, who see slices of their own lives made vivid. Majority-group readers may experience a jolt to the imagination that helps them to grasp something of the meaning of life to the minority, and also, if they are fortunate, gain insight into their own experience. We define these autobiographies too narrowly by noting them here as one expression of aggression against discrimination, but that is clearly one of their dimensions (see Brown 1965; Cleaver 1968; Lester 1969; Malcolm X 1966; Wilkins and Matthews 1982; Wright 1937).

8. An almost universal way of expressing aggression is humor. It may be used as a means of social control, to prevent individuals from following a disapproved course of action or to stop the action. It may have no effect on the objective situation but serves rather to make one's own role in that situation seem more desirable, or to make the whole situation seem less important—and therefore one's own disadvantaged role of less consequence. Humor may, however, contain a symbolic reversal of the social order, as Bergson (1956) saw it, or an attack on the system of control (Freud 1938, Book 4). Burma (1946) and Lomax (1961) emphasize humor as a minority-group weapon, making even tragic situations, as in "gallows humor," more bearable and helping to sustain morale.

Despite the numerous insightful interpretations, it is difficult to speak with confidence about the causes and the consequences of humor. Little is known about who invents humor, who communicates it to what audiences (Barron 1950). There is clearly an in-group dimension, involving morale and social control, but also expressing and seeking to handle self-hatred. More obviously there is an out-group dimension, involving both an effort at accommodation and conflict (Middleton and Moland 1959; Rinder 1965).

When status patterns are under sharp attack, humor is part of the arsenal. The comedian Godfrey Cambridge, for example, tells how he handles a major problem for Blacks—getting a taxi in New York. One of his methods is the try and look innocent method: I stand there with a big broad smile on my face. I remove my sunglasses so no one thinks I'm a drug addict. I try to show them I'm a white Negro, carrying my attaché case. I hail them with my attaché case. They think I'm an executive. (quoted by Hughes 1965)

Or Dick Gregory says: "There's only one difference between the North and the South. In the South, they don't care how close I get, as long as I don't get too big. In the North, they don't care how big I get, as long as I don't get too close" (Arnez and Anthony 1968, p. 341).

Humor may be used to blur a line of distinction, to expose our friendly as well as our unfriendly rigidities:

High noon in New York, August: The crowded bus jogged to a stop at Fourteenth Street. All the passengers got off, except two women who had been sharing a seat—one Negro, the other white. Both were stout. *If I move to another seat,* the white woman thought, *this Negro will think I don't want to sit by her.* Two stops later the Negro looked at her seatmate and said: "Honey, there's plenty room on this bus; why for then are you crowding me?" (Lomax 1961, p. 41)

Such lighthearted, barrier-crossing humor, it should be noted, can help to reduce hostility (O'Quin and Aronoff 1981).

Most people have experienced the feelings of solidarity, the release of tension, and the tightening of social control that come from humor. There is some experimental evidence to support personal insights and clinical observations. Freud's catharsis theory, for example, is given some support by an experimental study of the effects of hostile humor on tension. Negro respondents heard either a recording designed to mobilize aggressive impulses toward segregationists or a control recording of music. Then they heard Negro performers deliver hostile, antisegregationist humor, neutral humor, and a benign speech. For those subjects who were moderately aroused and involved by the stimulus, both the hostile and the neutral humor reduced aggression and tension, as measured by a mood check list. For those highly aroused, the hostile humor was particularly aggression reducing, and only the hostile humor reduced tension (Singer 1968; see also Dworkin and Efran 1967).

Displaced Aggression

In Chapter 6 we discussed some of the attitudes that members of minority groups develop with regard to their fellow group members. We also noted that much of the aggression that might be expected to be directed against the dominant group is redirected instead against one's fellows or other substitute targets. These two ideas need now to be combined briefly in order to observe the hostility and tensions that characterize the interaction *within* a minority group. Two cautions are necessary at this point. Along with the forces making for conflict within these groups there are, as we have seen, a number of other forces that encourage cohesion and group solidarity, the balance varying with many factors. Secondly, it should not be supposed that all the aggression within a minority group is displaced from the dominant group, which is the real target and cause of the hostility. Some of it is simply a product of the normal interaction *within* the group, the prejudice of the majority being at most an indirect factor.

Despite these qualifications, it seems apparent that some of the violence and hostility that, for example, Blacks show toward other Blacks is to be explained by displaced aggression and is properly included in this discussion of the aggressive response to prejudice and discrimination. Not knowing the true source of one's difficulties, or being unable to attack what one believes is the true source, one turns upon an easily accessible and relatively powerless fellow group member (Crain and Weisman 1972, Chapter 4). This person then receives not only the hostility that his or her own acts might have caused, but also the pent-up and blocked hostility that the accumulated experiences with the dominant group have caused. Insofar as this is true, then, a higher level of conflict within a minority group is to be seen as a product of prejudice and discrimination.

Having discussed the many ways in which Blacks in the United States express direct aggression, we do not want to exaggerate the extent to which aggression is displaced. By many important indexes, however, it seems clear that hostility is often expressed toward substitute targets near at hand—and less able to retaliate—rather than against a member of the dominant group (Wallace 1979). It is critical to note that most of the victims of black murderers are Blacks and that Whites kill Whites (Daniels 1982; Farley 1980).

The displacement may be not only toward one's immediate associates but also toward other minorities with whom one happens to be in contact. Again, though, a feeling of solidarity *with* other minorities may also be a product of prejudice.

Not all of the tendencies toward aggression, direct and displaced, of minority-group members are to be explained, of course, by prejudice and discrimination. Hostile feelings and impulses are part of the equipment of all human beings because of the gap between what they want and what they attain. Physical and biological laws of the universe, social rules, and competing desires all combine to frustrate to some degree even the best-satisfied individual. It is not necessarily true that a person of inferior status will have more aggressive tendencies than the one who is dominant over him, because there are so many sources of aggression, prejudice being only one. Moreover, a member of a minority group may make an avoidance or an acceptance adjustment instead. On the other hand, the tendencies for aggression in the minority-group member may be stronger than can be explained by the prejudice he has experienced. Personal maladjustment or failures from other causes may be blamed on discrimination. A Black, for example, may be sensitive not only to real racial barriers but to imagined ones, every act of a white person being interpreted in racial terms, every criticism being seen as an expression of prejudice, any failure to advance a sign of a categorical barrier. If such a person were white, he would find some reason other than race prejudice to explain his failure.

Variables Affecting Types and Extent of Aggression

In the last several pages we have seen that minority-group members can express their hostility toward the dominant group in a number of ways. It is important not to mistake the absence of overt aggression for a lack of feelings of hostility or for a lack of effects. If these effects are covert or heavily disguised, if they are obscured by external gestures of acceptance of an inferior status, they are nevertheless exceedingly important in the analysis of the tendencies of minority-group members. The powerful underlying feelings may be revealed overtly only in unusual circumstances—when anger overcomes fear, or a mob situation reduces the usual inhibitions—but the feelings are there at all times.

Important class, regional, age, and other group differences in expressing aggression exist because of different personality tendencies, different subcultural modes of expression of a particular minority group (Orum and Cohen 1973), different attitudes and culture patterns in the dominant group, different chances of success, and the chance factors of a specific situation:

> The weapons employed by lower-class Negroes in expressing hostility covertly may take the form of petty sabotage, unexplained quitting of jobs, gossip, pseudo-ignorant malingering. Middle-class Negroes are in a better position to use the economic weapon of controlled purchasing power. Upper-class Negroes may use this also, but in addition they find it effective to use the method of indirect attack on the offending institutions by arousing outside public opinion. (Johnson 1943, p. 302)

The general economic and political situation strongly influences the varieties and extent of aggression on the part of minority groups (Geschwender 1977; Szymanski 1978a). A growing sense of relative deprivation, even if their economic conditions have improved in absolute terms, increases the likelihood of militant responses among minority groups (Abeles 1976).

Acceptance of Status as a Form of Adjustment

Contemporary sociology and cultural anthropology have shown that people can learn to adjust to and even accept extremely diverse circumstances that seem strange, painful, or evil to those who have received different training. Standards of value by which the desirability of a given status is judged, as well as the status itself, are a product of society. A whole group may accept what to others seems to be an inferior role because it seems perfectly normal to them; it is taken for granted. Only contact with other standards, the acquisition of levels of aspiration that are blocked in the old status, may destroy acceptance of that status.

Types of Acceptance

1. Wholehearted. In some circumstances members of a minority may fairly wholeheartedly accept an inferior position. However, since unwillingness to accept one's status fully is one of the defining characteristics of a minority, as contrasted with a caste, as we are using these terms, wholehearted acceptance is always qualified, particularly in urban and mobile societies.

2. Specific. Far more common than acceptance of the whole status pattern is acceptance of some specific situation or some phase of a relationship

that implies inferiority, either out of belief or out of desire to escape some unwanted aspect of the relationship. In the latter case, acceptance borders closely on avoidance.

3. Unconscious. There is also a measure of acceptance in the attitude toward onself and one's group that we have discussed in the preceding chapter. Feelings of inferiority and even of self-hatred, often deeply unconscious or disguised by assertions to the contrary, may develop in some members of minority groups who have come to see themselves from the point of view of the majority.

It is clearly necessary to distinguish carefully among these three varieties of acceptance, for they have very different consequences. Nearly complete acceptance is closely correlated with resignation and passivity. It becomes the dominant factor in the life of the individual who follows this pattern. Acceptance of some specific situation that requires an inferior role is far more likely to be a conscious or even a rational decision. It tells little about the total personality. Were persons faced by a different situation they would make another mode of adjustment. Members of the dominant group may well misinterpret this kind of acceptance, mistaking it for passivity and a *general* acceptance. The unconscious adoption of feelings of inferiority and self-hatred produces ambivalence and tension that are important in behavior. It may arouse an extraordinary amount of striving and even of aggressiveness in order to overcome the feelings of inferiority. It may, however, be related to a disorganizing ambivalence, a tendency that is often found in the marginal man, to borrow Stonequist's phrase.

Variables Affecting Types and Extent of Acceptance

In acceptance, as in avoidance and aggression, one cannot speak of the reaction of *the* Hispanic, *the* Indian, or *the* Black. In each instance there are variations among classes, age groups, regions, educational levels, and other factors. Individual variations also affect the nature of the response. It is important to observe the interactions among these factors. Older persons may be more likely to accept a disadvantaged status (Brunswick 1970; Marx 1967a) but various qualifications are necessary to avoid misinterpreting this correlation. Age itself is probably not the important variable. It happens to be correlated with education, degree of urbanness, and

knowledge of "the American dream" and availability of contact with social movements and ideas that expose and oppose the old status patterns.

Whole-hearted acceptance of minority status is characteristically a product of isolation—physical and/or social. Or it may be based on a role that, despite the inferiority implied, brings security and a reflected glory (there are numerous parallel situations within the majority). A servant may feel rewarded by the friendly atmosphere, by the economic and personal security of the job, by a feeling of identification with the employers, and by a sense of pride when appreciation is shown for his or her work—although those conditions may, of course, be quite uncommon.

The number of people in the United States and, one may say with confidence, around the world who are willing to accept an inferior status, particularly in the whole-hearted sense, is declining sharply. Description of this response is important, not because it is a common type, but because it is an important part of the background out of which other types of response are emerging. Belief in inferiority may be gone, but one may still accept it, in one of the senses of acceptance we have described, to hold a job, to gain favor, or simply to avoid trouble.

It is well to recall again that seldom will a response be purely of an acceptance, reformist, aggressive, or avoidance variety. In studying acceptance one must particularly avoid mistaking surface accommodation for a thoroughgoing willingness to stay in one's "place." As Elkins (1959, pp. 132–133) reminds us, accommodation is morally and psychologically a very complex phenomenon, involving a principle of interpersonal relations that operates in many settings. The admixture of types of response is shown in

The principle of how the powerless can manipulate the powerful through aggressive stupidity, literal-mindedness, servile fawning, and irresponsibility. In this sense the immovably stupid 'Good Soldier Schweik' and the fawning Negro in Richard Wright's *Black Boy* who allowed the white man to kick him for a quarter partake of the same tradition. Each has a technique whereby he can in a real sense exploit his powerful superiors, feel contempt for them, and suffer in the process no great damage to his own pride. Jewish lore, as is well know, teems with this sort of thing. There was much of it also in the traditional relationships between peasants and nobles in central Europe.

Thus overt acceptance may hide opposition. It is well to note, moreover, the opposite situation: Overt expressions of hostility and aggression may hide a deep-seated sense of inferiority and acceptance of inferior status.

Reformism

Reformism can be distinguished analytically from each of the other three types of response to discrimination, yet it shares elements of each. There is acceptance, but of the system as capable of change and reform, not of one's own status in it. This shades off toward aggressive actions designed to take advantage of that capability. These actions differ from the kinds of aggression we have described because they express more hope, greater readiness to trust and work with members of the dominant group, and stronger feelings that life is satisfying. Insofar as reform is seen as implying more autonomy for minorities, it also contains elements of avoidance, but this is a minor theme. The main emphasis is on relatively hopeful actions expressing the belief that the system they live in is capable of improvement, that the deprivations suffered by minorities are not intrinsic to its very structure. Roy Wilkins, associated with the NAACP for over half a century, entitled his autobiography *Standing Fast* (1982); he wanted "to include Negro Americans in the nation's life, not to exclude them." This did not imply, however, any unwillingness to oppose discrimination vigorously, as in his encouragement to Martin Luther King, Jr., in the early days of King's civil rights movement, to press against segregation more militantly and in the more than two score suits opposing discrimination brought to the Supreme Court by the NAACP during his period of leadership.

Many of the paradoxes in the lives of minority-group leaders and the policies of minority-group movements come from the mixtures in their efforts at reform of acceptance—in the sense we are using that term here—aggression, and avoidance. DuBois, in his early work, Rudwick observes (1969, p. 36), "sought to prove Negroes were capable of developing their own 'superior' culture and he favored a separate racial social system. But he also repudiated 'the color line' and wanted to overturn racial barriers."

Efforts at reform are less visible, perhaps less "newsworthy" than hostile attacks against a system or movements declaring their autonomy. Under many circumstances, however, they receive wider support among minorities. When two national samples of America's black population were asked, in 1968, "As you see it, what's the best way for Negroes

to try to gain their rights?" over 93 percent answered either "use laws and persuasion" or "use non-violent protest" (Schuman and Hatchett 1974, p. 8).

Variables Affecting the Reformist Response

The history and culture of a society strongly influence the likelihood that minorities will respond to discrimination by reformist efforts. In some societies there can be an appeal to "our highest traditions." That has some impact in France, England, or the United States, for example, but little in South Africa or in nations long divided along conflicting cultural, religious, and economic lines.

The immediate experiences of members of minority groups are important. Those that increase hope, that strengthen the sense that discrimination is being reduced, lend support to reformist efforts, especially among those individuals who are in the best positions to benefit from the direction of change. When hopes are frustrated, reformist responses are weakened. In the context of the great controversy surrounding American involvement in the Vietnam war, which sharply reduced attention to the civil rights movement, and the change of administration in 1968, trust in government fell rapidly, especially among Blacks. The *Newsletter* of the Institute for Social Research (Spring-Summer, 1973) reported a shift among Blacks, on a "support" to "estrangement" scale from $+50$ in 1958 to a -40 by 1972. In the same period Whites moved from a $+50$ to a $+8$ (see also Schwartz and Schwartz 1976). Clemente and Sauer reported (1976) that Blacks had much lower levels of life satisfaction than Whites, although the difference was much smaller among the young. Of several variables related to life satisfaction, they found race to be the strongest predictor. These are the kinds of conditions under which reformist responses are weakened and avoidance and aggressive responses are strengthened.

Organized Protests and Social Movements among Minority Groups

One of the consequences of prejudice and discrimination for minority groups is the development of a wide variety of social movements and organized group pressures to escape from or to improve their status. These range from religious or nationalistic mass movements to the carefully planned use of legal, political, and economic weapons. We shall not at this point make a detailed study of such group effects, for they will be involved in a number of places in the analysis of social structure, and those that are especially concerned with social change will be discussed in Part III. Here, however, a brief statement of the general principles underlying such groups is necessary to relate them to the theme of this chapter.

Some of the social movements among minority groups are primarily attempts to escape or avoid the difficulties of their status; some are primarily aggressive protests against their lot; some, which on the surface may seem to be escape devices, are indirectly attacks upon the dominant group. All over the world in the twentieth century, minority groups have organized for more effective opposition to their status. The group factor has focused their individual feelings of frustration, has given them some measure of common objectives, has *intensified,* by the repricrocal exchange involved, their antagonism to specific situations. The resentment of inequality by individual Blacks is one thing; the same resentment focused through the organized legal activity of the NAACP or, in a different vein, the American Muslim Mission, is another; and both need analysis.

Studies of group patterns among Americans have almost universally agreed that participation increases with social status. Except for church and to some degree labor union membership, lower-class persons are more likely to interact within a narrow circle of family, friends, and neighbors than in organized groups. That is not true of Blacks, however, for they have a high rate of participation in voluntary associations (Williams, Babchuk, and Johnson 1973). The groups are primarily recreational and expressive, furnishing an opportunity for status recognition, leadership, and a release from the restrictions of the larger society.

Lower-class Blacks are more likely to belong to and participate actively in organizations than are their white counterparts, but this relationship is reversed in the upper class (Orum 1966). Olsen (1970) found that when class and age were controlled, Blacks were more active than Whites in every type of activity investigated. He postulates that the difference reflects an "ethnic community" influence among Blacks—a sense of sharing that encourages participation. This interpretation is supported by his finding that those Blacks who identify

with their group are more active than those who do not (see also Orum and Cohen 1973).

When these observations are applied specifically to political activity, controlling for differences in such background factors as class, region, and education, the effects of the ethnic community appear to be incomplete as an explanation of black–white differences. On the basis of his study of national samples, 1952-1972, Danigelis (1977, 1978) shows the effects also of what he calls the "political climate"—the formal and informal rules governing black political behavior and the attitudes of Whites and Blacks toward those rules. These varied quite widely during the twenty-year period. When the political climate was intolerant, black registration and voting were suppressed; when it was supportive they increased. The political climate had much less effect on less visible and less effective types of political activity than on registration and voting.

Blacks have long participated in protest organizations (DuBois 1962; Harding 1981; Rudwick 1969) and have helped to show the way for other minorities. Individual membership in the nationally prominent protest organizations is not common, probably fewer than one Black in ten being formally affiliated. The local associations are important, however, because of the opportunity they furnish for leadership experience and because they are a link in the chain of public opinion on which the national organizations depend.

Current Trends in Minority Responses

Although the dominant theme among minority groups continues to be the reduction of discrimination and the achievement of equal opportunity, the continuing emphasis among Native Americans and a growing emphasis among Blacks and, to a somewhat lesser degree, among Hispanics has been on pluralism and, in some measure, on sharper forms of separatism. Some are beginning to ask: What is so great about this society that Whites have built? Why should we struggle for middle-class status in a society of shady morality (expense-account living, income-tax evasion, and many forms of official violence), of mediocre artistic standards (witness the normal level of movies, television shows, and literary products), of doubtful ranking of values (cars seem so much more important than better schools or cleaner air, swimming pools and color television for the well-to-do than a basic minimum standard of living for the millions of poor), of disregard for the sanctity of the earth on which we all must live? Why break our backs, some are asking, to integrate with that? We can do better.

Even among the most self-confident who take this position there is doubtless some ambivalence. But in the current protest movements of Blacks, Hispanics, and Indians there are also genuine expressions of pride and self-confidence, and a reciprocal dismay at some of our society's foibles. Acceptance of inferior status has almost disappeared as a response, but avoidance responses— separation from the dominant group—continue to compete with the stronger efforts toward integration. We are thinking here not so much of the self-segregation in community and association that is found among many deprived ethnic and racial minorities, nor of nationalist groups, important as these phenomena are. Our reference, rather, is to a more classic pluralism that is expressed by some minority intellectuals, artists, professionals and musicians. Let us not, they say in effect, integrate ourselves out of existence. While joining fully in the economic and political life of the nation, let us maintain our distinctive identity.

With reference specifically to Blacks, what we are witnessing is a culture-building process. The extent of the contribution of the African background to North American Blacks is controversial. Some lingual patterns perhaps, some contribution to music and dance, to folk literature and religion have been incorporated. But on these beginnings new forms have grown. Their African community and tribal identities were broken, but Blacks have become a community of suffering. Their widely different origins and contemporary conditions are to an important degree obscured by their shared fate.

When they were powerless this community of suffering, although it created some major cultural products, was too split and demoralized to weld these products into a distinctive subculture. When they gained some power—but not much—they sought to eliminate the special burdens they carried, to win equality in an integrated society. Now some few, seeing integration bearing down upon them, are beginning to wonder if its full accomplishment will not mean the fading of a valued culture, a loss of recognition of special accomplishments, a reduced opportunity to wring from their vastly difficult experience a valuable and unique contribution to the total human endeavor, and a weakening of the sense of pride and identity that has been so painfully won.

Like Jews, Blacks have developed something of the commmunity of feeling that comes from having been through enormously destructive experiences together—and come out of them with something creative and valuable. Jazz is a widely heralded musical style that is predominantly Negro in origin; there has grown an insightful body of literature; drawing on their religious traditions, Blacks in their fight for equality are contributing to the culture of social change, and in the process are helping to bring the country more fully in touch with the contemporary world; they have vitally influenced the civil rights activities of other minorities; their contributions to sports are impressive.

We have no desire to exaggerate the strength of the movement toward pluralism. It is doubtless in its early stages as culture-building processes go and may not develop far if discrimination is rapidly reduced. It seems more likely, however, that it will grow in importance in the years ahead. We expect to hear more voices—not simply from the impoverished, but from the talented and creative—calling for the preservation of distinctive Black and Hispanic cultures and supporting associations, voices we have long heard from Native Americans. Short of an unexpectedly rapid integration of American society or the opposite, the renewal of massive segregation, we believe some of the most sensitive and creative of minority individuals and groups, as well as some of the angry, (who may be the same persons) will continue to emphasize the possibility and desirability of distinctive subcultures.

Is this a happy possibility? Perhaps in view of the speculative quality of this section we should indicate our own value perspective. We tend to be integrationist; but we also believe that a dash of pluralism in this large and complex society is desirable. From our point of view, if this perspective is maintained by only a few or becomes only a small part of the perspective of all, it may well add flexibility and enrichment to American society. As a strong movement, however, promoted by a slow pace in the elimination of injustice, it could contribute to a vicious circle by strengthening tendencies toward prejudice and schism rather than a pluralism sustained by mutual respect.

CHAPTER 8

The Consequences of Prejudice and Discrimination for Prejudiced Persons and Dominant Groups

So happily is the world designed, Adam Smith wrote in *An Inquiry into the Nature and Causes of the Wealth of Nations* (1776) that each person working diligently in his own interests will best serve the nation as a whole. No economic thesis has so powerfully influenced the Western world, particularly the United States, as Smith's, even down to the late twentieth century. This partial truth has often dominated public policy. Only slowly are we learning the relevance of a nearly opposite statement: So perversely is the world designed that each person working diligently in his own interests often injures not only himself but the community, the nation and, in these interdependent times, the world as a whole.

Studies of this latter statement come under a variety of names: The tragedy of the commons, the prisoner's dilemma, the critical mass. What they have in common is an emphasis on the turn of events that occurs when an action that one or a few persons could gain from is followed by others: "'The commons' has come to serve as a paradigm for situations in which people so impinge on each other in pursuing their own interests that collectively they might be better off if they could be restrained, but no one gains individually by self-restraint" (Schelling 1978, p. 111; see Hardin 1968).

There are, of course, individual, cultural, and

exchange restraints that, in any social order, prevent many potential spiraling tragedies (Kelley and Thibaut 1978). But many are not prevented, to individual and social detriment. Our concern in this chapter is to note some of the costs of discrimination and prejudice to members of the dominant group, even when they believe they are acting in their own interests.

We have seen in the preceding two chapters that prejudice and discrimination have important consequences for individual minority-group members and important influences on the nature of social movements among them. The consequences for the dominant group are no less significant. Again it is difficult to separate causes from effects. Once set in motion, many consequences become in their turn causes of further prejudice and discrimination. Discrimination in the form of segregated schools (partly an effect of prejudice) may, because it proves to be an expensive luxury for a community, set in motion a host of other events which increase prejudice. The effect thus becomes a cause: Segregation will minimize the kind of equal-status contact that reduces prejudice; blinding stereotypes will be perpetuated; levels of academic achievement will be lower (Weinberg 1975).

Before indicating some of the consequences of prejudice for members of the dominant group, we

155

must also point out that they are almost always discussed in terms of some value stand, implicit, or explicitly stated. One can speak, for example, of the gains and costs of prejudice. These may be gains and costs in terms of the values of the prejudiced person himself, or according to some scheme of generally agreed-upon values, or in light of the premises of the person making the judgment. Often these three value schemes will coincide, but they may not. There are conflicts of value within a society and particularly there are differences in the ranking of values. Freedom from contact with the members of a minority group may in itself become a value, high in the ranking of some people, of lower importance for others, and completely lacking for others.

The present authors do not see how the indication of value stands can be avoided in this discussion; nor do they see any reason to avoid them. The only requisite of a scientific approach in this regard is that the premises be made explicit. As we discuss the gains and the costs of prejudice and discrimination, we shall try to make clear to whom the particular consequence is a gain or a cost. Readers who have a different value stand or a different order in their hierarchy of values will, of course, make a different judgment. Description and analysis of the effects themselves, however, will, if they are valid, be agreed upon by all.

We must distinguish the gains or losses to individuals from those to groups—the community, nation, or world. We must remember that what is a gain to one member of the dominant group (granted his or her value hierarchy) would be a loss to another member of the dominant group with different preferences. And we must discriminate carefully between short-run and long-run consequences, for they may be very different—if not, indeed, opposites.

The Gains from Prejudice and Discrimination

It seems unlikely that human beings would show such an enormous capacity for prejudice and discrimination were it not for the gains they seem to acquire. To be sure, these may be primarily short-run individual gains, tied inextricably to serious long-run losses. Most of us, however, prefer a bird in the hand (the immediate gains) to two in the bush (the gains to the world society in the long run from abolishing categorical inequities), particularly if the concerted community action necessary for the long-run gain seems to be lacking. Moreover, the complicated interaction that makes prejudice costly in the long run is difficult to understand. The international consequences of my discriminatory treatment of Mexican migrant workers is far less apparent to me than the desirability of getting my crops picked as cheaply as possible. If this means gross underpayment, unsanitary living quarters, and great insecurity for the workers, a rationalizing prejudice will help me to justify the situation or see it as inevitable.

John Dollard (1937) described the three primary gains made by white people in the South in terms of economic, sexual, and prestige advantages, all closely related (and, it should be noted again, all tied to disadvantages). These are applicable to minority–majority situations in many times and places.

1. Almost all efforts to calculate economic gains refer to individual gains, summed across the majority group. This is essential because it locates the areas of vested interest in discrimination, where resistance to change is at a maximum. It should not lead us to forget, however, the possible—indeed probable—economic costs to the whole society, to which we shall refer later. The situation is analogous to private gain from the overcutting of forests, strip mining without environmental restoration, or dumping of wastes into public water ways—all likely to be profitable—set against the long-run public costs. We need a social budget and not simply a series of individual budgets to understand the full range of economic effects of discrimination.

With that distinction in mind, we can note that white men clearly profited from slavery (Fogel and Engerman 1974; Stampp 1965), that employers who can keep Mexican workers at a minimum-wage level reap larger profits (Grebler, Moore, and Guzman 1970, Chapter 10), that dominant groups are able to reduce the necessity for their own employment in heavy manual, monotonous, and poorly paid jobs if they keep minorities relatively powerless.

Thurow (1969, pp. 130–134), in a careful appraisal of the American situation, estimated that white workers gained (in 1969 dollars) about $15 billion (plus or minus $5 billion, for a precise calculation is impossible) per year from discrimination against nonwhite workers. This gain came from a combination of employment, wage, human capital, occupational, and labor monopoly discrimination.

The apparent economic gains are often reduced by the inefficiency of workers with low morale and the pseudo-ignorant malingering that we discussed in the preceding chapter, as well as by the long-run social costs we shall discuss later; but there remains a residue of economic advantage for those able to command the labor of minority-group members or otherwise take advantage of their relative powerlessness. When one rents or sells a house to a person of low status, he often is able to charge considerably more than he could get from a member of the dominant group because of the limited opportunities for housing available to the minority group member. It may be an immediate gain to an individual to reduce competition for jobs by branding minority groups inferior, keeping them out of unions, social clubs (where jobs are often found), medical associations (for this is not simply a practice of the lower classes), or limiting their chances for vocational and professional training.

2. Often, in the relationships between a dominant and an oppressed group, a pattern of sexual contact between the men of the majority and the women of the minority group develops that allows some of the men of the dominant group to gain an immediate sexual advantage. The total effects of this pattern are, of course, distinct from the immediate physical gratification. Sexual contacts between "superior" and "inferior" influence, in many important ways, the nature of the relationship between the dominant men and women, the family patterns of the majority and minority groups, the feelings and frustrations of the men of the oppressed group, the status position of the mixed offspring who may result, and so on. Some of the costs of the sexual gain—the price paid—we shall discuss in the next section. This advantage will be seen as actually part of a vicious circle (vicious in terms of the total values of the dominant men themselves) and thus very costly (Dollard 1937, pp. 134–72).

3. Most people enjoy the feeling that they are not just average members of society but are to some degree special and important. The enthusiasm with which most of us identify with a winning baseball team or a glamorous movie star indicates our appetite for prestige, vicarious as well as real. If my school is best, my community most attractive, and my nation all-powerful and all-wise, I somehow have gained in significance. If a whole group of fellow human beings can be kept in an inferior

position and especially if they can be made to give daily signs of deference and humility—and if I can persuade myself that they are really inferior—I can get a comfortable feeling of prestige that my own individual achievements might not command.

The gain in prestige of belonging to a group one defines as superior is seldom unambiguous; there are often self-doubts and doubts over the whole-hearted acceptance of one's status by the minority-group member. These lead to an almost compulsive need for reassurance in some instances and thus to a rigid insistence that all the forms of deference be followed to the letter (Dollard 1937, pp. 173–87; Doyle 1937). The long-run total consequences, moreover, may add up to losses that far exceed the prestige gain, as we shall see. From the point of view of day-to-day adjustments, however, the feeling of mastery and importance may seem to be a real gain. It also assists in achieving the economic and sexual advantages. And, particularly for those of the dominant group who are most frustrated and least successful, it may have an adjustment value that prevents their lot from seeming unbearable. The pseudosuccess of prejudice may allay the fear and sense of failure (even while it contributes to the likelihood of failure).

Therapists who fail to see this prestige gain, and the other gains as well, may attempt a head-on attack on prejudice instead of trying to create a situation in which prejudice is relatively useless. When individuals are given some chance at economic security and advancement, when sexual contacts within the approved cultural framework are free of anxieties, rigidities, and internal contradictions, when members of the minority group have genuine opportunities for achievement, however small, that will give them a feeling of self-confidence and worthiness—under these conditions prejudice will decline progressively and may come to be seen as a costly and inefficient way of achieving human values.

4. The nature of human society makes one gain of prejudice a peculiarly difficult one to reduce rapidly. Once established as a value, the sheer maintenance of a status system, even in the face of obvious costs, is considered desirable, an end in itself. The pattern of superiority–inferiority comes to be looked upon as good and right. To violate it is bad, an attack on one's sense of selfhood and feelings of solidarity with the community. Evidence that prejudice and discrimination are costly in terms of people's desires will not persuade them

to change, at least in a hurry, if they think they are essentially right. Few of us choose our course of action only after weighing the costs. This does not mean that such beliefs cannot be changed (see Part III of this volume), but it does mean that there will be a lag between the reduction of the functions of the prejudice and the reduction of prejudice itself. Many of us are capable of saying: That which is, is good—even if it is bad.

The Personality Costs of Prejudice

Our discussion of the gains from prejudice and discrimination was continually qualified by the need for referring to the concomitant losses. Seldom are the gains achieved without cost to the individual and to the group (see Bowser and Hunt 1981). The great *interdependence* of all people within a society, and today of all the people in the world, makes it impossible for a dominant group to inflict penalties on minority groups without being penalized itself. In the eloquent words of John Donne (1923, p. 98):

No man is an Iland, intire of it selfe; every man is a peece of the *Continent,* a part of the *maine;* if a *Clod* bee washed away by the *Sea,* Europe is the lesse, as well as if a *Promontorie* were, as well as if a *Mannor* of thy *friends* or of *thine owne* were; any man's *death* diminishes *me,* because I am involved in *Mankinde;* And therefore never send to know for whom the *bell* tolls; It tolls for thee.

Booker T. Washington expressed something of the same idea when he said that the white man could not keep the colored man in the ditch without getting down there with him. Or we might put the notion of interdependence in the no less vivid terms of *The New Yorker* cartoon: Three mountain climbers are tied together as they climb a steep canyon wall. The woman at the top begins to slip and the man in the middle calls to the man below him, "There she goes!" "What do you mean," comes the reply, "'There *she* goes'?" In a very real sense, the death of or the confining discrimination against any person "diminishes *me.*"

We cannot write with great confidence of the personality costs of prejudice, because of the lack of well-controlled studies and the difficulty of separating cause from effect (see Willie, Kramer, and Brown 1973). In such a situation, implicit value judgments are particularly likely to slip into the discussion and interfere with objective analysis.

(With the present authors, these would take the form of tendencies to exaggerate the personality damage that results from prejudice.) Keeping this danger in mind, we think that the evidence, nevertheless, indicates that prejudice is an expensive luxury *in terms of the prejudiced person's own total interests and values.* The cost will differ, of course, from individual to individual and from situation to situation. It is necessary to distinguish, for example, between the consequences of a prejudice that is taught to a child as a normal part of culture and of one that is seized upon by an insecure person as an attempted adjustment pattern. The former prejudice may create guilt, tension, and tendencies toward projection in a person who is simultaneously taught democratic ideas of nonprejudice; but it may not pervade the whole personality in such a way as to affect most aspects of behavior. The latter prejudice however, may result not only in guilt, tension, and projection but in a rigidity of mind and a compulsiveness in adjustment that block a realistic appraisal of one's problems.

The Cost of Ignorance

By definition, prejudice is a categorical prejudgment of an individual because he is classified as a member of a particular group. One of the inevitable effects, applying to a greater or lesser degree, is a loss of contact with reality. Rationality is highly valued by most people. It is contradicted by prejudice, which furnishes a greatly oversimplified or completely inaccurate explanation of one's difficulties and often also a program of action that is supposed to solve them. Because it is blind to the real causes, this program of action is unable to effect a real cure. Keeping minority groups in their place will somehow reduce our tensions, improve our economic position, and boost our shaky feelings of self-esteem. But what if this protection of our place in the status system actually has very little to do with our tensions, our economic insecurity, or our lack of self-confidence; what if, in fact, it is one of the *causes* of our difficulties (as we shall see below)? Then our prejudice blocks us from a realistic appraisal of the problems we face. Its program of action is a modern form of magic that manipulates symbols and follows rituals but knows nothing of the true course of events. When a great many Germans came to believe that most of their difficulties were caused by Jews, when they adopted a program of action dominated by anti-Semitism, they were blinded to the true causes of their problems. They were led then to accept leadership that was equally lacking (or uninterested) in understanding the basic forces at work, with the result that they soon faced the overwhelmingly greater problems of war. One pays a penalty for ignorance in interhuman relations as one does for ignorance of the physical world.

Myrdal speaks of "the convenience of ignorance." He refers to the almost studied lack of information and the misinformation with which many white Americans try to protect the status system and make it seem reasonable and moral:

It thus happens that not only the man in the street, but also the professional man, shows ignorance in his own field of work. One meets physicians who hold absurd ideas about the anatomical characteristics of the Negro people or about the frequency of disease among the Negroes in their own community; educators who have succeeded in keeping wholly unaware of the results of modern intelligence research; lawyers who believe that practically all the lynchings are caused by rape; ministers of the gospel who know practically nothing about Negro churches in their own town. In the North, particularly in such groups where contacts with Negroes are lacking or scarce, the knowledge might not be greater, but the number of erroneous conceptions seems much smaller. The important thing and the reason for suspecting this ignorance to be part of the escape apparatus is that knowledge is constantly twisted in one direction—toward classifying the Negro low and the White high. (Myrdal 1944, pp. 40–41)

Myrdal might as aptly have entitled this observation "the *in*convenience of ignorance." Serious problems result from faulty knowledge and attempts to make magical cures. When energies are directed by misinformation into activities that cannot possibly produce the desired result, the prejudice which helps to create that misinformation becomes a heavy cost.

The Cost of Moral Ambivalence

Another consequence of prejudice is the development of seriously ambivalent, mutually contradictory views of life that cause one to be at odds with oneself. What are the effects on the white child of being taught a democratic and Christian or Judaic ideology and then also being taught the contrary ideology of intergroup prejudice? The prejudice encourages the child to displace hostilities onto members of the presumably inferior groups, but the democratic and religious training prevents him or her from being quite sure. There

is a burden of guilt that will not, for the most part, be consciously recognized (although some of it may be revealed in the nature of the religion which a person accepts) but will be projected onto the minority group, with further feelings of hostility, more aggression, and intensified feelings of guilt. This vicious circle wastes one's resources and diverts one's energies into ineffective actions. Myrdal (1944, xliii) considers this moral ambivalence the most important factor in race relations in the United States.

Though our study includes economic, social, and political race relations, at bottom our problem is the moral dilemma of the American—the conflict between his moral valuations on various levels of consciousness and generality.

There has perhaps been a tendency to accept Myrdal's thesis too quickly. He did not clearly demonstrate that most Americans do in fact feel guilty about racial discrimination nor indicate what the range of variation was. For some persons, segregation is morally good and they defend it with moral fervor.

Westie (1965, p. 531) examined, among a random sample of Indianapolis households, the degree of agreement to a general value statement related to the American creed and then to a specific application of that value. For example: "Everyone in America should have equal opportunity to get ahead," and "I would be willing to have a Negro as my supervisor in my place of work." Of 1,030 item pairs, answers to 383 were inconsistent, with the general value being the one most frequently accepted. Westie noted that 81 percent of the American creed items were accepted, but only 56 percent of the specific valuations. Only 12.6 percent of his respondents were entirely consistent and thus did not share in the "American dilemma," as measured. There were many ways for the others to handle the inconsistencies, for example by repression ("what conflict?"), by appealing to the relativity of the value ("there are different kinds of brotherhood"), by projection ("a Negro juror would be prejudiced"). It is also interesting to note, however, that some felt obliged to explain their lack of prejudice, their unwillingness to discriminate:

Thus, people with no dilemma in Myrdal's sense seem to experience another type of dilemma: a conflict between their endorsement of democratic action and yet *another normative system,* which exists in the majority of American local communities: the system which says that one ought to discriminate. (Westie 1965, p. 538)

Such evidence qualifies the application of the thesis of the American dilemma and should make us cautious about the assumption of a homogeneous moral view regarding race relations at some basic level of the national conscience. There is little doubt, however, that many persons sense a contradiction between their religious and political ideology and their race relations practices. The moral ambivalence produced by prejudice is illustrated in an important way by the tensions and the sustaining beliefs that are created by sexual activity between majority- and minority-group members. Lillian Smith, in *Killers of the Dream*, has given an insightful account of the costs to white men and women of the race–sex situation in the South a generation ago. Although the patten of relationship has changed a great deal in the last several decades, many of the beliefs and attitudes of earlier days survive to affect significantly the personality development of those who share them. The effects of contact between the races were sharply influenced by the religious and moral teachings that white children received: God was a God of love, and yet of wrath. "We were told that He loved us, and then we were told that He would burn us in everlasting flames of Hell if we displeased Him" (Smith 1949, p. 79). They were taught that the black person was inferior and evil, yet many of their warmest relationships were with a colored nurse, and in adult life many white men found sexual pleasure with Negro women.

What a strange ugly trap the white race made for itself! Because these slaveholders were "Christian," they felt compelled to justify the holding of slaves by denying these slaves a soul, and denying them a place in the human family. Because they were puritan, they succeeded in developing a frigidity in their white women that precluded the possibility of mutual satisfaction....The white man's roles as slaveholder and Christian and puritan were exacting far more than the strength of his mind could sustain. Each time he found the back-yard temptation irresistible his conscience split more deeply from his acts and his mind from things as they are.

The race–sex–sin spiral had begun. The more trails the white man made to back yard cabins, the higher he raised his white wife on her pedestal when he returned to the big house. The higher the pedestal, the less he enjoyed her whom he had put there, for statues after all are only nice things to look at....Guilt, shame, fear, lust spiralled each other. Then a time came, though it was decades later, when man's suspicion of white woman began to pull the spiral higher and higher. It was of course inevitable for him to suspect her of the sins he had committed so pleasantly and often. *What if*, he whispered, and the words were never finished. *What if*....Too often white woman could only smile bleakly in reply to the unasked question. But white man mistook this empty smile for one of cryptic satisfaction

and in jealous panic began to project his own sins on to the Negro male. (Smith 1949, pp. 116–17)

Thus the white man confronted himself with guilt and fears that required a great deal of emotional energy to try to dispel—the fear of "mongrelization" (which he projected onto the black man); guilt over the rejection of some of his own children; confusion in trying to free himself from a deep-seated childhood affection for a colored nurse, a second mother; fear

lest their sons, and especially their daughters should feel the same attraction they felt and should perhaps continue the blending of races to which they and their forefathers had made such lavish contributions. And because they feared this, knowing the strength of temptation, they blocked their children's way by erecting as many barriers as possible, extracting energy from their own guilt to build fortifications of law and custom against what they considered an "irresistible sin." (Smith 1949, pp. 121–22)

This set of circumstances was shared directly by only a small minority perhaps, but a minority important in affecting the nature of southern society and culture. Others shared many of the traditional attitudes that grew up in this situation and participated by identification in its support. Although the elements in this pattern have all been modified, they survive with sufficient strength to be a primary factor in the personality development of many Whites as shown by the energy with which segregation has been defended.

Not only white men, of course, but also white women were strongly influenced by this whole pattern. There was a strong tendency for the cultural sex taboos to be referred primarily to white women; the repressed sex feelings were directed, whether in action or fantasy, toward Negroes. Sacred white womanhood came to symbolize not just a barrier to black males but part of the ambivalent attitude toward sex of white men as well. White women who were taught that sex was to be shunned, and who at the same time often experienced the loss of their own men, came to feel that sex was indeed largely an evil that split their homes. Their sexual unresponsiveness then encouraged their men to direct more of their sexual interest and to project more of their ideas of sexual vitality onto black people, which further enhanced the dogma of sacred white womanhood, which in turn further frustrated the white women and blocked them from a normal warm relationship with their husbands.

Our discussion of some of the personality consequences of prejudice has been only illustrative. It has shown that in a society in which rationality is prized and where the values of democracy and sexual fidelity are widely held, prejudice is a costly item. Further consequences could be discussed. Most people believe that a realistic appraisal of one's own worth and a lack of arrogance are to be prized. These are blocked by prejudice. Dominant individuals in a society characterized by discrimination bear an often overwhelming burden of fear and insecurity. White South Africans sometimes show an almost obsessive fear of revolt and violence from the repressed black men. Today many city residents have several locks on their doors and are afraid to walk the streets at certain hours and in certain neighborhoods. Thus a pattern of discrimination is supported only at the cost of much irrationality, moral confusion, arrogance, and fear.

The Economic Costs of Prejudice

It is impossible to designate in precise dollar figures how much it costs to maintain a pattern of prejudice and discrimination, although there have been careful estimates by economists that the costs due to wasted skills, lower production, fewer customers, and duplicated facilities runs to several tens of billions of dollars a year in the United States. We can, however, indicate some of the ways in which specific groups among the dominant members of society are injured economically and in related ways and how society as a whole suffers.

Prejudice that takes the form of segregated areas in housing and severe limitations on the economic opportunities of minority-group members is an important factor in the development and continuation of slums. Beyond the loss of skills and the loss of purchasing power that such a situation creates (Gibson 1978), there is the direct financial cost of large expenditures for public health, for fire protection, for police and courts, and for relief. These costs are much higher per capita in slum areas than in other parts of a community. The tax yield, moreover, is low. Discriminatory limitation on the supply of housing for minority groups means that owners of the houses that are obtainable have less incentive to maintain their property in decent conditions—they can rent anyway. This deterioration lowers the value of the bordering property and injures the whole community through the total costs of slums.

That prejudice and discrimination play a part in housing segregation has been well documented (see, e.g., Courant and Yinger 1977; Guest and Weed 1976; Jackman and Jackman 1980; Villemez 1980; J. Yinger 1976, 1979). What we want to emphasize here is that the resulting housing patterns and the higher costs to minorities, especially Blacks, have direct and indirect effects for the communities and the society at large.

Although segregation is only one factor, it is part of an interesting set of forces that increase the levels of fear, violence, crime, and civic disruption. These burdens fall mainly on those experiencing discrimination, but they spread to the communities at large. Charles Silberman (quoted in *The New York Times,* March 12, 1979, p. B10; see also Glaser and Possony 1979, pp. 213–214) notes:

After 350 years of fearing whites black Americans have discovered that the fear runs the other way, that whites are intimidated by their very presence....The taboo against expression of anti-white anger is breaking down, and 350 years of festering hatred has come spilling out.

We have already cited the finding by Blau and Blau (1982) that variations in criminal violence—with much higher rates among the black population—are largely due to economic inequality among the races: "High rates of criminal violence are apparently the price of racial and economic inequalities" (p. 126). Violation of a democratic ideology breeds alienation, despair, and conflict. It is the sense of relative deprivation in a society of conspicuous affluence that provokes attack and entails the high costs for society. (We are not forgetting the higher economic costs of "white collar crimes" committed by "respectables." But that is another story, with a different pattern of costs.)

One of the largest costs to society flowing from discrimination is the failure to employ to the full the talents of large segments of the population. That discrimination prevents the training and use of workers at their highest possible skill is shown not only in the failure to employ fully the trained carpenter or pilot or teacher if he or she belongs to the "wrong groups," but more particularly in the failure to train many individuals in the first place. Ginzberg (1960) stresses the importance of discrimination and segregation in affecting the way many Blacks prepare themselves for work. This influence stretches back into the family, where children first see the occupational world through the experience of their parents. Many minority children have access only to poorer schools in which the occupational world is not opened to them; nor are standards of achievement held up to them. Much of the minority potential goes to waste because it fails to be developed. Some individuals just coast through school; others drop out because they see no point in continuing; still others, because of a lack of opportunity, never become aware that they possess special aptitudes (Ginzberg 1960; see also Katz 1969; Semyonov and Tyree 1981).

This, of course, is a partial picture. Some students, both minority and majority, who have well-trained and well-motivated parents and who attend good schools drop out. Segregated schools often mean inferior education for dominant-group members as well as for minorities (Wynne 1977). Oppositely, some who attend schools that by most criteria are inferior and raised in families whose work patterns fit those described by Ginzberg nevertheless develop high skill and initiative (see Coles 1967, 1977, 1981; Stack 1974). There is also skillful adaptation to discrimination and poverty, as we noted in Chapter 6. These creative responses need emphasis but they must not cause us to forget the costs to society from talents undeveloped and hopes unaroused. These costs are partly expressed in the proportions of a population who are employed. Between 1950 and 1977 the proportion for most

male groups fell, especially among Blacks. The proportion rose among most female groups, with Puerto Ricans being an exception, as shown in Table 8-1.

These data are not easy to interpret. In part they reflect different age distributions; changes in percentages are partly due to increased school attendance; the increases in employment among Mexican Americans are largely in unskilled jobs and reflect fairly high employment among teenagers; there are business cycle effects. On balance, however, they show decreasing employment among minority males and lower increases of employment opportunities among minority females. Not only the individuals involved, but the nation as a whole carries heavy costs as a result of the failure to use its human resources to the full.

Both the economic costs and the economic gains of discrimination are clearly apparent in other parts of the world. In South Africa, for example, most of the dominant Whites are dedicated to a policy that keeps nonwhites in a subservient position. During the last 35 years, South Africa has experienced rapid economic growth. The standard of living for the 18 percent of the population that is White matches that of the Western European countries; but the per capita income of the colored and Indian population is only one-fifth as high, and for the two-thirds of the country who are of full African ancestry it is only 10 percent as high. Table 8-2 indicates the changes in relative incomes of the

Table 8-1. Percentage of the Population, 14 Years of Age or Older, Employed

	1950	1960	1970	1977
Males				
White	73.7	71.7	73.7	71.3
Black	69.4	63.7	62.8	58.6
Mexican American	66.8	69.7	70.5	73.0
Puerto Rican	62.7	69.2	67.3	60.4
Native American	53.6	47.8	53.0	NA
Females				
White	26.8	31.9	39.1	44.1
Black	34.0	38.1	43.7	42.3
Mexican American	19.3	25.9	33.4	37.3
Puerto Rican	34.7	32.2	28.8	26.1
Native American	15.4	22.2	31.6	NA

Adapted from Anderson and Cottingham 1981, p. 261.

Table 8-2. Comparative Per Capita Incomes in South Africa, 1946–1976 by Racial and Ethnic Group

	1946	1960	1976
Whites	100	100	100
English	144	126	114
Africaners	68	81	82
Coloreds	16	16	20
Asians	20	18	23
Africans	8	9	10

Adapted from Adam and Giliomee 1979, p. 174.

racial and ethnic groups, 1946–1976. Africans, Coloreds, and Asians improved their lot only slightly, while the Africaner Whites reduced by more than half the disparity between their per capita income and that of Whites of English descent.

It is clear from the comparative incomes that Whites have succeeded in preserving their advantages by *apartheid*. Although this term refers to a presumed long-run goal of separate but related communities of Europeans and Africans, in practice apartheid has meant massive oppression and restriction of nonwhites within the White-dominated society.

This oppression has not been without costs, however. There are direct costs to taxpayers to maintain the system of domination. Agencies of control and repression are not inexpensive (Savage 1977). South African goods are widely boycotted abroad, especially by the newer nations (with the ironic exception of some of the Black-led nations in southern Africa, whose economies are highly interdependent with the Union of South Africa). The political and moral climate entails rigid conformity for most of the Whites, isolation from the world, and authoritarian patterns throughout the society (Adam 1971; van den Berghe 1978). Commenting on the flight of young Blacks from South Africa after serious conflicts in 1976–77, an Afrikaans newspaper wrote:

This is the kind of investment we cannot afford. For it is an investment in hate and violence. There is a good chance that when South Africa again sees these young blacks it will be over the barrel of a gun. (Adam and Giliomee 1979, p. 5)

In a country that is rapidly industrializing, there is need for an expanding group of skilled workers, rationally organized into productive enterprises and sufficiently well paid to be able to afford the products of their own making. "As a result of its racial policies, South Africa has experienced shortages of skilled labor, low rates of productivity, a restricted domestic market, and high costs of law enforcement." (Wilensky and Lawrence 1979, p. 241; see also Feit and Stokes 1976).

Lack of training for skilled jobs is not the only economic cost of discrimination. Contemporary studies of industry have shown that failure to pay attention to the workers' need for being treated with respect leads to lower productivity, higher labor turnover and, in the last analysis, higher costs. Workers from minority groups are particularly likely to lack the sense of being treated with respect; hence this factor in the loss of efficiency applies especially to them. In Chapter 7 we noted that a partially intentional, partially unconscious inefficiency on the job was one of the aggressive responses to discrimination. It can be seen in the present context as one of the costs of discrimination.

Who in the Dominant Group Pays the Costs of Discrimination? It is sometimes believed that, although the upper classes—the employers and professional people—pay an economic price for discrimination and prejudice in the loss of consumers and reduced choice of employees, the workers who would face the most immediate competition from the labor of minority-group members profit from a system that protects their advantages in the job market. Beck (1980) reads the evidence to show that the families who are best off do pay a price in contexts of discrimination, while workers in the fourth quintile of income profit from discrimination. Examinations of split labor markets (see, e.g., Bonacich 1972, 1976; Cummings 1980; Marks 1981) suggest that the distribution of gains and costs among workers depends upon the range of skills needed in a job market and control of access to those skills. Villemez (1978) believes that in the American economy Whites at all levels gain by the subordination of Blacks, but Dowdall (1974) sees the gains to be "so minimal as to be imperceptible"—indeed to be negative for the least powerful of those in the majority group.

Marxists contend that the working class suffers from the use of discrimination because it is used by owners to divide workers (Nikolinakos 1973; Reich 1981; Szymanski 1976, 1978a). Workers from the dominant racial or cultural group are paid off in the coin of presumed superiority and small economic advantages while their employers extract "surplus value" from majority and minority alike.

Some conservatives and neoconservatives see a very different situation. The costs to society are due, in their view, not to discrimination but in a sense to the failure to discriminate—that is, to an excessive emphasis on equality (Steinfels 1979, pp. 214–47).

Such a range of views is doubtless inevitable in a complex situation strongly influenced by assumptions, values, and ideologies. We can scarcely resolve the contradictions among the interpretations. We would like to emphasize, however, that the results vary widely, depending on many variables, including the following: the size and number of minority groups; the nature of the economy; the nature and strength of labor unions; and the extent of competition among employers. Although owners and employers sometimes find that their interests are hurt by the presence of discrimination in the labor market (they cannot hire and fire freely), and although skilled workers sometimes find their positions threatened by discrimination (employers use it to weaken workers' influence over job opportunities), it is not only sometimes, but almost always that the least well off among the majority group pay the price for discrimination. Exploited minorities are most likely to be used in direct competition with these least powerful "dominants."

We need also to emphasize that changes in the sizes of the "pieces of the pie" (Lieberson 1980) served to various subgroups among the majority are often less important than the size of the whole pie. For the various reasons we are discussing in this chapter, total economic output is likely to be reduced by discrimination, even though some individuals and groups see themselves, in close-up comparisons, profiting by it. This is important because they also see themselves—at least in the short run often correctly—in a zero-sum situation. If the lot of others is improved, they will pay the price. All the solutions to our economic problems, Thurow writes (1981, p. 11) "have the characteristic that someone must suffer large economic losses. No one wants to volunteer for this role....Our political and economic structure simply isn't able to cope with an economy that has a substantial zero-sum element." The moral and policy implications of this situation with reference to minorities have to do with equitable ways to distribute the costs attendant upon minority gains. The sociological

task is to note who bears the costs of change, what their responses are, and the conditions under which long-run changes cancel out the zero-sum elements to produce potential gains for all.

Prejudice and the National Welfare: Politics

It is generally held that a nation unified by common purposes and a shared allegiance is greatly to be desired. In democratic societies, virtually everybody also defends a political system in which differences of interest are resolved in a process of discussion and by freely elected representatives. It is a truism to say that prejudice and discrimination attack these values, but some of the precise ways in which they injure the democratic process should be noted. Not everybody, of course, shares these values or gives them top priority. Some people have political power or hold office precisely because of prejudice and tend therefore to look upon the results that we mention below not as costs but as gains. A reader who takes this position will want to reverse the value orientation of the following discussion but will concur, if the analysis is accurate, on what the effects are.

One important political concomitant of prejudice has been the many devices used since the days of Reconstruction, especially in the South, for keeping Blacks disfranchised. These have largely been swept away by judicial decision and legislative enactment, so that we are now witnessing more residual than direct effects. We shall not at this point describe the role of minority groups in the political process (see Chapters 11 and 12), but simply note some of the costs of this situation for the majority. Not only have Blacks been prevented until recently from achieving the gains that they might have made by using the political instrument, but the great majority of *white people* of all classes have been injured. The lower-class Whites have been made politically ineffective by the prevailing systems. Even those who technically manage the governmental machinery have been affected by the limitation on issues that come to the fore in a political situation geared to protecting a status system. A political system whose key function, at least on the surface, is to keep a minority group from political influence puts a sharp limitation on the kinds of issues that will be discussed. There is a tendency for all candidates to center their claims around their enthusiasm for and their ability to enforce the status system. "Personalities" thus tend to be the "issues" of political campaigns. And the nation as a whole is vitally influenced in a federal system in which the votes of representatives from each area determine policies that affect citizens in every area.

Some of the laws that were devised to disfranchise Blacks had a similar effect on many of the Whites. If the poll tax stood as an economic barrier to black citizens, it was scarcely less of one to an even larger number of Whites (it is now outlawed). The poorer Whites were also affected to a minor degree by educational and property requirements in some states. Actual disfranchisement, however, is far less significant than a general political ineffectiveness.

It is often assumed that even if minorities and lower-class dominants suffer from an oligarchic political situation, at least the small group of upper-class dominants profit by the restricted party competition, the small electorate, and their own controlling position in political activity. Even this assumption is not entirely correct. They too suffer from a political system that easily gives power to persons who play upon hate, fear, and prejudice. They suffer from the support this gives to all the other costs of discrimination.

Today in the United States there is less actual disfranchisement of Blacks or other minority-group members. Representation is sometimes blocked, however, by gerrymandering—determining the boundaries of election districts in such a way that the vote of a minority group is cut into small segments, each too small to elect a candidate or to have much effect on policy. In the last few years, legal and judicial actions, the civil rights movement, and the further concentration of minorities in many cities have reduced these political effects. There are many more minority-group politicians and they are much less dependent on majority-group support and mass apathy—two powerful forces in earlier political processes. In the years immediately following the decennial census, however, it becomes apparent that the art of gerrymandering has by no means been lost.

A final political cost of prejudice and discrimination to the majority has not yet loomed large in the United States but in some circumstances grows in importance. This is the appeal to minority groups of political movements and ideologies that the dominant community considers highly objectionable and in some instances subversive and dangerous. Every imperialist nation in recent years has carried the burden of arms and often of battle against nationalist uprisings as a price for its discriminatory treatment of colonial peoples. Where discrimination has been strongest, the national protests have taken the form of a reflexive prejudice that has reduced the chances for peaceful and cooperative interchange after independence has been attained by a colony. Thus the relations of the nations of the West with the nations of Asia and Africa are complicated not simply by the desire for freedom but by the suspicion and the prejudice that many of the people of these continents continue to have for the nations of the West.

The situation in the United States is not entirely different, although it has not developed very far. In the last decade one segment of the protest movement among Native Americans has sought complete separation from the United States. Some Indians now speak of "Indian countries," not of reservations, believing that by historical right and by treaty they possess the powers of sovereignty and self-government. This is one expression of alienation from American society (Deloria 1974; Steiner 1968), as shown in the remark of Sid Mills, executive director of Survival of American Indians Association (Cleveland *Plain Dealer,* June 30, 1976, pp. 1, 14):

This country is destined for destruction, and there's nothing that's going to turn it back....We're never, ever going to be part of this melting pot, this American society....We don't ever intend to be. We can't be. We're different people. We're seeking our independence. We do have treaties with the United States. We do have a land base. We do have our own governments. We want to be developed without exploitation by the United States.

In Chapter 7 we noted political alienation among black Americans, as measured by the sharp reduction in their feelings of trust in government. The implications of this shift are not clear. Viewed over a period of several decades, only a small number of Blacks have become sufficiently radical to become communists, despite intensive efforts by the Communist Party to win them over. A big recruiting drive in 1930 persuaded several hundred to join, but many resigned after a few months. The total had not reached 3,000 by 1940, a figure representing less than ten percent of the membership. There may have been a few years in the early 1940s when the Negro membership constituted a little more than ten percent of the total (Glazer 1961, pp. 174–75). The Communist Party expelled members for signs of "white chauvinism" and promoted many blacks to responsible positions in its recruitment efforts, but with little success (Cruse 1967, pp. 147–70; Glazer 1961; Naison 1983; Painter 1979; Record 1951).

Comparing the experience of American Negroes to those from other parts of the world whom he met in Paris at a Conference of Negro-African Writers and Artists in 1956, James Baldwin wrote (1961, p. 20):

We had been born in a society, which, in a way inconceivable for Africans, and no longer real for Europeans, was open, and, in a sense which has nothing to do with justice or injustice, was free. It was a society, in short, in which nothing was fixed and we had therefore been born to a greater number of possibilities, wretched as these possibilities seemed at the instant of our birth. Moreover, the land of our forefathers' exile had been made, by that travail, our home.

However, it would be a mistake to conclude that black Americans have no difficulty in giving unqualified allegiance to a nation that makes them second-class citizens. Baldwin's ambivalence is shown by his remark, a few sentences after the statement quoted above (1961, p. 21): "We had been dealing with, had been made and mangled by, another machinery altogether." The highly disprivileged are the least supportive of civil liberties and the most likely to approve the use of violence. Despite legal and economic gains, Blacks were far less ready in the 1960s and 1970s than ever before to wait for some natural process of evolution or the reform of white men to bring them equality. Civil disobedience—the explicit and open violation of hated laws—became a major part of their civil rights campaign. This was mainly a highly disciplined and restrained violation of laws of doubtful constitutionality. To their opponents it threatened anarchy; to their defenders it expressed another step in America's continuing revolution, with strong kinship to a movement that goes back at least to the Boston Tea Party. But to all it documented the depths of their opposition to a segregated and discriminatory society.

If America has not yet faced the problem of a thoroughly restive political minority in her midst it is partly because of the inarticulateness of the masses of minority-group members, the compelling hope of the American dream, the progress toward equality that has been made in the last fifty

years, and the lack until recently, in the world outside, of a powerful and successful competing system. If these conditions change, as the first and last have already changed, one can look for sharper internal conflicts, with the costs they entail.

Discrimination, Prejudice, and the National Welfare: International Relations

The effects of discrimination and prejudice on the relationships among nations of different race and culture are of growing importance. In times of international tension these effects become a particularly heavy cost. It has been widely observed that American treatment of minority groups receives world-wide attention. During World War II the forced relocation of Americans of Japanese ancestry and discrimination against Blacks in the United States were exploited by Japan as propaganda among the nonwhite peoples of the world. Even Germany, whose basic policy was so cruelly discriminatory, played upon the theme of American hypocrisy. The propaganda often exaggerated or distorted the facts, but there were many instances of violence and injustice upon which to build, so that enemies had only to cite American papers to get evidence.

Communist policy makers and propagandists are given a great advantage among nonwhites around the world by past history and present incidents in American race relations and by the imperialism and color prejudice of many of the Western powers. The even more important problem of finding a road to international cooperation under law is confused by the barriers of prejudice. In a world that has become so thoroughly interdependent, white people dare not disregard the growing power and population of nations of predominantly Asian, African, or Indian ancestry.

It is almost a truism to note that world opinion of American race relations is highly negative. This opinion is not itself, of course, without bias. America has no special capacity for making invidious distinctions over and beyond the capacity so widely shared among the peoples of the world. But with power come both special visibility and responsibility, as well as opportunity. A well-trained and motivated black population in the United States, and of course matching populations of Hispanics,

Indians, and Asians, can be a great resource for peace.

Summary

We have examined only a few of the costs of prejudice for members of the dominant group. Although there may be some gains, there are far more losses in the long run. One could scarcely expect otherwise among a people who proclaim a democratic ideology with great fervor and in a highly interactive world of many races and religions. The threat to a democratic society—and the opportunity—are well put in the poetic words of James Baldwin (1963, pp. 119–20):

If we—and now I mean the relatively conscious whites and the relatively conscious blacks, who must, like lovers, insist on, or create, the consciousness of the others—do not falter in our duty now, we may be able, handful that we are, to end the racial nightmare, and achieve our country, and change the history of the world. If we do not now dare everything, the fulfillment of that prophecy, re-created from the Bible in song by a slave, is upon us: *God gave Noah the rainbow sign, No more water, the fire next time!*

Many people agree with Robert MacIver (1949, p. 6) that the greatest cost of discrimination is the loss of purpose and solidarity that are the strength of a people. His statement may well sum up the whole question:

Whatever is distinctive about this country, its spiritual heritage, comes from the recognition and the liberation of the universal in man, transcending division and harmonizing differences. It is this heritage, exalting the rights and the liberties of men, that more than anything else America must stand for if it stands for anything. It cannot stand on alien traditions but on this thing that is peculiar to its own being. Without that, we are spiritually impoverished, voiceless, and inarticulate before the world.

PART II

Minorities in the Social Structure

The Institutional Patterns of Intergroup Relations

In Part II we shall focus on the institutional patterns of intergroup relations in the United States in order to assess the extent of discrimination and the trends. Our attention will be given primarily to the most disadvantaged minorities—Blacks, Hispanics, and Native Americans. The analysis of institutional structures and changes, however, should be of value in the study of other groups. Within the most disadvantaged groups there is wide variation in the degree to which individuals face discrimination and among less disadvantaged there are some who face major categorical barriers. Even within the dominant majority pockets of deprivation exist in part because of discrimination.

· In 1980, the three groups of our major interest here constituted together approximately one-fifth of the American population (see Part II table). The one-fifth estimate is not precise because of the overlapping categories, some undercount in the census, and the heterogeneity of the "other" category. The total Hispanic population in 1980 was probably nearer 20 million than 14.6 million. Since some of these are Black as well as Hispanic, the Black population was higher than the 26.5 million given in the census. Among the Hispanics, about 65% are of Mexican origin and 15% are Puerto Rican. This does not include the nearly three million who live in Puerto Rico. The "other" category also includes a few Asians, Native Americans, and Africans.

169

Part II. American Population by Race (in thousands)

	1970		1980	
	n	Percentage	*n*	Percentage
Total	203,302	100.0	226,505	100.0
White	177,749	87.4	188,341	83.2
Black	22,580	11.1	26,488	11.7
American Indian, Eskimos and Aleut[1]	827	0.4	1,418	0.6
Asian and Pacific Islander	1,539	0.8	3,501	1.5
Other	517	0.3	6,757	3.0
Hispanics[2]	9,073	4.5	14,606	6.5

[1]Estimates of the American Indian population are not precise. In 1982, the Census published *Ancestry and Language in the United States*, based on the monthly *Current Population Survey* of November, 1979. From this survey of 56,500 households, estimates were made of the national size of various groups by standard techniques of projection. 2,053,000 thus identified themselves as American Indians. Those who gave that as one of two or more identities totalled 7,847,000 (*Newsletter*, American Ethnological Society, Feb., 1983, 7–8).

[2]The Hispanic category overlaps the others, since it is not based on race. 56% of Hispanics were classified as White in 1980, 93% in 1970. The "other" category, based on self-identification, was made up primarily of Hispanics, as determined by a separate question on origin (U.S. Bureau of the Census, *Supplementary Report PC 80-S1-1*, May, 1981).

CHAPTER 9

Minorities in the Economy of the United States

Part II of this book deals with the institutional aspects of majority–minority relations: economic life, political and legal processes, family structures and intermarriage, religious institutions, and education. Chapters 9 and 10 consider the roles of minorities in the American economy. Since we cannot include all racial and cultural minorities in the United States in this segment of the book, the focus here is mainly on the four groups who are most disadvantaged: Blacks, Mexican Americans, Puerto Ricans, and Native Americans.

Employment opportunities and size of income are important not only in the narrow economic sense but also in terms of their influence on the whole way of life of individuals and on the institutional structure of groups. The political influence of a group, its family patterns, its educational aspirations and achievements, even its possibilities of good health can be understood only when the place of that group in the total economy is studied. Similarly, the political, familial, educational, religious, and other institutional patterns affect the economic situation.

Blacks in Agriculture

The number of black farmers increased through 1920, when 925,000 were reported by the Census. The spread of the boll weevil in the early 1920s brought about a slow decline in the black farm population. Drought, depression, and the agricultural policies of the New Deal in the 1930s occasioned a further decline in numbers. By the early 1940s, there were fewer than 700,000 black farm operators (owners, part-owners, managers, and tenants, including sharecroppers). The draft and employment in defense industries during and after World War II reduced the number to fewer than 600,000. The growth of large-scale, highly capitalized farming added strongly to these trends, so that by 1978 only 57,000 black-operated farms remained. At the rate of loss at the end of the 1970s, there will be fewer than 10,000 black-operated farms at the end of the 1980s (U.S. Commission on Civil Rights, February, 1982, p. 176).

Farm operators constitute only a small part of the total farm population. Early in the nation's history, 80 percent of the total population and more than 90 percent of the black population lived on farms. By 1972, the total farm population of 9,600,000 was less than five percent of the total population, and Blacks made up less than nine percent of the farm population total. That was less than half the size of the black farm population of two million in 1960. The total farm population dropped by 1.4 million, or 14 percent, between 1970 and 1976. The loss was particularly great among Blacks. The number of Blacks living on farms fell from 900,000 to 500,000 in six years

171

(Cleveland *Plain Dealer,* April 15, 1977). Blacks currently comprise only 4 percent of the 6 million farm residents in the United States (U.S. Commission on Civil Rights, February, 1982, p. 44; U.S. Bureau of Labor Statistics 1983, p. 15).

Those Blacks who remain as farm residents in the agricultural labor force are overrepresented as wage and salary workers and underrepresented as self-employed workers. Approximately 63 percent of the 1.7 million farm residents employed in agriculture are self-employed, 20 percent are employed for wages and salaries, and 17 percent are unpaid family workers. Among Blacks, the respective proportions are: 27 percent, 67.5 percent, and 5 percent (U.S. Commission on Civil Rights, February, 1982, pp. 44–45).

Blacks who have remained in farming continue to be handicapped by the relatively small size of their marginal holdings. Economies of scale based on mechanization, priorities for agricultural research (supported largely by state and federal funds), and institutional lending practices all are connected to large-scale farming. Discrimination, past and present, perpetuates distrust on the part of Blacks of the legal system and lending institutions, discouraging some black farmers from seeking credit and expanding their operations. The Farmers Home Administration has not given priority to dealing with the current plight of black farmers. In 1981, Blacks received only 2.5 percent of the total amount loaned through FHA's farm credit program (U.S. Commission on Civil Rights, February, 1982, pp. 177–78).

The black farmer is a disappearing species, and the black population in rural areas is rapidly declining. Heavy out-migration on the part of rural Blacks over many decades has left a population with a large proportion of children and aged and proportionately fewer persons of working age. The result is a heavy burden on those who remain and work in rural areas, as well as a demand for services beyond the capability of most rural counties to support (*The New York Times,* May 8, 1977, pp. 1, 22; Reid 1974, p. 267; Wadley 1974, pp. 279–83).

Black Urbanization

In recent years, Blacks have continued to move from rural and nonmetropolitan sections of the country to central cities in metropolitan areas.

Increasingly, however, black migrants move from one metropolitan area to another, and this migration is largely from smaller to larger standard metropolitcan statistical areas (SMSA). On the whole, this shift is advantageous to the migrants. More black males in central cities in the largest metropolitan areas are found in better-paying, more esteemed white-collar occupations than are those in smaller SMSAs, but proportionately fewer Blacks live in low-income families in smaller metropolitan centers (Tucker and Reid 1977, p. 64).

In 1960, Washington, D.C., was the only metropolitan central city of at least 100,000 population where Blacks constituted more than half of the population. In 1980, there were nine such cities: Gary, Washington, Atlanta, Detroit, Newark, Birmingham, New Orleans, Baltimore, and Richmond (Reid 1982, pp. 7–8).

More than half of the nation's black population lives in the South, and because rural Blacks have the highest birth rates of any comparable segment of the national population, the potential for migration to the cities remains high. In recent years, fewer Blacks have been heading for the cities, and of those who do three out of every five now go to Southern cities. Because industry has begun settling in the rural South, job opportunities in the region's small towns and counties have been increasing faster than opportunities in Southern cities (*The New York Times,* May 8, 1977, pp. 1, 22).

Other noteworthy demographic trends are found in the return of southern Blacks to the South and in the number of northern-born Blacks who are moving to southern states. Until the civil rights movement got under way in the middle 1960s, about one of every three blacks who moved north went back home. By 1974, perhaps one of every two was returning. Also, it has been estimated that 15 to 20 percent of the overall southbound stream of Blacks is made up of persons who were born in the North, a rate believed to be three or four times as high as in earlier years (Cleveland *Plain Dealer,* June 23, 1974, p. A23). In 1979, the Census Bureau reported that the traditional migration of Blacks from the South was ending and that Blacks were leaving the Northeast. The Midwest and the South had about the same numbers of Blacks moving in as leaving between 1975 and 1978, and the West gained in Blacks (Cleveland *Plain Dealer,* June 19, 1979, p. 4).

Some reports of the return of Blacks to the South have given the impression that these migrants were returning to their rural origins. Careful study shows that this movement was mainly from northern cities to southern urban areas (Reid 1982, p. 3; see also the section on Black suburbanization in Chapter 12).

Employment and Unemployment of Black Workers

The proportion of the population of the United States age 16 and over employed, by race and sex, 1950–1981, is shown in Figure 9-1 (Farley 1982, p. B-35).[1] In 1950, 81 percent of the white men were employed, compared with 76 percent of the nonwhite men. Racial differences in employment were about the same in 1970, but since that year the proportion of men with jobs has decreased, with

[1] This and later references to Farley 1982 are now available in *Blacks and Whites: Narrowing the Gap?*, Harvard University Press, 1984, which has just appeared as this book goes to press.

the decline being greater among Nonwhites than among Whites. In 1981, the racial difference in the proportion of adult men with jobs increased to 11 percentage points (Farley 1982, p. B-34). According to Farley, approximately two-thirds of the decrease in the proportion of white men at work was due to less employment of men over 54. This drop was related to the expansion of Social Security benefits and the provision of better private pension programs. The employment of nonwhite men at ages over 54 has also dropped substantially, but this change accounts for only one-third of the decrease in the proportion of men with jobs. The proportion of women of both races holding jobs increased during the entire period 1950 to 1981, but the rise in employment has been larger among Whites (Farley 1982, pp. B-38–40).

Information provided by the Bureau of Labor Statistics on the reasons given by men 25 to 54 if they are neither working nor looking for work is shown in Table 9-1 (Farley 1982, p. B-39). It seems

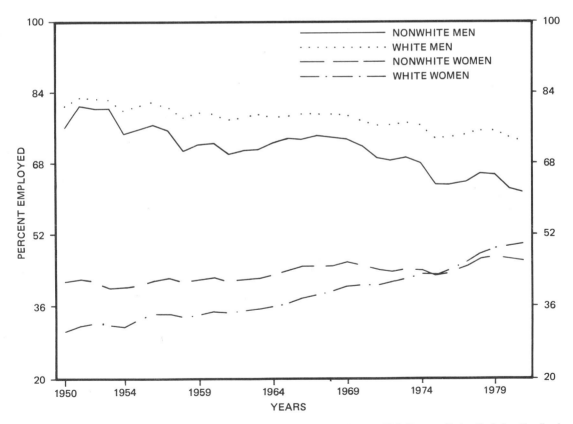

Figure 9–1. Proportion of population age 16 and over employed, 1950–1981. Sources: U.S. Bureau of Labor Statistics, *Handbook of Labor Statistics: 1978*, Tables 3 and 60; *Employment and Earnings*, Vol. 26, No. 1; Vol. 27, No. 1; Vol. 28, No. 1; and Vol. 29, No. 1.

Table 9-1. Reasons Given by Nonwhite and White Men Age 25 to 54 if Not Working or Looking for Work: 1970 and 1981

Major activity	Nonwhite Men			White Men		
	1970	1981	Change	1970	1981	Change
At work	88%	80%	−8%	94%	91%	−3%
Looking for work	4%	8%	+4%	2%	4%	+2%
Going to school	1%	1%	−	1%	1%	−
Unable to work	3%	3%	−	1%	2%	−
Keeping house	−	1%	+1%	−	−	−
Other reasons .	4%	7%	+3%	2%	2%	−
Total	100%	100%		100%	100%	

Source: U.S. Bureau of Labor Statistics; *Employment and Earnings*, Vol. 17, No. 7, Table A-1; Vol. 22, No. 7, Table 3.

likely that the increase in the proportion of nonwhite men not working for other reasons is due largely to declining employment prospects.

One measure of the employment of racial and cultural minorities in the United States is the rate of labor force participation. Table 9-2 shows the 1970 labor force participation rates by sex for a number of racial and ethnic groups. American Indians had the lowest rates for both sexes. It indicates also the differences in labor force participation among Spanish-speaking people and among Asian Americans, as well as the differences in participation by sex (Sullivan 1978, p. 167).

The long-run decline in labor force participation rates of nonwhite males has been accompanied by a more modest secular decline in the LFPR of white males. White female participation rates have

Table 9-2. Labor Force Participation Rates for Ten Racial-Ethnic Groups by Sex, 1970

Racial-Ethnic groups	Male	Female
Cuban	83.7	51.0
Japanese	79.3	49.4
Filipino	79.0	55.2
Hawaiian	77.9	48.5
Mexican	77.4	36.4
Korean	75.5	41.5
Puerto Rican	75.5	35.3
Chinese	73.2	49.5
Negro	69.8	47.5
American Indian	63.4	31.6
All Whites[a]	73.8	38.9

Source: Teresa A. Sullivan, 1978, p. 167.
[a]Includes Hispanic groups.

increased steadily since 1890, but the rates for nonwhite women dropped through the first five decades of this century and then increased. They have always exceeded the rates for white women. Several questions arise concerning these differences in participation rates, for example: Are nonwhite women "better off" than white women in the labor market? This interpretation has been given by some, especially with reference to college graduates. Are nonwhite men "worse off" in the labor market than white men now than they were in 1890 when the white labor force participation rate was 84.0 and the black rate was 86.6? An optimistic interpretation points out that declining male participation rates can be due to such developments as early retirement, longer schooling, and improved disability benefits. The pessimistic interpretation asserts that high unemployment leads to discouragement, that many Nonwhites withdraw from the labor force, and that some withdraw from what might be called the legitimate labor force in favor of clandestine or illegal activities. As Sullivan (1978, p. 170) remarks, the falling participation rate is a problem, both in the sense of its being a puzzle for social scientists and of its being a social detriment.

The labor force participation rates for 1960 to 1980 by race and sex are shown in Table 9-3.

A widely accepted belief holds that black women have had an advantage over black men in the labor market and that this is still true in the search for jobs. This belief is false; the evidence over past periods indicates that black men enjoy a clear economic superiority over black women and that there is a striking similarity between Whites and Blacks in this matter (Harwood and Hodge 1977, pp. 327–28).

Table 9-3. Civilian Labor Force Participation Rates by Race and Sex, 1960–1980

Race and sex	1960	1970	1975	1980
White	58.8	60.2	61.5	64.2
Male	83.4	80.0	78.7	78.3
Female	36.5	42.6	45.9	51.3
Black and Other	64.5	61.8	59.3	61.2
Male	83.0	76.5	71.5	70.8
Female	48.2	49.5	49.2	53.4
Total: 16 years old and over	59.4	60.4	61.2	63.8

Source: *Statistical Abstract of the United States: 1981*, p. 381. For a detailed table showing the labor force participation rate by sex, age, and race for December 1981 and December 1982, see Bureau of Labor Statistics, January 1983, pp. 15–16, Table A-4.

As black women have increased their participation in the labor force and upgraded their occupational status, their employment in the public sector has increased, whereas white women have tended to be employed in private business. In 1970, 22 percent of black women in the civilian labor force were employed in federal, state, or local government, compared with 18 percent of white women (Wallace 1980, p. 53).

Certain negative effects of the work situation for black women—racial discrimination, deficiencies in their human capital, inadequacy of the earnings of black husbands, black family structure, and characteristics of urban labor markets—tend to offset such recent gains as educational attainment, a noteworthy shift to full-time employment, improved opportunities through federally funded employment and training programs, and the carrying out of affirmative action programs (Wallace 1980, p. 99).

In the case of black women whose earnings are restricted by lack of education, skills, and work experience, many have concluded that the transfer system (including AFDC grants, food stamps, Medicaid, and subsidized housing) provides greater support for their families than their own work efforts. To change this system, market work would have to be made far more attractive for women (Wallace 1980, pp. 104–105, makes several suggestions that would not require major expenditures of funds).

Recent studies demonstrate the economic importance of illegal markets for young men in the central city. Mangum and Seninger (1978, pp. 76–78) point out that ghetto youth are not without

skills; in fact, they possess many traits that are highly esteemed by middle-class society: intelligence, highly developed verbal skills, leadership, courage, resourcefulness, tenacity, and ability to manage people. Unlike the lower-class white youth, however, the black youth, and especially the black male youth, has not been socialized in ways that enable him to identify with factory and office work. Experiencing a loss of self-esteem when he is found inadequate on a job, the street-skilled youth retreats to the street where his competencies are assets. Legal ghetto jobs are found mostly in low-asset, low-profit manufacturing and small retail trades that provide an atmosphere of discouragement for ghetto youth. The evidence seems to indicate that the poor want to work but that their desire is not realistic in view of the alternatives. Entertainers and athletes are admired, but the number who can succeed in these occupations is limited. In these circumstances, many ghetto youth turn to pool hustling, numbers running, and the more lucrative illegal activities—the production and sale of hard and soft drugs, prostitution, and pimping.

Unemployment among Blacks

Unemployment rates for white and nonwhite men, 1950 to 1981, are shown in Figure 9-2. In 1950, approximately 9 per cent of the nonwhite and 5 percent of the white men were unemployed. In 1981, 13 percent of the nonwhite and 6 percent of the white men were seeking work (Farley 1982, pp. B-29–30). In October, 1982, the unemployment rate in the United States rose to 10.4 percent—the highest since the Depression of the 1930s. Black unemployment rates were twice as high as the white rates: 20.2 percent compared with 9.3 percent for men and women combined; 19.8 percent compared with 8.8 percent for men over 20; 16.3 percent versus 7.6 percent among women over 20; and for teenagers, 46.7 percent for Blacks versus 21.7 percent for Whites (Reid 1982, p. 27).

Unemployment, as defined by the Bureau of Labor Statistics is based on the number of persons in the labor force actively looking for work and does not include the unemployed persons who have left the labor force as a result of long-term joblessness and who are no longer seeking employment. Prior to 1970, many thousands of older Blacks who had exhausted their unemployment insurance benefits, as well as a large number of young persons who had never entered the labor market, were not

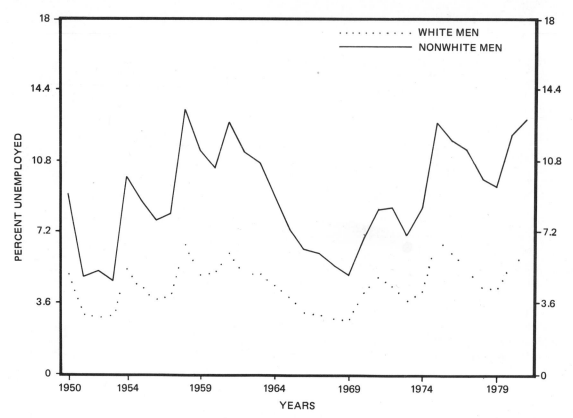

Figure 9–2. Unemployment rates for men by race, 1950–1981. Source: U.S. Bureau of Labor Statistics, *Handbook of Labor Statistics: 1978*, Tables 3 and 60; *Employment and Earnings*, Vol. 26, No. 1; Vol. 27, No. 1; Vol. 28, No. 1; and Vol. 29, No. 1.

included in official unemployment statistics. Many labor economists regarded those statistics as an understatement of actual employment conditions. Also, some population surveys of the United States Government have not enumerated a part of the working-age population. The undercount for black workers has been estimated to be 13 to 15 percent. Because of the estimated undercount, the true unemployment rate for black working-age males probably is significantly greater than reported in official publications.

Table 9-4 shows the unemployment rates for black and white women by marital status in March, 1978 (Wallace 1980, p. 45).

Wallace (1980, pp. 56–57) concluded that the various federally funded employment and training programs have not been effective for black women. Unemployment rates for black women are generally higher than for white men and women and black men.

According to the Bureau of Labor Statistics, a monthly survey of households showed a 14.1

Table 9-4. Unemployment Rates for Women by Marital Status, March 1978

Marital status	Black	White	Black/White ratio
Single	23.4	8.9	2.63
Married			
spouse present	8.1	4.8	1.69
spouse absent	14.8	8.7	1.70
Widowed	8.8	4.3	2.05
Divorced	8.1	6.3	1.29
Total	13.6	6.0	2.27

Source: U.S. Department of Labor, Bureau of Labor Statistics, *Marital and Family Characteristics*, March 1978.

percent jobless rate among all 16- to 21-year-old youth and a 28 percent rate among black youth of the same age in the spring of 1979. For the same period, a long-term survey by the Center for Human Research, Ohio State University, indicated that overall youth unemployment was 19.3 percent, while black youth unemployment was 38.8 percent. The latter report attributes the disparity between the long-term survey results and the monthly household survey to the fact that the youth involved were interviewed rather than the head of a household. The long-term survey tended to refute the widely held opinion that unemployment among young people, particularly those from minority groups, is high because they will not accept jobs considered menial. The majority of the young people, white and black, said they would be willing to take low-paying jobs in such areas as fast-food service and dishwashing, and many said that they would work at below the minimum wage (Cleveland *Plain Dealer,* February 29, 1980, p. 1B). Also in 1979, a Labor Department survey showed that the jobless rates for high school dropouts were 31.6 percent for black youths and 16.4 percent for Whites. For high school graduates the percentages were 21.3 for Blacks and 8.5 for Whites. For college graduates, the rates were 17.1 percent for Blacks and 4 percent for Whites, (Cleveland *Plain Dealer,* September 15, 1980, p. 22A). Black female teenagers (ages 15–19) have the highest unemployment rates and the lowest labor force participation rates of any group of workers (Wallace 1980, pp. 102–103).

The unemployment rates by sex and age for Blacks and persons of Hispanic origin for 1982 are shown in Table 9-5. In September 1984, the national unemployment rate stood at 7.4 percent. Large group differences remained, with rates of 6.4 percent for Whites, 10.7 percent for Hispanics, and 15.1 percent for Blacks.

Sources of Societal Changes and High Unemployment Rates among Blacks

High rates of unemployment among Blacks, and especially among black youths, in times of both prosperity and recession appear to be due largely to changes since World War I in the economy, the nation's social structure, and its political climate. Beyond continuing racial discrimination in the market place, some of the most important of specific causes are the following:

1. In the black-white split labor market between World War I and the New Deal, Blacks were used to undermine white workers and their unions. The price differential between two or more groups of workers includes wages and other costs associated with an employer's labor supply (housing, recruitment, training, and discipline). Even more important than wage differentials was a difference in militance—Whites were more likely to form unions, make demands, and engage in strikes. In the displacement phase Blacks were desirable employees relative to Whites but threatened the gains that Whites had made. Protective laws during the New Deal materially assisted in making the price of labor equal regardless of race, but they also increased labor costs and led capital to seek cheaper alternatives. During the 1950s and later, in the United States and abroad, machines and other low-cost labor groups have been substituted to a considerable extent for black labor (Bonacich 1976, pp. 34–51).

Table 9-5. Unemployment Rates by Sex, Race, Age, and Hispanic Origin for 1982

	Total	White	Black	Hispanic origin
Males:				
16 to 65 and over	9.9	8.8	20.1	13.6
16–19 years	24.4	21.7	48.9	31.2
Females:				
16 to 65 and over	9.4	8.3	17.6	14.1
16–19 years	21.9	19.0	47.1	28.2

Source: U.S. Bureau of Labor Statistics, *Employment and Earnings*, January 1983, p. 180, Table 51.

2. Business and industry have been moving out of central cities which have large black populations.
3. White women have been entering the labor market in large numbers.
4. Various interest groups, for example, the elderly, the handicapped, and ethnic groups, have become more militant in defending their positions, creating a situation which has made the advancement of Blacks more difficult.
5. Federal programs have apparently failed to reach those most in need, especially the hard-core unemployed.
6. Persons trained as professionals who have not been able to find jobs have taken lower-level jobs, both in the private realm and in public service (*The New York Times,* March 11, 1979, pp. 1, 44).

Occupations and Incomes of Blacks

Occupational Trends

By 1970 professional and related services had become a leading employer of black women. Although 32 percent of black women were in personal services, 29 percent were in professional and related services. Professional and related services, together with public administration, accounted for one-third of all black female employees, compared with 16 percent for black men. For black men, the most marked change occurred in manufacturing. The proportion engaged in this industry rose from 14 percent in 1940 to 28 percent in 1970. It became the leading source of employment for black men in the South. During the 1960s, black female employees in the South increased by 400,000, compared with an increase in 100,000 for black males. Also noteworthy was decrease of nearly 200,000 black women in personal services and increase of nearly 300,000 in professional and related services (Rhee 1974, pp. 295–297).

Despite these changes, in the 1970s many jobs were still widely regarded as "black" or "white," and those designated black were inferior in status and pay relative to those in the white category. Within prevailing conditions, occupation parity with Whites will not soon be achieved. Hill (1977, p. 32) points out that as certain industries decline or

as white workers are no longer available in sufficient numbers, black workers are able to move into vacated jobs. One example of such a shift came in the late 1960s when black workers became the last available source of cheap labor in the textile industry. Whites moved out of low-paying textile jobs into cleaner, higher paying industries, creating a labor shortage which black workers filled. Another example is the change which occurred in the telephone industry. According to a report presented by an AT&T vice president: "What a telephone company needs to know is who is available for work paying as little as $4,000 to $5,000 a year. It is...just a plain fact that in today's world, telephone company wages are more in line with black expectations. . . . It is therefore perfectly plain that we need nonwhite employees" (Hill 1977, p. 32).

Figure 9-3 shows trends in the occupations of employed workers in the period 1950–1975 (Farley 1977b, pp. 196–198). The United States censuses and monthly labor force reports use eleven major categories of workers. Persons in each category are assigned a prestige score ranging from laborers with a score of 7 to professionals with a score of 75. The figure shows the first and third quartiles of the occupational prestige distribution. Indexes of occupational dissimilarity are also shown.

Concerning Figure 9-3 Farley (1977b, 196–98) comments:

Between 1950 and 1970, the first and third quartiles of the white distribution changed very little, but among Nonwhites the first and third quartiles rose. Particularly sharp jumps at the first quartile point occurred in the 1960s as Nonwhites moved out of low prestige jobs as farm laborers or factory workers. As a result, the occupational distributions of white and nonwhite men became increasingly alike. The dissimilarity index for men fell from 43 in 1940 (not shown) to 37 in 1960, to 31 at the end of that decade, and to 26 in 1975. The relative improvements in the occupational status of nonwhite women were even greater than those for nonwhite men. In 1940, three-quarters of employed black women moved into service jobs, clerical and sales positions. By 1975, only 10 percent worked as domestic servants or on farms.

During the 1960s and 1970s the number of Nonwhites employed in nonmanual jobs or as craftsmen grew more rapidly than the number of Whites in those occupations. It should be emphasized, however, that the gains registered by Blacks in the 1960s and 1970s did not eliminate the large differences between the occupations followed by Whites and Nonwhites. The average prestige score for nonwhite workers in 1975 was inferior to that

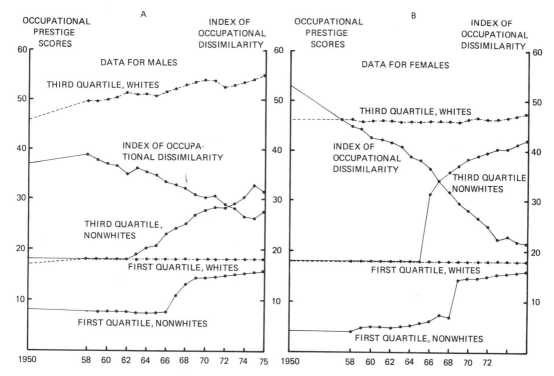

Figure 9–3. First and third quartiles of occupational prestige and indexes of occupational dissimilarity, 1950–1976. Source: Reynolds Farley, "Trends in Racial Inequalities: Have the Gains of the 1950s Disappeared in the 1970s?" *American Sociological Review*, April 1977, p. 197. Based on U.S. Bureau of the Census reports, and reports on employment and earnings, U.S. Bureau of Labor Statistics.

of white workers in 1940 (Farley 1977a, p. 198). Figure 9-4 shows the average annual growth rates for occupations by sex for Whites and Nonwhites for 1970 to 1981 (Farley 1982, p. B-51). In 1980, Blacks comprised about ten percent of the total civilian labor force. They were underrepresented in certain occupations: managerial and professional speciality occupations (6 percent), and technical, sales, and administrative support occupations (8 percent). In certain occupations, Blacks were overrepresented. For example, they constituted fourteen percent of all operators, fabricators, and laborers, and eighteen percent of all service workers (U.S. Bureau of the Census, July 1983, p. 11).

Incomes of Blacks

The most frequently cited statistics concerning the economic status of Blacks are those of family incomes. Table 9-6 shows the trends in the incomes of black and white families from 1947 to 1975. In 1947, the income of Whites was approximately double that of Blacks. In 1975, the median income for black families was 62 percent of the average income for white families. By 1981, the median black family income was 56 percent of the white median, even lower than the nonwhite level of 57 percent in 1960 (Reid 1982, pp. 29–30).

A second measure of income trends is seen in the overlap of black and white income distributions, that is, in the indexes of income dissimilarity shown in the accompanying table. Between 1947 and 1975, this index declined from 38.3 to 26.3, indicating a growing overlap (Farley 1977b, pp. 198–199). The indexes of dissimilarity measuring the overlap between the income distributions of black and white families declined more slowly in the 1970s than in the 1960s.

The strong relationship between social class background and the structure of the black family is shown in Table 9-7. Although 80.3 percent of all black families with incomes of less than $4,000 and 63.8 percent of those with incomes between $4,000 and $6,999 were headed by women in 1978,

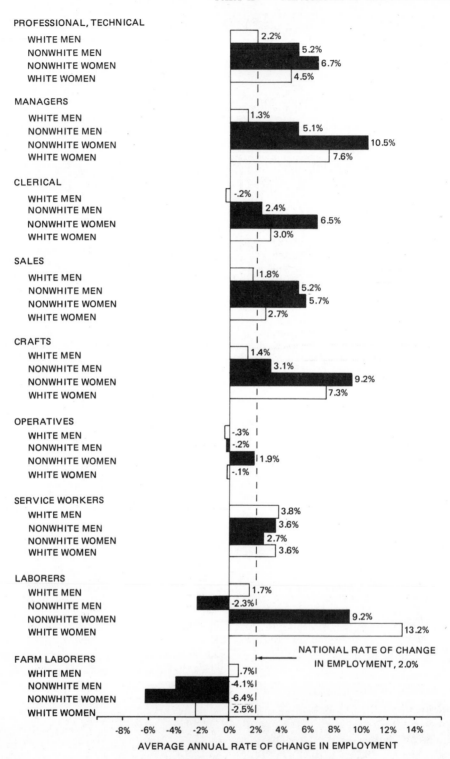

Figure 9–4. Average annual growth rates for occupations for race-sex groups, 1970–1981. Sources: U.S. Bureau of Labor Statistics, *Employment and Earnings*, Vol. 17, No. 7 (Table A-17); Vol. 29, No. 1 (Table 22).

Table 9-6. Trends in the Income of White and Black Families: 1947 to 1975

Year	Median family income in constant dollars[a]		Black median income as percentage of White	Index of dissimilarity[b]
	Blacks	Whites		
1947	3,888	7,608	51	38.3
1950	4,178	7,702	54	36.8
1955	5,113	9,271	55	34.7
1960	5,871	10,604	55	31.7
1965	6,812	12,370	55	32.8
1967	7,859	13,273	59	31.0
1968	8,292	13,826	60	29.1
1969	8,807	14,379	61	28.9
1970	8,703	14,188	61	27.3
1971	8,558	14,182	60	28.2
1972	8,831	14,858	59	28.0
1973	8,804	15,254	58	29.3
1974[c]	8,737	14,633	60	27.8
1975	8,779	14,268	62	26.3

Sources: U. S. Bureau of the Census, Current Population Reports, Series P-60, No. 103, Table 4.
[a]Amounts shown in constant 1975 dollars. Data for 1947 to 1965 refer to Whites and Nonwhites.
[b]Indexes of dissimilarity computed from seven-category constant dollar income distributions.
[c]Revised 1974 income figures. For details see Current Population Survey, Series P-60, No. 103, Table 4.

Table 9-7. Proportion of Families by Race, Income Level, Female Head, and Metropolitan Residence in 1978

Subject	All families (in percentages)	Female heads (in percentages)	Families in metropolitan areas (in percentages)	Metropolitan families with female heads (in percentages)
Black				
Under $4000	15.9	80.3	71.1	85.1
$4000 to $6999	16.2	63.8	74.7	71.2
$7000 to $10,999	18.3	46.2	74.8	50.7
$11,000 to $15,999	16.7	28.9	76.3	31.8
$16,000 to $24,999	19.2	15.3	82.7	15.4
$25,000 and over	13.4	7.7	88.5	7.6
White				
Under $4000	4.3	42.1	53.3	50.2
$4000 to $6999	4.7	27.6	56.2	33.7
$7000 to $10,999	12.7	19.5	57.7	21.8
$11,000 to $15,999	16.9	13.4	59.9	16.7
$16,000 to $24,999	28.8	7.2	66.0	8.5
$25,000 and over	29.5	2.9	75.4	3.1

Source: U.S. Bureau of the Census, *Current Population Reports,* Consumer Income, Series P-60, No. 23 (Washington, DC: U.S. Government Printing Office, 1980).

only 15.3 percent with incomes between $16,000 and $24,999 and 7.7 percent with incomes of $25,000 and more were headed by women (Wilson 1981, pp. 35–37).

Another way of comparing family income by race is to consider type of family. Table 9-8 shows median income of white and black families by type and average rates of change for three years: 1959, 1969, and 1975. Data are given for total families, families which include both spouses, and families headed by women (figures are not presented for the approximately 3 percent of the families headed by a man who did not have a wife present). The median incomes of husband–wife and female-headed black families increased more during the 1960s than they did for comparable white families. From 1969 to 1975 the median income of husband–wife black families rose more slowly, but the rate of increase was greater than for similar white families. During those years the median income for female-headed black families remained the same while that of similar white families fell by 0.9 percent annually (Farley 1977b, p. 199–200).

The median income of the most common types of black families—husband–wife and female-headed—increased or remained unchanged from 1969 to 1975, and for these types the racial difference in purchasing power decreased considerably. In the same period, the median income for all black families declined and the racial difference in purchasing power remained essentially the same at approximately $5,500. The explanation of this situation is found in the changing distributions of families by type. The lowest-income families—female-headed families—became a larger part of total black families. increasing from 28 percent to 36 percent in 1975, while husband–wife families declined from 68 to 60 percent. The study of family income trends must, therefore, consider the shifting living arrangements of adults and children (Farley 1977b, p. 200).

The income gains of black families slowed during the 1970s compared to the 1960s relative to the gains of white families. According to the Census Bureau, black families had median incomes about 60 percent of those of white families in 1970,

Table 9-8. Median Incomes (in Constant 1975 Dollars) of White and Black Families by Type and Average Rates of Change: 1959, 1969, and 1975

	Median income (in dollars)			Average annual rate of change (percentage)	
	1959[a]	1969	1975	1959 to 1969	1969 to 1975
Total Families					
Black	5,837	8,807	8,779	+ 4.2	− 0.1
White	10,885	14,379	14,268	+ 2.8	− 0.1
Dollar difference	− 5,048	− 5,572	− 5,489		
Ratio of medians	.54	.61	.62		
Husband-Wife Families					
Black	7,314	10,744	11,526	+ 4.7	+ 1.2
White	11,247	15,014	15,125	+ 2.9	+ 0.1
Dollar difference	− 4,537	− 4,270	− 3,599		
Ratio of medians	.60	.72	.76		
Female-headed families					
Black	3,201	4,897	4,898	+ 4.3	0.0
White	6,535	8,063	7,651	+ 2.1	− 0.9
Dollar difference	− 3,333	− 3,165	− 2,753		
Ratio of medians	.49	.61	.64		

Sources: U.S. Bureau of the Census, Census of Population: 1960, PC(1)-1D, Table 224; Current Population Reports, Series P-60, No. 75, Table 17; No. 103, Tables 1, 3, and 4.
[a]Data for 1959 refer to Whites and Nonwhites.

but by 1977 the median for Blacks had declined to 57 percent. Separation and divorce affected both groups during the 1970s, but black families apparently suffered more and by 1977, the median income for Blacks had declined to 57 percent.

Because of the special difficulties faced by black husbands in the labor market—greater frequency of unemployment, lower participation in the labor force, and limited wage increases—working black wives have tended to emphasize the maximization of family income, and their earnings constitute a large part of black family income. In 1978, the labor force participation of working black wives (58 percent) was more than double that of 1940. About two-thirds of black husband–wife families had a working wife in 1976, compared with two-fifths in 1965 (Wallace 1980, p. 64).

The earnings of black wives approximate those of their husbands more closely than is the case among white couples. Also, black women's earnings are much closer to white women's earnings whereas black men earn considerably less than white men. In 1976, black married women who worked full-time year-round had median earnings that were 73 percent of the median earnings of black married men who worked in that way. White married women earned only 54 percent as much as white married men. It should be pointed out that in 1976 black wives contributed 34 percent of the family income, compared with 26 percent for white wives (Wallace 1980, pp. 64–65).

If the definition of relative economic status includes income from all sources, significant differences are found between white and black women. More income is received by white women from social security, private pensions, annuities, and alimony than by black women. More public assistance and welfare payments are received by black than white women. For both Blacks and Whites, however, earnings make up the largest part of money income (Wallace 1980, pp. 65–66).

Trends in Personal Earnings of Blacks. The study of differences in the trends of majority–minority earnings is of great importance and has many facets. A number of these trends and their ramifications are examined in the following summaries of recent analyses.

A study of income data for males from 1954–1974 to determine the pattern of reduction in black–white inequality and the concomitant variation of those reductions with changes in the size distribution of black income shows that the general tendency in the industrial non-South has been for the distribution of income in the black sector to become more inequitable as black–white income inequality lessened. This study (Villemez and Wiswell 1978, pp. 1019-1032) indicates that most black economic gains have occurred at the top of the black economic distribution.

In his extensive study of social indicators based on 1980 census data, Farley (1982, p. D-30) shows that economic gains were widespread for Blacks in the 1960s and 1970s. This evidence is contrary to the hypothesis that those who benefited most were young Blacks or highly educated Blacks or those who were employed in government. Farley's analysis shows that the actual earnings of black men rose more rapidly than those of white men during those decades. Gains for black women in most categories of education, region of residence, class of work, type of industry, and age group rose at least as rapidly as those of either white or black men.

According to Farley (1982, pp. D-31–32), a variety of overlapping reasons may account for the decline in racial differences in earnings after 1960: (1) the likelihood that Blacks as individuals and through civil rights organizations were more insistent upon their rights; (2) the Civil Rights Act of 1964 and federal court decisions which overturned discriminatory employment practices and ordered affirmative action programs guaranteeing jobs for Blacks and for women; and (3) the changing attitudes of Whites.

Farley (1982, pp. D-33–34) suggests three possible explanations why the earnings of black women have risen much faster than those of white women and why the gap which separates the earnings of black women from those of white men has narrowed while the white woman–white man gap has remained large or increased: First, the duration and quality of work experience is different for black and white women and that the changes which have occurred over time in this variable have not been the same for both groups. Second, black women are more likely to head their own families than are white women, perhaps leading more black women than white to maximize their earnings by capitalizing upon their training and experience. Third, because of the requirements of the Equal Opportunity Commission, many court decisions, and various affirmative action programs, being a black woman may be a benefit in today's labor market.

Despite the fact that 1960–1979 was a generally

prosperous period for Blacks and Whites of both sexes, there were racial differences in the rates of gain. During this period Blacks were gradually catching up—the average income of black men rose by 1.9 percent annually and that of black women 3.0 percent. For Whites, the yearly gain was about 1.2 percent. Racial differences in income, however, remained substantial in 1979 (Farley 1982, p. C-41). The incomes of black men were only five-eighths those of white men while black women's incomes were about 94 percent as great as white women's.

By the 1970s, young black college-trained men had attained impressive gains in job opportunities and income. For the first time, large corporations were actively recruiting them. Increased income and the achievement of equality in starting salaries had made the rate of return to black male college graduates to exceed that of Whites, and the return to investments in graduate training also surpassed that of Whites (Freeman 1976, p. 216).

The occupational returns to schooling for Blacks with no college education have been considerably below those in the majority population. Although the rewards for additional college training have been more comparative in recent years, the effects of increments of higher education are misleading in that the largest returns for such training are limited to black graduates and postgraduates. According to Featherman and Hauser (1978, p. 365), the black minority has had to complete more schooling than their white counterparts in order for the incremental gains of education to approach equality with the majority.

In his study of continuing black–white income differentials, Masters (1975, pp. 110–111) found that differences in years of schooling accounted for about 10 percent of the differences in racial earnings. The effect of discrimination in the labor market is believed to account for at least 30 percent of the difference, and the residual is attributed to other aspects of productivity (quality of training, lack of effort, and so forth) not captured in as gross a measure as years of schooling.

Another study of racial inequality (Parcel 1979, pp. 262–265) focuses upon the influence of areal labor market characteristics (the social and economic organization of markets) on the earnings attainment of Blacks and Whites. The argument here is that a high-wage export industry (one which produces goods for export outside the SMSA) not only benefits its own workers by paying them high wages, but that it also indirectly helps other workers by raising wages in the local service sector through interarea competition.

In a study of the full-time white-collar federal civilian work force, considerable salary difference was found to exist between nonminority men and other minority/sex groups (Taylor 1979, p. 472). Variables such as age, years of federal service, education, and a number of other employment-related variables were controlled. On the average, minority males earned $1,994 less than nonminority males; nonminority females earned $3,476 less than nonminority males; and minority females earned $5,172 less than nonminority males.

Taylor (1979, p. 478) indicates that as much as one-half of the salary disparities between minority/sex groups could be eliminated in future cohorts of federal employees by modifications in employer practices alone, especially in the placement of individuals into particular job streams. Such "tracking" in the past may have operated to segregate women into low-paid clerical occupations and minorities into technical occupations. Once hired into a particular job stream, internal staffing regulations may "track" employees as long as they are employed by the federal government.

This study supports the contention that institutional discrimination alone does not explain inequalities among groups. By institutional discrimination is meant the equal application of universalistic criteria to groups that meet these criteria unequally. Examples of such discrimination would include denial of admission of black students to college because of low scores on standardized tests, payment of lower salaries to women than to men because they have less on-the-job experience, and withholding employment or promotion to Hispanics because they lack the educational requirements of the position. Although the use of universalistic criteria may be quite proper at times—for example, utilizing aptitude tests for employment selection—the application of such criteria at the discretion of the individual decision maker may be a pretext for employer discrimination (Taylor 1979, p. 478).

An interesting aspect of the Taylor study is the indirect evidence it brings about returns to education and quality of schooling. Presumably, the quality of minority male education is not substantially higher than the quality of minority female education, and similarly for nonminority males and females. The returns to schooling, however, vary more by sex within one minority group than within either sex group (Taylor 1979, p. 477).

Among women, the earnings of black women are approaching those of white women. On the evidence now available, it appears that from one-third to one-half of the racial difference in the earnings of black and white men is due to discrimination. A number of studies indicate that reductions in economic inequality are small compared to the remaining racial differences and that the forces creating the racial differences will be difficult to eliminate (Farley 1977b, p. 206; Featherman and Hauser 1978, pp. 422–423; Institute for the Study of Educational Policy 1976, pp. 195–196; Masters 1975).

Mexican Americans

Mexico as a Source of Labor for the United States

Since the 1920s Mexico has been the chief source of low-wage labor for the United States. Persons who have crossed the Rio Grande River from Mexico and entered the United States without legal inspection have been known popularly as "wetbacks." Those who have crossed the international border where there is no river, for example, at San Diego, California or El Paso, Texas, are also called wetbacks. If they have cut a fence in crossing they may be called *alambristas* (Samora 1971, p. 6). Although it is a felony to be a wetback, it has not been against the law to employ these persons. Employers looking for cheap labor are willing to employ wetbacks.

Temporary contract farm workers who have come from Mexico are known as *braceros*. They came under an international agreement between Mexico and the United States which provided that Mexico would supply seasonal farm laborers to help in the war effort during World War II. After the war, the State Department advised Mexico that the agreement would be terminated within three months. Through the influence of agricultural interests the agreement was extended until 1951, when Congress enacted Public Law 78. The *bracero* program was finally phased out in 1964 (Samora 1971, pp. 7, 19).

It seems unlikely that the *bracero* program will be revived. There is opposition to that proposal in the Mexican American community, and important agricultural interests also oppose it. In South Texas,

many of the crops that were harvested in the past by hand are now harvested by machine. Some agribusiness operators in the Lower Rio Grande Valley say they now have no trouble obtaining an adequate work force. Others are not interested in using *braceros* because they believe the federal government would impose strict regulations concerning housing and pay for such workers.

Commuters are persons from Mexico who have acquired an immigrant visa (Form I-151) which entitles them to reside and work in the United States as legal resident aliens. Because of custom, the visa has in effect become a work permit, and "green-carders" actually live in Mexico and commute to the United States to work. Thousands of people cross each day into El Paso and at such border crossing points as Tijuana, Mexicali, Nogales, Piedras Negras, Nuevo Laredo, Reynosa, and Matamoros. Many of the commuters are United States citizens—perhaps one fourth of the group, who prefer to live in Mexico and work in the United States. In addition to the *green-carders*, there are *blue-carders* who are permitted to enter the United States legally but whose residency is limited to not more than seventy-two hours at one time. Many persons who hold these border-crossing cards enter the United States legally but violate the law by working as domestics or in other types of employment. Since the end of Public Law 78, commuters have done much of the work performed earlier by *braceros*.

Three different systems of migrant labor exist in California. Migrants who circulate between Mexico and California constitute a system of *external migrant labor*. Aliens who reside in California throughout the year constitute a system of *internal migrant labor*. The third system, *migratory labor*, is a domestic labor force which migrates from place to place in search of employment (Burawoy 1976, p. 1066).

Growers seem to prefer a system of migrant labor, but at times, especially during depressions, migrant labor has hardly existed. In a recent period, the organization of migratory labor in the United Farm Workers Union and the discontinuation of the *bracero* program resulted in an increase in the use of domestic labor. Burawoy (1976, p. 1067) points out that the interests of the state, as seen in such factors as the level of employment and the political power of domestic groups, interact with the interests of growers in determining the relative importance of each labor system.

Unemployed domestic labor is maintained during the off season by the distribution of relief, a type of assistance which is immediately suspended when jobs appear in the fields. This procedure ensures that labor will be available during the busy season. Thus there is twin dependency upon the state and the employer in the mobilization and distribution of labor to meet the changing demands of the economy. Relief, then, is the functional equivalent of migrant labor (Burawoy 1976, p. 1069).

Migrant workers earn lower wages than domestic workers because they require fewer resources to sustain the renewal process, that is, the replacement of workers. If a supply of migrant labor is not available, industry may migrate to areas where the cost of reproducing laborers is lower. Migration by capitalists relieves them of responsibility for meeting the social and political costs of a migrant labor supply. At the same time, however, when a host country takes responsibility for regulating the labor force, entrepreneurs are subjected to political and economic uncertainties (Burawoy 1976, p. 1082).

The higher wages and improved working conditions which have come from union representation in the grape industry in California encourage farm owners to replace manual employees with a vineyard picking machine that can harvest a row of grapes in fifteen minutes instead of the two days that two workers require to complete the task. The increasing mechanization of agriculture will continue to displace large numbers of rural people.

A special question pertaining to Mexican American agriculturalists living in northern New Mexico is land tenure. According to one estimate, between 1854 and 1930, Spanish Americans lost a minimum of 2,000,000 acres of privately owned lands, 1,700,000 acres of communal or *ejido* lands, and 1,800,000 acres of land taken by the federal government without remuneration. The loss of this land destroyed the economic basis of Spanish American rural villages (Knowlton 1973, p. 335).

The Alianza Federal de Mercedes (Federal Alliance of Land Grants) was formed in 1963 to campaign for the return of or compensation for land it claims was wrongfully acquired by the federal government. This claim is based on the Treaty of Guadalupe Hildago of 1848 which followed the war between Mexico and the United States. The treaty conferred citizenship on Mexicans who stayed in the conquered areas and provided that land grants made to New Mexicans by the Spanish and Mexican governments were to be recognized in the courts of the United States. Those courts invalidated 94 percent of the land claims made by Mexican Americans, and these decisions led to their expulsion from the land (Griego and Merk 1973, pp. 388–389).

Mexican Americans believe that the Departments of Interior and Agriculture are responsible for the land that Spanish American subsistence farmers located along the rivers of New Mexico have lost. Thousands of people were driven from their lands because they could not afford to meet the financial charges levied upon their small farms by the development of the main irrigation and flood control districts of the state (Knowlton 1973, p. 335).

Knowlton has suggested that a government committee be appointed by the Departments of Interior and Agriculture to study in depth the land question in New Mexico, southern California, western Texas, and neighboring areas. Such a committee would consider Spanish and Mexican landowning customs that were practiced in New Mexico, the impact of American conquest upon the Spanish Americans, and the causes of land loss from that time until today. The Alianza is concerned mainly with the village land grants that were owned communally by the heirs of the original grantees. It does not lay claim to the land grant acreage now owned privately, but it is concerned with the land appropriated by the federal government, much of it now in the national forest. If the villages could obtain the grazing and timber lands taken from their *ejidos*, their incomes could be increased through grazing and forest activities. In addition, other revenue might come to the villages if they were assisted in catering to the recreational interests of the larger society, and if industries suitable to the natural environment were encouraged to come into the region (Knowlton 1973, pp. 335, 339; Griego and Merk 1973, p. 389).

Urbanization of Mexican Americans

In 1940, the majority of people with Spanish surnames in the Southwest lived in rural areas. The Census of 1960 showed that the majority of Mexican Americans were urban residents—an important demographic shift over a period of twenty years. The 1970 and 1980 censuses show a continuation of this trend to the cities. Today, the Mexican

American population is more than four-fifths urban. Evidence of the earlier Mexican-American orientation to rural life, however, is seen in the fact that the occupations of Chicanos are less highly urbanized than their place of residence. A relatively large proportion of those who live in cities work in agriculture, using their urban residence as a center for migratory work (Grebler, Moore, and Guzman 1970, p. 16; Hirsch 1973, p. 11; Peñalosa 1973a, p. 269).

The shift to urban centers has often been a move to California, in particular to Los Angeles, San Francisco, and San Diego. Los Angeles has a larger population of persons of Mexican descent than any other city except Mexico City. One and one half million citizens of Mexican ancestry live there and perhaps half a million more illegal immigrants. There are more Mexican American than black or Anglo-American children in the Los Angeles school system.

Employment of Mexican Americans

In discussing black employment and unemployment, some comparisons were made with other racial and cultural minorities. Where comparisons were not made, we considered a number of points concerning Blacks that apply as well to Mexican Americans, Puerto Ricans, and American Indians: undercounts of working-age population, labor force participation rates, differences between white and minority unemployment rates, the effects of split labor markets, the movement of industries out of central cities, continuing discrimination against racial and cultural minorities in the marketplace, the entrance of majority group women into the labor market in large numbers, competition with such interest groups as the elderly, the handicapped, and various nationality groups for economic assistance, the failure of federal programs to reach those most in need, and the willingness of persons trained for higher-level jobs to take lower-level jobs.

In the late 1960s, many localities in the Southwest were rated average in unemployment rates for the total labor force, but from 7 to 10 percent of the male Mexican American labor force might be unemployed at a given time. In Los Angeles in that period, unemployment rates of 12 to 25 percent were found in some Mexican American neighborhoods. During the low point in agricultural production in the Lower Rio Grande, the Salt River valley, and the central valley of California, some

communities had a male unemployment rate of one-third. Mechanization in canneries and other food-processing plants had eliminated thousands of jobs. For decades, these cannery jobs had been regarded as the next step up from farm labor. In the cities, mechanization in laundering, car washing, and other fields had eliminated jobs that had provided employment for many Mexican Americans (Galarza, Gallegos, and Samora 1969, pp. 32–34).

Under the Mexican Border Industries Program of 1965, the Mexican government created a free trade industrial zone which extended twelve miles in from the border along its entire length. In that year, American tariff regulations were revised as compensation for the cessation of the *bracero* program referred to earlier in this chapter. The "offshore operations" of American- or Mexican-owned assembly plants were assessed only a 10 percent tax on the value added to products in Mexico. Since most of the work consisted of assembling electrical component parts and textile products, wages made up most of the value added. Because the prevailing minimum wage in Mexico was low, the assembly costs to American manufacturers were considerably reduced. Mexico did not apply any duty on these exports. Under this arrangement, unassembled goods were shipped from American plants to Mexico for final assembly and then brought back into the United States market. This program is often called the "twin plants" program. By 1971, 333 plants, almost all of which were American-owned, were involved in the program. Among these companies were Bendix, Zenith, Lockheed, RCA, Honeywell, and Samsonite. It was estimated that 40,000 Mexicans were employed in these enterprises (Briggs 1973, pp. 45–46). By 1977, some 500 twin plants had been set up just across the border by United States companies seeking to take advantage of wage rates about one-fourth the average in this country. Labor union officials charge that this arrangement hurts American workers. The operators of these factories argue that their facilities support tens of thousands of jobs in the United States that would otherwise be transferred to Hong Kong, Taiwan, Japan, and South Korea, where wage rates are more competitive (*The New York Times,* April 3, 1977, p. 44).

In 1970, about 39 percent of all married Mexican American women were employed at some time during the year. This proportion is only slightly lower than the percentage of all Mexican American women who were employed. Although their rate of labor force participation is below the 50 percent rate of other white women, these figures refute the stereotype of the Mexican American woman as one who is not gainfully employed. At the same time, the unemployment rate for Mexican American women was rather high (11.5 percent). Their educational attainment and employment earnings are lower than those of Mexican American men or Anglo men and women, and the income gap persists even among Mexican American women who have acquired more skills and education.[2]

Mexican American women are most likely not to enter the labor force where there are children under 18 years of age in the family. Where there are not children under that age, women in this group are as likely to be employed outside the home as other women. The increase in labor force participation of females in the past two decades, especially in urban areas, suggests that there has been a considerable diminution of cultural influences that formerly kept Mexican American women from seeking outside employment (Briggs, Fogel, and Schmidt 1977, p. 32).

The labor force participation rates for Mexican Americans for 1975 and 1980 were: males, 79.8 percent and 83.2 percent; females, 42.1 percent and 49.5 percent (*Statistical Abstract 1981,* p. 384, Table 641).

In seeking employment, Chicanos are at a disadvantage in the "queuing process" where each prospective worker tries to get the most desirable job and where employers select those people who they think will perform best. Workers who are not chosen for the most desirable jobs then get in line for less desirable ones until they are selected for employment. The disadvantages of Mexican Americans are: lack of schooling and technical skills, lack of facility in English and familiarity with labor markets, and discrimination by some employers. As a result of these disadvantages and the queuing process, numbers disproportionate to their population and qualifications find employment with low-wage employers and in the less desirable occupations in high-wage firms (Briggs, Fogel, and Schmidt 1977, p. 69).

[2]U.S. Department of Labor, *Employment and Training Report of the President,* 1976, p. 149; U.S. Bureau of the Census, "Persons of Spanish Origin in the United States, March, 1976," *Current Population Reports,* Series P–20, No. 310 (July, 1977); Mirandé and Enríquez 1979, pp. 120, 130, 135; Alvirez and Bean 1976, pp. 282–283.

Unemployment among Mexican Americans

A federal census report in 1976 showed that unemployment and general economic conditions among Americans of Spanish-speaking origin were considerably worse than those for Whites but slightly better than those for Blacks. In March, 1976, the unemployment figures were 11.5 percent for Hispanics, compared with 6.8 percent for Whites and 13 percent for Blacks (*The New York Times,* December 12, 1976, p. 40).

The unemployment rate for persons of Mexican origin in 1982 was 13.9 percent. For males 20 and over, it was 12.2 percent, and for females in that age group, 12.5 percent. For both sexes, 16 to 19 years, the unemployment rate was 28.8 percent (U.S. Bureau of Labor Statistics, January 1983, 176, Table 45).

Testimony by employers about the widespread use of aptitude tests, high school diplomas, honorable military discharges, physical examinations, and records of no arrests as employment screening devices without asking whether these requirements had any relation to job performance has been given to the Equal Employment Opportunity Commission (EEOC). Without performance validation, these practices serve to deny Chicanos and other excluded groups from consideration for employment and promotion. Briggs, Fogel, and Schmidt (1977, pp. 99, 101–102) assert that there is a great need in the Southwest "to demonstrate to Chicano youth that it is possible to advance on the basis of the content of one's character and the skill one possesses."

Occupations of Mexican Americans

Table 9-9 shows that Mexican Americans are disproportionately overrepresented in blue-collar occupations—one-half compared with one-third. For operatives (except transport) and for nonfarm labor the ratio is 2:1. At the same time, in the professional and technical fields Mexican Americans are underrepresented by a ratio of nearly 3:1 in comparison with the general population (Pachon and Moore 1981, p. 117).

Earlier in this chapter we referred to the great shift since 1940 of the Mexican American population from rural areas and agricultural work to urban residences and occupations. For example, the Mexican American population in California no

Table 9-9. Employed Persons of Mexican Origin and the General Population by Occupation, 1978 Annual Average

	Mexican	General population, 16 years and older
Total employed		
Number, in thousands	2665	94,373
Percentages	100.00	100.00
White collar, in percentages	27.5	50.00
Professional and technical	5.6	15.1
Managers and administrators	5.4	10.7
Sales	3.0	6.3
Clerical	13.5	17.9
Blue collar, in percentages	49.9	33.4
Craft and kindred	14.6	13.1
Operatives, except transport	21.0	11.5
Transport equipment operatives	4.5	3.8
Nonfarm labor	9.8	5.0
Service, in percentages	16.5	13.6
Farm, in percentages	6.1	3.0

Source: Bureau of Labor Statistics, U.S. Department of Labor, unpublished data.

Note: Numbers may not add up to 100 due to rounding.

longer engages to any significant extent in migratory labor. Less than 15 percent of the Mexican American labor force there is employed in agriculture, forestry, or fisheries, and only one-eighth is employed as farm laborers or foremen. Mexican American field hands were largely displaced during World War II and the postwar period by the flow of *braceros* (contract laborers) from Mexico. The *bracero* program was discontinued in 1964, and, for various reasons, Mexican Americans have not returned to agricultural employment (Peñalosa 1973a, p. 259).

The principal occupational opportunities for urban Mexican Americans have been in the garment industries; the construction industry; domestic services; building maintenance; hotels and restaurants; trucking, gardening and landscaping;

and retail selling (Gallarza, Galegos, and Samora 1969, p. 30). In dual or segmented labor market theory, most of the jobs in these industries pay low wages, provide little security, and offer limited opportunities for advancement. The other labor market, the primary sector, offers high wages, security, better working conditions, and chances for advancement. Some Mexican American workers return to Mexico, others remain in the dead-end jobs. The children of the latter often drop out of school or become functional illiterates; some make their way into primary sector jobs (Pachon and Moore 1981, pp. 118–120).

Although Hispanics remain underrepresented in the more skilled, higher paying occupations, their occupational status has improved since 1973. Hispanic women have made more gains than Hispanic men. According to Davis, Haub, and Willettee (1983, p. 36), a marked improvement in occupations will require a substantial increase in the educational attainment of Hispanics that will meet the demands of the age of high technology.

Incomes of Mexican Americans

Mexican Americans are disproportionately employed in low-paying or marginal firms. Companies which pay standard wages or higher often reject Chicano applicants because they do not meet job qualification standards or because of their minority group membership. Mexican Americans are overrepresented among those who have the least schooling, quantitatively and qualitatively, and this characteristic affects them adversely in the job selection process (Grebler, Moore, and Guzman 1970, p. 22; Moore 1970, p. 63).

The median family income of Mexican Americans in 1970 was $6,002, compared with $5,879 for Puerto Ricans and $7,891 for the total population (Sowell 1975b, p. 111). In 1976, the median income was $6,450 for Chicano men, but $2,750 for Chicano women. The median income for Puerto Rican men in that year was $6,687, and $3,837 for women. The percentages for workers with incomes less than $5,000 annually were: 39 for Mexican American men, 75.2 for Mexican American women; 34.5 for Puerto Rican men, and 68.6 for Puerto Rican women. Only .8 percent of Puerto Rican men earned more than $25,000 per year in 1976, while 1.2 percent of Chicano men were in that income category. In family income, the median for Chicanos was $9,546 in 1976, compared with the median family income of $7,291 for Puerto Ricans and $8,200 for Blacks (Blackwell 1978, p. 4). For 1979, median income for Mexican American families was $12,835, compared with $17,912 for families of non-Hispanic origin. This income gap of $5,077 was twice as large as the gap between Mexican American families and majority families in 1969. According to Current Population Survey figures for 1978, however, 34.9 percent of all Mexican American families gave their income as $15,000 or more (Pachon and Moore 1981, p. 118).

In five Southwestern states, when income was adjusted for schooling differentials, Mexican American males showed larger earnings than any nonwhite group, even the Japanese in California. Probably Mexican Americans experience less discrimination in employment than most racial and cultural minorities. Large income gaps, however, have persisted between Mexican Americans and the majority population. Even when differences in schooling are taken into account, substantial disparities between Chicanos and Anglos are shown. Grebler, Moore, and Guzman (1970, pp. 197, 201) attribute some of these disparities to variations in the quality of education obtained by the two groups.

The income of Mexican Americans in relation to the majority population varies among states and metropolitan areas. These differences are much greater than those for Anglos, even when the schooling gap is considered and adjustments are made by age, sex, and locality. In these comparisons, Texas shows the largest differences between Mexican Americans and Anglos, and between Chicanos and the whole population. In Texas, the Spanish-surname population is concentrated in the low-income southern part of the state. Mexican American workers living there are more seriously affected by commuters who live across the border than those in any other part of the Southwest. Mexican Americans who live in Colorado and New Mexico are faced with the problems of declining industries. As yet, most have not acquired the skills required for higher-paying jobs in those states.

In most comparisons, California shows the smallest differences in income between Chicanos and the majority population. The movement of Mexican American people toward California accelerated region-wide improvements in the population's relative position (Grebler, Moore, and Guzman 1970, pp. 28, 201–202). Conditions for

workers in California's industries are not, however, ideal. The California Division of Labor Enforcement surveyed 999 companies in the garment industry and found that only 8 percent were paying the minimum wage of $2.90 an hour; the state issued 616 citations for child labor law violations and found a third of the companies did not have workmen's compensation coverage to aid employees on the job. In an investigation of other businesses that employed alien workers, it found that 64 percent were not paying minimum wages or state-mandated overtime (*The New York Times*, February 18, 1979, pp. 1, 16).

Although the relative income of Chicanos is improving throughout the Southwest, the income figures for California's Mexican American population showed no improvement over a ten-year period, and the statistics for family income showed a decline (Briggs, Fogel, and Schmidt 1977, p. 60). This lack of gains in California may indicate that equality of Mexican American income with that of Anglos will not come rapidly. There seem to be two possible explanations for this situation. First, although Chicanos have gained craft and clerical jobs, they may not be able to move into the high-paying managerial and professional positions because of discrimination and educational deficiencies. Second, the high incomes (absolute and relative) in California have attracted many less well qualified Chicanos from Texas and other parts of the Southwest (both legal and illegal immigrants), and these workers must start at the bottom of the economic structure. These migrants tend to hold down the average incomes of the whole Mexican American population, even though some in the group are gaining high-salaried jobs.

A factor of major importance in examining differences in income among racial and cultural minorities is the average age between groups. Americans of Irish and Italian descent have a median age of 36 years, while Mexican Americans and Puerto Ricans have a median age of 18 years. The median age of the black population is 23, while that of Japanese Americans is 29. Since employment and earnings are correlated with experience, groups whose average age is higher would have higher earnings even if there were no differences in the qualifications of workers or in the ethnic preferences of employers. Average annual income for individuals in the same age group vary much less from one minority group to another than group averages.

Puerto Ricans on the Mainland

Population Distribution of Puerto Ricans

In 1982, there were 1,215,000 persons of Puerto Rican origin in the civilian noninstitutional population of the United States (Bureau of Labor Statistics, 1983, p. 176). There are Puerto Ricans living in every state, with the greatest concentration in New York City. This population grew from 612,000 in 1960 to 800,000 in 1970, and to approximately 1,100,000 in 1980.

Within New York City, Puerto Ricans have spread into every section. Large concentrations of them are found in East Harlem, in the South Bronx, South Central Bronx, on Manhattan's Lower East Side, and in the Williamsburg section of Brooklyn (Fitzpatrick 1970, p. 301; Fitzpatrick 1971, pp. 55, 57). In nearby Newark, the 27,443 Puerto Ricans constituted 7.1 percent of the population in 1970 (Wagenheim 1975, p. 50). Puerto Ricans now live in half the towns and districts of New Jersey. Usually, they are commuters who work in New York (Tovar 1970, p. 58).

Estimates of the Puerto Rican population on the mainland do not include seasonal farm laborers who emigrate from Puerto Rico. In 1973, the Migration Division of the Puerto Rican government supervised the contracts of 20,000 laborers, and it was estimated that 30,000 to 40,000 more were working without formal contracts (Wagenheim 1975, p. 5).

The great majority of Puerto Ricans have lived here less than 15 years, and nearly half of that population is under 21 years of age. Also, among those Puerto Ricans born in the United States of Puerto Rican parents, four-fifths are under 14 years of age.

Puerto Ricans in the United States are sometimes thought of as consisting of three groups. In the first group are those who were born, brought up, and educated in Puerto Rico. These persons have made adjustments to their new environment, but their values, ways of thinking, and emotional reactions are still rooted primarily in Puerto Rico. In the second group are those who were born in Puerto Rico, spent part of their lives there, and received part of their education in the Commonwealth, but migrated at an early enough age to complete their education on the mainland. Also, they have lived in cities for a number of years and have acquired more of the values and behavior patterns of the United States than have those in the first group. In the third group are those who were born on the mainland of Puerto Rican parents. These young people have been enculturated in the United States and have been strongly influenced by the culture of its cities, as well as by their forebears' experience here. By 2000 this new generation will have an important part in determining the nature of Puerto Rican life in the United States (Tovar 1970, pp. 270–271).

The Farm Labor Problem

The main difficulty associated with the farm labor program has been the problems Puerto Ricans face when they try to establish themselves permanently in small towns in farm areas. These towns are not prepared to provide ordinary community services and recreation to people of different language and cultural background. In addition, many Puerto Ricans are defined on the mainland as black and therefore meet with color prejudice. If a group of Puerto Ricans settles in or near a small town, tensions may develop immediately over questions of schooling, employment, recreation, public order, and welfare. The Office of the Commonwealth devotes much of its effort toward resolving local community tensions (Fitzpatrick 1971, p. 19). The farm work program has received considerable publicity, but apart from attracting Puerto Ricans who later settled in the cities, it has been marginal to the Puerto Rican experience on the mainland. An insignificant part of the Puerto Rican group lives in rural sections.

Color, Race, and Prejudice on the Mainland

The proportion of Puerto Ricans on the mainland who are classified as nonwhite declined from 13 percent in 1940 to 8 percent in 1950, and to 4 percent in 1960. Beyond 1960 there appears to be no difference in the proportion of nonwhite. The shift in 1960 seems to have been the result of the change in enumeration procedures. In 1940 and 1950 the enumerators classified the respondent; in 1960, the respondent classified himself. Although these data indicate the self-perception of color of Puerto Ricans, they do not show how the host community regards the color of the Puerto Rican. This perception by the host community, however, may be one of the most important factors in the Puerto

Rican's adjustment to life in the United States. In Puerto Rico a person's color is of minimal importance. On the mainland, it is critical (Macisco 1970, p. 257). As a people, Puerto Ricans here do not wish to be identified with Blacks. For this reason, those with dark skins often do not want to learn English, preferring to be considered foreigners (Tovar 1970, p. 24). Prejudice exists in Puerto Rico, but it is expressed primarily between individuals rather than on an institutionalized basis. Although Puerto Ricans are citizens, many Americans regard them as foreigners. In addition, they are regarded as a racial group, and as such they are not understood either by Whites or Blacks in the United States. To black men, Puerto Ricans are trying to "pass." They do not understand why Puerto Ricans have not participated more militantly in the black revolution. To many Whites, the Puerto Rican is seen as a nonwhite person, one who is somehow not a full-scale American entitled to share the rights, opportunities, and duties of other Americans.

Since the end of World War II, an estimated 800,000 Puerto Ricans, approximately one-third of the island's population, has migrated to the United States. With the exception of 1974, however, more Puerto Ricans returned to the island from 1972 through 1977 than came to the mainland. In 1972, the net flow to Puerto Rico was 34,000; in 1977, it was 27,000 people.

Employment and Unemployment of Puerto Ricans

In our previous discussion of Puerto Ricans, we have referred to a number of points pertinent to the discussion of employment of Puerto Ricans: the farm labor problem, the youthfulness of this population, its concentration in urban areas, and the importance of color and color prejudice on the mainland.

In the labor force participation rates for ten racial-ethnic groups in the United States in 1970 (see Table 9-2), Puerto Rican men, with 75.5 percent, were tied for sixth place with Koreans. Below them in participation rates were Chinese men (73.2 percent), black men (69.8 percent), and American Indian men (63.4 percent). Puerto Rican women, with 35.3 percent, were lowest in labor participation rate among women in the ten racial-ethnic groups, and lower in participation than the females in the "all whites" groups (which included Hispanic

groups) with 38.9 percent. The labor force participation rates for Puerto Ricans for 1975 and 1980 were: males, 73.4 percent and 72.5 percent; females, 33.5 percent and 34.8 percent (*Statistical Abstract 1981,* p. 384).

Puerto Ricans have been greatly affected by the number of jobs that have shifted to suburban locations in recent years, reducing work opportunities in the cities. For example, between 1969 and 1974, according to the Bureau of Labor Statistics, New York City lost 316,500 jobs.

Puerto Ricans have the highest unemployment rates of most, perhaps all, of the racial and ethnic groups in the United States. The percentage of Puerto Rican men and women reported as looking for work usually has been one and a half times as high as for the total population. The true picture is more serious because the rate of unemployment refers to that part of the civilian labor force that is jobless. That does not mean the entire working-age population; it includes only those persons who are working or actively seeking work. It does not include disabled persons, and those who are not actively seeking work because of lack of skills or lack of employment opportunity in geographic area, or because they have lost hope (Wagenheim 1975, pp. 27–28; Bonilla and Campos 1981, p. 157).

The unemployment rate for persons of Puerto Rican origin in 1982 was 17.6 percent. For males 20 and over, it was 15.3 percent, and for females in that age group, 15.8 percent. For both sexes, 16 to 19 years, the unemployment rate was 40.7 percent (U.S. Bureau of Labor Statistics, January, 1983, p. 176, Table 45).

Occupations of Puerto Ricans on the Mainland

In March, 1973, 22.6 percent of Puerto Rican men aged 16 years and over were engaged in white-collar occupations, compared with 40.2 percent of males in the total population. For blue-collar workers, the respective percentages were 56.2 and 46.9; for farm workers, the respective percentages were 1.1 and 4.5; and for service workers, 21.1 and 8.2. (U.S. Bureau of the Census, May, 1974, p. 5).

Table 9-10 shows the increase in the number of Puerto Ricans employed in mainland United States and the distribution of these workers by occupational group in 1960 and 1976. Especially noteworthy are the large increases in the number of

Table 9-10. Puerto Ricans in the United States by Employment and Major Occupational Group

	1960[a]		1976[a]	
	Male	Female	Male	Female
Employed				
Thousands	194	91.3	309.6	189.4
Percent	100	100	100	100
Productive workers—percent	83.0	78.1	72.8	60.2
Craft and kindred workers	11.3	1.9	18.9	.6
Operatives, including transport	41.4	66.5	24.3	37.0
Service workers	18.4	8.5	18.8	20.8
Laborers, excluding farm	8.7	0.9	—	—
Farm laborers and supervisors	3.2	0.3	10.8	1.8
Unproductive workers—percent	17.0	21.9	27.2	39.8
Professional, technical and kindred workers	2.9	4.0	7.0	5.8
Managers and administrators	3.4	1.2	7.2	3.2
Sales workers	2.9	2.8	4.3	4.2
Clerical and kindred workers	7.8	13.9	8.7	26.6

Source: Frank Bonilla and Ricardo Campos, *Daedalus*, Spring 1981, p. 133–176. Based on U.S. Bureau of the Census, 1950, 1960, 1970. The 1976 figures are from that year's Survey of Income and Education.
[a]For those 14 years and over.

female workers and the shifts in the proportion of both male and female unproductive workers.

Statistical reports fail to convey the importance of Puerto Ricans in the New York City job market. In the hotel and restaurant trade, employers would now be helpless without them. In the garment industry, Puerto Rican women especially make up a significant part of the labor force. Among other major employers of Puerto Ricans are laundries, bakeries, confectioneries, construction companies, warehouses, retail stores, canning plants, and maritime services; and manufacturers of electronic components, television sets, luggage, paperboard boxes, paints and varnishes, photographic supplies, jewelry, and toys (Padilla 1977, p. 161).

Incomes of Puerto Ricans

The Puerto Rican family has the lowest income of any major racial and cultural minority in the United States. In 1959, the median family income for Puerto Ricans was $3,811, or less than 65 percent of the median white family income in the United States, $5,893. In 1971, the median family income for Puerto Ricans was $6,135, compared with $6,440 for Blacks, $10,672 for Whites, and $7,548 for all families of Spanish origin. By 1976, the estimated income for Puerto Rican families had increased to $7,669, but the median white family

income had risen to $15,178 (Bonilla and Campos 1981, p. 160; LaRuffa 1975, p. 227; Wagenheim 1975, p. 30).

The median income of Spanish-origin families in 1977 was: total, Spanish-origin, $11,421; Mexican, $11,742; Puerto Rican, $7,972; Cuban, $14,182; Central or South American, $11,280; and other Spanish, $12,855. For families not of Spanish origin, the median family income was $16,284 (U.S. Bureau of the Census, June, 1979, p. 13).

In 1979, the median money income by race and Spanish origin was: White, $17,333; Black, $10,216; Spanish-origin, $13,423 (*Statistical Abstract 1981*, p. 432).

American Indians

The American Indian Population

Currently, American Indians are increasing faster than the general population.[3] The 1950 Census listed approximately 350,000 Indians; the 1960 Census, nearly 525,000; the 1970 Census, about 792,000; and the 1980 Census, 1,418,195 American Indians, 42,149 Eskimos, and 14,177 Aleuts (U.S. Bureau

[3]For various conceptions of race and several definitions of American Indians, see Chapter 2.

of the Census, July, 1981, p. 6). In addition to the continuing increase in the American Indian population, a major change in the distribution of this population has occurred. Instead of the stable, rural community of 1950 sending individuals into the mainstream, nearly half of those who call themselves Indian live in towns and cities. Many tribal groups now have more members living in towns and cities than in rural communities and reservations. Almost half of the migrants to urban centers live in large metropolitan areas. Several cities have larger Indian populations than any reservation except the Navajo—Los Angeles, Tulsa, Oklahoma City, San Francisco, Phoenix, and New York City (Stanley and Thomas 1978, pp. 113, 116; Levitan and Johnston 1975, p. 3).

The nine states with over 10,000 Indians in 1970 in which urban Indians constituted less than half of the population in 1970 were: North Dakota, 13.3; North Carolina, 14.0; Arizona, 17.4; New Mexico, 18.7; Montana, 19.2; South Dakota, 24.4; Alaska, 29.2; Utah, 35.0; and Wisconsin, 39.6 (Tax 1978, p. 131).

In general, the migrants to the cities are culturally more marginal than those who did not migrate. They are younger, more competent in English, have better education and more skills. Those in the rural communities consist of older, culturally more conservative people and an almost equal number of young people under age 20. Indians off the reservation have much lower unemployment rates; two-thirds have greater average family income, fewer dependent children, and less than half the chance of being in poverty as those on reservations. By such standards as family income, male labor force participation, proportion of high school graduates, dependents per breadwinner, and poverty status, Indians in metropolitan areas are better off than metropolitan Blacks (Stanley and Thomas 1978, p. 113; Levitan and Johnston 1975, p. 3).

There are more than 280 Indian reservations, the largest of which is the Navajo reservation with 22,000 square miles in Arizona, New Mexico, and Utah. This is slightly larger than Massachusetts, Connecticut, and Rhode Island combined. Most reservations are considerably smaller, ranging from the 8,000 Sioux who live on 2,600 square miles at Pine Ridge, South Dakota, to many small reservations of a few hundred acres or less. Most tribes have their own reservations, but some tribal groups share lands with others. Altogether, Indian lands total approximately 52 million acres, or 2.3 percent

of the land area of the nation (Levitan and Johnston 1975, p. 2).

Agriculture

Three categories of farming and ranching provide significant sources of Indian income. Grazing, the least intensive land usage, occurs on approximately 45 million acres of land. Dry farming is practiced on 1.6 million acres, and 600,000 acres are irrigated. A large proportion of the most productive land is leased to non-Indians. The returns per acre are smaller on farms operated by Indians than reservation farms operated by non-Indians. Lower productivity on Indian farms is due to poorer land quality, inefficient management, inadequate education and technical assistance, and the lack of agricultural traditions on the part of most tribes. In addition, Indians lack sufficient capital to invest in machinery, feed, fertilizer, and buildings. The revolving farm loan fund of the Bureau of Indian Affairs (BIA) amounted to only $12 million in 1973, but the needs for agriculture were said to be more than $89 million (Sorkin 1978a, pp. 10–11).

Land ownership has become fractionalized since the 1887 allotment act, and many Indian landholdings are too small to be efficient. Only 40 percent of allotted Indian lands have only one owner, and 17 percent have 11 or more. Federal programs to improve Indian agricultural productivity include technical assistance, range management, and legal assistance in the consolidation of separated landholdings. Irrigation projects represent the most important attempts to improve agriculture. By 1978, 600,000 acres were irrigated, and the BIA estimated that another 400,000 could be profitably irrigated (Sorkin 1978a, p. 11).

The land given American Indians when the reservations were established was land thought to be useless. Much of it consisted of the most nonarable, nongrazable land in the United States. Because white ranchers have diverted much of the water, irrigation is often almost impossible. The Dawes Act of 1887—the Allotment Act—divided Native American lands into individual parcels. The effects of this act make farming or ranching difficult. Much Indian land passed into white hands, and a large share of the remaining land has been divided and subdivided by inheritance to a confusing extent. This may leave the individual with small pieces of land all over a reservation. As a result, the joint heirs to a parcel of 100 acres or so usually lease their land to a white farmer, and each heir receives a check for a portion of the land. (Beuf 1977, pp. 25–26).

Indians must have the approval of the BIA for any land-lease transaction, and the rates set by the Bureau are often below those of other lands in the area. Stock raising and commercial farming are now big business and provide opportunities for only a relatively few experienced operators on the limited lands of most reservations (Fuchs and Havighurst 1972, p. 29; Jorgensen 1971, pp. 80–82).

In recent years, the bulk of the income from mineral leases on Indian land has come from oil and gas leases, with much smaller returns coming from coal, asbestos, phosphate, uranium, vanadium, and copper. Income from minerals is unevenly distributed among the reservations, with nine receiving 85 percent of the oil and gas royalties. Recent energy shortages may lead to increasing income for Indian tribes from mineral deposits (Sorkin 1978a, pp. 11–12). The BIA estimates that farm production could be increased by one-third if soil conservation was widely followed and that the income from timber, mineral, and surface leases could be doubled under aggressive development and careful management (Levitan and Johnston 1975, pp. 20–21).

Occupations of American Indians

Although the American Indian labor force is concentrated in the lowest paying positions, the occupational status of Indians is somewhat more favorable than that of Blacks. Table 9-11 shows that higher percentages of the former are classified as professionals, managers, and craftsmen, and smaller percentages as operatives, laborers, and service workers than the latter.

Among Indians, the most striking occupational change has been the sharp decline in agricultural employment. In 1940, almost half of all Indian males were engaged as farmers or farm managers, but only 2 percent were in that classification in 1970. Sorkin attributes this decline mainly to the competition of non-Indian farmers, who have greater capital resources and technical skill. Indian farmers earn about 60 percent as much as reservation Indian males following other occupations. This differential has stimulated a movement away from agriculture and the leasing of a substantial part of the most productive land owned by Indians to Whites (Sorkin 1978a, pp. 3–4).

The proportion of Indians employed as skilled and semiskilled workers has increased greatly. Between 1940 and 1970, the percentage of all Indian males employed as craftsmen or operatives rose from 12 to 46. This growth has been related to the migration from the reservations to the cities. Many of these migrants received training and assistance from the relocation program operated during the 1960s and later by the Bureau of Indian Affairs (Sorkin 1978a, p. 4).

In 1940, less than 4 percent of Indian men were employed as professional workers or managers or proprietors compared to 14 percent in 1970. Many of the Native American professionals are school teachers on the reservations or in cities where large numbers of Indian children are enrolled. (In reservation schools, only about one-sixth of the teachers are Indian.) More than one-third of the well-paid professional positions in the Bureau of Indian Affairs and the Indian Health Service are now held by Indians (Sorkin 1978a, pp. 4–5). Jobs available to Indians on reservations show the dominant influence of government. Nearly half of all reservation jobs are state, local, and federal positions. This proportion is three times the national average for government employment (Levitan and Johnston 1976, p. 16).

Unemployment among American Indians

The unemployment rates for Native Americans are several times those of non-Indians. Throughout the 1958–1975 period the unemployment rate of reservation Indians was far higher than the rate for men during the Depression of the 1930s, which reached 25 percent in 1933. A comparison of unemployment rates for Indian, black, and white men during the period 1940–1975 is shown in Table 9-12.

Jobs in areas near reservations are scarce and temporary, and, for persons equally qualified, the Indian is usually the last person hired. Nonreservation Indians have unemployment rates from 10 to 15 percent higher than Blacks. Both of these groups are highly urbanized and have similar types of employment and income levels. Despite a large migration from the reservations to the cities in the period 1950–1970, the unemployment rate for nonreservation Indians fell almost 40 percent. According to Sorkin (1978a, p. 6), this drop reflects some tendency for migrants to enter cities with relatively tight labor markets. In 1973, the Bureau of Indian Affairs estimate, which counts all those able to work but not working as unemployed, was that more

Table 9-11. Percentage Distribution of Indian, Black, and White Males by Occupation Group, 1940, 1960, 1970

Occupation group	Indian					Black			White		
	1940	1960	Total 1970	Urban 1970	Rural 1970	1940	1960	1970	1940	1960	1970
Professional and technical	2.2	4.9	9.2	11.4	6.8	1.8	3.4	5.7	5.9	11.6	14.9
Managers, officials, and proprietors except farmers	1.4	2.8	5.0	5.8	4.2	1.3	1.9	2.8	10.7	12.1	12.4
Clerical and sales	2.0	4.9	8.1	7.3	3.9	2.0	7.0	10.0	14.0	15.1	14.8
Craftsmen and foreman	5.7	15.5	22.1	23.1	20.9	4.4	10.7	15.4	15.7	21.1	21.9
Operatives	6.2	21.9	23.9	25.6	22.1	12.6	26.7	29.5	18.9	20.1	18.8
Laborers	11.4	20.2	13.2	10.8	15.8	21.4	22.2	16.1	7.5	6.0	6.0
Service workers	2.6	6.3	10.4	10.8	10.1	15.3	16.0	15.9	6.0	5.7	7.3
Farmers and managers	46.7	9.5	2.3	0.2	4.6	21.2	4.7	0.9	14.1	5.8	2.8
Farm laborers	21.7	14.0	5.7	1.8	10.2	19.9	7.5	3.6	7.0	2.5	1.5

Source: Alan L. Sorkin, "The Economic Basis of Indian Life," *Annals*, March, 1978, p. 4.

Table 9-12. Unemployment Rates, Indian, Black, and White Males, 1940–1974[a] (in percentage)

Year	Indians All	Urban	Reservation[b]	Blacks	Whites
1940	32.9			18.0	14.8
1950		15.1		9.6	5.9
1958			43.5	13.8	6.1
1960	38.2	12.1	51.3	10.7	4.8
1962			43.4	10.9	4.6
1965			41.9	7.4	3.6
1967			37.3	6.0	2.7
1970	28.6	9.4	41.0	8.2	4.0
1973			36.5	7.6	3.7
1975			39.8	13.7	7.2

Source: Alan L. Sorkin, "The Economic Basis of Indian Life," *Annals*, March, 1978, p. 5. (Based on reports of the Department of Labor and the Bureau of Indian Affairs.)

[a]Data for Indians 1940–1970 and Blacks and Whites in 1940 include those 14 years and over; all other data include males 16 years old and over.

[b]The Bureau of Indian Affairs considers an individual who is not in school or working as unemployed whether the person is actually looking for a job or not. The Department of Labor, in its calculation of national unemployment rates, excludes persons who are not looking for work from the labor force.

than a third of all Indians were without jobs. On some reservations, half of all Indians were jobless.

A question in connection with the high unemployment rates of Native Americans is the possibility of expanding reservation industries by American Indians or by outside corporations who would employ Native Americans. Several problems have arisen in connection with attempts to persuade corporations to establish plants on reservations. One of these is the lack of water and in some cases of electricity on the reservation. These lacks necessitate large investments in setting up power and plumbing systems. Many reservations are geographically isolated, making them inaccessible to markets. Frequently, there is a lack of paved roads and landing strips, requiring further investments by the corporation. Also, if a large number of American Indians are to be employed, an investment must be made in a training program. A few corporations have made the improvements essential to establish a going concern. In some cases, the results have been unfortunate, most notably because some companies have failed to keep their promise of hiring a large number of unemployed Native Americans who reside on the reservation. Often, these corporations have proceeded to hire fewer American Indians than non-Indians, pay substandard wages, and relegate Indians who are hired to the least desirable jobs (Beuf 1977, pp. 26–27).

Table 9-13 shows the employment of Indians and non-Indians in factories on reservations from 1957 to 1974.

American Indian Incomes

Table 9-14 brings together data on median family income and other characteristics of Indians on reservations, Indians in SMSA, Blacks in SMSA, and all races in SMSA in 1970 (Levitan and Johnston 1975, p. 5). On median family income, median years of education (persons over 25), male labor force participation, and proportion of high school graduates (persons 25 and over), Indians in SMSA had better averages that year than Blacks. The male unemployment rate (age 16 and over) was 2 percent higher for Indians in SMSA than for Blacks, but for reservation Indians it was nearly three times as high as for Blacks in SMSA. The number of children under 18 per family head is significantly higher for reservation Indians than for Indians and for Blacks in SMSA, and the proportion of the reservation population in poverty is twice as high as for Blacks in SMSA and more than twice as high as for Indians in SMSA.

In the past three decades, many relatively well educated and skilled Indians have migrated from reservations to cities. Their better-paying jobs have

Table 9-13. Factories on Indian Reservations and Total Employment, 1957–1974

Year	Plants established	Plants closed down	Total plants in operation (end of year)	Total employment (end of year) Indian	Total employment (end of year) Non-Indian
1957–59	4	1	3	391	171
1960	3	0	6	525	156
1962	5	1	14	887	600
1964	14	7	25	1668	2286
1966	21	4	57	3044	3244
1968	36	3	110	4112	4365
1970	28	4	162	6443	7051
1972	37	1	225	7339	9093
1974	21	4	250	6173	9390

Source: Alan L. Sorkin, "The Economic Basis of Indian Life," *Annals*, March, 1978, p. 8.

widened the income gap between reservation Indians and urban Indians. Reservation Indians are heavily dependent on government for jobs. In 1972, nearly 40 percent of the earnings of reservation Indians came from the federal government, and an additional 20 percent was accounted for by tribal, state, and local government. Another fifth of the incomes of these Indians was obtained from commercial and industrial employment, 12 percent from agriculture, and 8 percent from forestry, minerals, and outdoor recreation. In addition to earned income, about one-fifth of all Indian families receive some type of welfare (money) income compared with 5 percent for the whole United States population. The average income provided by this source was $1,200 in 1974 (Sorkin 1978a, p. 2).

The Poverty Level among Blacks, Mexican Americans, Puerto Ricans, and American Indians

Certain groups within the most disadvantaged racial and cultural minorities—husband–wife families, the college-educated, gainfully employed women, and those in the middle-class—have made

Table 9-14. Characteristics of Indians on Reservations and in Standard Metropolitan Statistical Areas Compared with Other Races, 1970

	Indians on reservations[a]	Indians in SMSA	Blacks in SMSA	All Races in SMSA
Median family income	$4,088	$7,566	$6,832	$10,474
Number of children under 18 per family head	3.0	1.8	1.9	1.4
Median years of education (persons over age 25)	7.6	11.5	10.4	12.1
Population in poverty	54.9%	23.3%	28.2%	10.9%
Male labor force participation (age 16 and over)	50.3%	73.0%	72.0%	78.3%
Male unemployment rate (age 16 and over)	18.6%	8.4%	6.3%	3.8%
High school graduates (persons age 25 and over)	21.9%	42.5%	36.7%	55.3%

Source: U.S. Bureau of the Census, *1970 Census of the Population, American Indians*, PC(2)1F (June 1973), Tables 11–14; idem, *General Economic and Social Characteristics*, PC(1)C1 (June 1973), Tables 107–29.
[a]Averages for Indians living within the boundaries of the 115 largest reservations.

economic advances in recent years. Nevertheless, the four groups emphasized in Part II of this book—Blacks, Mexican Americans, Puerto Ricans, and American Indians—are overrepresented in the statistics on the uneducated, school dropouts, the unskilled, the underemployed, the unemployed, and the poor, regardless of how poverty is defined. Improving the economic status of these minorities depends mainly upon getting people whose incomes are lowest out of poverty.

A frequently used concept of the poverty line is that level which is regarded in the United States as the minimum necessary to meet basic needs in modern society. In 1978, poverty was defined by the Census Bureau as a money income of less than $6,662 for a nonfarm family of four. This included any welfare checks or other money benefits but did not count food stamps or any payments in goods. Among white families, the Census Bureau said in that year, 6.9 percent were living in poverty. For black families, the figure was 27.5 percent, and for families of Spanish origin, 20.4 percent (*The New York Times*, November 25, 1979, p. 44).

In 1981, the average poverty level for a family of four was $9,287. Almost 2 million black families (30.8 percent of the total) were living in poverty, compared to 4.7 million white families (8.8 percent) in the poverty group. More than half (52.9 percent) of the black households headed by a female with no husband present were below the poverty level in 1981. For such households among Whites, the rate was 27.4 percent (Reid 1982, p. 30).

Farley's study (1982, Chapter D) shows economic gains for all groups of black workers during the 1960s and 1970s and a decline in racial differences in purchasing power. However, the actual changes in family income and poverty do not indicate a racial convergence (Farley 1982, p. E-1).

Blacks in poverty declined from 55 percent in 1959 to 32 percent in 1969, but there was little change after 1969 and throughout the 1970s slightly less than one-third of the black population was impoverished (Farley 1982, p. E-3).

Changes in racial differences in the income of families and in poverty are more difficult to determine than those of workers and need to take three trends into account (Farley 1982, p. E-48). First, in the 1960s and 1970s, the earnings of black workers and black individuals have generally risen faster than those of Whites, tending to reduce racial differences in poverty. Second, a change has occurred in the family living arrangement associated with the highest income levels—a shift away from hus-

band–wife families. This change has resulted in a rapid increase in the proportion of women who are family heads for a part of their adult lives. Compared to husband–wife families, these families have very low incomes and high rates of poverty. The changes in family living arrangements have been much greater among Blacks than among Whites. By 1980, a majority of black births were occurring to unmarried women and a minority of adult black women were married and living with a husband. Third, fertility rates have declined. According to the National Center for Health Statistics, if the fertility rates of 1960 had continued, the typical black woman would have completed her childbearing with 4.5 offspring, and the typical white woman with 3.5. By 1978, these rates had fallen to 2.3 offspring for black women, and 1.7 for white women. As Farley (1982, p. E-49) comments, the change in fertility rates in the 1970s (largely a decrease in childbearing within marriage) tended to reduce poverty and raise per capita income levels. Higher earnings for employed Blacks and lower fertility appear not to have offset the effects of shifts in family structure. Thus, the racial gap in per capita income did not decline during the 1970s, and there was little change in poverty in the black population.

A government sampling report estimated that 23.2 percent of all persons of Spanish origin in the United States lived below the poverty level as defined by the Bureau of the Census in 1974. That was twice as high as the proportion of 11.6 percent in that category for the population as a whole. For Mexican American residents, the proportion was 24.3 percent. For Puerto Ricans, the proportion was especially high—32.6 percent (*The New York Times*, September 7, 1975, p. 30). By 1979, 20.8 percent of all persons of Mexican origin were living below the poverty level, and 38.8 percent of all persons of Puerto Rican origin were below that level (*Statistical Abstract 1981* p. 448).

About 17 percent of all families of Mexican origin were headed by a woman in 1970, and about 58 percent of these households were below the poverty level as defined by the Census Bureau (Mirandé and Enríquez 1979, p. 135). In 1978, nearly half (45.9 percent) of all Mexican American families headed by a woman were below the poverty level (Pachon and Moore 1981, pp. 118–19).

Poverty in the Puerto Rican community on the mainland is related in part to the economic situation in New York City, where more than a half million unskilled and semiskilled jobs have been lost since

1970. But it also derives in part from the educational level of Puerto Ricans. The Puerto Rican population is very young, and a large proportion has not yet reached high school age. In 1976, 26.5 percent of all Hispanic families in New York City were below the poverty level. However, 57.8 percent of female-headed families were below it (Fitzpatrick and Parker 1981, p. 107).

As we pointed out earlier in this chapter, nearly two-fifths of the earnings of reservation Indians come from employment by the federal government, and an additional one-fifth comes from jobs provided by tribal, state, and local government. Despite the impact of these government monies, approximately 55 percent of all Indians on reservations live in poverty, compared with less than a quarter of the Indians living in SMSAs. These proportions compare with approximately 11 percent of the whole population living in poverty (Levitan and Johnston 1975, p. 19).

Critics of the Census Bureau figures on poverty point out that in some years the people considered poor are the prime beneficiaries of many types of important nonmoney income, three of the most important of which are food stamps, housing subsidies, and Medicaid.

The definition of poverty has been in dispute for many years. The federal government spends three dollars in noncash benefits for every two it spends in cash payments, but it continues to define poverty only in terms of cash income. "Official poverty level" is an important definition because it determines eligibility for many aid programs. In 1980, Congress asked the Census Bureau to determine how the poverty statistics might be changed if noncash benefits were included. The Bureau suggested three approaches: money income alone; money income plus food and housing; and money income plus food, housing, and medical care. In 1979, the proportion of the population in poverty would have been between 6.4 and 8.9 percent if noncash benefits had been counted, instead of 11.1 percent, the official figure based on cash income only (*The New York Times*, April 18, 1982, p. E1).

In recent years, a distinction has often been made between the poor, those living below the poverty line, and America's underclass. According to the federal census, in 1980 there were 29.3 million Americans living in poverty. If the temporarily poor are distinguished from those who are caught in long-term poverty, estimates of the size of the latter group vary from 30 to 45 percent of the poor. The

"acutely poor" are those who are poor five years out of every seven. As Auletta (1982, pp. 27, 266) observes, poverty may have declined, but an American underclass has grown.

Racial and Cultural Minorities in Labor Unions

The role of labor organizations in encouraging or discouraging black, Mexican American, Puerto Rican, and American Indian members is an important part of the industrial and agricultural experience of these groups. In earlier years the techniques used by labor unions to retard the employment of persons in these groups included withholding membership by means of constitutional provisions, or ritual pledges, or as an unwritten policy of the international or local union; accepting members but discriminating against them in referrals; hindering the upgrading of members of these minorities; and sponsoring the employment and upgrading of minority group members in plants in which the union had no bargaining agreements, while failing to correct discrimination in plants in which the union had an agreement.

For more than 50 years there have been differences between the policies toward racial and cultural minorities of trade or craft unions on the one hand and industrial unions on the other. Over a long period of years, many craft unions, particularly the mechanical building trades (electricians, plumbers, sheet-metal workers, iron workers, operating engineers, and elevator constructors), practiced racial and ethnic exclusion. Membership in the mechanical crafts was limited largely to relatives of members. Nepotism kept the composition of these unions constant over a long period of years.

In the 1960s and 1970s, pressure by civil rights groups was exerted on the federal government to open admission to unions to all groups equally. As a result, objective standards resembling the credentials required by large private employers—written examinations, high school diplomas, no-arrest records, and physical examinations—have been established. To some extent, the "cult of credentialism" has replaced open exclusionism as the obstacle to overcome in seeking employment (Briggs, Fogel, and Schmidt 1977, pp. 99–100).

Unions of the industrial type include all workers

in a mass-production industry regardless of craft, skill, or lack of skill. In general, the industrial unions have been more favorable to the admission of racial and cultural minorities than have the trade unions. Also, these unions have been much more likely to have members of these groups on executive boards and as officers and job stewards than have the craft organizations.

In the past decade or so, the labor movement's response to the plight of racial and cultural minority workers has been ambivalent. Today the issues in disputes between minorities, especially Blacks, and both the industrial and the craft unions are: (1) restrictions on admission to apprenticeship programs jointly administered with employers and unions (industrial and craft); (2) the refusal to grant journeyman cards to qualified black unionists; (3) denial of membership to Blacks, even though no union now includes a formal color bar in its constitution or by-laws; (4) the use of segregated or auxiliary locals for Blacks; (5) the maintenance of separate seniority lines which prohibit or discourage transfers by Blacks into relatively better paying jobs held by Whites; and (6) the absence of Blacks and other minorities from important elected and appointed positions within the unions (Gould 1977, p. 16).

The enumeration of confrontations between unions and members of minority groups that follows does not mean that minorities have not benefitted from some policies and actions of the leaders of the labor movement. The principles of collective bargaining and of negotiation in grievance-arbitration machinery affords protection to minority as well as majority workers. Often, unions have provided valuable training for minority-group leadership. In addition, unions have given support to a number of social and economic reforms and to civil rights legislation. The AFL–CIO has advocated the elimination of racial discrimination in voting, housing, education, and employment. (After the enactment of civil rights legislation that the AFL–CIO has supported, that organization has not implemented fair employment policies that would make it possible to eliminate union discrimination in this generation.) Unions in the public sector, such as the American Federation of State, County and Municipal Employees, where Blacks constitute a large part of the work force, have given the greatest amount of attention to the position of minority-group employees (Gould 1977, pp. 16–17).

Title VII of the Civil Rights Act of 1964 and Labor Unions

Any discussion of labor unions and minorities today must include a reference to Title VII (Employment) of the Civil Rights Act of 1964. Title VII declares it to be unlawful for an employer "to fail or refuse to hire or to discharge any individual, or otherwise to discriminate against any individual with respect to his compensation, terms, conditions, or privileges of employment, because of such individual's race, color, religion, sex, or national origin." It established a commission to investigate alleged discrimination and use persuasion to end it. It authorizes the Attorney General to sue if he believes any person or group is engaged in a "pattern or practice" of resistance to the title, and to ask for trial by a three-judge court. With its amendments of 1972 and 1973, Title VII prohibits unlawful forms of discrimination in private and public employment and makes such discrimination by employers or by labor unions a federal offense. The amended title covers the employment practices of employers and labor organizations with more than fifteen employees or members, as well as employment agencies servicing employers covered by the act. As amended in 1972, the law gives the Civil Service Commission authority to enforce equal employment opportunities within the federal government and also covers state and local government agencies and most educational institutions (Hill 1977, p. 47).

Until the amendments of 1972, authorizing the Equal Employment Commission to initiate lawsuits, Title VII was a weak law. The Equal Employment Opportunity Commission was engaged primarily in conciliation and negotiation. It lacked enforcement powers that some state agencies possess. The Attorney General was authorized to sue if he believed any person or group was engaged in a pattern or practice of resistance to the title and to ask for trial by a three-judge court. The Department of Justice filed few suits in the years immediately following the passage of Title VII. The EEOC could not initiate litigation; cases were handled by a joining of privately initiated litigation with legal support from the EEOC, that is, the commission provided investigative reports and filed *amicus curiae* briefs. When Congress amended Title VII in 1972, EEOC was again denied direct enforcement through cease-and-desist powers, but it was authorized to initiate lawsuits (Hill 1977, pp. 47–49).

A decade after the passage of the Civil Rights Act of 1964, it was quite clear that employers and labor unions in many industries frequently made a joint defense in Title VII lawsuits and employed a joint legal strategy in resisting compliance. Certain differences, however, have developed in the types and degree of resistance of industry and labor. Employer resistance has reflected the racial and ethnic prejudices of American society, but it also stems from the objections of management to government interference. To a considerable extent, the resistance of organized labor is based on the reluctance of white workers to give up or to get fewer of the benefits in employment which have come from the existence of an exploited class of black labor that has been prevented from moving into all-white occupations. Eliminating racial disadvantages in employment means that white workers must compete with black workers and members of other minority groups. Many white male workers believe that their "rights" (finding a job, job status, promotion, seniority, and liability of layoffs)—all of his employment expectations—are at stake (Hill 1977, pp. 28–29). Some idea of the magnitude of the resistance of certain labor unions to equal employment opportunities for Blacks is shown in the number of complaints against these organizations. From July 2, 1965, the date that Title VII went into effect, until the end of 1968, the EEOC received more than 4,200 complaints about unions. According to Hill, the commission entered a finding of reasonable cause in almost 70 percent of the complaints investigated, but it was unable to secure compliance through conciliation procedures in many of these cases (Hill 1969, pp. 203–204).

Minority Workers, the CIO, and the AFL–CIO

The CIO, organized in 1935, began its campaign to organize steel workers in February, 1936. In 1942, the SWOC (The Steel Workers Organizing Committee, a joint CIO and Amalgamated Association of Iron, Steel, and Tin Workers, AFL) became the United Steelworkers of America (USA–CIO). Because of their previous experiences with labor unions, many black workers were skeptical about the CIO during its early years. Eventually, thousands of Blacks in industry came to accept the organization, but within a short time they found that they were being subjected to new types of discrimination. In the southern steel industry, fewer

job assignments were available to Blacks than before unionization. In many industries, collective bargaining agreements regularized seniority practices in which job assignment, promotion, and dismissal were determined by race. These discriminatory practices were enforced through union contracts. In the South this end was accomplished by specifying racial lines of job promotion, in the North, through the use of a variety of devices and through departmental seniority. The segregated seniority lines that were openly labeled "white" and "colored" have been eliminated, but separate lines of advancement are retained in subtle ways. Testing devices and other qualifications unrelated to work, although seemingly nondiscriminatory, are utilized to keep black workers out of desirable jobs. Some industrial unions have actively prevented the elevation of Blacks and other minorities to positions of leadership within the organization, and have failed to process the grievances of black workers (Hill 1977, pp. 23–25). According to Gould (1977, pp. 19–20), the AFL–CIO has never lessened its opposition to the reform of seniority systems that have discriminated against Blacks in the past. The important point here is that the AFL–CIO has been adamant in its insistence that the Civil Rights Act does not in any way interfere with existing job rights. During economic recessions, the rigid application of "last in, first out" principles under seniority systems that have been in place for many years has undone many of the gains black men and women had made under the Civil Rights Act. In refusing to consider share-the-work plans at such times, cutbacks in employment have decimated the ranks of those who have joined the work force recently. Gould does not advocate discarding the seniority system, but he does call for changes that would provide for greater union allegiance to the principle that unions represent all workers regardless of color, not just senior workers—most of whom are white.

Litigation on Employment Practices and Labor Unions

Before referring to traditions of racial discrimination in particular labor unions, it should be mentioned that courts are increasingly aware of the need to view discriminatory acts in employment in a broad context of social behavior. In the first decade of litigation under Title VII, the federal courts did what state fair employment commissions and previous rulings failed to do: to confront the entire structure of discriminatory practices instead of simply providing limited relief for individual plaintiffs. The courts now consider that acts of employment discrimination are not isolated, individual events but are only elements in widespread institutionalized patterns. Equally important, in numerous cases the courts have held that intent is irrelevant, that the important thing is the consequences of employment practices, regardless of who is responsible for the discrimination (Hill 1977, pp. 53, 62).

Litigation under Title VII has had significant consequences upon the International Association of Machinists. This union has continued to resist change, but the use of the law by Blacks and other minority workers is slowly bringing a long tradition of racial exclusion and discrimination to an end (Hill 1977, p. 217).

From 1965 to 1980 the construction industry produced one of the largest volumes of charges filed by black workers against building trade unions and contractors with the Equal Employment Opportunity Commission. Numerous court decisions indicate the continuing resistance by employers in this industry and labor organizations to the conditions specified by civil rights laws and federal executive orders (Hill 1977, p. 247).

Trucking is another industry in which employers and unions have resisted efforts to eliminate racial discrimination (Hill 1977, p. 259).

The clothing industry, a labor-intensive industry, has been shifting from the East toward the Southwest, in part because of the low-wage supply made up of Mexican Americans, border commuters, and immigrants from Mexico. The difficulties of unionizing such a labor supply are shown in the year-and-a-half strike for union recognition against the Farah Company. The plants of this company, located in Texas and New Mexico near the Mexican border, employ 10,000 workers, 90 percent of whom are Mexican Americans and 85 percent women (Briggs, Fogel, and Schmidt 1977, p. 42; Kaplan 1977, pp. 306–307).

Compared with most other labor unions, the United Automobile Workers is known for its formal commitment to civil rights. According to Hill (1977, p. 270), in the 1960s and 1970s its black members tended to view this commitment as an abstraction lacking in specific application. In this union, the racial question continues to be a source of conflict.

Perhaps the union with the most impressive record on interracial matters is the United Packinghouse Workers. From its inception, black workers have shared in the leadership of the union, and it has often promoted the interests of black workers against the opposition of white members, especially in the South. As Hill (1977, p. 273) comments, "The uniqueness of this union was that it perceived itself not merely as a collective bargaining agent that provided certain services to its members in return for dues but rather as a labor organization involved in social change."

Government's Role in the Collective Bargaining Process

The role of government in the collective bargaining process has increased greatly in recent decades. In addition to conferring legal authorization upon a union to act as exclusive bargaining agent and providing protection from competing unions, it can require employers to engage in collective bargaining and arrange the filing of unfair labor practice charges with the National Labor Relations Board. Governmental agencies intervene in labor disputes, require reports of union election proceedings and expenditures, mediate labor conflicts, and influence labor–management relations through the awarding of contracts, as well as through the formulation of broad economic policies (Hill 1977, p. 26).

The National Labor Relations Board, formed more than forty years ago, is the major governmental agency involved in labor–management affairs. This agency has not used its authority to pursue problems of racial discrimination in a vigorous manner. Hill (1977, p. 169) thinks this will continue to be the case until the courts compel the board to take such action.

The Equal Employment Opportunity Commission came into existence in 1965. In its first decade, it was a weak administrative agency with a monumental backlog of unsettled complaints and little support from the White House. Under the leadership of Eleanor Holmes Norton, the record of the commission improved markedly by the end of the 1970s.

Minority workers have found it necessary to bring actions in the federal courts to secure enforcement of their legal rights. The courts, rather than the administrative agencies of government, have played the major role in interpreting and enforcing Title VII (Hill 1977, p. 27).

Labor Unions and Apprenticeship Programs

In a number of industries, apprenticeship programs are administered jointly by employers and unions. In the construction industry in many cities, unions establish the selection criteria for apprentices. Often, contractors are too divided to exercise enough bargaining power to counteract union wishes concerning apprentices. Although the employer has the final word in hiring, the craft unions have played a major role in permitting access to the labor market prior to the time when an employer may turn an apprentice away from a job. Before a worker can be considered for a job, he or she must gain entrance to, and graduate from, an apprenticeship. In this respect, the building and construction trades especially have great power (Gould 1977, p. 18).

Black workers constituted a much higher percentage among apprentices than they did in the membership of unions reporting on apprenticeship programs to the Equal Economic Opportunity Commission in the middle 1970s. "Spanish Americans" (as defined by the EEOC), however, had a smaller proportion in apprenticeship programs (3.1 percent) than they had in the total membership of the referral unions that administered the program (3.9 percent). This difference suggests that Chicanos more frequently become journeymen through informal channels. Both in union membership and apprenticeship, their representation is largest in the roofing and trowel trades rather than the mechanical trades. For both Mexican Americans and Blacks, there is an inverse relationship between skill level of an occupation and the participation they have in it (Briggs, Fogel, Schmidt 1977, pp. 39–40).

Minorities and Leadership Roles in Unions in the Future

Black trade unionists have had some success in gaining leadership positions in the UAW, Amalgamated Meat Cutters, the American Federation of State, County, and Municipal Employees, the International Longshoremen Workers Union, and the National Education Association. The American Federation of State, County and Municipal Employees played a leading role in the formation of the Coalition of Black Trade Unionists, an organization that may help to increase the number of Blacks in positions of leadership. Some unions with large minority memberships such as the Teamsters, the International Ladies Garment Workers Union, United Steelworkers, United Rubberworkers, and the Amalgamated Transit Union have few, if any, blacks and other minorities in top positions. Due to stirrings among the black rank and file, it is possible that changes in the policies of some of the major unions may occur in the 1980s. Discontent in the UAW has already produced a larger number of black local union presidents and staff, and some changes have taken place even in the United Steelworkers (Gould 1977, pp. 425–426).

Farm Workers Union

The attempts to organize seasonal farm workers, most of whom were Mexican Americans, in the late 1940s and the 1950s were defeated. Through the efforts of César Chavez in the 1960s, farm workers eventually met with a measure of organizational success. In December, 1965, the National Farm Workers Association began a boycott of grapes grown by Schenley farms. The grape boycott spread and became nationwide. By July of 1970, twenty-five grape growers of Delano, California had signed three-year contracts with UFWOC (Samora and Simon 1977, pp. 189–190). AFWOC's victory brought about major changes in the socioeconomic structure of California agriculture, but it also contributed to a decline in the demand for farm laborers. The unionization of farm workers has accelerated the trend toward mechanization (Meier and Rivera 1972, pp. 269–270).

The union faced major difficulties in 1974 when it attempted to sign new contracts with the grape and lettuce growers. The Teamsters Union had begun to sign contracts with growers who had not signed with the UFW and with growers whose contracts with UFW were terminating (Samora and Simon 1977, p. 190). Within a few years, this conflict was resolved when the Teamsters withdrew from organizing farm workers.

In March, 1980, twenty-two of the thirty-four lettuce and vegetable growers in California that had been struck fourteen months earlier by the UFW signed contracts on terms only slightly below those originally demanded by the union, terms which the growers had said would "devastate" agriculture in the state. The contracts made UFW members the highest-paid agricultural laborers in the United States. In addition, growers agreed to double their contributions to the union's medical and pension plans and to pay for full-time union representatives on the job (Cleveland *Plain Dealer,* March 16, 1980, p. A3).

CHAPTER 10

Minorities in the Economy of the United States (Continued)

Minority Businesses

Black Businesses

Most black businesses in the United States have been small businesses, and nearly all are single proprietorships in retail and service trades. The most numerous businesses have been personal services: hairdressing and barbering, luncheonettes and restaurants, and funeral services. A protected market for the provision of these services evolved within the black community. In businesses that sell to the general public, such as hardware and department stores, blacks have not made much progress. The desegregation movement of the 1960s opened most public accommodations to minorities and thereby resulted in an erosion of the position of many black businessmen. Especially hard hit were hotels and restaurants which had previously catered to Blacks (Brimmer 1970, p. 6).

Studies of the Census Bureau and the Internal Revenue Service, which compared data gathered in 1972 and 1977, the last time a census of black business was taken, show American black businesses growing in number, gross revenues and average revenue per business but lagging behind the overall trend for business except in one respect. The number of businesses operated by Blacks has increased more than the total number of businesses (*The New York Times,* July 26, 1981, p. 13). There

were 231,203 black businesses in 1977, an increase of 23.2 percent from the number of black businesses in 1972. Gross sales of black-owned businesses rose from $5.5 billion in 1972 to $8.6 billion in 1977, but the percentage of total sales revenues of all businesses in the nation remained the same, at two-tenths of one percent.

According to the Small Business Administration, only 716 black-owned firms had receipts of more than $1 million in 1977, and a number of those, such as automobile agencies, have since gone out of business. About 94 percent of black-owned businesses were sole proprietorships, 2 percent were corporations, and 4 percent were partnerships. For all American businesses 15.2 percent were corporations, 7.9 percent were partnerships, and 76.4 percent were sole proprietorships (*The New York Times,* July 26, 1981, p. 13).

Evidence of the relative insignificance of black-owned businesses is seen in the total sales of the top ten American black companies in 1972. These companies had combined sales that year of $195 million, a figure that fell short of the $203.7 million recorded by the 500th corporation of the *Fortune* "500" listing. In the insurance field, the combined assets of the top five black companies in the United States were approximately $300 million, slightly more than one percent of Prudential's total assets (Coleman and Cook 1976, p. 44). It should be noted, however, that the sales volume for the Black

205

Enterprise Top 100 companies quadrupled in the decade 1972–1982, with three firms exceeding the $100 million mark in 1982 (Cleveland *Plain Dealer,* September 14, 1983).

During the 1960s and early 1970s, much was said and written about "black capitalism," "community-owned businesses," and "ghetto industries." The purpose of these slogans varied, but some Blacks hoped that replacing white merchants with black merchants would result in lower prices or more honest business policies. Another hope was that the presence of black merchants would stimulate racial pride. Some advocates felt that the ghetto could be made into an economically independent community which would utilize the best talents of Blacks instead of losing them to the larger society (Sowell 1975a, p. 59). On the whole, these hopes have not materialized.

Differences in the total service provided, plus the much quicker turnover of goods at the supermarket, enable the larger stores to sell at lower prices. High-efficiency chains (groceries, restaurants, drug stores) now tend to avoid the ghetto. In middle-class suburbs, supermarkets can operate at lower costs because they can attract efficient workers, management, capital, and low-cost insurance. These stores are forced to operate at lower cost because there are so many firms competing with one another (Sowell 1975a, p. 59; 1975b, pp. 174–178).

In an analysis of black capitalism, Andrew Brimmer (1970, p. 6), a black economist and former member of the Federal Reserve Board, said that the low incomes, high unemployment rates, and poor financial position of urban black families provide a poor economic setting for business investment. One aspect of this situation is the tendency on the part of black families in the ghetto who make economic advances to move to other areas or at least to prefer to consume in the more diverse national economy. Increased economic status for families living in segregated sections does not, therefore, necessarily improve the profit prospects of neighborhood businesses.

According to Brimmer (1970, p. 6), an even more basic reason for questioning the value of the strategy of black capitalism is its premise of self-employment. In modern economy, self-employment in the managerial occupations is a declining factor because salaried positions offer greater financial rewards. The promotion of black capitalism may discourage many from participating in the national economy, with its greater range of opportunities, and thus retard the general economic advancement of Blacks. Further comment on this point is made later in this chapter in the section on black economic development.

The prosperity of Whites and the poverty of Blacks cannot be seen simply as the robbing of the latter by the former. Some white merchants in the ghetto and some slum landlords do prosper by cheating black people, "but the prosperity of the white 90 percent of the country can hardly be explained by what they take from the black 10 percent" (Sowell 1975a, p. 62). Moreover, it cannot be assumed that cheating and abuse are limited to merchants and employers of only one color. The real exploitation of minorities lies in denying them the opportunities to develop their potential in technical and scientific skills and managerial experience (Sowell 1975a, p. 62).

Recent surveys have found that the question of who owns local businesses is of little importance to most black residents. In the Hough area of Cleveland, only 10 percent preferred a black rather than a white storeowner, and in a study of 15 cities only 18 percent of all Blacks thought that stores in a black neighborhood should be owned and operated by Blacks (Aldrich 1978, p. 1423).

Minority Contractors. The virtual exclusion over a long period of years from apprenticeship programs and membership in building craft unions and the continuing resistance by employers in this industry to the conditions specified by civil rights laws and federal executive orders has made it extremely difficult for black workers to acquire the skills to enter the construction business. The normal channel is to go from skilled worker and foreman to small-scale contracting and later into large-scale work. It has also been almost impossible for black contractors to have available the number of skilled workers necessary for large enterprises. In addition, the black contractor lacks access to financing. For these reasons, black contractors are frequently unable to qualify for surety bonds needed for participation in most government-insured projects and in public construction work. An officer of the Refine Construction Company, Inc., one of the largest minority construction firms in New York City, said of his dilemma: "They tell me I can't get bonding for that amount because I don't have a track record on the bigger jobs. But the reason I don't have a track record on the bigger jobs is that I can't get bonding on the bigger jobs" (*The New*

York Times, December 25, 1977, p. 1). According to the chairman of the Metropolitan New York Council of Minority Builders, there were 330 minority contractors in New York City in 1967. By the end of 1977, there were fewer than 150, and fewer than 10 of those were viable. Nevertheless, the prospects for minority contractors were enhanced at the end of 1977 by the promise of billions of dollars in publicly financed projects. The federal government ordered 10 percent minority participation in these projects (*The New York Times,* December 25, 1977, pp. 1, 30).

Black Car Dealers. The automobile industry's efforts to put Blacks into the car business has been characterized by many disappointments and some successes. In 1970, there were only about 10 black dealers among the 27,000 showroom owners in the United States. Six years later there were approximately 80, and six of the top 20 black-owned businesses were automobile agencies. General Motors had 28, the Chrysler Corporation had 24, and Ford Motor Company, 18 (*The New York Times,* February 8, 1976, pp. 1, 9).

Franchising. The field of franchising—automobile dealerships, gas stations, restaurants, shoe stores, ice cream stores, and other types of business—offers opportunities for minority business people. Franchising provides a system of management aid, including helping the owner to select a site, apply for a loan, prepare advertising, and learn inventory. Such outlets need not be limited to the minority community, as demonstrated by Howard Johnson restaurants and Holiday Inn motels.

Hispanic Businesses

Much that has been said about black businesses could also be said about Mexican American and Puerto Rican businesses. Among Mexican Americans, a small merchant sector has emerged. The typical *barrio* businessman is a grocer, restaurant keeper, building contractor, publisher of a newspaper with limited circulation, self-employed mechanic, or craftsman. Bakeries and *tortillerias* also provide opportunities for small-scale investments. A few larger processors and manufacturers located in major cities supply materials and equipment for these consumer services (Galarza, Gallegos, and Samora 1969, pp. 34–35). The small insurance and banking interests which have long been a part of the black community are largely absent among Mexican Americans. The more

wealthy Chicanos have tended to go into the professions and are in business only part-time, relying on investments for income. The Mexican American community has been slow, therefore, in accumulating the essential capital for businesses, and, according to Moore (1970, pp. 64–65), there is some evidence that the few wealthy people tend to disappear into the Anglo community.

The small scale of minority-owned businesses is seen in the 1977 Survey of Minority-Owned Enterprises conducted by the Bureau of the Census. The 219,000 business units held by persons of Spanish origin had average receipts of $48,000 per business annually. Of these firms, 41,000 had a total of 206,000 employees; 178,000 firms owned by Hispanics had no paid employees. The 231,000 black-owned businesses had average receipts of $38,000 per business annually. Of these firms, 40,000 had a total of 164,000 employees; 191,000 firms owned by Blacks had no paid employees (*Statistical Abstract, 1982–83,* p. 530).

Black Banks

Of the more than 13,000 commercial banks in the United States, only a small number are black-owned. In 1963, there had not been a national bank charter awarded to black people for forty years. In 1962, there were only 10 black banks, but the number grew to 27 in 1970, to 50 in 1976, to an estimated total of 60 in 1978, and more were being formed (Bates and Bradford 1979, p. 172; Irons 1976, p. 18).

The president of the Seaway National Bank of Chicago says that black banks have problems that are not found in many other banks—more traffic, more account activity, more problem accounts because their customers are not used to banking, and more fraud. When this bank opened ten years earlier, 70 percent of the individuals who opened checking accounts had never had them before. The recession of 1973 had reduced the support that large corporate supporters had given the bank, the federal government's campaign to increase deposits for black banks had subsided, and the black banks in Chicago were attempting to persuade city and county agencies to place deposits with them. In the 1973–1975 period, other black banks experienced problems as they sought new capitalization (*The New York Times,* February 23, 1975).

Despite the problems that black banks have encountered, they have had an impact inside and outside their communities. Before Seaway opened, the community banks in the Chicago area were paying as little as 2 percent interest on savings accounts at a time when the maximum a bank could pay was 4 percent. Seaway and another black bank both offered 4 percent interest, and Chicago's majority banks immediately raised their payments to 4 percent. This bank and other black banks have provided minorities with opportunities in banking that they would have had to wait years for at a white bank. In 1975, twelve banks, eleven of which were black banks, pooled their resources in extending a $1.5 million line of credit to Aetna Life Insurance Company (*The New York Times,* February 23, 1975).

Two influential analyses of black commercial banks appeared in 1970s. Brimmer (1970) asserted that black banks are poorly managed institutions which suffer from high operating costs and loan losses. He contended that these banks are handicapped by (a) a severe shortage of management and (b) a local market that is a risky place for small banks to lend money. In addition, Brimmer asserted that black banks invest a disproportionate share of their total resources in federal government securities and may thus inadvertently divert resources from the black community into the financing of the national debt. The research of Boorman and Kwast in 1974, however, shows that those minority banks chartered from 1963 through 1965 were operating as efficiently in the early 1970s as comparable nonminority banks. The importance of this research is that it separates the start-up problems of young banks from those traits characteristic of black banks.

On the question of whether black banks are incapable of helping to finance economic development of their communities, the evidence summarized by Bates and Bradford (1979, pp. 107–108, 173) indicates that the group of black banks organized since 1963 "cannot be characterized as risk adverse, or as being unwilling to finance the loan demands of businesses and households located in their communities."

Black Savings and Loan Associations. For the 15-year period ending December 31, 1974, the number of black savings and loan associations grew from 28 to 41, and from $184.8 million to $476.6 million in total assets. At that time, however, these associations represented .99 percent of the total savings and loan industry and held only .17 percent of the industry's assets (Bates and Bradford 1979, p. 170). Nevertheless, black savings and loan

companies are important because they perform general financial intermediary services and provide housing capital to minority communities. To evaluate the performance of black savings and loan associations, Bates and Bradford (1979, Chapters 2–4, pp. 170–171) analyzed financial data on 28 black savings and loans and a matched sample of white savings and loans, covering the period 1968 through 1974. They found that the black savings and loans participated in financing inner-city housing to a much greater extent than the matched sample of white savings and loans. In fact, the proportion of assets invested by the black companies in FHA–HUD mortgages averaged more than three times that of the white organizations. In addition, the black associations had participated in other types of socially valuable financing (home improvement loans, education loans, and so forth) to a greater extent than their white counterparts.

Black Economic Development

According to one definition, black economic development "is the process by which the total quantity and quality of resources available in and to the black or minority community is increased in relation to the total resources of the white or majority community" (Cash and Oliver 1975, p. xv). Some economists hold that to achieve this objective the existing as well as the new businesses in the black community must be owned and controlled by Blacks. Others conceive of black economic development in terms of expanding businesses and financial institutions owned and controlled by Blacks regardless of whether such organizations are located in the ghetto community or the larger community. A still wider conception of black or minority economic development involves increasing human capital as well as financial capital—the accumulation of skills through expenditures on education, on-the-job training, and medical care, and in addition the expansion of social capital. Social capital consists of the collective savings of a society in colleges and universities, schools, libraries, parks, hospitals, playgrounds, and so forth. Access to such facilities facilitates the acquisition of human capital, and it reduces the cost of doing business. Blacks have had less access to such facilities than Whites, and the inadequacies have increased as the tax base has eroded following the movement of large numbers of prosperous Whites to the suburbs. Not the least of the forms of social capital is the stock of knowledge that is transmitted informally from father to son, and among friends at clubs, luncheons, and social gatherings. Lack of this type of knowledge has compelled firms employing ghetto youths to provide counseling services which are not usually necessary (Blackman 1975, pp. 127–128).

Some economists, activists, and politicians advocate "keeping money in the community," meaning that community savings should be invested in community businesses instead of being employed to finance enterprises elsewhere. But, as Sowell (1975a, p. 61) points out, just as ghetto residents will not become better off by working in the ghetto at wages lower than those they could earn outside the ghetto, so the use of black capital at a lower rate of return inside the ghetto than elsewhere will not promote prosperity. Capital goes wherever the rate of return is highest. It should be noted that financial capital from savings of families is substantially less among Blacks than among Whites, so less is available to black firms than to white firms. Financial capital may be borrowed, but, with more collateral assets, Whites are better risks than Blacks (Blackman 1975, p. 127).

Some black entrepreneurs have enjoyed monopoly profits within the protected "black" market where they face a relatively inelastic demand curve. The narrowness of such a market, however, imposes a lower ceiling on earnings than in the situation of the white entrepreneur. Most Blacks who are wealthy by national standards have become prosperous by providing services in the national market and in entertainment and sports. Narrow markets contribute to higher costs for black industry, and lower sales prevent black companies from benefiting from the economies of scale. Moreover, white firms have an absolute cost advantage over black firms. Where the scale of production is similar for both black and white companies, the fixed costs of operating in black neighborhoods, where most black firms are located, are higher than in white neighborhoods, where most white companies are found. Police protection, sanitation, and general utility services are deficient in black areas, so much so in some cases that insurance is unavailable at any cost to the black businessman, and bank loans are hard to secure and costly when obtainable. Another factor which increases the costs of black entrepreneurs is the input of labor. The quality of the labor force available in most black neighborhoods is inferior to that available in white neighborhoods, in considerable part because educated Blacks can earn

more in the national labor markets. In addition, greater capital and managerial resources enable white industry to employ more advanced technology. Because the experience of Blacks in managing large corporations is very limited, the efficiency of black firms relative to white firms decreases as the scale of operation increases. Blackman (1975, pp. 124–125) draws two inferences from this type of analysis: first, black enterprise must increase its productivity (lower its cost of production) if it is to compete successfully with white businesses; and second, attempts at black economic development must include the entry of black firms into the national markets.

The formation of smaller industrial firms using the cooperative type of organization is a possibility for getting around the difficulties of increasing economic power through the creation of black-owned, large-scale industrial enterprises. Cooperative activities on a significant scale might prove successful in fields such as banking, milling, real estate, and factories (Henderson and Ledebur 1975, p. 185).

Preferential Lending to Minority Businesses. In economic growth theory, increased productivity results from the greater use of capital relative to labor inputs. Black firms tend to be less efficient than white companies because they use relatively fewer inputs of capital. Since black capital inputs tend to be quantitatively and qualitatively less than white capital inputs, black enterprises are unable to employ the most advanced technology. A strategy for black economic development necessarily involves increasing the quantity and quality of capital inputs—financial capital, human capital, and social capital (Blackman 1975, pp. 126–127).

Minority capital deficits are unlikely to be overcome without special assistance programs. One form of preferential treatment of minorities involves lending. An early experiment in more liberal lending policies for black businesses was the "6 × 6" Pilot Loan and Management Program started in Philadelphia in 1964 by the Small Business Administration (SBA). Under this program, loans up to $6,000 for six years were made to very small businesses, and management training and counseling were provided. In the first year, 219 loans were approved; 98 were made to Blacks. Sixty-eight of the latter loans went to established businesses and thirty to new black businesses. Traditional bank barriers were overcome by considering loan applicants principally on character, integrity, and ability to repay the loan from earnings, rather than on collateral. This program provided the basis for the Economic Opportunity Loan program (EOL) that was authorized in 1965 under Title IV of the Economic Opportunity Act. The EOL program increased the maximum loan to $25,000 and the maximum loan maturity to 15 years. During the following year, Title IV was amended to include people above the poverty level. By July, 1968, minorities had received approximately 40 percent of the number and amount of these loans. Before 1968, nearly all SBA loans to minorities were EOLs, and from 1969 through fiscal 1975, nearly two-thirds of the 47,911 SBA loans to minorities were in that category; the others were regular SBA business loans. This program produced very high default rates, largely because it required that black loan recipients be bad credit risks. Abandoning this lending rule and adopting a flexible cut-off point would produce more salutary results.

Another program of the late 1960s consisted of "seed money" grants made by the Economic Development Administration of the United States Department of Commerce to selected trade associations representing the black business community, including the National Bankers Association, the National Insurance Association, and the National Business League (Irons 1969, p. 222). Also, a number of construction programs were administered by the Department of Housing and Urban Affairs (HUA; HUD) to provide opportunities for black contractors and black employees and for the economic development of ghettos.

There was, therefore, a vast expansion in government and banking industry programs for financing black enterprise in the late 1960s. Bates and Bradford (1979, pp. 113–114) have analyzed a sample of 554 black firms that received SBA loans between 1967 and 1970. In this study, an important distinction is made between traditional and emerging lines of business. The distribution of black-owned firms in selected lines of business is shown in Table 10-1. These researchers conclude that greater availability of long-term credit enables black business people to depart from their traditional lines of small, labor-intensive, service types of enterprise. If capital markets remain open, they predict that black businesses of the future may be represented by a relatively larger number of sizable firms competing effectively in all lines of business. The

Table 10-1. Percentage of Black-Owned Firms in Selected Lines of Business

Lines of black enterprise	Pierce's survey[a]	SBA's sample[b]
Traditional		
Barber shops and beauty parlors	30.2	4.2
Restaurants	19.2	8.3
Groceries	7.6	7.9
Cleaning and pressing	7.4	5.6
Shoe shine and repair	4.7	.5
Funeral homes	3.3	.7
Total	72.4	27.2
Emerging		
Manufacturing	1.6	10.1
Wholesaling	.1	4.5
Contracting services	.6	12.6
Retail apparel	.3	7.0
Retail furniture	.3	3.6
Total	2.9	37.8

Sources: Bates and Bradford (1979, p. 114; Pierce, 1947).
[a] 3866 firms.
[b] 554 firms.

estimated rate of return on net investment in traditional lines of black enterprise is extremely low. On emerging black-owned businesses, the estimated rate of return on net investment is approximately 16 percent, but their liquid asset positions are typically very weak (Bates and Bradford 1979, pp. 114, 120).

Guaranteed Markets. One means of furthering minority economic development is through the provision of a guaranteed market for new businesses and industries. For many years the Department of Defense and other federal procurement agencies have followed the practice of reserving certain contracts for exclusive bidding by small business and have required prime contractors to demonstrate attempts to subcontract to small business. The Small Business Administration's "8 Program," begun in 1969, channels federal contracts without competitive bidding to selected companies whose owners are "socially and economically disadvantaged." Originally started to aid black businesses, it was expanded to include other minority groups. In May, 1981, the SBA began a review of the 2,130 companies in the program. The program has been criticized on the ground that very few businesses, once they begin to receive the preferential federal business, ever leave to compete without governmental assistance. The administrator of the program said that it had been mismanaged in the past, adding that 2 percent of the companies in the program had received 31 percent of the dollar volume, while 681 others in the program had not received any awards. Another 600 companies had applied for admission to the program, but none were to be admitted until new policy rules were adopted. Under the most important change to be put into effect, companies would be admitted only for a specified number of years, ranging from three to five. Following that, they would have to stand on their own. Also, the practice of admitting coal brokers and oil brokers into the program was to be discontinued (*Wall Street Journal,* May 4, 1981).

The Carter administration selected the Department of Defense for special attention as it attempted to triple the dollar volume of federal business given to companies owned by minorities and women. In 1981, the administrator said that he would lessen pressure on the department to award noncompetitive contracts to companies in the program. He indicated also that he did not expect much growth in the dollar volume of awards made to companies in the program during the Reagan administration and that a larger number of smaller contracts would be awarded. Complaints were made that some minority-owned concerns had been given contracts that were too large for them to handle (*Wall Street Journal,* May 4, 1981).

Some have advocated that government set-aside programs for minorities be made at local, state, and federal levels on a transitional basis. If such a policy were followed also in the private sector by foundations, trade associations, private industry, educational and religious institutions, and social organizations, a guaranteed market of considerable size would come into existence. Thus far, this has not occurred, and it seems unlikely that it will be adopted to a significant extent in the 1980s.

The Training of Managers. The training of managers to operate minority enterprises is a matter of great importance. For managers other than small entrepreneurs, three techniques have been suggested. The first technique necessitates formal training, and work beyond the undergraduate level may be required. In the case of plants that are set up as independent profit centers, it is necessary to train other people in such areas as accounting, marketing, and finance to assist the manager. A second technique in managerial preparation places a minority person in training with an experienced majority employee from within the corporation to run the plant until the minority person learns the operating methods. Learning in these circumstances is regarded as difficult at best and the results are often unsatisfactory. The third technique is an accelerated program that assesses the new manager's weaknesses in relation to the job he will have and then designs a program that will enable him to acquire the skills that he needs. Many companies have established programs of this type, and some management experts think this may be the most efficient way rapidly to train a minority manager.

Some schools of business, including those at Harvard University, Columbia University, and New York University, have established consulting services to assist minority entrepreneurs of small businesses. Atlanta University, a black institution, includes a graduate school of business, and Florida A. & M. University's School of Business and Industry has sought for several years to make the school one of the nation's most important suppliers of black business graduates. Indiana, Rochester, The University of Southern California, Washington University, Stanford, the University of Massachusetts, and Wisconsin are among the predominantly white universities that have sought graduates from predominantly black colleges and offered them the opportunity to study for a master's degree in business.

White Corporate Support for Black Business. Even if discrimination against Blacks were suddenly to stop, the problem of capital deficit would still remain. White cooperation is crucial if this deficit is to be drastically reduced. As we have stated earlier in this discussion of black economic development, in addition to cash transfers (financial capital), programs must be developed to increase the educational level and technical skills in the black community. As Blackman (1975, p. 129) comments, the black community cannot make significant progress in the face of white hostility or even intransigence. The black community has much to do, but "the white community also has a grave responsibility to remove barriers to black entry into the national market and to come up with measures for closing, in as short a time as possible, the gap between capital resources of the black and white communities."

American Indian Economic Development

Despite efforts made during the 1970s to improve the attractiveness of Indian lands for plant locations by expanding public utility systems (water, sewage and infiltration systems, power and communication systems, and so forth), reservations are among the least inviting locations for business establishments in the United States. During the past two decades, a combination of technical assistance, feasibility studies, on-the-job training subsidies, guaranteed contracts, credit assistance, and political pressure have been used in attempts to overcome the considerable obstacles that are inherent in reservations and to bring new businesses onto them. Before 1961, there were only six firms located in Indian labor force areas. By the end of 1972, 230 plants were operating on or near reservations employing 7,460 Indians, with an annual payroll of over $30 million. Indian industrial development has not, however, been without its problems, including the limited degree of Indian investment in and ownership of new plants. Also, the services and small businesses near reservations—restaurants, automobile agencies, liquor and food stores—are almost entirely white-owned (Levitan and Johnston 1975, pp. 30–32).

In addition to public works grants, the Economic Development Administration (EDA) makes public works and business loans at below-market interest rates, and the latter loans are made on a 25-year repayment basis. Much of the public works funding totaling nearly $150 million in the years 1966 to 1975 was utilized for the development of industrial parks. Despite these expenditures, including $17,000,000 for industrial parks, not more than 2,000 Indians were employed in 1976 due to EDA efforts, including 1,213 working in industrial parks. Indian tribes provide assistance of various types to potential manufacturers. In some cases, tribal land is made available as an industrial site, and a plant may be built to the owner's specifications at no cost to the company. The building and land are then leased to the firm. No property tax is paid by these companies because the lands are held in trust by the federal government and are exempt from this tax. Some tribes have invested capital in industrial enterprises (Sorkin 1978a, pp. 8–9).

The Indian Business Development Fund was started in 1971 with a $3.4 million appropriation. Its purpose was to further Indian entrepreneurship and employment by making nonreimbursable capital grants to Indian individuals, associations, and tribes to create Indian-owned businesses. This grant, intended to provide equity financing to encourage lenders to provide Indian business loans, was successful in generating capital from customary lenders. In the first year, nearly five dollars in loans was obtained for every dollar of grant money. Moreover, in that year the program generated 3,000 Indian jobs at less than one-fourth of the cost of the EDA industrial development program. Suspended for two years, the IBDF was reestablished in 1974 following passage of the Indian Financing Act. In 1975, it received an appropriation of $10 million. (A 1972 survey by the Bureau of Indian Affairs indicated that there were 773 Indian-owned businesses employing 5,819 Native Americans [Sorkin 1978a, p. 101.])

Economic Power: Economic Development or Infiltration?

Some economists have suggested that a more effective way for minorities to secure economic power might be through the development of management personnel to enter at the sources of power in industry and the government. The argument here is that the structure of American industry is expanding horizontally rather than through the creation of new industries and that the constraints upon minority participation in management training and job opportunities have decreased greatly in recent years (Henderson and Ledebur 1975, p. 183).

No one has stated the case for recognizing that the world of work is an integrated world better than W. Arthur Lewis. Concerning the "myth" of black capitalism, Lewis (1969, p. 9) writes:

American economic life is dominated by a few large corporations which do the greater part of the country's business; indeed, in manufacturing, half the assets of the entire country are owned by just 100 corporations. The world of these big corporations is an integrated world. There will be black grocery shops in black neighborhoods, but in your lifetime and mine there isn't going to be a black General Motors, a black Union Carbide, a black Penn-Central Railway, or a black Standard Oil Company. These great corporations serve all ethnic groups. American economic life is inconceivable except on an integrated basis.

Our conclusion is that it is unnecessary to see the possibilities of increasing minority economic power as a matter of either/or. One need not decide whether it is more advisable to advocate building up black business or to favor entering the industrial establishment and the government. Both strategies will contribute to economic progress in minority communities.

Black Executives in White Businesses

In 1979, 1.6 million Blacks held professional and managerial jobs. A large segment of this group held well-paying administrative positions in the public sector—federal, state, and local governments, health-care facilities, and social service organizations.

Middle-management private-sector jobs provide training, experience, and opportunities for advancement to executive leadership. These managers, however, confront situations that are unknown to most white managers. Some find that they are excluded from channels of informal communication and separated from white peers by differences in background, tastes, and personal values (*The New York Times,* February 4, 1979, p. E19; *The New York Times Magazine,* Dec. 12, 1982, pp. 36 ff).

Many of the black managers and executives in corporate America are assigned to race-related areas such as community affairs, minority affairs, consumer affairs, urban affairs, and special markets. They seldom hold line positions concerned with developing products or competing with their white peers for important promotions. These created jobs provide less security than line positions. Corporate decision makers often expect blacks to be moderate and "balanced" on racial issues. As a consultant to private corporations on affirmative action, Clark (1981, p. 30) frequently found that black affirmative-action officers tended to be more cautious in their actions than many Whites in similar positions (see section in Chapter 7 of this volume on acceptance of status as a form of adjustment to prejudice). Many black directors on corporate boards seem not to be involved in advocating employment practices beyond racial tokenism. According to Clark, they appear to have little influence on decisions concerning Blacks in white-controlled corporations with which they are affiliated.

In contrast to the pessimistic views of some observers, a survey of approximately 100 black managers in 1977 expressed optimism concerning their experiences in large organizations. Most felt confident that they could master the corporate environment and attain executive positions within one or two decades. This widely shared optimism was accompanied, however, by the view that advancement is limited by the lack of confidence that white officers have in Blacks' ability at all levels of management. This survey also found that seventy of these black managers considered themselves reasonably well paid or better, while thirty gave negative views on the fairness of their salaries. Another finding was that close sponsoring relationships, which are of great importance to managers, may be less common for black than for white managers (America and Anderson, *The New York Times,* September 4, 1977, pp. 1, 10).

During the last two decades, the increasing demand for white-collar salaried employees and the pressures of government for effective affirmative action programs have resulted in major attempts to recruit and hire educated Blacks. Rapidly expanding industries, including IBM, American Telephone and Telegraph, Lockheed, Goodyear, Western Electric, Radio Corporation of America, and Texas Instruments have regularly visited black colleges to recruit engineers, scientists, mathematicians, and sales and managerial personnel (Wilson 1978, pp. 100–102).

Racial and Cultural Minorities in Government Service

The Civil Service Act of 1883 ended half a century of the spoils system. Blacks had not been the recipients of many jobs under the spoils regime, and at the time of the creation of the Civil Service Commission only 620 Blacks were employed by the government in Washington. As the total number of government employees grew, there was an increase in black employees, but the number of Blacks in responsible jobs declined. In 1912, Blacks held more than 19,000 jobs in the federal service, including a number of important positions as collectors of customs, collectors of ports, postmasters, paymasters, and diplomats which had carried over from previous years.

During the administration of Woodrow Wilson, Blacks were completely eliminated from responsible government positions. Two procedures were used during that administration to keep Blacks out of desirable civil service jobs. The first method, the "rule of three," dating back to the early years of the civil service, allowed the appointing officer to choose among the three highest eligibles. The second method was the requiring of a photograph. These practices were continued under Harding, Coolidge, and Hoover. The number of Blacks employed by the government steadily increased, but the jobs were mainly those of custodians.

During the depression of the 1930s, President Roosevelt and other white government officials attempted to get a fair share of employment for Blacks. Most of the black appointees under Roosevelt, however, were not regular federal jobholders, but advisers dealing exclusively with black problems. The rank and file of black workers in the federal government continued to be overwhelmingly in custodial categories. In 1938, Blacks constituted 8.4 percent of a total of 115,552 federal employees in Washington.

President Roosevelt issued Executive Order 8802 on June 25, 1941, and the Committee on Fair Employment Practice was appointed. In March, 1942, Roosevelt authorized the FEPC to obtain employment data from all government agencies and departments. On July 31, 1943, Blacks constituted 12 percent of all federal workers as compared with 9.9 percent in 1938. The utilization of Blacks in terms of classifications and grades within these classifications varied greatly among the agencies and departments during World War II.

The number of Blacks in federal service increased markedly during the 1960s, as did the proportion of Blacks holding positions of high rank and salary. In 1961, approximately 1,000 Blacks were employed in GS-12 to GS-18 categories. Executive agencies added 1,411 Blacks to these categories between June, 1962, and early 1966, an increase of more than 100 percent. Of the 18,420 federal employees added in one year, June, 1964, to June, 1965, more than half were black. During 1965, President Johnson appointed 50 Blacks to positions paying from $19,000 to $35,000. Many of these appointees acquired the ability to influence the pattern of hiring and promotion in government.

On February 24, 1966, the Civil Service Commission issued new regulations designed to open more federal jobs to Blacks and other minorities. These regulations included, for the first time, procedures for appealing grievances concerning racial discrimination to the commission from the agencies where they originate (Cleveland *Plain Dealer*,

February 25, 1966). By May, 1970, minority groups (Blacks, Spanish-surnamed Americans, Asian Americans, and American Indians) held 19.2 percent of federal jobs (*The New York Times*, January 24, 1971).

In November, 1975, 79,917 persons of Spanish origin were employed by the federal government. They constituted 3.3 percent of the total number of federal employees, up from 3.0 percent in 1972. In November, 1975, there were 37 Hispanic employees in the top three career grades (GS-16, 17, and 18). For Hispanics, implementation of court decisions and affirmative action plans has been slow.

In Puerto Rico, government provides jobs for a substantial number of workers, but on the mainland it is still a low-penetration sector for immigrants even in areas such as New York City where there is a large Puerto Rican population. According to the *1976 Survey of Income and Education* by the Bureau of the Census, two-thirds of Puerto Rican workers in the professional and government sectors occupied subprofessional jobs. Many held clerical, food-service, and cleaning jobs. Most of the workers designated professional in government and other services were employed in social action, health technology, personnel and labor relations, or recreation positions. Some were librarians, elementary-school teachers, and clergymen. The sample included no scientists, lawyers, physicians, dentists, engineering technicians, airline pilots, radio or television announcers, editors, architects, reporters, veterinarians, or urban planners.

Despite the advances made by racial and cultural minorities in federal service during the 1960s, two inquiries in 1975 showed that the government's record on nondiscriminatory employment was in some respects dismal. First, according to a series of reports by the Civil Service Commission, several federal agencies had disregarded the civil service and equal employment rules intended to insure that federal jobs are awarded by merit rather than patronage or race. Among the agencies cited here the Small Business Administration, the National Science Foundation, and the Equal Opportunity Commission. Second, the General Accounting Office, which oversees the performance of the executive branch and reports back to Congress, charged a number of federal agencies with failure to enforce the 1965 executive order prohibiting government contractors from using discriminatory employment practices. Especially conspicuous in this inquiry was the Office of Federal Contract Compliance in the Department of Labor. This agency sets policy for eleven employing agencies which are required to determine that all aspects of a company's employment practices conform to the rules before a contract for $1 million or more is signed. The absence of affirmative action from the President or the Secretary of Labor meant that the pressure for compliance on both enforcement of government contracts and on government employment policies, if any, had to come from Congress through hearings of such committees as the House Subcommittee on Equal Opportunity (*The New York Times,* May 11, 1975).

On January 11, 1979, the Garcia Amendment to the Civil Service Reform Act of 1978 became effective. This amendment required the *immediate* development of a continuing program intended to eliminate employment underrepresentation of minorities in the federal government. On July 17, 1979, the Office of Personnel Management (OPM) established the Federal Equal Opportunity Recruitment Program (FEORP) and announced guidelines giving assistance to other federal agencies in their attempts to comply with the law. Under this amendment, each agency is required to develop its own recruitment program based on the underrepresentation of minorities and women in its work force in relation to minorities and women in the national civilian labor force. It requires the OPM to report annually on its effectiveness, beginning in January, 1980 (U.S. Commission on Civil Rights, *The State of Civil Rights: 1979,* January, 1980, pp. 27–28).

Because of increasing concern about alleged discriminatory effects of major federal employment examinations, the House Subcommittee on Civil Service conducted a hearing in May, 1979, on the use of the Professional and Administrative Career Examination (PACE), a test used in filling many professional positions in the federal government. Evidence was presented by representatives of federal agencies and civil rights organizations which purported to show that PACE contains racial and ethnic bias and that it screens out a disproportionate number of minority applicants, especially Blacks and Hispanics, for federal jobs. Witnesses charged that the examination had not been demonstrated to be job-related and that minorities were relegated to nonprofessional positions by virtue of PACE's discriminatory effect. In view of the testimony from the General Accounting Office (GAO), the Commission on Civil Rights stated that PACE should be replaced and recommended that alternatives be "thoroughly explored." Also, the Office of Personnel Management reported that it was searching "for valid alternative means of examining competitive applicants that will have less adverse impact on minority applicants" than PACE. Ultimately, the Garcia Amendment may result in alternatives to PACE through the establishment of new recruitment techniques, hiring procedures, and entrance tests (U.S. Commission on Civil Rights, *The State of Civil Rights: 1979,* January, 1980, p. 28).

The experience of the Federal Deposit Insurance Corporation (FDIC) is instructive. When the agency relied on PACE for its entry-level bank examiners, 13.2 percent of the white applicants but only 1.2 percent of the minority applicants received scores that were high enough to be hired. Under newly adapted procedures, Whites are passing at the old rate (14 percent), but minorities have moved to a rate of 7 percent. FDIC abandoned the written test in favor of job-related criteria. Applicants who meet basic eligibility requirements (degree from an accredited four-year college with a major in business or accounting, with at least 12 class hours of accounting) are asked to show in writing their knowledge of accounting principles, their analytical judgment, and their communications skills. Thus far, the hiring rate for minorities who have applied is only half the rate for Whites and much too low to meet the U.S. District Court consent decree to stop using PACE and its requirement that white and minority applicants be hired in approximately the proportions in which they apply. However, the FDIC's procedure is markedly better than PACE in its ability to find qualified minorities. In addition, FDIC officials say that minorities who pass the examining panels have been as successful on the job as those hired under PACE. Whether the federal civil service can use some variation of FDIC's procedure as a merit-based replacement for PACE, and one which does not discriminate against Blacks and Hispanics, has not been determined (Cleveland *Plain Dealer,* December 5, 1981, p. A24).

Racial and Cultural Minorities in the Professions

The Legal Profession

Before World War II the practice of black lawyers was limited largely to civil cases or divorce and to the affairs connected with black churches and fraternal orders. In the South, a black attorney had little chance of winning a case; protection by a white person usually counted more for a black client that would even the best representation by a black lawyer. In the North before 1950, the black lawyer in private practice usually worked as a neighborhood attorney in black communities. Most black attorneys were sole practitioners. Many Blacks in the border areas and in some northern cities gave legal work to white attorneys, and some important black lawyers refused to take a case to court without having a white practitioner as an associate. The black public's conception of the black lawyer, however, was changing; an increasing number of Blacks believed that black lawyers were competent and that they would be able to get a fair hearing in court.

In the 1960s, black lawyers played a leading part in the drive to expand the civil rights of Blacks. Blacks were appointed to federal judgships and appointed or elected as judges in municipal courts, and this trend has continued. Opportunities for Blacks to be more active in politics, both in the North and in the South, has helped to enhance the status of black lawyers (Lewinson 1974, p. 97).

White law firms and large companies began to hire black attorneys in the mid-1950s, but it is still exceptional for black lawyers to work in integrated offices. More black lawyers are specializing in such areas as taxation, labor law, and corporate financing. Many black attorneys are moving from neighborhood to downtown locations, and the practice of a number of black lawyers is composed in considerable part of white clients. Black attorneys have been elected to the boards of major corporations, and many predominantly white law schools now have black faculty members (Schneider 1977, pp. 135–136).

In 1970, Blacks comprised 1.1 percent of lawyers in the United States labor force. In 1970, Blacks constituted 2.7 percent of the new entrants to the legal labor force. If current trends continue, it is projected that by 1985 Blacks will increase their representation to 8 percent of new entrants to the legal labor force and that black participation in the legal profession will increase to 4.5 percent (Schneider 1977, p. 151). In 1981, the American Bar Association reported that 4.4 percent of the 125,397 students enrolled at the nation's 171 accredited law schools were black. Hispanic Americans, not including those enrolled in law schools in Puerto Rico, numbered 3,024, or 2.4 percent (*The New York Times,* May 3, 1981, p. 15).

A study of employment patterns of 21,000 graduates of 150 American law schools in 1978 found that graduates who were members of minority groups were accepting jobs with government agencies at a considerably higher rate than other lawyers. Also, minority lawyers were being hired by law firms at a much lower rate. Although 53 percent of the white graduates had entered private practice within a year after finishing law school, only 28.2 percent of minority lawyers had done so. While 15.5 percent of the Whites had been employed as government lawyers, 28 percent of the minority lawyers had taken government employment. In part, the low percentage of minority lawyers entering private practice has been attributed to racial discrimination. (*The New York Times,* May 3, 1981, p. 15). The author of this study, an assistant dean of the Delaware Law School in Wilmington, commented on the hiring patterns: "It is hard not to attribute the low percentage entering private practice to racial discrimination" (*The New York Times,* May 3, 1981, p. 15).

In 1981 the nation's 50 largest law firms, which had a total of 10,679 partners and associates, had 171 black lawyers, including 40 partners, and 51 Hispanic lawyers, including 11 partners. Blacks constituted only 1.6 percent of all the lawyers at the 50 firms, and Hispanic Americans made up only .5 percent. Leaders of the legal profession deny that there is a pattern of discrimination on the part of major law firms and attribute the small number of members of minority groups in these firms to the relatively small numbers, until recently, of those groups in the nation's law schools (*The New York Times,* May 3, 1981, p. 15).

Reliable statistics on the number of nonblack minority students enrolled in law schools are not available for years before the late 1960s. Table 10-2 shows the enrollments of Chicanos, Puerto Ricans, and American Indians in American Bar Association-Approved Law Schools for the period 1969–1976.

In 1975–76, Chicanos represented only one percent of the total law school enrollment. The ratio of Anglo attorneys to Anglo citizens is about 1 to 500, but the ratio of Spanish-descended (Mexican Americans, Puerto Ricans, Cubans, South Americans, and all other Spanish-related Americans) attorneys is 1 to 9,000 Spanish-descended citizens (Schneider 1977, p. 138).

In 1975, in law, engineering, medicine, and education, Puerto Ricans constituted less than 1 percent of New York City's total employment in those occupations. In New York State, it is estimated that there are fewer than 70 Puerto Rican

Table 10-2. Minority Enrollments in ABA-Approved Law Schools, 1969–70 through 1975–76[a]

Group	Year	Enroll-ment	Group enrollment as percentage of total
Chicano	1969–70	412	.60
	1971–72	883	.95
	1972–73	1,072	1.05
	1973–74	1,259	1.19
	1974–75	1,357	1.23
	1975–76	1,297	1.11
Puerto Rican	1969–70	61	.09
	1971–72	94	.10
	1972–73	143	.14
	1973–74	180	.17
	1974–75	263	.24
	1975–76	333	.28
American Indian	1969–70	72	.11
	1971–72	140	.15
	1972–73	173	.17
	1973–74	222	.21
	1974–75	265	.24
	1975–76	295	.25

Source: Law School & Bar Adminission Requirements: A Review of Legal Education in the United States—Fall 1975 (Chicago: American Bar Association, 1976), pp. 42, 44.
[a]Data for 1970–71 are not available.

lawyers in the Puerto Rican population of more than one million. New Jersey's Spanish-speaking population of more than 300,000 was served by three Puerto Rican lawyers in 1975 (Schneider 1977, pp. 140–141).

Engineering

Because of its importance as a profession and because frequently it is a means of entering corporate management positions as well as leadership positions in government, education, and industrial research, Schneider (1977, p. 15) calls engineering a key profession. Racial and cultural minorities, however, have been greatly underrepresented in this field. Although Blacks, Mexican Americans, Puerto Ricans, and American Indians constituted 14.4 percent of the nation's population in 1970, these groups had a representation of 2.8 percent of the engineers.

In 1970, Blacks constituted approximately one percent (.95 percent for black men and .03 percent for black women) of the engineering labor force. The number of new entrants to the total engineering labor force is expected to grow from 52,200 in 1970 to 59,500 in 1985. During that time it is projected that the proportion of Blacks in the new entrants will increase from 347 (344 males and 3 females) to 1,963 males and 88 females, or from .67 percent to approximately 3.5 percent of the new entrants. Assuming present trends in recruitment and graduation from engineering schools and entrance into the labor force, Blacks will constitute somewhat less than 2 percent of the country's engineers in 1985 (Schneider 1977, pp. 15, 40–42).

In 1974, American Indians represented .55 percent of those in the field of engineering, roughly equivalent to their proportion in the general population. In 1974–75, Native Americans were awarded 44 bachelor's degrees in engineering, 3 master's degrees, and two doctorates. Among the Spanish-surnamed, the numbers receiving those degrees in that year were, respectively: 1,060, 185, and 28, or 2.8 percent, 1.2 percent, and .9 percent of the engineering degrees awarded in the United States in that year (Schneider 1977, pp. 26–27).

Since 1973 efforts have been made by a cross section of industry, engineering schools, state and federal governments, professional engineering societies, foundations, and minority groups to increase the number of minority engineers. The Committee of Minorities in Engineering (COME) conducted a survey in 1974 of the schools and colleges with the largest minority enrollments. These schools included six traditionally black schools and forty-five predominantly white schools, institutions which made up more than half of the total undergraduate minority enrollment (Blacks, Spanish-surnamed, Asians, and American Indians) in engineering. This survey found that the major problems in minority engineering programs are: identifying and motivating minority youth to choose engineering as a career, recruiting minority youth, assisting those with weak scholastic backgrounds, and supporting enrolled students financially, academically, and socially until they receive an engineering degree (Schneider 1977, pp. 33–34).

The Ministry

The ministerial profession was the first to be established among Blacks in the United States, and for many years ministers were the principal leaders of this group. Increasingly in the last several decades of the twentieth century this leadership has been shared with lawyers, physicians, social workers, teachers, journalists, government officials, businessmen, and labor union leaders. Nevertheless, the ministry has continued to be an important profession in the black group, and clergymen are second in numbers only to teachers among black professional people. The clientele of black ministers, like that of black teachers and lawyers, is limited mainly to the black group.

On the whole, the religions of Blacks in the United States have tended to reinforce the social and political status quo, but nearly everywhere some religious leaders and groups have sought to change existing structures. This was true during the periods of slavery and Reconstruction, and during recent decades the role of priest–political leader has been played with considerable success by such ministers as Adam Clayton Powell, Martin Luther King, Jr., Jesse Jackson, and Andrew Young. In the late 1960s and early 1970s, many pastors of black churches emerged as leaders of the black rebellion.

Black clergymen in white denominations often hold second-class status, earning less than their white colleagues, being limited generally to black congregations, and finding that they are relegated to lesser positions in the hierarchies, if they are included at all. There are exceptions to these policies—black bishops in the Methodist and Episcopal churches, interracial ministerial staffs in a number of churches, and vigorous support for civil rights on the part of many white clergymen. Nevertheless, churches have not made major progress in eliminating separation and discrimination. Further attention is given to the black clergy in Chapter 14.

The Teaching Profession

In the black group, the number of persons engaged in teaching exceeds that in other professions. In the past, the development of black teachers was complicated by the low salaries offered, racial wage discrimination, racial differentials in teaching loads, lack of professional training, and the strong control on black teachers by the white community. Depending upon the nature of the school system and the school, the status and role of the black public school teacher changed to a greater or lesser degree in the 1960s and the 1970s.

Some of these changes are discussed in Chapter 16.

In the early 1980s, when there was a general shortage of positions in college and university teaching, the supply of blacks trained for such positions was inadequate to meet the demand for them. Blacks with doctorates constitute about 4 percent of all sociologists holding the doctorate, 5 percent of psychologists with doctorates, 2 percent of the economists, and less than 1 percent of the historians, mathematicians, physicists, biologists, and chemists. The number of black college students has increased rapidly since the mid-1960s, as has racial integration in institutions of higher education in the United States. The demand for black professors has led to competition among predominantly white colleges and universities, and between white and black institutions, for black teachers and administrators (Blackwell 1975, pp. 189–190).

Health Care

Medicine. In 1971–1972, there were 108 medical schools in the United States with 43,650 students, of whom 2,055 (4.7 percent) were black Americans. In 1975–76, there were 114 medical schools with 55,818 students, of whom 3,456 (6.2 percent) were black Americans. The 12,168 new places in six new medical schools represented an increase of 27.8 percent, compared with an increase in black medical students of 1,401 (68 percent), up to 6.3 percent of total first-year enrollment during this period (Sullivan 1977, p. 181).

The minority recruitment effort was at its height in the decade 1967–76, but black and other minority students occupied less than 10 percent of the places in medical schools. Although American minority groups comprise nearly one-fifth of the nation's total population, fewer than 7 percent of the first-year medical students in 1976–77 were Black, Mexican American, Mainland Puerto Rican, or American Indian (Sullivan 1977, p. 181). According to the Association of American Medical Colleges, the proportion of Blacks applying to medical schools rose from 2.7 percent in 1968 to 7.5 percent in 1974 and fell to 6.7 percent in 1977 (*The New York Times*, December 11, 1977, p. 41).

The efforts of individual medical schools in recent years to recruit minority students have been hindered principally in three ways: the small number of minority applicants with the requisite academic backgrounds; competition among schools for minority students; and reductions in federal loan and scholarship funds (Schneider 1977, p. 221).

The National Chicano Health Organization sponsors minority recruitment, admission, and retention programs for Chicanos entering the health professions. The National Boricua Health Organization performs similar functions for disadvantaged mainland Puerto Ricans, and the Association of American Indian Physicians operates programs to increase the proportion of Native Americans in medicine (Schneider 1977, p. 227).

In 1965, black physicians comprised only 2 percent of the profession in the United States, compared with 10.7 percent in the field of social welfare, 7.8 percent of the teachers, and 3 percent of the college teachers (Bond 1966, pp. 579–80). In 1972, black doctors still constituted only 2 percent of the profession and by 1977 2.5 percent. The projection for 1985, assuming the rates of admission and graduation prevailing in 1977, was 4.5 percent (3.98 percent black men and .6 percent black women). The 11-fold increase in black entrants into the medical labor force from 1970 to 1985 (from 140 male and 13 female physicians in 1970 to 1454 male and 349 female physicians in 1985) will result in only a two-fold increase in representation in the profession (Schneider 1977, pp. 232–233). Table 10-3 shows the total enrollments in schools of medicine in the United States by racial and ethnic category for the years 1968–69 through 1979–80.

The proportion of black physicians in relation to the black population is extremely important because these doctors provide services mainly to Blacks. Approximately 87 percent of the black doctors serve black patients, and 90 percent of the nonblack physicians serve the white population when analyzed in ambulatory medical care patient visits (Darity and Pitt 1979, p. 142).

In 1981, Blacks in the medical profession became concerned about the move to slow down the number of new physicians in the United States, a move favored by many white doctors, and the apparent acceptance by some federal health planners of the claim that there are too many physicians in this country. According to the National Association of Deans of Minority Medical Schools, acceptance of the premise that fewer doctors are needed could hinder attempts to increase the numbers of black physicians, dentists, pharmacists, and veterinarians and could occasion decreases in federal assistance that could threaten the existence of some black medical schools. Specifically cited are two new black medical institutions, Morehouse, which opened in 1977, and Drew, a postgraduate medical center which began an undergraduate program in 1980. Both are using federal and state aid to construct new campuses. These officials believe that improving health care among black Americans remains the province of black physicians, and they see the ratio of black doctors (2 percent) in relation to the black population of the country (12 percent) as a matter of equity (Cleveland *Plain Dealer*, January 11, 1981, p. C17).

According to Sidel (1974, pp. 264–268), physicians have shown little inclination toward practice in the ghetto or sympathy for the health problems of its citizens. There is no assurance that medical students drawn from the lower socioeconomic classes will later enter ghetto practice—in fact, such evidence as is available suggests that the majority of ghetto recruits go into the same types of nonghetto practices as their colleagues.[1]

Racial discrimination in the gaining of admission to hospital staffs by black physicians was still prevalent as recently as 1968. Such discrimination had been reduced, but had not completely disappeared a decade later, and it was not limited to the South (*The New York Times*, April 22, 1979, p. 26).

Dentistry. In 1969, minorities, including Blacks, Puerto Ricans, Mexican Americans, American Indians, and Asians, constituted 2.2 percent of all enrolled dental students. By 1975–76, a significant change had occurred, with minorities comprising 11.1 percent of first-year enrollments, 9.7 percent of total enrollments, and 7.5 percent of graduates from United States dental schools. During 1975–76, Howard University and Meharry Medical College enrolled 23 percent of the total minority students in dentistry. The other fifty-seven dental schools had a minority enrollment of only 7.6 percent. Only sixteen dental schools had minority enrollments of more than 10 percent, and several schools reached that proportion by enrolling a large number of Asian students, many of whom were not disadvantaged (Schneider 1977, p. 248). Table 10-4 shows the number of graduates from American dental schools by racial and ethnic category for the years 1972–1976.

In 1977, 2 percent of the nation's 120,000 dentists were black. There is one dentist for every 1,750 Americans, but only one black dentist for

---

[1]For suggestions on several possibilities of attracting physicians into the ghetto, see Sidel 1974, pp. 267–68.

Table 10.3 Total Enrollments in Schools of Medicine in the United States, by Racial/Ethnic Category: Academic Years 1968–69 through 1979–80

Academic year	Total enroll- ments[c]	Total U.S. minority	Under-rep- resented minority[a]	Racial/ethnic category					
				Black American	American Indian	Hispanic American[b]	Asian American	Other American minority	White American
				Number of students					
1968–1969	35,833	1,275	854	783	9	62	421	—	34,558
1969–1970	37,690	1,630	1,178	1,042	18	118	452	—	36,060
1970–1971	40,238	2,294	1,723	1,509	18	196	571	—	37,944
1971–1972	43,650	3,072	2,425	2,055	42	328	647	—	40,578
1972–1973	47,366	3,918	3,102	2,582	69	451	718	98	43,448
1973–1974	50,751	4,840	3,765	3,049	97	619	883	192	45,911
1974–1975	53,554	5,974	4,738	3,355	159	1,224	959	277	47,580
1975–1976	55,818	6,361	5,101	3,456	172	1,473	1,022	238	49,457
1976–1977	57,765	6,787	5,351	3,517	189	1,645	1,177	262	50,978
1977–1978	60,039	7,260	5,838	3,587	201	2,050	1,422	—	52,779
1978–1979	62,213	7,596	6,004	3,537	202	2,265	1,592	—	54,617
1979–1980	63,800	8,128	6,351	3,627	212	2,512	1,777	—	55,672
				Percentage					
1968–1969	100.0	3.6	2.4	2.2	d	0.2	1.2	—	96.4
1969–1970	100.0	4.3	3.1	2.8	d	0.3	1.2	—	95.7
1970–1971	100.0	5.7	4.3	3.8	d	0.5	1.4	—	94.3
1971–1972	100.0	7.0	5.6	4.7	0.1	0.8	1.5	—	93.0
1972–1973	100.0	8.3	6.5	5.5	0.1	1.0	1.5	0.2	91.7
1973–1974	100.0	9.5	7.4	6.0	0.2	1.2	1.7	0.4	90.5
1974–1975	100.0	11.2	8.8	6.3	0.3	2.3	1.8	0.5	88.8
1975–1976	100.0	11.4	9.1	6.2	0.3	2.6	1.8	0.4	88.6
1976–1977	100.0	11.7	9.3	6.1	0.3	2.8	2.0	0.5	88.3
1977–1978	100.0	12.1	9.7	6.0	0.3	3.4	2.4	—	87.9
1978–1979	100.0	12.2	9.7	5.7	0.3	3.6	2.6	—	87.8
1979–1980	100.0	12.7	10.0	5.7	0.3	3.9	2.8	—	87.3

Source: "U.S. Medical Student Enrollment 1968–69 Through 1972–79," *Journal of Medical Education* 48(1973): pp. 293–297; U. S. Department of Health and Human Services, *Health of the Disadvantaged*, 1980, p. 100. Note: Percents may not add to total and subtotals due to independent rounding.

[a]Includes Black Americans, American Indians, and Hispanic Americans.
[b]Beginning in 1977–78, the fall enrollment questionnaire was revised to reflect DHEW suggested racial/ethnic classifications. The general "other" category was dropped and a Hispanic classification was added, which is defined to include any person of Spanish culture or origin, regardless of race. This would account for part of the increase for the Hispanic group from 1974–75 to later years.
[c]Includes also all foreign students.
[d]Less than 0.05 percent.

Table 10-4. Number of Graduates from U.S. Dental Schools by Racial/Ethnic Category, 1972–1976

Year	Total graduates	Racial/ethnic category						
		Minority	Black	Puerto Rican	Mexican American	Amerian Indian	Oriental	Other
1972	3,961	167	74	3	9	1	61	19
1973	4,230	241	110	3	22	1	73	32
1974	4,515	335	154	—	31	2	113	35
1975	4,969	368	187	6	33	5	107	30
1976	5,336	467	213	1	49	3	158	43

Source: Stephen A. Schneider, *The Availability of Minorities and Women for Professional and Managerial Positions, 1970–1985.* Industrial Research Unit, The Wharton School, University of Pennsylvania, 1977, p. 249.

every 11,500 black Americans. As recently as 1951, black applicants were not considered for admission to sixteen of the then forty accredited dental schools. In 1964, only eight dental schools in the United States had blacks enrolled; in 1975–76, fifty-five of the fifty-nine accredited schools had black students enrolled. Howard University and Meharry Medical College had 44 percent of the total black student enrollment, and these two schools produced half of the total number of dental school graduates in 1975–76. In more than a century, fewer than 2 percent of all black dentists have graduated from schools other than Meharry and Howard (Schneider 1977, pp. 239, 246).

By 1978–1979, 977 black Americans were enrolled in dental schools. They represented 4.4 percent of total dental school enrollments, compared with 3.5 percent in 1971–72. In that year, Hispanic Americans comprised 1.9 percent of total dental enrollments, compared with .5 percent in 1971–72. There were only 8 American Indian dental students enrolled in 1971–72, but 64, or .3 percent, in 1978–79 (U.S. Department of Health and Human Services 1980, p. 106).

In recent years, Meharry Medical College and Howard University have had difficulty recruiting qualified applicants. The difficulty is attributed to three factors: high cost and time commitment for dental training; the problems that average students have in meeting admission standards; and competition with industry in attracting students. Although most admission barriers have been removed, Schneider (1977, p. 247) says that attitudinal bias remains a problem with some students, faculty, and administrators in dental schools. Currently, programs by the W. K. Kellogg Foundation and the Robert Wood Johnson Foundation provide scholarships or loan awards to increase the number of minority students in dental schools. The National Chicano Health Organization sponsors recruitment, admission, and retention programs to increase the number of Chicano students in medical, dental, pharmacy, nursing, and public health schools. Several universities sponsor summer programs or academic reinforcement programs to prepare high school and college students for the health professions. Among these institutions are Harvard University, Howard University, University of Illinois, Haverford College, and the Harvard–Yale–Columbia Intensive Summer Study Program (Schneider 1977, p. 254).

The Allied Health Professions. Blacks constitute about 2 percent of all allied health professionals. Shortages exist in the fields of occupational therapy, medical data assistants, hospital and clinical staff members, pharmacology, food nutrition, toxicology, health-care administration, radiology and radio therapy, and biomedical science. Black registered nurses constitute approximately 7 percent of all registered nurses, 15 percent of all practical nurses, and 50 percent of all nurses' aides in the United States. These figures indicate the unequal distribution of black professionals in the health services field (Blackwell 1975, p. 188).

In 1970, the Hispanic population constituted approximately 6 percent of the total population in the United States. In the health occupations, the Spanish-origin group has been best represented among midwives and dental laboratory technicians. According to the Bureau of the Census (May 1981a, p. 2), 60 percent of the population of Spanish-origin is made up of Mexican Americans, 14 percent of Puerto Ricans, 8 percent of Central or South Americans, 6 percent of Cubans, and 12 percent of other Spanish. Health services are not equally available to these groups within the population of Spanish origin, nor are the several Hispanic groups equally represented in the personnel of the health services occupations. Mexican Americans and Puerto Ricans are the most disadvantaged economically among Hispanics, and they are least well represented and served in the health services. In areas wherein Mexican American poor are concentrated, the incidence of tuberculosis, poor dental hygiene, and alcoholism are greater than in the community at large. In these places, the shortages of personnel and facilities, compounded by cultural and communications barriers, constitute major obstacles to adequate health. Cabrera (1971, p. 22) suggests that a wholesale recruitment of medical aides with some medical training—admittedly not a full answer to present deficits—could complement available health services in these communities. Such services would also provide paramedical training and jobs.

Because of the importance of health care, we append to this discussion of the medical field the following sections on trends in the health of racial and cultural minorities, and on the extent to which minorities are underserved in health services. Disparities in morbidity and mortality rates and in the financing of health care between racial and cultural minorities and the majority population indicate another of the costs of minority status.

Trends in Black Health. Adjusted census data show that heart disease is the leading cause of death among Blacks as well as among Whites. In 1979, 31 percent of all deaths among Blacks were attributed to this cause. Cancer was the second leading cause for both races, males and females. The third leading cause of death for the whole population was stroke, but accidents are the third leading cause of death for black and white men. Table 10-5 shows that Blacks are 1.27 times as likely as Whites to die from heart disease and more than twice as likely to die from diabetes. The death rate for diseases of early infancy is more than twice as high for Blacks as for Whites. Census data show also that the infant mortality rate for Blacks is 1.9 times the white rate—the same differential as in 1960 when the rate for Blacks was 44.3 and 22.9 for Whites (Reid 1982, pp. 16–17).

Thanks to the high degree of control now exercised over infectious diseases, the death rate of Blacks has declined steadily in recent decades. In 1900, the leading causes of death were influenza

Table 10-5. Ratio of Black to White Age-Adjusted Death Rates for the 12 Leading Causes of Death: 1979

Rank	Causes of death	Ratio of Black to White
1	Heart Diseases	1.27
2	Cancer	1.32
3	Stroke	1.80
4	Accidents	1.20
5	Chronic obstructive pulmonary disease	0.75
6	Pneumonia and influenza	1.61
7	Diabetes	2.21
8	Chronic liver disease	1.90
9	Atherosclerosis	1.09
10	Suicide	0.60
11	Disease of early infancy	2.14
12	Homicide and legal intervention	6.26

Source: National Center for Health Statistics, Advance Report of Final Mortality Statistics, 1979. "*Monthly Vital Statistics Report.*" Vol. 31, No. 6, Supplement, 1982, Table C.

and pneumonia, tuberculosis, and gastritis; diphtheria, now nearly nonexistent, ranked tenth. All of these diseases took higher tolls among Blacks than among Whites. As a result of greater control of these diseases, more children survived and diseases of older ages became more prevalent for both Blacks and Whites. Heart disease, stroke, and cancer are responsible for 70 percent or more of the deaths of Whites today, but only approximately 55 percent of the deaths of black men and 60 percent of the deaths of black women (Reid, Lee, Jedlicka, and Shin 1977, p. 112).

A major difference in the causes of deaths by sex and race is the high rate of deaths from violence among black males. About 16 percent of the deaths of black males are due to accident, suicide, or homicide. Six percent are from homicide alone. The rates for adolescents and young adults are much higher. For black males aged 15–34, nearly one-third of the deaths are due to homicide, and approximately one-sixth of the deaths of black females of those ages are from that cause (Reid et al. 1977, p. 112).

Male–female differentials in death rates among Blacks resemble those for nearly every group throughout the world, that is, the decline in the death rate for women has been greater than that for men. For the major cardiovascular diseases, black men have death rates about 40 percent higher than those for black women. For cancer, the difference is 60 percent. Death rates from accidents and suicide are three times higher for black men as for black women and six times as high for homicide (Reid et al. 1977, pp. 113–114).

Hypertension has been called the killer disease among Blacks. The death rate for diseases related to high blood pressure is 58.4 per 100,000 for Blacks, compared with the white rate of 27.1. Among men in the age group 25–44, the death rate for Blacks is 15 times greater than it is for Whites. Among black women the death rate for blood pressure-related diseases is 17 times greater than for white women (Yabura 1977, p. 196).

In 1940, the maternal mortality rate (deaths of mothers in the period immediately following childbirth) was 770 per 100,000 live births for Blacks and other races and 320 for Whites—a differential ratio of 242 percent. In 1976, it was 9.0 for Whites and 26.5 for Blacks and others, a rate 2.9 times higher (National Urban League 1980, pp. 131, 240).

In 1920, the difference in life expectancy at birth was 8.6 years for white males, compared with black males, and 10.4 for white females, compared with black females. Since that year, there has been a continuing difference of five or six years in life expectancy between Whites and Blacks and other minorities. In 1979, the most recent year for which such data are available, life expectancy at birth for Blacks was 68.3 years, and the gap between Whites and Blacks was 6.1 years (National Urban League 1980, pp. 131–32; Reid 1982, p. 15; Wilson, Feldman, and Kovar 1978, pp. 149–51).

Nonwhite admission rates to all psychiatric outpatient services exceed those for Whites by about one half. In 1975, Blacks constituted 11 percent of the United States civilian resident population but comprised 22 percent of all inpatient admissions to public mental hospitals. Utilization of mental hospitalization, like outpatient services, is not distributed evenly across racial groups. For example, in 1971, 36 percent of Whites were admitted to private facilities and 64 percent to public, compared with 11 percent and 88 percent among Nonwhites. As Cannon and Locke (1977) point out, the higher utilization rates of mental health facilities by Blacks than Whites is not solely a function of higher rates of mental illness among Blacks. In part, the higher rates among Blacks result from a lack of early intervention or continued clinic

treatment for the black psychiatric patient, resulting in a greater need for hospitalization, longer hospitalization, and chronic conditions. Cannon and Locke (1977, pp. 413, 414, 417, 427–428) attribute the high prevalence of mental disorders among Blacks to stressful social conditions such as denial of respect, dignity, and courtesy, experiences of loss or failure, being viewed as inferior, and other effects of racism.

Mexican American Health Problems. Infant mortality is one-third higher among Chicanos than among Anglos. Mexican Americans are twice as likely as Anglos to die of accidents, influenza, or pneumonia. In 1975, life expectancy for Chicanos was 56.7 years, compared with 67.5 years for Anglos. Mexican-Americans have a lower physician-visitation rate per person per year (2.3) than Blacks (3.7) or Anglos (5.6). Because Chicanos are less likely to hold an insurance policy (a sample of Chicano, black, and Anglo populations showed insurance rates of 39.7, 45.8, and 58.1 respectively), health care costs are a greater burden on the Mexican American community (Weaver 1976, p. 134).

In many areas of Chicano concentration, health providers and facilities are scarce, and those that are available are overloaded or substandard or both. As a result of unawareness on the part of many health care personnel of the preferences, problems, and style of life of large numbers of Chicanos, or a disregard for the needs and expectations of their patients, together with a lack of information in the community about what services are available, a large part of the Chicano population is inadequately served by the health care system (Weaver 1976, p. 134).

On the question of whether ethnicity is independently related to the health problems of Chicanos, the evidence is not clearcut. The findings of a number of sociologists and anthropologists indicate that some Chicanos have dietary and curative practices, as well as hostile attitudes toward scientific medical providers, that prevent them from using preventive and remedial services. Such traits are found especially in isolated rural areas and among recent arrivals from rural Mexico (Cabrera 1971, pp. 23–24; Fernandez, Haug, and Wagner 1976, pp. 279–280; Weaver 1976, p. 135). These persons do not constitute the majority of the disadvantaged among Mexican Americans. Many thousands of Chicanos who are poor are city dwellers of the third and fourth generation who do not adhere to folk health beliefs and practices and yet have serious health problems. Lack of fluency in English and embarrassment when faced with the formality of modern medical facilities may inhibit the exchange of information between medical personnel and the patient (Cabrera 1971, pp. 23–24; Fernandez et al. 1976, pp. 279–280; Schreiber and Homiak 1981, pp. 264–336; Weaver 1976, pp. 135–146).

Health Problems of Mainland Puerto Ricans. Table 10-6 shows the annual mortality rates according to chief causes for Puerto Rican-born New Yorkers and all New York residents for the years 1969–1971.

A further breakdown shows that although the total mortality rate for Puerto Rican-born New Yorkers was much lower than for all New Yorkers, Puerto Ricans under the age of 45 died at a considerably higher rate than the same cohort in the total population. In this age group, the chief causes of death of the Puerto Rican-born were not diseases but accidents, homicide, and drug dependence. In this age range, these causes together accounted for 39 percent of all deaths. Harwood (1981, p. 406) assumes that mortality from homicide and drug dependence are higher in New York City than elsewhere but that disease-caused mortality differs little

from other East Coast cities where sizable populations of predominantly poor Puerto Ricans live.

Low income, substandard housing, and poorly designed medical services contribute to the epidemiology and the medical usage patterns of Puerto Ricans. Cultural conceptions of illness and treatment, their language preferences, their customary patterns of social interaction, and their expectations of medical care are important to the therapeutic outcome (Harwood 1981, p. 467).

Health Problems of American Indians. In 1954, when the U.S. Public Health Service took over the Indian Health Service from the Bureau of Indian Affairs, the major causes of mortality and morbidity among Indians were infectious diseases (Mail 1978, p. 43; Stewart 1977, p. 517). A campaign conducted by the Division of Indian Health personnel during the next two decades resulted in a marked reduction of the infectious diseases, as shown in Table 10-7.

More Native Americans are dying now from accidents and chronic conditions. In 1971, the Indian Health Service listed as the ten leading causes of death for Indians: accidents, diseases of the heart, malignant neoplasms, cirrhosis of the liver, cerebrovascular disease, influenza and pneumonia, diseases of infancy (unspecified), diabetes mellitus,

Table 10-6. Average Annual Mortality Rates for Chief Causes, Puerto Rican-Born and Total Populations, New York City, 1969–1971

Chief causes in rank order[a]	Puerto Rican-born population		Total population		
	Average annual rate[b]	Percentage	Average annual rate	Percentage	Rank
All ages					
Heart diseases	152.4	25.3	440.2	39.6	1
Malignant neoplasms	94.4	15.6	225.1	20.2	2
Cirrhosis of the liver	45.4	7.5	36.5	3.3	5
Cerebrovascular disease	35.0	5.8	78.4	7.1	3
Accidents	29.3	4.9	27.8	2.5	7
Influenza and pneumonia	20.5	3.4	44.5	4.0	4
Other diseases of digestive system	17.7	2.9	29.4	2.6	6
Diabetes mellitus	17.7	2.9	25.4	2.3	8
All other	191.3	31.7	204.7	18.4	—
Total	603.7	100.0	1,112.1	100.0	—

Source: Harwood ed. (1981: p. 407).
[a]The eight leading causes of death in order of importance for Puerto Ricans.
[b]Rates per 100,000 U.S. Census (New York City) population.

Table 10-7. Indian Health Service Program Accomplishments

Health Improvements	1955 rate	1974 rate	Percentage decrease
Death Rates			
Infant	62.5	18.7	70
Neonatal	22.7	9.4	59
Postneonatal	39.8	9.3	77
Maternal	82.6	16.4	80
Influenza and pneumonia	89.8	29.7	67
Certain diseases of infancy	67.7	21.0	69
Tuberculosis, all forms	55.1	7.5	86
Gastroenteritis, etc.	39.2	6.6	83
Congenital malformations	19.0	8.5	55
Incidence Rates			
New active tuberculosis	257.7[a]	79.8	69
Trachoma	1712.7[b]	388.8	77

Source: Indian Health Service, Analysis and Statistical Branch, "Program Accomplishments." (A package of charts and materials prepared for the congressional budget hearings of March 8 and March 10, 1976.)
[a]1962 rate.
[b]1966 rate.

homicide, and suicide (Beuf 1977, p. 37; Mail 1978, p. 43–44).

Four of the top causes of death among Indians are related to the heavy use of alcohol among reservation residents: accidents, cirrhosis, homicide, and suicide. Recently, dealing with the chronic diseases and mental health problems has become increasingly important in the work of medical professionals and paraprofessionals. Much remains unknown about the major health problem of alcoholism. The Indian Health Service has no overall policy for dealing with this problem. Mail (1978, p. 45) and others suggest that "it is time to stop the body count of abusers and begin to develop comprehensive, community-based approaches to the problem which incorporate prevention, early identification and intervention, effective treatment, follow-up and rehabilitation, with all of the attendant services implied by these concepts."

Health and medical care for Native Americans is provided in 24 western states by 51 hospitals, 83 health centers, and more than 300 health stations. By 1975, the Indian Health Service had a staff of 7,400 individuals and an annual appropriation of over $200 million. Legislation in 1974 provided a separate authorization for the construction of sanitation facilities on reservations which had previously had no running water or sanitary

waste disposal (Mail 1978, p. 42; Levitan and Johnston 1975, p. 56).

Corrective dental treatment (fillings and dentures) and preventive measures, including water fluoridation and fluoride treatments, are provided by Indian Health Service facilities. In Indian communities and in school programs, public health nurses encourage the acceptance and use of medical care. In 1972, approximately 20,000 Indian women were accepting birth control assistance—a matter of considerable importance considering the great population pressure on Indian reservations (Levitan and Johnston 1975, pp. 56–57).

Cultural differences affect the utilization of health services, and it has been suggested that an increase in the number of indigenous personnel, especially therapists to deal with emotional and social problems, might contribute to the improvement of Indian health. Medical health care delivery would be more effective if health professionals were able to modify their concepts of causation of psychosocial disturbances and if traditional practitioners could acquire a better understanding of modern medical concepts and be assisted in combining these with indigenous concepts of disease causation (Mail 1978, p. 45).

In 1968, a training center and research station was established near Tucson, Arizona, to provide basic training to tribal outreach workers known as Community Health Representatives. Ways to facilitate the delivery of health services to remote parts of reservations were explored. In 1970, the Indian Health Service established a Community Health Medic training program to produce Indian physician assistants. In addition to the programs within the federal government, Indian outpatient and social service programs have been started in many cities with substantial Indian populations. In Los Angeles, San Francisco, Seattle, Chicago, and Minneapolis, Indian clinics, often started by volunteers, have obtained state and federal funding (Mail 1978, pp. 46, 48).

Although emphasizing that Indian health has improved vastly in the past three decades, Mail (1978, pp. 48–49) says that it will not be equivalent to that of the majority population "until unemployment, poverty, isolation, discrimination, poor housing, inadequate and inferior education, and federal paternalism give way to genuine Indian participation, management, and assumption of administrative responsibility by trained Indian people."

Minorities Are Underserved in Health Services. Living in run-down dwellings in densely populated ghettos and barrios, the poor face many dangers to health. Air pollution, infectious diseases, and occupational hazards are constant threats. For example, the rate of newly detected cases of tuberculosis is several times as high in Central Harlem as it is in the Flushing area of New York City, and in Watts compared with the rest of Los Angeles County. The rates for diphtheria, brucellosis, polio, typhoid, hepatitis, mumps, measles, and rheumatic fever are disproportionately high in ghettos. Increasing rates of cancer are being reported for Blacks. The third national cancer survey of the National Cancer Institute found the following rates of cancer: black males: 397.2 per 100,000; Anglo males: 342.6; black females: 256.8; and Anglo females: 270.3. The increasing rates for Blacks may be due to better record keeping, or it may reflect the impact of environmental pollution and of food preservatives and processing on the increasingly urbanized black population. As early as 1966, reports indicated that the likelihood of heart disease with hypertension is greater for Blacks than for Whites. Research in Detroit shows that blacks who live in high stress areas have higher rates of blood pressure than Blacks living outside these areas (Weaver 1976, pp. 72–73).

The type of health care provider varies by race. Blacks rely disproportionately on public clinics and emergency rooms for service and regardless of income level are less likely to have a continuing relationship with a physician. Many low-income people use clinics and emergency rooms because internists, pediatricians, and other specialists are not available privately in their neighborhoods.

Black women are less inclined to utilize preventive services. They were twice as likely as white women to have begun prenatal care in the third trimester of pregnancy or to have had no care at all. Further, white mothers were more likely to have had their children immunized against measles than black mothers (U.S. Department of Health and Human Services 1980, p. vi).

The financing of health care is of extreme importance for Blacks in the United States since more than a fifth of that population is in poverty and another fifth is at the near-poverty level. About four-fifths of the white population under 65 years of age is covered by private hospital insurance, but less than three-fifths of the nonwhite population is so covered. The same disparities exist in hospital insurance coverage and employment status. For the white employed group, nine-tenths were covered and four-fifths of the nonwhite population was covered. Among the unemployed, approximately 63 percent of the white population is covered, compared with about 38 percent of the nonwhite (Darity and Pitt 1979, p. 146).

Minorities in the Armed Forces

During World War II, the racial policy of both the United States Army and the United States Air Force consisted of a 10 percent quota on enlisted men, segregated units, and severely limited job opportunities. After President Truman's Executive Order 9981 was issued in 1948, the new air force policy provided that there be no strength quotas of minority groups on a troop basis; that qualified black personnel be assigned to any position vacancy; that all individuals, regardless of race, be given equal opportunity for appointment, advancement, professional improvement, promotion, and retention in all components of the air force.

Integration in the army, begun in Europe in 1951, went ahead swiftly in 1952. The Marine Corps was the last of the services to admit Blacks at all, but its last two all-black units were integrated by the summer of 1952.

After discriminating widely against Blacks for many years, in 1946 the United States Navy lifted all restrictions on types of assignments for which black personnel were eligible and ordered that no special or unusual provisions were to be made in housing, mess, and other facilities for the accommodation of Blacks.

The Proportion of Blacks in the Armed Forces, 1944–1981

At the time of the Truman order in 1948, Blacks constituted 8.8 percent of the army personnel. In 1964, the proportion was 12.3 percent. Blacks serving in the air force increased from less than 5 percent in 1949 to 8.6 percent in 1964. The proportion of black personnel in the navy remained around 5 percent for the period 1944–1964. After integration was begun in the Marine Corps, the proportion of Blacks increased from 2 percent in 1949 to 8.2 percent in 1964. On March 31, 1969, Blacks constituted 9 percent of the armed forces, 11 percent of those serving in Southeast Asia, and 12 percent of those who died in Vietnam. At that time, Blacks made up 2 percent of all officers in the armed forces and 3 percent of the officers stationed in Southeast Asia. Approximately 3 percent of the Blacks in the armed services were officers compared with 13 percent of the Whites (U.S. Bureau of the Census 1969, pp. 85–86).

The proportion of Blacks in the armed forces grew during the 1970s, reaching nearly 20 percent of total enlisted personnel and attaining all-time highs of 33 percent and 22 percent in the army and marines, respectively, by the end of the decade. By the end of fiscal 1981, nearly one-fifth of all those on active duty in the armed services were black, a higher proportion than those who had advocated an all-volunteer force had anticipated (Binkin and Eitelberg 1982, pp. 6, 43).

The proportion of black enlisted volunteers in the army reached its highest point in 1979 (36.7 percent), nearly three times the proportion of Blacks in the general youth population (approximately 13 percent). Enlistments of Blacks declined to about 30 percent in 1980 and 27.4 percent in 1981. Binkin and Eitelberg (1982, pp. 44–45) suggest several

reasons for the drop: an increase in white enlistments as a result of the decline in the job market, increases in entry-level pay, enlistment incentives that may favor Whites (including educational benefits which Whites may be better able to take advantage, and special efforts by Army recruiters to enroll white enlistees in response to criticism about the racially unbalanced army). The proportion of all *reenlistments* in the army (first-term and career personnel) doubled between 1972 and 1981, and one-third of all army reenlistments were black.

Race and Occupational Mix

On military aptitude tests, Blacks have not performed as well as Whites. For selected years in the period 1953–81, on the Armed Forces Qualification Test (AFQT), less than 9 percent of the nonwhite male enlisted recruits placed above categories I and II (above average), compared to approximately 39 percent of the white males. About one-sixth of the Whites and one-half of the minority male enlisted entrants scored in category IV (below average) (Binkin and Eitelberg 1982, p. 46).

An ad hoc study group in the army secretariat has questioned the validity of the standardized tests used in the armed services. This group has suggested that the army change from a "norm-referenced" system to a "criterion-referenced" system. Instead of comparing one candidate with another, the latter system would compare the candidate "with a describable constant standard of performance." Binkin and Eitelberg (1982, pp. 89–93) say that one side sees the ASVAB (Armed Services Vocational Aptitudes Battery) as the best instrument available for selection purposes, whereas the other side argues that the present testing discriminates against Blacks and other minorities. It seems likely that the current standardized entry tests will continue to be used to screen potential military recruits.

Because Blacks score relatively poorly on the armed services' entry tests and because the tests are used to assign individuals to jobs, a disproportionate number of Blacks have always served in nontechnical jobs where training is minimal and advancement usually is slow. In 1981, more than half of all black army enlisted men were assigned to supply administration (55.4 percent) and 57.8 percent of linemen (telephone) were black. Blacks were slightly underrepresented in the infantry, but 45 percent of all men assigned to artillery and gunnery groups were black. In several so-called soft skills—unit supply, food service, administration, and personnel—Blacks constituted more than 40 percent of army enlisted personnel. Less than 16 percent of the military police were black, and blacks were underrepresented in armor and amphibious, combat operations control, combat engineering, track vehicle repair, and aircraft positions (Binkin and Eitelberg 1982, pp. 55–57).

In 1981, 90 percent of Blacks entering military service for the first time were high school graduates, compared to 65 percent in 1972. In all of the Department of Defense, almost 9 out of 10 black recruits during 1981 were high school graduates compared to about 8 out of 10 white recruits (Bureau of the Census 1983, p. 24).

In the officer corps, Blacks were almost unrepresented until the end of World War II, and in 1981 they still accounted for a relatively small proportion of officers in all four branches of the armed services. Black officers tend to be concentrated in the lower ranks and to be found mainly in occupations that do not provide the same career progression opportunities as others—supply, procurement, and administration. Army officials maintain that affirmative action plans designed to increase the proportion of minority officers are only starting to succeed since such plans are influenced by seniority. Civilian competition with the army for minority college graduates has been strong, as have the efforts by universities to enroll minorities who might otherwise be attracted to precommission programs (Binkin and Eitelberg 1982, pp. 59, 61).

Binkin and Eitelberg (1982, p. 158) recommend that greater attention be given to the imbalance between officers and enlisted men, adding that attracting more black officers will remain difficult if a college degree continues to be an important requirement. The expansion of commissioning programs, including officer candidate schools, academy preparatory schools, and direct appointments, to increase the opportunities for Blacks who are not college graduates offer possibilities.

Benefits of Military Service

Up to 80,000 young black men and women have entered the armed forces annually in recent years, and many of them have achieved an economic position better than they would have attained in the private sector. For black teenagers in large cities, the unemployment rate was estimated at nearly 60 percent. At the same time, the rate for white teenagers was 19.3 percent. In addition to higher pay, the military provides job training, educational assistance, and other benefits that would not be available in the inner city (Binkin and Eitelberg 1982, pp. 65, 69).

Skeptics have argued that the benefits of military service to minorities have been exaggerated. For example, Binkin and Eitelberg (1982, p. 73) quote the *New York Times* (February 5, 1975):

The myth that Army service can help by training deprived Blacks for civilian jobs is little borne out by the facts. Usable civilian skills are least likely to be acquired in the ground combat forces, where most Blacks are, while they are under-represented in the technical and support services, a vastly better training ground.

Racial Mix and Allegiance of Troops

Some observers have watched the increase in the proportion of Blacks in the armed services with trepidation, questioning whether black troops might be willing to obey orders in certain domestic situations—a suggestion that is vigorously rejected by many members of the black community. Binkin and Eitelberg (1982, p. 156) remark that this thought cannot be dismissed out of hand, citing the British policy of not sending Irish regiments into Northern Ireland during the 1970s as an example of withholding troops that share an ethnic bond with an adversary. In foreign involvements, with the exception of an unlikely American intervention on the side of Whites against Blacks, it seems improbable that black allegiance would be tested (for a comparative reference, see Enloe 1980).

Special Race Relations Programs in the Armed Forces

Recognizing the importance of complaints of underrepresentation and overrepresentation of minorities in the armed forces, with allegations of increases in racial tensions and management problems, the Department of Defense has established special race relations programs to reduce racial conflict (Hope 1979, pp. 64–65, 86, 106; U.S. Army Research Institute for the Behavioral and Social Sciences 1975a).

CHAPTER 11

Racial and Cultural Minorities and the American Political and Legal Processes

The study of the place of racial and cultural minorities in the social structure must give careful attention to the ways in which these groups influence and are influenced by political decisions and legal processes. In this chapter, our concern will be to compare the status of racial and cultural minorities with that of the majority population in voting, office-holding, and political influence in American life.

Political Activity of Blacks

Legal Status of Blacks before 1900

In the matter of voting, even free Blacks were disfranchised throughout the South and in most of the North and West as of 1860. New England, with the exception of Connecticut, permitted Blacks to vote. New York required Blacks who wished to vote to own a certain amount of property, a qualification that did not hold for Whites. Wisconsin granted the suffrage to Blacks in 1849. Other northern and border states disfranchised them as follows: Delaware in 1792, Kentucky in 1799, Maryland in 1809, Connecticut in 1818, New Jersey in 1820, Virginia in 1830, Tennessee in 1834, North Carolina in 1835, and Pennsylvania in 1838. Other

states in the South and West did not permit Blacks to vote (Mangum 1940, pp. 371–372).

After the adoption in 1865 of the Thirteenth Amendment abolishing slavery and involuntary servitude, except as a punishment for crime after due conviction, special restrictive legislation was enacted in the southern states. These laws, which became known as the Black Codes, virtually reintroduced the slave codes (laws pertaining to slaves in states of the Old South in the antebellum period, including discipline by masters, property-holding by slaves, mating, criminal justice, education, and use of the courts). The Black Codes covered apprenticeship, labor contracts, migration, vagrancy, civil and legal rights (Frazier 1957b, pp. 126–127). The passage of the Black Codes brought about the adoption of the Fourteenth Amendment containing the famous statement:

No State shall make or enforce any law which shall abridge the privileges or immunities of citizens of the United States; nor shall any State deprive any person of life, liberty, or property, without due process of law; nor deny to any person within its jurisdiction the equal protection of the laws.

The Fifteenth Amendment—"The right of the citizens of the United States to vote shall not be denied or abridged by the United States or by any State on account of race, color, or previous condition of servitude"—was also a reaction to the Black Codes, as was the federal Civil Rights Act of 1875. Blacks were elected to Congress for the first time during the forty-first session (1870–71). H. K. Revels of Mississippi came to fill the senate seat of Jefferson Davis; Jefferson F. Long was a representative from Georgia. From 1870 to 1901, twenty blacks were seated as representatives and two as senators. The largest number elected for any one Congress during these 30 years was seven (1876–1877).

Many interesting developments occurred during the Reconstruction period following the Civil War. The famous "Bargain of 1876," however, restored white supremacy to the South. The Republicans agreed not to oppose the election of Democrats to state office in South Carolina, Louisiana, and Florida and to withdraw troops from these states; the Democrats agreed to hand Hayes the presidency that Tilden had won. The bargain carried with it the nullification of the Civil War amendments insofar as Blacks were concerned. From then on Blacks were to be "eliminated from politics" (McWilliams 1951, p. 265; Woodward 1955). The Civil Rights Act was declared unconstitutional in 1883, and soon thereafter the southern states began to enact segregative legislation.

The Disfranchisement and Reenfranchisement of Blacks

To assure the permanent elimination of Blacks from political affairs in the South, various devices were invented. "Grandfather clauses" were included in a number of disfranchising constitutions adopted by southern states in the 1890s. The Louisiana constitution of 1898 provided that one might register permanently before September 1, 1898, if he was entitled to vote in any state on January 1, 1867, or if he was as the son or grandson of a person so entitled and 21 years of age or over in 1898. North Carolina included a "grandfather clause" in her revised statutes of 1905. These clauses excluded Blacks from voting while permitting white persons of all kinds to vote. The United States Supreme Court held these clauses to be unconstitutional in 1915.

Between 1889 and 1908, ten southern states (Alabama, Arkansas, Florida, Louisiana, Mississippi, North Carolina, South Carolina, Tennessee, Texas, and Virginia), through constitutional provision or statutory law, adopted a poll tax requirement for voting. North Carolina eliminated the poll

tax from her voting requirements in 1920 and later four other states eliminated this qualification. The tax existed in five states—Alabama, Mississippi, Arkansas, Texas, and Virginia until 1964, when the required 38 states had ratified an amendment to the Constitution that would prohibit such taxes as requirements for voting in a federal election. In a test case of the Twenty-fourth Amendment, the Supreme Court unanimously struck down a Virginia law requiring voters in federal elections to pay a poll tax or file a certificate of residence. On March 24, 1966, the Court ruled unconstitutional Virginia's poll tax law on state elections. Other states affected by this ruling were Alabama, Mississippi, and Texas.

Another device for disfranchising Blacks was the white primary. Since nomination in the Democratic primary usually was equivalent to election in the South, exclusion from the primary election meant the removal of Blacks from participation in the democratic process. In 1923 Texas passed the first white primary law, in which it was stated that "in no event shall a Negro be eligible to participate in a Democratic party primary election held in the state of Texas." This statute came to the Supreme Court in 1927 in *Nixon* v. *Herndon* (273 U.S. 536), and the Court ruled that it violated the equal protection clause of the Fourteenth Amendment. A new statute was passed empowering every political party in the state through its executive committee "to prescribe the qualifications of its own members" and permitting it to determine "who shall be qualified to vote or otherwise participate in such political party." The state executive committee quickly adopted a resolution which read, "All white Democrats who are qualified under the Constitution and laws of Texas and none others are to be allowed to participate in the primary elections." By a vote of five to four the Court held the second Texas law unconstitutional (*Nixon* v. *Condon*, 286 U.S. 73, 1932). The state Democratic convention then voted to exclude all but Whites from the primary. In 1935, the Supreme Court held that a vote of the state convention of a political party to restrict participation in the primary of that party did not violate the Fourteenth and Fifteenth amendments, provided the expenses of such primaries were paid by the party and not by the state.

On April 3, 1944, the Supreme Court reversed its 1935 ruling on the white primary. The court held that when primaries become a part of the machinery for choosing state and national officials, the same tests for discrimination apply to a primary as to a general election.

In 1898, the Supreme Court had held that Mississippi's requirement that electors be able to read any section of the state constitution or to understand it when read did not, on its face, discriminate between the races and did not violate the equal protection clause of the Fourteenth Amendment. However, state and federal courts placed limitations on the use of literacy tests as a qualification for voting. After 1949, registrars were no longer legally free to ask any questions they desired. In the case of *Davis* v. *Schnell* (1958) a three-judge federal district court held unconstitutional the Alabama law requiring a prospective elector to be able to understand and explain any article of the Constitution of the United States.

The Civil Rights Act of 1964 prohibited registrars from applying different standards to white and black voting applicants and from disqualifying applicants because of inconsequential errors on their forms. It required that literacy tests be in writing and that any applicant desiring one be given a copy of the questions and his answers. A basic feature of the 1964 law was its provision of a statistical formula to define discrimination. This provision made it unnecessary to bring a particular county official to trial and convince a judge of his misconduct. According to the law, a state or county was practicing discrimination if *both* of these conditions were present: (1) less than 50 percent of the voting-age population was registered as of November, 1964, or voted in the presidential election of that year and (2) any "test or device" was required of prospective voters. The phrase "test or device" was defined to mean: "any requirement that a person as a prerequisite for voting or registration for voting: (1) demonstrate the ability to read, understand, or interpret any matter; (2) demonstrate any educational achievement or his knowledge of any particular subject; (3) possess good moral character; or (4) prove his qualification by the voucher of registered voters or members of any other class."

To overcome the ineffectiveness of Title I (Voting) of the 1964 Civil Rights Act, Congress enacted the Voting Rights Act of 1965. The two basic features of the 1965 law are: (1) the suspension of a variety of tests and devices that have been used to deny citizens the right to vote because of race or color and (2) provision for the appointment of federal examiners to list voters in those areas where tests and devices have been suspended.

The Voting Rights Act of 1965 provided for a "freeze" on state voting requirements for five years. That law provides also for the appointment of federal examiners in those counties where local officials refuse to comply, or do not expand their facilities and working hours to accommodate the new black applicants. The Attorney General was given virtually unlimited discretion in the assignment of registrars. By June, 1967, federal examiners had been sent to a total of 60 counties: 13 in Alabama, 4 in Georgia, 9 in Louisiana, 32 in Mississippi, and 2 in South Carolina. In June, 1970, the 1965 law was amended and extended for five years, and in June 1982 it was extended, with minor modifications, for twenty-five years.[1]

The effects of the Voting Rights Act of 1965 are seen in some before-and-after figures. In Alabama as a whole, only 23.6 percent of the voting-age Blacks were registered before the law was passed. This figure more than doubled within seven months, and by April, 1966, nearly half of the black adults in the state were registered. In Mississippi, only 6.7 percent of the black adults were registered in August, 1965. By 1968 the proportion was 59.4. In the six states wholly covered by the Voting Rights Act (Alabama, Georgia, Louisiana, Mississippi, South Carolina, and Virginia), black registration increased from 30.9 percent to 57 percent in three years. In 1968, white registration for these states was 79.2 percent of those of voting age (Wall 1969, p. 6). In these six states plus Texas, black voter registration increased between 1964 and 1980 from 1,294,000 to 2,895,000 (*The New York Times*, May 3, 1981, p. E2). These gains occurred despite poor compliance with the Voting Rights Act in some jurisdictions. The U.S. Civil Rights Commission has reported (*Civil Rights Update*, October, 1982) that in just three states (Alabama, Georgia, and Mississippi) 536 election law changes on the state or county level which should have been submitted for preclearance were not submitted.

Registration for Blacks in the 1982 congressional elections totaled 10.4 million persons; 7.6 million or 73 percent of those registered reported voting compared with 76 percent of registered Whites. The overall participation rate (number voting divided by the number of voting age persons)

---

[1] For a comprehensive report on the status of minority voting rights in jurisdictions covered by the provisions of the Voting Rights Act of 1965, as amended, see U.S. Commission on Civil Rights, The Voting Rights Act: Unfulfilled Goals, 1981c.

for Blacks was 43 percent and that of Whites was 50 percent (Bureau of the Census, 1983, p. 23). Table 11-1 shows the percent reported registered and reported voted, by citizenship status, according to race, Spanish origin, and age, in the election of November, 1980.

The substantial increase in the registration of black voters has become a challenge to the established Democratic organizations. One political observer commented (*The New York Times,* January 24, 1971, p. E10): "Realizing that without the black vote their preeminence is seriously jeopardized, many white political leaders have begun *counting* the black vote and consequently changing their tune."

Obstacles to Voting by Blacks

Although black citizens have registered in large numbers and constitute substantial portions of the electorate in the South, in many places barriers have continued to limit black participation in the electoral process. According to the Voter Education Project of Atlanta, obstacles to black voting in the South include: inconvenient hours and locations of registration facilities, a lack of minority

registrars and election board officials, uncooperative and hostile registrars, fear of economic retaliation, and the failure of local boards to appoint deputy registrars or other additional personnel to accommodate minority registration drives (Cleveland *Plain Dealer,* December 21, 1975, p. 4).

An important barrier to black voting is the at-large voting district. Where multiple districts within a county might permit a concentrated black population to elect a black representative to the county legislature, at-large county-wide voting enables the white majority to outvote the black minority for every legislative post. For constitutional challenges to such at-large electoral schemes to be successful, it has had to be shown that a particular system of voting had been created on the basis of race. From 1973 to 1980, the courts ruled that such intent could be inferred from an accumulation of various factors, including a history of official racial discrimination, particularly in registering and voting; a disproportionally low number of Blacks elected to office; a lack of responsiveness by elected officials to the needs of the black community; and election law rules requiring election by an absolute majority. On April 22, 1980, in the *City of Mobile* v. *Bolden,* the U.S. Supreme Court ruled that it is no longer sufficient to infer the intent to discriminate

Table 11-1. Percentage Reported Registered and Reported Voted, by Citizenship Status: November, 1980

Race, Spanish origin, and age	Percentage reported registered		Percentage reported voted	
	All persons	All persons, excluding, noncitizens[a]	All persons	All persons, excluding noncitizens[a]
Race				
White	68.4	70.8	60.9	63.1
Black	60.0	61.7	50.5	52.0
Spanish origin[b]	36.3	53.6	29.9	44.1
Age				
18 to 24 years	49.2	51.8	39.9	41.9
25 to 44 years	65.6	69.0	58.7	61.7
45 to 64 years	75.8	78.2	69.3	71.5
65 years and over	74.6	76.4	65.1	66.7
Total	66.9	69.7	59.2	61.7

Source: *Bureau of the Census, Voting and Registration in the Election of November 1980,* April, 1982, p. 5.
[a]Includes a relatively small percentage of persons (3 percent) with no report on citizenship status.
[b]Persons of Spanish origin may be of any race.

from the presence of such factors. According to this decision, plaintiffs will now have to prove that an at-large voting system was explicitly adopted or maintained for its adverse effect upon Blacks. Such proof was offered in a suit by eight black voters brought against Burke County, Georgia. In July, 1982, the Supreme Court ruled in their favor, holding that the election system "was maintained for the invidious purpose of diluting the voting strength of the black population" (Cleveland *Plain Dealer,* July 2, 1982, p. 1). This ruling weakens the restrictive implications of the *Bolden* decision. It is the 1982 renewal of the Voting Rights Act, however, which seems more likely to protect the rights of black voters.

Some jurisdictions have tried to annex predominantly white areas or areas zoned for middle-income housing for the purpose of decreasing minority voting in the annexing jurisdiction. Other jurisdictions have refused to annex predominantly minority areas when these areas have requested annexation. Also, jurisdictions have drawn boundaries in order to dilute minority voting strength or have designed redistricting plans in which minority strength in the new districts is less than in existing districts (U.S. Commission on Civil Rights, September, 1981, p. 90).

Characteristics of Black Voting

Among other characteristics of black voting, three are of special interest: Blacks tend to register and vote as Democrats, to vote in a bloc, and to vote at a relatively high rate once they are registered. In 1976, 83 percent of the 8.7 million Blacks who were registered actually went to the polls, compared with 89 percent among Whites. The showing of Blacks who actually voted in comparison to the number eligible to vote, registered and unregistered, is poorer. The percentage in 1964 was 58, compared with 61 among Whites, but in 1976, only 49 percent of all eligible black voters actually cast votes, compared with 61 percent of eligible white voters. In 1980, the percentages were 61 for Whites and 51 for Blacks. In 1982, however, the percentage of black voters was higher in some districts than the percentage of white voters. Voter participation among Blacks tends to increase as educational levels rise. In 1972, approximately 55 percent of Blacks with four years of high school voted; the rate was 80 percent for those with four

years or more of college (National Urban League 1980, p. 210).

At the state and local level, the tendency of black voters to support individual candidates rather than political parties has benefited Republican moderates and liberals. Following Watergate, black voters saved a number of moderate and liberal Republican incumbents from defeat in the election of 1974. In 1978, the black vote remained heavily Democratic, but it gave significant support, and in some instances the margin of victory, to Republican candidates for Congress in Pennsylvania, Illinois, Michigan, Tennessee, and Arkansas (Williams 1979, pp. 65–66).

The Significance of Black Voting

Two generations ago, black political behavior differed little from white political behavior in the North. Blacks voted in almost the same proportion as Whites, they were not tied to one party, and they went along with the machines rather than with third parties and reformers. However, Blacks carefully appraised the attitudes of candidates and parties toward their group. Professional politicians quickly realized the potentialities in the black vote and organized Blacks as they had formerly done with the Irish, the Germans, the Poles, and other newcomers to city life. Blacks developed their own ward machines and in return demanded concessions for support.

From the beginning of the New Deal until 1952, 75 to 80 percent of the black voters cast their ballots for Democratic presidential candidates. Some change occurred in the elections of 1952, and in 1956 the black vote dropped to between 60 and 65 percent. In 1960, it is estimated that nearly 80 percent of the black voters voted for John F. Kennedy. That vote played a crucial role in the election. In 1964, almost all southern black precincts supported Lyndon B. Johnson. Some heavily black precincts in New York, Pennsylvania, Maryland, and Ohio showed a better than 90 percent vote for Johnson. Blacks were crucial in swinging Virginia, Tennessee, and Florida back to the Democrats after several years of Republican control (*The New York Times,* November 4, 1964, p. 26). Although the Nixon–Agnew ticket won the 1968 presidential election, it received 10 percent or less of the black vote.

In the presidential election of 1976, black voters apparently contributed to Jimmy Carter's margin of victory in all states of the Deep South except Virginia. In Georgia, Whites and Blacks both favored Carter. In the other southern states, about 55 percent of the white voters preferred Gerald R. Ford, but more than 95 percent of the black voters favored Carter. In earlier years, the almost unanimous vote for Carter would not have mattered, but in 1976, when 63 percent of registered voters, black and white, voted, it was highly significant (*The New York Times,* November 14, 1976). Of the black voters, 82 percent voted for Carter, both in 1976 and in 1980.

In November 1984, exit polls showed that nationwide 88 percent of Blacks voted for Mr. Mondale; 65 percent of Whites voted for Mr. Reagan. In the South, Mr. Reagan got 71 percent of the white vote; 90 percent of Blacks voted for Mr. Mondale. Approximately 9 percent fewer white southerners voted for the Democratic ticket in 1984 than in 1980. Blacks provided more than half of the Mondale vote in the South. Some observers believe that increases in black registration and turnout in 1984 were at least offset by a movement of Whites into the Republican column (*Washington Post,* November 8, 1984, p. 46; November 12, 1984, p. A16.)

The black vote is important to black political aspiration, and not only in presidential election years. More than 15 million blacks are of voting age and represent 10 percent of the national electorate. For the most part, they reside in major metropolitan centers in states with large blocs of electoral votes. Blacks constitute at least 10 percent of the voting-age population in 18 states; at least 20 percent of that population in 89 cities with a population of 50,000 or more; and 50 percent or more of that group in 103 counties, mainly in the South. Blacks are, therefore, in a position to exert considerable influence at the ballot box. A high registration rate causes political candidates to take black views into account (National Urban League 1979, p. 55).

Although the number of Blacks actually voting may not be particularly high in some elections, it has been sufficient to provide the margin of victory for some candidates. Several examples of the potential of the black vote are seen in the elections of 1978. In Mississippi, Mayor Charles Evers of Fayette ran as an independent for the seat vacated by Senator James O. Eastland. Evers lost, but he

received 95 percent of the black vote and 23 percent of the total vote, thus taking enough votes from the Democratic candidate to permit Mississippi Republicans to win their first statewide election since the Reconstruction period. In Arkansas, the Republican candidate in the Second Congressional District received 44 percent of the black vote and won by 3,000 votes. In New York, Governor Hugh L. Carey won reelection by 283,000 votes, with 83 percent of the black vote. In Florida, Governor Robert Graham defeated his Republican opponent by 282,000, with 84 percent of the black vote (*The New York Times,* April 1, 1979, p. E5).

In Houston, Blacks played an important role in the election of a white mayoral candidate, Kathy Whitmore, who received more than 90 percent of the black vote in the November 17, 1981, mayoral election (*The New York Times,* November 22, 1981, p. E5). Also in the fall of 1981, black voters helped to reelect Mayor Maurice Ferre in Miami, and in Birmingham, Mayor Richard Arrington was reelected due to a strong black turnout. The black vote also helped elect Charles Robb as governor of Virginia in 1981. In 1982, a record black vote was an important factor in the defeat of Mayor Edward Koch in New York's gubernatorial contest (Cleveland *Plain Dealer,* September 14, 1983). Black turnout was a decisive factor in the defeat of four conservative Republican incumbents in Congress in the November, 1982 election: Albert Lee Smith of Alabama, Eugene Johnston of North Carolina, John Napier of South Carolina, and Robert Daniel of Virginia (*The New York Times,* November 14, 1982, p. E6).

The changing composition of a number of central cities in the United States has given Blacks an opportunity to obtain control of urban political systems. Nine cities—Washington, D.C., Gary, Atlanta, Detroit, Newark, Birmingham, New Orleans, Baltimore, and Richmond—now have a majority black population. Several other major cities have populations that are one-third or more black. In Chicago, the black population increased from one-seventh to one-third of the total population from 1950 to 1972, and to 40 percent in 1980. These rises in numbers have enabled an increasing number of black politicians to win political office.

Political observers have often assumed that the vote will automatically give southern Blacks influence over public policy commensurate with their numbers. They have held that when Blacks voted in substantial numbers, southern state and local officials would respond to black demands or suffer at the polls. In this view, by means of political leverage, governments will be forced to eliminate many types of discrimination.

Whether in the North or the South, the exercise of the franchise by Blacks or other racial and cultural minorities will not guarantee equal justice under the law. As Burns (1981, p. 228) comments: "It will help, but since this group is, by definition, in the minority, it does not have the numbers to control the politics of rights." Even with the use of the franchise and increased representation in government, "minorities must depend on just laws and the Constitution fairly enforced to avoid Toqueville's 'tyranny of the majority.'"

Black Elected Officials

Between Reconstruction and the mid-fifties, Blacks held only two seats in Congress—for New York's Harlem and Chicago's South Side. The change in the pattern came when the civil rights movement of the 1960s resulted in new antidiscrimination laws and stronger political consciousness among black voters. Blacks won seats from various places across the country, and in 1972, the South elected its first Blacks to Congress in almost a hundred years—Andrew Young from Atlanta and Barbara Jordan from Houston. By 1982, 21 Blacks sat in the House of Representatives. Few Blacks, however, have been able to win districts with a majority of white voters. Of the 15 voting members of the 1980 Black Caucus, only one, Representative Ronald V. Dellums, Democrat of California, represented a district that is less than 40 percent black.

In 1967, Carl Stokes (Cleveland) and Richard Hatcher (Gary, Indiana) became the first Blacks to become mayors of major American cities. By 1977, there were 152 black mayors, a large number of them in small southern cities. Sixteen (15 men and 1 woman) were mayors of cities with populations of 50,000 or more, and 40 were in cities with white majorities. At that time, major cities with black mayors included Washington, D.C., Los Angeles, Detroit, Newark, Gary, and Atlanta. Harold Washington was elected mayor of Chicago and Wilson Goode in Philadelphia in 1983.

In 1974, three Blacks became state executives, including two lieutenant governors, making a total of seven Blacks chosen for political office by state-wide electorates (Massachusetts, Michigan, Pennsylvania, Colorado, Connecticut, and two in California).

Table 11-2 shows the number of black elected officials by office from 1970 to 1979 by regions and states of the United States. The figures for July, 1981, are: total, 4,890; United States Congress and state legislatures, 326; city and county offices, 2,832; law enforcement, 526; and education, 1,206 (*Statistical Abstract 1981*, p. 495). By November, 1982, the number of Blacks in state legislatures had increased to 337 (*The New York Times*, November 14, 1982, p. E6). According to the Joint Center for Political Studies, 4,912 black elected officials held office in 1980 in 43 states, the District of Columbia, and the Virgin Islands. Of that number, 976 (20 percent) were women (Cleveland *Plain Dealer*, December 17, 1980).

The principal interacting factors in the increased number of elected black officials in the United States seem to be: (1) the Voting Rights Act of 1965, (2) voter education and registration campaigns, (3) more black candidates seeking office, (4) perception by Blacks of enhanced chances for success in the election of black candidates, (5) the black power movement, and (6) United States Supreme Court decisions in the reapportionment cases forcing state legislators to draw congressional district lines so that Blacks will have a better opportunity to send representatives from their communities to the U.S. House of Representatives.

The number of black elected officials in the South increased 19 percent in the 1980 election, but Blacks are still underrepresented in the region (*The New York Times*, April 26, 1981, p. 16). Blacks constitute about 20 percent of the South's population but hold only 3 percent of the region's 79,000 elective offices. In 1981, 607 blacks served as mayors, county commissioners, state legislators, and U.S. Representatives in 11 southern states. State senators in the South now number 15 out of 457 (about 3 percent). Of 1,352 state representatives in the region, about 8 percent (112) are Black.

Most elected officials in the South are not mayors. Typically, they are members of a white-controlled city council, county board, or state legislature. Although they are not without power, most find it necessary to select the right time to grant or withhold support on issues that closely divide the white majority. State Senator Julian Bond of Atlanta considers the black caucuses that have

Table 11-2. Black Elected Officials, by Office, 1970 to 1979, and by Regions and States, 1979

Year, region, and state	Total	U.S. and State legislatures[a]	City and county offices[b]	Law enforcement[c]	Education[d]
1970 (Feb.)	1,472	182	715	213	362
1972 (Mar.)	2,264	224	1,108	263	669
1973 (Apr.)	2,621	256	1,264	334	767
1974 (Apr.)	2,991	256	1,602	340	793
1975	3,503	299	1,878	387	939
1976 (Apr.)	3,979	299	2,274	412	994
1977 (July)	4,311	316	2,497	447	1,051
1978 (July)	4,503	316	2,595	454	1,138
1979 (July)	4,584	315	2,647	486	1,136
Northeast	541	55	193	80	213
North Central	985	89	542	105	249
South	2,768	147	1,828	233	560
West	290	24	84	68	114
Ala.	208	16	131	39	22
Alaska	2	—	1	—	1
Ariz.	13	2	4	2	5
Ark.	226	4	136	1	85
Calif.	227	[e]12	63	55	97
Colo.	16	3	4	5	4

State	Total	U.S. and State leg.[a]	City and county offices[b]	Law enforcement[c]	Education[d]
Kansas	28	5	14	1	8
Ky.	76	4	47	11	14
La.	334	10	197	39	88
Maine	3	—	3	—	—
Md.	85	[g]21	52	10	2
Mass.	17	6	3	—	8
Mich.	272	[h,j]18	118	36	100
Minn.	8	1	1	3	3
Miss.	327	6	203	56	62
Mo.	132	[g]16	92	12	12
Nebr.	7	1	1	—	5
Nev.	7	3	1	1	2
N.H.	1	1	—	—	—
N.J.	143	5	77	—	61
N. Mex.	3	—	2	—	1
N.Y.	195	[h]18	32	35	110
N.C.	240	4	168	7	61
Ohio	177	[g]13	100	20	44
Okla.	71	4	48	1	18
Oreg.	6	1	2	2	1
Pa.	129	[g]17	45	44	23

State	Total	[a]	[b]	[c]	[d]
Conn.	46	7[f]	28	1	10
Del.	14	3	9	—	2
D.C.	247	1[g]	238	—	8
Fla.	91	4	71	7	9
Ga.	237	23	162	8	44
Hawaii	1	1	—	—	—
Ill.	276	24[h]	167	25	60
Ind.	62	7	42	5	8
Iowa	6	—	—	1	5
R.I.	7	1	5	—	1
S.C.	222	13	125	22	62
Tenn.	109	13[g]	76	7	13
Tex.	174	15[g]	70	19	70
Va.	88	5	79	4	—
Wash.	15	2	7	3	3
W.Va.	19	1	16	2	—
Wis.	17	4[i]	7	2	4

As of July 1979, no Black elected officials had been identified in Idaho, Montana, North Dakota, South Dakota, Utah, Vermont, or Wyoming.

Source: Joint Center for Political Studies, Washington, D.C., *National Roster of Black Elected Officials*, Table 848. Bureau of the Census, *Statistical Abstract of the United States*, 1980, p. 514.

—Represents zero. [a]Includes elected State administrators and directors of State agencies. [b]County commissioners and councilmen, mayors, vice mayors, aldermen, regional officials, and other. [c]Judges, magistrates, constables, marshals, sheriffs, justices of the peace, and other. [d]College boards, school boards, and other. [e]Includes 3 U.S. Representatives and 1 State Superintendent of Public Instruction. [f]Includes 1 State Treasurer. [g]Includes 1 U.S. Representative. [h]Includes 2 U.S. Representatives. [i]Includes 1 Comptroller. [j]Includes 1 Secretary of State.

been organized in southern capitals a sign of growing maturity among black elected officials. Bond says that black politicians at all levels—state, city and county—realize increasingly that patient labor and shrewd compromise are essential to success, not the confrontation and unyielding militancy of the 1960s (*The New York Times,* November 6, 1977, p. E3).

Black political participation in the South has been manifest in the takeover of political units larger than municipalities, specifically in counties with strong black majorities. Heavy migration to the cities has reduced the number and strength of such majorities, but where they exist they offer Blacks the potential for maintaining communities in which they have some self-determination and economic independence. Since the counties where Blacks are in the majority are almost always the poorest counties in their states, the task of developing them is difficult. Perhaps the most notable example of such counties is Green County, Alabama, where a full slate of black officials was elected in the middle 1970s (Browne 1975, p. 74).

In Florida, according to former governor Reuben Askew, Blacks, Hispanics, and other minorities constitute less than 2 percent of all elected officials despite the fact that minorities make up a quarter of the state population. There are no members of minority groups among the statewide elected officials, and among the 160 members of the state legislature, there are only five Blacks and one Hispanic (Cleveland *Plain Dealer,* September 9, 1980, p. A23).

Although there are instances of racial intimidation, a lack of motivation and organization is largely responsible for the relatively few offices held by Blacks in the South. Mayor A. J. Cooper, of Pritchard, Alabama, the chairman of the National Conference of Black Mayors, said that Blacks lost some of their zeal after the first election victories of the 1960s. According to Cooper, "black folks suddenly discovered that politics is grinding work that requires tremendous organization. You have to find candidates, register voters, get them to turn out, then produce results that will please people whose expectations were probably unrealistic to begin with" (*The New York Times,* November 6, 1977, p. E3).

Black Officials in Northern Cities. The role of Blacks in the political life of New York City has increased in recent years and will continue to increase, but it will never be as great as in some smaller cities. Blacks make up about one-fifth of the city's population. No Black has been a serious contender for the mayoralty in New York. A Black running for mayor could not base his campaign wholly or even primarily upon the black community, although the combined backing of Blacks and Hispanics would provide a significant base.

In Detroit in 1977, there were four Blacks on the nine-member City Council, compared with one ten years earlier. Seven of the 13 independent school board members were black; a decade earlier, there were two out of seven. The police department was 21 percent black, against about 5 percent in 1970. The positions of mayor and county sheriff were held by Blacks, which was not the case ten years earlier when Blacks comprised roughly 35 percent of the population as against 50 percent in 1977 (*The New York Times,* July 24, 1977, p. 31).

In California in 1980, Blacks comprised 7.6 percent of the population; the census figure for those of Spanish origin was 19 percent. In Los Angeles, 17 percent are black, and 29 percent of the city's residents identify themselves as of Spanish origin. In 1981, Thomas Bradley, a black politician, won a third term as mayor (he was defeated, however, in a close race for United States Senator in 1982). Two black politicians have won statewide offices. Wilson Riles was elected Superintendent of Public Instruction in 1970 and reelected in 1974 and 1978. State Senator Mervyn Dymally was elected Lieutenant Governor in 1974 and later became a member of the United States House of Representatives. Two of California's state senators are black. Willie L. Brown, Jr., is Speaker of the Assembly, where five others of the eighty members are black. Mayor Lionel Wilson of Oakland is black, and there are many black county supervisors and city council members in the state (*The New York Times,* July 26, 1981).

Cole's study (1976, pp. 11–13) of black elected officials in New Jersey is illuminating. Sixteen cities in New Jersey with populations of twenty-five thousand or more include substantial black populations, at least 15 percent of each city's total. These cities are governed from 123 elected executive and legislative offices, and during 1972, 135 individuals filled these offices. Thirty-one Blacks served, but there were never more than 27 at one time. Cole draws these conclusions, among others, from his study (pp. 232–34): (1) black elected officials responded to the needs of the black community as well as to those of their entire city; (2)

these officials retained the loyalty of the black citizenry while gaining increasing support from the white electorate; (3) white elected officials were divided over whether black officials placed the interest of Blacks ahead of the city's; (4) the relationships between white and black officials were devoid of racial implications in most communities most of the time. Cole concluded that whether black officials could continue to satisfy both communities was uncertain. In these cities much will depend on whether the economic and social gaps between the races cease to converge, whether the quality of the first wave of black officials persists among their successors, and whether the interests of the two races come to be seen as inherently conflicting.

Black Mayors in Detroit and Atlanta: A Comparison. Eisinger (1980, pp. 5–6) calls the election of black mayors in Detroit, Atlanta, and elsewhere, the key event in "ethnoracial transition." The capture of the mayoralty by a member of a formerly subordinate ethnic group does not mean, however, that all of the old patterns of influence and power have inevitably been altered.

Demographics are important in race relations. Detroit grew rapidly around World War I, drawing mainly on European immigrant labor until the 1920s and then on increasing numbers of Blacks from the South. The city's black population doubled between 1940 and 1950, and the proportion of Blacks in the city grew from 16 percent in 1950 to a majority in 1973. As Detroit began to lose population in the 1950s, Atlanta began to grow rapidly as a regional center. Table 11-3 shows the black population growth in these two cities between 1910 and 1975.

The response to black rule among the elites in the white communities of Detroit and Atlanta indicates that important resources controlled by Whites have been available to the city and city government under black mayors as they were under white rule. Some politically prominent Whites withdrew from politics, but the adjustments that were made in the legal, business, and financial sectors were predominantly cooperative in nature. Few people or firms suggested leaving the city or trying to challenge the new mayors electorally or of obstructing their administrations.

Black representation in all appointive positions in both cities prior to 1973 fell far short of reflecting their proportion in the population. Both in Detroit and in Atlanta, the black mayors asked black men and women to fill nearly half of the appointive positions in city government. Increased affirmative action on appointive positions in city government was considered important to ensure the representation of black interests, but also to create job opportunities for Blacks in city agencies (Eisinger 1980, pp. 159–162).

Ethnoracial transitions in the United States do not result in drastic transformations of the socio-economic-political structure. Given the limits of politics in America, city governments, or other governments, probably cannot put into effect policies that will deal quickly with such large problems as poverty, discrimination, unemployment, and housing. This does not mean that government can do nothing about these major problems, but that these problems are addressed through incremental policies aimed at the public and private sectors.

Black Power

In the mid-1960s, a political concept known as "black power" began to develop. Stokely Carmichael was one of the first to use the term. From 1966 on, the meaning of these words was widely debated. Carmichael used the term to mark a departure from the civil rights movement. He called upon black people to reject coalitions with Whites. This interpretation of black power was at once rejected by many civil rights leaders, including Roy Wilkins, Martin Luther King, Jr., and Bayard Rustin.

An influential advocate of the black power position said that it was concerned "with organizing the rage of black people and with putting new, hard questions and demands to white America" (Hamilton 1968, p. 79). Black power, Hamilton asserted, must deal with the alienation of black people and their distrust of the institutions of American society, work to build a new sense of community and of belonging, and work to establish new institutions that make participants out of people traditionally excluded from "the fundamentally racist processes of this country." The ghetto was looked at from the standpoint of "internal" and "external" problems. Internal problems were said to range from exploitative merchants, to absentee landlords, to inferior schools and arbitrary law enforcement, to the inability of black people to develop their own independent economic and political bases.

Some advocates of black power in those years took a "provincialistic" posture, advocating precedence to a quality—skin color—over actual performance of black Americans. They justified this position with the claim that racial discrimination

Table 11-3. Black Population Growth in Atlanta and Detroit

Year	Atlanta Total population (in thousands)	Total Black (in thousands)	Percentage Black	Detroit Total population (in thousands)	Total Black (in thousands)	Percentage Black
1910	154	51	33	495	5	1
1920	200	62	31	993	40	4
1930	270	90	33	1,568	120	7
1940	302	104	35	1,623	149	9
1950	331	121	37	1,849	303	16
1960	487	186	38	1,670	487	29
1970	496	255	51	1,511	660	44
1975 (est.)	470	265	56	1,385	770	56

Source: U.S. Bureau of the Census.

had so retarded black Americans that only a few Blacks could perform competitively with white Americans. Historic handicaps, it was said, can be overcome only by separation from Whites, at least temporarily, and by preferential treatment (Hamilton 1968, p. 81; Rohrer 1970, pp. 133–134).

At the height of the black power movement, it was assumed that white decision makers would yield nothing without a struggle and a confrontation by organized power. Black people, it was claimed, would make gains only through their ability to organize bases of economic and political power, that is, through boycotts, electoral activity, rent strikes, work stoppages, and pressure-group bargaining.

Black power advocates did not want Whites in decision making or leadership positions in the institutions of the black community. New welfare and development agencies, public and private, were criticized for ignoring existing black organizations and trying to do the job of delivering social services themselves. Comer (1968, p. 81) commented that often such agencies "have storefront locations and hire some 'indigenous' workers, but the class and racial gap is difficult to cross."

Black power advocates recognized the need for the help of Whites, mainly in technical and financial matters. In addition, Whites were frequently asked to attack white racism (prejudice). Specific objectives outside the black community that were suggested for concerned Whites included bringing pressure on local and national decision makers to adopt open housing policies and to expand job opportunities for minorities. Comer (1968, p. 83) said that white people of good will with interest, skills, and funds were needed and "contrary to the provocative assertions of a few Negroes—are still welcome in the Negro community." A related view held (Hamilton 1968, p. 81):

It is not necessary that Blacks create parallel agencies—political or economic—in all fields and places. Richard Hatcher did so in Gary, but he first had to organize black voters to fight the Democratic party machine in the primary. . . . At some point it may be wise to work within the existing agencies, but this must be done only from a base of independent, not subordinated, power.

Political Activity of Hispanic Americans

In general, political participation is closely related to education, and members of the linguistic minorities are poorly educated (with the exception of Japanese Americans, whose literacy rate is above the national average). In 1975, of all the Hispanic citizens over 25 years old, one-fifth had not completed the fifth grade (*The New York Times*, July 27, 1975).

Voting by Mexican Americans

Among both Anglos and Mexican Americans it is widely believed that Mexican Americans are indifferent to exercising their right to vote. Although they make up about 7 percent of the American population, they were only 2 percent of the voters in 1980, an election in which they divided their votes 54 percent for Carter, 36 percent for Reagan, and 7 percent for Anderson (they had split 75–24 for Carter and Ford in 1976 according to the *New York Times*–CBS Poll, November 9, 1980). In November, 1984, exit polls showed that Mr. Mondale received 56 percent of the Hispanic vote to 44 percent for Mr. Reagan. In Texas, Mexican Americans voted 79 percent for Mondale, compared with 21 percent for Reagan. In Los Angeles, Mondale received 68 percent of the votes of Mexican Americans; Reagan received 32 percent. In New York City, the predominantly Puerto Rican Hispanic population voted 67 percent for Mondale and 33 percent for Reagan. In Miami, Cuban American Americans voted 9-1 for Reagan. It is estimated that the Hispanic vote increased from 3.4 million in 1980 to 4.5 million in 1984 (*Washington Post*, November 8, 1984, p. 46).

An important factor diluting the potential political strength of Mexican Americans is the illegal status of some members of the group. A survey by Grebler, Moore, and Guzman (1970, p. 570) found however, that the rate of voter registration in Los Angeles County was within the range of United States norms and the actual voting rate was not much below average. Here, the effects of a relatively open environment were clearly evident. Lower rates of participation in San Antonio, Texas, reflect the greater isolation of Mexican Americans and their depressed economic status in that city.

Until a Texas law was declared unconstitutional by the United States Supreme Court in 1967, Texas citizens were required to pay a poll tax in order to vote. This tax applied to all citizens, but it was particularly harsh for Mexican Americans because most of them had relatively low incomes. When the tax was eliminated, the number of Mexican American voters increased rapidly. In 1966, only 53 percent of eligible Mexican Americans registered to vote; in 1968 and 1970, registration increased to 65 and 70 percent, respectively. Before 1970, the only citizens who could vote in California were those who were literate in English. This law disfranchised large numbers of Mexican Americans who were taxpayers, productive workers, and persons who accepted all the responsibilities of citizenship (de la Garzo 1979, p. 107).

Taking the Hispanic group as a whole, only 44.4 percent were registered for the 1972 presidential election compared with 73.4 percent for those of European origin. Also, Hispanic registration lags behind black registration nationally (*The New York Times,* July 27, 1975).

Voter participation rates among population groups are closely related to the proportion of the population that registers to vote. Not being a citizen is a strong barrier to registration, especially for persons of Spanish origin. Table 11-1 shows that the exclusion of those identified as noncitizens (6.3 million) in computing voting and registration rates raises the registration rate for the nation from 67 to 70 percent and the voter participation rate from 59 to 62 percent. For persons of Spanish origin, however, the registration rate rose from 36 to 54 percent and the voter participation rate increased from 30 to 44 percent when the reported number of noncitizens are removed in calculating the voting rate (U.S. Bureau of the Census, April, 1982, p. 5).

One measure of Mexican American political power is seen in presidential politics. In 1960 Mexican Americans played an important role in the campaign, "Viva Kennedy," and in 1968 they provided the swing vote in carrying Texas for the Democratic candidate. In the presidential elections since that time, both political parties have tried to capture the Mexican American vote. Tactics at the national level now include the appointment of Mexican Americans to visible positions in the federal government (Pachon and Moore 1981, p. 123).

Obstacles to Mexican American Voting

Politicians have employed a variety of legal tactics to discourage Mexican American voting. Mexican Americans have been confronted with official indifference, insults, and embarrassments when attempting to vote. At times, they have had to risk economic retaliation in the form of loss of employment or of welfare benefits or food stamps when they have tried to vote. Such tactics were alleged to be widespread in Texas prior to the 1972 election. Gerrymandering and multiple-member districts are other devices used to dilute the voting strength of Mexican Americans. A city in which the minority is about to become a majority can annex a new territory from the suburbs; in 1972, San Antonio added additional white neighborhoods for that reason. At-large elections were designed originally to escape the corruption of machine politics, but in many cities of the Southwest at-large elections have served to decrease the probability of Mexican Americans winning local office. In such elections, all voters in the city vote for all councilmen, but in ward or district elections each ward or district nominates and elects its own candidates (*The New York Times,* July 27, 1975; de la Garzo 1979, pp. 107–108).

According to a 1979 report of the Federal Election Commission on the conduct of bilingual elections, local officials in parts of California and of the Southwest have provided little or no compliance with the 1975 amendments to the federal Voting Rights Act of 1965. Thirty states are affected by the law, which requires the holding of bilingual elections according to a formula worked out by the Justice Department that considers the number of non-English-speaking voters in each county as well as illiteracy rates and levels of participation in past elections. In some states, including New York, only a few counties are affected, but in Alaska and Texas all political jurisdictions are covered by the law (*The New York Times,* July 8, 1979, pp. 1, 17).

Four-fifths of the linguistic minorities in the United States are of Hispanic origin, and these minorities are most heavily concentrated in Texas, New Mexico, Arizona, Colorado, and California. Of the five states, only New Mexico had a bilingual election rule prior to 1975. Over all, the Federal Election Commission found California to have been "most responsive" to the law and Texas least, with the other three states next. Only half of the jurisdictions covered by the law said they had started special programs to register voters who could not speak English, and the Commission found that many of these programs were "modest efforts indeed." In one-fifth of the jurisdictions, the bilingual assistance required by the Justice Department seemed not to have been provided to voters at the polls, and in many places registration and voting materials printed in more than one language were not distributed within minority communities but could be obtained only at a central office. In nearly every case, the requirement for the availability of bilingual ballots was met (*The New York Times,* July 8, 1979, p. 17).

Mexican American Office Holders

For years, Mexican Americans were most likely to be chosen to serve on police advisory commissions, welfare advisory councils, and advisory committees on employment. Occasionally they were asked to serve on highway or public utilities commissions or on official bodies dealing with city planning, finance, or commerce. They were seldom appointed to positions in federal agencies. They have been more acceptable as the recipients of services in such departments as Health and Human Welfare and in the United States Commission on Civil Rights than as administrators and technicians. Even as recipients, the Mexican American community has been frustrated by a middle layer of political power that may intervene between itself and federal programs. This layer consists of the networks of state and local officials that presumably are ready to carry out the national programs. When these offices are held by persons who are indifferent or hostile to a minority, those programs can be stymied or rejected (Galarza et al. 1969, pp. 53–54, 68–69).

In New Mexico, Chicano political participation along conventional lines is high compared to that in other states. Approximately one-third of the state legislature is Mexican American, and two Hispanic politicians, Dennis Chavez and Joseph Montoya, have served in the United States Senate. In 1966, Jerry Apodaca became New Mexico's first Spanish-named Governor in fifty years, and Raul Castro, a native of Mexico, was elected Governor of Arizona. In 1980, Mr. Castro resigned to become United States Ambassador to Argentina, and Mr. Apodaca was unable to run in the primary election because of a one-term limit in his state (Moore 1973a, p. 366). In November, 1982, Tony Anaya became the nation's only Hispanic governor by winning in New Mexico.

In small towns and villages of southern Colorado and northern New Mexico, some Chicanos have been active politically for many years. Where they have been in the majority, they have dominated the politics of the county or community. In Texas, however, even when Mexican Americans have been in the majority in rural areas and towns, they have seldom been able to control local governments. Until recently, they have met with little success politically in the cities of the Southwest and Midwest (Samora and Simon 1977, p. 196). In the spring of 1981, Henry Cisneros ran a pro-business campaign for mayor of San Antonio and won in a landslide—the first Mexican American in this century to head a major city (*The Wall Street Journal,* May 14, 1981).

In 1979–80, there were 1,138 Hispanic elected officials in Arizona and Texas, the two states covered under the preclearance provisions of the 1975 amendments to the Voting Rights Act of 1965. (Preclearance requires jurisdictions to prove to the

U.S. Department of Justice or the U.S. District Court for the District of Columbia that any changes in voting procedures are not discriminatory in purpose or effect.) Hispanics constitute approximately 13 percent of all elected officials in Arizona and 6 percent in Texas (U.S. Commission on Civil Rights, September 1981, pp. 16, 89).

If political effectiveness is judged by Mexican American representation in national and state legislatures, the contrast between California and Texas is striking. By all other indicators, the relative position of Mexican Americans is better in California than Texas, but the Texans have much better political representation than the Californians. This is true despite the fact that Chicanos have approximately equal numerical strength in the two states, despite the less open social system in Texas, and despite the much lower rate of voter participation as shown in surveys in San Antonio and Los Angeles. The higher proportion of Mexican Americans in the population of the Rio Grande valley of Texas than in any other region of California seems to explain most of the difference in political representation in the two states (Grebler et al. 1970, pp. 569–570).

In 1971, less than 2 percent of all elected and appointed officials in California were Mexican Americans. Until 1974, the state which is the most progressive for Chicanos had no Mexican American state senators and only five state representatives (de la Garzo 1979, pp. 109–110). There were, however, 15 mayors, 56 city councilmen, and 20 school board members throughout the state, mainly in southern California (Peñalosa 1973a p. 261). In contrast, the Texas legislature has had as many as ten Mexican Americans, and a Chicano was elected to the state senate (Grebler et al. 1970, p. 561). Table 11-4 shows the growth in the number of

Table 11-4. Mexican American State Legislators in Five Southwestern States, 1950–79

	1950	1960	1965	1974	1979
Arizona	0	4	6	11	11
California	0	0	0	8	11
Colorado	0	1	1	6	7
New Mexico	20	20	22	33	33
Texas	0	7	6	15	20
Total	20	32	35	73	82

Source: Harry P. Pachon and Joan W. Moore, "Mexican Americans." *Annals*, March, 1981, p. 123.

Mexican American officials at the state level from 1950 through 1979.

There were eight Hispanics in Congress in 1980, including two nonvoting representatives from the Virgin Islands and Puerto Rico. These eight Congressmen were reelected in 1982, and, with the three newly elected Hispanics, brought the total to 11—three from California, three from Texas, two from New Mexico, and one each from New York, Puerto Rico, and the Virgin Islands. Since there are 40 districts in eight states with Hispanic populations over 20 percent, and 9 over 50 percent, further increases in Hispanic representation are to be expected (Fessler 1982, p. 2805; Gurwitt 1982, pp. 2708–2709). In the November 1984 elections, Hispanics gained one seat in the House with the election of Albert G. Bustamante (D) in Texas.

Despite the small number of federal elected Mexican American officials, Chicano political activity at the national level is significant. Active organizations include the Mexican American Legal Defense and Education Fund (MALDEF), the National Council of La Raza, and the Southwest Voter Registration Project. In addition, the Congressional Hispanic Caucus and the National Association of Latino Elected and Appointed Officials (NALEO) seek to unite with other Hispanic groups, including Puerto Ricans and Cubans, to present Hispanic concerns at the national level (Pachon and Moore 1981, p. 123).

Voting by Puerto Ricans

Puerto Ricans constitute 10 percent or more of New York City's population, but their political strength is much less. One voter registration campaign showed that less than one third of the Puerto Ricans of voting age were registered. In New York City, the Puerto Rican population is spread throughout the city, but even in areas where Puerto Ricans comprise the majority, they have often seemed apathetic politically or have run opposing Puerto Rican candidates who split the bloc vote, allowing a minority of the voters to elect their candidate (Wagenheim 1975, pp. 42–43).

On the question of voter apathy among Puerto Ricans, it has been pointed out that most residents of voting age in New York were born and raised on the island and do not identify with local issues and candidates on the mainland. However, a second group, born in Puerto Rico but raised and educated in New York, has many members who are active in politics. A third group born in the United

States is, for the most part, too young to vote. Some observers expect that as these young people reach voting age, they will exhibit a different political style (Wagenheim 1975, p. 43).

In New Jersey, persons of Hispanic background make up about 10 percent of the population, but their share of political power has been extremely slight. The Byrne administration sought Hispanics for state offices in 1978 but encountered a considerable amount of factionalism. There seemed to be no one person or group that commanded the support of the Puerto Rican community, even in such heavily Hispanic counties as Hudson, Essex, Union, Bergen, and Passaic. Infighting has been common in Puerto Rican communities in New Jersey and frequently it has been difficult to get a coordinated effort behind a political candidate (*The New York Times*, July 16, 1978).

Puerto Rican Officials

The smaller number of Puerto Ricans in many districts in New York City, together with their low proportion of registered voters, left the community with no elected representatives in the city government in 1970, and with only four elected representatives in the New York State legislature, one Senator, and three Assemblymen. All of the Assemblymen came from the South Bronx. In 1980, Puerto Ricans had one Congressman, two New York State senators, and four members of the state assembly. In addition, they had one representative on the New York City Council (Fitzpatrick 1971, p. 58; Fitzpatrick and Parker 1981, p. 107).

In 1978, Nancy Muñiz was sworn in as a member of the Perth Amboy, New Jersey City Council, the first Puerto Rican member of the council and the first Puerto Rican woman to win elective office of any kind in the state. Besides her, there were only two other Hispanics in local government, Felix Montes, a Camden City Councilman since 1975, and Robert Sosa, a new member of Weehawken's governing commission. In 1975, the Reverend Fernando Colon had won a place on the county level when he was elected to the Hudson County Board of Chosen Freeholders. However, the form of government was changed ten months later and he declined to run again. Neither house of the state legislature has had a Hispanic member (*The New York Times*, July 16, 1978).

During the Carter administration (1977–1980), a large number of Puerto Ricans were appointed to important positions in the federal government, including chief of protocol for the United States at the United Nations; assistant secretary of education; and regional director in New York of the Department of Health and Human Services (Fitzpatrick and Parker 1981, p. 107).

Puerto Rican Organizations and Community Services

Fitzpatrick (1971, p. 62) says that it is difficult to see how the Puerto Rican community in New York City is structured and how it operates. Highly dispersed and comprised of a high proportion of poor people, the community has not yet developed the kinds of organizations which have been effective in older, more established groups. The Puerto Rican population in New York City is about 40 percent of the size of the entire population of Puerto Rico, but it lacks a visible leader. It is a community which has continually lost experienced persons to the island in return migration and has replenished its poorest ranks with newcomers from the island (Fitzpatrick 1971, pp. 62, 70–71).

One result of the relative lack of community organization among Puerto Ricans is that they have received little political patronage in New York City. In addition, Puerto Ricans, like other racial and cultural minorities, typically receive less in the way of community services than the majority population. If there are inadequate schools, libraries, garbage collection, police protection, or other services in a middle-class neighborhood, protests pour in by mail, phone, and personal visits and are supplemented by publicity in the press, pressure on politicians, and lawsuits. As Sowell (1975a, p. 195) points out, majority interests, and especially middle-class interests, tend to be taken care of first, even if this means that less will remain to take care of other citizens using the same public services. Disadvantaged minorities have fewer votes and lower voting records. Typically, they lack the knowledge and experience to use other forms of political pressure effectively.

In California, the Puerto Rican community is dispersed throughout the state. Although there are major concentrations of Puerto Ricans in the Los Angeles–Long Beach and San Francisco–Oakland areas, even there they are not concentrated in any one neighborhood or section. Puerto Rican organizations in California are structured along social club lines and are involved mainly in activities that support the culture and language. In most cases, the organizations are not directed toward solving community problems.

For the most part, Puerto Ricans in California have been ignored by public officials because, typically, Puerto Rican problems are lumped under the Hispanic category. Puerto Ricans are often mislabeled as Mexican aliens. Puerto Ricans in California claim that there is a lack of awareness by federal and state agencies as to the existence of a Puerto Rican population in the state. They allege that the nature of their daily concerns has not been understood and considered by public officials and agencies (U.S. Commission on Civil Rights, January 1980a, p. 19).

Within the Puerto Rican community in New York City, however, the second generation is developing a new style—a more assertive style politically. It seems likely that the members of this generation will differ in significant ways educationally, economically, and socially from the first (Fitzpatrick 1971, p. 72). Aspira, organized to promote educational opportunity and excellence, has become an important advocate on educational issues in New York and on the national level. The Puerto Rican Family Institute provides citywide family services in New York City. The Puerto Rican Legal Defense and Education Fund has been successful in the class-action suits in which it represents Puerto Ricans (Fitzpatrick and Parker 1981, pp. 107–108).

American Indian Political Activity

There are 315 Indian tribal groups in 26 states operating under treaty status as quasi-sovereign nations. The tribes range from the Navajos with some 130,000 population and 16 million acres of land to the Mission Creek of California with 15 members and a minute piece of land. More than half of the Native American population now resides in urban areas. The problem of defining *tribe* is, therefore, difficult. Traditionists favor the old type of organized band governed by open council instead of elected officials, one in which chiefs and medicine men dominate the tribal policies. In opposition to that viewpoint, at least in some areas, is the National Congress of American Indians, which represents officially elected tribal governments organized under the Indian Reorganization Act of 1934 as Federal corporations (Deloria 1971, pp. 499, 504).

Native Americans who live on or near reservations occupy a special wardship status. Their tribal governments have only limited control over tribal resources and affairs. Ultimately, authority is vested in the Secretary of the Interior, with local employees of the Bureau of Indian Affairs exercising lesser authority over many aspects of their lives. Reservation Indians, then, are subject to local, state, and federal governments, like everyone else, plus special institutions in the form of tribal governments. In addition, the Secretary of the Interior and the House Committee on Interior and Insular Affairs have decision-making power to intervene in the affairs of Indians (Jorgensen 1977, p. 187).

Krueger (1973, p. 79) has suggested major differences between the Indians' political behavior and that of residents of urban-industrial areas, using Pimas to exemplify Native Americans. Pima political life is said to be consensus-oriented, while urban-industrial life is majority-rule-oriented. Pimas emphasize persons; urban-industrial people are concerned with things. Political roles among the Pimas are functionally diffuse, whereas urbanites prefer specific political roles. Pima Indians have a fluid concept of leadership and authority, but urban people have assigned leadership. Politically, Pimas are nonhierarchical; the urban-industrial way is hierarchical. In this analysis, Pima and urban-industrial political norms are not held to be strictly dichotomous, but to tend toward different poles. In concrete cases, the tendency may seem to be reversed, but these cases are viewed as exceptions rather than the rule. Exceptions are increasing with the incorporation of individuals into the political life style of urban-industrial citizens.

American Indians governed themselves for centuries, but self-government on the European model originated in the Indian Reorganization Act of 1934. Reservations were encouraged to adopt constitutions and bylaws and to function as federal corporations for most purposes. Until the 1960s, most political activities on reservations consisted of local social and ceremonial occasions. When tribal governments became eligible to sponsor poverty programs, tribal governmental functions expanded greatly through federal funding. The idea of tribal sovereignty became more popular as Indians acquired greater political sophistication through dealing with state and federal agencies. Instead of creating corporations through the use of sovereign political powers, however, most tribes initially asked the tribal councils to act as the housing authority, the school board, the community action board, and other entities that were necessary to qualify for federal funds. With more experience and confidence, many tribes established separate organizations to carry out these functions for reservation residents (Deloria 1981, p. 146).

In recent years, the management of rich mineral resources has required tribal governments to seek expert advice. Dealing with these problems has led to a much wider awareness of economic and political factors than ever before. As Deloria (1981, p. 147) comments: "Whether Indians like it or not, they have become a part of the American political spectrum and must now learn how to exploit this status."

What has been called "the ethnic renascence" of Indians began a century ago but became a major movement about twenty years ago. In addition to reservation and band administrations, approximately one-hundred Indian political organizations have appeared in the United States and Canada. Many of these organizations publish periodicals, and together these publications form an information network. Important news items spread rapidly through this network, and this literature contributes to the integration of an Indian ethnic group (Price 1976, p. 269).

American Indian voting has lagged because of a lack of knowledge of issues and candidates, experience in the mechanics of voting, and effective organization. Largely because of the development and growth of their own organizations, tribal and intertribal, marked increases have been made in registering and voting on many Indian reservations and in urban areas during the past twenty-five years. Although the Amerian Indian population is small, the Indian vote has been a decisive factor in some elections in Montana, Idaho, Colorado, Washington, Oregon, North Dakota, Utah, Minnesota, Nebraska, and Alaska.

Minority–Majority Political Coalitions

Since minorities seldom are dominant numerically anywhere in the United States, north or south, usually it is necessary for them to enter into coalitions with at least some majority politicians and voters. Some of these coalitions are tacit, though unorganized, and often the alliances are conflicting. Nationally, organized labor may support civil

rights and income-transfer programs, but locally it may go along with segregated housing and economy in government. Religious groups are effective on voting rights but less effective on economic questions. Upper-class business interests may support black voting claims in southern cities and black-oriented public works programs in northern cities, but nationally they tend to oppose large-scale income redistribution (Wilson 1965, pp. 960–961).

Black Voters and Coalitions

In the 1960s and 1970s, it was not uncommon for black leaders and black social scientists to distinguish between political independence and coalition politics. It was said that the emphasis on independence was not just a matter of separatism, but a strategy that was in the tradition of American politics. As examples of this strategy, the Irish, Germans, and Italians were cited. It was claimed that Blacks needed first to consolidate; otherwise the relationship would be of the patron–client type. A political group seeking to enhance its influence must be able to punish an ally if the partner's word is not kept. Thus, if any ally does not support what your group is interested in, the next time your group does not support what the other party wants. In this view, a coalition must be based on issues, not just on organization. Examples of such issues are unemployment insurance, national health insurance, and social security benefits (Charles V. Hamilton, lecture at Oberlin College, April 30, 1979).

The precondition that Carmichael and Hamilton insisted upon before Blacks join coalitions with Whites—"The coalition deals with specific and identifiable—as opposed to general and vague—goals"—has largely been ignored by black elected officials in New Jersey. Cole (1976, pp. 54–55) found that these officials had successfully entered coalitions but that their programmatic aims were developed after they attained office.

Black-Hispanic Coalitions

In 1978, a meeting of leaders from twenty black, Mexican American, Puerto Rican, and Cuban civic organizations formed a coalition called the Working Committee on Concerns of Hispanics and Blacks (National Urban League 1980, p. 74). Issues suggested then and later around which Blacks and Hispanics could coalesce included unemployment, housing, and greater political representation. There are, however, forces at work within and between these populations, including feelings about alien workers, which promote suspicion and hostility and serve to retard political coalitions.

The Renewal in 1982 of the Voting Rights Act of 1965

The law of 1965 was renewed in 1970 and in 1975. The section that requires certain states with a history of discrimination to get advance approval from either the Justice Department or a federal court for any change in election rules was due to expire in August, 1982. That requirement, known as preclearance, was included in the law because southern states had found new forms of discrimination as fast as the courts ruled against the old ones. New discriminatory techniques have included the use of multimember legislative districts with at-large voting, racial gerrymandering designed to split up concentrations of black voting strength, annexing white suburbs to dilute the minority vote in a city, building low-income housing for Blacks just outside city limits in predominantly white counties so that the black vote is diluted, relocation of polling places, and changing from election to appointment of public officials (*The New York Times,* May 3, 1981, p. E2).

Features of the voting law other than preclearance are permanent and apply throughout the United States. They prohibit poll taxes and establish criminal penalties for anyone intimidating a person trying to vote.

The 1975 amendment extended the Voting Rights Act for another seven years and expanded its original coverage beyond black Americans to include language minority groups who could not speak or write English. This amendment required the following jurisdictions to "preclear" any election changes with the U.S. District Court in Washington, D.C., or with the U.S. Attorney General:

1. all state, county and local units of government in Texas
2. three counties and any governmental unit within those counties in California
3. all state, county, and local units of government in Arizona
4. one county and any governmental unit within that county in Colorado

5. three counties and any governmental unit within those counties in New Mexico

The nine states and scores of towns and counties around the nation that are required to get federal approval of proposed election-law changes are shown in Table 11-5.

The act also provided for bilingual elections in those states or counties that:

1. have 5 percent or more single language minority citizens of voting age (18 or over)
2. have an illiteracy (failure to complete fifth grade) rate for single-language minority that is higher than the national average (*Maldef Newsletter,* December, 1975, pp. 1–2).

In 1980, bilingual elections helped to increase Chicano voter registration 64 percent in Texas and 41 percent in Colorado. In the election of November, 1980, twenty percent more Hispanics took part than in the 1978 elections (*Maldef Newsletter,* Spring, 1980, p. 8).

On June 23, 1982, Congress passed a twenty-five year renewal of the Voting Rights Act of 1965.

Table 11-5. Jurisdictions Requiring Federal Approval of Election Law Changes

Alabama	Statewide
Alaska	Statewide
Arizona	Statewide
California	4 Counties
Colorado	1 County
Connecticut	3 Towns
Florida	5 Counties
Georgia	Statewide
Hawaii	1 County
Louisiana	Statewide
Massachusetts	9 Towns
Michigan	2 Townships
Mississippi	Statewide
New Hampshire	9 Towns, 1 Township
New Mexico	2 Counties
New York	3 New York City Counties
North Carolina	39 Counties
South Carolina	Statewide
South Dakota	2 Counties
Texas	Statewide
Virginia	Statewide
Wyoming	1 County

Minorities and the American Political and Legal Processes (Continued)

The Civil Rights of Minorities

Political rights, such as the right to vote, may be distinguished from civil liberties (freedom of speech, freedom of the press, freedom of assembly, religious freedom, the right to bear arms, the right to security against unreasonable searches and seizures, security against double jeopardy and excessive bail, the right to trial by jury, security against self-incrimination, and other rights mentioned in the Bill of Rights), and from civil rights. The term *civil rights* refers to rights to employment and to accommodations in hotels, restaurants, common carriers, and other places of public accommodation and resort.

Landmark Civil Rights Court Decisions: 1883–1956

The Civil Rights Act of 1875 was declared unconstitutional in 1883. This act, which provided that Blacks should have full equality in the use of theaters, hotels, and public conveyances, was part of the legislation designed to give the former slaves the status of free people. In 1896 the Court, in *Plessy* v. *Ferguson* (163 U.S., 537), confirmed a Louisiana law requiring racial segregation on common carriers. This ruling held that separate but equal accommodations did not violate the equal protection clause of the Fourteenth Amendment. Later this principle was extended to cover schools, parks, playgrounds, hotels, places of amusement, restaurants, and all types of public transportation facilities.

The "separate but equal" doctrine held that the separation of Blacks and Whites in public places prevented conflicts, insured better race relations, and was therefore a proper exercise of the state's police power. The northern states used their police powers through civil rights laws to forbid the segregation that southern states required. In several decisions the Court's interpretation of the Fourteenth Amendment was that "mathematical" equality in the treatment of segregated groups was not required, but only "substantial" equality. In some cases very little equality was considered to be "substantial."

By 1914, the Court had begun to tighten its definition of equality in segregation cases. In that year it decided that an Oklahoma law did not provide equal accommodations when railroads were allowed to offer sleeping, dining, and chair cars for Whites without furnishing them on demand for Blacks. In 1946, the Supreme Court ruled against segregation on interstate buses, and also in 1946, a federal court of appeals in the District of Columbia held unconstitutional the segregation of interstate black passengers by a railroad company. In the same year, a United States district court of southern California enjoined school authorities from establishing separate grade schools for "Mexicans."

In 1953, the Supreme Court upheld an 1873 law that required District of Columbia restaurants to serve persons of any race provided they are well behaved. During that year, the main theaters in downtown Washington began to admit Blacks, and two legitimate theaters soon opened on a nonsegregated basis. Later, neighborhood theaters began to admit Blacks.

The public school decision of the Supreme Court in 1954 (*Brown* v. *Board of Education of Topeka*) opened the way for further legal attacks on segregated facilities. On March 14, 1955, the United States Fourth Circuit Court of Appeals in Richmond, Virginia, reversed a decision of the federal district court at Baltimore which had held that segregation in public recreational facilities was permissible if both races were given equal facilities. The Circuit Court said that the May 17, 1954, decision of the Supreme Court "swept away" as well any basis for separating the races in public parks or playgrounds.

On July 14, 1955, the Circuit Court of Appeals in Richmond, Virginia, held in a Columbia, South Carolina, bus case that the Supreme Court decree outlawing public school segregation "should be applied in cases involving transportation." On June 5, 1956, a three-judge U.S. district court panel in Montgomery, Alabama, ruled segregation on Montgomery and Alabama public conveyances unconstitutional. The U.S. Supreme Court upheld this ruling on November 13, 1956.

Federal Civil Rights Legislation

The Civil Rights Act of 1957 was the first civil rights legislation to come from Congress since the Civil Rights Act of 1875, an interval of 82 years. This act gave the federal government power to protect and enforce the right to vote with court orders and provided for jury trials in certain federal court criminal cases. Within six years, thirty-seven voter registration cases were brought by the federal government under this act. Eleven of these suits were brought in Mississippi; the others were brought in Louisiana, Georgia, Alabama, and Tennessee. The

cases included discrimination in registration, restoration of Blacks to registration rolls, and economic boycotts against black voters.

In 1960, Congress passed a second civil rights statute, strengthening and extending the 1957 Act. This law provided that states, as well as the registrar, may be sued for discriminatory voting practices. Under Title III, the 1960 act required the preservation of voting records and empowered the U.S. Attorney General to inspect them. Also, Title VI of this act introduced the possibility of federal voting referees to see that persons who have been improperly disfranchised are in fact registered where a court finds a "pattern or practice" of discrimination.

A more substantial civil rights law was passed by Congress in 1964. Title VII of this act banned discrimination because of race, color, sex, religion, or national origin on the part of employers and labor unions. It established a commission (Equal Economic Opportunity Commission) to investigate alleged discrimination and use persuasion to end it. The Attorney General was authorized to sue any person or group he believed was engaged in a pattern or practice of resistance to the title. (This title is discussed more fully in Chapter 9 in the section on "Title VII of the Civil Rights Act of 1964 and Labor Unions.") Other sections of the Civil Rights Act of 1964 dealt with voting (Title I), which is discussed in Chapter 11; public accommodations (Title II); public facilities (Title III); public school desegregation (Title IV); and federal aid (Title VI). Title VI provides that no person shall be subjected to racial discrimination in any program receiving federal aid.

The Role of the Executive Branch on Employment Discrimination: 1946–1980

The federal wartime Fair Employment Practice Committee was discontinued in 1946. Two years after the refusal of Congress to enact permanent federal fair employment practice legislation, President Truman issued Executive Order 9980 to provide machinery for implementing fair employment policy and redressing the discrimination evident in the federal government.

In January, 1955, President Eisenhower abolished the Fair Employment Board of the Civil Service Commission and established a committee of five to carry out a nondiscrimination order. The new committee was asked to report directly to the President. The committee, recognizing the limited role that complaints could play in the nondiscrimination effort, instituted a program of information and persuasion for top-level administrators and personnel officers. Mainly this program consisted of conferences on nondiscrimination policy established by departments and agencies. President Eisenhower issued two executive orders (10479 in 1953 and 10557 in 1954) which expanded the obligations of federal contractors, but the President's Committee on Governmental Contracts, chaired by then Vice President Richard M. Nixon, acted only by issuing public relations statements. These pronouncements had no effect on the situations faced by minority workers (Hill 1977, pp. 379–380).

Action was taken during the Kennedy administration on enfranchising southern Blacks, but action against job discrimination was ineffective. President Kennedy issued Executive Order 10925 in 1961 requiring equal employment opportunity within federal agencies and in the firms of government contractors, and he established the President's Committee on Equal Employment Opportunity. In 1963, he issued Executive Order 11114 covering federally assisted construction. The President's committee had greater enforcement powers than previous agencies, but reliance was placed upon voluntary compliance through such approaches as "Plans for Progress." Sanctions were not used and these executive orders were not enforced (Hill 1977, p. 380).

President Lyndon B. Johnson issued Executive Order 11246 on October 24, 1965, further extending the obligations of federal contractors and establishing the Office of Federal Contract Compliance within the Department of Labor. Again, voluntary compliance instead of enforcement was relied upon. The use of federal executive orders to reduce employment discrimination has been of little value (Hill 1977, p. 380).

In 1978, the Leadership Conference on Civil Rights, a coalition of civil rights organizations, issued a statement on what the Carter administration had done up to that point. The Equal Employment Opportunity Commission had been reorganized, and more money and personnel had been put into civil rights enforcement. New guidelines had been established for combating discrimination in colleges and universities. The Justice Department had upheld enforcement of affirmative action in hiring and admissions of minorities. Blacks had been appointed to high positions in the administration. The conference said that the administration had been lax, as previous administrations had been, in enforcing the 1968 Fair Housing Act to ban discrimination in housing and in other areas, including veterans' affairs. The Carter administration pushed through Congress in 1977 a $12 billion program of jobs in public works and additional programs to spur economic development in the central cities, and it proposed in 1978 to "target" many federal programs on inner-city areas in greatest need. According to the conference, these policies did not have much effect on the inner-city poor. Mr. Carter's cutback on social programs to balance the budget and attack inflation in 1980 brought criticisms from civil rights leaders. Attempts to meet these criticisms were made in his reelection campaign with a "reindustrialization" program (*The New York Times* September 7, 1980, p. E3).

The failure of administrative agencies to obtain compliance with the law has made it necessary to seek enforcement through litigation.[1]

State and Local Civil Rights Laws

Civil rights statutes covering racial and religious discrimination in places of public accommodation have been enacted by about four-fifths of the states in the United States. In some of these states, violation of these laws is a misdemeanor and is punishable by fine and imprisonment. Other states permit the aggrieved individual to sue for damages. On the whole, the sections of these laws pertaining to public accommodations have not been effective, but there have been some notable exceptions. Some public prosecutors consider such offenses insignificant and are unwilling to prosecute unless provided with unquestionable cases.

About forty states have laws against discrimination in employment. These laws have been enacted mainly because the state FEPC has certain areas of operation that cannot be covered by a national law. One reason for this situation is the shift to employment in the service industries and the distributive trades. Also, a substantial number of persons are employed in public and semipublic utilities. These branches of industry are not reached

[1]Additional discussions of federal civil rights activity are found in Chapters 10, 15, 16, and 18.

by a federal employment agency, which is limited to firms engaged in interstate commerce.

More than 50 cities have enacted fair employment practices laws. Among the cities prohibiting discrimination in public and private employment are Chicago, Philadelphia, Minneapolis, Cleveland, San Francisco, Milwaukee, and Des Moines.

During the past two decades, there has been a tendency to charge the state commission handling fair employment practices with the enforcement of laws against discrimination in housing (public and publicly assisted housing, FHA and VA-aided housing, and privately owned housing), places of public accommodation, and, in some cases, education. In the face of continuing discrimination in employment, critics have asked what the state and municipal agencies have been doing since they were created. The answer seems to be that they have been processing complaints. In terms of expanding opportunities for racial and cultural minorities, the effects of this processing have been minimal.

Affirmative Action

The term *affirmative action* first appeared in the 1964 Civil Rights Act, and in 1965 President Johnson incorporated it in Executive Order 11246. Under this order, the duties of government contractors remained essentially the same as those given in President Kennedy's Executive Order 10925 of March, 1961. Contractors were to undertake to refrain from discrimination, but in addition they were to promise to "take affirmative action to ensure that applicants were employed, and that employees were treated during employment, without regard to their race, creed, color, or national origin." Since 1965, the concept of affirmative action has been used frequently in legislative acts, executive orders, and court decisions pertaining to equal opportunities in education and employment for racial and cultural minorities and women.

Various remedies have been used by the courts and government agencies to end discrimination. Injunctions have been issued, and the courts have ordered employers to: disseminate job information directed at the group discriminated against; keep records to insure nondiscriminatory hiring; employ and provide back pay for those who have been discriminated against; provide pretest tutoring for job applicants; expand apprenticeship and training

programs; and pay punitive damages. Where these remedies have proved to be inadequate, some governmental agencies have utilized affirmative action plans, consent decrees, and conciliation agreements, and some courts have ruled that some form of preferential remedy is needed to enforce equal employment opportunity where there has been a long record of discrimination (Edwards 1977, p. 91).

Preferential remedies have taken a number of forms. Courts have required employers to hire on the basis of ratios of minority to majority employees. Or the employer may be asked to use the ratio until a certain percentage of the total work force consists of minority workers, or to follow the ratio until a specified number of minority workers are hired. Another remedial preferential is "fictional seniority," that is, providing minority workers with more seniority protection against layoff or giving them preferences in promotions by giving them more seniority than they would have attained under existing practices. All of these remedies are defined as temporary and are to be used only until the practice of discrimination has been overcome (Edwards 1977, pp. 91–92).

Objections to the Principle of Affirmative Action

Strong objections to preferential remedies have been made by some scholars who have specialized in the study of minorities. In opposition to affirmative action, the term *reverse discrimination* has been used, and there have been demands for "color blindness" in employment (Borgatta 1976; Glazer 1978). Glazer (1978, 1983, pp. 161–62, 207) has also used the term *affirmative discrimination* to distinguish between "reaching out" to recruit blacks and other minorities through advertising, recruiting, and training from setting statistical goals. The latter type of affirmative action is called affirmative discrimination. Glazer argues that "result-oriented" sounds good, but if it means that we are capable of establishing accurate figures of availability, it fosters illusion. The evidence on the economic status of racial and cultural minorities in the United States (see Chapter 9) shows, however, that the effects of discrimination over a long period of time cannot be broken solely through the principle of color blindness. As Edwards (1977, p. 92) points out, ordering an offender to discontinue a discriminatory practice is ineffectual without providing affirmative relief (see also the section on affirmative action in higher education in Chapter 16).

The arguments used against preferential remedies include the following: (1) despite the preference that has been shown white males in the past, to give job preference now to minorities (and to women) would unfairly punish innocent white males for the actions of their predecessors; (2) white males should not suffer today for the discrimination of certain employers in the past; and (3) because minorities and women who may be given preferences now are not the same individuals who were discriminated against in the past, they are being rewarded for the wrongs to their ancestors. These arguments fail to take certain points into consideration: (1) court-ordered preferential remedies are not so widespread as opponents have suggested; (2) where the preferences have been ordered and enforced, the remedies have usually been carefully circumscribed; (3) preferential remedies are designed to favor one group temporarily in order to open all levels of the job market to all qualified applicants; and (4) in the absence of affirmative action, minorities and women are routinely passed over in favor of less well qualified white males (Edwards 1977, pp. 93–94; *The New York Times,* January 10, 1982, p. F3).[2]

It should be added that in March, 1981, the Supreme Court struck down a lower court decision which said that employers accused of bias must prove that they chose the "better qualified" applicant for a job or a promotion. The court said that the employer is given "discretion to choose among equally qualified candidates, "provided there is no proof that the choice was made to discriminate against females or minorities." This ruling means that employers may choose to hire a white male instead of a minority person or a woman if all are equally qualified (Cleveland *Plain Dealer,* March 5, 1981, p. E2).

Civil rights advocates argue that the selection of an applicant partially on the basis of race, as a means of breaking the cycle of inferior education, unemployment, and poverty, has as much or more moral justification than many of the criteria that are widely used. Among such criteria are: tenure for professors, seniority rights for industrial workers, the union shop, veterans' preferences, devices

used to obtain a geographically or otherwise diverse student body, admission to college of children of wealthy families, and word-of-mouth recruitment to help a friend or relative gain admission to a school (Greenberg 1976).

Criticisms of Affirmative Action Programs

Many personnel managers claim that equal-rights regulation is vague and ambiguous, and they object to federal "invasion" of their domains. Some contend that enforcement of affirmative action legislation is lax at the upper levels of industry and government, but harsh with less influential employers. Also, employers and supervisors are concerned over the disciplining or firing of minorities and women, fearing that they will claim they were discriminated against. Litigation in such cases is lengthy and expensive, especially for small companies. If management wins, individuals alleging discrimination may use extralegal methods of appeal, especially appeals to human rights organizations. If employers and supervisors do not discipline minority and women employees who do not meet expected standards, other workers may resent such preferential treatment. Preferential treatment of any kind—in hiring or promotion; tolerance of idiosyncratic work behavior, including tardiness and absenteeism; special training; adjustments in working conditions; and circumvention of traditional seniority systems—causes hostility toward those who are favored and stiffens the resistance to job equality (Kaplan 1977, pp. 310–311). Also some minority group members who qualify apart from special programs have expressed concern that their appointments will be attributed, at least in part, to special consideration on the basis of race or ethnicity.

A review of the U.S. Civil Service Commission (CSC) by the U.S. Commission on Civil Rights in the middle 1970s showed that the CSC had not been very zealous in promoting equal employment opportunities among the civilian personnel of the federal government, which employs 4 percent of the labor force in the nation. It is the responsibility of the Civil Service Commission to ensure that federal employment practices are nondiscriminatory. The report of the U.S. Commission on Civil Rights stated that the CSC maintained it did not have to adhere to Title VII Equal Economic Opportunity Commission guidelines, which apply to all other employers, nor did it have to comply with

---

[2]For a discussion of judicially imposed limitations on the use of preferential remedies for employment discrimination, the problem of "last hired, first fired," and alternative solutions to fictional seniority, see Edwards 1977, pp. 94–117.

affirmative action rules which apply to federal contractors. Also, the Commission on Civil Rights said that the CSC had failed to show that many of its employee selection techniques related to minorities and women are associated with job performance[3] (USCCR 1975, vol. 5, p. 619; Kaplan 1977, p. 299).

At the same time, the USCCR criticized the Office of Federal Contract Compliance. This Office was responsible for removing employment discrimination on the basis of race, creed, color, sex, and national origin by federal contractors, subcontractors, and construction contractors handling federally assisted construction projects under authority of Executive Order 11246 (1965), as well as the amendments contained in Executive Order 11375 (1967) (USCCR 1975, vol. 5, p. 635; Kaplan 1977, pp. 300–301).

Laxness in enforcing affirmative action programs has also been reported for federal nonconstruction contractors. In 1974, these contractors were awarded more than $50 billion in federal contracts involving 25 million employees. The General Accounting Office (GAO) found the Department of Labor remiss in its administration of Executive Orders 11246 and 11375 (General Accounting Office 1975a, p. 7).

A 1974 report of the U.S. Commission on Civil Rights criticized the Federal Communications Commission, the Interstate Commerce Commission, the Civil Aeronautics Board, the Federal Power Commission, and the Securities and Exchange Commission for their weak efforts in eliminating employment discrimination in the industries they regulate. Of all these agencies, only the FCC, which regulates the radio and television, cable television, and telephone and telegraph communications industries, had promulgated rules forbidding job discrimination to its licensees. The commission pointed out, however, severe deficiencies in FCC's enforcement of its rules (USCCR 1974a, vol. 1, pp. 222–225; Kaplan 1977, p. 302).

A General Accounting Office report issued in 1975 criticized the efforts of the Department of Health, Education, and Welfare to enforce affirmative action programs in colleges and universities. A public college or university which had 50 or more employees and a government contract of

$50,000 or more was required to submit an acceptable affirmative action program with HEW before May 19, 1973. Between 1,100 and 1,300 colleges and universities came under this regulation (General Accounting Office 1975b; Kaplan 1977, p. 303).

The Value of Affirmative Action

Establishing goals, timetables, and recruitment programs has increased the participation of minorities and women in education, business, and the professions. Affirmative action programs have enhanced the education of members of the majority population by exposing them to diversity.

Approximately 1 percent of law students in the United States were members of minority groups in 1964. By 1981, the proportion was 10 percent. In 1969, about 3 percent of medical students was minority; now the proportion is more than 10 percent. The ratio of black undergraduates to black population is now about the same as the ratio of white undergraduate enrollment to white population.

Progress has been made, but opportunities for racial and cultural minorities are still far from being equal. Minority managers are concentrated on the lower levels, and the percentage of minority professionals remains below 10 percent. A disproportionate number of minorities attend two-year colleges or fail to graduate from four-year colleges. Affirmative action programs have not enabled a large number of ghetto Blacks to find regular employment (Greenberg 1981, p. 19A; Killian 1981, p. 54; Wilson 1978, p. 151).

The Supreme Court Decisions in the Bakke and Weber Cases

Two decisions in the late 1970s are outstanding among the court cases on affirmative action. In the Bakke case in 1978, the United States Supreme Court struck down the admissions program of the medical school of the University of California at Davis (see Chapter 16).

On June 27, 1979, the U.S. Supreme Court refused to order an employer and a union to admit Brian F. Weber, a white factory worker, to an on-the-job craft-training program. The program had set aside one-half the slots for minority workers. The craft-training program at Kaiser Aluminum & Chemical Corporation plant in Gramercy, Louisiana, excluded white workers from 50 percent of

---

[3]See the discussion of PACE (the U.S. Civil Service Commission's Professional and Administrative Career Examination) in Chapter 10.

the places in the plan, but the Court held that it did not concern the constitutional guarantee of equal protection because no action by the state or federal government was involved. The Kaiser program was viewed by the court as a voluntary agreement between the corporation and the United Steelworkers of America, private parties whose actions are not regulated by the Fourteenth Amendment.

Kaiser and the steelworkers union had bargained collectively to set up affirmative action plans at fifteen plants across the country. The programs were to remain in effect until the number of Blacks in skilled jobs reached the proportion of Blacks in the labor force in the community. At Gramercy, the work force was 39 percent black, but Blacks made up less than 2 percent (5 out of 273) of the skilled workers at the plant. The new training program had thirteen openings. Weber lacked sufficient seniority to win one of the six places reserved for Whites, but two of the Blacks accepted had less seniority than he did.

The Supreme Court ruled, 5 to 2, that hiring and promotion preference do not necessarily violate Title VII of the Civil Rights Act of 1964. That act forbids discrimination in employment on the basis of race. Weber had charged that a training program in a steel mill intended to increase the number of Blacks in skilled jobs constituted discrimination against Whites in violation of Title VII. He had argued also that affirmative action plans could not be adopted until an employer or union had been found guilty of discrimination.

In his majority opinion, Justice Brennan wrote:

It would be ironic indeed if a law triggered by the nation's concern over those who had been "excluded from the American dream for so long" constituted the first legislative prohibition of all voluntary, private, race-conscious efforts to abolish traditional patterns of racial segregation and hierarchy.

By focusing on the need to improve the opportunities of those discriminated against, the Court interpreted Title VII to encourage voluntary remedies to employment discrimination. Although Title VII prohibits the federal government from *requiring* employers to give preferential treatment to minorities to redress an imbalance in their work forces, the Court held that the act does not prohibit such *voluntary* efforts (U.S. Commission on Civil Rights 1980b, p. 22).

The Supreme Court's decision in Weber reversed two lower federal courts. It is an important ruling for those who favor increased integration of the

work place. Prior to the decision, companies and unions were in a difficult situation. If they voluntarily adopted affirmative action programs, they were liable to "reverse discrimination" suits like Weber's; if they did not adopt such programs, they faced damage suits by minorities and the possible loss of federal contracts. By upholding the Kaiser plan, the Court ruled that private institutions such as companies and unions may voluntarily remedy the consequences of racial bias without the requirement that one or more parties first be found guilty of discrimination (*The New York Times,* June 28, 1979, pp. 1, B12). Concerning the interests of white workers, Justice Brennan wrote that the plan "does not unnecessarily trammel the interests of white employees. The plan is a temporary measure. It is not intended to maintain racial balance but simply to eliminate a manifest racial imbalance."[4]

The Reagan Administration and Civil Rights

During its first year in office, the Reagan Administration reversed many of the civil rights policies of its recent predecessors, criticized laws and court decisions put into effect over twenty years, and began to dismantle much of the federal government's machinery for enforcing the rights of minorities and women. At the important enforcement agencies—the Justice Department, the Equal Employment Opportunity Commission, the Office of Federal Contract Compliance, and the Office for Civil Rights in the Department of Education—enforcement activities were slowed down or discontinued (*The New York Times,* July 26, 1981; *The New York Times,* January 24, 1982, p. 1; Blackwell and Hart 1982, Chapter 8).

Criticism against the Reagan administration's policies on minorities began to mount with the announcement that the twelve-year-old government policy of witholding tax exemption from private schools that discriminate against Blacks would be revoked. Strong protests caused Reagan to retreat from that position. In fact, he then announced that he would ask Congress for legislation forbidding exemptions for schools that discriminate. Such legislation would do what the Internal Revenue Service has done since 1969 under a body of law,

[4]Kaiser expected the Gramercy program to take about thirty years, until the proportion of craft employees reached 39 percent (*The Nation,* vol. 228, May 26, 1976, p. 602).

policy, and precedent (*The New York Times,* January 24, 1982, p. 16).

After the Supreme Court ruling in the Weber case, the Labor Department prepared guidelines based on the decision. President Reagan, unfamiliar with both the decision in Weber and his Justice Department's opposition to it, said at a news conference December 17, 1981, that he approved of an arrangement if it was voluntary. Later the White House issued a statement saying that Reagan agreed with the Justice Department that the Weber case had been "wrongly decided" and with Assistant Attorney General William B. Reynolds that raising the rights of groups over the rights of individuals was "at war with the American ideal of equal opportunity for each person." According to Reynolds: "This Administration is firmly committed to the view that the Constitution and laws protect the right of every person to pursue his or her goals in an environment of racial and sexual neutrality" (*The New York Times,* January 24, 1982, p. 16).

A comprehensive attack on affirmative action came in the new guidelines for the Office of Federal Contract Compliance announced in August, 1981, which reduced drastically the number of contractors required to prepare affirmative action plans. The new guidelines require written plans of contractors employing at least 250 workers and having a $1 million contract, rather than of those with 50 or more employees and $50,000 in contracts. In addition, the former practice of aggregating contracts to determine who must file plans was abandoned. According to this policy, firms with millions of dollars in federal contracts, but no single million dollar grant, no longer have to prepare affirmative action plans. The Department of Labor estimates that three-fourths of the contractors who had been submitting affirmative action plans would be exempt under the new regulations (Huber 1981, p. 2).

Among universities, the exempt proportion is even higher. Of the 272 colleges and universities required to file plans in 1980, about one-fifth will do so under the new regulations. Moreover, even where affirmative action plans are still mandatory, a compliance review would no longer be required before the contract is awarded, and an institution would be exempt for five years after a review is made. Under the new rules, the written affirmative action plan would no longer be the means of self-evaluation that it was before. Although complaints by employees can be made at any time under the new regulations, these can not be filed as class actions. Goals and timetables are no longer required

in employment discrimination suits; active efforts to recruit minorities and women are sufficient (Huber 1981, pp. 2–3).

By early 1982, major changes in the federal civil rights enforcement mechanism had been proposed by the Reagan administration whereby all enforcement efforts would be centralized within the Justice Department. At the same time, the Labor Department's Office of Federal Contract Compliance Programs would be abolished and the Equal Employment Opportunity Commission would be considerably shrunk (Jordan and Jacob 1982, p. vii; Blackwell and Hart 1982, pp. 181–212).

Barring rapid shifts throughout the judiciary, it seems unlikely that the judicial position on affirmative action will change. Cutting funding for enforcement by the executive branch could have an adverse effect, but it would not limit lawsuits by civil rights groups or private lawyers. If a presidential executive order were to revoke affirmative action, it would be limited to certain areas under presidential control, such as government contracts, and would not change voluntary programs or Title VII, state laws, or court-imposed requirements (Greenberg 1981, p. 19A; and see section on Affirmation in Chapter 16).

On school integration, the Reagan administration is in direct opposition to a long series of Supreme Court decisions. Assistant Attorney General Reynolds announced November 19, 1981, that the Justice Department would no longer try to desegregate entire school districts but would concentrate on specific schools where there is evidence of intentional, state-enforced segregation. Also, the Reagan administration opposes busing to bring about desegregation, and this position has encouraged the introduction of antibusing bills (*The New York Times,* January 24, 1982, p. 16).

Effect versus Intent in Discrimination Cases

In earlier civil rights cases, notably *Brown* v. *Board of Education of Topeka* (1954), an explicit racial classification existed which on its face had a discriminatory purpose and effect. Later, the Supreme Court overruled laws which transparently excluded Blacks even though there was no explicit classification by race. In 1960, in *Gomillion* v. *Lightfoot,* an Alabama law redrawing the boundaries of Tuskegee was held to be unconstitutional because it had the "inevitable effect" of excluding Blacks from the city and of depriving them of the right to vote. In southern school cases, the Supreme Court has used the effects, not the purpose, of the actions of school boards, holding that the officials had a duty to dismantle school systems that result from intentional segregation in the past. This approach of focusing on discriminatory effects, rather than intentions, is seen clearly in the Supreme Court's landmark decision in *Griggs* v. *Duke Power Company*. The Court stated (401 U.S. 424, 1971; see also Edwards 1977, p. 90; Masters 1975, p. 155):

> The objective . . . of Title VI is . . . to . . . remove barriers that have operated in the past to favor an identifiable group of white employees. Under the Act, practices, procedures, or tests neutral on their face, and even neutral in terms of intent, cannot be maintained if they operate to "freeze" the status quo of prior discriminatory employment practices. . . . Congress directed the thrust of the Act to the consequences of employment practices, not simply the motivation.

Actually, there are two standards, and these overlap to some degree. The basic rule followed by the Supreme Court is that "proof of racially discriminatory intent or purpose is required to show a violation" of the Constitution, particularly the Fourteenth Amendment, which guarantees "equal protection of the laws." The Court has held, however, that in specific situations, Congress may go beyond the Constitution and prohibit practices that merely have a discriminatory effect. For example, the Court ruled that Title VII of the Act of 1964 outlaws employment practices that in effect exclude Blacks and that are not clearly related to job performance. In another case, the Court required San Francisco schools to provide remedial instruction to 1,800 students of Chinese descent who did not speak English. That decision was based on Title VI of the 1964 Civil Rights Act, which forbids discrimination on the ground of national origin in any program receiving federal aid. The Court held this in order to prohibit practices that had the effect of discrimination.

The Court has said that statistical evidence showing the effects of discrimination may help to show discriminatory purpose. But statistical disparities alone are not sufficient to show that a policy is unconstitutional. Such disparities must be considered along with surrounding circumstances, including the legislative history of a law. In different kinds of cases, the courts have given different weight to statistics. For example, courts have generally held that pervasive underrepresentation of Blacks or Mexican Americans on juries creates a presumption of intentional discrimination (*The New York Times,* April 19, 1981, p. 16).

Beginning in the late 1970s, Congress and the courts at times seemed to reemphasize the need for Blacks, Hispanic Americans, and women to prove intentional discrimination in lawsuits claiming violations of civil rights. In cases wherein school boards have not had a previous record of discrimination, the Court has said that there is no violation of the Constitution without discriminatory intent (*Washington* v. *Davis* in 1976). In the District of Columbia, the Court upheld the use of a written test in appointing police officers even though Blacks failed the test at a higher rate than Whites. Similarly, in 1977 the Court upheld a refusal by the village of Arlington Heights, Illinois, to rezone land for low- and moderate-income housing, finding no racially discriminatory purpose. In 1980, in a case from Mobile, Alabama, in which the black plaintiffs had complained that at-large elections diluted the strength of their votes, the Supreme Court ruled it would be necessary to show that the local election laws had a discriminatory purpose (*The New York Times,* April 19, 1981, pp. 1, 16).

Evidence of intent is more difficult to prove, and lawyers for minority groups and women prefer to use a test based on the effects of a given practice. Deborah Bachrach, a civil rights specialist in the office of the New York State Attorney General, comments that the standard of intent is "a tremendously difficult, if not impossible, burden" for litigants to meet in most voting and employment cases. Owen M. Fiss, of the Yale University law school, says that the intent test is "an attempt to individualize or personalize an evil or wrong that is basically an institutional wrong." For example, he said, "all the evils that can be attributed to school segregation exist independently of whether or not the superintendent or school board members intended them" (*The New York Times,* April 19, 1981, p. 16).

Housing for Minorities: Occupancy Characteristics; Residential Segregation and Integration

Housing is both an essential commodity and one that provides numerous emotional satisfactions or dissatisfactions. Housing deprivations consist of physical shortcomings in dwelling units and of the inability to enter a neighborhood of one's choice. Housing opportunities, together with educational and employment opportunities, are central areas of concern to racial and cultural minorities in the United States. The importance of housing is seen clearly in the school segregation–desegregation situation. Desegregation of the public schools proceeds slowly or actually declines, in part because of the concentration of racial and cultural minorities within metropolitan areas. Residential segregation is also the *de facto* segregation underlying segregation in stores, places of employment, and other institutions. Each of these other types of segregation has additional support from general racial and cultural prejudice in the society and from specific patterns of social interaction of long standing (Taeuber 1969, p. 186).

Earlier, housing discrimination included Irish, Italians, and other European immigrants, but today those most affected are Blacks, Mexican Americans, Puerto Ricans, and American Indians. As we indicate below, Blacks face the greatest amount of discrimination. They are confronted with exclusion in every city, except in a relatively small number of neighborhoods. In addition, the housing available to Blacks is for the most part inferior to that of Whites. Both the housing and the neighborhoods in which Blacks live are more deteriorated; amenities are fewer; mortgages are harder to obtain; private investment in new buildings is rare; overcrowding is greater; schools, hospitals, and recreation facilities are inferior; and Blacks often get less housing value for their money than do Whites (see Jackman and Jackman 1980; Villemez 1980; Wienk et al. 1979; J. Yinger 1975, 1979).

Housing Occupancy Characteristics for Puerto Ricans and Chicanos

According to HUD, of the Hispanic groups in the United States, the Puerto Ricans, followed by Chicanos, are most disadvantaged in finding adequate housing. The units in which Puerto Ricans and Chicanos live are more often flawed than those of Hispanics generally, and these two groups have the most difficulty among Hispanics in affording adequate, uncrowded housing. HUD estimates that by spending a fourth of their income on housing, 80 percent of all American families should be able to obtain unflawed, uncrowded housing. Among Hispanics, Cubans almost meet the same standard, and Central and South Americans closely approach

it. However, only about 71 percent of all Hispanic households are able to get adequate housing for one-fourth of their income. And only 48 percent of Puerto Ricans and 73 percent of Chicanos can obtain adequate housing without exceeding the one-fourth-of income standard (U.S. Department of Housing and Urban Development January, 1978, p. 23).

Housing Occupancy Characteristics of Female-Headed Households

In 1979, one-parent families constituted nearly a fifth of all families with children present. Most of these were headed by women, 46 percent of black families and 14 percent of white families. This was a sharp increase over the 1970 figures of 31 percent for black families and 8 percent for white families (Kitagawa 1981, p. 16).

On average, female-headed households live in somewhat less adequate housing than the population as a whole. These household units have a few more flaws, they are somewhat older, and they are more likely to be rented than owned. However, averaging distorts the picture. The Annual Housing Survey makes clear that race and ethnic background, as well as household size and income, strongly affect how well female-headed households are housed. If a woman is black, if she is Hispanic, or if she heads a large family, there are great disparities between her housing situation and the nation as a whole. And adequate housing costs a woman head of household a much larger proportion of her income than it costs the average American (U.S. Department of Housing and Urban Development December, 1978, pp. 1, 4–5).

Housing for American Indians

Indian reservations have often been referred to as "open air slums." On several occasions, the Indian Health Service has testified before Congress that many Native American families live under such poor housing conditions that many of the deaths and injuries of children in these families are directly attributable to unsafe housing. The IHS has also found that the high infant mortality rate among American Indians, as well as the high mortality rates resulting from infectious diseases, are associated with inadequate housing, especially among the Navajo population (U.S. Commission on Civil Rights December, 1975b, p. 159).

For American Indians who have left reservations to live in urban areas, housing conditions tend to be of the poorest quality. For example, in a residential section of Rapid City, South Dakota that is predominantly Native American, over 14 percent of the homes had to be torn down by the city because they could not meet minimum code standards. In 1974, only 41 percent of the homes in this area met city building code standards. One report on the housing problems faced by American Indians when they leave reservations states: "Practically every Indian family lives in an old shack or old run-down apartment. This is the only thing they can get. . . . Landlords generally say: 'There's no use fixing it up, because we just rent to Indians'" (U.S. Commission on Civil Rights December 1975b, pp. 159–160). Native Americans are frequently charged exorbitant rents for substandard housing.

The BIA and the Department of Housing and Urban Development have both sponsored programs intended to improve housing conditions for Indians. Federal law has permitted Indian tribes to form housing authorities to secure financing for low-rent public housing and mutual help construction projects. In the low-rent programs, HUD has supplied supplements to low-income families which have allowed them to rent or purchase housing units built with federally backed financing. In the mutual help housing and construction program, HUD has worked with the BIA to supply a small number of homes for purchase by Indians. The BIA has also operated a housing improvement program for the construction and renovation of Indian homes. In one year (1974), the Bureau spent nearly $13 million to remodel 4,400 homes and to construct about 500 new homes. In that year, federal housing assistance was given to approximately 11,000 Indian families, or about one-sixth of those estimated to be in need (Levitan and Johnston 1975, pp. 65–66).

Racial Separation and Concentration in Housing

A comprehensive report on racial residential segregation for 109 cities in the United States, 1940 to 1970, gives indexes of dissimilarity[5] on the basis

of city blocks. For 1940, 1950, 1960, and 1970, indexes are shown for Whites versus Nonwhites; for 1970, indexes are given also for White versus Blacks. In Table 12-1 indexes of dissimilarity from the Sorensen, Taeuber, and Hollingsworth study (1975, pp. 125–142) are given for the 25 cities with the highest degree of segregation and the 25 cities with the lowest indexes of black–white separation among these 109 cities in 1970.

Residential segregation in urban areas by race is considerably greater than separation by social class. The principal findings of an important study of twenty-nine cities (Farley 1977a, pp. 497–518) may be summarized as follows:[6]

1. Controlling for social class, Blacks are highly segregated from Whites. The extent of this racial residential segregation does not vary by occupational prestige, educational achievement, or income. In any social class category, Whites are more segregated from Blacks in that category than they are from Whites in other social class categories.

2. In the typical metropolis, to eliminate residential segregation of Blacks with no years of schooling from Whites without schooling, it would be necessary to shift 87 percent of either group to other census tracts. To eliminate the residential segregation among those

---

[5]The index of dissimilarity ranges from 0 to 100. If the distributions by city blocks (or by census tracts) of two racial groups are identical, the index has a value of zero, indicating no residential segregation at the tract (or block) level. This would

be true, for example, if each block in a city that is 80 percent White and 20 percent Black were also 80–20. If no tract (or block) contains both racial groups, the groups would be maximally segregated, and the index would be 100. The index "equals the minimum proportion of either group who would have to be shifted to bring about an equal distribution of the two groups by tract (or block), that is, a situation of no residential segregation" (Farley 1977a, p. 500).

A substantial body of literature discusses the usefulness and the weaknesses of the index of dissimilarity. It is quite easy to interpret and is unaffected by the relative numbers of the groups involved. However, this latter advantage—for some purposes—becomes a disadvantage when the comparative sizes of majority and minority groups are of interest as well as the pattern of distribution. Although our reference here is to the index of dissimilarity, for discussions of various indexes interested readers will want to consult Cortese, Falk, and Cohen 1976; Duncan and Duncan 1955; Falk, Cortese, and Cohen 1978; Jahn, Schmidt, and Schrag 1947; Lieberson 1980, pp. 253–291; Taeuber and Taeuber 1965; Winslip 1977, 1978.

[6]Data were obtained from the 1970 Census for New York, Los Angeles, Chicago, Philadelphia, Detroit, San Francisco, Boston, Washington, Cleveland, St. Louis, Pittsburgh, Minneapolis, Houston, Baltimore, Dallas, Milwaukee, Seattle, Miami, San Diego, Atlanta, Cincinnati, Kansas City, Buffalo, Denver, San Jose, New Orleans, Portland, Indianapolis, and Providence.

Table 12-1. Indexes of Residential Segregation between Whites and Nonwhites, 1940 to 1970, and between Whites and Blacks, 1970 for 50 Cities.

City	White versus Black 1970	White versus Nonwhite			
		1970	1960	1950	1940
Shreveport, LA	97.8	97.4	95.9	93.2	90.3
Dallas, TX	95.9	92.7	94.6	88.4	80.2
Oklahoma City, OK	95.6	81.8	87.1	88.6	84.3
Fort Worth, TX	95.4	92.6	94.3	90.4	81.3
Winston-Salem, NC	94.6	94.0	95.0	93.8	92.9
Tulsa, OK	94.5	76.4	86.3	91.2	84.6
Jacksonville, FL	94.3	92.5	96.9	94.9	94.3
Augusta, GA	93.8	93.3	93.0	88.9	86.9
Charlotte, NC	93.7	92.7	94.3	92.8	90.1
Montgomery, AL	93.6	93.2	·94.7	90.5	86.8
Norfolk, VA	93.5	90.8	94.6	95.0	96.0
Chicago, IL	93.0	88.8	92.6	92.1	95.0
Greensboro, NC	93.0	91.4	93.3	93.5	93.1
Wichita, KS	93.0	85.0	91.9	93.3	92.0
Houston, TX	92.7	90.0	93.7	91.5	84.5
Roanoke, VA	92.7	91.8	93.9	96.0	94.8
Memphis, TN	92.4	91.8	92.0	86.4	79.9
Knoxville, TN	92.2	89.6	90.7	89.6	88.6
Miami, FL	92.0	89.4	97.9	97.8	97.9
Tampa, FL	92.0	90.7	94.5	92.5	90.2
Atlanta, GA	91.9	91.5	93.6	91.5	87.4
Birmingham, AL	91.8	91.5	92.8	88.7	86.4
Savannah, GA	91.8	91.2	92.3	88.8	84.2
Mobile, AL	91.5	91.0	91.9	89.4	86.6
Dayton, OH	91.1	90.1	91.3	93.3	91.5
Jersey City, NJ	79.0	75.6	77.9	80.5	79.5
Washington, DC	78.8	77.7	79.7	80.1	81.0
New Bedford, MA	78.7	72.7	81.6	86.8	83.4
Trenton, NJ	78.1	77.2	79.6	83.0	81.9
Harrisburg, PA	77.3	76.2	85.7	89.8	87.2
New York, NY	77.3	73.0	79.3	87.3	86.8
Charleston, WV	77.0	74.3	79.0	79.6	80.3
East St. Louis, IL	76.9	76.8	92.0	94.2	93.8
Providence, RI	76.8	72.0	77.0	85.5	85.8
Rochester, NY	76.5	73.8	82.4	86.9	85.5
Newark, NJ	76.4	74.9	71.6	76.9	77.4
Youngstown, OH	75.9	74.9	78.5	83.5	80.0
Berkeley, CA	75.4	62.9	69.4	80.3	81.2
New Rochelle, NY	75.1	70.7	79.5	78.9	80.6
San Francisco, CA	75.0	55.5	69.3	79.8	82.9

Continued

Table 12-1. (*continued*)

City	White versus Black	White versus Nonwhite			
	1970	1970	1960	1950	1940
Bridgeport, CT	73.5	71.7	69.7	74.4	78.8
Yonkers, NY	73.1	68.0	78.1	81.7	82.0
Paterson, NJ	72.0	70.3	75.9	80.0	79.8
New Haven, CT	71.5	69.1	70.9	79.9	80.0
Sacramento, CA	71.1	56.3	63.9	77.6	77.8
Wilmington, DE	70.5	69.8	79.8	86.2	83.0
Oakland, CA	70.4	63.4	73.1	81.2	78.4
Camden, NJ	68.3	67.4	76.5	89.6	87.6
Cambridge, MA	63.4	52.6	65.5	75.6	74.3
East Orange, NJ	61.4	60.8	71.2	83.7	85.3

Source: Sorensen, Taeuber, and Hollingworth 1975.

who had completed five years or more of college, a shift of 85 percent of either the Blacks or the Whites would be required. For families with incomes under $1,000, the average racial segregation index was 85.

3. Residential segregation of socioeconomic groups is moderate. For an educational group, or a family income category, about one-fourth of that group would have to be shifted if they were to be residentially distributed in a way similar to all other families or individuals.

4. Among Whites, levels of social class residential segregation are similar in central cities and suburbs. Among Blacks, social class segregation is somewhat greater in suburbs than in central cities.

Improvements in the social and economic status of Blacks and in white attitudes toward Blacks, that occurred between 1960 and 1970 did not result in large-scale advances in racial integration. Segregation levels in SMSAs (Standard Metropolitan Statistical Areas) in the United States remained almost unchanged in that decade. It is possible, of course, that ten years is too short a time to produce appreciable declines in segregation as a result of economic or attitudinal changes (Van Valey, Roof, and Wilcox 1977, pp. 842–843).

A study of 35 southwest cities (Grebler et al. 1970, pp. 274–276) showed marked variations in the residential segregation of black and Spanish-surname persons. The index of segregation of the total minority population from Anglos ranged from 39 in Laredo, Texas, to 83 in Dallas, Texas. The segregation index of Spanish-surname persons from Anglos varied from 30 in Sacramento, California, to 76 in Odessa, Texas. The segregation of Blacks from Anglos ran from 57 in Pueblo, Colorado, to 94 in Lubbock, Texas. The segregation of Blacks from Spanish-surname persons ranged from 29 in Odessa, Texas, to 89 in Lubbock, Texas. The segregation of Spanish-surname persons from "other Nonwhites" ranged from 10 in Santa Barbara, California, to 89 in San Angelo, Texas.[7]

A comparison of two of the principal cities in the Southwest, San Antonio and Los Angeles, showed that San Antonio is far more segregated (Grebler et al. 1970, pp. 286–287, 312). Approximately 10 percent of the Mexican Americans in Los Angeles live in census tracts that were more than three-fourths Mexican American, compared with more than 50 percent in San Antonio. Judged by educational attainment, incomes, and occupational distribution, as well as residential segregation, the

[7]The composition of the "Other nonwhite" population differs from state to state. In Arizona and New Mexico, it is predominantly American Indian. In California, it is predominantly Asian. In most areas in the region, blacks are relative newcomers compared with other minorities.

social isolation of Mexican Americans in San Antonio is far greater than it is in Los Angeles.

A study of residential segregation of Blacks and Spanish Americans in the United States (Massey 1979, pp. 1015–1022) shows the effects of socioeconomic factors in ten urbanized areas with large Spanish populations (Chicago, Dallas, Denver, Houston, Los Angeles, Miami, San Diego, San Francisco, San Jose, and Washington, D.C.). Indexes of dissimilarity within social classes, defined on the basis of education, family income, and occupation, showed a negative relationship between socioeconomic status and degree of Spanish-Anglo segregation. Such segregation clearly decreased when measured in terms of education, income, or occupation. Black-white and Spanish-black segregation were high across all socioeconomic classes. Spanish-Anglo segregation, however, declined 33 points from the lowest to the highest educational category. The level of Spanish-black segregation was generally somewhat less than that of black-white separation. Spanish-Anglo residential segregation also decreased with increases in occupational status, but the pattern was less clear than with educational status. There was no apparent decline in either Spanish-black or black-white segregation across occupational groups. These findings are shown in Figures 12-1 to 12-4, together with a figure showing the quite different effect of social class for persons of Puerto Rican birth or parentage in New York. The latter figure shows that there is no indication of decline in Puerto Rican-Anglo segregation with increasing social class. It shows also that the level of Puerto Rican-Anglo segregation is significantly higher than that of Puerto Rican-black segregation. The same patterns were found when income and occupation were used as indicators of social class. Massey (1979, p. 1018) says that it is not clear whether these findings indicate the uniqueness of the New York metropolitan area or the Puerto Ricans as a Hispanic population.

Reasons for Racial Residential Segregation. According to a purely economic argument, racial residential segregation occurs mainly because Blacks cannot afford more integration. Although black family income is somewhat less than two-thirds that of white families, Blacks can afford to purchase or rent housing in white areas of central cities or in suburban rings to a much greater extent than they did in the 1970s. Nevertheless, high-income Whites and high-income Blacks live in different neighborhoods—as, for the most part, poor

Whites and poor Blacks do. Blacks in all income brackets tend to live in central cities, whereas Whites in all income categories are well represented in the suburbs (Farley, Bianchi, and Colasanto 1979). "Only a small part of the relative concentration of Blacks can be explained by their relatively low socioeconomic status" (J. Yinger 1979, p. 449).

A second view attributes racial residential segregation to a combination of discriminatory policies and practices. Unquestionably, real estate agents, apartment managers, landlords, and suburban developers have denied Blacks access to housing in white areas. In his study of real estate brokers, John Yinger (1981, p. 604) concludes, "The welfare gains from government intervention in the market for real estate broker services could be substantial." This is based on the influence that a multiple-listing service open to all brokers, minority and majority alike, would have on the market. The lending policies of banks and other financial institutions have contributed to racial residential separation. Through their control of zoning, building rules, and land development regulations, local governments have furthered segregation, as have the FHA and VA regulations of the federal government (U.S. Commision on Civil Rights 1977, pp. 21–34). For many years, restrictive covenants in deeds were used to keep Blacks out of white areas, and at times violence has been used to exclude Blacks and other minorities. The passage of the Civil Rights Act of 1968, which bars discrimination in the sale or rental of most housing, and a number of important decisions of the Federal courts have had relatively little effect on exclusionary tactics (U.S. Commission on Civil Rights 1980b, pp. 8–9). In addition, more subtle tactics, especially the selective steering of Blacks and other minorities to some neighborhoods and majority Whites to others, have been adopted. The "web of discrimination" continues to operate despite the reports in national samples that Whites are willing to accept black neighbors and the growing recognition by Whites that they do not have the prerogative of excluding Blacks (Farley et al. 1979).

A third view is that residential segregation is largely the result of a preference on the part of Blacks to live in black neighborhoods. This belief is not supported by empirical studies. For example, a national sample in 1969 found that three-fourths of the black families wished to live in integrated neighborhoods, but only one-sixth preferred an all-black area (Pettigrew 1973, p. 44). In a study of

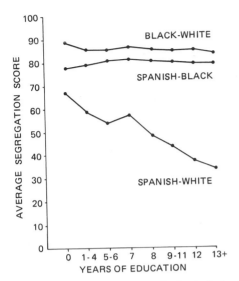

Figure 12–1. Average segregation by level of education, 10 urbanized areas. Source: D. S. Massey, "Effects of Socioeconomic Factors on the Residential Segregation of Blacks and Spanish Americans in U. S. Urbanized Areas." *ASR*, December 1979, p. 1017.

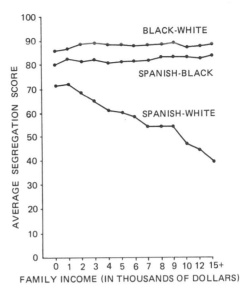

Figure 12–2. Average segregation by level of family income, 10 urbanized areas. Source: Massey, *ASR*, December 1979, p. 1018.

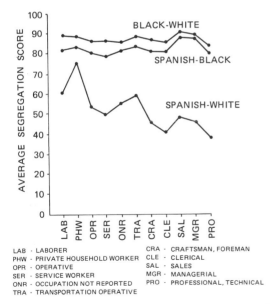

LAB · LABORER
PHW · PRIVATE HOUSEHOLD WORKER
OPR · OPERATIVE
SER · SERVICE WORKER
ONR · OCCUPATION NOT REPORTED
TRA · TRANSPORTATION OPERATIVE
CRA · CRAFTSMAN, FOREMAN
CLE · CLERICAL
SAL · SALES
MGR · MANAGERIAL
PRO · PROFESSIONAL, TECHNICAL

Figure 12–3. Average segregation by occupational groups, 10 urbanized areas. Source: Massey, *ASR*, December 1979, p. 1018.

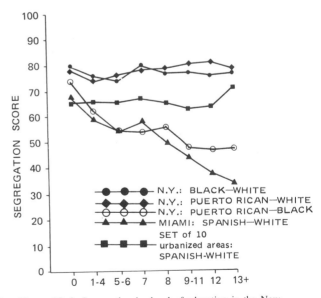

Figure 12–4. Segregation by level of education in the New York urbanized area compared to Miami and a set of 10 urbanized areas. Source: Massey, *ASR*, December 1979, p. 1018.

Detroit Blacks, the proportion who preferred mixed neighborhoods increased from 57 to 62 percent between 1968 and 1971 (Schuman and Hatchett 1974, Table 1).

Interviews obtained from a sample of 1134 households (734 Whites and 400 Blacks) in the Detroit area in 1976 showed that the residential preference by race of the respondents differed considerably. Sixty-three percent of the Blacks preferred to live in a neighborhood that has an equal number of black and white residents, and an additional one-fifth gave this as their second choice. The third most popular choice was a neighborhood in which Blacks are in the majority. The least attractive to the majority of Blacks was the all-white neighborhood, but the all-black neighborhood was also unpopular. The latter was selected by only 17 percent as their first or second choice (Farley, Bianchi, and Colasanto 1979).

The Whites in the Detroit study were less favorable to residential integration than Blacks. Three-fourths of the Whites said they would feel comfortable with one black family in their neighborhood, 59 percent would be comfortable with three black families, 44 percent if Whites were slightly in the majority, and 26 percent if there were more Blacks than Whites. In sum, marked differences were found in the neighborhood preferences of Blacks and Whites. Blacks favored integrated neighborhoods, but Whites regarded desirable levels of racial integration as neighborhoods in which Whites were the overwhelming majority (Farley et al. 1979).

The Detroit area housing study of 1976 showed what other investigations of attitudes toward racial segregation have failed to show, namely, that Whites are not very accepting of residential integration. The procedures in this study enabled respondents to go beyond reacting to general values and to indicate what they would do in specific situations. When asked if they would actually try to move out of a neighborhood of fifteen houses if it contained one black family, 7 percent of the white respondents said they would. Twenty-four percent said they would attempt to move if there were three black families. If the neighborhood was one-third black, 41 percent would try to leave, and 64 percent would leave the majority black area. It would be difficult not to conclude on the basis of this evidence that residential segregation results to an important degree from the preferences of many Whites for segregated neighborhoods (Farley et al. 1978).

As a result of discrimination in housing, minorities have only limited access to improved housing outside segregated neighborhoods. Also, housing discrimination has important consequences on whether Blacks and other minorities can be equal participants in labor markets, education, and other social institutions (U.S. Department of Housing and Urban Development 1979, p. 200).

Redlining. When 127 of 180 savings and loan associations in the Chicago area responded to a request of the Federal Home Loan Bank in 1974 for information concerning the geographic locations of their home mortgages and savings deposits, it was found that older neighborhoods were receiving far less than their deposit dollar in mortgage loans than the expanding suburban areas. The predominantly white areas in the newer southwest and northwest sections of Chicago were receiving 4.5 times more in new mortgage loans than the redlined, depressed black areas of the city. Also, these newer areas were receiving new mortgage loans that were disproportionately small relative to their savings deposits in comparison to the loans made to the outlying suburbs (Bates and Bradford 1979, p. 12).

Redlining is the practice of denying a loan on the basis of race, where the purpose of the loan is to finance the purchase of a home in an integrated neighborhood. There are degrees of redlining. The first phase involves increasing the difficulty of obtaining a home mortgage by demands for high down payments, charging high interest rates, and writing mortgages with maturities of less than twenty years. Typically, in this phase, neighborhood property values decline. In the second phase, conventional mortgages are cut off to a community. Prospective home owners must find financial institutions that will approve FHA-guaranteed mortgage loans. When conventional mortgages disappear, home improvement loans decline. Some mortgage bankers who handle FHA loans do not deal in home improvement loans or will not deal in home improvement loans in neighborhoods that are redlined from conventional mortgages. Thus, property in redlined neighborhoods falls increasingly into disrepair (Bates and Bradford 1979, p. 13).

A federal law, the Community Reinvestment Act (CRA) or Title VIII of the Housing and Community Development Act of 1977, became effective November 6, 1978. Designed as a step toward eliminating redlining, this law requires all lenders to demonstrate that they are following affirmative action programs to assist in meeting the credit needs of their communities, including low- and moderate-income neighborhoods (Cleveland *Plain Dealer,* February 4, 1979, Section 7, 1).

Black Suburbanization. In 1979, HUD (February 1979, 3) examined questions of population movement within metropolitan areas. This study, based on annual housing survey samples and data from the 1960 and 1970 censuses, considered migration by race in nineteen of the nation's largest SMSAs, including the fourteen with largest black populations in 1970.

Trends in white and black intrametropolitan movement from 1955 to 1976 vary greatly among these metropolitan areas. Although a national reversal occurred in net migration of Blacks from central cities, black suburbanization increased very little from 1970 to 1976 in more than half of the SMSAs. (U.S. Department of Housing and Urban Development 1979, p. 26). In the last half of the 1970s, however, black suburbanization increased at a more rapid rate. In the nation as a whole, Blacks made up 4.7 percent of the suburban population in 1960, 4.8 percent in 1970, and 6.1 percent in 1980 (Long and DeArc 1981, p. 16). One in five was a suburban dweller by 1980, as compared with two in five of the entire population (Glick 1981, p. 111).

The number of Blacks living in metropolitan suburbs rose from 4.3 million in 1970 to 6.2 million in 1980. Despite this increase, Blacks comprised only 6.1 percent of the suburban population in the United States in 1980, a smaller proportion than the 8.9 percent living in city suburbs in 1900 (Reid 1982, pp. 7–8). From 1960 to 1980, the black metropolitan population residing in suburbs increased from 23 percent to 29 percent (in 1980, two-thirds of all Whites living in SMSAs were in the suburbs). The much publicized "suburbanization" of Blacks in the 1970s needs to be examined carefully. A 1982 study concluded: "Our findings suggest that (this) is more an indication of 'spillover,' or the extension of segregated city neighborhoods into deteriorating inner suburbs, than of black upward mobility into racially integrated suburbs." (Joint Center for Political Studies 1982, p. 5; Long and DeArc 1981, pp. 18–21; Logan and Schneider 1984; see also the section on black urbanization in Chapter 9).

Problems of the Inner Suburb. In the middle 1970s, officials of both races in the municipalities studied by Cole (1976, pp. 189–190) were optimistic about the future of their cities. Dwellers in the suburban rings of these urban centers were less optimistic, and city residents least optimistic of all. In the case of the white residents of integrated suburbs, pessimism slightly exceeded optimism. Cole says that the inner suburbs contend with racial antagonism, increased crime, decreasing white population, and disproportionate black enrollment in the public schools. In short, the problems of the inner city have spread to the inner suburb.

When housing is open to Blacks only in a few suburbs, the pressure on these communities mounts. Local governments alone cannot prevent the deterioration of multiracial communities. Proposals to maintain residential balance have included providing resources attractive to Whites such as a college or research park, government subsidies to biracial communities, or residential quotas. In one view, the simplest and fairest approach "is to ensure that no municipality exempts itself from sharing responsibilities with its suburban neighbors" (Cole 1976, p. 191). How long racial balance can be maintained may depend more on state or regional actions than on local attitudes.

Prospects for Housing Integration

Enforcement Problems. Federal fair housing enforcement efforts in the late 1970s generally failed to provide minorities with housing opportunities without encountering discrimination. After examining the detailed evidence of continuing housing discrimination, HUD stated (1979, p. ES29; see also Leigh 1981, pp. 158–59; U.S. Commission on Civil Rights 1979, pp. 71–72, USCCR 1980a, p. 5):

Efforts to combat racial discrimination have not been completely successful. . . . One can only conclude that the sanctions imposed on discriminators are insufficient, or that the probability of detecting discriminatory behavior is too low, or both.

Since the Department of Housing and Urban Development has the authority only to try voluntary conciliation, people who feel discriminated against must bring their own lawsuits in federal court, a costly process. In 1980 the House of Representatives voted to allow administrative law judges, attached to HUD, to assess fines and order compensation. However, the measure bogged down in the Senate, where conservative members preferred to keep enforcement in the courts. Another issue arose over the amount of proof an alleged victim must present. The House bill favored having to demonstrate only that there are few, if any, members of a given minority group in a neighborhood. Others insisted on evidence of discriminatory intent (*Wall Street Journal,* May 6, 1981, p. 25).

In the light of the conservative mood of the country in the early 1980s, and the seeming determination of the Reagan administration drastically to reduce all types of social programs and to transfer many functions of the federal government to the states under the "new federalism," it seems likely that fair housing enforcement will continue to diminish.

Rent Control. Because price increases in many cities have raised rents above the means of tenants, a new round of rent control measures (the first was post-World War II) was started in the late 1970s. However, rent control, with limited profits for landlords, has furthered the conversion of many buildings to condominiums and cooperatives. Such conversion of rental units to another form of ownership often leads to the displacement of low-income, elderly, and minority tenants who cannot afford the prices. Some cities have added anti-speculation clauses to their rent control legislation, and a bill to stop condominium and cooperative conversions (H.R. 5175, the Condominium-Cooperative Conversion Moratorium Act) was introduced during the first session of the 96th Congress (1979–80). At that time the federal government continued to study the problem of affordability as required under Section 902 of the HCD Act of 1978 (Leigh 1981, pp. 156–157) without taking any action.

Preferences of Whites for Segregated Neighborhoods. As noted above in the section on "Reasons for Racial Segregation," there is evidence to indicate that racial residential segregation results largely from the preferences of many Whites for segregated neighborhoods. Racial attitudes seem to be involved in this preference, but fiscal and ecological features of metropolitan areas are also important (Frey 1979). "White flight" is significantly affected by tax rates, fiscal instability, poor amenities, and urban pollution. There seems to be little likelihood that because of increases in educational attainment or because more conservative whites will be replaced soon by younger and more liberal residents attitudes about neighborhood integration will change in the near future (Farley et al. 1978).

Housing Programs at the Local Level. Quite a number of cities in the United States have carried on fair housing activities. These programs have brought pressure on the real estate industry to follow fair housing practices. They have also provided black homeseekers with general information on housing and on homes and apartments that were available (Grier and Grier 1978, pp. 14–15; Saltman 1978). Most of the services offered by these organizations provide only a limited means to reduce residential segregation, and their activities are confined largely to the more affluent segment of the minority market.

Fair housing councils, many of which were 70 percent federally funded, were in trouble in 1981 because the Reagan administration proposed to make drastic financial cutbacks. Also, the proposals of this administration to allow greater leeway to the states in spending the approximately $4 billion in HUD community block grant money is expected to result in large cuts in fair housing assistance (*Wall Street Journal,* May 6, 1981, p. 25).

In some cities, voluntary neighborhood stabilization campaigns have been organized. However, these plans have tended to slow down racial transition and keep the change orderly rather than to stop it completely.

Finally, groups of private citizens interested in attempting to reduce residential segregation have exerted political pressure in favor of antidiscrimination housing legislation and comparable governmental action. The National Committee Against Housing Discrimination is a federation of several dozen religious, civil rights, labor, and civic organizations concerned with the problems of race on a national level.

The Effectiveness of Legislation, Administrative Action, and Judicial Decision in the Field of Civil and Human Rights

At the federal level, we believe that the laws pertaining to employment, housing, voting, and public accommodations through the 1964 Civil Rights Act, the 1965 Voting Rights Act, and the 1968 Civil Rights Act (with their amendments) are reasonably adequate instruments for the ends they are intended to attain. The main legislative problem is the appropriation by Congress of sufficient funds to implement the existing laws in more than a token way. It seems likely that the "new federalism" policies, with the transfer to the states of responsibility for many social programs will, in a number of states, adversely affect the poor and minorities.

At the state level, the legislative trend has been toward strengthening the earlier laws, as well as the enactment of antidiscrimination laws by additional states. Some of these laws are now quite strong, but the great lacks at the state level are overcautiousness on the part of state commissioners, insufficient funds and staff, lack of support from some state administrations, and the absence of such legislation in the southern states.

Some earlier American sociologists, Sumner in particular, tended to minimize the influence of the legal pattern and to emphasize the importance of the mores in race relations. Increasingly, sociologists and legal scholars have concluded that legislation can be effective in reducing discrimination. This view does not hold, however, that law, particularly in a nonauthoritarian society, is all-powerful (Ball, Simpson, and Ikeda 1962).

Court decisions reflect the climate of opinion, and from 1868 until 1936 the rulings of the Supreme Court functioned to support the prevailing racial system. The narrow and legalistic interpretations of the Court during these years had the effect of reducing to a minimum some of the liberties guaranteed by the Constitution. During this period the Court played an important part in "keeping the Negro in his place." Supreme Court decisions, however, modify as well as reflect opinion, and the decisions from 1937 to 1970 greatly influenced public opinion and prepared the way for legislative and executive action.

Important decisions have been handed down in the fields of education, housing, voting, and public accommodations by the U.S. Supreme Court, the lower federal courts, and many of the state courts. The Supreme Court has had to assume the task of revealing the unfairness of some American institutions because other branches and levels of government have not spoken with authority and justice on these issues. The "Warren Court" of the 1960s is often called an "activist" court because of its inclination toward social change. The "Burger Court" of the 1970s and 1980s may come to be known as a "strict constructionist" court. Chief Justice Burger has said that the courts should not be regarded as instruments for bringing about social change. Despite legal ideologies and trends,

however, it is clear that the Supreme Court's decisions have considerable impact on national life, as, for example, the effects of the 1954 school cases in the rearrangement of American cities.

Beginning with President Roosevelt's Executive Order 8802 in 1941 dealing with the employment of workers in defense industries, significant presidential orders have been issued concerning a number of civil rights, particularly employment and housing. The enforcement records of federal administrative agencies have not, on the whole, been impressive. Through the efforts of a few departments and agencies, some advances have been made in education, public accommodations, voting, and hospital services, but discrimination is widespread in housing and employment where the federal government has the power but not the will to enforce the law.

Changing the Rules

Housing discrimination is more difficult to attack than discrimination in employment or education. Discrimination occurs in individual transactions and must usually be fought on a case-by-case basis. In a white neighborhood, a real estate agent may work harder for a white client than for a black customer. The seller may choose a white over a black buyer even when there is no economic basis for his choice. Bank lenders may demand more from black than from white buyers, and it is difficult to prove such discrimination. Also, it is hard to enforce a law or change a practice if many persons are opposed to it and if the rights of some people may have to be sacrificed (Levitan and Johnston 1975, pp. 289–290).

Despite these difficulties, some gains have been made. The rights of Blacks to get into almost any section they select are now protected by law, and grievance procedures are available if their rights are disregarded. Nevertheless, housing segregation continues, and, in many places, is becoming more marked.

Although the results obtained in combating discrimination vary considerably in the areas of education, employment, and housing, some common themes of rule changing may be discerned (Levitan and Johnston 1975, pp. 291–292).

1. Progress depends upon the level of public support. Equal employment opportunity and the integration of southern schools have been

favored; busing and housing laws have lacked favor.

2. In individual cases of flagrant violation, enforcement is easier to obtain than where there is less obvious racial imbalance. Completely segregated schools have been more easily eliminated than those where separation was less extreme.

3. The courts have been more effective in implementing the principles of nondiscrimination than have legislatures and executive agencies.

4. Financial penalties for violating the law provide more effective leverage in applying court decisions than threats of lawsuits and appeals to the consciences of those who control institutions. One example is seen in the possibility of cutoffs of water, sewer and other grants to communities which practiced discrimination in their subsidized housing. Another instance is the reaction of school systems to the possibility of losing federal funds, compared with the threat of legal actions. And employers responded faster to the threats of class action suits with expensive settlements for past discrimination than to the conciliation efforts by the Equal Employment Opportunities Commission.

In 1972 we said (Simpson and Yinger 4th edition, p. 451) that for many black people the emphasis had shifted from equality of opportunity to equality of results, and that an important question was whether the mood of most white Americans matched the change of concern on the part of Blacks. Economic conditions and the mood of the populace in the early 1980s preclude an affirmative answer to that question.

Criminal Justice and Minorities

Crime Rates

Although Blacks constitute approximately 12 percent of the population of the United States, they account for about one-third of all arrests tabulated in the Uniform Crime Index of the FBI. More than 40 percent of the 306,602 inmates of federal prisons in 1978 were black, as were 48 percent of the prisoners in state prisons. Hispanic people and American Indians also have higher rates of arrest,

incarceration, and victimization than those for Whites, but their rates are lower than the black rates. It should be pointed out that these rates are high in part because of the disproportionate number of individuals in those age brackets where the crime rate is high.

Crime rates vary with types of offense. Homicide consists of two categories: (1) murder and nonnegligent manslaughter and/or felonious murder and (2) manslaughter by negligence. Approximately three-fifths of all persons arrested for murder are Blacks, and two-fifths are Whites. Oppositely, more than three-fourths of those arrested for manslaughter by negligence are white, but less than one-fourth are black (Blackwell 1975, p. 247).

Young persons predominate among those arrested for robbery (theft in victim's presence); approximately 55 percent are under the age of 21, and nearly one-third (32 percent) are under 18. Blacks constitute two-thirds of those arrested for robbery throughout the nation (Blackwell 1975, p. 254).

Burglary is defined as unlawful entry into a structure, not involving force, for the purpose of committing a felony or theft. Whites are arrested twice as often for burglary as are black Americans. Also, by a two-to-one ratio, Whites outnumber Blacks in arrests for larceny-theft (the wrongful taking and carrying away of personal goods of another with intent to convert them to the taker's own use), as well as arrests for auto theft (Blackwell 1975, pp. 254–55).

Street Crime versus White Collar Crime. Although crime has multiplied in recent years, a very few antisocial and/or traumatized street criminals are responsible for most violent crimes. "Career criminals," most of whom are between the ages of 16 and 25 and who have a record of repeated arrests and convictions, are defiantly hostile and have chosen crime as their vocation. In the borough of Manhattan, about 500 of these individuals commit 70 percent of the street robberies. Also, career criminals comprise just 6 percent of those arrested for violent crimes in Manhattan, but they are responsible for a third of these crimes (Auletta 1982, p. 45).

Street crime, including robbery, mugging, murder, rape, and assault, is committed more frequently by the Black and the poor than by the White and the nonpoor. In 1978, the FBI reported that urban Blacks constituted 49.7 percent of all arrests for violent crimes and 32.7 percent of all arrests

YET WHITE -COLLAR CRIMES -ARE ON THE SAME LEVEL W/STREET CRIMES THAT IS THE DIFFERENCIATION IS ONLY BETWEEN ECONOMIC position

CHAPTER 12 • MINORITIES AND POLITICAL AND LEGAL PROCESSES (CONTINUED) 269

for property crimes—a total of 36 percent of all arrests. White-collar crime, including bribery, embezzlement, consumer fraud, corruption, and so forth, is committed mainly by Whites. According to the FBI, Whites constituted 72.4 percent of those arrested for embezzlement while Blacks made up 26.5 percent. For the most part, Blacks do not commit white-collar crime because they lack opportunities to do so (Mendez 1981, pp. 220–21).

The U.S. Chamber of Commerce estimates that white-collar crime costs the nation about $200 billion annually, compared to an estimated $88 billion for street crime. White-collar criminals who steal large sums of money often receive small fines and/ or suspended sentences, whereas a poor Black who steals a few hundred dollars worth of property often is sent to prison (Mendez 1981, p. 221).

Since the poor are more often victims of crime than the nonpoor, Blacks are more likely than Whites to be victimized by violent crime. Fifty-five of every one hundred murder victims in the United States are black. Murder is the fifth leading cause of death among black male adults. Black women are less likely to be homicide victims, but the loss of life for this group from homicide is greater than that caused by all types of infections or parasitic diseases. Given current rates, the probability that a black male will eventually be a homicide victim is nearly five percent and that for a black female is about one percent. Homicide reduces black male life expectancy at birth by about one and a half years and causes a greater loss of years of life expected than cancer (Blackwell 1975, p. 250; Shin, Jedlicka, and Lee 1977, p. 407).

American black males living in metropolitan communities are ten times as likely as American white males to be murder victims. A New York City study showed that intraracial homicides constituted more than four-fifths of the total. Forty-eight percent of the murders involved Blacks killing Blacks; 21 percent were Hispanics killing Hispanics; and 13 percent involved Whites killing Whites. During the study years, three-fifths of all those arrested for murder in New York City were Blacks; and half of the victims were black (Blackwell 1975, pp. 250–51).

In property crimes, the black victimization rates are higher than those for Whites. This is true for black households and burglary (71.2 per 1,000 population, compared to 40.0 for white households) for all income groups; for larceny, the rates

are 58.7 percent per 1,000 Blacks, compared with 50.8 per 1,000 for Whites. Also, Blacks with incomes over $10,000 have a rate of victimization for motor vehicle theft that is approximately twice as high as the white rate (Mendez 1981, pp. 222–23).

In any discussion of criminal statistics, it is necessary to recognize their limitations and deficiencies. As Wolfgang and Cohen (1970, p. 100) say:

We do not know with certainty the actual amount of crime among whites, Negroes, Puerto Ricans, or any other group. We do know that persons of all groups commit many offenses that are unrecorded. We cannot be sure of the degrees of seriousness of even the recorded crime without further study. . . . Among offenses for which non-whites as well as whites are arrested, crimes of homicide, rape, and other assaultive acts represent a small proportion compared to drunkenness, gambling, disorderly conduct and other relatively minor offenses against the public order. Interracial assaults are rare and no more threatening to whites than to non-whites.

Related to the point that minor offenses against the public order constitute the majority of offenses is the dramatic difference in arrests for these offenses according to racial and ethnic background. Drunk driving arrests provide an example. According to Morales (1971, p. 177), more police are present to observe drinking infractions of the law in the East Los Angeles area, with a large Mexican American population, than in areas where the residents are almost entirely white and without Spanish surnames. Arrests for drunkenness and drunk driving increase as the number of police per population unit and square mile increases. Mexican Americans appear not to drink more than their more affluent neighbors. One indicator is the Department of Public Health report of an identical ratio of alcoholism per 100,000. Where the population was white, 50 percent to 60 percent Spanish-surname, there were 13.5 officers per square mile and 9,676 drunk and drunk driving arrests per year. In neighboring areas that were 95 percent white, non-Spanish-surname, there were 3.5 officers per square mile and 1,552 arrests per year for drunkenness and drunk driving. With the exception of three or four Alcoholics Anonymous groups in East Los Angeles and a small outpatient public health agency, there were no detoxification or professional services available to Mexican Americans with drinking problems. The community has lacked an efficient system for processing drinking behavior which includes the system of criminal justice and social agencies (Morales 1971, p. 178).

Incarceration. An estimated 210,000 persons were confined in local jails in the United States on June 30, 1982. This rate was one-third higher than in February, 1978, and matched the rate of increase of the prison population during the same period. Jails held one inmate for every two inmates held in state and federal prisons (U.S. Department of Justice, Bureau of Justice Statistics, February, 1983, pp. 1–2). Jails differ from prisons in that they hold unconvicted as well as convicted persons serving sentences for lesser offenses. The majority of prison inmates are serving maximum sentences of more than a year for the commission of felonies.

On December 31, 1982, the number of prisoners under state and federal jurisdiction per 100,000 population was 183. For Whites, the detention rate was 114 per 100,000 population, compared with a rate of 716 for Blacks (U.S. Department of Justice, Bureau of Justice Statistics, March–April, 1984, Table 9). On June 30, 1982, the number of inmates in local jails per 100,000 population was 90. For Whites, the detention rate was 50 per 100,000 population, compared with a rate of 304 per 100,000 population for Blacks.

Young men constitute the largest group of prisoners. About three-fourths of all adult prisoners in the United States are under 34 years of age. In 1975, one white man between 18 and 34 was in prison for every 153.6 white men in that age group in the total population. For nonwhite males, one between 18 and 34 was in prison for every 22.4 nonwhite men in that age group in the nation (Mendez 1981, p. 225).

Minorities are overrepresented in prisons in the United States, but in some reports minorities mean only Blacks. In its decennial census of prison populations, the U.S. Census did not list Mexican Americans, but included them as White. This practice makes it difficult to document the extent to which Chicanos are overrepresented in the nation's prisons. One estimate gave the incarceration rates for black men in California in the age group 25–44 as seven times that of white men of the same age. The rate for Chicanos was about twice as high as for Whites (Moore 1978, pp. 95–96).

The Native American Rights Fund estimates that there are 800 Indian inmates in the state penitentiaries of five states (Montana, South Dakota, North Dakota, Nebraska, and Minnesota) and another 500 in federal penitentiaries for the same area. With an Indian population of approximately 100,000, more than one out of 100 Indians is in prison in these five states (Stanley and Thomas 1978, p. 118).

Race, Minority Status, and Crime Causation

Crime causation is the most difficult aspect of the study of illegal behavior. Students of criminality have suggested a number of factors to account for criminal actions and differential crime rates, and each of these explanations has some merit. To us the most satisfactory interpretation of crime causation lies in the interaction of three major variables: cultural, socioeconomic, and psychological. This approach is useful in understanding the high crime rates of members of racial and cultural minorities, as well as high rates of crime victimization in these groups.

Available data indicate that poor young black men disproportionately commit such crimes as homicide, assault, rape, and robbery. However, other groups are overrepresented in other kinds of violence, crime, and deviance. For example, older white middle-class men are disproportionately involved in white-collar crime and political corruption. When all types of crimes are considered, it is difficult to say that a racial group with certain social class, age, and sex attributes is more deviant than a racial group with a different set of such characteristics (Curtis 1975, p. 49). In any case, the majority of the black population, and of other minorities in the United States, like the majority of American people, are law-abiding citizens. Others, for a variety of reasons, deviate from societal norms in one or a number of ways (Blackwell 1975, p. 244).

The Cultural Factor in Black Crime. Curtis (1975, pp. 37, 45) hypothesizes that poor young urban black males follow and approve of violent contraculture patterns more than most attribute groups (for example, poor black females, or older middle-class white males) when a kind of average group index is used. The violent contraculture patterns of some poor young black males are interpreted by Curtis as an adaptation to poverty and racism. In this view, these patterns are seen as a redirection and exaggeration of expressions of certain types of masculinity—behaviors which are less stymied by powerful figures in the dominant culture than other expressions.[8] As part of this hypothesis,

---

[8] Although full agreement does not exist on the meaning of black contraculture—a violent contraculture—a hypothesized cluster of values and behaviors might include emphasis on physical prowess, emphasis on sexual power and exploitation, emphasis on shrewdness and manipulativeness, and emphasis on thrill seeking and change versus safeness and sameness (Curtis 1975, pp. 8–9, 12, 24).

Curtis sees certain stimuli (especially pursuit of status change) from the dominant culture combining with the role-modeling influences of the violent contraculture in the socialization of young black males in the urban community.

The Socioeconomic Factor in Crime Causation. In our view, the second major interacting factor in crime causation is socioeconomic conditions. Nine-tenths of the black population in the North and West lives in cities, and nine-tenths of these live in, or adjacent to, disorganized slum areas. Unemployment, poverty, overcrowding, vice, crime, and social disorder characterize these areas (Yongsock, Jedlicka, and Lee 1977, pp. 399, 406). Silberman (1978, pp. 89–90) comments that to children growing up in lower-class neighborhoods, crime is an occupational choice in the way that law, medicine, or business are for adolescents who live in affluent suburbs. Many youngsters in slum areas possess detailed knowledge concerning robbery, burglary, "fencing," the sale and use of drugs, prostitution and pimping, the "numbers" business, loan-sharking, and other crimes and rackets (see also Curtis 1975, p. 6).

As we noted earlier, Blau and Blau (1982, p. 114), utilizing data on the largest metropolitan areas (SMSA's) in the United States, found that socioeconomic inequality between races, as well as economic inequality generally, increases rates of criminal violence. However, when economic inequalities were controlled, poverty did not influence violent crime rates, nor did location in the South, and the ratio of Blacks in the population had only a small effect. According to Blau and Blau, these results imply that the roots of criminal violence are pronounced inequalities, particularly if they are associated with ascribed position.

To these aspects of the socioeconomic factor in crime causation and differential crime rates may be added the role of gangs. Gang-related crimes increased during the 1970s. In several major cities, hundreds of deaths have been attributed to juvenile and young-adult gangs. For many jobless and homeless minority youths who have become alienated from society, these gangs provide a sense of belonging. However, equipped with more effective weapons than earlier gangs, these groups have provided protection for drug dealers and drug users. Some gang members have become expert hustlers, operating confidence games, pimping for prostitutes, and perpetrating various types of fraud (Blackwell 1975, p. 258).

Until relatively recently, black gangsters worked for white mobsters who controlled gambling, prostitution, loan-sharking, organized burglary, narcotics selling, bookmaking, the numbers game, and other kinds of organized crime. Black mobsters now play more important roles in organized crime, and some police officials say that these individuals are trying to gain control over this type of activity in the black community. "Playing the numbers" is widespread in the black community, with an estimated 40 percent of the black and Puerto Rican communities in New York City participating in the "policy game." The highly organized numbers system involves about $2 billion in annual receipts and like other types of organized crime can exist only with some form of corruption of law enforcement agents (Blackwell 1975, p. 259).

A study of Chicano gangs in Los Angeles found that most gang members use drugs and that the gang has been the main context for the marketing successively of marijuana, heroin, inhalants, and PCP. The norms of the neighborhood Chicano youth gangs persist among the men of the barrios who go to prison in California and reappear in self-help groups which have been formed in those institutions (Moore 1978, pp. 11, 36, 75).

According to Moore (1978, p. 167) barrio residents live within a tripartite survival economy of secondary jobs, welfare programs, and illegal activities. These residents believe that jobs and training for decent jobs are urgently needed for youths and ex-convicts, but Moore (chapter 1) suggests that such a search is bound to meet a degree of failure. There are not enough good jobs in the legal economy to go around, and in Chicano Los Angeles, the illegal economy, dominated by the drug trade, seriously hinders any rational development of the skills of the people of the barrios.

Despite the destructive aspects of youth gangs in the barrios of Los Angeles, some residents maintain optimism about their neighborhoods. Both standard and deviant orientations to life are found in the cohorts of the Chicano fighting gangs. The self-help groups that have developed in and away from the prisons into barrio social movements, with little help from established social agencies, may encourage the adoption of the square identity (Moore 1978, p. 179).

Many tribal people, as well as federal officials, hold alcohol abuse to be a major health problem among American Indians. Competent observers regard this abuse as symptomatic of economic, environmental, acculturative, and other stresses which prevail in Indian communities (Mail 1978, pp. 44–45).

An important study of excessive Indian drunkenness sought an explanation in terms of structural and psychological variables that pertain also to non-Indian drinkers (Graves 1971, pp. 274–311; 1970, pp. 35–54). Among other variables, attention was given to parental role models, premigration training for successful urban employment, and marital status. The average Indian migrant comes to Denver with limited education and a limited ability in English. More than half of the migrants stay in the city less than six months. Navajos with better education who stay on the reservation obtain the best jobs there. Thus many migrants experience a cycle of frustration—migration to the city, return, and personal failure ending in drunkenness. Married migrants who had adapted to urban life and who were not associated socially with the drinking cliques of single Navajos had arrest rates similar to those of other minority groups in the city—rates which were only a fraction of the overall Navajo rate.

The Indian arrest rate in Denver, almost always for a drinking related offense, is considerably higher than for other American minority groups and for the majority population. However, the arrest rate for serious crimes, personal and property, is clearly lower than that for the total population of the city.

Another study showed that nearly one-third of the Mexican American migrants in Denver had fathers who were employed as semiskilled wage laborers or better. Most Navajo wage labor of the last generation was unskilled manual labor. Approximately one-third of the Mexican American migrants also had had eleven years or more of high school training, compared with 14 percent of the Navajo migrants. Eighty-eight percent of the Mexican American migrants were married, compared with one-fifth of the Navajo migrants. The first job in Denver was skilled for 15 percent of the Mexican American migrants, compared with 6 percent for the Navajo. If these differences between Indian urban migrants and other working-class groups were controlled, differences in drinking behavior would be small (Graves 1971, p. 306).

The Psychological Factor in Crime Causation. In our interpretation of crime causation and differential racial crime rates, the third major variable is psychological. One facet of this factor is the encouragement of illegal behavior produced by the barriers inflicted upon minorities. As Pettigrew

(1964, p. 194) says, crime may be utilized "as a means of escape, ego-enhancement, expression of aggression, or upward mobility." Poussaint (1974) asserts that racially engendered rage and self-hatred play an important role in black crime. He claims that many black street criminals reveal a strong subconscious drive toward self-destruction in that they ignore the great probability of their being caught. Poussaint says that many lower-class Blacks are primed for violent outbursts by the problems of daily life and, to a greater extent than middle-class people, lack ways to defuse their rage.

An interesting aspect of robbery (theft with force) is the motivation behind a crime. Typically, "professional" robbers are in their mid-twenties, have middle- or working-class backgrounds, steal for a living, plan their thefts carefully, carry firearms, and try to obtain large sums of money, especially from institutions. "Opportunist" robbers, who are more numerous, are younger, have lower-class backgrounds, steal for small sums to use in maintaining style rather than to gain a living, often rob randomly on the street without much planning, usually do not carry firearms, and more often use force than professionals. Conklin (quoted in Curtis 1975, p. 92) found that Blacks tend to fall in the opportunist category.

A New York City study showed that nearly three-fourths of those arrested for murder were either unemployed (39 percent) or were laborers (34 percent). The others were students, housewives, drivers of taxicabs, trucks, or buses, or businessmen. Blackwell (1975, p. 251) asserts: "This occupational profile supports the theoretical position that intrarace murders originate in frustrations related to economic deprivation or alienation." In this view, frustrations arising from conditions in the social structure may be displaced and directed against members of the ingroup. The minority offender may even have come to believe that offenses against members of his own group will be less severely punished than offenses against majority persons.

In considering the psychological factor in crime causation, self concept is important. Once labeled a criminal, the individual may come to regard himself as a criminal and therefore to reorder his behavior in ways that conform to that social expectation (Blackwell 1975, p. 262).

Drawing on social scientific and psychological studies, Silberman (1978, chapter 5) presents an explanation of black criminal violence similar to the interpretation given here. Until forty years ago,

Blacks, with rare exceptions, were locked into the lower class. Without regard to individual merit, humiliation and embarrassment were a part of black daily experience. Gradually, Blacks developed new outlets to control their anger and to preserve their sense of personal worth. In lower-class black neighborhoods, and particularly among lower-class black men, verbal contests—word play, "signifying," "playing the dozens," boasts, jokes, insults, and "toasts"—played important roles from the late nineteenth century until recently as substitutes for physical violence.[9]

The toasts are built upon inverted stereotypes. Through folklore, black men have turned white morality upside down and converted their own supposed unusual sexuality, physical strength, and alleged inability to control their impulses into positive characteristics. As Christina and Richard Milner (quoted in Silberman 1978, p. 149) comment:

> If being Black means one is the "bad guy" according to White majority culture, the question becomes how can one turn "badness" into "goodness" without either "acting White" or destroying oneself. . . . The man who asserts his masculinity and refuses to bow before authority is therefore "good." Thus a "bad nigger" is one who is so "bad" he is "good"; he is admirable in his defiance.

The toasts, and black folklore in general, have served to transform black rage into entertainment, but according to Silberman (1978, pp. 152–56), the process no longer works as it did in former years. Toasts and other elements of black folk culture continue to provide role models for black adolescents to emulate, but young Blacks have begun to act out their aggression: "It is this shift from the mythic to the real—from toasting, signifying, and playing the dozens to committing robbery, murder, rape, and assault—that underlies the explosive increase in criminal violence on the part of black offenders."

The Police

Recruitment. In 1968, the National Advisory Commission on Civil Disorders found that Blacks were underrepresented in every police department for which statistics were available. Of 80,621 personnel in 28 major cities, only 7,046 were nonwhite.

During the next fifteen years substantial increases in the number of black policemen were made in a number of major American cities. In 1980, 23 percent of the police force in Chicago was black; in Philadelphia, 19 percent; in Memphis, 18 percent; in Baltimore, 17 percent; in Detroit, 62 percent; and in San Francisco, 14 percent. In some cities the proportion has declined. In Tampa, only 19 of 559 officers were black, fewer than were on the force during the 1967 riot in that city. New Orleans has a Hispanic population of 120,000, but by May, 1980, it had been unable to recruit a single Spanish-speaking officer (*The New York Times,* May 25, 1980, p. 16).

In the economic recession of the summer of 1980 in Detroit, the city laid off 690 police officers, 18 percent of its patrol force. This action seriously affected an affirmative action program that had placed a higher percentage of Blacks and women on the force than in any other major city in the country. Approximately one-fourth of the department's black officers were laid off. Of the 690 police officers who were furloughed, 44.4 percent were black men, 29.8 percent were black women, 16.2 percent were white men, and 9.4 percent were white women. The layoffs received considerable attention, in part because some officials feared that the loss of a large number of Blacks and women would reverse an improvement in police–community relations that had been attributed to the affirmative action program (*The New York Times,* September 7, 1980, pp. 1, 13).

Police–Community Relations. Much of the activity of the police department in a large city is concerned with attempts to detect crime through undercover work, a communications network, preventive patrols, regular patrols, and so on. Inevitably, much of the energy of the department is directed toward the ghetto (Cooper 1980, p. 50).

The American police system has a subculture with interests, norms, and ideals which differ from those of other subcultures, with the result that prejudice, fear, and conflict are constantly generated. The relations of racial and cultural minorities, as well as of political and social dissenters of various kinds, to the police often are characterized by anger, hatred, and violence. The police are seen as thugs whose behavior is upheld by the larger community. Ghetto citizens often feel that they have no means of redress to police actions and many seek police officers only in situations of great necessity (Cooper 1980, p. 52; Glasgow 1980, pp. 100–101).

---

[9]Silberman's account of verbal contests among lower-class blacks as a surrogate for actual violence is based largely on Abrahams 1970, Jackson 1974, and C. and R. Milner 1972.

In the relations between a policeman and a ghetto resident, protecting one's "honor" is important. The policeman on the beat may do this by getting the resident to honor his authority, by getting the ghetto citizen to show him respect. A ghetto resident who is hostile to the authority structures of society may consider that resisting police authority is one of the most honorable ways he can behave (Alex 1969, pp. 200–210; Cooper 1980, p. 73).

In playing their role in the ghetto, the police tend to adhere strongly to the rules and to develop a rule-book mentality. Some observers of ghetto life see the police as more bureaucratic than the teachers, social workers, or parole and probation officers. Cooper (1980, pp. 99, 123) asserts that, regardless of race, all police who work in the ghetto try to become emotionally detached from their job. The job is a means to an end—the middle-class way of life, job security, and a pension.

Because of his color, a black officer may be thought to have no authority, no legitimate role. In the ghetto he may be seen simply as an agent of the white establishment, and as such he is hated. In the 1960s, some city officials believed that black officers could be a calming force in the ghetto, but by 1980 this belief was less widely held (Cooper 1980, pp. 111–112). The black policeman who follows the wishes of politicians and community-minded Blacks may be charged by his white colleagues with being soft on crime. If he behaves otherwise, Blacks in the community may accuse him of disloyalty (Cooper 1980, pp. 111–12, 126).

Despite the frequently somewhat unfavorable characterizations of the black policeman, undoubtedly the police serve an important role for the ghetto with the social services they perform. Police spend much of their time breaking up fights in bars and stadiums and settling disputes between spouses, lovers, neighbors, landlords and tenants, and other strangers and friends (Silberman 1978, p. 203). "Without such services," Cooper says, "the ghetto would be a much more downtrodden, volatile place for those who live there." These services, then, often produce ambivalent feelings on the part of the residents toward the police.

Other reports in the years following the tumults of the 1960s describe a "new" type of black policeman. This officer is said to share the sensitivity of his friends and neighbors to police excesses and to show the confidence that goes with increasing numbers of Blacks in the forces of many of the country's large cities. The number of so-called new black policemen is a matter of dispute. No doubt many of Cooper's comments about the black policeman are accurate, but the beginnings of change can be discerned. The reorientation of police work is seen in the goals of the Chicago-based National Black Police Association, a coalition of state and local organizations. The reformist approach also has started to gain substantial backing at the highest levels of the police department and city officialdom in some cities, including Detroit (*The New York Times,* August 11, 1974, pp. 1, 35).

Antagonism between black and white policemen is not uncommon when Blacks first appear in numbers on the force, but "salt-and-pepper" patrols are now relatively common and accepted by black and white officers, especially among the younger members. Black policemen are sometimes reported to have a restraining influence on white colleagues who might otherwise tend to act in a prejudiced manner (*The New York Times,* August 11, 1974, p. 35).

Following the riots of the 1960s and early 1970s, many police departments in the United States developed new techniques for dealing with community unrest; police officers were given training in better understanding of minorities, and in many cases Blacks and members of other minorities were added to the police force and elected to governing positions in city hall (*The New York Times,* May 25, 1980, p. 16).

In the spring of 1980, conflicts between the police and minority neighborhoods intensified again. A serious riot occurred in Miami during the weekend of May 17, and disturbances were reported in Wichita, Baltimore, and Los Angeles. Tensions were reported to be somewhat less in Detroit, Atlanta, and Newark, where Blacks have considerable political power, but even in these cities strong antagonisms were evident (*The New York Times,* May 25, 1980, p. 16). Conflicts arose again in December, 1982.

Mexican Americans and the Police in the Southwest. Reports of federal commissions reveal biased treatment of Mexican Americans by law enforcement agencies in the Southwest. This treatment includes verbal abuse, beatings, unwarranted arrests, improper use of bail, underrepresentation in law enforcement agencies and juries, and a lack of serious investigation into these allegations at all levels of government. Juveniles as well as adults have been treated with a lack of sensitivity. The

U.S. Commission on Civil Rights found that this treatment had produced an attitude of distrust and fear on the part of the Chicano community toward law enforcement agencies. Tensions between the police and the Mexican American community have been aggravated by the inability of many Spanish-speaking residents to communicate with officers who understood only English (Fernandez, Haug, and Wagner 1976, p. 84).

Psychological brutality toward Mexican Americans on the part of police officers is reported to be more widespread than physical brutality. The President's Crime Commission reported the feeling that police are condescending and paternalistic in addressing Mexican Americans and that there is excessive patroling in Mexican American districts and unwarranted frisking of adults and youths (Rowan 1977, p. 39).

Discrimination in the Administration of Criminal Justice

A government advisory body, the National Minority Advisory Council on Criminal Justice, stated in October, 1980:

> Minorities are not only more likely to be suspected of crime than whites, they are also more likely to be arrested and less likely to secure bail. Further, after being arrested, minorities are more likely to be indicted than whites, and are less likely to have their cases dismissed. If tried, minorities are more likely to be imprisoned and more likely to serve full terms without parole. (Cleveland *Plain Dealer*, October 18, 1980, p. 10A)

The extent of racial discrimination in the administration of criminal justice, however, is difficult to determine. Clearly, poor people are at a disadvantage in hiring legal representation and in obtaining bail, and a very high proportion of Blacks and other minorities are poor people. With less ability to secure legal aid, Blacks are often not apprised of due process and are not so successful in having felonious murder charges reduced to less serious crimes (Blackwell 1975, p. 247). Unquestionably, racial and cultural minorities encounter prejudice on the part of some judges and members of juries who sit in judgment upon them.

Savitz (1973, p. 493) says that there is a widespread view, especially among Blacks, that police are prejudiced and frequently discriminate against Blacks. Also, police have been found to verbalize hostile ideas about Blacks. Nevertheless, he adds:

There is little evidence that this, in turn, influences such police behavior as field interrogations, searches, seizures, and arrests. There is little empirical support to the contention that police systematically discriminate against blacks. The evidence is that they are more severe and less justified in some of their practices in their encounters with lower-class whites.

Black–black crimes produce less official concern than do white–white crimes. There is some evidence to show that law enforcement agencies react overseverely toward black–white offenses. However, the much greater number of intraracial offenses makes it likely or at least arguable that a more scrupulous criminal justice system would result in a larger number and proportion of black offenders that become known to the police and the courts (Savitz 1973, pp. 484, 505).

An interesting study of the adjudication of homicide defendants in a large urban jurisdiction in the northeastern United States suggests that the stereotype of the violent offender constitutes an official imagery influencing legal decisions (Swigert and Farrell 1977, pp. 16–32). The diagnostic category of the "normal primitive" employed by the evaluation clinic attached to the court specifies persons whose violent behavior is regarded as normal within their own social setting. This study shows that the race and occupational prestige of defendants contribute materially to the designation "normal primitive." Blacks and those of lower occupational prestige are more likely to be designated "primitive" than are Whites or higher-status individuals.

Race and social class have often been considered the most important factors in studies of the adjudication of criminal defendants. The financial ability to retain private counsel aside, higher social status tends to merit a defendant a more lenient conviction. In the imagery surrounding legal decisions, the offender is to be penalized in proportion to the severity of his offense, but also so that he will consider the advantages and disadvantages of committing offenses in the future. The lower-class defendant appears to have little to lose except freedom from incarceration. The higher-status person is said to have suffered greatly as a result of arrest, the loss of status in the community, personal and familial trauma, and, perhaps, loss of professional license or practice. Thus, Swigert and Farrell (1977) make an important distinction between overt discrimination on the basis of race and class and conformance with an institutionalized imagery. In their analysis, race did not exert immediate influence on legal processing; the only significant effects of race were its strong associations with social class and the conception of certain types of criminality as "normal primitiveness."

Indian tribes have been limited by the U.S. Supreme Court and the U.S. Congress in dealing with serious crimes committed on reservations. The responsibility of the federal government for law enforcement on Indian reservations is not being fully met. Procedures vary from reservation to reservation for investigating felony offenses. In the general pattern, tribal police share responsibility for law enforcement with the BIA police and with BIA special officers. When a crime is committed, a tribal officer or BIA patrol officer is usually first to investigate. If it is a serious offense, the officer calls in a BIA special officer who conducts an investigation and notifies the FBI. Usually, the FBI conducts an independent investigation and presents the case to the United States attorney for prosecution. Ordinarily, no serious action will be taken against an offender if the United States attorney takes none. Indian organizations, the U.S. Commission on Civil Rights, and the American Indian Policy Commission appointed by Congress to evaluate federal policies and programs in relation to Indians have been highly critical of federal investigation and prosecution of offenses in Indian country (U.S. Commission on Civil Rights, June, 1981b, pp. 185–86).

Proposals for Changes in the System of Criminal Justice

The Police. Police department consultants have suggested that the police could do more to "change the climate" between them and minority communities. Ways of improving relations with these communities might include responding to neighborhood complaints, such as abandoned cars and buildings and uncollected trash, that are not their responsibility. Thus, the police could tell residents that they do not have responsibility over these matters but at the same time could help them negotiate the bureaucratic maze of city government to get action. Providing such assistance would offset the view that the police are agents of a hostile society and help establish them as guardians of the community.

Other recommendations that have been made for the improvement of police operations include: increases in both salaries and training of policemen, including more training in human relations;

promotion of minority officers to leadership positions on the force; the creation of citizen advisory committees to work with local police precincts; better procedures for evaluating complaints against the police; the development of policy guidelines for the exercise of discretion by police officers; stress on sensitivity and ability to deal with people as requisites for promotion; increased use of local civilians, male and female, for parking-meter patrol, school crossing guard duty, and similar tasks; expanded early-warning systems for reporting accidents, disorders, and community tensions; the use of more police in high-crime areas; and assigning priority in law enforcement to crimes of violence and to breaking up the syndicates behind the narcotics trade and other crimes that victimize the poor.

Silberman (1978, p. 252) questions the hypothesis that delegating more responsibility to patrol officers would increase their effectiveness. What is needed, he says, "is not more hardware, communications equipment, or personnel, but more research and experimentation." In the meantime, discarding the belief that there is a police solution to the problem of criminal violence might be helpful.

The Judicial System. The National Minority Advisory Council on Criminal Justice asserts that minorities are often denied their constitutional right to be judged by a jury of their peers because of the systematic exclusion of prospective minority jurors. Voter registration lists that are used to draw jury panels include relatively fewer minority names because minorities do not vote as frequently as nonminorities. The council advocates the use of driver's license lists as a better source of public records to secure diversity in the pool of prospective jurors (Cleveland *Plain Dealer*, October 18, 1980, p. 10A).

One of the main problems with juvenile courts is not too great leniency but that judges in these courts spend the bulk of their time on juveniles charged with "status offenses." Offenses such as "incorrigibility," truancy, and running away from home make up at least 50 percent, and perhaps two-thirds, of juvenile court time. The result is that there is little time to deal with those juveniles who are involved in serious crimes (Silberman 1978, pp. 311–12). A major question, therefore, is how to find more effective ways of handling minor forms of youthful offenses, before and after these young people are arrested.

Silberman (1978, pp. 367–368) suggests that a

revised juvenile code should specify statutory maximum dispositions for each offense or group of offenses. Incarceration should be prohibited for such offenses as vandalism and shoplifting, and a strong presumption should prevail against incarceration of first or second offenders of any nonviolent crime. In this approach, courts would have jurisdiction over juveniles only when they engage in behavior that would be criminal if committed by an adult. A revised code should provide, however, for short-term intervention in clearly defined and sharply limited crisis situations—for example, holding a runaway for twenty-four hours until parents can be reached, or using the court's power to obtain psychiatric help for a suicidal youngster. In addition, juvenile court jurisdiction might be extended to make provisions for parents or others to rebut the presumption of nonintervention in situations wherein a child's mental state indicates that a "hands-off" policy would be damaging to the child.

Other proposed changes in the judicial system include: the appointment of many more qualified judges from the membership of minority groups, as well as the recruitment of minority-group lawyers, probation officers, and others concerned with the administration of justice; increasing free legal services; and reducing delays in the courts (see Silberman 1978, pp. 296–308).

Silberman's conclusion concerning the criminal courts is far from pessimistic. He says:

What is remarkable is not how badly, but how well, most criminal courts work. Inefficient and unjust as they appear to be, criminal courts generally do an effective job of separating the innocent from the guilty; most of those who should be convicted are convicted, and most of those who should be punished are punished.

(This generalization does not apply to the juvenile courts). Silberman thinks there is no reason to believe that any of the reforms in criminal court procedures now being advocated would produce any noticeable reduction in criminal violence. What is wrong with the judicial process, he argues, is the shabby, haphazard way in which it is conducted. To contribute to a reduction in crime, courts will have "to become models of fairness and due process." In short, courts will have to encourage respect for law by treating human beings with decency and concern.

Corrections. A six-year follow-up of arrests by the FBI found that two-thirds of those arrested had been rearrested at least once. Nine out of ten arrestees whose cases were dismissed or acquitted were rearrested, as were 40 percent of those who received a fine or probation; and 60 percent of those eventually paroled after serving prison sentences were also rearrested. Levitan (1975, pp. 324–25) attributes part of this poor record to the nature of the correctional system. Removing offenders from society and concentrating them in an environment with other offenders may exacerbate criminal tendencies. But in Levitan's view, much of the problem is a matter of resources—the costliness of maintaining the police, judicial, and correctional systems. Since most correctional systems operate without adequate funding, little can be done except catch, sentence, and incarcerate offenders. The overwhelming majority of jails and workhouses, which contain approximately 40 percent of the institutionalized population, have no educational facilities, and a high proportion make no provision for recreation. A small minority of state prisons offer vocational training to a minor fraction of inmates, and the small majority offering educational courses provide them for a small minority of inmates. Federal prisons contain about one-tenth of all prisoners, but a majority of releasees from these institutions have not participated in any training or education.

Because of these shortcomings, the courts rely heavily on noninstitutional treatment. In a typical year, the number of probationers equals the number of prisoners, and the ratio is expected to increase. In addition, there have been trends toward earlier parole, partial release for work, or release to community institutions. The treatment received during parole and probation, however, is of doubtful value. On the average, an adult probation officer has a caseload of over one hundred, an assignment that permits little except the most sketchy counseling and services (Levitan 1975, p. 325).

Pretrial intervention programs work with first or second offenders to keep them out of the prison system. Projects in Washington, D.C., New York, and other cities have found jobs for these offenders, improved their wages, and reduced the rate of recidivism for several months after participation. Also, some efforts have been made to help ex-offenders through bonding under government subsidy, increasing parole staffs, and the funding of a variety of groups to furnish halfway house treatment and placement services to persons released from prison. These latter projects have not met with notable success (Levitan 1975, p. 326).

Other recommendations for changes in the correctional system include: raising standards for recruitment, selection, and training of correctional personnel; expansion of psychological and educational testing of inmates, and provision of a wider variety of educational and vocational opportunities; provision of in-service human-relations training for all correctional personnel; establishing machinery for receiving prisoner complaints; the use of better means of screening out insensitive, sadistic, and racially biased correction workers; making salaries of correctional personnel competitive with other civil-service jobs; and developing pre-release centers.

General Proposals for the Reduction of Crime. Numerous measures have been suggested, and some have been tried, in the field of community action, ranging from volunteer neighbor street patrols and drives for better street lighting to businessmen's committees to find job and training opportunities for high-school dropouts and young people returning to their neighborhoods from military service, juvenile detention, or prison terms.

In the late 1970s and the early 1980s, demands were frequently made by citizens for safer communities and stricter enforcement of the law, longer fixed sentences for offenders, use of the death penalty, trying juveniles as adults for certain crimes, and expanded correctional facilities. In this philosophy, the emphasis is on the punishment of offenders, an approach that opponents assert has never deterred crime or made society safer (Mendez 1981, pp. 227–31). An alternate approach advocates taking drastic steps to combat the underlying causes of criminal behavior by improving the quality of the inner-city public schools, expanding job training and job opportunities, providing quality health care services and adequate housing for all groups in the population, and reducing the social and psychological isolation of racial and cultural minorities from the society as a whole.

In the long run, the answer to the problem of reducing criminal violence is clear enough: the elimination of poverty, inequality, and racial discrimination as important factors in American life. A large part of the high level of criminal violence among persons of the lower class is related to poor black and Hispanic youths' feeling of impotence and exclusion, and their search to be *somebody*—to believe that they are persons of worth. Clearly, social changes of greater magnitude, more sustained economic growth than that of the 1970s and the early 1980s, and greater effort than any recent administration has shown would be required (Silberman 1978, pp. 169–70).

CHAPTER 13

Minority Family Patterns and Intermarriage

Family institutions govern the biological reproduction of a society, and through them many of the economic and emotional needs of human beings are met. Much of the interaction in the families of racial and cultural minorities parallels that in other American families, but minority status does have some effects on family life. In this chapter, following a discussion of fertility levels, we shall consider black families, Mexican American families, Puerto Rican families, American Indian families, and finally intermarriage.

Fertility Levels for Racial and Cultural Minorities

The fertility of certain racial and cultural minorities in the United States ranges from very high levels for southern rural Blacks, American Indians, and Mexican Americans to moderate levels for southern urban Blacks and Blacks living outside the South, to low levels for Japanese and Chinese Americans (Rindfuss and Sweet 1977, p. 89). The Mexican American birthrate is exceptionally high, considerably higher than that of any other group, and about 50 percent greater than that of the total population (Rowan 1977, p. 37).

When age-specific fertility rates for the years 1955–1969 were calculated for six groups—Mexican Americans, American Indians, Blacks, Whites,

Chinese Americans, and Japanese Americans—substantial declines in fertility were found for every group considered. There was, however, little change in the relative positions of the six groups with regard to the level of fertility. Substantial declines in marital fertility were found for every racial and cultural group examined. The largest declines were found among the black population, and this was true for both marital fertility and overall fertility (Rindfuss and Sweet 1977, p. 115). The data in this study by Rindfuss and Sweet support two seemingly contradictory hypotheses: (a) as a minority group acquires the social, demographic, and economic characteristics of the majority group, its fertility behavior will tend to resemble that of the majority group; and (b) even when groups are similar socially, demographically, and economically, minority group membership will continue to exert an effect on fertility.

On the second point, among the effects exerted by group membership are age patterns of fertility. Formerly, American Indians, Mexican Americans, Blacks, and Whites began childbearing early and reached their peak level of fertility by their early twenties, but this has changed in recent years, especially among Whites. The Chinese Americans and Japanese Americans begin their childbearing substantially later and do not attain their peak level of childbearing until their late twenties. For the early fertility groups, between 40 and 50 percent of their childbearing occurs before age 25; among Chinese Americans and Japanese Americans, the proportion is one-fourth. With the exception of American Indians and Mexican Americans, differences in fertility past age 27 are minimal; these two groups have comparatively high levels of fertility at virtually every age (Rindfuss and Sweet 1977, pp. 145, 148).

In 1970, Puerto Ricans living in mainland United States had a fertility rate that was somewhat higher than that of urban Whites. Lower than average fertility is found for Puerto Rican couples, however, if both spouses were born in the United States or for couples where the wife was born in the United States and the husband was born outside the United States. The highest rates are found for couples in which the wife was born outside continental United States and the husband was born within the country. The relationship between income and fertility is inverse if adjustment is not made for factors such as education, marriage duration, and age of marriage. When such factors are included, the relationship between income and recent marital fertility is virtually eliminated (Cooney, Rogler, and Schroder 1981, pp. 1094–1113; Rindfuss and Sweet 1977, pp. 137, 139).

With the exception of southern rural Blacks, where there is a very small relationship, there is a consistent inverse relationship between fertility and education for all groups considered. The American Indian, Puerto Rican American, Mexican American, and rural farm white population all have coefficients approximating that for the urban white population. For urban Blacks, the relationship is about half the level of the white rate; Chinese Americans and Japanese Americans also have a lower relationship between fertility and education than do urban Whites (Rindfuss and Sweet 1977, p. 150).

One-third of all Puerto Ricans reside in mainland United States (Rindfuss and Sweet, p. 174). Rather surprisingly, there is virtually no difference between the current fertility of urban island residents and of recent migrants to the mainland, when age, education, and occupation of husband are controlled. Also, no significant difference was found between these two groups and long-term residents of the mainland. Substantial differences in fertility do exist between these three groups and rural island residents, and these differences may be a function of urban residence rather than of migration to the mainland (Rindfuss and Sweet 1977, p. 183).

The pervasiveness of the fertility trends across racial and cultural groups in the United States since the end of World War II suggests that the causes must be broad and historical. Such causes would include the relative prosperity of the 1950s, increases in education, more women in the labor force, the introduction of the pill, and the growing impact of the women's movement (Rindfuss and Sweet 1977, p. 192).

The median age of the Hispanic population is 22, compared with 25 for Blacks and over 31 for Whites. The median for the total population is 30. Prominent among the reasons for high population growth among Hispanics are the relatively large number of women of childbearing age and the cultural and religious resistance to birth control (*The New York Times,* February 2, 1979, p. 16).[1]

Black–White Fertility Rates

Births to Nonwhites rose to 599,000 annually in 1954 and stayed above 600,000 from 1955 to 1972, with slight drops in 1967 and 1968. The fertility rate of black women declined sharply along with that of white women in the mid-1960s. The white fertility rate decreased to 1.7 births per woman in 1975 and remained there until rising to 1.8 in 1979. The decline in the black fertility rate was less rapid, but by 1970 it was down to 3.1 and has remained around 2.3 since 1973 (Reid 1982, p. 10).

Education and fertility are correlated in both races—the higher the educational level, the lower the fertility. The lowest fertility of any group is found for black women with a college degree or more education—a rate of 1,730 births per 1,000 women, compared to 1,857 for white women of similar education. Fertility is correlated also with income—the larger proportion of families in poverty among Blacks compared to Whites is related to their higher overall fertility (Reid 1982, pp. 10–11).

Although the black fertility rate has fallen steadily to the present level of 2.3 births per woman, completed fertility for Blacks remained one-third higher than that of white women in 1981—1,887

---

[1] Finding that Mexican Americans had larger families than Anglos in every income category, Grebler, Moore, and Guzman (1970, pp. 185–186) concluded that differential family size may not be simply a function of low-income status. Other studies have shown that the relationship between fertility and ethnic background persists even after socioeconomic status has been controlled. It appears that to understand Mexican American fertility, further research is needed on factors other than socioeconomic ones (Alvirez and Bean 1976, p. 282).

births per 1,000 black women aged 18–44 compared to 1,414 per 1,000 for white women. The difference in fertility between the two groups may be due in part to the differences in contraceptive use among black and white married women (Reid 1982, pp. 13–14). For women 18 and 19, the average fertility for Blacks (411 per 1,000) was more than three times the average for Whites (128 per 1,000). Reid (1982, p. 11) comments that if teenage fertility as well as unwanted births could be materially lowered, black fertility probably would approximate white fertility in a short time.

Reid (1982, p. 14) says that the fact that Blacks are obtaining abortions more often than Whites may reflect their having more unplanned pregnancies. Among the factors that may account for this difference are the following: a greater increase in sexual activity among Blacks than among Whites (not true of teenagers), use of less effective methods of contraception among Blacks, and coercive pressures on black women to seek abortions rather than carry their pregnancies to term.

Black Families

Black Families Today

In 1980, 86 percent of black families were comprised of married couples with or without children or a single parent living with one or more of his or her own children under age 18. In the total population, 93 percent are found in one of these categories. Single parents with children constituted nearly one-third (31 percent) of black families in 1980, compared to one-tenth in the total population. For black families with children, approximately half were headed by single parents, compared with less than one-fifth for the whole population. For single-parent families of all races, 90 percent are headed by the mother; for Blacks the proportion is 94 percent. Among Blacks, female-headed families almost doubled during the 1970s. More black children under age 18 were living with their mother only in 1980 (44 percent) than with two parents (42 percent). Among Whites, 83 percent of the children under 18 were living with two parents and 14 percent with their mother only (Reid 1982, pp. 21–22).

During the 1970s unmarried-couple households increased rapidly, but by 1980 only 2 percent of all households maintained by adults regardless of race were of this type. In 1980, Blacks maintained 11 percent of all households, but they maintained 19 percent of all unmarried-couple households. Because households of this type increased eight times as fast during the 1970s as other types of households among persons of other races, compared with three times as fast among Blacks, the gap between Blacks and others in this respect has been narrowing (Glick 1981, p. 113).

The pattern of delaying marriage longer by young adult Blacks, compared to young Whites, became more pronounced by 1980. In part, this trend may be attributed to the higher employment rates and the faster increasing college enrollment rates among Blacks. A demographic factor in the amount of marriage postponement in the 1960s and 1970s was the "marriage squeeze." Since women are usually a few years younger than men at marriage, a woman born when the birth rate has risen (1947, for example) would be likely to marry a man born two or three years earlier when the birthrate was lower. As a result, about twenty years later, there was an excess of women in the most marriageable age group. By 1970, the number of black men 20–26 years of age was only 82 percent of the number of black women 18 to 24. For persons of all races in 1970 the percentage was 93. By 1980, the percentage for Blacks had risen to 89, compared with 98 for all races (Glick 1981, p. 116).

The Black Nuclear Family

The 1970 Census showed that 75 percent of black families fell into one of three nuclear categories: husband–wife, husband–wife–children, or man or woman and children. For Whites, the proportion was 90 percent (Heiss 1975, p. 22).

A tabulation of household relationship and presence of parents for persons under 18 years old by race and Spanish origin in March, 1981, showed that for all children under 18 years, 42.7 percent of black children were living with both parents, 43.3 percent with mother only, 2.5 percent with father only, and 11.1 percent with neither parent. Comparable proportions for Whites were: 82.3 percent, 13.7 percent, 1.8 percent, and 1.9 percent. For persons of Spanish origin, the proportions were 68.8 percent, 23 percent, 2.4 percent, and 4.1 percent (Bureau of the Census, June, 1982, pp. 29–30).

Attention should be called to the presence of "extraneous" adults—adults other than husband and wife within husband–wife families. Two categories of relatives may be distinguished—adult children of the couple and other relatives. In white husband–wife families, 20 percent have another adult present. For Blacks and Spanish-surname families, this proportion is approximately 30 percent. Usually, the adult is a child of the couple. In white husband–wife families, only 7 percent have a related adult other than own children of the household heads. For Blacks, the proportion is about two and a half times higher (18 percent), and among southern Blacks it is about one-quarter. Mexican Americans, Puerto Ricans, and American Indians all have proportions between 12 and 15 percent (Sweet 1979, p. 245).

In modern industrial societies, many of the functions of the extended kin are lost, and the economically self-sufficient nuclear family becomes the ideal family mode (Martin and Martin 1978, p. 101; Scanzoni 1971, pp. 323–324). At present, however, many urban Blacks are abandoning the extended family without having the economic resources to establish stable nuclear families. They have adopted urban values but are not permitted to become full participants in the modern economy. These individuals struggle to survive in the streets of the ghetto or depend on welfare programs provided by the government. Usually, family members do not exert pressure on a better-off member to help those who are less fortunate, but he will be expected to make some contributions to his parents, especially to his mother. Dependent family members may be seen as parasites. Elderly family members may be given institutional care. Family members are expected to raise their own children. Those who are employable may be forced to look after themselves. Such attitudes may alienate a middle-class person from his relatives (Martin and Martin 1978, pp. 75–76, 100).

In many black homes where the husband and wife are present, women appear to have assumed the major responsibility for the family. Frequently, however, the husband makes decisions in the household which his wife implements. In other families, the wife makes important decisions but with the permission of the man. He has the ultimate authority and exercises it whenever he wishes. In still other families, the husband defers to his mate in certain decisions because she has more formal education than he has, or because she is more familiar with the operations of white bureaucracies than he is. In any case, the black woman is unlikely to

make any decisions which he actively opposes (Staples 1977a, pp. 182–183).

Staples (1973, pp. 149–150) points out that the child-rearing practices in lower-class black families often conflict with contemporary theories about child development. Most middle-class black women are recent entrants to that class and therefore tend to raise their children in the same way that their mothers or grandmothers did. The black mother often works, has more children, and less time to devote to child care. Nevertheless, many black mothers have transcended many hardships and reared their children effectively. Their affection has given their children much support. Staples (1973, pp. 151–152) asserts that black children are less likely to develop the neurotic traits associated with some of the rigid child-rearing practices characteristic of some members of the white middle class. Some observers have claimed that neglect and abuse of children in welfare families are more frequent among Whites than Blacks.

Many black fathers are devoted to their children, but paradoxically the black father who most nearly approximates the middle-class ideal of fatherly behavior may do his children a disservice by inculcating the child with middle-class values and skills. If the father ignores the coping mechanisms essential to survival in the ghetto, the child who is unable to leave the ghetto may become marginal to both social worlds (Staples 1973, p. 151).

The marginal economic status of many black families in the lower and working classes is an important factor in sexual behavior. High rates of unemployment and underemployment among black males force many black women into employment outside the home, resulting in little parental supervision of the children. The absence of the parents from the home is a major factor in the strong influence of the peer group (Staples 1973, pp. 45–46).

A Washington, D.C., study sought to identify two types of poor families among Blacks: the effective copers and the ineffective copers (McQueen 1979; see also Willie 1976, pp. 135–142). In the first group were the families that fed and clothed their members well, paid their rent on time, and were "future-oriented." Those in the second group ranked low on these variables. Families in both groups tended to be large, averaging about seven persons per household, but the "troubled" families were somewhat larger, and more of them included relatives and nonrelatives. Eighty-five percent of the effectively coping families had male heads, compared with 65 percent of the ineffective copers. Three times more wives worked in the future-oriented families than in the troubled families, and only 6 percent of these families received some form of welfare, compared with more than a fifth of the other families. McQueen suggests five hypotheses to account for the differences in stability and capabilities between these two groups of very poor families: (1) strong family orientation, (2) mobility aspirations, (3) quest for respectability, (4) planning, and (5) self-reliance.

McAdoo (1979) found that black middle-class families in Washington, D.C., and the suburban "new town" of Columbia, Maryland, fifteen miles from the capitol, have retained networks of mutually helpful family and kin. About 15 percent of these 178 families were not newly arrived but had been middle class for a generation or more. Seventy-two percent of this sample were two-parent families. More than three-fourths of the mothers worked, and for both urban and suburban families the average combined income was $33,000.

Only 6 percent of these middle-class parents lived in extended families, but the others had not cut themselves off from their kin or emotionally separated themselves. A majority lived within a one-hour drive of their relatives. More than half said their parents and kin helped them by providing child care, financial assistance, emotional support, help with repairs or chores, or gifts of clothes and furniture. Only 20 percent reported that no one helped them regularly. Two percent said that community agencies were a primary source of help. Eighty-one percent of the families gave the same kinds of help they received. Contrary to some reports, this study found that the old patterns of handling problems within the family continue to be strong. According to McAdoo, Blacks still do not perceive community social agencies as particularly sensitive or helpful, but it cannot be assumed that black families will "take care of their own" so well that they need no services. She suggests that existing networks be augmented rather than replaced.

The Black Family and Social Class[2]

In his "new look" at black families, Willie (1976, 1981) examined 200 middle-class and working-class

households. Omitted in his analysis were upper-class and upper-middle-class families, as well as those of the under class (under $3,000 income). The three class levels analyzed by Willie are middle class (income $10,000–$20,000), working class (income $6,000–$10,000), and lower class (income $3,000–$6,000). The families examined in this study are said to be representative of approximately 75 percent of all black families in America (Willie 1976, pp. 11–12). If income and educational levels are used, from 25 to 30 percent of black families in the United States would be in the middle-class category.

Although there are variations in the life-styles of black middle-class families, they may be described in general terms. They tend to be nuclear households, consisting of husband and wife and two or three children. Frequently, their middle-class status is a result of employment of both husband and wife, with heavy reliance on the public sector for jobs. The parents are seldom involved in community affairs, or at least they are not extensively involved in such movements. Willie found that members of the black middle class are success-oriented, upwardly mobile, materialistic, and equalitarian. Property, especially residential property, symbolizes success for these affluent conformists (Willie 1976, pp. 12, 19, 22–23, 58).

According to Willie, the parents in black working-class families are literate, but their education is limited. Some are high-school dropouts, and few have more than high-school education. They desire high-school education for their children but may hope that one or two will go on to college. The jobs they envision for their children require only a high-school or junior college education. Cooperation is essential in black working-class families, and the husband–wife relationship tends to be of the equalitarian variety. The husband tends to make decisions about financial expenditures and to act as advisor for the boys. The mother tends to be responsible for the household tasks, but she may delegate some of this work to the children. She acts as advisor for the girls and serves as the link between the family and the school, and in some cases with the church. In times of crisis, these roles may change. Black working-class families have also internalized the basic values of American society. They are success-oriented, but their symbol

[2]For a discussion of competing theoretical frameworks for the study of black families: structural-functional, interactional-situational, developmental (life cycle), cultural equivalent, cultural deviant, and cultural variant, see Allen (1978), Mathis (1978), and Nobles (1978).

of success is the welfare of the whole family. Such families are successful if they are respectable, and a family is respectable "when its members are well-fed, well-clothed, and well-housed, and do not get into trouble with the police" (Willie 1976, pp. 60, 63, 93–94).

Movement is a prominent characteristic of lower-class Blacks. Jobs, residences, cities, spouses, boyfriends, and girlfriends are often changed. Marriage may occur early, and the first child may be born before the first marriage. Others come along rapidly, until some families have eight or more children. First marriages may be dissolved within a few years, and other marriages or liaisons may follow. When illness and unemployment strike, and the burdens of a large family continue to increase, the man in the family may move out (Willie 1976, p. 96). Black lower-class families are more likely to be one-parent households than are black middle-class or black working-class families. Some of these households are extended families consisting of grandmother, mother, and children. One-parent families often have a male present—a boyfriend who visits frequently, helps support the family, and is attentive to the children (Willie 1976, p. 13). Faced repeatedly with disappointment and failure, black lower-class families tend to withdraw. This retreatist behavior does not necessarily mean a rejection of basic societal goals. Willie (1976, pp. 169–170) rejects the concept of a "culture of poverty" or a "subculture of the poor" which reinforces and perpetuates itself, including the condition of poverty.

The Black Extended Family[3]

A recent study (Martin and Martin 1978, p. 1) gives a comprehensive definition of a black extended family:

A multigenerational, interdependent kinship system which is welded together by a sense of obligation to relatives; is organized around a "family base" household; is generally guided by a "dominant family figure"; extends across geographical boundaries to connect family units to an extended family network; and has a built-in mutual aid system for the welfare of its members and the maintenance of the family as a whole.

In her work in Chicago, Aschenbrenner found that the black family "is extended in character, often

[3]Our discussion of the black extended family and the black nuclear family in this chapter does not include a consideration of dating and courtship. The most extensive statement on these topics is found in Staples 1973 (reprinted 1978), pp. 43–62.

showing a bilateral tendency, but more frequently oriented toward the maternal side" (Aschenbrenner 1975, p. 3).

There are limits, however, on what the black extended family can do for its members. Unemployment was widespread in the families observed by Martin and Martin (1978, p. 15), and many of those who were working did not earn enough money to provide for their dependent children. Family members can encourage children to stay in school and can teach them the value of work, but the means to economic self-sufficiency and advancement are largely outside the influence of the extended family. This type of family is geared mainly toward survival and security, including emotional security. For some, the strengths of the group also constitute its weakness; they become so dependent on the economic security of the extended family that their initiative to become self-sustaining is blocked (Martin and Martin 1978, p. 15, 29, 37, 38).

Although many urban Blacks rely on relatives for help, they depend more upon government assistance than rural Blacks do. Members of extended families in the city become involved with programs which provide welfare checks, food stamps, medical care, counseling, birth control information, day nurseries, foster homes, legal services, housing services, homes for the aged, consumer education, and other services. Greater reliance on government services for survival and family stability means relinquishing some of the control that the extended family has had in the past. Also, because government assistance programs are more numerous and generous in urban communities, rural Blacks who are having economic difficulties are encouraged to migrate to overcrowded and financially troubled cities. Usually the welfare grants received by low-income people "are in amounts insufficient either to allow family members to become independent of extended family aid or to break their chain of dependency on government assistance" (Martin and Martin 1978, p. 87).

The base household of a black extended family may include the nuclear family plus one or more grandparents, cousins, aunts, uncles, nieces, or nephews. When sons and daughters marry, they usually leave home, but they may remain in the same neighborhood as their parents (Aschenbrenner 1975, p. 3). An extended family may include a boyfriend of the principal female instead of a husband. This man may serve as a quasi-father who (1) supports the family regularly over long periods of time; (2) shows his concern for the children in the household by giving them spending money, disciplining them, and taking them to places of entertainment; (3) visits the family during the week, and may or may not reside with them. This relationship is not hidden but is conducted with the knowledge of relatives on both sides. In return, the boyfriend receives meals, washing and ironing, sexual satisfaction, and familial companionship. In short, he is not simply arranging a sexual relationship but is "seeking intimacy in the context of a family" (Schulz 1969, p. 137; Shimkin, Louie, and Frate 1978, pp. 53, 72–73).

The main problem in the single-parent household, usually a household headed by a mother, is the burden of socialization, and often of support, which must be borne by that parent. Such responsibility may put a heavy strain on the mother–child relationship, even if help is received from grandparents, aunts, uncles, sisters, and brothers in rearing the children (Aschenbrenner 1975, p. 85; see also Stack 1974).

Despite the efforts of relatives to maintain the extended family in the city, such families are likely to deteriorate in that locale. At the same time, members of extended families find it difficult to form self-sustaining nuclear families there. Individuals tend to focus on their own lives and to depend more and more on their nearest relatives and close friends. Abortion, the formal adoption of children, delinquency and crime, and the institutionalization of care for the aged show that the extended family is not fulfilling many of its traditional functions in the city. Nevertheless, the extended family "is still useful in sustaining its members as full participation in the American economy continues to elude them" (Martin and Martin 1978, pp. 83–84, 91, 100).

Is the Black Extended Family Female-Dominated? Since the term *matriarchal* has often been applied to the black family in the United States, attention must be given to the meaning of this concept. In social anthropology, *matriarchy* refers to (a) female-headed households and (b) wife dominance. On the first point, it is true that the proportion of female households heads is larger among Blacks than Whites. On the second point, if the concept of matriarchy is limited to wife dominance in husband–wife families, it appears that matriarchy is most evident in white, professional families where the wife is not gainfully employed. Intact lower-class black families may be even more patriarchal than such families among Whites.

Equalitarianism seems to be most characteristic of working-class and middle-class families, black and white (Jackson 1973, pp. 437–438).

Although the dominant figures in the black extended family are frequently females, ranging in age from 65 to 85, this type of family should not be thought of as a matriarchal structure. Most of these elderly females have simply outlived their husbands. When living, their husbands were either dominant family figures or shared the dominant role with their wives. When shared, the husband's duties included helping to provide for the family and regulating the moral behavior of family members. While her husband was alive, the wife's main responsibilities were domestic (teaching younger members how to cook, how to care for children, how to handle money, how to get along with relatives) and also serving as a provider as well. In short, the husband served as a stabilizer, while the wife served primarily as an organizer of the extended family (Martin and Martin 1978, pp. 19–20).

In virtually all of the extended families that Martin and Martin observed in two small towns in central Missouri and southern Florida and in two cities, Cleveland and Kansas City, the dominant figure was elderly. Dominant family figures help members of the group develop a "sense of family," assist in the allocation of scarce family resources among needy family members, facilitate communication among relatives, help socialize the children, arbitrate family disputes, supervise joint family activities (reunions, holiday celebrations, and so forth), transmit family history, and pass on the black heritage. The dominant family figure is not a dictator; the heads of sub-extended families are the principal managers of their own families. (Martin and Martin 1978, pp. 17–19).

Since Emancipation, it has often been more difficult for black men than for black women to obtain employment. Frequently, this denial to men of an opportunity to work has made it necessary for black women to assume the role of family provider. The marginal economic position of the black male has, therefore, reinforced the pattern of female-headed families (Staples 1977, p. 136). It is well to emphasize again the point made by Gutman (1976, pp. 461–75): Slavery did not leave the black family in shambles. Nor was it in shambles in the early twentieth century. The most serious difficulties it now faces reflect what Gutman calls a Modern Enclosure Movement, forcing Blacks off the land by the millions just when the urban economy is losing many of the lower-skilled jobs by means of which earlier migrants had been integrated into the urban labor force.

A sub-extended family household with the father absent appears to be a broken home, but actually it may be part of a strong extended family. In the female-headed family, a number of male relatives may be influential. An older brother, an uncle, a male cousin, or a boyfriend may play a supportive role and serve as a father figure to the children (Martin and Martin 1978, p. 9; Staples 1977b, p. 138).

Adoption ("Absorption Mechanism") in the Black Extended Family. Because of age, sickness, unemployment, or other reasons, homeless family members and those unable to care for themselves may be taken into the household of a relative. Within the black extended family, this "absorption mechanism" is an important feature of mutual aid. Usually such arrangements are temporary until the family members become independent again, but if the mechanism is to be effective the base household and the sub-extended family household must be open at all times to dependent family members. If these households cannot absorb those who become dependent, those individuals must try to survive on the streets or rely on public or private assistance. If the extended family rigidifies, the likelihood that its members will be absorbed by public welfare agencies, prisons, foster homes, nursing homes, and correctional agencies will increase (Martin and Martin 1978, pp. 39–41).

One of the main features of the absorption mechanism is the informal adoption of children. A principal reason for such adoption is economic necessity, the sheer inability of a parent or parents to provide for a child or children. Among other reasons are: children create strain on a mother who is pregnant; one or both parents die; the natural parents cannot discipline their children; family members do not want their children; or a child is the victim of neglect or abuse by his parents. In some cases, children are given to family members who are living alone and want to rear a child. Still another reason is that family members may be reluctant to see children adopted by nonrelatives or put up for legal adoption (Martin and Martin 1978, pp. 41–43).

In some ways, the extended family's informal adoption of children is dysfunctional. This system makes it easier for females to have children outside of marriage and for males to abandon their wives and children. When a male abandons his children, little or no pressure is exerted on him by the extended family to be responsible economically for them. Also, the extended family does not usually try to force its own male members to care for the children and the women they have abandoned or divorced; it is reluctant to absorb the children its males have fathered. As a rule, the dependent children are provided for by the extended families of the females. However, at least one study found that far more men support their children than do not (Martin and Martin 1978, pp. 62–63).

Since the majority of black households are headed by men, illegitimate and orphaned children, especially in less populated areas of the South, are often cared for in the households of the paternal grandfather, a paternal uncle, a maternal uncle, or a maternal great uncle. Young found that responsibility for a son's illegitimate children, as well as a daughter's, may be taken over by older stable couples. In "Georgetown" (Young's fictionally named town in Georgia), family and emotional ties through men, as well as mother–daughter ties, are socially important. This is not to say that there are not "many illegitimate births, multiple sequential marriages, and frequent dissolution of marriage; practices the prevailing literature on the American Negro associates with family breakdown and the female-headed family (Young 1970, p. 272)."

Dependent children born into the extended family network strain the resources of the family, and when it can no longer absorb them, members are more likely to seek abortions or to place their children in foster homes (Martin and Martin 1978, p. 45).

Out-of-Wedlock Childbearing. In 1979, the proportion of out-of-wedlock births for all women of childbearing age was 55 percent for Blacks and 9 percent for Whites. Despite the decline in total births and overall fertility rates for both black and white teenagers in recent years, rates of out-of-wedlock childbearing in that age group have increased to about one-half. From 1976 to 1979, the proportion of out-of-wedlock births among Blacks rose from 71 to 79 percent for women 18 and 19 and from 90 to 93 percent for women 15–17. The increase for white teenagers was from 19 percent to 24 percent for 18- and 19-year-olds and from 36 to 42 percent for white women 15–17.

The fact that a large majority of births (85 percent) to black teenage mothers are out of wedlock is of great importance; the health, social, and economic consequences are, for the most part, adverse.

Black leaders are concerned that the increasing numbers of teenage pregnancies and fatherless families threaten to jeopardize the progress that Blacks have made in recent decades. Recently, leading black organizations have sought to involve middle-class Blacks in finding community-based solutions to the problem of high rates of black teenage fertility and out-of-wedlock childbearing (Auletta 1982, p. 69; Reid 1982, pp. 12–13).

Is There a Distinctive Black Family System? There are three major points of view concerning the lower-class black family. Among others, E. Franklin Frazier (1939, 1966), and Daniel P. Moynihan (1965) have portrayed this kind of family as disorganized and dysfunctional. Others, including Herskovits (1941), Young (1970), and Aschenbrenner (1975), have asserted that there is a distinctive black family. Still others discern no distinctiveness in the black family (Heiss 1975; Jackson 1973; and Scanzoni 1971). Since we regard the first viewpoint largely in error, as do most students of black families, we shall not elaborate on it here.

Young's fieldwork in the southeastern United States led her to conclude that black childhood and family constitute a distinctive complex institutionally and behaviorally. She accepts Herskovits's thesis of the retention of African cultural elements among New World Blacks. The distinctive forms of behavior that Young (1970, p. 286) found include:

The indulgence of the baby, the constant human environment, linking of aggression and love, the simultaneous encouragement and control of aggressiveness, the early entry into the children's gang and the devotion of childhood to baby-tending and to the cooperative group of brothers and sisters.

Although American white culture may dominate in those aspects of life where Blacks participate in general American institutions, in small groups the organizational style of many American Blacks is different. Independence in sexual behavior and marriage, comparability of role of husband and wife, and the supplementing of the nuclear family by ties to the grandparents are consistent with an American black social structure characterized by "an unorganized network of loose social groupings with a high level of communication and a low level of authority and coercion" (Young 1970, p. 286).

Some of the families in Aschenbrenner's study of black families in Chicago were relatively affluent, others poor. Although there were individual differences, underlying similarities in opinions and values were found among informants. Several points support the view of this study that life in the black community is in many ways a unique way of life (Aschenbrenner 1975, p. 7). First, the casual attitude toward legal marriage and divorce may be derived in part from African social forms in which separation and remating are accepted and in which marriage is an agreement between families. Second, the traditions associated with the patrilateral, matrilateral, and bilateral extended families, as well as lineages, found in African societies continue to have an influence in contrast to those of the truncated conjugal family which is a part of Northern European culture. The emphasis on consanguinity has been documented especially among lower-income black families and those in the rural South (Sudarkasa 1981, p. 49). It seems unlikely that black people completely lost the African concept of family, then reinvented it as an adaptation to economic conditions in the New World. Third, black families are not usually as child-centered as white conjugal families. Fourth, in the organization of extended families, a humanistic value—"that of deep involvement in the lives of many people" is a prominent feature. Although the demands of relatives sometimes cause resentments, the sense of obligation to family members is strong, as seen in sharing which takes the form of small loans and gifts of money and services, and of moral support through sympathy and concern. This practice is common to black and white families, despite some structural differences. Thus, black people are seen as developing and maintaining a way of life and a system of values that is much more than a series of strategies for survival (Aschenbrenner 1975, pp. 136–139, 143–144; Sudarkasa 1981, p. 49).

Those who hold the third position, that family patterns among Blacks in the United States have no distinctiveness, point out that there is considerable variation within the group. They observe that within similar economic levels, black and white families tend to resemble each other more than do those of different socioeconomic status. As the level of income rises, the number of male-headed families increases. In 1970, at an income level of $15,000 and over, the proportion of male-headed households was comparable to that for white families. If families reconstituted by a second marriage are combined with those never broken, 69 percent of black children lived in families with both a father and mother present. (U.S. Bureau of the Census, 1972). This position recognizes that race is still one of the important determinants of social class in the United States and that it is difficult to make meaningful comparisons of familial attitudes and behaviors. Nevertheless, such variables as education, income, and family size are regarded as more influential than race upon family organization and ideology (Jackson 1973, pp. 437–438).

Marital Stability for Blacks and for Whites. Most blacks who have ever been married continue to live with their spouses. The divorce and separation rates for Blacks in the United States are, however, considerably higher than they are for Whites.

Delayed marriage is also more marked among Blacks. In 1980, 69 percent of black women aged 20–24 were still unmarried, compared with 50 percent for all women that age. This greater tendency to postpone marriage may be related to the higher unemployment rates of young black women and to faster increasing college enrollment rates (Reid 1982, p. 22).

In the 25–34 group, 28 percent of black women (double the percent for all women that age) and 13 percent of black men said in 1980 that they were divorced or separated. At the same time, less than half of black women in that age bracket were living in intact marriages compared to 84 percent among white women. Of all race–sex groups in 1981, black women were the most likely to be divorced—289 divorced black women for every 1,000 black women who were married and living with their spouses. For black men, the number was 178, for white women 118, and for white men 82 (Reid 1982, pp. 22–23).

The high black divorce rate reflects a conflict in black subculture, a conflict whose origin has been attributed in part to conditions created by white society. Lower-class black males face the problems of unemployment and underemployment which confront many white males, but the rates are higher among Blacks. Rather recently the "man in the house" provision has been removed from the rules on welfare support, but men who are unemployed continue to be a burden to their families. The economic impotence of the lower-class black male may ultimately affect family structure and interactions within the family more than does the so-called poverty culture. In addition to the problem of finding employment, the black male has to contend with racial prejudice and discrimination. Frustrations generated by racial prejudice constitute an additional source of many black male–black female

conflicts (Glasgow 1980, pp. 181–182; Staples 1973, pp. 5, 113).

Interviews conducted by the Panel Study of Income Dynamics, Institute of Social Research, University of Michigan, showed that "once income, home ownership, and family size differences are taken into account, all of which are relatively highly correlated with race, the percentage of black families experiencing divorce or separation is 6 percentage points less than for Whites." This finding suggests that it is the economic characteristics of Blacks that lead to separation and divorce rates that are higher than those of Whites (Duncan and Morgan Vol. III, 1975).

Broken families appear to have a more devastating effect upon white than upon black children. Several studies have indicated that black mothers without husbands have greater coping abilities than white mothers have. In view of the greater excess of females among Blacks than Whites, the gradually increasing proportion of black female-headed households is not likely to be reversed in the near future. The recent trend of excessive females among Whites may lead to a similar increase in the proportion of female-headed households in the majority population. Perhaps one indication of such a trend can be seen in the slowly increasing rate of illegitimacy among Whites (Jackson 1973, pp. 438–439).

Few students of the family would contend that broken families are more advantageous than intact families. Intact families tend to promote greater educational and occupational achievements and less social disorganization, but the broken home does not necessarily lead to all of the consequences that are often attributed to it. The idea is not new, but intact homes can be perceived as bad and broken homes as good. The contrast between the good intact family and the bad broken home is too extreme (Heiss 1975, p. 146; Jackson 1973, pp. 438–439).

The assertion that a parental broken home results in poor adjustment and low income rests upon at least two questionable assumptions. The first assumption is that breakup of the parental home is necessarily traumatic and productive of emotional disturbance. Often this is the case, but in many instances the difference between broken and unbroken families may be minimal. Where there is continuous conflict, a parental separation may be a relief. Heiss points out that limited evidence from Whites indicates that the children of broken homes are better adjusted than those living in conflict-filled homes. Also, many black women without spouses and many remarried women provide good homes for their children. In short, the effects of broken homes do exist, but they are more complex and less strong than is generally assumed (Heiss 1975, p. 116).

The second assumption is that the breakup of the family home is the cause of the lower income of Blacks. In Heiss's study of black families in northern cities, the family variables accounted for little of the variance on income. For lower-status black males, it was somewhat better to have come from a stable home and one which the mother dominated, but the main advantage for these males came from obtaining more education. Among the variables tested in this study were age, age at marriage, number of siblings, maternal control score, parental marriage unbroken, parental socioeconomic status, education, and urban birth. The general conclusion was that changes in black family structure had had little influence on the income of black men. Reducing the economic difficulties of Blacks does not lie, Heiss asserts, in changing the structural features of the family. The opposite relationship is more nearly true. As far as the differential distribution of income by race is concerned, intact parental homes has little to do with the lower income of Blacks. If all people, black and white, came from unbroken homes, the gap between the races in family income in the middle 1970s would have been $327 less than it was (Heiss 1975, pp. 139, 142).

On the question of whether a break in the parental home affects marital stability, Heiss found this to be true primarily among those of higher status background. In this group, a break at an early age seems to have greater effect, but only for women. Only small differences exist between those whose parental home was broken by conflict and those whose home was broken by death. Household composition after the break was irrelevant (Heiss 1975, p. 115).

Conclusions on the Black Family

Much has been written about the black family as an adaptive institution. Aschenbrenner's distinction between *adaptive* and *adaptable* is important. The black family is not merely a strategy for survival. It is not simply a part of what has been called the culture of poverty. In fact, the essentially

negative concept of a culture of poverty is of doubtful value. As Aschenbrenner says, "The strength of black people stems from a social organization that has been created in the face of adversity, and is not merely an adjustment to it." The black family has been adaptable in the rural South, during migration to southern and northern cities, and in urban communities in recent years (Aschenbrenner 1975, pp. 7, 140). It is one aspect of a black subculture in American society.

We think that there is no inconsistency between the view just expressed and the conclusion reached by Heiss (1975, p. 77) that in northern metropolitan areas family dynamics among Blacks and Whites are similar but not identical. Economic improvement will contribute to changes in the lower-class black family, but small increases in income will not bring about major changes immediately. Such changes will occur gradually as more general conditions change, especially political conditions (Heiss 1975, pp. 228–230; Scanzoni 1971, pp. 324, 327).

Mexican American Families

The acculturative process has been occurring at a slower rate among Mexican Americans and American Indians than among the Chinese and Japanese, European ethnic groups, and, perhaps, Puerto Ricans. In the Mexican American population, changes have been greatest in material culture.

Generalizations about Mexican American family life, or *the* family in any racial or cultural minority, are difficult to make. There is no Mexican American family *type*. Families differ in income, in whether Spanish is the exclusive language spoken in the home or is never spoken, in the length of time they have been in the United States, in ancestry (Spanish forefathers or Mayan, Zapotec, Toltec, or Aztec forefathers), and in many other factors (Murillo 1976, pp. 15–16).

The characterization of the Mexican American woman as being chronically depressed, self-denying, and overly submissive, and of the Mexican American man as being passive and dependent— one who compensates for his feelings of weakness and inferiority with exaggerated masculine behavior—has been questioned. Such men and women are said to represent exceptions rather than the rule (Hernández, Haug, and Wagner 1976, p. 4). Mirandé and Enríquez (1979, p. 12) refer to the "triple oppression" of Chicanas due to their membership in a subordinated cultural group, the status accorded women cross-culturally, and the burden of oppression within a group that tends to be dominated by males (see also Gallegos y Chávez 1979, pp. 67–69).

Major characteristics of the contemporary Chicano family—the emphasis on familism and the importance given to members of the extended family, the expectation that the individual will subordinate his needs to collective needs, the stress put upon respect and deference to elders and to men, and the norms of feminine virtue (chastity, modesty, honor, cleanliness, and willingness to minister to the needs of her husband and children) are said to have their counterparts in Aztec society (Mirandé and Enríquez 1979, p. 98).[4]

Mexican American families are large. Spanish-surname families in the Southwest average 4.77 persons, compared with 3.39 for Anglos and 4.54 for Nonwhites. These differences are found whether all families or only urban families are considered, or husband–wife versus broken families, or persons in the age group 35–44 years; the rank order of family size is always Mexican American, Nonwhite, Anglo. The average size of Mexican American families (4.4) is approximately one person per family larger than that of the total population in the United States (Alvirez and Bean 1976, pp. 280–281).

The Mexican American Extended Family

The Mexican American family includes the extended as well as the nuclear family. Grandparents, uncles, aunts, and cousins, as well as husband, wife, and children, are important, but somewhat greater importance may be attached to the father's side of the family. The family may also include compadres, the godparents of the children. Parents and compadres maintain the same kind of relationship as that between parents and other adult relatives. Visiting and sharing characterize the relationships among extended family members. The strength of the family lies in the security it provides for its members. The sharing of material things

often puzzles Anglos, especially welfare workers who discover that a family they are trying to assist is sharing what they have with persons outside the immediate family (Murillo 1976, pp. 20–21).

In the Spanish-surname population in the Southwest, the incidence of families other than the husband–wife type is much greater than among Anglos, but smaller than among Nonwhites. This is true for the percentage of female heads of families, and for "other male" heads (other than husband with wife present). These rank orders hold true for the Southwest as a whole as well as for its urban areas, and the data for separate age classes indicate that the differences are not a function of age differences. As Grebler et al. (1970, pp. 129–130) have pointed out, broken families may have different implications in different cultural minorities:

> In the case of Mexican-Americans, the deserted wife's brother or another close relative may more often represent the "other male" and assume the absent husband's role in the family; or the core family may be reconstituted by grandparents living with the woman and her children. If so, the psychological and economic effects of a broken family on mother and children may be substantially modified.

Chicano Child-Rearing. A perceptive observer states that Chicano children are brought up, in most cases, in homes that could be called authoritarian and patriarchal (Coles 1977, pp. 350–351), terms which many Chicano fathers and mothers would not find objectionable. Fathers insist that they must be strict or tough, especially with older children, and mothers agree. Actually, mothers constantly make decisions and administer punishment to their children; the father is the ultimate arbiter of conflict. His name, or the priest's, may at times be mentioned as the source of what is right, but usually mothers take their own stands, saying: "I am your mother, and I know," or sometimes "I am a woman and I know." When the husband is dead or seriously ill, a grandfather, an uncle, or a priest exerts moral and psychological guidance.[5]

When children are young, the home is usually child-centered. Parents tend to be permissive and indulgent with younger children, but the children are not allowed to be disrespectful within the home (Murillo 1976, pp. 21–22).

Chicanos have been more isolated than the Irish, Italians, or Poles. When they move to Los Angeles,

---

[4]For a criticism of many social science depictions of the authoritarian Mexican American family constellation, as well as an attempt to give a "more realistic and sympathetic interpretation" of the contemporary Chicano family, see Mirandé and Enríquez (1979, 108–117).

[5]Although Coles does not state explicitly that most of the children he worked with were not middle class children, one gets the impression that that was the case.

San Antonio, or Albuquerque, they tend to remain apart and to retain their language and values. One factor in the slower rate of integration of Mexican Americans into contemporary life in the United States is the fact that for the most part they live in a section of the country (the Southwest) which has until recently resisted the encroachment of urban industrial culture.

Coles found that Chicano children of six or seven learn about their "fate" and develop a feeling of loyalty to their people. They become less and less individualistic and less and less ambitious, more deferential to one another rather than to their teachers—whom they obey rather than respect. Psychologically, they feel defenseless, feeling that it is best to go along with the Anglo rather than to challenge him. They become psychologically part of a people, sensing that Mexican American culture offers them support in coping with the Anglo-dominated world (Coles 1977, p. 380). In a world that is often perceived as hostile, the Spanish language is of great importance. Spanish provides a private world for its speakers.

Although group pride and loyalty have increased greatly in recent years, the erosion of the use of Spanish in the Chicano population continues. Retention of the Spanish language is much more common among Mexican Americans of lower socioeconomic status (SES). In one study 42 percent of the respondents reported using Spanish in the home, compared to 8 percent among high SES families (Alvirez and Bean 1976, p. 288); the same percentages were found by Grebler et al. (1970, p. 332). Also, 24 percent of lower SES respondents spoke primarily English, compared to 61 percent in the higher category (Alvirez and Bean 1976, p. 288).

Changes in Mexican American Families

Generations of Mexican American families change at different rates in different parts of the Southwest. Changes tend to occur more rapidly in the bigger cities, but there is variation among urban communities. Generally, second-generation residents of Los Angeles are more acculturated than second-generation persons in a Texas city, for example, Corpus Christi. Change proceeds so slowly in some agricultural towns that it is hardly noticeable from one generation to another. Also, little change toward urban American relationships and values has occurred among old-family Spanish Americans who live in northern New Mexico and southern Colorado (Moore 1970, p. 100).

Familism is declining in the large cities of the Southwest. Public services in the city tend to diminish family responsibilities. More jobs are available, and welfare services reduce the obligation to assist indigent relatives. In a survey by Grebler et al. (1970, p. 355), only slightly more than half of the respondents in Los Angeles admitted that they had received financial aid from relatives (a proportion similar to that found in a general sample in Cleveland), and only a third of the San Antonio sample had received such aid. The lower figure for San Antonio probably reflects the lower average income for that city; other data indicate greater traditionalism in San Antonio. The survey showed that two-thirds of the Los Angeles respondents and approximately 40 percent of the San Antonio respondents claimed that they had provided financial help to relatives. These percentages probably indicate that giving increases with family income.

Studies in Los Angeles and San Antonio show that the nuclear family is the normal household, at least in the urban setting. In the shift away from kinship structures which emphasize one-sex relationships in the extended family (mother–daughter, sister–sister, and so forth) toward the husband–wife relationship, the Mexican American family is following the change found in studies of upwardly mobile individuals in other groups (Grebler et al. 1970, pp. 357–358).

Another change in Mexican American family life is found in revised conceptions of family roles, especially in the husband's role. It seems doubtful that the father's control over family matters, including the budget, was ever as great as tradition holds. Survey data indicate that ideas about the father's role among younger, better paid, and less ghettoized individuals are less rigidly patriarchal than those portrayed in many reports. Masculinity is said to be "not quite so associated with dominance as it may have been in the past" (Grebler et al. 1970, p. 362). Mexican American men in Los Angeles are less embarrassed to assist with child care than the traditional norms indicate. Also, Chicano husbands in that city are more inclined to share decision-making with their wives than are those in Albuquerque and San Antonio. Moore (1970, p. 117) suggests that the changes in familism are not due simply to television and other mass stimuli, but rather to "the increased visibility of a variety of styles of intrafamily relationships that a city as large and as complex as Los Angeles offers."

A third significant change in Mexican American family life is the much greater approval of birth control, at least in interview replies, than would be predicted in a Catholic group. The rate of acceptance in Los Angeles corresponded with that in a nationwide sample, but the rate for San Antonio was lower (Grebler et al. 1970, p. 582).

A fourth kind of change has been occasioned by radio and television programs. Almost all Chicano families possess sets which bring Anglo culture into the home. As a result of being bombarded by many contradictory stimuli, boys and girls experience a number of conflicts: "The tension between a rural, mystical, emotional Catholic faith and an agnostic, urban, materialistic culture, occasionally wrapped in fundamentalist Protestantism, but, in the clutch, committed to Mammon" (Coles 1977, p. 376).

Marital Stability

Two-thirds of the respondents in the surveys conducted by Grebler et al. in Los Angeles and San Antonio were brought up in intact families. Many of the others were reared by their mothers alone, and the rest were brought up predominantly by one or another relative—grandparents, or the father alone, or a collateral relative on either the mother's or the father's side. The high proportion of individuals not brought up by both parents is explained by a high rate of desertion or divorce in the parental generation. The disorganizing effects of immigration and poverty made desertion in the 1930s a common occurrence in both rural and urban communities. Studies made of that period contradict the widely accepted view that the Mexican American family has been unusually stable. Later studies showed that divorce was increasingly common among Mexican Americans; frequently these reports erroneously contrasted then current divorce rates with a presumed earlier stability, both in the United States among older persons and in Mexico (Grebler et al. 1970, pp. 358–359).

Currently, family stability among Mexican Americans is somewhat greater than among Anglos. The number of divorced men per 1,000 married men is 16 for Mexicans and 39 for other Whites. The number of divorced women per 1,000 currently married Mexican American women is 50,

compared with 57 for all white women. Evidence available at present is not, however, sufficiently strong to show that Mexican Americans manifest greater family cohesiveness than Anglos. The question is complicated by the indeterminate number of unreported desertions (Alvirez and Bean 1976, p. 282).

Conclusions on the Mexican American Family

The extensive survey of Mexican American families, especially in Los Angeles and San Antonio, conducted by Grebler, Moore, and Guzman, the observations of Robert Coles on Chicanos, and the papers by Murillo, Peñalosa, Mirandé and Enríquez, and others show that Chicano families differ considerably from the patterns presented in the earlier literature. In recent years, the extended family household has become extremely rare, and there is reason to believe that this type of family was never as prevalent and as deep-rooted as its reputation has held. Perhaps this type of family structure may have been a part of the adaptation of an economically poor population which had little access to sources of help outside the group. Taking in destitute relatives and doubling up with other families were often regarded as onerous obligations; nevertheless, they were met. As Grebler et al. (1970, p. 368) comment: "Poverty sometimes emphasizes kinship obligations, but the general upgrading of material welfare in the population means that the more stressful obligations could be allowed to wither."

Conceptions of the proper roles for husband and wife are undergoing modification, seemingly in the direction of less emphasis on patriarchy and masculine dominance. The shift from rural to urban residence has brought the usual personal stresses of adjustment to city life, heightened in the case of Mexican Americans by the problems of minority status, language handicaps, and poverty. A high incidence of broken families indicates that the new social environment often has a disruptive effect on family life (Grebler et al. 1970, pp. 112, 369, 582).

Puerto Rican Families

Puerto Ricans living in Puerto Rico have a deeper sense of family than Puerto Ricans living on the mainland. Individualism is less prevalent on the island than in the United States, and those who advance in business or public office feel obligated to aid their relatives.

Fitzpatrick (1971, pp. 83–84) has suggested a fourfold classification of Puerto Rican families on the island and the mainland. Extended families include a wide range of natural or ritual kin. These families, based on regular or consensual marriages, are characterized by strong bonds of kinship and frequent interaction among their members. Grandparents, parents, and children may live in the same household or may live in separate households but visit frequently. Second, the nuclear family is becoming more common as Puerto Ricans acquire middle-class status. Here husband, wife, and their children tend not to live close to relatives and to have relatively weak bonds to the extended family. The third type includes husband, wife, their children, and the children of another union or unions of husband or wife. The fourth type is one headed by the mother, with children of one or more men, but with no permanent consort in the home.

An important aspect of Puerto Rican family structure is the consensual union. Such a union is relatively stable, but its members have not gone through a civil or religious marriage ceremony. After living together and rearing children, they may or may not have a marriage ceremony performed. These unions are not the same as common-law marriages in the English legal system. In Puerto Rico, the Roman law tradition has prevailed, a tradition which does not recognize a union as a marriage unless it was regularized ceremonially but does acknowledge the state wherein two people live together without getting married. This state, concubinage, does not have the unfavorable connotations in Roman law tradition that it has in English tradition (Fitzpatrick 1971, p. 84).

The proportion of consensual unions among Puerto Rican families on the mainland has been dropping sharply. Fitzpatrick (1971, p. 85) attributes this decline to three factors: first, an increase in religious programs has created a desire for religious marriage; second, substantial economic benefits are associated with regular marriages—social security, family aid, widow's pensions, eligibility to public housing projects; and third, the middle class has increased in size. At the same time, the proportion of out-of-wedlock children is increasing in New York State. In 1957, only 11 percent of Puerto Rican births in that state were out of wedlock, but by 1967 this rate had increased

to 22 percent and by 1969 to 30 percent. This was considerably higher than the 20 percent rate in Puerto Rico in 1970 (Fitzpatrick 1976, p. 209).

In 1972, women headed 24.1 percent of Puerto Rican families in the United States, compared with 13.7 percent of other families of Spanish heritage, 27.4 percent of black families, and 11.6 percent of all families. It is rather surprising that this high rate of Puerto Rican families on the mainland having a female head continues in the second generation, in which 26 percent of the families are of this type (Fitzpatrick 1976, p. 209). In 1970, the Public Health Survey estimated that 30.9 percent of Puerto Rican families and 33.9 percent of black families in New York City were headed by a woman, compared with an average for the city of 17.3 percent (Wagenheim 1975, p. 13). Since Puerto Rican mothers have a very low participation in the labor force, and those who work earn low wages, the average Puerto Rican family headed by a woman is at a considerable economic disadvantage.

The birthrates of Puerto Ricans on the mainland have important social implications. Although the Puerto Rican birthrate is higher than that for the population as a whole, United States-born Puerto Rican women have fewer children than migrant women born on the island, and women in the age bracket 25–44 years old have fewer children than the average American woman. Among other pressures involved in bringing about this phenomenon are the high rents and scarcity of living space in urban areas where most Puerto Ricans live. Wagenheim (1975, p. 15) predicts a considerable growth of the Puerto Rican population, with a gradual tapering off of the rate of growth as United States-born Puerto Rican women become a larger factor (see also Cooney et al. 1981, pp. 1094–1113).

Changes in Puerto Rican Family Life

The roles of husband and wife undergo change on the mainland. Frequently, it is easier for Puerto Rican women to obtain jobs than Puerto Rican men. Employment outside the home gives the wife greater economic independence, and if the husband is unemployed while his wife is working, a reversal of roles may occur. Also, greater involvement in social and political activities outside the home on the part of lower-class Puerto Rican women encourages them to adopt the cultural patterns of the mainland (Fitzpatrick 1971, pp. 94–95).

The role of the Puerto Rican child also changes

on the mainland. On the island, children are more submissive than American children are. In the United States, parents lament the behavior even of boys who do not get into serious trouble. They consider the young to be aggressive, competitive, and disrespectful. When girls reach the early teens, they desire the freedom that American girls have— to go to dances without a chaperone and to associate freely with girls and boys in their neighborhoods and schools (Fitzpatrick 1971, pp. 95–96). Complicating the relationships between the generations is the question of identity. We point out in Chapter 2 that the question of race is more complex for Puerto Ricans on the mainland than for other Americans. In the United States Blacks are counted as Blacks regardless of the amount of African ancestry they have. Racial membership is less important on the island, and racial lines are less sharply drawn. Many Puerto Rican migrants are shocked to discover the racial distinctions that are made on the mainland. Persons of mixed descent with Caucasian features find it advantageous to be regarded as white. Aligning themselves with Whites may mean painful separations from some family members and friends.

As the mobility, economic and spatial, of Puerto Rican families in the United States increases, the bonds of the extended family tend to be weakened. In time of need, departments of Social Service provide assistance. In the early 1970s, approximately 35 percent of the Puerto Rican population in New York City received assistance from the Aid to Families With Dependent Children, a situation which one observer calls "an extremely serious social, political, and moral problem for the Puerto Rican and for the city" (Fitzpatrick 1971, p. 159). Also, as regulations in schools, housing, courts, consumer loans, and other aspects of life press upon urban dwellers, the family becomes less and less effective.

Judged by statistics on divorce, family instability among Puerto Ricans on the mainland is higher than for the whole population, but lower than for the Mexican American group. For those 15 years and older, the percentages of the divorced for the three groups respectively are 5.6, 5.2, and 4.6 (*Statistical Abstracts 1981*, p. 36).

American Indian Families

Although there are nearly five hundred identifiable American Indian tribes in the United States, half of all Native Americans belong to nine tribes, some of which are divided into subgroups (Levitan and Johnston 1975, p. 1). Differences in Indian political and social structures are reflected in family life. Maternal lineages and extended clan relationships are still important in some tribes; in others, indigenous social structures have disappeared. In urban areas, the family life of many Indians is indistinguishable from that of most non-Indians. Nevertheless, some general patterns are found. Indian family structure is more stable than that of other minorities, but less stable than white family structure. In 1970, 18 percent of all Indian families were headed by women, a proportion about two-thirds of that for Blacks (28 percent), but double the rate for Whites (9 percent).

Indian families tend to be larger than those of Blacks or Whites. Nineteen percent of all Indian families have seven or more persons, compared with 15 percent of black and 5 percent of white families. The Indian rate of natural increase of 3 percent per year is the highest of any of the subpopulations in the United States. The number of children born per thousand Indian women ages 15 to 44 in 1970 was 155, nearly a third higher than the nonwhite rate of 114, and almost twice that of the white rate of 84. High birth rates mean that the average age of reservation populations is much younger than for the total population—a median age of 18 compared to 28 in 1970. For each potential Indian male worker between the ages of 25 and 54, there are 4.1 potential dependents under 19 years of age, compared with 2.2 for the whole population. For economically disadvantaged reservation Indians, this is a significant statistic (Levitan and Johnston 1975, pp. 53–55).

Child-Rearing in Traditional Indian Families

Robert Coles, a pediatrician and child psychiatrist, found that Indian parents, especially among the Hopi and Pueblo peoples, begin early to direct their children's attention outward—"toward the land, the sky, the tribe and its history, its customs and traditions" (Cole 1977, p. 520). Because Indian parents believe that a child does not belong to a certain family but to a tribe, a people, and to a segment of the natural world, they do not respond as immediately to the cries and demands of their children as do other American parents. Indian children come to feel at home in that world and to appreciate its demands.

The socialization of Pueblo children is permissive. Weaning and toilet training are gradual and there is little explicit disciplining until children are more than two years of age. Emphases then are on hard work, enduring discomfort, and not wasting food. Disobedient children are threatened with whips by masked disciplinarians. Boys and girls are initiated into a *kiva* (religious society) between the ages of 6 and 9 with strict physical and dietary restrictions (Price 1976, p. 261).

Indian parents do not provide inquirers with lengthy analyses of their ways of rearing children. In general, parents encourage their children "to be sensitive to their kin, their tribe, and to their land, but not to themselves as individuals possessed of a discrete mind, a discrete 'personality,' a discrete bundle of assets and liabilities, gifts and conflicts" (Coles 1977, p. 522).

The Acculturative Process in the Rearing of Indian Children

The rearing of children is closely related to the kind of response an Indian community has made in the confrontation between its culture and Western culture. In their study of the Menominee of Wisconsin, the Spindlers found four major adaptations (Spindler and Spindler 1978, pp. 74–85): (1) the native-oriented, consisting of attempts to revitalize and maintain as much as possible of the traditional way of life; (2) the Peyote or Native American Church, a synthesis of beliefs and rituals taken from traditional Indian and white cultures; (3) the transitional, a combination of Indian and white ways, but, unlike the Peyote cult, lacking a systematic synthesis of cultural elements; and (4) the acculturated, consisting of individuals who are largely white culturally and who compete with Whites on their terms.

The native-oriented group wanted to remain Indian:

They held ceremonies, used medicine bags, spoke Menominee, raised their children to think as they did, brought them into positions on the Drum as soon as possible, and lived well off the main roads in substandard housing without electricity, built of tar-paper and bent saplings in the shape of the old wigwam. (Spindler and Spindler 1978, p. 80)

Most members of the Peyote cult (Native American Church) had grown up in traditional Menominee families. These individuals had had considerable experience with Whites and had acquired doubts about the validity of native beliefs. All had had some exposure to Catholicism, and a few had been baptized in the church. The Peyote Church helped to resolve the conflicts of those who felt suspended between two ways of life. Peyotism, as a type of accommodation, seems to be dying out among the Menominee as young people favor more militant stands.

The transitionals among the Menominee were often people who had retreated into apathy or alcoholism. Many of their children, however, have been asserting their Indianness militantly and seeking redress of grievances (Spindler and Spindler 1978, pp. 79–83).

Some of the Menominee began to be acculturated individually as soon as they arrived on the reservation. This minority included technicians, supervisors, entrepreneurs, and skilled workers whose incomes, speech, and behavior closely resembled that of Whites (Spindler and Spindler 1978, p. 83). The acculturated elite tend to live in a community that differs from that of the traditionals. Their homes are similar to those of business and professional people in neighboring Euro-American communities. They are active in the Catholic Church, play golf or bowl, and do not speak Menominee. Although they are oriented toward American culture, they retain some identity with their Menominee heritage (Price 1976, p. 263).

Instead of growing up in families in which their parents attempted to perpetuate traditional ways, or to create a synthesis of Indian and white beliefs in Peyote, or to withdraw into apathy or to seek relief in alcohol, many children of the present generation have been conditioned to recognize the necessity of getting along with Whites or have come to believe in militancy as a means of redressing grievances (Spindler and Spindler 1978, pp. 83–85).

Indian Family Composition and the Processes of Social Change

In white America, the nuclear, conjugal-pair, and single-person family types predominate. The composition of many Indian households is somewhat different. Among the Hopi, marriage is monogamous, but men join their wives' households and support them economically while retaining ritual, leadership, and disciplinary roles in their natal households. They discipline their sisters' children but play a passive role in their wife's household. This combination of roles contributes to a high divorce rate among the Hopi (Price 1976, p 261).

In California, 30 percent of all Indian households are composite, and they include combinations such as grandchildren, nieces and nephews, brothers or sisters of the husband or wife, a married child with spouse or children or both, and in-laws (Jorgensen 1971, p. 78). Studies among the Salt River Pima–Papago of Arizona, the Blackfeet of Montana, and the Shoshones and Utes on five reservations in Idaho, Wyoming, Colorado, and Utah show that there are relatively more composite Indian households outside California than in that state and that those outside are larger. Jorgensen (1971, p. 78) comments that this is to be expected, given the greater average family income for California Indians.

American Indian composite households have adjusted to poverty by sharing funds from diverse sources: welfare assistance (Aid for Dependent Children, Old-Age Assistance, Federal Aid to the Blind), per capita payments from Indian Claims Commission judgments, wages from part-time labor, income from leased land, cash from piece work, and hunting and fishing (Jorgensen 1971, p. 79).

The composition of Indian family households tends to change from composite to nuclear. A son who finds regular employment moves out of his father's home and, with his wife and children, establishes a separate household. Within fifteen to twenty years, this nuclear family may become a composite household if the man's or his wife's parents move in, or if his own married children establish residence in the household on a temporary basis. Neither the composite household nor the family household cycle are retentions of aboriginal customs but are the results of low and unstable incomes and lack of skills (Jorgensen 1971, p. 79).

In some ways, the Indian family seems to be little affected by migration from the reservation to the city. Proportions of female-headed families, women without husbands, and children living with both parents differ little in urban and rural areas. Urban Indian families are smaller, with an average of 3.9 compared with 4.9 for rural Indian families (Levitan and Johnston 1975, pp. 53–54).

Levitan and Johnston found little evidence among Indians of the trend toward deterioration of the family unit noticeable for other minorities in the

1960s. During that decade, the proportion of female-headed Indian families increased only 2 percent, while the proportion of women who were single, widowed, divorced, or separated declined.

The process of urbanization has been greatly furthered by the Employment Assistance Program of the Bureau of Indian Affairs. More than 100,000 Indians have been assisted in relocating from reservations to urban areas, and urban-oriented vocational training has been provided for over 25,000 household heads. The major incentive for this migration is to find a job or higher wages and to improve living conditions (Price 1976, p. 264).

Although the long-time trend in American Indian family life seems to be the increasingly predominant pattern of the bilateral, patrilineal-based, nuclear family, some residual differences may be discerned between even urbanized Native Americans and the larger society. According to Price (1976, p. 268), these differences include less child-centeredness in family life, and less emphasis on toilet training, cleanliness, punctuality, competition, and material achievement.

Intermarriage

Rates of intermarriage are sensitive indexes of social distance, the nature of intergroup contact, the strength of group identification, the comparative size of groups, the heterogeneity of a population, and the processes of integration in a society. In a study of intermarriage in the 125 largest American metropolitan areas, Blau, Blum, and Schwartz (1982) show that members of small groups are more likely to outmarry and that areas with heterogeneous populations have higher rates, at least those areas that are heterogeneous in national origins, mother tongue, birth region, industry, and occupation. Racial heterogeneity is not associated with this latter effect because "great socioeconomic differences between races consolidate racial boundaries and thereby counteract the influence of heterogeneity on intermarriage" (Blau, Blum, and Schwartz 1982, p. 45). When controls are introduced for income differences, however, "racial heterogeneity and intermarriage are positively related."

In this chapter we consider sexual relations and intermarriages of Blacks and Whites, Chicanos and

Table 13-1. Black–White Marriages in the United States, 1960 and 1970

	1960	1970	Percentage change 1960 to 1970
United States: Total	51,409	64,789	+ 26.0
Husband black, wife white	25,496	41,223	+ 61.7
Husband white, wife black	25,913	23,566	− 9.1
North and West: Total	30,977	51,420	+ 66.0
Husband black, wife white	16,872	34,937	+ 107.1
Husband white, wife black	14,105	16,483	+ 16.9
South: Total	20,432	13,369	− 34.6
Husband black, wife white	8,624	6,286	− 27.1
Husband white, wife black	11,808	7,083	− 40.0

non-Chicanos, Puerto Ricans and non-Puerto Ricans, and American Indians and non-Indian Americans.[6]

The Prevalence of Intermarriage in the United States

Black–White Marriages. Table 13-1 shows the number of black–white marriages in the United States according to the censuses of 1960 and 1970 (Heer 1974, p. 247). The 26 percent increase in the total of black–white marriages in this ten-year period exceeded the increase in the total number of married couples in the United States, which increased 10.1 percent. There were, however, important differences by type of marriage: the number of married couples in which the husband was black and the wife white increased 61.7 percent, but a decrease of 9.1 percent occurred in black–white couples where the husband was white and the wife black. Also, in the North and West black–white marriages increased by 66.0 percent, compared with a decline of 34.6 percent in the South. Heer hypothesizes that a high percentage of the black–white marriages in the South in 1960 and 1970 were consensual unions since the Supreme Court did not hold the miscegenation laws formerly found in every southern state unconstitutional until 1967.

Table 13-2 shows that the number of married couples in the United States increased from 44,597,000 to 48,765,000 between 1970 and 1980, but the number of interracial married couples nearly doubled—from 310,000 to 613,000. The number of all black–white married couples increased by 100,000, from 65,000 to 166,000. Other interracial married couples increased by 200,000 from 245,000 to 447,000. Although interracial marriage continues to increase, it is still relatively rare. In 1977, it accounted for only 1 percent of all married couples, and in 1980 for 1.3 percent (Bureau of the Census December 1978, p. 7).

In all likelihood, the Census figures underestimate the extent of racial intermarriage. Enumerators have always failed to count a disproportionate number of Blacks, and members of mixed households are not always accurately identified. Most of the figures for earlier censuses are based on marriage licenses and are inaccurate. According to Sickels (1972, p. 127), in the District of Columbia some couples listed as interracial on marriage licenses have been found not to be, and some light-skinned Blacks have written "white" in the space for "color" (rather than "race") on the district application; in New York City, some applicants have specified "chartreuse," "red," "flesh" and so forth. In the census report on intermarriage published in 1969, eleven states were not included because they maintain no statewide file on marriage certificates, and of the thirty-six reporting states many no longer require information on the race of the applicants. New York, California, and Michigan have eliminated race from marriage certificates (Day 1977, pp. 200–201).

Statistics on the marriages of Blacks and Whites give little idea of the extent of sexual life between the members of these racial groups in the United States. During the period of slavery, an unknown

---

[6]For discussions of these topics with reference to European nationality groups in the United States, Asians, and Catholics, Protestants, and Jews, see, e.g., Gordon 1964; Greeley 1970; Mindel and Habenstein 1976; Monahan 1973; Peach 1980; Rosenthal 1978; Yinger 1979.

Table 13-2. Interracial Married Couples: 1970 to 1980

Item	Number		Percentage	
	1970	1980	1970	1980
Total married couples	44,597,000	48,765,000	100.0	100.0
Interracial married couples	310,000	613,000	.7	1.3
All black-white married couples	65,000	166,000	21.0	27.0
Husband black, wife white	41,000	120,000	63.0	72.0
Wife black, husband white	24,000	46,000	37.0	28.0
Other interracial married couples	245,000	447,000	79.0	73.0
Husband black	8,000	18,000	3.0	4.0
Wife black	4,000	14,000	2.0	3.0
Husband white	139,000	254,000	57.0	57.0
Wife white	94,000	161,000	38.0	36.0

Source: *Statistical Abstract 1981*, p. 41.

number of black women served as the concubines of white men. In addition to sexual relationships through concubinage, interracial mating occurred during slavery as a result of free Blacks intermarrying, liaisons between black male slaves and white female indentured servants, extramarital unions in southern and northern cities, and prostitution. Williamson observes (1980) that mulattoes have not always been assigned black status. Before 1850 free mulattoes were a kind of third class. Relations with Whites, Williamson notes, "had a distinct West Indian flavor." Some married Whites, especially in South Carolina and Louisiana; but by 1850, intermarriage was strongly opposed by Whites. Along the same line, Porterfield states (1978) that laws opposed to miscegenation during colonial times were passed precisely because marriage between white female indentured servants and black male slaves was regarded as too frequent a practice.

It should be remembered, however, that many, perhaps a majority of those who are regarded as black today and who regard themselves as black in this country, are not the offspring of persons of African ancestry and persons of European ancestry, but of persons who are themselves of mixed ancestry. Such matings might be regarded as secondary rather than primary race crossings.

In his study of the percentage of persons classified as white in the United States that have African ancestry (genes received from an African ancestor), Stuckert (1976, pp. 135–139) found that 2 percent of the white population in 1790 had some degree of African ancestry but that in 1970 the percentage had increased to 23.9. During the same

period he estimates that the proportion of the black population that had some non-African ancestry increased from 19 percent to 80.5 percent. If 42,368,000 "white" persons had some African ancestry in 1970, the majority of the persons with African ancestry are classified as white. According to these figures, some 64,000,000 persons (42,000,000 Whites and 22,000,000 Blacks), or approximately 29 percent of the population of the United States, have some African ancestry. These data show that racial purity in the white race is a myth. •

A recent work on race mixing in the United States points out that mating between Blacks and Whites is minimal and asserts that it has been so since 1865. After emancipation, race mixing virtually ceased, but the mixing of Blacks and mulattoes began at a high rate. Studies cited by Williamson (1980, pp. 113, 188–191) state that the great majority of Blacks have some white ancestry and estimate the "gene pool" of Blacks to be about one-fifth white. Among Whites, the "gene pool" is thought to be about 1 percent black.

Some increase in interracial marriage occurred during the civil rights movement of the 1960s, almost entirely because of an increase in the number of white women marrying black men. Unlike the majority of interracial marriages in earlier years, most of those who intermarried in this period were of the middle and upper class. Nevertheless, the proportion of interracial marriages in the total population remained exceedingly small. According to Williamson (1980, p. 189), through 1965 fewer than two out of every 1,000 marriages in this country were between Whites and Blacks. Pressures in the white group continued against interracial dating and marriage, as did opposition in the black community. Many Blacks, especially women, were critical of Blacks who dated and married across the race line, charging opportunism against those who did so.

The 125,000 black–white married couples in the United States in 1977 were almost twice the number in 1970: 65,000. These couples represented about 3.6 percent of all black married couples and .3 percent of all white married couples (Glick 1981, p. 119).

Chicano Intermarriage. The marriage of persons of Spanish origin to persons of other ethnic backgrounds is considerably more frequent than interracial marriage (Jaffe, Cullen, and Boswell 1980, pp. 63–68). Of the 48 million married couples in the United States in 1977, there were 762,000 couples in which one spouse was of Spanish origin and one was not. In approximately one half of these couples, the wife was of Spanish origin. These 762,000 couples constituted less than 2 percent of all married couples, but they accounted for 31 percent of the 2.4 million couples in which the husband and/or wife were of Spanish origin (Bureau of the Census, December 1978, p. 7).

As Chicanos attain middle-class status, ethnicity tends to be diluted. Middle-class status brings increased participation in the activities of the larger society, with the result that the Spanish language is used less and contact with the extended family decreases. Associates at work tend to be less and less of Mexican descent. Upward mobility often means geographical mobility, and hence more contact with Anglos, especially for those who move outside of the Southwest (Murguía 1982, pp. 14–25).

In the three states where sufficient data to make comparisons are available, the highest rates of exogamy occur in California, followed by New Mexico, and the lowest rates are in Texas. The highest rate of exogamous individuals found in Texas was 16 percent in Bexar County (San Antonio) in 1973. In California, the highest rate recorded was 38 percent for the entire state in 1962. In New Mexico, the highest rate was 31 percent in Bernalillo County (Albuquerque) in 1967. In general, outmarriage has been increasing in these three states, but in areas where the highest rates of exogamy have prevailed (Bernalillo County, New Mexico, and the state of California) rates appear to have stopped increasing

significantly. The most likely factor in the apparent stabilization of outmarriage seems to be the large in-migration from Mexico, but the Chicano movement's emphasis on ethnic consciousness may have had some effect (Murguía 1982, p. 47).

Finding the concept of assimilation insufficient when likelihood of majority individuals marrying minority persons is being considered, Murguía (1982, pp. 60, 80–110) uses the concept of "breaking of ties" in his study of intermarriage in three Texas counties and one county in New Mexico. Both minority and majority individuals are seen as being bound to generally homogeneous subsystems. The extent to which individuals of each group will outmarry is said to depend on individual characteristics which encourage contact with outgroups.

Murguía (1982, pp. 112–13) points out that certain facts about the situation of Chicanos in the United States reduce the possibility of complete absorption into the majority society. First, most Mexican Americans have physical characteristics that distinguish them as at least partially non-Caucasian. Second, because of the history of the Southwest, there is an emphasis in the region on some aspects of Mexican culture, among them architecture and cuisine. Third, the size of the Mexican American population in the Southwest slows both the acculturative process and social integration. Fourth, the relatively small distances between southwestern cities and major Mexican cities help to maintain contacts between Mexican Americans and Mexicans. Fifth, the economic opportunities in the United States will continue to attract immigration of Mexicans, both documented and undocumented, reinforcing the culture of the group. Despite these facts of Chicano life, there has been a considerable amount of Chicano cultural and structural assimilation. Rates of Chicano–Anglo intermarriage have stabilized in recent years. If there is general acceptance of Chicanos by Anglos and significant opportunities for upward mobility, Murguía expects that rates of intermarriage will increase. An increase in prejudice and discrimination, with the isolation of Chicanos in barrios and the lower social classes, would result in a decrease in intermarriage rates.

Intermarriage among Puerto Ricans. More than 80 percent of Puerto Rican migrants marry Puerto Ricans, but among their children born on the mainland only slightly more than half marry Puerto Ricans (Wagenheim 1975, p. 9). The 1970 Census showed that 34 percent of second-generation women, married and living with their spouses, are married to non-Puerto Ricans. Rates outside New York are considerably higher: 68 percent of second-generation Puerto Rican men and 65 percent of women, married and living with their spouses, were married to non-Puerto Ricans. The 1970 census reports do not distinguish between non-Puerto Rican spouses who are Hispanic and those who are not (Fitzpatrick 1976, pp. 214–215).

Intermarriage among American Indians. On the basis of a small sample (28 couples) of Spokane reservation Indians, Roy (1972) estimated that between 80 and 90 percent of the individuals on the reservation manifest some form of amalgamation. Tribal rolls indicate the amount of Indian ancestry for each member; the average proportion of Indian ancestry for the men was 55 percent, for the women 59 percent. Only eight of the twenty-eight marriages were between Indian full bloods. The other marriages involved part Indians with part Indians, part Indians with Whites, or part Indians with full-blood Indians. Walker's (1967, pp. 155–156) analysis of the reduction of Nez Percé breeding isolation in the Plateau area showed that interbreeding with other Indian groups and racial minorities of Euro-American society is increasing. In a study of migration of American Indians to Los Angeles, Price (1972) found that 64 percent of the marriages within the generation of the respondent's parents were within the tribe, but only 39 percent of the marriages within the respondent's generation were within the tribe. Approximately one-third of the married respondents had married Whites. The offspring of these marriages, although sometimes legally definable as Native American, seem likely in most instances to move toward assimilation with Whites (Wax 1971, pp. 191–92).

Factors Influencing Intermarriage and Interracial Sexual Practices

Since the period of slavery, interracial marriages of prominent people have occurred in states without antimiscegenation laws, and some of them have been highly publicized. Frederick Douglass, a leading spokesman for Blacks in the years following the Civil War, married a white suffragist in 1884. Father Divine, religious cult leader of the 1920s and 1930s; Walter S. White, the long-time Executive Secretary of the NAACP; Adam Clayton

Powell, clergyman and Congressman; LeRoi Jones, the black poet; Richard Wright, the novelist; former Senator Edward W. Brooke of Massachusetts; James Farmer, former head of CORE and later an Assistant Secretary of Health, Education, and Welfare; and entertainers Pearl Bailey, Harry Belafonte, Sammy Davis, Jr., Chubby Checker, Eartha Kitt, Leslie Uggams, and Lena Horne have married white persons (Sickels 1972, p. 124). According to Sickels, the marriages of black celebrities symbolize social emancipation for the Black mainly, while the marriage of Margaret Rusk, daughter of former Secretary of State Rusk, to a black man symbolizes emancipation for the White. Today, the older pattern of black political leaders, entertainers, and other notables marrying Whites may be at a low ebb. The time when black entertainers could attain upward mobility by taking a white spouse has passed. Some black activists regard intermarriage as backsliding (Sickels 1972, p. 125).

Among others, Napper (1973, pp. 82–83) has pointed out that one of the most destructive themes among Blacks, induced by slavery and continued by racial prejudice since that time in the United States, is the casting of black men and black women as adversaries. The conditions which produced the image of the black man as a prolific breeder and an irresponsible liability for his mate also tended to make the black woman self-reliant.

No estimates are available on black–white dating (Staples 1973/1978, pp. 265–269). A large proportion of college students now live off campus, and administrative offices keep no score on interracial dating. Black–white couples are reported by faculty and students on every integrated campus in the northern, eastern, and western states, and in the southwest—for example, at the University of Texas (Day 1972, p. 11).

More people are involved in interracial dating than in marriage, but some new trends are observable. According to Day (1977, p. 205), two decades ago mixed couples were most likely to meet at work, where both were low-income employees—frequently in domestic service. In many cases, the white spouses were foreign-born. Now young Blacks and Whites who mix and sometimes marry usually are native-born Americans and often meet on college campuses or in pursuing their careers. Typically, both have at least a high school education, and they belong to the middle class. Of those who marry, the partners tend to be older than those who marry within their own race, and frequently it is a second marriage for one or both partners.

Numerous factors, and the interaction of these factors, influence interracial dating and marriage. These variables include: sex ratios; the size of groups; life conditions within the group; opportunities for association in the workplace, residential areas, recreational sites, and educational facilities; social mobility; community attitudes toward interracial associations; institutional controls over social life; and cultural similarities of potential dating or marriage partners (Blackwell 1977, pp. 234–235; see also Aldridge 1978; Stember 1976). No research has yet shown that one of these factors is more influential than the others in bringing about the decision to date or marry interracially.

We pointed out earlier that whereas the United States Censuses of 1960 and 1970 showed the presence of an almost equal number of husband black–wife white and husband white–wife black marriages in 1960, the intermarriages of the first type exceeded those of the second type by more than 60 percent in 1970. This trend continued between 1970 and 1980. In 1977, 74 percent of the black–white married couples, as compared to 63 percent in 1970, had a black husband and a white wife (Glick 1981, p. 119). Two main hypotheses have been suggested to account for these differences. In one explanation, black men of high socioeconomic status marry white women of low status, thereby exchanging higher social position for the preferred color status of the white female. According to the second (accessibility) hypothesis, black men have had little social access to white women; legitimate sexual liaisons have come mainly through marriage. This has not been true of white males in their relations with black women. Porterfield's investigation of mixed marriages (1978, pp. 96–97) and other research appears to support the second hypothesis. At present, individuals who intermarry racially tend to be quite similar in social, educational, and occupational characteristics.

In the eastern states, numerous groups of people of mixed descent reside. These *mestizos* are known by such names as Jackson Whites (New York and New Jersey), Moors and Nanticokes (Delaware), Wesorts (Maryland), Guineas (West Virginia), and Melungeons (Tennessee). In Virginia, there are many groups known as Rumps, Issues, Cubans,

and Brown People, as well as those who claim descent from Indian tribes, including the Chickahominy, Mattapony, Pamunkey, Nansemond, and Rappahannock. Numerous groups of this type live in North Carolina: 30,000 Lumbees of Robeson County, and the Haliwas, Portuguese, and Smilings. In South Carolina, these people include the Brass Ankles, Croatans, Redbones, Redlegs, Buckheads, and Yellowhammers. They are numerous also in Louisiana: in the southern part of the state, these are Houma Indians, known also as Sabines. In western Louisiana, a large group known as Redbones are found. Alabama has mestizos known as Creoles and Cajuns, Florida has Dominickers, Ohio has a Carmelite community, Rhode Island has Narragansetts, and Massachusetts has Gay Heads and Mashpees (Berry 1972, pp. 191–192). Many Mestizos think of themselves as Whites and resent any suggestion that they are not white. Marriage to a white person is strongly approved, whereas marriage to a Black results in ostracism. Many Mestizos have chosen to identify themselves with Indians, including, perhaps, those who have despaired of being considered as Whites. For example, the Sabines in Lousiana insist that they are Houma Indians. Some mestizo communities have disappeared, mainly because their members have moved to other states or to such cities as New York City, Baltimore, Washington, and Akron. Berry (1972, p. 211) thinks that some who leave home eventually marry into and identify themselves with the black community but that probably most pass into the white population.

Unlike the tendency found in black–white marriages, the exogamy rate for Mexican American men and women indicates that women are more exogamous than men with rates of 27 percent and 24 percent respectively (Grebler et al. 1970, p. 408). Sex differences exist within each generation, with the highest rate of exogamy found among third-generation women (32 percent) and the lowest rate (13 percent) among first-generation men. Similar findings were discovered in a two-generational analysis of Puerto Rican exogamy; in both cases the results were interpreted within a social class context, that is, higher-status individuals were most likely to marry outside the group. Also, in a milieu that permits freer social interaction, the roles of the cultural minority and of the family as prime sources of identity tend to be weakened (Grebler et al. 1970, pp. 581–582; Schoen and Cohen 1980, pp. 359–66). It should be added that among Mexican Americans, second- and third-generation individuals are more likely to marry Anglos than immigrants from Mexico. In the third generation, the chances are higher for both men and women that they will marry Anglos than either first- or second-generation Mexican Americans.

In a study of intermarriage among Puerto Ricans, La Ruffa (1975, p. 220) asserts that it is difficult in the context of Puerto Rican society to view interracial marriage as it is generally understood in the social science literature. Puerto Ricans do not constitute a single people; the population on the island and on the mainland is comprised of three categories: *los blancos* (Whites), *los trigueños* (Mulattoes), and *los morenos* (Blacks). Interracial marriage, as that term is used in the United States, is relatively frequent in Puerto Rico. The frequency of such marriages, however, does not mean that race is not an important factor in Puerto Rican life. Puerto Ricans are extremely race-conscious, socially and culturally. This awareness is based in part on the large number of *trigueños* in the population of the island, persons who vary greatly in shades of skin color and in hair texture. Consciousness of race is seen especially in the "ideal of whiteness" when members of the middle and upper classes marry. In recent years, the influence of race has grown with an increase in the size of the middle class, a change that has come about with the industrialization of the island. The ideal of whiteness is important to migrants and their descendants in New York City. As in the island, *trigueños* represent the majority of the Puerto Rican population of New York, and they tend to identify with white rather than black Puerto Ricans (La Ruffa 1975, pp. 224–225; see also Gurak and Fitzpatrick 1982, pp. 921–34).

We referred earlier to studies which have indicated the prevalence of intermarriage and the increasing tendency to intermarry among American Indians. Walker's analysis (1967, pp. 150–152) of the reduction of Nez Percé breeding isolation in the Plateau area showed that interbreeding with other Indian groups and racial minorities of Euro-American society is increasing but that Whites are contributing most of the reduction of Nez Percé genes at present. The predominance of Whites in these intermarriages is due in part to the fact that this is the largest non-Nez Percé group to which the Nez Percés are exposed. Part of the explanation lies, however, in the disapproval of Nez Percés of intermarriage with Blacks, Latin Americans, and Shoshonean-speaking peoples to the south in the Great Basin. Walker found also that there are marked variations in outbreeding among different segments of the Nez Percé population. The off-reservation segment possesses fewer Nez Percé genes than does the on-reservation group. Also, the Lapwai people on the reservation are more outbred than the Kamiah population, largely because of the preference among the latter, almost totally Presbyterianized, for endogamous marriages.

The Legal Aspects of Intermarriage

The legal history of intermarriage in the United States is fascinating. Until relatively recently, Mississippi had a criminal statute providing for the punishment of anyone who published, printed, or circulated any literature in favor of or urging interracial marriage or "social equality."

So much intermixture had occurred in Louisiana that it was said that a marriage license would be refused only in cases where mixture was obvious from the appearance of the person making the application. Ordinarily the marriages of white persons to individuals with a small amount of African ancestry were questioned only by those interested in property succession, and the courts dealt lightly with children of mixed ancestry (Barron 1948, pp. 50–58; Johnson 1943, pp. 162–169; Klineberg 1944, pp. 358–364; Mangum 1940, Chapter 10).

A number of legislatures in southern and western states had enacted statutes expressly punishing members of different races and sexes for living in a state of concubinage or for indulging in acts of sexual intercourse with one another, whether it be fornication or adultery. Illicit interracial relationships were also punishable under ordinary statutes prohibiting unlawful cohabitation generally. Louisiana had a statute that penalized cohabitation between a Negro and an Indian. Texas punished the continuance of a cohabitation between a white person and a Negro after a marriage in or out of the state, but the marriage was an essential element of the offense and had to be averred and proved (Mangum 1940, pp. 256–257).

The evidence that was admissible in trying to establish the race of anyone accused of miscegenation or of his or her accomplice is extremely interesting. Certain types of testimony were held to be acceptable, including bringing either the defendant or his or her paramour into court for the jury to view and to ascertain whether or not this individual was a Black. The same could be done with respect to "the immediate direct or collateral kindred of the person involved." It was even considered as proof, with or without photographs, of Negro ancestry if "one of the party's none-too-distant ancestors had kinky hair and other racial characteristics of the Negro" (Mangum 1940, pp. 262–263).

At one time or another, 41 states had miscegenation laws. In the 1940s, 30 states prohibited, through constitutional provision or statutory law or both, the marriage of white persons and those who were defined in varying ways as "Negro." By 1963, through the repeal of statutes prohibiting interracial marriages or their nullification by state court decisions, the number was reduced to 21.[7] In the 1940s, 15 states possessed laws that expressly or impliedly prohibited the marriage of Caucasians and Mongolians, 10 states did likewise for Whites and Malays, and five forbade the marriage of Whites and Indians. Louisiana and Oklahoma prohibited unions of Indians and Negroes, and North Carolina banned the marriage of Cherokee Indians of Robeson County with persons of Negro ancestry through the third generation. Maryland forbade the marriage of Malays and Negroes. States differed with respect to the amount of Negro ancestry that would prevent a person from entering a valid marriage with a white person (Mangum 1940, Chapter 10).

California's antimiscegenation law was declared unconstitutional by the State Supreme Court in 1948. Until that time, no state or federal court had found an antimiscegenation law unconstitutional on any ground. The decision in *Perez* v. *Lippold* struck down, as a violation of the guarantee of equal protection of the laws, a section of the state's civil code which stated: "All marriages of white persons with Negroes, Mongolians, members of the Malay race or mulattoes are illegal and void." The petitioners, one black and one white, had argued that as Roman Catholics they had a right to marry under the constitutional guarantee of free exercise of religion and that the county clerk should not have refused them a marriage license. The attorneys for the clerk argued that there was no discrimination because all groups were equally affected, that is, both Whites and Blacks were subject to the terms of the law. The court replied that individuals have a right to equal treatment under the law, and that if a white man can marry a white woman a black man should be able to also. The clerk's attorneys cited an old Missouri case in which the judge had said: "It is stated as a well authenticated fact that if the issue of a black man and a white woman, and a white man and a black woman intermarry, they cannot possibly have any progeny, and such a fact sufficiently justifies those laws which forbid the intermarriage of blacks and whites, leaving out of view other sufficient grounds for such enactments." The court countered with the statement that modern opinion disagreed with this "fact" as well as with an 1869 Georgia opinion quoted by the county's attorneys: "The amalgamation of the races is not only unnatural, but is productive of deplorable results. Our daily observation shows us that the offspring of these unnatural connections are . . . inferior in physical development and strength to the full blood of either race." The court said that it would make no difference as a question of law if the theories in Missouri and Georgia were correct. To the clerk's assertion that miscegenationists come from the "dregs of society" and that their progeny would become a burden on the community, the court answered that no law may forbid marriage among the dregs of society (Sickels 1972, pp. 98–99).

In 1964, the United States Supreme Court unanimously struck down a Florida law that made it a crime for persons of different races to cohabit (*The New York Times,* March 13, 1966, p. E12). And the Court's final and definitive word on the matter came in June, 1967, in the case of *Loving* vs. *The Commonwealth of Virginia. The United States Law Week* wrote (June 13, 1967, pp. 4679–4682; see also Sickels 1972, pp. 104–122):

When the U.S. Supreme Court ruled against state laws prohibiting interracial marriage, 17 states still had such laws. The final decision of the Court against the state laws came in the case of the Lovings versus the Commonwealth of Virginia. Richard Terry Loving and his part Negro, part Indian wife, Mildred Jeter Loving, were married in Washington, D.C., in 1958, because they could not get a license in Virginia. They returned to their home state, were indicted for violation of the antimiscegenation law, and pleaded guilty. They were sentenced to one year in jail, but the prison term was suspended for a period of 25 years upon the condition that they leave the state and not return together for 25 years. In announcing the suspension of the sentence, the trial judge stated: "Almighty God created the races white, black, yellow, malay, and red,

---

[7]The states prohibiting Negro-white marriages were: Alabama, Arkansas, Delaware, Florida, Georgia, Idaho, Indiana, Kentucky, Louisiana, Mississippi, Missouri, Nebraska, North Carolina, Oklahoma, South Carolina, Tennessee, Texas, Utah, Virginia, West Virginia, and Wyoming.

and he placed them on separate continents. And but for the interference with his arrangement there would be no cause for such marriages. The fact that he separated the races shows that he did not intend for the races to mix." They left for a time, but in 1963 returned to challenge the conviction. In March, 1966, the Supreme Court of Appeals of Virginia held that nothing in the federal courts decisions of the previous 15 years had infringed upon the "overriding state interest in the institution of marriage." To upset the law in the courts would be "judicial legislation in the rawest sense of that term," the court said. It suggested that any change would have to come from the legislature. The decision left the conviction of the Lovings in effect, but said that they could return to Virginia at the same time, as long as they did not cohabit.

In June, 1967, the U.S. Supreme Court held that the Virginia law to prevent marriages between persons solely on the basis of racial classification violated the Equal Protection and Due Process Clauses of the Fourteenth Amendment.

With the striking down of the states' laws, the only barriers against interracial marriage are social and psychological. Contrary to the predictions of those who supported the antimiscegenation laws for a century, lifting the barriers did not result in a stampede of Blacks for white partners (B. Day 1972, p. 14).

Attitudes toward Racial Intermarriage

Polls in recent years have shown marked change in the public attitude toward black–white intermarriage. Answers have varied quite widely, depending on how the question was asked. For example, a national poll in 1965 showed that nearly half of the respondents favored making interracial marriage a crime. Six years later, a Harris poll found a general acceptance of both interracial dating and marriage, but considerable concern and doubt was expressed about the probable success of such relationships (B. Day 1972, pp. 16–17). In 1972, the National Opinion Research Center asked a carefully selected sample of the adult population, in its General Social Survey: "Do you think there should be laws against marriages between (Negroes/ Blacks) and Whites?" Three percent said "Don't know," 39 percent said yes, and 61 percent said no. When the same question was asked in 1982, the percentages were 30 percent yes and 70 percent no.

It must be remembered that often there is a difference between verbal reactions and actual behavior; also, differences exist between attitudes toward the intermarriage of close relatives and intermarriage in general. On the verbal level at least, an

increasing number of Whites are becoming more receptive, or more tolerant, of these marriages.

A study of thirty black families in two small towns in Missouri and Florida, and in Cleveland and Kansas City, showed that few of the informants favored the marriage of an individual in their extended family to a White. Disapproval seemed to be based on a basic mistrust of white people in general. Other reasons for opposing interracial marriage were: such marriages show a lack of racial pride; members of their family would be subjected to humiliation by Whites and to ostracism by Blacks; the emergence, in time, of racial prejudice between the spouses; and resentment by black women of having to compete with white women for black men. A few condoned interracial marriage on the grounds that marriage is a personal matter, something that is of concern only to the two parties involved (Martin and Martin 1978, p. 67).

Blackwell (1977, pp. 236–237) refers to the strong negative sanctions against black male–white female unions, whether dating or marrying. Black males involved in such relationships have, at times, been viewed as demeaning other Blacks. Some of these individuals have been socially isolated, insulted, and discriminated against in housing and job opportunities. Blackwell points out that the unequal sex ratio between black women and black men reduces the number of black men available for dating and marriage. The situation is further complicated by the fact that the pool of highly educated black men is smaller than that of educated black women, and by the disproportionate number of black men in prisons. These reasons lead frequently to strong disapproval by black women of relationships between black men and white women.

Some of the Effects of Interracial Dating and Marriage

In a context of changed laws and changing attitudes but of lingering opposition, interracial dating and marriage face various special circumstances and problems (see Blumberg and Roye 1979; Tseng, McDermott, and Maretzki 1977).

Family Relationships in Black–White Marriages. Black–white marriages are likely to be a second marriage for one or both partners, and typically the partners are older than those who marry within their own race (B. Day 1972, p. 16). Liberation movements have changed the life-styles and role integration for black and white families.[8] The larger part that men are taking in the rearing of children is less of a change for black than for white households. Despite some reluctance to do chores at home when he feels that he is discriminated against on his job, the chances are that the black man and his family have all participated in role sharing and role changing (B. Day 1972, p. 297).

Day found that all of the interracial couples she interviewed either already had, or intended to have, a family, something that studies of mixed couples a decade earlier had not found. Later, Day (1977) wrote that in contrast to the high percentage of childless mixed couples of a generation ago, the couples now marrying probably will have children.

The availability of adequate contraceptive devices and the relaxation of abortion laws have affected the average size of families—black, white, and black–white. In both black husband–white wife and white husband–black wife marriages, the average number of children ever born was fewer in 1970 than in homogeneous black marriages and was similar to that among couples where both husband and wife were white. The proportion of childless wives in the two types of interracial marriage was greater in every age group than among homogeneous white couples and among homogeneous black couples provided that the wife was less than 45 years of age. Exact data on the number of children born with racially mixed parentage cannot be provided because it is not known whether the children born in 1970 to a racially heterogeneous marriage were born during their mother's then current marriage. In a substantial number of racially mixed marriages, one of the marriage partners had been married more than once; some of the wives in such marriages in 1970 may have borne some or all of the children in a previous racially homogeneous marriage. Heer (1974, pp. 251, 256–257) concludes that fertility in black–white marriages is less than in homogeneous black marriages.

One of the most interesting studies of children of black–white marriages (Teicher 1968, pp. 146, 249–256) found that these mixed children experience greater identity problems than do the children of black couples. Teicher found that many of these

children feel that black is devalued in this society and, resenting both parents, cannot identify with either. Resentment occurs also with respect to siblings who have different racial characteristics. Further study may provide insights concerning problems affecting children in all-black families whose physical characteristics may be strikingly different.

The parents of children of mixed descent often attempt to prepare their children for some of the questions they may encounter. Several of the couples interviewed by B. Day (1972, p. 303) stated that they had looked for other black–white couples with children, thinking that the children would not perceive having one black parent was strange or unusual and believing that knowing other children of their own intermediate color would be desirable.

A Jewish woman who was married to a black artist and later married a white man, said that her teen-aged interracial daughter seemed confused about her identity even though she got along well with her stepfather. The girl had no contact with her own father, and it seemed difficult for her to accept two Whites as her parents (B. Day 1972, p. 308). Day adds that the Jewish-black child must decide whether he wishes to consider himself part of the Jewish or of the black community. According to Day (pp. 309–310), social acceptance appears to be greater for legitimate Jewish-black children if the black parent either converts to Judaism or offers no objection to Jewish education for the children.

Like black children, interracial children find that their social problems increase with age, especially during the teenage period when dating begins. Even children who have played together earlier tend to separate at adolescence (B. Day 1972, p. 306).

An interesting question concerns whether the combination of a white father and black mother might provide a better start to upward mobility, other things being equal, than the combination of a black father and a white mother. Heer (1974, p. 257) suggests that this would follow if it were assumed that the role of the father were more important than that of the mother in facilitating access to jobs obtainable through family connections and if it were further assumed that white mothers provided no advantage over white fathers in matters of inheritance and instruction concerning the nature of the white social world. It is possible, however, that marriages of a white man and a black women may more often be consensual unions and

---

[8]For an interesting discussion of the daily family life (entertainment, spending money, nonverbal communication, emotional expression, husband–wife roles) of black–white couples, see B. Day 1972, 233–250.

that the consensually married (common law) white husband may be relatively less interested in his children.

Interracial Adoption. There has been a considerable increase in interracial adoption in recent years (see, e.g., Blumberg and Roye 1979; Ladner, 1977; Simon and Alstein 1977). In 1970, 2,200 nonwhite babies were so adopted, a figure three times as high as in 1968. More than one-fourth of these adoptions occurred in the states of Oregon, Washington, and California. The number of Asian children adopted mainly by white parents increased, according to the Immigration and Naturalization Service, from 1,672 in 1971 to 5,044 in 1976. In transracial adoption, the greatest objection comes from relatives, especially grandparents, neighbors, and from some black spokesmen who oppose having a black child reared by a white family. Adoptive agencies consider such situations from the viewpoint of the child, holding that it is more important to provide the child with a home and parents than to preserve racial or cultural origins by having the child languish in an institution (B. Day 1972, pp. 310, 312).

Problems of Interdating and Intermarrying. The social costs of interracial dating and marriage vary greatly from one locale to another. The white or the black woman who considers dating interracially must be aware of possible damage to her reputation. In many places, the belief is that interracial dating necessarily involves interracial sexual relations, so the girl who dates interracially may be regarded as sexually promiscuous (Blackwell 1977, p. 237).

With the exception of neighborhoods near some of the largest universities in the United States and "the more liberally inclined" sections of New York City and other metropolitan areas, black–white couples experience the same rejection by landlords that all-black couples face. Middle-class couples often resolve this problem by moving into a neighborhood that is changing from white to black or vice versa and trying to identify with the numerically predominant group, not always a satisfactory solution (B. Day 1972, p. 224). According to Porterfield (1978, p. 149), there seems to be less of a problem if the wife is black. Some hostility exists toward mixed families in both black and white communities, but it appears to be least in public apartment buildings.

Reliable data on the use of economic sanctions against those who intermarry racially are scarce,

but such sanctions may be declining. A majority of the 40 intermarried couples studied by Porterfield (1978, pp. 149–150) in Urbana, Illinois, Cambridge, Ohio, Birmingham, Alabama, and Jackson, Mississippi, had had no difficulties in the area of employment, but a small number reported losing their jobs because of their marriages.

Interracial married couples have found that some friendships ended after their marriage but that the closest friends remained friends. Friendships are less likely to be affected if the wage earner of the family is employed in civil rights work, the theater, teaching, or social work. B. Day (1972, pp. 227–228) found that the life-style of interracial couples depends in part on the city in which they reside. In Chicago, Detroit, and New York, mixed couples tend to get together socially; in Philadelphia, they do not.

It is not unusual for mixed couples to have humiliating experiences for years after their marriage. White parents and relatives tend not to alter their negative attitudes, whereas kinsmen of black spouses tend to be more receptive to mixed marriages (Porterfield 1978, p. 123).

During the decade 1960 to 1970, existing black–white marriages showed a higher rate of attrition than racially homogeneous marriages. Sixty-three percent of the marriages involving a black husband and white wife contracted in the ten years prior to the 1960 Census were still in existence in 1970 and of those involving a white husband and a black wife 47 percent (Heer 1974, p. 256). When marital difficulty arises, it may be difficult to discover whether the racial factor is directly or indirectly involved. Few studies control for class, education, residence, or other variables that influence the stability of marriages. Hence it is difficult to measure the possible impact of the factor of intermarriage. Although interracial marriages produce a higher rate of dissolution than do homogeneous marriages, one must take into consideration the fact that a considerable number of intermarriages are remarriages. Studies of Jewish-Gentile marriage and divorce show that remarriages are not so enduring as first marriages and that the probability of divorce rises with each successive marriage (Rosenthal 1967, p. 262). A similar tendency may be present in remarriages involving Blacks and Whites.

Intermarriage requires adjustments on the part of the partners in addition to the adjustments which must be made by spouses in a racially homogeneous marriage. Social pressures and value differences, as well as ordinary personality differences, produce stresses which some individuals cannot tolerate. An awareness of the importance of such pressures and differences may help to prevent the development of conflict, or to understand and manage it if it arises (Kiev 1973).

Summary and Conclusions

1. The number of black–white marriages contracted annually is not large, but it is increasing. At present, probably not more than 5 percent of the black population is interracially married (Staples 1976, p. 235) and not more than 1 percent of the black population marries interracially annually.

2. In 1970, there were nearly twice as many black husband–white wife marriages as there were white husband–black wife marriages and the 1980 Census reported more than 2½ times as many interracial marriages of the first type as of the second type.

3. The U.S. Census figures underestimate the extent of black–white marriages.

4. Statistics on black–white marriages give little idea of the extent of sexual life between the members of these racial groups in the United States.

5. In 1970, approximately one-fourth of the population of the United States of Hispanic origin were married to people of non-Hispanic origin.

6. Only half of the children born of Puerto Ricans living on the mainland marry Puerto Ricans.

7. Figures on intermarriage among American Indians as a whole are not available, but such marriages are increasing. A study in Los Angeles showed that approximately one-third of the married respondents had married Whites.

8. The kinds of sexual behavior that have occurred between Blacks and Whites in the United States cannot be attributed mainly to any one factor, but rather to the interplay of several variables.

9. Mexican American women are more exogamous than Mexican American men.

10. In marrying, the "ideal of whiteness" is important to Puerto Ricans on the island and the mainland.

11. The legality of intermarriage is an important aspect of equal civil rights. In 1967, the U.S. Supreme Court struck down the laws forbidding interracial marriages in the 17 states that still had such legislation.

12. During the past decade and a half, polls have shown an increase in tolerance on the part of Whites toward racial intermarriage. Such marriages are disapproved by many in the black community, but some condone them on the grounds that marriage is a personal matter.

13. Black–white marriages are likely to be a second marriage for one or both partners, and typically the partners are older than those who marry within their own race.

14. The children of black–white marriages may experience greater identity problems than do the children of black couples.

15. The problems of black–white couples continue along the lines of earlier years: finding satisfactory housing, retaining employment, maintaining friendships that existed prior to marriage, and facing the negative attitudes of parents and relatives, especially on the white side.

16. In the long run, it appears likely that the social, economic, and political changes of recent decades will lead to higher rates of all types of intermarriage.

CHAPTER 14

Minority–Majority Relations and Religion

Whether a society is religiously homogeneous or has adherents of several different faiths, its religious patterns are a sensitive index of the majority–minority situation. The religious beliefs and institutional structures of a group not only show intrinsic religious aspects but also indicate secular positions and secular problems as well.

Are Religious People More or Less Prejudiced?

Judging solely on ideological grounds, one might suppose that highly religious people would be less prejudiced against minorities than would nonreligious people. The relationship is difficult to test, however, because they may also be different in other ways—in education, age, and occupation, for example—that must be taken into account. The strength and nature of religious attachment and of prejudice are difficult to measure. It is also true that on this, as on so many social scientific questions, it is mainly Christians and American Jews who have been studied, and therefore generalizations are rather severely limited. From a distance one might assume that Muslims, because their tradition opposes race prejudice, were immune from majority–minority problems. Yet in many Muslim societies, women are clearly a minority and religious prejudice is severe. Hinduism draws no sharp

race lines and is religiously tolerant, but it is integrally associated with a caste system in most interpretations. Although Buddhism is highly tolerant, devout Buddhists have often withdrawn from the societies in which they live and shown little concern for rigid class systems. These lines are not written to prove that every religion and every individual is equally likely to be prejudiced, but to emphasize the need for careful, comparative study.

Studies of the relationship between individual religiosity and prejudice are extremely sensitive to the questions asked, the sample, and the measures of religiosity. In virtually every instance, verbal, not behavioral measures of the dependent variable are used. It remains problematic whether there is a close link between attitudes and behavior in this area. Behavioral measures for the independent variable (church attendance, for example) are more commonly employed. Samples are often fairly small, moreover, so that controls for critical variables, particularly age and education, are often impossible (Cygnar, Noel, and Jacobson 1977).

In a review of over 100 studies of the possible relationship between Christianity and prejudice, Gorsuch and Aleshire (1974) noted the widely varying ways of measuring both variables. Many studies identified the "religious" persons solely on the basis of church membership. Half to two-thirds of church members, however, are inactive. When their prejudice scores are lumped together with those of active members, the results are difficult to interpret because a number of studies have found a curvilinear relationship between religion and prejudice (Hoge and Carroll 1973). "The highly committed religious person is—along with the nonreligious person—one of the least prejudiced members of our society" (Gorsuch and Aleshire 1974, p. 287).

Keeping these methodological problems in mind, we can profitably examine some of the continuing research on religion and prejudice.

In their follow-up of a well-known study by Stouffer (1955), Nunn, Crockett, and Williams (1978, p. 128): observe:

> Those who identify with a particular religious institution, with the exception of Jews, and those who attend religious services are less likely to be tolerant of nonconformists than citizens who claim no affiliation and do not participate in religious services.

We should note that all groups had become more tolerant since the 1954 study, but the differences among groups had increased (see also J. A. Davis 1975; Steiber 1980). Although these studies are not concerned specifically with racial or ethnic intolerance, other studies make that the focus of attention. Glock and Stark (1966, pp. 208–209) argue:

> the causal chain that links Christian belief and faith to secular anti-Semitism begins with orthodoxy—commitment to a literal interpretation of traditional Christian dogma. Orthodoxy, in turn, leads to particularism—a disposition to see Christian truth as the only religious truth. . . . This process—orthodoxy to particularism to religious hostility—culminates in secular anti-Semitism.

Since they do not have data indicating which of these beliefs comes first, we think the causal connection cannot be easily established. A substantial proportion—perhaps half, depending upon the measure being used—even of the orthodox and particularistic have low scores on the anti-Semitism scale. Controlling for age, education, and race, Martire and Clark (1982, p. 76) found that the correlation of Christian orthodoxy with anti-Semitism disappeared.

Christian belief is not only not a sufficient cause of anti-Semitism; it is not a necessary cause in the contemporary world. Nevertheless, some kinds of Christian teaching for some people in some contexts do give additional support to anti-Semitic beliefs that are sustained by other forces as well. This is shown more clearly perhaps in a follow-up

study of 1,580 clergymen in California, over half of whom are mildly or strongly anti-Semitic, according to the measures used (Stark et al. 1971).

It is essential in any interpretation of the influence of "religiosity" on prejudice to ask how religiosity has been measured, other than by church membership or the frequency of church attendance. Often it is only highly traditional or orthodox measures that are used. The religious are those who think like Cotton Mather—to put it a bit too severely. Since they are also more likely to be rural, older, and less well educated, the causal connections are obscure. Fundamentalist views, moreover, are unrelated to some measures of racism. For example, Powell and Steelman (1982) found that unwillingness to vote for a black candidate nominated by one's party for president was not correlated with fundamentalism.

How can we interpret these diverse findings? It is impossible to speak of the effects of religion on prejudice as if religion were a wholly homogeneous phenomenon. The first need, of course, is for careful controls that eliminate the influence of other variables. Religion may have nothing at all to do with the relationship. Middle-class people seem by some measures to be more anti-Semitic in our society than lower-class people; they are better educated; they are more likely to attend church and to be "religious"; but they are also in more direct economic competition with Jews. To say that middle-class people are more anti-Semitic because they have received more education or because they go to church more often, when other variables have not been controlled, is clearly unwarranted. Nor can we assume that this might not be true. To make the issue absurdly clear—or perhaps just absurd—middle-class people are fatter than lower-class people, and also more anti-Semitic; therefore, corpulence leads to prejudice. Descriptive studies can be of use in science only when they are related to a general theory that prevents one-sided, possibly spurious explanations.

After the application of controls we may find that the relationship between religion and prejudice is still complex. We need in addition, therefore, an analysis of the kind of religious training a person has received, a study of why and how he is religious.

In a valuable study, Roof (1974) found evidence that to an important degree the correlation between religious orthodoxy and prejudice reflects the effects of *localism*—of limited experience—on interracial views. He does not argue that orthodoxy is uninvolved but that it must be studied in conjunction with the effects of localism. Thus his multiple-regression analysis leads him, not to interpretation one or two, but to interpretation three:

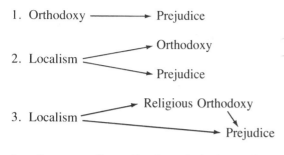

1. Orthodoxy ⟶ Prejudice

2. Localism ⟨ Orthodoxy / Prejudice

3. Localism ⟨ Religious Orthodoxy / Prejudice

Localism, according to Roof's analysis, has a direct influence on the level of prejudice, and that influence is heightened when it is combined with religious orthodoxy.

One persistent finding that throws doubt on the religiosity–prejudice relationship is that the clergy, at least in this period in American history, are less prejudiced, on the average, and more likely both to support and to participate actively in civil rights efforts than are laymen (Hadden 1969; Quinley 1974b). Clergy make up a high proportion of those who have participated in civil rights marches and have organized conferences to protest racial injustice; in opinion polls dealing with race relations, ministers take more liberal views than laymen in most instances.

It is not enough, of course, simply to assume that a stronger religious interest accounts for the clergy's actions. Various attitudinal, structural, and role factors are also involved. In a survey of 1,580 parish clergy in California, those whose responses placed them near the "modernism–liberalism" end of a scale designed to measure their attitudes were much more likely to have been involved in civil rights activities than those near the "traditionalism" end (Quinley 1974a). Among a sample of Protestant ministers in five cities, Nelsen, Yokley, and Madron (1973) found that those who defined their roles as "problem-solving" and who took liberal theological and political positions were most likely to be favorably inclined toward protest activities in efforts to improve the lot of racial minorities.

Related to comparisons of clergy and laymen are various comparisons of type of religiosity. Gordon Allport (1960, p. 264) drew a distinction between extrinsic beliefs that are used simply as instruments of self-interest by insecure persons and

intrinsic beliefs that are the results of normal socialization and security. A child who has deep feelings of insecurity and distrust may tie his religion to prejudice: I am of the elect (which implies that many others are not); God is partial to me. Such beliefs in the insecure lead easily to categorical condemnation of outgroup members in an effort to bolster a shaky security. A secure person, on the other hand "does not need to look on people as threats to his well-being." One does not need to use religious revelation or the doctrine of election to downgrade others in order to bolster oneself. Indeed, capacity for reciprocity of perception—seeing the world from another's point of view—encourages the use of religion to emphasize a common humanity rather than for self-defense.

Although Allport recognized that the extrinsic-intrinsic concept referred to a range of possibilities, not to a sharp either–or contrast, he examined its potential influence on prejudice by describing the end points on the range (Allport 1960, pp. 257–67; Allport and Ross 1967) Wilson (1960) made the concept more useful by devising an "extrinsic religious values" scale to measure motives for affiliating with religious groups. He found a significant positive correlation between the scores on this scale and an anti-Semitism scale among 10 small, rather diverse groups.

The extrinsic-intrinsic idea is useful. Unfortunately, efforts to employ it in research have yielded contradictory results. From a total sample of 497 college students, Allen and Spilka (1967) selected the 210 who were "most religious" on the basis of their rated importance of religion, frequency of church attendance, religious identity, and attitudes toward the church. These were then given a 16-item prejudice scale, on the basis of which those highest in prejudice ($n = 29$) and those lowest in prejudice ($n = 32$) were selected for further study. This further study consisted of extensive tape-recorded interviews in which the aim was to determine the extent to which their religious views were "committed" or "consensual" (a distinction related to intrinsic-extrinsic). Neither interviewers nor those who rated the subjects from the tapes knew the prejudice or religious scores of the respondents. The results, in brief, were that a strong correspondence was found between committed religion and low prejudice, and between consensual religion and high prejudice. Allen and Spilka did not find, however, that the Extrinsic Religious Values scale used by Wilson successfully distinguished between their subjects holding a committed or consensual orientation. The measurement processes and instruments used by Allen and Spilka are, in our judgment, somewhat richer and more likely to be valid than Wilson's; but in this line of research each scale must be used with caution until more extensive validation has been undertaken. (See also Dittes 1971; Hunt and King 1971; Kahoe 1977; Roof and Perkins 1975).

We are a long way from the use of validated instruments on standardized populations, hence all generalizations in this area are subject to doubt. Batson, Naifeh, and Pate (1978) found, for example, that religion defined as *quest*—the pursuit of ultimate questions rather than ultimate answers—was significantly correlated with tolerance, even after controls, much more strongly than the intrinsic quality of religion. At this time we believe that two statements are justified: the nature of one's religious belief as a personality tendency (intrinsic-extrinsic or some other measure) is largely a dependent variable, reflecting most directly, perhaps, the degree of inner security. Second, the extrinsic or intrinsic quality of one's religious beliefs is partly a cultural phenomenon, as is the linkage or lack of linkage between prejudice and religion. These things may simply be taught to one as part of his cultural training: God ordained that races shall be separate, or God ordained brotherhood. On this level, it is cultural analysis, not personality analysis, that is most fruitful.

Segregation and the Churches

When we shift our attention from individual attitudes and behavior to institutional practices, we find the same mixed picture. American churches are substantially segregated by race. This fact requires careful study, however, for there is wide variation among churches. A trend toward integrated churches exists alongside tendencies toward separation and resegregation.

Segregation and Integration in Protestant Churches

Shortly after World War II, Loescher (1948) found that perhaps 6 percent of black Protestants belonged to predominantly white denominations; and of these not more than 8,000 attended integrated local churches. The usual pattern in Protestantism, then and now, is initial resistance to the coming of black members; but when the transition has occurred, the church property is sold to a black group. This is not invariably the case, however. There may be a prolonged period of integration; a black and a white church may join together (Davis and White 1980; Pugh 1977).

Gradually, barriers to church integration have been lowered. In 1952, the Presbyterian Church in the United States (southern) voted to absorb the Negro congregations into the regional synods. In 1952 the Methodist Church began the abolition of its segregated Central Jurisdiction for Negro churches. Several general conferences, which meet every four years, reemphasized this policy but also spoke of "reasonable speed" and emphasized voluntary procedures, as noted in the *Doctrines and Disciplines of the Methodist Church,* 1964. This reflected, to an important degree, the large southern membership of the Methodist Church. After 20 years, the Central Jurisdiction was officially disbanded by voluntary action of the Annual Conferences. Opposition to the national policy of integration continued, however, on the local and state levels, in the form of reduced support for race relations work, reduced use of Methodist literature, formation of a Methodist Layman's Union to resist integration, and the like (Wood and Zald 1966).

In 1956, the United Presbyterian Church of North America voted for "complete integration of all churches, agencies, and institutions" (Mays 1957, pp. 51–52) and in 1964 elected a black moderator (the membership is 95 percent white). The Protestant Episcopal Church and the Methodist Church have black bishops serving mainly white constituencies. In 1977 Joseph Kibira, a black bishop from Tanzania, was elected head of the Lutheran World Federation; and Sterling Cary, a black minister, has served as president of the National Council of Churches.

Although such changes are modifying the segregation structure, it is doubtless still true that the majority of black Protestants are in separate denominational organizations. There are equivalent changes at the local congregational level. It is difficult to speak with precision on this matter, but it can be estimated reasonably that 10 to 15 percent of northern and western Protestant churches are interracial to some degree (with a denominational range of perhaps 5 to 20 percent). The number of individuals involved is small. Probably no more than one or two percent of Blacks are in interracial churches. Interracial ministerial staffs or appointment of black ministers to predominantly white churches is uncommon. Looked at another way, however, the interracial element in Protestant churches seems stronger. Using the 1978 and 1980 surveys of the NORC, Hadaway, Hackett and Miller (1984, p. 208) found that 32 percent of white Protestants attend churches with Blacks.

Continuation of racially homogeneous churches is not simply a sign of prejudice in the churches. To some degree it reflects housing segregation (often defended, of course, by church people). It also signifies denominational loyalty and a desire for separate churches on the part of some nonwhites.

There have been strenuous efforts by national church leaders and conferences to break down racial barriers, both in the churches and in other institutions. In 1963, Catholic, Jewish, and Protestant leaders joined in a National Conference on Religion and Race in an effort "to increase the leadership of religion in ending racial discrimination in the United States." For many spokesmen in the churches, "Racism is our most serious domestic evil" and "the number-one scandal of the church" (see Ahmann 1963; Pope 1957). Churches, deeply involved as they are in the institutional structure of society, are seldom leaders in social reform; yet they are often important in carrying a movement along and conditioning the process by which change is accomplished.

Churches in one society are also affected by the situation in other societies. The growing influence of "liberation theology" in Latin America, for example, highlights problems in the United States to which some church leaders and laymen are sensitive and helps to focus their efforts. The New York Circus, an interethnic and ecumenical ministry based in Manhattan's upper west side, relates liberation theology to the problems of poverty and discrimination faced by Hispanic immigrants and refugees in New York (*The New York Times,* December 5, 1982, p. 36).

Segregation and Integration in Catholic Churches

In Catholic countries generally, the race line has been drawn less sharply than in predominantly Protestant countries. The emphasis on liturgy and worship in Catholicism, compared with the more informal social patterns found in many Protestant churches, has supported an interracial perspective. And the hierarchical, rather than local, control removes some decisions from the influences of local prejudices. On the other hand, Catholic churches are affected by the values and prejudices of their constituents and by the traditions and practices of the communities of which they are a part. Catholics exhibit about the same range of prejudices as Protestants, and local traditions and pressures affect decisions concerning the time and place to integrate.

Although most black Americans are Protestants, there are over a million black Catholics, with heaviest concentrations in Louisiana and in six cities (Washington, New York, Chicago, Philadelphia, Galveston–Houston, and Los Angeles). Fifty percent of white Catholics attend church with black Catholics (Hadoway, Hackett, and Miller 1984, p. 208). The Catholic Church participated in and was influenced by the civil rights movement, but whether in the depth demanded by the critical issues involved is a matter for dispute. During the height of that movement one could see such contrasting headlines as: "Gain by Catholics on Race Bias Seen," and "Negro Catholics Say Church Fails" (*The New York Times,* October 4, 1970, p. 46 and August 24, 1970, p. 21).

We know of no way to measure the rate of change confidently or to state precisely how strongly the Roman Catholic Church has participated in the movement to reduce racial discrimination in the United States; but our strong impression is that the Roman Catholic Church, like the other churches, has not played an important part. On the one hand we should note the important contributions of individual Catholic leaders, such as Father John LaFarge and Father Theodore Hesburgh. We should also call attention to the establishment, in 1961, of the National Catholic Conference for Interracial Justice, an outgrowth of the Catholic Interracial Council movement begun by Father LaFarge in New York in 1934. Under the leadership of its director, Mathew Ahmann, the conference played a critical role, along with the National Council of Churches and the Synagogue Council of America, in the creation of the Conference on Religion and Race (Ahmann 1963).

It is also important to note that in the early days of school desegregation, Roman Catholic schools often took the lead, especially in southern and border states. In 1925, Xavier University in New Orleans was opened to Negroes, with an integrated faculty; Catholic University, in Washington, D.C., admitted Negro sisters in 1933 and other Negro students to the undergraduate and graduate programs in 1936. In 1944 St. Louis University began the first integration on the college level in Missouri, and in 1947 the archdiocese of St. Louis began school desegregation. Seven high schools and 32 elementary schools in Virginia were desegregated in 1958, at that time the only integrated schools below the college level in the state. By 1959, Catholic schools in most southern states had been desegregated (Foy 1962, pp. 105–107).

At the same time, the number of black priests has increased slowly. The ratio of black priests to black communicants is scarcely one-tenth of the ratio of white priests to white communicants (the latter being about one to one thousand). Although there are over 100,000 Negro Catholics in New York City, it was not until 1968 that the first black priest was appointed to head a parish in the New York archdiocese. The 700 black women among the 130,000 Catholic nuns constitute scarcely more than one-half of one percent of the total (Cleveland *Plain Dealer,* July 12, 1980, p. B15).

The first black bishop in the United States was named in 1965. By 1982 there were six black members of the National Conference of Catholic Bishops (*The New York Times,* November 21, 1982, p. 23).

Churches in the South

The pervasive "dilemma of the churches" (Yinger 1970, pp. 234–39), is nowhere more clearly shown than in the activities of southern churches during the most active days of the civil rights movement. A few comments on the religion–segregation picture in this region can serve as a useful case study of the way in which churches and church leaders seek to deal with a set of mutually contradictory demands—in this case, between religious norms of brotherhood and sisterhood on one hand and the structures of a highly segregated society on the other.

Southern religious history broke with that of the rest of the nation over the slavery issue in the 1830s, and has continued since then to be somewhat distinctive. In the Methodist Church, despite a national bureaucratic structure, regional and local forces are very strong. Interregional migration, instead of reducing contrasts, tends to increase them, as the more liberal clergy leave the South and, to a lesser degree, more conservative clergy from the North move in (Rymph and Hadden 1970). We do not disagree substantially with Frady's judgment (1967, p. 37) of the largest Protestant church: "Here in the South the moral challenge of the post-1954 civil rights movement was mounted—and here it was for the most part ignored, sidestepped, and in some

cases opposed by the churches of the Southern Baptist Convention." A few years after the Supreme Court school desegregation decision, Waldo Beach (1956, p. 30) noted that some persons were using religion to defend racism on religious grounds, but "the great majority of the churches are in the middle, maintaining a troubled uncertain silence."

There were evidences of religious opposition to segregation. Many black ministers, of course, took the lead in the civil rights movement, but we should also note that white ministers were not absent from the scene. In 1957, 74 Protestant clergymen in Atlanta issued "a statement on race relations calling for obedience to law, preservation of public schools, protection of free speech, and maintenance of communication between white and Negro leaders" (*The New York Times,* November 3, 1957, p. 84). This both reflected and helped to set the tone for changes beginning in Atlanta. When desegregation began in New Orleans schools, white students at first boycotted the integrated schools. At William Frantz School ten white children joined one Negro child during the second week. Seven of those ten were children of clergymen. Ministerial associations in several cities supported school board plans for school desegregation. In 1963, 28 young Methodist ministers in Mississippi issued a manifesto proclaiming their belief in "freedom of the pulpit" and "opposing racial discrimination in the state of their birth." All were subjected to boycotts by their congregations or other forms of harassment (*The New York Times,* June 30, 1963, p. E8).

But these were fairly isolated incidents. The troubled, uncertain silence of which Beach wrote or outright opposition to desegregation was the norm among southern churchmen. During the period of crisis in the desegregation of schools in Little Rock, ministers of all faiths cooperated in arranging for special church services to pray for a calming of the fever of racial passion—in segregated services! Eight of a group of clergymen who had been among those in January, 1963, to sign "An Appeal for Law and Order and Common Sense" in dealing with racial problems in Alabama wrote Martin

We are now confronted by a series of demonstrations by some of our Negro citizens, directed and led in part by outsiders. . . . We do not believe that these days of new hope are days when extreme measures are justified in Birmingham. We commend the community as a whole, and the local news media and law enforcement officials in particular, on the calm manner in which these demonstrations have been handled. (*Liberation,* June 1963, p. 9)

Luther King, Jr., in May urging him to call off demonstrations in Birmingham.

This statement struck King, who was then in jail, as somewhat ironic, since order had been kept in part by the use of dogs, who had bitten six demonstrators, by vigorous use of firehoses, and by the jailing of hundreds of persons.

The most systematic study of the dilemma of southern churchmen and their ambivalent behavior was made in Little Rock by Campbell and Pettigrew (1959). On the basis of interviews, they classified 25 Protestant ministers (representing largely the more prominent churches) and two rabbis into three groups: five segregationists, 16 inactive integrationists, and 8 active integrationists. Campbell and Pettigrew note that different "reference systems" pulled the men in varying directions. Typically the self-reference system—personal values and training—pulled them toward integration. The professional reference system—the regional and national church—rewarded a minister for keeping up membership and attendance. Finally, the membership reference system, his own congregation, encouraged segregation or inaction. Pulled by these diverse forces, most of the clergymen took the ambivalent position of inactive integrationism. They felt little guilt, for their sense of worth was based largely on success in managing their churches; they readily assumed that a slow process of education was what was needed, and "you can't teach those you can't reach"; they avoided commitment by reference to "deeper issues"—humility, brotherly love; and they felt rather courageous in the little bit they did toward integration because stanch segregationists attacked the clergy for being race-mixers. Among those who attacked them were the ministers of the fundamentalist sects, all of whom were vigorous segregationists (Campbell and Pettigrew 1959, Chapter 3).

If the southern scene continues to change, as we believe it will, the dilemma will become less sharp, and churchmen who did not make the first moves may be involved significantly in the less dramatic task of consolidating and extending the gains, because the social context of their work is rapidly changing. If the church as a sociological type is accommodated to its social setting—not without some sectarian deviants in its midst—it should be emphasized that the social setting is being rapidly urbanized and industrialized. Blacks have become a significant force in politics. School desegregation, although far from complete, has moved a long way past the complete separation of the races before 1954. Churches will move toward desegregation as the rest of society moves, affecting and being affected by the other forces at work.

The Churches' Interest in the Integration of Other Institutions

When we examine the evidence of the role of churches in promoting an integrated society, we find the same mixed picture that we found in the church situation itself, with support of segregation or indifference on the one hand and the beginnings of vigorous efforts to promote integration on the other (Simpson 1978, pp. 224–28). It is not difficult to find church defense of slavery, for example; but churches were also the source of much of the abolitionist movement. Using a multiple regression model, Hammond shows that religious revivals in Ohio before the Civil War independently increased antislavery voting. That is, the connection between revivals and antislavery voting was not spurious; it was not due to socioeconomic status, to membership in a particular religious organization, or to group identification, but to the revivals themselves. Hammond notes (1974, p. 175) that "revivals preached a new doctrine which demanded active opposition to slavery. . . . The revivals transformed the religious orientations of those who experienced them, and this transformation affected their voting behavior." The religious element in the antislavery movement did not begin with the revivals, Hammond observes. The Methodist Church condemned slavery in 1780 and the Presbyterians in 1818.

Religious Opposition to Inequality in Latin America

The complex relationship between religion and systems of social stratification is especially clearly shown today in Latin America. A brief reference to that situation can help us develop a comparative perspective that will contribute to our understanding of the United States and elsewhere. The conflicts in Latin America are not usually defined as minority–majority or racial conflicts. Class conflicts or peasant–landowner struggles are more commonly described. In many instances, however, the peasants are mainly Indians or mestizos; in others they are of African ancestry. As objects of collective, categorical discrimination, they are relevant to our concerns. The blurring of class and minority status is especially evident in Latin America.

In his well-known study, *The Natural History of Revolution* (1927), Lyford Edwards discussed the opposition of intellectuals to the established regime as one of the master symbols of a potential revolutionary situation. We believe this may also be true of religious leaders. Revolutions may not occur, due to the range of forces against them; but in many parts of the world there are strong protest movements, among the leaders of which are church men and women. This is true in South Africa, South Korea, the Philippines, and—our interest here—in Latin America. (Each reader will have to decide for herself or himself whether this development is a happy one.)

Because the Church has been so much a part of the establishment in Latin America, revolutionary movements, such as Mexico's in 1910 and thereafter, sought to curtail its power and to take over part or all of its enormous land holdings. It requires some effort of the imagination, therefore, to see some elements in the Church today as strong participants in movements opposed to the established powers (see Eagleson 1975; Kenworthy 1983; Lernoux 1982; Levine 1981; Lewy 1974, Chapter 20). Students of this movement may tend to exaggerate the extent of the shift, but there is little doubt that "liberation theology"—binding religious thought closely to questions of justice and equality—has strongly influenced the place of the Church in Latin America. This is attested to by the strong opposition it has aroused among political and military rulers. Lernoux estimates (1982, xvii) that as of 1982 there have been 950 religious martyrs, in Chile, Bolivia, and most recently in El Salvador.

"Viewed historically," Lernoux writes (1982, p. 10) "the Latin-American Catholic Church would seem the least likely institution to oppose the military regimes. From the moment Columbus set foot in the New World, cross and sword had been indistinguishable. Priests and conquistadors divided the plunder in people and land—it was a toss-up which was the greedier." But she goes on to describe in detail the shifts that occurred after 1960. "In any number of cases bishops who started out by mildly scolding the regime for failing to respect human rights ended up at war with the military" (Lernoux 1982, p. 11). "The ideological and political link

between the church and the defenders of privilege is being severed" (Lewy 1974, p. 504). Opposition comes from more than a few church leaders. "Christian *communidades de base* (grassroots congregations often led by laity) have served functions comparable to those provided in the U.S. civil rights movement by the black church: legitimating 'illegal' challenges to the dominant order while offering sanctuary to those who make this challenge their praxis" (Kenworthy 1983, p. 73). Lernoux estimates that several hundred thousand persons participate in these grassroots congregations.

Religious Influence on the Civil Rights Movement in the United States

The important changes that have occurred in the churches' roles in Latin America should help us avoid overly simple interpretations of the connection perceived as usual between religion and systems of stratification. Probably the dominant theme in the United States during most periods has been a verbal emphasis on the dignity and worth of each individual accompanied by charitable activities, but with little attention to the structural roots of discrimination. There have been important exceptions to this generalization, however, in the abolitionist movement, the "social gospel" during the late nineteenth and early twentieth centuries, and the civil rights movement of the 1960s and early 1970s.

In the twenty-year period before the Depression, the Protestant churches were almost completely silent on the subject of race relations. The number of resolutions increased during the 1930s, but these pronouncements were quite general and dealt mainly with the gross aspects of the disabilities and injustices that Negroes experience.

In the 1940s, religious opposition to segregation and discrimination became stronger, although more at the level of pronouncements from national organizations than more direct opposition at the community level. In 1946 the Federal Council of Churches of Christ in America declared that it renounced "the pattern of segregation in race relations as unnecessary and undesirable and a violation of the Gospel of love and human brotherhood." Subsequently, four denominations adopted the statement as their own, and three other denominations, without adopting the council statement, recommended that their churches welcome Negroes (Loescher 1948, p. 42).

At the top organizational level, north and south, there was almost unanimous approval of the Supreme Court decision calling for desegregation of the schools. Catholic leaders and the National Council of Churches had repeatedly declared that discrimination and segregation were evil. In 1963, the World Council of Churches issued its strongest statement condemning racism. Reaffirming a 1954 declaration that "any form of segregation based on race, color or ethnic origin is contrary to the Gospel and is incompatible with the Christian doctrine of man, and with the nature of the Church of Christ," they added that "wherever and whenever any of us Christians deny this, by action or inaction, we betray Christ and the fellowship which bears his name" (*The New York Times,* September 1, 1963, p. 40).

Some religious groups have gone beyond pronouncements. Protestant churches, which have left the inner city by the hundreds when neighborhoods have shifted from white to nonwhite, have established new programs in several cities. These inner-city parishes are deeply involved in the full range of community life, not simply in religion. Their role in a period of emphasis on local community control, however, has become problematic.

Thousands of Catholic, Jewish, and Protestant ministers took part in the freedom rides, sit-ins, and protest marches of the civil rights movement in the 1960s—and dozens were sent to jail for their efforts. Various "social action" groups of Protestant denominations have directed their efforts toward desegregation in housing, an activity that Quakers and other sects have engaged in for some time. For example, the American Baptist Convention, Disciples of Christ, Methodist Church, Presbyterian Church, U.S.A., and United Church of Christ are seeking in a combined effort to supply professional leadership in study-action programs concerned with housing.

Such activities are not without their costs, in the form of public criticism and reduced support. These are most visibly directed against the National Council of Churches and the World Council of Churches; but social activism also plays a part in causing loss of membership in the "mainline" Protestant denominations in a period, beginning about 1970, of increasing public conservatism (see Kelley 1972; *The New York Times,* October 8, 1975, p. 48). Under a Program to Combat Racism, the World Council of Churches has given over three million dollars to groups in thirty countries. These include, in the United States, the American Indian Movement, Coalition for Black Americans, and the Malcolm X Liberation University. Sharpest criticism, however, has been directed at the support the program has given to guerrillas in Rhodesia (now Zimbabwe) and Namibia. Critics claim that "terrorists" use the money, despite the ostensible humanitarian purposes for which it was given to them, in attempts to overthrow the governing regimes. Critics do not mention that these charges are poorly documented and that most of the WCC budget is allocated to ongoing humanitarian and religious programs (Brown 1983). Nor do they observe that the governing regimes have used massive violence to keep power in the hands of the small dominating elites—a fact that scarcely justifies the violence of the guerrillas but needs examination within the same framework. (A segment of the television program "Sixty Minutes," January 23, 1983, examined the response to this Program to Combat Racism in a local church in Indiana; it was sharply critical and at the same time strongly editorialized in opposition to the World Council of Churches. See also Ernest Lefever in *The Wall Street Journal,* May 21, 1980.)

The "keep religion out of politics" theme is a strong one in the United States. It is used by the left when it wants to oppose the Moral Majority or similar groups from "imposing their narrow views of morality on the rest of us." It is used by the right when it wants to block religious progressives from seeking to promote social change. Our concern in this section has been to emphasize that churches, normally not much concerned directly with racial and ethnic discrimination, under some conditions are drawn into the public controversies over such discrimination, and at times are led from pronouncement, to protest, to direct action. Small segments, indeed, have often taken the lead in opposing what they see as injustice.

The Churches of Black Americans

One does not speak accurately of *the* Black church, for there are many varieties, indicating the wide differences among Blacks in all the forces that affect religious life—occupation, residence, education, secular group memberships, and the like. NORC national polls revealed that 87 percent of nonwhite respondents (about ninety percent of whom are Black) listed a Protestant preference in 1957 and 84 percent in the 1972–73–74 surveys. Seven percent gave a Catholic preference in 1957, nine percent in 1972–73–74. Among Blacks alone, NORC found 86 percent Protestant and 4 percent Catholic in 1980. Among the Protestants, most were Baptists or Methodists, with 55 percent of the total in the 1972–73–74 surveys preferring the former, 16 percent the latter (Glenn and Gotard 1977, p. 444). Similar figures appear in twelve pooled Gallup surveys: 87 percent of black respondents were Protestant, 8 percent Catholic (Welch 1978). All of these data refer to religious preference, not to membership. Although exact figures are not available, at least two-thirds of black Americans, who belong to religious groups in somewhat higher proportion than do Whites, are members of various churches. The "other" category, which includes numerous Muslim and other non-Christian groups, was preferred by 1.5 percent in 1957, by 2.3 percent in 1972–73–74, and by 1.4 percent in 1980.

Rural Black Churches

Religious gatherings were the first forms of association permitted under the slave system, and the first black leaders were religious teachers. Doctrines and practices were a subtle mixture of adaptation to the enormous power of the planters and of attack on that power. In Chapter 7 we noted Powdermaker's (1943) interpretation of black religion, along with other cultural forms, as partly deflected and controlled hostility. She interpreted the self-effacing humility of most slaves and the freedmen as an attempt to rescue victory from defeat—one's suffering was only a prelude to ultimate victory and reward; one got power from suffering. Meek Negroes, moreover, Powdermaker argued, had feelings of guilt because of their hostile feelings toward Whites. They had taken the Christian injunctions against hatred seriously yet were continuously faced with situations that produced hatred. The meekness was a way of appeasing their own guilt feelings.

Christian missionaries of pre-Civil War days emphasized the rewards for humility and the glories of the future life. This emphasis stemmed partly from their own doctrines and partly from the insistence of planters that they preach only that kind of

religion (see Simpson 1978, pp. 219–21). By giving it their own interpretations, Blacks found that it fit their needs, considering the status they were caught in: The meek shall inherit the earth; the suffering shall be rewarded; the ultimate victory shall be given to the faithful, not to the powerful.

Recent studies of slavery have emphasized the adaptive and indeed aggressive elements in black religion (see, e.g., Genovese 1974, pp. 232–84; Harding 1969; Raboteau 1978; Willmore 1973, chapters 1–4). There developed what Raboteau interprets as "a distinctive form of Christianity," or what we would see as a blend of European and African elements forged together by the American experience. In Genovese's words (1970, pp. 34–35): "the slaves developed a religious life that enabled them to survive as autonomous human beings with a culture of their own within the white master's world," and at the same time armed them with the ability to protest, for "we must be struck by the appearance of one or another kind of messianic preacher in almost every slave revolt on record."

After emancipation, the church developed into the cornerstone of the black community (DuBois 1903; Frazier 1963; Johnson 1941; Winter 1977, pp. 265–91). Despite the relative lack of an explicit protest theme in the churches of the small towns and the rural South in the decades after the Civil War, there was nourished an ability to withstand great hardship. When this was combined with the momentum of the civil rights movement in the 1950s, recently urbanized Blacks and those still rural proved to have a religiously sustained courage of great importance in breaking the patterns of segregation.

Urban Black Churches

Urbanization of a majority of Blacks in the United States has influenced their religious life in many ways, and their religious beliefs and practices have affected the nature of their responses to life in the city. These are among the consequences: (1) Some have become "unchurched." The city has shattered their older beliefs, and they feel alienated from the existing churches—that some look upon as just another "racket." (2) For a majority, however, the church remains an important force. It is the association to which they are most likely to belong and in which they actively participate. (3) The urban world furnishes a wide variety of forms of belief and worship: small sects and cults like those in rural areas, denominations that are similar to the established churches of the white population, and dramatically new religious movements that depart widely—although not completely—from the Christian tradition. (4) In the city one finds the beginnings of a racially integrated church, in which lines of class, education, and residence determine membership more than does race (see Childs 1980; Drake and Cayton 1963 [1945]; Frazier 1963; Hannerz 1969).

A purely descriptive approach to the religion of minority-group members may cause us to overlook the ways in which religion is involved in the pursuit of life's values. If, on one occasion, it is a tranquilizer, on another it is a stimulant. There are some among the oppressed who use religion as a shield against the misfortunes of life, but others are armed with righteous anger. The student of majority–minority relations must attempt to discover the conditions under which these various patterns occur.

In briefest terms, those whose deprivation is so severe that even hopes and dreams for improvement of their earthly lot are denied them will be drawn to a religion that promises them a shield, and rewards in another life. Such persons are characterized by a particularly intense form of "status crystalization." Not only are they consistently low on measures of income, power, and prestige, but they have also been denied hope that their situation can be improved. In situations wherein income, power, and prestige are beginning to improve, however, hope will soar. Status becomes decrystallized for those who can hope, and religious values are among the clearest indicators of their inconsistencies of status.

Expressed in terms of a general sociology of religion, the former situation tends to promote withdrawal or avoidance sects, the latter to stimulate the development of aggressive sects that challenge not only the established religious structures, but the secular order as well (Yinger 1970, Chapters 14 and 15). Seldom is a situation so uniform that sects of only one type appear among a minority group. Hope can break through in the most discriminatory of circumstances, due to accidents of personal biography or some variation in the structure that decrystallizes the lives of some members of a minority.

Religion and Protest

Our attention here will be directed mainly to the protest theme in black religion. The most widely held view, however, has been, in the words of Benjamin Mays (1938), that the Negroes' idea of God "kept them submissive, humble, and obedient." Such a view, as Mays recognized, is subject to serious misinterpretation if it is not put alongside the evidences of radical religious protest. These evidences are found not only in the lives of Denmark Vesey, Nat Turner, Frederick Douglass, Harriet Tubman, John Brown, and others who became well known; but also in the lives of the rank and file who came to believe in a gospel of freedom. This is well documented by Vincent Harding (1969) in his careful review of the theme of religion and resistance. He notes, for example (p. 182) that in 1800

South Carolina's legislature indicated a keen awareness of the possible connections between black rebellion and black religion, an awareness that was apparently the property of many southern white persons. In that year the legislature passed one of the first of those countless 19th century laws restricting black religious services. This one forbade Negroes "even in company with white persons to meet together and assemble for the purpose of . . . religious worship, either before the rising of the sun or after the going down of the same."

Bracey, Meier, and Rudwick (1970, pp. 3–17, 123–55) provide similar documentation.

Protest themes have become more common in black religion, but the change should not be exaggerated. There are still strong tendencies toward avoidance. Most movements are a mixture, as we shall see in our examination of several recent and current trends in the "black power" movement, broadly defined. We shall focus on four such trends: the formation of new religions; heightened pressures from black ministers and laymen against the "white" church; the development of a "black theology"; and religious leadership in the civil rights movement generally.

The American Muslim Mission—The Black Muslims. New religions, or the transfer of loyalty to a new religion, are likely to occur under conditions of prolonged suffering, where the dominant religion appears implicated in the suffering and where hope has been aroused. Scores of religious groups have appeared, especially among black Americans. Some of them are predominantly Christian, others marginally so, and some clearly

WE SHALL OVERCOME

not. Despite their differences they make a common testimony to the burden of oppression.

The Black Muslims—now the American Muslim Mission—are one of the largest and most important of these groups, and we shall use them to illustrate the "revitalization process" (Wallace 1956) in religious movements.[1] Because they have moved into a second generation with new leadership, their doctrines and actions have evolved, along with the circumstances of their members and the nature of race relations in America. We shall comment first on their "nationalistic" or "black power" period, which lasted from their beginnings in the mid-1930s until the early 1970s. We shall use the name they were first known by—Black Muslims—at this point and write in the past tense in order to call attention to the changes that have occurred, despite a significant degree of continuity.

In their strongly puritanical code of behavior, their opposition to racial discrimination, and their search for security and dignity, the Black Muslims were similar to such groups as the cult of the late Father Divine. There were, however, important differences. They were more ascetic, more energetic in their pursuit of educational and economic improvement, more hostile to Whites (Essien-Udom 1962; Lincoln 1961). The Black Muslims attacked integrationist Negroes as lackeys of the white man. They called, as did Marcus Garvey, for a separate Negro nation, but unlike Garvey they preferred to establish it in the United States, in a region set aside for that purpose or in Muslim sections of cities and states, where they could run their own farms and businesses.

Muslims in New York and Chicago and elsewhere developed and operated hundreds of businesses. Although most of these were small, they represented a substantial increase in the number of black-owned businesses in the central cities. The Muslims also gave increasing attention to education. Curricula and methods in their schools tended to be traditional and stern, and the school year was 50 weeks long.

There is also a more psychological revitalization quality to the Black Muslim movement. It fits closely Wallace's definition of such a movement as a deliberate and organized effort "to construct a more satisfying culture" (see Laue 1964). In their effort to cast aside the punishing meaning of their identities as Negroes, they declared: We are the lost nation of Islam; salvation will come from a rediscovery of that tradition. All science stems from the work of twenty-four original black scientists, thousands of years ago. It is the black man, not the white man, who is good, and right, and powerful—or he can be, if he abides by the tenets of the faith, follows the stern requirements of self-denial and hard work, and breaks away from the evil ways of the white man.

There was a harshness about the way the Black Muslims spoke, built up a quasi-military arm (called "The Fruit of Islam"), and ridiculed nonviolent integrationist efforts that shocked most Whites. It is startling to hear a Muslim minister proclaim as a goal: "To get the white man's foot off my neck, his hand out of my pocket and his carcass off my back. To sleep in my own bed without fear, and to look straight into his cold blue eyes and call him a liar every time he parts his lips" (quoted by Lincoln 1961, p. 27).

For 25 years, Muhammad's Black Muslim movement grew only slowly; but by 1960 it was gaining strength and membership quite rapidly. Growing contact with "the American dream" (and growing frustration because it was being realized so slowly for them), disillusionment with Christian churches, the inadequacy of alternatives to religious response (political action or individual effort, for example), the rise to independence of the African states, and doubtless the publicity—some of it quite fearful—given to the cult by the mass media were among the influences promoting its growth. Even those Blacks—probably a large majority (see Marx 1967a)—who opposed its message and its strategy recognized the appeal of the movement.

But who were the dedicated followers? Those who joined were mostly young men, lower-class, often functionally illiterate. Some were converted in prison. These are persons ill-equipped to struggle for status in the urban world; they are poorly trained; they face discrimination. They may seek to escape the trap by use of drugs, alcohol, and mental illness, as some do. They may attack the frustrating society by random aggression or criminality, as some do. They may, by happy chance, get a good start in family and school, seize the rare opportunity, and win success by the dominant

[1]For discussions of other sects and cults, from a variety of perspectives, see Baer 1981; Lincoln and Mamiya 1980; Riley 1975; Simpson 1978, pp. 253–273; Snow and Machalek 1982; Washington 1972; Wilmore 1973, pp. 228–261. Although Jim Jones, leader of the People's Temple, was white, many of its members were black. It warrants study by those interested in race relations. See, e.g., Levi 1982; Richardson 1980.

group's own criteria, as a few do. But for some, the former responses are unacceptable and the latter unattainable. They join such movements as the Muslims. We should not be misled by the antiwhite tone. Far more importantly, the Black Muslim movement was a radical attack on the inferiority complex and sense of powerlessness of Negroes.

Like many other religious groups, the Black Muslims have a tendency to schism. Malcolm X, who was suspended as the New York leader in December, 1963, at first talked of organizing a "black nationalist party," presumably to promote a sharper attack on discrimination, with implications of mounting violence. After a trip to Mecca, however, and other parts of the Islamic world, he proclaimed himself an orthodox Muslim, denounced black racism, and broke sharply with Elijah Muhammad.

His murder a few months later leaves unresolved the question of how he might have developed these ideas organizationally. He has become a hero to quite contrasting kinds of people, because in his lifetime he stood for sharply contrasting kinds of goals and means. But above all, he stood for unmitigated attack on racial discrimination; he challenged "whitey." And by the strength of that challenge he has become a saint to many of the most militant participants in the black power movement (see Malcolm X 1966; P. Goldman 1979).

The tendency toward schism did not end with Malcom X. He was ahead of most persons in the sect with his belief that it should become a more standard or orthodox Muslim group, rather than a separatist and nationalistic American group. Those ideas began to be adopted, however, first by moves of reconciliation with black Christians and then, when Wallace Muhammad became the leader upon the death of his father in 1975, by similar moves toward Whites. The name was changed to American Muslim Mission; the emphasis on business ventures has been reduced; Whites are admitted to membership; the quasi-military Fruit of Islam has been disbanded; and, altogether, the emphasis is on being, or becoming, a branch of Sunni Muslim orthodoxy (see Goldman 1979; Mamiya 1982; Muhammad 1980; Whitehurst 1980). The title of the official publication is now *Bilalian News,* rather than *Muhammad Speaks,* named for Bilal, an Ethiopian who had been the caller to prayer in the Prophet Muhammad's first Muslim community (Mamiya 1982, p. 139).

Thus, like so many sects before it, the former Black Muslims are denominationalizing, or, to use the well-known concepts of Troeltsch, they are moving from sect to church (Whitehurst 1980). With the rapid growth of a black middle class, the partial success of the civil rights movement, the death of early leaders, the growing prosperity of the group, and other contextual changes, their harsh separatism has been modified significantly. That is not the end of the story, however. A new schism has developed, led by Louis Farrakhan, who had succeeded Malcolm X as leader of the Harlem mosque but was transferred to Chicago by Wallace Muhammad. Farrakhan is seeking to rebuild the Nation of Islam and to return to its earlier doctrines. There have been few economic gains for black Americans since 1970; the pace of educational and political gains has slowed; unemployment remains at twice the level of Whites and hovers around 50 percent for young black males. These are the conditions that brought converts to the early Black Muslims. They give strength to Farrakhan's renewed emphasis on separation and alienation from American society; he finds his recruits among the black masses (Mamiya 1982). He could see the reason for the changes being made by Wallace Muhammad, Farrakhan has remarked, "if the white man had improved just a little. But the devil hasn't changed. If anything, he's gotten worse" (Cleveland *Plain Dealer,* November, 15, 1978, p. A27). Similar harsh rhetoric during the Democratic primary campaign in 1984 brought nationwide publicity and condemnation to Farrakhan.

In discussing the Black Muslims in the 1972 edition of this book, we wrote:

If the aspirations of the Black Muslims continue to be seriously frustrated, the potential for violence that the movement carries may grow. If, on the other hand, the United States removes the special burdens imposed on Negroes, the Black Muslims may prove to be an effective instrument for the development of discipline, thrift, responsibility, and stable family patterns. Norms of behavior that are unlikely to be adopted when they are seen as the coercive demands of white men become deep commitments when they are seen as commandments of a specifically black man's religion. The divisiveness of the sect's approach to Whites may also decline.

What we see now is that both of these things have occurred. A largely middle class Muslim community has developed that is still Black—Bilalian—but not harshly separatist. The conditions that produced the original Black Muslims are still widespread, however. The Farrakhan schism may not persist, but similar angry religious and other kinds of protest will surely occur if those conditions are not removed.

Black Religious Protests within Predominantly White Churches. Today there are more black participants in predominantly white churches than ever before, more black leaders in those churches, more cooperation and integration between formerly separate denominations. (More, however, is still not very much.) There have also been some sharp challenges to the continuing evidences of prejudice, although these have not been frequent since the 1960s and early 1970s. It is not uncommon for challenges to occur even as changes are occurring: A few changes, won at what seems the cost of great effort, open up the vision of much more extensive change. Against this vision, the new, slightly improved situation is even less acceptable than the old.

Breaking into public view in 1967, black challenges to the churches began to crystallize into black caucuses of clergymen and laymen. These vary widely in size and degree of support, but the Black Methodists for Church Renewal, Union of Black Clergymen and Laymen of the Episcopal Church, Black Affairs Council of the Unitarians, and various other caucuses and organizations among Lutherans, Roman Catholics, and others express a decisive new aspect of the American "Social Gospel" movement. Some of these caucuses reflected the influence of the National Council of Black Churchmen, a group that was first organized to help white clergy deal with the idea of black power and to respond openly to radical black clergy. The leadership of the National Council came from clergy in largely white denominations—a handicap at a time when the black church was, as Lincoln expresses it (1974, p. 128) becoming "more self-conscious about its blackness."

There are various demands and goals, but perhaps they center on the following: more positions of responsibility for black clergymen; greater support from the churches for the economic, educational, and housing needs of blacks; incorporation of elements of black Christianity into worship, church-school, and music programs; control of inner-city activities by Blacks, to replace what are seen as well-meaning but ineffectual white efforts. As these themes are developed in conferences and pronouncements, two basic sectarian styles emerge: There is an element of aggressive prophecy, seeking to bring the church to justice, to make it an instrument of radical change. "We must stop worshipping a cute white baby and recognize the adult, black revolutionary that Christ was" (*The New York Times,* November 9, 1970, p. 30, quoting a speaker at a black caucus). There is also a withdrawal theme, indicating another sectarian approach rooted deep in Christian history. Some caucus members are seeking to achieve a purely black fellowship, a situation in which a "black religious experience" can be achieved without bending to white styles and dominance. It is not surprising that "soul" should be sought in the churches, as elsewhere.

Although protest and avoidance themes are mixed in most activities of black churchmen, some express one or the other predominantly. The prophetic-aggressive approach was vividly expressed in the demands for $500 million in "reparations" from white churches and synagogues. With a little change of wording, James Forman's Black Manifesto could be attributed to Gerrard Winstanley, that uncompromising seventeenth-century English radical, for whom Christ "is the true and faithful leveller."

The Manifesto was presented to a meeting of the Black Economic Development Conference in Detroit, April 1969. It achieved a great deal of national publicity in May, 1969, when Forman repeated the demands at Riverside Church, New York, from a pulpit that had been vacated by the church's ministers; (although the Rev. Ernest Campbell returned later and spoke favorably of the idea of restitution). Some of Forman's supporters attracted further attention, and opposition, when they occupied national offices of the Presbyterian church in an effort to attain some of the goals of the Manifesto (see Lecky and Wright 1970; Lincoln 1974, pp. 130–33, 179–90). Forman's accusations and demands shocked most white churchmen. He called for "total control" of their own lives by black people and declared that their hearts went out to the Vietnamese, who like themselves suffered under the domination of a racist America. The accusations, the radicalism, the economic costs, the very idea of reparations were not likely to win support from major church bodies. The Roman Catholic Archdiocese of New York, for example, rejected the Manifesto completely. The Council of Bishops of the United Methodist Church in a "message on reconciliation" stated, "The violent Marxism of the black manifesto is utterly unacceptable to United Methodists" (Cleveland *Plain Dealer,* November 14, 1969). The National Council of Churches discussed the issue carefully, but without the aid of experts who might have examined its economic implications. Two years after the Manifesto was issued, the document had largely been forgotten.

There was some support, it should be noted, for the idea of reparations (see, for example, the chapters by William Stringfellow, James Lawson, and Harvey Cox in Lecky and Wright 1970). The manifesto appealed to the prophetic-sectarian elements that are not unimportant in the contemporary American church. But the church as a whole is not likely to begin to act like a sect. The effects of such protest on programs and the allocation of funds are likely to be indirect and moderate.

Black Theology. Crises that drastically disorganize or reorganize the lives of a group of people are usually accompanied by a body of thought that seeks to bring the new experience into a framework of systematic religious interpretation. Among minority-group members, theology often interprets disprivilege as a peculiar sign of God's grace, of the special mission of the group, of its unique insight based on its unique experiences. The theology cuts two ways: As the "suffering servant," the persecuted group has been chosen to bring a message to all mankind; but as a group treated unjustly, the minority is told by some of its theologians that they are destined to prevail in a holy war. Thus they hear, "If God is for you, must you not also be for yourself" (C. Eric Lincoln) but also, when Jesus said walk a second mile, "he meant only with your brother" (Albert B. Cleage Jr.). These messages mingle in the work of many contemporary black theologians.

Theology is not immune from the pressures toward polarization during a time of crisis, when the "he who is not for us is against us" mentality prevails. Even the more universalistically inclined are pushed toward one pole or the other. One can note a shift, for example, in the thought of Martin Luther King, Jr., toward more support for disruptive resistance, by comparing *Stride Toward Freedom* (1958) with *Why We Can't Wait* (1963) and *The Trumpet of Conscience* (1968). Vincent Harding (1968, p. 7) raises a critical question with regard to the polarization: "An interim goal is how to make white men 'invisible' while black men are brought into the light. Can it be brought off by blacks with any less poisoning of the spirit than occurred in whites who invented 'tuning out'?"

Black theology is being given some attention in predominantly white Protestant seminaries; it is the focus of an Institute for Black Ministries,

established in Philadelphia in 1970; and it has been developed in a large number of books and articles. We shall not try to examine the wide range of materials, but a few quotations may indicate some of its dimensions.

> What is Black Theology? . . . It is black people reflecting religiously on the black experience, attempting to redefine the relevance of the Christian Gospel for their lives. . . . To study theology from the perspective of Black Theology means casting one's mental and emotional faculties with the lot of the oppressed so that they may learn the cause and the cure of their humiliation. . . . Black Theology is revolutionary in its perspective. . . . Relating this concept to our contemporary situation in America, Black Theology affirms that the church of the Oppressed One must be a black church. (Cone 1970, p. 53)

Theological work everywhere is filled with effort to state the integral, true, authentic expression of a religious tradition. It may include a universalistic dimension: "Black theology will need to give full expression to the particularity of the black experience while not neglecting the universal character of religion" (Roberts 1974, p. 47). But it is sometimes quite particularistic: "Our theology must emerge consciously from an investigation of the socioreligious experience of black people, as that experience is reflected in *black* stories of God's dealings with black people in the struggle of freedom" (Cone 1975, p. 16). Black theology is the religious expression of black power. Ironically, these revolutionaries, these Marxists, as some have called them, have somehow failed to get the message that "religion is the opiate of the people."[2]

Black Religion and the Protest Movement. Preceeding sections have indicated many ways in which religion is involved in the civil rights movement, but it may be useful to conclude this discussion of religion and protest with a few more general observations. Although the message of solace is still the predominant one in many black churches, it would be a mistake to overlook two important qualifications: Many leading churches and clergymen have occupied and occupy major roles in the movement to end discrimination; and even the most otherworldly of approaches has implications for a system of repression.

There may be a strong cultural continuity between the "aggressive meekness" of the plantation Negro and the nonviolent resistance movement that appeared in the 1950s. The relation of Martin

---

[2]In addition to the works cited above, see Cleage 1968; Cone 1969, 1970; Lincoln 1974, pp. 135–52.

Luther King's methods to those of Gandhi has been often remarked. It may be equally or more to the point to note that King was a Christian minister, heir of a tradition which, for all of its ambivalences, has always contained an explosive potential, often expressed in sectarian movements (Ansbro 1982). The nature of the protest is strongly influenced by the hopes of the participants, their educational level and other resources, and the potentialities of the situation. There are, therefore, important differences between the forms of religious "attack" used by an illiterate peasantry and by a literate, urban group with strong middle-class leadership. But in observing these differences we should not overlook the continuity.

The theme of aggression that underlies much of the "otherworldly" emphasis in the religion of lower strata can break out into the open when hope rises and movements appear to create rallying points. "What the South experienced between 1955 and 1960 was a revival of Black religion—a revival that broke out not with sawdust trails and mourners' benches, but with picket lines, boycotts, and marches" (Wilmore 1973, p. 243).

Almost all the largest urban black churches have become "race churches"; they are involved in the civil rights movement, they support black businessmen, and they exert pressure against discriminatory white businesses (Sullivan 1969). In no other institution can so many Blacks be reached and mobilized to action so quickly. The ministry was the first profession to gain recognition, and black preachers became the principal race leaders. Ministers have a great deal of freedom of action. They answer to no one except their congregations and they are expected to be real "race men."

Black ministers no longer hold the great preponderance of leadership positions because civil rights workers, lawyers, physicians, teachers, journalists, social workers, businessmen, and politicians have come increasingly to the fore. Experts in these secular fields, often with more academic training than the ministers, are rendering many services formerly performed only by preachers. A call to preach no longer guarantees respect and influence. There has been an absolute as well as a relative decline in the number of black clergymen (Glenn and Gotard 1977, p. 447). Nevertheless, clergymen remain among the most important black leaders. Probably only a minority of them are militant, but the ratio is much higher among the younger

and better educated clergy (see, e.g., Childs 1980; Hamilton 1972; Lincoln 1974, pp. 65–153; Nelsen and Nelsen 1975; Turner 1973).

The scores of separate black churches differ widely in their approach to discrimination. A detailed examination would require, for example, that one distinguish carefully between the African Methodist Episcopal Church and the African Methodist Episcopal Church Zion, between the National Baptist Convention and the Progressive National Baptist Convention that split away from it in 1961 in protest against its conservative approach to social change (see Childs 1980). There are those who see even the liberal churches involved mainly in conventions and pronouncements, not effective campaigns, and other churches "imprisoned by conservatism and parochialism, mired in an outdated rural ethos, its ministers unable to deal with the increasingly difficult social problems" (*The New York Times,* January 6, 1980, p. E5).

Others see, with Lincoln, a much more active church:

> The "Negro Church" that Frazier wrote about no longer exists. It died an agonized death in the harsh turmoil which tried the faith so rigorously in the decade of the "Savage Sixties," for there it had to confront under the most trying circumstances the possibility that "Negro" and "Christian" were irreconcilable categories. . . . Out of the ashes of its funeral pyre there sprang the bold, strident, self-conscious phoenix that is the contemporary Black Church. (Frazier and Lincoln 1975, pp. 105–106)

Both of these views are, in our judgment, exaggerations—undoubtedly intendedly so. What is probably of greatest interest in terms of our topic is the extent to which an active and even a protest approach has spread among black churches. The African Methodist Episcopal Church is quite conservative, on the whole, yet twelve of its bishops have declared: "Lockheed gets bailed out, the railroads get bailed out, it's socialism for the rich and rugged individualism for the poor" (*The New York Times,* February 27, 1973, p. 23). An activist minister, the Rev. Theodore Jemison, has replaced the Rev. Joseph Jackson, a conservative, as president of the National Baptist Convention (*The Washington Post,* October 16, 1982, p. C9), perhaps influenced by the fact that the Progressive National Baptist Convention had grown, by 1982, to one-and-a-half million members. The seven largest black churches have taken steps toward a united front to combat economic, social, and political ills. Church leaders have met behind the scenes since 1978 and in 1982 moved ahead in a conference to forge the Congress of National Black Churches (*The New York Times,* December 12, 1982, pp. 1, 20).

When we focus attention on individuals rather than religious organizations we find the same range from quietism to protest. Using a national sample of Blacks and various single measures of religion, Gary Marx (1967a) found that the more "religious" a person was, the less likely it was that he would be militant in civil rights; or, the more subjective importance he assigned to religion, the less likely he was to support militant activities. When Marx specified the variable "religiosity," however, by distinguishing between those who interpret religion in otherworldly terms and those who believed it involved interest in the "here and now," a sharp difference appeared. Among those who rated high on the "otherworldly" religious scale, only 15 percent were militant; of those who rated high on the "temporal" religious scale, 39 percent were militant.

Further study has shown the need to specify the relationship between religiosity and militancy in additional ways. Alston, Peek, and Wingrove (1972, p. 252) found that in a national sample "among younger black adults, females and members of denominations other than Baptists, the relationship was reversed: the more religious were slightly *more* militant." The five years separating the two studies were years of active protests, often led by ministers—an influence that may well have caused some shift in attitudes. Additional studies by Nelsen, Madron, and Yokley (1975) and by Hunt and Hunt (1977) indicate the necessity of taking denomination and the extent of sectlike separation into account. Black religion both stimulates and inhibits civil rights militancy.

When opportunities improve, when hope rises, aggression begins to be focused on segregation and discrimination. James Baldwin has described the remark of Dr. Marcus James, a priest of the Anglican church, to a Conference of Negro-African Writers and Artists in Paris. Dr. James quoted the old saying that when Christians arrived in Africa they had the Bible and the Africans had the land; but after a while, Africans had the Bible and Christians had the land. Sharing this sentiment, the group responded with laughter; but James went on to say "that the African not only has the Bible but has found in it a potential weapon for the recovery of his land" (Baldwin 1961, pp. 38–39). So it is in the United States: under some conditions, black churches have been bulwarks of segregation; less commonly, yet importantly, they have been the focal points of opposition to segregation and discrimination.

The Religions of Hispanic Americans

A very high proportion of Americans of Spanish-speaking background are, at least nominally, Catholic. Their origins are diverse, but most of them come from societies within which the Church, until recently, was identified strongly with the middle and upper classes. To those at the bottom of the status ladder, the Church was not—as with the Irish—their great defender, but part of an oppressive regime. For many, their religion was a mixture of folk elements, the festival aspects of Catholicism, and marginal participation in a parish church. Unlike many other immigrant groups, few priests were among the Puerto Ricans and Mexicans, the two Hispanic groups we shall be discussing. Many of the priests who served them in the United States did not speak Spanish and regarded the syncretist beliefs and practices of their parishoners as heretical or superstitious.

These broad generalizations must be qualified, of course, with respect both to the lands of origin and to the United States. There have always been segments of the Church concerned with the needs of the Hispanic poor. Liberation theology, to which we referred earlier, is attracting some attention in the United States. More Spanish-speaking priests have been trained. And such organizations as Catolicos Por La Raza (Catholics for the People) are urging the Church to be more responsive to the needs of Spanish-speaking poor (see Vigil 1980; *The New York Times,* January 9, 1983, p. E10).

Mexican American Religion

Americans of Mexican descent are highly diverse, ranging from those whose ancestors lived in the Southwest, especially in New Mexico, when it was part of Old Mexico to undocumented aliens who have few roots in any American community. Our comments will refer to the larger middle group of recent immigrants and those whose parents or grandparents were immigrants. Most are baptized

Catholics but do not feel close identification with the Church. Separated by language, ethnicity, and poverty from the established institutions, they have not benefited from a religious organization concerned primarily with their situation, as many immigrant groups have done. Grebler et al. (1970, p. 449) describe the circumstances well:

The role of the Catholic Church in the lives of Mexican Americans has been importantly conditioned by two factors. One is the clergy's prevailing view of these people as uninstructed and deficient in their adherence to the general norms of Church practice. The other is the inadequacy of resources available to the Church in the Southwest.

Although the Catholic Church has been quite traditional in dealing with its members of Mexican background, one should not disregard the exceptions to that statement. Long before governmental and educational institutions began to think about their special problems, the churches (both Catholic and Protestant) had tried, even if not very successfully, to design programs for them. There was little experience to go on, resources were limited, but perhaps most importantly, there were, and are, disagreements over methods and goals which limited the success of these programs. Grebler et al. (1970, pp. 461–69) describe the continuum from conservative to liberal in church policy—from pastoral to social action among Catholics, from evangelical to social gospel among Protestants. When agricultural workers sought, by strikes and the organization of unions, to improve their working conditions, some priests supported them. Most of those who did, however, were from outside the areas involved. The Cursillo Movement, brought to America from Spain in the late 1950s—built around three-day periods of intensive religious renewal—tended to encourage social action, although it was not specifically focused on that aim.

Protestant missionary activity among Hispanics, especially in Texas, began before the middle of the nineteenth century. Perhaps 5 percent of Americans of Mexican descent are now Protestant, most of them members of fundamentalist churches. Those in the middle class, however, are more likely to belong to mainline Protestant churches (Madsen 1973), and it is such churches that are most likely to be active in intergroup relations (Weigert, D'Antonio, and Rubel 1971). The Protestant social action ministry among Mexican Americans goes back more than half a century. The National Council of Churches (then the Federal Council) established its Council on Spanish-American Work in 1912. A "migrant ministry" program, started in 1920, was a response to the extremely difficult conditions of farm workers of Mexican descent. Many of its members were direct participants in the unionization campaign of Cesar Chavez (see Grebler et al. 1970, Chapter 20). Most Mexican American Protestants, however, are members of fundamentalist sects oriented more toward individual salvation and achievement than social action. Only in recent years have they begun to get involved in civil rights activities.

Religion among Puerto Ricans

As among Mexican Americans, Americans of Puerto Rican background, whether residing on the island or on the mainland, blend Catholicism with folk religious beliefs and practices. Among Puerto Ricans it is Africa that is the primary source of the folk tradition, although Indian elements, as in Mexico, are also present (see Steiner 1974, pp. 475–86). Some see *spiritism,* to use this term to refer to a variety of folk elements, as a strong competitor with Catholicism, others see it as something of a healing cult within Catholicism. In New York City, where it is strong (*The New York Times,* November 11, 1977, p. 57), spiritism is not simply an import from Puerto Rico, but an urban mode of adaptation to the strains that result from migration out of a basically preindustrial situation into an urban-industrial setting.

In recent years, Puerto Rican Catholicism has begun to expand beyond its basically middle-class orientation to include more concern with the circumstances of the larger number of persons of lower status. This is not a major trend, however; there are few Puerto Rican priests; "national parishes" were not created by the Church, as they had been for other immigrant groups (Steiner 1974, pp. 464–75), a decision that strengthened the sense of alienation.

Ten percent or more of Puerto Ricans are Protestants, most of them in Pentecostal or other fundamentalist groups (Parsons 1965; Poblete and O'Dea 1960). Although some middle-class Puerto Ricans have joined mainline Protestant churches and these churches have supported some inner-city activities and missions, this has not been a major concern (Costas 1982). Pentecostalism, however, as Garrison argued (1974, pp. 321–322), can be seen as a revitalization movement. She is using

Wallace's term (1956) to describe an adaptive technique often found among people who are disillusioned with the dominant model of the world:

Given the prevailing conditions in the Puerto Rican slum and the available alternatives, Pentecostalism appears to provide a means of access to the resources of the larger society as well as providing, through its own informal channels, the pooled resources of the Pentecostal network. . . . They have also not given up hope of reforming society, or a part of it. They believe in radical individual change through conversion to Christ and gradual social change through the conversion of many individuals, but they do not believe in radical secular methods to bring about social change.

In a manner similar to the Black Muslims, the Pentecostals seek out the marginal members of society for conversion, although these do not make up the largest part of the membership. And like the Muslims, they have had some success in reducing alienation.

The Religions of Native Americans

Pre-Columbian Americans had a wide variety of religions. There was a great deal of similarity, however, in their world views—images of a world inhabited by many kinds of beings bound together in an integrated whole, of which humankind was a part. We shall not examine these religions[3] but will refer briefly to some of the religious effects of contact with Europeans before turning to the recent and contemporary situation.

Persons brought up on the doctrine of the separation of church and state and the experience of numerous congregations, denominations, and religions within a society find it difficult to recognize the inseparable bond of religion with the whole of life. That bond is most readily seen when it begins to be broken, as happened among Native Americans, due to the superior economic and military power of the Europeans. Through the generations, some of the most important adaptations to that power have been religious. Often based on the reports of revelations from a Creator God, they brought messages of a new way of life, yet one based on ancient ways and virtues. Christian elements were frequently incorporated, as in Handsome Lake's Great

[3]For studies of aboriginal Indian religions and some of their adaptations to contact with Europeans, see Hultkrantz 1979; Jorgensen 1972; Neihardt 1979; Powers 1977; Underhill 1965; Wallace 1970; Wax and Wax 1978.

Message to the Iroquois (Wallace 1970) a revitalization movement that is of continuing importance after more than a century and a half.

The influence of Christianity was more muted in the Ghost Dance among the Plains Indians, in the years following 1870 and 1890, because it was more strongly an effort to protect and restore a sociocultural order rapidly being destroyed by Whites. The Ghost Dance represented a renaissance of Indian culture to the Pawnee, "the very flame of new hope to the Sioux." That hope was nearly lost, however, because conflicts over the dance precipitated the events that led to the 1890 Battle of Wounded Knee, in which more than 200 Indians and sixty white soldiers were killed. And with them died the Dance among the Sioux (see Carroll 1975; LaBarre 1972; Mooney 1965; Thornton 1981).

Among the many native American religious movements we will mention only one more, the Peyote Cult, now known as the Native American Church of North America. Unlike the Ghost Dance, which sought to restore a lost dominance, the Native American Church has pulled back from confrontation. It incorporates many Christian beliefs, rituals, and ethical principles but builds them into religious forms that are fundamentally Indian (see Aberle 1982; B. Wilson 1973, pp. 414–49). The practice most visible, and most controversial, to the outside world is the use of the peyote cactus button to induce mild disorientation and heightened perceptions of sound and color. "Those who consume it during religious activities claim that it enhances concentration and highlights central truths with vivid imagery. Far from producing irreverence or promiscuity, peyote users say that it induces a solemn respect for spiritual power and serious moral behavior" (Bowden 1981, p. 209). After a series of court tests, the Native American Church's use of peyote has been excluded from the legal prohibitions against drug use. About 250,000 Indians from many tribes now belong to the Native American Church, making it, as Hertzberg (1971) put it, a kind of "Pan-Indianism of the reservations." They find in it an affirmation of their shared cultural identity while still adhering to many Christian beliefs and practices and living at peace with the larger society.

Christianizing the Indians has been on the agenda of European settlers almost from the beginning of contact (Bowden 1981). At the start of the reservation period after the Civil War, specific denominations were given permission, or assigned the responsibility, to give religious instruction on specific reservations. This decision was made by the government, with little or no participation by the Indians themselves. The results have been diverse, ranging from full allegiance to white Christianity, to strong opposition. Most commonly, however, the result has been participation in a Christianity strongly influenced by Indian beliefs and practices. Some Whites as well as Indians have come to look on this blending as not only possible but desirable (Deloria 1969, 1974; Starkloff 1971). In a study by the National Council of Churches, 51 percent of the Protestant missionaries to the Indians who responded to a questionnaire said they found some native values worth preserving; 31 percent of the Catholics supported a blending of cultural patterns. These rather general statements from an imprecise sample, however, must be seen against the fact that "on the whole, missionaries continue to denounce religious toleration" (Bowden 1981, pp. 220–201).

On the other side is a renewed emphasis on ancestral religion (see Begay 1979; Steiner 1981).

Vine Deloria, Jr., one of the most articulate of contemporary Indian leaders, criticizes the exaggerated expression of such views while emphasizing the richness of Indian religion:

Among the Indian activists a tremendous interest in tribal religions manifested itself early in the movement. Attendance at tribal ceremonies became almost as necessary as attendance at protests. The American Indian Movement became so attached to the tribal religious ceremonies that more experienced Indians began referring to them as the Indian version of the 'Jesus freaks.' But few Indians realized the extent to which the world had changed since the days of Chief Joseph. . . . Tribal religions thus face the task of entrenching themselves in a contemporary Indian society that is becoming increasingly accustomed to the life-style of contemporary America. While traditional Indians speak of reverence for the earth, Indian reservations continue to pile up junk cars and beer cans at an alarming rate. . . . [And yet] within the traditions, beliefs, and customs of the American Indian people are the guidelines for mankind's future. . . . Who will find peace with the lands? . . . Who will listen to the trees, the animals and birds, the voices of the places of the land? As the long-forgotten peoples of the respective continents rise and begin to reclaim their ancient heritage, they will discover the meaning of the lands of their ancestors. That is when the invaders of the North American continent will finally discover that for this land God is Red. (Deloria 1973, pp. 66, 260, 300–301)

CHAPTER 15

The Education of Racial and Cultural Minorities in the United States

In a world in which status and social mobility are more and more affected by levels of education, students of minority–majority relations must examine carefully the distribution of educational opportunities, the trends, and the outcomes. As we focus on the most deprived of America's minorities, we hope to suggest principles and facts that demonstrate the significance of education in maintaining or, as can be the case, weakening patterns of inequality.[1] We are convinced that "schools make a difference" (see Summers and Wolfe 1977).[2] It is

essential for students of minority–majority relations to study the conditions under which they reinforce the structures of inequality and when they promote equality.

Elementary and Secondary Education of Black Students

School Attendance and Quality of Schooling

Our emphasis in the first section of this chapter is on school desegregation, with special reference to black students. It should be noted first, however, that progress has been made in school attendance. In 1870, less than 10 percent of southern Blacks from 5 to 20 were enrolled in school. The proportion had increased to 58.5 percent by 1930, compared with the two-thirds enrolled among Whites in that age group in the South. By 1980, for the country as a whole, school attendance rates for Blacks and Whites were practically the same (Reid 1982, p. 24).

Changes in black school enrollment during the past century do not mean that parity or near parity with Whites has been attained. The quality of

---

[1] For a range of views on the stratification–education links, see Bowles and Gintis 1976; R. Collins 1979; Jencks et al. 1972; Juster 1975; Ogbu, 1978.

[2] Coleman, Hoffer, and Kilgore have recently argued (1982) that Catholic and other private schools make a bigger difference, are educationally richer, even after controlling for resources, classes of students, and the levels of their entering abilities. This does not seem unlikely. They cannot, however, control for the self-selectivity of the families and students, who may be more predisposed to sacrifice for education, nor can they control for the fact that public schools are less able to enforce adequate performance by threat of dismissal. Thus it is not clear how much the fact of being private or public or public produces the observed results.

Since minority students make up a small proportion of private school enrollments, it is essential for the student of minority-majority relations to examine this issue carefully. In addition to Coleman, Hoffer, and Kilgore, see the papers in Hallinan 1982.

schooling available to Blacks has generally been inferior to that provided to Whites. The most recent evidence of this disparity is found on scores for black and white college-bound seniors who have taken the Scholastic Aptitude Tests. Some improvement in schooling for Blacks and other minorities was shown in the contribution they made to the rise in overall SAT scores between 1981 and 1982—the first such upturn since 1963. However, scores for Blacks were still at least 100 points below those of Whites on both the verbal and the mathematics scores. These disparities give some indication of the extent to which minority students are being short-changed (Reid 1982, pp. 24–26).

The Supreme Court's Decisions of May 17, 1954, and May 31, 1955 on School Desegregation

On May 17, 1954, the decisions of the U.S. Supreme Court, consolidating cases arising in Delaware, Kansas, South Carolina, and Virginia, ruled unanimously that the separate-but-equal doctrine (*Plessy* v. *Ferguson*) which had been used to exclude Negro children from public schools maintained for white children was unconstitutional. The Court held (*Brown* v. *Board of Education of Topeka*) that the plaintiffs, by being required on the basis of race to attend separate schools, were deprived of the equal protection of the laws assured by the Fourteenth Amendment. In a related case, the Supreme Court ruled on the same day that the separate-but-equal doctrine when applied to exclude black children from admission to the public schools of the District of Columbia violated the due-process clause of the Fifth Amendment. The Court found that education today is not merely social as in 1896 but "is perhaps the most important function of state and local governments" and "is a principal instrument in awakening the child to cultural values, in preparing him for later professional training, and in helping him to adjust normally to his environment." The Court concluded that racially separate schools have "a tendency to retard the educational and mental development of Negro children and to deprive them of some of the benefits they would receive in a racially integrated school system." The 1954 decision said that to separate grade-school and high-school children from others solely because of race "generates a feeling of inferiority as to their

status in the community that may affect their hearts and minds in a way unlikely ever to be undone."

In the District of Columbia case, the Court held that "segregation in public education is not reasonably related to any proper governmental objective."

The Supreme Court invited the attorneys of the separate-school states to submit proposals in the fall of 1954 for accommodating their school systems to the new legal principle. The Court's second unanimous decision, handed down on May 31, 1955, stated: "All provisions of federal, state or local law requiring or permitting such discrimination must yield to this [the May 17, 1954] principle." Trial courts (federal district courts) that had originally heard the cases were instructed to order a "prompt and reasonable" start toward desegregation with a view to "good faith compliance at the earliest practicable data." No deadline was set for the desegregation of the public schools, but the Court said that it should be carried out "with all deliberate speed."

What did the 1954 decisions mean? In the simplest terms, the historical decisions of 1954 meant that the rigid and arbitrary separation of the races in the public schools solely on the basis of race was no longer legal. An explanation of the Court's decisions was given in Judge Bryan's memorandum in the Arlington school cases of 1956:

It must be remembered that the decisions of the Supreme Court of the United States in Brown v. Board of Education, 1954 and 1955, 347 United States 483 and 349 United States 294, do not compel the mixing of the different races in the public schools. No general reshuffling of the pupils in any school system has been commanded. The order of that court is simply that no child shall be denied admission to a school on the basis of race or color.

School Desegregation, 1954–1967[3]

The public-school decisions were welcomed enthusiastically by supporters of civil liberties, liberal political leaders in both major parties, and spokesmen for minority-group organizations. Prosegregationists criticized the decisions and the justices of the Supreme Court. Between 1956 and

[3]For a review of attempts to integrate the public schools and studies of particular school districts, see Farley 1978, pp. 16–24; Kalodner and Fishman 1978; Mills 1979; Pettigrew 1975, pp. 224–239; Raffel 1980; Stephan and Feagin 1980; Weinberg 1977, pp. 11–139; Wolf 1980.

1963 denunciations of the ruling came from state officials in several southern states, and 19 senators and 82 representatives from 11 states signed a manifesto against the decision. Opposition to school desegregation appeared in the form of legislative acts and resolutions, amendments to state constitutions, and decisions by state supreme courts. In many parts of the South, White Citizens' Councils were organized to intimidate Blacks who supported desegregation.

Before 1964, no systematic data on the implementation of *Brown* were collected and analyzed. Students of desegregation estimated that fewer than one percent of all black children in the 11 southern states attended desegregated schools. A strong civil rights bill was passed by Congress in 1964. Title IV of this act provided federal assistance for districts undergoing desegregation and authorized the Attorney General to act as plaintiff in such litigation. Discrimination in education was forbidden and the withholding of public funds from segregated school systems was authorized. Title VI authorized all federal agencies which made grants or loans to refuse payment of the monies if potential beneficiaries were subject to discrimination on the basis of race, color, or national origin. This provision was augmented the next year with the passage of the 1965 Elementary and Secondary Education Act. During the early 1960s, federal funds for local schools had been restricted, totaling about a half billion dollars annually. The 1965 law provided federal funds to low-income areas such as the rural South. In the next two years, federal disbursements to school districts quadrupled (Farley 1975, p. 5; Rist 1979a, p. 4).

In 1965, 80 percent of all white children in the United States were attending schools that were from 90 to 100 percent white. About 65 percent of all black students attended schools in which 90 percent of the students were black. Segregation was the norm wherever the proportion of Blacks was large. The Office of Education survey found that Mexican Americans, American Indians, Puerto Ricans, and Oriental Americans were also segregated, but to a lesser extent than Blacks. A report of the U.S. Commission on Civil Rights (1967) pointed out that national and regional averages do not show the full extent of school segregation. The Commission's investigation indicated that in metropolitan areas, where two-thirds of both the black and white populations live, school segregation is more extreme than the national averages suggest. Racial concentration, especially in elementary schools, is severe within central cities. In these areas, three-fourths of the black students were in elementary schools with enrollments that were nearly all-black (90 percent or more black), and 83 percent of the white students were in all-white schools. Approximately nine-tenths of the black elementary school students attended majority-black schools.

National statistics on school desegregation in 1968–69 showed that 23.4 percent of all black students were in majority white schools, compared with 18.4 percent in the South. Two years later the South had 40.5 percent of all black students in majority white schools and the national average was 33.1 percent. In 1974–75, the proportions for the South and the nation were 44 percent and 33 percent, respectively.

Court-ordered School Integration since 1968

In the period 1968–1973, the Supreme Court and federal district courts handed down rulings that furthered the desegregation of schools. Four of these decisions were especially important (Farley 1978, pp. 23–24). Under pressure from HEW, a Virginia county had adopted a freedom of choice plan, and some black children had chosen the previously white school at the opposite end of the county. No Whites, however, had enrolled in the black school. In *Green v. New Kent County* (391 U.S. 430, 1968), the Supreme Court declared that freedom of choice plans were acceptable only if they achieved actual desegregation of schools. Failing that, district federal courts were obliged to order more effective programs.

In *Alexander v. Holmes* (396 U.S. 19, 1969), thirty Mississippi school systems were told to integrate at the beginning of the fall term of 1969. Their appeal for a delay was granted by the Fifth Circuit Court of Appeals, but the Supreme Court overruled the stay, stating that *the principle of integration "with all deliberate speed" was no longer constitutionally permissible.* The Court ruled that school districts must terminate dual systems (racially identifiable schools) *at once* and provide only unitary schools from then on.

In *Swann v. Charlotte-Mecklenburg* (402 U.S. 1, 1971), the Supreme Court upheld an integration order of a district judge requiring that the ratio of black to white students be about the same at all schools in Charlotte and that children be bused to achieve this end. This ruling by the Supreme Court legitimized the use of busing and racial ratios as a means of bringing about integration.

In *Keyes* v. *School District No. 1, Denver* (396 U.S. 1215, 1973), the Supreme Court ruled that, because school administrators were partly responsible for the segregation of Blacks in the northeast section of Denver, a city-wide busing program was a legitimate remedy. This decision was important because litigants outside the South had had a more difficult time obtaining favorable court decisions (the *Brown* ruling of 1954 dealt with states in which school segregation was legally mandated). Suits in Cincinnati, Gary, and Kansas City had not produced integration orders because the courts believed that school desegregation resulted mainly from residential patterns. In the Denver case, the plaintiffs argued that school boards segregated black students by gerrymandering attendance zones, allowing Whites to transfer away from black schools, and by the method used to select sites for new school buildings. This decision has been cited as a precedent in integration orders elsewhere in the North and West—Boston, Dayton, Detroit, Milwaukee, Minneapolis, and Omaha.

Between 1974 and 1978, court-ordered integration was begun or expanded in Baltimore, Boston, Detroit, Houston, Louisville, and Milwaukee. Federal courts in Cleveland and Columbus and state courts in Los Angeles and San Diego held that those districts were responsible for racial segregation, and some type of integration orders were issued (Farley 1978, p. 44).

Judicial retreat from facilitating equal educational opportunity for urban minorities or the elimination of differential systems of resource allocation is evident in some of the decisions of the Supreme Court in the 1970s. In *San Antonio Independent School District* v. *Rodriquez* (1973), the Court reversed the district court and upheld the common system of financing public education. The Court held in this case that educational opportunities in central-city schools need only be "adequate," that there is no compelling reason why they must be equal to suburban opportunities (Showell 1976, p. 108). It is interesting to recall that the separate-but-equal doctrine enunciated by the Supreme Court in *Plessy* v. *Ferguson* in 1896 was long used to justify separate but equal schools. This doctrine

was repudiated by the Court in *Brown* v. *Board of Education* (1954). The *Rodriquez* decision legitimated the doctrine of separate and *unequal* schools.

In 1974, the Supreme Court in *Milliken* v. *Bradley* (S. Ct. 73–74, 1974) refused to accept the metropolitan approach to the desegregation of the Detroit schools. The Court decided in favor of local autonomy, saying:

No single tradition in public education is more deeply rooted than local autonomy over the operation of the schools; local autonomy has long been thought essential both to the maintenance of community concern and support for pubic schools and to the quality of the educational process.

In his remarks on the 1974 decision, Justice Stewart said (see U.S. Commission on Civil Rights, February, 1977, pp. 87–101):

This is not to say, however, that an inter-district remedy of the sort approved by the Court of Appeals would not be proper, or even necessary, in other factual situations. Were it to be shown, for example, that state officials had contributed to the separation of the races by drawing or redrawing school district lines . . .; purposeful, racially discriminatory use of state housing or zoning laws, then a decree calling for transfer of pupils across district line or for restructuring of district line might well be appropriate.

In the case of Detroit, Justice Stewart found no evidence to suggest that school officials either in or outside Detroit had been involved in any of these activities.

A new development in Supreme Court decisions began in 1976, a development which may make it more difficult to gain approval for large-scale busing programs. In two instances, the Court held that plaintiffs in desegregation cases must prove intent. In Washington, D.C., the police department had given a verbal ability test to officer candidates, and many more Blacks than Whites failed the test. In Arlington Heights, Illinois, city officials refused to rezone an area to permit the building of moderate-income housing. The effect of this action made it more difficult for Blacks to move into the suburb. In both cases, the plaintiffs asserted that the actions had had adverse effects upon Blacks and requested that the courts overrule the verbal ability test and require rezoning. The Supreme Court recognized the adverse consequences of the examination and the zoning decision but held that this was not sufficient to declare them unconstitutional. Instead, the plaintiffs would have to show that those who chose the test or refused to change the zoning intended to discriminate. In the next two years, the Court dealt with segregation cases in four cities and in each case raised questions concerning whether or not large-scale busing programs were needed in view of the principles set forth in the Washington, D.C., and Arlington Heights cases (Farley 1978, p. 45).

When Dayton school authorities challenged a city-wide busing order, the Supreme Court in 1977 remanded the case, saying that judges must determine "how much incremental segregative effect" the alleged violations had on the current racial distribution of students "compared to what it would have been in the absence" of such violations. It said also that the remedy "must be designed to redress that difference, and only if there has been a system-wide impact may there be a system-wide remedy." To some this ruling seemed to indicate a reversal of the Keyes presumption that an entire system is illegally separated if only a substantial portion is found to be segregated. On July 2, 1979, however, the Court, finding abundant evidence that the Dayton and Columbus schools were illegally segregated by official intent, before and after 1954, declared that they still had the "affirmative duty" to rectify that separation (*The New York Times*, July 8, 1979, p. E6). These decisions upheld the systemwide, crosstown busing plans for Dayton and Columbus schools. They place a burden on northern school boards operating schools attended predominantly by one race to show that the segregation is not the result of past actions of the authorities—actions such as the drawing of attendance zones that produced segregation in districts that never maintained legally established dual systems.

As we point out below, these decisions did not change the fact that substantial integration cannot be achieved now in most large northern cities without the tabooed metropolitan remedy. In the first place, Washington's schools are 96 percent minority, Chicago's 75 percent, Philadelphia's 68 percent, and New York City's 67 percent. And second, the costs of proving intentional segregation in a large school system are so great that no group can think of suing for a city-wide busing plan.

Nevertheless, the Supreme Court reaffirmed the legitimacy of busing in January, 1983, keeping it on the agenda of those seeking school integration.

Measuring School Desegregation

The index of dissimilarity measures school segregation independently of the racial composition of the school district. If all Blacks and all Whites attend racially homogeneous schools, the index is 100; if every school has the same racial composition, the index equals zero. This index indicates whether black and white children attend the same schools, and its numerical value shows the proportion of students of either race who would have to be moved from one school to another to eliminate segregation—to produce an index of zero. In the second decade after the landmark decisions of the 1954 U.S. Supreme Court, many southern cities and some in the North were led by federal court orders and pressure from HEW to reduce segregation in their school systems significantly. Attendance zones were redrawn, busing was increased, and other changes were instituted. Large reductions were made in pupil segregation in Memphis, where the index fell from 95 to 51, and in Jacksonville, Nashville, Fort Worth, and Oklahoma City. In the North, the largest changes came in cities where the courts had ordered desegregation—Indianapolis and San Francisco. A major effort to integrate might be considered to be a decrease of 20 or more in the index of dissimilarity. Such drops were more common in the South than elsewhere; 63 percent of the southern central cities and approximately one-fourth of the northern cities showed that amount of school desegregation between 1967 and 1974 (Farley 1978, p. 29).

Many school districts experienced modest decreases in segregation in the years just mentioned. These were districts where the index of dissimilarity fell from 6 to 19 points. Approximately one-fourth of the southern and one-third of the northern cities were in this category. These districts brought about some integration by closing some all-black schools, redrawing attendance lines, establishing magnet schools, or busing modest numbers of pupils. At the same time, many northern and a few southern cities made little headway in reducing segregation. Central-city school districts where the index of pupil segregation increased or decreased by less than six points fell in this category. According to this measure, 10 percent of the southern and 40 percent of the northern cities had schools that were as segregated in 1974 as they had been nearly a decade earlier. In general, school segregation was declining in those years, but seventeen northern cities, including New York, Newark, Chicago, Cleveland, Cincinnati, Philadelphia, and St. Louis, had schools that were more segregated by race than they were in 1967 (Farley 1978, p. 30).

White enrollments in central cities declined rapidly during the 1970s, due in part to fertility trends. For example, in 1976 the number of white births was only 70 percent as large as in 1957. Decreases in white enrollments also reflect the outmigration of Whites. In 1975, Coleman et al. suggested that desegregation programs then in effect in central-city schools were not effective because they encouraged whites to take their children out of public schools. Other investigators, however, have shown that white enrollments are falling markedly both in cities where schools have been integrated and in cities whose schools remain segregated. Trends from 1967 to 1974 showed that in the largest cities school integration is related to loss of white students. A major integration order, that is, one that reduced the index of dissimilarity by 20 points or more in a city of at least 300,000 where one-third of the students are black, resulted in an incremental loss of white students equal to one year's normal loss of Whites (Farley 1978, pp. 37–38).

Typically, in a large northern city, approximately three-fourths of the white students but fewer than one-fifth of the black students attend suburban schools. Milwaukee represents an extreme case; 65 percent of the Whites, but only 1 percent of the Blacks attend suburban schools. In the typical southern metropolis, however, approximately three-fifths of the white, compared to one-fifth of the black students go to suburban schools (Farley 1978, p. 38).

In relating residential segregation to school segregation, Farley (1978, pp. 42–44) predicts that the basic tendency toward a concentration of Blacks in central cities and Whites in suburbs will not soon change. By 1975, two-thirds of the white students in metropolitan areas went to suburban schools, but only 30 percent of the black students in the metropolitan areas were enrolled in those schools. In many metropolises, the shift of Whites to the suburbs is the main factor in preventing school integration. Nevertheless, racial residential segregation slowly declined in 109 central cities outside the South after 1950 and within the South since 1960. Notable declines in segregation were found in smaller cities and in those having relatively few black residents.

By 1978, approximately 76 percent of the students in public elementary and secondary schools nationally were Whites who were not of Spanish origin (U.S. Bureau of the Census, 1981b: Table 1), but in Washington D.C., only 4 percent were White; in Atlanta 10 percent, in San Antonio 13 percent, and in Detroit and New Orleans, 14 percent. In many metropolitan centers, many white public-school students live in the suburban ring. Unless cities and suburbs are consolidated into single school districts, many areas, including New York, Boston, Chicago, Los Angeles, Detroit, and Philadelphia, will have public schools nearly as segregated racially as those which were constitutionally permitted before the *Brown* decision of 1954 (Farley 1982, pp. B26–27).

The Effects of Educational Policies on Pupils in Desegregated Schools[4]

Black children entering interracial schools are often behind white students in academic skills. Many racial and cultural minority parents are opposed to the tracking of their children. Once tracked, it is unlikely that a child will be transferred to another group. Tracking, then, often leads to resegregation (Alexander, Cook, and McDill 1978; Rosenbaum 1976; Schofield 1979; Shavit 1984). The alternative—heterogeneous classroom grouping—virtually ensures that a large proportion of black students will, at least initially, do less well than white students (Schofield and Sagar 1979, pp. 159–160).

Even if a formal tracking process is not used, informal sorting, by counseling and labeling, may have similar effects (Erickson 1975; McDermott 1977; Rist 1970). In a middle school in a large northeastern city, a tracking system is not used. There are, however, two highly segregated groups of students in the school. More than 80 percent of the students in the eighth-grade scholars' program are white, and nearly 90 percent of the children in educable mentally retarded (EMR) classes are black (Schofield and Sagar 1979, p. 159). Some teachers

[4]For studies concerned with the subtleties of interrelationships between students and teachers, between Blacks and Whites, and between administrators and parents in various sites, see Gouldner 1978; Metz 1978; Rist 1979a; Schofield, 1981; Summers and Wolfe 1977.

in this school have divided their classes into three groups. In one teacher's three academically homogeneous groups, Group A was all white, and Group C was all black except for one white male. Group B was a racially balanced middle group in which the social learning opportunities, considered in isolation from the rest of the class, seemed ideal. Black and white students worked in close association on the same material at the same time and at the same general level of skill. To observers this appeared to be a learning situation on an equal-status, reciprocal basis. When the class as a whole was considered, however, the social cost of this type of tracking appeared to be high. Schofield and Sagar (1979, p. 184) remark that the higher-achieving black students must have noticed that they had been paired with white students who were in the lower half of the white contingent. Also, students in the racially homogeneous upper and lower groups had hardly any more opportunity for interaction than those in classes which were more completely segregated.

Putting black and white children in the same classrooms does not insure positive educational experiences. They may bring sharply contrasting control expectations, with black students used to strict authority and white students used to more permissive or open classes (Metz 1978). Either control method might work, but clashing expectations might block the effectiveness of both. The policies that teachers adopt in matters such as seating and instructional strategies strongly affect the kind of interaction children of different racial or cultural groups have with each other. In instruction, the approaches vary from traditional to individualized to group-oriented. Often, teachers are not adequately trained or are not strongly motivated to consider the effects of their attitudes and behavior on students in an interracial or intercultural situation. Because of the heavy demands placed upon them to produce gains in academic performance, they may not have time to consider how the social experiences of students affect their academic development. When children are free to work out their own relationships without guidance, the results may consist mainly of misunderstandings, defensiveness, and conflicts. If children have little or no direct contact with one another, stereotypes may be reinforced. In some classes, however, contacts are maintained under conditions which seem to build positive relationships despite differences in background (Schofield and Sagar 1979, p. 196).

Magnet Schools and School Desegregation

The first alternative programs were begun as special options within regular school systems. Among the urban school districts that offer some degree of option in educational programs are Berkeley, California, Cincinnati, Minneapolis, Dallas, Seattle, Philadelphia, and Boston. Multiple-option systems gained support from the movement which arose in the 1960s for greater parental participation in the educational process. The strongest support for these systems, however, has come from those seeking voluntary desegregation methods. Magnet schools were seen as strategies to avoid large-scale desegregation. In the case of *Green* v. *New Kent County* (1968), the Supreme Court ruled that although there was no inherent problem with the basic concept, such plans were unacceptable when they did not produce adequate results. Later, the federal courts mandated or recommended the use of magnet schools in a number of desegregation orders as a part of school desegregation plans.

The programs offered as the focus of an entire school or as a specialization within a school vary greatly. Those that appear most frequently include the creative and performing arts, ecology, fundamental curriculum, open structured classes, schools without walls, and career exploration programs (Warren 1978, pp. 1–2).

The use of magnet schools or projects in school desegregation involves several difficult problems. They cannot alone bring about district-wide desegregation. First, location is still an important factor in parental choice, especially in large, urbanized districts. Second, if a magnet school attracts students away from other schools and thereby leaves behind racially isolated schools, it has simply complicated the problem. Third, if enough students from both minority and nonminority groups are not attracted and racial methods are used to fill student places the idea of the magnet concept is undermined. In some cases, this has meant that magnet schools have had to operate at enrollments below the desired level. Fourth, a more serious problem is that of resegregation within racially balanced schools. When several optional programs are offered within one school, one of the special options may become the preserve of the group that is better prepared academically, while another special program may be more attractive to those less well prepared. Fifth, these schools may draw support services and attention away from nonmagnet schools also being desegregated. Sixth, there is the problem of providing adequate information for parents to make the best choices for their children's future. Despite these problems, magnet schools have several positive aspects. They provide a wider variety of learning experiences to children than can be offered in a single-approach school, and they enable a school district to deal with children whose interests or learning styles work against their success in conventional schools.

In Detroit, the 21 magnet high-school programs were said by an assistant superintendent not to be working because they were not different enough from the regular schools with which they were competing for pupils. This school official asserted that the degree of desegregation the high-school magnet programs fostered was about 1 percent. In contrast, the middle-school magnets in Detroit have been so successful that parents stand in line overnight to get their children enrolled. According to the assistant superintendent, the difference was that the middle schools were totally modified in function when they became magnets, whereas the high school programs were simply embellished with a few special courses (Cleveland *Plain Dealer,* January 29, 1979).

Busing for School Desegregation

Busing is shorthand for a policy of assigning children to a school outside their own neighborhood, on the basis of their race, for the purpose of bring about school desegregation (see Blalock 1979, pp. 87–107; Coleman 1975; Finger 1976; McClendon and Pestello 1983; Orfield 1978). Thirteen of the twenty largest cities in the United States now have school systems with minority enrollments of more than 50 percent, and in nine of these cities minority enrollment is more than two-thirds of total enrollment—Washington, D.C, Detroit, Chicago, St. Louis, Baltimore, San Francisco, Memphis, Philadelphia, and New York. It is in these cities that the most serious problems have arisen in connection with school desegregation, especially with busing where it has been used to reduce segregation. (It should be pointed out that two-thirds of the nation's seven million black pupils do not go to school in urban districts where Blacks are a majority of the enrollment. It is also true that 70 percent of the black students who are

in all-minority schools are in 19 cities—north, south, east, and west (*The New York Times,* December 21, 1975, p. E3).

The districts where busing has been most successful are small cities, as well as the countywide school districts in Florida, where desegregation is not only countywide but statewide. Among these small cities are Des Moines, Iowa; Rockford, Illinois; Las Vegas, Nevada; and Wichita, Kansas— in general, cities which have less than 20 percent black enrollment (*The New York Times,* December 21, 1975, p. E3).

Two main issues are involved in the resistance to busing to achieve school desegregation. First, it is claimed that it promotes white flight, ruining the cities and threatening the fiscal base of school systems. Second, it is asserted that busing does not increase the quality of education and may be detrimental to it. Frequently in these discussions, James Coleman's work is cited. The Coleman study of 1966 found that the scholastic achievements of various racial and ethnic groups are enhanced as the proportion of white students is increased. This survey showed also that white pupils do not suffer academically when mixed with black students in predominantly white schools. Although Coleman had not endorsed mandatory busing, and his research did not deal with the impact of desegregation upon the racial composition of cities, he had appeared to be a proponent of busing. In 1975, Coleman announced his opposition to mandatory busing. One of the most important findings in his new research was that "the loss of Whites did increase when there was a reduction of school segregation" (Coleman 1975, pp. 76–77). Four qualifications were attached to this general finding: (1) the loss of Whites was smaller in small cities than in large cities; (2) the loss of Whites was greater when the city had a high percentage of Blacks; (3) the loss of Whites was greater when there was a large disparity in racial composition between city and adjoining suburbs; and (4) the loss of Whites due to desegregation appears to be a one-time effect, limited to the year of desegregation. Coleman concluded: "Ironically, 'desegregation' may be increasing segregation. . . . Eliminating central city segregation does not help if it increases greatly the segregation between districts through accelerated white loss."

On the basis of his 1975 conclusion, Coleman recommended that school desegregation policy should concentrate on slowing the movement of

Whites from central cities; that the courts should limit their actions to eliminating *de jure* segregation; that mandatory within-district busing should be discontinued; that mandatory cross-district busing not be started; and that school desegregation might proceed by permitting children in metropolitan areas to attend schools in the area that have a lower percentage of the child's race than the neighborhood school (Robin and Bosco 1976, pp. 47–48).

Coleman argued that this policy of voluntary busing preserves the right of the parents to select their child's school by residential selection and adds the right of school selection under specified conditions. Robin and Bosco (1976, p. 56) point out that this recommendation, if implemented, would encounter difficulties. Schools regarded as better would receive an influx of students and become overcrowded, requiring them to be enlarged in order to resolve the conflict that would arise between a child's right to attend a neighborhood school and his or her right to attend a preferred one. In a period of resistance to bond issues and tax increases, it seems unlikely that school officials and boards would request monies to expand the preferred schools so that they could be further desegregated and so that the underused educational facilities could be left increasingly vacant.

On the question of white migration to the suburbs, it should be pointed out that this shift cannot be attributed solely, or even mainly, to busing to achieve school desegregation (see, e.g., Clotfelter 1979; Farley, Richards, and Wurdock 1980; Pettigrew and Green 1976). It began on a large scale more than three decades ago because white families wanted to get out of the city, to acquire suburban homes to enhance their social status, and for other reasons. Busing for school desegregation is only one factor in white flight. Federal housing policies had more to do with this populational movement than busing (see U.S. Commission on Civil Rights 1977, pp. 20–25). Black housing became increasingly segregated from 1934 to 1948. From the beginning of the FHA until the Supreme Court ruled against racial covenants in the latter year, FHA policies emphasized racial unity as a condition for the highest evaluations of neighborhoods and insisted that racial homogeneity was essential to a neighborhood's financial stability. Even after FHA ruled that it would no longer insure mortgages on properties that had had covenants placed on

them after February, 1950, it continued to insure properties on which covenants existed before that date. The Housing Act of 1954 amended existing housing laws, putting major emphasis upon urban renewal. The FHA's 221 program of assisting private industry in building rental projects for lower- to middle-income families was almost entirely a central-city program. Because of the high degree of residential segregation in urban areas, these projects often reinforced existing concentrations. Also, for many years, approval for FHA loans on new homes in the suburbs was more easily obtained than for loans on existing homes in the city.

Often a matter of considerable importance in the resistance to busing as a means to achieve school desegregation goes unmentioned, namely the racial prejudice of white parents. Twenty million pupils in the United States are transported to school daily by buses for purposes other than desegregation without arousing controversy. Approximately 3 percent of all bused students are transported to schools to further school desegregation. In 1972, Metropolitan Applied Research Center, New York, reported that both white and black students were being transported greater distances for a longer time and at greater cost to racially segregated than to desegregated schools (MARC 1972, p. 10). The prejudice of white parents, which seems to be mainly of the "symbolic racism" variety (see Chapter 5), persists even in the face of a significant increase in tolerance of school desegregation (Smith 1981b).

Recognizing the complexity of the issue and the wide variation in conditions among school districts, we tend nevertheless to agree with Orfield (1978, p. 7): "Desegregating big city schools through busing is not an ideal or even a natural solution to segregation, but it is quite simply the only solution if there is to be substantial integration in this generation." We would emphasize, however, the interdependence of busing with housing policy and with the question of metropolitan school districts—interdependence that we shall comment on below.

Obstacles in the Way of School Desegregation

Segregation in the schools of a large city is exceedingly complex. Among its major aspects are the following: the questionable academic caliber of some of the public schools; the rising poverty of the children in the school system; uncertainty concerning the legal status of the segregation, due in part to the inability of civil rights organizations to pursue expensive litigation in the courts; alleged racial discrimination in faculty hiring and assignment practices; alleged discrimination in disciplinary practices; and segregation of children into racially isolated classrooms. In addition, most desegregation programs place more of the burden on black and Puerto Rican children than on Whites. Children from minority groups travel more than Whites (Lesley Oelsner, *The New York Times*, November 20, 1977, p. 64).

The increase in the number of private and parochial schools and the marked growth in enrollments in these schools since the late 1960s represents a new trend. Attendance at these schools no longer constitutes evidence of membership in the social elite or in a group of the devoutly religious. Race is only one factor, but an important one, in this development. Other reasons include dissatisfaction with the quality of education and the feeling that discipline is lacking in the public schools, as well as a greater interest recently in the moral side of education and in religious instruction. In the North, Catholic parochial school enrollments, which had been declining, appear to have stabilized. A large majority of students in these schools are white Catholics, but non-Catholic and often black and Hispanic pupils are turning more frequently to parochial schools. In the South, many of the new church-based (Protestant) schools appear to be capable of successful, long-term competition with the public school systems. In 1976, 92,000 pupils were enrolled in Hebrew day schools in the United States, 54,000 of them in New York City (*The New York Times,* September 19, 1976; Coleman, Hoffer, and Kilgore 1982).

Many Blacks have come to question the value of integration—or the value of most integration that has occurred. Numbers of black parents are concerned about sending their children to schools where they are not welcome. Some black leaders believe that the white community does not intend to integrate the schools and that further efforts are a waste of time. A number of all-black or mostly black private schools have been established around New York City, and many of these schools emphasize black culture (*The New York Times,* November 20, 1977, p. 64).

The situations in southern cities are somewhat different from those in the North. This is due in part to the *de jure* pattern of segregation before 1954. This was easier to attack by court order than the *de facto* segregation in the North. In medium-sized southern cities, desegregation has proceeded quite a long way, despite strong resistance. In Little Rock, for example, Central High School became known throughout the world when nine students broke the school's color bar. Black students had to be protected for a year, and tension continued during the 1960s and into the 1970s. By 1976, however, this high school had become one of the most effectively desegregated schools in the nation. Enrollment at Central had become almost 50–50, with a slight majority for Blacks. Racial violence had almost disappeared, and something approaching racial harmony prevailed. Many student organizations, athletic teams, and squads of cheerleaders had become integrated, and elective offices were about evenly divided between Blacks and Whites.

Several factors seem to have contributed to the changed atmosphere at Central High School. By the late 1970s, the black and white students attending the school had been going to classes together since the early grades. (Little Rock began massive desegregation with busing in 1971.) The new principal, the second black principal since the school was desegregated, enjoyed unusual rapport with black and white students. Counseling rooms had been opened in every school in the district where angry students were sent to "cool off" and discuss their problems. Efforts had been made to improve basic educational skills, and the academic gap between Blacks and Whites had been narrowed. Some white families had moved to the western part of the city, and some of their children had left Central. Many of Central's white students, however, were being bused in from those same suburbs (Cleveland *Plain Dealer,* October 3, 1976, Section 4, p. 4).

Desegregation has proceeded less successfully in Memphis. When the federal district court ordered the Memphis schools to desegregate in 1972, white parents reacted negatively, but nonviolently. Nearly 35,000 white pupils were withdrawn from a school population of 120,000 and sent to white academies. During this process, the competition for rewards and the building of racial boundary-maintenance systems were revealed, as shown in a study of desegregation in "Crossover" High School (Collins 1979, pp. 90 ff.).

After nearly twenty years of litigation for school desegregation, this high school was paired with a black high school about eight blocks away. The black school was converted into a junior high school and the students who had attended the black school were ordered to attend Crossover. When the pairing began, most of the white students then in school decided to stay rather than transfer to a private school. Most of the white students who were bused to "Feeder" (the formerly black high school that had been converted into a biracial junior high) chose to leave the system.

At first, the white students already enrolled at Crossover had the advantage—they knew the territory and they were well organized. Black students who participated in extracurricular activities were given minor roles to play, and they had to confrom to white norms in dress, hairstyles, and use of standard English, and aspirations for future achievement. For a time, the Whites were able to maintain control of many student activities, including student government, clubs, ROTC, and the yearbook, even though these areas were desegregated. As the Blacks took over areas such as sports and cheerleading, the status of these was downgraded by Whites. A rigid boundary-maintenance system between the two racial groups had evolved. Competition in extracurricular activities developed in favor of the black students as they increased numerically over Whites—from roughly 50–50 in 1972–73 to 72 percent black and 28 percent white in 1976–77. One student observed: "Desegregation has only brought Blacks and Whites together under one roof, but segregation remains." Since they had lost control of the student subsystem, after five years the upper status Whites chose to withdraw from the school (Collins 1979, pp. 102–113).

The Metropolitan Solution[5]

Racial boundaries are seen most clearly in the United States in housing segregation patterns. During the past three decades the largest cities have been transformed from being predominantly white to a situation in which seven of the ten most populous have black populations of one-third or more. In the suburban rings around the cities, the population remains overwhelmingly white. Cities like Racine, Wisconsin; Portland, Oregon; or Des

Moines, Iowa, with black populations of approximately 5 percent, have problems that are different from cities like Washington, D.C., or Detroit, where the black populations exceed 70 percent. All have one characteristic in common—residential segregation. In all of these cities, a policy of neighborhood schools would result overwhelmingly in white children going to school with white children and black children going to school with black children. The first three cities mentioned above could successfully desegregate their schools within the boundaries of the city, but this could not be done in Washington, Detroit, or St. Louis. In the latter schools, the only solution to racial separation may be metropolitan consolidation (Rist 1976, pp. 118–119). This view is not shared by Coleman:

I believe it's not entirely lower-class blacks that middle-class whites are fleeing. They are fleeing a school system that they see as too large, as unmanageable, as unresponsive, to find a smaller, more responsive system. If the system is made even larger, covering the whole metropolitan area, many parents will find ways to escape it, either by moving even further out or by use of private schools. (Cleveland *Plain Dealer,* June 19, 1975)

St. Louis's school desegregation plan went into effect in September, 1980, after eight years of litigation and under a court-ordered busing plan. However, it included only city schools, which enroll 59,000 students of whom four-fifths are black. When a federal judge found that area housing authorities and the state had furthered segregation, he ordered a cross-district desegregation plan involving the city and suburbs. Fifteen districts joined the plan. In February, 1983, just before a hearing that would have led to court-ordered busing, the remaining districts (22 of 23 suburbs) proposed their own voluntary busing program, the first involving a large city and its metropolitan area. The agreement provided that 15,000 black students from predominantly black school districts in the city and northern suburbs would transfer to predominantly white schools in the southern suburbs. Over a period of five years, each district must reach a black enrollment of at least 15 percent but not more than 25 percent. The plan is designed to attract white students to city schools that offer advanced or specialized programs (*The New York Times,* February 27, 1983, p. E7).

The Supreme Court acted in a decision dealing with Louisville and its surrounding county in 1975, and its results are worth noting. Louisville and

[5]For a comprehensive report on all aspects of metropolitan school desegregation, see U.S. Commission on Civil Rights (February 1977).

Jefferson County desegregated their schools without incident in 1956, two years after the Supreme Court's *Brown* decision. Although federal district courts had overruled metropolitan plans for school desegregation in Richmond and in Detroit, the courts found such a remedy acceptable for Louisville and Jefferson County. The latter decision was made because the city and the county had once operated legally segregated school systems. After this ruling, black children were bused from the inner city to the suburbs and white children were transported the opposite way to achieve over-all racial balance in the schools of the metropolitan area. Sentiment against busing was strong among Whites of all classes, and there was vandalism and rioting by 2,500 white antibusing protestors during the first weekend after school opened in 1975. Blacks, most of whom live in the west part of the city, were quiet during the early stages of busing. Middle-class blacks who live in the suburbs sent their children to the desegregated schools in large numbers.

Observers of the Louisville plan say that it meets at least three of the conditions essential for success in metropolitan busing. First, Whites have no place to flee to escape busing. The plan involves the entire region. Second, the city-suburban school system is less than 30 percent black. Third, the federal judge who administers the plan is vigilant about letting any school within the district become predominantly black, or even more than 30 percent black. It is believed that larger proportions of black students in one or more schools would destabilize the system and lead to the movement of Whites to avoid predominantly black schools. (This is, of course, a controversial policy, seeming to some to continue to carry overtones of prejudice. Others believe that it is a wise policy, helping to support continuing school integration.) In addition to these factors, another must be added—the long tradition of moderation and tolerance in Louisville. That tradition of tolerance was reflected in the response of public officials in 1975. When the busing decision was handed down, an effort was made to obey the law and make busing work. No official attempted to stir up antibusing feelings publicly once the issue was decided (*The New York Times*, September 14, 1975, Section 4, p. 1).

School Reforms

The Coleman report (1966) and later studies have shown lower average scores for Blacks on standard achievement tests than for Whites at twelfth grade and earlier, but there are considerable differences by social class and region for both races (U.S. Commission on Civil Rights, 1967, Vol. 1, p. 91; Sewell 1971, pp. 793–809; Blackwell 1978, p. 7). Dropout rates are almost twice as high for black as for white adolescents, but racial differences are sharply reduced when type of parental occupation and other socioeconomic factors are considered.

Many attempts have been made to improve the quality of education for disadvantaged children. Remedial instruction gives intensive assistance to students in academic difficulty. Techniques include a low student–teacher ratio, tutors to help students during and after school, counseling, and the use of special teaching materials to increase basic skills. The cultural enrichment approach offers activities that go beyond those traditionally given to students. Such programs provide access to museums, concerts, and theater, other schools, and college campuses. Another type of program attempts to overcome attitudes that inhibit learning. Here efforts are made to increase self-esteem through black studies or similar programs and to instill confidence through academic success and recognition. Still another program is preschool education. This approach makes use of some of the elements in the other approaches as it tries to increase the verbal skills of the disadvantaged child and to provide cultural enrichment activities for him before he enters primary school. All of these programs try to involve parents in the various activities, and in some cases adult education is offered in connection with them. Among the federal educational programs launched in recent years with the goal of improving skills and motivation of children in a number of minority groups are Head Start (preschool), Follow Through (primary grades), Talent Search (high school), and Upward Bound (high school).

Alternative schools designed specifically to deal with black students, including those who have failed in the regular schools, have attained some notable successes (see Henry 1980; Wagner 1977). Since minority students seem to experience even more strongly than majority students the serious decline in academic competence so widespread during the summer months (see Heyns 1978), programs designed to keep and increase school-year momentum have proved of value (Yinger, Ikeda, Laycock, and Cutler 1978).

In 1982, the superintendent of schools in Baltimore, who is black, pointed to a reversal of the trend in the results of standardized tests administered in the schools of his city. He attributed the change to three factors: (1) tightened standards, (2) improved instruction, and (3) improved attitudes of faculty, parents, and the community, particularly among Blacks. Well-defined goals and objectives had replaced the educational fads of the 1960s. In addition, he stressed the presence of black superintendents in such cities as Newark, Detroit, Atlanta, Memphis, St. Louis, Minneapolis, Washington, and Richmond, who "partly because they know the political ropes and partly because they are black, can hold black children responsible in ways that many white superintendents could not, for fear of being accused of racism" (*The Cleveland Plain Dealer,* August 15, 1982). That Baltimore is not alone in experiencing these gains is shown by national test results. In 1970, the test scores of black children were 18 percent below those of Whites. By 1980, the gap had been reduced to 13 percent (*New York Times,* April 18, 1982, p. 33).

School reforms may play an important part in improving the school performance of minorities, but more important is the elimination of barriers in employment, education, and housing so that Blacks and similarly placed minority groups can attain the same social and occupational positions now offered to Whites for their ability and training. As Ogbu (1978) emphasizes, equality of educational opportunity must be related to social structure beyond the school. His evidence suggests that Blacks and members of certain other minority groups fail to work hard in school because such efforts have not traditionally benefited members of their group. This accounts for the "mental withdrawal" of school children in these groups, a tendency found to be strong among children in other castelike societies, as he calls them.

In this thesis, the concept of equality of educational opportunity must be redefined to include equality of access to postschool rewards of formal education as well as equality of access to school resources and equality of school performance.

Summary and Conclusions on School Desegregation

1. The issue is not the hindering of academic achievement for either majority or minority children.

Studies of desegregating school systems show that racial mixture in the schools has no negative effects for majority group pupils. When central-city children are bused to outlying communities, there is no significant difference in achievement between children in schools that do and those that do not receive bused pupils (Rist 1980, pp. 122–125).

2. Black children entering biracial schools are often behind white students in academic skills. What happens in such situations depends in part on the educational policies followed by the school. Homogeneous grouping often leads to resegregation; heterogeneous grouping usually results in a large proportion of black students doing less well, at least initially, than white students. The social cost of tracking seems to be high, and many racial and cultural minority parents oppose it. When heterogeneous grouping is used, the seating of pupils, the instructional strategies that are employed, and the training and attitudes of teachers all affect the kind of interaction that occurs in the classroom.

3. Busing *per se* is not the issue. More than half of the public school students ride buses to school daily. Only 7 percent are bused for purposes of school desegregation.

4. A distinction must be made between desegregation (a certain racial mix of students) and integration (interracial acceptance). In five different desegregated settings from New York to Memphis, the industrial Northeast, the Midwest, and the Deep South, Rist (1979a, p. 8) says that although the student populations may have been desegregated, none of the sites was integrated.

5. Attitude studies show that the majority of white parents have no objection to sending their children to schools where black students constitute half or less of the student body (Rist 1980). Perhaps this point should be qualified by evidence (Armor 1980, pp. 214–16; and Stinchcombe and Taylor 1980, pp. 179–80) showing that most Whites may be willing to have their children attend integrated schools provided that they go to schools they have already chosen for their children.

6. Despite the exodus of Whites to the suburbs, it is possible to achieve racial balance in school districts, but it is not possible to put all children in predominantly white schools. The options, therefore, appear to be: desegregate portions of the city school system but not all; include the suburbs in the desegregation plan; regard any school that enrolls students of two or more racial groups as

desegregated regardless of their proportions; and, under some conditions do nothing.

Mexican American Schooling

So now lack of achievement is correlated to lack of cultural emphasis — Fuck you

Enrollments

A tradition of learning is not characteristic of Mexico's population as a whole, and Mexican Americans have put less emphasis on education than many of the racial and cultural minorities in the United States. For example, Blacks average more years of schooling than Mexican Americans and are functionally illiterate approximately half as often. Also, Mexican Americans attend college less often than either black or white Americans (Sowell 1975, p. 112).

Table 15-1 shows the deficiencies in the education of Spanish-surname children and compares the educational level of Mexican Americans with that of other groups in 1950, 1960, and 1970 in five southwestern states. The problem of retention of Mexican American children in school has not improved in recent years. In the late 1970s, about the same proportion in the age group 16 to 24 were not attending high school. Furthermore, more Mexican American students were attending segregated schools in 1980 than in 1970 (Pachon and Moore 1981, p. 121).

Among persons of Spanish origin 25 years old and over, Mexican Americans had the highest proportion (23.9 percent) of those who had completed less than five years of school in 1979. Of those of Spanish origin, Puerto Ricans (38.6 percent) and Mexican Americans (34.9 percent) had the smallest percentages who had completed four years of high school or more (see "The Academic Achievements of Puerto Ricans" later in this chapter).

Segregation, Tests, Curriculum, and Dropouts

For a few years, the *Brown* decision of the U.S. Supreme Court (May 17, 1954) had only a slight effect on the segregation of black students. Mexican Americans were affected even less. Under *Plessy (Plessy v. Ferguson,* 163 U.S. 537), Mexican Americans had sought the legal status of Caucasians in order to claim equal school rights. For a decade or so after *Brown,* school administrations used them as sham Caucasians. When desegregation of black schools could no longer be avoided, federal courts in Texas accepted plans that put black and Mexican American students in the same schools. Anglo students continued to attend separate schools, now with the approval of federal courts. Mexican American students were used as Whites in order to avoid Anglo desegregation (Weinberg 1977, p. 169).

The findings of the U.S. Commission on Civil Rights (1971–1974) found a continuity in Mexican American education along these lines: (1) a high degree of segregation, (2) low academic achievement, (3) exclusionary practices by schools, and (4) a discriminatory use of public finance. This educational pattern is similar to that imposed on black children (Weinberg 1977, p. 177).

Table 15-1. Median School Years Completed[a]

| | 1950 | | | 1960 | | | 1970[b] Spanish | |
	Spanish	Total white	Non-white	Spanish	Total white	Non-white	Male	Female
Arizona	6.1	10.6	5.5	7.9	11.7	7.0	9.8	9.5
California	7.6	11.8	8.9	9.0	12.1	10.5	10.5	10.4
Colorado	6.4	10.9	9.8	8.6	12.1	11.2	10.3	10.4
New Mexico	7.4	9.5	5.8	8.4	11.5	7.1	10.3	10.3
Texas	3.6	9.7	7.0	6.1	10.8	8.1	8.4	8.1

Source: Samora and Simon, 1977, 165, and U.S. Bureau of the Census, 1970 Census of Population—subject reports—"Persons of Spanish Surname," June, 1973, Table 8, 32–41.
[a]By Spanish surname, total white, and nonwhite populations for five southwestern states, 1950 and 1960, and for male and female Spanish surname, 1970.
[b]Comparable statistics not available.

Mexican Americans were legally segregated in California schools as recently as 1946 and in Texas schools until 1948 (Murguia 1975, p. 54). Segregation is now illegal, but separation remains. *De facto* separation, and Anglo opposition to sending their children to school with Mexican Americans, based upon patterns of residential segregation, is still common in the Southwest. One survey showed that 57 percent of Spanish-surname children in eight large districts (50,000 or more children) in California attended "minority schools." In a sample of smaller districts in California, 30 percent of the Mexican American children were found to be attending such schools. Spanish-surname teachers were also segregated; in the larger districts 51 percent were assigned to minority schools (Moore 1970, p. 79). In the East Los Angeles ghetto, more than two-thirds of the population is Mexican American and its high school population is more than 80 percent Mexican American (Dworkin 1972, p. 173).

In comparison with standardized achievement of Anglos in the metropolitan Northeast, Chicanos fell increasingly behind from grades one through twelve. In verbal ability the differential in grades was 2.0 years at the end of the sixth grade, 2.3 years at the end of the ninth grade, 3.5 years at the end of the twelfth grade. The differential in reading comprehension was 2.4 years at the end of the sixth grade, 2.6 years at the end of the ninth grade, and 3.3 years at the end of the twelfth grade; in mathematics it was 2.2 at the end of the sixth grade, 2.6 years at the end of the ninth grade, and 4.1 years at the end of the twelfth grade. It was not claimed that these tests were culturally fair, but it was said that their content measured knowledge which many employers felt was important for success in American society (Briggs 1973, pp. 15–16). Other studies have found similar results. For example, a national appraisal of the educational performance of American students with a Spanish heritage, conducted by the Education Commission of the States, showed that, at 17, more than a third of the Hispanic students were still in the tenth grade or below, compared with about 10 percent of white students. This report indicated also that Hispanic students in the Northeast, with New York City students being the majority in this group, lagged behind Hispanic students in the West in many categories (*The New York Times,* May 22, 1977).

For many years Mexican American children have been given IQ tests standardized on Anglo children and administered in English. The result of such testing has been to classify a large proportion of Mexican American children as EMR ("educable mentally retarded"). According to one report (Gomez 1973, p. 111) approximately 5 percent of Anglo children were categorized as EMR (IQ of 75 or below), but 13 percent of Mexican American children were so classified. About 25 percent of Anglo children were listed as slow learners (IQ of 75–90), but 50 percent of Mexican American children were placed in this category. Fifty percent of Anglo children were categorized as average or normal (IQ of 90–100), compared with 25 percent of Mexican American children.

When a guidance counselor for the San Francisco schools arranged for a group of Hispanic children to be tested in Spanish, 80 percent did well enough to show that they had been wrongly identified as retarded. The psychologist pointed out that this result was obtained despite the fact that the test that was given had been designed for use in Puerto Rico and was written in the island's vernacular, some of which is alien to Mexican Americans and people of other Hispanic backgrounds. According to the president of the National Association for Bilingual Education, in New York State a conservative estimate is that about 25 percent of Hispanic children in classes for the retarded are there in error. Clifton Shryock, an official of the California Board of Education, has said that the state is prepared to agree that all minority children would be tested in their primary language (*The New York Times,* September 16, 1979, pp. 1, 66).

To put these data in perspective, let us recall our discussion of race and ability in Chapter 2. There we noted that the quota principle embodied in the so-called permanent immigration law of the United States in 1924 was rationalized on the basis of tests of presumed innate ability developed by psychologists which showed that Italians, Poles, Russians, and Jews scored 25 or 30 IQ points lower than those whose forebears came earlier from northwestern Europe.

In addition to being segregated in minority schools, Mexican American children are sometimes separated by a special curriculum. Various types of ability grouping or "tracking" are used, especially in the Southwest. In the main, children from economically poor homes have lower scores in school achievement. Mexican Americans are, therefore, overrepresented in the lower track in southwestern schools. By junior high school, most children are tracked and by high school it is virtually impossible for a student to be retracked (Moore 1970, p. 80).

The U.S. Commission on Civil Rights (1974, p. 4) found that the curriculum in the schools of the Southwest does not meet the needs of Chicano students. Instead, it is "geared for the white, middle-class monolingual, English-speaking child, excluding the language and culture of Mexican American children" (Mirandé and Enríquez 1979, p. 139).

A study of the Los Angeles school system suggests that an urban area with substantial resources can provide more uniformity between the Mexican American schools and the Anglo schools. Nevertheless, the southwestern pattern is evident in Los Angeles. This study found that the most consistent and important factor affecting the performance of Mexican American children in the Los Angeles system was the educational level of the family; the economic level was less important. Other factors influencing performance were the use of English in the home, pupil attitudes and values, and the ethnic composition and social class level of the school (Moore 1970, p. 84).

In the Southwest, at least 17 percent of all public-school children are Mexican Americans. The proportion would be nearly twice as high except for the dropout rates that eliminate almost half of all Chicano students. Of these students, 9 percent have dropped out by the eighth grade and 40 percent by the twelfth grade (Gomez 1973, p. 102). Nationwide, for every 100 Hispanic children who graduate from high school, 51 drop out (*The New York Times,* April 22, 1979, p. E19). These educational deficits of the early 1970s appeared to Carter and Segura (1978) to have been reduced scarcely at all by 1978.

Coles (1977, p. 360–361) asserts that the imprint of poverty and social discrimination upon Chicano children is obvious. The aloofness and self-restraint that some Anglo teachers have noticed in Mexican American children are related to the attitudes that these teachers have toward their pupils. Judgments that Chicano children speak poorly, are hard to understand, uninterested in learning, unpromising, and not very bright are expressed every day in casual remarks, facial expressions, and the general indifference of these teachers. Children tend to live up to the expectations that others have of them. Chicano children are not exceptions; they tend to perform according to the negative and pessimistic

views of their abilities that many of their teachers hold. In time, a further judgment may be made, namely, that a Mexican American child cannot learn because he or she lacks the intelligence.

Widely held stereotypes affect the way teachers, school officials, and employers interact with Mexican Americans. In an image of long standing, Mexican Americans are a nonmotivated, backward, lackadaisical people who are committed to dozing in the sun, attending festivals, and praying in the churches a great deal. Whereas both Burma and Nova (in Burma 1970) state that those segments of the Mexican American group which are most likely to hold value orientations most like the traditional Mexican culture are those who live in rural areas along the Mexican border, a study by three rural sociologists at Texas A & M University produced quite different conclusions. Wright, Salinas, and Kuvlesky (1973, pp. 46–47) found the youth from three counties selected to fit the criteria mentioned by Burma and Nova—rural, proximity to Mexico, predominantly Mexican American, and agriculturally dependent, to be highly success-oriented. According to these authors, Mexican American young people have high educational goals, and they believe that the parents of these young people endorse such goals. Since many Mexican American families live at or near the poverty level, and since so few adults in the group have had experience with high school and college education, these parents are at a disadvantage in helping to prepare their children to attain their goals and in some cases fear estrangement from them as a result of their superior training.

During the years when the Southwest was primarily agricultural, Mexican immigrants met the need for a reservoir of cheap labor. In society's view, these people had little need for education. Their minimal educational needs were met by schools which turned out pupils who were destined to work in the fields. It is within the framework of this adaptation that language and cultural problems become serious and tend to persist (Ogbu 1978, p. 225). Those who were denied an equal education were thought to be incapable of learning and could logically be assigned a lower status in society. The unequal hierarchy of jobs and income on the basis of group membership was at least as decisive in determining what children would do in later life as were curricula or the efforts of even the best teachers and school administrators. An important reason for the high dropout rate for Chicanos is the realistic view that the school experience is irrelevant to their future jobs, income, and status (Gomez 1973, pp. 104–105; Weinberg 1977, p. 177).

English as a Second Language, Bilingualism, and Biculturalism

Because of their early childhood experience, Mexican Americans sometimes have acquired English as a second language. A decade or more ago, and even more recently, under a kind of linguistic imperialism in the Southwest, penalties have been imposed upon Chicano students for speaking Spanish in the schools or their environs. In many Southwestern schools a form of punishment called Spanish detention existed until at least the early 1970s. This is afterschool detention for having broken the "no-Spanish" rule. This practice produces resentment on the part of Spanish-speakers and causes them to feel that Spanish is an inferior language. Some Anglo-American educators have spoken of Spanish-speaking Mexican Americans as being "illiterate in two languages", without realizing that for many Mexican Americans learning to read Spanish was a part of learning their first language (Cabrera 1971, pp. 126, 437–438).

The limited exposure that many Chicano children have to English often becomes the basis of conflict when they become school pupils. Enrique H. Lopez, a consultant to the Ford Foundation, describes the situation as "schizolingual" (Briggs 1973, p. 17):

Many of us are not really bilingual but schizolingual. We actually speak an amalgam of English and Spanish that creates special problems in education. For every human being, the greatest period of learning is from birth to age 5 and for the Chicano child that learning is taking place in this schizolingual amalgam, which is mostly Spanish. This is the child's principal cognitive tool but the day he enters school it is snatched away from him. You may as well perform a partial lobotomy on him. He's so severely traumatized at a crucial period in kindergarten. When he is forbidden to talk his own language he gets a terrific sense of inferiority and guilt. He begins to dislike himself and his parents and everyone else.

In the 1960s, many schools adopted the "Teaching of English as a Second Language" approach in a effort to help young Mexican American youth learn the English language. In the main, this approach has failed to live up to expectations, and often it has deteriorated into perfunctory drill. The theory behind TESL is that in training children in the basic skills necessary for mobility, Spanish is used initially with children who speak the language at home, but as soon as possible English becomes the primary language and Spanish the secondary one. The hope is that students will continue to study Spanish so that they will become truly bilingual. The assumptions of those who advocate going beyond routine drill in bilingual education are that mastery of English is basic for optimal opportunities in the United States but that Spanish is still needed to provide security, identity, and pride (Cabrera 1971, pp. 60–61; Ortego 1971, p. 132).

Today, the tendency is to regard TESL as a valuable component of bilingual-bicultural education. It is not, however, a bilingual program, nor can it replace a true bilingual program. The practice of never using the child's first language in the classroom, usually because the teacher could not speak it, is now considered less effective than the approach whereby the child is greeted and complimented in Spanish and where respect is shown for his native language and culture (Guerra 1979, p. 129).

In 1968, Congress enacted the Bilingual Education Act, which provided financial help for interested school districts with sizable numbers of people who do not speak English. In 1974, the United States Supreme Court issued a unanimous ruling in *Lau* v. *Nichols,* a case involving Chinese students in San Francisco, that it is a violation of civil rights to teach in English pupils who cannot understand the language. Later in 1974, the Federal District Court of Appeals for the Tenth Circuit confirmed the decision of the District Court of Appeals in Albuquerque that Chicano children attending schools in Portales, New Mexico, School District have a right to bilingual education under Title VI of the 1964 Civil Rights Act. MALDEF (Mexican American Legal Defense and Educational Fund, Inc.) had argued that Chicano children were not receiving an effective education as shown by the high dropout rate of 50 percent, as well as low achievement and reading scores of the children compared with Anglo children, and that these children were thus denied equal protection of the laws as assured by the Fourteenth Amendment. MALDEF also argued that bilingual education was the only acceptable remedy and was to be preferred to ESL (English as a Second Language). Both the lower court and the Tenth Circuit Court agreed.

The lower court held for the school children on the grounds of equal protection, and the Tenth Circuit Court affirmed that decision on the basis of Title VI of the 1964 Civil Rights Act which provides that no person shall be subjected to racial discrimination in any program receiving federal aid. Implicit in the *Serna* v. *Portales* decision is the important point that when a school district has non-English-speaking children it has an obligation to apply for bilingual monies, federal or state (*MALDEF News Letter,* October, 1974, p. 1; *The New York Times,* January 30, 1977).

In the United States as a whole, however, relatively few bilingual teachers had been trained by the fall of 1979 and the requirement that bilingual education be provided for non-English-speaking children had been waived in school districts across the country (*The New York Times,* September 16, 1979, pp. 1, 66).

In 1980, the federal government allocated $170 million to support programs in which a child's first language is used in instruction while help is given in learning English. That sum was more than matched by local and state spending. In addition, support has come from private sources. For example, the Carnegie Corporation has provided $2.6 million for projects related to bilingual education (*The New York Times,* June 22, 1980, p. 39).

A dispute arose in August, 1980, over the rules proposed by the Secretary of the new Department of Education for teaching children with limited or no ability to speak English. The proposed federal rules stipulated that children who have a primary language other than English and score below the fortieth percentile on an English test must be taught required subjects in both English and their native language. The Secretary said that 3.5 million children in the United States had limited English proficiency. Seventy percent of those children are Hispanic. Her staff estimated that 1.3 million would qualify for bilingual education at a cost to the public schools of from $176 million to $592 million. At that time, it was estimated that the schools already spent $169 million to $325 million on special language instruction for 831,000 children, mostly in English as a second language courses rather than in bilingual classes. Leaders of several groups, including the National School Boards Association, the Council of Chief State School Officers, the American Federation of Teachers, and the national associations of elementary and secondary school principals opposed a federal mandate to require schools to teach pupils in their native language.

Conclusion on Public Schools and Mexican Americans

Although there have been some substantial achievements, many Mexican Americans are not well served by the public schools. The problems of Mexican Americans cannot, however, be attributed entirely to education. Their needs are related to politics, jobs, income, housing, and recreation. Education may be the prime agent for the alleviation of many of the conditions faced by a large proportion of Mexican Americans, but if changes in the educational system are to be effective, they must be accompanied by economic and political changes resulting in a more equal distribution of wealth and power in society (Cabrera 1971, p. 13; Brischetto and Arciniega 1973, pp. 41–42).

The Schooling of Puerto Ricans on the Mainland

The Academic Achievements of Puerto Ricans

Puerto Ricans have less formal education than Whites, Blacks, or other Spanish-speaking groups. In 1970, Puerto Ricans had completed about the same average number (8.6) of school years as the United States population had completed forty years earlier. In 1979, 17.6 percent of persons of Spanish origin 25 years old and older had completed less than five years of school. Among Hispanics, Mexican Americans had the highest proportion (23.9 percent) in this educational group, and those of Puerto Rican origin constituted 14.4 percent, of Cuban origin 6.9 percent, and of other Spanish origin 6.7 percent. In the population not of Spanish origin, 2.8 percent had not completed five years of schooling. Of those of Spanish origin in the United States, Mexican Americans and Puerto Ricans had the smallest percentages, 34.9 and 38.6 respectively, of those who had completed four years of high school or more. In comparison, the proportion for the total group of Spanish origin was 42 percent; for those of Cuban origin, 50.4 percent;

other Spanish origin, 60.8 percent; and not of Spanish origin, 68.9 percent (U.S. Bureau of the Census 1980, p. 5).

Educational Problems among Puerto Ricans

In New York City's school system, the nation's largest, 71 percent of the 950,000 pupils are Blacks or Hispanics. Nearly two-thirds of all Spanish-surnamed students in the city's schools were in schools with 99–100 percent minority student enrollments. In East Harlem, 90 percent of the students are Blacks or Puerto Ricans. More than one-third of the pupils in New York City schools are Spanish-speaking— Puerto Ricans, Cubans, Dominicans, and other Latin Americans; approximately five-sixths of that third are Puerto Ricans. In Boston, twelve schools are one-half Puerto Rican and three are all Puerto Rican. In Chicago in 1970, there were 444,631 public school students who spoke only Spanish. Nationally, Latino children are now as concentrated in schools with more than 70 percent minority children enrolled as are black students (Rist 1980, p. 129; Tovar 1970, pp. 62–64; Wagenheim 1975, pp. 60–61; *The New York Times,* October 21, 1979, p. E6).

Dropping out of school is a major problem for Puerto Ricans in the United States. In 1970, among all Puerto Ricans on the mainland, ages 16 to 21, 55 percent were not in school and 36 percent of these dropouts were jobless. Among Puerto Ricans born in the United States, the dropout rate was lower, 39 percent, but 43 percent of these young people were unemployed. In the age group 16 to 21, the dropout rate for all Americans in the Northeast was 32 percent, with an unemployment rate for dropouts of 16 percent. Although Puerto Ricans represented only 3 percent of the males, ages 16 to 21, in the Northeast, they constituted 5 percent of the school dropouts and over 12 percent of the unemployed (Wagenheim 1975, p. 20).

In 1979, the 112 high schools in the New York City system had a dropout rate of about 45 percent. Approximately 55 percent of the black students and 65 percent of the Puerto Rican students drop out before the twelfth grade (*The New York Times,* October 12, 1979, p. 6E). In Chicago, it is estimated that 70 percent of all Puerto Rican and Mexican American children who enter the public schools never graduate from high school (Wagenheim 1975, pp. 61–62).

In New York City, about 100,000 of the Hispanic students have a poor command of English, and 86 percent are below normal in reading levels for their age and grade. In the early 1970s, the city had 22 bilingual programs, but only 4,000 children were enrolled. More than 100,000 Hispanic children who needed linguistic help were unaffected. At that time, a Board of Education study stated that 4,200 bilingual classroom teachers were needed, but the city had only 800. According to Wagenheim (1975, pp. 24–25) and Fuentes (1974, pp. 18–19), the powerful teachers' union in New York City showed that it was more concerned with its own survival and maintaining the status quo than in facing this educational crisis.

A Boston study (Wagenheim 1975, p. 60) claims that "not one guidance counselor" in the entire school system could speak Spanish, that only 4 of 5,800 teachers were Puerto Rican, and that the Boston schools had no secretaries, administrators, clerical workers, reading specialists, science specialists, art specialists, truant officers, librarians, or janitors from the Spanish-speaking community.

Many Puerto Ricans have believed that school authorities have been determined not to educate their children. Many Puerto Rican students have believed that teachers and other school staff are prejudiced against them. After sustained community pressure and two federal court decisions on the absence of black and Puerto Rican principals, the New York system modified its policy and undertook a more affirmative program of recruitment of Puerto Ricans and Blacks as supervisory personnel (Weinberg 1977, p. 258).

The Schooling of American Indians

Indian Pupils and Their Schools

Indian children attend school in a variety of settings ranging from isolated rural areas to major urban centers. These settings vary with respect to employment opportunities, language spoken in the home, degree of Indian ancestry, the proportion of non-Indians in attendance at school, and the types of schools attended. In 1978 there were approximately 275,000 Indians between the ages of 6 and 17, and about 90 percent of them were enrolled in school. Estimates of the number of children in four types of schools attended by Indians are presented in Table 15-2 (Fuchs and Havighurst 1972, p. 38; Havighurst 1978, p. 17).

The usual argument in favor of the federal boarding schools is that the size of the Navajo reservation, from which 20,000 of the pupils come, and that the isolation of families precludes the attendance of children at BIA day schools.

Indian leaders are aware of the problems associated with Indian boarding schools: curricula, teacher training, personnel services for pupils, dormitory arrangements, and locations of the schools, and they have made many suggestions for change. They acknowledge, however, that the boarding schools function in important ways, including the offering of programs for the special needs of many Indian children, the employment of Indian people, and the provision of food, clothing, shelter, and medical care to many children whose families have difficulty providing for them. Also, the federal schools symbolize the commitment of the federal government to Indian education (Fuchs and Havighurst 1972, p. 244).

Los Angeles has the largest urban Indian population in the United States, as well as the largest number of Indian children and youth in school—more than 2,000. Minneapolis–St. Paul has the next largest number of urban Indian residents, with approximately 8,000 Indians and 1,700 Indian pupils in school. Other major urban centers with large Indian populations include the San Francisco Bay area, Oklahoma City, Tulsa, Phoenix, and Chicago (Fuchs and Havighurst 1972, p. 275).

As we indicate later in this section, advances have been made in recent years in Indian education, but the educational level of Indians remains below that of the general population. For all Indians under federal supervision, the average educational attainment is less than six years. The dropout rates of Indian children are twice the national average (Stewart 1977, p. 518).

Achievement and Underachievement of Indian Pupils

As a group, Indian pupils stand below national averages on standard tests of school achievement. Beginning with the third grade, Indian children attain a level about one year below national averages, and at the senior high school ages they are approximately two years below national averages (Havighurst 1978, p. 18).

Fuchs and Havighurst (1972, p. 119) point out that the factors which depress American Indian school achievement are complex, involving ability, the family, the school itself, the community, culture change, and the relations of native Americans to the larger society. These investigators attribute a large part of the school achievement of pupils to factors other than the school. For example, many Indian children live in homes and communities in which there are major differences between the cultural expectations of parents and those of teachers and school officials. The Coleman report cites cultural deprivation as a major factor influencing the

Table 15-2. Estimates of the Number of Children in Four Types of Schools

	Enrollment	Percentage of total group
Schools with practically all-Indian enrollment:		
BIA-operated boarding and day schools	47,000	17
Indian-controlled School Boards: Contract with BIA		
(estimated)	2,500	1
Mission or other private schools	9,000	3
Public schools operating on or contiguous to reservations	30,000	11
Public Schools with 50 to 90 percent Indian enrollment:		
Contiguous to Indian reservations or in Indian		
communities	105,000	38
Public schools with 10 to 50 percent Indian enrollment:		
Mainly in rural communities and small cities	50,000	18
Public schools with 1 to 10 percent Indian enrollment:		
Mainly in large cities	30,000	11

academic achievement of Indian children, but cultural differences rather than cultural deprivation would be a more accurate term. In addition to cultural differences, conditions of poverty, isolation, nonparticipation in urban-industrial society, and language differences also affect performance on the usual tests of academic achievement (Beuf 1977, pp. 32–33; Fuchs and Havighurst 1972, p. 299). Citing several studies based on intelligence tests which do not require reading ability, Havighurst comments that the relatively low academic achievement of Indian children is not attributable to an average intelligence lower than that of white children (Havighurst 1978, p. 18).

Curricula, Language, and Teachers

In most BIA schools, the curriculum has followed Anglo culture, and in the public schools the curriculum is the same for Indians and non-Indians. Since Indian parents want nothing less for their children than the curriculum offered to other Americans, they tend to accept the curriculum as offered. However, many would like the schools to give some recognition to Indian identity (Fuchs and Havighurst 1972, p. 221).

As is the case in the education of Mexican Americans and Puerto Ricans, the language problem is important in the schooling of Native Americans, especially in the reservation situation. Children who have spoken a tribal language or "reservation English" until first grade, find themselves in classrooms where basic instruction is conducted in a language they may find hard to understand. When these children are tested, their performance is judged on national norms (Beuf 1977, p. 30).

The Bilingual Education Act, part of the Elementary and Secondary Education Act since 1967, provides funds for the employment of teachers who speak the local language in Indian and Eskimo communities. This act emphasizes the use of the pupil's home language when he is learning to read. This method has been used with Navaho children; a Navaho orthography has existed for some time, and children's books have been printed in that language. Soon after Navaho students enter school, they begin to learn English as a second language. This procedure enables them to progress in reading as rapidly as Anglo pupils can. Indian children who speak English at home use the tribal language as a second language to be learned after the student has used English in the school. In a community where English predominates, bilingual education uses teachers who accept whatever language the child prefers and who begin a program of the native language, as a second language, when pupils are nine or ten years old. If the native language is predominant in the community, bilingual teachers emphasize English in the school when the children are about the same age (Havighurst 1978, pp. 24–25).

Closely related to the question of language in the schools is the study of Indian history and culture. Indian students need to acquire skills which will help them occupationally, learn their civil and political rights, find out how to obtain necessary social services, and understand how to deal with employers, credit managers, and salespeople. To accompany these and other skills, the inclusion of Indian culture and history in the school curriculum would allow the student to develop a positive Indian identity. The achievement of such an identity would increase his chances of being able to function in either the Indian community or the larger society (Chadwick 1972, p. 132). Students of Indian education also advocate such studies as a means of promoting mutual understanding and appreciation of the various native cultures by the bearers of these cultures. In schools where Indian pupils constitute the majority, Indian youth can be helped to understand their own tribal history and culture by reading material that deals with the local tribal group and by utilizing tribal elders to tell stories and exhibit crafts which they know. In teaching Indian history and cultures accurately, serious problems may arise when attempts are made to make the material interesting and effective for Anglo pupils and for the wide variety of American Indian tribes. As yet, very few textbooks for use in grade school or in high school which present accurate information are available. The BIA offers an optional course on Native American cultures for its teachers, but few take the opportunity to learn about the societies from which their students come. History in these schools is taught from the white perspective, which means that Indian children are exposed to the same colorful but distorted portrayal of their own people as white children (Beuf 1977, p. 34).

Approximately 15,000 elementary and secondary schoolteachers teach at least two Indian pupils daily. About 7,000 of these teachers are engaged in teaching classes with a preponderance of Indian boys and girls—1,800 in Bureau of Indian Affairs boarding and day schools; 4,900 in public schools located on or near Indian reservations; and 300 teachers in mission and other private schools. About 3,000 teach in public schools with five to fifteen Indian pupils in their classes, mainly in towns and rural areas. Another 5,000 teach in cities over 50,000, with two to five Indian pupils (Fuchs and Havighurst 1972, pp. 191, 203).

It should be emphasized that the majority of Indian pupils attend public schools with white students and are taught in classes with white children by the same teachers. A long-time student of Indian education thinks that these teachers are probably a cross-section of teachers in towns and rural sections of the country west of the Mississippi, as well as in the twenty or more large cities that have relatively large Indian populations (Havighurst 1978, pp. 18–19).

The Funding of Indian Education

The most important law providing for federal–state cooperation in Indian affairs is the Johnson–O'Malley Act of April 16, 1934 (48 Stat. 596). Under this law the Secretary of the Interior is authorized to enter into contracts with states and private institutions "for the education, medical attention, agricultural assistance, and social welfare, including relief of distress of Indians in each State or Territory, through the qualified agencies of each State or Territory" (Haas 1957, p. 19). Under the Johnson–O'Malley Act, public schools in which Native American children are enrolled may receive payments from the Bureau of Indian Affairs for every Indian child in the school. Although one of the purposes of this act was to improve the quality of Indian education through the use of these funds for remedial language programs and other programs of special help to Native American children, there has been flagrant violation of this intent. Schools have used Johnson–O'Malley funds for various purposes, for example, for pianos and new football fields which Indian children have never used. It is only recently that legislation has given tribal groups control over their own Johnson–O'Malley funds (Beuf 1977, p. 35).

Levitan and Johnston conclude that the elementary and secondary education of Indian children is more than adequately funded, if not adequately targeted, particularly when it is compared with that of other disadvantaged pupils throughout the United States. For example, in 1974, public school systems with approximately 135,000 children enrolled received $52 million in ESEA (Elementary and Secondary Education Act) funds, $42 million in federal aid to impacted areas, and $42 million under the Indian Education Act, in addition to $25 million in Johnson–O'Malley funds. These allocations amounted to a supplement of about $1,200 per Native American child, compared with state and local education funds that averaged about $1,200 per child in fiscal 1973 in the reservation states. The problem in this funding is that some of the funds intended for the education of Indian children do not reach their pupils; sometimes they are diluted among all children in these districts (Levitan and Johnston 1975, pp. 41–42).

In the early 1970s, the federal government provided funds to assist Native Americans in revising and directing their educational systems. The Indian Education Act of 1972 and the Indian Self-Determination and Educational Assistance Act of 1975 provide funds and require Indian direction for the design of educational programs. The Bilingual Education Act, a part of the Elementary and Secondary Education Act since 1967, provides money to employ teachers who speak the local language in Indian and Eskimo communities (Havighurst 1978, pp. 20–21).

Under the Indian Education Act and for fiscal 1976, approximately $18 million was allocated to school and tribal education projects through 210 separate grants. These projects were intended to supplement existing education programs and to train Indian personnel for work in schools. These funds made possible the expansion of the program started in the late 1960s whereby the Bureau of Indian Affairs contracted with a reservation school board to provide the money that would have been used to operate a BIA school to the Indian Board, with this body assuming the responsibility for the school. The first of these contract schools was the Rough Rock school on the Navaho Reservation. This school begins teaching in the Navaho language and emphasizes Navaho tradition and arts (Havighurst 1978, p. 22).

The expenditure of money is necessary for the improvement of Indian education, but, as Fuchs and Havighurst (1972, p. 298) point out, money alone will not solve the problem. The problem of Indian education is complex and requires consideration of the total Indian–White situation, including factors that are not located in the schools and over which the schools have little control. These external factors include the kind of relationships that exist in the community between Indians and non-Indians, as well as the socioeconomic context within which Indians live. Merely spending more money on the education of Indian children in their present schools seems unlikely to produce much improvement in the educational performance of Native Americans.

Among the steps which have been suggested for modifying the relationships between Indians and non-Indians is to include Indian parents on the local school board and give them an influential voice in policy decisions. Reservation schools serving only Indians could be turned over to the tribe when the members have the ability and interest in operating them. Such actions would increase the influence of Indians on the curricula and this parental interest might increase student interest and motivation (Chadwick 1972, p. 142).

The possibilities for Indian control of the schools that Indians attend vary greatly from community to community. It is important that plans for local control be flexible and responsive to the heterogeneity of Indian community life. Many Indian communities are divided by factions advocating different educational policies. Community leaders on the reservations and in the towns near reservations expect the school system to contribute to improvement in the economic position of Indians, but they also favor increased teaching of Indian culture and history. Usually they are more critical of the schools than are the parents but do not demand revolutionary change. Increased responsibility in policy decisions in the local school system by community leaders would tend to cause them to support programs of relatively conservative change (Fuchs and Havighurst 1972, pp. 189–190, 321–22).

A second step for improving the academic performance of Indian students is the development of their own adult education program. Among the possibilities that have been suggested are brief workshops in prenatal care, a program in operating heavy construction equipment, and a course in development planning in connection with the establishment of a particular industry on the reservation. The planning and operation of an adult education program by Indian people might lead to a greater appreciation of the practical benefits of education, increased interest in educational achievement, and greater facility in English by parents and children (Chadwick 1972, p. 142).

A third step which might improve Indian education would be the provision of guidance counselors for the whole community. Preferably, such counselors would be well-trained Indians who could provide assistance concerning legal aid, vocational guidance and placement, marital conflict, and alcohol and drug problems (Chadwick 1972, pp. 142–43).

Some encouraging developments in Indian education are discernible. Indians are staying in school longer, a larger proportion is graduating from high school, and more Native Americans are attending college. More Indian teachers are available to teach in Indian schools. Congress has appropriated increased funds for Indian schooling. The quality of educational services appears to be improving, in part due to greater parental and tribal involvement in school systems, especially in communities where federal funds have been channeled through Indian organizations (Levitan and Johnston 1975, p. 45).

CHAPTER 16

The Education of Racial and Cultural Minorities in the United States (Continued)

During the last generation, several factors have increased the enrollment of minority students in colleges and universities. Urbanization, changes in the occupational world that require more training, the growth of the middle classes, private efforts, and governmental programs are among those factors. These have collided with a number of forces that we shall be discussing as we examine the changes in the levels and kinds of higher education among Blacks, Hispanics, and Native Americans.

Black Americans and Higher Education

In 1960, approximately 16 percent of the white men in the United States 25 to 29 and 5 percent of the black men said they were college graduates. This difference increased gradually and, in 1979, 27 percent of the white men compared to 13 percent of the black men had completed college. Similarly, a gap existed between the proportion of white and black women finishing college, but the rise was greater among white women. These differences are shown in Figure 16-1 (Farley 1982, pp. B–68).

In recent years, the college enrollment rates for Blacks have generally risen more rapidly than for Whites. The proportion of Blacks in the age group 18–24 enrolled in colleges almost doubled from 1965 to 1981—from 10.3 percent to 19.4 percent. During that time, the proportion among Whites stayed at approximately 26 percent (Reid 1982, p. 24).

During the 1970s, the enrollment rates of white men began to fall while those of black men and women continued to rise at least through 1976. As a result of those changes, racial differences in college enrollment rates in the late 1970s were somewhat smaller than in the 1960s. Enrollment rates at the college level will not converge soon; in the fall of 1980, about 28 percent of the white men 18–24 were in college, compared to 18 percent of the black men. Black women are approaching white women in college attendance more rapidly than black men are approaching white men. These differences are shown in Figure 16-2 (Farley 1982, pp. B9–11).

Black Students in Predominantly White Colleges

Less than half of the black high-school seniors who aspire to enter college actually enroll, compared with two-thirds of the white seniors aspiring to college who actually enroll (Institute for the Study

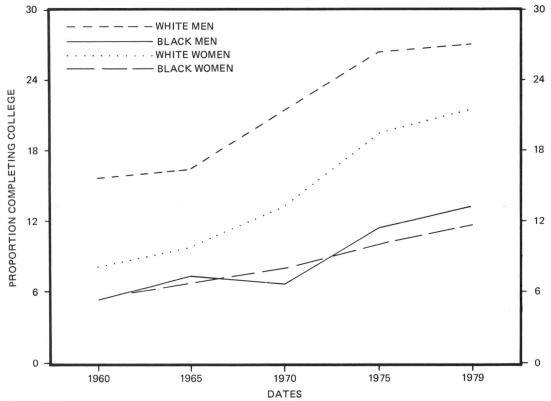

Figure 16–1. Proportion of persons 25 to 29 who completed 4 or more years of college by race and sex,1960–1979. Sources: U. S. Bureau of the Census, *Census of Population: 1960*, Vol. 1, Part. 1, Table 173; *Census of Population: 1970*, Vol. I, Part 1, Table 199; *Current Population Reports*, Series P-20, No. 158, Table 4; No. 294, Table 1; No. 356, Table 1. Data for 1960 refer to Whites and Nonwhites.

of Educational Policy 1976, p. 46). Nevertheless, black college enrollment has doubled and redoubled in the past twenty years. In 1960, there were about 200,000 black college students; in 1982, there were over one million (although some declines began in that year). More than half the black college students in 1960 attended the historic black colleges (Monro 1978, p. 13). Now over four-fifths of black students attend predominantly white colleges (*Wall Street Journal*, March 8, 1982, p. 1).

Public universities in the United States enroll a higher percentage of low-income Whites than low-income Blacks, and a higher proportion of bright, poor Whites than bright, poor Blacks. The American Council on Education reported in 1973 that public universities enrolled only 27 percent of white freshmen with grade-point averages of B plus or better from families with incomes under $4,000 and 30 percent from families with incomes under $6,000. They enrolled only 7 percent and 10

percent, respectively, of equally bright and economically disadvantaged black freshmen (Fairfax 1978, p. 40).

Viewing the educational system as a pipeline, Astin (1982, pp. 174–75) identifies five "leakage" points at which disproportionately large numbers of minority group students drop out: completion of high school, entry to college, completion of college, entry to graduate or professional school, and completion of graduate or professional school. Figure 16-3 shows the educational pipeline for four minorities, compared with Whites. The loss of minorities at these transition points strongly influences their large underrepresentation in positions of influence in American life.

New York State has been outstanding in increasing the number of minority students in the postsecondary system. Various opportunity programs make it possible for economically and educationally disadvantaged persons to enroll at a state university, a city university in New York City, or one

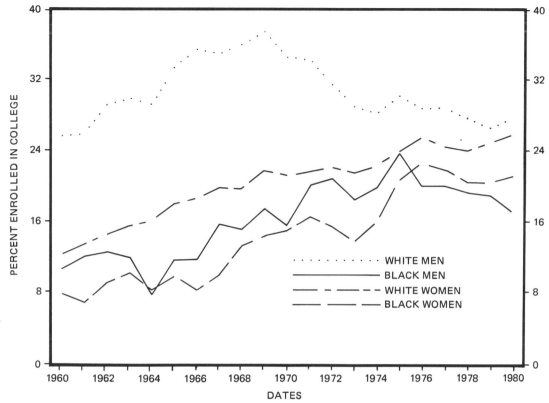

Figure 16–2. College attendance of persons 18 to 24 by race and sex, 1960–1980. Sources: U.S. Bureau of the Census, *Current Population Reports,* Series P-20, Nos. 110, 117, 126, 129, 148, 162, 167, 190, 206, 222, 241, 260, 272, 286, 303, 319, 333, 346, 360, 362.

of the private colleges and universities in the state. Grants from these programs enable colleges to admit and subsidize disadvantaged minority students who do not meet the institution's regular admissions requirements. In the late 1970s, 16 percent of the total number of entering freshmen were from various minority groups, a higher percentage than the proportion of minority persons in the traditional college-age population (Nyquist 1978, p. 25). No other state has matched this record.

Black students are most underrepresented in the total enrollment of large public universities and private four-year colleges and best represented in public four-year and two-year colleges (Institute for the Study of Educational Policy 1976, 65–66). The attrition rate of Blacks and other minority students in community colleges is exceedingly heavy. One study found that these colleges experienced a drop between freshmen and sophomore years of about two-thirds—more than double the rate for all community college students (Weinberg 1977,

p. 325). This study and similar findings by others indicate that equal opportunity programs require effective remediation for past educational disadvantage.

Increased Number of Black Students in White Colleges. In the period 1968–1970, when predominantly white institutions of higher learning began to increase the enrollment of black students, many white administrators and faculty members soon learned that it was not enough simply to bring black students to the campus and assume that they would survive and thrive. Many white colleges, like the thirteen institutions studied by a University of Michigan research group, recruited black students with backgrounds unlike the middle- or upper-class backgrounds from which the small numbers of black students previously on these campuses had come. Most of the new students came from working-class families or from disadvantaged families in urban ghettos. Typically, they were the first in their families to attend college. Competition for

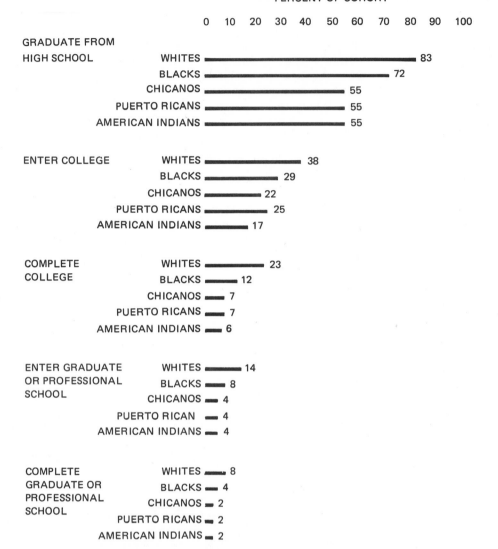

Figure 16–3. The educational pipeline for minorities. Source: A. W. Astin, *Minorities in Higher Education: Recent Trends, Current Prospects, and Recommendations.* Jossey-Bass, 1982,p. 174.

students, especially in moderately and minimally selective colleges, frequently led to accepting whoever could be enrolled (Gamson 1978, pp. 163–64).

In more recent years, colleges and universities have given more attention to their recruiting programs, trying not to enroll students who are unable to cope with college work even with adequate financial aid and efficient support programs (Proctor and Johnston 1978, pp. 66–67). Such efforts have not always been sufficient to find qualified minority students.

Monro (1978, p. 15) asserts that 10 to 15 percent of the entering class at Miles College, an open-door college in Birmingham, Alabama, could do the work required by the more selective colleges and universities. With little or no remedial work, these students proceed to college-level work, often succeeding with honors. The barriers between these students and the more selective institutions are acquaintance, student and family aspirations, finances, and entrance tests.

Critics of the model of selective admissions based on test scores and prior grades advocate selecting students who are likely to be influenced by the educational process, regardless of their entering performance level. This is the "value-added" approach to the goals of higher education. In the case of advanced professional education such as medicine and law, these critics believe that a careful analysis should be made of how much additional time the less well prepared minority student will require to complete certification standards, how much the dropout rate will increase, and how much would be needed in additional resources. In our view, it is realistic to expect that the standardized test and the predictive model of admissions will continue to be widely used for the foreseeable future. However, unless some changes are made, these admissions procedures will continue to constitute serious barriers to the educational development of many minority students (Astin 1982, p. 149).

Characteristics of Black Students in Predominantly White Colleges. Boyd (1974, p. 5–6) found that 90 percent of the black students in colleges with largely white enrollments were graduates of public high schools. Most black students go to college in their home areas, and most maintain at least a C average. Usually, black students obtain adequate help with their financial problems by combining the resources available to them (Boyd 1974, p. 5). From two-thirds to three-quarters of black students share several important characteristics. Financial aid (loans, scholarships, and veterans' benefits) is the primary source of funds for 68 percent of the students. Whatever their primary source of money is, most black students supplement it by working. Seventy-three percent said that they currently held at least one job. Of these students, 54 percent reported working from eleven to twenty hours per week, and one-third thought that working had a negative effect on their college experience.

As this is written, federal budget policy and a serious recession have weakened the support programs for minority and other low-income students. The effects began to be felt in the autumn of 1982 (*The New York Times*, November 18, 1982, p. 1). How persistent those effects are depends, of course, on many economic and policy factors.

Four other distinctions among black students in Boyd's study (1974, p. 8) are of special interest.

Neither parent of 59 percent of the students had attended college. Fifty-six percent came from large cities. Family incomes of 54 percent were less than $10,000. Fifty-two percent considered their preparation for college as fair or poor, and half felt that they were "special admits."

Boyd reports several significant differences between black men and women at predominantly white colleges. These differences, similar to those between white men and white women, pertain to family and educational backgrounds, as well as academic behavior and opinions related to background. Black women in predominantly white colleges tend to come from richer and more highly educated families than black men. Boyd comments that the pattern of differences between men and women probably creates tensions in the black student population, adding that unfavorable reciprocal stereotypes of the black man and the black woman can be minimized by recruiting black men and women who are similar in background (Boyd 1974, pp. 18–19).

In the University of Michigan study, a high proportion of the minority students at thirteen colleges and universities received financial aid; in some cases this aid was close to 100 percent. Black students needed academic and social support as well as financial support. The thirteen institutions provided the nonfinancial support in a variety of forms: one-to-one tutoring, special courses or sections of regular courses, and precollege courses; academic, career, and personal counseling; day-care provisions; medical and dental services; and cultural programs (Gamson 1978, p. 174).

Tensions on White Campuses with Increase in Black Students. When black students were recruited in larger numbers at the end of the 1960s, white students assumed that they would want to be integrated with white students. This assumption proved to be fallacious in many instances. Administrators and faculty members assumed further that most Blacks, regardless of their educational background, would perform satisfactorily in the existing academic environment, or, when this was not the case, with small amounts of remedial work. It was thought also that the new students would be satisfied with the courses and programs already in existence. Very few faculty members and administrators had thought of a course in black studies, or a major, a department, or a degree in black studies. It was expected that the admission of black students into white middle-class institutions would be accepted with gratitude. Such was not the case (Blackburn, Gamson, and Peterson 1978, pp. 310–311).

Large sums of money became available for minority programs and financial aid in the late 1960s and early 1970s, and black enrollments increased rapidly. The new students did not adjust quietly to the programs and standards of the white colleges. They demanded more, challenging norms of rational debate, organizing sit-ins, sometimes taking over buildings, and often rejecting white support and advice. The atmosphere was charged; top administrators were placed in negotiating roles, and faculty members questioned the legitimacy and status of new courses and programs that were proposed or introduced (Blackburn et al. 1978, p. 311).

Many of the predominantly white colleges and universities tried to minimize conflict by establishing separate student organizations and separate support services, and in some cases, separate academic programs. Because of the diversity of interests among Blacks and increased enrollment of other minority groups, these arrangements caused serious problems. Separate programs and organizations for every minority meant a duplication of effort and was expensive. Combining programs also presented problems. Nonblack minorities were reluctant to join a larger unit in which they felt themselves to be a minority within a minority. Because of different staffing needs, the joint "ethnic studies" approach was difficult to implement (Blackburn et al. 1978, p. 319).

On the whole, the response to increased numbers of black students on predominantly white campuses during the late 1960s and the early 1970s was not encouraging. White students, faculty members, and administrators expected to see integrated student bodies and programs. The first groups of black students were more militant than anticipated. Considerable hostility and tension arose between black and white students, and many separate black clubs, organizations, and living patterns were created (Peterson and Davenport 1978, p. 207). Tensions between black students and white faculty members in all thirteen institutions in the University of Michigan study were not so extensive as the report of tensions between black and white students (Peterson 1978b, p. 221).

Boyd (1974, p. 13) criticizes the assertion by both Whites and Blacks that Blacks want to withdraw as completely as possible from contact with Whites and that they should be allowed or encouraged to do so while studying in predominantly white institutions. Boyd challenges the belief of many Whites that black dormitories, black student organizations, black tables or areas in the student union, and Black Studies programs indicate that most black students are separatists. When institutional climates are based on false assumptions, however, the situation may become one in which most black students become separatists. Boyd found evidence that separatism is a minority viewpoint among black students. For example, his findings on preferred living arrangements in forty colleges and universities are presented in Table 16-1.

With college enrollments beginning to decline, the effects of inflation on college finances, less zeal on the part of the students for social reform and more concern about their personal interests, affirmative action, and minority programs in general began to slow down in the late 1970s and early 1980s. Racial conflicts on college campuses were infrequent and relatively minor. The most extended disorder, in which a black-led group of approximately seventy students held an eight-day sit-in, took place at Amherst College. The chairman of the Black Student Union and other black students at Amherst insisted that the Ivy League schools "had no serious and continuous commitment to the needs of black students." At Harvard, student protestors linked the issues of black studies and divestiture of stocks in companies doing business in South Africa. Blacks said that without this linkage, the cooperation of white students on the black studies issue could not have been obtained (*The New York Times*, May 20, 1979, p. 47).

In four predominantly white colleges in upstate New York, black students reported that white students tended to treat them as if they were invisible

Table 16-1. Actual and Preferred Living Arrangements of 979 Black Students

	Housing (Percentage)	
	Actual	Preferred
Dorm that mixed Whites and Blacks	48%	20%
All Black, or minority dorm, floor, or wing	4%	15%
Private, off-campus apartment or room	24%	46%
Parent's Home	18%	9%

and to insist that they conform to the norms of the majority. Trust between black and white students appears to decrease with increased contact on predominantly white college campuses. Willie (1981, p. 76) comments that an understanding of what to expect initially from the coming together of previously estranged populations should prevent disillusionment.

Black Colleges

Of the 111 predominantly black colleges and universities in the United States in 1982, 39 are public and 72 are private. Approximately two-thirds of the colleges are fully accredited by the appropriate regional agencies. Although only four-tenths of the black students were enrolled in predominantly black colleges in the 1970s, the majority of black college graduates earned their degrees from these colleges. The proportion was about 35 or 40 percent by 1982 despite the fact that the historically black colleges enrolled less than 20 percent of the black students (*The New York Times*, March 28, 1982, p. 14), indicating that a higher proportion of black students completed their degree programs from those colleges than from the predominantly white schools.

Teaching is emphasized in black colleges. Less time is spent by faculty members on research and writing than in other colleges, and more time on classroom activities, personal counseling, and sponsoring student organizations (Thompson 1978, p. 190). The task of providing compensatory aid or development services is a formidable one in most black colleges. Attempts must be made to provide such assistance without reducing the quality of the academic experience and without engendering in the students a feeling of inferiority and resentment. This is a requirement because the majority of the students have been "prepared" in overcrowded, understaffed, and underequipped schools (Ford 1973, pp. 46–47).

With the exception of the student bodies in the dozen or so more selective private and public black colleges, the majority of students in black colleges have been inadequately prepared for entrance upon college work. Monro (1978, p. 15) writes about the students in Miles College, a so-called open-door college:

In Birmingham, where most of our students come from, we see and deal firsthand with all the problems of poor preparation and low-level aspiration that the Howard (Howard University, *Equal Educational Opportunity for Blacks: An Assessment*, 1976) statistics sketch out. Half of the 300 students in our entering class read at the eighth-to-ninth grade level or below. They have had little mathematics and no science. They know little of the world around them because they do not read newspapers or magazines. They have never been pressed to solve intellectual problems at home or in school and, thus, in Jean Piaget's terms, are still deep in a "concrete" mode of mental operations. Most of the students have never been more than 50 miles from home. Most of their parents did not get through high school. To become an accountant or a policeman or to get a federal job in social security, those are major career goals for even the most gifted. Our freshmen take the ACT (American College Testing Program Assessment) but most score in the range of 6 to 10; the state university usually requires a composite score of 18 for admission.

In terms of interest, and of knowledge of ways to bridge the gap between the educational backgrounds of black students and the skills essential for doing college-level work, black schools generally are better equipped than predominantly white schools to assist the poorly prepared student. An important aspect of this question is English language instruction. Although black English is surrounded by political and social controversy, the general operating principle at Miles College in teaching English has been that the instructional task is to teach standard English—vocabulary, sentence structure, paragraph formation. It is thought that teachers who are thoroughly familiar with black English can help the student in their use of language. Monro (1978, p. 246) cites the case of a class that undertook to translate scenes from *Oedipus Rex* into black English and to stage the scenes in dialect, calling it "a marvelous exercise in translation."

Economic pragmatism may be more of a problem among students in black colleges than in white colleges. Thompson (1978, p. 187–188) says that only a few of the students he has known regard higher education as inherently good and satisfying in itself and that this rather extreme pragmatism often militates against their success academically because they become bored in required courses which seem to have little relevance to their occupational goals. It is often claimed, however, that black colleges are more flexible in combining the liberal arts and vocationally oriented courses than white colleges are (Willie and MacLeish 1978, p. 143).

In 1967, Jencks and Riesman (p. 48) stated that typically the sixty "obscure" private black colleges were small, with only one or two enrolling more than 1,000 students, and most having fewer than 500. Most of these colleges were said to have a small faculty and a budget of around half of a million dollars. This is not the full pictures, however. Less than ten years later, Willie and Mac-Leish (1978, p. 134–37) studied twenty-one of eighty-eight four-year schools in the National Association for Equal Opportunity in Higher Education. The average size of the student body in fifteen black colleges which provided detailed statistical data was 2,800. Only five of these fifteen colleges had student bodies under 1,000, and all of these had enrollments of more than 500. The average size of the full-time faculty was 154; only three of these fifteen schools had fewer than fifty faculty members. Total budgets ranged from $1.8 million to $28.6 million, with an average of $9.9 million. Their average instructional budget was $4.1 million; none had a total budget, or even an instructional budget, of less than $500,000.

The forty-one predominantly black colleges and universities constituting the membership of the United Negro College Fund are private, fully accredited, four-year institutions (three offer graduate degrees). These schools enroll approximately 50,000 students from 50 states and 62 countries. The majority of students attending these colleges require financial aid. No discrimination because of race, creed, or color exists in these schools. The faculties have always been biracial, and the student bodies are becoming more so. Nearly one-fifth of the graduates go on to graduate schools.

Among their achievements, black colleges and universities have produced a large majority of the black leadership in America. About 85 percent of the black physicians and dentists, approximately 80 percent of the black lawyers, more than 70 percent of the black elected officials, over 80 percent of the black military officers, and thousands of college professors, teachers, librarians, social workers, ministers, and trained businessmen are graduates of these schools (Robinson 1978, p. 158; Ford 1973, p. 47).

In 1978, 74 percent of the students in black colleges came from families whose annual income was less than $12,500, while the annual family income of approximately 71 percent of all college students was $12,500 and over (Thompson 1978, p. 187).

During the 1970's, a number of black private colleges experienced serious financial crises. In 1972, several of these colleges could not meet their monthly payrolls. In two cases, drastic cuts in teaching and nonteaching personnel were announced for the following year. Among the colleges in difficulty were two of the four that the Ford Foundation had selected as the most promising of the private group with the promise that each would be given annually more than a million dollars for the following six years (Ford 1973, p. 172). The scarcity of funds available at the black colleges is seen in the size of the gross combined endowments of the forty-one members colleges of the United Negro College Fund. The total, about $100 million dollars in 1974, is much less than the endowment of many of the prestigious white institutions (Robinson 1978, p. 158).

Sixteen states have separate land-grant colleges for Whites and Blacks. Historically, great inequities have existed in the appropriations made by states in support of the two sets of schools. For example, in fiscal year 1971, the white schools were allocated approximately $87 million by the Department of Agriculture. The black schools, through their main source of federal agricultural funding, were allocated $286,000, or about $18,000 per school. When combined with matching funds from state and local governments, funds for the sixteen white colleges for the year ending on June 20, 1972, were $267.7 million for research and extension work, compared with a total of $16.8 million received by the black schools for programs related to agriculture (*The New York Times*, October 17, 1976, p. 34).

As we have noted, black colleges now enroll less than 20 percent of black students. Although foundations and corporations have provided considerable funds to predominantly white colleges for campaigns to recruit black students, black private colleges have been unsuccessful in obtaining large grants to provide scholarship money to attract white students. In the South, white students attend predominantly black colleges in significant numbers only if there are no predominantly white colleges in the community or if the predominantly black colleges are public institutions with low tuition rates (Willie and MacLeish 1978, p. 142). A study of Whites on predominantly black college campuses (Standley 1978) found that Whites were receiving a career-oriented and liberal arts education from competent teachers. These students hoped that the schools would recruit more Whites, wished that their extracurricular and social experiences were as comfortable as their educational programs, and expressed doubts about the sincerity of and intentions of the schools' administrators (Willie 1981, p. 84).

A dilemma of many black colleges in recent years is that of recruiting and retaining enough black faculty to balance nonblack personnel. These colleges are now flooded with applications from Whites who are highly trained and experienced and who are willing to accept lower salaries than Blacks of similar training and experience (Ford 1973, p. 45). A special problem is seen in the underrepresentation of Blacks in the sciences. A National Science Foundation report (1975) indicated that in 1972 there were approximately 9,700 black scientists, fewer than 2 percent of the total of 496,000 scientists in the United States. Among the 143,000 scientists holding the doctorate, there were 1,300 Blacks, fewer than 1 percent of the total holding doctorates in science. There were four black scientists per 10,000 total black population, compared with twenty-seven white scientists per 10,000 total white population (McBay 1978, p. 216).

The Future of Black Colleges. In the past, appropriations for black public institutions have been minuscule compared with those for buildings, equipment, teaching, and research in the white public colleges, and these inequalities are not likely to change markedly.

The private black colleges will probably continue to have serious financial problems, as well as enrollment and staffing difficulties. Foundaiton and corporate support for current and capital operations is problematic. Private gifts may or may not increase, but student aid for black students and institutional aid from the federal government has been reduced. It is doubtful whether substantial grants to provide scholarship money for white students to enroll in black schools (in the way that funds have been obtained for black students to attend predominantly white colleges) will be available from any source.

Nevertheless, if history is any guide, most of the private and public black colleges will survive in the 1980s demonstrating again their resilience; some will disappear. The faculties of most predominantly black schools will continue to be diversified. These institutions will continue to accept students of all backgrounds. Changes in the composition of the student body will not, in most cases,

eliminate the orientation of these schools toward the black heritage and the black community. Black colleges will continue to do what many white colleges are beginning to do, namely, combine liberal arts with vocationally oriented courses (Willie and Cunnigen 1981, pp. 177–198).

Black Studies Programs

Objectives and Organization. Ford, who studied 200 Black Studies programs in both black and white colleges, found that the objectives of black studies courses can be grouped under six headings (Ford 1973, pp. 55–63).

1. To provide black students with a feeling of personal identity, personal pride, and personal worth
2. To enhance black pride through a knowledge of black history and culture
3. To promote interest and involvement in the improvement of the black community (local, national, and worldwide)—to raise the black awareness level of the black community
4. To reform American education by attacking underlying racist assumptions
5. To train black students in the philosophy and strategy of revolution, that is, the present state of American race relations—the "Negro revolution"
6. To provide programs that are as rigorous intellectually and as scholarly as the average program in its particular college or university.

Black Studies programs are organized according to three major patterns: the interdisciplinary program, the independent or semiautonomous department, and the semiautonomous school. In the first pattern, the director, coordinator, or chairman of the Black Studies Committee usually administers the program, with regular departments of the college supplying faculty members to offer courses. Nearly three-fourths of all programs operate in accordance with this plan. Less than one-fourth of the programs are organized as independent or semiautonomous departments. Those who favor departmental status argue that it indicates that the college recognizes Black Studies as a legitimate academic field. Critics claim that departmental status encourages emphasis on ideological goals opposed to rigorous scholarship. Ford (1973, pp. 69–73) cites Malcolm X College in Chicago and the ethnic studies programs in all state colleges and universities in California (1973, pp. 74–75) as examples of the semiautonomous school with the same privileges and responsibilities as other such units in a university, municipal, or state system.

Although Malcolm X College had not been designated as a school of black studies by the Chicago Junior College Board, it was always regarded as such by the president, the faculty, the students, and the community, as is clearly seen in President Hurst's assertion (*The Christian Science Monitor*, May 7, 1971):

We had to create an image of the ability of black people to develop and administer an institution. Our faculty is now around 65 percent black and heading very rapidly toward 80 percent. The administration is 85 percent black and will probably stay right about there. I would say this, it's 100 percent black in thinking and ideology.

Among the students there are only a few Whites.

Reactions of black educators in Chicago who are not associated with Malcolm X College are mixed. Some consider the college's program to be more pertinent for Blacks than any they know about, and they approve of the uncompromising leadership of the president. Others say the programs are innovative but question the educational value of the innovations and lament the unqualified loyalty which the president demands to his concept of education for Blacks (Ford 1973, p. 73).

The ethnic studies in all state colleges and universities in California consist of an organized program in each of the major ethnic cultures or a series of individual courses in each culture. All of the programs in the state institutions except one follow the interdisciplinary or the departmental pattern. The exception is the Third College, a part of the University of San Diego. This college is not designated as a school of black studies, but it is regarded as such because the largest of its ethnic components is black. In the 1970s, the provost was black, as was half of the faculty, administrative personnel, and students. The other half of the student population was made up of Mexican Americans, Asian Americans, and white Americans (Ford 1973, pp. 74–75).

The fifteen most popular types of courses in black studies programs are, in percentages: history,

21; sociology, 19; literature, 17; political science, 12; anthropology, 6; art, 5; psychology, 4; music, 4; economics, 3; African languages, 3; speech and rhetoric, 2; religion, 2; geography, 1; mass media, 1; and others, 1; (percentages rounded up or down from .5 percent). Approximately two-thirds of the courses offered in the total number of black studies programs that Ford investigated were in the social sciences, with most of the remainder in humanities (Ford 1973, p. 79).

Black Studies Courses and Black Political Consciousness during the Period of Student Unrest. In the late 1960s and early 1970s, a number of black students saw Black Studies courses as a device to get through college with minimal effort. Many of the students who held that view felt that they knew all there is to know about black people and therefore saw no need to attend classes regularly. Also, a number of black students argued that extensive reading and the writing of papers, if they were required, were a "white man's thing." Claiming that Blacks are an "oral people," many used this argument in an attempt to avoid doing arduous work for the course. Often such students claimed that they were "working in the community" and should be graded for that activity rather than academic work. Although the desire to get through a course, as well as the offhand measures often used to achieve this end, are not a monopoly of black students, concern was expressed with the way in which the idea of blackness was used by some students as a means to satisfy their academic goals. Napper says: "For these students, 'revolution by any means necessary' has been replaced by 'a grade by any means necessary'—except perhaps, by studying" (Napper 1973, pp. 113–14).

By 1973, it was Napper's (1973, pp. 114–115) impression that despite all the political rhetoric and alleged political consciousness, black students at the University of California, Berkeley, tended to view the world in much the same way as their predecessors of ten or twenty years earlier. His reference here is to the problem of individualism and indifference toward the lot of the great majority of the black population. Despite the revolutionary slogans that characterized their earlier demonstrations and strikes, there appeared to be a sense of well-being regarding the accommodations provided for black students by the university.

Problems of Black Studies Programs. Thomas Sowell (1973, pp. 261–262), a black economist, asserts that some colleges were willing in the early 1970s to put incompetent Blacks in charge of black studies departments at white institutions "for the sake of 'representation' on the assumption that they are a temporary necessity and will be replaced by capable blacks as such become available." According to Sowell, when this policy was followed in black colleges, the incompetents drove out (or kept out) the competents. In reply to the fear that independent departments of black studies would necessarily lower academic standards, Blauner (1972, pp. 292–293) points out that at the University of California, Berkeley, new departments in other fields are begun if there is a core of interested faculty and a student demand. These departments "are not expected to become eminent bodies overnight, either as teaching units or as groups of scholars. In other contexts it is recognized that its takes time to produce an institution or program of high quality; yet many faculty members have opposed Black Studies departments because that quality is not available in the beginning."

Among the thirteen colleges and universities studied by the University of Michigan group, a study that is cited earlier in this chapter, several Black Studies programs have been understaffed and poorly supported (Gamson 1978, p. 193). Even those which received greater financial support had not gained control over faculty recruitment or promotion. Their full acceptance and institutionalization, unlike supportive services (recruitment, financial aid, counseling, tutoring, and so forth), rest with faculties. Even the well-supported programs encounter difficulty in times of budget cuts. (See also Hechinger 1980 with regard to the Harvard Black Studies Program.)

Important questions concerning black studies programs, especially those with majors, are entrance to graduate schools and finding employment. Both from the standpoint of the career interests of most black students and in terms of the influence of the black community on the life of the nation, Sir W. Arthur Lewis (1969, pp. 34–45, 39) an internationally known economist, thinks it is of great importance that the number of specialists in Afro-American studies be rather small in comparison with black scientists, engineers, accountants, and doctors. Oppositely, the advocates of black studies hope that these programs will provide a favorable environment for the emergence of able black leaders.

The Future of Black Studies Programs. In 1972, there were about 500 black studies programs in colleges and universities in the United States. By 1977 the number had declined to about 300, and by 1980 to approximately 250. This decrease came about for several reasons, including budget cuts, declining pressure on administrators, lack of permanent funding, and the general trend away from the humanities and the social sciences and toward more "practical" courses (*The New York Times*, June 19, 1977, p. 38; and April 13, 1980, p. 48).

The number of majors has fallen off in some schools, at Ohio State and Harvard, for example, and in most schools the number of students in the field is fewer than a dozen or so. Many black students now choose a double major, combining Afro-American studies with history, sociology, economics, or a premedical course.

By 1980, black studies programs were doing well on a number of campuses, including Yale, the University of North Carolina, the University of California, Berkeley, and the University of Detroit. Courses based on the ideological slogans of black power have disappeared, and in many universities hundreds of students, Whites as well as Blacks, enroll in the programs. Schools offering master's degrees in black studies include Yale, Harvard, Boston, Atlanta, and Ohio State (*The New York Times*, June 19, 1977, p. 38, and December 2, 1979, p. E22; Hechinger 1980, pp. 50, 62, 64, 66–68).

The National Council for Black Studies, founded in 1975 at the University of North Carolina, has organized summer workshops along scholarly lines. Half a dozen new scholarly journals were started in the 1970s, including the *Journal of Black Studies* at the University of Buffalo.

In periods of financial stringency, reduced enrollments, and less concern for minorities, the number of students taking Afro-American courses may continue to decline. Some programs in this field will disappear or be merged with courses in regular departments. In time, many of the present programs may be incorporated in other departments. Nevertheless, scholars in the field of black studies predict that extensive changes will not occur for a long time (Hechinger 1980, p. 76). Meanwhile, black studies will serve as an instrument through which power relationships between Blacks and Whites are balanced on predominantly white campuses (Willie 1981, p. 120).

Mexican Americans and Higher Education

In higher education, next to American Indians, Chicanos are the least well represented among minority groups. One of the main obstacles to substantial numbers of Mexican American youth obtaining a college education is the language problem. Some Mexican American youths are discouraged from entering college by their deficiency in English; others who do enter are handicapped by that deficiency, which existing bilingual programs have been insufficient to overcome.

Even when Mexican American youth decide to seek a college education, they tend to enter a school near home, thus perpetuating their isolation from the larger society. For example, the major state universities in Texas have an average of 2 percent or less of Mexican Americans in their student bodies. Exceptions to this rule are Texas A & M University, Pan American University, and the University of Texas at El Paso, schools which are located in sections of Texas where the population is predominantly Mexican American (Wright, Salinas, and Kuvlesky 1973, p. 48).

Another noteworthy aspect of Mexican Americans in higher education is the concentration of students in community colleges. A number of studies have shown that between 70 and 75 percent of the Chicanos enrolled in postsecondary education have entered these colleges (de los Santos, Jr. 1978, p. 70).

The College Board Panel on Financing Low-Income and Minority Students in Higher Education has reported that less selective two-year and four-year community colleges have the highest attrition rate for both majority and minority students. Astin has reported (see Figure 16-3) that only about one out of three Chicano students who enroll in college graduates, compared with more than one out of two Anglos. In addition to the problems faced by students in general, the bilingual, bicultural student has some unique problems: cultural differences, shortcomings in the English language, and the effects of low-income status.

Among the policies suggested for increasing the number of Mexican American students in higher education, as well as enhancing their chances of completing their courses, are the following: seeking out potential college students in high school, modifying admission standards, providing tutorial assistance and special counseling, giving more attention in curricula to Mexican American cultural contributions, and offering more financial support (Grebler et al. 1970, p. 592). In connection with the need for more adequate counseling, de los Santos, Jr. (1978, p. 71) suggests that colleges and universities begin to prepare more Chicanos to serve as professional counselors. Meanwhile, Chicano students might be used as peer counselors and tutors, an approach that has proved successful in a number of places.

Mexican American Studies

At the end of the 1960s, articulate and angry Chicano college and university students formulated resolutions and demands concerning the need for Mexican American studies at both undergraduate and graduate levels. As a result of these student pressures, Chicano studies programs and departments were organized in a number of colleges throughout the Southwest and in other areas where there were concentrations of Mexican Americans. Most of these programs were staffed by young Chicano professionals with support from the Mexican American community (Meier and Rivera 1972, p. 255).

Mexican American Studies programs are designed to serve two groups. The first, Chicano youth, has utilized these programs for several purposes, including entry and continuation in courses leading toward occupational and personal goals, a search for identity and self-esteem, and the discovery of the group's heritage. For the second target of Chicano studies, all other students, the value of these studies consists of acquiring knowledge and understanding about Mexican Americans, as well as contributing to respect and acceptance of Chicanos. In terms of the desired goals, the effectiveness of these programs has not yet been established (Cabrera 1971, pp. 19–20).

Considerable variations are found in the Chicano studies programs and personnel among the eight campuses of the University of California system. Berkeley established a Chicano Studies Division within a Department of Ethnic Studies. Davis formed a Chicano Studies Program with faculty members from traditional departments teaching Chicano courses. Irvine set up a Comparative Cultures Program with a Chicano component. At UCLA, a Chicano Studies Center has served primarily as an academic research center. Riverside's interdisciplinary Mexican American Studies Program utilizes faculty members from existing departments. Santa Barbara has a Department of Chicano Studies and a Chicano Research Center. Santa Cruz has developed a Chicano program within a new Urban Studies College. San Diego's program of Chicano Studies is a component of its Third College. Berkeley, Irvine, Riverside, and San Diego offer majors in Ethnic, Cultural, or Chicano Studies (Stoddard 1973, pp. 208–209).

The limited number of Mexican Americans with formal academic credentials has made it difficult to expand their participation on university faculties. In the early 1970s, only thirty of the 5,730 assistant, associate, and full professors on the eight campuses of the University of California were Mexican American, and only nine of those had tenure. Twenty-five untenured instructors, associates, and lecturers brought the total to fifty-five for the entire system. At the University of Texas at El Paso, only thirteen of the 314 assistant, associate, and full professors were Mexican American. Three of the 246 tenured members of that faculty were Mexican American; an additional eight Chicanos were employed as instructors, mostly in specially funded programs. The University of Texas at El Paso claimed that it enrolled nearly one-eighth of the total Mexican American students in the United States, but its prestige and salary schedule have been unable to compete with the University of Texas at Austin, UCLA, Notre Dame, and other well-known institutions that are better situated financially (Stoddard 1973, pp. 210–211). The problems which arose in staffing Black Studies programs in the first years after their establishment have also characterized Chicano Studies programs.

Puerto Ricans and Higher Education

Puerto Rican Students in Mainland Colleges and Universities

The number of college graduates in the Puerto Rican population on the mainland is very small, scarcely more than one percent. College attendnace, however, is increasing. A study of the mainland Puerto Rican college student suggests the following composite: The student is more likely to be male than female, to come from a low-income family, to be somewhat older than most students,

and to be the first in his family to go to college. He is majoring in the social sciences, education, Spanish, or social work. The Puerto Rican student is unlikely to complete an educational program in a two- or four-year period but will drop out for one or more semesters and return later (U.S. Commission on Civil Rights 1976, p. 123).

Like black students, Puerto Rican students have tended to be concentrated in community colleges rather than in the senior colleges of the City University of New York. By 1972, however, the City College of New York had enrolled 800 Puerto Rican students, a larger number than any college outside Puerto Rico. More than half of the open admissions freshmen needed intensive help in reading and writing, but many failed to obtain enough aid to enable them to continue. In the community college, attrition rates were in excess of one-third (Weinberg 1977, p. 345; see also Lavin, Alba, and Silverstein 1981).

The installation of open admissions in CUNY was preceded by close cooperation between Puerto Rican and black students. Public statements were issued in the name of black and Puerto Rican students, and a number of faculty members from both groups worked with the students.

The SEEK Program of City University of New York. SEEK (Search for Education, Elevation, and Knowledge) began in 1966 as a program to open the doors of City College to students who otherwise would have had little or no access to higher education (Lavin et al. 1981). The program was intended also to further racial intergration of the university. By 1977–78 the program had 11,000 students, 90 percent of whom were black or Puerto Rican. SEEK offered remedial, developmental, and compensatory courses, tutoring and counseling services, and the award of stipends averaging approximately $500 annually. The cost of the program, about $15 million in 1977–78, was shared equally by the city and the state.

From the beginning of the program, a series of city, university, and state reports questioned the effectiveness and the integrity of the system. These reports claimed that there were substantial numbers of ineligible students in the program, inappropriate expenditures, large amounts of improperly awarded financial aid, and inadequate management. One study showed that SEEK students failed to graduate at a higher rate than other similarly disadvantaged students admitted under the university's open-admissions policy. Both groups graduated one in six students after five years (*The New York Times*, December 18, 1977, p. 34). A 1984 City University report showed that 43 percent of those accepted to the four-year colleges under open admissions in 1970 had finally earned their degrees (*The New York Times,* April 8, 1984, p. E6).

Outside New York City, most Puerto Rican students were enrolled in community colleges. In Chicago, Puerto Rican enrollment in the city's community colleges may have equaled such enrollment in the remainder of public higher education in the state of Illinois (Weinberg 1977, p. 346).

American Indians in Higher Education

Figures on American Indian attendance in institutions of higher education prior to 1970 are incomplete. Excluding Alaska and Hawaii,the total enrollment of Native Americans in full-time undergraduate, graduate, and professional study in 1970 was 28,456. Of that number 5,678 were in California, 3,679 in Oklahoma, 1,926 in Texas, 1,378 in New York, 1,274 in Illinois, 1,047 in Pennsylvania, 1,011 in Washington, and 12,463 in other states (Weinberg 1977, p. 338).

Among the one-fifth of all American Indian undergraduate students enrolled in California institutions, dropout rates are high, but exact figures are not available. Like Blacks and Puerto Ricans, American Indian students are concentrated in community colleges where dropout rates are significantly higher than for the other schools, particularly for minority students (Weinberg 1977, p. 339).

The proportion of American Indians going on to college has risen in recent years, but the percentage, as indicated in Figure 16-3, is still considerably below that for Whites and for Blacks. The increase in college enrollment has been due in large part to the availability of increased funds for scholarships, loans, and other subsidies to Indian youth through the Bureau of Indian Affairs and other federal agencies.

Because of high dropout rates from high school, lower proportions of college attendance, and high unemployment rates, many reservation Indians are candidates for intensive retraining programs. Federal programs of this type are sponsored by the Department of Labor, the Bureau of Indian Affairs, and the Department of Health and Human Welfare.

More than $100 million was spent in 1974 for adult education and training programs: Department of Labor, $50 million; Bureau of Indian Affairs, $36.5 million; and HEW, $14.6 million. Despite these efforts in educational upgrading, a serious problem remains in that even the most qualified trainees cannot be assured of finding jobs in the depressed labor markets on Indian reservations. We discuss this situation in Chapter 9, but it may be briefly characterized here. Most of the industrial enterprises which have been established on Indian reservations are designed to employ low-skilled or unskilled employees. The main job openings for skilled or professional workers are in the social service agencies operated by the government. Indians who have acquired skills that are not related to these jobs find it necessary to relocate in urban areas to find openings. The Bureau of Indian Affairs supports such relocation by paying for transportation and temporary support for family units. Levitan and Johnston (1975, p. 46–48) point out that training programs on the reservation will have little effect on employment opportunities there unless they are related directly to postgraduation job chances.

Navajo Community College was founded in 1968. After one year of its existence, the president of the college stated: "This is an Indian owned and an Indian operated institution, and we certainly don't want any people other than Indian to dictate to us what is good for us." By 1970, the faculty was 40 percent Indian, one-third Navajo.

One of the major emphases in the curriculum at Navajo Community College is Navajo Studies. This program offers a three-semester course in Navajo history and culture given in Navajo, with one section presented in English. The final semester has dealt with current tribal problems. Among other offerings are courses in the Navajo language, Navajo culture change, Navajo arts and crafts, and Navajo creative writing. Other courses have been given in the history of Indian affairs and in Anglo-Indian relations, all organized from an Indian point of view. The college has attempted to prepare the students for alternative career paths: first, transfer to a four-year institution; second, seeking a job on the reservation. For the former goal, the curriculum has offered courses to meet the requirements of four-year colleges, but it has been felt important to emphasize also the Navajo Studies program in the preparation of these students. Through the latter program, the aim has been to prevent an identity crisis when the students enter Anglo society. For the second group of students, NCC offers courses in nursing, secretarial training, welding, auto mechanics, agriculture, commercial art, drafting, and related fields. NCC has tried to improve upon the vocational training program of the Bureau of Indian Affairs (Szasz 1974, pp. 178–179).

An interesting attempt to launch a program of American Indian Studies is seen at the University of Minnesota. Created in 1969, this department has two goals: first to provide knowledge of the complexity of Indian affairs for the thousands of non-Indians who comprise the overwhelming majority of the university and of the state; and second, to offset the legacy of low self-esteem and alienation among many Indian groups occasioned by three hundred years of disastrous culture contact. This program has differed somewhat from many Black Studies programs in that the latter have placed a stronger emphasis on the special academic needs of black students. The Minnesota program has sought "to cooperate with the Indian people in a common effort to develop their communities and to improve education at all levels, for Indians and non-Indians alike" (Miller 1971, pp. 312–342).[1] It is no longer a separate department.

Minority Graduate and Professional Students

Although graduate school enrollments have increased steadily since the end of World War II, minority graduate students still make up a small proportion of the total number of graduate students in the United States. Blacks, the largest minority in the nation, constitute about 12 percent of young adults but represent about 6 percent of all graduate students.

More than half of black college students expect to pursue some type of graduate education either full time (45 percent) or along with work (10 percent). Because only one-fourth of black students have average grades of B or above, it seems unlikely that many of these students will be able to realize their aspirations. According to Boyd (1974, p. 9), many of the unrealistic aspirants would be less concerned about obtaining graduate credentials if

Blacks could secure satisfying jobs and earn as much as Whites without having to complete additional years of education.

Among Blacks planning postbaccalaureate education, Boyd (1974, p. 9) found that 10 percent expected to pursue Ph.D. degrees. Other preferences were as follows: law (21 percent), medicine (21 percent), social sciences (18 percent), education (9 percent), and business (7 percent). Boyd comments that black students are not taking advantage of the entire range of options available to them, adding that with decreased job opportunities in fields such as education and social sciences and increased chances in science and engineering, educators should re–examine their views.

In 1970, 40 percent of the undergraduate degrees of black students were in education. By 1978, the United Negro College Fund reported that more black undergraduates were majoring in business than in education. On the graduate level, however, that trend is much less visible. The maldistribution in fields of study among Blacks who earn doctorate degrees is seen in the record for 1975: 61.2 percent of the recipients of these degrees were in education, 16.1 percent in the social sciences, 5.6 percent in life sciences, 3.6 percent in the physical sciences, 1.1 percent in engineering, and 3.5 percent in "professional and other" (Blackwell 1978, p. 6). A National Science Foundation report showed that in 1972 there were approximately 9,700 black scientists in the United States, less than 2 percent of the total pool of 496,000 scientists. Of 143,000 scientists holding the doctorate, less than 1 percent (1,300) were black (McBay 1978, p. 216).

By 1977 only slight changes had occurred in the distribution of doctoral degrees conferred by race (Table 16-2).

In 1972, Blacks enrolled in medical schools made up 5.4 percent of total enrollment. Their proportions rose to 6.3 percent (3,355 students) in 1974–75 and declined to 5.7 percent in 1978–79 (3,548 students). The number of black students in medical schools declined in 1978–79 despite an increase in the total medical school enrollment, and the proportion of Blacks in the first-year class was the lowest it had been since 1970. Black students made up 6.4 percent of the freshman class in the 124 medical schools in the United States in 1978–79, compared with 6.7 percent in 1977–78. The pool of black applicants to medical school remained virtually unchanged in size from 1972–73, when there were 2,382 black applicants. In 1977–78, 2,482

---

[1] For a comprehensive report of recommendations on the higher education of minorities, especially blacks, Mexican Americans, Puerto Ricans, and American Indians, see Astin 1982, pp. 187–212.

Table 16-2. Doctoral Degrees Conferred by Field and Race, 1977

Subject	Percent of total white recipients	Percent of total black recipients
Agriculture and natural resources	2.2	.9
Biological sciences	10.3	4.2
Business and management	2.5	1.0
Education	24.7	54.7
Engineering	5.8	1.8
Fine and applied arts	2.2	1.7
Foreign languages	2.3	1.1
Health fields	1.6	1.1
Letters-humanities	7.2	4.8
Mathematics	2.3	.8
Physical sciences	9.8	3.6
Psychology	9.2	8.4
Social Sciences	11.5	9.3
Theology	3.5	1.7

Source: National Center for Educational Statistics and *The New York Times*, April 20, 1980, p. 25 (Educ.).

blacks sought admission. During that time, the total number of applicants rose from 36,135 to 42,155.[2] The proportion of Blacks in the applicant pool increased by only about 1 percent during the 1970s (*The New York Times*, December 3, 1978, p. 45).

The number of Chicano medical students doubled in the period 1972 to 1976, increasing from 361 students (0.8 percent) to 638 students (1.2 percent) in 1974 and to 780 students (1.4 percent) in 1976–77 (Blackwell 1978, p. 6). Puerto Ricans represented 0.2 percent (90 students) of the total enrollment in medical schools in 1972, 0.3 percent (172 students) in 1974, and 0.4 percent (232 students) in 1976–77. American Indians constituted 0.2 percent (69 students) in 1972, 0.3 percent (159 students) in 1974, and the same proportion in 1976 (186 students).

In 1978–79, the total medical school enrollment in the country was 62,242, and 86.4 percent of the students were white Americans. Other students included: 5.7 percent, black Americans; 2.6 percent, Asian Americans; 3.6 percent, Hispanic descent (including those enrolled in medical school in Puerto Rico); 0.3 percent, American Indian; and 1.4 percent, foreigners.

In 1973–74, the representation of racial and cultural groups among 19,369 students enrolled in dental schools in the United States was as follows: black, 4.5 percent (872); Asian American, 2.5 percent (490); Mexican American, 0.8 percent (174); Puerto Rican, .06 percent (12); American Indian, 0.1 percent (28); other minority, 0.4 percent (80); Non-minorities, 91.4 percent (17,713) (*Annual Report, Dental Education 1973–74*, American Dental Association, p. 4; quoted in Institute for the Study of Educational Policy 1976, p. 292).

Between 1969–70 and 1975–76, minority enrollments in law schools approved by the American Bar Association increased signficantly. The enrollment of black students more than doubled during that period, increasing from 2,128 to 5,127. The number of Chicano law students more than tripled, rising from 412 to 1,297. Puerto Rican law students increased five times—from 61 to 333, and the number of American Indian law students quadrupled—from 72 to 295. During those years, total law school enrollment more than doubled. By 1976–77, however, the number of black law students dropped below 5,000 and the proportion of black to white students was less than 10 percent. In that year black first-year admissions decreased, and fewer Blacks were graduating. Similar declines were occurring for other minority students (Blackwell 1978, p. 5).[3]

In 1976, Blacks constituted about 2 percent of the nation's 350,000 physicians and about the same proportion of the 355,000 lawyers. Until the middle 1960s, about 80 percent of the physicians and 74 percent of the black doctoral degree holders came from the historically black colleges. Until that time, a high proportion of the country's black lawyers also came from black colleges.

---

[2]In discussions of the number of applicants for admissions to selective colleges and to professional schools, it should be remembered that total figures are inflated by the practice on the part of many students of making multiple applications.

[3]A problem of growing concern in the late 1970s and early 1980s was the increasing emphasis placed upon the Law School Admission Test (LSAT) as a major criterion for admission. The same concern was expressed about the Medical College Admission Test (MCAT). To assist students in preparing for these tests, cram courses are offered by preparatory schools at a cost of from $75 to $500. Many minority students come from low-income families and cannot afford to pay such fees, thus putting them at a disadvantage in competition with those who can afford them (Blackwell 1978, p. 5).

Preferential Treatment in Admission to Professional Schools

The DeFunis Case

Marco DeFunis, a 1970 graduate of the University of Washington, was twice denied admission to the university's law school. In 1971, DeFunis sued the university, charging that only six of the forty-four minority students among the 150 students admitted to the law school that year had academic records better than his. The qualifications of the minority applicants—Blacks, Spanish-surname, Asian American, and Filipino Americans—had been considered in a separate group, rated against each other rather than combined with white applicants. DeFunis maintained that this admissions policy violated the Fourteenth Amendment's guarantee of equal protection of the laws. The Washington Superior Court ruled in favor of DeFunis and he was admitted to the law school. Eventually, the case reached the U.S. Supreme Court, where the lower court was reversed and the school's policy upheld. A stay of that ruling by Justice William O. Douglas kept DeFunis in school. He had almost finished by the time the Supreme Court was ready to hear the appeal. The justices declared the case moot, and DeFunis graduated in 1974.

The Bakke Case

The Allan P. Bakke case arose when Mr. Bakke, a white engineer, was denied entry to the University of California Medical School at Davis in 1973 and 1974. In those years a special admissions program set aside 16 of its 100 places for minority students—Blacks, Chicanos, and Asians. Bakke charged that this policy was unconstitutional and said that he was better qualified than some of the students admitted under the special program. In November, 1974, Judge F. Leslie Manker of the Yolo County Superior Court ruled that the university's program was invalid on the grounds that it discriminated against Bakke because of his race. Judge Manker, however, did not order the university to admit Bakke, saying only that he was entitled to have his application reconsidered without regard to race. Both Bakke and the university appealed the decision. Without waiting for a state

appeals court to hear and decide the case, the California Supreme Court agreed to hear the case. On September 16, 1976, this court ruled that the university's affirmative action program was unconstitutional because it violated the equal-protection rights of Whites. The court ordered the university to admit Bakke in the fall of 1977. In December, 1976, the university sought a review by the United States Supreme Court, and that review was granted in February, 1977.

The long-awaited decision of the Supreme Court was handed down on June 28, 1978. Five members of the Court found the affirmative action program of the Davis Medical School too rigid. Decided on constitutional grounds, the plan was held to disregard individual rights as guaranteed by the 14th Amendment, which states that "no state shall . . . deny to any person within its jurisdiction the equal protection of the law." Since the medical school is a state institution, its admission program involves actions by the state of California. In his opinion, Justice Powell, who wrote the main opinion, said that the Davis program used an explicit racial classification "never before countenanced by this Court. It tells applicants who are not Negro, Asian or 'Chicano' that they are totally excluded from a specific percentage of the seats in the class." The Court upheld that part of the decision of the California Supreme Court which held the Davis program unlawful and directed that the respondent be admitted to the medical school.

The Supreme Court reversed, however, that portion of the California court's judgment which enjoined the Davis Medical School from giving any consideration in its admissions process to race. A majority of the Court disagreed with the petitioner's argument that a dual admissions program is the only effective means of insuring diversity in a student body. Justice Powell wrote that this program, "focused solely on ethnic diversity, would hinder rather than further attainment of genuine diversity." The more flexible Harvard University admissions plan was then cited with approval. In that plan, such qualities as exceptional personal talents, unique work or service experience, leadership potential, maturity, demonstrated compassion, a history of overcoming disadvantage, ability to communicate with the poor, or other qualifications are considered important. Such a policy considers race only as one factor and is said to treat each applicant as an individual in the admissions process and to prevent a candidate from losing out on the last available seat to another applicant simply because he was not the right color or had the wrong surname.

Four justices of the Supreme Court concluded that Section 601 of Title VI of the Civil Rights Act of 1964 prohibits programs such as that at the Davis Medical School. The language of this section states: "No person in the United States shall, on the ground of race, color, or national origin be excluded from participation in, be denied the benefits of or be subjected to discrimination under any program or activity receiving Federal financial assistance." On that statutory basis alone, they held that Bakke's rights had been violated and that he must be admitted to the medical school. Another four justices concluded that the affirmative action program at Davis was constitutional and favored reversing the judgment of the California Supreme Court in all respects. Joining the second group in its view that some uses of race in university admissions are permissible, Justice Powell provided the fifth vote reversing the California Supreme Court's judgment insofar as it prohibited the university from establishing programs in the future which take race into account.

The question of the validity legally of racial classifications is of special interest. Five of the justices held that racial distinctions are inherently suspect. In order "to justify the use of a suspect classification, a state must show that its purpose of interest is both constitutionally permissible and substantial and that its use of the classification is 'necessary to the accomplishment' of its purpose of the safeguarding of its interest." Cases cited by the petitioner (the University of California) to show that the Court had approved preferential classifications were held to be materially different from the facts in the Bakke case. These cases were drawn from three areas: school desegregation, employment discrimination, and sex discrimination. According to Justice Powell, the school cases "each involved remedies for clearly determined constitutional violations. Racial classifications thus were designed as remedies for the vindication of constitutional entitlement." The employment discrimination cases involved persons who had been victims of discrimination by the respondents, not just by society at large. Gender-based distinctions were said to be less likely to create analytical and practical problems since there are only two possible classifications, and Justice Powell pointed out that

the Court had never viewed such classification as inherently suspect or as comparable to racial or ethnic classifications for the purpose of equal-protection analysis.

What the Bakke Decision Means. The Supreme Court's decision in *Bakke* means that rigid racial quotas in admitting students to colleges and universities are unconstitutional. The majority held that a university cannot use such means to remedy "the past effects of societal discrimination." Justice Powell pointed out that special preference for Blacks was not what the majority meant when it said that race could be considered in an admissions policy. He wrote about the need for diversity, for Asian-Americans, Mexican-Americans, people from rural as well as urban areas.

Apparently, a university that has never discriminated on the basis of race will not be required to have race as a factor in an affirmative action program. For universities that have discriminated in the past, race can be considered as a factor in flexible admissions plans. Harvard has long included such factors as geographic origin, class, and professional and extracurricular interests in the admissions process. Race as a factor has been added only in recent years. Only 150 or so places are allocated in each entering class solely on the basis of academic merit. The rest, a large pool of also academically qualified students, are selected for those who could bring some diversity to the student body in the belief that such diversity contributes to the educational process. Formerly, Harvard had only a handful of minority students, but under the present admissions policy 8.1 percent of those admitted to the freshman class in the fall of 1978 were Black, 4.6 percent were of Hispanic origin, and 0.4 percent were Native Americans.

The Court rejected the suggestion of the California Supreme Court that the best way to promote affirmative action among minority students was under racially blind programs for economically disadvantaged students. Most college administrators regard such programs as unworkable because, as one administrator said: "You'd have to take in 32 more white students in order to get 16 black ones" (*The New York Times*, June 29, 1978, p. A23). While a much higher proportion of black students come from educationally disadvantaged families the absolute number of white students from such families is more than twice as large.

Since most universities have not had systems as rigid as Davis's, their affirmative action programs will not be greatly affected by the Court's decision. Race can be taken into account as one, but not the only, factor in admissions procedures. Open to question is whether colleges will be charged with making arbitrary and capricious choices by those qualified students who are nonetheless rejected.

The Court's decision in *Bakke* is expected to have little effect on efforts to increase minority representation in various federal programs. In Health and Human Services, 95 percent of the department's efforts cover cases in which previous discrimination has been found. Former Secretary Joseph A. Califano believes that affirmative action can be effective without unyielding quotas. Eleanor Holmes Norton, former chairman of the Equal Employment Opportunity Commission, predicts that *Bakke* will have no impact on EEOC decisions since the commission deals primarily with correcting past discrimination. Drew S. Days, 3rd, former Assistant Attorney General for Civil Rights, points out that the 10 percent set-aside for minorities in certain public works programs is not rigid in practice. According to Days: "It is flexible in the sense that if a grantee, let's say a city, is not able to locate adequate numbers of minority contractors who can do the job, they can seek waivers."[4] (See also the sections on affirmative action in Chapters 9, 12, and 18).

The Effects of Preferential Admissions Policies and Enrollments in Medical and Law Schools

In 1967–68, the last year before special admissions programs began to be significant, there were 735 Blacks in medical schools. Of that number, 71 percent had been admitted in ways that could not be called "racially neutral": they were at Howard University and Meharry Medical College, the country's two predominantly black medical schools. In the one hundred other medical schools, the 211 Blacks constituted only 0.6 percent of the total enrollment.

By the fall of 1977, there were 3,000 Blacks, 5 percent of the total, in the mainly white medical schools. Observers assert that if these predominantly white schools were required to follow "racially neutral" admissions policies, the number of Blacks would drop back to about where it was

in 1968. They believe also that a similar effect would occur in other professional schools and in selective colleges. This view is based on the wide gaps that still exist in economic, educationnal, and social advantage. As Bundy (1977, pp. 44–45) points out, Whites as a group outnumber Nonwhites at all levels of advantage and disadvantage, and on any criteria that are genuinely nonracial they will receive all but a few places.

Spurred by the racial conflicts of the late 1960s and the early 1970s, many law schools initiated programs to increase the proportion of minority students they admitted. At first, some of the legal education opportunity plans were crash programs, and often the early results were disastrous. For example, of the 14 minority students admitted by the Law School at the University of California, Los Angeles in 1967, 11 were graduated, 10 took the bar examination, and 2 passed it. Of the class of 1971, only 12 of the 39 minority members admitted went on to be admitted to the bar. In the class of 1973, 64 minority students were admitted, 40 were graduated at the end of three years, and 9 had passed the bar examination by April, 1974. Nearly all of the colleges and professional schools that went ahead quickly with minority recruiting programs had similar experiences.

In 1974, between 75 and 80 percent of the white law graduates of the country went on to pass the bar examinations, but the proportion for Blacks was less than half that (*The New York Times*, April 7, 1974).

Many white students and their parents have accused the professional schools of discriminating in reverse by favoring minority applicants with grades and test scores lower than theirs. A number of professional men and women of all races have argued that the campaign to enroll minorities has led to a decline in professional standards.[5]

Those who favor preferential treatment in admissions for racial and cultural minorities claim that those who fall short on the measurements are not necessarily less qualified.[6] They say that scores

---

[4]Cleveland, *The Plain Dealer*, July 3, 1978, p. A9; *The New York Times*, July 2, 1978, p. E1, and April 22, 1979, p. 35.

[5]For a criticism of affirmative action programs in higher education, see Borgatta, 1976, pp. 62–72; two replies: Duster 1976, pp. 73–78, and Keller 1976, pp. 79–82; and Borgatta's rejoinder, *ibid.*, pp. 82–85.

[6]The social and cultural bias of standardized tests, including the Scholastic Aptitude Test (SAT), (LSAT), and (MCAT), has often been noted. Tollett (1978, p. 49) comments that such discussions are necessary for the self-esteem of Blacks, adding that it is hardly surprising that tests developed by the dominant group would reflect their values and skills. Tollett says that

and records indicate a great deal about those at the upper and lower margins and that they are relatively reliable indicators of academic performance. For this reason, admissions officers usually do not exclude those near the top nor admit those near the bottom. In trying to identify promise and quality of all kinds, an important question in recent years has been whether race itself should be taken into consideration. This question was the basic issue in the *Bakke* case discussed earlier in this chapter.

The admission of white men to medical and law schools has been more affected in recent years by the number of women of all races entering these schools than by the number of specially admitted black or Hispanic men. Since 1968 the number of women entering medical schools has risen from 8 percent to 25 percent, and a similar increase has occurred in law schools. Since the women admitted have had generally competitive records on the usual measures, no constitutional issue has been raised by this change. In the fall of 1977, 4,000 young women entered medical school, and this number had more to do with the rejection of the white males who were not admitted than any special admissions program for minorities (Bundy 1977, p. 49–50).

In part because of the troubles that many minority students had in completing their professional training and becoming licensed to practice, applications have declined in recent years, especially in some of the East Coast schools. Attempts to change the situation now include campaigns by civil rights organizations to recruit promising applicants, more selective admissions policies by professional schools, and programs after admission of counseling and tutoring of minority students.

Federal Laws, Court Orders, and Programs Prohibiting Racial Discrimination against Students in Higher Education

The major federal law is the Civil Rights Act of 1964, Title VI. As Title VI applies to higher education, it is enforced by the Office for Civil Rights, Department of Education. As it applies to proprietary schools, the enforcement of Title VI comes under the Veterans Administration. In addition to Title VI, an Internal Revenue Service Ruling (71–447) prohibits private tax-exempt schools from discriminating against students on the basis of race (Institute for the Study of Educational Policy 1976, pp. 216–217).

In 1969, after investigations by federal officers had revealed the existence in ten states of separate dual systems of public education, these states were asked to submit plans for achieving racial equality. The states were: Alabama, Arkansas, Florida, Georgia, Louisiana, Mississippi, North Carolina, Oklahoma, Pennsylvania, and Virginia. In 1970, the Legal Defense Fund of the NAACP and the Washington law firm of Rauh and Silard sued HEW in a federal district court for failure to obtain state plans of desegregation in public higher education and for failing to withhold federal aid to the ten states. The plantiffs' lawyers argued that HEW's failure to implement the 1964 civil rights ruling ensured racism and a dual system of public higher education that was expensive and wasteful. In 1973, the plaintiffs won their case over an appeal by the defendants of the district court's decision of 1972. The court then ordered HEW to obtain desegregation plans from the ten states and to notify the states of HEW's acceptance or rejection of the plans by April 30, 1974, but later extended the deadline to June 30 (*Adams* v. *Richardson*). Nine of the ten states submitted plans for desegregating their public colleges and universities by June, 1974. HEW accepted eight of the ten plans; Mississippi's plan was rejected, and Louisiana refused to comply. The plans that were accepted were said by HEW to provide for progress in the recruitment and retention of students from minority groups, equal-resource allocations to all state colleges and universities (with additional funds to make up for past injustices), and hiring minority faculty members (Browning and Williams 1978, pp. 88–89).

The plans that were accepted were not uniform, but HEW required that they be "comprehensive and statewide, that they enhance through equalization rather than threaten the existing black colleges, and that they provide substantial desegregation of all institutions." These criteria were intended to develop an "adequate remedy for segregation and discrimination in public higher education," to maximize the capacity of black colleges to provide an education of good quality, and to increase the black

"our scores do not look good" and that "we must work at improving our performance on these tests." Meanwhile, as he has remarked to his black law students: "Black English is lively, expressive, and groovey, but I suggest that you write your pleadings, compose your briefs, and make your oral arguments in standard English. You are more likely to succeed that way."

presence in higher education. In accepting the plans, HEW agreed to monitor the process of dismantling the dual systems (Browning and Williams 1978, p. 89).

In April, 1976, Federal District Judge John Pratt ordered HEW to prepare guidelines for the desegregation of universities in six southern states— Arkansas, Florida, Georgia, North Carolina, Oklahoma, and Virginia. He asked HEW to "take into account the unique importance of black colleges." HEW said that desegregation of the white institutions must precede desegregation of black colleges and asked state colleges systems to give black colleges priority when instituting new courses or degree programs. The guidelines, issued in July 5, 1977, also state: "The department does not take this language to mean that black institutions are exempt from the Constitution" or from federal civil rights laws. Because some stipulations in the guidelines are favorable to black schools, some interpreted them as guarantees for the survival of the black institutions. An official of HEW said on July 9, 1977, that was not the case and that the presidents of black colleges did not expect such guarantees. According to this official, the administrators wanted only an equal chance to compete for students within the state college system. He said further that the government could not insure that the thirteen black schools involved would be able to compete successfully for students when predominantly white colleges were opened to large-scale black enrollment, adding that black colleges would have to stand or fall on their merits as educational institutions (*The New York Times*, July 10, 1977, p. 22).

The guidelines established by HEW required that faculty, students, and college governing boards be mostly desegregated in five years. In an effort to show special consideration for black colleges, mandatory desegregation in them did not begin until 1979. The guidelines covered publicly supported colleges enrolling 1.1 million students, including 46,500 students in the thirteen black colleges (*The New York Times*, July 10, 1977, p. 22). In June, 1981, Education Secretary T. H. Bell announced an agreement with the State of North Carolina providing for increased funds from the state for its five predominantly black colleges and the creation of 29 new academic programs at the schools to attract white students. The agreement set goals of 10.6 percent black enrollment at white schools and 15 percent white enrollment at the black schools by December 31, 1986. In addition, the agreement

guarantees continued integration of the faculty and staffs of the black and white schools. The Education Department has ordered more than a dozen other states to correct similar but less serious civil rights violations (*The New York Times*, June 21, 1981, p. 13).

In October, 1981, the Justice Department and the state of Louisiana entered into an agreement whereby Louisiana, and other states like North Carolina and South Carolina, will enlarge present open-admission programs by allocating funds for new buildings and new educational projects. South Carolina State College was to receive a business administration building, as well as $2.1 million for faculty salaries and $7.8 million to establish new courses. Florida promised to set up nine unduplicated learning programs at Florida A & M University in order to attract white students. North Carolina, confronted with a $10 million withholding of federal support, ended its eleven-year legal battle by agreeing to establish a new graduate center at Winston-Salem and upgrade its traditionally black institutions. The state agreed to a set of guidelines whereby black students are expected to constitute 10 percent of the total enrollment at the white institutions by 1986, and white students 15 percent of enrollment at black schools (*Time*, October 12, 1981).

In the fall of 1979, the United States Supreme Court refused to review a Sixth Circuit Court of Appeals decision which required that the Nashville Branch of the University of Tennessee be merged into the predominantly black Tennessee State University in Nashville. The University of Tennessee sought Supreme Court review. Enrollment at Tennessee State after the merger was 59.8 percent black, 34.4 percent white, and 5.8 percent other races. In 1978, the student population was 12 percent white (*LDF Report, NAACP*, October, 1979, p. 2). There are two reasons for the special interest in the Tennessee case: first, usually when state authorities are required to desegregate institutions of higher learning, they try first to eliminate the predominantly black schools; and second, a predominantly black school was found by the courts to be worthy of becoming the base in a merger with a predominantly white school. The higher courts upheld the finding of the U.S. District Court (1977) that the predominantly white institution was a "newly created branch" and that "neither the record nor the historical facts would support placing the merged institution under the University of Tennessee Board of Trustees." This court found that the predominantly black institution was a "land-grant university with a sixty-year history" and that for the University of Tennessee to take over the merged institution would mean the "elimination of Tennessee State University as an educational institution with all the concomitant losses entailed therein" (Willie 1981, pp. 95–96). Since there are fourteen areas in the United States in which black and white public colleges are located close together (nine of these pairs are in the same cities), the Tennessee case assumes even greater importance.

In the light of the *Adams* v. *Richardson* decision of the Supreme Court in 1973, which requires unitary school systems for higher education, the racial composition of the student body of black colleges and universities is of considerable interest. In the study of black colleges by Willie and MacLeish (1978, pp. 134–137) referred to earlier in this chapter, three of the fifteen schools had no white enrollment, and twelve reported white enrollments ranging from two to 845 students. The average number of white students attending these institutions was 275, 9.6 percent of the combined student populations. In this study, seven of the eight private institutions had a white student enrollment of fewer than twenty. The number of white students in the state-supported schools varied from 200 to 845. The latter figure was 15 percent of the total enrollment of Prairie A & M University in Texas, the largest white enrollment of any of the southern colleges included in the study. The situation is quite different in some of the predominantly black colleges in the North. Delaware State University has a 40 percent white enrollment (Willie and MacLeish 1978, p. 144–145); other black schools which have had substantial numbers of white students include West Virginia State College, Lincoln University (Missouri), Bluefield College (West Virginia), and Kentucky State University.

If the federal government and the states provide financial support to improve the black public institutions, including the expansion of present programs and the introduction of new curricular offerings, the white enrollment in some of them may increase significantly. One cannot be certain that such support will be forthcoming, however, in a time of decreasing enrollments and budget cuts. In 1983, the United States Office of Civil Rights reported, for example, that only five of the eleven new programs planned to enhance Florida A & M University, a largely black school, in order to attract more white students, had been implemented. White enrollment had declined from 620 in 1978–79 to 519. (*St. Petersburg Times*, February 14, 1983, p. B2).

Under Title VI of the Civil Rights Act of 1964, the government is required to withhold federal funds from colleges and universities that are segregated. Although this has never been done, HEW has forced several states to modify their systems of higher education to comply with the law. The situation in Texas is interesting. Among the findings of a study made by officials from the regional office of the Department of Health, Education, and Welfare in Dallas were the following:

At most of the 38 state-supported senior colleges and universities and 47 community colleges in Texas, the student body is either overwhelmingly white or overwhelmingly black.

At the University of Texas at Austin, there were 28,213 white undergraduates in the 1976–77 school year, 721 blacks, and 2,277 Hispanic-Americans. (In 1970, the population of Texas was 12 percent black and 18 percent Hispanic.)

At Texas A & M, there were 21,766 undergraduates in 1976–77. Only 66 were black, and, of those students, 50 were athletes.

Hispanic-Americans were grouped on certain campuses, particularly at Pan American University. There were relatively few Mexican-Americans at most of the other schools.

The white schools are better financed than the black ones. The physical facilities at Prairie View A & M, an almost entirely black school, are the worst of any college in the state.

Faculty members are better paid at white schools.

Texas officials conceded that the statistics seemed to indicate racial segregation, but they asserted that their admissions policy was color-blind and that the preponderance of Whites at some colleges and Blacks at others was a result of the wishes of applicants. They claimed also that major steps have been taken in recent years to equalize expenditures and facilities. The initial report was returned to the Dallas office because of "deficiencies" in the evidence. The final report was filed in the summer of 1979 (*The New York Times*, December 16, 1979). Next steps were up to the Secretary of Education.

Federal programs that play important roles in higher education of minorities fall into four main categories: (1) institutional aid programs: Strengthening Developing Institutions program, the Tribally Controlled Community College Program, and Land-Grant College Appropriations, (2) student financial aid programs, the largest of which are the Pell Grants (formerly the Basic Educational Opportunity Grant program), the College Work–Study Program, and the Guaranteed Student Loan Program, (3) special programs to promote access and persistence, which embrace such well-known programs as Upward Bound, Talent Search, and Special Services for Disadvantaged Students, (4) professional training and human resource development programs, which comprise, among others, bilingual education programs (the largest in this category), Minority Biomedical Support, Minority Access to Research Centers, and the Graduate and Professional Opportunities Program (Astin 1982, pp. 116–17).

During the 1970s, federal, state, and institutionally supported, campus-based assistance and outreach programs for disadvantaged or high-risk students multiplied. In 1977, 95 percent of the pub-lic community colleges and 77 percent of the public senior colleges provided one or more special services for disadvantaged students—tutoring, counseling, financial aid. Extensive evaluations of these programs found that they are generally effective and do contribute to increased access and persistence (Astin 1982, p. 126).

The Civil Rights Act of 1964 (Title VI) and the Education Amendments of 1972 and later have had a positive influence on equal opportunity for minorities in higher education, especially at the undergraduate level. Financial aid for minorities in graduate and professional schools has been less readily available than for undergraduates. A central issue for the 1980s is the extent to which such programs will continue and will be improved on the basis of past experience.

Prejudice, Discrimination, and Democratic Values

Most persons who study majority—minority relations, we believe, have moral and political interests as well as scientific curiosity about the topic. Certainly the present authors do. We approach the issue created by this dual concern in the tradition of Max Weber: Recognize, do not deny, these different levels of interest. Try to minimize the negative impact each may have for the other—scientism dulling one's moral sensibilities or moral fervor blurring the sharpness of one's understanding. To the degree that we are successful in Part III, there will be no ambiguity about our goal—the elimination of discrimination and prejudice; but that goal will not obscure our observations and analysis as we examine the individual, group, and societal factors that block and those that contribute to social change.

CHAPTER 17

The Reduction of Prejudice and Discrimination
CHANGING THE PREJUDICED PERSON

In the first two parts of this volume we have followed the tangled patterns of relationship that
develop between dominant groups and minority
groups. We have examined the causes of prejudice
and discrimination and described their results, for
the individuals involved and for the social structure. Throughout this analysis, we have attempted
to maintain an objective approach. Our own value
stand has not been disguised, but we have tried to
prevent it from distorting the picture.

In turning to the analysis of strategies that are
effective in reducing prejudice and discrimination,
our value stand becomes more explicit. We believe
that the categorical judgment and treatment of
human beings according to ethnic background not
only is evil in itself but brings with it a host of
other evils. Having stated that premise, we shall
attempt to analyze strategies on a thoroughly objective basis. The surgeon cannot afford to be
sentimental.

Even in this section our concern is not simply
with social-action programs, although we shall hope
that this discussion is relevant to them. One of the
most effective ways of learning about the nature
of intergroup hostility is to study the techniques
that are effective and those that are ineffective in
reducing it; for such a study to be valid, it must
be concerned with the causes and functions of that
hostility.

Variables to Consider in the Development of Strategies

Effective strategy is based on a precise knowledge of the goals one wants to achieve and on a
thorough understanding of the obstacles in the
way. We need to consider (1) types of goals for
which different groups are striving; (2) types of
persons to be affected, in terms of their relation to
prejudice and discrimination; and (3) types of situations, in time and place, to which strategy must
adjust.

The strategies of a given period reflect assumptions about these issues, but the assumptions are
often unexamined. The result is less effective action.
We want again to emphasize strongly, as we have
throughout our discussion, the *system* quality of
prejudice and discrimination. They express cultural
norms; they are embedded in institutional and interpersonal structures; they are related to the motives,
needs, and anxieties of majority- and minority-group
members. Strategies, unhappily, often focus on one
element of the system. Perhaps we can illustrate
this by a partially imaginary historical sequence,
in which we will note major shifts in strategy.

The first stage in the breakup of patterns of
dominance–submission is a slowly increasing readiness of dominants to admit some among the minority into relative equality of status if. . . . If, that

379

is, they "improve themselves," take on "proper" attitudes and styles of behavior, and the like. The underlying theory is: Disprivilege is caused by the inadequacies of minorities. Hence sound strategy requires the removal of those inadequacies. There is often generous and well-meaning help from the dominants, in the form of educational support, for example. Considering the feedback mechanisms in complex social systems, one should not set this "cause" aside; but it is a third-level cause and becomes meaningful only when preceeding "causes" are recognized and acted upon.

The next stage of strategic effort, with its underlying theory, shifts major concern to the majority-group member: Minority-majority relations are full of conflict because of the prejudices of those on top. A major campaign of education and persuasion must be mounted to help them see, and to set aside, their own prejudices and the culture on which they rest. This approach is also valuable; but insofar as its fails to see how prejudices are tied into the social system—in particular, into the system of discriminations which the dominant-group members participate in regularly—it cannot be very effective.

It is exactly this system of discriminations that is the focus of attention in the next stage. The institutions of a racist society must be transformed, whether by organized legal and political action or by violent protest (the contrast, of course, is significant). According to those who take this approach, dominant-group prejudices are unimportant; at most they are reflections of the basic causes of injustice. And attention to the behavior of the minority-group members is a travesty, for it seems to blame them for being victimized. It is essential, of course, to deal with the structure of discrimination. If the reenforcements to that structure which come from culture and character are overlooked, however, gains that are won by costly effort may fade out as the homeostatic forces in the total system bring it back to "normal."

In all this, there is room for strategic specialists who prefer to work on one part of the total system. There are times and situations when one part of the system of discrimination is more vulnerable, suggesting that scarce resources should be expended there. There are no conditions, however, in which the several forces we have been dealing with are not operative, a fact that a general theory adequate to strategic requirements must emphasize. And in the long run, structure, culture, and character must all change.

Strategic disagreements sometimes rest on inadequate examination of conflicting goals, of variation among individuals in their readiness for change, and of differing situations. Hence we must comment on the dilemmas and problems that these circumstances present.

Types of Goals

Those who are seeking to reduce prejudice and discrimination do not all agree on the immediate or long-run objectives. Some believe that peaceful co-existence is most desirable. Others are willing to accept and work for economic and political equality and integration but are opposed to social equality (there is a vague and shifting line separating economic and political from social). Still others are working for complete integration, for a situation in which each individual will be judged and treated as an individual and not in any way as a member of a *supposed* or functionless group. Functional group membership will continue to be important; it would be foolish to treat physicians as if they were engineers. Prejudice and discrimination, however, are characterized precisely by the fact that they disregard function; they treat the black physician and engineer and farm laborer and machine operator and teacher and unskilled worker as if they were all alike.

The present authors believe in the third goal mentioned above—complete equality and integration. This goal is harmonious with peaceful coexistence or pluralism, provided that the pluralism is chosen by individuals of the minority group as a matter of right and not enforced on them by the majority as a categorical requirement. Plural rights are limited, of course, by the legitimate needs for security and integration of the whole society. One of the great problems of modern society is the determination of differences that are allowable and are harmonious with the principle of the greatest good to the greater number. We believe these differences can be very broad—broader than most societies, in this day of crisis, are permitting. Differences in language, in religion, in belief in the best methods for achieving life's values—these are not only permissible but necessary for a society that is eager to find better ways to solve its problems. *Active allegiance* to a system of law that opposes the democratic method for settling disputes is doubtless beyond the range of differences that an integrated society may permit. Advocacy of such a system is less dangerous to democracy than its suppression; but active programs may well represent "a clear and present danger." Unfortunately, in the difficult and important task of separating advocacy from active programs, a legitimate and necessary pluralism has been weakened. Opposition to those who are working for an undemocratic state has been extended, by some, to opposition to those who have different ideas, believe different religious doctrines, have different conceptions of the proper extent of governmental activity, and trace descent from different ancestors. Thus reaction and prejudice frequently have been joined in our society. We believe that America can prosper only by encouraging the integration of all groups while permitting a wide and diversified pluralism.

In day-by-day moral decisions, one often has to decide between two values. Is it better to make the maximum number of public housing units available to disprivileged black families, or to promote housing integration even at the cost of turning away some of the families in greatest need? This raises the difficult question of quotas. Can they be "benign," as Dodson, Cohen, and others have asked? That is, can they be designed to guarantee, in housing for example, that a neighborhood that has become integrated racially will not rather quickly be resegregated? (Cohen 1960; Dodson 1960). In some circumstances, neighborhoods that are 70 percent white and 30 percent black will become entirely black within a few years if actions are not taken to prevent it: "If whites want to be at least three-fourths and blacks at least one-third, it won't work" (Schelling 1978, p. 142). Those actions may require that the preservation of an integrated neighborhood be preferred to a policy of equal access. We think it is desirable to have far more integrated neighborhoods. We also support a policy of equal access. In such a dilemma, to make an informed policy or moral decision one must know: Who pays the costs? Blacks denied access to an integrated neighborhood in an effort to preserve its integration must find their housing in a more restricted market. They pay more. We also must know whether and how both integration and equal access can be maintained. By seeing that many neighborhoods are open? By supporting amenities that make them attractive to both whites and blacks? It is essential for students of intergroup relations to study such collisions of values.

In the early days of the desegregation movement in the United States, there was not a great deal of disagreement over goals or over priorities because there was so much to do that any step seemed right. After a few gains, however, value priorities begin to emerge, and serious dilemmas, within and between persons, are revealed. Is it better to promote justice even at the cost of conflict, or to promote peace even at the risk of some injustice?

Is liberty the primary goal—making certain that everybody has a fair start, that each has a choice among reasonable alternatives and the right to participate in decisions affecting his welfare, or, in a definition closer to John Stuart Mill, that everyone is free from tyranny of leaders and from constraints by the majority when those constraints are unnecessary for the larger good? Liberty has perhaps been the first goal of liberal societies during the last two centuries. For others, however, the first goal is equality. They believe, with R. H. Tawney, that liberty is impossible without equality, that the democratic society, therefore, must strive to achieve a relative equality in the distribution of scarce goods. Some would say that this is so important that equality should be sought even at the sacrifice of some liberty. Still others emphasize fraternity as the fundamental goal. In Max Weber's terms, this might be defined as relative similarity in the distribution of social honor, creating a situation in which people are not separated by rank. Each is therefore the brother or sister—perhaps more precisely, a potential brother-in-law or sister-in-law—of every other.

Goode (1976) has recently examined some of the consequences of the choices of goals and has concluded that the good society will more equally distribute not only income but also esteem. We do not need differences in rewards as large as we now have to maintain striving:

And if the rewards at lower levels were higher, many more people at those levels would strive harder. Second, if people at lower levels were esteemed more, the esteem they give to others would be worth more, so that the total amount given to the upper levels (if not the discrepancy between their share of respect and that of others) would be as large as, perhaps even larger than, at present. (p. 378)

Although there are many zero-sum elements in American society (Thurow 1981)—perhaps in any society—some of these are only short run. In the long run, all can gain by greater equality (see Goode 1978, Chapter 14).

It would take a long philosophical treatise to discuss the relationships among these goals. The French Revolution, and to an important degree the

American revolution as well, assumed that they were not incompatible, but indeed mutually supportive. Many persons, however, would argue that they are mutually limiting, that efforts to attain one will reduce the chances of attaining the others, not because of their incompatibility but because of the selective use of time and resources. Still others see them as mutually exclusive. In the United States, for example, there has always been an underlying tension between the goals of liberty and of equality, with the former being more strongly supported, and fear being expressed that too much equality means the end of liberty. Today, the pluralism–integration question raises the issue of fraternity in a crucial way. The goal of subgroup fraternity is receiving new emphasis, as for example in some phases of the Black Power movement.

We will not undertake the philosophical treatise required, but perhaps we may be permitted a moral aside. It is possible that each of the three values can be carried to self-defeating limits? Ought the goal to be to maximize not any one of the values but the *product* value of the three? Ought we not to ask, in moral discourse about these goals, whether or not gain in any one of them contributes also to gain in the others? If not, perhaps the first gain has been pushed too far.

However one answers these questions, *some* answer is essential before meaningful strategic action is possible.

Types of Persons

Those who declare that *the* way to eliminate prejudice is education or law or more contact between peoples, or those who oppositely declare that prejudice cannot be eliminated because *the* prejudiced person is torn by a deep-seated anxiety that is basic to his ego—all make the mistake of failing to distinguish among the many different types of persons who show intergroup hostility. The reduction of prejudice and discrimination demands that we make such distinctions, for a different strategy will be effective for each of the different types of persons.

Robert Merton (in MacIver 1949, p. 99–126) has devised a useful classification of four types of persons for each of whom a different group of strategies is appropriate.

1. The unprejudiced nondiscriminator, or all-weather liberal; the person who accepts the American creed in both belief and action. Such a person must be the spearhead of any effective campaign to reduce prejudice and discrimination, but his force is reduced by several errors. There is the "fallacy of group soliloquies." "Ethnic liberals are busily engaged in talking to themselves. Repeatedly, the same groups of like-minded liberals seek each other out, hold periodic meetings in which they engage in mutual exhortation, and thus lend social and psychological support to one another." The fallacy of group soliloquies produces the illusion that there is consensus on the issue in the community at large and thus leads to the "fallacy of unanimity." The all-weather liberal mistakes discussion in like-minded groups for effective action and overestimates the support for his position. His isolation from other points of view also produces the "fallacy of privatized solutions."

These fallacies lead to the paradox of the passive liberal's contributing, to some degree, to the persistence of prejudice and discrimination by his very inaction. They may be overcome by having the liberal enter groups that are not composed solely of fellow liberals (giving up the gratifications of consistent group support); by realization that discrimination brings rewards—or seems to—and that exhortation, therefore, is not enough if the social environment is not changed at the same time; and by action on the part of the militant liberal to show the passive liberal how he contributes to prejudice and discrimination by his inaction (see Pinkney 1968).

2. The unprejudiced discriminator, or fair-weather liberal. This is the person who, despite his own lack of prejudice, supports discrimination if it is easier or profitable. He may show the expedience of silence or timidity or discriminate to seize an advantage. The fair-weather liberal suffers from some degree of guilt and is therefore a strategic person for the all-weather liberal to work on. The need is to bring him into groups of all-weather liberals, where he will find rewards for abiding by his own beliefs.

3. The prejudiced nondiscriminator, or fair-weather illiberal. This is the reluctant conformist, the employer who discriminates until a fair employment practices law puts the fear of punishment and loss into him, the trade-union official who, though prejudiced himself, abolishes Jim Crow because the rank and file of his membership demands it, the bigoted businessman who profits from the trade of minority-group members. The fair-weather illiberal can be kept from discrimination, not by appeal to his value creed, but by making discrimination

costly or unpleasant while rewarding tolerance (Griffitt and Garcia 1979). Legal controls, strictly administered, may at first increase his prejudice—or at least his verbalization of it—but they will reduce his discrimination.

4. The prejudiced discriminator, or all-weather illiberal. He is consistent in belief and practice. He believes that differential treatment of minority groups is not discrimination, but discriminating. Strategy in dealing with such persons must vary from region to region. In some subcultures of the United States the all-weather illiberal is a conformist, supported by the group norms; if he were to change, he would be alienated from the people important to him. In other cultures he is isolated and a change in his attitudes and behavior would help to bring integration with people significant to him. He can be moved toward type three. Change of the illiberal who is supported by group norms requires legal and administrative controls and large-scale changes in the economic supports to prejudice.

It is important to understand the distribution of these various types and to realize the kinds of strategies that are effective with each. To try to appeal to all of them in the same way, or to assume that a given proportion of each type is found, when they are in fact very differently distributed, is to make serious strategic errors. We must note that such a classification has little reference to the intensity dimension; two all-weather illiberals, for example, may have very different patterns of behavior because prejudice and discrimination occupy an important place in the personality organization of one and an unimportant place for the other. One cannot assume, moreover, that the same distribution would be true for each minority. In a given community one might find discrimination against both an Indian and a black group, but most of the white population may be fair-weather liberals toward the Indians and all-weather illiberals toward the blacks.

Levinson (in Adorno et al. 1950, p. 60) draws a valuable distinction between the openly antidemocratic individual and the pseudodemocratic individual. The former is nearly the equivalent of Merton's all-weather illiberal, except that Levinson emphasizes the deep-seated irrational sources (a specialized causal explanation that Merton might not share entirely). The pseudodemocratic person is somewhat similar to the fair-weather liberal; but Levinson places a useful emphasis on the ambivalence of such a person's feelings: he discriminates but has some sense of guilt about it; he is prejudiced but also believes in democratic values.

Because of their ambivalence, pseudodemocratic individuals are relatively unaffected by current literature that attacks prejudice as "un-American" or "un-Christian," for they have disguised their prejudice from themselves by a group of rationalizations that seem to square behavior with value creed. Strategy must find a way not simply of exposing those rationalizations (for the problem is not essentially a rational one with the individual) but of lowering the need for prejudice while strengthening the belief in democratic values.

Types of Situations

When one has distinguished the types of goals and types of persons involved, one has a great deal of information about a situation in which prejudice and discrimination are found. But other factors must also be considered if strategy is to be effective. What is the legal pattern? Does it support discrimination or condemn it? Does the law condemn it ideologically but fail to provide enforcement techniques? To try the same strategy in a situation in which one can count on legal support as one tries in a situation in which the law is weak or actually supports discrimination is to be ineffective.

Is the situation one that requies immediate action, or is there time for more deliberate analysis? What is called for in one would be foolish in the other. Schermerhorn (1949, p. 519) distinguishes between emergency problems and tractable problems and emphasizes the need to deal with them in different ways. Strategic errors have been made in both directions. In a time of critical hostility a community may "appoint a committee" when what is most needed is training for their police in how to disperse a mob with the least violence. Or, oppositely, a group may "call in the cops," may throw down the gauntlet to discriminators when what is most needed is the careful analysis of causes, the skillful rallying of allies, and the creation of a more favorable environment for change. No easy formula can separate emergency problems from tractable problems, but to neglect to take account of their differences is to invite failure.

Is the discrimination supported mainly by lower-class members of the dominant group, themselves insecure and hoping to climb a little higher on the backs of minority-group members? Or is the pattern primarily set by powerful groups who are exploiting prejudice to maintain their authority? Or, more accurately, how are these two supports interrelated? Associated with this is the question of power in a community. Who makes the key decisions; whose support is vital? Much strategic counsel is based on the assumption that major support for change must come from "the conservative power elite." McKee argues, however, (1958–9, p. 198), that this leads to failure to create "support for new policies by building a constituency in the community who have a genuine stake, personal or ideological, in effecting changes in the community's policies." In some contexts, a coalition can be built up among organized black groups, Hispanics, an active liberal middle-class group, the Jewish community, some church groups, and women's organizations. In many instances, when such a coalition is mobilized, such "power elite" as there is may then find participation more desirable. Under other conditions, of course, this procedure may mobilize opposition. The need is for flexibility of judgment.

Many aspects of a society can be important situational influences. One must ask: What is the level of unemployment, the degree of tension and frustration, the extent of status dissatisfaction? What subtle cues are people receiving on issues wholly unrelated to intergroup relations that influence their readiness for various kinds of intergroup behavior. In the United States, for example, the vast majority of motion pictures, television shows, and advertisements show few native Americans, Hispanics, or Blacks; or they use them only in stereotyped roles. In the last several years, however, minority persons have appeared as parts of casual crowds, juries, or as professionals. The number of storylines featuring Blacks in soap operas has increased quite rapidly, due partly to the success of such television programs as "Roots" and the potential size of the black audience (*The New York Times*, July 4, 1982, II-1, 21). An increasing proportion of advertisements show Blacks and Whites (Greenberg and Mazingo 1976). Were this trend to develop, what Americans come to look upon as normal may be slightly affected.

Mapping Out a Program

Having defined one's goals and analyzed the kinds of persons and situational factors to be dealt with, the strategist is in a position to plan an anti-hostility program. Unfortunately, planning and testing are not common.

Well-intentioned but unguided programs can be useless or even harmful. When they fail, many people may conclude, as Robin Williams points out, that intergroup hostility is inevitable. Others may decide that such hostility is so deeply embedded in our society that only revolutionary change can produce results. Assumptions of these kinds can be tested only by action that is guided by research. The effects of such action "should be to develop realistic confidence and to stabilize expectations in such a way as to reduce the dangers of unchecked utopianism on the one hand and fatalistic disillusionment on the other (Williams 1947, p. 10).

One of the functions of research is to discover the points at which prejudice and discrimination can be attacked most successfully. Myrdal (1944, pp. 60–67) refers to the white man's "rank order of discriminations" toward the Negro, with particular reference to the South. He believes the white man is most willing (although not necessarily very willing) to grant economic and political gains to Negroes and is least willing to grant what he calls social equality. The Negro, on the other hand, is primarily concerned with just the concessions the white man will make most readily. This seems to carry the obvious strategic implication that action programs should center upon economic and political discriminations.

Evidence on this question is not decisive, for there is variation in time and place (see Blackwell and Hart, 1982). Behavior may differ from the answers to interview questions (few Americans, for example, will verbally deny the right to freedom of economic activity, but their actions often speak more loudly); and rankings depend on what the actual situation is (if the right to vote has been won by Blacks, Whites may not state high opposition to it even though they had earlier strongly supported the disfranchising situation). It is also important to note with Killian and Grigg (1961) that the rank order tells you nothing about the absolute level of discriminatory tendency—which may be the more significant fact.

Black and white student responses in a southern university confirmed Myrdal's finding, on the whole (Wilson and Varner 1973). Williams and Wienir (1967) found, in a study of student attitudes at three universities, that there was a consistent ordering but that it varied somewhat from the pattern described by Myrdal. Myrdal hypothesized (on the basis, as he noted, of observation, and not controlled study) the following order, with the relationships on which the white man was least willing to yield given first: intermarriage, personal relations, public facilities (schools, churches, means of transportation), politics, legal and judicial activities, and economics. For the three student groups, the order was: intermarriage, personal relations, economics, public facilities, politics, and legal and judicial activities. The placement of economic privilege is undoubtedly crucial in understanding any given minority–majority situation.

Matthews and Prothro (1966) also show the need for qualifying the Myrdal thesis. They found that Negro political demands in the eleven southern states were sharply· in opposition to what Whites were willing to grant. They also added a time dimension and found that Negroes were expecting extremely rapid progress, whereas Whites were just beginning to get comfortable with the thought of glacial speed in changes of race relations. We should observe, however, that their study would not have served as a good basis for prediction of the actual speed at which change in southern politics actually occurred. National political factors of course were critical in effecting this change.

Despite these qualifications, knowledge of the strong and weak points of opposition is essential to sound strategy. This does not mean that weak points should always be attacked first, for greatest opposition may be found on issues of greatest importance, which therefore must be confronted in spite of the difficulty. Only by knowedge of which issues are most difficult can a rational decision on this question be made.

In addition to knowing the relative importance of various issues to the interacting individuals and groups, one must know, in mapping out a program, how a given type of strategy will be viewed by all those involved. Do they regard it as a legitimate way to express a grievance or as a deviation from the accepted standards? Or, as is commonly the case in societies under serious stress, is a given strategy accepted by some—whatever their views of the goals being sought—and rejected by others? In America, various forms of public protest are applauded by some as necessary and right, while others see them as acts of rebellion against legitimate authority. Olsen (1968, p. 299) has designed a scale to measure the extent to which respondents grant legitimacy to various acts and has tested it with a largely upper-middle-class, urban, white group. The questions form a Guttman scale (coefficient of reproducibility = 96.6 percent):

If a group of people in this country strongly feels that the government is treating them unfairly, what kinds of actions do you think they have a right to take in order to try to change the situation? . . . Which of these actions do you think groups have a right to take in our country?
1. Hold public meetings and rallies. (92%)
2. March quietly and peacefully through town. (70%)
3. Take indirect actions such as economic boycotts or picketing. (60%)
4. Take direct action such as strikes or sit-ins. (46%)
5. Stage mass protest demonstrations. (41%)

That 59 percent of this highly educated group of respondents opposed mass protest demonstrations is perhaps not so striking as the fact that 30 percent opposed the right to "march quietly and peacefully through town." In any event, for those seeking change, it is necessary to know probable responses to various strategies.

Turner has extended our knowledge on this question by asking: Under what conditions will acts of disruption and violence be viewed as forms of legitimate protest and when will they be considered crime and rebellion? He defines protest as an action with the following elements: it expresses a grievance, wrong, or injustice; protesters are unable to correct the condition directly by their own efforts; they seek to call attention to the grievance, to provoke ameliorative steps by some target groups; and some combination of sympathy and fear is invoked. The same act can be defined in many different ways, and the subsequent course of events is strongly affected by the definition that emerges. Those who define a disorder as a protest, in Turner's use of the term, see it as a form of communication. If they define it as deviation, they see it as an individual criminal act. When it is called rebellion or revolution, the disorder is seen not as an effort to communicate with others or to change the system but as an effort to destroy it.

What conditions support these various definitions; in particular, when will a more or less legitimate protest definition emerge? Turner notes the following conditions: Protesters must be seen as a major part of a group whose grievances are well known, who seem powerless to correct those grievances, and who seem deserving of support because they are customarily law-abiding and restrained in their methods. The appeal message must command attention; a combination of threat and appeal is required: "When the threat component falls below the optimal range, the most likely interpretation is deviance; above the optimal range, preoccupation with threat makes rebellion the probable interpretation" (Turner 1969, p. 821). As Turner notes further: "Official protest interpretations can serve as an effective hedge only in societies and communities where humanitarian values are strong relative to toughness values, so that failure of official action in the service of humanitarianism is excusable" (Turner 1969, p. 828; see also Lipsky 1968; Robert Fogelson in Connery 1968, pp. 25–41).

Knowledge of the conditions under which conflictful or potentially conflictful action can win a protest definition—and thus presumably win attention while activating less resistance—is still rudimentary. What is clear is that acts formerly defined as deviant are now carried out under claims of legitimacy. This is well described by Horowitz and Liebowitz (1968) as a process of bringing various social problems out of the welfare arena and into the political arena. In the former, various forms of deviation are defined as public problems to be handled by social agencies according to various norms of administrative policy. In the latter, deviation (in matters of our interest, let us say black welfare parents demanding by disruptive means a voice in policy) is defined as a political problem to be fought out among the contending parties in an open and public process. Thus, to cite an extreme contrast, if welfare mothers organize to demand an increase in welfare payments, saying they cannot feed their children on what they receive, they are defined as deviant, outside the legitimate process for reviewing and ameliorating such problems. If cotton farmers organize to demand a payment for not growing cotton (some of them receive over $1 million each in a year from the government), this is not deviant activity seeking welfare, since their efforts are carried out through political channels. Perhaps this issue can be stated in its most general terms in the following way:

When the distinction between deviation and political competition is easily drawn, we have:

1. Illegitimate deviation according to the powerful majority, and therefore control by administrative means
2. Legitimate dissent accepted as such by majority and minority, and therefore decision by political competition

But when decisive power of the majority or consensus breaks down:

1. Powerful minorites may rise to say: "Our view is legitimate" and try to push it into the political arena: e.g., black parents seeking control over welfare policies.
2. Powerful groups arise to say, of formerly accepted dissent: "Your views are illegitimate" and try to push it out of the political arena into the deviation category: e.g., the abortion controversy.

It is difficult to develop an objective statement of this situation, since long-run consequences are more difficult to see than the immediate actions of those with whom one feels much or little sympathy. Perhaps the more common error in the general public is the belief that the boundary between administrative control and political control is fixed and obvious, while the more common error among intellectuals is the belief that everything ought to be politicized, that there is little consensus to build on, and that therefore all issues should be made matters of public controversy.

Whatever one's views on the value questions involved in this issue, it is clear that effective strategy requires an assessment of the various definitions of the situation made by those who will be affected by one's actions. Since individuals are often ambivalent, more favorable rather than less favorable responses can be drawn out by actions appropriate to the tendency one wishes to encourage. And since this is a time of rapid change of views regarding the legitimacy of both means and goals, continuous appraisal is required.

Strategies with Major Emphasis on Changing the Personality

It has been noted frequently that attempts to reduce intergroup hostility can focus either on the prejudiced individual or on those aspects of the situation that allow and encourage discrimination. The former strategies try to change the values, the attitudes, the needs of individuals. They are sometimes based on the oversimplified theory that majority-minority conflict "fundamentally" rests on personality factors. But they are sometimes consciously chosen specialties that are used in full awareness of the value and necessity of other approaches.

We shall describe and evaluate five kinds of approaches that emphasize the need for changing the persons who show prejudice and discrimination: exhortation, propaganda, contact, education, and personal therapy. These are not analytically precise and mutually exclusive categories, but one can draw useful distinctions among them.

Propaganda is the manipulation of symbols on a controversial topic when the controversial element is disguised, emotional appeals are used, some or all of the relevant facts are left out or distorted, and the motives of the propagandist and/or the sources of the propaganda are hidden. Education is the transmission of noncontroversial information (it may or may not be true, but it is generally regarded as true in the society involved); or it is the handling of controversial topics by recognizing them as controversial, using an objective approach, bringing all relevant facts to bear, and noting clearly the sources and motives of the educator. *No empirical act will be simply propaganda or education.* We are describing pure types that may never be found. Each event can be placed along the continuum on the basis of the criteria used.

Exhortation seems ordinarily to be at about the midpoint between propaganda and education. It often minimizes the controversial nature of the topics with which it deals and uses emotional appeals; but it frequently marshals a great many facts and makes no effort to disguise its motives or its sources. Efforts to encourage contact between minority- and majority-group members are also near the midpoint, although perhaps somewhat more educational than propagandistic, as we have defined those terms. They are partially propagandistic because they frequently distort the facts in the guise of studying facts, for the contacts are selected on the basis of their ability to change attitudes, not according to their typicality.

Exhortation

Exhortation is perhaps the most frequently used method in trying to reduce intergroup hostility. Appeal to people's better selves; revivify belief in their value creed; change their hearts and they will change their ways. Despite the frequency with which this approach is used, its value has not been tested in any way that permits one to speak with confidence about the degree of its effectiveness. Myrdal's famous work has brought a strong emphasis on the importance of the "American creed" as an ideological weakness of the prejudiced person. There is a moral struggle going on *within* most Americans, says Myrdal, that prevents race relations from being worse than they are and makes an ideological approach to their improvement feasible. "The American Negro problem is a problem in the heart of the American." Because he believes in democracy, in the rights of the common man, in the rightness of free enterprise (no barriers to freedom of economic activity), the American cannot believe, without some mental gymnastics, that prejudice and discrimination are justified. The strategy of exhortation tries to bring this contradiction to the forefront of our attention, to revitalize the creed.

Although exhortation sounds quite old-fashioned, it is essentially the strategy of many current activities, from demonstrations and rallies to "guerrilla theater." In this last, the players attempt, by a surprise dramatic event, to call vivid attention to an issue and to persuade those who see (or experience) the "play" that a given moral view is right. The theater group may stage a severe interracial argument on a bus: then speak words of reconciliation (see Brustein 1971).

Participants in these contemporary forms of exhortation doubtless feel quite secular in most instances. In many ways, however, such events are modernized versions of sermons, not lacking in surrogates for hell-fire and brimstone, followed by descriptions of the true road to salvation. As with all sermons, the central questions remain: are the sinners in the pews; are they listening? Such evidence as that found in Crawford's paper (1974), "Sermons on Racial Tolerance," indicates that the impact is small.

In the context of other changes, exhortation may help to reduce prejudice, particularly by increasing the enthusiasm of those who are already convinced. It may also inhibit the discriminations, although it may not affect the prejudices, of many fair-weather illiberals who do not want to violate the community standards openly. It is easy, however, to exaggerate the influence of exhortation. It may raise one's guilt feelings, which are then allayed by a blinder defensiveness, by new discriminations that actually furnish new justification for the prejudices. One must also recognize a contrary creed—a moral code that justifies prejudice and discrimination.

Effective strategy appears to indicate that exhortation can play only a modest role in the total efforts to reduce prejudice and discrimination. The moral premises on which it rests are not universally shared and are alloyed with countervalues; most of us are skilled at compartmentalizing our professions of belief and our other actions, overlooking any contradictions; and those who are most likely to show hostility to minority-group members are probably those who are least often reached by exhortation.

Propaganda

The success of the mass campaigns of persuasion by modern nations and the skill with which commercial propaganda (advertising) has converted cigarettes and chewing gum into necessities make us believe that a tremendously powerful instrument for controlling human behavior has been created. Why not turn this instrument to the purpose of reducing intergroup hostility?

Before examining attempts to use propaganda to control intergroup behavior, it may be wise to state briefly the contemporary answer to the question, How effective is propaganda? As we have learned more and more about the problem, we have seen that there is no *general* answer. The question must be more complicated: How effective is a specific propaganda campaign with a stated group of people in a particular situation? Gradually it has become apparent that far more limits are imposed on the power of propaganda than was generally believed to be true a few years ago.

Modern societies, to be sure, are more susceptible to propaganda than stable, "sacred" societies. The entrance of more and more questions into the area of controversy, because of the breakup of traditional answers, concomitant personal insecurities that make many people eager for some simple answer to life's problems, the spread of mass media of communication, capable of bringing simultaneous stimuli to millions of people, and even the rise of the sciences of man—these and other factors have made propaganda more likely and more powerful than before.

Propaganda is limited, however, even under such favorable conditions. It is limited by knowledge of the facts on the part of propagandees; it is limited by counterpropaganda; and above all, it is limited by the already existing values, needs, and hopes of the persons to whom it attempts to appeal. To put this point oppositely: Propaganda is most effective when it is dealing with a poorly informed public, when it has a monopoly in the field of communication (censorship), and when it either is working in an area in which the values and needs of the public are diffuse and poorly structured or ties its appeals closely to well-structured needs and values.

Propaganda may have wholly unexpected and unintended effects, for ultimately it is interpreted by specific individuals whose own values and needs are brought to bear. Unintended or "boomerang" effects of propaganda are particularly likely to occur when one tries to influence a heterogenous group.

Propaganda to Reduce Intergroup Hostility. Literally millions of leaflets, pamphlets, cartoons, comic books, articles, and movies have been issued in the struggle against intergroup hostility. How effective are they? Flowerman (1947) suggests that this question can be answered only when we have the following information: To what degree do protolerance groups control the media of communication? What is the level of saturation—the proportion of a population that is reached by the appeals? What is the attention level? Does the propaganda conform to group standards? (If it does not, it can have little effect. And those standards may include prejudice.) What is the sponsorship? Is it held in high esteem?

The evidence appears to suggest that on many of these counts antiprejudice propaganda has not been very effective. For the most part it reaches those who already agree with it.

In some instances individuals have been confronted with antiprejudice propaganda involuntarily. Some fight it, openly or covertly; a few may accept it; but many evade it by managing to misunderstand its message. A number of studies have been made of the effects of a "Mr. Biggott" series of cartoons, designed to show an absurd man exhibiting ridiculous prejudices. "In each of them, Mr. Biggott, the central character, is shown as a cantankerous and unattractive man of middle age and moderate income. In each of them he displays the antiminority attitudes from which he earns his name" (Patricia Kendall and Katherine Wolfe, in Lazarsfeld and Stanton 1949, p. 158). Three cartoons are used in the study by Kendall and Wolf. One shows Mr. Biggott glowering at an "honor roll" billboard on which the community war heroes are listed. He says, "Berkowitz, Fabrizio, Ginsberg, Kelly—disgraceful!" In another cartoon, Mr. Biggott, lying sick in bed, says to a somewhat startled doctor, "In case I should need a transfusion, doctor, I want to make certain I don't get anything but blue, sixth-generation American blood!" In an "Indian" cartoon Mr.Biggott says to a humble American Indian, "I'm sorry, Mr. Eaglefeather, but our company's policy is to employ 100 percent Americans only."

The assumption behind the cartoons was that the picturing of an absurd man exhibiting absurd ideas would lead the observer to reject his own prejudices. Cooper and Jahoda (1947) found, however, that prejudiced persons created many mechanisms of evasion. Understanding may be "derailed" by avoiding identification with Mr. Biggott (despite the sharing of prejudice). Mr. X, on seeing the blood transfusion cartoon, looked upon Mr. Biggott as an inferior *parvenu*: "I'm eighth generation myself. . . . He may not be the best blood either." Then Mr. X leads off into other subjects. Having understood the cartoon at first ("He don't want anything but sixth-generation American blood! Ha! That's pretty good."), he then felt it necessary to disidentify. Many observers believe that the television show "All in the Family" is subject to the same multiple interpretations. A liberal viewer regards it as an exposé of foolish prejudices; but others may identify with Archie Bunker and in so doing are given an opportunity to "rehearse" a variety of prejudices.

Because of the difficulties of reaching the audience for whom the propoaganda would be most useful and because of the ease with which its points can be evaded, we cannot rely heavily on propaganda as a strategy. To be sure, a cartoon series is a brief stimulus. We do not know what the effects of an intensive, long-run propaganda campaign would be. A movie is a stronger stimulus, on which we have some information. There have been many studies to test the effects of movies on attitudes; and, partly on the basis of the results obtained, several movies (some propagandistically and others educationally inclined) have aimed at the reduction of prejudice. Our knowledge of the total long-run effects of movies, however, is still far from adequate because of several methodological weaknesses. Sampling problems have not been given much attention (school populations are so readily available to the researcher); the distortions in evidence produced by the "before-after" type of experiment (the kind that has been most often used) have not been explored adequately; and the relation between pencil-and-paper responses and other kinds of behavior usually has not been studied.

Despite these weaknesses, it seems fair to say that many movies do have a measureable effect on attitudes as recorded in verbal tests. Three hundred twenty-nine students at a southern state university were shown *Gentleman's Agreement*, a successful Hollywood picture that took a strong stand against anti-Semitism. They had first recorded their attitudes on a ten-item anti-Semitism and ten-item anti-Negro scale. After seeing the film they were again asked to record their attitudes. Sixty-nine percent had lower scores; 31 percent showed no change or higher scores. This compares with 42 percent lower scores and 58 percent the same or higher scores among the 116 who had not seen the film. This difference is significant at the .001 level. Interestingly, anti-Negro scores also fell among those who saw the film ($p = .05$). Largest absolute gains were made by those whose anti-Semitism scores were highest at the beginning (they had more room in which to change), but those whose original scores were low showed the largest change when it is calculated as a percentage of possible change. Those persons low in status concern also had signficantly greater reductions in their scores (see Middleton 1960).

With the limits set by the present evidence it seems unwise to say either that antiprejudice propaganda is powerless or that it can by itself effect extensive changes. Flowerman (1947, pp. 434–35) points out these minimum requirements if it is to have any influence: The propaganda must be received under favorable conditions, so that it will be looked at or heard; it must attract and hold the attention of the propagandee; it must be enjoyable, not bring pain; it must be understood, not evaded by misunderstanding. None of these is easy to accomplish. Propaganda usually is seen only by the already converted; if prejudiced persons happen to see it, they usually turn away; if they do not turn away, they often find it painful (because of guilt feelings or a sense of hostility); and if they do not find it painful, they frequently misunderstand its point. It is with the mildly prejudiced and the neutral, particularly with children, that these disadvantages are at a minimum.

How Should Prejudiced Propaganda Be Handled? Wise strategy must understand not only the possible uses of propaganda but also the techniques that are most effective in counteracting prejudiced propaganda. There has been a vigorous debate, and sharp differences in action, between those who believed that "hate-mongers" should be exposed, ridiculed, and made to stand in the glare of public attention and those who contended that they should be disregarded and offset by positive action. One must pay careful attention to destructive rumors or propaganda against minorities; but they should usually be opposed indirectly, by positive action, not directly, by exposing them and pointing out their errors. If one tries to prove a rumor wrong by repeating it and then describing the truth, many listeners may hear only the rumor, if that is all they want to hear. Thus one accomplishes the opposite of what one intends. If one ignores the rumor but supplies truthful information, those who have not heard the rumor may to some degree be "vacinnated" against it. When the British movie production of *Oliver Twist* was brought to the United States, several groups opposed its release because *one* of the antagonists of the story is a Jew. They thought seeing the movie might increase anti-Semitism. Their opposition made it more likely that the movie would be widely attended and that those with mild or latent anti-Semitism would be sensitized to the unfavorable Jewish character. Violent anti-Semites, moreover, were given the rare opportunity of parading as defenders of civil liberties—upholding free speech and opposing censorship. These rules may help to guide one' decisions:

1. Do not overlook the importance of hate propaganda.
2. Where possible, deal with it indirectly, by furnishing true information, by developing people immune to prejudice, not by direct attack.
3. Do not exaggerate the extent of the rabble-rouser's following or the strength of his influence.
4. Stress the injury his actions bring to the whole society, not to some "poor, oppressed minority."

Contact

No factor has received more attention among strategies for reducing prejudice and discrimination than the effects of contact between the members of different groups. It is often said, "If there were only more contact, if people only knew each other better, there would be less prejudice." Yet it is also known that prejudice often seems most intense in areas where there is most contact. How effective is contact with members of a minority group in changing attitudes and behavior toward that group? This question requires careful study, for there are many factors that affect the results.

Converging evidence from the sociology of knowledge, expectations states theory, and the psychology of perception shows that experience is situational. What we see or hear, what we believe, how we think are all dependent upon the total situation in which these actions occur and upon our total mental context. We never see an isolated unit of human behavior; we see behavior in a larger situation through the perspectives we have acquired. Most of us can look a fact squarely in the face and, if we already have a frame of reference that involves it, turn it completely around.

The ambiguity of many aspects of human behavior makes it possible to perceive such behavior in a way that harmonizes with an already established belief. When a person greets you warmly, it is possible that he is a true friend, but it is possible that he is busily engaged in opposing you behind your back and wants to prevent you from suspecting it. If you already "know" which is true, you will interpret his behavior in that light.

A strong prejudice can have an almost paralyzing effect on observation and rational judgment. Whatever the behavior involved, it can be explained by the prejudice. Even opposite kinds of behavior are used as proof of a supposed trait, as is well illustrated in the statement of General J. L. DeWitt concerning the evacuation of the Japanese from the West Coast in 1942:

In the war in which we are now engaged racial affinities are not severed by migration. The Japanese race is an enemy race and while many second and third generation Japanese born on United States soil, possessed of United States citizenship, have become "Americanized," the racial strains are undiluted. . . . That Japan is allied with Germany and Italy in this struggle is no ground for assuming that any Japanese, barred from assimilation by convention as he is, though born and raised in the United States, will not turn against this nation when the final test of loyalty comes. It, therefore, follows that along the vital Pacific Coast over 112,000 potential enemies of Japanese extraction are at large today. There are indications that these are organized and ready for concerted action at a favorable opportunity. The very fact that no sabotage has taken place to date is a disturbing and confirming indication that such action will be taken.[1]

---

[1] From United States Army Western Defense Command and Fourth Army, *Japanese in the United States, Final Report: Japanese Evacuation from the West Coast*. Washington, D.C.: U.S. Government Printing Office 1943, pp. 33–34.

The conclusion, the attitude, is found in the first part of this statement. The last sentence shows how *any* fact, even one that to the naive observer must seem to be an exact refutation of the conclusion, can be made to seem to support it. Contact with the members of a minority group can scarcely weaken a prejudice that is so impervious to experience. Behavior that does not harmonize with the prejudice may not be seen at all; our perceptions are made selective and partial by the prejudice itself, which thus becomes self-confirmatory. Or if the behavior is seen, it is treated as an exception: "Some of my best friends are Jews," but—they are not typical.

Contact with members of a minority group may of course, be of an unpleasant variety. This is sometimes held to be a cause of prejudice—that attitude is simply a generalization from a few unfortunate experiences. Unpleasant experience with individual members of a minority group, however, can scarcely be the cause of prejudice, because that experience would not be generalized to the whole minority group unless the prejudice were already there. Moreover, we cannot be certain that persons who report more unpleasant memories of contact with members of minority groups have actually had more such contacts. Memory is selective; they may remember (or invent) such contacts *because* they already have a stronger than average prejudice.

Thus we find that prejudice is sometimes explained as a result of the *lack* of contact with members of a minority group and sometimes explained as the result of the *presence* of such contact. Both theories explain only surface relationships.

Such observations do not mean, however, that one's experiences with individual members of a minority group have no effect on attitudes toward that group. Prejudice does not entirely precede and coerce the interpretation of experience. Unpleasant contacts probably increase the strength of prejudice. Oppositely, *certain kinds of contact* are effective in reducing the strength of prejudice and the likelihood of discrimination.

Allport (1954, pp. 262–63) prepared a valuable outline of the variables that we should have in mind in any analysis of the effects of contact between members of different groups.

Quantitative aspects of contact:
  a. Frequency
  b. Duration
  c. Number of persons involved
  d. Variety

Status aspects of contact:
  a. Minority member has inferior status.
  b. Minority member has equal status.
  c. Minority member has superior status.
  d. Not only may the individuals encountered vary thus in status; but the group as a whole may have relatively high status (e.g., Jews) or relatively low status (e.g., Negroes).

Role aspects of contact:
  a. Is the relationship one of competitive or cooperative activity?
  b. Is there a superordinate or subordinate role relation involved; e.g., master–servant, employer–employee, teacher–pupil?

Social atmosphere surrounding the contact:
  a. Is segregation prevalent, or is egalitarianism expected?
  b. Is the contact voluntary or involuntary?
  c. Is the contact "real" or "artificial"?
  d. Is the contact perceived in terms of intergroup relations or not perceived as such?
  e. Is the contact regarded as "typical" or as "exceptional"?
  f. Is the contact regarded as important and intimate, or as trivial and transient?

Personality of the individual experiencing the contact:
  a. Is his initial prejudice level high, low, medium?
  b. Is his prejudice of a surface, conforming type, or is it deeply rooted in his character structure?
  c. Has he basic security in his own life, or is he fearful and suspicious?
  d. What is his previous experience with the group in question, and what is the strength of his present stereotypes?
  e. What are his age and general education level?
  f. Many other personality factors may influence the effect of contact.

Areas of contact:
  a. Casual
  b. Residential
  c. Occupational
  d. Recreational
  e. Religious
  f. Civil and fraternal
  g. Political
  h. Goodwill intergroup activities

Even this list of variables that enter into the problem of contact is not exhaustive. It does, however, indicate the complexity of the problem we face (see also Amir 1969, 1976; Williams et al. 1964, Chapter 7; 1977, pp. 264–80). After one of the most intensive reviews of the effects of contact, Williams (1964, pp. 167–68) concludes:

In all the surveys in all communities and for all groups, majority and minorities, the greater the frequency of interaction, the lower the prevalence of ethnic prejudice. (Note that the same correlation can be stated: the less the frequency of ethnic prejudice, the more frequent is the interaction.)

Williams does not stop with this statement of a simple correlation. By the introduction of several test variables, he is able to strengthen a causal inference. "*If* contacts can be established"—an interesting and important qualification—even quite marked prejudices cannot nullify the prejudice-reducing influence of interaction.

Availability of contacts is not simply a matter of propinquity. Interracial contact in the United States continues to be infrequent in most communities despite the spread of nonwhites throughout the country. Attitudes have changed, however, indicating the strengthening of one of the ingredients necessary to favorable contact. In 1972 the General Social Survey of the NORC asked a cross-section of American adults: "How strongly would you object if a member of your family wanted to bring a (Negro/Black) friend home to dinner?" Twenty-nine percent answered "strongly" or "mildly," 71 percent said "not at all." When the same question was asked of the 1982 sample, 20 percent said "strongly" or "mildly" and 80 percent answered "not at all." When this question was first asked, by the Survey Research Center in 1963, only 50 percent had said "not at all" (Smith 1980, p. 62).

Behavior is governed by many factors in addition to attitudes, however; the change of verbal readiness for contact has not been matched by a similar change in behavior. It has often been remarked that "eleven o'clock Sunday morning is the most segregated time of the the week," but Molotch (1969) found that eleven o'clock Saturday evening was even more segregated. In those few situations wherein interracial activity was quite common, as for example a city commission for civic activities, there were status contrasts and, within the commission, contrasts in power (for the Blacks were chosen as "representatives," not because of their personal expertise or influence). Such contacts are as likely to confirm stereotypes as they are to create greater sensitivity to members of another race.

Individual experiences of contact affect and are affected by the community atmosphere. Suburban Whites, Warren notes (1970) are not only individually isolated from Blacks, a situation that encourages race tension, but also share a community atmosphere that reenforces that isolation and tends to furnish a community response to the conflict situation. Primary lack of contact generates a secondary, community-sustained lack of contact.

Effects of Equal-status Contact. The influence that has been most carefully explored in recent research is the degree of status equality or status difference among the participants in intergroup relations. In exploring this issue we must remember how resistant stereotypes are to evidence. Yet they are not entirely resistant. If they are disconfirmed time after time, revisions of belief may occur, in a kind of "bookkeeping" process, as Myron Rothbart calls it (in Hamilton 1981, Chapter 5). Or, he adds, a powerful conversion experience, a few highly salient contacts, may break the hold of a stereotype.

Equal-status contacts may involve competition or conflict that gets attached to racial or ethnic differences, even though those differences have nothing to do with the conflict or competition (Katz 1955; Tsukashima and Montero 1976). This is especially likely when the surrounding environment in which the equal-status contact occurs does not support the implications of equality.

Nevertheless, there is good evidence that what might be called stereotype-breaking contacts reduce prejudice. A somewhat unusual experience of this sort occurred in the U.S. Army in Europe during the winter and spring of 1945. The army at that time was substantially segregated. In March and April, however, several Negro rifle platoons were attached to white companies. Two months later, the Information and Education Division of the Army Service Forces conducted a survey to discover the response of white officers and men to this change. Five trained interviewers asked all available white company grade officers and a representative sample of platoon sergeants in twenty-four companies that contained Negro platoons, "Has your feeling changed since having served in the same unit with colored soldiers?" The responses were as follows: Seventy-seven percent of the white officers and the same percentage of white noncoms said that their feelings had become more favorable. Eighty-four percent of the white officers and 81 percent of the white noncoms answered "Very well" (the most favorable answer on a four-point scale) to the question, "How well did the colored soldiers in this company perform in combat?"[2]

Alongside these findings, however, it should be noted that in the last several years contact in the American armed forces has been associated with extensive interracial conflict, indicating again the complexity of the issue with which we are dealing. We shall only note the following variables as among those involved: (1) Conflict is brought quickly to public attention, friendly contact is not; hence we do not know how sharply the present situation contrasts with the earlier one. (2) A separatist mood affects some current contacts. (3) There is a high ratio of black noncommissioned officers now; thus the contact is not always equal status (and there are elements of status inconsistency for members of both races). (4) The current situation creates more general frustration than did World War II because of motivational factors. (5) The ratio of Black to White is much higher than it was in the period studied (see, e.g., Binkin and Eitelberg 1982; Hayles and Perry 1981).

In many contact studies, there are methodological problems of self-selection and limitation to verbal behavior. Deutsch and Collins (1951, Chapter 11) report the interesting results of different patterns of interracial housing in which these problems are minimal. In two housing projects black and white families were assigned to apartment buildings regardless of race (the integrated pattern); in two other projects different buildings or different parts of the project were used for Blacks and Whites (the segregated biracial pattern). Interviews with the women in these situations revealed that the integrated pattern reduced prejudice much more sharply.

In the integrated projects only one-third as many women spontaneously expressed prejudice in the interviews as in the segregated projects (13 percent and 10 percent compared with 35 percent and 31 percent). About two of the women wanted to be friendly for every one who wanted to avoid contact

with Blacks in the integrated arrangement, but in the segregated situation there were ten who wanted to avoid contact for each one who wished to be friendly. It is particularly interesting to note that 67 percent and 71 percent of the women in the integrated projects had positive attitudes toward the interracial aspects of their communities, many having come to like it more; but in the segregated projects most of the women liked the interracial aspects less than they did before they moved into the community.

Similar contrasts can be found as a result of court rulings on school desegregation. Parents whose children were involved became strong supporters of desegregation and busing, Jacobson found (1978). Those without children in schools or with children in parochial schools became more resistant to the court action. In this case, contact led to adjustive responses, not to opposition.

The effects of the types of contact describe by Deutsch and Collins would not be the same, of course, on persons whose prejudices were so strong that they would not join an interracial community; but among families who did accept housing on a biracial basis persons assigned (without regard to their original attitudes, for the type of arrangement was an administrative decision, not an individual choice) to integrated patterns discovered that their prejudices were very inadequate modes of adjustment. Those in the segregated projects had no such opportunity to revise their atittudes.

In a follow-up study of the effects of interracial housing, Wilner, Walkley, and Cook (1955) furnish evidence that supports many of the findings of Deutsch and Collins, but they also introduce some qualifications. In interracial neighborhoods, "the assumption that segregation is right and inevitable is challenged" by the authority of the community project; and the white resident is confronted with the problem of reconciling the evidence concerning the behavior of actual minority-group members with his stereotypes. They note, however, that proximity and contact must be distinguished; and initial attitudes, the general social climate, and the racial proportions must be taken into account.

The four housing projects studied by Wilner et al. had a small proportion of Negro residents; none had more than 10 percent. The white women who lived near Negroes perceived, more often than those living farther away, that the opinions of other white women in the project were favorable to interracial

[2]Information and Education Division, U.S. War Department, "Opinions about Negro Infantry Platoons in White Companies of Seven Divisions." Reprinted in Newcomb and Hartley 1947, pp. 542–46.

contact. They also held Negroes in higher esteem and were more likely to believe that the races were equal in such things as cleanliness, manners, intelligence, and ambition. Although the attitudes toward Negroes that the white women had when they entered the project affected their responses, they were less important than proximity in the project.

Similar results occur in some neighborhoods of individual, private homes. Hamilton and Bishop report (1976) that initial negative reactions to black neighbors changed into acceptance and more favorable racial attitudes, due, they believe, to the persistent disconfirmation of what they expected—that is, contradictions of their stereotypes," "widely shared myths—that blacks will not take care of their property, that their' yards will be messy, that they pose a threat to personal safety, that their children will be 'rough,' that property values will decline, etc." (Hamilton and Bishop 1976, p. 66). Over time, many of these expectations are refuted by the facts.

One uncontrollable aspect of these and most other studies of contact is the lack of any measures of selectivity of black participants. Are they more "contact-prone"? Would the same results occur if a different pattern of selectivity prevailed? A study undertaken in Los Angeles may throw some light on these questions (although there are risks in making inferences through time and space back to the housing studies we have examined). Bullough (1969) wondered why there had been a comparatively weak response to the growing opportunities for integrated housing among Blacks. Comparing two samples of Blacks in integrated neighborhoods ($n = 224$) with one in a solidly black area ($n = 106$), she found that the latter were signficantly higher in feeling of powerlessness and anomia. Without panel data, we cannot tell whether these feelings reflect or cause the housing patterns. From our interest here, however, they indicate the need to take account of black as well as white attitudes in studies of the effects of contact. Ford also found (1973) that the white women in an interracial housing project were more tolerant than those in a segregated project but that this was not the case with the black women, who "objected to the lack of social recognition and the contentious attitudes some of their white neighbors held toward them and the members of their families" (Ford 1973, pp. 1442–43). They also felt isolated from other black women and believed they were being cast in the role of intruders. In a similar way, white teachers who participated in an institute preparatory to joining

an integrated school staff showed lower levels of prejudice. The prejudice scores of the black teachers, however, were not influenced. They did not perceive the situation as one of equal status (Robinson and Preston 1976). Clearly there are many subtle nuances in the experience of equal-status contact.

This is true among children as well as adults. In a valuable study of intergroup relations in a boys' camp, Muzafer Sherif and his associates (1961) reveal the tension-building and stereotype-creating processes and then indicate how harmony may be established or reestablished. Although this research has no direct interest in majority-minority relations, it skillfully reveals more general principles of intergroup relations that are of wide applicability. The subjects were twenty-two eleven-year-old middle-class boys. There were no problem children among them; each had a good school record; and all were strangers to one another at the start. So far as possible they were matched into pairs on weight, height, skills, and previous camping experience and then assigned randomly into two groups. For a week the two groups lived separately at an isolated camping site. They were then brought into frequent competitive and often frustrating interaction. At the end of this second stage, there were strong reciprocal prejudices and stereotypes; members of the two groups did not want to associate; there was name-calling and conflict.

How could these expressions of tension and disharmony be reduced? One might make appeals to a common "enemy," break up the groups by individual reward and rivalry, or shift attention to intergroup leaders. Sherif rejected these, however, in favor of an effort to reduce friction by introducing "superordinate goals"—a series of tasks that required, for a mutually esteemed outcome, intergroup cooperation. These task were preceded by seven unstructured contact situations. By themselves, these contacts did little to break down the group lines, reduce stereotypy, or end the conflict. When the two groups had to work together, however, to raise enough money to bring a movie to camp or to get water flowing again (after the staff had devilishly disrupted the supply), group lines blurred, antipathies receded, and the differential rating of in-group and out-group disappeared.

Here is group-building and attitude-formation before our eyes. Undoubtedly new variables are introduced, however, when one deals with group identities that have lasted for years, not weeks. This is true of a far more important "experiment" that is taking place in recently desegregated schools, where hundreds of thousands of white and black children, as well as other minority children, are seeing each other for the first time as fellow students. The results are exceedingly complex, varying with the attitudes of school and government officials, the responses of parents, the talents and tensions of the white and black children, the grade level, and many other factors. The transition from a segregated to an integrated school is undoubtedly somewhat easier for first-graders than for high-school students. Nevertheless, changes of attitudes can occur even among some of the more segregationist-minded adolescents.

A useful way to examine the effects of interracial contact in schools is to apply the "theory of status characteristics and expectation states," a theory we commented on in Chapter 4. "This theory explains how the power and prestige order in a newly constituted group of high- and low-status members comes to parallel the relative ranking on a status characteristic initially held by members of the group" (Cohen and Roper 1972, p. 643; see also Berger, Rosenholtz, and Zelditch 1980; Cohen 1982; Humphries and Berger 1981; Riordan and Ruggiero 1980). Research on expectation states is significant for studies of contact because it is exploring a variable that can strongly influence the effects of contact, including equal-status contact. Two persons who may seem to be of equal status, using many socioeconomic, educational, and personal variables, may in fact be unequal at a strategic point—their expectations of each other. We should note that the evidence to date also shows "that it is somewhat easier to modify the expectations for the low-status members's performance held by *high-status members* than it is to change the expectations low-status members hold for themselves" (Cohen 1982, p. 216). When, in an experiment (or classroom activity), those expectations are modified by training the lower-status person in a skill, she or he will be perceived as more competent and will be more equally participant in other activities, even those for which the skill is irrelevant. Based on their series of experiments, Cohen and Roper conclude (1972, p. 656): "The most impressive and important finding is the need to treat both black and white expectations to attain 'equal status interaction' in the intergrated group." Unless they are treated, even the most friendly and egalitarian environment may be insufficient in its influence to overcome the effects of the diffuse status characteristics (such as race) brought into the interaction by the participants. Typically, white students will talk more, get more leadership positions, and generally dominate the interaction.

The effects of contact, it is clear, vary widely. To use it as a quick and easy antidote for those factors poisoning intergroup relations can only mean disappointment. Study after study has shown the complexity of effects in interracial classrooms, for example. In a sample of twenty desegregated classrooms, Hallinan found (1982, p. 56):

> Blacks showed a stronger tendency than whites to segregate racially in the selection of friends regardless of the racial composition of the classroom. Both blacks and whites were most integrated in their friendships in majority white classrooms. Segregation by whites decreased over the school year while black segregation remained constant. Blacks were found to be friendlier toward both races than whites, with the greatest difference in black and white friendliness occurring in majority white classrooms.

In an interesting finding, Longshore notes (1982) that white hostility toward Blacks was greatest in schools with 40 to 60 percent black enrollment, and the hostility was lower when the percentage was either higher or lower. (For studies that indicate the wide variety of influences of contact in desegregated classrooms, see Cohen 1975; Hunt 1977; McConahy 1978; Metz 1978; Prager, Longshore, and Seeman 1983; Schofield 1979.)

From the results of such studies as we have reported and the larger number we have cited we cannot conclude that a decrease in discrimination and prejudice is the inevitable result of contact, whether equal-status or otherwise. It is true, however, that some kinds of contact do in fact have that result. By being aware of the variety, if not the contradictory quality, of the findings, we can begin to identify the variables that interact with contact to produce the observed results. For example, when are there too few members of a minority to break stereotypes (a few can be regarded as "exceptions"), and when are there so many that a sense of threat develops? The "solo" literature we discussed in an earlier chapter can help us to answer that question (see Kanter 1977; Taylor 1981). To what degree do "weak ties," if not strong bonds of friendship, develop as a result of school desegregation or other kinds of contact (see Granovetter 1983, 1973); and what are the effects of those weak ties on prejudice, on the perceptions of status, on the opening up of opportunities? What is the impact on different levels of personal insecurity on the experience of equal-status contact (Mussen 1950)? We must be aware that individuals vary in their responses, depending in part on their self-regard and self-confidence.

One can perhaps sum up the present knowledge about the effects of contact on prejudice in these four related propositions:

1. Incidental, involuntary, tension-laden contact is likely to increase prejudice.

2. Pleasant, equal-status contact that makes it unnecessary for the individuals to cross barriers of class, occupational, and educational differences as well as differences in symbolic (nonfunctional) group membership represented by such symbols as race is likely to reduce prejudice.

3. Stereotype-breaking contacts that show minority-group members in roles and having characteristics not usually associated with them reduce prejudice. It must be added, however, that many people have little capacity for experiencing the members of minority groups as individuals; their stereotypes easily persist in the face of contrary evidence.

4. Contacts that bring people of minority and majority groups together in functionally important activities reduce prejudice. This is particularly true when those activities involve goals that cannot be achieved without the active cooperation of members of all the groups.

Do We Want Contact, Equal-status or Otherwise? In recent years there has been some increase in separationist sentiments in the United States, some of it in the name of pluralism—both black and white—but much of it renewing established prejudices. This takes us back to a topic we dealt with in Chapter 1 and elsewhere, but our interest in it here is in connection with the study of contact. In a valuable paper Pettigrew (1969) summarizes the reasons often given by Whites today to support racial separation: (1) Each race feels awkward and uncomfortable in the presence of the other and benefits from separation. (2) Since Whites are superior, they will lose by integration (in schools, for example). (3) Contact increases conflict. Black separationists have somewhat matching assumptions: (1) Yes, each race does feel awkward and uncomfortable in the presence of the other; we are more comfortable by ourselves. (2) Most Whites *think* they are superior, so white liberals should spend their time working on white racists, not worrying over integration. (3) Yes, contact does mean conflict, and it will continue to do so until after a period of autonomy, when Blacks can enter into interaction on a fully equal basis.

It is true, Pettigrew notes, that some interracial contacts are awkward, that intraracial contacts may seem more comfortable. But, he asks, at what cost do we gain this comfort? Isolation leads to mutual misinformation and, more important, it promotes differences. There has been a sharp reduction in racist beliefs in the United States during the last generation; wise policy should not be based on assumptions of its prevalence or increase. Contact does, under some conditions, increase conflict; but lack of conflict is no sign of progress: "One of the quietest periods in American racial history, 1895–1915, for example, witnessed the construction of the massive system of institutional racism as it is known today." (Pettigrew 1969, p. 57).

Many people argue, Pettigrew notes, that in the long run full integration may be desirable but that for the immediate and foreseeable future separation is necessary and wise. The white desegregationist, using some mixture of the three reasons given above, supports some public desegregation, but not extensive integration. This is basically a moderate version of the older segregationist view. Perhaps more interesting is the argument of some black leaders

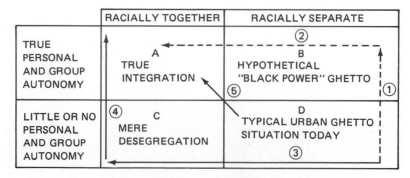

Figure 17–1. Schematic diagram of autonomy and contact-separation.

that autonomy must come first, then integration may be possible. The various positions are charted by Pettigrew as shown in Figure 17-1. Pettigrew marshalls substantial evidence to support "route 5." With reference to the "3-1-2" route," for example, he writes (1969, pp. 58–59):

The black separatist route has a surprising appeal for an untested theory; besides those whites who welcome any alternative to integration, it seems to appeal to cultural pluralists, white and black, to militant black leaders searching for a new direction to vent the ghetto's rage and despair, and to Negroes who just wish to withdraw as far away from whites as possible. Yet on reflection the argument involves the perverse notion that the way to bring two groups together is to separate them further. One is reminded of the detrimental consequences of isolation in economics, through "closed markets," and in "genetic drift." In social psychology, isolation between two contiguous groups generally leads to: (a) diverse value development, (b) reduced intergroup communication, (c) uncorrected perceptual distortions of each other, and (d) the growth of vested interests within both groups for continued separation. American race relations already suffer from each of these conditions; and the proposal for further separation even if a gilded ghetto were possible, aims to exacerbate them further.

Pettigrew may exaggerate the favorable outcomes of contact and overlook some of the costs (see Eisenman and Pettigrew 1969). But, in our judgment, he weighs the balance correctly.

Education

Most Americans have a good deal of faith in the power of education (often accompanied by an antiintellectualism that exalts the practical man, the man of action, and disdains the expert and the intellectual). It is frequently declared that education (empirically shading off into programs of contact, exhortation, and propaganda) could reduce prejudice and discrimination sharply. Discussion of the value of education frequently fails to distinguish two levels of argument. One proposition might state: *If we were able to have* a scientifically adequate and nationwide program of education in majority-minority relations, prejudice would be reduced. But the most frequent declaration is simply: Education can reduce prejudice.

The latter statement pays no attention to the obstacles in the way of getting an adequate program of education in intergroup relations. There is no likelihood that schools, communities, adult education programs, and the like will suddenly develop adequate and widespread studies of discrimination and prejudice, for they are part of the total society,

largely reflecting its traditions and power structure—and its prejudices.

Effective strategy requires that we distinguish these two problems in developing a program of education to reduce prejudice and discrimination: (1) What are the barriers to setting up such a program? Who will oppose it, and how may their opposition be reduced? Who will finance it? (2) After one has set up the program, what techniques are most effective in changing the atitudes of different groups of people?

We perhaps know more about the second problem than about the first. One is justified in a modest optimism that when a program has been set in motion, particularly with children, it can be fairly effective in preventing or reducing prejudices. But in what circumstances will an educational program be set in motion? In March 1971, the United States Department of Defense announced the creation of an institute to train, within a year, 1,400 instructors to staff a program in race relations. Classes were to be required of every person who enters the service, with six-hour refresher courses each year thereafter (*The New York Times*, March 6, 1971, pp. 1, 14). The goal of this Defense Race Relations Institute was to change behavior in the armed services through education. By 1979, the training period for Institute personnel had been extended from six to sixteen weeks.

Two surveys have been conducted to evaluate the first six classes conducted at the Institute. The judgments of the graduates of the Institute program and of the commanders were generally positive in the first survey and even more positive in the second, as shown in Table 17-1.

These favorable results are not matched by the assignments given to the institute graduates. Since 1974 most DDRI graduates have devoted little time to giving race relations instruction. They reported strong satisfaction with their training as preparation for instructional assignments but are less satisfied with that training as preparation for carrying out tasks related to equal opportunity programs, administration, and supervision (Hope 1979, pp. 64–65).

Few institutions can match the armed forces in creating an extensive program by a decision from the top. Yet the school system is also an area in which some action is possible. Despite the close connection between formal education and the rest of society, there is a measure of autonomy in the school system. This autonomy is easy to exaggerate, but it is a strategic error to dismiss it altogether.

Table 17-1. Effects of Race Relations Education on Interracial/Ethnic Relations on Military Installations (in percentage)

	Graduates' judgments		Commanders' judgments	
	1974	1975	1974	1975
Significant improvement	11	20	19	26
Some improvement	44	56	49	52
Little improvement	13	14	9	11
No improvement	2	1	4	2
Made things worse	1	1	1	1
Do not know	28	8	18	9

Sources: Hope, 1979, p. 66. Based on Defense Race Relations Institute *Graduate Commander Field Survey Reports*, 1974 and 1975.

Those professionally connected with education, because of their functional role in society, are somewhat more concerned with the pursuit of truth, a little less likely to be provincial (Lacy and Middleton 1981). In our society they are also inclined to be somewhat more liberal than the average, although some are timid and others are emotionally identified with the upper classes. Coles (1963, p. 17) observed, even among teachers who were unhappy with desegregation, "a kind of adherence in the end to professional responsibilities and obligations . . . a deep sense of professional integrity, of identity as teachers which transcended their private feelings about race."

Although efforts to increase intergroup education have been expanded, this modest resource has been used only slightly. Few teachers are trained specifically in the analysis of majority–minority relations; teachers from minority groups are underrepresented; and few courses treat their material in a way designed to reduce prejudice.

What Kind of Education? The first job of strategy, in making use of education, is to determine the areas—such as schools and unions—wherein programs are most likely to be adopted. But that is only half the job. Having cleared the ground, one must decide how to proceed. Is it a matter simply of transferring information, for knowledge leads to action? Or are the ways in which the knowledge is acquired, the total situation of learning, as crucial as the facts themselves? More and more we see that the latter is the case. How one learns an idea is important to his mastery of it, to his acceptance of the idea as valid, and to the likelihood of his acting upon it. The total personality is involved in the learning process. One

type of situation may stimulate a personality "set" that makes a person unable to acquire new knowledge. Or knowledge may be learned on a symbolic level but be so compartmentalized that it does not affect other ideas or overt behavior. At the very least, when one gives up a prejudice one admits an error, and most of us are reluctant to do this. Fineberg (1949, pp. 183–184) illustrates the way in which sensitivity to the feelings of the prejudiced person contributes to reeducation:

Mrs. Tenney, a brilliant young woman active in community relations work, had remained silent at a dinner party when a woman whom she and her husband were meeting for the first time spoke of members of another race as mentally inferior to white people. It was an incidental remark. The conversation quickly drifted to something else.

Driving home, Mr. Tenney said to his wife, "I was watching you when Mrs. Hammond put in that nasty crack about colored people. Why didn't you speak up?"

"And spoil the chance of ever changing her mind?" asked Mrs. Tenney. "Had I spoken up, Mrs. Hammond would have defended her opinion. If I had won the argument, it would have been to my satisfaction but not to hers. She would have disliked me for embarrassing her among her new acquaintances. She looks like a sincere, capable person. I think we can change her views on several things. When she made that quip about racial inferiority, I put it down in my little mental notebook. And what do you think I did while we were getting our wraps?"

Mr. Tenney smiled. "Knowing you as I do, I'd say you made a date with Mrs. Hammond."

"Right! When we know each other better, I'll introduce Mrs. Hammond to Dr. Sanford and to Mrs. Taylor, who are as intelligent as any white person she has ever met. One of these days Mrs. Hammond will be working for our Interracial Commission. That's not a promise, John, but I'll try hard."

In less than two months Mrs. Hammond had abandoned the notion of racial inferiority without having been forced to recant, apologize, or even to recall the invidious remark. Her mentor, Mrs. Tenney, is one of the few—there are altogether too few—

who are concerned enough about racial and religious prejudice and astute enough to undertake the *reeducation* of mildly prejudiced individuals.

It is widely believed that misinformation and lack of information are among the factors that lead to discrimination and prejudice. Although it is difficult to demonstrate the connection empirically, we share that belief. We must emphasize, however, that misinformation or lack of information may be the dependent variable. That is, it may be the result of other factors that are the stronger forces supporting discrimination and prejudice. Under these conditions, ignorance is convenient, as we noted earlier, and not easily overcome simply by presenting the facts. For some people, nevertheless, and probably for all people to some degree, a rich diet of information and knowledge can increase their tolerance. Thus, Farley, Bianchi, and Colasanto (1979) list these items among those that would encourage residential integration: Make Whites aware that other Whites are not as prejudiced as they may think; make Whites aware that Blacks of equal status would be their new neighbors; make Blacks aware that Whites are not so hostile to residential integration as they may think; emphasize the illegality of discrimination in renting or selling a house (about half did not know that). We are all aware of situations in which we have made the wrong decision because of misinformation or lack of information, decisions we have been able to change when we became better informed. There is no reason why race relations should not be subject to the same corrective procedures, if we recognize, with Alexander Pope, that "a little learning is a dangerous thing" and get beyond surface information.

Out of Kurt Lewin's studies has come the emphasis on the involvement of the total personality in the educative process. This has led to the development of several principles: Create an informal situation; see education as a group process, not simply an individual process; maximize the individual's sense of participation in getting new ideas (see Lewin 1948).

We are not expounding a general theory of education. We are concerned with the learning process in an area in which emotional attitudes and stereotypes affect observation and the acceptance of evidence. The degree to which different principles are involved in different learning situations is a problem that cannot be examined here.

Intergroup Education in the Schools. With the great increase in public awareness of intergroup relations and tensions since World War II, schools at every level have begun to pay more attention to interracial, intercultural, interfaith, and international questions. Specific courses have been introduced in a number of cities, and teacher-training programs, literature designed for specific age levels, and some attention to intergroup relations in the total life of schools have increased.

Several obstacles and weaknesses have become apparent in the short history of deliberately planned intergroup education. Intergroup instruction is distorted if minority groups are poorly represented on the teaching staff, a situation that is slowly being changed. (Most of these teachers, of course, on all levels of education, teach subjects other than intergroup relations. Their influence on that topic is indirect and informal.)

A second type of difficulty lies in the attitudes of teachers. Intergroup education has no possibility of being effective unless those who are charged with carrying it out are competent and sympathetic. Routine performance of an assigned program accomplishes little or nothing. Subtle or obviously prejudiced remarks or acts on the part of the teacher outside the program itself may more than offset that which is included in formal instruction. Many pupils come from homes where prejudice is strong. If the teacher also harbors prejudice, the results of intergroup education are likely to be negligible. Some school systems now include interest and skill in intergroup relations among the criteria used in the selection of new teachers. These generalizations apply to school situations in many parts of the world (see, e.g., Musgrove 1982, on Britain).

Closely related to teachers attitudes are school policies with regard to pupil assignment. In the matter of ability level, schools are confronted with a dilemma: In some ways it is more effective to teach relatively homogeneous groups because methods and materials can be adapted to their particular needs. On the other hand, grouping and tracking tend to create self-fulfilling prophecies, to create expectations in the minds of students and teachers alike about levels of performance. The result is that those in slow tracks remain slow, those in fast tracks are given further support and encouragement.

Much tracking is unintended and unplanned. Nevertheless, labelling, steering, and counseling can sort out minority students as surely as explicit tracking, if teachers "know" in advance that those students are capable only of less demanding work. Although there are problems of interpretation in their study, Rosenthal and Jacobson (1968) have demonstrated their major point that teacher expectations affect not simply the grading of pupils but the pupils' actual performances. In a controlled study, they showed that teachers, without realizing it, sent cues to presumed slow learners and fast learners that tended to reenforce their original tendencies. No amount of formal attention to intergroup relations will reduce the effects of such subtle and unintended discrimination. The policy of ability grouping is the subject of a great deal of controversy, in educational circles and among parents. The sharpness of the dilemma it presents will encourage pendulum swings as one or another force becomes stronger, until creative educational programs are designed that serve both the well prepared and the less well prepared student.

Policies and actions, whatever their intentions, that perpetuate the educational disadvantages of many minority students can only deprive majority students of the possibility of learning, through their educational experiences, what the costs and the injustices of inadequate opportunities are. Fortunately, a substantial body of research now documents the prevalence of educational "steering," furnishing the opportunity to reduce its destructive impact (see, e.g., Alexander et al. 1978; Erickson 1975; McDermott 1977; Rist 1970; Rosenbaum 1976).

Minority–majority education is strongly influenced also by the textbooks and other school materials available. Until recently these sources tended either to overlook minorities or to treat them in a stereotypical way. The momentum of the civil rights movement, however, has led to the publication of a wide range of materials designed to make minorities both visible and better understood.

Some of the problems in intergroup education found on the primary and secondary levels also characterize college work. Many general college programs are concerned with studying the democratic tradition and strengthening belief in the democratic heritage, but few have the specific aim of reducing prejudice, nor have they used techniques appropriate to that end. There are, of course, hundreds of courses in departments of sociology, anthropology, history, and social psychology concerned with minorities and prejudice. These are usually elective courses, dealing with self-selected students, and they therefore face different problems in reducing prejudice. The changing of attitudes, if it is recognized at all, is only one aim, although that hope probably lies behind most of the courses. Since the reducing of prejudices is not explicitly sought—and methods appropriate to that aim are not adopted—one does not judge the effectiveness of a course by measuring changes in attitude. Nevertheless, such measurements as have been made reveal that one of the results—perhaps a by-product—of the study of minorities and prejudice may be an increase in tolerance. The results, however, are far from definite. Some of the courses produced no change of attitude. The studies vary widely, moreover, in the degree to which they have controlled variables and eliminated the effects of self-selection that so often distort the analysis of human behavior. Their total weight gives some support to the hypothesis that knowledge may reduce prejudice.

Not all the educational needs vis-à-vis majority–minority relations are found among members of the majority. A significant development is the appearance of black studies programs in many schools. They are being followed by demands for, and to some degree action on, Puerto Rican, Mexican, Indian, and other programs. Jewish studies have long been a part of traditional curricula, but are now being developed in some places somewhat more along the "ethnic group" line of the newer programs.

The implications of these developments for the topic of this chapter are not clear. Black students, for example, make up the vast majority of students in black studies programs. They are presented with materials and educational philosophies ranging from scholarly emphasis on black history, literature, music, art, and experience to action programs designed to speed the destruction of "imperialistic societies." With such contrasts in basic premises, inevitably there are sharp disputes among those who design and work in these programs. Some see them as a necessary and appropriate way to emphasize black contributions to American culture and society, and others work to make the programs agents of black separation.

As we noted in Chapter 16, judgments vary widely on the consequences of black studies and other ethnic programs. We see two opposite possibilities. Courses that promote the growth of pride and the strengthening of self-identity may reduce prejudice. On the other hand, some of the materials and approaches seem likely to reduce the sense of common humanity, to promote stereotypes, and to create a world picture as inaccurately imaginary as the one under which white students have long suffered. The balance, we suspect, will be determined not only by struggles among the staffs and the schools where they work but also by the total national setting. Slow progress in reducing discrimination and granting full rights to all citizens will support the chauvinistic elements in ethnic studies. Rapid progress will support their broader humanistic potential and thus help to break the vicious circle of majority–minority relations.

The Influence of Language Differences.[3] Some of the issues connected with ethnic-studies programs are found also in connection with bilingual programs. Having discussed bilingualism in Chapters 6 and 15, we will refer to it here only in connection with its potential as an educational method for reducing prejudice and discrimination.

The critical questions are: Does a skillfully managed bilingual program reduce the prejudice and discrimination of dominant group members? Does it reduce the vulnerability of the minorities? Does it reduce the reciprocal prejudices of the minorities? Does it weaken the structural conditions on which discrimination rests? And, basic to each of these, what are the qualities of a "skillfully managed" bilingual program?

We cannot give confident answers to those questions. Our hope is to persuade readers to think seriously about them in the belief that this will help us move toward those answers and toward the policies needed to act upon them.

Through the centuries, language supremacy and the "purity" of the dominant language have been focal points of struggle over power and over national or ethnic group identity in many lands. Patterns of stratification are often clearly revealed, and reenforced, by variations in language and dialect. It is against this background that we should think about bilingualism in American schools.

Three policies, not usually clearly articulated, compete in the public arena:

1. Resist the growth of bilingual training. This is a one-language country, to everyone's advantage.

2. Recognize as a temporary fact that for some students English is not the native language.

[3]This section is adapted from Yinger in Prager, Longshore, and Seeman 1983, pp. 391–94.

Bilingual policy should be to create a bridge over into English.

3. Accept bilingualism as a fact of life in the United States and as an advantage for the country. Pluralism in language as in other qualities is desirable. In areas in which many people do not speak English other languages should be given some kind of official recognition.

Since the Bilingual Education Act of 1968, indeed on a state and local basis for several years before then, official policy has approximated statement two. This was made quite explicit in the Bilingual Education Act of 1974, in its definition of a bilingual education program as:

instruction given in, and study of, English and to the extent necessary to allow a child to progress effectively through the educational system, the native language of the children of limited English-speaking ability, and such instruction is given with appreciation for the cultural heritage of such children, and, with respect to elementary school instruction, such instruction shall, to the extent necessary, be in all courses or subjects of study which will allow a child to progress effectively through the educational system. (quoted by Cafferty 1982, p. 119)

Agreement on the goals described in the Bilingual Education Acts is far from complete. Indeed it may have decreased, for bilingual education has become a major civil rights issue among some groups even while resistance to it has also grown, as in Texas, Florida, and New Jersey (Burke 1981). Part of the resistance is fiscal (several language groups may make claims), part is opposition to separatism (pluralism to its supporters) that is involved, and part is based on educational grounds.

In our view, the need for bilingual education is unquestionable (for a different view see Glazer 1983, pp. 145–56). Without some kind of attention to the fact that for many, English is not the primary language, equal educational opportunity is impossible. This is the position taken by the Supreme Court in 1974 (*Lau* v. *Nichols*) and put into law by the Congress in one of the sections of the Equal Opportunity Act of 1974. The question is; What kind of attention? What educational programs will open up opportunities to non-English-speaking minorities rather than closing them off from full participation in society? Do bilingual programs set groups apart, emphasizing their differences; or do they furnish opportunities for more communication and interaction?

It is important to remember that it is one thing to teach English as a second language (there are numerous ESL programs) by providing supplementary training in English. It is something else to teach bilingualism, on the premise that maintaining and improving competence in the first language is a goal complementary to the goal of mastering English. Once again this raises the question of the nature and extent of pluralism that will best serve American society. Some fear that a robust bilingualism is more likely to divide the country than to reduce discrimination. (Few oppose ESL or other programs designed to help people learn English more rapidly.) Others see bilingual education, at least as presently used, as incapable of serving the needs of those for whom English is not the native language (Epstein 1977).

In our judgment, the fragmentary evidence available indicates that the bilingual programs presently in use—only a fraction of non-English speakers are involved—do facilitate the learning of English and educational attainment in other subjects as well. And they do not tend to reenforce or increase divisions within the country. They are not likely to maintain Spanish or other languages as primary for those involved because the need for English is too great. Hispanics are shifting to English at a rate similar to earlier groups (most speak English predominantly by the third generation). Because the proportion of first and second generation remains high, however, and because discrimination and limited opportunity frustrate their entry into full participation in American society, some native Spanish speakers "may be electing to bypass the process of acculturation and assimilation that turned previous immigrant groups into English-speaking Americans" (Nunis 1981, p. 29). Bilingual programs are not the cause of this tendency, it should be emphasized; and insofar as they increase the opportunities available to those who are trained bilingually, they should have the opposite result.

Issues similar to those connected with bilingualism refer to dialects rather than languages. In many ways, dialectical differences are less easily dealt with than lingual differences. Nonstandard dialects are more often clear signs of socioeconomic differences; fewer people grant them authenticity as languages. With desegregation of schools, however, they have become a fact to be dealt with. Early students (e.g., Bernstein 1966) stressed, however sympathetically, the limiting influence of what they saw as restricted dialects on cognition. Language deprivation = cognitive deprivation. His

critics (e.g., Labov 1972) believe that he missed the richness of nonstandard dialects, with their own syntax, grammar, and vocabulary. These critics sometimes failed to note that dialects adapted to restricted settings may not be good media if one wants to move freely in wider circles. Nor did they note that to some degree they were antilanguages, in Halliday's sense (1976), designed to oppose the larger society while communicating with one's group. The kinds of quasi experiments with black ghetto English carried on in Ann Arbor schools need to be extended and enriched by both survey and ethnographic studies if dialectical differences are not to continue to weaken seriously the efforts to improve educational opportunity and to reduce discrimination.

Federal Judge Charles Joiner ruled that the Ann Arbor School Board had violated the civil rights of eleven black students by not recognizing their different manner of speech as a fact to be dealt with in teaching, not a criterion for judging the quality of students. Responses to his decision varied widely. Carl Rowan believed that the ruling was "dubious at best," an invitation to an alibi, until we "do something about the absences from school, until we make more black parents understand the value of reading in the home, until more teachers force ghetto students to read newspapers and magazines and at least try to resist peer-pressures to downgrade standard English" (quoted by Newell 1981, p. 27). William Raspberry saw it differently. He read the decision to say: "What we are talking about is teaching children to read without turning them off, without teachers deciding on the basis of their speech patterns that they cannot learn" (in Newell 1981, p. 29).

The latter interpretation appears to be closer to Judge Joiner's intent. He sought to remove a barrier to learning—an often unconscious negative attitude of teachers toward the home language of some of their black students. They need to recognize the existence of that language "and to use that knowledge," he wrote, "as a way of helping the children to learn to read standard English" (in Newell 1981, p. 28).

Rowan's fears may be justified, or Judge Joiner's hopes may prove to be well founded. What we need to know is the range of outcomes of various policies toward dialects, particularly those closely correlated with minority backgrounds and deprivation, under a variety of conditions. We greatly need research that shows the conditions under which differences of language and dialect stand as barriers to the reduction of discrimination in schools and the kinds of school policy that can overcome those barriers. It seems possible to deal with language differences in such a way that they even become, in the process of reduction, integrative.

Does Education in Itself Promote Tolerance? Related to the question of the efficacy of intergroup education as such is the question of the general influence of education on antiminority attitudes and behavior. Public opinion polls almost always show that better educated people are more tolerant and less likely to express antiminority views. This relationship holds up even when other variables, such as income and age, are controlled, as shown in a recent study of a national sample by Kluegel and Smith (1982).

Many observers see the greater tolerance found rather generally throughout the population as somehow one-dimensional—not penetrating to the depths of their beliefs:

Underlying this work is the common thesis that the reduction in overt racial bigotry and opposition to legal and normative denial of rights to blacks have not been accompanied by any broader change in white racial attitudes and beliefs. . . . While racial prejudice has markedly waned in the last three decades, we find little or no evidence of a growing recognition of structural limits to blacks' opportunity. (Kluegel and Smith 1982, p. 523; see also Kinder and Sears 1981; A. W. Smith 1981a)

We have written about this in an earlier chapter in connection with our discussion of the concept of symbolic racism, which can be seen more as a shift in the basis of criticism of minorities than a reduction of that criticism.

Kluegel and Smith found in their examination of perceptions of Blacks' opportunities that the better educated continued to show greater sensitivity. Although they do not use these terms, it seems fair to say from their evidence that education is negatively correlated not only with overt racial bigotry but also with symbolic racism. We cannot stop at this point, however. It is not nearly so clear that education is negatively correlated with discrimination. Educated persons are among the chief beneficiaries of the structures of disadvantage that minorities face. Education does not produce this relationship, but it does not effectively challenge it. This is said not to downgrade the value of education but to emphasize that it works in a structural and cultural context that strongly constrains its influence.

Achieving Tolerance through Therapy

If prejudice and discrimination are frequently manifestations of personal insecurities or of a basic personality instability, then an effective program of strategy must be concerned with the reduction of emotional disturbance. The prevention and treatment of personality disorganization is a very large area that we can only touch upon; but we must examine some of the general principles involved as they refer to our problem. We must avoid, as some specialists fail to do, exaggerating the effectiveness of personal therapy as a strategy. The authors of *The Authoritarian Personality* (Adorno et al. 1950, p. 973) write, "The major emphasis should be placed, it seems, not upon discrimination against particular groups, but upon such phenomena as stereotypy, emotional coldness, identification with power, and general destructiveness." Such a statement is the result of an inadequate theory of the causes of prejudice and discrimination. There are far too many feelings of rancor, prejudice, and snobbery among the mentally healthy and, as Coles notes (1967, p. 353) among the analyzed—and even those who analyze—to allow any longer such an easy interpretation. There are some situations, in the view of the present authors, in which personality factors are relatively unimportant, others in which they loom large; but more often the several factors are closely interlocked, and none should be chosen for major emphasis.

Personal Therapy. Therapy is frequently most effective when the reduction of prejudice is simply a by-product of the larger goal of a stable personality. In this field, as in so many others, prevention is far more effective than cure. The creation of a society and of an interpersonal situation that make possible the maximum satisfactions of needs will reduce the likelihood of intergroup hostility. There is the danger in this strategy, as in education, of our adopting a "boot-strap" kind of thinking—asking unstable persons living in a prejudice-prone society to devise situations in which personal stability and tolerance prevail more widely. We have here no cure-all, but simply one approach among many that may contribute to the reduction of hostility. With this limitation in mind, we may say that anyone who contributes to the development of a strong economy, to a political situation that gives each individual some sense of control over his government, to a satisfying recreational program, to the growth of less restrictive and frustrating personal relations, particularly between parents and children—such a person is assisting, directly or indirectly, in the reduction of prejudice.

Even an extensive program of prevention, however, would be inadequate. For a long time to come we must be equally concerned with a program of cure—of treatment for insecure persons who use prejudice and discrimination as modes of adjustment to their insecurities. Therapy may concentrate primarily on the tendencies of the individual or on the situations that are activating those tendencies. The latter approach is too often disregarded by psychiatrists and others concerned with personality reorganization; yet to treat "society as the patient" (Frank 1948) is frequently a more effective approach than the intensive analysis of each individual (who, in any case, can be understood only by examining the situational factors as well as individual tendencies).

In the treatment of problem children particularly—children who may exhibit prejudice among other manifestations of insecurity—a change in the situation around them is often far more effective than direct attention to their problems. Often, in fact, the child can be disregarded completely.

When personal insecurities are more deeply set, the situational approach is less likely to be effective. The responses of the individual may take on a rigidity that coerces the interpretation of every situation into the same mold. Alongside the therapeutic approaches that seek to modify the tension-laden situations, therefore, we need the direct treatment of unstable persons. This treatment can range from friendly counseling (simply listening, frequently) to intensive psychoanalysis. Techniques that help an individual to face the causes of his hostility help to reduce its sharpness.

Public attention has been directed mainly to problems of therapy for members of the dominant group. There is some tendency, in fact, to regard their prejudices and hostilities as pathological and those of minority-group members are normal responses to abuse. This may be good strategy at certain points in history, or a relatively harmless error in dealing with a thoroughly oppressed group. When a pattern of discrimination is breaking down, however, and the anxieties and hatreds of the oppressed are being released from repression, we need a more tough-minded analysis of the therapeutic problems and possibilities among them. Minority anxieties and hatreds are also inimical to social welfare.

We are not referring, of course, to more or less rationally chosen opposition to discrimination, but to the unconscious problems that express themselves in ways unlikely to affect social practices, except negatively. Perhaps most important of these are the various paranoid symptoms. As Grier and Cobbs note (1968, p. 161):

> For a black man survival in America depends in large measure on the development of a "healthy" cultural paranoia. He must maintain a high degree of suspicion toward the motives of every white man and at the same time never allow this suspicion to impair his grasp of reality. It is a demanding requirement and not everyone can manage it with grace. . . . Of all the varieties of functional psychosis, those that include paranoid symptoms are by far the most prevalent among black people. The frequency of paranoid symptoms is significantly greater among mentally ill blacks than it is among mentally ill whites.

Direct and indirect methods of therapy to reduce minority anxieties are a necessary part of a total strategic plan to reduce racial animosities.

Group Therapy. Individual therapy is certainly a strategy that any complete program must use, particularly in the treatment of persons having deep-seated prejudices. It suffers, however, from two disadvantages. It is costly in time and energy, and it is inadequate to cut the supports of prejudice that derive from groups.

Group therapy tries to overcome these disadvantages. It is an attempt to produce changes in the personality by using the knowledge of the effects of groups on attitudes and behavior. The activities of therapeutic groups may range all the way from doing simple rhythmic actions together—a major step for some isolated schizophrenics—to enacting a plot that contains the anxiety-laden problem, to discussions in which fellow "patients" get insight into their own problems by studying those of another. Group therapy has a long implicit history in religion, in drama, in other group practices; but as an explicit method of treatment for disorganized persons it is quite new, and as a strategy in the reduction of prejudice it is even newer.

The underlying theory is that the feeling of belonging of group members breaks down their feelings of isolation, facilitates interaction among them, and encourages role-taking and self-knowledge. The sharing of symptoms and problems with others bring a sense of security and a lowering of guilt tensions—"I'm not the only one who faces this difficulty." The therapist attempts to create a situation that is thoroughly permissive and informal. Individuals are allowed to express their feelings of hostility freely, for self-discovery can scarcely occur in situations that require inhibition and concealment. Thus group therapy is closely related to the approach to education that we have discussed above. It is based on the same conception of change as a group process.

Illness, of course, as well as therapy, has a group dimension. Treatment is ineffective if this is not understood. One aspect of the group dimension of illness is that societies and smaller groups have culturally defined "sick roles," indicating how a person should (and may) behave when he is ill and how he should be treated. The process of assignment of a person to the sick role, referring specifically now to mental illness, may begin when his behavior deviations are minor. The assignment is part of the adjustment process of others who interact closely with him; it expresses efforts to handle their own anxieties and guilt, for example. The result may be to solidify the minor symptoms of the first person. In this sense, it is not the individual who is ill and needs treatment, but the group process, although individual differences in vulnerability are also involved of course. In the same way, prejudice is anchored in group processes and can be cured only by attention to group as well as to individual factors.

CHAPTER 18

The Reduction of Prejudice and Discrimination

STRATEGIES WITH MAJOR EMPHASIS ON CHANGING SITUATIONS

Patterns of discrimination and segregation that had lasted for three quarters of a century after the abolition of slavery began to break up in the 1940s. These patterns have become the target of a powerful movement, involving a larger share of black Americans than had ever before participated in organized protests, as well as substantial numbers of Chicanos, Puerto Ricans, Native Americans, and Whites.

The movement has evolved through several stages, with different strategies, different participants, and different kinds of conflict. Although there have been some overlapping and accumulation of strategies, rather than sharply divided periods, we might call 1944–1954 the constitutional stage, marked at the beginning by the Supreme Court ruling against white primaries and at the end by the Court ruling against *de jure* school segregation. (This is not to imply, of course, that opposition to discrimination was lacking before 1944.)

The next stage had two related but distinct parts. It was a period of nonviolent but active protest against discrimination by private individuals and groups. It was also a time of extensive statutory changes that registered the same protest. The beginning of the private campaign can be marked by the Montgomery bus boycott, 1955–56 and its

conclusion by the March on Washington, 1963, when 210,000 persons, black and white, joined Martin Luther King, Jr., to proclaim "I have a dream" of a society without discrimination and prejudice. Both frequency and intensity of protests had been mounting since 1955, and by 1963 there were, within a few months, over 1,000 demonstrations, marches, sit-ins, and protest meetings that demanded equality of treatment. These actions registered themselves politically in a series of unprecedented legal actions by the U.S. Congress (state legislative action had begun as early as 1945). In a series of civil rights bills, 1957–65, the Congress removed any doubt that might have been left by the Supreme Court decisions that racial, religious, or ethnic discrimination that in any way involved public actions, officials, or monies was illegal.

The third stage also had various elements. We might call it the "black power period," but with the involvement of numerous minorities it became polychrome. It burst onto the scene, not without some preliminary noise elsewhere, in the form of the 1965 Los Angeles Watts riot and in a succession of other riots in Chicago, Cleveland, Detroit, Newark, and elsewhere, leaving scores dead, thousands wounded, and hundreds of millions of dollars of damage. Out of the ashes black power emerged as a rallying cry and to some degree as a strategy. Legal and political efforts were downgraded (as it turned out, only temporarily); cooperation with Whites was sharply reduced; Blacks were seen by some as a colony within the nation, unlikely to get out of their colonial status without militancy.

This stage began to lose momentum by 1968 and by the early 1970s was no longer dominant. National attention and energy were deflected by the controversies surrounding the war in Vietnam; a series of recessions kept the economy sputtering along; and a shift toward more conservative views occurred among those groups who were comparatively well off, but felt insecure as the prosperity of the 1960s leveled off and by the mid-1970s began to decline slightly. We say slightly but must add that a small decline, seen against the experience of steady improvement over the previous several years and the hopes of even greater gains, is felt as a large decline. There is nothing more painful, Veblen wrote years ago, than a retreat from a standard of living. Perhaps we can call this period, which persisted at least into the early 1980s, as the stage of quiescence and retrenchment (Anderson 1977).

Several different currents are being carried into the 1980s. It is not yet clear which one or ones will constitute the mainsteam. The slight economic decline which we noted above had become, by 1982, a drastic decline for perhaps a third of the American population. This included not only a substantial part of the minority population but also several million Whites. For all of these, recurrent recessions have meant persistent depression. Families below the poverty line, as one measure, increased between 1976 and 1981 from 1.62 million to 1.97 million (from 27.9% to 30.8%) among Blacks and from 3.56 million to 4.67 million (from 7.1% to 8.8%) among Whites (Reid 1982, p. 31). The extent of poverty is most dramatically shown by the figure of twelve million unemployed in 1983, to whom should be added the two million or more discouraged workers who had dropped out of the labor force. Over half of these, it should be remembered, are part of the "dominant majority." Their economic woes strongly influence their attitudes and actions toward the even more disadvantaged minorities—in some measure raising barriers but partly creating a sense of shared fate.

We are not implying that in this fifth stage no pressures toward change exist or that no changes

in majority–minority relations are occurring or will occur. Important laws and judicial decisions remain, although not consistently enforced. Experience and seniority are slowly building among minority workers. A substantial minority middle class documents the expanded range of opportunities.

On the other hand, the 50 percent or more of the population that has scarcely been touched by recession and inflation has become adept at "crying poor"— judging their current situations against the wants stimulated by many years of prosperity. (In fact, per capita income after taxes, in constant dollars, went up, although slowly, even in the 1979–82 period.) Many of them are less sympathetic to the movement designed to increase opportunities among minorities and to eliminate injustices. From minority leaders and movements we hear stronger calls for independent action. This reflects both growing self-confidence and strength and also a recognition that at this stage there are fewer allies in the majority population. Black and perhaps expanded minority caucuses in Congress allied with the large number of black mayors are likely to be increasingly influential in the years ahead. In several recent elections, minority participation has increased, sometimes to a higher rate than that of the majority. If this were to become a trend, the 1980s may be remembered as the stage of political action. The current situation contains many volatile forces, however. Federal inaction plus economic stagnation plus inner-city desperation can add up to tragedy, both for individuals who bear most of the costs and for the society.

Compromise versus Contention

What strategic lessons emerge from study of the current balance of forces? What resources are available for mobilization, within society at large and among minority groups? Which obstacles can be removed most readily? In facing problems of discrimination against members of minority groups, the wise strategist will try to decide to what degree the practices should be opposed directly and immediately and to what degree they should be attacked indirectly by eroding away their supports. Enthusiastic supporters sometimes defend a particular approach as *the* strategy, as if a willingness to compromise or a flat refusal to compromise with discriminatory practices were wise in every situation. The problem is to determine when a vigorous program is likely to be successful *despite* the opposition it will arouse in some people, and when compromise is required *despite* the short-run sacrifice of some aspects of one's ultimate goal. It is scarcely necessary to note that the latter is more necessary when one has few allies, when prejudices are widespread, when the discriminatory practices are deeply embedded in the social structure.

There can be compromise that represents almost complete capitulation—"We mustn't raise that issue, for it will arouse too much hostility; we need a program of education"—and there can be compromise that keeps long-run goals clearly in mind while making necessary day-by-day adjustments. There can be contention that effectively prevents the very thing it is trying to do, by arousing hostile opposition; and there can be contention that destroys a discriminatory pattern. Ineffective contention is often the kind that attacks individuals, that blames them for their discriminations, rather than trying to understand them. It is usually necessary to secure the cooperation of the discriminator in changing an unhappy situation. This is not likely to be accomplished by exposing him to ridicule, attacking him as a person, and generally threatening his security. Opposition to discriminators is very different from opposition to discrimination.

The Place of Law and Administration

In recent years there have been substantial efforts to reduce discrimination through the use of law and administrative decisions. These efforts, many of which we have described in previous chapters, are indications that many people—including most social scientists—now challenge an earlier belief that law was impotent to enforce interracial justice. In this challenge, there has sometimes been a failure to seek out the conditions under which law is most likely to be effective. Some observers have simply reversed the earlier dogma to affirm that law is the crucial weapon in the fight to improve intergroup relations. The scientific task, however, is not to assert one position or the other but to analyze factors involved in the variation in the effectiveness of an approach through law. In our judgment it can best be described as a middle strategy. It is unnecessary to wait until everybody in a society is ready for a change before it can be incorporated into law. On the other hand, to pass a law that has little support in other institutional patterns is a relatively ineffective move, although it may not be entirely

meaningless. The fate of efforts in the United Nations to protect minorities shows that it is too early to hope to reduce discrimination substantially by international legal action. This does not mean that the efforts are not worth while; but it means that far more preparation by way of economic strength for minorities, shared values, the reduction of stereotypes and traditional prejudices, the relaxation of fear of war, and the like is necessary before international legal action to protect minorities can be particularly helpful. Within the United States and many other societies, however, the necessary preparation for improving intergroup relations through the organized political community is well advanced.

What will be effective in one setting may fail in another; and in virtually every case a variety of approaches is required. An effort that might fail by itself can be a valuable element in a larger strategy. Education and conciliation, for example, may leave the tough institutional structure of discrimination undisturbed; but in a situation wherein vigorous direct action is also undertaken they may smooth the process of change. Legal action by itself may run into massive resistance or reluctant compliance that returns at once to the old patterns when surveillance is removed. This is well documented in a report by the Citizens Commission on Civil Rights (1982) that describes in detail various "Congressional efforts to curb the federal courts and to undermine the Brown decision," to use the language of the report's title.

In a situation in which educational and conciliatory processes have also been at work, however, gains won by legal coercion may gradually get the support of personal conviction and institutional practice.

Underlying this statement on strategy is our belief that on the level of theory we also need a blend of separate, even superficially contradictory, views—a theory of conflict resolution, but also a theory of conflict. In our view, the aim of policy should not be the elimination of conflict, but its redirection into constructive channels. The relatively open and public conflict of a strike may be preferable to the covert sabotage and demoralization of workers who have no way of expressing their grievances. A massive assault on segregation barriers by freedom marchers and crowds may be preferable to the self-destructive bitterness and the lack of motivation of the dispossessed. What we need, therefore, is a complex theory both of conflict resolution and of the consequences of various forms of conflict.

Affirmative Action

Having discussed some of the facts of affirmative action in connection with economics and education, we want here to examine it in more general terms, with special attention to strategic and policy issues. Is affirmative action an effective way to reduce discrimination? Is it a zero-sum policy, shifting advantages to some persons while others pay an equivalent price; or is there a net social gain? If there are costs, who pays them?[1]

It is difficult, on this topic, to keep sociological, ethical, and policy aspects separate. The social facts under various sets of conditions, the desirable state of affairs according to stated ethical criteria, and the plans and actions needed to move toward that desirable state of affairs under the conditions being faced—these sociological, ethical, and policy perspectives, although interdependent, must be kept analytically separate.

The sociology of affirmative action is not well developed; that is, we do not have empirically well-grounded answers to important questions. If one asks: Who within a society supports, who opposes affirmative action; and is this distribution associated with the social locations of opponents and proponents? The answer is likely to be imprecise. To be sure, public opinion polls indicate that a very large majority, even of black respondents, oppose giving a qualified black person a job over a somewhat better qualified white person, which is the way the Gallup poll asked the question (Lipset and Schneider 1978, p. 143). The Harris poll found a similarly large majority opposed to "giving blacks a preference." One can only wonder what the results might have been had the sample been asked: "Assuming that the candidates are qualified, ought jobs to be filled in a way that helps to rectify prevailing disadvantages of blacks or other minorities?" A majority might still oppose affirmative action; but only by careful attention to the way the question is asked can we improve our measures.

It is also necessary to be aware of the different meanings, especially the emotion-laden connotations, that a word may have for different groups.

Quoting 200 national black leaders, Oliphant (1979, p. 20) records the different feelings aroused by the word *quota*: "The term quota, which traditionally meant the *exclusion* of Jews, is now being used by many Jews to warn against attempts to *include* blacks in aspects of our society and economy from which they were previously excluded."

Some persons regard affirmative action as a zero-sum situation: What one person gains, the other loses. Seen on an individual level, this is true of any job or educational decision involving more applicants than openings, whether or not affirmative action is involved. The critical sociological question is the extent of agreement on the criteria of selection. What to some is a "special admissions" program is to others the addition of criteria that had been neglected. "Affirmative action, properly understood, is much more than an attempt to rectify injustice to groups by bestowing rewards on some of their members; it is fundamentally an attempt to get interests, needs, skills, and ideas that have previously been ignored spoken for throughout the social order" (Green 1981, p. 191). One thinks of the injustices to which black lawyers may be especially sensitive or the linguistic problems that Hispanic teachers may be best able to identify.

The question of criteria can lead us to ask: What are the consequences of *not* having an affirmative action program in a society with a history of extensive discrimination and with minorities whose aspirations have been greatly increased? Can opponents suggest an alternative that has increased or might be expected to increase minority representation significantly throughout the educational, occupational, and other parts of society? That was one of the tests of the "Brennan group" of the Supreme Court in the *Bakke* case. Of the 452 applicants admitted to the University of California—Davis Medical School, 1970–74, 29 were Black and 39 Mexican American. Without the affirmative action provisions of the admissions policy, only one Black and six Mexican Americans would have been admitted (Sexton 1979, p. 315). The deans of the four publically supported law schools in California pointed out, in their brief filed with the Supreme Court in that case, that without "special admissions" programs the great underrepresentation of minority persons in law (and, we can add, in professions generally) will continue. In 1970, 1.08% of lawyers were black. The ratio of Mexican Americans was even lower. As Griswold notes (1979, p. 57): "Law and medicine are inevitably involved in politics in the broad sense, and minority groups

[1] A vast literature expressing diverse views deals with this issue from sociological, legal, economic, and philosophical perspectives. See, e.g., Bell 1982; Borgatta 1976; Bundy 1978; Burns 1981; Burstein 1979; Davis and Hope 1979; Dovidio and Gaertner 1981; Duster 1976; Garcia et al. 1981; Glazer 1978; A. Goldman 1979; Green 1981; Griswold 1979; Keller 1976; Kluegel and Smith 1983; Lipset and Schneider 1978; Maguire 1980; Massey 1981; McCormack 1978; Sexton 1979; Sowell 1981; U.S. Commission on Civil Rights 1982.

will be underrepresented in the political process if their members cannot gain admission to the professions."

Ethical questions repeatedly emerge from a sociological examination of affirmative action. It would be desirable if our various judgments of fairness could be made by application of John Rawls's criterion (that is fair which is agreed upon by well-informed persons of good faith who do not know to which group they will belong), but our judgments are more primordial—buried deep within our biographies and group histories. It is perhaps not too great an oversimplification to say that discussions of affirmative action once more involve judgments about the comparative importance of liberty and equality and the nature of the interactions between them. Are they mutually exclusive, so that movement toward one implies movement away from the other; or are they integral, so that only by advancing both can we advance either; or are they relatively unconnected, with various relationships possible, depending on circumstances?

Tension between liberty and equality has persisted throughout American history. A century ago, writing for the majority of the Supreme Court, Justice Joseph Bradley declared: "When a man has emerged from slavery, and by the aid of beneficent legislation has shaken off the inseparable concomitants of that state, there must be some stage in the progress of his elevation when he takes the rank of a mere citizen and ceases to be the special favorite of the laws" (quoted by Bell 1982, p. 855). This seems, again, to be the dominant view, as opposed to Justice Harlan's minority dissent in opposition to Justice Bradley's view that it is "scarcely just to say that the colored race has been the special favorite of the laws" (Bell 1982, p. 856). Justice Bradley's philosophy, Bell observes (1982, p. 863), "for better or worse . . . presently influences corporate, institutional, and governmental power in the United States" in the belief "that individualism is the appropriate prescription for slavery in the past and racism in the present."

The United States Commission on Civil Rights has emphasized that discrimination can scarcely be reduced by remedies that ignore its existence. In our judgment the commission is correct in declaring:

Despite civil rights laws and a noticeable improvement in public attitudes toward civil rights, continued inequalities compel the conclusion that our history of racism and sexism continues to affect the present. A steady flow of data shows unmistakably that most of the historic victims of discrimination are still being victimized and that more recently arrived groups have also become victims of ongoing discriminatory attitudes and processes. (U.S. Commission on Civil Rights 1982, Vol. 2, p. 4).

The steady flow of data also indicates that affirmative action has made a significant contribution to the increase of minority enrollments in undergraduate and graduate programs, in professional and managerial jobs, on police and fire-fighting forces, and, perhaps to a lesser degree, in blue-collar jobs. These gains are not large, nor are they securely held under conditions of administrative opposition and recession. Numerous dilemmas must be faced, as in *Boston Firefighters Union* v. *Boston Chapter, N.A.A.C.P.*, a case pitting the principle of seniority against affirmative action. The Federal District judge had ruled that layoffs must not be used to reduce the percentage of minority and women employees. By the time the case had reached the Supreme Court in 1983, it had become moot, since workers who had been laid off had been rehired as a result of action by the Massachusetts legislature. In June, 1984, however, the Supreme Court ruled, in a 6–3 vote in its *Firefighters* v. *Stotts* decision, that an employer (in this case the Memphis Fire Department) could lawfully use its seniority rules rather than an affirmative action program designed to increase the percentage of minority workers.

Dilemmas such as this clash of the seniority principle with the affirmative action principle pose difficult policy problems. Let us note several others: What adaptations have to be made to design a policy that is within the realm of possibility, that stretches and strains and changes discriminatory patterns as far as they will go without leading to a reactionary countermovement? The Supreme Court, in the *Bakke* case, rejected an admissions plan containing a fixed quota but allowed the legitimacy of taking race into account—in effect permitting a racially mixed student body to be one of the goals. A goal, rather than a quota, is a soft, ambiguous, flexible, and therefore politically acceptable target. It is criticized from the right for being a full-fledged quota and from the left for being a pious promise without authoritative backing. If one goes simply on the basis of past American experience, the latter judgment seems more nearly correct. The response, however, ought not to be to move to a quota but to increase the intensity of the review to see to it that idle promises are not serving as policies.

Another serious policy question: How to see to it that the gains from affirmative action are made available to the least privileged of the target groups as well as the better-trained, who are more likely to be able to take advantage of new opportunities? America faces the danger that its minority populations will be split between a small proportion for whom opportunities are opening and the larger proportion for whom present policies are of little avail. In this regard, the *Weber* and *Fullilove* decisions of the Supreme Court, involving minority workers and small businesses, may have dealt with a more important issue than the *Bakke* decision. Their effects on policy may reach farther out toward the disadvantaged.

We will mention only one additional policy question: How to prevent the less well off among the presumably privileged majority from bearing most of the immediate costs of affirmative action? The upper middle class and upper class are pretty well insulated against the shifts of opportunity. (In fact, it is when that insulation wears thin for *them* that affirmative action policies are brought under most severe pressure.) Slowly we are learning how to spread the risks of social change—unemployment insurance, labor unions, social security systems, adult education programs, and the like are involved—but little serious attention has been given to spreading the risks associated with affirmative action. When a college resolves to admit more students from minority backgrounds, most of them requiring financial aid, majority students from middle-income families, not the wealthy, are the first to feel the pinch.

We cannot defend affirmative action programs by disregarding such problems. Quite clearly, present procedures have many flaws; some are inherent and must be seen as inevitable costs, others are due to inadequacies of design and administration. But neither can we attack such programs by contrasting them with utopia. Seen against the realities of the future if we do not support affirmative action in America today, our present policies deserve support, careful study, and improvement.

The Strategy of Change

A new context for intergroup relations has been created in the United States—and indeed throughout the world. We must be careful not to give our sole attention to the militant protest movements or the extensive legal changes, for they have been going on during a quiet revolution that has weakened the foundations of the earlier structures

of discrimination. The multiple forces at work—demographic, economic, international, religious, educational, and many others—have been remaking views of the world held by minorities, and at the same time they have significantly changed the structures within which intergroup relations occur. It is within this rapidly changing context that strategic choices are being made (Williams 1977, Chapters 8–12).

With both hopes and power raised, it has been inevitable that minorities would protest the continuing patterns of discrimination and would seek to enlarge their gains. Much of the initiative has been shifted to the minorities (Scott 1976).

Nonviolent Resistance

When Mrs. Rosa Parks refused to give her seat to a white man on a Montgomery bus, she precipitated a series of events that have yet to run their course. In the months that followed, Blacks combined the strategy of economic boycott with a philosophy of nonviolent protest in a way that proved to be highly effective. The fact that they succeeded in winning nonsegregated seating on Montgomery buses, after many months of struggle, was less significant in the long run than the solidarity of purpose, the testing of method, the strengthening of self-respect, and the discovery of leadership that came from the dispute.

Under what conditions are such nonviolent protests likely to be effective? (see Bruyn and Rayman 1979; Kuper 1957 and 1974, pp. 255–74; Oppenheimer 1969). The most general factor is the extent to which potential opponents are divided or unified, both individually and collectively. If some are individually ambivalent, sharing values and goals with the protesters, while also holding contrary views, they are more likely to be persuaded by nonviolence. They may indeed not be ambivalent but may sympathize wholeheartedly with the protest, yet need an effective argument to disidentify with the dominant position of their own group.

"The principal virtue of nonviolence as a strategy is that it does not serve the opponent by unifying his force and intensifying his anger, as does an aggressive or violent act" (Coleman 1969, p. 316). It is a critical question, therefore, how members of a minority envisage the dominant group. If they see no moderates when in fact there are some, they are unlikely to act in such a way as to exploit the resources available to nonviolent protests. Those who themselves have been violent—on whatever side—are unlikely to recognize moderation on the other side because it makes their own actions seem less reasonable or civilized. A different series of interactions characterizes some white activists and intellectuals today, as during most times of crisis: For fear of being thought unsympathetic to a just protest or insensitive to injustice, they describe a thoroughly racist society.[2] *But poor appraisal of the actual situation means poor strategy.* Sweeping generalizations may be emotionally simpler, but their effects are negative.

Applying this point of view to the Montgomery bus boycott as an illustration, we find several factors that contributed to its success. The interdependent economy of the city meant that many Whites were ambivalent. The bus company needed black riders; and white women, many of them working for $75 a week (these were 1955 dollars), needed their maids, whom they paid $20 a week. The quiet technique of the Reverend Martin Luther King and his coworkers was ideally suited to win the support of moderates and weaken the opposition, who were put in the position of extremists. In these circumstances, the restrained but insistent demand for equal services by the use of legal processes was effective.

What is the origin of this strategy of nonviolence? It has often been referred to as a Gandhian technique, and there is no doubt that the early leaders of CORE, SCLC, and others had been influenced by study of Gandhi and his work in South Africa and India (Bell 1968). This is an inadequate explanation, however, particularly of the alacrity with which nonviolent resistance was adopted by thousands of Blacks, young and old, North and South, lower class and middle class, most of whom doubtless knew Gandhi only as a remote historical figure. The total explanation would certainly be complex, but these factors are probably involved: Relatively powerless groups, who would inevitably be overcome in any open contest of force, have often found nonviolent resistance a way of maximizing their strength in dealing with an opponent who has some respect for law and a conscience. In a sense, this is a way of getting part of the dominant force over on the minority's side. (This is a tactic, of course, in interpersonal as well as intergroup relations. We will leave it to the reader's memory to identify the conditions under which children employ it successfully.)

To this perhaps humanwide source of nonviolent resistance one must add the Christian tradition. It comes as a natural part of the cultural training of most Blacks to believe that they can achieve through suffering, that they should turn the other cheek, that the enemy can better be overcome by love than by force.

Narrowing the sources of this movement further, we would note the American tradition as one of the essential ingredients. Half a century before Gandhi began his work, Henry David Thoreau was advising civil disobedience of laws that were an offense to one's conscience, and there was ample precedent for his advice (although the nonviolent quality gets lost) in the Boston Tea Party or the American Revolution itself. It is perhaps not too much of an exaggeration to say that there is a touch of the anarchist in every American: hateful laws and offensive authorities are not to be obeyed. This is both the glory and the problem of a free society.

In reply to a letter from eight Alabama ministers who expressed regret over the vigor of the protest against segregation in Birmingham, Martin Luther King wrote (1963a, pp. 12–13):

> You express a great deal of anxiety over our willingness to break laws. . . . An unjust law is a code inflicted upon a minority which that minority had no part in enacting or creating. . . . I submit that an individual who breaks a law that conscience tells him is unjust, and willingly accepts the penalty by staying in jail to arouse the conscience of the community over his injustice, is in reality expressing the very highest respect for law. We can never forget that everything Hitler did was "legal"

---

[2]There are scores of books and articles today dealing with the concept of *racism*. It is not a new term—Ruth Benedict made significant use of it in 1940 in her classic *Race: Science and Politics*—but it has recently come into prominence. In many ways it is a useful shorthand way of saying: a complex of discriminations and prejudices directed against an alleged inferior race. Nevertheless, we have made only minimal use of the term for two related reasons: Racism tends to be a "swearword," not an analytic term; as such, in most of its present uses, it freezes the mind and perpetuates a vocabulary of praise and blame that we think reduces our ability to understand, and therefore to reduce, intergroup hostilities and injustices. The second reason is closely related. Racism is often used as an explanation, rather than a description of a situation: "White racism is essentially responsible for the explosive mixture which has been accumulating in our cities since the end of World War II" (*Report of the National Advisory Commission on Civil Disorders* 1968, p. 10). This does not take us very far. It is equivalent to saying that we are having a serious epidemic because many people have been infected by a virus. How does the virus work to cause the disease? Who is vulnerable, who immune? What situations harbor it? The tragedies associated with intergroup hostility are too severe to permit us the luxury of "medieval" explanations by naming or by lodging the cause in individual choice.

and everything the Hungarian freedom fighters did in Hungary was "illegal."

This sounds as much like Patrick Henry as Gandhi. But more than that, in the course of his long letter, King cited, among others, the eighth-century prophets, Socrates, St. Paul, St. Thomas, Thomas Jefferson, Abraham Lincoln, Martin Buber, and Paul Tillich, not to mention Shadrach, Meshach, and Abednego. Such is the reach of the goals and strategy of freedom.

We shall not undertake to describe the wave of nonviolent protests that swept across the United States, particularly in the early years of the 1960s. There were thousands of boycotts, sit-ins, freedom rides, picketing, and mass rallies. Some of these were designed to win a specific goal, to secure jobs or to open facilities from which nonwhites had been barred; others were primarily symbolic affirmations of the need for an open society.

Sit-ins and freedom rides involve a great deal of courage and self-discipline, for their purpose is to persuade people without violence to abide by a law that they have long been disregarding, usually with support from the dominant community and the police. These protests started with restaurants and lunch counters and spread out to parks, libraries, art galleries, swimming pools, churches, and transportation facilities, all of which were substantially segregated in the South in 1960. There were wade-ins, read-ins, and pray-ins. Violence broke out in many cases, and many of the protesters were injured and thousands more were jailed. Several were killed. The total effect, nevertheless, was the desegregation of many public facilities, but more importantly, the dramatization of segregation and discrimination so vividly that they can never again be taken for granted in the United States.

Violent Resistance

Almost everybody admires at least one revolution—usually one distant in time if the person is comfortable and a contemporary one if he is not. The staunchest defenders of law and order recognize the role of coercion in human affairs, but they want the use of violent coercion limited to the official representatives of society. For those who deeply believe, however, that they suffer from that society—and at the hands of those representatives—such a restriction on the use of violence is unacceptable. Coercion is monopolized only under those

rare conditions when the locus of legitimacy is unanimously agreed upon. Clearly that is not the situation in most societies today. Minorities in many places are saying: Why should we simply capitulate to *their* violence? It is less moral than our own.

We cannot discuss here the conditions under which such loss of legitimacy is likely to occur (see Graham and Gurr 1969; Nieburg 1963; see also footnote one in Chapter 7). Briefly, it is the product of a cycle of causes; rising aspirations and a sharply increased sense of relative deprivation on the part of minorities; pressure against the system; reaction by the dominant group, some of it violent (violence may actually decrease, but it is more visible and probably more "official" because the informal social control mechanisms prove to be inadequate); stronger pressure against the system, with supporting ideologies now justifying reciprocal violence (we are an internal colony, with every right to break free).

For the dominant group it is clear that violence is successful in maintaining allegiance only when it is used minimally. Greater use may maintain sullen and unwilling compliance, but not allegiance. A related principle applies to minorities: Minimal violence used to underline a neglected legitimacy may get support, or not arouse major retaliation. When the conflict is heightened, counterviolence is increased and it becomes more difficult to maintain a publicly accepted definition that the minority violence was an understandable (if unfortunate) protest (Fogelson 1968).

It is, of course, difficult to draw a line between violence and nonviolence. Gamson (1975, p. 74) defines violence as "deliberate physical injury to property or persons." Yet, one wonders, is it violent to hurt a child personally, but nonviolent to support a system that causes the child to be malnourished as an infant so that he does not fully develop, physically or mentally? Is it violent to smash the windows in a man's store and loot his shelves, but nonviolent to picket his business so that his economic loss is as great as it would have been had he been looted? Those who justify opposition to violence on moral grounds must be certain they are not drawing a distinction without a difference.

Important as these moral questions are, the focus of our attention in this chapter is on strategy. In this light, a minority appropriately asks how the willingness or unwillingness to use violence increases the resources at its disposal and reduces the deficits. In a relatively open society the marshaling of resources is more dependent on the mutual trust within the minority than on their persuading or coercing the majority to make concessions. Effective action requires the *accumulation* of resources. Politically, this means the use of flexible and focused voting that can be brought to bear on particular issues and elections, rather than scattered and competitive politics that divides the minority vote. Economically, it means the building up, out of funds that are individually too small, of resources that jointly are adequate to accomplish a given purpose. Geertz (1962) describes the "revolving credit associations" that exist in many villages and towns of Southeast Asia and Africa. The associations are circles of friends and neighbors who make periodic contributions to a common fund. Each member, in an order determined by lot or by some prearranged method, has his turn in using the fund for some major purpose. Similar arrangements are not uncommon among minority communities in the United States and elsewhere.

What has this to do with the question of violence? Violence is an outward strategy. It is based on the assumption that coercing the majority is the primary need. Although it is sometimes justified as a source of minority community solidarity, it tends in fact to tear the fabric of trust on which community solidarity depends. Whenever a situation has developed in which discrimination by the majority has fallen off, and new procedures to take advantage of new openings are called for, violence deflects energy and wastes resources. It is one of the ironies of history that violence is most likely to erupt precisely when, and partly because, new opportunities are opening; and it may persist into the period when techniques for exploiting newly available opportunities are the chief need.

Interpretations of the impact of violence differ widely, not only because of differing moral premises, but also because the situation is extremely complex, as emphasized by recent research (see Button 1978; Gurr 1980; Kelly and Snyder 1980; Mirowsky and Ross 1981; Stark et al. 1974; Useem 1975). One must be alert to long-run, and not only short-run, consequences, to all the unintended as well as to the intended effects. Among interpretations of the riots in American cities during the 1960s, for example, one finds such contrasting notions as these: Riots increase hatred, confirm prejudices; action to remedy grievances must not follow riots or it will appear that lawlessness and

hostility are being rewarded. Yet others argue that desperately needed action seems to come only after a riot, which smashes complacency and exposes the problem as nothing else has been able to do. The assessment is difficult. It does seem clear that in some circumstances riots are heard as a cry of pain. They may help to transform private trouble into a public issue, to use a theme developed by C. Wright Mills in another connection, by flooding the media of communication with the importance of the problem. Yet riots, in addition to the immediate losses and costs, tend to confirm mutual stereotypes, to increase segregation by speeding the flight of Whites to the suburbs, and to give the participants a sense that they have struck a blow for freedom when in fact they have only indicated the need for freedom while leaving the basic difficulties intact.

We agree with B. L. R. Smith (in Connery 1968, p. 128) that extensive use of violence tends to spread through a society a "revolutionary myth" that has serious unanticipated, long-run costs:[3]

The costs are partly visible in such things as an increased sense of fear in the community shared by whites and blacks alike, the greater salience of politics for people's lives in a society which has usually resisted the encroachments of political attitudes into the sphere of basic human relationships, and the prospect that, since the stakes of politics are higher, ruling elites in the future may seek to manage conflict by excessive resort to force. Violence begets more violence and ultimately will leave deep scars on the nation's image of itself, profoundly alter life styles, and change the temper of the American mind.

Barrington Moore (in Connery 1968, p. 6) suggests that violence fails to work "mainly when revolutionary rhetoric outruns the real possibilities inherent in a given historical situation," that is, when a group underestimates the opposition. We believe it also fails, in the sense that it entails great costs without concomitant gains, when it overestimates the opposition, when it fails to see possibilities that are available in a situation at much lower cost than that required by violence.

[3]That myth, we scarcely need to add, is scarcely the invention of minority groups seeking redress. Violence is widely accepted among dominant-group members as a way of trying to deal with difficult disputes, and it becomes a prime strategy among marginal members of the dominant society, as in the Ku Klux Klan. Despite the small revival of the Klan (see King 1980; Suall 1980–81; Turner et al. 1981), however—it presently has about 10,000 members, with perhaps 100,000 sympathizers who attend some rallies, compared with the three or four million members in the 1920s—its version of the myth of violence has few believers.

In his careful study of fifty-three groups that challenged what they regarded as an injust situation, Gamson (1975, p. 82) found that most used violence not as a primary tactic but as something incidental to strikes, bargaining, and propaganda. In his view, about 60 percent of the groups were successful in their protests: either they were accepted as expressing legitimate interests or attained half or more of their goals. The cause–effect relationship, however, is difficult to determine. Such groups may appear when history seems to be furnishing an opening for change. It is necessary to distinguish short-run and long-run effects, local and national changes. In their study of recent racial disorders in the United States, Kelly and Snyder observe (1980, p. 739):

> Our results consistently indicate no relationship between racial violence and black socioeconomic gains at the local level. These findings suggest that earlier evidence of reform responses to disorder in some cities may have reflected efforts to cool out black protest but did not result in substantive changes. Our conclusions on the effects of racial violence therefore parallel those on causes: if there were socioeconomic consequences, they must have operated at the national level and affected blacks uniformly across local communicities.

(See also Isaac and Kelly 1981; Isaac, Mutran, and Stryker 1980; and for a somewhat different view Jennings 1983.).

Minority protests, some of them with violent aspects, cannot escape the limitations on power imposed by more normal strategies of change. Rebellion, Gamson observes, "is simply politics by other means" (1975, p. 139). And Zelditch argues (1978, pp. 1515–1514) "Movements are violent and coercive because they are the politics of the disprivileged, the unrepresented. . . . Normal politics is the politics of recognized, established interests, the politics of 'members.' " Movements are the politics of "nonmembers."

Resource Mobilization

Minority group strategies often contain an implicit, if not an explicit, theory of resource mobilization, that is, a theory of the best ways to draw in and activate members, to aggregate their resources into an effective size and strength, and to secure outside help.

In recent years, a more general theory (or a set of partially competing theories) of resource mobilization has been developed, primarily in connection with studies of social movements and collective behavior. That theory can be of great value in understanding and strengthening minority efforts to oppose discrimination and to improve their situation (see, e.g., Coleman 1971; Gamson 1975; Gamson, Fireman, and Rytina 1982; Kriesberg 1979; Leifer 1981; McCarthy and Zald 1977; Tilly 1978; Zald and McCarthy 1979). This work, it should be noted, can be distinguished from but is related to the work on status attainment. This latter focuses on individuals, on the background factors and individual activities—education, for example—most likely to lead to status improvement (see, e.g., Blau and Duncan 1967; Featherman and Hauser 1978; Kerckhoff and Jackson 1982; Sewell and Hauser 1975). Perhaps we can think of this emphasis as the study of the factors that lead to the accumulation of resources, one element involved in the mobilization process.

Minority resources, however, are not simply those possessed by individuals and relevant to their individual status improvement, such as skill, money, courage, and readiness to endure pain and sacrifice. Interpersonal resources are also vital. We have noted the importance of community cohesion and trust. Relationships among minority organizations and with the media and authorities in the society at large must also be considered (McCarthy and Zald 1977). This is true because we are dealing with "the problem of how a distinct subgroup in society, with little power and without direct resources for gaining more power, can nevertheless come to gain those resources" (Coleman 1971, p. 1). He is using the term *power*, Coleman goes on to note, "not in the sense of power over another group but a position in society having as much power over one's own life and over community and national actions as other citizens."

Resource mobilization theorists believe that protest movements are not well explained by reference to individual frustrations or perceptions of individual interests. Feelings of solidarity with the group seeking change are essential in order to deal, among other things, with the "free rider" problem. This refers to the fact that changes that are won often benefit those who did not work for them as well as those who did (see Bruce Fireman and William Gamson in Zald and McCarthy 1979, pp. 15–18). If many try to be free riders, of course, there will not be any ride; hence the need to emphasize shared interests and a nearly exclusive identity—we versus they. Such an identity is reinforced both positively and negatively: Positively, we are bound together by kinship and friendship and common values. Negatively, we are kept together by the barriers to our social mobility, imposed by the majority. Those barriers may be exaggerated by the leaders of a social movement—the functions of pessimism—in efforts to maintain solidarity and reduce the number of free riders. There is a delicate problem of balance in this aspect of resource mobilization: How to increase cohesion without at the same time increasing the cohesion of a majority opposed to the goals being sought (this is sometimes called backlash) and, as a corollary, how to emphasize an exclusive identity without losing ties to those in the majority who can be valuable allies, bringing resources of their own to the efforts to reduce discrimination. We urge readers to think about various minority groups seeking to mobilize their resources and to ask: How skillfully do they manage to balance the need for solidarity and a strong group identity with the need to prevent the sense of an exclusive solidarity growing among members of the majority?

Changing the Minority-Group Member. Where causes are cyclical and mutually reenforcing it is not sufficient to pay attention only to group mobilization. Resources must be increased, and this requires attention to the skills and attitudes among the oppressed. Built into the personality systems and group structures of minorities are some of the consequences of *past* discrimination. These may persist into situations that are less discriminatory, lowering the possibilities that present opportunities will be exploited. Thus the responses of minority-group members to prejudice and discrimination frequently lend support to further hostility. One line of approach that strategy may take, therefore, is to discover ways of changing some of the responses of the minorities.

In a time of sharp controversy this point is difficult to make. If members of the dominant group call attention to the behavior of minority-group members—whatever the cause—and the support that behavior gives to oppression, they are liable to criticism for blaming the victim for having the weaknesses that mistreatment has forced upon him. If one of the minority-group itself calls attention to the need for discipline and self-improvement, he runs the risk of being called an "Uncle Tom" or "Uncle Tomahawk," a traitor to the cause.

Nevertheless the point should be made, for there is great need for further study of the conditions that promote the perpetuation of minority subcultures and personality tendencies which prevent the entrance of minority-group members into the full range of community life even when barriers have been lowered. Perhaps recriminations can be avoided if one puts the issue not in terms of a vocabulary of praise and blame, but in terms of cause and effect. One then asks a strategic question: To what degree is emphasis on changes in the motivation, values, behavior, and group structures of minorities effective as a complement to changes in patterns of dominant-group discrimination and segregation, in the effort to remove inequities? There is little that one can say with confidence in answer to this question, but we would suggest that the further desegregation has proceeded the stronger should be the emphasis on minority change. In some aspects of American life, we may be reaching the point at which a call for expanded opportunities meets an embarrassing shortage of persons qualified to use those opportunities.

Minority-group norms and character structures are to some degree tuned to a discriminatory society; they reflect efforts to adjust to or deal with that society. When discrimination declines, minority-group members may not be fully ready to seize new opportunities. Protected islands may be demanded, or built (and perhaps are needed during a period of transition), and the system may still be blamed. If, however, this blame is poorly placed, if it does not identify the true situation, it will be an expensive luxury.

Following this line of argument, we are led into one of the great issues of social change: What force is powerful enough to transform people, to create individuals ready and able to respond effectively to a new world? Some argue, as we have noted, that violence can do this, that it is, to repeat Sartre's words "man recreating himself." But this does not ask what he is recreating himself for. Oppenheimer asks (1969, p. 65) "whether this therapeutic effect stems from violence or from the effect of struggling against oppression." And Fanon (1963), even as he exalts violence, also notes its great psychic costs, for the individual, his family, and the total community.

Are there less costly ways to achieve necessary personal transformations? The power of some religious movements to revitalize their adherents has often been studied. (This is not necessarily in contradistinction to violence, it should be noted, since violence may be heightened by the belief that one is fighting for a sacred cause.) When this thesis is applied to race relations in the United States, without specifically religious connotations, it may be "that the real benefit [one of the benefits?] of the civil rights movement is the psychological change it has produced and is producing in those Negroes who are active in it" (Coleman 1969, p. 295).

Whatever one may regard as the most effective method for achieving this goal, it is clear that some personality reorganization, not only of the majority-group member, but of the minority-group member as well, is necessary as part of the process whereby resources are mobilized and majority–minority systems transformed.

Organizations Opposing Discrimination

The *Civil Rights Directory, 1981,* issued by the United States Commission on Civil Rights, lists 41 federal governmental agencies involved in the enforcement of civil rights, nearly 400 state and local agencies, and over 300 private agencies seeking to protect and extend and/or to study the civil rights of racial and cultural minorities, of women, the handicapped, the elderly, and others. As the directory observes, this is by no means a complete list.

Protest organizations and movements have a long history in the United States (Franklin and Meier 1982; Harding 1981; Meier and Rudwick 1976). Black opposition to slavery, the abolition movement, and immigrant protective associations were important in the nineteenth century. Requisites for effective organization, however, were often lacking. Literacy, trained leadership, some economic power in the hands of minorities, and a growing awareness of the costs of discrimination in the dominant group create a situation in which opposition to disprivilege can be much more effective. Those influences have grown, and by 1940 an environment favorable to a strong attack on discrimination had emerged.

As more and more people have been drawn into the field of intergroup relations as a full-time occupation, it has gone through the process of professionalization. A body of principles has developed to guide their work, a program of training for staff members, coordinating organizations for the exchange of experience, and professional publications for research and information. This process is by no means complete. It will doubtless be some

time before we have graduate schools of intergroup relations to match our medical schools (or more probably, departments of intergroup relations in professional schools of conflict resolution). But steps in this direction have been taken at several universities, and it seems highly probable that further development along this line will take place.

A focal point of this professionalization is the National Association of Intergroup Relations Officials (NAIRO), an organization founded in 1947. In its *Journal of Intergroup Relations* (Autumn 1961, p. 291), NAIRO describes itself as "an organization of individuals concerned with advanced intergroup relations knowledge and skills, improving the standards of professional intergroup relations practice, and furthering acceptance of the goals and principles of intergroup relations work."

Public and Quasi-Public Agencies in Intergroup Relations

We cannot begin even to list the numerous agencies and departments of government now concerned with racial and cultural relations. Some of them may be called quasi-public, for they are primarily advisory and have no official status. But there are hundreds established by ordinance, staffed professionally, and financed out of public funds.

State and local agencies are known by a variety of titles, Civil Rights Commission, Community Relations Commission, Human Relations Commission being among those commonly used. There are also administrators of public housing, school officers, and advisers in various branches of the government. They vary in their investigative and enforcement powers, but the emphasis is on conciliation and education. A fairly standard description of responsibilities and powers is this one referring to the Ohio Civil Rights Commission: "The Commission is concerned with discrimination in employment, housing, credit, and public accommodations based on race, color, religion, sex, national origin or ancestry, and age. It receives, initiates, and investigates complaints, holds hearings (with subpoena power), creates advisory councils, issues publications, conciliates, issues cease and desist orders, and grants compensatory damages" (U.S. Commission on Civil Rights, 1981a, p. 236).

The municipal and state agencies have handicaps as forces in the movement to reduce discrimination, but they also have some significant strengths and accomplishments. Most of them work on small budgets, although that is not true in the larger cities and states. They are often affected by the local political situation. This can be an advantage insofar as minority groups are in a balance-of-power position. More often, however, it is a disadvantage, because those seeking to hold or gain political power will give only token support to the agency if powerful interests oppose the agency's recommendations on housing, recreation, or job opportunities. This is not to criticize the skill of the various committees, but only to suggest that they work within the framework of an often difficult political structure, as do agencies on the federal level.

Despite the obstacles faced by local and state groups, they have made important contributions to intergroup relations. They have countered violence and the threat of violence with firmness, with facts and open discussion. They have helped to reduce discrimination in city employment, particularly by increasing minority employment in police departments, schools, and public transportation. There is little doubt that these agencies occupy a strategically important place in the efforts to reduce discrimination in American cities.

It is difficult to select the most important federal agencies, but the list should certainly include the following, along with their regional offices: Department of Education, Office for Civil Rights; Equal Employment Opportunity Commission; Department of Health and Human Services, Office for Civil Rights; Department of Housing and Urban Development, Office of Fair Housing and Equal Opportunity; Department of Justice, Civil Rights Division; Department of Labor, Office of Federal Contract Compliance Program. All of these are strongly influenced by the political climate of a given administration. Somewhat more autonomous and the most important of the federal agencies is the United States Commission on Civil Rights. Its mandate is extremely broad, with its emphases changing from year to year as the national situation changes. Its present (1984) chairman, Clarence Pendleton, and staff director, Linda Chavez, express the more conservative views of President Reagan. The mandate, however, remains the same:

The U.S. Commission on Civil Rights is a temporary, independent, bipartisan agency established by Congress in 1957 and directed to:

Investigate complaints alleging that citizens are being deprived of their right to vote by reason of their race, color, religion, or national origin, or by reason of fraudulent practices;

Study and collect information concerning legal developments constituting a denial of equal protection of the laws under the Constitution;

Appraise Federal laws and policies with respect to equal protection of the laws;

Serve as a national clearinghouse for information in respect to denial of equal protection of the laws; and

Submit reports, findings, and recommendations to the President and the Congress. (U.S. Commission on Civil Rights 1969, p. ii)

Private Organizations in the Field of Racial and Cultural Relations

Complementing the official agencies are many private associations dedicated wholly or in part to the reduction of prejudice and discrimination and the enlargement of opportunities for minorities. Some are concerned with civil rights generally, others with the special problems of particular minority groups. Some emphasize education, others are involved in action programs. Here we will mention only a few in order to note the range and importance of their programs.[4]

National Association for the Advancement of Colored People. The NAACP, founded in 1909, works for the elimination of segregation and discrimination against Blacks and other Americans. For the most part, it seeks its objectives through court and legislative action, although it has participated to some degree in the demonstrations and protest marches of the civil rights movement and has given legal and financial support to others in this movement. Campaigns for equality have been waged in the fields of housing, employment, education, recreation, law, travel, the armed forces, voting, and officeholding. Efforts have also been made to ban residential segregation, to secure passage of antilynching laws, and to bring about cooperation between religious organizations and the NAACP. The Research Department has compiled a large quantity of material on race relations and civil rights, and the national office has published a monthly journal, *The Crisis,* since 1910 (see

[4] Figures for budgets, membership, and staff change from year to year. Those interested in the data for the current year may consult standard reference works and the current official publications of the agencies themselves. See also *The Civil Rights Directory, 1981,* the current issue of the *American Jewish Yearbook,* and the *Encyclopedia of Associations; National Organizations of the U.S.,* 1977.

Hughes 1962; Lewis 1964; White 1948; Wilkins and Matthews 1982).

At the local level the NAACP serves as a legal-aid society, but in fighting for the rights of black Americans at the national level it selects cases for their strategic importance, and insofar as possible enters the courts only where there is good chance of success. In earlier chapters we have discussed some of the outstanding cases that the NAACP has taken to the U.S. Supreme Court. The NAACP has won most of the several dozen cases it has argued before the Supreme Court, most recently a victory in defense of its own activities. In 1982 the Supreme Court upheld its right to urge boycotts of merchants who discriminated against Blacks, overturning a judgment in favor of a group of white businessmen in Mississippi who, in 1976, had won a judgment of $1.2 million against the NAACP in the lower courts.

The NAACP is an interracial organization, but its membership is preponderantly Black. The influence of white members and officers has declined in recent years. There are about 1,700 branches, youth councils, and college chapters, with a total membership of 450,000. In 1977 Benjamin L. Hooks succeeded Roy Wilkins as executive director.

The NAACP Legal Defense and Education Fund, founded by the NAACP in 1939, is an associated but now legally separate organization with a staff of lawyers headed by Jack Greenberg. Disagreements between the two organizations have increased in recent years, mainly over fund raising, but their goals remains very similar.

The NAACP has been the subject of criticism from both the left and the right. Some regard it as being too militant, others as too conservative. In our judgment, the NAACP has been and continues to be an unusually effective organization in the fields of civil rights and civil liberties. We would emphasize the need for several types of organization. Too closely unified a movement would be weaker than present diversity.

The NAACP has endorsed and to some degree participated in nonviolent action programs. It has sharply criticized national administrations, particularly those of Presidents Nixon and Reagan, for their lax enforcement of civil rights laws. And it works alongside other groups in voter registration drives. In 1982, the NAACP identified 105 congressional districts where Blacks are 15 percent or more of the voting pool, indicating its intention of promoting registration and voter turnout. The higher than usual level of voting by Blacks and the increase in the number of black congressmen and of others supportive of civil rights indicate the effectiveness of these activities.

Throughout these developments, the NAACP has maintained its essentially integrationist approach.

National Urban League. The National Urban League, founded in 1910, has operated primarily as a social work agency. A large part of its work is devoted to the extension of economic opportunities to Blacks in industry, business, and the professions and to the improvement of housing. This objective is sought through discussions and conferences with business executives, industrialists, and labor union officials. Many Urban Leagues now provide clients with expert testing and counseling services in the professional, technical, clerical, skilled, and semiskilled job categories. Other activities include providing information about Blacks, serving as adviser to governmental agencies and industry on health, welfare, and employment matters affecting Blacks, developing programs to provide for the adjustment and social needs of immigrant workers, and assisting in the interracial planning of social services and community projects.

The Urban League maintains nearly 100 branches in cities throughout the country. Its professional staff is the largest of the predominantly black civil rights groups. Although the League took little direct part in the protest demonstrations of the 1960s, preferring to specialize in job training and placement and various social welfare programs, it has taken a militant stand on economic issues. The late Whitney Young, Jr., executive director for ten years, proposed programs for Blacks similar to veterans' benefits to compensate for the years of disprivilege, or a domestic "Marshall Plan" to bring Blacks rapidly into the mainstream of American society. The plan would guarantee a job for everyone willing and able to work and called for the building of one million low- and medium-income housing units a year to eliminate slums.

Young did not accept the label "moderate," declaring that the "moderate versus militant" contrast was imaginary. He thought of the Urban League as militant rather than extremist (see Young 1964, 1969).

Young died in March, 1971. From 1972 until 1982, the Urban League was directed by Vernon Jordan, Jr., a lawyer with experience in the United Negro College Fund and the Voter Education

Project. He continued the emphasis on job opportunities and, with his successor, John Jacob, a minister and social worker, criticized the Reagan
administration for drastically weakening those
opportunities. In the 1982 annual report of the Urban
League they wrote of the "broad feeling of isolation,
of a turning back of the clock, of a retreat from
civil rights policies and social service programs"
throughout Black America (Williams 1982, p. i).

**Southern Christian Leadership Confer-
ence.** In 1955–56 the Montgomery Improvement
Association in Alabama successfully carried through
a long and difficult boycott of city buses. The well-
disciplined nonviolent technique of the group
attracted national attention and brought its leader,
the Reverend Martin Luther King, Jr., into the front
ranks of the civil rights movement. To extend the
use of nonviolent but direct resistance to segregation and discrimination, King and others formed
the Southern Christian Leadership Conference.
Beginning with the sit-ins of 1960, the freedom
rides of 1961, and the crescendo of protests in
1963, SCLC leaped to prominence. King had
become, by almost any reckoning, the most influential black leader of the day, not as an administrator of an organization, but as a charismatic leader
and the most articulate voice of the civil rights
movement.

The approach of the SCLC is well expressed in
the following statement (from a leaflet, "This is
SCLC," quoted in Meier, Rudwick, and Broderick
1971, pp. 303–305):

The basic tenets of Hebraic-Christian tradition coupled with
the Gandhian concept of *satyagraha*—truth force—is at the
heart of SCLC's philosophy. Christian nonviolence actively
resists evil in any form. It never seeks to humiliate the opponent,
only to win him. Suffering is accepted without retaliation. Internal violence of the spirit is as much to be rejected as external
physical violence. At the center of nonviolence is redemptive
love. Creatively used, the philosophy of nonviolence can restore
the broken community in America.

SCLC sees civil disobedience as a natural consequence of
nonviolence when the resister is confronted by unjust and immoral
laws. This does not imply that SCLC advocates either anarchy
or lawlessness. The conference firmly believes that all people
have a moral responsibility to obey laws that are just. It recognizes, however, that there also are injust laws. From a purely
moral point of view, an unjust law is one that is out of harmony
with the moral law of the universe, or, as the religionist would
say, out of harmony with the Law of God. More concretely,
an unjust law is one in which the minority is compelled to
observe a code which is not binding on the majority. . . . In
the face of such obvious inequality, where difference is made
legal, the nonviolent resister has no alternative but to disobey
the unjust law. In disobeying such a law, he does so peacefully,

openly and nonviolently. Most important, he *willingly* accepts
the penalty for breaking the law.

Although King preached nonviolence throughout his career, which ended with his murder in
1968, he did adopt a more militant stance in the
last two years. He spoke of civil disobedience to
disrupt American society; urged black control and
ownership of the ghettos; and used a rhetoric that
was close to that of Black Power advocates. He
continued to call for cooperation with Whites, however, and for the attainment of an integrated society. In an article written shortly before he was
killed, he opposed those who were suggesting that
rioting was a necessary and valuable strategy (in
Meier, Rudwick, and Broderick 1971; see also
Garrow 1978; King 1958, 1963a, 1968; and for
more critical perspectives, Lewis 1970 and Lincoln
1970).

Some observers, particularly those who take a
radically militant point of view, believe that King's
approach reached its peak in 1963 and was replaced
by a nonintegrationist black power strategy in the
mid-1960s. The evidence does not support this
belief. A *Newsweek* poll (June 30, 1969, pp. 14–
15), for example, showed that King remained a
dominant figure. "King, in death, remains by far
the most revered Negro leader—and . . . no one
alive is even close. King's standing today has passed
from hero-worship to beatification; he is rated
favorably by 95 percent of the sample, excellent
by 83 percent." In 1983, his birthday was declared
a national holiday.

Nevertheless, the SCLC, like a variety of very
different types of organizations, was to some degree
a product of its times. The Rev. Ralph Abernathy,
who succeeded King as president, was more successful in holding the group together than many
thought possible, considering the overriding symbolic importance of King. Disagreements over
strategy, however, and some competition for leadership affect its work. The Rev. Jesse Jackson, a
more charismatic and aggressive leader, challenged
Abernathy for authority, and after a few years broke
away to found People United to Save Humanity,
PUSH. The current president, the Rev. Joseph
Lowery, is seen by some to represent a middle-
class perspective that overlooks the needs of working-class Blacks.

Perhaps the most influential of the outgrowths
of SCLC is the Martin Luther King, Jr., Center
for Social Change, of which Coretta Scott King is

the president. It is committed to the perpetuation of King's nonviolent movement for social change.

People United to Save Humanity (PUSH). An opinion poll among black Americans in 1980 found that the Rev. Jesse Jackson, president of PUSH, was ranked as the nation's leading black figure (Cleveland *Plain Dealer,* July 18, 1980, p. 4). Coretta Scott King, Shirley Chisholm, Maynard Jackson, and Tom Bradley were next in order. Jesse Jackson describes black America as one of the richest "underdeveloped" nations in the world— the best educated and most skilled of the Third World nations. Its potential, however, he sees as little used through a lack of disciplined education among the great majority and of organized pressure on corporate America. His Push-Excel program in schools is primarily exhortative and its long-run results difficult to measure, but it has been adopted in dozens of schools. The program is designed to involve not only students and teachers but also parents, community leaders, and the media in a resolve to increase hours of study, increase order in the schools, eliminate drug use, and relate education to a broader range of occupations. It has received several million dollars of federal and local support and a great deal of praise. "High-schools in Los Angeles report that Push-Excel has increased attendance, cut down on vandalism and otherwise improved the atmosphere of the schools" (*The New York Times,* March 4, 1979, p. 38). Some believe that its effects are temporary if not superficial. We believe that a program of this kind is a highly beneficial part of a situation in which opportunities are expanding more rapidly than the training and the attention of minorities. Under more difficult conditions, when "payoffs" are few, it is less effective.

Faced with growing national conservatism in economic and social affairs, PUSH, along with the NAACP and NUL, has begun to turn to the private sector and to urge a tactic that, at times, has been effective—the economic boycott. They seek jobs and support of black-owned businesses through the threat of loss of black patronage.

PUSH has reached agreement with the Seven-Up Company to invest $61 million over a five-year period to develop black businesses. A similar agreement, involving $360 million, was arranged with Heublein Corporation as was a $34 million agreement to expand black participation in the Coca Cola Company (*Boston Globe,* July 18, 1982, p. 5).

Religious Organizations and Intergroup Relations

Many organizations among Protestants, Catholics, and Jews are devoted primarily to the reduction of prejudice and discrimination. These are too numerous even to list, but mention at least must be made of the existence of specialized intergroup agencies or staff members in other agencies. Among Protestants these are found particularly among the Methodist, Presbyterian, Episcopal, United Church, Unitarian-Universalist, and Quaker organizations. Extensive activity is carried out by the National Council of Churches of Christ (Department of Racial and Cultural Relations) and the World Council of Churches. As we noted in Chapter 15, the NCC and WCC are among the groups most willing to oppose structures of discrimination as well as individual prejudices.

In the Catholic Church, the primary organization working to reduce discrimination is the National Catholic Conference for Interracial Justice. Other groups include the United States Catholic Conference—Department of Social Development and World Peace and the National Catholic Welfare Conference—Social Action Department.

Of the dozens of Jewish organizations interested in intergroup relations, perhaps the leading ones are the American Jewish Congress, the Anti-Defamation League of B'nai B'rith, and the American Jewish Committee. Their interests range from the enforcement of legal sanctions against discrimination to research. A number of Jewish agencies have joined together to form the National Jewish Community Relations Advisory Council in order better to coordinate their various programs and to undertake some common projects to protect and enhance equal rights and equal opportunities. The Council is composed of eleven Jewish organizations, of varying interests and differing strategies, and over one hundred state and local affiliates. They are united by the conviction that the problem of discrimination is indivisible.

Groups of Importance in the Recent Past

Some minority protest and reform groups have lasted several generations, although with ups and downs in their effectiveness. Others reflect more specific sets of circumstances. They last only a few years, and then, because of changes in the larger society, sharp disputes over policy among their members, strategies that arouse redoubled opposition, or controversial leadership, they disband or fade away. We shall mention a few such groups because their activities and their declines can teach us a great deal about the processes of change in minority–majority relations. In particular, they demonstrate the way in which violent rhetoric (physical violence was seldom used by these groups) can, at first, attract and activate some members of a minority and then can become a divisive force within the groups and a stimulus to repression and opposition from some members of the majority.

Student Nonviolent Coordinating Committee. Following the dramatic and successful desegregation of lunch counters in Greensboro, North Carolina, in February, 1960, student groups throughout the South adopted the nonviolent method of seeking equal treatment in parks, restaurants, theaters, swimming pools, and other facilities. In April, Martin Luther King called together leaders of various student groups, meeting at Shaw University, Raleigh, North Carolina, and out of their conversations came the Student Nonviolent Coordinating Committee. Although intended, perhaps, as an arm of SCLC, SNCC soon broke away. There was some rivalry over leadership, some disagreements over the timing and coordination of protests between the student leaders and King. After a few months SNCC was more formally organized, established a central office in Atlanta, and became separate not only from SCLC but also from the informal student groups on college campuses. By 1963 it had a staff of about seventy people, headed by John Lewis, many of them drawing only subsistence pay, and a budget of $160,000. It was particularly effective in voter registration, often in the "hard-core" areas least influenced by the integration movement.

Disagreements over strategy and goals became more severe within SNCC during the mid-1960s. It was caught up in the Black Power movement, Stokely Carmichael became its chairman in 1966, and the nonviolent philosophy was set aside. H. Rap Brown, Carmichael's successor as chairman, was even more vehement in his verbal attacks. The organization continued to support voter registration effectively but began to organize all-Negro parties, as in Lowndes County, Alabama, under the Black Panther emblem (Carmichael and Hamilton 1967, Chapter 5). In 1970, the name of the organization was changed to the Student National Coordinating Committee, but by that time it had faded out as a major national organization, its militant approach

having been taken up by CORE and in a more extreme way by the Black Panthers (see Lester 1968; Meier et al. 1971; Stoper 1977; Zinn 1966).

Congress of Racial Equality. Founded in 1942, CORE had quietly applied the techniques of nonviolence and the sit-in, largely in the North, for many years before it was brought into prominence by the black revolt of the 1960s. CORE was established first as a committee of the pacifist Fellowship of Reconciliation in an effort to apply Gandhian techniques of vigorous, nonviolent resistance to American race relations. It pioneered in the training of interracial groups for peaceful picketing, sit-ins, and negotiation.

The first president was James Farmer, one of the original organizers, a conscientious objector during World War II, and a disciple of Gandhi. During its first fifteen years, CORE was primarily a middle-class organization; but with the success of the Montgomery bus boycott in 1956 under King's leadership black organizations throughout the country began to see possibilities in mass action. CORE began to move quite rapidly in that direction with the sharp increase in sit-in protests and freedom rides in 1961. Thus King, who had been influenced by CORE and its nonviolent programs, in turn brought CORE, somewhat paradoxically, into a more militant phase of the civil rights movement. The transformation from an integrationist, nonviolent, yet very active and uncompromising organization, into a separatist, angry, and highly militant if not violent organization, took place over a period of just a few years.

By 1964 CORE was primarily a black nationalist, not an integrationist organization (although its separate chapters varied in the extent and timing of this change). Its membership, which had been predominantly white, was by that time mainly black. Some Whites remained, however, on the advisory committee. Floyd McKissick became the national director in 1966 and Roy Innis in 1969, both more separatist than Farmer (see Farmer 1966; Meier and Rudwick 1973). It is ironic that CORE, a pioneer in breaking down walls of segregation, in 1970 proposed separate schools for Blacks and Whites, with each race controlling its own. Innis said that CORE had talked with the governors of Georgia, Alabama, Mississippi, and Louisiana, and "all conceded that the plane could fly, that their side could live with it" (Cleveland *Plain Dealer,* March 6, 1970), p. A2). Thus, for some, had the civil rights movement come full circle.

By the late 1970s, what the Rev. Jesse Jackson had once called "the very soul of the civil rights movement" was sharply split. Farmer declared that Innis had become a dictator; charges of threats and violence were made against him by several members—charges that led to convictions of some of his supporters; and CORE's substantial fund-raising abilities—over four million dollars in 1976—seemed to lead to fewer and fewer programs along with larger expense accounts (Zehner 1979). In 1980, Waverly Yates was chosen to be chairman in an election that Innis's supporters deemed fraudulent.

The Black Panthers. For about five years, the left wing of the black protest movements was occupied by the Black Panthers. Reference to the period when they were subjects of public attention and controversy may be of value in suggesting some of the consequences of harsh confrontation as a way of trying to increase interracial justice.

The organization was founded in Oakland, California, in 1966. It began as a group of liberal antipoverty workers and evolved into a nationalist movement. It was the product in some measure of the split in strategy of SNCC, or it was at least illustrative of the radicalizing of one segment of the black nationalist movement. It was never a large group, having reached a peak of about 5,000 members in 1968 and dropping to perhaps 1,000 by 1971 (*The New York Times,* March 1, 1971, pp. 1, 14). The aims of the Blacks Panthers were similar to those of other black nationalist groups, except perhaps for the explicit demands that the government furnish jobs and decent income for all.

From the beginning there were differences over strategy and aims among the Black Panthers, as there are in any sectarian group. These differences became sharper in the context of intense public opposition to the severity of Panther rhetoric and their violent stance. By 1971 the Black Panthers, led by Huey Newton, had begun a major shift in methods. Confrontations with police were to be avoided; emphasis was placed on strengthening black communities—tactics and ideology that clashed with the call for intensified guerrilla activity against America being made by Eldridge Cleaver, who had fled to Algeria.[5]

[5]To get something of the underlying feelings and the range of views of Black Panthers, as well as opposition to them, see Anthony 1970 (an attack by an ex-officer of the group); Cleaver 1968; Meier, Rudwick, and Broderick 1971, pp. 491–515; Seale 1970; *The New York Times,* February 6, 1971, p. 11 and March 21, 1971, p. 61.

One of the most difficult questions in the assessment of the efforts of the Black Panthers to reduce discrimination has to do with the rhetoric and reality of their violent guerrilla activity, particularly in dealing with the police, and the degree to which the police tried to crush them. It is impossible to describe the Black Panther–police interaction in general terms; the details of each encounter require examination. Perhaps this much, however, can be said to indicate our judgment about the context. In a day of sharp interracial conflicts, stereotypes hardened on both sides, creating a strong tendency toward mutual self-fulfilling prophecies. Police, seeing the Black Panthers through the prism of violent rhetoric and riots, often acted first and looked for specific law violations second or not at all. Members of the Black Panthers, seeing the world through years of discrimination, excessive use of police repression, and frustrated hopes, talked hatred, gathered weapons, and in some instances, employed violence. They also fed some hungry children.

Several court decisions in the spring of 1971 found the Black Panthers innocent of charges or found insufficient evidence even for an indictment. In a long and costly trial in New York, for example, thirteen Black Panthers were acquitted on charges of conspiracy to bomb stores and murder police (*The New York Times,* May 14, 1971, pp. 1, 20). In light of these trials it seems clear that police actions during the preceding several years were much more repressive against the Panthers than was warranted or than the law allowed. Documents obtained under the Freedom of Information Act in 1980 revealed that the F.B.I. "tried to use black journalists, anonymous telephone calls and forged letters to disrupt the New York chapter [and other chapters]" (*The New York Times,* October 19, 1980, p. 1). In 1982, after a thirteen-year court fight, Chicago, Cook County, and federal authorities agreed to a $1.85 million settlement with nine plaintiffs—relatives of two Black Panthers who were slain in a raid and survivors of the raid (*The New York Times,* November 11, 1982, p. 35). It had become clear that in the "fierce gun battle with the Panthers" almost all of the shots had been fired by the police.

Thus the courts have recognized, in some instances slowly, the rights of Panthers to scream with pain and to demand change. This is not to say that the police were not sometimes under duress nor that reports of the confrontations accurately stated the number of Panthers killed. Although evidence is incomplete and difficult to interpret, it seems probable that the number of deaths was exaggerated in the press (Epstein 1975, pp. 33–77). The extent of official surveillance and harassment, however, was probably understated until recently.

For us, the basic question remains: Did the Black Panthers help to jolt the United States into action against discrimination or frighten it into retrenchment? The importance of this one organization should not be exaggerated; its approach and activity are more symbolic than causal. In our judgment, however, the 1968–69 confrontation period caused retrenchmore more than change; it helped to elect reactionary politicians, slowed implementation of law designed to achieve equality, and broke up essential alliances.

Black Power. Black power, of course, is not an organization but a movement, or perhaps a style. Some see it as the successor to the civil rights movement, or it can be thought of as one of the forms that the rights movement took beginning about 1964. Although black power has a wide variety of meanings, we can identify it as a movement that emphasizes confrontation strategies and nationalistic (separatist) goals more strongly than did most previous movements: "We must fill ourselves with hate for all white things." Such white things include the American political and economic system to some advocates of black power: "We must destroy both racism and capitalism" (Huey Newton).

It is not clear from such writings as Carmichael and Hamilton's *Black Power,* just what policies are called for. Nevertheless, the term designates a mood that it is very important to understand. The background, the perspective, and the ambiguities are well caught up in the statement by Christopher Lasch (1969, pp. 128–29):

Black Power represents, among other things, a revival of black nationalism and therefore cannot be regarded simply as a response to recent events. Black Power has secularized the separatist impulse which has usually (though not always) manifested itself in religious forms. Without necessarily abandoning the myth of black people as a chosen people, the new-style nationalists have secularized the myth by identifying black people in America . . . with the contemporary struggle against colonialism in the Third World. Where earlier nationalist movements, both secular and religious, envisioned physical separation from America and reunion with Islam or with Africa, many of the younger nationalists propose to fight it out here in America, by revolutionary means if necessary, and to establish—what? a black America? an America in which black people can survive as a separate "nation"? an integrated America?

As an explicit theme, black power faded out after a few years. Some of its emphasis was expressed in more orthodox radicalism, as in Amiri Baraka's Revolutionary Communist League. Some of its leaders, notably Stokely Carmichael, developed an ideology of pan-Africanism. Others moved to the right: Eldridge Cleaver is a "born-again Christian" and a supporter of Sun Myung Moon. A combination of increasing opportunities on one hand and dominant conservative trends on the other, from the late 1960s into the 1980s, encouraged the use of less separatist and conflict-oriented forms of protest. The increase in the number and visibility of black mayors, congressmen and congresswomen, and state legislators has furnished alternative routes for those seeking redress.

The gains in politics, still quite small, are not matched by economic gains, and the gap is a critical aspect of the current scene. The seeds of black power types of protest still lie in American soil.

Native American Organizations

American Indians have been fighting and negotiating for their rights for nearly 500 years, but we shall not try to tell that important story here (see Barsh and Henderson 1980). Suffice it to say that they were pushed back into small enclaves; their population was sharply reduced from perhaps one million to 210,000 in 1910 (it had increased to 1.4 million by 1980); and opportunities either to live as Indians or in the larger society were seriously limited. Even after the "Indian Wars" [sic] were over, the land base on which Indians lived declined, from 146 million acres in 1897 to 56 million acres in 1970 (since 1970, several million acres have been added). Federal policy vacillated but reached what some thought was a final stage in 1953 with the passage of the Termination Act. This was designed "to get the United States out of the Indian business," by permitting sale of reservation lands and developing various training and educational plans for individuals.

The treaty-making process had come to an end in 1871. Dorris observes (1981, p. 49) that the content of the treaties was not of major importance since all were eventually broken by the "Europeans." What was significant was that the treaties were made at all. "The very act of treaty-making imparted a European version of nationhood to the Native party, and as a result, established at least a legal parity, in terms of co-equal sovereignty, between aboriginal and European states."

This, then, is the context within which Native American organizations seek to deal with their current situation: a background of warfare and broken treaties, population pressure on a limited land base, an inconsistent federal policy, the strong sense of separate and autonomous tribes, and—within most tribes—political divisions reflecting different visions of what the tribal course of action and goals should be.

The year 1961 can be regarded as another important turning point in Indian affairs. Stimulated by the civil rights movement generally, the American Indian Chicago Conference brought representatives of 210 tribes together to draft a statement of principles and aims. There was, of course, a wide range of judgments, varying from an emphasis on detribalized assimilation to the belief that Indians are citizens of independent nations, not of the United States. But there was overwhelming support for the principle that decisions about the best course of action should be made by Indians. Most participants supported the position of the National Congress of American Indians, that reforms could come from within the system by working with the Bureau of Indian Affairs, provided that it could be made into an instrument for the expression of Indian judgments and interests.

The National Congress of American Indians, founded in 1945, is perhaps the most important group working for Indian rights. Sometimes called the "United Nations of the tribes," the NCAI represents about one hundred groups and approximately three-fourths of the Indians of the United States. It has sought to develop intertribal consensus and to influence national and state policy on Indians, principally by lobbying. It has tried to exert pressure on the goals and tactics of the Bureau of Indian Affairs and the Department of the Interior, has opposed legislation that proposed to transfer federal functions concerning Indians to the states, has demanded that the Indian land base be protected, and has sought to improve educational opportunities for Indians (Day 1972, pp. 506–507; Stewart 1977, p. 519).

One of the products of the American Indian Chicago Conference was the organization of the National Indian Youth Council, a militant, intertribal organization. Confederations among Indian tribes go back, of course, to the seventeenth century (the League of the Iroquois and perhaps some Pueblo intertribal organizations preceded contact

with Europeans), but tribal autonomy has been much the stronger force. The NIYC was formed because many young Indians were frustrated with the shifts in national Indian policy, with the paternalism of the Bureau of Indian Affairs, and with the cautious tactics, as they saw them, of the NCAI leaders. Members of the NIYC outlined a policy of self-determination and self-help (Day 1972, pp. 506–507).

The year 1961 also marked the beginning of yet another change in government policy. President Kennedy halted termination and began to bring more Indians into the Bureau of Indian Affairs. (On the BIA see Raymond Butler and James Officer in Yinger and Simpson 1978, p. 50–72.) It was not until 1966, however, that an Indian was named commissioner, a policy that has continued (the title itself was changed in 1977 to Assistant Secretary of the Interior for Indian Affairs.) Bit by bit the Termination Act of 1953 has been modified in other ways. In 1946, Congress set up the Indians Claims Commission in an effort to resolve the myriad of unresolved disputes over land and other issues. By 1977, $657 million had been awarded to Indian claimants, mainly for lands taken without adequate compensation (Lurie 1978). The shift in attitude that led to the Indians Claims Commission was also shown in various acts of Congress that restored land to the Taos, Menominee, and other tribes.

Even as these modifications of the conservative Termination Act were occurring, militant Indian groups were formed—the Indian versions of the civil rights campaign of the 1960s—the most prominent of which is the American Indian Movement (AIM). By the early 1970s, many elements in the "Red Power" movement were seeking to achieve a reservation-based "tribal nationalism." The tactics of these groups included fish-ins, the closing of beaches, rivers, and highways on reservation land, demands for legal protection and financial aid, blockage of dam construction, and—most visibly to the general public—occupation of the BIA offices, Alcatraz (California), Fort Lewis (Washington), and—symbolic of earlier conflicts—the village of Wounded Knee (South Dakota). The aim of Red Power was to create self-reliant, Indian-controlled, tribal "nations" within the United States (Day 1972, p. 507; see also Collier 1970; Deloria 1969; Levine and Lurie 1970; Stewart 1977).

Several developments in recent years have carried Native Americans into still another stage in their efforts to eliminate discrimination and to win greater control over their own affairs. The rapidly growing population, its urbanization (half now live in cities), and the rather sudden realization that they own enormous natural resources have combined with the expanded activism to create a new set of groups and strategies. "The Great American Desert, thought to be the ideal out-of-the-way spot to locate Indians in the nineteenth century, turns out to have more in common with Arabia than anyone at the time imagined" (Dorris 1981, p. 63). Indian lands contain nearly two-thirds of the low-sulpher coal, much of the uranium, and oil, gas, copper, and geothermal resources. In 1975, the leaders of the twenty-five largest western reservations formed the Council of Energy Resource Tribes (CERT)—what some have called an Indian OPEC—in an effort to control the development of these resources and to try to prevent their being funneled away, once again, from Native Americans. By 1982, thirty-seven tribes held membership.

The resources potentially available to some tribes may lead many Americans to overlook the continuing high rates of infant mortality, the unemployment, the inadequate educational opportunities, and the continuing struggle over treaty obligations that Indians face. Recent court decisions granting land and fishing rights to Indians, based on treaties, have aroused strong opposition among non-Indians. In addressing a meeting of representatives of more than 120 tribes, gathered to create a coordinating group called the Native American Treaty Rights Organization, Peter MacDonald, then Navajo tribal chairman, observed:

If you believe what you read, we are all millionaires. We are taking back the whole Eastern United States, starting with Maine and working our way down the Eastern Seaboard. We are destroying tourism in the Northwest by asserting our fishing rights. We are holding the entire Southwest hostage with our water rights and energy resources.

This kind of belief, he went on,

wipes out any need to feel guilt or concern; it provides a justification for taking our resources, destroying our tribal sovereignty and ignoring our problems. The media projects our feeble efforts to pull ourselves up by our own bootstraps as the biggest menace since Little Big Horn. (*The New York Times,* April 16, 1978, p. 24)

It is not only the federal government and non-Indians that must be dealt with. Intertribal cooperation has been notoriously difficult because of the strong emphasis on tribal sovereignty. And intratribal disagreements over goals and methods are often sharp. Peterson Zah, who defeated Peter MacDonald for the Navajo tribal chairmanship in 1982, is uncertain whether or not to remain in the Council of Energy Resource Tribes. He sees it as more concerned with developing resources than dealing with the interests of the tribe (*The New York Times,* November 21, 1982, p. 20).

What new structures are needed to insure Indian rights while guaranteeing the integrity of the nation? Do they need to be as drastically different as that proposed by Barsh and Henderson (1980) to give tribes, by constitutional amendment, something akin to statehood? Considering the extensive dispersal and urbanization of Indians, the number and small size of most tribes, and the great internal conflict within tribes over what they would like the future to bring, we think this proposal quite unrealistic. Yet it forces us to realize that the enormous variety of actions and policies, by Indians and non-Indians alike, has not produced an adequate model and has allowed, if not directly produced, many injustices. It seems likely that the current fairly high awareness of Indian grievances among the general public will continue to influence federal policy, as will the increase in the number of educated Indian leaders, trained to protect Indian rights. In this period of emphasis on Indian nationalism, however, we may forget to ask: What degree of intertribal cooperation can be maintained? Who will control the resources, in the interest of what classes and in the support of what policies? What will be the interests and aims of the increasing number of intermarried Indians (presently over 30 percent) and their children? What will be the impact of the entry of more and more Indians, as individuals, into the national economy?

These are questions the student of racial and cultural minorities must ask, alongside questions related to tribal Native Americans.

Hispanic Civil Rights Organizations

Although for many decades there have been mutual benefit and culturally oriented associations among Hispanics in the United States, especially those of Mexican background (La Alianza Hispano Americana was founded in 1894), it was not until after World War II that various political, economic, and civil rights became major objects of their attention. There are now dozens of such groups, local, regional, and national. We shall only illustrate the range of their interests. Some of them are focused almost entirely on concerns of one of the Hispanic groups, but most, in their statements of purpose, refer to all Hispanics and many to "all persons regardless of race or national background."

After World War II, Mexican American veterans organized the GI Forum, to encourage greater political participation, a goal supported by La Raza Unida Party. The Political Association of Spanish-Speaking Americans (PASSO) in Texas, the Community Service Organization (CSO), and the Mexican-American Political Association (MAPA) in California had a more regional focus. They supported voter registration drives and helped to defeat legalized restrictive covenants in housing, California's antimiscegenation law, and laws requiring segregated schools and public accommodations. *De facto* segregation and discrimination, we must add, continued.

As among Blacks earlier and Native Americans, Hispanic groups have become more nationalistic and militant, within a legal and political framework. The League of United Latin American Citizens (LULAC), formed in the 1920s, at first was concerned primarily with educational and welfare activities, but by the 1960s was joining other groups in lawsuits challenging discrimination in jury selection, fighting school segregation, and working to defeat the poll tax. It now has over 100,000 members.

Between 1974 and 1979, COPS (Communities Organized for Public Service) registered 18,000 new voters in San Antonio, forced the city to rechannel federal community block grant moneys to neighborhoods where parks, drainage, and housing had been neglected for generations, and challenged business leaders' promotion of the city as a center of cheap labor. In the East Los Angeles *barrio*, in four years of operation, UNO (United Neighborhoods Organization) forced several major automobile firms to reduce their insurance rates by 38 percent. Because of Los Angeles's poor mass transit, UNO leaders said auto insurance was a "survival budget issue." Behind COPS and UNO, and similar groups in some 20 cities across the country, lie the family and the church. Seed money is collected from the Catholic Church's Campaign for Human Development and similar organizations of Episcopalians, Presbyterians, Methodists, and the United Church of Christ. Nonviolent confrontations are used as one of the techniques of these organizations (Cleveland *Plain Dealer*, May 14, 1979, p. A17).

Several forces encouraged the development of this more political and protest-oriented approach. Among these are the rapid growth and urbanization of the Hispanic population, the general civil rights movement, the example set by black Americans, and the legal and administrative recognition of Hispanics as a group to be dealt with in various governmental programs. This last meant that there were economic and political advantages in being organized as a Hispanic group. In 1967 the federal government set up the Inter-Agency Committee on Mexican American Affairs to coordinate programs directed at Mexican Americans (G. Cohen 1982, p. 178).

Private organizations have also contributed to these developments. In 1968, the Ford Foundation provided the initial grant for the formation of MALDEF (Mexican American Legal Defense and Education Fund) for Mexican Americans of the Southwest. This organization was modelled after the NAACP Legal Defense and Education Fund. At the same time, additional money was provided for the support of legal education of minority students—Mexican Americans, Blacks, and American Indians. Between 1969 and 1977, MALDEF assisted more than 300 Chicano law students at a cost of over half a million dollars. Its program of litigation has included cases in the fields of equal educational opportunity, political access, land and water rights, equal employment opportunity, rights of political association and expression, and abuses of authority by prison officials, the police, the Immigration and Naturalization Service, and health and welfare agencies (Grebler et al. 1970, p. 546; Samora and Simon 1977, p. 221).

The United Farm Workers of America under the leadership of Cesar Chavez is the best known of Mexican American groups that focus primarily on economic questions. Chavez's campaign of "militant nonviolence" has won union recognition and some improvement of wages and working conditions for the fruit and vegetable pickers in the West. The union was a major force behind the passage of the California Labor Relations Act, probably the most effective statute protecting the right of agricultural workers to organize and bargain collectively. Membership ranges from 30,000 to 100,000 or more, depending upon whether one includes only the work force under contract throughout the year or the larger group who are employed sometime during the year (*The New York Times*, December 6, 1981, pp. 1, 40). The frequently drawn parallel between Chavez and Martin Luther King is, we believe, a useful one, not only because of their common emphasis on Gandhian techniques, but also because of their similar charismatic quality of leadership (Mathiessen 1970). This quality, of course, is not for everyone—not for the farm owners and managers, nor for the Teamsters Union that has been competing with the United Farm Workers of America, but also not for those who have shifted toward more nationalistic goals. Some conflicts within the union reflect the dissatisfaction of some with what they see as slow gains and insufficient militancy.

Puerto Rican Americans have also formed hundreds of organizations, many of them in New York but others along the Eastern seaboard and in the Midwest and elsewhere, designed to improve the working, living, and educational experiences of Puerto Ricans (Bonilla and Campos 1981; Fitzpatrick and Parker 1981). These include the National Puerto Rican Coalition, the Puerto Rican Legal Defense and Education Fund, the Puerto Rican Forum, the National Association for Puerto Rican Civil Rights, the Puerto Rican Family Institute, and Aspira (primarily concerned with increasing educational opportunities).

The larger of the Puerto Rican groups, like the Mexican American, speak of serving "other Hispanics" or "all persons regardless of race or national origin." So far, however, differences in national and cultural backgrounds, different centers of geographical concentration, and different kinds of relationship between the United States and lands of origin or of ancestry (compare, e.g., the very different kinds of relationship of the United States to Mexico, Puerto Rico, and Cuba), have meant that Hispanic organizations in the general sense have been mainly loose federations. Undoubtedly the need for maintaining organizations for particular Hispanic groups remains strong. Nevertheless, we expect that common interests and the increased political and economic strength that can come from closer coordination will lead to stronger alliances in the years ahead. Indeed, some persons are working for alliances across an even wider circle. If rates of unemployment among minorities remain high and income, education, and political power continue significantly below the level of the majority, we are likely to see interminority hostility, but also some action on such suggestions as this (Cleveland *Plain Dealer,* April 30, 1983, p. B3):

Hispanics and blacks should put aside petty differences and work together for equal opportunities and against federal cutbacks in social and health services, an affirmative action conference was told here yesterday. David F. Montoya, president of Image, Inc., a Hispanic advocacy organization in Washington, said if Hispanics and Blacks got together to cooperate on national and local issues they could represent a potential of 50 million or more Americans who are a part of the two groups.

The Field Context of Equality[6]

In Chapter 5 we summarized our discussion of the major sources of discrimination in a figure entitled "The Field Context of Discrimination." We described the set of sources as if together they made up a closed, self-perpetuating system, and in Part II we examined some of the expressions and the consequences of that system. As we noted, the system is not, in fact, closed. If it were, changes could come about only as a result of its own internal contradictions and tensions. Tough as it is, the system of discrimination is an open system, influenced by the larger context within which it operates. Minority groups, despite their relative lack of power, possess some actual and a great deal of potential strength that can be mobilized to their own advantage. Moreover, the advantages of dominant groups and the discriminatory system in which they are embedded are not consistent: individual ambivalences, cultural contradictions, and structural diversities represent potential strengths for movements seeking to change inequitable arrangements.

Perhaps these points can best be made by drawing a figure that is, in a sense, the mirror image of "The Field Context of Discrimination" (Figure 5–1). We shall call it "The Field Context of Equality." To begin with, we shall also treat it as a closed system, as if its own feedback processes kept it going, regardless of the situation within which it exists. That, of course, is not the case; hence we will not only have to put the two systems together, but also see them in the larger environment of which they are a part.

In this interdependent world, poorly trained and motivated workers, poverty-stricken customers, and alienated citizens are recognized by dominant groups, in some contexts, as costly burdens rather than exploitable resources. In this system, the gains

[6]This section is adapted from Yinger 1983.

from equality, as suggested at point 1a (Figure 18–1), not gains from exploitation, are emphasized.

Interdependence gives minorities economic and political power when individual resources are aggregated. In the southwest of the United States, for example, even illegal aliens, mainly of Mexican origin, are unionizing and striking to improve their status (*The New York Times,* April 4, 1978, p. E20). Black voters in the United States in recent years have occupied decisive balance-of-power positions in many elections, including the presidential elections of 1960 and 1976 and several of the congressional contests in 1982 and 1984.

On the individual level, point 2a, humankind is seen not simply as "the imperial animal" dominated by aggressive impulses, but also as a "prosocial" creature selected for survival in part by the capacity for altruism and cooperation and trained to exercise that capacity (Caplan 1978; Wispé 1972; Yarrow, Scott, and Zahn-Waxler 1973).

Powerful religious and political ideologies, point 3a, consolidate these tendencies into norms and values that stress cooperation and helpfulness (Campbell 1975; Myrdal 1944). To some degree, at least, these norms and values not only are

expressed in individual actions but become embodied in institutions (5a), thus acquiring greater continuity and influence. We have examined some of their impact in the chapters on politics and religion. Thus we have not only "institutional racism" but also "institutional humanitarianism"—leaving open the question of their comparative strength in specific settings.

Point 6a in figure 18–1 suggests that from the perspective of this "equality system," individual members of minority groups cannot be seen simply as helpless victims, governed by feelings of powerlessness and hopelessness (Louden 1981; Rosenberg 1979). The dominant institutions and policies as well as the talents and perceptions of minority-group members support aspirations for change. Minor improvements in opportunities may stimulate major improvement of effort (Coles 1967). We have seen that even the crushing conditions of slavery in the United States did not prevent active—even if often disguised—resistance and creative adaptations on the part of the oppressed. In the contemporary scene, dominant groups may be ready to permit, even to encourage, the training and ambition of individual minority-group members,

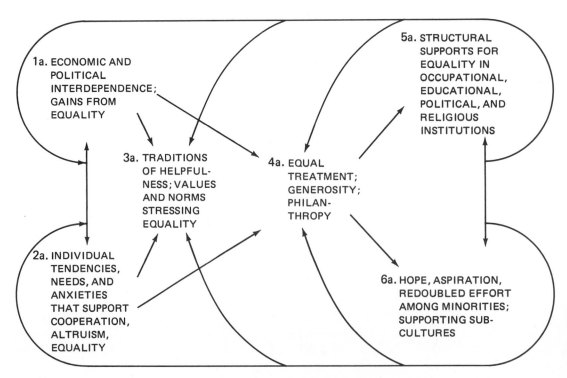

Figure 18–1. The field context of forces supporting equality.

even when they are far less supportive of significant changes in the social structure.

The equality system suggests a beneficent cycle, not a vicious cycle. A series of interacting forces keeps alive the possibility, and to some degree the reality, of change toward greater equality (see Williams 1977, Chapter 1). To realize the potential of this system often requires that individual resources be aggregated by a group. Many of the religious and political movements among minorities are efforts to attain such aggregation.

The Larger Context of the Systems of Discrimination and Equality

The two closed systems we have described are, of course, imaginary. Not only are they in reality open to the influence of each other, but together they also interact in a large field of forces. Technical, economic, demographic, ecological, and international changes all influence the unfolding of the patterns of minority–majority relations. Figure 18–2 is an attempt to suggest this larger field. We believe that efforts to reduce discrimination are strongly dependent on our understanding of the interdependencies and interactions within this field. Strategies for change that focus on only one or a few of the factors are unlikely to be effective. In a given setting at a particular time, one or another approach may deserve greatest effort, but it can be successful only as the several interdependent factors are taken into account.

It is almost useless, for example, to try to reduce the discriminatory tendencies and prejudices of members of the dominant group (point 2) if institutional discrimination and minority group demoralization (points 5 and 6) are strong. Or, the most powerful attack on the system of discrimination will be insufficient in a context in which we disregard major ecological and demographic problems. We shall only illustrate the numerous policy and theoretical implications of these interdependencies. We urge readers to study this complex set of forces and to apply the interpretation we are suggesting to settings and problems of major interest to them.

The members of minority groups are likely to be mobilized only for symbolic movements of social transformation if their aspirations and hopes are raised without an increase in opportunities and a reduction of institutional discrimination. It is somewhat more difficult to make an opposite point: An increase in the strength of the structural and cultural supports for equality can finally be effective, we noted earlier, only if there are matching personality changes. Because of some reduction in discrimination and some increase in opportunities, it is now possible for a person like the Reverend Jesse Jackson to emphasize "self-development"—personality changes that keep pace with structural changes. He writes (1976, p. 13):

The thrust of my argument is that black Americans must begin to accept a larger share of responsibility for their lives. For too many years we have been crying that racism and oppression have to be fought on every front. . . . Many leaders who are black, and many white liberals will object to my discussing these things in public. But the decadence in black communities—killings, destruction of our own businesses, violence in the school—is already in the headlines; the only question is what we should do about it. Others will object that to demand that we must meet the challenge of self-government is to put too much pressure on the victims of ancient wrongs. Yet in spite of these objections, in spite of yesterday's agony, liberation struggles are built on sweat and pain rather than tears and complaints.

Such a message is one ingredient necessary in the mobilization of a disadvantaged group for change. Not only its content, but its "social movement" quality affects the response. Mobilization of resources is not simply drawing from some social banking account. It must engage shared dreams and frustrations, giving them the energy of collective purpose (see Geschwender 1978a). Insofar as Jackson's movement is successful it will strengthen the process of structural change that, to a degree, made it possible. It is a strong group, one that is experiencing a growing self-confidence and some increase in opportunities that will produce and listen to such a message. In the absence of continuing expansion of opportunities, however, it would soon be seen, as Jackson recognizes, as a meaningless message if not indeed a hoax.

Effective mobilization in any setting requires an accurate appraisal of the balance between each item in the system of discrimination with its matching item in the system of equality. We might imagine scales ranging from -1.0 (maximum discrimination) to $+1.0$ (maximum equality), with the zero point indicating an equal degree of influence. We do not have the information, of course, to use such scales, but we would guess that in most societies all the comparisons between the two systems are negative—that is, below zero. The discrimination system seems tougher than the equality system.

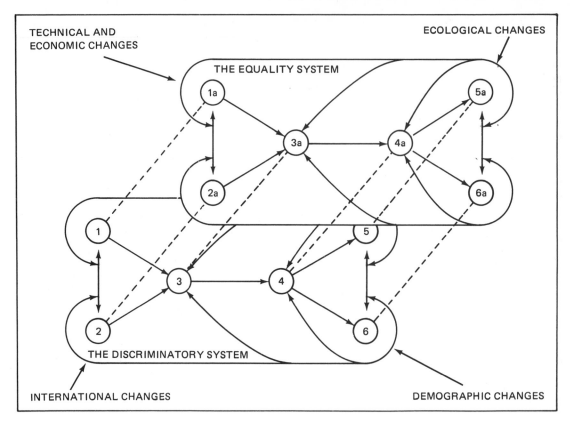

Figure 18–2. The field context of two open systems, one supporting discrimination, the other supporting equality.

This does not mean, however, that resources for equality are lacking. Such resources are there to draw upon and are being drawn upon. Referring to the United States, we believe the evidence shows that the balance in the last twenty-five years has shifted upward in each segment of the diagram, even if the balance is still negative (Jones 1981). For example, the following comparisons appear to be appropriate with reference to Figure 18–2:

1 and 1a: Economic and political interdependence is now more clearly recognized.
2 and 2a: Individual prejudice has declined.
3 and 3a: Cultural supports and justifications for discrimination are weaker.
5 and 5a: Significant reductions in the strength of the structures of institutional discrimination have occurred.
6 and 6a: Individual members of ethnic minorities have grown in self-confidence, skill, and morale. Their collective

efforts are more powerful, with better aggregation of political and economic resources.

Because we were arguing that the whole system, not just one part of it, must be shifted, the fact that several related changes have occurred is significant.

Yet there are serious lags that keep feeding discriminatory influences back into the system, weakening the impact of the changes toward equality. In the United States, established patterns of discrimination that rest less on individual prejudice or perceived self-interest than on customary ways of doing things, on the effects of past discrimination, and on inertia continue to operate in the full range of institutional life. They too have declined, but less than other parts of the system of discrimination.

Shifting to forces outside the two systems, we find other influences that tend to perpetuate discrimination, although their impact is not entirely one-sided. Important changes in the structure of the occupational system in industrialized societies, for example, have increased the economic advantages of the more educated and skilled parts of the population. Many members of the more severely disadvantaged minorities are unemployed, require welfare support, and are seriously demoralized, not simply because of institutional discrimination or the prejudices of the majority, but also because of these shifts in the occupational structure. Until more effective attention is paid to such impersonal forces, the most energetic efforts to marshal the resources of minorities can be neutralized (Lieberson 1980).

In a similar way, a significantly higher birth rate among a minority can continuously deny educational and occupational gains that would otherwise be possible, because the financial and perhaps the social resources of the large families are depleted. Thus population policies, even if they are made without reference to those comparative advantages of minority and majority groups, affect those advantages.

The most advantaged members of a minority group are unlikely to be strongly affected by these structural and demographic trends. Those trends, in fact, may create a sharp split within a minority that hinders the aggregation of its resources and sharpens the dilemma—individual versus group struggle—so common in minority movements (see Dillingham 1981; Moore 1981; Pettigrew 1981b; Wilson 1978).

Figure 18-2 is not so complicated as it may appear when first seen. We believe that it becomes clear if the flow of influence within each system is first studied, then the interaction between the systems, and finally the impact of the forces that create the larger context within which that interaction occurs. The dotted lines between the matching factors in the two systems represent the need for assessing the comparative strength of the factors in each pair.

Social change toward greater equality can be effectively blocked, despite a favorable legal and political situation, increasing goodwill among the majority and higher levels of self-confidence and skill among the minorities, until the impersonal structural forces are precisely identified, their effects recognized, and suitable action taken to offset their impact.

No general formula can determine the best balance of emphasis on structural, cultural, and personality change. Each situation has its own set of possibilities and limitations. In the final analysis, however, social change toward greater equality requires modification of the whole system.

Conclusion

The freedom movement of the last decades has brought inescapably to the attention of white Americans the plight and the demands of the nation's minorities. Probably more important, it has galvanized the minorities themselves into action and has increased their self-respect and the sense that they can struggle with their difficult conditions with some chance of success. America can go on with her revolution, broadening the base of participation, or she can go through a long period of tension, conflict, and repression. Whichever route is taken, the relatively stable majority–minority system, with its great inequities, has been drastically modified.

This does not mean that new patterns will emerge smoothly, automatically, peacefully. The speed of change, the degree of conflict which accompanies it, the extent to which attitudes change along with behavior, depend upon the strategic skill of the contending groups and upon the way in which America deals with various problems before her that have nothing directly to do with majority–minority relations. Two of these problems are basic: international tensions and economic instability and inequity. Although disputes with other nations to some degree tend to reduce lines of separation within a country, there are also powerful forces on the other side: not only does a vast military budget deprive us of many of the resources with which we might deal with internal problems, but international tensions also give the bigot an opportunity for attacking minority groups as somehow threatening to the nation.

Economic questions are also of vital importance. There are some 25 million persons in the United States who, by almost any definition, live in poverty. Two-thirds of them are white. Since World War II, per capita personal income has doubled, in dollars adjusted for inflation; but tens of millions of persons have been left behind. Many of them are caught in a vicious circle of low income, poor health, poor schools, and low motivation that has become more difficult to escape because of changes in the economy. So long as the United States fails to deal successfully with this problem, she may open up opportunities for the well-trained among her minorities, but for many, lack of legal or customary obstacles will not be enough. So long as they are caught in poverty's vicious cycle they will not be able to take advantage of the opportunities now formally, and painfully, being opened to them.

Throughout this analysis we have emphasized the interactive and cumulative nature of the forces influencing intergroup relations. The interlocking of the many factors that affect majority-minority relations greatly complicates the work of the student and of the social engineer. We have all too often tried to untangle this complexity by oversimplified theories and strategies.

The Need for Research. Only a small proportion of the time and energy spent in trying to improve intergroup relations is devoted to research—to analysis of the effectiveness of specific programs and to the study of the total causal complex; hence much of the work may be inefficient or even harmful. In many areas of modern life, extensive research is considered indispensable. In industry, in medicine, in the development of military weapons, no important program is adopted before vast sums have been spent to develop the most efficient means. It is only in a partial sense, however, that this is a scientific age. Many people, faced by the confusion and anxiety of modern life, have developed a prideful antiscientism when it comes to understanding human beings. They cannot accept qualifications that science demands, the painstaking research, the refusal to declare unqualifiedly that this or that is true, regardless of conditions.

In the field with which we are concerned we must demand of every proposition its methodological credentials: What is the evidence? What variables are involved? How were they controlled? How does this harmonize with, or contradict, existing theoretical positions? It may seem like tedious business to some, although to others it is exciting adventure, but there is no easier way to understanding and control.

Science and Values. It is sometimes said that science cannot contribute to the solution of such moral problems as discrimination because its predictions are of the "if and when" variety; they tell us only what will happen when certain specified variables are controlled, not what will occur in a

particular situation. True, science cannot make concrete predictions; it must state its predictions for specific situations in terms of probability limits, depending upon the degree to which certain variables are operative. Nevertheless, as we isolate more and more of the influencing factors and learn more about their interaction, we can greatly narrow the probability of limits.

The discouraging aspects of the concepts of interaction, of the vicious circle and the self-fulfilling prophecy, have led some to believe that science, in describing these processes, has deepend our pessimism and injured the will to action. But science does not say that these things are inevitable; it says they will occur if certain variables do not change:

In the world laboratory of the sociologist, as in the more secluded laboratories of the physicist and chemist, it is the successful experiment which is decisive and not the thousand-and-one failures which preceded it. More is learned from the single success than from the failures. A single success proves it can be done. Thereafter, it is necessary only to learn what made it work. (Merton 1968, p. 436)

It is often said that social science is deterministic in the sense that it makes any human effort useless. Humans behave the way they do because of what they are. They are products of heredity and environment; since nature cannot be changed, nothing can be done.

This is not the sense, however, in which science is deterministic. Science does state that events have a natural pattern and that humanity is part of the natural world, a creature of law. *If* certain forces are operative, these will be the results. But it may well be (and it is at this point that science is deterministic, but not predeterministic) that an understanding of the nature of events is a new variable that changes the results. Natural laws indicate that if one eats certain kinds of foods in excess and fails to brush his teeth, one is liable to tooth decay. *Knowledge of those facts is a new variable that may prevent that result.* The laws are still true—*if.* Knowledge can help to free us; it does not blind us to the inevitable *application* of the natural laws. Those who demand the millennium day after tomorrow will be frustrated by this slow process. But many may find in the promise of this difficult road a quiet confidence that modern people sorely need.

Bibliography

Abeles, Ronald P., "Relative Deprivation, Rising Expectations, and Black Militancy." *Journal of Social Issues* Spring (1976): 119–37.

Abell, Troy, and Lyon, Larry. "Do the Differences Make a Difference? An Empirical Evaluation of the Culture of Poverty in the United States." *American Ethnologist* August (1979): 602–20.

Aberle, David. *The Peyote Religion Among the Navaho*. 2nd ed. Chicago: University of Chicago Press, 1982.

Abrahams, Roger D. *Deep Down in the Jungle*. 1st rev. ed. Hawthorne, NY: Aldine, 1970.

Abudu, Margaret J. G.; Raine, Walter J.; Burbeck, Stephen L., and Davison, Keith K. "Black Ghetto Violence: A Case Study Inquiry into the Spatial Pattern of Four Los Angeles Riot Event-Types." *Social Problems* Winter (1972): 408–26.

Adam, Barry D. "Inferiorization and 'Self-Esteem'." Social Psychology March (1978): 47–53.

Adam, Heribert, and Giliomee, Hermann. *Ethnic Power Mobilized: Can South Africa Change?* New Haven, CT: Yale University Press, 1979.

Adam, Heribert. *Modernizing Racial Domination: South Africa's Political Dynamics*. Berkeley: University of California Press, 1971.

Adorno, T. W., Frenkel-Brunswik, Else; Levinson, D. J. and Sanford, R. N. *The Authoritarian Personality*. New York: Harper & Row, 1950.

Ahmann, Mathew, ed. *Race: Challenge to Religion*. Chicago: Henry Regnery, 1963.

Alba, Richard D. "Social Assimilation among American Catholic National-Origin Groups." *American Sociological Review* December (1976): 1030–1046.

Aldrich, Howard. "White-Owned Businesses in Black Ghettos." *American Journal of Sociology*, May (1978): 1422–25.

Aldridge, Delores P. "Interracial Marriages." *Journal of Black Studies* March (1978): 355–68.

Alex, Nicholas. *Black in Blue: A Study of the Negro Policeman*. New York: Meredith, 1969.

Alexander, Karl L., Cook, Martha, and McDill, Edward L. "Curriculum Tracking and Educational Stratification: Some Further Evidence." *American Sociological Review* February (1978): 47–66.

Alfert, Elizabeth. "Are Social Stereotypes Vanishing: A Study of a Non-College Population." *Journal of Social Issues* (1972): 89–99.

Alland, Alexander, Jr. *Human Diversity*. New York: Columbia University Press, 1971.

Allen, Russell O., and Spilka, Bernard. "Committed and Consensual Religion: A Specification of Religion–Prejudice Relationships." *Journal for the Scientific Study of Religion* Fall (1967): 191–206.

Allen, Vernon L., Issue Editor. "Ghetto Riots." *Journal of Social Issues* Winter (1970).

Allen, Vernon L., and Wilder, David A. "Categorization, Belief Similarity, and Intergroup Discrimination." *Journal of Personality and Social Psychology* (1975): 971–77.

Allen, Walter R. "The Search for Applicable Theories of Black Family Life." *Journal of Marriage and the Family*. February (1978): 117–29.

Allport, Gordon W. *The Nature of Prejudice*. Reading, MA: Addison-Wesley, 1954.

Allport, Gordon W. *Personality and Social Encounter*. Boston: Beacon, 1960.

Allport, Gordon W. "The Religious Context of Prejudice." *Journal for the Scientific Study of Religion* Fall (1966): 447–57.

Allport, Gordon W., and Ross, J. Michael. "Personal Religious Orientation and Prejudice." *Journal of Personality and Social Psychology* (1967): 432–43.

Allvine, Fred C. "Black Business Development." in William L. Cash, Jr., and Lucy R. Oliver (eds), *Black Economic Development*. Ann Arbor: University of Michigan Press, 1975, pp. 256–68.

Alston, Jon P., Peek, Charles W., and Wingrove, C. Ray. "Religiosity and Black Militancy: A Reappraisal." *Journal for the Scientific Study of Religion* September (1972): 252–61.

Alvarez, Rodolfo. "Psycho-Historical and Socio-Economic Development of Chicanos." In Carol A. Hernandez, Marsha J. Haug, and Nathaniel N. Wagner, eds., *Chicanos: Social and Psychological Perspectives.* Boston: Mosby, 1976.

Alvirez, David, and Bean, Frank D. "The Mexican American Family." In Charles H. Mindel and R. H. Habenstein, eds., *Ethnic Families in America.* New York: Elsevier, 1976, pp. 271–92.

America, Richard F., and Anderson, Bernard E. "Getting Ahead in the Corporation." *The New York Times,* September 4, 1977, pp. 1, 10.

Amersfoort, Hans von. *Immigration and the Formation of Minority Groups: The Dutch Experience, 1945-1975.* Cambridge: Cambridge University Press, 1982.

Amir, Yehuda. "Contact Hypothesis in Ethnic Relations." *Psychological Bulletin* May, (1969): 319–42.

Amir, Yehuda. "The Role of Intergroup Contact in Change of Prejudice and Ethnic Relations." In Phyllis Katz, ed., *Towards the Elimination of Racism.* Elmsford, NY: Pergamon, 1976, pp. 245–308.

Anderson, Bernard E. and Cottingham, Phoebe H. "The Elusive Quest for Economic Equality." *Daedalus* Spring (1981): 257–74.

Anderson, S. E. "Black Students: Racial Consciousness and the Class Struggle: 1960-1976." *The Black Scholar* January–February (1977): 35–43.

Angell, Robert C. "Preference for Moral Norms in Three Problem Areas." *American Journal of Sociology* May (1962): 650–60.

Ansbro, John J. *Martin Luther King, Jr.: The Making of a Mind.* Maryknoll, NY: Orbis Books, 1982.

Anthony, Earl. *Picking up the Gun: A Report on the Black Panthers.* New York: Dial, 1970.

Antonovsky, Aaron. "The Social Meaning of Discrimination." *Phylon* Spring (1960): 81–95.

Apostle, Richard A., Glock, Charles Y., Piazza, Thomas, and Suelzle, Marijean. *The Anatomy of Racial Attitudes.* Berkeley: University of California Press, 1983.

Aptheker, Herbert. *The Negro People in America.* Introduction by Doxey A. Wilkerson. New York: International Publishers, 1946.

Archdeacon, Thomas J. *Becoming American: An Ethnic History.* New York: The Free Press, 1983.

Armor, David J. "White Flight and the Future of School Desegregation." In Walter G. Stephan and Joe R. Feagan, eds., *School Desegregation: Past, Present, and Future.* New York: Plenum Press, 1980, 187–226.

Arnez, Nancy Levi, and Anthony, Clara B. "Contemporary Negro Humor as Social Satire." *Phylon* Winter (1968): 339–46.

Arrow, Kenneth J. *Some Models of Racial Discrimination in the Labor Market.* Santa Monica, Calif: Rand Corporation, 1971.

Aschenbrenner, Joyce. *Lifelines: Black Families in Chicago.* New York: Holt, Rinehart, and Winston, 1975.

Ashmore, Richard D. "Sex Stereotypes and Implicit Personality Theory." In David L. Hamilton, ed., *Cognitive Processes in Stereotyping and Intergroup Behavior.* Hillsdale, NJ: Lawrence Erlbaum Associates, 1981, Chapter 2.

Ashmore, Richard D., and Frances K. DelBoca. "Psychological Approaches to Understanding Intergroup Conflict." In Phyllis A. Katz, ed., *Towards the Elimination of Racism.* Elmsford, NY: Pergamon Press, 1976, pp. 73–123.

Ashmore, Richard D., and DelBoca, Frances K. "Sex Stereotypes and Implicit Personality Theory: Toward a Cognitive-Social Psychological Conceptualization." *Sex Roles* (1979): 219–48.

Astin, Alexander W. *Minorities in Higher Education: Recent Trends, Current Prospects, and Recommendations.,* San Francisco: Jossey-Bass, 1982.

Auletta, Ken. *The Underclass.* New York: Random House, 1982.

Azrael, Jeremy R. (ed.). *Soviet Nationality Policies and Practices.* New York: Praeger, 1978.

Backman, Carl W. "Attraction in Interpersonal Relations." In *Social Psychology: Sociological Perspectives.* New York: Basic Books, 1981, pp. 235–268.

Baer, Hans A. "Black Spiritual Churches: A Neglected Socio-Religious Institution." *Phylon* Fall (1981): 207–23.

Bagley, Christopher, "Race Relations and Theories of Status Consistency," *Race,* January (1970): 267–88.

Bagley, Christopher, and Verma, Gajendra K. *Racial Prejudice, the Individual, and Society.* New York: Saxon House, 1979.

Bagley, Christopher, Verma, Gajendra K., Mallick, Kanka, and Young, Loretta. *Personality, Self-Esteem and Prejudice,* New York: Saxon House, 1979.

Bahr, Howard M., Chadwick, Bruce A., and Day, Robert C. eds. *Native Americans Today: Sociological Perspectives.* New York: Harper and Row, 1972.

Baker, John R. *Race.* Oxford: Oxford University Press, 1974.

Baker, Paul T. "The Biological Race Concept as a Research Tool." *American Journal of Physical Anthropology* (1967): 21–25.

Baldwin, James. *Notes of a Native Son.* New York: Beacon Press, 1955.

Baldwin, James. *Nobody Knows My Name.* New York: Dell, 1961.

Baldwin, James. *The Fire Next Time.* New York: Dial, 1963.

Ball, Harry V., Simpson, George E., and Ikeda, Kiyoshi. "Law and Social Change: Sumner Reconsidered." *American Journal of Sociology* March (1962): 532–40.

Ball, Richard A. "A Poverty Case: The Analgesic Subculture of the Southern Appalachians." *American Sociological Review* December (1968): 885–95.

Banfield, Edward C. *The Moral Basis of a Backward Society.* Chicago: University of Chicago Press, 1958.

Banfield, Edward C. *The Unheavenly City: The Nature and Future of Our Urban Crisis.* Boston: Little, Brown, 1968.

Banton, Michael. *The Idea of Race.* Boulder, CO: Westview Press, 1977.

Banton, Michael. *Racial and Ethnic Competition.* New York: Cambridge University Press, 1983.

Baraka, Amiri (LeRoi Jones). *Selected Poetry of Amiri Baraka/LeRoi Jones.* New York: William Morrow, 1979.(a)

Baraka, Amiri (LeRoi Jones). *Selected Plays and Prose of Amiri Baraka/LeRoi Jones.* New York: William Morrow, 1979.(b)

Barker, Lucius J., and McCorry, Jesse L. Jr. *Black Americans and the Political System.* Englewood NJ: Winthrop, 1976.

Barrera, Mario. *Race and Class in the Southwest.* Notre Dame, IN: University of Notre Dame Press, 1979.

Barron, Milton L. *People Who Intermarry.* Syracuse, NY: Syracuse University Press, 1948.

Barron, Milton L. "A Content Analysis of Intergroup Humor." *American Sociological Review* February (1950): 88–94.

Barron, Milton L. "Recent Developments in Minority and Race

Relations." *Annals of the American Academy of Political and Social Sciences* July (1975): 125–76.

Barsh, Russel Lawrence, and Henderson, James Youngblood. *The Road: Indian Tribes and Political Liberty.* Berkeley: University of California Press, 1980.

Bass, Bernard M. "Authoritarianism or Acquiescence." *Journal of Abnormal and Social Psychology* November (1955): 616–23.

Bates, Timothy, and Bradford, William. *Financing Black Economic Development.* New York: Academic Press, 1979.

Batson, C. Daniel, Naifeh, Stephen J., and Pate, Suzanne. "Social Desirability, Religious Orientation, and Racial Prejudice." *Journal for the Scientific Study of Religion* March (1978): 31–41.

Bayton, James A. "The Racial Stereotypes of Negro College Students." *Journal of Abnormal and Social Psychology* January (1941): 97–102.

Beach, Waldo. "Storm Warnings from the South." *Christianity and Crisis* March 19, 1956, 27–30.

Beck, E. M. "Discrimination and White Economic Loss: A Time Series Examination of the Radical Model." *Social Forces* September (1980): 148–68.

Becker, Gary S. *The Economics of Discrimination.* 2nd ed. Chicago: University of Chicago Press, 1971.

Becker, Howard P. *Man in Reciprocity.* New York: Praeger, 1956.

Beeghley, Leonard and Butler, Edgar W. "The Consequences of Intelligence Testing in the Public Schools Before and After Desegregation." *Social Problems* June (1974): 740–54.

Begay, Jimmie C. "The Relationship between People and the Land." *Arwesasne Notes* Summer (1979): 28–29.

Bell, Derrick A., Jr. "Preferential Affirmative Action: A Review of *A New American Justice* by Daniel C. Maguire." *Harvard Civil Rights–Civil Liberties Law Review* Winter (1982): 855–73.

Bell, Inge Powell. *CORE and the Strategy of Non-violence.* New York: Random House, 1968.

Benedict, Ruth. *Race: Science and Politics.* Bridgeport, CT: Modern Age Books, 1940.

Benitez, Joseph S. "Dimensions for the Study of Work-Related Values in Mexican-American Culture." In H. Roy Kaplan, *American Minorities and Economic Opportunity.* Itasca, Ill.: F. E. Peacock, 1977.

Berger, Joseph, Rosenholtz, Susan J., and Zelditch, Morris, Jr. "Status Organizing Process." *Annual Review of Sociology* (1980): 479–508.

Bergson, Henri. "Laughter." In Wylie Sypher (ed.), *Comedy.* New York: Doubleday Anchor Books, 1956, 61–190.

Berk, Richard A., and Aldrich, Howard E. "Patterns of Vandalism During Civil Disorders as an Indicator of Selection of Targets." *American Sociological Review* October (1972): 533–47.

Berkowitz, Leonard and James A. Green, "The Stimulus Qualities of the Scapegoat," *Journal of Abnormal and Social Psychology* April (1962): 293–301.

Bernstein, Basil. "Elaborated and Restricted Codes: Their Social Origins and Some Consequences." In *The Ethnography of Speaking (American Anthropologist,* Special Publication 22 (1966): 55–69).

Berreman, Gerald D. "Social Categories and Social Interaction in Urban India." *American Anthropologist* (June): 1972, 567–86.

Berry, Brewton. *Almost White.* New York: Macmillan, 1963.

Berry, Brewton. "America's Mestizos." In Noel P. Gist and A. G. Dworkin (eds.), *The Blending of Races: Marginality and Identity in World Perspective.* New York: Wiley, 1972, pp. 191–212.

Béteille, André. *Caste, Class, and Power: Changing Patterns of Stratification in a Tanjore Village.* Berkeley: University of California Press, 1965.

Bettelheim, Bruno, "Individual and Mass Behavior in Extreme Situations." *Journal of Abnormal and Social Psychology* October (1943): 417–52.

Beuf, Ann H. *Red Children in White America.* Philadelphia: University of Pennsylvania Press, 1977.

Binkin, Martin, and Eitelberg, Mark J. *Blacks and the Military.* Washington, D.C.: The Brookings Institution, 1982.

Blackburn, Robert T., Gamson, Zelda F., and Peterson, Marvin W. "The Meaning of Response: Current and Future Questions." In Marvin W. Peterson et al., *Black Students on White Campuses.* Ann Arbor: Institute for Social Research, University of Michigan, 1978, pp. 309–21.

Blackman, Courtney N. "An Eclectic Approach to the Problem of Economic Development." In William L. Cash, Jr., and Lucy R. Oliver, eds., *Black Economic Development: Analysis and Implications.* Ann Arbor: Graduate School of Business Administration, University of Michigan, 1975, pp. 114–33.

Blackwell, James E. *The Black Community: Diversity and Unity.* New York: Harper & Row, 1975.

Blackwell, James E. "Social and Legal Dimensions of Interracial Liaisons." in D. Y. Wilkinson and R. L. Taylor (eds.), *The Black Male in America.* Chicago: Nelson-Hall, 1977.

Blackwell, James E. "Racial Factors Affecting Educational Opportunity for Minority Group Students." In *Beyond Desegregation: Urgent Issues in the Education of Minorities.* New York: College Entrance Examination Board. 1978, pp. 1–10.

Blackwell, James E. *Mainstreaming Outsiders: The Production of Black Professionals.* Bayside, NY: General Hall, 1981.

Blackwell, James E., and Janowitz, Morris, eds., *Black Sociologists: Historical and Contemporary Perspectives.* Chicago: University of Chicago Press, 1974.

Blackwell, James E. and Hart, Philip S. *Cities, Suburbs, and Blacks: A Study of Concerns, Distrust and Alienation.* Bayside, NY: General Hall, 1982.

Blair, Thomas L. *Retreat to the Ghetto: The End of a Dream?* New York: Hill and Wang, 1977.

Blalock, Hubert M. Jr. *Toward a Theory of Minority-group Relations.* New York: Wiley, 1967.

Blalock, Hubert M., Jr. *Black–White Relations in the 1980s: Toward a Long-Term Policy.* New York: Praeger, 1979.

Blalock, Hubert M., Jr. *Race and Ethnic Relations.* New York: Prentice-Hall, 1982.

Blau, Judith, and Blau, Peter M. "The Cost of Inequality: Metropolitan Structure and Violent Crime." *American Sociological Review* February (1982): 114–29.

Blau, Peter M. "A Macrosociological Theory of Social Structure." *American Journal of Sociology* July (1977): 26–54.

Blau, Peter M., and Duncan, O. D. *The American Occupational Structure.* New York: Wiley, 1967.

Blau, Peter M., Blum, Terry C. and Schwartz, Joseph E. "Heterogeneity and Intermarriage." *American Sociological Review* February 1982: 45–62.

Blau, Peter M., Beeker, Carolyn and Fitz-Patrick, Kevin M.

"Intersecting Social Affiliations and Intermarriage." *Social Forces*, March (1984): 585–606.

Blau, Zena Smith. *Black Children/White Children: Competence, Socialization, and Social Structure*. New York: Free Press, 1981.

Blauner, Robert. "Internal Colonialism and Ghetto Revolt. *Social Problems* Spring (1969): 393–408.

Blauner, Robert. *Racial Oppression in America*. New York: Harper & Row, 1972.

Bloom, Leonard, and Riemer, Ruth. *Removal and Return: The Socio-economic Effects of the War on Japanese Americans*. Berkeley: University of California Press, 1949.

Bloom, Richard, Whiteman, Martin, and Deutsch, Martin. "Race and Social Class as Separate Factors Related to Social Environment." *American Journal of Sociology* January 1965: 471–76.

Blue, John T., Jr. "Patterns of Racial Stratification: A Categoric Typology." *Phylon* Winter (1959): 364–71.

Blum, Howard. "Illegal Aliens: The Hidden New Yorkers." *The New York Times* March 18, 1979, pp. 1, 40 and March 19, 1979, pp. 1,B6.

Blumberg, Rhoda G. and Roye, Wendell, James, eds. *Interracial Bonds*. Bayside, NY: General Hall, 1979.

Blumer, Herbert. "Race Prejudice as a Sense of Group Position." *Pacific Sociological Review*, 1958 (1): 3–7.

Bogardus, Emory S. *Immigration and Race Attitudes*. Lexington, MA: D. C. Heath, 1928.

Bogardus, Emory S. "Racial Distance Changes in the United States During the Past Thirty Years." *Sociology and Social Research* November–December (1958): 127–35.

Bogardus, Emory S. "Race Reactions by Sex." *Sociology and Social Research* July-August, (1959): 439–41: (a)

Bogardus, Emory. "Racial Reactions by Regions." *Sociology and Social Research* March-April (1958): 286–90.

Bonacich, Edna. "A Theory of Ethnic Antagonism: The Split Labor Market." *American Sociological Review* October (1972): 547–59.

Bonacich, Edna. "A Theory of Middleman Minorities." *American Sociological Review* October (1973): 583–94.

Bonacich, Edna. "Abolition, the Extension of Slavery, and the Position of Free Blacks: A Study of Split Labor Markets in the United States, 1830-1863." *American Journal of Sociology* November (1975): 601–28.

Bonacich, Edna. "Advanced Capitalism and Black/White Relations in the United States: A Split Labor Market Interpretation." *American Sociological Review* February (1976): 34–51.

Bonacich, Edna, and Modell, John. *The Economic Basis of Ethnic Solidarity: Small Business in the Japanese American Community*. Berkeley: University of California Press, 1980.

Bond, H. M. "The Negro Scholar and Professional in America." In John P. Davis, ed., *The American Negro Reference Book*. New York: Prentice-Hall, 1966, pp. 579–80.

Bonilla, Frank, and Campos, Ricardo. "A Wealth of Poor: Puerto Ricans in the New Economic Order." *Daedalus* Spring (1981): 133–76.

Boorman, John T. "The Prospects for Minority-Owned Commercial Banks: A Comparative Performance Analysis." In William L. Cash, Jr., and Lucy R. Oliver (eds.), *Black Economic Development*, Ann Arbor: University of Michigan Graduate School of Business Administration, 1975, pp. 200–23.

Boorman, John T. and Kwast, M. "The Start-up Experience of

Minority-owned Commercial Banks: A Comparative Analysis." *The Journal of Finance* (1974): 1123–42.

Borgatta, Edgar F. "The Concept of Reverse Discrimination and Equality of Opportunity." *The American Sociologist* May (1976): 62–72, 82–85.

Bowden, Henry Warner. *American Indians and Christian Missions: Studies in Cultural Conflict*. Chicago, University of Chicago Press, 1981.

Bowles, Samuel, and Gintis, Herbert. *Schooling in Capitalist America*. New York: Basic Books, 1976.

Bowser, Benjamin P., and Hunt, Raymond G. (eds.). *Impact of Racism on White Americans*. Beverly Hills, CA: Sage, 1981.

Boyd, William B., II. *Desegregating America's Colleges: A Nationwide Survey of Black Students*. New York: Praeger, 1974.

Boyd, William C. "Genetics and Human Races." *Science* (1963): 1057–65.

Bracey, John H., Jr., Meier, August, and Rudwick, Elliott, eds. *Black Nationalism in America*. New York: Bobbs-Merrill, 1970.

Brashler, William. "The Black Middle Class: Making It." *The New York Times Magazine*, December 3, 1978, 34 ff.

Brewer, M. B., and Campbell, Donald T. *Ethnocentrism and Intergroup Attitudes: East African Evidence*. Beverly Hills, CA: Sage, 1976.

Briggs, Vernon M., Jr. *Chicanos and Rural Poverty*. Baltimore: John Hopkins University Press, 1973.

Briggs, Vernon M., Jr., Fogel, W., and Schmidt, F. H. *The Chicano Worker*. Austin: University of Texas Press, 1977.

Brigham, Carl, *A Study of American Intelligence*. Princeton: Princeton University Press, 1923.

Brigham, John C. "Ethnic Stereotypes." *Psychological Bulletin* July (1971): 15–38.

Brigham, John C., Woodmansee, John J., and Cook, Stuart W. "Dimensions of Verbal Racial Attitudes: Interracial Marriage and Approaches to Racial Equality." *Journal of Social Issues* Spring (1976): 9–21.

Brimmer, Andrew. "Black Capitalism." *South Today* March (1970): 6.

Brink, William, and Harris, Louis. *The Negro Revolution in America*. New York: Simon and Schuster, 1964.

Brischetto, Robert, and Arciniega, Tomás. "Examining the Examiners: A Look at Educators' Perspectives on the Chicano Student." In R. O. de la Garza, Z. A. Kruszewski, and T. A. Arciniega, eds., *Chicanos and Native Americans*. New York: Prentice-Hall, 1973, pp. 39–42.

Brody, Erness B., and Brody, Nathan. *Intelligence: Nature, Determinants, and Consequences*. New York: Academic Press, 1974.

Brower, Michael, and Little, Doyle. "White Help for Black Business." In William L. Cash, Jr., and Lucy R. Oliver, eds., *Black Economic Development*. Ann Arbor: University of Michigan Graduate School of Business Administration, 1975, pp. 89–99.

Brown, Claude. *Manchild in the Promised Land*. New York: New American Library, 1965.

Brown, Cynthia. "N. C. C. Under Fire: The Right's Religious Red Alert." *The Nation* March (1983): 289, 303–6.

Brown, David L., and Fuguitt, Glenn V. "Percent Nonwhite and Racial Disparity in Nonmetropolitian Cities in the South." *Social Science Quarterly* December (1972): 573–82.

Brown, George H., Rosen, Nan H., Hill, Susan T., and Olivas,

Michael A., *The Condition of Education for Hispanic Americans*. Washington, D.C.: National Center for Education Statistics, 1980.

Brown, Roger W. "A Determinant of the Relationship between Rigidity and Authoritarianism." *Journal of Abnormal and Social Psychology* October (1953): 469–76.

Browne, Robert S. "The Constellation of Politics and Economics: A Dynamic Duo in the Black Economy." In William L. Cash, Jr., and Lucy R. Oliver, eds., *Black Economic Development: Analysis and Implications*. Ann Arbor: School of Business Administration, University of Michigan, 1975, pp. 71–9.

Browning, Jane E., and Williams, John B. "History and Goals of Black Institutions of Higher Learning." In Charles V. Willie and R. R. Edmonds, eds., *Black College in America*. New York: Teachers College Press, 1978, pp. 68–93.

Bruce, James D., and Rodman, Hyman. "Black–White Marriages in the United States: A Review of the Empirical Literature." In I. R. Stuart and L. E. Abt, eds., *Interracial Marriage*. New York: Grossman, 1973, pp. 147–59.

Brunswick, Ann F. "What Generation Gap? A Comparison of Some Generational Differences among Blacks and Whites." *Social Problems* Winter (1970): 358–71.

Brustein, Robert. *Revolution as Theatre: Notes on the New Radical Style*. New York: Liveright, 1971.

Bruyn, Severyn, and Rayman, Paula M., eds. *Nonviolent Action and Social Change*. New York: Halsted, 1979.

Bryce-Laporte, Roy S., ed. *Sourcebook on the New Immigration: Implications for the United States and the International Community*. New Brunswick, NJ: Transaction Books, 1980.

Bullough, Bonnie. *Social-Psychological Barriers to Housing Desegregation*. Univ. of California, Housing, Real Estate and Urban Land Studies Program and Center for Real Estate and Urban Economics, Special Report, No. 2, 1969.

Bundy, McGeorge. "The Issue before the Court: Who Gets Ahead in America?" *The Atlantic Monthly* November, (1977): 41–54.

Bundy, McGeorge. "Beyond Bakke: What Future for Affirmative Action?" *The Atlantic Monthly* November (1978): 69–73.

Burawoy, Michael. "The Function and Reproduction of Migrant Labor: Comparative Material from Southern Africa and the United States." *American Journal of Sociology* March (1976): 1050–87.

Burke, Fred G. "Bilingualism/Biculturalism in American Education: An Adventure in Wonderland" *Annals of the American Academy of Political and Social Science* March (1981): 164–77.

Burke, Peter J. "Scapegoating: An Alternative to Role Differentiation." *Sociometry* June (1969): 159–68.

Burma, John H. "Humor as a Technique in Race Conflict." *American Sociological Review* December (1946): 710–15.

Burma, John H., ed. *Mexican Americans in the United States*. Cambridge, MA: Schenkman, 1970.

Burns, Haywood. "From *Brown* to *Bakke* and Back: Race, Law, and Social Change in America." *Daedalus* Spring (1981): 219–31.

Burstein, Paul. "Equal Employment Opportunity Legislation and the Income of Women and Nonwhites." *American Sociological Review* June (1979): 367–91.

Bustamante, Jorge A. "The 'Wetback' as Deviant: An Application of Labeling Theory." *American Journal of Sociology* January (1972): 706–18.

Bustamante, Jorge A. "Undocumented Immigration from Mexico: Research Report." *International Migration Review* Summer (1977): 149–77.

Button, James W. *Black Violence: Political Impact of the 1960 Riots*. Princeton: Princeton University Press, 1978.

Byrne, Donn, and Wong, Terry J., "Racial Prejudice, Interpersonal Attraction, and Assumed Dissimilarity of Attitudes." *Journal of Abnormal and Social Psychology* October (1962): 246–53.

Cabrera, Y. Arturo. *Emerging Faces: The Mexican Americans*. Dubuque, IA: William C. Brown, 1971.

Caditz, Judith. "Ethnic Identification, Interethnic Contact, and Belief in Integration." *Social Forces* March (1976): 632–45.

Cafferty, Pastora San Juan. "The Language Question: The Dilemma of Bilingual Education for Hispanics in America." In *Ethnic Relations in America*, edited by Lance Liebman. New York: Prentice-Hall, 1982, pp. 101–27.

Cain, Glen G. "The Challenges of Segmented Labor Market Theories to Orthodox Theory: A Survey." *Journal of Economic Literature* December (1976): 1215–57.

Camilleri, Santo F. "A Factor Analysis of the F-Scale." *Social Forces* (1959): 316–23.

Campbell, Angus. *White Attitudes Toward Black People*. Ann Arbor: Institute for Social Research, 1971.

Campbell, Donald T. "On the Genetics of Altruism and the Counter-Hedonic Components in Human Culture." *Journal of Social Issues* 28, 3 (1972): 21–37.

Campbell, Donald T. "On the Conflicts Between Biological and Social Evolution and Between Psychology and Moral Tradition." *American Psychologist*. December (1975): 1103–26.

Campbell, Ernest Q. "Moral Discomfort and Racial Segregation—An Examination of the Myrdal Hypothesis" *Social Forces* March (1961): 228–34.

Campbell, Ernest Q., and Pettigrew, T. F. *Christians in Racial Crisis: A Study of Little Rock's Ministry*. Washington, D.C.: Public Affairs Press, 1959.

Cannon, Mildred S., and Locke, Ben Z. "Being Black Is Detrimental to One's Health; Myth or Reality?" *Phylon* December (1977): 410–28.

Caplan, Arthur L., ed. *The Sociobiology Debate: Readings on Ethical and Scientific Issues*. New York: Harper & Row, 1978.

Carmichael, Stokely, and Hamilton, Charles. *Black Power*. New York: Vintage Books, 1967.

Carr, Leslie G. "The Srole Items and Acquiescence." *American Sociological Review* April (1971): 287–93.

Carroll, Michael P. "Revitalization Movements and Social Structure: Some Quantitative Tests" *American Sociological Review* June (1975): 389–401.

Carter, Thomas P. "Mexican Americans; How the Schools Have Failed Them." In Livie I. Duran and Russell Bernard, eds., *An Introduction to Chicano Studies*. New York: Macmillan 1973, pp. 447-59.

Carter, Thomas P., and Segura, Roberto D. *Mexican Americans in School: A Decade of Change*. New York: College Entrance Examination Board, 1978.

Cash, William L., Jr., and Oliver, Lucy R., eds., *Black Economic Development: Analysis and Implications—An Anthology*. Ann Arbor: University of Michigan Graduate School of Business Administration, 1975.

Catton, William R., Jr. "The Functions and Dysfunctions of

Ethnocentrism: A Theory." *Social Problems* Winter (1960–61): 201–11.

Caudill, William, and DeVos, George. "Achievement, Culture and Personality: The Case of the Japanese Americans." *American Anthropologist* December (1956): 1102–126.

Cauthen, Nelson R., Robinson, Ira, and Krauss, Herbert. "Stereotypes: A Review of the Literature 1926–1968." *Journal of Social Psychology* June (1971): 103–25.

Cedrix X (Clark) issue editor. "The White Researcher in Black Society." *Journal of Social Issues* 29,1 (1973).

Chadwick, Bruce A. "The Inedible Feast." In H. M. Bahr, B. A. Chadwick, and R. C. Day, eds., *Native Americans Today: Sociological Perspectives*. New York: Harper & Row, 1972, pp. 131–45.

Chamberlain, Houston Stewart. *The Foundations of the Nineteenth Century*. Menlo Park, CA: J. Lane Co., 1914.

Chapman, Loren J., and Campbell, Donald T. "The Effect of Acquiescence Response-Set upon Relationships among the F Scale, Ethnocentrism, and Intelligence." *Sociometry* June (1959): 153–61.

Chase, Philip H. "A Note on Projection." *Psychological Bulletin* July (1960): 289–90.

Cheng, Lucie and Bonacich, Edna (eds.), *Labor Immigration under Capitalism: Asian Workers in the United States before World War II*. Berkeley: University of California Press, 1984.

Childs, John Brown. *The Political Black Minister: A Study in Afro-American Politics and Religion*. Boston: G. K. Hall, 1980.

Chisholm, Shirley. *Unbought and Unbossed*. Boston: Houghton-Mifflin, 1970.

Christie, Richard, and Cook, Peggy. "A Guide to Published Literature Relating to the Authoritarian Personality Through 1956." *Journal of Psychology* April (1958): 171–99.

Christie, Richard, and Jahoda, Marie, eds. *Studies in the Scope and Method of "The Authoritarian Personality."* New York: The Free Press, 1954.

Christie, Richard, Havel, Joan, and Seidenberg, Bernard. "Is the F Scale Irreversible?" *Journal of Abnormal and Social Psychology* March (1958): 143–59.

Citizens Commission on Civil Rights. *"There Is No Liberty…" A Report on Congressional Efforts to Curb the Federal Courts and to Undermine the Brown Decision*. Washington, D.C.: Citizens Commission on Civil Rights, 1982.

Clark, Kenneth B. *Dark Ghetto: Dilemmas of Social Power*, New York: Harper & Row, 1965.

Clark, Kenneth B. "The Role of Race," *The New York Times* October 1981, p. 30.

Clark, Kenneth B., and Clark, Mamie P. "Racial Identification and Preference in Negro Children." In *Readings in Social Psychology*, edited by T. M. Newcomb and E. L. Hartley. New York: Holt, 1947, pp. 169–78.

Claude, Inis L., Jr. *National Minorities: An International Problem*. Cambridge: Harvard University Press, 1955.

Cleage, Albert B., Jr. *The Black Messiah*. New York: Sheed and Ward, 1968.

Cleaver, Eldridge, *Soul on Ice*. New York: Dell, 1968.

Clemente, Frank, and Sauer, William J. "Racial Differences in Life Satisfaction." *Journal of Black Studies* September (1976): 3–11.

Clotfelter, Charles T. "School Desegregation as Urban Public Policy." In Peter Mieszkowski and Mahlon Straszheim, eds., *Current Issues in Urban Economics*. Baltimore: Johns Hoplins University Press, 1979, pp. 359–87.

Cohen, Abner, ed. *Urban Ethnicity*. Kennebunkport, ME: Tavistock Publications, 1974.

Cohen, Albert K., and Hodges, Harold M., Jr. "Characteristics of the Lower-Blue-Collar-Class." *Social Problems* Spring (1963): 303–34.

Cohen, Elizabeth G. "The Effects of Desegregation on Race Relations." *Law and Contemporary Problems* 39 (1975): 271–99.

Cohen, Elizabeth G. "Expectations States and Interracial Interaction in School Settings." In Ralph H. Turner and James F. Short, Jr., eds., *Annual Review of Sociology*, Annual Reviews (1982): 209–35.

Cohen, Elizabeth G., and Roper, Susan S. "Modification of Interracial Interaction Disability: An Application of Status Characteristic Theory." *American Sociological Review* December (1972): 643–57.

Cohen, Gaynor. "Alliance and Conflict among Mexican Americans." *Ethnic and Racial Studies* April (1982): 175–95.

Cohen, Oscar. "The Case for Benign Quotas in Housing." *Phylon* Spring (1960): 20–29.

Cohen, Rosalie A. "Conceptual Styles, Culture Conflict, and Nonverbal Tests of Intelligence." *American Anthropologist* October (1969): 828–56.

Cohn, Norman. *Warrant for Genocide*. New York: Harper & Row, 1967.

Cole, Leonard A. *Blacks in Power: A Comparative Study of Black and White Elected Officials*. Princeton: Princeton University Press, 1976.

Coleman, James S. "Implications of the Findings in Alienation." *American Journal of Sociology* July (1964): 76–78.

Coleman, James S. "Race Relations and Social Change." In Irwin Katz and Patricia Gurin, eds., *Race and the Social Sciences*. New York: Basic Books, 1969, pp. 274–341.

Coleman, James S. *Resources for Social Change: Race in the United States*. New York: Wiley, 1977.

Coleman, James S. "Racial Segregation in the Schools: New Research with New Policy Implications." *Phi Delta Kappan* October (1975).

Coleman, James S., Campbell, Ernest Q., Hobson, Carol J., McPartland, James, Mood, Alexander M., Weinfeld, Frederick D., and York, Robert L. *Equality of Educational Opportunity*, Washington, D.C.: U. S. Office of Education, 1966.

Coleman, James S., Kelly, Sara D. and Moore, John A. *Trends in School Segregation, 1968-73*. Washington, D.C.: The Urban Institute, 1975.

Coleman, James S., Hoffer, Thomas, and Kilgore, Sally. *High School Achievement: Public, Catholic, and Private Schools Compared*. New York: Basic Books, 1982.

Coleman, L. S., Jr., and Cook, S. C. "The Failures of Minority Capitalism: The Edapco Case." *Phylon* March (1976): 44–48.

Coles, Robert. *The Desegregation of Southern Schools: A Psychiatric Study*. New York: Anti-Defamation League and Southern Regional Council, 1963.

Coles, Robert. *Children of Crisis: A Study of Courage and Fear*. Boston: Little, Brown, 1967.

Coles, Robert. *Eskimos, Chicanos, Indians*. Boston: Little, Brown, 1977.

Coles, Robert. "Minority Dreams, American Dreams," *Daedalus* Spring, (1981): 29–41.

Colfax, J. David, and Sternberg, Susan Frankel. "The Perpetuation of Racial Stereotypes: Blacks in Mass Circulation Magazine Advertisements." *Public Opinion Quarterly* Spring (1972): 8–18.

College Entrance Examination Board. *Beyond Desegregation.* New York: 1978.

Collier, Peter. "The Red Man's Burden." *Ramparts* February (1970): 23–38.

Collins, Randall. *Conflict Sociology.* New York: Academic Press, 1975.

Collins, Randall. *The Credential Society: An Historical Sociology of Education and Stratification.* New York: Academic Press, 1979.

Collins, Thomas W. "From Courtrooms to Classrooms: Managing School Desegregation in a Deep South High School." In Ray C. Rist, ed., *Desegregated Schools.* New York: Academic Press, 1979, pp. 89–114.

Comer, James P. "The Social Power of the Negro." In Floyd B. Barbour, ed., *The Black Power Revolt.* Boston: Porter Sargent, 1968, pp. 72–84.

Commission on Wartime Relocation and Internment of Civilians. *Personal Justice Denied.* Washington, D.C.: U.S. Government Printing Office, 1982.

Condram, John G. "Changes in White Attitudes Toward Blacks, 1963–1977," *Public Opinion Quarterly* Winter (1979): 463–76.

Cone, James H. *Black Theology and Black Power.* New York: Seabury Press, 1969.

Cone, James H. *A Black Theology of Liberation.* Philadelphia: Lippincott, 1970.

Cone, James H. *God of the Oppressed.* New York: Seabury Press, 1975.

Connery, Robert H., ed. *Urban Riots: Violence and Social Change.* New York: The Academy of Political Science, 1968.

Connor, Walter D. *Socialism, Politics, and Equality.* New York: Columbia University Press, 1979.

Connor, Walker. *The National Question in Marxist-Leninist Theory and Strategy.* Princeton, NJ: Princeton University Press, 1984.

Coon, Carleton S. *The Origin of Races,* New York: Knopf, 1962.

Coon, Carleton S., Garn, S. M., Birdsell, J. B. *Races.* Springfield, IL: Charles C Thomas, 1960.

Cooney, Rosemary Santana, Rogler, Lloyd H., and Schroder, Edna. "Puerto Rican Fertility: An Examination of Social Characteristics, Assimilation, and Minority Status Variables." *Social Forces* June (1981): 1094–113.

Cooper, Eunice, and Jahoda, Marie. "The Evasion of Propaganda: How Prejudiced People Respond to Anti-Prejudice Propaganda." *Journal of Psychology* January (1947): 15–25.

Cooper, John L. *The Police and the Ghetto.* Port Washington, NY: Kennikat Press, 1980.

Cornelius, Wayne A. "Mexican Migration to the United States: Causes, Consequences, and U.S. Responses." Cambridge: Center for International Studies, MIT, 1978.

Cortese, Charles, Falk, R. Frank, and Cohen, Jack C. "Further Considerations on the Methodological Analysis of Segregation Indexes." *American Sociological Review* August (1976): 630–37.

Coser, Lewis A. *The Functions of Social Conflict.* New York: The Free Press, 1954.

Coser, Lewis A. *Continuities in the Study of Social Conflict.* New York: The Free Press, 1967.

Coser, Lewis A. "Unanticipated Conservative Consequences of Liberal Theorizing." *Social Problems* Winter (1969): 263–72.

Coser, Lewis A., issue editor "Collective Violence and Civil Conflict." *Journal of Social Issues* 28,1 (1972).

Costas, Orlando E. "The Hispanics Next Door." *Christian Century,* August 15–22, 1982, pp. 851–6.

Courant, Paul N., and Yinger, John, "On Models of Racial Prejudice and Urban Residential Structure." *Journal of Urban Economics* 4 (1977): 272–91.

Coutu, Walter. *Emergent Human Nature: A Symbolic Field Interpretation.* New York: Knopf, 1949.

Covello, Vincent T., ed. *Poverty and Public Policy: An Evaluation of Social Science Research.* Cambridge, MA: Schenkman, 1980.

Coward, Barbara E., Feagin, Joe R., and Williams, J. Allen Jr. "The Culture of Poverty Debate: Some Additional Data." *Social Problems* June (1974): 621–34.

Cox, Keith K. "Changes in Stereotyping of Negroes and Whites in Magazine Advertisements." *Public Opinion Quarterly* Winter (1969–70): 603–6.

Cox, Oliver L. *Caste, Class and Race: A Study in Social Dynamics.* New York: Doubleday, 1948.

Crain, Robert L., and Weisman, Carol Sachs. *Discrimination, Personality, Achievement: A Survey of Northern Blacks.* New York: Seminar Press, 1972.

Crawford, Thomas J. "Sermons on Racial Tolerance and the Parish Neighborhood Context." *Journal of Applied Social Psychology* 4,1 (1974): 1–23.

Crawford, Thomas J., and Naditch, Murray. "Relative Deprivation, Powerlessness, and Militancy: The Psychology of Social Protest." *Psychiatry* May (1970): 208–23.

Crewdson, John: *The Tarnished Door: The New Immigrants and the Transformation of America.* New York: Times Books, 1983.

Cronon, David E. *Black Moses: The Story of Marcus Garvey and the Universal Negro Improvement Association.* Madison: University of Wisconsin Press, 1955.

Crosbie, Paul V. "Effects of Status Inconsistency: Negative Evidence from Small Groups." *Social Psychology Quarterly* June (1979): 110–25.

Cruse, Harold. *The Crisis of the Negro Intellectual.* New York: William Morrow, 1967.

Cruse, Harold. *Rebellion or Revolution.* New York: Morrow, 1968.

Cummings, Scott. "White Ethnics, Racial Prejudice, and Labor Market Segmentation." *American Journal of Sociology* January (1980): 938–50.

Curtin, Philip D. *The Atlantic Slave Trade: A Census.* Madison: University of Wisconsin Press, 1969.

Curtis, Lynn A. *Violence, Race, and Culture.* Lexington, MA: Heath, 1975.

Cutler, Stephen J. "Cohort Changes in Attitudes about Race Relations." Unpublished manuscript, 1983.

Cutright, Phillis. "The Civilian Earnings of White and Black Draftees and Nonveterans." *American Sociological Review* June (1974): 317–27.

Cygnar, Thomas E., Noel, Donald L., and Jacobson, Cardell K. "Religiosity and Prejudice: An Interdimensional Analysis." *Journal for the Scientific Study of Religion* June (1977): 183–91.

Dadrian, Vahakn N. "The Common Features of the Armenian and Jewish Cases of Genocide: A Comparative Victimological Perspective." In Israel Drapkin and Emilio Viano, eds., *Victimology: A New Focus*. Vol. 4. *Violence and Its Victims*. D. C. Heath, 1975a, pp. 99–120.

Dadrian, Vahakn N. "A Typology of Genocide," *International Review of Modern Sociology* Autumn, (1975b): 201-212.

Dadrian, Vahakn N. "The Victimization of the American Indian." *Victimology: An International Journal* Winter (1976): 517–37.

Dahrendorf, Ralf. *Class and Class Conflict in Industrial Society*. Palo Alto, CA: Stanford University Press, 1959.

Daniels, Lee A. "Black Crime, Black Victims." *The New York Times Magazine,* May 16, 1982, pp. 38–44 ff.

Danigelis, Nicholas L. "A Theory of Black Political Participation in the United States." *Social Forces* September (1977): 31–47.

Danigelis, Nicholas L. "Black Political Participation in the United States: Some Recent Evidence." *American Sociological Review* October (1978): 756–71.

Darity, William A., and Pitt, Edward W. "Health Status of Black Americans." In J. B. Williams, ed., *The State of Black America*. New York: National Urban League, 1979, pp. 125–56.

Davidson, Chandler, and Gaitz, Charles M. "'Are the Poor Different?' A Comparison of Work Behavior and Attitudes among the Urban Poor and Nonpoor." *Social Problems* December (1974): 229–45.

Davis, Abram L., and Hope, Corrie. "Some Notes on Reverse Discrimination." *The Review of Black Political Economy* Winter (1979): 199–207.

Davis, Allison W., and Havighurst, Robert J. *Father of the Man: How Your Child Gets His Personality*. Boston: Houghton-Mifflin, 1947.

Davis, Brion David. "Slavery and the Post-World War II Historican." *Daedalus* Spring (1974): 1–16.

Davis, Cary, Haub, Carl, and Willette, JoAnne. "U. S. Hispanics: Changing the Face of America." *Population Bulletin,* Vol. 38, June 1983: whole issue.

Davis, Frank G. "Problems of Economic Growth in the Black Community: Some Alternative Hypotheses." In William L. Cash, Jr., and Lucy R. Oliver, eds., *Black Economic Development*. Ann Arbor: University of Michigan Graduate School of Business Administration, 1975, pp. 134–62.

Davis, James A. "Communism, Conformity, Cohorts, and Categories: American Tolerance in 1954 and 1972–73." *American Journal of Sociology* November (1975): 491–513.

Davis, James H., and White, Woodie W. *Racial Transition in the Church*. Nashville, TN: Abingdon Press, 1980.

Dawidowicz, Lucy S. *The War Against the Jews, 1933–1945*. New York: Holt, Rinehart & Winston, 1975.

Day, Beth. *Sexual Life Between Blacks and Whites*. Mountain View, CA: World, 1972.

Day, Beth. "The Hidden Fear." In D. Y. Wilkinson and R. L. Taylor, eds., *The Black Male in America*. Chicago: Nelson-Hall, 1977.

Day, R. C. "The Emergence of Activism as a Social Movement." In H. M. Bahr, B. A. Chadwick, and R. C. Day, *Native Americans Today*. New York; Harper & Row, 1972, pp. 506–16.

Dearman, Nancy B., and Plisko, Valena White. *The Condition of Education*. Washington, D.C.: U.S. Department of Education (National Center for Education Statistics), 1981.

Della Fave, L. Richard. "The Culture of Poverty Revisited." *Social Problems* June (1974): 609–21.(a)

Della Fave, L. Richard. "Success Values: Are They Universal or Class-Differentiated?" *American Journal of Sociology* July (1974): 153–69.(b)

Della Fave, L. Richard. "The Meek Shall Not Inherit the Earth: Self-Evaluation and the Legitimacy of Stratification." *American Sociological Review* December (1980): 955–71.

de la Garzo, Rudolph O. "The Politics of Mexican Americans." In Arnulfo D. Trejo, ed., *The Chicanos*. Tucson, AZ: University of Arizona Press, 1979, pp. 107–18.

Deloria, Vine, Jr. *Custer Died for Your Sins*. New York: Macmillan, 1969.

Deloria, Vine, Jr. "This Country Was a Lot Better Off When the Indians Were Running It." In H. M. Bahr, B. A. Chadwick, and R. C. Day, eds., *Native Americans Today*. New York: Harper & Row, 1972, pp. 498–506.

Deloria, Vine, Jr. *God Is Red*. New York: Dell, 1973.

Deloria, Vine, Jr. *Behind the Trail of Broken Treaties*. New York: Delacorte Press, 1974.

Deloria, Vine, Jr. "Native Americans: The American Indian Today." *Annals of the American Academy of Political and Social Science* March (1981): 139–49.

de los Santos, Alfredo G., Jr., "Differential Career Counseling of Mexican American Students." In *Beyond Desegregation*. New York: College Entrance Examination Board, 1978, pp. 70–1.

Dennis, Ruth E. "Social Stress and Mortality Among Nonwhite Males." *Phylon* September (1977): 315–28.

Derbyshire, Robert, and Brody, Eugene. "Social Distance and Identity Conflict in Negro College Students." *Sociology and Social Research* April (1964): 301–14.

Despres, Leo A. ed. "Ethnicity and Resource Competition in Plural Societies." Hawthorne, NY: Mouton, 1975.

Deutsch, Morton, and Collins, Mary Evans. "Interracial Housing. A Psychological Evaluation of a Social Experiment." Minneapolis: University of Minnesota Press, 1951.

Deutscher, Irwin. *Why Do They Say One Thing, Do Another?* Morristown, NJ: General Learning Press, 1973.

DeVos, George, and Romanucci-Ross, Lola, eds. *Ethnic Identity*. Palo Alto, CA: Mayfield, 1975.

Diab, Lutfy N. "Factors Affecting Studies of National Stereotypes." *Journal of Social Psychology* February (1963): 29–40.

Dickstein, Morris. *Gates of Eden: American Culture in the Sixties*. New York: Basic Books, 1977.

Dignan, Don. "Europe's Melting Pot: A Century of Large-Scale Immigration into France." *Ethnic and Racial Studies* April (1981): 137–52.

Dillingham, Gerald L. "The Emerging Black Middle Class: Class Conscious or Race Conscious?" *Ethnic and Racial Studies* October (1981) 432–51.

Dittes, James E. "Typing the Typologies: Some Parallels in the Career of Church–Sect and Extrinsic–Intrinsic." *Journal for the Scientific Study of Religion* (1971): 375–83.

Dobzhansky, Theodosius. "Race Equality." In *The Biological and Social Meaning of Race,* edited by Richard H. Osborne. San Francisco: W. H. Freeman, 1971, pp. 21 ff.

Dobzhansky, Theodosius. *Mankind Evolving*. New Haven: Yale, 1962.

Doctors, Samuel I., and Lockwood, Sharon "New Directions for Minority Enterprise." In William L. Cash, Jr., and Lucy R. Oliver eds., *Black Economic Development,* Ann Arbor:

University of Michigan Graduate School of Business Administration 1975, pp. 357–74.

Dodson, Dan W. "Can Intergroup Quotas Be Benign?" *Journal of Intergroup Relations* Autumn (1960): 12–17.

Dollard, John. *Caste and Class in a Southern Town.* New Haven: Yale, 1937.

Dollard, John, Miller, Neal E., Dobb, L. W., et al. *Frustration and Aggression.* New Haven: Yale University Press, 1939.

Donne, John. *Devotions upon Emergent Occasions.* Cambridge: Cambridge University Press, 1923.

Dorris, Michael A. "The Grass Still Grows, the River Still Flows: Contemporary Native Americans." *Daedalus* Spring (1981): 43–69.

Douglass, Frederick. *The Life and Times of Frederick Douglass.* St. Paul, MN: Park, 1882.

Dovidio, John F., and Gaertner, Samuel L. "The Effects of Race, Status, and Ability on Helping Behavior." *Social Psychology Quarterly* September (1981): 192–203.

Dowdall, George W. "White Gains from Black Subordination in 1960 and 1970." *Social Problems* December (1974): 162–83.

Doyle, Bertram. *The Etiquette of Race Relations in the South.* Chicago: University of Chicago Press, 1937.

Drake, St. Clair, and Cayton, Horace R. *Black Metropolis.* New York: Harcourt, Brace, Jovanovich, 1945/1963.

Dreger, Ralph Mason. "Intellectual Functioning." In Kent S. Miller and Ralph M. Dreger, eds., *Comparative Studies of Blacks and Whites in the United States.* New York: Seminar Press, 1973, pp. 185–229.

Dreyfuss, Joel. "Such Good Friends: Blacks and Jews in Conflict." *Village Voice,* August 27, 1979, pp. 11–12.

Dubey, Sumati N. "Blacks' Preference for Black Professionals, Businessmen and Religious Leaders." *Public Opinion Quarterly* Spring (1970): 113–16.

DuBois, W. E. B. *The Negro Church.* Atlanta: Atlanta University Press, 1903.

DuBois, W. E. B. *Black Reconstruction in America.* Mountain View, CA: World, 1962.

Duncan, Greg J., and Morgan, James N., eds. *Five Thousand American Families: Patterns of Economic Progress.* Ann Arbor: University of Michigan Institute of Social Research, 1975.

Duncan, O. D., and Duncan, Beverly. "A Methodological Analysis of Segregation Indices." *American Sociological Review* April (1955): 210–17.

Duncan, O. D., Featherman, David L., and Duncan, Beverly. *Socioeconomic Background and Achievement.* New York: Seminar Press, 1972.

Duster, Troy. "The Structure of Privilge and Its Universe of Discourse." *The American Sociologist* May (1976): 73–8.

Dworkin, A. G. "The Peoples of La Raza." In Noel P. Gist and A. G. Dworkin, eds., *The Blending of Races.* New York: Wiley, 1972.

Dworkin, Earl S., and Efran, Jay S. "The Angered: Their Susceptibility to Varieties of Humor." *Journal of Personality and Social Psychology* (1967): 233–36.

Eagleson, John, ed. *Christian and Socialism: The Christians for Socialism Movement in Latin America.* Translated by John Drury. Maryknoll, NY: Orbis Books, 1975.

Easterlin, Richard A. *Birth and Fortune: The Impact of Numbers on Personal Welfare.* New York: Basic Books, 1980.

Easton, David. *A System Analysis of Political Life.* New York: Wiley, 1965.

Edwards, Harry T. "Race Discrimination in Employment: What Price Equality?" in Victor J. Stone, ed., *Civil Liberties and Civil Rights.* Urbana: University of Illinois Press, 1977, pp. 71–144.

Edwards, Lyford P. *The Natural History of Revolution.* Chicago: University of Chicago Press, 1927.

Edwards, Richard C., Reich, Michael, and Gordon, David M. *Labor Market Segmentation.* Lexington, MA: Heath, 1975.

Ehrenhalt, Alan. "Pulling Away from Racial Gerrymander." *Perspectives* Winter–Spring (1983): 32–37.

Eells, Kenneth, Davis, Allison, Havignurst, Robert J., Herrick, Virgil E., and Tyler, Ralph W. *Intelligence and Cultural Difference.* Chicago: University of Chicago Press, 1951.

Ehrlich, Howard J. *The Social Psychology of Prejudice.* New York: Wiley, 1973.

Ehrlich, Paul R., Bilderback, Loy, and Ehrlich, Anne H. *The Golden Door: International Migration, Mexico and the United States.* New York: Ballantine, 1979.

Eisenman, Russell, and Pettigrew, Thomas F. "Comments and Rejoinders." *Journal of Social Issues* Autumn (1969): 199–206.

Eisinger, Peter K. *Patterns of Interracial Politics: Conflict and Cooperation in the City.* New York: Academic Press, 1976.

Eisinger, Peter K. *The Politics of Displacement: Racial and Ethnic Transition in Three American Cities.* New York: Academic Press, 1980.

Eitzen, D. Stanley. "Status Inconsistency and Wallace Supporters in a Midwestern City." *Social Forces* June (1970): 493–98.

Elder, Glen H., Jr. "Intergroup Attitudes and Social Ascent among Negro Boys." *American Journal of Sociology* January (1971): 673–97.

Elkins, Stanley M. *Slavery: A Problem in American Institutional and Intellectual Life.* Chicago: University of Chicago Press, 1959.

Encyclopedia of Associations: National Organizations of the U.S. 11th ed., vol. 1. Detroit: Gale, 1977.

Enloe, Cynthia. *Ethnic Conflict and Political Development.* Boston: Little, Brown, 1973.

Enloe, Cynthia H. *Ethnic Soldiers: State Security in Divided Societies.* Athens, GA: University of Georgia Press, 1980.

Epstein, Edward Jay. *Between Fact and Fiction: The Problem of Journalism.* New York: Random House, 1975.

Epstein, Noel. *Language, Ethnicity, and the Schools: Policy Alternatives for Bilingual-Bicultural Education.* Washington, D.C.: Institute for Educational Leadership, 1977.

Erickson, Frederick. "Gatekeeping and the Melting Pot." *Harvard Educational Review* February (1975): 44–70.

Essien-Udom, E. U. *Black Nationalism: A Search for Identity in America.* Chicago: University of Chicago Press, 1962.

Fairfax, Jean. "Current Status of the Adams Case: Implications for the Education of Blacks and Other Minorities. In *Beyond Desegregation,* New York: College Entrance Examination Board, 1978, pp. 36–44.

Falk, Frank R., Cortese, Charles F., and Cohen, Jack. "Utilizing Standard Indices of Residential Segregation: Comment on Winship." *Social Forces,* vol. 57, December (1978): 713–16.

Fallows, James. "Immigration: How It's Affecting Us." *Atlantic Monthly* November (1983): 85–106.

Fanon, Frantz. *The Wretched of the Earth.* Preface by Jean-Paul Sartre. New York: Grove Press, 1963.

Fanshel, David. *Far from the Reservation: The Transracial Adoption of American Indian Children.* Methuen, N.J.: Scarecrow Press, 1972.

Farley, Reynolds. "Residential Segregation and Its Implications for School Desegregation." Symposium on the Courts, Social Science, and School Desegregation (Part I). *Law and Contemporary Problems* (Duke University School of Law) Winter (1975): 187–193.

Farley, Reynolds. "Residential Segregation in Urbanized Areas of the United States in 1970: An Analysis of Social Class and Racial Differences." *Demography* November (1977a): 497–518.

Farley, Reynolds. "Trends in Racial Inequalities: Have the Gains of the 1960s Disappeared in the 1970s?" *American Sociological Review* April (1977b), 189–208.

Farley, Reynolds. "School Integration in the United States." In Frank D. Bean and W. Parker Frisbee, eds. *The Demography of Racial and Ethnic Groups.* New York: Academic Press, 1978, pp. 22–45.

Farley, Reynolds. "Homicide Trends in the United States." *Demography,* May (1980): 177–88.

Farley, Reynolds. *Catching Up? An Analysis of Recent Changes in the Social and Economic Status of Blacks.* The Population Studies Center, Department of Sociology, University of Michigan, Ann Arbor, MI, 1982. A later version of this study is *Blacks and Whites: Narrowing the Gap?,* Harvard University Press, 1984.

Farley, Reynolds, Schuman, Howard, Bianchi, Suzanne, Colasanto, Diane, and Hatchett, Shirley. "Chocolate City, Vanilla Suburbs: Will the Trend Toward Racially Separate Communities Continue?" *Social Science Research* December (1978): 319–44.

Farley, Reynolds, Bianchi, Suzanne, and Colasanto, Diane. "Barriers to Racial Integration of Neighborhoods: The Detroit Case." *Annals of the American Academy of Political and Social Science* (1979) March 97–113.

Farley, Reynolds, Richards, Toni, and Wurdock, Clarence. "School Desegregation and White Flight: An Investigation of Competing Models and Their Discrepant Findings." *Sociology of Education* July (1980): 123–39.

Farmer, James. *Freedom—When?* New York: Random House, 1966.

Fay, Keith. *Developing Indian Employment Opportunities.* Washington, D.C.: Bureau of Indian Affairs, 1974.

Feagin, Joe R., and Hahn, Harlan. *Ghetto Revolts: The Politics of Violence in American Cities.* New York: Macmillan, 1973.

Featherman, D. L., and Hauser, R. M., *Opportunity and Change.* New York: Academic Press, 1978.

Fein, Helen. *Accounting for Genocide: National Response and Jewish Victimization During the Holocaust.* New York: Free Press, 1978.

Feit, Edward, and Stokes, R. G. "Racial Prejudice and Economic Pragmatism: A South African Case Study. *Journal of Modern African Studies* 14,3 (1976): 487–506.

Fendrich, James M. "Perceived Reference Group Support: Racial Attitudes and Overt Behavior. *American Sociological Review* December (1967a): 960–70. (a)

Fendrich, James M. "A Study of the Association among Verbal Attitudes, Commitment and Overt Behavior in Different Experimental Situations." *Social Forces*, Vol. 45, March (1967b): 347–55.

Fernandez, C. A., Haug, J. M., and Wagner, N. N. *Chicanos.* St. Louis, MO: C. V. Mosby, 1976.

Feshbach, Seymour, and Singer, Robert. "The Effects of Personal and Shared Threats upon Social Prejudice." *Journal of Abnormal and Social Psychology* May (1957): 411–16.

Fessler, Pamela. "Women, Minorities Gain Seats in Congress." *Congressional Quarterly* November 6, 1982, 2805.

Field, Geoffrey G. *Evangelist of Race: The Germanic Vision of Houston Stewart Chamberlain.* New York: Columbia, 1981.

Fine, Morris, and Himmelfarb, Milton, eds. *American Jewish Yearbook* 1975. New York: American Jewish Committee and Jewish Publishing Society of America, 1974–75.

Fineberg, S. A. *Punishment Without Crime.* New York: Doubleday, 1949.

Finestone, Harold. "Cats, Kicks, and Color." July (1957): 3–13.

Finger, John A., Jr. "Why Busing Plans Work." *School Review* May (1976): 364–72.

Finnerty, Frank A., Jr. "Hypertension is Different in Blacks." In A. Shiloh and I. Selawan, eds., *Ethnic Groups of America: Their Morbidity, Mortality, and Behavior Disorders.* Vol. 2, *The Blacks.* Charles C. Thomas, 1974, pp. 100–103.

Fishbein, Martin, and Ajzen, Icek. *Belief, Attitude, Intention, and Behavior: An Introduction to Theory and Research* Reading, MA: Addison-Wesley, 1975.

Fishman, Joshua. *Bilingual Education: An International Sociological Perspective.* Rowley, MA: Newbury House, 1976.

Fitzpatrick, Joseph P. "The Integration of Puerto Ricans." In F. R. Tovar, ed., *Handbook of the Puerto Rican Community.* New York: Plus Ultra Educational Publishers, 1970.

Fitzpatrick, Joseph P. *Puerto Rican Americans: The Means of Migration to the Mainland.* New York: Prentice-Hall, 1971.

Fitzpatrick, Joseph P. "The Puerto Rican Family." in C. H. Mindel and R. W. Habenstein, eds., *Ethnic Families in America.* New York: Elsevier, 1976.

Fitzpatrick, Joseph P., and Parker, Lourdes Travieso. "Hispanic-Americans in the Eastern United States." *Annals of the American Academy of Political and Social Science* March (1981): 98–110.

Flores, Juan, Attinasi, John, and Pedraza, Pedro, Jr. "La Carreta Made a U-Turn: Puerto Rican Language and Culture in the United States." *Daedalus* Spring (1981): 193–217.

Flowerman, S. H. "Mass Propaganda in the War against Bigotry." *Journal of Abnormal and Social Psychology* October (1947): 429–39.

Fogel, Robert William, and Engerman, Stanley L. *Time on the Cross.* 2 vols. Boston: Little, Brown, 1974.

Fogelson, Robert M. "Violence as Protest." In Robert Connery, ed., *Urban Riots: Violence and Social Change.* Proceedings of the Academy of Political Science. New York: Columbia University Press, 1968, 25–41.

Fogelson, Robert M. *Big-City Police.* Cambridge: Harvard, 1977.

Ford, Nick A. *Black Studies.* Port Washington, NY: Kennikat Press, 1973.

Ford, W. Scott. "Interracial Public Housing in a Border City: Another Look at the Contact Hypothesis." *American Journal of Sociology* May (1973): 1426–47.

Foy, Felician A., ed. *National Catholic Almanac*, 1962. Patterson, NJ: St. Anthony's Guild, 1962.

Frady, Marshall, "God and Man in the South." *Atlantic,* January (1967): 37–42.

Francis, E. K. *Interethnic Relations: An Essay in Sociological Theory,* New York: Elsevier, 1976.

Frank, L. K. *Society as the Patient.* New Brunswick, NJ: Rutgers, 1948.

Franklin, John Hope, and Meier, August, eds. *Black Leaders of the Twentieth Century.* Urbana: University Press of Illinois, 1982.

Frazier, E. Franklin. *The Negro Family in the United States.* Rev. ed. Secaucus, NJ: Citadel Press, 1966.

Frazier, E. Franklin. "Sociological Theory and Race Relations. *American Sociological Review* June (1947): 265–71.

Frazier, E. Franklin. *Black Bourgeoisie* Glencoe, Ill.: Free Press, 1957.(a)

Frazier, E. Franklin. *The Negro in the United States.* New York: Macmillan, 1957.(b)

Frazier, E. Franklin. *The Negro Church in America.* New York: Schocken Books, 1963.

Frazier, E. Franklin and Lincoln, C. Eric. *The Negro Church in America: The Black Church Since Frazier.* New York: Schocken Books, 1974.

Fredrickson, George M. *The Black Image in the White Mind: The Debate on Afro-American Character and Destiny, 1817–1914.* New York: Harper & Row, 1971.

Freeman, Gary P. *Immigrant Labor and Racial Conflict in Industrial Societies: The French and British Experience, 1945–1975.* Princeton: Princeton University Press, 1979.

Freeman, Richard B. *Black Elite.* New York: McGraw Hill, 1976.

Freud, Sigmund. *The Basic Writings of Sigmund Freud.* Edited by A. A. Brill. New York: Random House, 1938.

Frey, William H. "Central City White Flight: Racial and Nonracial Causes." *American Sociological Review* June (1979): 425–48.

Friedman, L. J. *Sex Role Stereotyping in the Mass Media.* Macon, GA: Garland, 1977.

Frisbie, W. Parker, and Neidert, Lisa. "Inequality and the Relative Size of Minority Populations: A Comparative Analysis." *American Journal of Sociology* March (1977): 1007–30.

Fuchs, Estelle, and Havighurst, Robert J. *To Live on this Earth: American Indian Education.* New York: Doubleday, 1972.

Fuentes, Luis. "Puerto Rican Children and the New York City Public Schools." In Edward Mapp, ed., *Puerto Rican Perspectives.* Metuchen, NJ: Scarecrow Press, 1974, pp. 18–19.

Funk, Sandra G., Horowitz, Abraham D., Lipshitz, Raanan, and Young, Forrest W. "The Perceived Structure of American Ethnic Groups: The Use of Multidimensional Scaling in Stereotype Research." *Sociometry* June (1976): 116–30.

Furnivall, J. S. *Colonial Policy and Practice.* Cambridge: Cambridge University Press, 1948.

Gabriel, John, and Ben-Tovim, Gideon. "The Conceptualization of Race Relations in Sociological Theory." *Ethnic and Racial Studies* April (1979): 190–212.

Gage, N. L., Leavitt, George, and Stone, George. "The Psychological Meaning of Acquiescence Set for Authoritarianism." *Journal of Abnormal and Social Psychology* July (1957): 98–103.

Galarza, Ernesto, Gallegos, Herman, and Samora, Julian. *Mexican Americans in the Southwest.* Santa Barbara, CA: McNally & Loftin, 1969.

Gallegos y Chávez, Ester. "The Northern New Mexican Woman: A Changing Silhouette." In Arnulfo D. Trejo, ed., *The Chicanos: As We See Ourselves.* Tucson: University of Arizona Press, 1979, pp. 67–79.

Gamson, William A. *The Strategy of Social Protest.* Homewood, IL: Dorsey, 1975.

Gamson, William A., Fireman, Bruce, and Rytina, Steven. *Encounters with Unjust Authority.* Homewood, IL: Dorsey, 1982.

Gamson, Zelda F. "Programs for Black Students, 1968–1974." In Marvin W. Peterson et al., *Black Students on White Campuses.* Ann Arbor: Institute for Social Research, University of Michigan, 1978, pp. 163–93.

Gans, Herbert J. "The Positive Functions of Poverty." *American Journal of Sociology* September (1972): 275–89.

Garcia, Luis T., Erskine, Nancy, Hawn, Kathy, and Casmay, Susann R. "The Effect of Affirmative Action on Attributions about Minority Group Members." *Journal of Personality* December (1981): 427–37.

Garn, Stanley. *Human Races,* 3rd ed. Springfield, IL: Charles C. Thomas, 1971.

Garrison, Howard H. "Education and Friendship Choice in Urban Zambia." *Social Forces* June (1979): 1310–24.

Garrison, Vivian. "Sectarianism and Psychosocial Adjustment: A Controlled Comparison of Puerto Rican Pentecostals and Catholics." In Irving Zaretsky and Mark Leone (eds.), *Religious Movements in Contemporary America.* Princeton University Press, 1974, 298–329.

Garrow, David J. *Protest at Selma: Martin Luther King, Jr., and the Voting Rights Act of 1965.* New Haven: Yale, 1978.

Garza, Joseph M. "Race, the Achievement Syndrome, and Perception of Opportunity." *Phylon* Winter (1969): 338–54.

Gast, D. "Minority Americans in Children's Literature." *Elementary English* 44 (1967): 12–23.

Gecas, Viktor. "The Self-Concept." In Ralph H. Turner and James F. Short, Jr., (eds.), *Annual Review of Sociology* (1982): 1–33.

Geertz, Clifford. "The Rotating Credit Association: A 'Middle Rung' in Development." *Economic Development and Cultural Change* April (1962): 241–63.

Geis, Gilbert, and Stotland, Ezra, eds. *White Collar Crime: Theory and Research.* Beverly Hills, CA: Sage, 1980.

Gelb, Joyce. *Beyond Conflict. Black-Jewish Relations: Accent on the Positive.* New York: Institute on Pluralism and Group Identity, 1980.

Gendzier, Irene L. *Frantz Fanon: A Critical Study.* New York: Pantheon, 1972.

General Accounting Office. *The Equal Employment Opportunity Program for Federal Nonconstruction Contractors Can Be Improved.* Report for the Subcommittee on Fiscal Policy of the Joint Economic Committee., U. S. Congress. 1975a.

General Accounting Office. *More Assurance Needed That Colleges and Universities Provide Equal Employment Opportunities: Departments of Labor and Health, Education and Welfare,* 1975b.

Genovese, Eugene D. *The Political Economy of Slavery.* New York: Pantheon, 1965.

Genovese, Eugene D. *The World the Slaveholders Made.* New York: Pantheon, 1969.

Genovese, Eugene D. "American Slaves and Their History." *New York Review of Books* December 3, 1970, 34–43.

Genovese, Eugene D. *Roll, Jordan, Roll: The World the Slaves Made*. New York: Pantheon, 1974.

Geschwender, James A. "Status Discrepancy and Prejudice Reconsidered." *American Journal of Sociology* March (1970): 863–65.

Geschwender, James A. *Class, Race, and Worker Insurgency: The League of Revolutionary Black Workers*. Cambridge: Cambridge University Press, 1977.

Geschwender, James A. "On Power and Powerlessness: Or with a Little Help from Our Friends." In J. Milton Yinger and Stephen J. Cutler, eds., *Major Social Issues: A Multidisciplinary View*. New York: The Free Press, 1978, pp. 439–54.(a)

Geschwender, James A. *Racial Stratification in America*. Dubuque, IA: Wm. C. Brown, 1978.(b)

Gibson, D. Parke. *$70 Billion in the Black: America's Black Consumers*. New York: Macmillan, 1978.

Giddens, Anthony. *The Class Structure of Advanced Industrial Societies*. New York: Barnes and Noble, 1973.

Gilbert, G. M. "Stereotype Persistence and Change among Black Students." *Journal of Abnormal and Social Psychology* April (1951): 245–54.

Giles, Michael W., Gatlin, Douglas S., and Cataldo, Everett F. "Racial Class Prejudice: Their Relative Effects on Protest Against School Desegregation." *American Sociological Review* April (1976): 280–88.

Ginzberg, Eli. "Segregation and Manpower Waste." *Phylon* Winter (1960): 311–16.

Gist, Noel P., and Dworkin, Anthony Gary. *The Blending of Races*. New York: Wiley, 1972.

Glaser, Kurt, and Possony, Stefan T. *Victims of Politics: The State of Human Rights*, New York: Columbia University Press, 1979.

Glasgow, Douglas G. *The Black Underclass: Poverty, Unemployment, and Entrapment of Ghetto Youth*. San Francisco: Jossey-Bass, 1980.

Glassner, Barry. *Essential Interactionism: On the Intelligibility of Prejudice*. Boston: Routledge and Kegan Paul, 1980.

Glazer, Nathan. *The Social Basis of American Communism*. New York: Harcourt, Brace & World, 1961.

Glazer, Nathan. "Blacks and Ethnic Groups: The Difference, and the Political Difference It Makes." *Social Problems* Spring (1971): 444–61.

Glazer, Nathan. *Affirmative Discrimination: Ethnic Inequality and Public Policy*. New York: Basic Books, 1978.

Glazer, Nathan. *Ethnic Dilemmas 1964–1982*. Cambridge: Harvard University Press, 1983.

Glazer, Nathan, and Moynihan, Daniel P. eds. *Ethnicity: Theory and Experience*. Cambridge: Harvard University Press, 1975.

Glenn, Norval D., and Gotard, Erin. "The Religion of Blacks in the United States: Some Recent Trends and Current Characteristics." *American Journal of Sociology* September (1977): 443–51.

Glick, Paul C., "A Demographic Picture of Black Families." In Harriette Pipes McAdoo, *Black Families*. Beverly Hills, CA: Sage, 1981, pp. 106–126.

Glock, Charles Y., and Stark, Rodney. *Christian Beliefs and Anti-Semitism*. New York: Harper & Row, 1966.

Glock, Charles Y., Wuthnow, Robert, Piliavin, Jane Allyn,

and Spencer, Metta. *Adolescent Prejudice*. New York: Harper & Row, 1975.

Gobineau, Arthur de. *The Inequality of Human Races*. translated by Adrian Collins. New York: Putnam's, 1915.

Goering, John M. "Changing Perceptions and Evaluations of Physical Characteristics Among Blacks: 1950–1970." *Phylon* Fall (1972): 231–41.

Goldman, Alan H. *Justice and Reverse Discrimination*. Princeton: Princeton University Press, 1979.

Goldman, Peter. *The Death and Life of Malcolm X*. 2nd ed., Urbana: University of Illinois Press, 1979.

Goldstein, Jack A. "The Weakness of Organization: A New Look at Gamson's *The Strategy of Social Protest*. *American Journal of Sociology* March (1980): 1017–42.

Goldstein, Rhoda L. "Comments on the January (1971) Issue, 'American Sociology and Black Americans.'" *American Journal of Sociology* November (1971): 547–79.

Gomez, D. F. *Somos Chicanos: Strangers in Our Land*. Boston: Beacon, 1973.

Goode, William J. *The Celebration of Heroes: Prestige as a Control System*. Berkeley: University of California Press, 1978.

Goodman, Mary Ellen. *Race Awareness in Young Children*. Rev. ed. New York: Collier Books, 1964.

Gordon, Albert I. *Intermarriage*. Boston: Beacon, 1964.

Gordon, Chad. *Looking Ahead: Self-Conceptions, Race and Family Factors as Determinants of Adolescent Achievement Orientations*. Washington, D.C.: American Sociological Association, 1973.

Gordon, Edmund W., and Green, Derek. "An Affluent Society's Excuses for Inequality: Developmental, Economic, and Educational." in Ashley Montagu, ed., *Race and IQ*. New York: Oxford, 1975, pp. 90–97.

Gordon, Milton M. *Assimilation in American Life*. New York: Oxford University Press, 1964.

Gordon, Milton M. *Human Nature, Class and Ethnicity*. New York: Oxford University Press, 1978.

Gorsuch, Richard L., and Aleshire, Daniel. "Christian Faith and Ethnic Prejudice: A Review and Interpretation of Research." *Journal for the Scientific Study of Religion* September (1974): 281–307.

Gould, Stephen Jay. "Racist Arguments and IQ." In Ashley Montagu, ed., *Race and IQ*. New York: Oxford University Press, 1975, 147–49.

Gould, Stephen Jay. *The Mismeasure of Man*. New York: W. W. Norton, 1981.

Gould, William B. *Black Workers in White Unions*. Ithaca, NY: Cornell, 1977.

Gouldner, Alvin W. "Stalinism: A Study of Internal Colonialism." *Telos* Winter (1977): 5–48.

Gouldner, Helen P. *Teachers' Pets, Troublemakers, and Nobodies: Black Children in Elementary School*. Westport, CT: Greenwood, 1978.

Gove, Walter R., ed. *The Labelling of Deviance*. New York: Wiley, 1975.

Grabb, Edward G. "Working-Class Authoritarianism and Tolerance of Outgroups: A Reassessment." *Public Opinion Quarterly* Spring (1979): 36–47.

Graham, Hugh Davis, and Gurr, Ted. R. eds., *Violence in America: Historical and Comparative Perspectives*. Washington, D.C.: National Commission on Causes and Prevention of Violence, 1969.

Granovetter, Mark. "The Strength of Weak Ties." *American Journal of Sociology* May (1973): 1360–80.

Granovetter, Mark. "The Strength of Weak Ties: A Network Theory Revisited." In Randall Collins, ed., *Sociological Theory 1983*. San Francisco: Jossey-Bass, 1983, Chapter 7.

Grant, Madison. *The Passing of a Great Race*. New York: Scribner's, 1916.

Grant, Peter R., and Holmes, John G. "The Integration of Implicit Personality Theory Schemas and Stereotype Images." *Social Psychology Quarterly* June (1981): 107–15.

Graves, Theodore D. "The Personal Adjustment of Navajo Indian Migrants to Denver, Colorado." *American Anthropologist* February (1970): 35–54.

Graves, Theodore D. "Drinking and Drunkenness Among Urban Indians." In J. O. Waddell and O. M. Watson, eds., *The American Indian in Modern Society*. Boston: Little, Brown, 1970, pp. 274–311.

Graves, Theodore D. "Urban Indian Personality and the 'Culture of Poverty.'" *American Ethnologist* February (1974): 65–86.

Grebler, Leo, Moore, Joan W., and Guzman, Ralph C. *The Mexican-American People: The Nation's Second Largest Minority*. New York: Free Press, 1970.

Greeley, Andrew M. "Religious Intermarriage in a Denominational Society. *American Journal of Sociology* May (1970): 949–52.

Green, Philip. *The Pursuit of Inequality*. New York: Pantheon Books, 1981.

Greenberg, Bradley S., and Mazingo, Sherrie L. "Racial Issues in Mass Media Institutions." In Phyllis A. Katz, ed., *Toward the Elimination of Racism*. New York: Pergamon, 1976, pp. 309–39.

Greenberg, Jack. "Affirmative Action, Quotas, and Merit." *The New York Times*, February 7, 1976.

Greenberg, Jack. "Don't Discard Equality Tool." *The Cleveland Plain Dealer*, January 12, 1981, p. 19A.

Greenberg, Stanley B. *Race and State in Capitalist Development: Comparative Perspectives*. New Haven: Yale, 1980.

Greenstein, Fred I., ed. "Personality and Politics." *Journal of Social Issues* July (1968): whole issue.

Greer, Edward. *Big Steel: Black Politics and Corporate Power in Gary, Indiana*. New York: Monthly Review Press, 1979.

Griego, Richard, and Merk, Gilbert W. "Crisis in New Mexico." In R. Rosaldo, R. A. Calvert, and G. L. Seligmann, eds., *Chicanos: The Revolution of a People*. Minneapolis, MN: Winston, 1978, pp. 388ff.

Grier, Eunice, and Grier, George. *Black Suburbanization at the Mid-1970s*. Washington, D.C.: National Committee Against Discrimination in Housing, April 1978.

Grier, William H., and Cobbs, Price M. *Black Rage*. New York: Basic Books, 1968.

Griffitt, William and Garcia, Luis. "Reversing Authoritarian Punitiveness: The Impact of Verbal Conditioning." *Social Psychology Quarterly* March (1979): 55–61.

Grimshaw, Allen D. "Relationships Among Prejudice, Discrimination, Social Tension, and Social Violence." *Journal of Intergroup Relations* Autumn (1961): 302–10.

Grimshaw, Allen D. *Racial Violence in the United States*. Chicago: Aldine, 1969.

Griswold, Erwin N. "The Bakke Problem—Allocation of Scarce Resources in Education and Other Areas." *Washington University Law Quarterly* Winter (1979): 55–80.

Grodzins, Morton. *Americans Betrayed*. Chicago: University of Chicago Press, 1949.

Groves, W. E., and Rossi, Peter H. "Police Perceptions of a Hostile Ghetto: Realism or Projection." *American Behavioral Scientist* 13 (1970): 727–44.

Guerra, Manuel H. "Bilingualism and Biculturalism: Assets for Chicanos." In Arnulfo D. Trejo, ed., *The Chicanos: As We See Ourselves*. Tucson: University of Arizona Press, 1979, pp. 129ff.

Guest, Avery M., and Weed, James A. "Ethnic Residential Segregation: Patterns of Change." *American Journal of Sociology* March (1976): 1088–1111.

Guilford, J. P. "Racial Preferences of a Thousand American University Students." *Journal of Social Psychology* May (1931): 179–204.

Guillemin, Jeanne. *Urban Renegades: The Cultural Strategy of American Indians*. New York: Columbia, 1975.

Gurr, Ted R. *Why Men Rebel*. Princeton: Princeton University Press, 1970.

Gurr, Ted R., ed. *Handbook of Conflict Theory and Research*. New York: Free Press, 1980.

Gurwitt, Rob. "Widespread Political Efforts Open New Era for Hispanics." *Congressional Quarterly* October 23, 1982, 2707–2709.

Gutiérrez, A. G. "Institutional Completeness and La Raza Unida Party." In R. O. de la Graza, Z. A. Kruszewski, and T. A. Arciniego, eds., *Chicanos and Native Americans*. New York: Prentice-Hall, 1973, pp. 118ff.

Gutman, Herbert G. *The Black Family in Slavery and Freedom, 1750–1925*. New York: Pantheon, 1977.

Haas, Michael. "Filipinos in Hawaii and Institutional Racism." Unpublished manuscript February, 1978.

Haas, Theodore H. "The Legal Aspect of Indian Affairs from 1887 to 1957." *Annals of the American Academy of Political and Social Science* May (1957): 12–22.

Hadaway, C. Kirk, Hackett, David G., and Miller, James F. "The Most Segregated Institution: Correlates of Interracial Church Participation," *Review of Religious Research*, March (1984): 204–219.

Hadden, Jeffrey K. *The Gathering Storm in the Churches*. New York: Doubleday, 1969.

Hagan, John. "Labelling and Deviance: A Case Study in the 'Sociology of the Interesting.'" *Social Problems* Spring (1973): 447–58.

Hall, Raymond L. *Black Separatism in the United States*. Hanover, NH: University Press of New England, 1978.

Halliday, M. A. K. "Anti-Languages." *American Anthropologist* September (1976): 570–84.

Hallinan, Maureen T. "Classroom Racial Composition and Children's Friendships." *Social Forces* September (1982), 56–72.

Hallinan, Maureen T., issue editor. "Public and Private Schools." *Sociology of Education* April–July (1982).

Hamilton, Charles V. "An Advocate of Black Power Defines It." *The New York Times Magazine*, April 14, 1968, pp. 79ff.

Hamilton, Charles V. *The Black Preacher in America*. New York: Wm. Morrow, 1972.

Hamilton, David L. "A Cognitive-Attributional Analysis of Stereotyping." In Leonard Berkowitz, ed., *Advances in Experimental Social Psychology*. Vol. 12. New York: Academic Press, 1979, pp. 53–84.

Hamilton, David L., *Cognitive Processes in Stereotyping and*

Intergroup Behavior. Hillsdale, NJ: Lawrence Erlbaum Associates, 1981.

Hamilton, David L., and Bishop, George D. "Attitudinal and Behavioral Effects of Initial Integration of White Suburban Neighborhoods." *Journal of Social Issues* 32, 2 (1976): 47–67.

Hamilton, Gary. "Pariah Capitalism: A Paradox of Power and Dependence." *Ethnic Groups* 2 (1978): 1–15.

Hammond, John L. "Revival Religion and Antislavery Politics." *American Sociological Review* April (1974): 175–86.

Han, Wan Sang. "Two Conflicting Themes: Common Values Versus Class Differential Values." *American Sociological Review* October (1969): 679–90.

Handlin, Oscar. *The Uprooted*. Boston: Little, Brown, 1951.

Hannerz, Ulf. *Soulside: Inquiries into Ghetto Culture and Community*. New York: Columbia University Press, 1969.

Hansen, Niles. *The Border Economy: Regional Development in the Southwest*. Austin: University of Texas Press, 1981.

Hardin, Garrett. "The Tragedy of the Commons." *Science*, December 13 (1968): 1243–48.

Harding, John, and Proshansky, Harold, Kutner, Bernard, and Chein, Isidor. "Prejudice and Ethnic Relations." In Gardner Lindzey and Elliott Aronson, eds., *The Handbook of Social Psychology*. Reading, MA: Addison-Wesley, 1969, pp. 1–77.

Harding, Vincent. "The Religion of Black Power." In Donald Cutler, ed., *The Religious Situation*. Boston: Beacon Press, 1968, pp. 3–38.

Harding, Vincent. "Religion and Resistance among Anti-Bellum Negroes, 1800–1860." In August Meier and Elliott Rudwick, eds., *The Making of Black America*. New York: Atheneum, 1969, pp. 179–97.

Harding, Vincent. *There Is a River: The Black Struggle for Freedom in America*. New York: Harcourt Brace Jovanovich, 1981.

Harlan, Louis R. *Booker T. Washington*. 2 vols. New York: Oxford University Press, 1972, 1983.

Harrington, Charles C. "Bilingual Education, Social Stratification, and Cultural Pluralism." *Equal Opportunity Review* Summer (1978): 1–4.

Harris, Marvin. "Caste, Class, and Minority." *Social Forces* March (1959): 248–54.

Hartley, Eugene L. *Problems in Prejudice*. New York: King's Crown Press, 1946.

Harwood, Alan. "Mainland Puerto Ricans." in Alan Harwood, ed., *Ethnicity and Medical Care*. Cambridge: Harvard University Press, 1981, pp. 397–487.

Harwood, Edwin, and Hodge, Clair C. "Jobs and the Negro Family: A Reappraisal." In. D. Y. Wilkinson and R. L. Taylor, eds., *The Black Male in America*. Chicago: Nelson-Hall, 1977, pp. 325–28.

Havighurst, Robert J. "Indian Education Since 1960." *Annals of the American Academy of Political and Social Science* March (1978): 13–26.

Havenman, Robert H., ed. *A Decade of Federal Antipoverty Programs: Achievements, Failures, and Lessons*. New York: Academic Process, 1977.

Hawley, Willis D., ed. *Effective School Desegregation*. Beverly Hills, CA: Sage, 1981.

Hayles, Robert, and Perry, Ronald W. "Racial Equality in the American Naval Justice System: An Analysis of Incarceration Differentials." *Ethnic and Racial Studies* January (1981): 44–55.

Hearnshaw, L. S. *Cyril Burt: Psychologist*. London: Hodder and Stoughton, 1979.

Hechinger, Fred M. "Black Studies Come of Age." *The New York Times Magazine*, April 13, 1980, pp. 48ff.

Hechter, Michael. "Response to Cohen: Max Weber on Ethnicity and Ethnic Change." *American Journal of Sociology* March (1976): 1162–68.

Hechter, Michael. *Internal Colonialism: The Celtic Fringe in British National Development, 1536–1966*. Berkeley: University of California Press, 1977.

Heer, David M. "The Prevalence of Black–White Marriages in the United States, 1960 and 1970." *Journal of Marriage and the Family* 36 (1974): 246–58.

Heiss, Jerold. *The Case of the Black Family*. New York: Columbia University Press, 1975.

Heiss, Jerold, and Owens, Susan. "Self-Evaluations of Blacks and Whites." *American Journal of Sociology* September (1972): 360–70.

Henderson, William L., and Ledebur, Larry C. "Programs for the Economic Development of the American Negro Community: The Moderate Approach." In William L. Cash, Jr., and Lucy R. Oliver, eds., *Black Economic Development*. Ann Arbor: University of Michigan Graduate School of Business Administration, 1975, pp. 169–85.

Henry, Diane. "Love and Discipline Spawn Education in the Midst of Despair." *The New York Times*, November 16, 1980, p. 14.

Hentoff, Nat. "The Integrationist" [Kenneth B. Clark]. *The New Yorker*, August 23, 1982, pp. 37–73.

Hermalin, Albert I., and Farley, Reynolds. "The Potential for Residential Integration in Cities and Suburbs: Implications for the Busing Controversy." *American Sociological Review* October (1973): 595–610.

Hermann, Janet Sharp. *The Experiment at David Bend: The Pursuit of a Dream*. Oxford: Oxford University Press, 1981.

Hernández, C. A., Haug, M. J., and Wagner, N. N., eds. *Chicanos: Social and Psychological Perspectives*. St. Louis, MO: Mosby, 1976.

Hernton, Calvin C. *Sex and Racism in America*. New York: Grove, 1968.

Herskovits, Melville J. *The Myth of the Negro Past*. New York: Harper & Brothers, 1941.

Herskovits, M. J. *The Human Factor in Changing Africa*. New York: Knopf, 1962.

Hertzberg, Hazel W. *The Search for an American Indian Identity: Modern Pan-Indian Movements*. Syracuse: Syracuse University Press, 1971.

Hewitt, John P. *Social Stratification and Deviant Behavior*. New York: Random House, 1970.

Heyns, Barbara. *Summer Learning and the Effects of Schooling*. New York: Academic Press, 1978.

Higginbotham, A. Leon Jr. *In the Matter of Color*. Oxford: Oxford University Press, 1978.

Hill, Herbert. "Black Labor in the American Economy." In Patricia W. Romero, ed., *In Black America*. Garden City, NY: United Technical Publications, 1969, pp. 179–215.

Hill, Herbert. *Black Labor and the American Legal System*. Washington, D.C.: Bureau of National Affairs, 1977.

Hill, Herbert, and Greenberg, Jack. *Citizen's Guide to Desegregation*. Boston: Beacon Press, 1955.

Hill, Martha S., and Ponza, Michael. "Poverty and Welfare Dependence Across Generations." *Economic Outlook USA* Summer (1983): 61–64.

Hill, Richard J. "Attitudes and Behavior." In Morris Rosenberg and Ralph H. Turner, eds., *Social Psychology: Sociological Perspectives*. New York: Basic Books, 1981, pp. 347–77.

Hill, Robert A., ed., *Marcus Garvey and the Universal Improvement Association*. Berkeley: University of California Press, 1983.

Himes, Joseph S. *Conflict and Conflict Management.*, Athens, GA: University of Georgia Press, 1980.

Hirsch, Herbert. "Political Scientists and Other Comrades: Academic Myth-Making and Racial Stereotypes." In Rudolph O. de la Garza, Z. Anthony Kruszewski, and Tomas A. Arciniega, eds., *Chicanos and Native Americans*. New York: Prentice-Hall, 1973, pp. 11ff.

Hirsch, N. D. "A Study of Natio-Racial Mental Differences." *Genetic Psychology Monographs* 1 (1926): 394–47.

Hirschman, Charles. "Prior U.S. Residence Among Mexican Immigrants." *Social Forces* June (1978): 1179–1201.

History Task Force, Centro de Estudios Puertorriqueños. *Labor Migration Under Capitalism: The Puerto Rican Experience*. New York: Monthly Review Press, 1979.

Hitler, Adolph. *Mein Kampf*. New York: Reynal and Hitchcock, 1940.

Hodge, Robert W., and Treiman, Donald J. "Occupational Mobility and Attitudes Toward Negroes." *American Sociological Review* February (1966): 93–102.

Hodson, Randy, and Kaufman, Robert L. "Economic Dualism: A Critical Review." *American Sociological Review* December (1982): 727–39.

Hogben, Lancelot. *Genetic Principles in Medicine and Social Science*. New York: Knopf, 1932.

Hoge, Dean R., and Carroll, Jackson W. "Religiosity and Prejudice in Northern and Southern Churches." *Journal for The Scientific Study of Religion*, June (1973): 181–97.

Hope, Keith. "Models of Status Inconsistency and Social Mobility Effects." *American Sociological Review* June (1975): 322–43.

Hope, Richard O. *Racial Strife in the U.S. Military*. New York: Praeger, 1979.

Horowitz, Irving L. *Genocide: State Power and Mass Murder*. New Brunswick, NJ: Transaction Books, 1976.

Horowitz, Irving L., and Liebowitz, Martin. "Social Deviance and Political Marginality: Toward a Redefinition of the Relation Between Sociology and Politics." *Social Problems* Winter (1968): 280–96.

Horowitz, Ruth. "Racial Aspects of Self-Identification in Nursery School Children." *Journal of Psychology* January (1939): 91–99.

Hourwich, Isaac A. *Immigration and Labor*. New York: G. P. Putnam, 1912.

House, James S., and Harkins, Elizabeth B. "Why and When Is Status Inconsistency Stressful?" *American Journal of Sociology* September (1975): 395–412.

Howard, John W., and Rothbart, Myron. "Social Categorization and Memory for In-Group and Out-Group Behavior." *Journal of Personality and Social Psychology* February (1980): 301–10.

Howell, Frank M., and Freese, Wolfgang. "Educational Plans as Motivation or Attitude? Some Additional Evidence." *Social Psychology Quarterly* September (1981): 218–36.

Howton, Louise G. "Genocide and the American Indians." In Bernard Rosenberg, Israel Gerver, and F. William Howton, eds., *Mass Society in Crisis*. 2nd ed. New York: Macmillan, 1971, pp. 144–50.

Huber, Bettina J. "Gutting Affirmative Action—New Policy in Action." *American Sociological Association Footnotes*, December (1981): 2–3.

Hughes, Langston. *Fight for Freedom. The Story of the NAACP*. New York: W. W. Norton, 1962.

Hughes, Langston, ed. *The Book of Negro Humor*. New York: Dodd, Mead, 1965.

Hultkrantz, Ake. *The Religions of the American Indians*. Berkeley: University of California Press, 1979.

Humphreys, Paul, and Berger, Joseph. "Theoretical Consequences of the Status Characteristic Formulation." *American Journal of Sociology* March (1981): 953–83.

Hunt, Janet G. "Assimilation or Marginality? Some School Integration Effects Reconsidered." *Social Forces* December (1977): 604–10.

Hunt, Larry L., and Hunt, Janet G. "Black Religion as Both Opiate and Inspiration of Civil Rights Militance: Putting Marx's Data to the Test." *Social Forces* September (1977): 1–14.

Hunt, Larry L., and Hunt, Janet G. "A Religious Factor in Secular Achievement Among Blacks: The Case of Catholicism." *Social Forces* June (1975): 595–605.

Huxley, Julian S., and Haddon, Alfred C. *We Europeans*. New York: Harper & Row, 1936.

Hyman, Herbert H. *Political Socialization*. New York: Free Press, 1959.

Hyman, Herbert H., and Wright, Charles R. *Education's Lasting Influence on Values*. Chicago: University of Chicago Press, 1979.

Indian Health Service Task Force on Alcoholism. *Alcoholism: A High Priority Health Problem*. HEW Pub. no. (HSM) 73–12002. Washington, D.C.: U.S. Government Printing Office, 1972.

Innis, Roy. "Separatist Economics: A New Social Contract." In William F. Haddad and G. Douglas Pugh, eds. *Black Economic Development*. New York: Prentice-Hall, 1969.

Institute for the Study of Education Policy. *Equal Opportunity for Blacks in U.S. Higher Education: An Assessment*. Washington, D.C.: Howard University Press, 1976.

Irelan, Lola M., Moles, Oliver C., and O'Shea, Robert M. "Ethnicity, Poverty, and Selected Attitudes: A Test of the 'Culture of Poverty' Hypothesis. *Social Forces* June (1969): 405–13.

Irons, E. D. "Black Entrepreneurship: Its Rationale, Its Problems, Its Prospects." *Phylon* March (1976): 18.

Irons, Peter. *Justice at War: The Story of the Japanese Internment Cases*. New York: Oxford University Press, 1984.

Isaac, Larry, and Kelly, William R. "Racial Insurgency, the State, and Welfare Expansion: Local and National Level Evidence from the Postwar United States." *American Journal of Sociology* May (1981): 1348–86.

Isaac, Larry, Mutran, Elizabeth, and Stryker, Sheldon. "Political Protest Orientations Among Black and White Adults." *American Sociological Review* April (1980): 191–213.

Jacobson, Frank N. and Salomon Rettig, "Authoritarianism and Intelligence." *Journal of Social Psychology* September (1959): 213–19.

Jackman, Mary R. "Education and Prejudice or Education and Response-Set?" *American Sociological Review* June (1973): 327–39.

Jackman, Mary R. "Education and Policy Commitment to Racial Education." *American Journal of Political Science* May (1981): 256–69.

Jackman, Mary R., and Jackman, Robert W. "Racial Inequalities in Home Ownership." *Social Forces* June (1980): 1221–34.

Jackman, Mary R., and Muha, Michael J. "Education: Moral Enlightenment or Intellectual Refinement." Manuscript, January, 1983.

Jackman, Mary R., and Senter, Mary S. "Images of Social Groups: Categorical or Qualified?" *Public Opinion Quarterly* Fall (1980): 341–61.

Jackson, Bruce. *Get Your Ass in the Water and Swim Like Me: Narrative Poetry from Black Oral Tradition.* Cambridge: Harvard University Press, 1974.

Jackson, Douglas N., Messick, S. J., and Solley, C. M. "How 'Rigid' is the 'Authoritarian'?" *Journal of Abnormal and Social Psychology* January (1957): 137–40.

Jackson, Elton F., and Curtis, Richard F. "Effects of Vertical Mobility and Status Inconsistency: A Body of Negative Evidence." *American Sociological Review* December (1972): 701–13.

Jackson, Esther Merle. "The American Negro and the Image of the Absurd." *Phylon* Winter (1962): 359–71.

Jackson, Jacquelyne J. "Family Organization and Ideology." In K. S. Miller and R. M. Dreger, eds. *Comparative Studies of Blacks and Whites in the United States.* New York: Seminar Press, 1973.

Jackson, Jesse L. "Give the People a Vision," *The New York Times Magazine,* April 18, 1976, pp. 13, 71–3.

Jacobson, Cardell K. "Separation, Integrationism, and Avoidance Among Black, White, and Latin Adolescents." *Social Forces* June (1977): 1011–27.

Jacobson, Cardell K. "Desegregation Rulings and Public Attitude Changes: White Resistance or Resignation?" *American Journal of Sociology* November (1978): 698–705.

Jacobson, Frank N. and Rettig, Salomon, "Authoritarianism and Intelligence," *Journal of Social Psychology* September (1959): 213–19.

Jaffe, A. J., Cullen, Ruth M., and Boswell, Thomas D. *The Changing Demography of Spanish Americans.* New York: Academic Press, 1980.

Jahn, Julius A., Schmidt, Calvin F., and Schrag, Clarence. "The Measurement of Ecological Segregation." *American Sociological Review* April (1947): 293–303.

Jencks, Christopher, and Riesman, David. "The American Negro College." *Harvard Educational Review* Winter (1967): 3–60.

Jencks, Christopher, et al. *Inequality: A Reassessment of the Effect of Family and Schooling in America.* New York: Basic Books, 1972.

Jencks, Christopher, et al. *Who Gets Ahead? The Determination of Economic Success in America.* New York: Basic Books, 1979.

Jennings, Edward T., Jr. "Racial Insurgency, the State, and Welfare Expansion: A Critical Comment and Reanalysis. *American Journal of Sociology* May (1983): 1220.

Jensen, Arthur R. "How Much Can We Boost IQ and Scholastic Achievement?" In *Environment, Heredity, and Intelligence.* Harvard Educational Review Reprint Series 2, 1969.

Jensen, Arthur R. *Educability and Group Differences.* New York: Methuen, 1973.

Jensen, Arthur R. "Race and Mental Ability." In *Racial Variation in Man* edited by F. J. Ebling. New York: Wiley, 1975, pp. 80–105.

Jensen, Arthur B. *Bias in Mental Testing.* New York: Free Press, 1980.

Johnson, Charles S. *Shadow of the Plantation.* Chicago: University of Chicago Press, 1934.

Johnson, Charles S. *Growing Up in the Black Belt.* Washington, D.C.: American Council on Education, 1941.

Johnson, Charles S. *Patterns of Negro Segregation.* New York: Harper & Row, 1943.

Johnson, Guy B. "Personality in a White–Indian–Negro Community. *American Sociological Review* August (1939): 516–23.

Johnson, Norman J., and Sanday, Peggy R. "Subcultural Variations in an Urban Poor Population. *American Anthropologist* February (1971): 128–43.

Joint Center for Political Studies. *Blacks on the Move: A Decade of Demographic Change.* Washington, D.C.: 1982.

Jones, Faustine C. "External Crosscurrents and Internal Diversity: An Assessment of Black Progress, 1960–1980." *Daedalus,* Spring (1981): 71–101.

Jones, Maldwyn. *American Immigration.* Chicago: University of Chicago Press, 1960.

Jones, Sherman J., and Weathersby, George B. "Financing the Black College." In C. V. Willie and R. R. Edmonds, eds., *Black Colleges in America.* New York: Teachers College Press, 1978, pp. 100–131.

Jordan, Vernon E., and Jacob, John E. Introduction to *The State of Black America.* New York: National Urban League, 1982.

Jorgensen, Joseph G. *The Sun Dance Religion: Power for the Powerless.* Chicago: University of Chicago Press, 1972.

Jorgensen, Joseph G. "Indians and the Metropolis." In Jack O. Waddell and O. Michael Watson, eds., *The American Indian in Modern Society.* Boston: Little, Brown, 1971.

Jorgensen, Joseph G. "Poverty and Work Among American Indians." In H. R. Kaplan, ed., *Minorities and Economic Opportunity.* Itasca, IL: F. E. Peacock, 1977, pp. 170–97.

Juster, Thomas, ed. *Education, Income and Human Behavior.* New York: McGraw-Hill, 1975.

Kahoe, Richard D. "Intrinsic Religion and Authoritarianism: A Differentiated Relationship." *Journal for the Scientific Study of Religion* June (1977): 179–82.

Kallen, David J., ed. *Nutrition, Development, and Social Behavior.* Washington, D.C.: Department of Health, Education, and Welfare, 1973.

Kalodner, Howard I., and Fishman, James J., eds. *Limits of Justice: The Court's Role in School Desegregation.* New York: Ballinger, 1978.

Kamin, Leon. "IQ Tests as Instruments of Oppression—From Immigration Quotas to Welfare." *South Today* July (1973): 6, 10.

Kamin, Leon J. *The Science and Politics of IQ.* New York: Wiley, 1974.

Kann, Robert A. *The Multi-National Empire.* 2 vols. New York: Columbia University Press, 1950.

Kanter, Rosabeth Moss. "Some Effects of Proportions on Group Life: Skewed Sex Ratios and Responses to Token Women." *American Journal of Sociology* March (1977): 965–90.

Kaplan, H. Roy. "The Road Ahead: Prospects for Equality in the World of Work." In H. R. Kaplan, ed., *Minorities and Economic Opportunity.* Itasca, IL: F. E. Peacock, 1977. pp. 279–318.

Kapsis, Robert E. "Black Streetcorner Districts." *Social Forces* June (1979): 1212–28.

Kardiner, Abram, and Ovesey, Lionel. *The Mark of Oppression: A Psychological Study of the American Negro.* New York: W. W. Norton, 1951.

Karlins, Marvin, Coffman, Thomas L., and Walters, Gary. "On the Fading of Social Stereotypes: Studies in Three Generations of College Students." *Journal of Personality and Social Psychology* 13,1 (1969): 1–16.

Karlovic, N. L. "Internal Colonialism in a Marxist Society: The Case of Croatia." *Ethnic and Racial Studies,* vol. 5, July (1982): 276–99.

Kasschau, Patricia L. "Age and Race Discrimination Reported by Middle-Aged and Older Persons." *Social Forces* March (1977): 728–42.

Katz, David, and Braly, Kenneth. "Racial Stereotypes of One Hundred College Students. *Journal of Abnormal and Social Psychology* October-December (1933): 280–90.

Katz, Irwin. *Conflict and Harmony in an Adolescent Interracial Group.* New York: New York University Press, 1955.

Katz, Irwin. "A Critique of Personality Approaches to Negro Performance, With Research Suggestions." *Journal of Social Issues* Summer (1969): 13–28.

Katz, Irwin. *Stigma: A Social Psychological Analysis.* Hillsdale, NJ: Lawrence Erlbaum Associates, 1981.

Katz, Irwin, and Gurin, Patricia, eds. *Race and the Social Sciences.* New York: Basic Books, 1969.

Katz, Phyllis A., ed. *Towards the Elimination of Racism.* New York: Pergamon Press, 1976.

Katz, Phyllis A., and Zalk, S. R. "Doll Preferences: An Index of Racial Attitudes?" *Journal of Educational Psychology* 66 (1974): 663–68.

Katz, Shlomo, ed. *Negro and Jew: An Encounter in America.* New York: MacMillan, 1967.

Keller, Suzanne. "Reply to Borgatta's 'The Concept of Reverse Discrimination and Equality of Opportunity.' " *The American Sociologist* May (1976): 79–82.

Kelley, Dean. *Why Conservative Churches Are Growing.* New York: Harper and Row, 1972.

Kelley, Harold H., and Thibaut, John W. *A Theory of Interdependence.* New York: Wiley, 1978.

Kelly, William R., and Snyder, David. "Racial Violence and Socioeconomic Changes Among Blacks in the United States. *Social Forces* March (1980): 739–60.

Kelman, Herbert C. "A Social-Psychological Model of Political Legitimacy and Its Relevance to Black and White Student Protest Movements." *Psychiatry* May (1970): 225–46.

Kelman, Herbert C. "Violence Without Moral Restraint: Reflections on the Dehumanization of Victims and Victimizers." *Journal of Social Issues* 29,4 (1973): 25–61.

Kennedy, Theodore R. *You Gotta Deal with It: Black Family Relations in a Southern Community.* New York: Oxford, 1980.

Kenworthy, Eldon. "Dilemmas of Participation in Latin America." *Democracy* Winter (1983): 72–83.

Kerckhoff, Alan C., and Jackson, Robert A. "Types of Education and the Occupational Attainments of Young Men." *Social Forces* September (1982): 24–45.

Kerlinger, Fred and Rokeach, Milton. "The Factorial Nature of the F and D Scales." *Journal of Personality and Social Psychology* (1966): 391–99.

Kershaw, David, and Fair, Jerilyn. *The New Jersey Income-Maintenance Experiment.* New York: Academic Press, 1976.

Kiev, Ari. "The Psychiatric Implications of Interracial Marriage." In Irving R. Stuart and L. E. Abt, eds., *Interracial Marriage.* New York: Grossman, 1973.

Killian, Lewis M. "Optimism and Pessimism in Sociological Analysis." *American Sociologist* 6 (1971): 281–86.

Killian, Lewis M., "Black Power and White Reactions: The Revitalization of Race-Thinking in the United States," *Annals of the American Academy of Political and Social Science* March (1981): 42–54.

Killian, Lewis M., and Grigg, Charles M. "Urbanism, Race, and Anomia." *American Journal of Sociology* May (1962): 661–65.

Kilson, Martin. "The Black Experience at Harvard." *The New York Times Magazine*, September 2, 1973, pp. 13ff.

Kinder, Donald R., and Sears, David O. "Prejudice and Politics: Symbolic Racism Versus Racial Threats to the Good Life." *Journal of Personality and Social Psychology* 40, 3 (1981): 414–31.

King, Haitung, and Locke, Frances B. "Chinese in the United States: A Century of Occupational Transition." *International Migration Review* Spring (1980): 15–42.

King, Martin Luther, Jr. *Stride Toward Freedom: The Montgomery Story.* New York: Harper & Row, 1958.

King, Martin Luther, Jr. *Strength to Love.* New York: Harper & Row, 1963. (a)

King, Martin Luther, Jr. *Why We Can't Wait.* New York: Harper & Row, 1963. (b)

King, Martin Luther, Jr. "Letter from a Birmingham Jail." *Liberation* June (1963): 10–16, 23. (c)

King, Martin Luther, Jr. *The Trumpet of Conscience.* New York: Harper & Row, 1968.

King, Robert R. *Minorities Under Communism: Nationalities as a Source of Tension Among Balkan Communist States.* Cambridge: Harvard University Press, 1983.

King, Wayne. "The Violent Rebirth of the Klan." *The New York Times Magazine,* December 7, 1980, pp. 150–60.

Kirscht, John P., and Dillehay, Ronald C. *Dimensions of Authoritarianism: A Review of Research and Theory.* Lexington: University of Kentucky Press, 1967.

Kitagawa, Evelyn M. "New Life-Styles: Marriage Patterns, Living Arrangements, and Fertility Outside Marriage." *Annals of the American Academy of Political and Social Science* January (1981): 1–27.

Kitagawa, Evelyn M., and Hauser, Philip M. *Differential Mortality in the United States: A Study in Socioeconomic Epidemiology.* Cambridge: Harvard University Press, 1973.

Kitano, Harry H. L. *Japanese Americans: The Evolution of a Subculture.* 2nd ed. New York: Prentice-Hall, 1976.

Klineberg, Otto. *Race Differences.* New York: Harper & Brothers, 1935. (a)

Klineberg, Otto. *Negro Intelligence and Selective Migration.* New York: Columbia University Press, 1935. (b)

Klineberg, Otto, ed. *Characteristics of the American Negro.* New York: Harper & Row, 1944.

Kluckhohn, Clyde, Murray, H. A., and Schneider, David, eds. *Personality in Nature, Culture, and Society.* Rev. ed. New York: Knopf, 1953.

Kluegel, James R., and Smith, Eliot R. "Whites' Beliefs About Blacks' Opportunity." *American Sociological Review* August (1982): 518–532.

Kluegel, James R., and Smith, Eliot R. "Affirmative Action Attitudes: Effects of Self-interest, Racial Affect, and Stratification." *Social Forces* March (1983): 797–824.

Knoke, David. "Community and Consistency: The Ethnic Factor in Status Inconsistency." *Social Forces* September (1972): 23–33.

Knowles, Louis L., and Prewitt, Kenneth. *Institutional Racism in America.* New York: Prentice-Hall, 1969.

Knowlton, Clark. "Recommendations for the Solution of Land Tenure Problems Among the Spanish Americans." In R.

Rosaldo, R. A. Calvert, and G. L. Seligmann, eds., *Chicanos: The Revolution of a People*. Washington, D.C.: Winston, 1973, pp. 335–39.

Knutson, Jeanne N. *The Human Basis of the Polity*. Chicago: Aldine, 1972.

Knutson, Jeanne N., ed. *Handbook of Political Psychology*. San Francisco: Jossey-Bass, 1973.

Kofsky, Frank. *Black Nationalism in Music*. San Diego, CA: Pathfinder Press, 1970.

Kohn, Melvin. "Social Class and Parental Values." *American Journal of Sociology* January (1959): 337–51.

Kohn, Melvin L., and Williams, Robin M. Jr. "Situational Patterning in Intergroup Relations." *American Sociological Review* April (1956): 164–74.

Kovar, Mary G. "Mortality of Black Infants in the United States." *Phylon* December (1977): 370–97.

Krech, David, and Crutchfield, Richard S. *Theory of Problems of Social Psychology*. New York: McGraw-Hill, 1948.

Kriesberg, Louis, ed. *Research in Social Movements, Conflicts and Change: A Research Annual* Vol. 2. Greenwich, CT: JAI Press, 1979.

Kronus, Sidney. *The Black Middle Class*. Columbus, OH: Charles E. Merrill, 1971.

Krueger, D. W. "The Effect of Urban-Industrial Values on the Indian Life Style." In de le Garza, R. O., Kruszewski, Z. A., and Arciniega, T. A., eds. *Chicanos and Native Americans*. New York: Prentice-Hall, 1973.

Krug, Robert E. "An Analysis of the F Scale: I. Item Factor Analysis." *Journal of Social Psychology* April (1961): 285–91.

Krug, Robert E., and Moyer, K. E. "An Analysis of the F Scale: II. Relationship to Standardized Personality Inventories." *Journal of Social Psychology* April (1961): 293–301.

Kuper, Leo. *Passive Resistance in South Africa*. New Haven: Yale University Press, 1957.

Kuper, Leo. *Race, Class, and Power: Ideology and Revolutionary Change in Plural Societies*. Chicago: Aldine, 1974.

Kuper, Leo. *The Pity of It All*. Minneapolis: University of Minnesota Press, 1977.

Kuper, Leo. "Theories of Genocide." *Ethnic and Racial Studies* July (1981): 320–33.

Kuper, Leo. *Genocide: Its Political Use in the Twentieth Century*. New Haven: Yale University Press, 1982.

Kuper, Leo, and Smith, M. G., eds. *Pluralism in Africa*. Berkeley: University of California Press, 1969.

Kurokawa, Minako. "Mutual Perceptions of Racial Images: White, Black, and Japanese Americans." *Journal of Social Issues*: 27,4 (1971): 213–35.

LaBarre, Weston. *The Ghost Dance: The Origins of Religion*. New York: Dell, 1972.

Labov, William. *Language in the Inner City: Studies in the Black English Vernacular*. Philadelphia: University of Pennsylvania Press, 1972.

Lacy, William B., and Middleton, Ernest. "Are Educators Racially Prejudiced? A Cross-Occupational Comparison of Attitudes." *Sociological Focus* January (1981): 87–95.

Ladner, Joyce A. *Tomorrow's Tomorrow: The Black Woman*. New York: Doubleday, 1971.

Ladner, Joyce A. *The Death of White Sociology*. New York: Random House, 1973.

Ladner, Joyce A. *Adopting Across Racial Boundaries*. New York: Anchor Press, 1977.

Lampe, Philip E. "Ethnic Labels: Naming or Name Calling?" *Ethnic and Racial Studies* October (1982): 542–48.

Landry, Bart. "The Economic Position of Black Americans." In H. Roy Kaplan, ed. *American Minorities and Economic Opportunities*. Itasca, IL: F. E. Peacock, 1977, pp. 109–47.

Lane, Robert E. *Political Life: Why People Get Involved in Politics*. New York: Free Press, 1959.

Lanternari, Vittorio. "Ethnocentrism and Ideology." *Ethnic and Racial Studies* January (1980): 52–67.

La Ruffa, Anthony. "Interracial Marriage Among Puerto Ricans." In I. R. Stuart and L. E. Abt, eds., *Interracial Marriage*. New York: Grossman, 1975.

Lasch, Christopher. *The Agony of the American Left*. New York: Random House, 1969.

Lasswell, Harold. *Psychopathology and Politics*. Chicago: University of Chicago Press, 1930.

Laue, James H. "A Contemporary Revitalization Movement in American Race Relations: The 'Black Muslims.' " *Social Forces* March (1964): 315–23.

Laughlin, William S. "Race: A Population Concept." *Eugenics Quarterly* 13 (1966): 326–40.

Laumann, Edward O., and Segal, David R. "Status Inconsistency and Ethnoreligious Group Membership as Determinants of Social Participation and Political Attitudes." *American Journal of Sociology* July (1971): 36–71.

Lavin, David, Alba, Richard D., and Silberstein, Richard A. *Right Versus Privilege: The Open Admissions Experiment at the City University of New York*. New York: Free Press, 1981.

Lazarsfeld, Paul F., and Stanton, Frank N., eds. *Communications Research, 1948–49*. New York: Harper and Row, 1949.

Leach, Edmund R. "Cultural Components in the Concept of Race." In F. J. Ebling, ed., *Racial Variation in Man*. New York: Wiley, 1975, pp. 25–30.

Lecky, Robert S., and Wright, E. Elliot. *Black Manifesto: Religion, Racism and Reparations*. New York: Sheed and Ward, 1970.

Lefton, Mark. "Race, Expressions, and Anomia." *Social Forces* March (1968): 347–52.

Lehner, J. Christopher, Jr. *A Losing Battle: The Decline in Black Participation in Graduate and Professional Education*. Washington, D.C.: National Advisory Committee on Black Higher Education and Black Colleges and Universities, October, 1980.

Lehrman, R. L. *Race, Evolution, and Mankind*. New York: Basic Books, 1966.

Leifer, Eric M. "Competing Models of Political Mobilization: The Role of Ethnic Ties." *American Journal of Sociology* July (1981: 23–47.

Leigh, Wilhelmina. "Changing Trends in Housing." In *The State of Black America, 1980*. New York: National Urban League, 1981, pp. 149–97.

Leighton, Alexander Hamilton. *The Governing of Men*. Princeton: Princeton University Press, 1945.

Lenski, Gerhard E. "Status Crystallization: A Non-Vertical Dimension of Social Status." *American Sociological Review* August (1954): 405–12.

Lenski, Gerhard. *Power and Privilege: A Theory of Social Stratification*. New York: McGraw-Hill, 1966.

Lenski, Gerhard. "Marxist Experiments in Destratification: An Appraisal." *Social Forces* December (1978): 364–83.

Lenski, Gerhard E., and Leggett, John C. "Caste, Class, and Deference in the Research Interview." *American Journal of Sociology* March (1960): 463–67.

Léons, M. B. "Race, Ethnicity, and Political Mobilization in the Andes." *American Ethnologist* August (1978): 484–94.

Lernoux, Penny. *Cry of the People: The Struggle for Human Rights in Latin America—The Catholic Church in Conflict with U.S. Policy.* New York: Penguin, 1982.

Lester, Julius. *Look out Whitey, Black Power's Gon' Get Your Mama.* New York: Dial Press, 1968.

Lester, Julius. *Search for the New Land.* New York: Dial Press, 1969.

Levi, Ken, ed. *Violence and Religious Commitment: Implications of Jim Jones's People's Temple Movement.* State College: Pennsylvania State University Press, 1982.

Levine, Daniel H. *Religion and Politics in Latin America.* Princeton: Princeton University Press, 1981.

Levine, Gene M., and Rhodes, Robert C. *The Japanese-American Community: A Three Generation Study.* New York: Praeger, 1981.

Levine, R. A., and Campbell, Donald T. *Ethnocentrism: Theories of Conflict, Ethnic Attitudes and Group Behavior.* New York: Wiley, 1972.

Levine, Stuart, and Lurie, Nancy Oestreich, eds. *The American Indian Today.* New York: Penguin, 1970.

Levitan, Sar A., and Johnston, William B. *Indian Giving: Federal Programs for Native Americans.* Baltimore: Johns Hopkins University Press, 1975.

Levitan, Sar A., Johnston, William B., and Taggart, Robert. *Still a Dream: The Changing Status of Blacks Since 1960.* Cambridge: Harvard University Press, 1975.

Levy, Jerrold E. *Indian Drinking: Navajo Practices and Anglo-American Theories.* New York: Wiley, 1974.

Lewin, Kurt. *A Dynamic Theory of Personality.* New York: McGraw-Hill, 1935.

Lewin, Kurt. *Resolving Social Conflicts.* New York: Harper & Row, 1948.

Lewinson, Edwin R. *Black Politics in New York City.* Boston: Twayne, 1974.

Lewis, Anthony. *Portrait of a Decade: The Second American Revolution.* New York: Random House, 1964.

Lewis, David L. *King: A Critical Biography.* New York: Praeger, 1970.

Lewis, Hylan. " 'Tough' Aspects of Higher Education." *Phylon* Fourth Quarter (1949): 359–61.

Lewis, Michael. *The Culture of Inequality.* Amherst: University of Massachusetts Press, 1978.

Lewis, Oscar. *Five Families: Mexican Case Studies in the Culture of Poverty.* New York: Basic Books, 1959.

Lewis, Oscar. *The Children of Sanchez.* New York: Random House, 1961.

Lewis, Oscar. "The Culture of Poverty." *Scientific American* October 1966(a): 19–25.

Lewis, Oscar. *La Vida: A Puerto Rican Family in the Culture of Poverty.* New York: Random House, 1966b.

Lewis, W. Arthur. "The Road to the Top is Through Higher Education—Not Black Studies." *The New York Times Magazine,* May 11, 1969, pp. 34–5, 39.

Lewy, Guenter. *Religion and Revolution.* Oxford: Oxford University Press, 1974.

Li, Peter S. *Occupation Mobility and Kinship Assistance: A Study of Chinese Immigrants in Chicago.* San Francisco: R & E Research Associates, 1978.

Lieberson, Stanley. "A Societal Theory of Race and Ethnic Relations." *American Sociological Review* December (1961): 902–10.

Lieberson, Stanley. *A Piece of the Pie: Blacks and White Immigrants Since 1880.* Berkeley: University of California Press, 1980.

Lieberson, Stanley. "Stereotypes: Their Consequences for Race and Ethnic Interaction." In Robert Hauser, David Mechanic, Archibald Haller, and Taissa Hauser, eds., *Social Structure and Behavior: Essays in Honor of William Hamilton Sewell.* New York: Academic Press, 1981, pp. 47–68.

Liebow, Elliot. *Tally's Corner: A Study of Negro Streetcorner Men.* Boston: Little, Brown, 1967.

Lifton, Betty Jean. "The Cruel Legacy: The Children Our GIs Left Behind in Asia." *Saturday Review* November 29, 1975, pp. 10–11, 59.

Light, Ivan. *Ethnic Enterprise in America.* Berkeley: University of California Press, 1972.

Light, Ivan. "Numbers Gambling Among Blacks: A Financial Institution." *American Sociological Review* December (1977): 892–904.

Lincoln, C. Eric. *The Black Muslims in America.* Boston: Beacon Press, 1961; rev. ed., 1973.

Lincoln, C. Eric, ed. *Martin Luther King, Jr.* New York: Hill and Wang, 1970.

Lincoln, C. Eric, ed. *The Black Experience in Religion.* New York: Anchor Press, 1974.

Lincoln, C. Eric, and Mamiya, Lawrence H. "Daddy Jones and Father Divine: The Cult as Political Religion." *Religion in Life* Spring (1980): 6–23.

Lind, Andrew W., eds. *Race Relations in World Perspective.* Honolulu: University of Hawaii Press, 1955.

Linn, Lawrence S. "Verbal Attitudes and Overt Behavior: A Study of Racial Discrimination." *Social Forces* March (1965): 353–64.

Linton, Ralph, ed. *Acculturation in Seven American Indian Tribes.* New York: Appleton-Century, 1940.

Linton, Ralph, ed. *The Science of Man in the World Crisis.* New York: Columbia University Press, 1945.

Lipset, Seymour M. "Democracy and Working-Class Authoritarianism." *American Sociological Review* August (1959): 482–501.

Lipset, Seymour M., and Raab, Earl. *The Politics of Unreason.* New York: Harper Torchbooks, 1970.

Lipset, Seymour M., and Schneider, William. *From Discrimination to Affirmative Action: Public Attitudes, 1935–77.* Unpublished manuscript, 1978.

Lipsitz, Lewis. "Working-Class Authoritarianism: A Re-Evaluation." *American Sociological Review* February (1965): 103–9.

Lipsky, Michael. "Protest as a Political Resource." *American Political Science Review* December (1968): 1144–58.

Lipsky, Michael. *Protest in City Politics.* New York: Rand McNally, 1970.

Liu, William T., Lamanna, Maryanne, and Murata, Alice K. *Transition to Nowhere: Vietnamese Refugees in America.* New York: Charter House Publishing, 1981.

Locke, Alain, and Stern, B. J., eds. *When Peoples Meet.* Rev. ed. New York: Hines, Hayden & Eldridge, 1946.

Loehlin, John C., Lindzey, Gardner, and Spuhler, J. N. *Race Differences in Intelligence.* San Francisco: W. H. Freeman, 1975.

Loescher, F. S. *The Protestant Church and the Negro*. New York: Association Press, 1948.

Logan, John R. and Schneider, Mark. "Racial Segregation and Racial Change in American Suburbs, 1970–1980." *American Journal of Sociology* January (1984): 874–888.

Logan, Rayford W., and Winston, Michael R., eds. *Dictionary of American Negro Biography*. New York: W. W. Norton, 1983.

Lomax, Louis E. *The Negro Revolt*. New York: Harper and Row, 1962.

Lomax, Louis E. "The American Negro's New Comedy Act." *Harper's* June (1961): 41–6.

Long, Larry H. "Poverty Status and Receipt of Welfare Among Migrants and Nonmigrants in Large Cities." *American Sociological Review* February (1974): 46–56.

Long, Larry, and DeArc, Diana. "The Suburbanization of Blacks." *American Demographics* September (1981): 16–21, 44.

Longshore, Douglas. "Race Composition and White Hostility: A Research Note on the Problem of Control in Desegregated Schools." *Social Forces* September (1982): 73–8.

Lopez, Adalberto, and Petras, James, eds. *Puerto Rico and Puerto Ricans: Studies in History and Society*. Cambridge, MA: Schenkman, 1974.

López, David E. "The Social Consequences of Chicano Home/School Bilingualism." *Social Problems* December (1976): 234–46.

Lorenz, Gerda. "Aspirations of Low-Income Blacks and Whites: A Case of Reference Group Processes." *American Journal of Sociology* September (1972): 371–98.

Louden, Delroy. "A Comparative Study of Self-Concepts Among Minority and Majority Group Adolescents in English Multi-Racial Schools." *Ethnic and Racial Studies* April (1981): 153–74.

Ludwig, Ed, and Santibañez, James. *The Chicanos: Mexican American Voices*. New York: Penguin, 1971.

Lurie, Nancy Oestreich. "The Indian Claims Commission," *Annals of the American Academy of Political and Social Science* March (1978): 97–110.

Lutterman, Kenneth G., and Middleton, Russell. "Authoritarianism, Anomia, and Prejudice." *Social Forces* June (1970): 485–92.

Lyman, Stanford M. *Chinese Americans*. New York: Random House, 1974.

Lyman, Stanford M. *The Black American in Sociological Thought*. New York: Putnam, 1972.

Macartney, C. A. *National States and National Minorities*. Oxford: Oxford University Press, 1934.

MacCrone, I.D. *Race Attitudes in South Africa*. Oxford: Oxford University Press, 1937.

MacGregor, Gordon. *Warriors Without Weapons*. Chicago: University of Chicago Press, 1946.

Macisco, John J. "Assimilation of the Puerto Ricans on the Mainland." In F. R. Tovar, ed., *Handbook of the Puerto Rican Community*. New York: Plus Ultra Educational Publications, 1970.

MacIver, R. M. *The More Perfect Union*. New York: Macmillan, 1948.

MacIver, R. M., ed. *Discrimination and National Welfare*. New York: Institute for Religious and Social Studies, Harper & Row, 1949.

Mackie, Marlene. "Arriving at 'Truth' by Definition: The Case of Stereotype Inaccuracy." *Social Problems* Spring (1973): 431–47.

MacKinnon, William J., and Centers, Richard. "Authoritarianism and Urban Stratification." *American Journal of Sociology* May (1956): 610–20.

Madsen, William. *Mexican-Americans of South Texas*. 2nd ed. New York: Holt, Rinehart, and Winston, 1973.

Maguire, Daniel C. *A New American Justice*. New York: Doubleday, 1980.

Maher, Brendan. "Personality, Problem Solving, and the Einstellung Effect." *Journal of Abnormal and Social Psychology* January (1957): 70–4.

Mail, Patricia D. "Hippocrates Was a Medicine Man: The Health Care of Native Americans in the Twentieth Century." *Annals of the American Academy of Political and Social Science* March (1978): 40–49.

Malcom X with Alex Haley. *The Autobiography of Malcolm X*. New York: Grove Press, 1966.

Malinowski, Bronislaw. *Myth in Primitive Society*. New York: W. W. Norton, 1926.

Malof, Milton, and Lott, Albert J. "Ethnocentrism and the Acceptance of Negro Support in a Group Pressure Situation." *Journal of Abnormal and Social Psychology* October (1962): 254–58.

Mamiya, Lawrence H. "From Black Muslim to Bilalian: The Evolution of a Movement." *Journal for the Scientific Study of Religion* June (1982): 138–52.

Mangum, C. S., Jr. *The Legal Status of the Negro*. Chapel Hill: University of North Carolina Press, 1940.

Mangum, Garth L., and Seninger, Stephen F. *Coming of Age in the Ghetto*. Baltimore: Johns Hopkins University Press, 1978.

Mannheim, Karl. *Ideology and Utopia*. New York: Harcourt, Brace & World, 1936.

Mapp, Edward. *Puerto Rican Perspectives*. Metuchen, NJ: The Scarecrow Press, 1974.

Marks, Carole. "Split Labor Markets and Black-White Relations, 1865–1920." *Phylon* Winter (1981): 293–308.

Marshall, Ray. "The Economics of Racial Discrimination: A Survey." *Journal of Economic Literature* September (1974): 849–71.

Martin, Elmer P., and Martin, Joanne M. *The Black Extended Family*. Chicago: University of Chicago Press, 1978.

Martin, James G. *The Tolerant Personality*. Detroit: Wayne State University Press, 1964.

Martin, Philip L. *Guestworker Programs: Lessons from Europe*, U.S. Department of Labor, Bureau of International Labor Affairs. Washington, D.C.: U.S. Government Printing Office, 1980.

Marvick, Dwaine, ed. *Harold D. Lasswell on Political Sociology*. Chicago: University of Chicago Press, 1977.

Martire, Gregory, and Clark, Ruth. *Anti-Semitism in the United States: A Study of Prejudice in the 1980s*. New York: Praeger, 1982.

Marx, Gary. *Protest and Prejudice: A Study of Belief in the Black Community*. New York: Harper and Row, 1967. (a)

Marx, Gary. "Religion: Opiate or Inspiration of Civil Rights Militancy Among Negroes. *American Sociological Review* February (1967): 64–72. (b)

Marx, Gary T. "Civil Disorder and the Agents of Social Control." *Journal of Social Issues* 26 (1970): 19–57.

Marx, Gary, ed. *Racial Conflict: Tension and Change in American Society*. Boston: Little, Brown, 1971.

Marx, Karl. *The Eighteenth Brumaire of Louis Napoleon.* New York: International Publications, 1963.

Massey, Douglas S. "Effects of Socioeconomic Factors on the Residential Segregation of Blacks and Spanish Americans in U.S. Urbanized Areas." *American Sociological Review* December (1979): 1015–22.

Massey, Douglas S. "Dimensions of the New Immigration to the United States and the Prospects for Assimilation." In Ralph H. Turner and James F. Short, Jr., eds., *Annual Review of Sociology* Annual Reviews 7 (1981): 57–85.

Massey, Stephen J. "Rethinking Affirmative Action." *Social Theory and Practice.* Spring (1981): 21–47.

Masters, Stanley H. *Black–White Income Differentials: Empirical Studies and Policy Implications.* Institute for Research on Poverty Monograph Series. New York: Academic Press, 1975.

Mathiessen, Peter. *Sal Si Puedes: Cesar Chavez and the New American Revolution.* New York: Random House, 1970.

Mathis, Arthur. "Contrasting Approaches to the Study of Black Families." *Journal of Marriage and the Family* November (1978): 668–72.

Matthews, Donald R., and Prothro, James W. *Negroes and the New Southern Politics.* New York: Harcourt, Brace Jovanovich, 1966.

Matza, David, and Sykes, Gresham. "Juvenile Delinquency and Subterranean Values." *American Sociological Review* October (1961): 712–19.

Mayer, Kurt B. "Intra-European Migration During the Past Twenty Years." *International Migration Review* Winter (1975): 441–47.

Maykovich, Minako Kurokawa. "Reciprocity in Racial Stereotypes: White, Black, and Yellow." *American Journal of Sociology* March (1972): 876–97.

Mays, Benjamin E. *The Negro's God As Reflected in His Literature.* New York: Chapman and Grimes, 1938.

Mays, Benjamin E. *Seeking to Be Christian in Race Relations.* New York: Friendship Press, 1957.

McAdoo, Harriette Pipes. "Black Kinship." *Psychology Today* May (1979): 67ff.

McBay, Shirley M. "Black Students in the Sciences: A Look at Spelman College." In C. V. Willie and R. R. Edmonds, eds. *Black Colleges in America.* New York: Teachers College Press, 1978, pp. 216–28.

McCall, George J. "Symbiosis: The Case of Hoodoo and the Numbers Racket." *Social Problems* Spring (1963): 361–71.

McCarthy, John D., and Yancey, William L. "Uncle Tom and Mr. Charlie: Metaphysical Pathos in the Study of Racism and Personal Disorganization." *American Journal of Sociology* January (1971a): 648–72.

McCarthy, John D., and Yancey, William L. "Reply to Washington." *American Journal of Sociology* November (1971b): 590–91.

McCarthy, John D., and Zald, Mayer N. "Resource Mobilization and Social Movements: A Partial Theory." *American Journal of Sociology* May (1977): 1212–41.

McClendon, McKee J., and Pestello, Fred P. "Self-Interest and Public Policy Attitude Formation: Busing for School Desegregation." *Sociological Focus* January (1983): 1–12.

McClosky, Herbert, and Schaar, John H. "Psychological Dimensions of Anomy." *American Sociological Review* February (1965): 14–40.

McConahay, John B. "The Effects of School Desegregation upon Student Racial Attitudes and Behavior: A Critical Review of the Literature and a Prolegomenon to Future Research." *Law and Contemporary Problems* 42,3 (1978): 77–107.

McConahay, John B., and Hough, Joseph C., Jr. "Symbolic Racism." *Journal of Social Issues* Spring (1976): 23–45.

McCormack, Wayne, ed. *The Bakke Decision: Implications for Higher Education Admissions.* Washington, D.C.: American Council of Education and the American Association of American Law Schools, 1978.

McDermott, R. P. "Social Relations as Contexts for Learning in School." *Harvard Educational Review* May (1977): 198–213.

McDonald, J. R. "Labour Immigration into France 1946–65." *Annals of the Association of American Geographers* 59 (1969): 116–34.

McKay, Claude. *Harlem Shadows.* New York: Harcourt, Brace, 1922.

McKay, Claude. *Selected Poems of Claude McKay.* Boston: Twayne, 1953.

McKee, James B. "Community Power and Strategies in Race Relations." *Social Problems* Winter (1958–59): 195–203.

McQueen, Albert J. "The Adaptations of Urban Black Families: Trends, Problems, Issues." In David Reiss and Howard A. Hoffman, eds. *The American Family.* New York: Plenum Press, 1979, pp. 79–101.

McWilliams, Carey. *Prejudice—Japanese-Americans: Symbols of Racial Intolerance.* Boston: Little, Brown, 1944.

McWilliams, Carey. *A Mask for Privilege: Anti-Semitism in America.* Boston: Little, Brown, 1948.

McWilliams, Carey. *Brothers Under the Skin.* Rev. ed. Boston: Little, Brown, 1951.

Meier, August. "Black Sociologists in White America: A Review of *Black Sociologists: Historical and Contemporary Perspectives* by James E. Blackwell and Morris Janowitz. *Social Forces* September (1977): 259–70.

Meier, August, and Rudwick, Elliott. *Along the Color Line: Explorations in the Black Experience.* Urbana: University of Illinois Press, 1976.

Meier, August, Rudwick, Elliott, and Broderick, Frances L. eds. *Black Protest Thought in the Twentieth Century.* 2nd ed. New York: Bobbs-Merrill, 1971.

Meier, Matt S., and Rivera, F. *The Chicanos.* New York: Hill and Wang, 1972.

Mendez, Garry A. "Crime: A Major Problem in Black America." *The State of Black America, 1980.* New York: National Urban League, 1981, pp. 219–33.

Mercer, Jane R. *Labelling the Mentally Retarded.* Berkeley: University of California Press, 1973.

Merton, Robert K. *Social Theory and Social Structure.* Rev. and enlarged ed. New York: Free Press, 1968.

Merton, Robert K. "Insiders and Outsiders: A Chapter in the Sociology of Knowledge." *American Journal of Sociology* July (1972): 9–47.

Merton, Robert K., and Nisbet, Robert A., eds. *Contemporary Social Problems.* 2nd ed. New York: Harcourt, Brace, and World, 1966.

Messick, Samuel, and Jackson, Douglas. "Authoritarianism or Acquiescence in Bass's Data." *Journal of Abnormal and Social Psychology* May (1957): 424–27.

Metropolitan Applied Research Center, *Fact Book on Pupil Transportation,* New York: rev. ed. 1972, p. 10.

Metz, Mary Haywood. *Classrooms and Corridors: The Crisis of Authority in Desegregated Secondary Schools.* Berkeley: University of California Press, 1978.

Metzger, L. Paul. "American Sociology and Black Assimilation: Conflicting Perspectives." *American Journal of Sociology* January (1971): 627–47 (a)

Metzger, L. Paul. "Reply to Goldstein and Washington by Metzger." *American Journal of Sociology* November (1971): 587–90. (b)

Middleton, Russell. "Ethnic Prejudice and Susceptibility to Persuasion." *American Sociological Review* October (1960): 679–86.

Middleton, Russell. "Regional Differences in Prejudice." *American Sociological Review* February (1976): 94–117.

Middleton, Russell, and Moland, John. "Humor in Negro and White Subcultures: A Study of Jokes among University Students." *American Sociological Review* February (1959): 61–9.

Midgley, Elizabeth. "Immigrants: Whose Huddled Masses?" *Atlantic Monthly* April (1978): 6–26.

Miles, Robert, and Phizacklea, Annie, eds. *Racism and Political Action in Britain*. London: Routledge and Kegan Paul, 1979.

Miller, Arthur G. ed., *In the Eye of the Beholder: Contemporary Issues in Stereotyping*. New York: Praeger, 1982.

Miller, Frank C., "Involvement in an Urban University." In J. O. Waddell and O. M. Watson, eds. *The American Indian in Modern Society*. Boston: Little, Brown, 1971.

Miller, Kent S., and Dreger, Ralph, eds. *Comparative Studies of Blacks and Whites in the United States*. New York: Seminar Press, 1973.

Miller, Roy A., Jr. "Are Familists Amoral? A Test of Banfield's Amoral Familism Hypothesis in a South Italian Village." *American Ethnologist* August (1974): 515–35.

Miller, S. M., and Riessman, Frank. "Working-class Authoritarianism: A Critique of Lipset." *British Journal of Sociology* 12 (1961): 263–76.

Miller, Walter B. "Lower Class Culture as a Generating Milieu of Gang Delinquency." *Journal of Social Issues* 14,3 (1958): 5–19.

Mills, Nicolaus, ed. *Busing U.S.A.* New York: Teachers College Press, 1979.

Milner, Christina and Richard. *Black Players*. Boston: Little, Brown, 1972.

Milosz, Czeslaw. *The Captive Mind*. New York: Knopf, 1953.

Mindel, Charles H., and Habenstein, Robert W. *Ethnic Families in America*. New York: Elsevier, 1976.

Mirandé, Alfredo, and Enríquez, Evangelina. *La Chicana: The Mexican-American Woman*. Chicago: University of Chicago Press, 1979.

Mirowsky, John, and Ross, Catherine E. "Protest Group Success: The Impact of Group Characteristics, Social Control, and Context." *Sociological Focus* August (1981): 177–92.

Miyamoto, Frank. "The Forced Evacuation of the Japanese Minority during World War II." *Journal of Social Issues* 29,2 (1973): 11–31.

Molnar, Stephen. *Races, Types, and Ethnic Groups*. New York: Prentice-Hall, 1975.

Molotch, Harvey. "Racial Integration in a Transition Community." *American Sociological Review* December (1969): 878–93.

Monahan, Thomas P. "Some Dimensions of Interreligious Marriages in Indiana, 1962–67." *Social Forces* December (1973): 195–203.

Monro, John U. "Teaching and Learning English." In C. V. Willie and R. R. Edmonds, eds. *Black Colleges in America*. New York: Teachers College Press, 1978, pp. 235–60.

Montagu, Ashley. *An Introduction to Physical Anthropology*. Springfield, IL: Charles C. Thomas, 3rd ed. 1960.

Montagu, Ashley. "The Concept of Race." *American Anthropologist* October (1962): 919–28.

Montagu, Ashley. "Sociogenic Brain Damage." *American Anthropologist* October (1972): 1045–61. (a)

Montagu, Ashley. *Statement on Race*. 3rd ed. Oxford: Oxford University Press, 1972. (b)

Montagu, Ashley. *Man's Most Dangerous Myth: The Fallacy of Race*. 5th ed. Oxford: Oxford University Press, 1974.

Montagu, Ashley, ed. *Race and IQ*. Oxford: Oxford University Press, 1975.

Montero, Darrel. *Japanese Americans: Changing Patterns of Ethnic Affiliation over Three Generations*. Boulder, CO: Westview Press, 1980.

Montero, Darrel, and Levine, Gene M., issue eds. "Research Among Racial and Cultural Minorities: Problems, Prospects, and Pitfalls." *Journal of Social Issues* 33,4 (1977).

Mooney, James. *The Ghost Dance and the Sioux Outbreak of 1890*. Chicago: University of Chicago Press, 1965.

Moore, Jesse Thomas, Jr. *A Search for Equality: NUL, 1910–1961*. State College: Pennsylvania State University Press, 1981.

Moore, Joan W. *Mexican Americans*. New York: Prentice-Hall, 1970.

Moore, Joan W. "Colonialism: The Case of the Mexican American." In *Introduction to Chicano Studies* edited by L. I. Duran and R. Bernard. New York: Macmillan, 1973a.

Moore, Joan W. "Some Constraints on Sociological Knowledge: Academics and Research Concerning Minorities," *Social Problems* Summer (1973b): 65–77.

Moore, Joan W. "American Minorities and 'New Nation' Perspectives." *Pacific Sociological Review*, October (1976): 447–67.

Moore, Joan W. *Homeboys: Gangs, Drugs, and Prison in the Barrios of Los Angeles*. Philadelphia: Temple University Press, 1978.

Moore, Joan W. "Minorities in the American Class System." *Daedalus* Spring (1981): 275–299.

Moore, Joan W., and Pachon, Harry. *Mexican Americans*. 2nd ed. New York: Prentice-Hall, 1976.

Morales, A. "Police Deployment Theories and the Mexican American Community." In V. Romano, ed. *Voices*. Berkeley: Quinto Sol Books, 1971, pp. 177–78.

Morton, N. E., Chung, C. S., and Mi, M. *Genetics of Interracial Crosses in Hawaii*. White Plains, NY: Karger, 1967.

Moynihan, Daniel P. *The Negro Family: The Case for National Action*. Washington, D.C.: U.S. Department of Labor, 1965.

Mughan, Anthony, and McAllister, Ian. "The Mobilization of the Ethnic Vote: A Thesis with Some Scottish and Welsh Evidence," *Ethnic and Racial Studies* April (1981): 189–204.

Muhammad, Wallace Deen. *As the Light Shineth from the East*. Cedarhurst, NY: WMD Publications, 1980.

Mukabe, Tomoko. "The Theory of the Split Labor Market: A Comparison of the Japanese Experience in Brazil and Canada." *Social Forces* March (1981): 786–809.

Muraskin, William. "The Moral Basis of a Backward Sociologist: Edward Banfield, the Italians, and the Italian-Americans." *American Journal of Sociology* May (1974): 1484–96.

Murguía, Edward. *Assimilation, Colonialism, and the Mexican American People.* Austin: University of Texas Press, 1975.

Murguía, Edward. *Chicano Intermarriage: A Theoretical and Empirical Study.* San Antonio, TX: Trinity University Press, 1982.

Murillo, Nathan. "The Mexican American Family." In C. A. Hernández, M. J. Haug, and N. N. Wagner, eds. *Chicanos: Social and Psychological Perspectives.* St. Louis: Mosby, 1976, pp. 15–24.

Musgrove, Frank. *Education and Anthropology: Other Cultures and the Teacher.* New York: Wiley, 1982.

Mussen, Paul H. "Some Personality and Social Factors Related to Changes in Children's Attitudes Toward Negroes. *Journal of Abnormal and Social Psychology* July (1950): 423–41.

Myers, Alonzo F. "The Colleges for Negroes." *The Survey* May (1950): 234–36.

Myrdal, Gunnar, with the assistance of Richard Sterner and Arnold Rose. *An American Dilemma: The Negro Problem and Modern Democracy.* 2 vols. New York: Harper & Row, 1944.

Naison, Mark. *Communists in Harlem During the Depression.* Urbana: University of Illinois Press, 1983.

Napper, George. *Blacker Than Thou: The Struggle for Campus Unity.* Grand Rapids, MI: William B. Eerdmans, 1973.

National Advisory Commission on Civil Disorders. *Report.* New York: Bantam Books, 1968.

National Committee Against Discrimination in Housing. *Trends in Housing.* Washington, D.C.: August, 1981.

National Commission on the Causes and Prevention of Violence. *To Establish Justice, To Insure Domestic Tranquility.* Washington, D.C.: U.S. Government Printing Office, 1970.

National Opinion Research Center. *General Social Surveys, 1972–1980: Cumulative Codebooks.* Chicago: Norc, 1982.

National Urban League. *The State of Black America, 1979.* New York: January, 1980.

National Urban League. *The State of Black America, 1980.* New York: January, 1981.

National Urban League. *The State of Black America, 1982.* New York: January, 1982.

Negrón, Frank. "Affirmative Action in Higher Education." In Edward Mapp, ed., *Puerto Rican Perspectives.* Metuchen, NJ: Scarecrow Press, 1974.

Neihardt, John G. *Black Elk Speaks: Being the Life Story of a Holy Man of the Oglala Sioux,* Lincoln: University of Nebraska Press, 1979.

Nelsen, Hart M., and Nelsen, Anne K. *Black Church in the Sixties.* Lexington: University of Kentucky Press, 1975.

Nelsen, Hart M., Madron, Thomas W., and Yokley, Raytha L. "Black Religion's Promethean Motif: Orthodoxy and Militancy." *American Journal of Sociology* July (1975): 139–46.

Nelsen, Hart M., Yokley, Raytha L., and Madron, Thomas W. "Ministerial Roles and Social Actionist Stance: Protestant Clergy and Protest in the Sixties." *American Sociological Review* June (1973): 375–86.

Newcomb, Theodore, and Hartley, Eugene. *Readings in Social Psychology.* New York: Holt, Rinehart & Winston, 1947.

Newell, R. C. "Giving Good Weight to Black English." *Perspectives* Spring (1981): 25–9.

Nichols, Lee. *Breakthrough on the Color Front.* New York: Random House, 1954.

Nieburg, H. L. "Uses of Violence." *Journal of Conflict Resolution* March (1963): 43–54.

Nikolinakos, Marios. "Notes on an Economic Theory of Racism." *Race* April (1973): 365–81.

Nobles, Wade W. "Toward an Empirical and Theoretical Framework for Defining Black Families." *Journal of Marriage and the Family* November (1978): 679–88.

Noel, Donald L., ed. *The Origins of American Slavery and Racism.* Columbus, OH: Charles E. Merrill, 1972.

Nunis, Doyce B., Jr. "American Identities." *Society* November–December (1981): 29–30.

Nunn, Clyde A., Crockett, Harry J., Jr., and Williams, J. Allen, Jr. *Tolerance for Nonconformity: A National Survey of Americans' Changing Commitment to Civil Liberties.* San Francisco: Jossey-Bass, 1978.

Nyquist, Ewald B. "Shifts in Policies and Attitudes Toward Minority Education." In *Beyond Desegregation.* New York: College Entrance Examination Board, 1978, pp. 24–5.

Ogbu, John. *Minority Education and Caste.* New York: Academic Press, 1978.

O'Gorman, Hubert J. "Pluralistic Ignorance and White Estimates of White Support for Racial Segregation." *Public Opinion Quarterly,* Fall (1975): 313–30.

Oliphant, Thomas. "Blacks and Jews: A Strained Alliance." *Boston Globe,* August 26, 1979, pp. 1, 20–1.

Olsen, Marvin E. "Social and Political Participation of Blacks." *American Sociological Review* August (1970): 682–97.

Olsen, Marvin E. "Perceived Legitimacy of Social Protest Actions." *Social Problems* Winter (1968): 297–310.

Oppenheimer, Martin. *The Urban Guerrilla.* New York: Quadrangle Books, 1969.

O'Quin, Karen, and Aronoff, Joel. "Humor as a Technique of Social Influence." *Social Psychology Quarterly* December (1981): 349–57.

Orfield, Gary. *Must We Bus?* Washington, D.C.: Brookings Institution, 1978.

Oretego, Philip D. "Some Cultural Implications of a Mexican Border Dialect of American English." In Livie I. Duran and Russell Bernard, eds., *Introduction to Chicano Studies.* New York: Macmillan, 1973, pp. 435–41.

Ortego, Philip D. "Montezuma's Children." In V. Romano, ed. *Voices.* Berkeley: Quinto Sol Publications (1971): 126–32.

Orum, Anthony M. "A Reappraisal of the Social and Political Participation of Negroes." *American Journal of Sociology* July (1966): 32–46.

Orum, Anthony, and Cohen, Roberta S. "The Development of Political Orientations Among Black and White Children." *American Sociological Review* February (1973): 62–74.

Pachon, Harry P., and Moore, Joan W. "Mexican Americans." *Annals* March (1981): 111–24.

Padilla, Elena. "Concepts of Work and Situational Demands on New York City Puerto Ricans." In H. R. Kaplan, ed. *American Minorities and Economic Opportunity.* Itasca, IL: F. E. Peacock, 1977.

Painter, Nell Irvin. *The Narrative of Hosea Hudson: His Life as a Negro Communist in the South.* Harvard: Harvard University Press, 1979.

Parcel, Toby L. "Race, Regional Labor Markets and Earnings." *American Sociological Review* April (1979): 262–79.

Parker, Seymour, and Kleiner, Robert J. *Mental Illness in the Urban Negro Community.* New York: Free Press, 1966.

Parker, Seymour, and Kleiner, Robert J. "The Culture of Poverty: An Adjustive Dimension." *American Anthropologist* June (1970): 516–27.

Parsons, Anne. "The Pentecostal Immigrants." *Journal for the Scientific Study of Religion* June (1965): 183–97.

Pasamanick, Benjamin. "Some Misconceptions Concerning Differences in the Racial Prevalence of Mental Disease." *American Journal of Orthopsychiatry* January (1963): 72–86.

Pascal, A. H., ed. *Racial Discrimination in Economic Life.* Lexington, MA: Heath, Lexington Books, 1972.

Patterson, G. James. "A Critique of 'The New Ethnicity.' " *American Anthropologist* March (1979): 103–5.

Patterson, James T. *America's Struggle Against Poverty 1900–1980.* Cambridge: Harvard University Press, 1981.

Patterson, Orlando. *Ethnic Chauvinism: The Reactionary Impulse.* New York: Stein and Day, 1977.

Patterson, Orlando. *Slavery and Social Death.* Cambridge: Harvard University Press, 1982.

Patterson, Sheila. *Immigrants in Industry.* Oxford: Oxford University Press, 1968.

Peabody, Dean. "Authoritarian Scales and Response Bias." *Psychological Bulletin* (1966): 11–23.

Peach, Ceri. "Which Triple Melting Pot? A Re-Examination of Ethnic Intermarriage in New Haven." *Ethnic and Racial Studies* January (1980): 1–16.

Peñalosa, Fernando. "The Changing Mexican American in Southern California." In R. Rosaldo, R. A. Calvert, and G. L. Seligmann, eds. *Chicanos: The Revolution of a People.* Minneapolis, MN: Winston, 1973a, pp. 259ff.

Peñalosa, Fernando. "Toward an Operational Definition of a People." In R. Rosaldo, R. A. Calvert, and G. L. Seligmann, eds., *Chicanos: The Revolution of a People.* Minneapolis, MN: Winston, 1973b, pp. 439ff.

Peñalosa, Fernando. "Recent Changes Among the Chicanos." In R. Rosaldo, R. A. Calvert, and G. L. Seligmann, eds., *Chicanos: The Revolution of a People.* Minneapolis, MN: Winston, 1973c.

Peres, Yochanan. "Ethnic Relations in Israel." *American Journal of Sociology* May (1971): 1021–47.

Perry, Ronald W. *Racial Discrimination and Military Justice.* New York: Praeger, 1977.

Peterson, Marvin W. "Environmental Forces: The Crucial Context." In Marvin W. Peterson et al., *Black Students on White Campuses.* Ann Arbor: Institute of Social Research, University of Michigan, 1978, pp. 105–25. (a)

Peterson, Marvin W. "Impacts on Administrative, Faculty, and Organizational Structures and Processes." In Marvin W. Peterson et al., *Black Students on White Campuses.* Ann Arbor: Institute of Social Research, University of Michigan, 1978, pp. 209–33. (b)

Peterson, Marvin W., and Davenport, Roselle W. "Student Organizations and Student Life." In Marvin W. Peterson et al., *Black Students on White Campuses.* Ann Arbor: Institute of Social Research, University of Michigan, 1978, pp. 195–208.

Peterson, Marvin W., Blackburn, Robert T., Gamson, Zelda F., Arce, Carlos H., Davenport, Roselle W., and Mingle, James R. *Black Students on White Campuses: The Impact of Increased Black Enrollments.* Ann Arbor: Institute for Social Research, University of Michigan, 1978.

Peterson, William. *Japanese Americans: Oppression and Success.* New York: Random House, 1971.

Pettigrew, Thomas F. "Personality and Sociocultural Factors in Intergroup Attitudes: A Cross-National Comparison." *Journal of Conflict Resolution* March (1958): 29–42.

Pettigrew, Thomas F. *A Profile of the Negro American.* New York: Van Nostrand, 1964.

Pettigrew, Thomas F. "Racially Separate or Together?" *Journal of Social Issues* January (1969): 43–69.

Pettigrew, Thomas F. "Attitudes on Race and Housing: A Social Psychological View." In A. H. Hawley and V. P. Rock, eds., *Segregation in Residential Areas.* Washington, D.C.: National Academy of Sciences, 1973, pp. 43–58.

Pettigrew, Thomas F. *Racial Discrimination in the United States.* New York: Harper & Row, 1975.

Pettigrew, Thomas F. "Placing Adam's Argument in a Broader Perspective: Comment on the Adam Paper." *Social Problems* March (1978):58–61.

Pettigrew, Thomas F. "The Ultimate Attribution Error: Extending Allport's Cognitive Analysis of Prejudice." *Personality and Social Psychology Bulletin,* 5, (1979): 461–76.

Pettigrew, Thomas F. "Extending the Stereotype Concept." In David L. Hamilton, ed., *Stereotyping Cognitive Processes and Intergroup Behavior.* Hillsdale, NJ: Lawrence Erlbaum Associates, 1981a, pp. 303–31.

Pettigrew, Thomas F. "Race and Class in the 1980s: An Interactive View." *Daedalus* Spring (1981b): 233–55.

Pettigrew, Thomas F., and Green, Robert L. "School Desegregation in Large Cities: A Critique of the Coleman 'White Flight' Thesis." *Harvard Educational Review* February (1976): 1–53.

Phillips, U. B. *American Negro Slavery.* New York: D. Appleton and Co., 1918.

Phillips, U. B. *Life and Labor in the Old South.* Boston: Little, Brown, 1929.

Pinkney, Alphonso. *The Committed: White Activists in the Civil Rights Movement.* New Haven, CT: College and Universities Press, 1968.

Pinkney, Alphonso. *The American Way of Violence.* New York: Random House, 1972.

Pinkney, Alphonso. *Red, Black and Green: Black Nationalism in the United States.* New York: Cambridge University Press, 1976.

Poblete, Renate, and O'Dea, Thomas. "Anomie and the 'Quest for Community': The Formation of Sects Among the Puerto Ricans of New York." *American Catholic Sociological Review* Spring (1960): 18–36.

Podhoretz, Norman. "My Negro Problem—and Ours." *Commentary* February (1963): 93–101.

Poggie, John H., Jr. *Between Two Cultures: The Life of an American-Mexican.* Tucson: University of Arizona Press, 1973.

Ponting, J. Rick, and Gibbins, Roger. *Out of Irrelevance: A Socio-Political Introduction to Indian Affairs in Canada.* Woburn, MA: Butterworths, 1980.

Poole, W. C., Jr. "Social Distance and Personal Distance." *Journal of Applied Sociology* 11 (1927): 114–20.

Pope, Liston. *The Kingdom Beyond Caste.* New York: Friendship Press, 1957.

Porter, Judity R. *Black Child, White Child: The Development of Racial Attitudes.* Cambridge: Harvard University Press, 1971.

Porter, Judith R., and Washington, Robert E. "Black Identity and Self-Esteem: A Review of Studies of Black Self-Concept, 1968–1978." In Alex Inkeles, James Coleman, and Ralph

H. Turner, eds., *Annual Review of Sociology* Annual Reviews 5 (1979): 53–74.

Porterfield, Ernest. *Black and White Mixed Marriages*. Chicago: Nelson-Hall, 1978.

Portes, Alejandro, ed. "Illegal Mexican Immigrants to the United States." *International Migration Review* Winter (1978): whole issue.

Portes, Alejandro, Parker, Robert N., and Cobas, José A. "Assimilation or Consciousness: Perceptions of U.S. Society Among Recent Latin American Immigrants to the United States. *Social Forces* September (1980): 200–24.

Pouissant, Alvin. "Building a Strong Self-Image in the Black Child." *Ebony* August (1974): 136–43.

Pouissant, Alvin F., and Lewis, Toye Brown. "School Desegregation for Racial Equality." In F. H. Levinson and Benjamin D. Wright, eds., *School Desegregation: Shadow and Substance*. Chicago: University of Chicago Press, 1976, pp. 23ff.

Powdermaker, Hortense. *After Freedom: A Cultural Study in the Deep South*. New York: Viking Press, 1939.

Powdermaker, Hortense. "The Channeling of Negro Aggression by the Cultural Process." *American Journal of Sociology* May (1943): 750–58.

Powell, Brian, and Steelman, Lala Carr. "Fundamentalism and Sexism: A Reanalysis of Peek and Brown." *Social Forces* June (1982): 1154–58.

Powers, William K. *Oglala Religion*. Lincoln: University of Nebraska Press, 1977.

Prager, Jeffrey, Longshore, Douglas, and Seeman, Melvin (eds.). *Advancing the Art of Inquiry in School Desegregation Research*. Santica Monica, CA: System Development Corp., 1983.

President's Committee on Equality of Treatment and Opportunity in the Armed Services. *Freedom to Serve*. Washington, D.C.: U.S. Government Printing Office, 1950.

Price, H. D. *The Negro and Southern Politics: A Chapter of Florida History*. New York: New York University Press, 1957.

Price, John A. "The Migration and Adaptation of American Indians in Los Angeles." In H. M. Bahr, B. A. Chadwick, and R. C. Day, eds., *Native Americans Today: Sociological Perspectives*. New York: Harper & Row, 1972.

Price, John A. "North American Indian Families." In C. H. Mindel and R. W. Habenstein, eds., *Ethnic Families in America*. New York: Elsevier, 1976, pp. 248–70.

Proctor, Samuel D., and Johnston, Gladys Styles. "The Significance of Education for Blacks." In *Beyond Desegregation*. New York: College Entrance Examination Board, 1978, pp. 66–7.

Prothro, E. Terry, and Jensen, John A. "Comparison of Some Ethnic and Religious Attitudes of Negro and White College Students in the Deep South." *Social Forces* May (1952): 426–8.

Pugh, Jeanne. "Three Churches Merge in Spirit of Brotherhood." *Crossroads, St. Petersburg Times,* February 26, 1977, pp. 1,4.

Pye, Lucian W. "China: Ethnic Minorities and National Security." In Nathan Glazer and Daniel P. Moynihan, eds., *Ethnicity: Theory and Experience*. Cambridge: Harvard University Press, 1975, 489–512.

Quinley, Harold E. "The Dilemma of an Activist Church: Protestant Religion in the Sixties and Seventies." *Journal for the Scientific Study of Religion* March (1974a): 1–21.

Quinley, Harold E. *The Prophetic Clergy: Social Activism Among Protestant Ministers*. New York: Wiley, 1974b.

Quinley, Harold E., and Glock, Charles Y. *Anti-Semitism in America*. New York: Free Press, 1979.

Raboteau, Albert J. *Slave Religion: "The Invisible Institution" in the Antebellum South*. Oxford: Oxford University Press, 1978.

Raffel, Jeffrey A. *The Politics of School Desegregation: The Metropolitan Remedy in Delaware*. Philadelphia: Temple University Press, 1980.

Rainwater, Lee. "Crucible of Identity: The Negro Lower-Class Family." *Daedalus* Winter (1966): 172–216.

Rainwater, Lee. "The Problem of Lower Class Culture." *Journal of Social Issues* Spring (1970): 133–48.

Rakowska-Harmstone, Teresa. "Ethnicity in the Soviet Union." *Annals of the American Academy of Political and Social Science* September (1977): 73–87.

Ransford, H. Edward. "Blue-Collar Anger: Reaction to Student and Black Protest." *American Sociological Review* June (1972): 333–46.

Ransford, H. Edward. *Race and Class in American Society: Black, Chicano, Anglo*. New York: Schenkman, 1977.

Rawick, George P. *From Sundown to Sunup: The Making of the Black Community*. Westport, CT: Greenwood, 1972.

Rawley, James A. *The Transatlantic Slave Trade: A History*. New York: W. W. Norton, 1981.

Ray, John J. "Authoritarianism in California 30 Years Later—With Some Cross Cultural Comparisons." *Journal of Social Psychology* June (1980): 9–17.

Record, C. Wilson. *The Negro and the Communist Party*. Chapel Hill: University of North Carolina Press, 1951.

Reich, Michael. *Racial Inequality: A Political-Economic Analysis*. Princeton: Princeton University Press, 1981.

Reid, John D. "Black Urbanization of the South." *Phylon* September (1974): 260–67.

Reid, John D. "Black America in the 1980s." *Population Bulletin* December (1982): 1–39.

Reid, John D., and Lee, Everett S. "A Review of the W. E. B. DuBois Conference on Black Health." *Phylon* December (1977): 341–51.

Reid, John D., Lee, Everett S., Jedlicka, Davor, and Shin, Yongsock. "Trends in Black Health." *Phylon* June (1977): 105–16.

Reimers, David M. "Post-World War II Immigration to the United States: America's Latest Newcomers." *Annals of the American Academy of Political and Social Science* March (1981): 1–12.

Reinhold, Robert. "Government 'Minority' Category Growing to Include More Groups." *The New York Times*, July 30, 1978, pp. 1, 33.

Reitzes, Dietrich C. "Institutional Structure and Race Relations." *Phylon* Spring (1959): 48–66.

Renshon, Stanley Allen. *Psychological Needs and Political Behavior*. New York: Free Press, 1974.

Rex, John. *Race Relations in Sociological Theory*. London: Routledge and Kegan Paul, 1983.

Rex, John, and Tomlinson, Sally. *Colonial Immigrants in a British City: A Class Analysis*. London: Routledge & Kegan Paul, 1979.

Reynolds, Vernon. "Sociobiology and the Idea of Primordial Discrimination." *Ethnic and Racial Studies* July (1980): 303–15.

Rhee, Jong Mo. "The Redistribution of the Black Work Force

in the South by Industry." *Phylon* September (1974): 295–97.

Richardson, James T. "People's Temple and Jonestown: A Corrective Comparison and Critique." *Journal for the Scientific Study of Religion* September (1980): 239–55.

Richmond, Anthony H. *Migration and Race Relations in an English City.* Oxford: Oxford University Press, 1973.

Riding, Alan. "Silent Invasion: Why Mexico Is an American Problem." *Saturday Review,* July 8, 1978, pp. 14–17.

Riley, Clayton. "The Golden Gospel of Reverend Ike." *The New York Times Magazine,* March 9, 1975, pp. 12, 26–38.

Rinder, Irwin D. "Strangers in the Land: Social Relations in the Status Gap." *Social Problems* Winter (1958–59): 253–60.

Rinder, Irwin D. "A Note on Humor as an Index of Minority Group Morale." *Phylon* Summer (1965): 117–121.

Rindfuss, Ronald R., and Sweet, James A. *Postwar Fertility Trends and Differentials in the United States.* New York: Academic Press, 1977.

Riordan, Cornelius, and Ruggiero, Josephine. "Producing Equal-Status Interracial Interaction: A Replication." *Social Psychology Quarterly* March (1980), 131–36.

Rist, Ray C. "Student Social Class and Teacher Expectations: The Self-Fulfilling Prophecy in Ghetto Education." *Harvard Educational Review* August (1970): 411–51.

Rist, Ray C., "School Integration: Ideology, Methodology, and National Policy." In F. H. Levinson and B. D. Wright eds., *School Desegregation.* Chicago: University of Chicago Press, 1976.

Rist, Ray C. *Guestworkers in Germany: The Prospects for Pluralism.* New York: Praeger, 1978. (a)

Rist, Ray C. *The Invisible Children.* Cambridge: Harvard University Press, 1978. (b)

Rist, Ray C., ed. *Desegregated Schools.* New York: Academic Press, 1979. (a)

Rist, Ray C. "Guestworkers in Germany: Public Policies as the Legitimation of Marginality."*Ethnic and Racial Studies* October (1979): 401–15. (b)

Rist, Ray C. "On the Future of School Desegregation: A New American Dilemma." In Walter G. Stephan and Joe R. Feagin, eds., *School Desegregation: Past, Present, and Future.* New York: Plenum Press, 1980, pp. 117–31.

Roberts, A. H., and Rokeach, Milton. "Anomie, Authoritarianism, and Prejudice: A Replication." *American Journal of Sociology* January (1956): 355–58.

Roberts, J. Deotis. *A Black Political Theology.* Philadelphia: Westminster Press, 1974.

Robin, Stanley S., and Bosco, James J. "Coleman's Desegregation Research and Policy Recommendations." In F. H. Levinson and B. D. Wright, eds., *School Desegregation.* Chicago: University of Chicago Press, 1976, pp. 46–56.

Robinson, Jerry W., Jr., and Preston, James D. "Equal-Status Contact and Modification of Racial Prejudice: A Reexamination of the Contact Hypothesis." *Social Forces* June (1976): 911–24.

Robinson, Prezell R. "Effective Management of Scarce Resources: Presidential Responsibility." In C. V. Willie and R. R. Edmonds, eds., *Black Colleges in America.* New York: Teachers College Press, 1978, pp. 155–66.

Rodman, Hyman. "The Lower-Class Value Stretch." *Social Forces* December (1963): 205–15.

Roen, Sheldon R. "Personality and Negro–White Intelligence." *Journal of Abnormal and Social Psychology* (1960): 148–50.

Rogler, Lloyd. *Migrant in the City: The Life of a Puerto Rican Action Group.* New York: Basic Books, 1972.

Rohrer, John H., and Edmonson, Munro S., eds., with Harold Lief, Daniel Thompson, and William Thompson, co-authors. *The Eighth Generation: Cultures and Personalities of New Orleans Negroes.* New York: Harper & Row, 1960.

Rohrer, Wayne C. *Black Profiles of White Americans.* New York: Davis, 1970.

Rokeach, Milton. "Generalized Mental Rigidity as a Factor in Ethnocentrism." *Journal of Abnormal and Social Psychology* July (1948): 259–78.

Rokeach, Milton, "Political and Religious Dogmatism: An Alternative to the Authoritarian Personality." *Psychological Monographs,* 70, no. 18, 1956.

Rokeach, Milton. *The Open and Closed Mind.* New York: Basic Books, 1960.

Rokeach, Milton. *Beliefs, Attitudes, and Values.* San Francisco: Jossey-Bass, 1968.

Roof, Wade Clarke. "Religious Orthodoxy and Minority Prejudice: Causal Relationship or Reflection of Localistic World View?" *American Journal of Sociology* November (1974): 643–64.

Roof, Wade Clark, and Perkins, Richard B. "On Conceptualizing Salience in Religious Commitment." *Journal for the Scientific Study of Religion* June (1975): 111–128.

Rorer, L. G. "The Great Response-Style Myth." *Psychological Bulletin* 63 (1965): 129–56.

Rose, Peter I., ed. *Americans from Africa: Slavery and Its Aftermath.* New York: Atherton Press, 1970.

Rose, Peter I. *"Nobody Knows the Trouble I've Seen": Some Reflections on the Insider–Outsider Debate.* Northampton, MA: Smith College, 1978.

Rose, Peter I. "Blacks and Jews: The Strained Alliance." *Annals of the American Academy of Political and Social Science* March (1981): 55–69.

Rosenbaum, James E. *Making Inequality: The Hidden Curriculum of High School Tracking.* New York: Wiley, 1976.

Rosenberg, Morris. *Conceiving the Self.* New York: Basic Books, 1979.

Rosenberg, Morris, and Simmons, R. G. *Black and White Self-Esteem: The Urban School Child.* Washington, D.C.: American Sociological Association, 1972.

Rosenberg, Morris, and Turner, Ralph H. eds. *Social Psychology: Sociological Perspectives.* New York: Basic Books, 1981.

Rosenstein, Carolyn. "The Liability of Ethnicity in Israel." *Social Forces* March (1981): 667–86.

Rosenthal, Bernard. "Development of Self-Identification in Relationship to Attitudes Towards the Self in the Chippewa Indians." *Genetic Psychology Monographs* August (1974): 44–141.

Rosenthal, Erich. "Jewish Intermarriage in Indiana." *American Jewish Yearbook* 68 (1967): 262ff.

Rosenthal, Erich. "Intermarriage Among Jewry: A Function of Acculturation, Community Organization, and Family Structure." In Bernard Martin, ed., *Movements and Issues in American Judaism.* Westport, CT: Greenwood Press, 1978.

Rosenthal, Robert, and Jacobson, Lenore. *Pygmalion in the Classroom.* New York: Holt, Rinehart, and Winston, 1968.

Rosenthal, Robert, Bernard, Bruce, Dunne, Faith, and Ladd,

Florence. *Different Strokes: Pathways to Maturity in the Boston Ghetto*. Boulder, CO: Westview Press, 1976.

Rosenthal, Steven J. "Symbolic Racism and Desegregation: Divergent Attitudes and Perspectives of Black and White University Students." *Phylon* September (1980): 257–66.

Rossi, Peter H. *Ghetto Revolts*. Chicago: Aldine, 1970.

Rotter, J. B. "Generalized Expectancies for Internal Versus External Control of Reinforcement." *Psychological Monographs* 80,1 (1966).

Rowan, Carl. "Blacks and Hispanics: Allies or Foes." *The Cleveland Plain Dealer,* July 15, 1979, section 7, p. 4.

Rowan, Helen. "Mexican Americans in the Southwest." In R. A. Garcia, ed., *The Chicanos in America 1540–1974*. Dobbs Ferry, NY: Oceana, 1977.

Roy, Prodipto. "The Measurement of Assimilation: The Spokane Indians." In H. M. Bahr, B. A. Chadwick, and R. C. Day, eds., *Native Americans Today: Sociological Perspectives*. New York: Harper & Row, 1972.

Rubin, Zick, and Peplau, Anne. "Belief in a Just World and Reactions to Another's Lot; A Study of Participants in the National Draft Lottery." *Journal of Social Issues* 29,4 (1973): 73–93.

Rubovits, P. C., and Maehr, M. L. "Pygmalion Black and White." *Journal of Personality and Social Psychology* 25 (1973): 210–18.

Rudwick, Elliott M. *W.E.B. DuBois: Propagandist of the Negro Protest*. New York: Atheneum, 1969.

Rush, G. B. "Status Consistency and Right-Wing Extremism." *American Sociological Review* February (1967): 86–92.

Ryan, Sally, and Bronfenbrenner, Urie. *A Report on Longitudinal Evaluations of Preschool Programs*. 2 vols. Washington, D.C.: Department of Health, Education, and Welfare, pub. nos. (OHD) 72–75, 1974.

Ryan, William. *Blaming the Victim*. New York: Vintage Books, 1971.

Rymph, Raymond C., and Hadden, Jeffrey K. "The Persistence of Regionalism in Racial Attitudes of Methodist Clergy." *Social Forces* September (1970): 41–50.

Sagarin, Edward, ed. *The Other Minorities*. Lexington, MA: Ginn, 1971.

Saltman, Juliet. *Open Housing: The Dynamics of a Social Movement*. New York: Praeger, 1978.

Samora, Julian, with the assistance of Jorge Bustamante and Gilbert Cardenas. *Los Mojados: The Wetback Story*. Notre Dame, IN: University of Notre Dame, 1971.

Samora, Julian, and Simon, Patricia V. *A History of the Mexican-American People*. Notre Dame, IN: University of Notre Dame Press, 1977.

Samuels, Howard. "How to Even the Odds." *Saturday Review,* August 23, 1969, p. 23.

Sánchez, Ricardo. *Canto y Grito Mi Liberación*. New York: Anchor Books, 1973.

Sanford, Nevitt. "Authoritarian Personality in Contemporary Perspective." In Jeanne N. Knutson, ed., *Handbook of Political Psychology*. San Francisco: Jossey-Bass, 1973, pp. 139–70.

Savage, Michael. "Costs of Enforcing Apartheid and Problems of Change." *African Affairs* July (1977): 287–302.

Savitz, Leonard D. "Black Crime." In K. S. Miller and R. M. Dreger, eds., *Comparative Studies of Blacks and Whites in the U.S.* New York: Seminar Press, 1973, pp. 484–505.

Scanzoni, John H. *The Black Family in Modern Society*. Boston: Allyn & Bacon, 1971.

Scheff, Thomas. "The Labelling Theory of Mental Illness." *American Sociological Review* June (1974): 444–52.

Schelling, Thomas C. *Micromotives and Macrobehavior*. New York: W. W. Norton, 1978.

Schermerhorn, R. A. *These Our People: Minorities in American Culture*. Lexington, MA: Heath, 1949.

Schermerhorn, R. A. "Minorities: European and American." *Phylon* Summer (1959): 179–85.

Schermerhorn, R. A. *Comparative Ethnic Relations: A Framework for Theory and Research*. New York: Random House, 1970.

Schermerhorn, R. A. *Ethnic Plurality in India*. Tucson: University of Arizona Press, 1978.

Schneider, Stephen A. *The Availability of Minorities and Women for Professional and Managerial Positions, 1970–1985*. Philadelphia: The Wharton School, University of Pennsylvania, 1977.

Schofield, Janet Ward. "The Impact of Positively Structured Contact on Intergroup Behavior: Does It Last Under Adverse Conditions?" *Social Psychology Quarterly* September (1979): 280–84.

Schofield, Janet Ward. *Behind Closed Doors: Race Relations in an American School*. New York: Praeger, 1981.

Schofield, Janet Ward, and Sagar, H. Andrew. "The Social Context of Learning in an Interracial School." In Ray C. Rist, ed., *School Desegregation*. New York: Academic Press, 1979, pp. 157–98.

Schreiber, Janet M., and Homiak, John P. "Mexican Americans." In Alan Harwood, ed., *Ethnicity and Medical Care*. Cambridge: Harvard University Press, 1981, pp. 264–336.

Schreike, B. *Alien Americans: A Study of Race Relations*. New York: Viking Press, 1936.

Schulz, David. *Growing Up Black: Patterns of Ghetto Socialization*. New York: Prentice-Hall, 1969.

Schuman, Howard, and Converse, Jean M. "Effects of Black and White Interviewers on Black Responses in 1968." *Public Opinion Quarterly* Spring (1971): 44–69.

Schuman, Howard, and Harding, John. "Prejudice and the Norm of Rationality." *Sociometry* September (1964): 353–71.

Schuman, Howard, and Hatchett, Shirley. *Black Racial Attitudes: Trends and Complexities*. Ann Arbor: Institute for Social Research, University of Michigan, 1974.

Schuman, Howard, and Johnson, Michael P. "Attitudes and Behavior." *Annual Review of Sociology* 2 (1976): 161–207.

Schusky, Ernest L., ed. *Political Organization of Native North Americans*. Washington, D.C.: University Press of America, 1980.

Schwartz, David C. *Political Alienation and Political Behavior*. Chicago: Aldine, 1973.

Schwartz, Sandra Kenyon, and Schwartz, David C. "Convergence and Divergence in Political Orientations Between Blacks and Whites: 1960–1973." *Journal of Social Issues* Spring (1976): 153–68.

Scott, Joseph W. *The Black Revolts: Racial Stratification in the USA*. Cambridge: Schenkman, 1976.

Seale, Bobby. *Seize the Time: The Story of the Black Panther Party*. New York: Random House, 1970.

Seeman, Melvin. "On the Meaning of Alienation." *American Sociological Review* December (1959): 783–91.

Seeman, Melvin. "Alienation and Social Learning in a Reformatory." *American Journal of Sociology* November (1963): 270–84.

Seeman, Melvin. "Alienation Studies." In Alex Inkeles, James

Coleman, and Neil Smelser, eds., *Annual Review of Sociology,* Annual Reviews (1975): 91–123.

Seeman, Melvin. "Some Real and Imaginary Consequences of Social Mobility: A French-American Comparison." *American Journal of Sociology* January (1977): 757–82.

Seeman, Melvin. "Intergroup Relations." In Morris Rosenberg and Ralph H. Turner, eds., *Social Psychology: Sociological Perspectives.* New York: Basic Books, 1981, pp. 378–410.

Seitz, S. T. "Firearms, Homicides and Gun Control Effectiveness." *Law and Society Review* 6 (1972): 595–613.

Selznick, Gertrude J. and Steinberg, Stephen. *The Tenacity of Prejudice: Anti-Semitism in Contemporary America.* New York: Harper and Row, 1969.

Semyonov, Moshe, and Tyree, Andrea. "Community Segregation and the Costs of Ethnic Subordination." *Social Forces* March (1981): 649–66.

Senior, Clarence. *Strangers—Then Neighbors.* New York: Freedom Books (Anti-Defamation League of B'nai B'rith), 1961.

Sewell, William. "Inequality of Opportunity in Higher Education." *American Sociological Review* October (1971): 793–809.

Sewell, William, and Hauser, Robert M. *Education, Occupation, and Earnings: Achievement in the Early Career.* New York: Academic Press, 1975.

Sewell, William H., Hauser, Robert M., and Featherman, David L. eds. *Schooling and Achievement in American Society.* New York: Academic Press, 1976.

Sexton, John. "Minority-Admissions Programs after Bakke." *Harvard Educational Review* August (1979): 313–39.

Shapiro, E. Gary. "Racial Differences in the Value of Job Rewards." *Social Forces* September (1977): 21–30.

Shavit, Yossi. "Tracking and Ethnicity in Israeli Secondary Education." *American Sociological Review* April (1984): 210–220.

Sheehan, Edward R. F. "Europe's Hired Poor." *The New York Times Magazine,* December 9, 1973, pp. 36–7, 70–82.

Sherif, Muzafer. *An Outline of Social Psychology.* New York: Harper & Row, 1948.

Shibutani, Tamotsu. *The Derelicts of Company K: A Sociological Study of Demoralization.* Berkeley: University of California Press, 1978.

Shibutani, Tamotsu, and Kwan, Kian M. *Ethnic Stratification: A Comparative Approach.* New York: Macmillan, 1965.

Shils, Edward A. *Center and Periphery: Essays in Macrosociology.* Chicago: University of Chicago Press, 1975.

Shimkin, D. B., Louie, G. J., and Frate, D. A. "The Black Extended Family: A Basic Institution and a Mechanism of Urban Adaptation." In D. B. Shimkin, E. M. Shimkin, and D. A. Frate (eds.)., *The Extended Family in Black Societies.* Hawthorne, NY: Mouton, 1978, pp. 25–147.

Shin, Yongsock, Jedlicka, Dover, and Lee, Everett S. "Homicide Among Blacks." *Phylon* December (1977): 399–406.

Short, James, Rivera, Ramon, and Tennyson, Ray. "Perceived Opportunities, Gang Membership, and Delinquency. *American Sociological Review* February (1965): 56–67.

Shosteck, Herschel. "Respondent Militancy as a Control Variable for Interview Effect." *Journal of Social Issues* 33,4 (1977): 36–45.

Showell, Betty. "The Courts, the Legislature, the Presidency, and School Desegregation Policy." In Florence H. Levinson and Benjamin D. Wright, eds., *School Desegregation.* Chicago: University of Chicago Press, 1976, pp. 95–110.

Sickels, R. J. *Race, Marriage, and the Law.* Albuquerque: University of New Mexico Press, 1972.

Sidel, Victor W. "Can More Physicians Be Attracted to Ghetto Practice?" In A. Shiloh and I. Selavan eds., *Ethnic Groups in America* Vol. 2. Springfield, IL: Charles C Thomas, 1974, pp. 258–70.

Sieber, Sam D. *Fatal Remedies: The Ironies of Social Intervention.* New York: Plenum Press, 1981.

Silberman, Charles E. *Criminal Violence, Criminal Justice.* New York: Random House, 1978.

Silberstein, Fred B. and Seeman, Melvin. "Social Mobility and Prejudice," *American Journal of Sociology* November (1959): 258–64.

Silverman, Sydel. "Agricultural Organization, Social Structure, and Values in Italy: Amoral Familism Reconsidered." *American Anthropologist* 70 (1968): 1–20.

Simmel, Georg. *Conflict.* Translated by Kurt Wolff. New York: Free Press, 1955.

Simon, Rita J., and Altstein, Howard. *Transracial Adoption.* New York: Wiley, 1977.

Simpson, George E. "Political Cultism in West Kingston, Jamaica." *Social and Economic Studies* June (1955): 133–49.

Simpson, George E. "Assimilation." in *International Encyclopedia of the Social Sciences.* New York: Macmillan and Free Press, (1) 1968, pp. 438–44.

Simpson, George E. *Black Religions in the New World.* New York: Columbia University Press, 1978.

Simpson, George E., and Yinger, J. Milton. *Racial and Cultural Minorities.* 4th ed. New York: Harper & Row, 1972.

Simpson, Miles. "Authoritarianism and Education: A Comparative Approach." *Sociometry* June (1972): 223–34.

Singer, David L. "Aggression Arousal, Hostile Humor, Catharsis." *Journal of Personality and Social Psychology* January (1968): 1–14.

Smith, A. Wade. "Racial Tolerance as a Function of Group Position." *American Sociological Review* October (1981): 525–41. (a)

Smith, A. Wade. "Tolerance of School Desegregation, 1954–77." *Social Forces* June (1981): 1256–74. (b)

Smith, James P., and Welch, Finis. "Race Differences in Earnings: A Survey and New Evidence." In Peter Mieszkowski and Mahlon Straszheim, eds., *Current Issues in Urban Economics.* Baltimore: Johns Hopkins University Press, 1979, pp. 49–73.

Smith, Lillian. *Killers of the Dream.* New York: W. W. Norton, 1949.

Smith, M. Brewster. "Opinions, Personality, and Political Behavior." *American Political Science Review* March (1958): 1–17.

Smith, M. G. "Ethnicity and Ethnic Groups in America: The View from Harvard." *Ethnic and Racial Studies* January (1982): 1–22.

Smith, Tom W. *A Compendium of Trends on General Social Survey Questions.* Washington, D.C.: National Opinion Research Center, 1980.

Smith, Tom W. "Hardship, Hard Times, and Hard Hearts." *Perspectives* Summer–Fall (1981): 27–9.

Smock, David R., and Smock, Audrey C. *The Politics of Pluralism: A Comparative Study of Lebanon and Ghana.* New York: Elsevier, 1975.

Smooha, Sammy. *Israel: Pluralism and Conflict.* Berkeley: University of California Press, 1978.

Sniderman, Paul M. *Personality and Democratic Politics.* Berkeley: University of California Press, 1975.

Snow, David A., and Machalek, Richard. "On the Presumed Fragility of Unconventional Beliefs." *Journal for the Scientific Study of Religion* March (1982): 15–26.

Solomon, Barbara Miller. *Ancestors and Immigrants.* Cambridge: Harvard University Press, 1956.

Sorensen, Annemette, Taeuber, Karl E., and Hollingsworth, Leslie J., Jr. "Indexes of Racial Residential Segregation for 109 Cities in the United States, 1940–1970." *Sociological Focus* April (1975): 125–42.

Sorkin, Alan L. "The Economic Base of Indian Life." *Annals of the American Academy of Political and Social Science* March (1978): 1–12. (a)

Sorkin, Alan L. *The Urban American Indian.* Lexington, MA: Heath, 1978. (b)

Sowell, Thomas. *Black Education.* New York: David McKay, 1973.

Sowell, Thomas. "Economics and Black People." in William L. Cash, Jr., and Lucy R. Oliver, eds., *Black Economic Development: Analysis and Implications.* Ann Arbor: School of Business Administration, University of Michigan, 1975, pp. 52–65. (a)

Sowell, Thomas. *Race and Economics.* New York: David McKay, 1975(b).

Sowell, Thomas. *Markets and Minorities.* New York: Basic Books, 1981.

Spangler, Eve, Gordon, Marsha A., and Pipkin, Ronald M. "Token Women: An Empirical Test of Kanter's Hypothesis." *American Journal of Sociology* July (1978): 160–70.

Spencer, Robert F., and Jennings, Jesse D., et al. *The Native Americans* 2nd ed. New York: Harper & Row, 1977.

Spicer, Edward. *Cycles of Conquest: The Impact of Spain, Mexico, and the United States on Indians of the Southwest, 1553–1960.* Tucson: University of Arizona Press, 1962.

Spiegelman, Mortimer, and Erhardt, Carl. "Mortality and Longevity in the United States." In Carl L. Erhardt and Joyce E. Berlin, eds., *Mortality and Morbidity in the United States.* Cambridge: Harvard University Press, 1974, pp. 1–20.

Spilerman, Seymour. "The Causes of Racial Disturbances: A Comparison of Alternative Explanations." *American Sociological Review* August (1970): 627–49.

Spilerman, Seymour. "Structural Characteristics of Cities and the Severity of Racial Disorders." *American Sociological Review* October (1976): 771–793.

Spindler, George D., and Spindler, Louise S. *Dreamers Without Power: The Menomini Indians.* New York: Holt, Rinehart, and Winston, 1971.

Spindler, George D., and Spindler, Louise S. "Identity, Militancy, and Cultural Congruence: The Menominee and Kainai." *Annals of the American Academy of Political and Social Science* March (1978): 73–85.

Srinivas, M. N. *Caste in Modern India and Other Essays.* Bombay: Asia Publishing House, 1962.

Srinivas, M. N. *Social Change in Modern India.* Berkeley: University of California, 1969.

Srole, Leo. "Social Integration and Certain Corollaries: An Exploratory Study." *American Sociological Review* December (1956): 709–16.

Stack, Carol B. *All Our Kin: Strategies for Survival in a Black Community.* New York: Harper & Row, 1974.

Stamler, J., Berkson, D. M., Lindberg, H. A., and Hall, Y. "Racial Patterns of Coronary Heart Disease." In A. Shiloh

and I. Selavan, eds., *Ethnic Groups of America: Their Morbidity, Mortality, and Behavior Disorders.* Vol. 2. *The Blacks.* Springfield, IL: Charles C Thomas, 1974, pp. 84–99.

Stampp, Kenneth. *The Peculiar Institution: Slavery in the Ante-Bellum South.* New York: Knopf, 1965.

Standley, Nancy V. *White Students Enrolled in Black Colleges and Universities.* Atlanta, GA: Southern Regional Educational Board, 1978.

Stanley, Sam, and Thomas, Robert K. "Current Demographic and Social Trends Among North American Indians." *Annals of the American Academy of Political and Social Science* March (1978): 111–20.

Staples, Robert. "The Black American Family." In C. H. Mindel and R. W. Habenstein, eds., *Ethnic Families in America.* New York: Elsevier, 1976, pp. 221–47.

Staples, Robert. "The Myth of the Black Matriarchy." In Doris Y. Wilkinson and R. L. Taylor, eds., *The Black Male in America.* Chicago: Nelson-Hall, 1977, pp. 187ff. (a)

Staples, Robert. "The Myth of the Impotent Black Man." In Doris Y. Wilkinson and R. L. Taylor, eds., *The Black Male in America.* Chicago: Nelson-Hall, 1977. (b)

Staples, Robert. *The Black Woman in America.* Chicago: Nelson-Hall, 1973, 1978.

Stark, Margaret J. Abudu, Raine, Walter J., Burbeck, Stephen L., and Davison, Keith K. "Some Empirical Patterns in a Riot Process." *American Sociological Review* December (1974): 865–76.

Stark, Rodney, Foster, Bruce, Glock, Charles, and Quinley, Harold. *Wayward Shepherds: Prejudice and the Protestant Clergy.* New York: Harper & Row, 1971.

Starkloff, Carl F. "American Indian Religion and Christianity: Confrontation and Dialogue." *Journal of Ecumenical Studies* Spring (1971): 317–40.

Starr, Paul D., "Continuity and Change in Social Distance: Studies from the Arab East—A research Report," *Social Forces,* June, (1978): 1221–27.

Steiber, Steven R. "The Influence of the Religious Factor on Civil and Sacred Tolerance, 1958–71." *Social Forces* March (1980): 811–32.

Stein, Barry N., and Tomasi, Silvano M., eds. "Refugees Today." *Internation Migration Review* Spring–Summer (1981): whole issue.

Stein, David D. "The Influence of Belief Systems on Interpersonal Preference: A Validation of Rokeach's Theory of Prejudice." *Psychological Monographs: General and Applied* 80,8 (1966).

Steinberg, Stephen. *The Ethnic Myth: Race, Ethnicity, and Class in America.* New York: Atheneum, 1981.

Steiner, Ivan D., and Johnson, Homer H. "Authoritarianism and Conformity." *Sociometry* March (1963): 21–34.

Steiner, Ivan D. and Vannoy, J. "Personality Correlates of Two Types of Conformity Behavior." *Journal of Personality and Social Psychology,* 4 (1966): 307–15.

Steiner, Stan. *The New Indians.* New York: Dell, 1968.

Steiner, Stan. *The Islands: The Worlds of the Puerto Ricans.* New York: Harper & Row, 1974.

Steiner, Stan. "Sacred Objects Secular Laws." *Perspectives* Summer–Fall (1981): 13–15.

Steinfels, Peter. *The Neoconservatives: The Men Who Are Changing America's Politics.* New York: Simon & Schuster, 1979.

Stember, Charles H. *Education and Attitude Change: The Effect of Schooling on Prejudice Against Minority Groups.* Old Bethpage, NY: Institute of Human Relations Press, 1961.

Stember, Charles H. *Sexual Racism: The Emotional Barrier to an Integrated Society.* New York: Elsevier, 1976.

Stephan, Walter G., and Feagin, Joe R., eds. *School Desegregation: Past, Present, and Future.* New York: Plenum Press, 1980.

Stern, C. G., Stein, M. I., and Bloom, B. S. *Methods in Personality Assessment.* New York: Free Press, 1956.

Stewart, Don, and Hoult, Thomas. "A Social-Psychological Theory of the Authoritarian Personality." *American Journal of Sociology* November (1959): 274–79.

Stewart, Kenneth M. "American Indian Heritage: Retrospect and Prospect." In Robert F. Spencer, Jesse D. Jennings, et al., *The Native Americans: Ethnology and Backgrounds of the North American Indians.* 2nd ed. New York: Harper & Row, 1977, pp. 501–22.

Stewart, R. A., Powell, G. E., and Chetwynd, S. J. *Person Perception and Stereotyping.* New York: Saxon House, 1979.

Stiglitz, Joseph E. "Approaches to the Economics of Discrimination." *American Economic Review* May (1973): 287–295.

Stinchcombe, Arthur L., and Taylor, D. Garth. "On Democracy and School Integration." In Walter G. Stephan and Joe R. Feagin, eds. *School Desegregation: Past, Present, and Future.* New York: Plenum Press, 1980, pp. 157–86.

St. John, Nancy H. *School Desegregation Outcomes for Children.* New York: Wiley, 1975.

Stockton, William. "Going Home: The Puerto Ricans' New Migration." *The New York Times Magazine.* November 12, 1978, pp. 20–22, 88–93.

Stoddard, Ellwyn R. *Mexican Americans.* New York: Random House, 1973.

Stoddard, Ellwyn R. "A Conceptual Analysis of the 'Alien Invasion': Institutionalized Support of Illegal Mexican Aliens in the U.S." *International Migration Review* Summer (1976): 157–89.

Stoddard, Lothrop. *The Rising Tide of Color Against White World-Supremacy.* New York: Scribner's, 1920.

Stone, John. "Introduction: Internal Colonialism in Comparative Perspective." *Ethnic and Racial Studies* July (1979): 255–59.

Stone, William F. *The Psychology of Politics.* New York: Free Press, 1974.

Stone, William F. "The Myth of Left-Wing Authoritarianism." *Political Psychology* Fall–Winter (1980): 3–19.

Stonequist, Everett V. *The Marginal Man: A Study in Personality and Culture Conflict.* New York: Scribner, 1937.

Stoper, Emily. "The Student Nonviolent Coordinating Committee: The Rise and Fall of a Redemptive Organization." *Journal of Black Studies* September (1977): 13–34.

Stouffer, Samuel A. *Communism, Conformity, and Civil Liberties.* New York: Doubleday, 1955.

Stouffer, Samuel A., Suchman, Edward, DeVinney, Leland, Star, Shirley, and Williams, Robin, Jr. *The American Soldier: Adjustment During Army Life.* Princeton: Princeton University Press, 1949.

Stryker, Sheldon. "Social Structure and Prejudice." *Social Problems* Spring (1959): 340–54.

Stuckert, Robert P. " 'Race' Mixture: The Black Ancestry of White Americans." In Peter B. Hammond, *Physical Anthropology and Archaeology.* New York: Macmillan, 1976, pp. 135–39.

Suall, Irwin J. "The Ku Klux Klan Malady Lingers On." *Perspectives* Fall–Winter (1980): 11–15.

Sudarkasá, Niara. "Interpreting the African Heritage in Afro-American Family Organization." In Harriette Pipes McAdoo, *Black Families.* Beverly Hills, CA: Sage 1981, 37–53.

Sue, Stanley, and Kitano, Harry H. L., issue eds. "Asian Americans: A Success Story?" *Journal of Social Issues* 29,2 (1973).

Sullivan, Leon H. *Build Brother Build.* New York: Macrae-Smith, 1969.

Sullivan, Louis D. "The Education of Black Health Professionals." *Phylon* June (1977): 181–93.

Sullivan, Patrick L., and Adelson, Joseph. "Ethnocentrism and Misanthropy." *Journal of Abnormal and Social Psychology* April (1954): 246–50.

Sullivan, Teresa A. "Racial-Ethnic Differences in Labor Force Participation." In F. D. Bean and W. P. Frisbie, eds. *Racial and Ethnic Groups.* New York: Academic Press, 1978, pp. 167–82.

Summers, Anita A., and Wolfe, Barbara L. "Do Schools Make a Difference?" *American Economic Review* September (1977): 639–52.

Sumner, William Graham. *Folkways.* Lexington, MA: Ginn, 1906.

Sutherland, Robert L. *Color, Class and Personality.* Washington, D.C.: American Council on Education, 1942.

Suttles, Gerald D. *The Social Order of the Slum: Ethnicity and Territory in the Inner City.* Chicago: University of Chicago Press, 1968.

Sutton, Gordon F. "Assessing Mortality and Morbidity Disadvantages of the Black Population of the U.S." In A. Shiloh and I. Selavan, eds., *Ethnic Groups of America: Their Morbidity, Mortality, and Behavior Disorders.* Vol. 2. *The Blacks.* Springfield, IL: Charles C Thomas, 1974, pp. 18–35.

Sweet, James A. "Indicators of Family and Household Structure of Racial and Ethnic Minorities in the United States." In F. D. Bean and W. P. Frisbie, eds., *Demography of Racial and Ethnic Groups.* New York: Academic Press, 1979, pp. 241–46.

Sweet, James A., and Bumpass, Larry L. "Differentials in the Marital Instability of the Black Population: 1970." *Phylon* 35 (1974): 323–31.

Swigert, Victoria L., and Farrell, Ronald A. "Normal Homicides and the Law." *American Sociological Review* February (1977): 16–32.

Szasz, Margaret. *Education and the American Indian.* Albuquerque: University of New Mexico, 1974.

Szymanski, Albert. "Racial Discrimination and White Gain." *American Sociological Review* June (1976): 403–14.

Szymanski, Albert. *The Capitalist State and the Politics of Class.* Englewood, NJ: Winthrop, 1978. (a)

Szymanski, Albert. "White Workers' Loss from Racial Discrimination: Reply to Villemez." *American Sociological Review* October (1978): 776–82. (b)

Taeuber, Karl E. "Negro Population and Housing: Demographic Aspects of a Social Accounting Scheme." In Irwin Katz and Patricia Gurin, eds., *Race and the Social Sciences.* New York: Basic Books, 1969.

Taeuber, Karl E., and Taeuber, Alma F. *Negroes in Cities.* Chicago: Aldine, 1965.

Tajfel, Henri. "Cognitive Aspects of Prejudice." *Journal of Social Issues* Autumn (1969): 79–97.

Tajfel, Henri. "Social Psychology of Intergroup Relations." In

Mark Rosenzweig and Lyman Porter, eds., *Annual Review of Psychology,* Annual Reviews 33 (1982): 1–39.

Tandon, Yash. *Problems of a Displaced Minority: The New Position of East Africa's Asians.* London: Minority Rights Group, 1973.

Tax, Sol. "The Impact of Urbanization on American Indians." *Annals of the American Academy of Political and Social Science* March (1978): 121–36.

Taylor, Marylee C., and Walsh, Edward J. "Explanations of Black Self-Esteem: Some Empirical Tests." *Social Psychology Quarterly* September (1979): 242–53.

Taylor, Patricia A. "Income Inequality in the Federal Government." *American Sociological Review* June (1979): 468–78.

Taylor, Ronald L. "The Black Worker in Post-Industrial Society." In D. Y. Wilkinson and R. L. Taylor, eds., *The Black Male in America.* Chicago: Nelson-Hall, 1977.

Taylor, Ronald L. "Black Ethnicity and the Persistence of Ethnogenesis." *American Journal of Sociology* May (1979): 1401–23.

Taylor, Shelley, E. "A Categorization Approach to Stereotyping." In David L. Hamilton, ed., *Cognitive Processes in Stereotyping and Intergroup Behavior.* Hillsdale, NJ: Lawrence Erlbaum Associates, 1981, Chapter 3.

tenBroek, Jacobus, Barnhart, Edward N., and Matson, Floyd W. *Prejudice, War, and the Constitution.* Berkeley: University of California Press, 1954.

Tenhouten, Warren D. "Race and Family Power Structure." In Irving R. Stuart and Lawrence E. Abt, eds., *Interracial Marriage.* New York: Grossman, 1973, pp. 81–109.

Thernstrom, Stephan, ed. *Harvard Encyclopedia of American Ethnic Groups.* Cambridge: Harvard University Press, 1980.

Thomas, Dorothy S. *The Salvage.* Berkeley: University of California, 1952.

Thomas, Gail E., ed. *Black Students in Higher Education in the 1970s.* Westport, CT: Greenwood, 1981.

Thompson, Daniel C. "Black College Faculty and Students: The Nature of Their Interaction." In C. V. Willie and R. R. Edmonds, eds., *Black Colleges in America.* New York: Teachers College Press, 1978, pp. 180–94.

Thompson, E. T., ed. *Race Relations and the Race Problem.* Durham, NC: Duke University Press, 1939.

Thornberry, Patrick. "Minority Rights, Human Rights and International Law." *Ethnic and Racial Studies* July (1980): 249–63.

Thornton, Russell. "Demographic Antecedents of a Revitalization Movement: Population Change, Population Size, and the 1890 Ghost Dance." *American Sociological Review* February (1981): 88–96.

Thurow, Lester, C. *Poverty and Discrimination.* Washington, D.C.: Brookings Institution, 1969.

Thurow, Lester, C. *The Zero-Sum Society.* New York: Penguin Books, 1981.

Tilly, Charles. *From Mobilization to Revolution.* Reading, MA: Addison-Wesley, 1978.

Tobin, James. "On Improving the Economic Status of the Negro." *Daedalus* Fall (1965): 878–98.

Tollett, Kenneth D. "Implications of the Bakke Case and Similar Cases for the Higher Education of Minorities." In *Beyond Segregation.* New York: College Entrance Examination Board, 1978, pp. 49ff.

Tomlinson, T. M. "Determinants of Black Politics: Riots and the Growth of Militancy." *Psychiatry* May (1970): 247–64.

Tovar, Federico, ed. *Handbook of the Puerto Rican Community.* New York: Plus Ultra Educational Publishers, 1970.

Toynbee, Arnold J. *A Study of History.* Vol. 1. Oxford: Oxford University Press, 1934.

Treiman, Donald J. "Status Discrepancy and Prejudice." *American Journal of Sociology* May (1966): 651–64.

Trejo, Arnulfo D. *The Chicanos: As We See Ourselves.* Tucson: University of Arizona Press, 1979.

Tseng, Wen-Shing, McDermott, John F., Jr., and Maretzki, Thomas W., eds., *Adjustment in Intercultural Marriage.* Honolulu: University of Hawaii Press, 1977.

Tsukashima, Ronald Tadao, and Montero, Darrel. "The Contact Hypothesis: Social and Economic Contact and Generational Changes in the Study of Black Anti-Semitism." *Social Forces* September (1976): 149–65.

Tuch, Steven A. "Analyzing Recent Trends in Prejudice Toward Blacks: Insights from Latent Class Models." *American Journal of Sociology* July (1981): 130–42.

Tucker, C. Jack, and Reid, John D. "Black Urbanization and Economic Opportunity: A Look at the Nation's Large Cities." *Phylon* March (1977): 55–68.

Turner, Castellano B., and Wilson, William J. "Dimensions of Racial Ideology: A Study of Urban Black Attitudes." *Journal of Social Issues* Spring (1976): 139–52.

Turner, Jonathan H., and Singleton, Royce, Jr. "A Theory of Ethnic Oppression: Toward a Reintegration of Cultural and Structural Concepts in Ethnic Relations Theory." *Social Forces* June (1978): 1001–18.

Turner, John, Stanton, Bill, Vahala, Mike, and Williams, Randall. *The Ku Klux Klan: A History of Racism and Violence.* Montgomery, AL: Southern Poverty Law Center, 1981.

Turner, Ralph H. *The Social Context of Ambition.* New York: Chandler, 1964.

Turner, Ralph H. "The Public Perception of Protest." *American Sociological Review* December (1969): 815–30.

Turner, Ralph H., and Killian, Lewis M. *Collective Behavior.* New York: Prentice-Hall, 1957.

Turner, Ronny E. "The Black Minister: Uncle Tom or Abolitionist?" *Phylon* March (1973): 86–95.

Udry, J. Richard, Bauman, Karl E., and Chase, Charles. "Skin Color, Status, and Mate Selection." *American Journal of Sociology* January (1971): 722–33.

Underhill, Ruth. *Red Man's Religion: Beliefs and Practices of the Indians North of Mexico.* Chicago: University of Chicago Press, 1965.

United Nations Subcommission on Prevention and Protection of Minorities. *Yearbook of Human Rights for 1950.* New York: United Nations, 1952.

U. S. Army Research Institute for the Behavioral and Social Sciences. *Improving Race Relations in the Army—Handbook for Leaders.* Washington, D.C., 1975a, pp. 600–16.

U. S. Army Research Institute for the Behavioral and Social Sciences. "Research on Race and Ethnic Relations in the Army." *Research Problem Review,* 75–2 (June) 1975b.

U. S. Army Research Institute for the Behavioral and Social Sciences. *Measuring Changes in Institutional Racial Discrimination in the Army* April, 1977, pp. 600–43.

U. S. Bureau of the Census. *The Social and Economic Status of Negroes in the United States,* 1969.

U. S. Bureau of the Census. "The Social and Economic Status of the Black Population in the United States." *Current Population Reports,* P-23, No. 42, 1972.

U. S. Bureau of the Census. *Persons of Spanish Origin in the United States.* March, 1973, May, 1974.

U. S. Bureau of the Census. "Persons of Spanish Origin in the United States, March, 1976." *Current Population Reports,* P-20, No. 310, July, 1977.

U. S. Bureau of the Census. "Perspectives on American Husbands and Wives." *Current Population Reports,* P-23, No. 77, December, 1978.

U. S. Bureau of the Census. "Persons of Spanish Origin in the United States: March 1978." *Current Population Reports,* P-20, No. 339, June, 1979. (a)

U. S. Bureau of the Census. *The Social and Economic Status of the Black Population in the United States: An Historical View, 1790–1978.* P-23, No. 80, 1979. (b)

U. S. Bureau of the Census. *Persons of Spanish Origin in the United States: March, 1979.* P-20, no. 354, October, 1980.

U. S. Bureau of the Census. *Current Population Reports,* P-20, No. 361, May, 1981a.

U. S. Bureau of the Census. "School Enrollment—Social and Economic Characteristics of Students: October 1980." Advance Report. *Current Population Reports,* P-20, No. 362, May, 1981b.

U. S. Bureau of the Census. *1980 Census of Population. Supplementary Reports,* PC-80, S1-3, 6, July, 1981c.

U. S. Bureau of the Census. *Statistical Abstract of the United States 1981.* December, 1981d.

U. S. Bureau of the Census. "Population Profile of the United States: 1981." *Current Population Reports,* Series P-20, No. 374, September, 1982.

U. S. Bureau of the Census. "Marital Status and Living Arrangements: March 1981." *Current Population Reports,* P-20, No. 372, June, 1982.

U. S. Bureau of the Census. "Voting and Registration in the Election of November 1980." *Current Population Reports,* P-20, No. 370, April, 1982.

U. S. Bureau of the Census, *America's Black Population, 1970–1982.* Washington, D.C.: Government Printing Office, 1983.

U. S. Bureau of Labor Statistics. *Employment and Earnings,* January, 1983.

U. S. Commission on Civil Rights. *Racial Isolation in the Public Schools* (1), 1967.

U. S. Commission Civil Rights. *For All the People . . . By All the People,* 1969.

U. S. Commission on Civil Rights. *The Federal Civil Rights Enforcement Effort—1974.* (1) *To Regulate the Public Interest,* 1974. (a)

U. S. Commission on Civil Rights. *Toward Quality Education for Mexican Americans: Report VII: Mexican American Study,* 1974. (b)

U. S. Commission on Civil Rights. *Mexican American Education Study.* 6 vols. 1971–74.

U. S. Commission on Civil Rights. *The Federal Civil Rights Enforcement Effort—1874.* (5) *of To Eliminate Employment Discrimination,* 1975a.

U. S. Commission on Civil Rights. *Twenty Years After Brown.* December, 1975b.

U. S. Commission on Civil Rights. *Puerto Ricans in the Continental U.S.: An Uncertain Future.* October, 1976.

U. S. Commission on Civil Rights. *Statement on Metropolitan School Desegregation.* February, 1977.

U. S. Commission on Civil Rights. *The State of Civil Rights: 1977.* February, 1978.

U. S. Commission on Civil Rights. *The Federal Fair Housing Enforcement Effort.* March, 1979.

U. S. Commission on Civil Rights. *Puerto Ricans in California.* January, 1980a.

U. S. Commission on Civil Rights. *The State of Civil Rights, 1979.* 1980b.

U. S. Commission on Civil Rights. *Success of Asian Americans: Fact or Fiction?* September, 1980c.

U. S. Commission on Civil Rights. *The Tarnished Golden Door: Civil Rights Issues in Immigration.* September, 1980d.

U. S. Commission on Civil Rights. *Civil Rights Directory 1981.* 1981a.

U. S. Commission on Civil Rights. *Indian Tribes: A Continuing Quest for Survival.* June, 1981b.

U. S. Commission on Civil Rights. *The Voting Rights Act: Unfulfilled Goal.* September, 1981c.

U. S. Commission on Civil Rights. *Consultations on the Affirmative Action Statement* of the U.S. Commission on Civil Rights. 2 Vols. 1982.

U. S. Commission on Civil Rights. *The Decline of Black Farming in America.* February, 1982.

U. S. Committees on the Judiciary, Senate and House of Representatives. *U.S. Immigration Policy and the National Interest.* 1981.

U. S. Department of Health and Human Services. *Health of the Disadvantaged.* Chart Book II, DHHS Pub. No. (HRA) 80–663, September, 1980.

U. S. Department of Housing and Urban Development. *Hispanic Americans in the United States: A Selective Bibliography, 1963–1974.* Washington D.C.: Government Printing Office, 1974.

U. S. Department of Housing and Urban Development. *How Well Are We Housed? (2) Female-Headed Households.* December, 1978.

U. S. Department of Housing and Urban Development. *How Well Are We Housed? (1) Hispanics.* January, 1978.

U. S. Department of Housing and Urban Development. *How Well Are We Housed? 3. Blacks.* December, 1979a.

U. S. Department of Housing and Urban Development. *Discrimination Against Chicanos in the Dallas Rental Housing Market.* August, 1979b.

U. S. Department of Housing and Urban Development. *Measuring Racial Discrimination.* May, 1979c.

U. S. Department of Housing and Urban Development. *Recent Suburbanization of Blacks: How Much, Who and Where.* Annual Housing Survey Studies. February, 1979d.

Useem, Michael. *Protest Movements in America.* New York: Bobbs-Merrill, 1975.

Valentine, Betty Lou. *Hustling and Other Hard Work: Life Styles in the Ghetto.* New York: Free Press, 1978.

Valentine, Charles A. *Culture and Poverty.* Chicago: University of Chicago Press, 1968.

Valentine, Charles A. *Black Studies and Anthropology: Scholarly and Political Interests in Afro-American Culture.* Reading, MA: Addison-Wesley, 1972.

Van den Berghe, Pierre. *Race and Ethnicity: Essays in Comparative Sociology.* New York: Basic Books, 1970.

Van den Berghe, Pierre. *Race and Racism: A Comparative Perspective.* 2nd ed. New York: Wiley, 1978.

Van Valey, Thomas L., Roof, Wade C., and Wilcox, Jerome E. "Trends in Residential Segregation: 1960–1970." *American Journal of Sociology* January (1977): 826–44.

Vaughan, G. and White, K. "Conformity and Authoritarianism

Reexamined." *Journal of Personality and Social Psychology*, 3, 1966, 363–66.

Vickery, William E. and Opler, Morris E. "A Redefinition of Prejudice for Purpose of Social Science Research." *Human Relations*, 1948, *1*, 419–28.

Vigil, James Diego. *From Indians to Chicanos: A Sociocultural History*. St. Louis: C. V. Mosby, 1980.

Villemez, Wayne, J. "Black Subordination and White Economic Well-Being." *American Sociological Review* October (1978): 772–76.

Villemez, Wayne, J. "Race, Class, and Neighborhood: Differences in the Residential Return on Individual Resources." *Social Forces* December (1980): 414–30.

Villemez, Wayne J. and Wiswell, Candace Hinson. "The Impact of Diminishing Discrimination on the Internal Size Distribution of Black Income: 1954–74." *Social Forces* June (1978): 1019–34.

Wadley, Janet K. "The Disappearance of the Black Farmer." *Phylon* September (1974): 276–83.

Wagenheim, Kal. *A Survey of Puerto Ricans on the United States Mainland in the 1970s*. New York: Praeger, 1975.

Wagley, Charles, and Harris, Marvin. *Minorities in the New World*. New York: Columbia University Press, 1958.

Wagner, Jon. *Misfits and Missionaries: A School for Black Drop-outs*. Beverly Hills, CA: Sage, 1977.

Waldron, Sidney R. "Ethnicity and Refugees in Africa." *Cultural Survival* Spring (1981): 1–6.

Walker, Deward E., Jr. "Measures of Nez Percé Outbreeding and the Analysis of Cultural Change." *Southwestern Journal of Anthropology* Summer (1967): 155ff.

Wall, Marvin. "Black Votes." *South Today* August (1969): 6–7.

Wallace, Anthony F. C. "Revitalization Movements." *American Anthropologist* April (1956): 264–81.

Wallace, Anthony F. C. *The Death and the Rebirth of the Seneca*. New York: Knopf, 1970.

Wallace, Michele. *Black Macho and the Myth of the Superwoman*. New York: Dial, 1979.

Wallace, Phyllis A. *Black Women in the Labor Force*. Cambridge: MIT Press, 1980.

Warner, Lyle G., and DeFleur, Melvin L. "Attitude as an Interactional Concept." *American Sociological Review* April (1969): 153–69.

Warner, Lyle G., and Rutledge, Dennis M. "Prejudice Versus Discrimination: An Empirical Example and Theoretical Extension." *Social Forces* (1970): 473–84.

Warren, Constancia. "The Magnet School Boom: Implications for Desegregation." *Equal Opportunity Review* Spring (1978): 1–4.

Warren, Donald I. "Suburban Isolation and Race Tension: The Detroit Case." *Social Problems* (1970): 324–39.

Washington, Joseph R., Jr. *Black Sects and Cults*. New York: Doubleday, 1972.

Washington, Robert. "Further Comments on 'American Sociology and Black Americans.' " *American Journal of Sociology* November (1971): 580–87.

Watson, Wilbur H. "The Idea of Black Sociology: Its Cultural and Political Significance." *The American Sociologist* May (1976): 115–23.

Watts, Harold W. "Why, and How Well, Do We Analyze Inequality?" In J. Milton Yinger and Stephen J. Cutler, eds., *Major Social Issues*. New York: Free Press, 1978, 126–40.

Watts, Harold W., and Rees, Albert, eds. *The New Jersey Income-maintenance Experiment*. Vol. 2. *Labor-supply Responses*. New York: Academic Press, 1977a.

Watts, Harold W., and Rees, Albert, eds. *The New Jersey Income-maintenance Experiment*. Vol. 3 *Expenditures, Health, and Social Behavior, and the Quality of the Evidence*. New York: Academic Press, 1977b.

Wax, Murray L. *Indian Americans: Unity and Diversity*. New York: Prentice-Hall, 1971.

Wax, Murray L., and Wax, Rosalie H. "Religion among American Indians." *Annals of the American Academy of Political and Social Science* March (1978): 27–39.

Waxman, Chaim I. *The Stigma of Poverty: A Critique of Poverty Theories and Policies*. Elmsford, NY: Pergamon, 1977.

Weatherford, Willis D., and Johnson, Charles S. *Race Relations: Adjustment of Whites and Negroes in the United States*. Lexington, MA: D. C. Heath, 1934.

Weaver, Jerry L. *National Health Policy and the Underserved: Ethnic Minorities, Women, and the Elderly*. St. Louis, MO: C. V. Mosby, 1976.

Weglyn, Michi. *Years of Infamy: The Untold Story of America's Concentration Camps*. New York: Morrow, 1976.

Weigert, Andrew J., D'Antonio, William V., and Rubel, Arthur J. "Protestantism and Assimilation Among Mexican Americans: An Exploratory Study of Ministers' Reports." *Journal for the Scientific Study of Religion* Fall (1971): 219–32.

Weil, Frederick D. "Tolerance of Free Speech in the United States and West Germany, 1970–79: An Analysis of Public Opinion Survey Data." *Social Forces* June (1982): 973–92.

Weimann, Gabriel. "On the Importance of Marginality: One More Step into the Two-step Flow of Communication." *American Sociological Review* December (1982): 764–773.

Weinberg, Meyer. "The Relationship Between School Desegregation and Academic Achievement: A Review of the Research." *Law and Contemporary Problems* Spring (1975): 241–70.

Weinberg, Meyer. *A Chance to Learn*. Cambridge: Cambridge University Press, 1977.

Weisbord, Robert G., and Stein, Arthur. *Bittersweet Encounter: The Afro-American and the American Jew*. Westport, CT: Negro Universities Press, 1970.

Welch, Michael R. "The Unchurched: Black Religious Non-Affiliates." *Journal for the Scientific Study of Religion* September (1978): 289–93.

Wellman, David T. *Portraits of White Racism*. Cambridge: Cambridge University Press, 1977.

Weppner, Robert S. "Urban Economic Opportunities: The Example of Denver." In J. O. Waddell and O. M. Watson, eds., *The American Indian in Modern Society*. Boston: Little, Brown, 1971, p. 244–73.

West, Stanley A., and Macklin, June, eds. *The Chicano Experience*. Boulder, CO: Westview, 1979.

Westie, Frank R. "Negro–White Status Differentials and Social Distance." *American Sociological Review* October (1952): 550–58.

Westie, Frank R. "The American Dilemma: An Empirical Test." *American Sociological Review* August (1955): 527–38.

Westie, Frank R., and Westie, Margaret L. "The Social-Distance Pyramid: Relationships Between Caste and Class." *American Journal of Sociology* September (1957): 190–96.

Wheeler, Geoffrey. *Racial Problems in Soviet Muslim Asia*. 2nd ed. Oxford: Oxford University Press, 1962.

White, Ralph K., and Lippitt, Ronald. *Autocracy and Democracy: An Experimental Inquiry.* New York: Harper & Row, 1960.

White, Walter. *A Man Called Whites.* New York: Viking, 1948.

Whitehurst, James E. "The Mainstreaming of the Black Muslims: Healing the Hate." *Christian Century* February 27 (1980): 225–29.

Wienk, Ronald E., Reid, Clifford E., Simonson, John C., and Eggers, Frederick J. *Measuring Racial Discrimination in American Housing Markets: The Housing Market Practices Survey.* U.S. Department of Housing and Urban Development, April, 1979.

Wilder, David A. "Perceiving Persons as a Group: Effects on Attributions of Causality and Beliefs." *Social Psychology* March (1978): 13–23.

Wilensky, Harold L., and Edwards, Hugh. "The Skidder: Ideological Adjustments of Downward Mobile Workers." *American Sociological Review* April (1959): 215–31.

Wilensky, Harold L., and Lawrence, Anne T. "Job Assignment in Modern Societies: A Re-examination of the Ascription–Achievement Hypothesis." In Amos H. Hawley, ed., *Societal Growth: Processes and Implications.* New York: Free Press, 1979, pp. 202–48.

Wiley, Norbert. "The Ethnic Mobility Trap and Stratification Theory." *Social Problems* Fall (1967): 147–59.

Wilhelm, S. M. "Some Reflections Upon Work and the Work Ethic in Contemporary America." In H. R. Kaplan, ed., *Minorities and Economic Opportunity.* Itasca, IL: F. E. Peacock, 1977.

Wilkins, Roy, and Matthews, Tom. *Standing Fast: The Autobiography of Roy Wilkins.* New York: Viking, 1982.

Wilkinson, Doris Y., and Taylor, Ronald L., eds. *The Black Male in America: Perspectives on His Status in Contemporary Society.* Chicago: Nelson-Hall, 1977.

Williams, Eddie N. "Black Political Participation in 1978." *The State of Black America.* New York: National Urban League, 1979, pp. 41–77.

Williams, J. Allen, Jr., and Wienir, Paul L. "A Reexamination of Myrdal's Rank Order of Discriminations." *Social Problems* Spring (1967): 443–54.

Williams, J. Allen, Jr., Babchuk, Nicholas, and Johnson, David R. "Voluntary Associations and Minority Status: A Comparative Analysis of Anglo, Black, and Mexican Americans." *American Sociological Review* October (1973): 637–46.

Williams, James D., ed. *The State of Black America 1982.* New York: National Urban League, 1982.

Williams, John E., and Morland, J. Kenneth. *Race, Color, and the Young Child.* Chapel Hill: University of North Carolina, 1976.

Williams, Robin M., Jr. *The Reduction of Intergroup Tensions.* New York: Social Science Research Council, 1947.

Williams, Robin M., Jr. *Mutual Accommodation: Ethnic Conflict and Cooperation.* Minneapolis: University of Minnesota Press, 1977.

Williams, Robin M., Jr., Dean, John P., and Suchman, Edward A. *Strangers Next Door,* New York: Prentice-Hall, 1964.

Williamson, Joel. *New People: Miscegenation and Mulattoes in the United States.* New York: Free Press, 1980.

Willie, Charles V. *The Ivory and Ebony Towers: Race Relations and Higher Education.* Lexington, MA: Lexington Books, 1981a.

Willie, Charles V. *A New Look at Black Families.* Bayside, NY: General Hall, 1976, 1981b.

Willie, Charles V., and Cunnigen, Donald. "Black Students in Higher Education: A Review of 1965–1980." *Annual Review of Sociology* 7 (1981): 177–98.

Willie, Charles V., and Edmonds, Ronald R., eds. *Black Colleges in America.* New York: Teachers College, 1978.

Willie, Charles V., and Greenblatt, Susan L. "Four 'Classic' Studies of Power Relationships in Black Families: A Review and Look to the Future." *Journal of Marriage and the Family.* November (1978): 691–93.

Willie, Charles V., and MacLeish, Marlene Y. "The Priorities of Presidents of Black Colleges." In C. V. Willie and R. R. Edmonds, eds. *Black Colleges in America.* New York: Teachers College, 1978.

Willie, Charles V., Kramer, Bernard M., and Brown, Bertram S., eds. *Racism and Mental Health.* Pittsburgh: University of Pittsburgh, 1973.

Wilmore, Gayraud S., Jr. *Black Religion and Black Radicalism.* New York: Doubleday, 1973.

Wilner, Daniel M., Walkley, Rosabelle P., and Cook, Stuart W. *Human Relations in Interracial Housing.* Minneapolis: University of Minnesota, 1955.

Wilson, Bryan R. *Magic and the Millennium.* New York: Harper & Row, 1973.

Wilson, Cody. "Extrinsic Religious Values and Prejudice." *Journal of Abnormal and Social Psychology* March (1960): 286–91.

Wilson, Franklin D. *Residential Consumption, Economic Opportunity, and Race.* New York: Academic Press, 1979.

Wilson, James. *The Original Americans: U.S. Indians.* London: Minority Rights Group, 1976.

Wilson, James Q. "The Negro in Politics." *Daedalus* Fall (1965): 949–73.

Wilson, Kenneth L. "Status Inconsistency and the Hope Technique, I: The Grounds for a Resurrection." *Social Forces* June (1979): 1229–47.

Wilson, Ronald W., Feldman, Jacob J., and Kovar, Mary G. "Continuing Trends in Health and Health Care." *Annals of the American Academy of Political and Social Science* January (1978): 179–205.

Wilson, Warner and Varner, William. "The Rank Order of Discrimination." *Phylon* March (1973): 30–42.

Wilson, William J. *Power, Racism, and Privilege: Race Relations in Theoretical and Sociohistorical Perspectives.* New York: Macmillan, 1973.

Wilson, William J. *The Declining Significance of Race: Blacks and Changing American Institutions.* Chicago: University of Chicago Press, 1978.

Wilson, William J. "The Black Community in the 1980s: Questions of Race, Class, and Public Policy." *Annals of the American Academy of Political and Social Science* March (1981): 26–41.

Winship, Christopher. "A Revaluation of Indexes of Residential Segregation." *Social Forces* June (1977): 1058–66.

Winship, Christopher. "The Desirability of Using the Index of Dissimilarity or Any Adjustment of it for Measuring Segregation: Reply to Falk, Cortese, and Cohen." *Social Forces* December (1978): 717–20.

Winter, J. Alan. *Continuities in the Sociology of Religion: Creed, Congregation, and Community.* New York: Harper & Row, 1977.

Wirth, Louis. "Race and Public Policy." *Scientific Monthly* April (1944): 302–12.

Wirth, Louis. "The Problem of Minority Groups." In Ralph Linton, ed., *The Science of Man in the World Crisis.* New York: Columbia University Press, 1945, pp. 347–72.

Wispé, Lauren G., ed. "Positive Forms of Social Behavior." *Journal of Social Issues* (1972): whole issue.

Wolf, Eleanor P. *Trial and Error: The Detroit School Segregation Case.* Detroit: Wayne State University Press, 1980.

Wolfgang, Marvin E., and Cohen, Bernard. *Crime and Race.* Old Bethpage, NY: Institute of Human Relations, 1970.

Wood, James R., and Zald, Mayer N. "Aspects of Racial Integration in the Methodist Church: Sources of Resistance to Organizational Policy." *Social Forces* December (1966): 255–65.

Woodrum, Eric. "An Assessment of Japanese American Assimilation, Pluralism, and Subordination." *American Journal of Sociology* (1981): 157–69.

Woodward, C. Vann. *The Strange Career of Jim Crow.* Oxford: Oxford University Press, 1955.

Woodward, C. Vann. "Review of *Time on the Cross.*" *New York Review of Books,* May 2, 1974, pp. 3–6.

Word, Carol O., Zanna, Mark P., and Cooper, Joel. "The Nonverbal Mediation of Self-Fulfilling Prophecies in Interracial Interactions." *Journal of Experimental Social Psychology* March (1974): 109–120.

Wright, D. E., Salinas, E., and Kuvlesky, W. P. "Opportunities for Social Mobility for Mexican-American Youth." In R. O. de la Garza, Z. A. Kruszewski, and T. A. Arciniego, eds., *Chicanos and Native Americans.* New York: Prentice-Hall, 1973, p. 48–59.

Wright, James D. "The Working Class Authoritarianism and the War in Vietnam." *Social Problems* Fall (1972): 133–50.

Wright, James D. *The Dissent of the Governed: Alienation and Democracy in America.* New York: Academic Press, 1976.

Wright, Richard. *Black Boy.* New York: Harper & Brothers, 1937.

Wright, Roy Dean, and Wright, Susan N. "A Plea for a Further Refinement of the Marginal Man Theory." *Phylon* 33,4 (1972): 361–68.

Wuthnow, Robert. "Anti-Semitism and Stereotyping." In Arthur G. Miller, ed., *In the Eye of the Beholder.* New York: Praeger, 1982, pp. 137–87.

Wylie, Ruth. *The Self Concept.* Rev. ed. Lincoln: University of Nebraska, 1979.

Wynne, Edward A. *Growing Up Suburban.* Austin: University of Texas Press, 1977.

Yabura, Lloyd. "Health Care Outcomes in the Black Community." *Phylon* (1977): 194–202.

Yancey, William L., Rigsby, Leo, and McCarthy, John D. "Social Position and Self-Evaluation: The Relative Importance of Race." *American Journal of Sociology* September (1972): 338–59.

Yancey, William L., Ericksen, E. P., and Juliani, R. N. "Emergent Ethnicity: A Review and Reformulation." *American Sociological Review* June (1976): 391–402.

Yarrow, Marian R., Scott, Phyllis, and Zahn-Waxler, Carolyn. "Learning Concern for Others." *Developmental Psychology* 8 (1973): 240–60.

Yinger, John. *The Black–White Price Differential in Housing: Some Further Evidence.* Madison: Institute for Research on Poverty, University of Wisconsin, December, 1975.

Yinger, John. "Racial Prejudice and Racial Residential Segregation in an Urban Model." *Journal of Urban Economics* 3 (1976): 383–96.

Yinger, John. "Prejudice and Discrimination in the Urban Housing Market." In Peter Mieszkowski and Mahlon Strazheim, eds., *Current Issues in Urban Economics.* Baltimore: Johns Hopkins University Press, 1979, pp. 430–68.

Yinger, John. "A Search Model of Real Estate Broker Behavior." *American Economic Review,* September (1981): 591–605.

Yinger, J. Milton. "Interethnic Attitudes in Hawaii." Unpublished manuscript, 1961.

Yinger, J. Milton. *A Minority Group in American Society.* New York: McGraw-Hill, 1965a.

Yinger, J. Milton. *Toward a Field Theory of Behavior.* New York: McGraw-Hill, 1965b.

Yinger, J. Milton. "A Research Note on Interfaith Marriage Statistics." *Journal for the Scientific Study of Religion* Spring (1968): 97–103.

Yinger, J. Milton. *The Scientific Study of Religion.* New York: Macmillan, 1970.

Yinger, J. Milton. "Anomie, Alienation, and Political Behavior." In Jeanne N. Knutson, ed., *Handbook of Political Psychology.* San Francisco: Jossey-Bass, 1973, pp. 171–202.

Yinger, J. Milton. "Ethnicity in Complex Societies." In Lewis A. Coser and Otto N. Larsen, eds., *The Uses of Controversy in Sociology.* New York: Free Press, 1976, pp. 197–216.

Yinger, J. Milton. "Toward a Theory of Assimilation and Dissimilation." *Ethnic and Racial Studies* July (1981): 249–64.

Yinger, J. Milton. *Countercultures: The Promise and Peril of a World Turned Upside Down.* New York: Free Press, 1982.

Yinger, J. Milton. "Ethnicity and Social Change: The Interaction of Structural, Cultural, and Personality Factors." *Ethnic and Racial Studies* October (1983): 395–409.

Yinger, J. Milton, and Cutler, Stephen J., eds. *Major Social Issues: A Multi-disciplinary View.* New York: Free Press, 1978.

Yinger J. Milton, and Simpson, George E., eds. "American Indians Today." *Annals of the American Academy of Political and Social Science* March (1978): whole issue.

Young, Crawford. *The Politics of Cultural Pluralism.* Madison: University of Wisconsin Press, 1976.

Young, Kimball. *Social Psychology.* 3rd ed. New York: Appleton-Century-Crofts, 1956.

Young, Virginia H. "Family and Childhood in a Southern Community." *American Anthropologist* 72 (1970): 269–288.

Young, Whitney M., Jr. *To Be Equal.* New York: McGraw-Hill, 1964.

Young, Whitney M., Jr. *Beyond Racism: Building an Open Society.* New York: McGraw-Hill, 1969.

Yuchtman-Yaar, Ephraim and Semyonov, Moshe. "Ethnic Inequality in Israeli Schools and Sports: An Expectation-States Approach." *American Journal of Sociology* November (1979): 576–90.

Zald, Mayer N., and McCarthy, John D., eds. *The Dynamics of Social Movements: Resource Mobilization, Social Control, and Tactics.* Englewood, NJ: Winthrop, 1979.

Zawadski, Bohdan. "Limitations of the Scapegoat Theory of Prejudice." *Journal of Abnormal and Social Psychology* April (1948): 127–41.

Zehner, Harry. "How Roy Innis Ravaged Core." *Saturday Review* April 28 (1979): 21–24.

Zelditch, Morris, Jr. "Review Essay: Outsiders' Politics" (Review of *The Strategy of Social Protest* by William A. Gamson). *American Journal of Sociology* May (1978): 1514–20.

Zeligs, R. and Hendrickson, G. "Racial Attitudes of 200 Sixth-Grade Children." *Sociology and Social Research*, September–October (1933): 26–36.

Zinn, Howard. *SNCC: The New Abolitionists*. Boston: Beacon, 1966.

Zurcher, Louis A., Jr. *The Mutable Self: A Self-Concept for Social Change*. Beverly Hills, CA: Sage, 1977.

Zurcher, Louis A., and Wilson, Kenneth L. "Status Inconsistency and the Hope Technique, II: A Linear Hypothesis About Status Enhancement, Status Detraction, and Satisfaction with Membership." *Social Forces* June (1979): 1248–64.

Name Index

Subject Index